Trademarks, Unfair Competition, and Business Torts

ASPEN CASEBOOK SERIES

Trademarks, Unfair Competition, and Business Torts

Barton Beebe
Professor of Law
Co-Director, Engelberg Center on Innovation Law and Policy
New York University School of Law

Thomas F. Cotter
Briggs and Morgan Professor of Law
University of Minnesota Law School

Mark A. Lemley
William H. Neukom Professor of Law
Director, Stanford Program in Law,
Science and Technology
Stanford University

Peter S. Menell
Professor of Law
Director, Berkeley Center for Law and Technology
University of California at Berkeley

Robert P. Merges
Wilson, Sonsini, Goodrich, and Rosati
Professor of Law and Technology
University of California at Berkeley

Wolters Kluwer
Law & Business

AUSTIN BOSTON CHICAGO NEW YORK THE NETHERLANDS

www.wolterskluwerlb.com

To contact Customer Care, e-mail customer.care@aspenpublishers.com, call 1-800-234-1660, fax 1-800-901-9075, or mail correspondence to:

Aspen Publishers
Attn: Order Department
PO Box 990
Frederick, MD 21705

Printed in the United States of America.

1 2 3 4 5 6 7 8 9 0

ISBN 978-0-7355-8877-6

Library of Congress Cataloging-in-Publication Data

Trademarks, unfair competition, and business torts / Barton Beebe . . . [et al.].
p. cm.—(Aspen casebook series)
Includes index.
ISBN 978-0-7355-8877-6
1. Trademarks—Law and legislation—United States. 2. Competition, Unfair—United States.
3. Casebooks I. Beebe, Barton Carl, 1969-

KF3180.T737 2011
346.7304′88—dc22

2010054592

About Wolters Kluwer Law & Business

Wolters Kluwer Law & Business is a leading provider of research information and workflow solutions in key specialty areas. The strengths of the individual brands of Aspen Publishers, CCH, Kluwer Law International and Loislaw are aligned within Wolters Kluwer Law & Business to provide comprehensive, in-depth solutions and expert-authored content for the legal, professional and education markets.

CCH was founded in 1913 and has served more than four generations of business professionals and their clients. The CCH products in the Wolters Kluwer Law & Business group are highly regarded electronic and print resources for legal, securities, antitrust and trade regulation, government contracting, banking, pension, payroll, employment and labor, and healthcare reimbursement and compliance professionals.

Aspen Publishers is a leading information provider for attorneys, business professionals and law students. Written by preeminent authorities, Aspen products offer analytical and practical information in a range of specialty practice areas from securities law and intellectual property to mergers and acquisitions and pension/ benefits. Aspen's trusted legal education resources provide professors and students with high-quality, up-to-date and effective resources for successful instruction and study in all areas of the law.

Kluwer Law International supplies the global business community with comprehensive English-language international legal information. Legal practitioners, corporate counsel and business executives around the world rely on the Kluwer Law International journals, loose-leafs, books and electronic products for authoritative information in many areas of international legal practice.

Loislaw is a premier provider of digitized legal content to small law firm practitioners of various specializations. Loislaw provides attorneys with the ability to quickly and efficiently find the necessary legal information they need, when and where they need it, by facilitating access to primary law as well as state-specific law, records, forms and treatises.

Wolters Kluwer Law & Business, a unit of Wolters Kluwer, is headquartered in New York and Riverwoods, Illinois. Wolters Kluwer is a leading multinational publisher and information services company.

For Nancy Pastor Beebe

B.B.

For Karin and Alec, for their love and support

T.F.C.

For Rose

M.A.L.

For Claire, Dylan, and Noah

P.S.M.

For my family

R.P.M

Summary of Contents

Contents

Preface

This casebook is the culmination of a substantial effort on the part of its coauthors to create a text that brings together a variety of related bodies of law, many of which until now were only rarely covered in much depth (if at all) in the typical law school curriculum. Our motivation in writing the book therefore was threefold: (1) to expose students to rich new theoretical, analytical, and empirical insights into the law of trademarks, unfair competition, and business torts; (2) to integrate the important (and often overlooked) bodies of state unfair competition law; and (3) to emphasize the growing challenges posed by the Internet and digital technology. Law professors can use this casebook to teach for a variety of two- or three-credit courses within the law school curriculum, including courses primarily devoted to trademark or advertising law; to unfair competition and business torts; or to any combination of these subjects. The casebook makes ample use of problems, many of them derived from real cases. In some instances, to highlight how related legal doctrines can sometimes impact the same set of facts, students are asked to reconsider a problem found in an earlier chapter in light of the material discussed in a later chapter.

The following is a synopsis of the casebook contents:

Chapter 1. Introduction. In this chapter, we briefly outline the different bodies of law discussed in later chapters. We also present readings and problems designed to introduce students to the various policy rationales for, and critiques of, each of these bodies of law. In particular, we hope that students come away from this chapter with a basic understanding (to be explored at greater depth throughout the course) of the difficulty of distinguishing "fair" from "unfair" competition, and of the tension that sometimes arises between some applications of these bodies of law and the First Amendment.

Chapters 2-8. Trademarks. These chapters expand upon and update the coverage of trademark law found in Chapter 5 of Robert P. Merges, Peter S. Menell, and Mark A. Lemley, *Intellectual Property in the New Technological Age* (5th ed. 2009). Chapter 2 briefly surveys the history of trademarks and trademark law and the theoretical bases for trademark protection. Chapters 3 and 4 consider what can qualify for trademark protection and how trademark rights are established. Chapter 4 in particular includes enhanced coverage of genericness, trade dress, and functionality doctrine and of the registration process at the U.S. Patent and Trademark Office. Chapter 5 addresses trademark infringement and provides thorough coverage of the multifactor test for the likelihood of consumer confusion, courts' application of the new Trademark Dilution Revision Act, and secondary liability in trademark law. Chapter 6 reviews defenses to trademark infringement, such as abandonment and fair use. Chapter 7 briefly considers international aspects of trademark protection, while Chapter 8 covers remedies for trademark infringement.

Chapter 9. False Advertising. This chapter provides thorough coverage of the law of false advertising and related doctrines under various common-law and statutory systems. It begins with an overview of the economics of advertising, and then contrasts the common law's skeptical take on false advertising suits initiated by competitors to the Lanham Act's (somewhat) more permissive approach. The chapter also includes substantial coverage of a parallel body of false advertising law developed and enforced by the Federal Trade Commission (FTC) and a brief discussion of analogous state laws (the so-called Baby FTC Acts). The chapter continues with a discussion of the related tort of commercial disparagement under the common law and the Lanham Act, and with materials on litigants' attempts to use the Lanham Act to create a federal right of attribution. The chapter concludes with an extended discussion of possible First Amendment constraints on the law of false advertising and disparagement; a brief survey of international issues; and remedies for false advertising.

Chapter 10. Right of Publicity. This chapter presents detailed coverage of state law rights of publicity and related claims for false endorsement. The chapter covers the historical development of the right and differences among the various state law approaches. The chapter also includes extensive discussion of the tension between the right of publicity and the First Amendment, and various courts' and commentators' efforts to reconcile the two.

Chapter 11. Trade Secrets. Like chapters 2-8, this chapter expands upon coverage of a topic presented in *Intellectual Property in the New Technological Age*. The chapter provides a comprehensive overview of the law of trade secrets, including both its civil and criminal law aspects, as well as the related body of law on employee covenants not to compete. The chapter includes extensive problems designed to flesh out the meaning of the often ambiguous language of the relevant statutes, and like the two preceding chapters incorporates extensive discussion of related First Amendment issues.

Chapter 12. Legal Protection for Facts, Uncopyrightable Factual Compilations, and Ideas. This chapter covers a variety of still-evolving bodies of law, including the once-dormant "hot news" doctrine that now appears, for better or worse, to be making a modest comeback in the Internet age; the enforceability of shrinkwrap and clickwrap agreements; and a topic of interest to aspiring screenwriters everywhere, the enforceability of contracts allegedly relating to the confidential submission of ideas.

Chapter 13. Cybertrespass. This chapter explores how courts in the digital age have looked to the antique law of personal property to fashion remedies for conduct such as unauthorized access to websites and transfers of domain names. Are these common-law analogies apt when applied to a very different setting from that in which they arose?

Chapter 14. Tortious Interference and RICO. This chapter introduces students to two commonly pled business torts (which sometimes arise in connection with other bodies of law discussed elsewhere in the book, as well as independently of those bodies of law). The chapter begins with a discussion of the related torts of tortious interference with contract and tortious interference with prospective business advantage. It concludes with a brief discussion of common-law fraud and of modern-day civil claims arising under the federal RICO statute.

Chapter 15. Preemption. Preemption issues pervade many of the topics covered elsewhere in the book. Professors who wish to do so could teach portions of chapter 15 in connection with these other chapters, or they may leave the topic of preemption to separate class periods towards the end of the semester as a way of tying the various materials together. The chapter excerpts the leading U.S. Supreme Court cases on federal preemption of state intellectual property and unfair competition claims, as well as recent appellate court decisions addressing the preemption of hot news, shrinkwrap, and right of publicity claims. The chapter concludes by presenting contrasting views on the preemption of state law claims by other state law, namely the Uniform Trade Secrets Act.

Barton Beebe
Thomas F. Cotter
Mark A. Lemley
Peter S. Menell
Robert P. Merges

January 2011

Acknowledgments

Many people have contributed to the completion of this project, both before and after we decided to go forward with the creation of a casebook in 2009. We are also grateful to the many students to whom we have taught from earlier versions of the materials presented herein, and whose suggestions for improvement have often proven very helpful. We thank John Devins and Troy Froebe at Aspen for shepherding this project through to completion. Thanks also to Theresa Stadheim and Nicholas Tymoczko for excellent research assistance.

Note: We have selectively omitted citations and footnotes from cases without the uses of ellipses or other indications. All footnotes are numbered consecutively within each chapter, except that footnotes in cases and other excerpts correspond to the actual footnote numbers in the published reports.

Many of the problems in the text are taken from actual cases. In many instances we have altered the facts of the case. In some cases we have also altered the names of the parties involved, though in other instances we thought it was important to the problem to use the name of the product or company with which the reader would be familiar. Readers should understand that the problems are hypothetical in nature and that we do not intend them to represent the actual facts of any case or situation.

Trademarks, Unfair Competition, and Business Torts

1

Foundations of Trademark and Unfair Competition Law

Free-market economic systems such as the U.S. economy in the early twenty-first century are characterized by intense economic competition. Firms compete aggressively to generate and bring to market new ideas and technologies, to gain market share and expand the scope of their markets, to persuade potential customers to buy their products rather than a competitor's on the basis of price, quality, or other characteristics, and to build commercial goodwill. Though the competition is fierce, it is also economically and socially salutary. It is not a "zero sum" game, in which any gain is offset by a countervailing loss. On the contrary, the free-market system is based on the premise that robust competition leads to positive sum outcomes in the form of lower prices, higher quality, a greater selection of products, more efficient allocation and use of resources, and rapid innovation.

An additional premise of the free-market system is that economic competition produces the greatest gains to general welfare when it is subject to certain basic rules that distinguish between permissible and impermissible forms of competition. A "no holds barred" brand of economic competition may very well produce some general economic or social advancement, but experience and theory suggest that unrestrained competition will not produce the greatest gains to general welfare that are possible. These basic rules of economic competition and the experience and theory underlying them are the subject of this book.

While nearly all would agree that some forms of economic competition should not be permitted, determining precisely which commercial practices fall into this category has troubled courts and policymakers for centuries and continues to do so. It is well accepted, for example, that one firm may not simply break into a competitor's factory in order to learn the secrets of the competitor's manufacturing process, but can the firm hire a pilot to fly over the factory and take high-resolution photos of the factory that will yield the same information? *See* E.I. duPont deNemours & Co. v. Rolfe Christopher et al., 431 F.2d 1012 (5th Cir. 1970), *infra*, Chapter 11. Rather than hire a pilot, can the firm seek to hire away one of the competitor's key engineers and then learn from that engineer how the competitor produces its products? What if the engineer signed a contract in which she agreed not to work for any competing firm for a specified period of time following her employment? *See* Edwards v. Arthur Andersen LLP, 81 Cal. Rptr. 3d 282 (Sup. Ct. 2008). Or can the firm simply purchase one of the competitor's products and reverse engineer it to determine how it was made? *See* Kadant, Inc. v. Seeley Machine, Inc., 244 F. Supp. 2d 19 (N.D.N.Y. 2003), *infra*, Chapter 11. Alternatively, what if the firm sought to tarnish its competitor's reputation by making the false claim in advertisements that its competitor was affiliated with and forwarded a substantial portion of its profits to the Church of Satan? *See* Procter & Gamble Co. v. Haugen, 222 F.3d 1262 (10th Cir. 2000), *infra*, Chapter 9. Or, if failing to beat its competitor, the firm in some sense sought to join it, by selling its products under a trademark or in packaging strikingly similar to its competitor's? *See* Chapters 2-8.

Such questions arise across the spectrum of modern-day commercial conduct. A friend tells you his brilliant idea for the plot of a new movie. Because he pitches it to you at a high level of generality, it is not protectable under copyright law. Is there any principle of law preventing you from simply taking his idea and selling it to the highest bidder, and how do you prevent the bidders from "stealing" the idea from you just as you did from your friend? *See* Desny v. Wilder, 46 Cal. 2d 715 (Cal. Sup. Ct. 1956), *infra*, Chapter 12. A famous singer refuses as a matter of principle to allow her voice to be used in television commercials. Undaunted, a major American company hires a "sound alike" to impersonate her. Does the singer have any legal recourse? *See* Midler v. Ford Motor Co., 849 F.2d 460 (9th Cir. 1988), *infra*, Chapter 10. A company designs a "software robot" that overrides an auction Web site's "robot exclusion headers" and systematically scours the site for price information. Its technological efforts having failed, can the auction site invoke any principle of law to prevent this conduct? *See* eBay, Inc. v. Bidder's Edge, Inc., 100 F. Supp. 2d 1058 (N.D. Cal. 2000), *infra*, Chapter 13. Finally, a newspaper publishes news stories online. A competitor hires writers to rephrase the copyrightable elements of the newspaper's articles but otherwise presents the uncopyrightable facts from those articles on its own Web site. Unable to sue under copyright law, does the newspaper have any legal recourse? What if the competitor simply copies the newspaper's arguably uncopyrightable headlines with a hyperlink to the newspaper's stories? *See* International News Service v. Associated Press, 248 U.S. 215, 240 (U.S. 1918), *infra*, Chapter 12.

All of these questions fall within the general area of unfair competition that this book covers. Yet they implicate far broader questions about why we permit certain kinds of commercial conduct and forbid others. This chapter has two principle purposes. It first explores the principal theoretical foundations for the prevention of unfair competition. Many of these will be familiar to readers already conversant with the justifications for real and intellectual property protection. Understanding the reasons why we prevent unfair competition — and how those reasons draw from and differ from the justifications for real and intellectual property — will help the reader grasp the details of the many legal rules that follow in this book. The second section provides a comparative overview of the principle areas of unfair competition. Understanding the unfair competition landscape requires thinking about each area of unfair competition law not just in isolation, but as it interacts with others. This is especially true because unfair competition disputes typically involve multiple parts of this landscape at once.

A. THEORETICAL PERSPECTIVES

"Unfair competition" is the general heading that has for centuries been given to the body of law covered in this book, including trademark law and business torts. The phrase implies that ethical or moral standards of fairness guide courts' and policymakers' judgments of what conduct is permissible and impermissible. To be sure, in speaking of unfair competitive conduct, courts often couch their judgments in ethical and moral terms. *See, e.g.*, Water Gremlin Co. v. Ideal Fishing Float Co., 401 F. Supp. 809, 811 (D. Minn. 1975) ("[T]he essence of the law of unfair competition is fair play."); Mars Inc. v. Kabushiki-Kaisha Nippon Conlux, 24 F.3d 1368, 1373 (Fed. Cir. 1994) ("The common law concept of 'unfair competition' has not been confined to any rigid definition and encompasses a variety of types of commercial or business conduct considered 'contrary to good conscience.'" (citing International News Service v. Associated Press, 248 U.S. 215, 240 (U.S. 1918)); Leon Finker, Inc. v. Schlussel, 469 F. Supp. 674, 680 (S.D.N.Y. 1979) ("Unfair competition encompasses a broad range of conduct (much like negligence), and may, in the final analysis, consist of selling goods by means that shock the judicial senses."). But concepts of fairness often provide little guidance as to what conduct the law actually forbids and why. That some form of commercial conduct is "unfair" often merely designates a legal conclusion rather than the analytical basis for that conclusion. *See* E.I. duPont deNemours & Co. v. Federal Trade Comm'n, 729 F.2d 128, 137-38 (2d Cir. 1984) ("The term 'unfair' is an elusive concept, often dependent upon the eye of the beholder. A line must therefore be drawn between conduct that is anticompetitive and legitimate conduct that has an impact on competition.").

To reach the conclusion that a particular form of conduct is "unfair," courts and policymakers employ a wide variety of theoretical perspectives. These perspectives touch upon timeworn justifications for real property and intellectual property as well as more recently developed economic theories of efficient markets. As you read through the following discussion of these perspectives, consider which ones are limited to specific areas of unfair competition law (as reflected in the various questions asked above) and which ones apply more broadly across the entire landscape. We first consider two closely related economic perspectives on unfair competition law, one which seeks to ensure the integrity of the marketplace, the other which seeks to preserve incentives for innovation and creativity.

1. The Integrity of the Marketplace

The efficiency of the marketplace depends critically upon the quality of information available to consumers. In markets in which the quality of goods is uniform or easily inspected at the time of purchase, consumers can determine the attributes themselves and no information problem arises. In many markets, however — such as used automobiles, computers, watches — an information asymmetry exists: Sellers typically have better information about the products or services being offered than buyers can uncover without buying the product. *See* George A. Akerlof, *The Market for "Lemons": Quality Uncertainty and the Market Mechanism*, 84 Q.J. Econ. 488 (1970).

Unscrupulous sellers will be tempted to make false or misleading product claims or copy the trademark of a rival producer known for superior quality. It is often easier to copy a trademark than to duplicate production techniques, quality assurance programs, and the like. For example, two watches that look the same on the outside may have very different mechanical features, manufacturing quality, and composition of materials used.

Proliferation of unreliable information in the marketplace increases consumers' costs of search and distorts the provision of goods. Consumers will have to spend more time and effort inspecting goods, researching the product market, and actually testing products. Manufacturers will have less incentive to produce quality goods as others will be able to free-ride on such reputations. In markets for products where quality is costly to observe, high-quality manufacturers might not be able to survive without effective mechanisms for policing the source of products and the accuracy of claims relating to unobservable product characteristics.

Trademarks, as precise and unequivocal indicators of the source (e.g., Apple) and the nature (e.g., iPhone 4) of particular goods, counteract the "market for lemons" problem by communicating to consumers the enterprise responsible for the goods and, in some cases, for the specifications of the goods. The brand name Coca-Cola, for example, informs the consumer of the maker of the soft drink beverage as well as the taste that they can expect. If the product lives up to or exceeds expectations, then the trademark owner gains a loyal customer who will be willing to pay a premium in future transactions; if the product disappoints, then the trademark owner will have more difficulty making future sales to that consumer (or will have to offer a discount to attract their business). In this way, trademarks implicitly communicate unobservable characteristics about the quality of branded products, thereby fostering incentives for firms to invest in product quality, even when such attributes are not directly observable prior to a purchasing decision. Sellers who enter the high-quality segment of the market must initially invest in building a strong reputation. Only after consumers become acquainted with the attributes of their brand can they recoup these costs. As this process unfolds, high-quality items can sell for a premium above their costs of production, since consumers will expect them to be of high quality. Trademarks also facilitate efficient new business models, such as franchising, which generate economies of scale and scope in marketing and facilitate rapid business diffusion across vast geographic areas.

Prohibitions against deceptive forms of advertising similarly work to preserve the quality of information available to consumers. Though the overall effect of advertising on general welfare remains the subject of debate (as we discuss in Chapter 9), there can be little doubt that certain forms of advertising greatly aid consumers in making their purchasing decisions and facilitate competition among producers over price, product quality, and innovative product characteristics. These beneficial effects of advertising will only result, however, if the advertising is truthful. Consumers who rely on false advertising may waste resources in purchasing a product that does not meet their needs, while the producer of the product that they would otherwise have bought is also harmed by the lost sales. Possibly worse, such consumers may grow weary of all advertising, so even truthful advertising will fail to benefit them. Prohibitions against false advertising help to prevent this "lemonization" of commercial advertising.

COMMENTS AND QUESTIONS

1. *Comparative Institutional Analysis.* In addition to private rights of action for trademark infringement and false advertising, several other mechanisms are available to provide and regulate market information, such as deceit and fraud common law causes of action and privately enforced consumer protection statutes, public regulation and public enforcement of unfair competition laws, and industry self-regulation and certification organizations. How do these institutions compare with trademark protection? Should they supplement or substitute for trademark protection?

2. *Status Goods.* Some trademarks also serve a more ambiguous function: signaling status or identity for some consumers. Some have referred to such commodities as "Veblen" goods, reflecting Thorstein Veblen's theory of conspicuous consumption. *See* THORSTEIN VEBLEN, THE THEORY OF THE LEISURE CLASS: AN ECONOMIC STUDY OF INSTITUTIONS (1899). This theory posits that, unlike normal goods, demand for status goods actually increases with their price. Purchasers of such goods may be interested in being associated with a particular brand — such as a Rolex watch, a T-shirt with the name and colors of a particular university, or a corporate brand — possibly apart from whether it is authentic or the quality associated with the authentic good. Some purchasers of such goods may well prefer a less expensive, counterfeit version. They presumably would not be confused when purchasing such goods (e.g., a Rolex watch sold on a street corner for $10).

The marketing of less expensive, lower-quality imitations of status goods creates the possibility of separate harm to the sellers and purchasers of authentic goods. The availability of counterfeit articles could well divert some consumers who would otherwise purchase the authentic article, although this effect is likely to be relatively small due to the large price differential and the availability of the authentic goods for those who are interested. The lower quality of the counterfeit goods could, however, erode the goodwill associated with the authentic manufacturer through post-sale confusion — on-lookers who mistake the shoddier counterfeit good for the authentic good and are thereby less inclined to purchase the authentic version, thereby reducing sales by the trademark owner. In addition, due to the proliferation of non-easily recognized "fakes," prior and potential purchasers of the authentic "status" goods may be less interested in owning a much less rare commodity. The value of ownership may be sullied. In essence, status goods exhibit a negative network externality, whereby proliferation of such goods erodes the value to prior purchasers. Should trademark law be concerned with this effect?

3. *Advertising and Consumer Demand.* Will Rogers memorably defined advertising as "the art of convincing people to spend money they don't have for something they don't need." Should this be of concern to false advertising law? Are consumers so susceptible to the persuasive power of advertising? For a discussion of various theoretical approaches to consumer persuasion, see Barton Beebe, *Search and Persuasion in Trademark Law*, 103 MICH. L. REV. 2020 (2005).

4. *Anti-Dilution Protection.* In 1996, Congress expanded trademark protection beyond the prevention of consumer confusion to safeguard famous marks — such as Coca-Cola, Nike, Rolls Royce, Disney, and Tiffany's — against blurring (loss of distinctiveness) and tarnishment of brand identity. As consumers develop their mental lexicon of brands, they associate both specific products and general attributes with

particular trademarks. For example, Rolls Royce connotes both the source of a luxury automobile as well as a brand of uncompromising quality and ornate styling (as well as high cost). If another company were to introduce Rolls Royce candy bars, it is unlikely that many (if any) consumers would believe that the automobile manufacturer was the source. Whether intended or not, the candy company might benefit from the particular general attributes that the consuming public associates with the Rolls Royce brand. They might also gain some "status" equity to the extent that consumers value the signal associated with a mark. Thus, adopting the Rolls Royce name enables the newcomer some ability to free-ride on the general brand reputation of the famous trademark owner.

Such use, however, might impose some costs on consumers and the owner of the famous trademark. As this new use of the Rolls Royce term gained popularity, the association between the mark and a particular source would become blurred. Furthermore, as more companies in unrelated markets adopt this moniker — Rolls Royce tennis racquets, Rolls Royce landscaping, Rolls Royce tacos — the distinctive quality of the mark would become further eroded. Over time, consumers would lose the non-product-specific identity (i.e., Rolls Royce as a brand of uncompromising quality and ornate styling) that the original Rolls Royce mark once evoked. Arguably this raises consumers' search costs: Consumers' mental lexicon has become more difficult to parse. *See* Stacey L. Dogan & Mark A. Lemley, *The Merchandising Right: Fragile Theory or Fait Accompli?*, 54 EMORY L.J. 461 (2005).

As another example, Disney has developed a strong reputation for wholesome, family entertainment. If a pornographic film maker were to brand its films Disney Smut Productions, it is unlikely that many consumers would be confused as to the source of such films. Nonetheless, consumers' shopping lexicon would arguably be distorted because the Disney name would trigger associations with both family-oriented content and pornography. Such a negative association could well injure the Disney Corporation's brand equity.

Anti-dilution protection prevents this erosion of the distinctive quality of a mark by prohibiting famous marks from being used by others — even in unrelated product markets and in non-confusing ways. This preserves distinctive brands and affords the owners exclusive rights to carry their brand names into wholly new markets (or not). We see examples of such brand migration in many markets. Sony Corporation, for example, which honed its reputation in the consumer electronics marketplace, has now developed products in the sound recording and motion picture marketplaces. Cross-branding, such as the marketing of a Barbie doll adorned with Coca-Cola's logo and a distinctive red ensemble, is also increasingly common.

What are the costs of anti-dilution protection? Is the harm to consumers of non-confusing, diluting uses of famous marks likely to be significant? Would scaling back or eliminating anti-dilution protection significantly weaken the incentives of firms to invest in and maintain their brand equity?

5. *"Truthful" Advertising?* According to a recent industry report, 95 percent of consumers surveyed indicated that they did not trust advertising, and only 8 percent said that they believe "what the company says about itself." Alterian, *Your Brand: At Risk or Ready for Growth?* (2010), *available at* http://www.alterian.com/resource-links/campaigns/brandsatrisk/brands-at-risk. In light of consumer attitudes towards advertising, is it realistic to believe that consumers rely on advertising to make purchasing decisions? Notwithstanding false advertising law, has advertising long since become a "market for lemons"?

2. Incentives for Innovation and Creativity

Certain areas of unfair competition law, such as trade secret protection, the "law of ideas," and the tort of misappropriation, if not also trademark law and the right of publicity, are closely aligned with conventional incentive justifications for the protection of intellectual property. The U.S. Constitution expressly conditions the grant of power in the Patent and Copyright Clause on a particular end, namely "to Promote the Progress of Science and useful Arts." U.S. CONST., art. I, cl. 8. As the Supreme Court explained in Mazer v. Stein, 347 U.S. 201 (1954):

> "The copyright law, like the patent statutes, makes reward to the owner a secondary consideration." United States v. Paramount Pictures, 334 U.S. 131, 158. However, it is "intended definitely to grant valuable, enforceable rights to authors, publishers, etc., without burdensome requirements: 'to afford greater encouragement to the production of literary [or artistic] works of lasting benefit to the world.' " Washington Pub. Co. v. Pearson, 306 U.S. 30.
>
> The economic philosophy behind the clause empowering Congress to grant patents and copyrights is the conviction that it is the best way to advance public welfare through the talents of authors and inventors in "Science and useful Arts." Sacrificial days devoted to such creative activities deserve rewards commensurate with the services rendered.

To understand why the Framers thought exclusive rights in inventions and creations would promote the public welfare, consider what would happen absent any sort of intellectual property protection. Invention and creation require the investment of resources—the time of an author or inventor, and often expenditures on facilities, prototypes, supplies, etc. In a private market economy, individuals will not invest in invention or creation unless the expected return from doing so exceeds the cost of doing so—that is, unless they can reasonably expect to make a profit from the endeavor. To profit from a new idea or work of authorship, the creator must be able either to sell it to others or to put it to some use that provides her with a comparative advantage in a market, such as by reducing the cost of producing goods.

But ideas (and writings, for that matter) are notoriously hard to control. Even if the idea is one that the creator can use herself, for example, to boost productivity in her business, she will reap a reward from that idea only to the extent that her competitors don't find out about it. A creator who depends on secrecy for value therefore lives in constant peril of discovery and disclosure. Competitors may steal the idea or learn of it from an ex-employee. They may be able to figure it out by watching the creator's production process or by examining the products she sells. Finally, they may come upon the idea on their own or discover it in the published literature. In all of these cases, the secrecy value of the idea will be irretrievably lost.

The creator who wants to sell her idea is in an even more difficult position. Selling information requires disclosing it to others. Once the information has been disclosed outside a small group, however, it is extremely difficult to control. Information has the characteristics of what economists call a "public good"—it may be "consumed" by many people without depletion, and it is difficult to identify those who will not pay and prevent them from using the information. *See* Kenneth J. Arrow, ***Economic Welfare and the Allocation of Resources for Invention***, *in* THE RATE AND DIRECTION OF INVENTIVE ACTIVITY: ECONOMIC AND SOCIAL FACTORS 609, 614-16 (Nat'l Bureau of Economic Research ed., 1962). Once the secret of a manufacturing process is disclosed, others can imitate it easily. Once a news story is made public, others can copy it at low cost. It is difficult to exclude nonpurchasers from sharing in the benefits of the information.

Ideas and information can also be used by many without depleting the enjoyment of others. Unlike an ice cream cone, a manufacturing process or a news story can be used by many without diminishing their utility.[1]

If we assume that it is nearly costless to distribute information to others — an assumption that was once unrealistic but now much more reasonable with advances in digital technology (including the Internet) — it will prove virtually impossible to charge for information over the medium run in the absence of effective intellectual property or some other means of protection, such as unfair competition law. If the author of a book charges more than the cost of distribution, hoping to recover some of her expenditures in writing the work, competitors will quickly jump in to offer the book at a lower price. Competition will drive the price of the book toward its marginal cost — in this case the cost of producing and distributing one additional copy. In such a competitive market, the author will be unable to recoup the fixed cost of writing the book. Similarly, if a newspaper charges more than the nominal cost of newsprint to recover their costs of collecting the news, competitors are well positioned to undercut the newspaper. The problem is made worse online. Competitors may be able to appropriate and repost its news stories through automated software at exceptionally low cost. The result, according to economic theory, would be an underproduction of news and of other works of invention and creation with similar public goods characteristics.[2]

Information is not the only example of a public good. Economists generally offer lighthouses and national defense as examples of public goods, since it is virtually impossible to provide the benefits of either one only to paying clients. It is impossible, for example, to exclude some ships and not others from the benefits of a lighthouse. Furthermore, the use of the lighthouse by one ship does not deplete the value of its hazard warning to others. As a result, it would be inefficient to exclude nonpayers from using the lighthouse's warning system even if we could, since consumption of this good is "nonrivalrous" (meaning that everyone can benefit from it once it is produced). For these reasons, the market will in theory undersupply such goods because producers cannot reap the marginal (incremental) value of their investment in providing them.[3]

Can you see why broadcast television signals, beautiful gardens on a public street, and national defense are also public goods?

By contrast, markets for pure private goods, such as ice cream cones, feature exclusivity and rivalrous competition — the ice cream vendor provides the good only to those who pay the price, and the consumer certainly depletes the amount of the good available to others. Thus the market system provides adequate incentives for the creation of ice cream cones: Sellers can exact their cost of production, and the value of the product is fully enjoyed by the purchaser.

In the case of national defense (and most lighthouses), we avoid the underproduction that would result from leaving it to the market by having the government step

1. To some extent this statement oversimplifies the problem by ignoring possible second-order distorting effects. In practice, if you taught several hundred million people to fish, the result might be depletion of a physical resource (fish) that would otherwise not have occurred. Similarly, wide dissemination of information may have particular effects on secondary markets, depending on the information.

2. *See, e.g.*, F.M. Scherer, Industrial Market Structure and Economic Performance 444 (2d ed. 1980) ("If pure and perfect competition in the strictest sense prevailed continuously . . . incentives for invention and innovation would be fatally defective without a patent system or some equivalent substitute."). Professor Scherer goes on to note, however, that natural market imperfections may give advantages to first movers, reducing the need for intellectual property protection. *Id.* at 444-45.

3. Ronald Coase has offered evidence casting doubt on the economic assumption that lighthouses must be publicly provided. *See* Ronald H. Coase, *The Lighthouse in Economics*, *in* The Firm, the Market, and the Law (1988).

in and pay for the public good. For a variety of good reasons, going mainly to the advantages of decentralized market ordering over central planning, we have not gone that route with many forms of information. Instead, government has created intellectual property rights in an effort to give authors and inventors control over the use and distribution of their ideas, thereby encouraging them to invest in the production of new ideas and works of authorship. Thus the economic justification for intellectual property lies not in rewarding creators for their labor but in ensuring that they (and other creators) have appropriate incentives to engage in creative activities.

Unfortunately, this approach comes at a cost. Granting authors and inventors the right to exclude others from using their ideas necessarily limits the diffusion of those ideas and so prevents many people from benefiting from them. In economic terms, intellectual property rights prevent competition in the sale of the particular work or invention covered by those rights, and therefore may allow the intellectual property owner to raise the price of that work above the marginal cost of reproducing it. This means that in many cases fewer people will buy the work than if it were distributed on a competitive basis, and they will pay more for the privilege. A fundamental principle of our economic system is the proposition that free market competition will ensure an efficient allocation of resources, absent market failures. In fact, the principal thrust of the antitrust laws serves precisely this goal. In this limited sense, then, intellectual property rights appear to run counter to free market competition: They limit the ability of competitors to copy or otherwise imitate the intellectual efforts of the first person to develop an idea. These rights enable those possessing intellectual property rights to charge monopoly prices or to otherwise limit competition, such as by controlling the use of the intellectual work in subsequent products.

Because intellectual property rights impose social costs on the public, the intellectual property laws can be justified by the public goods argument only to the extent that they do on balance encourage enough creation and dissemination of new works to offset those costs. One of the reasons that intellectual property rights are limited in scope, duration, and effect is precisely in order to balance these costs and benefits. For example, the limited term of intellectual property rights ensures that inventions will be freely available after that fixed term. The key to economic efficiency lies in balancing the social benefit of providing economic incentives for creation and the social costs of limiting the diffusion of knowledge.

COMMENTS AND QUESTIONS

1. Does the conventional incentives justification for intellectual property protection apply equally as well to areas of unfair competition law with intellectual property characteristics, such as the tort of misappropriation or the protection of trade secrets? Does it affect your answer that there is no limit on the term of protection for trade secrets, and that facts, such as news items, may be protected by the tort of misappropriation? Is there any reason to create incentives for the production of trademarks? False advertising law seeks in some sense to incentivize the production of truthful advertising, but is its rationale for doing so the same as intellectual property law's rationale for incentivizing the production of inventions and works of authorship? For an argument that the incentive story should play no part in trademark and unfair competition law, see Mark A. Lemley & Mark P. McKenna, *Owning Mark(et)s*, MICH. L. REV. (forthcoming 2011).

2. Several kinds of intangible commercial assets protected by unfair competition law might also or instead qualify for copyright or patent protection. For example, a method of manufacturing protected by trade secret law could instead receive protection under patent law, provided that the method meets the patent requirements of novelty, non-obviousness, and usefulness. However, if the company seeks to patent the method, it will be required to disclose the method to the public and its property right will be limited in time. The disclosure and the eventual dedication of the method to the public domain at the end of the patent term represents a substantial gain to general welfare. Why should companies be given the option instead of protecting their secret in perpetuity by means of trade secret law?

Two other theories that are sometimes advanced in support of property rights generally — and of intellectual property rights in particular — are derived, respectively, from the writings of John Locke and of Immanuel Kant and Georg W.F. Hegel. Consider how well these theories apply to the law of unfair competition.

3. The Natural Rights Perspective

Starting from the theological premise that, at the beginning of time, God created the world and gave it to human beings to enjoy in common, John Locke in his *Two Treatises on Government* (1698) asked whether the move from this primordial state of nature to a system of private property rights could be justified, consistent with Locke's understanding of natural law. To answer this question, Locke began with what he considered to be the self-evident propositions that "every man has a 'property' in his own 'person'" and that "[t]he 'labour' of his body and the 'work' of his hands . . . are properly his. Whatsoever, then, he removes out of the state that Nature hath provided and left it in, he hath mixed his labor with it, and joined to it something that is his own, and thereby makes it his property. It being by him removed from the common state Nature placed it in, it hath by this labour something annexed to it that excludes the common right of other men. For this 'labour' being the unquestionable property of the labourer, no man but he can have a right to what that is once joined to, at least where there is enough, and as good left in common for others." As Locke understood it, then, human beings by mixing their labor with the commons acquired a property interest in the fruit of their appropriation. In this manner, private property rights were consistent with natural law, as long as the appropriator left in the commons enough and as good for others to appropriate for their own needs, and did not commit waste. To illustrate his thesis, Locke imagined a person gathering apples or acorns for his own future consumption. Someone who takes the apples or acorns from the gatherer in effect appropriates the gatherer's labor without consent and, in doing so, commits a moral wrong.

Locke wrote little specifically about *intellectual* property, which was still in its infancy in his day.[4] For some people today, however — including some who do not necessarily subscribe to Locke's theological starting point — the intuition that the

4. *See* Justin Hughes, Copyright and Incomplete Historiographies: Of Piracy, Propertization, and Thomas Jefferson, 79 S. CAL. L. REV. 993, 1012 (2006) (discussing Locke's proposal of a limited term of copyright protection).

creator of a new invention or work of authorship acquires a moral entitlement to prevent others from free-riding upon the fruit of her (intellectual) labor seems appealing. Scholars have debated whether Locke's theory makes sense on its own terms and, if so, whether the extension of the theory to intellectual property is persuasive. One possible problem is that the intangible products of our minds are (as discussed in the preceding section) unlike real and personal property in that they tend to be nonrivalrous and nonexcludable. Depriving the gatherer of the acorns he was about to eat surely makes him worse off because it prevents the gatherer from consuming them; using his idea for a new way of harvesting acorns, on the other hand, does not deprive him of the use of that idea. For further discussion of the possible applicability of, and problems with, the Lockean paradigm as applied to intellectual property, *see, e.g.*, William W. Fisher III, *Theories of Intellectual Property*, *in* New Essays in the Legal and Political Theory of Property (Stephen Munzer ed., 2001); Wendy J. Gordon, *A Property Right in Self-Expression: Equality and Individualism in the Natural Law of Intellectual Property*, 102 Yale L.J. 1533 (1993).

To the extent, if any, that the Lockean theory is relevant to the law of intellectual property, its most obvious applications would be to the law of patents and copyrights. But the Lockean theory also could have some relevance to at least a few of the unfair competition doctrines discussed in this casebook: for example, the law of trade secrets, the "hot news" doctrine, and the right of publicity could derive some justification by virtue of the labor the owner has invested in developing (respectively) commercially valuable secret information, time-sensitive factual information, or a marketable persona. The Lockean theory is, at any rate, no weaker as applied to these types of subject matter than as applied to patents and copyrights — though whether it is more persuasive than the applicable utilitarian justifications (or persuasive at all, for that matter) remains fodder for debate. The theory would seem to have little if anything to do with some of the other doctrines we discuss in subsequent chapters, however, such as the law of false advertising and of tortious interference with contract.

Does Locke's theory shed any light on the law of trademarks? In particular, what would Locke say to Jessica Litman's argument that most famous trademarks have achieved their fame not simply through the labor of their owners, but also through the labor of their consumers:

> The building of a brand that becomes its own product is a collaborative undertaking; the investment of both dollars and imagination flows both ways. There is no particularly good reason to adopt a rule permitting the producers of the brands to arrogate all of that collaboratively created value to themselves. The icons that embody the persuasive force of those brands, I suggest, should properly be viewed as collectively owned. The public's use of those icons is no more a case of free riding than is Warner Brothers's use of the customer base for Batman-branded products to extract a license fee for Batman's guest appearances on Kellogg's cereal boxes or MCI phone cards.

Jessica Litman, *Breakfast with Batman: The Public Interest in the Advertising Age*, 108 Yale L.J. 1717, 1734 (1999). Surely if Locke considered the working of land and raw materials to be "labor" that justified ownership of the resulting product, he would have considered collective labor toward the creation of a cultural icon to be equally deserving of protection. The proviso poses a problem we will see throughout the course: how to delimit the rights of a creator (for example, of a trade secret or a submitted idea) in the face of claims by consumers, competitors, and other members of the public at large.

4. The Personhood Perspective

Another perspective that may inform some aspects of intellectual property law is sometimes referred to as the "personhood" theory. The theory builds on ideas proposed by the philosophers Kant and Hegel in the late eighteenth and early nineteenth centuries, and to a large extent forms the philosophical basis for much of copyright law in continental Europe. At some risk of oversimplifying, the key idea is that the author or artist invests something "internal" to herself—her unique will or personality, her autonomous self, her individuality—in her creative work. The respect society owes to the autonomous individual in turn entails a degree of respect for the creative work in which that individuality is imprinted. Like other things that are internal to the human actor, however—such as one's religion or sexuality—the author's will or personality morally cannot be commodified; it must be, in some sense, inalienable, even though it comes to be embodied in some external thing such as a manuscript or a canvas.

As the preceding account suggests, the personhood theory's principal application to the law of intellectual property resides in the domain of copyright. *See, e.g.*, Neil Weinstock Netanel, *Copyright Alienability Restrictions and the Enhancement of Author Autonomy: A Normative Evaluation*, 24 RUTGERS L.J. 347 (1993); *compare* Amy Adler, *Against Moral Rights*, 97 CAL. L. REV. 963 (2009). The theory has made only limited inroads in American copyright law, however, most notably in the area of authors' moral rights for qualifying works of visual art. *See, e.g.*, Copyright Act § 106A. The personhood theory's relevance to the law of unfair competition appears to be confined mostly to two subjects. First, although many countries accord authors a moral right of attribution (e.g., to be properly attributed as the author of a work the author created, and not to be attributed as the author of a work the author did not create or that has been distorted in such a way that it no longer reflects the author's vision), U.S. copyright law only grants explicit attribution rights to a limited class of original works of visual art. *See* Copyright Act § 106A(a)(1), (2). Some courts nevertheless have made creative use of the author's copyright right to prepare derivative works, *see id.* § 106(2), and of the Lanham Act's prohibitions on false attributions of origin and false advertising, to craft something like a moral right of attribution in creative works. Whether any such applications of the Lanham Act survive the Supreme Court's 2003 decision in *Dastar Corp. v. Twentieth Century Fox Film Corp.* remains an open question. *See infra* Chapter 9.F. Second, many states grant individuals the right to prevent the unauthorized use of their names, likenesses, and other indicia of identity for purposes of trade. One of the possible justifications for this "right of publicity" is a variation of the personhood rationale. *See infra* Chapter 10.

B. OVERVIEW OF TRADEMARK, UNFAIR COMPETITION, AND BUSINESS TORTS LAW

Trademark law, unfair competition law, and business torts law have traditionally been taught in separate courses, with trademark law typically playing the role of the eccentric cousin in intellectual property survey courses that focus on patent and copyright law, while the various areas of unfair competition law and business torts law are covered in advanced specialty courses, if they are covered at all. Yet contemporary commercial realities increasingly require attorneys to have a thorough and integrated understanding of these areas of law. High-technology and media companies now routinely confront novel and complex issues at the intersection of trade secrets doctrine, the law of ideas, and cybertrespass, while issues in trademark and false advertising law as well as in business torts law are raised throughout the modern economy.

For this reason, our book integrates the various areas of trademark law, unfair competition law, and business torts law in a functional manner. Nonetheless, it is still necessary to devote significant time to mastering each of these distinct areas. Therefore, Part I of this book addresses trademark law in detail. Part II then provides chapter-length treatments of false advertising law, the right of publicity, trade secrets law, legal protection for uncopyrightable facts and ideas, cybertrespass, and business torts.

Before we begin this more detailed study, however, a brief survey of the overall landscape of unfair competition law is in order. The following section sketches the elements of each of the principal areas of law covered in this book.

1. Trademark

Trademarks are protected by federal statute, although the source of constitutional authority is different from that of the Patent and Copyright Acts. Rather than deriving from a specific grant of constitutional power, federal power to regulate trademarks and unfair competition derives from the Commerce Clause of the Constitution, which authorizes Congress to regulate interstate commerce. Unlike patent and copyright protection, trademark law did not evolve from a desire to stimulate particular types of economic activity. Rather, its original purpose was to protect consumers in a world of mass merchandising from unscrupulous sellers attempting to fly under the banner of someone else's well-known logo or identifying symbol. Only in recent years has trademark law begun to embrace the incentive, personhood, and natural rights rationales. The Lanham Act (the federal trademark statute) protects words, symbols, and other attributes that serve to identify the nature and source of goods or services. Examples of marks protectable under the Lanham Act include corporate and product names, symbols, logos, slogans, pictures and designs, product configurations, colors, and even smells. Not all such marks are protectable, however. To receive trademark protection, an identifying mark need not be new or previously unused, but it must represent to consumers the source of the good or service identified. It cannot be merely a description of the good itself or a generic term for the class of goods or services offered. Further, the identifying mark may not be a functional element of the product itself but must serve a purely identifying purpose. Since 1996, famous marks also receive federal protection against "dilution" by blurring or tarnishment. Finally, trademark protection is directly tied to the use of the mark to identify goods in commerce. Trademarks do not expire on any particular date but continue in force until they are "abandoned" by their owner or become unprotectable.

The United States Patent and Trademark Office (PTO) examines trademark applications and issues trademark registrations that confer significant benefits upon the registrants, including prima facie evidence of validity; constructive notice to others of the claim of ownership; federal subject matter jurisdiction; incontestability after five years, which confers exclusive right to use the mark; authorization to seek treble damages and attorney fees; and the right to bar importation of goods bearing the infringing mark. Federal trademark registration, however, is not necessary to obtain trademark protection. A trademark owner who believes that another is using the same or a similar mark to identify competing goods can bring suit for trademark infringement. Infringement turns on whether consumers are likely to be confused as to the origin of the goods or services. If so, the trademark owner is entitled to an injunction against the confusing use, damages for past infringement, and in some cases the seizure and destruction of infringing goods.

2. False Advertising

When a seller makes materially false statements about its own products or services, the common law may afford protection to defrauded buyers under the common law of contracts or fraud. A separate body of false advertising law only began to take root in the early to mid-twentieth century, and at present this body of law takes three principal forms. First, since the 1950s courts have construed §43(a) of the Lanham Act as affording a cause of action not only for trademark infringement but also for false advertising. Consistent with the standard for proving trademark infringement, the Lanham Act (in a departure from early twentieth-century common law) generally requires a plaintiff only to prove prospective harm—that is, a likelihood that the alleged misrepresentation will deceive consumers. Significantly, though, courts have interpreted the Lanham Act as conferring standing only on the defendant's competitors or others with an analogous financial interest; consumers do not have standing to pursue Lanham Act false advertising claims. Second, the Federal Trade Commission Act, as enacted in 1914 and amended in 1938, confers authority upon the Federal Trade Commission (FTC) to investigate and prosecute unfair and deceptive trade practices, including false advertising, that occur in interstate commerce. The FTC's standards for evaluating alleged false advertising differ in some important ways from the standards that courts have developed in the Lanham Act context, though courts sometimes look to FTC policy for guidance in evaluating Lanham Act claims. Third, most states have enacted so-called Little or Baby FTC Acts. Although the particulars of these acts differ from state to state, many of them authorize state officials and consumers to pursue remedies for false advertising and other forms of consumer fraud.

Other types of claims that can be analogized to false advertising include claims for commercial disparagement (materially false statements about a competitor's goods or services, as opposed to about one's own goods or services) and for false attribution of the authorship of creative works. Commercial disparagement claims can be litigated either at common law or, since 1989, under §43(a) of the Lanham Act; the requirements under each body of law differ to some extent. False attribution claims, once viewed as a means for safeguarding authors' "moral rights" to proper attribution, were curtailed by a 2003 U.S. Supreme Court decision, *Dastar Corp. v. Twentieth Century Fox Film Corp.* The question for now is the extent to which some such claims may survive as straightforward false advertising claims.

Finally, because false advertising and related claims involve the regulation of speech, courts sometimes must consider whether the First Amendment guarantees defendants any protections beyond those conferred by common law or statute.

Although the government may ban false commercial speech and may regulate truthful commercial speech (subject to a form of intermediate scrutiny), courts sometimes must consider questions such as whether the speech at issue properly qualifies as "commercial speech," whether broadly worded injunctions against false advertising encroach upon some forms of protected speech, and whether constitutional limits on the law of defamation apply in the context of commercial disparagement.

3. Right of Publicity

Many states confer upon individuals a right to prevent the unauthorized use of their names, likenesses, or other indicia of identity for purposes of trade. Although this body of law originally arose as an aspect of the right of privacy, many states today also recognize publicity rights as a type of property interest that can be assigned or licensed and that can pass to one's heirs. Because there is no federal right of publicity, however, protection can vary significantly, both in scope and duration, from one state to another. And while some fact patterns would appear to involve relatively straightforward violations of the right of publicity (for example, the unauthorized use of a celebrity's name to advertise products), others push the boundaries of what constitutes "indicia of identity" and "purposes of trade." Does the right of publicity forbid the unauthorized use of a soundalike recording of a celebrity's voice in a television commercial, for example, or of an athlete's image on mass market posters or T-shirts? Is there an exception for parodies, or for the inclusion of a real person's name or image in a work of fiction?

At present, no consensus exists as to the philosophical justifications for recognizing publicity rights. Although many would agree that personal privacy interests provide a compelling rationale for preventing a seller from using a private citizen's name or picture to advertise products without that person's consent, once we move beyond this limited context significant differences of opinion emerge. Does the privacy rationale justify extending the right of publicity to persons who seek the limelight (i.e., celebrities)? Does a personhood or autonomy rationale, similar to the rationale that underlies authors' moral rights in some foreign copyright regimes, support a broader application of the right of publicity? Are there compelling instrumental justifications, such as encouraging people to invest in creating memorable personas, in efficiently managing their fame, or in preventing consumer deception? Enforcement of publicity rights also sometimes gives rise to difficult First Amendment problems and, as discussed in a subsequent chapter, problems relating to the scope of federal copyright preemption.

4. Trade Secrets

Trade secret laws are state law doctrines that protect against the misappropriation of certain confidential information. As such, they are more akin to traditional tort and contract law than to patent or copyright law. While protection for trade secrets has long been a part of the common law, most states today protect trade secrets by statute, namely the Uniform Trade Secrets Act. The basic purpose behind protecting trade secrets is to prevent "theft" of information by unfair or commercially unreasonable means. In essence, trade secret law is a form of *private* intellectual property law under which creators establish contractual limitations or build legal "fences" that afford protection from misappropriation.

The definition of subject matter eligible for protection is quite broad: business or technical information of any sort. To benefit from trade secret protection, the information must be a secret. However, only relative and not absolute secrecy is required. In addition, the owner of a trade secret must take reasonable steps to maintain its secrecy. Trade secrets have no definite term of protection but may be protected only as long as they are secret. Once a trade secret is disclosed, protection is lost.

There is no state agency in charge of "issuing" (or even registering) secrets. Rather, any information that meets the above criteria can be protected. Courts will find misappropriation of trade secrets in two circumstances: where the secrets were obtained by theft or other improper means, or where they were used or disclosed by the defendant in violation of a confidential relationship. However, trade secret laws do not protect against independent discovery or invention. Nor do they prevent competitors from "reverse engineering" a legally obtained product in order to determine the secrets contained inside. Violations of trade secret law entitle the owner to damages and in some cases injunctions against use or further disclosure—though in some rare instances, the First Amendment may limit courts' abilities to enjoin the publication of alleged trade secret information. There also are, from time to time, criminal prosecutions for trade secret misappropriation, mostly under the federal Economic Espionage Act.

5. Legal Protection for Uncopyrightable Facts and Ideas

Federal copyright law confers protection on an author's original expression, selection, or arrangement of facts and ideas, but not on the facts or ideas themselves; for copyright purposes, facts and ideas are viewed as fundamental building blocks to which other authors must have access to create their own original works. Nevertheless, in some instances a person who has invested substantial resources in gathering factual material, or who has confidentially disclosed her original idea to another, may invoke various legal protections against the unauthorized use of such facts and ideas. In 1918, the Supreme Court affirmed the Associated Press's common law right to prevent a rival news organization from misappropriating facts gathered by the AP until the value of those facts as news had dissipated. Decades later, organizations including the AP, the National Basketball Association, and various financial service firms have continued to invoke this so-called "hot news" doctrine against new forms of content distribution, with mixed results. Alternatively, publishers sometimes invoke contract law to limit unauthorized dissemination; in recent years, controversies have centered on issues such as whether mass market license terms contained inside a package of software or at the bottom of a Web page are enforceable. Analogously, people who claim to have developed new ideas for subject matter such as movies or tv shows, toys, or theme parks, and to have confidentially disclosed those ideas to others in an effort to market them, sometimes invoke common law and contract doctrine in an effort to prevent unauthorized or uncompensated use. As with efforts to protect uncopyrightable facts, efforts to protect uncopyrightable ideas raise difficult questions such as whether the principal purpose of unfair competition law should be to promote fairness or economic efficiency; whether fairness or economic efficiency requires more or less protection for content providers in a given setting; and to what extent freedom of speech and principles of copyright preemption should limit content providers' ability to invoke common law protections for uncopyrightable facts and ideas.

6. Cybertrespass

In some instances, new technologies have breathed life into the arcane law of personal property. In recent years, plaintiffs have invoked the venerable doctrine of trespass to chattels in cases involving the unauthorized interference with computer systems and Web sites, with mixed results. In other instances, plaintiffs have looked to the common law of conversion to seek redress for more substantial interferences with intangible property such as domain names. Whether the heralded flexibility of the common law makes these doctrines good candidates for adaptation to the needs of a new technological era, or whether more targeted statutory responses would be preferable, remains a lively topic of debate.

7. Business Torts

Related to all of the above doctrines — and often pleaded in the alternative in cases involving these doctrines — are the common law doctrines of tortious interference with contract and with prospective business advantage, and the more recently invented cause of action for violation of the federal Racketeer Influenced and Corrupt Organizations (RICO) Act. The interference torts aim to discourage others from interfering with existing contractual relations between two parties or, sometimes, with future contractual or business relations between those parties. As such, and absent further delimiting principles, these torts might seem to stand in tension with some aspects of standard contract doctrine (which, for example, limits contract damages to those foreseeable at the time of contract and, in the opinion of some scholars, encourages "efficient breaches"), and with the tenets of a competitive economy (under which one firm generally is free to "steal" customers from another by offering a better deal). As with many of the other doctrines discussed throughout this book, the interference torts pose difficult questions about the competing roles of fairness and economic efficiency in regulating business behavior. Analogously, the civil RICO statute expands the confines of the common law of fraud by offering plaintiffs the prospect of treble damages for injuries suffered as a consequence of a "pattern" of fraudulent activity. In a series of cases since the early 1980s, the Supreme Court has expounded on the meaning of some (but not all) of the ambiguous terms of this federal statute, which today is pleaded in many complex commercial disputes.

PROBLEMS

Problem 1-1. VerdaPaco (VP) is a nonprofit, tax-exempt organization "that uses peaceful direct action and creative communication to expose global environmental problems and to promote solutions that are essential to a green and peaceful future." People who support VP's mission can become members of the organization by making contributions in any amount. At present, VP has about 200,000 members in the United States and many more worldwide. Bombono Inc. (Bombono) is a multinational corporation, headquartered in New Jersey, that makes and distributes various food products, including the popular SnikSnak brand of chocolate candy bar. One of the ingredients Bombono uses to make SnikSnak bars is palm oil, which makes up about 5 percent of a bar by both weight and volume.

In 2010, VP began investigating rumors that Bombono was buying some of the palm oil it uses for SnikSnak bars from Gummo S.A. (Gummo). Gummo is a company headquartered in the nation of Fredonia, and since 1990 Gummo has cleared about 15 percent of the Fredonian rain forest to establish and maintain the palm plantations from which Gummo derives palm oil. On March 1, 2011, VP called a press conference at its office in Washington, D.C., to announce the nationwide publication of a VP report detailing the results of its year-long investigation of Bombono. According to the report, from 2005 through at least the end of 2010 Bombono purchased some of its palm oil from Gummo. As a result, the report states, Bombono "has contributed to the destruction of the Fredonian rain forest, potentially exacerbated global warming, and endangered the orangutan population that is native to Fredonia." That same day, VP posted a video on YouTube. The video begins with a mock SnikSnak commercial showing an office worker opening a SnikSnak candy wrapper and snacking on (what is identified to be) a bloody orangutan finger. The video ends with an announcer stating "We need to save the orangutans, the rain forests they inhabit, and the world we all inhabit. Donate today and become a member of VerdaPaco. We're on the web at http://www.vp.org." Assume (1) that by clearing 15 percent of the Fredonian rain forest, Gummo has indeed endangered the orangutan population that is native to Fredonia; and (2) that most climate scientists would agree that Gummo's clearing of 15 percent of the Fredonian rain forest likely has exacerbated global warming, though to what degree is difficult to quantify.

Bombono learned about the YouTube video a day after it was posted and asked YouTube to take it down, citing copyright and trademark infringement. YouTube complied, but the video has continued to spread on the Web on many other sites. It is estimated that, as of April 30, 2011, over 1 million people worldwide (several hundred thousand in the United States alone) have viewed the video. During this same time period (March 1-April 30), worldwide donations to VP exceeded worldwide donations to VP for all of 2010. Meanwhile, Bombono's sales of SnikSnak bars are 50 percent lower (both in terms of quantity of bars sold, and revenue derived from sales) than they were from January 1 to February 28, 2011. If the current sales pace continues through the rest of this year, 2011 will be the worst year for sales of SnikSnak bars since 1978. In addition, U.S. Olympic gold medalist Fawn Lindsay pulled out of negotiations to appear in a series of television and print advertisements for SnikSnak bars.

In response, Bombono commenced a public relations campaign to refute VP's claims. In particular, in early May 2011, Bombono took out full-page ads in the *New York Times*, *Wall Street Journal*, and other national newspapers asserting the following: (1) as of January 1, 2011, Bombono ceased buying palm oil from Gummo; (2) from 2005 to 10, Gummo supplied only 1.25 percent of the palm oil Bombono used, and this amount constituted only about 0.5 percent of Gummo's output of palm oil during those years; and (3) Bombono is working toward buying only "environmentally sustainable" palm oil and is pressuring its current suppliers to "scrutinize their supply chains." These three assertions are all literally true. It is, however, *possible* that some of the 50 or so worldwide suppliers that Bombono currently uses to obtain ingredients for SnikSnak bars are obtaining a portion of the palm oil they sell to Bombono from Gummo.

a) Based on the overview presented in this chapter, do you think that Bombono should have a viable claim for trademark infringement or dilution? VP's report and video, after all, refer to SnikSnak bars by name. Are consumers likely to believe that the producer of SnikSnak bars is also the source or sponsor of the report or the YouTube video? Are the report and the video likely to tarnish the goodwill associated with the SnikSnak trademark? Even if so, how would you reconcile Bombono's interest in its trademark with VP's interest in engaging in a form of political speech?
b) Alternatively, do you think Bombono should have a viable claim for commercial disparagement? Won't people realize that the bloody orangutan finger is just an exaggeration? Should courts consider Bombono to be a "public figure" subject to a heightened burden of proof, as in defamation cases?
c) Should the law provide Bombono with a remedy for the loss of the Fawn Lindsay endorsement? How certain should it be that Lindsay was going to agree to endorse SnikSnak bars? Should it matter whether VP was aware of the contract negotiations between Lindsay and Bombono?
d) Do you think VP should be allowed to assert a claim against Bombono for false advertising, based on Bombono's responsive ad campaign? Bombono's ad is literally true, after all, though it omits some possibly relevant information. What would be the costs and benefits of imposing liability under these circumstances? Is the ad more in the nature of commercial speech or political speech, and why might this be relevant?

Problem 1-2. Early in 2009, Ty Inc. (the maker of Beanie Baby and Ty Girlz dolls) publicly announced plans to market two new 12-inch-tall dolls under the names "Sweet Sasha" and "Marvelous Malia." The dolls did not closely resemble President Obama's daughters Sasha and Malia (ages seven and ten, respectively, at the time), in terms of their physical features. Some commentators nevertheless expressed the opinion that the dolls were inspired by (and would evoke in the minds of many consumers) Sasha and Malia Obama for several reasons, including the similarity of the dolls' names to the Obama daughters' names; the fact that dolls depict two female children, one of whom (though of indeterminate fictional age) appears to be slightly older than the other; the fact that the dolls were the first African-American dolls Ty had included in its 30-doll line of Ty Girlz dolls; and the fact that Ty publicly announced the new dolls within a week of President Obama's inauguration. In February 2009, Ty announced that it was changing the names of the dolls to "Sweet Sydney" and "Marvelous Mariah."

a) Based on the overview presented above, and assuming that Ty had not changed the names of the dolls, do you think the Obama children (or their parents) would have had a viable claim for violation of the children's right of publicity? Should it matter that the children are (arguably) public figures? Should it matter that Ty probably had a valid copyright in the design of the dolls? What about the fact Ty planned to use only the first names "Sasha" and "Malia" and not "Sasha and Malia Obama"?

Alternatively, given that the children are widely known to the general public, do you think that marketing the dolls under the names "Sweet Sasha" and "Marvelous Malia" would have conveyed a false message that the children or their parents endorsed or approved of the dolls? Should a famous person's name be considered a sort of trademark? Would the marketing of the dolls under these circumstances constitute false advertising? On the other hand, even if consumers did draw the incorrect impression that the Obama family endorsed the dolls, would this impression be likely to affect consumers' purchasing decisions?

b) Suppose that Mattel, a rival toy manufacturer, had already begun marketing a line of Sasha and Malia Obama dolls when Ty announced its own marketing plans. Would a decision by Ty to go ahead with its plans infringe any trademark rights belonging to Mattel? Should Mattel be allowed to assert trademark rights in the names Sasha and Malia Obama for a line of dolls if Mattel is the first in the marketplace with such a product? Would it make sense to afford Mattel with trademark rights in the appearance of the dolls themselves?

c) Suppose that Elmer, an employee of Mattel, first came up with the idea of a line of Sasha and Malia Obama dolls, but then instead of disclosing it to Mattel he disclosed it to Mattel's rival, Ty. Does Elmer owe Mattel a duty of loyalty and secrecy as long as he is employed by Mattel? What if Elmer only disclosed the idea to Ty after accepting a job offer from, and beginning employment with, Ty? Should it matter whether Elmer improved upon the basic idea after beginning work for Ty? Should it matter whether Elmer had signed a noncompete agreement while employed by Mattel? Should Elmer be enjoined from going to work for Ty even in the absence of an enforceable noncompete, based only on the probability of his using or disclosing Mattel trade secrets in his new job, or is such a restriction on employee mobility bad public policy?

Alternatively, suppose that Elmer's friend Marie was the originator of the idea for the dolls, and that she disclosed the idea to Elmer in confidence. Should Mattel be free to use the idea without compensating Marie? How original is the idea, and should that matter?

Problem 1-3. Cotco Inc. develops and licenses certain software programs to thousands of customers throughout the world. Cotco's license agreements with its customers "prohibit access to, or use of, any portion of the software not expressly licensed and paid for by the licensee, and any sublicense, disclosure, use, rent, or lease of the software to third parties." Cotco also makes much of its software available to its licensees through its Customer Connection Web site. The Web site's terms of use state that "the information contained in the Materials [on Customer Connection] is the confidential proprietary information of Cotco. You may not use, disclose, reproduce, transmit, or otherwise copy in any form or by any means the information contained in the Materials for any purpose, other than to support your authorized use of the Cotco Programs for which you hold a supported license from Cotco." Licensees access the Customer Connection Web site via their personal usernames and passwords. After logging in, licensees sometimes search the Customer Connection Web site for solutions to specific problems. When doing so, the Web site asks them "to click on a button after each search to indicate whether or not a particular search result helped solve the customer's problem. If the customer selects the 'No, continue search' option, the support system responds by offering the customer further options." Cotco compiles this data to assess whether its system helped customers resolve their support issues.

According to Cotco, in August 2010, Cotco discovered "huge, unexplained spikes in the number of customers on the online support website who had clicked the 'No, continue search' option." These clicks numbered in the thousands for several customers, and Cotco discovered that each response occurred in a matter of seconds. Cotco's experts believe that these click patterns showed that the users had employed an automated process to move rapidly through the entire library of Software and Support Materials on the Customer Connection Web site.

Cotco alleges further that its investigation has turned up evidence of a pattern under which Cotco licensees who had decided to switch their allegiance to TFC (a rival software developer) permitted TFC, during the last month or so of the licensee's contract with Cotco, to use the licensee's password to obtain software and support materials from the Customer Connection Web site. Specifically, "in the month before a customer's Cotco support expired, a user purporting to be that customer, employing the customer's log-in credentials, would access Cotco's system and download large quantities of Software and Support Materials, including dozens, hundreds, or thousands of products beyond the scope of the specific customer's licensed products and permitted access."

Cotco believes that the information allegedly accessed by TFC constitutes Cotco's trade secrets. Can the software and support materials at issue really be viewed as "secret," given the large number of Cotco customers who have valid access to this information? If so, should Cotco be allowed to pursue a trade secret misappropriation claim against its defecting customers as well as against TFC? In particular, should the defecting customers be bound by the confidentiality provision found in the Web site's terms of use — and if so, has TFC committed a separate tort by inducing the defecting customers to breach their confidentiality agreements or to forgo future business relations with Cotco? Could Cotco allege a trespass or conversion of its physical property (e.g., its computer system)?

What if instead Cotco was an investment adviser providing clients with confidential stock tips? Can this sort of information be a trade secret? Should courts invoke the "hot news" doctrine to preserve Cotco's incentive to provide time-sensitive, labor-intensive, but arguably non-copyrightable information? If so, how long should that protection last?

Part I

TRADEMARK LAW

2 Introduction

A. BACKGROUND

Trademarks have existed for almost as long as trade itself. Once human economies progressed to the point where a merchant class specialized in making goods for others, the people who made and sold clothing or pottery began to "mark" their wares with a word or symbol to identify the maker. Such marks — often no more than the name of the maker — have been discovered on goods from China, India, Persia, Egypt, Rome, Greece, and elsewhere, and date back as much as 4,000 years.[1]

These early marks served several purposes. First, they were a form of advertising, allowing makers to get their name in front of potential customers. Second, they may have been used to prove that the goods were sold by a particular merchant, thus helping to resolve ownership disputes. Third, the marks served as a guarantee of quality, since a merchant who identifies herself with her goods puts her reputation on the line.

These functions coalesced in modern practice, where trademarks are widely viewed as devices that help to reduce information and transaction costs by allowing customers to estimate the nature and quality of goods before purchase.

Even the earliest trademark law cases reflect an awareness of the need to provide a legal remedy against counterfeiting.[2] Under English common law, a party who used a trademark was entitled to prevent subsequent use of the same mark by others selling the same types of goods. *See, e.g.*, Sykes v. Sykes, 107 Eng. Rep. 834 (1824).

1. *See, e.g.*, William H. Browne, A Treatise on the Law of Trademarks 1-14 (1885) (tracing the history of trademarks).

2. *See* Frank Schechter, The Historical Foundations of the Law Relating to Trademarks (1925) (reviewing medieval origins of modern trademark law).

In the United States, statutory trademark law appeared late on the scene, particularly given the early legislative interest in patents and copyrights.[3] This was no doubt a function of the low volume of trade in finished goods early in the history of the Republic. As Lawrence Friedman has written,

> [T]rademark law . . . was relatively undeveloped in [the early-nineteenth century]. No trademark infringement case was decided in the United States before 1825. Joseph Story granted the first injunction for trademark infringement, in 1844, to protect the makers of "Taylor's Persian Thread." Congress provided neither guidance nor any machinery for registration. Legal protection for designers of trademarks had to be forged in the rough mills of the courts. The economy was still deeply rooted in land and its produce. Intellectual property, despite the name, was not valued for intellectual reasons at all, but because of mercantile and industrial applications. As such, this property was not a central concern of the law until the full-blown factory age.

LAWRENCE FRIEDMAN, A HISTORY OF AMERICAN LAW 257 (2d ed. 1985).

As Kenneth J. Vandevelde points out in *The New Property of the Nineteenth Century: The Development of the Modern Concept of Property*, 29 BUFFALO L. REV. 325, 341 (1980), trademarks in the eighteenth century were protected only by the common law of fraud. Beginning with Millington v. Fox, 3 My. & Cr. 338, 40 Eng. Rep. 956 (Ch. 1838), where a tradesman was permanently enjoined from using another's mark, dicta began to appear suggesting that marks were a form of property. Further support for the notion that trademark law served primarily to prevent consumer fraud can be found in Mira Wilkins, *The Neglected Intangible Asset: The Influence of the Trademark on the Rise of the Modern Corporation*, 34 BUS. & HIST. 66, 72 (1992), where the author writes: "[I]n the American colonies laws passed to maintain the quality of manufactured articles came to form the basis of the country's subsequent trademark legislation. . . . [B]ut not until the late 1840s was the first state law passed to 'prevent fraud in the use of false stamps and labels.' . . ."

Trademarks were protected at common law in the United States until 1870, when Congress enacted the first federal trademark statute. That statute, which grounded protection for trademark rights in the Patent and Copyright Clause of the Constitution, was struck down by the Supreme Court as beyond the powers of Congress. The Court reasoned that the Patent and Copyright Clause of the Constitution could not support the statute, since it protected all marks regardless of any novelty or originality. *Trade-Mark Cases*, 100 U.S. 82, 94 (1879). Congress reenacted limited federal trademark protection in the Act of 1881, this time basing the statute in the Commerce Clause. The trademark statute was significantly modified in the Act of 1905 and further changed by subsequent amendment in 1920. Today, trademarks are protected by the Lanham Act, 15 U.S.C. §§ 1051 et seq., which was enacted in 1946.

With few exceptions, the history of these statutory changes has been one of expansion of the rights of trademark owners. The Act of 1905 eliminated the requirements of identity and intention to deceive, substituting instead the more fluid test of likelihood of confusion. The Lanham Act further liberalized trademark law

3. By contrast, one commentator has traced the earliest common law American trademark decision as far back as 1584, to the decision in *Sandforth's Case. See* Keith M. Stolte, How Early Did Anglo-American Trademark Law Begin? An Answer to Schechter's Conundrum, 8 FORDHAM INTELL. PROP. MEDIA & ENT. L.J. 505 (1993).

by providing advantages to registration of trademarks and introducing a separate statutory prohibition against "unfair methods of competition" that afforded protection even to unregistered marks. 15 U.S.C. § 1125(a) (also referred to as Section 43(a) of the Lanham Act, following the original Act's sections). The result is that a broad class of "marks" now qualifies for Lanham Act protection.

Traditionally, there has been nothing in trademark law analogous to the desire to encourage invention or creation that underlies (at least in part) patent and copyright law. There is no explicit federal policy to encourage the creation of more trademarks.[4] Rather, the fundamental principles of trademark law have essentially been ones of tort: unfair competition and the tort of deception of the consumer.[5] *See* Mark McKenna, *The Normative Foundations of Trademark Law*, 82 NOTRE DAME L. REV. 1839 (2007). In this sense, trademarks may not be thought of as analogous to "property rights" at all. *See, e.g.*, Hanover Star Milling Co. v. Metcalf, 240 U.S. 403 (1916), and cases cited therein. Rather, they are rights acquired with the use of a trademark in commerce, and they continue only so long as that use continues.[6] In trademark parlance, the senior (that is, first) user of a mark may prevent junior (subsequent) users from employing the same or a similar mark, where there is a "likelihood of confusion" between the two marks.

Early trademark cases (and statutes) took a restrictive view of these rights. Trademark infringement originally was limited to the use of a name or mark identical to the trademark in the sale of identical goods, where the infringer's use was intended to deceive consumers. These cases were essentially an extension of common law misrepresentation principles. Normally, if retailer *R* misrepresents to buyer *B* that *R*'s goods are made by manufacturer *M*, then buyer *B* has a cause of action for misrepresentation against *R*. This would void any contract between *R* and *B*. *M* might also have a common law cause of action against *R*, but the *consumer's* interests can be directly protected at common law only through the misrepresentation cause of action.

One reading of these old common law unfair competition cases is that they conflated *B*'s and *M*'s discrete harms into a single cause of action. They in some sense allowed *M* to stand in *B*'s shoes and sue *R* for misrepresentation.

One way to analyze this "propertization" trend is to say that it vested rights in competitors in order to increase the likelihood that these causes of action would be brought in the first place. Individual consumers are isolated, and each generally purchases only a few of a given trademarked item. If we also consider the United States' elaborate system of interstate transportation, an individual consumer has very little

4. Some commentators discern in federal trademark law a purpose to promote interbrand competition by strengthening brands, thereby providing information to consumers and potential competitors. *See* William P. Kratzke, *Normative Economic Analysis of Trademark Law*, 21 MEMPHIS ST. U. L. REV. 199, 212-19 (1991). To the extent that this is true, trademarks may be thought of as comporting with federal competition policy, as embodied in the antitrust laws and elsewhere. *See* Continental T.V., Inc. v. GTE Sylvania, 433 U.S. 36 (1977) (policy of the antitrust laws is to promote brand strength in order to promote interbrand competition).

Further, many commentators believe that recent decisions are moving the Court in the direction of an incentive-based theory of trademark law. We discuss this trend *infra*.

5. These are two very different interests held by different parties, both protected by a trademark granted to one of the parties. This combination of producer and consumer interests in trademark protection is significant, and we return to it later in this chapter.

6. The Trademark Law Revision Act of 1988 changed this general principle in an important respect. Under that Act, it is now possible to register and protect a trademark based on an *intention* to use that mark in commerce at some time within the next three years. 15 U.S.C. § 1051(b) (1988). But the right remains inchoate until use actually occurs.

incentive to police trademark infringements. The difficulty of forming a class for purposes of class action remedies is simply too great.

Competitors — *M* in the story here — have a much greater incentive to police misuse of their marks. In this view, the legitimate trademark user's lower transaction costs in policing the mark are harnessed to the original, fundamental consumer protection rationale to obtain the modern trademark infringement suit. Trademark "ownership," in this view, essentially begins as something like a legal fiction that gives the trademark owner a cause of action he would not otherwise have, in order to benefit consumers and the competitive process.

Giving the originator of a mark the right to police counterfeiting also serves to protect three types of investment: (1) investment in the creation of the mark; (2) investment in advertising and promoting the product in association with the mark; and (3) product-related investments such as high-quality raw materials, production equipment, and quality assurance techniques.

B. A BRIEF OVERVIEW OF TRADEMARK THEORY

In the *Trade-Mark Cases*, 100 U.S. 82 (1879), the Supreme Court compared trademarks (often written at the time as "trade-marks" or "trade marks," as in British English to this day) to the two other most significant forms of intellectual property, copyrights and patents. The Court's comparison deserves to be quoted at length. While much of what the Court says about the acquisition of rights in unregistered trademarks has not changed, consider whether what Justice Miller wrote in 1879 about the development of brand names themselves is still accurate:

> The ordinary trade-mark has no necessary relation to invention or discovery. The trade-mark recognized by the common law is generally the growth of a considerable period of use, rather than a sudden invention. It is often the result of accident rather than design, and when under the act of Congress it is sought to establish it by registration, neither originality, invention, discovery, science, nor art is in any way essential to the right conferred by that act. If we should endeavor to classify it under the head of writings of authors, the objections are equally strong. In this, as in regard to inventions, originality is required. And while the word writings may be liberally construed, as it has been, to include original designs for engravings, prints, &c., it is only such as are original, and are founded in the creative powers of the mind. The writings which are to be protected are the fruits of intellectual labor, embodied in the form of books, prints, engravings, and the like. The trade-mark may be, and generally is, the adoption of something already in existence as the distinctive symbol of the party using it. At common law the exclusive right to it grows out of its use, and not its mere adoption. By the act of Congress this exclusive right attaches upon registration. But in neither case does it depend upon novelty, invention, discovery, or any work of the brain. It requires no fancy of imagination, no genius, no laborious thought. It is simply founded on priority of appropriation.

Id. at 94.

By 1942, the Court was describing trademarks and the role of trademark law in different terms. In Mishawaka Rubber & Woolen Mfg. Co. v. S.S. Kresge Co., 316 U.S. 203 (1942), Justice Frankfurter explained:

> The protection of trade-marks is the law's recognition of the psychological function of symbols. If it is true that we live by symbols, it is no less true that we purchase goods by them. A trade-mark is a merchandising short-cut which induces a purchaser to select what he wants, or what he has been led to believe he wants. The owner of a mark exploits this human propensity by making every effort to impregnate the atmosphere of the market with the drawing power of a congenial symbol. Whatever the means employed, the aim is the same — to convey through the mark, in the minds of potential customers, the desirability of the commodity upon which it appears. Once this is attained, the trade-mark owner has something of value. If another poaches upon the commercial magnetism of the symbol he has created, the owner can obtain legal redress.

Id. at 205.

By the 1980s, American courts were describing trademarks and trademark law in yet different terms, terms which still resonate today. Reflecting the rise of the Chicago School economic analysis of law, Judge Easterbrook described the economic benefits of trademarks and trademark protection in Scandia Down Corp. v. Euroquilt, Inc., 772 F.2d. 1423 (7th Cir. 1985):

> Trademarks help consumers to select goods. By identifying the source of the goods, they convey valuable information to consumers at lower costs. Easily identified trademarks reduce the costs consumers incur in searching for what they desire, and the lower the costs of search the more competitive the market. A trademark also may induce the supplier of goods to make higher quality products and to adhere to a consistent level of quality. The trademark is a valuable asset, part of the "goodwill" of a business. If the seller provides an inconsistent level of quality, or reduces quality below what consumers expect from earlier experience, that reduces the value of the trademark. The value of a trademark is in a sense a "hostage" of consumers; if the seller disappoints the consumers, they respond by devaluing the trademark. The existence of this hostage gives the seller another incentive to afford consumers the quality of goods they prefer and expect.

Id. at 1429-30.

Which description of trademarks most accurately reflects their characteristics in the present day? Are they often adopted as "the result of accident rather than design"? Can we say of the development of trademarks, as of the legal conditions leading to their protection, that "no fancy of imagination, no genius, no laborious thought" is required? Or is it rather that, through the development of a brand name, "[t]he owner of a mark . . . mak[es] every effort to impregnate the atmosphere of the market with the drawing power of a congenial symbol"? Is the consumer in some sense a victim of these machinations of the trademark owner, who through the "commercial magnetism" of the trademark "induces the purchaser to select what he wants, or what he has been led to believe he wants"? Or is it finally not consumers who are victims of the trademark, but the trademark who is a "hostage" of consumers, whom it serves by enabling them to find what they desire and to insist on "the quality of goods they prefer and expect"?

Of course, these differing accounts of the trademark and trademark law are probably all more or less true, depending on the trademark, product, and consumer at issue.

But it is well accepted that the last account, based on the economic analysis of law, is currently by far the dominant account of trademark law. In Qualitex Co. v. Jacobson Products Co., Inc., 514 U.S. 159 (U.S. 1995), Justice Breyer cited, among other sources, William Landes & Richard Posner, *The Economics of Trademark Law*, 78 TRADEMARK REP. 267, 271-72 (1988), in support of the following statement of the purposes of trademark law:

> [T]rademark law, by preventing others from copying a source-identifying mark, reduces the customer's costs of shopping and making purchasing decisions, for it quickly and easily assures a potential customer that this item—the item with this mark—is made by the same producer as other similarly marked items that he or she liked (or disliked) in the past. At the same time, the law helps assure a producer that it (and not an imitating competitor) will reap the financial, reputation-related rewards associated with a desirable product. The law thereby encourages the production of quality products, and simultaneously discourages those who hope to sell inferior products by capitalizing on a consumer's inability quickly to evaluate the quality of an item offered for sale.

Id. at 163-64 (citations omitted).

The orthodox view of trademarks, then, is that they (1) minimize consumer search costs, and (2) provide incentives to producers to produce consistent levels of product quality. This latter benefit of trademarks is especially important for certain types of products. In general, products may be understood to possess three types of characteristics: "search" characteristics, such as color or price, which can be inspected prior to purchase; "experience" characteristics, such as taste, which can only be verified through use of the product; and "credence" characteristics, such as durability, which can only be confirmed over time. *See* Phillip Nelson, *Advertising as Information*, 82 J. POL. ECON. 729 (1974). For products such as medicine, automobiles, or high-technology goods, the readily apparent "search" characteristics of which say little about the quality of the product, consumers may rely heavily on the trademark attached to the product in making their purchasing decision. It follows that in a market without reliable source-identification for such products, producers would have little incentive to invest in the production of products of high quality. This is because they would likely be undercut by competitors who would offer cheaper products of lower quality. *See* George A. Ackerlof, *The Market for "Lemons": Quality Uncertainty and the Market Mechanism*, 84 Q.J. ECON. 488 (1970). *See also* Peter S. Menell & Suzanne Scotchmer, *Intellectual Property Law, in* 2 HANDBOOK OF LAW AND ECONOMICS 1473 (A. Mitchell Polinsky & Steven Shavell eds., 2007) (reviewing the economic rationale for trademark protection).

As indications of quality, trademarks signify and allow firms to develop commercial *goodwill*. This concept encompasses the reputation of the firm and its products and the probability, based on this reputation, that consumers will continue to patronize the firm in the future. A nineteenth-century court described goodwill in these terms:

> When an individual or a firm or a corporation has gone on for an unbroken series of years conducting a particular business, and has been so scrupulous in fulfilling every obligation, so careful in maintaining the standard of goods dealt in, so absolutely honest and fair in all business dealings that customers of the concern have become convinced that their experience in the future will be as satisfactory as it has been in the past, while such customers' good report of their own experience tends continually to bring new customers

> to the same concern, there has been produced an element of value quite as important — in some cases, perhaps far more important — than the plant or machinery with which the business is carried on.

Washburn v. National Wall-Paper Co., 81 F. 17, 20 (2d Cir. 1897). Indeed, for many firms, particularly consumer products firms, their brand may be by far their most valuable asset. The story is often told of the Coca-Cola lawyer who spoke of the value of the company's goodwill as symbolized by its brand: "The production plants and inventories of The Coca-Cola Company could go up in flames overnight. Yet, on the following morning there is not a bank in Atlanta, New York, or anywhere else, that would not lend this Company the funds necessary for rebuilding, accepting as security only the inherent good will in its trademarks 'Coca-Cola' and 'Coke.' "[7] The lawyer was not exaggerating. In 2009, Interbrand estimated the value of the Coca-Cola brand to be $68.7 billion (as against a tangible asset base of approximately $6 billion).[8] *See also* Jerre B. Swann & Theodore H. Davis, Jr., *Dilution, An Idea Whose Time Has Gone: Brand Equity as Protectable Property, The New/Old Paradigm*, 1 J. Intell. Prop. L. 219, 229 (1994) (documenting key role played by famous trademarks — Nabisco, Winston, Miracle Whip, Burger King — in raising acquisition prices up to five times book value in various corporate mergers).

Yet the example of Coca-Cola and brands like it may lead many readers to doubt the sufficiency of the economic account of trademark law, focused as it is on search costs and incentives to produce quality goods. After all, many trademarks, such as Coke, do more than merely indicate the source of the goods to which they are affixed, and strictly speaking, some trademarks don't even do that. A T-shirt bearing the trademark "Arsenal" is not intended to indicate and is not read by consumers to indicate that Arsenal soccer players knitted the shirt themselves. The trademark primarily functions instead as a "badge of support for or loyalty or affiliation to the trademark proprietor." Arsenal Football Club plc v. Matthew Reed, Case C-206/01, [2003] ETMR 19, ¶15. This same function may be attributed to many trademarks, and not simply to high-fashion marks such as Polo or Prada, but also to more mundane marks such as Pepsi or Ford, whose owners have quite consciously sought to build "consumption communities"[9] around these brands. *See* Int'l Order of Job's Daughters v. Lindeburg & Co., 633 F.2d 912, 918 (9th Cir. 1980) (recognizing that "[w]e commonly identify ourselves by displaying emblems expressing allegiances. Our jewelry, clothing, and cars are emblazoned with inscriptions showing the organizations we belong to, the schools we attend, the landmarks we have visited, the sports teams we support, the beverages we imbibe"). In such situations, the mark itself is often the primary product characteristic the consumer wishes to acquire, and the underlying material good, if any, is merely a means of conveying that characteristic.[10]

Even when the consumer is interested in the quality of the material good, the trademark may contribute to deleterious "artificial product differentiation," as when consumers pay a premium for branded versions of pharmaceuticals when lower-cost generic versions are required by government regulation to meet exactly the same

7. Quoted in Thomas D. Drescher, *The Transformation and Evolution of Trademarks — From Signals to Symbols to Myth*, 82 Trademark Rep. 301, 301-02 (1992).

8. *See* Interbrand, Best Global Brands 2009 (2009).

9. Daniel J. Boorstin, Americans: The Democratic Experience 145 (1974).

10. For further discussion of the trademark "merchandising right," see Stacey L. Dogan & Mark A. Lemley, *The Merchandising Right: Fragile Theory or Fait Accompli?*, 54 Emory L.J. 461 (2005).

quality standards as the more expensive branded versions. This argument, which associates trademarks with the purported evils of some forms of advertising, first gained significant influence with the publication in 1933 of the economist Edward Chamberlin's book *The Theory of Monopolistic Competition*, which systematically formulated the artificial product differentiation view.[11] Chamberlin's work proved to be especially influential in mid-twentieth-century trademark commentary[12] and is reflected to some degree in Justice Frankfurter's discussion of trademarks in *Mishawaka Rubber*. Other courts sometimes picked up on Chamberlin's ideas. *See, e.g.*, Smith v. Chanel, Inc., 402 F.2d 562, 567 (2d Cir. 1968) (proposing that, through the trademark, "economically irrational elements are introduced into consumer choices; and the trademark owner is insulated from the normal pressures of price and quality competition. In consequence the competitive system fails to perform its function of allocating available resources efficiently.")

Starting in the 1960s and 1970s, however, economists have viewed trademarks and advertising in a much more positive light. *See* George Stigler, *The Economics of Information*, 69 J. POL. ECON. 213 (1961). The consensus view now is that advertising cheaply conveys information to consumers. *See* Phillip Nelson, *Advertising as Information*, 82 J. POL. ECON. 729 (1974). *Cf.* Thomas T. Nagle, *Do Advertising-Profitability Studies Really Show That Advertising Creates a Barrier to Entry?*, 24 J.L. & ECON. 333 (1981) (brand loyalty demonstrates the costliness of information; advertising and brand promotion lower these costs somewhat).

Since consumers cannot easily verify advertising about these aspects of a product, economists wondered why advertisers spend so much money on such advertising. They have come to believe that it serves a "signaling function." Jack Hirshleifer, *Where Are We in the Theory of Information?*, 63 AM. ECON. REV. 31, 35-38 (1973) (interpreting work of Nelson, *supra*); Paul Milgrom & John Roberts, *Price and Advertising Signals of Product Quality*, 94 J. POL. ECON. 796 (1986). That is, "[t]he primary information content of advertisements for experience goods is the information that the brand advertises." Nelson, *supra*, at 745. The idea is that advertising pays only when consumers become repeat purchasers; consumers know this about advertising; hence advertising signals a product that the producer believes will attract repeat buyers. *Cf.* Benjamin Klein & Keith Leffler, *The Role of Market Forces in Assuring Contractual Performance*, 89 J. POL. ECON. 615, 630-31 (1981) (advertising signals high "firm-specific selling costs," and a "high premium," hence signals presence of high-quality goods). The basic idea has borne up under recent empirical investigation. *See* I.P.L. Png & David Reitman, *Why Are Some Products Branded and Others Not?*, 38 J.L. & ECON. 207 (1995) (summarizing empirical research on branded versus unbranded sales of gasoline and other products at gasoline stations, which shows branding is more common where goods are hard to inspect and where consumer search costs are higher); Lee Benham, *The Effect of Advertising on the Price of Eyeglasses*, 15 J.L. & ECON. 337, 344-45 (1972) (advertising correlates with lower prices). *But see*

11. *See also* JOAN ROBINSON, THE ECONOMICS OF IMPERFECT COMPETITION 89 (1933).

12. *See generally* Glynn S. Lunney, *Trademark Monopolies*, 48 EMORY L.J. 367, 367-69 (1999) (discussing the influence of Chamberlin's work on trademark commentary). *See also* Sherwin Rosen, *Advertising, Information, and Product Differentiation*, *in* ISSUES IN ADVERTISING: THE ECONOMICS OF PERSUASION 161-91 (David G. Tuerck ed., 1978) (summarizing the artificial product differentiation view). *See generally* Beverly W. Pattishall, *Trademarks and the Monopoly Phobia*, 50 MICH. L. REV. 967 (1952) (criticizing the artificial product differentiation view).

John A. Rizzo, *Advertising and Competition in the Ethical Pharmaceutical Industry: The Case of Antihypertensive Drugs*, 42 J.L. & ECON. 89 (1999) (primary effect of advertising drugs is to reduce consumer price sensitivity). While there may be something to this idea, it is inherently self-limiting: If consumers take advertising as a signal of quality, makers of low-quality products will begin to advertise too, hoping to deceive consumers into purchasing their low-quality products.

Despite the current consensus in economic thought that advertising serves important informational functions in markets, criticisms of branding and advertising remain influential. *See, e.g.*, NAOMI KLEIN, NO LOGO: TAKING AIM AT BRAND BULLIES (2000); JULIET B. SCHOR, BORN TO BUY: THE COMMERCIALIZED CHILD AND THE NEW CONSUMER CULTURE (2005). For readers sympathetic to these criticisms, two questions arise with respect to trademarks and trademark law. First, is it fair to apply general criticisms of advertising to trademarks specifically? Though trademarks are usually central to most forms of advertising, aren't trademarks themselves mere informational devices? Second, and related, how, if at all, can trademark law be modified to limit the ability of trademarks to lead the consumer to purchase, in Justice Frankfurter's terms, "what he has been led to believe he wants"? Stated differently, how can trademark law protect the ability of marks to inform consumers without also contributing to their ability to persuade? Any serious criticism of the role that trademark law plays in perpetuating status consumption or introducing "economically irrational elements" into purchasing decisions should be able to answer this question. Perhaps limiting the scope of trademark rights or the kinds of commercial signifiers that can be protected as trademarks would lessen the persuasive impact of strong brands. But it may be that minor modifications to trademark law will not help to ameliorate the effects of deeply engrained consumption practices, and efforts to reform these practices will be more effective if undertaken elsewhere.

COMMENTS AND QUESTIONS

1. Note how the two economic approaches to trademarks—the older product differentiation theory (trademarks bad) and the newer product information theory (trademarks good)—follow from differing views of the economic role of advertising and promotional expenditure in general. Do you think advertising (1) communicates valuable price/quality information; (2) artificially creates demand for nonessential product features and product "image"; or (3) some combination of the two?

2. The "consumer protection" and "producer incentive" theories of trademark law often seem to be flip sides of the same coin. Yet, as we will see, the two theories may lead to different outcomes in certain cases. You can get a preliminary sense of this by considering a simple question: What if a producer has spent a great deal of money creating and advertising a mark, but the public has not yet begun to associate it with the product? Can a competitor use the mark on identical or similar goods? What incentives are created by a rule either way?

What if instead an accused infringer could demonstrate conclusively in a particular case that (i) the trademark owner invested nothing in the creation of the mark; and (ii) she has spent next to nothing promoting the mark or the product to which it is attached. Her success, in other words, has been entirely through repeat purchases and word of mouth. If an incentive/reward theory is at the heart of trademark, what would we be rewarding if we enforced the trademark in this case — *choice* of an effective trademark? (Note that the trademark chosen would appear to be highly successful in one sense: It fosters repeat business with little promotional spending.)

3. Why is a legal remedy necessary for false representations about the origins of consumer goods? If you hire a carpenter to fix your roof and he does a bad job, you will not hire him again. What are the differences between this scenario and products purchased less often from more diverse sources? *See* George A. Akerlof, *The Market for Lemons: Quality Uncertainty and the Market Mechanism*, 84 Q.J. ECON. 488 (1970), *reprinted in* AN ECONOMIC THEORIST'S BOOK OF TALES 7 (1984) (observing that under some conditions markets for goods such as used cars may not function effectively because buyers find it difficult to test the quality of the goods offered, giving sellers an incentive to sell poor-quality items, with a resultant diminution of activity across the entire market). Akerlof concludes that one way to stop the "market for lemons" dynamic, where bad (low-quality) sellers drive out good ones, is through the use of brand names.

> Brand names not only indicate quality but also give the consumer means of retaliation if the quality does not meet expectations. For the consumer will then curtail future purchases. Often too, new products are associated with old brand names. This ensures the prospective consumer of the quality of the product.

Id., *in* AN ECONOMIC THEORIST'S BOOK OF TALES, at 21. Akerlof identifies other institutions that serve the same purpose: guarantees; chain stores; and government licensing, as of doctors. Could all trademark law be eliminated by mandatory warranty terms? Would consumers necessarily trust them? Would such terms lower search costs as much as brand names? How about government certification programs — for example, "U.S. Grade A Refrigerators"? If the idea is that consumers need certification of quality levels, why wouldn't they prefer independent, third-party certification? Under what circumstances do consumers demand just that? Do they do so, for example, for airlines, doctors, lawyers? Why in some cases and not others? (Consider the costs of a bad product choice.)

Alternatively, private organizations might be expected to spring up to provide unbiased evaluation of products for a fee. Such organizations exist. Groups like Consumer's Union sell their evaluations of products, and their reputation depends on continued accuracy and integrity in product investigation. Other examples of private, third-party certification include *Good Housekeeping* magazine and Underwriters Laboratories, both of which give "seals of approval" to certain products and services that meet their standards for quality.

4. As you will see as you work your way through the trademark chapters of this book, trademark law has been expanding in recent years. Trade dress, anti-dilution protection, and other developments are all part of the trend. This expansion has moved trademark's conceptual center of gravity well beyond its traditional moorings in "consumer confusion." For cogent critiques of this movement — often called the "propertization" of trademark — see Mark A. Lemley, *The Modern Lanham Act and the Death of Common Sense*, 108 YALE L.J. 1687 (1999) and Glynn S. Lunney, Jr., *Trademark Monopolies*, 48 EMORY L.J. 367 (1999). Lunney summarizes things this way:

> [M]any courts and commentators succumbed to "property mania" — the belief that expanded trademark protection was necessarily desirable so long as the result could be characterized as "property." The result has been a radical and ongoing expansion of

> trademark protection, both in terms of what can be owned as a trademark and in terms of what trademark ownership entails. This expansion, and its associated reinterpretation of trademark's underlying policies, presents a serious threat to social welfare and has placed at risk the competitive balance that deception-based trademark law originally established. Like deception-based trademark protection, property-based trademark protection can enable a trademark owner to differentiate her product and exclude others from using the differentiating feature. It can thereby cede control over distinct product markets to individual producers and generate for a trademark owner the downward sloping demand curve of a monopolist. However, unlike deception-based trademark, property-based trademark has only a tenuous relationship to consumer deception, and therefore lacks the offsetting efficiency advantages associated with deception-based trademark's quality control and certification functions. As a result, property-based trademark appears presumptively anticompetitive—it generates market power and associated efficiency losses without the offsetting efficiency gains that are thought to justify deception-based trademark.

Id. at 372. Critics of expansive trademark law address one form of trademark expansion: the strengthening of the bundle of rights associated with a particular trademark. However, trademark owners often engage in another type of expansion: Once a trademark is established for one type of product, they try to "leverage the brand" by selling other products under the same trademark. This has become especially popular in recent years as businesspeople and consultants awake to the economic power that accompanies established brands. *See, e.g.*, BRANDS: THE NEW WEALTH CREATORS (Susannah Hart & John Murphy eds., 1998). Marketing studies suggest, however, that brand extensions succeed only in very limited circumstances. *See* Mark McKenna, *Testing Modern Trademark Law's Theory of Harm*, 95 IOWA L. REV. 63, 97-107 (2009) (reviewing these studies).

3

What Can Be Protected as a Trademark?

What exactly is a trademark? As noted above, the first trademarks were simply names or identifying symbols attached to goods. Names, symbols, and logos remain important trademarks, but they have been joined by a host of other sorts of trademarks. Company names now exist alongside product names. Slogans or phrases qualify for protection as trademarks. The design of a product itself or its packaging may be distinctive "trade dress" entitled to protection under the Lanham Act.

Of course, not all identifying marks are entitled to protection. If all a party needed to do to gain exclusive use of a mark or name was to use it, product comparisons would be virtually impossible because the very words that describe a product would be appropriated to a specific company. Suppose, for example, that Ford owned the exclusive right to describe its products as "cars" or "automobiles." Customers looking for automated means of ground transportation offered by other companies might encounter difficulty in knowing what to ask for. *See* Kenneth L. Port, ***Foreword: Symposium on Intellectual Property Law Theory***, 68 CHI.-KENT L. REV. 585, 596-98 (1993).

To avoid this problem, only certain trademarks are entitled to legal protection. Whether an identifying name or phrase may be trademarked at all, and the degree of protection accorded to it, both depend on the "strength" of the mark. This in turn depends on, among other things, the "classification" of the mark as either (1) fanciful, (2) arbitrary, (3) suggestive, (4) descriptive, or (5) generic. A fanciful mark is a coined word or phrase that bears no semantic relationship to the product to which it is attached (e.g., Exxon for motor fuel and related products; Kodak for photographic film and related products). An arbitrary mark similarly bears no semantic relationship to the product to which it is attached, but consists of a preexisting word or phrase (e.g., Sun for banking services, Congress for spring water). Arbitrary and fanciful marks are the strongest because any value they possess in terms of name recognition obviously comes from the corporate use of the name, rather than the natural association in people's minds between a name and a product. The other three categories decrease in strength as they increase in natural association: "suggestive" marks suggest a product in people's minds (e.g., Coppertone for suntan oil); "descriptive" marks describe the product or service offered (e.g., Lots a Suds for dishwashing liquid); "generic" designations are so associated with a particular product class that they have always been or have become the natural way to refer to that type of product (e.g., computers for computers, escalator for moving staircases).

A. TRADEMARKS, TRADE NAMES, AND SERVICE MARKS

To the layperson, trademarks are often thought of as the public name of a producer or other business. In fact, however, the Lanham Act distinguishes in form between several different types of marks. "Trademarks" are the words, phrases, logos, and symbols that producers use to identify their goods:

> **Trademark.** The term "trademark" includes any word, name, symbol, or device, or any combination thereof—
> (1) used by a person, or
> (2) which a person has a bona fide intention to use in commerce and applies to register on the principal register established by this Act,
> to identify and distinguish his or her goods, including a unique product, from those manufactured or sold by others and to indicate the source of the goods, even if that source is unknown.

Lanham Act §45, 15 U.S.C. §1127.

The term *trademark* does not cover another closely associated type of business identifier, the service mark. Service marks serve the same purposes as trademarks, but they are used to identify services rather than goods. The Act defines service marks as follows:

> **Service Mark:** The term "service mark" means any word, name, symbol, or device, or any combination thereof—
> (1) used by a person, or
> (2) which a person has a bona fide intention to use in commerce and applies to register on the principal register established by this Act,
> to identify and distinguish the services of one person, including a unique service, from the services of others and to indicate the source of the services, even if that source is unknown. Titles, character names, and other distinctive features of radio and television programs may be registered as service marks notwithstanding that they, or the programs, may advertise the goods of the sponsor.

Lanham Act §45, 15 U.S.C. §1127. In general, service marks are subject to the same rules as trademarks, for example, the rules on establishing priority of use. *See, e.g.*, Martahus v. Video Duplication Services, Inc., 3 F.3d 417 (Fed. Cir. 1993) (cancellation of service mark on grounds that similar service mark had priority).

One issue that sometimes arises involves attempts to register service marks for services that are closely related to the sale of goods. In general, where the services are "expected or routine" in connection with the goods, such registrations are rejected. The theory is that, otherwise, closely related registrations will proliferate, clogging the register. *See, e.g.*, In re Dr. Pepper Co., 836 F.2d 508 (Fed. Cir. 1987) (affirming trademark office rejection of service mark for conducting contests in connection with sale of soft drinks).

A third category of marks is trade names. Rather than goods or services, trade names identify the company itself. Unlike trademarks and service marks, trade names cannot be registered under the Lanham Act unless they actually function to identify the source of particular goods or services, rather than merely identifying a company. *See* Bell v. Streetwise Records, Ltd., 761 F.2d 67, 75 (1st Cir. 1985). However, trade names are generally registrable in state offices, and state and federal common law may provide protection against confusingly similar company names.

COMMENTS AND QUESTIONS

Although the Lanham Act defines both trade names and service marks, it allows registration of only the latter. Why?

B. CERTIFICATION AND COLLECTIVE MARKS

For the most part, the "source" identified by a trademark is a single company or individual. But for two special types of marks — certification and collective marks — this is not the case.

Lanham Act § 45 (15 U.S.C. § 1127) defines a certification mark as follows.

> The term "certification mark" means any word, name, symbol, or device, or any combination thereof—
>
> (1) used by a person other than its owner, or
>
> (2) which its owner has a bona fide intention to permit a person other than the owner to use in commerce and files an application to register on the principal register established by this chapter,
>
> to certify regional or other origin, material, mode of manufacture, quality, accuracy, or other characteristics of such person's goods or services or that the work or labor on the goods or services was performed by members of a union or other organization.

Certification marks are generally used by trade associations or other commercial groups to identify a particular type of goods. For example, the city of Roquefort, France, holds a certification mark in "Roquefort" as a sheep's milk cheese cured in the limestone caves of Roquefort, France. *See* Community of Roquefort v. William Faehndrich, Inc., 303 F.2d 494 (2d Cir. 1962) (enjoining use of the term "Imported Roquefort Cheese" on cheese not made in Roquefort, France). Certification marks cannot be limited to a single producer; they must be open to anyone who meets the standards set forth for certification.

Certification marks serve to certify conformity with centralized standards. *See, e.g.*, Levy v. Kosher Overseers Association of America Inc., 36 U.S.P.Q.2d 1724 (S.D.N.Y. 1995), *rev'd*, 104 F.3d 38 (2d Cir. 1997) (case involving plaintiff, Organized Kashruth Laboratories, suing another for infringement of its well-known kosher certification mark, the "circle K" found on many kosher foods). Because trademarks are thought by many to have grown out of trade guilds, which had much the same quality-control function, it could be argued that certification marks were the first true modern trademarks. *See* FRANK SCHECHTER, THE HISTORICAL FOUNDATIONS OF THE LAW RELATING TO TRADE-MARKS 47 (1925).

Certification marks are meant to bear the "seal of approval" of a central organization, so they can be cancelled on the ground that the organization no longer exercises sufficient control over its members to ensure consistent product standards. *See* 15 U.S.C. § 1064 (providing that a certification mark may be cancelled if not policed effectively); *see* American Angus Association v. Sysco Corp., 865 F. Supp. 1180 (W.D.N.C. 1993) (denying cancellation standing to trademark infringement defendant who sought to cancel plaintiff's beef quality certification mark).

Collective marks are defined as follows in § 45 of the Lanham Act (15 U.S.C. § 1127):

> The term "collective mark" means a trademark or service mark—
>
> (1) used by the members of a cooperative, an association, or other collective group or organization, or
>
> (2) which such cooperative, association, or other collective group or organization has a bona fide intention to use in commerce and applies to register on the principal register established by this chapter, and includes marks indicating membership in a union, an association, or other organization.

See also Aloe Creme Laboratories, Inc. v. American Society for Aesthetic Plastic Surgery, Inc., 192 U.S.P.Q. 170 (T.T.A.B. 1976), a decision denying an opposition to registration of a collective mark:

> There are two basic types of collective marks. A collective trademark or collective service mark is a mark adopted by a "collective" (i.e., an association, union, cooperative, fraternal organization, or other organized collective group) for use only by its members, who in turn use the mark to identify their goods or services and distinguish them from those of non-members. The "collective" itself neither sells goods nor performs services under a collective trademark or collective service mark, but the collective may advertise or otherwise promote the goods or services sold or rendered by its members under the mark. A collective membership mark is a mark adopted for the purpose of indicating membership in an organized collective group, such as a union, an association, or other organization. Neither the collective nor its members uses the collective membership mark to identify and distinguish goods or services; rather, the sole function of such a mark is to indicate that the person displaying the mark is a member of the organized collective group. For example, if the collective group is a fraternal organization, members may display the mark by wearing pins or rings upon which the mark appears, by carrying membership cards bearing the mark, etc. Of course, a collective group may itself be engaged in the marketing of its own goods or services under a particular mark, in which case the mark is not a collective mark but is rather a trademark for the collective's goods or service mark for the collective's services.

192 U.S.P.Q. 170, 173-74.

Collective marks of the first type—those attached to goods and services—are useful in franchising and related arrangements where individual stores or outlets are at least somewhat independent from the central organization holding the collective mark. For the most part, these types of collective marks are treated the same as ordinary trademarks. *See, e.g.*, Sebastian Int'l v. Long's Drug Stores Corp., 53 F.3d 1073 (9th Cir. 1995), *cert. denied*, 116 S. Ct. 302 (1995) (holding trademark "first sale" doctrine applicable to sales under a collective mark).

C. TRADE DRESS AND PRODUCT CONFIGURATIONS

Words or phrases that serve to identify a product are not all that the Lanham Act protects. The Act also protects "trade dress," the design and packaging of materials, and even the design and shape of a product itself, if the packaging or the product configuration serve the same source-identifying function as trademarks. It is possible to register both trade dress and product configurations as "trademarks" under the Lanham Act. (Indeed, such a registration was at issue in the *Qualitex* case discussed above—and which is excerpted below.) However, because of their complex and changing nature, most trade dress and product configurations are protected without registration under Section 43(a) of the Lanham Act, 15 U.S.C. § 1125(a).

§ 1125 [Lanham Act § 43]. False Designations of Origin and False Descriptions Forbidden

(a)(1) Any person who, on or in connection with any goods or services, or any container for goods, uses in commerce any word, term, name, symbol, or device, or any combination thereof, or any false designation of origin, false or misleading description of fact, or false or misleading representation of fact, which—

(A) is likely to cause confusion, or to cause mistake, or to deceive as to the affiliation, connection, or association of such person with another person, or as to the origin, sponsorship, or approval of his or her goods, services, or commercial activities by another person, or

(B) in commercial advertising or promotion, misrepresents the nature, characteristics, qualities, or geographic origin of his or her or another person's goods, services, or commercial activities,

shall be liable in a civil action by any person who believes that he or she is or is likely to be damaged by such act.

Section 43(a) is commonly referred to as providing "federal common law" protection for trademarks and related source identifiers—for a discussion of the mid-twentieth-century debate on whether Section 43(a) or Section 44 of the Lanham Act would serve as the basis for federal unfair competition law, see *infra* Chapter 9.C. In the next section, we discuss the requirements for protecting a trademark, either under the Lanham Act's registration procedures or under Section 43(a).

D. COLOR, FRAGRANCE, AND SOUNDS

Qualitex Co. v. Jacobson Products Co., Inc.
514 U.S. 159 (1995)

Justice Breyer delivered the opinion of the Court.

The question in this case is whether the Lanham Trademark Act . . . permits the registration of a trademark that consists, purely and simply, of a color. We conclude that, sometimes, a color will meet ordinary legal trademark requirements. And, when it does so, no special legal rule prevents color alone from serving as a trademark.

I

The case before us grows out of petitioner Qualitex Company's use (since the 1950's) of a special shade of green-gold color on the pads that it makes and sells to dry cleaning firms for use on dry cleaning presses. In 1989 respondent Jacobson Products (a Qualitex rival) began to sell its own press pads to dry cleaning firms; and it colored those pads a similar green-gold. In 1991 Qualitex registered the special green-gold color on press pads with the Patent and Trademark Office as a trademark. Registration No. 1,633,711 (Feb. 5, 1991). Qualitex subsequently added a trademark infringement count . . . in a lawsuit it had already filed challenging Jacobson's use of the green-gold color.

Qualitex won the lawsuit in the District Court. 21 U.S.P.Q.2d 1457, 1991 WL 318798 (CD Cal. 1991). But, the Court of Appeals for the Ninth Circuit set aside the judgment in Qualitex's favor on the trademark infringement claim because, in that Circuit's view, the Lanham Act does not permit Qualitex, or anyone else, to register "color alone" as a trademark. 13 F.3d 1297, 1300, 1302 (1994).

The courts of appeals have differed as to whether or not the law recognizes the use of color alone as a trademark. Compare NutraSweet Co. v. Stadt Corp., 917 F.2d 1024, 1028 (CA7 1990) (absolute prohibition against protection of color alone), with In re Owens-Corning Fiberglas Corp., 774 F.2d 1116, 1128 (CA Fed. 1985) (allowing registration of color pink for fiberglass insulation). . . . Therefore, this Court granted certiorari. . . . We now hold that there is no rule absolutely barring the use of color alone, and we reverse the judgment of the Ninth Circuit.

II

The Lanham Act gives a seller or producer the exclusive right to "register" a trademark . . . and to prevent his or her competitors from using that trademark. . . . Both the language of the Act and the basic underlying principles of trademark law would seem to include color within the universe of things that can qualify as a trademark. The language of the Lanham Act describes that universe in the broadest of terms. It says that trademarks "includ[e] any word, name, symbol, or device, or any combination thereof." §1127. Since human beings might use as a "symbol" or "device" almost anything at all that is capable of carrying meaning, this language, read literally, is not restrictive. The courts and the Patent and Trademark Office have authorized for use as a mark a particular shape (of a Coca-Cola bottle), a particular sound (of NBC's three chimes), and even a particular scent (of plumeria blossoms on sewing thread). See, e.g., Registration No. 696,147 (Apr. 12, 1960); Registration Nos. 523,616 (Apr. 4, 1950) and 916,522 (July 13, 1971); In re Clarke, 17 U.S.P.Q.2d 1238, 1240 (TTAB 1990). If a shape, a sound, and a fragrance can act as symbols why, one might ask, can a color not do the same?

. . . True, a product's color is unlike "fanciful," "arbitrary," or "suggestive" words or designs, which almost automatically tell a customer that they refer to a brand. . . . [S]ee Two Pesos, Inc. v. Taco Cabana, Inc., 112 S. Ct. 2753, 2757 (1992). The imaginary word "Suntost," or the words "Suntost Marmalade," on a jar of orange jam immediately would signal a brand or a product "source"; the jam's orange color does not do so. But, over time, customers may come to treat a particular color on a product or its packaging (say, a color that in context seems unusual, such as pink on a firm's insulating material or red on the head of a large industrial bolt) as signifying a brand. And, if so, that color would have come to identify and distinguish the goods—i.e. to "indicate" their "source"—much in the way that descriptive words on a product (say, "Trim" on nail clippers or "Car-Freshner" on deodorizer) can come to indicate a product's origin. . . . In this circumstance, trademark law says that the word (e.g., "Trim"), although not inherently distinctive, has developed "secondary meaning." See Inwood Laboratories, Inc. v. Ives Laboratories, Inc., 456 U.S. 844, 851 (1982) ("secondary meaning" is acquired when "in the minds of the public, the primary significance of a product feature . . . is to identify the source of the product rather than the product itself"). Again, one might ask, if trademark law permits a descriptive word with secondary meaning to act as a mark, why would it not permit a color, under similar circumstances, to do the same?

We cannot find in the basic objectives of trademark law any obvious theoretical objection to the use of color alone as a trademark, where that color has attained "secondary meaning" and therefore identifies and distinguishes a particular brand (and thus indicates its "source"). In principle, trademark law, by preventing others from copying a source-identifying mark, "reduce[s] the customer's costs of shopping and making purchasing decisions," 1 J. McCarthy, McCarthy on Trademarks and Unfair Competition § 2.01[2], pp. 2-3 (3d ed. 1994) (hereinafter McCarthy), for it quickly and easily assures a potential customer that this item—the item with this mark—is made by the same producer as other similarly marked items that he or she liked (or disliked) in the past. At the same time, the law helps assure a producer that it (and not an imitating competitor) will reap the financial, reputation-related rewards associated with a desirable product. The law thereby "encourage[s] the production of quality products," ibid., and simultaneously discourages those who hope to sell inferior products by capitalizing on a consumer's inability quickly to evaluate the quality of an item offered for sale. . . . It is the source-distinguishing ability of a mark—not its ontological status as color, shape, fragrance, word, or sign—that permits it to serve these basic purposes. See Landes & Posner, *Trademark Law: An Economic Perspective*, 30 J. Law & Econ. 265, 290 (1987). And, for that reason, it is difficult to find, in basic trademark objectives, a reason to disqualify absolutely the use of a color as a mark.

Neither can we find a principled objection to the use of color as a mark in the important "functionality" doctrine of trademark law. The functionality doctrine prevents trademark law, which seeks to promote competition by protecting a firm's reputation, from instead inhibiting legitimate competition by allowing a producer to control a useful product feature. It is the province of patent law, not trademark law, to encourage invention by granting inventors a monopoly over new product designs or functions for a limited time, 35 U.S.C. §§ 154, 173, after which competitors are free to use the innovation. If a product's functional features could be used as trademarks, however, a monopoly over such features could be obtained without regard to whether they qualify as patents and could be extended forever (because trademarks may be renewed in perpetuity). See Kellogg Co. v. National Biscuit Co., 305 U.S. 111, 119-120 (1938) (Brandeis, J.); *Inwood Laboratories, Inc., supra*, 456 U.S., at 863 (White, J., concurring in result) ("A functional characteristic is 'an important ingredient in the commercial success of the product,' and, after expiration of a patent, it is no more the property of the originator than the product itself") (citation omitted). Functionality doctrine therefore would require, to take an imaginary example, that even if customers have come to identify the special illumination-enhancing shape of a new patented light bulb with a particular manufacturer, the manufacturer may not use that shape as a trademark, for doing so, after the patent had expired, would impede competition — not by protecting the reputation of the original bulb maker, but by frustrating competitors' legitimate efforts to produce an equivalent illumination-enhancing bulb. See, e.g., *Kellogg Co., supra*, 305 U.S., at 119-120 (trademark law cannot be used to extend monopoly over "pillow" shape of shredded wheat biscuit after the patent for that shape had expired). This Court consequently has explained that, "[i]n general terms, a product feature is functional," and cannot serve as a trademark, "if it is essential to the use or purpose of the article or if it affects the cost or quality of the article," that is, if exclusive use of the feature would put competitors at a significant non-reputation-related disadvantage. *Inwood Laboratories, Inc.*, 456 U.S., at 850 n.10. Although sometimes color plays an important role (unrelated to source identification) in making a product more desirable, sometimes it does not. And, this latter fact — the fact that sometimes color is not essential to a product's use or purpose and does not affect cost or quality — indicates that the doctrine of "functionality" does not create an absolute bar to the use of color alone as a mark. See *Owens-Corning*, 774 F.2d, at 1123 (pink color of insulation in wall "performs no nontrademark function").

It would seem, then, that color alone, at least sometimes, can meet the basic legal requirements for use as a trademark. It can act as a symbol that distinguishes a firm's goods and identifies their source, without serving any other significant function. See U.S. Dept. of Commerce, Patent and Trademark Office, Trademark Manual of Examining Procedures 1202.04(e), pp. 1202-13 (2d ed. May, 1993) (hereinafter PTO Manual) (approving trademark registration of color alone where it "has become distinctive of the applicant's goods in commerce," provided that "there is [no] competitive need for colors to remain available in the industry" and the color is not "functional"); see also 1 McCarthy §§ 3.01[1], 7.26 ("requirements for qualification of a word or symbol as a trademark" are that it be (1) a "symbol," (2) "use[d] . . . as a mark," (3) "to identify and distinguish the seller's goods from goods made or sold by others," but that it not be "functional"). Indeed, the District Court, in this case, entered findings (accepted by the Ninth Circuit) that show Qualitex's green-gold press pad color has met these requirements. The green-gold color acts as a symbol. Having developed secondary meaning (for customers identified the green-gold color as Qualitex's), it identifies the press pads' source. And, the green-gold color serves no other function. (Although it is important to use some color on press pads to avoid noticeable stains, the court found "no competitive need in the press pad industry for the green-gold color, since other colors are equally usable." 21 U.S.P.Q.2d, at 1460, 1991 WL 318798.) Accordingly, unless there is some special reason that convincingly militates against the use of color alone as a trademark, trademark law would protect Qualitex's use of the green-gold color on its press pads.

III

Respondent Jacobson Products says that there are four special reasons why the law should forbid the use of color alone as a trademark. We shall explain, in turn, why we, ultimately, find them unpersuasive.

First, Jacobson says that, if the law permits the use of color as a trademark, it will produce uncertainty and unresolvable court disputes about what shades of a color a competitor may lawfully use. Because lighting (morning sun, twilight mist) will affect perceptions of protected color, competitors and courts will suffer from "shade confusion" as they try to decide whether use of a similar color on a similar product does, or does not, confuse customers and thereby infringe a trademark. Jacobson adds that the "shade confusion" problem is "more difficult" and "far different from" the "determination of the similarity of words or symbols." . . .

We do not believe, however, that color, in this respect, is special. Courts traditionally decide quite difficult questions about whether two words or phrases or symbols are sufficiently similar, in context, to confuse buyers. They have had to compare, for example, such words as "Bonamine" and "Dramamine" (motion-sickness remedies); "Huggies" and "Dougies" (diapers); "Cheracol" and "Syrocol" (cough syrup); "Cyclone" and "Tornado" (wire fences); and "Mattres" and "1-800-Mattres" (mattress franchisor telephone numbers). . . . Legal standards exist to guide courts in making such comparisons. See, e.g., 2 McCarthy § 15.08; 1 McCarthy §§ 11.24-11.25 ("[S]trong" marks, with greater secondary meaning, receive broader protection than "weak" marks). We do not see why courts could not apply those standards to a color, replicating, if necessary, lighting conditions under which a colored product is normally sold. . . .

Second, Jacobson argues, as have others, that colors are in limited supply. See, e.g., *NutraSweet Co.*, 917 F.2d, at 1028; Campbell Soup Co. v. Armour & Co., 175 F.2d 795, 798 (CA3 1949). Jacobson claims that, if one of many competitors can appropriate a particular color for use as a trademark, and each competitor then tries to do the same, the supply of colors will soon be depleted. Put in its strongest form, this argument would concede that "[h]undreds of color pigments are manufactured and thousands of colors can be obtained by mixing." L. Cheskin, Colors: What They Can Do For You 47 (1947). But, it would add that, in the context of a particular product, only some colors are usable. By the time one discards colors that, say, for reasons of customer appeal, are not usable, and adds the shades that competitors cannot use lest they risk infringing a similar, registered shade, then one is left with only a handful of possible colors. And, under these circumstances, to permit one, or a few, producers to use colors as trademarks will "deplete" the supply of usable colors to the point where a competitor's inability to find a suitable color will put that competitor at a significant disadvantage.

This argument is unpersuasive, however, largely because it relies on an occasional problem to justify a blanket prohibition. When a color serves as a mark, normally alternative colors will likely be available for similar use by others. See, e.g., *Owens-Corning*, 774 F.2d, at 1121 (pink insulation). Moreover, if that is not so—if a "color depletion" or "color scarcity" problem does arise—the trademark doctrine of "functionality" normally would seem available to prevent the anticompetitive consequences that Jacobson's argument posits, thereby minimizing that argument's practical force.

The functionality doctrine, as we have said, forbids the use of a product's feature as a trademark where doing so will put a competitor at a significant disadvantage because the feature is "essential to the use or purpose of the article" or "affects [its] cost or quality." *Inwood Laboratories, Inc.*, 456 U.S., at 850, n.10. The functionality doctrine thus protects competitors against a disadvantage (unrelated to recognition or reputation) that trademark protection might otherwise impose, namely their inability reasonably to replicate important non-reputation-related product features. For example, this Court has written that competitors might be free to copy the color of a medical pill where that color serves to identify the kind of medication (e.g., a type of blood medicine) in addition to its source. See id., at 853, 858, n.20 ("[S]ome patients commingle medications in a container and rely on color to differentiate one from another"); see also J. GINSBURG, D. GOLDBERG, & A. GREENBAUM, TRADEMARK AND UNFAIR COMPETITION LAW 194-195 (1991) (noting that drug color cases "have more to do with public health policy" regarding generic drug substitution "than with trademark law"). And, the federal courts have demonstrated that they can apply this doctrine in a careful and reasoned manner, with sensitivity to the effect on competition. Although we need not comment on the merits of specific cases, we note that lower courts have permitted competitors to copy the green color of farm machinery (because customers wanted their farm equipment to match) and have barred the use of black as a trademark on outboard boat motors (because black has the special functional attributes of decreasing the apparent size of the motor and ensuring compatibility with many different boat colors). . . . The *Restatement (Third) of Unfair Competition* adds that, if a design's "aesthetic value" lies in its ability to "confe[r] a significant benefit that cannot practically be duplicated by the use of alternative designs," then the design is "functional." RESTATEMENT (THIRD) OF UNFAIR COMPETITION § 17, Comment c, pp. 175-176 (1995). The "ultimate test of aesthetic functionality," it explains, "is whether the recognition of trademark rights would significantly hinder competition." Id., at 176.

The upshot is that, where a color serves a significant nontrademark function—whether to distinguish a heart pill from a digestive medicine or to satisfy the "noble instinct for giving the right touch of beauty to common and necessary things," G.K. CHESTERTON, SIMPLICITY AND TOLSTOY 61 (1912)—courts will examine whether its use as a mark would permit one competitor (or a group) to interfere with legitimate (nontrademark-related) competition through actual or potential exclusive use of an important product ingredient. That examination should not discourage firms from creating aesthetically pleasing mark designs, for it is open to their competitors to do the same. See, e.g., W. T. Rogers Co. v. Keene, 778 F.2d 334, 343 (CA7 1985) (Posner, J.). But, ordinarily, it should prevent the anticompetitive consequences of Jacobson's hypothetical "color depletion" argument, when, and if, the circumstances of a particular case threaten "color depletion."

Third, Jacobson points to many older cases—including Supreme Court cases—in support of its position. [The Court distinguishes these as arising before the Lanham Act of 1946.]

Fourth, Jacobson argues that there is no need to permit color alone to function as a trademark because a firm already may use color as part of a trademark, say, as a colored circle or colored letter or colored word, and may rely upon "trade dress" protection, under § 43(a) of the Lanham Act, if a competitor copies its color and thereby causes consumer confusion regarding the overall appearance of the competing products or their packaging, see 15 U.S.C. § 1125(a) (1988 ed., Supp. V). The first part of this argument begs the question. One can understand why a firm might find it difficult to place a usable symbol or word on a product (say, a large industrial bolt that customers normally see from a distance); and, in such instances, a firm might want to use color, pure and simple, instead of color as part of a design. Neither is the second portion of the argument convincing. Trademark law helps the holder of a mark in many ways that "trade dress" protection does not. See 15 U.S.C. § 1124 (ability to prevent importation of confusingly similar goods); § 1072 (constructive notice of ownership); § 1065 (incontestable status); § 1057(b) (prima facie evidence of validity and ownership). Thus, one can easily find reasons why the law might provide trademark protection in addition to trade dress protection.

IV

Having determined that a color may sometimes meet the basic legal requirements for use as a trademark and that respondent Jacobson's arguments do not justify a special legal rule preventing color alone from serving as a trademark (and, in light of the District Court's here undisputed findings that Qualitex's use of the green-gold color on its press pads meets the basic trademark requirements), we conclude that the Ninth Circuit erred in barring Qualitex's use of color as a trademark. For these reasons, the judgment of the Ninth Circuit is

Reversed.

COMMENTS AND QUESTIONS

1. The Court mentions "NBC's three chimes" as an example of a sound that is registered as a trademark under the Lanham Act. Another famous example is MGM's "lion's roar," usually heard at the beginning of an MGM film. *See also Harley Wants Roar of Engine Protected by a Trademark*, SACRAMENTO BEE, Mar. 27, 1996, at D6 (describing Harley-Davidson trademark application for engine sound opposed by competitors). Compare this with Section 43(a) cases alleging imitation of famous voices, for example, Midler v. Ford Motor Co., 849 F.2d 460 (9th Cir. 1988), *cert. denied*, 503 U.S. 951 (1992); *see* Chapter 6.

2. Justice Breyer asks, "If a shape, a sound, and a fragrance can act as symbols why, one might ask, can a color not do the same?" What about flavor or taste? Could (or should) the flavor of a product qualify for trademark protection? *See* In re N.V. Organon, 79 U.S.P.Q.2d 1639 (T.T.A.B. 2006) (affirming PTO examining attorney's refusal to register "an orange flavor" as a trademark for quick-dissolving

antidepressants in part on the ground that the flavor was not distinctive of source). What about the texture of a product? *See* U.S. Reg. No. 3,155,702, whose mark description reads: "The mark consists of a velvet textured covering on the surface of a bottle of wine. . . . The mark is a sensory, touch mark."

3. Justice Breyer's opinion for a unanimous Court in *Qualitex* is quite important, not only for resolution of the color issue but also as a statement of current Court thinking on the cutting-edge issue of the functionality defense. For more on this topic, see *infra*.

PROBLEM

Problem 5-1. AlertFive makes medical alert bracelets. The bracelets are designed to monitor an aspect of the wearer's medical condition, and trigger an alarm if the measurement indicates a dangerous condition. For example, AlertFive makes a bracelet that monitors heart rate and sounds an alarm if the heart rate goes above or below a certain range.

Aware that people in the modern world are bombarded by sounds and can come to tune them out, AlertFive sought to make the alarm associated with its bracelets unusual and memorable. Rejecting a standard beeping noise, it selected a trilling sound that increases in volume as it goes up the scale. AlertFive advertises its product on daytime television, and the ads feature a patient being saved in the nick of time because one of its bracelet alarms went off.

Can AlertFive prevent a competitor from selling a bracelet that makes a similar noise to alert a patient to an abnormal heart rate?

4 Establishment of Trademark Rights

To establish exclusive rights in a trademark, the trademark owner must show that the mark is "distinctive," specifically, that the mark is distinctive of the source of the goods or services to which it is affixed. In this chapter, we review the doctrine of trademark distinctiveness as it applies to source-distinctive words and images as well as to source-distinctive product packaging and product configuration. We also review the doctrine of trademark "functionality," which denies trademark protection to commercial signs (such as utilitarian product features) exclusive rights in which would unduly limit competition, even when such signs may otherwise be perceived by consumers as distinctive of a particular source. Finally, we consider how trademark owners establish temporal priority over competitors in ownership of a particular mark, how owners may register a mark at the United States Patent and Trademark Office, and the effect of establishing "incontestable" rights in a mark.

A. DISTINCTIVENESS

1. Classification of Marks and Requirements for Protection

When a trademark is immediately capable of identifying a unique product source, rights to the mark are determined solely by priority of use. (See, for example, the *Zazu Designs* case at the beginning of section D of this chapter.) Marks such as these are labeled "inherently distinctive," though for analytical completeness they are further subdivided into arbitrary, fanciful, and suggestive marks. For all other trademarks — those deemed not inherently distinctive — the Lanham Act requires proof of an additional element to secure trademark rights: secondary meaning.

The *Zatarain's* case that follows explores the hierarchy of trademark classifications and illustrates why classifications matter.

The most important type of word or symbol requiring proof of secondary meaning is the *descriptive* trademark. A descriptive mark is defined as "[a] word, picture, or other symbol that directly describes something about the goods or services in connection with which it is used as a mark." J. THOMAS MCCARTHY, MCCARTHY'S DESK ENCYCLOPEDIA OF INTELLECTUAL PROPERTY 119 (2d ed. 1995). Examples include: Tender Vittles for cat food, Arthriticare for arthritis treatment, and Investacorp for financial services.

In addition to descriptive marks, several other categories of marks require secondary meaning to acquire legal protection: most notably *geographic marks* (such as Nantucket soft drinks) and *personal name marks* (such as O'Malley's beer).[1]

Secondary meaning exists when buyers associate a descriptive term with a single source of products. Thus when consumers recognize the Tender Vittles brand of cat food — when they expect the can so labeled to be of that brand — this descriptive term is functioning as a trademark. To be sure, Tender Vittles retains its primary meaning as a product descriptor. But proof that it has acquired a secondary meaning as a source identifier elevates it to trademark status.

It is important to understand the nature of this secondary meaning. It does not mean that buyers need to know the *identity* of the source, only that the product or service comes from a *single* source. The phrase "single source" may thus be understood to mean "single though anonymous source." *See* A.J. Canfield Co. v. Honickman, 808 F.2d 291 (3d Cir. 1986). For example, purchasers of Tender Vittles cat food need not know the actual name of the product's manufacturer in order for Tender Vittles to qualify as a trademark; purchasers need merely know that any product bearing the Tender Vittles designation comes from or is manufactured under the auspices of this single, though anonymous, source.

The next case is a leading example of the application of these and related concepts.

Zatarain's, Inc. v. Oak Grove Smokehouse, Inc.
698 F.2d 786 (5th Cir. 1983)

GOLDBERG, Circuit Judge:

This appeal of a trademark dispute presents us with a menu of edible delights sure to tempt connoisseurs of fish and fowl alike. At issue is the alleged infringement of two trademarks, "Fish-Fri" and "Chick-Fri," held by appellant Zatarain's, Inc. ("Zatarain's"). The district court held that the alleged infringers had a "fair use" defense to any asserted infringement of the term "Fish-Fri" and that the registration of the term "Chick-Fri" should be cancelled. We affirm.

1. In addition, the following require proof of secondary meaning: titles of single literary works; descriptive titles of literary series; non-inherently distinctive designs and symbols; non-inherently distinctive trade dress and packaging; and product and container shapes. MCCARTHY, TRADEMARKS AND UNFAIR COMPETITION § 15.01[2].

I. Facts and Proceedings Below

A. *The Tale of the Town Frier*

Zatarain's is the manufacturer and distributor of a line of over one hundred food products. Two of these products, "Fish-Fri" and "Chick-Fri," are coatings or batter mixes used to fry foods. These marks serve as the entree in the present litigation.

Zatarain's "Fish-Fri" consists of 100% corn flour and is used to fry fish and other seafood. "Fish-Fri" is packaged in rectangular cardboard boxes containing twelve or twenty-four ounces of coating mix. The legend "Wonderful FISH-FR™" is displayed prominently on the front panel, along with the block Z used to identify all Zatarain's products. The term "Fish-Fri" has been used by Zatarain's or its predecessor since 1950 and has been registered as a trademark since 1962.

Zatarain's "Chick-Fri" is a seasoned corn flour batter mix used for frying chicken and other foods. The "Chick-Fri" package, which is very similar to that used for "Fish-Fri," is a rectangular cardboard container labelled "Wonderful CHICK-FRI." Zatarain's began to use the term "Chick-Fri" in 1968 and registered the term as a trademark in 1976.

Zatarain's products are not alone in the marketplace. At least four other companies market coatings for fried foods that are denominated "fish fry" or "chicken fry." Two of these competing companies are the appellees here, and therein hangs this fish tale.

Appellee Oak Grove Smokehouse, Inc. ("Oak Grove") began marketing a "fish fry" and a "chicken fry" in March 1979. Both products are packaged in clear glassine packets that contain a quantity of coating mix sufficient to fry enough food for one meal. The packets are labelled with Oak Grove's name and emblem, along with the words "FISH FRY" or "CHICKEN FRY." Oak Grove's "FISH FRY" has a corn flour base seasoned with various spices; Oak Grove's "CHICKEN FRY" is a seasoned coating with a wheat flour base.

B. *Out of the Frying Pan, Into the Fire*

Zatarain's first claimed foul play in its original complaint filed against Oak Grove on June 19, 1979, in the United States District Court for the Eastern District of Louisiana. The complaint alleged trademark infringement and unfair competition under the Lanham Act §§ 32(1), 43(a), 15 U.S.C. §§ 1114(1), 1125(a) (1976), and LA. REV. STAT. ANN. § 51:1405(A) (West Supp. 1982).

The district court found that Zatarain's trademark "Fish-Fri" was a descriptive term with an established secondary meaning, but held that Oak Grove and Visko's had a "fair use" defense to their asserted infringement of the mark. The court further found that Zatarain's trademark "Chick-Fri" was a descriptive term that lacked secondary meaning, and accordingly ordered the trademark registration cancelled.

Battered, but not fried, Zatarain's appeals from the adverse judgment on several grounds. First, Zatarain's argues that its trademark "Fish-Fri" is a suggestive term and therefore not subject to the "fair use" defense. Second, Zatarain's asserts that even if the "fair use" defense is applicable in this case, appellees cannot invoke the doctrine because their use of Zatarain's trademarks is not a good faith attempt to describe their products. Third, Zatarain's urges that the district court erred in cancelling the trademark registration for the term "Chick-Fri" because Zatarain's presented sufficient evidence to establish a secondary meaning for the term. For these reasons, Zatarain's argues that the district court should be reversed. . . .

III. The Trademark Claims

A. *Basic Principles*

1. Classifications of Marks

The threshold issue in any action for trademark infringement is whether the work or phrase is initially registerable or protectable. Vision Center v. Opticks, Inc., 596 F.2d 111, 115 (5th Cir. 1980); American Heritage Life Insurance Co. v. Heritage Life Insurance Co., 494 F.2d 3, 10 (5th Cir. 1974). Courts and commentators have traditionally divided potential trademarks into four categories. A potential trademark may be classified as (1) generic, (2) descriptive, (3) suggestive, or (4) arbitrary or fanciful. These categories, like the tones in a spectrum, tend to blur at the edges and merge together. The labels are more advisory than definitional, more like guidelines than pigeonholes. Not surprisingly, they are somewhat difficult to articulate and to apply. Soweco, Inc. v. Shell Oil Co., 617 F.2d 1178, 1183 (5th Cir. 1980); *Vision Center*, 596 F.2d at 115.

A generic term is "the name of a particular genus or class of which an individual article or service is but a member." *Vision Center*, 596 F.2d at 115; Abercrombie & Fitch Co. v. Hunting World, Inc., 537 F.2d 4, 9 (2d Cir. 1976). A generic term connotes the "basic nature of articles or services" rather than the more individualized characteristics of a particular product. *American Heritage*, 494 F.2d at 11. Generic terms can never attain trademark protection. William R. Warner & Co. v. Eli Lilly & Co., 265 U.S. 526, 528, 44 S. Ct. 615, 616, 68 L. Ed. 1161 (1924); *Soweco*, 617 F.2d at 1183; *Vision Center*, 596 F.2d at 115. Furthermore, if at any time a registered trademark becomes generic as to a particular product or service, the mark's registration is subject to cancellation. Lanham Act § 14, 15 U.S.C. § 1064(c) (1976). Such terms as aspirin and cellophane have been held generic and therefore unprotectable as trademarks. See Bayer Co. v. United Drug Co., 272 F. 505 (S.D.N.Y. 1921) (aspirin); DuPont Cellophane Co. v. Waxed Products Co., 85 F.2d 75 (2d Cir. 1936) (cellophane).

A descriptive term "identifies a characteristic or quality of an article or service," *Vision Center*, 596 F.2d at 115, such as its color, odor, function, dimensions, or ingredients. *American Heritage*, 494 F.2d at 11. Descriptive terms ordinarily are not protectable as trademarks, Lanham Act § 2(e)(1), 15 U.S.C. § 1052(e)(1) (1976); they may become valid marks, however, by acquiring a secondary meaning in the minds of the consuming public. See id. § 2(f), 15 U.S.C. § 1052(f). Examples of descriptive marks would include "Alo" with reference to products containing gel of the aloe vera plant, Aloe Creme Laboratories, Inc. v. Milsan, Inc., 423 F.2d 845 (5th Cir. 1970), and "Vision Center" in reference to a business offering optical goods and services, *Vision Center*, 596 F.2d at 117. As this court has often noted, the distinction between descriptive and generic terms is one of degree. *Soweco*, 617 F.2d at 1184;

Vision Center, 596 F.2d at 115 n.11 (citing 3 R. CALLMAN, THE LAW OF UNFAIR COMPETITION, TRADEMARKS AND MONOPOLIES § 70.4 (3d ed. 1969)); *American Heritage*, 494 F.2d at 11. The distinction has important practical consequences, however; while a descriptive term may be elevated to trademark status with proof of secondary meaning, a generic term may never achieve trademark protection. *Vision Center*, 596 F.2d at 115 n.11.

A suggestive term suggests, rather than describes, some particular characteristic of the goods or services to which it applies and requires the consumer to exercise the imagination in order to draw a conclusion as to the nature of the goods and services. *Soweco*, 617 F.2d at 1184; *Vision Center*, 596 F.2d at 115-116. A suggestive mark is protected without the necessity for proof of secondary meaning. The term "Coppertone" has been held suggestive in regard to sun tanning products. See Douglas Laboratories, Inc. v. Copper Tan, Inc., 210 F.2d 453 (2d Cir. 1954).

Arbitrary or fanciful terms bear no relationship to the products or services to which they are applied. Like suggestive terms, arbitrary and fanciful marks are protectable without proof of secondary meaning. The term "Kodak" is properly classified as a fanciful term for photographic supplies, see Eastman Kodak Co. v. Weil, 137 Misc. 506, 243 N.Y.S. 319 (1930) ("Kodak"); "Ivory" is an arbitrary term as applied to soap. *Abercrombie & Fitch*, 537 F.2d at 9 n.6.

2. Secondary Meaning

As noted earlier, descriptive terms are ordinarily not protectable as trademarks. They may be protected, however, if they have acquired a secondary meaning for the consuming public. The concept of secondary meaning recognizes that words with an ordinary and primary meaning of their own "may [after] long use with a particular product, come to be known by the public as specifically designating that product." Volkswagenwerk Aktiengesellschaft v. Rickard, 492 F.2d 474, 477 (5th Cir. 1974). In order to establish a secondary meaning for a term, a plaintiff "must show that the primary significance of the term in the minds of the consuming public is not the product but the producer." Kellogg Co. v. National Biscuit Co., 305 U.S. 111, 118 (1938). The burden of proof to establish secondary meaning rests at all times with the plaintiff; this burden is not an easy one to satisfy, for "[a] high degree of proof is necessary to establish secondary meaning for a descriptive term." *Vision Center*, 596 F.2d at 118 (quoting 3 R. CALLMAN, supra, § 77.3, at 359). Proof of secondary meaning is an issue only with respect to descriptive marks; suggestive and arbitrary or fanciful marks are automatically protected upon registration, and generic terms are unprotectable even if they have acquired secondary meaning. See *Soweco*, 617 F.2d at 1185 n.20.

3. The "Fair Use" Defense

Even when a descriptive term has acquired a secondary meaning sufficient to warrant trademark protection, others may be entitled to use the mark without incurring liability for trademark infringement. When the allegedly infringing term is "used fairly and in good faith only to describe to users the goods or services of [a] party, or their geographic origin," Lanham Act § 33(b)(4), 15 U.S.C. § 1115(b)(4) (1976), a defendant in a trademark infringement action may assert the "fair use" defense. The defense is available only in actions involving descriptive terms and only when the term is used in its descriptive sense rather than its trademark sense. *Soweco*, 617 F.2d at 1185; see Venetianaire Corp. v. A & P Import Co., 429 F.2d 1079, 1081-1082 (2d Cir. 1970). In essence, the fair use defense prevents a trademark registrant from appropriating a descriptive term for its own use to the exclusion of others, who may be prevented thereby from accurately describing their own goods. *Soweco*, 617 F.2d at 1185. The holder of a protectable descriptive mark has no legal claim to an exclusive right in the primary, descriptive meaning of the term; consequently, anyone is free to use the term in its primary, descriptive sense so long as such use does not lead to customer confusion as to the source of the goods or services. See 1 J. McCarthy, Trademarks and Unfair Competition § 11.17, at 379 (1973).

4. Cancellation of Trademarks

Section 37 of the Lanham Act, 15 U.S.C. § 1119 (1976), provides as follows:

> In any action involving a registered mark the court may determine the right to registration, order the cancellation of registrations, in whole or in part, restore cancelled registrations, and otherwise rectify the register with respect to the registrations of any party to the action. Decrees and orders shall be certified by the court to the Commissioner, who shall make appropriate entry upon the records of the Patent Office, and shall be controlled thereby.

This circuit has held that when a court determines that a mark is either a generic term or a descriptive term lacking secondary meaning, the purposes of the Lanham Act are well served by an order cancelling the mark's registration. *American Heritage*, 494 F.2d at 14.

We now turn to the facts of the instant case.

B. *"Fish-Fri"*[3]

1. Classification

Throughout this litigation, Zatarain's has maintained that the term "Fish-Fri" is a suggestive mark automatically protected from infringing uses by virtue of its registration in 1962. Oak Grove and Visko's assert that "fish fry" is a generic term identifying a class of foodstuffs used to fry fish; alternatively, Oak Grove and Visko's argue that "fish fry" is merely descriptive of the characteristics of the product. The district court found that "Fish-Fri" was a descriptive term identifying a function of the product being sold. Having reviewed this finding under the appropriate "clearly erroneous" standard, we affirm. See *Vision Center*, 596 F.2d at 113.

3. We note at the outset that Zatarain's use of the phonetic equivalent of the words "fish fry" — that is, misspelling it — does not render the mark protectable. *Soweco*, 617 F.2d at 1186 n.24.

We are mindful that "[t]he concept of descriptiveness must be construed rather broadly." 3 R. CALLMAN, supra, § 70.2. Whenever a word or phrase conveys an immediate idea of the qualities, characteristics, effect, purpose, or ingredients of a product or service, it is classified as descriptive and cannot be claimed as an exclusive trademark. Id. § 71.1; see Stix Products, Inc. v. United Merchants & Manufacturers, Inc., 295 F. Supp. 479, 488 (S.D.N.Y. 1968). Courts and commentators have formulated a number of tests to be used in classifying a mark as descriptive.

A suitable starting place is the dictionary, for "[t]he dictionary definition of the word is an appropriate and relevant indication 'of the ordinary significance and meaning of words' to the public." *American Heritage*, 494 F.2d at 11 n.5; see also *Vision Center*, 596 F.2d at 116. *Webster's Third New International Dictionary* 858 (1966) lists the following definitions for the term "fish fry": "1. a picnic at which fish are caught, fried, and eaten; . . . 2. fried fish." Thus, the basic dictionary definitions of the term refer to the preparation and consumption of fried fish. This is at least preliminary evidence that the term "Fish-Fri" is descriptive of Zatarain's product in the sense that the words naturally direct attention to the purpose or function of the product.

The "imagination test" is a second standard used by the courts to identify descriptive terms. This test seeks to measure the relationship between the actual words of the mark and the product to which they are applied. If a term "requires imagination, thought and perception to reach a conclusion as to the nature of goods," *Stix Products*, 295 F. Supp. at 488, it is considered a suggestive term. Alternatively, a term is descriptive if standing alone it conveys information as to the characteristics of the product. In this case, mere observation compels the conclusion that a product branded "Fish-Fri" is a prepackaged coating or batter mix applied to fish prior to cooking. The connection between this merchandise and its identifying terminology is so close and direct that even a consumer unfamiliar with the product would doubtless have an idea of its purpose or function. It simply does not require an exercise of the imagination to deduce that "Fish-Fri" is used to fry fish. See *Vision Center*, 596 F.2d at 116-17; *Stix Products*, 295 F. Supp. at 487-88. Accordingly, the term "Fish-Fri" must be considered descriptive when examined under the "imagination test."

A third test used by courts and commentators to classify descriptive marks is "whether competitors would be likely to need the terms used in the trademark in describing their products." Union Carbide Corp. v. Ever-Ready, Inc., 531 F.2d 366, 379 (7th Cir. 1976). A descriptive term generally relates so closely and directly to a product or service that other merchants marketing similar goods would find the term useful in identifying their own goods. *Vision Center*, 596 F.2d at 116-17; *Stix Products*, 295 F. Supp. at 488. Common sense indicates that in this case merchants other than Zatarain's might find the term "fish fry" useful in describing their own particular batter mixes. While Zatarain's has argued strenuously that Visko's and Oak Grove could have chosen from dozens of other possible terms in naming their coating mix, we find this position to be without merit. As this court has held, the fact that a term is not the only or even the most common name for a product is not determinative, for there is no legal foundation that a product can be described in only one fashion. *Vision Center*, 596 F.2d at 117 n.17. There are many edible fish in the sea, and as many ways to prepare them as there are varieties to be prepared. Even piscatorial gastronomes would agree, however, that frying is a form of preparation accepted virtually around the world, at restaurants starred and unstarred. The paucity of synonyms for the words "fish" and "fry" suggests that a merchant whose batter mix is specially spiced for frying fish is likely to find "fish fry" a useful term for describing his product.

A final barometer of the descriptiveness of a particular term examines the extent to which a term actually has been used by others marketing a similar service or product. *Vision Center*, 596 F.2d at 117; Shoe Corp. of America v. Juvenile Shoe Corp., 266 F.2d 793, 796 (C.C.P.A. 1959). This final test is closely related to the question whether competitors are likely to find a mark useful in describing their products. As noted above, a number of companies other than Zatarain's have chosen the word combination "fish fry" to identify their batter mixes. Arnaud's product, "Oyster Shrimp and Fish Fry," has been in competition with Zatarain's "Fish-Fri" for some ten to twenty years. When companies from A to Z, from Arnaud to Zatarain's, select the same term to describe their similar products, the term in question is most likely a descriptive one.

The correct categorization of a given term is a factual issue, *Soweco*, 617 F.2d at 1183 n.12; consequently, we review the district court's findings under the "clearly erroneous" standard of Fed. R. Civ. P. 52. See *Vision Center*, 596 F.2d at 113; *Volkswagenwerk*, 492 F.2d at 478. The district court in this case found that Zatarain's trademark "Fish-Fri" was descriptive of the function of the product being sold. Having applied the four prevailing tests of descriptiveness to the term "Fish-Fri," we are convinced that the district court's judgment in this matter is not only not clearly erroneous, but clearly correct. . . .

2. Secondary Meaning

Descriptive terms are not protectable by trademark absent a showing of secondary meaning in the minds of the consuming public.[5] To prevail in its trademark infringement action, therefore, Zatarain's must prove that its mark "Fish-Fri" has acquired a secondary meaning and thus warrants trademark protection. The district court found that Zatarain's evidence established a secondary meaning for the term "Fish-Fri" in the New Orleans area. We affirm.

The existence of secondary meaning presents a question for the trier of fact, and a district court's finding on the issue will not be disturbed unless clearly erroneous. *American Heritage*, 494 F.2d at 13; *Volkswagenwerk*, 492 F.2d at 477. The burden of proof rests with the party seeking to establish legal protection for the mark—the plaintiff in an infringement suit. *Vision Center*, 596 F.2d at 118. The evidentiary burden necessary to establish secondary meaning for a descriptive term is substantial. Id.; *American Heritage*, 494 F.2d at 12; 3 R. Callman, supra, § 77.3, at 359.

In assessing a claim of secondary meaning, the major inquiry is the consumer's attitude toward the mark. The mark must denote to the consumer "a single thing coming from a single source," Coca-Cola Co. v. Koke Co., 254 U.S. 143, 146 (1920); *Aloe Creme Laboratories*, 423 F.2d at 849, to support a finding of secondary meaning. Both direct and circumstantial evidence may be relevant and persuasive on the issue.

5. A mark that has become "incontestable" under section 15 of the Lanham Act, 15 U.S.C. § 1065 (1976), cannot be challenged as lacking secondary meaning, although it is subject to seven statutory defenses. See id. § 33(b), 15 U.S.C. § 1115(b). In order for a registrant's mark to be deemed "incontestable," the registrant must use the mark for five continuous years following the registration date and must file certain affidavits with the Commissioner of Patents. Id. § 15, 15 U.S.C. § 1065. No evidence in the record indicates that Zatarain's has satisfied the requirements of "incontestability"; consequently, we must determine whether proof of secondary meaning otherwise exists.

Factors such as amount and manner of advertising, volume of sales, and length and manner of use may serve as circumstantial evidence relevant to the issue of secondary meaning. See, e.g., *Vision Center*, 596 F.2d at 119; *Union Carbide Corp.*, 531 F.2d at 380; *Aloe Creme Laboratories*, 423 F.2d at 849-50. While none of these factors alone will prove secondary meaning, in combination they may establish the necessary link in the minds of consumers between a product and its source. It must be remembered, however, that "the question is not the extent of the promotional efforts, but their effectiveness in altering the meaning of [the term] to the consuming public." *Aloe Creme Laboratories*, 423 F.2d at 850.

Since 1950, Zatarain's and its predecessor have continuously used the term "Fish-Fri" to identify this particular batter mix. Through the expenditure of over $400,000 for advertising during the period from 1976 through 1981, Zatarain's has promoted its name and its product to the buying public. Sales of twelve-ounce boxes of "Fish-Fri" increased from 37,265 cases in 1969 to 59,439 cases in 1979. From 1964 through 1979, Zatarain's sold a total of 916,385 cases of "Fish-Fri." The district court considered this circumstantial evidence of secondary meaning to weigh heavily in Zatarain's favor.

In addition to these circumstantial factors, Zatarain's introduced at trial two surveys conducted by its expert witness, Allen Rosenzweig. In one survey, telephone interviewers questioned 100 women in the New Orleans area who fry fish or other seafood three or more times per month. Of the women surveyed, twenty-three percent specified Zatarain's "Fish-Fri" as a product they "would buy at the grocery to use as a coating" or a "product on the market that is especially made for frying fish." In a similar survey conducted in person at a New Orleans area mall, twenty-eight of the 100 respondents answered "Zatarain's 'Fish-Fri' " to the same questions. . . .

The authorities are in agreement that survey evidence is the most direct and persuasive way of establishing secondary meaning. *Vision Center*, 596 F.2d at 119; *Aloe Creme Laboratories*, 423 F.2d at 849; 1 J. McCarthy, supra, § 15.12(D). The district court believed that the survey evidence produced by Zatarain's, when coupled with the circumstantial evidence of advertising and usage, tipped the scales in favor of a finding of secondary meaning. Were we considering the question of secondary meaning de novo, we might reach a different conclusion than did the district court, for the issue is close.

Mindful, however, that there is evidence in the record to support the finding below, we cannot say that the district court's conclusion was clearly erroneous. Accordingly, the finding of secondary meaning in the New Orleans area for Zatarain's descriptive term "Fish-Fri" must be affirmed.

3. The "Fair Use" Defense

Although Zatarain's term "Fish-Fri" has acquired a secondary meaning in the New Orleans geographical area, Zatarain's does not now prevail automatically on its trademark infringement claim, for it cannot prevent the fair use of the term by Oak Grove and Visko's. The "fair use" defense applies only to descriptive terms and requires that the term be "used fairly and in good faith only to describe to users the goods or services of such party, or their geographic origin." Lanham Act § 33(b), 15 U.S.C. § 1115(b)(4) (1976). The district court determined that Oak

Grove and Visko's were entitled to fair use of the term "fish fry" to describe a characteristic of their goods; we affirm that conclusion.

Zatarain's term "Fish-Fri" is a descriptive term that has acquired a secondary meaning in the New Orleans area. Although the trademark is valid by virtue of having acquired a secondary meaning, only that penumbra or fringe of secondary meaning is given legal protection. Zatarain's has no legal claim to an exclusive right in the original, descriptive sense of the term; therefore, Oak Grove and Visko's are still free to use the words "fish fry" in their ordinary, descriptive sense, so long as such use will not tend to confuse customers as to the source of the goods. See 1 J. McCarthy, supra, § 11.17.

The record contains ample evidence to support the district court's determination that Oak Grove's and Visko's use of the words "fish fry" was fair and in good faith. Testimony at trial indicated that the appellees did not intend to use the term in a trademark sense and had never attempted to register the words as a trademark. Oak Grove and Visko's apparently believed "fish fry" was a generic name for the type of coating mix they manufactured. In addition, Oak Grove and Visko's consciously packaged and labelled their products in such a way as to minimize any potential confusion in the minds of consumers. The dissimilar trade dress of these products prompted the district court to observe that confusion at the point of purchase — the grocery shelves — would be virtually impossible. Our review of the record convinces us that the district court's determinations are correct. We hold, therefore, that Oak Grove and Visko's are entitled to fair use of the term "fish fry" to describe their products; accordingly, Zatarain's claim of trademark infringement must fail.

C. *"Chick-Fri"*

1. Classification

Most of what has been said about "Fish-Fri" applies with equal force to Zatarain's other culinary concoction, "Chick-Fri." "Chick-Fri" is at least as descriptive of the act of frying chicken as "Fish-Fri" is descriptive of frying fish. It takes no effort of the imagination to associate the term "Chick-Fri" with Southern fried chicken. Other merchants are likely to want to use the words "chicken fry" to describe similar products, and others have in fact done so. Sufficient evidence exists to support the district court's finding that "Chick-Fri" is a descriptive term; accordingly, we affirm.

2. Secondary Meaning

The district court concluded that Zatarain's had failed to establish a secondary meaning for the term "Chick-Fri." We affirm this finding. The mark "Chick-Fri" has been in use only since 1968; it was registered even more recently, in 1976. In sharp contrast to its promotions with regard to "Fish-Fri," Zatarain's advertising expenditures for "Chick-Fri" were mere chickenfeed; in fact, Zatarain's conducted no direct advertising campaign to publicize the product. Thus the circumstantial evidence presented in support of a secondary meaning for the term "Chick-Fri" was paltry.

Allen Rosenzweig's survey evidence regarding a secondary meaning for "Chick-Fri" also "lays an egg." The initial survey question was a "qualifier": "Approximately how many times in an average month do you, yourself, fry fish or other seafood?" Only if respondents replied "three or more times a month" were they asked to continue the survey. This qualifier, which may have been perfectly adequate for purposes of the "Fish-Fri" questions, seems highly unlikely to provide an adequate sample of potential consumers of "Chick-Fri." This survey provides us with nothing more than some data regarding fish friers' perceptions about products used for frying chicken. As such, it is entitled to little evidentiary weight.[10]

It is well settled that Zatarain's, the original plaintiff in this trademark infringement action, has the burden of proof to establish secondary meaning for its term. *Vision Center*, 596 F.2d at 118; *American Heritage*, 494 F.2d at 12. This it has failed to do. The district court's finding that the term "Chick-Fri" lacks secondary meaning is affirmed.

COMMENTS AND QUESTIONS

1. If you are familiar with the copyright law concept of "fair use," do not be misled by *Zatarain's* reference to the "fair use" of a trademark. The trademark "fair use" defense is a totally different and much more limited defense than its counterpart in copyright law. We discuss it in more detail in Chapter 6, Defenses.

2. In the course of its opinion, the court states: "Oak Grove and Visko's apparently believed 'fish fry' was a generic name for the type of coating mix they manufactured." A generic term is a term that indicates what *type* or *category* a product belongs to, rather than indicating the producer or other source of the product. A generic term for a product "tell[s] the buyer what it is, not where it came from." 2 J. Thomas McCarthy, McCarthy on Trademarks and Unfair Competition §12.01[1] (3d ed. 1992 & Supp. 1996). Examples would include "bed," "chair," and "pants." (Contrast these with "Eas-a-bed," "ComfortMax Chairs," and "Aunt's Pants"—all at least capable of indicating the source of a product.) A generic term has no distinctiveness vis-à-vis source, so it cannot serve as a trademark. For more on generic trademarks, including the process by which formerly distinctive terms become generic ("genericide"), see section A.2 *infra*.

3. Note that in the case, the survey sample seems to be drawn from a very small area—the New Orleans metropolitan region. Should secondary meaning in this area permit a descriptive mark to be enforced anywhere, or only in this area? Is this in effect a geographic limitation on the scope of a trademark that is not apparent from the statute—which provides ostensibly national protection for registered marks? How does this geographic limitation interact with the doctrines governing the conflict between junior common law users of a mark and a senior, federally registered mark owner?

Adray v. Adry-Mart, Inc., 76 F.3d 984 (9th Cir. 1996), *amending* 68 F.3d 362 (9th Cir. 1995), discusses geographical issues related to secondary meaning. The case centered around rival operators of electronics stores in Southern California (Lou Adray

10. Even were we to accept the results of the survey as relevant, the result would not change. In the New Orleans area, only 11 of the 100 respondents in the telephone survey named "Chick-Fri," "chicken fry," or Zatarain's "Chick-Fri" as a product used as a coating for frying chicken. Rosenzweig himself testified that this number was inconclusive for sampling purposes. Thus the survey evidence cannot be said to establish a secondary meaning for the term "Chick-Fri."

and Adry-Mart), both of whom used the name "Adray's." In 1979, Adry-Mart acquired from Lou Adray's relatives the right to use the Adray's trademark in stores in Los Angeles County. Lou Adray continued to operate his Orange County store, as he had since 1968. In 1989, however, Adry-Mart began to expand to areas first near, and then inside, Orange County.

In this appeal from Lou Adray's trademark infringement suit, the Ninth Circuit held that the district court was correct in instructing the jury that for Lou to receive damages he must show secondary meaning in the market areas in which Adry-Mart operated its Orange County stores. The court observed that there was no possibility that Lou could show national secondary meaning. Also, the court noted, the alleged infringer had not adopted its mark in bad faith in this case. The court went on to hold, however, that it was clear error for the district court to find that Adry-Mart's market included all of Los Angeles County; the evidence established that in some parts of the county Lou Adray had a bigger market share than Adry-Mart. Given the overlap of sales and advertising in these areas, it is likely that neither Lou nor Adry-Mart had secondary meaning there. On remand, the court ordered, the district court should reexamine the issue of where each party had established secondary meaning.

To achieve registration and therefore nationwide protection, the Trademark Office has generally required applicants for federal registration (which confers presumptively nationwide protection) to show more than secondary meaning in a limited area. *See* Philip Morris, Inc. v. Liggett & Myers Tobacco Co., 139 U.S.P.Q. 240 (TTAB 1963).

Compare *Adray* to another case, Fuddruckers, Inc. v. Doc's B.R. Others, Inc., 826 F.2d 837 (9th Cir. 1987). Here defendant Doc's negotiated with Fuddruckers for a Fuddruckers franchise, but the negotiations fell through and Fuddruckers found another franchisee. In mid-June of 1983, Fuddruckers announced plans to open a restaurant in Phoenix in December of that year. Defendants knew of Fuddruckers's plans but proceeded to open a restaurant in Phoenix with trade dress quite similar to that of Fuddruckers. As Fuddruckers's trade dress (restaurant décor) was not inherently distinctive, Fuddruckers was required to show that its trade dress had acquired secondary meaning in its action under §43(a) of the Lanham Act. The court ruled, however, that Fuddruckers did not have to show secondary meaning *in Arizona* prior to Doc's opening its restaurant there: "Fuddruckers is a national restaurant chain, and restaurant customers travel. Fuddruckers should be permitted to show that its trade dress had acquired secondary meaning among some substantial portion of consumers nationally." 826 F.2d at 844.

4. What is the proper role of "circumstantial evidence" of secondary meaning, such as advertising expenditures, the commercial success of the product, and attempts at imitation? Such evidence is generally allowed by courts in cases where secondary meaning is at issue. But should it be? If it is clear, for example, that advertising expenditures have been completely ineffective in swaying the public, is the fact of such expenditures relevant? The answer may depend on your views as to why we are protecting trademarks. If our goal is to provide incentives for businesses to invest in marks (and therefore in quality control), we may want to encourage such expenditures directly.

Note that some courts (particularly the Second Circuit) have explicitly done away with the need to prove secondary meaning where plaintiffs can point to some other equitable factor in their favor, such as intentional deception or "palming off" by the defendants. These courts reason that if the defendant is intentionally copying the plaintiff's mark, the defendant at least must think there is some accumulated goodwill to appropriate. This view is known as the New York rule, although there is some question as to its continued vitality in New York state courts. For a detailed discussion of the New York rule, *see* 2 McCarthy, McCarthy on Trademarks and Unfair Competition §§ 15.12-15.20. What does the New York rule suggest about the rationale for trademark protection? Is it incentive-based, property-based, or tort-based?

The test of "secondary meaning" is very fact-specific and relies on the reactions of consumers to a mark, generally as tested through consumer surveys. We will see the use of consumer reaction as a test again when we consider trademark infringement. Does it make sense to rely on such empirical evidence to establish a party's intellectual property rights, particularly given the problems with most consumer surveys? Is there a better alternative?

5. *Foreign Descriptive Terms.* In some circumstances, it may not even be clear what a descriptive term is. Consider the problem of terms that are descriptive in a language other than English. The doctrine of foreign equivalents holds that foreign words must be translated into English for purposes of determining their protectability. But application of this doctrine has been uneven. Is "La Posada" (Spanish for "inn") descriptive of lodging services? Does it matter whether a substantial portion of the clientele speaks Spanish? *See* In re Pan Tex Hotel Corp., 190 U.S.P.Q. 109 (T.T.A.B. 1976) (La Posada is not descriptive because it is unlikely that consumers will translate the name into English); Palm Bay Imports v. Veuve Clicquot, 396 F.3d 1369 (Fed. Cir. 2005) ("Veuve Clicquot" not confusingly similar to "The Widow," since most American consumers won't know that "veuve" is French for "widow"; "[t]he doctrine of foreign equivalents is not an absolute rule and should be viewed merely as a guidleline . . . applied only when it is likely that the ordinary American purchaser would stop and translate the word into its English equivalent."). *Compare* In re Tokutake Industry Co., Ltd., 87 U.S.P.Q.2d 1697 (T.T.A.B. 2008) ("Ayumi" and Japanese character version, meaning "walking," is descriptive of footwear); In re Hag Aktiengesellschaft, 155 U.S.P.Q. 598 (T.T.A.B. 1967) ("Kaba," meaning coffee in Serbian and Ukranian, is descriptive of coffee). Similarity of meaning in translation is important, but not determinative, in deciding the issue of descriptiveness. The relation in sight and sound between the English and foreign terms is also important; "a much closer approximation [between the meaning of the foreign term and the English equivalent] is necessary to justify a refusal to register on that basis alone where the marks otherwise are totally dissimilar." In re Sarkli, Ltd., 220 U.S.P.Q. 111, 113 (Fed. Cir. 1983).

6. *Acronyms.* One possible way around a finding that a term is descriptive (or generic) is to alter the term, either by misspelling it or by using an acronym. This, and not an intrinsic aversion to proper spelling, explains the profusion of product names with words like "Evr," "EZ" and "Klear." Acronyms are occasionally, but not normally, effective in creating a distinctive mark. The relevant question for the courts is whether the misspelling or acronym has the same connotation as the original descriptive or generic mark. If it does, the acronym is not entitled to protection. Thus, ROM is generic because it conveys the same meaning to the listener as "read-only memory." Intel Corp. v. Radiation, Inc., 184 U.S.P.Q. 54 (T.T.A.B. 1984). *See also* In re BetaBatt, Inc., 89 U.S.P.Q.2d 1152 (T.T.A.B. 2008) (finding that DEC is "routinely used" by relevant consumers as an abbreviation for "direct energy conversion" and is descriptive). By contrast, "L.A." was not merely descriptive of "low alcohol" beer. Anheuser-Busch, Inc. v. Stroh Brewery Co., 750 F.2d 631 (8th Cir. 1984) ("[I]f some operation

of the imagination is required to connect the initials with the product, the initials cannot be equated with the generic phrase, but are suggestive in nature, thereby rendering them protectable."). *See generally* McCarthy, McCarthy on Trademarks and Unfair Competition § 11.32.

7. *Personal Names.* Like descriptive marks, personal names (e.g., "Jones Antiques") need to acquire secondary meaning in order to obtain trademark protection. But does the acquisition of trademark status of a personal name by one enterprise preclude a second comer from using his or her own name? Although early cases recognized an absolute right to use one's name in business, "the more recent trend is to forbid any use of the name as part of the proprietor's trademark, permitting use only in a subsidiary capacity, and . . . with the first name attached [in equal size]. . . . In either event, the junior user has almost uniformly been bound to display negative disclaimers." Basile, S.p.A. v. Basile, 899 F.2d 35, 38 (D.C. Cir. 1990). *See, e.g.*, Gucci v. Gucci Shops, Inc., 688 F. Supp. 916 (S.D.N.Y. 1988) (enjoining Paulo Gucci, grandson of Guccio Gucci, from using Paulo Gucci as a trademark, but permitting him to identify himself as the designer of products marketed under an alternative trademark, provided that his name always appear after the alternative trademark, be no more prominent than the alternative trademark, and be accompanied by a disclaimer). Thus, the courts have developed a limited fair use defense tailored to personal names along the general contours of the fair use defense for descriptive terms discussed in *Zatarain's*.

8. *Geographic Marks.* Geographic marks must also generally establish secondary meaning in order to receive trademark protection. The issue of what constitutes a geographic mark, however, raises various complications. For example, is Philadelphia Cream Cheese a geographic mark if the product is not made in or sold primarily in Philadelphia? The Trademark Office and the courts have developed an elaborate structure distinguishing between descriptive and misdescriptive geographic names. We examine these doctrines in detail below, in section E.3 *infra*.

Even beyond the threshold for protection, can the establishment of trademark protection in a geographic mark through secondary meaning (e.g., "New York Times") prevent other companies from using geographic designations? As with descriptive names and personal names, the courts have developed a fair use doctrine for analyzing such uses, balancing a merchant's interest in accurately describing its location against the interest of the senior users and the consumer. The junior user must confine and adapt geographical usage so as to avoid likelihood of confusion. Courts will often accommodate these competing interests by requiring junior users to employ disclaimers, prefixes, suffixes, and other means of reducing confusion. *See generally* McCarthy, McCarthy on Trademarks and Unfair Competition § 14.14.

9. *Prefixes and Suffixes.* The Trademark Trial and Appeal Board has held that use of the letter "e" as a prefix in front of a commonly known and understood word—such as "eFashion"—yields a descriptive term for an online retailer. *See* In re Styleclick, 57 U.S.P.Q.2d 1445 (T.T.A.B. 2000). In a companion case, the T.T.A.B. held that use of the word "virtual" in front of a common word—as in "Virtual Fashion"—also results in a descriptive term. *See* In re Styleclick, 57 U.S.P.Q.2d 1523 (T.T.A.B. 2000). *See also* In re Zanova, Inc., 59 U.S.P.Q.2d 1300, 2001 WL 460111 (T.T.A.B. 2001) (finding that the letter "i" is a recognized abbreviation for "Internet."). Similarly, the Federal Circuit has held that the addition of the top level domain designation ".com" to an otherwise unregistrable designation will very rarely change the legal status of the designation. *See* In re Oppedahl & Larson LLP, 373 F.3d 1171, 1177 (Fed. Cir. 2004)

("The term patents.com merely describes patent-related goods in connection with the Internet. The two terms combined do not create a different impression. Rather, the addition of '.com' to the term 'patents' only strengthens the descriptiveness of the mark in light of the designation of goods in the application. 'Patents' alone describes one feature of the goods — that of tracking patent applications and issued patents. Adding '.com' to the mark adds a further description of the Internet feature of the identified goods.").

2. Genericness

For a term to serve the purpose of a trademark, it must be distinctive of a unique source. When a term refers instead to a general class of products, it is deemed "generic" and cannot serve as a trademark. "Kodak" is a source of products, a species; "camera" is a class of products — a genus.

Generic terms are either (1) "born generic," i.e., refused registration on the Principal Register or denied protection by the courts because they are generic *ab initio, see, e.g.*, Rudolph Int'l, Inc. v. Realys, Inc., 482 F.3d 1195, 1199 (9th Cir. 2007) (analyzing "disinfectable" for nail files that could withstand the disinfection process and concluding "disinfectable: not trademarkable"), or (2) they become generic over time through a process called "genericide," *see, e.g.*, Donald F. Duncan, Inc. v. Royal Tops Mfg. Co., 343 F.2d 655, 667 (7th Cir. 1965) (The term "yo-yo" "if not a generic term in the beginning . . . became such in the minds of the public and . . . plaintiff itself did much to educate the public in this respect."). The first case that follows considers whether the designation at issue was generic from the start. The second case discusses the issue of genericide.

Filipino Yellow Pages, Inc. v. Asian Journal Publications, Inc.
198 F.3d 1143 (9th Cir. 1999)

FLAUM, Circuit Judge:

We must decide whether the publisher of a telephone directory for the Filipino-American community can establish that the term "Filipino Yellow Pages" is protectible under trademark law.

I

[Defendant AJP publishes a telephone directory called the Filipino Consumer Directory.]

AJP's Filipino Consumer Directory has a white-pages section, which contains general reference information as well as a listing of people and organizations affiliated with the Filipino-American community. The Filipino Consumer Directory also has a yellow pages section containing information about businesses serving the Filipino-American community. AJP periodically uses the term "Filipino Consumer Yellow

Pages" in print advertisements directed at potential advertisers. These advertisements either reference the full name of the directory or are found within the Filipino Consumer Directory itself.

[Plaintiff FYP is the] publisher of a directory called the Filipino Yellow Pages. FYP's Filipino Yellow Pages, AJP's Filipino Consumer Directory, and [another publication,] the Filipino Directory of the U.S.A. and Canada[,] currently compete in the Filipino-American telephone directory market in California. A directory unaffiliated with FYP's directory, also called the Filipino Yellow Pages, is marketed to the Filipino-American community in the eastern United States by Kayumanggi Communications, Inc.

[On August 2, 1996, FYP filed a complaint against AJP alleging that FYP's use of the term "Filipino Yellow Pages" constituted, among other things, trademark infringement and unfair competition. AJP moved for summary judgment on the ground that "Filipino Yellow Pages" is generic. On November 26, 1997, the district court granted AJP's motion for summary judgment. FYP appealed.]

II

A

Before proceeding to the merits, a word on the burden of persuasion is appropriate. In cases involving properly registered marks, a presumption of validity places the burden of proving genericness upon the defendant. See 15 U.S.C. §1057(b) ("A certificate of registration of a mark . . . shall be prima facie evidence of the validity of the registered mark. . . ."). If a supposedly valid mark is not federally registered, however, the plaintiff has the burden of proving nongenericness once the defendant asserts genericness as a defense. . . . The case at bar involves a claimed mark that is unregistered; FYP has not yet been successful in its attempts to register "Filipino Yellow Pages" with the PTO. Thus FYP, as trademark plaintiff, bears the burden of showing that "Filipino Yellow Pages" is not generic.

B

. . . "A 'generic' term is one that refers, or has come to be understood as referring, to the genus of which the particular product or service is a species. It cannot become a trademark under any circumstances." Surgicenters [of America, Inc. v. Medical Dental Surgeries Co., 601 F.2d 1011,] 1014 [(9th Cir. 1979)]. As explained by one commentator, a generic term is "the name of the product or service itself—what [the product] is, and as such . . . the very antithesis of a mark." 2 J. Thomas McCarthy, Trademarks and Unfair Competition §12:1[1] (4th ed. 1997). . . .

In determining whether a term is generic, we have often relied upon the "who-are-you/what-are-you" test: "A mark answers the buyer's questions 'Who are you?' 'Where do you come from?' 'Who vouches for you?' But the [generic] name of the product answers the question 'What are you?' " Official Airline Guides, Inc. v. Goss, 6 F.3d 1385, 1391 (9th Cir. 1993) (quoting 1 J. Thomas McCarthy, Trademarks and Unfair Competition §12.01 (3d ed. 1992)). Under this test, "[i]f the primary significance of the trademark is to describe the *type of product* rather than the *producer*, the trademark [is] a generic term and [cannot be] a valid trademark." Anti-Monopoly, Inc. v. General Mills Fun Group, 611 F.2d 296, 304 (9th Cir. 1979) (emphases added).

Here the parties do not dispute that "Filipino" and "yellow pages" are generic terms. The word "Filipino" is a clearly generic term used to refer to "a native of the Philippine islands" or "a citizen of the Republic of the Philippines." WEBSTER'S NINTH NEW COLLEGIATE DICTIONARY 462 (1986). The term "yellow pages" has been found to be a generic term for "a local business telephone directory alphabetized by product or service." AmCan Enters., Inc. v. Renzi, 32 F.3d 233, 234 (7th Cir. 1994) (Posner, J.) (citing cases, and noting that "yellow pages," which originally was not a generic term, has become generic over time); see also WEBSTER'S NINTH NEW COLLEGIATE DICTIONARY 1367 (defining "yellow pages" as "the section of a telephone directory that lists businesses and professional firms alphabetically by category and that includes classified advertising"). The district court further noted, as shown by FYP's application for trademark registration, that the PTO requires the use of a disclaimer regarding rights to the term "yellow pages" whenever it is used as part of a registered trademark.

The issue then becomes whether combining the generic terms "Filipino" and "yellow pages" to form the composite term "Filipino Yellow Pages" creates a generic or a descriptive term. AJP argues, and the district court concluded, that "Filipino Yellow Pages" is generic based on this court's analysis in Surgicenters of America, Inc. v. Medical Dental Surgeries Co., 601 F.2d 1011 (9th Cir. 1979). In *Surgicenters*, we held that the term "surgicenter" was generic and that the plaintiff's registered service mark had to be removed from the trademark register. In our discussion in *Surgicenters*, we summarized (but did not explicitly adopt) the analysis of the district court in that case, which reasoned that "surgicenter," created by combining the generic terms "surgery" and "center," retained the generic quality of its components. Id. at 1015. We distinguished "surgicenter" from the composite term "Startgrolay," upheld as a valid mark for poultry feed, by noting that the combination of terms in "surgicenter" did not constitute a "deviation from normal usage" or an "unusual unitary combination." Id. at 1018. Nowhere in *Surgicenters* did we hold, however, that a composite term made up of generic components is automatically generic unless the combination constitutes a "deviation from normal usage" or an "unusual unitary combination."

In reaching our conclusion of genericness in *Surgicenters*, we placed significant but not controlling weight on the dictionary definitions and generic nature of "surgery" and "center." We explained that "[w]hile not determinative, dictionary definitions are relevant and often persuasive in determining how a term is understood by the consuming public, the ultimate test of whether a trademark is generic." Id. at 1015 n.11. But we also based our genericness finding upon detailed information in some 45 exhibits that, taken collectively, suggested that the consuming public considered the composite term "surgicenter" to mean a surgical center generally speaking, as opposed to a surgical center maintained and operated by the plaintiff specifically. See id. at 1017. These exhibits included letters from potential consumers and several publications that used the term "surgicenter" in a clearly generic sense. The finding of genericness in *Surgicenters* cannot be separated from the uniquely well-developed record in that case. See *Park 'N Fly*, 718 F.2d at 330-31.

In this case, the district court cited *Surgicenters* for the proposition that "a combination of two generic words is also generic, unless the combination is a 'deviation from natural usage' or an 'unusual unitary combination.' " The court then stated that "[u]nder this analysis, the term 'Filipino Yellow Pages' seems to be neither a 'deviation from natural usage,' nor an 'unusual unitary combination.' " The district court's reading of *Surgicenters* appears somewhat troubling insofar as it oversimplifies our opinion. First, it overlooks our explicit recognition that "words which could not individually become a trademark may become one when taken together." 601 F.2d at 1017 (internal quotation marks omitted). Second, it effectively makes dictionary definitions the crucial factor in assessing genericness, even though *Surgicenters* makes clear that such definitions are "not determinative" and that the "ultimate test" of genericnessness is "how a term is understood by the consuming public." Id. at 1015 n.11. Finally, it severs our *Surgicenters* analysis from its unique factual context, in which a wealth of exhibits supported a finding that the term "surgicenter" was generic even when taken as a whole (as opposed to the sum of generic parts).

Furthermore, reading the *Surgicenters* opinion for the rather broad (and somewhat reductionist) principle that "a generic term plus a generic term equals a generic term" would give rise to an unnecessary conflict between that decision and several other cases, decided both before and after *Surgicenters*, in which we have adopted a more holistic approach to evaluating composite terms.

In United States Jaycees v. San Francisco Junior Chamber of Commerce, 513 F.2d 1226 (9th Cir. 1975) (per curiam), decided a few years before *Surgicenters*, this court rejected the rather blunt "generic plus generic equals generic" approach to evaluating composite terms. The Jaycees court affirmed the district court's holding that "Junior Chamber of Commerce" was a descriptive mark with secondary meaning over a dissent arguing that "Junior Chamber of Commerce" was generic. The dissent relied upon the presence of "junior" and "chamber of commerce" in the dictionary to argue that both terms were generic and that "junior" modified "chamber of commerce" in a perfectly ordinary way, thereby creating a generic term. Id. at 1229 (Merrill, J., dissenting). The Jaycees court, in affirming over the dissent, implicitly rejected evaluating genericness of composite terms by breaking them down into their parts.

. . . In California Cooler, Inc. v. Loretto Winery, Ltd., 774 F.2d 1451 (9th Cir. 1985), we affirmed the district court's preliminary injunction enjoining the defendant from using the name "California Special Cooler" for its wine cooler products on the ground that it was confusingly similar to the plaintiff's registered trademark, "California Cooler." The defendant in *California Cooler* argued that because the generic terms "California" and "Cooler" could not qualify as valid marks individually, their combination, "California Cooler," was similarly generic. See id. at 1455. We rejected this argument: "California Cooler's mark is a composite term, and its validity is not judged by an examination of its parts. Rather, the validity of a trademark is to be determined by viewing the trademark as a whole. . . . Thus, the composite may become a distinguishing mark even though its components individually cannot." Id. (emphasis added).

. . . As the foregoing discussion illustrates, several pre- and post-*Surgicenters* cases have announced what could be described as an "anti-dissection rule" for evaluating the trademark validity of composite terms. *Official Airline Guides, Inc.*, 6 F.3d at 1392 (noting that under this rule, "the validity and distinctiveness of a composite trademark is determined by viewing the trademark as a whole, as it appears in the marketplace"). When *Surgicenters* is examined in light of these later cases, it becomes clear that

Surgicenters should not be read overbroadly to stand for the simple proposition that "generic plus generic equals generic." Rather, *Surgicenters* must be read in its proper context. First, it must be noted that *Surgicenters* explicitly recognizes that generic individual terms can be combined to form valid composite marks. See 601 F.2d at 1017. Second, it must be recalled that we found the term "surgicenter" generic based in large part on a well-developed record of 45 exhibits showing that the term "surgicenter," considered as a whole, was generic (i.e., understood by the consuming public as referring simply to a center at which surgery was performed).

In light of the foregoing discussion, the district court here may have oversimplified matters somewhat when it stated that "[t]he Ninth Circuit has held that a combination of two generic words is also generic, unless the combination is a 'deviation from natural usage' or an 'unusual unitary combination.' " Any arguable imprecision in the district court's application of *Surgicenters* was harmless, however, because the term "Filipino Yellow Pages" would be unprotectible in any event.

In finding "Filipino Yellow Pages" generic, the district court did not rely solely upon the generic nature and presence in the dictionary of "Filipino" and "yellow pages." The district court also considered other evidence tending to suggest that "Filipino Yellow Pages," even when considered as an entire mark, is generic with respect to telephone directories. The district court took note of the following facts. (1) [an office of FYP] himself appeared to use the term "Filipino Yellow Pages" in a generic sense in [an earlier] Shareholders' Buy Out Agreement . . . , when he "agree[d] not to compete in the Filipino Directory (Filipino Yellow Pages) in California"; (2) FYP did not bring suit to challenge the marketing of a second Filipino Yellow Pages to the Filipino-American community on the East Coast; and (3) a *Los Angeles Times* article, in discussing a trend toward specialized yellow pages, appeared to use the term in a generic sense; the article referred to a directory published by one Virgil Junio as "his Filipino yellow pages" instead of using the actual title of Junio's publication.

These three pieces of evidence are not as weighty as the 45 exhibits presented in *Surgicenters*, in which the record established generic use of the term "surgicenter" by *Newsweek* magazine, six medical publications, and the Department of Health, Education and Welfare. See 601 F.2d at 1013, 1017 n.17. An important difference between *Surgicenters* and the instant case should be noted, however. The mark at issue in *Surgicenters* was a federally-registered mark, and thus the burden of proving genericness rested upon the party challenging the mark's validity. See id. at 1012, 1014. The mark at issue in this case, in contrast, is not registered; thus FYP, as trademark plaintiff, must prove that "Filipino Yellow Pages" is not generic. It does not appear that FYP has offered evidence of nongenericness sufficient to rebut even the fairly modest evidence of genericness offered by AJP. In light of the evidence presented by AJP, it would seem that under the "who-are-you/what-are-you" test, the term "Filipino Yellow Pages" is generic. If faced with the question "What are you?," FYP's Filipino Yellow Pages, AJP's Filipino Consumer Directory, and the Filipino Directory of the U.S.A. and Canada could all respond in the same way: "A Filipino yellow pages." Giving FYP exclusive rights to the term "Filipino Yellow Pages" might be inappropriate because it would effectively "grant [FYP as] owner of the mark a monopoly, since a competitor could not describe his goods as what they are." *Surgicenters*, 601 F.2d at 1017 (internal quotation marks omitted). . . .

Affirmed.

The Murphy Door Bed Co., Inc. v. Interior Sleep Systems, Inc.

874 F.2d 95 (2d Cir. 1989)

MINER, Circuit Judge:

Defendants-appellants appeal from a judgment entered in the United States District Court for the Eastern District of New York [for] . . . plaintiff. . . . The judgment includes a permanent injunction enjoining all defendants from use of the Murphy name. . . .

We hold that "Murphy bed" is a generic term, having been appropriated by the public to designate generally a type of bed. Consequently, defendants could not have infringed on plaintiff's trademark, alleged to be Murphy bed, and the district court erred in finding trademark infringement. . . .

Background

At the turn of this century, William Lawrence Murphy invented and manufactured a bed that when not in use could be concealed in a wall closet. By using a counter-balancing mechanism, the bed could be lowered from or raised to a closet in a wall to which the bed is hinged. In 1918, the United States Patent Office granted Mr. Murphy a patent for a "pivot bed," which was substantially similar to the wall bed. Mr. Murphy incorporated in New York in 1925 as the Murphy Door Bed Company and began to sell the wall bed under the name of "Murphy bed." Since its inception, the Murphy Co. has used the words Murphy and Murphy bed as its trademark for concealed beds. Other manufacturers of wall beds generally describe their products as "wall beds," "concealed beds," "disappearing beds," "authentic adjustable hydraulic beds" and the like, but rarely as Murphy beds. In fact, at least twice, when independent companies marketed their products as Murphy beds, Murphy complained to them and, as a result, the companies refrained from further deliberate use of the term Murphy bed.

On March 23, 1981, and again on November 16, 1982, the Patent and Trademark Office ("PTO") denied the Murphy Co.'s application to register the Murphy bed trademark. The PTO examining attorney explained that the words "Murphy bed" had become generic and that the phrase Murphy bed was "merely descriptive of a characteristic of the goods." In August 1984, the Trademark Trial and Appeal Board ("TTAB") affirmed the denial of registration. See In re Murphy Door Bed Co., Inc., 223 U.S.P.Q. 1030 (TTAB 1984). The TTAB noted that "Murphy bed has for a long period of time been used by a substantial segment of the public as a generic term for a bed which folds into a wall or a closet." Id. at 1033.

In December 1981, [defendants] entered into a distributorship agreement with the Murphy Co. and became the exclusive distributor of the Murphy bed in . . . four Florida counties. . . . The agreement, in the form of a letter signed by both Murphy and Zarcone [on behalf of Interior Sleep Systems, Inc.], provided in part that:

> 5)—Whenever the Murphy name is used, it must be in capital letters and identified by the word trademark or TM adjacent to Murphy. Cabinets or other material not furnished by Murphy will not be promoted or sold as Murphy products. . . .

> 8)—Upon termination of this agreement Interior Sleep Systems, Inc. agrees to discontinue the use of the name "Murphy bed."

After learning of the TTAB's 1984 decision denying Murphy's application for trademark registration, [defendants formed a corporation with the term "Murphy Beds" in the title, and then filled certain orders with both beds of its own making and beds from the Murphy Company]. . . .

[The district] court ruled that the name Murphy was not generic because a "secondary meaning" had been attributed to it by the general public, and that the common law of trademark therefore protected the Murphy Co. . . . Thus, the court held that the burden was on the defendants to show abandonment of the Murphy trademark—i.e. that the trademark had lost its significance. . . . The court then found that defendants did not sustain their burden. . . .

Discussion . . .

We have held that "the burden is on plaintiff to prove that its mark is a valid trademark . . . [and] that its unregistered mark is not generic." Reese Publishing Co. v. Hampton Intl. Communications, Inc., 620 F.2d 7, 11 (2d Cir. 1980).

As the Murphy mark is unregistered, *Reese* suggests that the district court erred in shifting the burden of proof to the defendants. However, the words at issue in *Reese,* "Video Buyer's Guide," were of common use before the product developer applied them to his product, whereas here, the term Murphy bed was created for its purpose by the manufacturer and only thereafter was it adopted by the public as a matter of common use. See Gimix v. JS & A Group, Inc., 699 F.2d 901, 905 (7th Cir. 1983) (differentiating between term in common usage before application to product and coinage of term to suit product that is later expropriated). It was this genericness of an "invented" term that Learned Hand addressed when determining whether "aspirin," a coined word, had been so adopted by the lay public as to become generic. See Bayer Co. v. United Drug Co., 272 F. 505, 509 (S.D.N.Y. 1921); see also King-Seeley Thermos Co. v. Aladdin Indus., Inc., 321 F.2d 577, 579 (2d Cir. 1963) (widespread use of the word "thermos," despite having been invented by plaintiff for description of vacuum bottle, created genericness); DuPont Cellophane Co. v. Waxed Products Co., 85 F.2d 75, 81 (2d Cir.) (expropriation by public of word "cellophane" created genericness), *cert. denied,* 299 U.S. 601, 57 S. Ct. 194, 81 L. Ed. 443 (1936). We find this distinction important and hold that where the public is said to have expropriated a term established by a product developer, the burden is on the defendant to prove genericness. Thus, critical to a trial court's allocation of proof burdens is a determination of whether the term at issue is claimed to be generic by reason of common usage or by reason of expropriation. This presumption of nongenericness of a product name in the case of apparent public expropriation is justified by the commercial protection a developer of innovations deserves.

The Murphy Co. was the first to employ the word Murphy to describe a bed that could be folded into a wall closet. It is claimed that over time the public adopted, or, rather, expropriated, the term Murphy bed as a synonym for any bed that folds into a closet. Accordingly, the district court was correct in placing the burden of proof of genericness upon the defendants. We find, however, that [defendant] did indeed establish the genericness of the term Murphy bed.

The following factors combined lead us to conclude that [defendant] showed at trial that today the term Murphy bed, in the eyes of "a substantial majority of the public," *King-Seeley*, 321 F.2d at 579, refers to a species of bed that can fold into a wall enclosure. First, the decision of the PTO, and certainly the TTAB, is to be accorded great weight. . . . The district court explicitly rejected the decisions of the PTO and TTAB finding genericness, despite acknowledging their persuasive force. Second, the term Murphy bed is included in many dictionaries as a standard description of a wall-bed. See, e.g., WEBSTER'S THIRD NEW INTERNATIONAL DICTIONARY 1489 (1981). While dictionary definitions are not conclusive proof of a mark's generic nature, they are influential because they reflect the general public's perception of a mark's meaning and implication. . . . Third, [defendant] introduced as evidence numerous examples of newspaper and magazine use of the phrase Murphy bed to describe generally a type of bed. Again, such evidence is not proof positive, but it is a strong indication of the general public's perception that Murphy bed connotes something other than a bed manufactured by the Murphy Co. . . .

In finding a lack of genericness, the district court was influenced by Murphy's efforts at policing its mark. The court noted with approval instances where Murphy complained to those who had used the term Murphy bed to describe beds not necessarily produced by Murphy. . . . However, when, as here, the mark has "entered the public domain beyond recall," policing is of no consequence to a resolution of whether a mark is generic. *King-Seeley*, 321 F.2d at 579. . . .

We conclude that the defendants adequately demonstrated that the Murphy bed mark is generic. . . .

COMMENTS AND QUESTIONS

1. *Preventing and Policing Genericide.* Companies often fight vigorously to prevent their trademarks from becoming generic through casual usage. Consider the strong message sent by Xerox Corporation in the accompanying advertisement (Figure 4-1).

Apart from general advertising such as this, firms also police the uses of their marks via lawsuits. *See, e.g.*, Selchow & Righter Co. v. McGraw-Hill Book Co., 580 F.2d 25 (2d Cir. 1978) (granting Scrabble trademark holder preliminary injunction against publisher of "The Scrabble Dictionary," on grounds that publication would cause irreparable injury by possibly rendering trademark generic); Elliot Staffin, *The Dilution Doctrine: Towards a Reconciliation with the Lanham Act*, 6 FORDHAM INTELL. PROP. MEDIA & ENT. L.J. 105, 117 (1995) (collecting recent cases finding that dilution causes of action may lie against those employing a trademark in a way that threatens to make it generic). *Cf.* Ralph H. Folsom & Larry L. Teply, *Trademarked Generic Words*, 89 YALE L.J. 1323, 1346-47 n.110 (1980) (describing organized efforts of trademark attorneys to pressure dictionary publishers into excluding trademarked words and/or including disclaimers, and arguing that inclusion in a dictionary should not bear on genericide issue). This latter form of policing may explain a finding in William M. Landes & Richard A. Posner, *Trademark Law: An Economic Perspective*, 30 J.L. & ECON. 265, 296 (1987) ("Thus, although words held to be generic are more likely to show up in the dictionary than those held not to be generic, the difference in probabilities is small — 54% versus 41%.").

FIGURE 4-1
Xerox advertisement

Trademark lawyers also seek to prevent their clients' terms from being used as nouns or verbs, fearing that this will lead to their use as the generic term. Perhaps surprisingly, however, no court has ever held a mark generic for being used as a verb, and many companies actually encourage such use in their advertising slogans (e.g., "Do you Yahoo!?"). The real question is whether people are using the trademark as a verb to refer only to use of the company's product, or also to cover use of competing products.

Allowing trademark owners broad enforcement powers to police their marks against genericide—for example, by constraining the use of marks by the public, advertisers, and newspapers so as to prevent "dilution by genericization"—potentially conflicts with competition (comparative advertisement, consumer product reviews) and First Amendment (news reporting, free speech) values. It also may extend the trademark owners' power beyond the bounds of commercial use, one of the elements of trademark infringement.

2. Under the law of at least one state, a generic term already in public use can later acquire secondary meaning by virtue of a product developer's unique use, thus

warranting trademark protection. *See, e.g.*, Anti-Defamation League of B'Nai B'rith v. Arab Anti-Defamation League, 72 Misc. 2d 847, 855, 340 N.Y.S.2d 532, 534-44 (N.Y. Sup. Ct. 1972). Thus genericide may be reversible. Does this rule conflict with the federal trademark scheme?

By contrast, other courts have asked only whether a mark once became generic, reasoning that if it was generic that should deny protection even if it no longer is generic today. *See* Microsoft Corp. v. Lindows.com, Inc., 69 U.S.P.Q.2d 1863 (W.D. Wash. 2004). If consumers now associate a term such as "Windows" with a particular product, shouldn't the law validate that association?

3. In an omitted portion of the *Murphy Door Bed Co.* opinion, the court held that defendants breached their contractual obligation to refrain from using the term Murphy bed after termination of their distribution agreement with the Murphy Co., and that defendants engaged in unfair competition by passing off beds of their own manufacture as beds of the Murphy Co. Does it make sense to restrict the rights of the defendants—who had signed an agreement—to a greater degree than other competitors? Does this holding suggest that parties can "contract around" trademark genericness? What would be the effect of such agreements?

4. In Kellogg Co. v. National Biscuit Co., 305 U.S. 111, 116-18 (1938), Justice Brandeis set out a classic discussion of "genericide," though one infused also with elements of functionality and descriptiveness/secondary meaning:

> The plaintiff has no exclusive right to the use of the term "Shredded Wheat" as a trade name. For that is the generic term of the article, which describes it with a fair degree of accuracy; and is the term by which the biscuit in pillow-shaped form is generally known by the public. Since the term is generic, the original maker of the product acquired no exclusive right to use it. As Kellogg Company had the right to make the article, it had, also, the right to use the term by which the public knows it. . . . Ever since 1894 the article has been known to the public as shredded wheat. For many years, there was no attempt to use the term "Shredded Wheat" as a trade-mark. . . .
>
> Moreover, the name "Shredded Wheat," as well as the product, the process and the machinery employed in making it, has been dedicated to the public. The basic patent for the product and for the process of making it, and many other patents for special machinery to be used in making the article, issued to Perky. In those patents the term "shredded" is repeatedly used as descriptive of the product. The basic patent expired October 15, 1912; the others soon after. Since during the life of the patents "Shredded Wheat" was the general designation of the patented product, there passed to the public upon the expiration of the patent, not only the right to make the article as it was made during the patent period, but also the right to apply thereto the name by which it had become known. As was said in Singer Mfg. Co. v. June Mfg. Co., 163 U.S. 169, 185:
>
>> It equally follows from the cessation of the monopoly and the falling of the patented device into the domain of things public, that along with the public ownership of the device there must also necessarily pass to the public the generic designation of the thing which has arisen during the monopoly. . . . To say otherwise would be to hold that, although the public had acquired the device covered by the patent, yet the owner of the patent or the manufacturer of the patented thing had retained the designated name which was essentially necessary to vest the public with the full enjoyment of that which had become theirs by the disappearance of the monopoly.
>
> It is contended that the plaintiff has the exclusive right to the name "Shredded Wheat," because those words acquired the "secondary meaning" of shredded wheat made at Niagara Falls by the plaintiff's predecessor. There is no basis here for applying the doctrine of secondary meaning. The evidence shows only that due to the long period in which the plaintiff or its predecessor was the only manufacturer of the product, many

> people have come to associate the product, and as a consequence the name by which the product is generally known, with the plaintiff's factory at Niagara Falls. But to establish a trade name in the term "shredded wheat" the plaintiff must show more than a subordinate meaning which applies to it. It must show that the primary significance of the term in the minds of the consuming public is not the product but the producer. This it has not done The showing which it has made does not entitle it to the exclusive use of the term shredded wheat but merely entitles it to require that the defendant use reasonable care to inform the public of the source of its product.

The Court cites Singer Mfg. Co. v. June Mfg. Co., 163 U.S. 169, 185 (1896), for the proposition that once a patent on a device expires, the name by which that device has been sold also enters the public domain. Surely that is not always the case. Numerous products that once were patented are still sold under the same trademark. And this result — that patent expiration does not automatically end trademark protection — is also consistent with the purposes behind the two laws, which are very different. The key to *Singer*'s holding may lie in its expressed concern that "the owner of the patent . . . had retained the designated name which was essentially necessary to vest the public with the full enjoyment of" the product. Thus it is only when the name itself is "essentially necessary" to sales of the product — that is, when the name is generic — that trademark protection should not survive the expiration of a patent.

5. While most genericness cases involve word marks, trade dress and product configurations can also be generic. *See, e.g.*, Kendall-Jackson Winery v. E. & J. Gallo Winery, 150 F.3d 1042 (9th Cir. 1998), where the court held that an autumnal grape leaf featured on both plaintiff's and defendant's wine bottles was generic in the wine industry. *See also* Sunrise Jewelry Mfg. Corp. v. Fred, S.A., 175 F.3d 1322 (Fed. Cir. 1999) (holding that generic product configuration may be cancelled notwithstanding "incontestable" status; remanding for determination of genericness).

6. When a court declares a trademark generic, it destroys a right built up with considerable investment. Is this the same as instances where government decrees destroy private property; that is, should "just compensation" be paid for this "taking"? Does your answer depend on whether trademarks are viewed as property or instead as an unfair competition or consumer protection right? *See* Stephen L. Carter, *Does It Matter Whether Intellectual Property Is Property?*, 68 Chi.-Kent L. Rev. 715 (1993) (speculating about the desirability of such an arrangement); *compare* Ruckelshaus v. Monsanto Co., 467 U.S. 986 (1984) (government required to compensate trade secret owner when it compels disclosure of the secret).

The Second Circuit has periodically suggested that even generic marks are entitled to protection against some forms of unfair competition. *See, e.g.*, Genesee Brewing Co. v. Stroh Brewing Co., 124 F.3d 137, 150 (2d Cir. 1997) (plaintiff's mark for "Honey Brown Ale" was generic, but defendant could still be liable if it did not use "every reasonable means to prevent confusion" as to the source of the products); Forschner Group Inc. v. Arrow Trading Co., 124 F.3d 402 (2d Cir. 1997); Home Builders Ass'n of Greater St. Louis v. L & L Exhibition Mgmt., Inc., 226 F.3d 944 (8th Cir. 2000) (holding that a generic mark that has acquired secondary meaning may require that other users take steps to avoid confusion). Does it defeat the point of genericness if it can be undone? *See* Stacey L. Dogan & Mark A. Lemley, *A Search-Costs Theory of Limiting Doctrines in Trademark*, 97 Trademark Rptr. 1223 (2007) (arguing that refusing to give any protection to generic marks can hurt consumers who associate the term with a particular company).

7. Some commentators have noticed that trademarks have come to serve a more expressive role in addition to their original function of identifying a source for a commercial product. People make use of trademarks and taglines in conversation without any attempt to identify a source, or even specifically connect the source to a commercial product. Such expressions have salience precisely because the owners of the mark have blanketed our culture with them. In this sense the communicative content of trademarks such as Barbie and Marlboro — the unique images and associations these terms call to mind — are an unintended offshoot of the advertiser's commercially motivated saturation campaigns. Even so, these associations are very real.

This is not news to many owners of well-recognized marks. Many of them have instigated aggressive licensing campaigns to take advantage of their unique image in markets far beyond those they originally served. Thus logos such as "NBA" and "NFL," though they may have originally identified unique "brands" (high-quality sports leagues), now appear almost everywhere. Surely no one looks for the NBA logo on toy balls or teddy bears to assure herself of getting a well-made ball or toy. Rather, the buyer is seeking a piece of the NBA image.

Rochelle Dreyfuss questions whether trademark doctrine has kept up with these developments in popular culture. Rochelle C. Dreyfuss, *Expressive Genericity: Trademarks as Language in the Pepsi Generation*, 65 NOTRE DAME L. REV. 397 (1990). She suggests a number of ways trademark law should be adjusted. Her primary suggestion is to extend traditional concepts of genericness to encompass the realm of expressive (as opposed to commercial, or what she calls "competitive") uses of trademarks. "[C]ourts," she writes,

> would first decide whether there is an expressive component to the challenged use and then consider how central the trademark is to the usage. If the mark is found to be rhetorically unique within its context, it would be considered expressively — but not necessarily competitively — generic, and the trademark owner would not be permitted to suppress its utilization in that context. . . . [T]he suggested analysis would permit courts to drop the fiction of consumer confusion, and instead focus on the primary concern, which is the expressive significance of the mark.

Dreyfuss, at 418-19.

8. *Generic.com.* The function of domain names as both unique cyberspace addresses and sources of goods and services has reversed the traditional dynamics of genericide. Many generic terms (e.g., escalator) begin their existence as product names of a particular manufacturer, but over time become identified with a particular good, thereby losing protection. By contrast, domain names (e.g., pets.com) begin as descriptive terms with a generic suffix (.com) but then build source identification and goodwill over time because of the uniqueness of the cyberspace address. Should courts protect this goodwill? *See* In re Reed Elsevier Properties, Inc., 77 U.S.P.Q.2d 1649 (T.T.A.B. 2005) ("lawyers.com" is generic).

9. Terms that were once trademarks but have since become generic include several that have passed into universal usage, including aspirin, elevator, escalator, and thermos. More recent rulings have held "bottled at the source" generic for bottled water, CG Roxane LLC v. Fiji Water Co., 569 F. Supp. 2d 1019 (N.D. Cal. 2008), and "duck tours" generic for amphibious city tours, Boston Duck Tours, LP v. Super Duck Tours, LLC, 531 F.3d 1 (1st Cir. 2008).

Note on Genericide, Language, and Policing Costs

It might seem that the notion of genericide does not make much sense. Why should a mark pass into the public domain because it has come to signify a category of products rather than a single product/source combination? If a trademark owner has "invented" a trademark, there is a clear sense in which the genericness doctrine takes away some rights that the creator was endowed with because of her creativity. Should trademark protection be permanent, or should we attempt a rough "calibration," along the lines of patent and copyright, to adjust the incentive to call forth the optimum (or at least desirable) level of this activity? *Cf.* William M. Landes & Richard A. Posner, *Trademark Law: An Economic Perspective*, 30 J.L. & Econ. 265, 270 (1987) (trademark protection offers a modest incentive to create new commercial terms).

Does it make sense that the very success of a trademark should be its undoing? In some ways, this is analogous to the argument that copyright protection on a software user interface should "lapse" when the interface becomes an industry standard. *Cf.* Lotus Dev. Corp. v. Borland Int'l, Inc., 49 F.3d 807 (1st Cir. 1995), *aff'd by equally divided court*, 516 U.S. 233 (1996). The unifying theme is the notion that the success of certain kinds of creative works is largely a result of the need for a single standard, rather than the creative brilliance of the work itself. Economists speak of these works as creating "network externalities": users benefit from the fact that others use the work. Widely used computer protocols, such as the TCP/IP standard allowing exchange of data over the Internet, are advantageous because they make a wide variety of content available to all users. Thus each new person who adopts a protocol benefits all current users of the protocol.

Some courts and legal scholars point out that under such a dynamic, the success of works of this kind is attributable more to the *collective labor* of the users than to the labor of the work's creator. *See, e.g.*, Lotus Devel. Corp. v. Borland Int'l, Inc., 49 F.3d 807, 821 (1st Cir. 1995) (Boudin, J., concurring) (accused infringer's product was "merely trying to give former Lotus users an option to exploit their own prior investment in learning. . . . [I]t is hard to see why customers who have learned the Lotus menu and devised macros for it should remain captives of Lotus because of an investment in learning made by the users and not by Lotus."). They argue that the efforts of the users in learning a new work, such as the computer protocol in the example above, rather than the efforts of the creator in designing the work, account for the success of these kinds of works. It follows from this argument that the claims of the work's creator must give way to those of the users in some cases. This logic is applied directly to generic trademarks in the following passage:

> Giving ownership in intellectual products that have come to serve as standards, such as West citations or generic trademarks, would not ordinarily leave "enough, and as good" [in the Lockean sense]. There may be room in the world for only one of a given type of thing, or a long-lived artifice may become a mode of communication. It is the nature of a standard that nothing "as good" is available. For these reasons, the [Lockean] proviso would be violated if the courts gave those who create standards in nonfungible goods a right to prevent people from utilizing them.

Wendy J. Gordon, *A Property Right in Self-Expression: Equality and Individualism in the Natural Law of Intellectual Property*, 102 Yale L.J. 1533, 1600 (1993) (footnote omitted). *See also* Justin Hughes, *The Philosophy of Intellectual Property*, 77 GEO. L.J. 287, 315-23 (1988) (suggesting that ownership of most intellectual products will easily satisfy the Lockean proviso, though "extraordinary ideas" like generic trademarks should remain open for all to use). The *public* contributes to the success of strong trademarks. *See* Steven Wilf, *Who Authors Trademarks?*, 17 CARDOZO ARTS & ENT. L.J. 1 (1999). Should they have an ownership interest too?

Economists have observed that human languages exhibit network externalities. Professor Gordon's argument just above in effect extends the network externalities argument to individual words. When a word comes to describe a genus or class of goods, i.e., enters general use, it takes on some of the properties of the computer protocol described earlier. It becomes the standard shorthand descriptor for a complex, multi-attribute product type. Past a certain point, any alternative descriptor becomes clearly second-best. Requiring consumers and competitors to use this second-best descriptor entails costs. *See* Ralph H. Folsom & Larry L. Teply, *Trademarked Generic Words*, 89 YALE L.J. 1323, 1340-41 (1980). Though difficult to quantify, these costs may be substantial. See also Landes & Posner, *supra*, at 280, 292 (discussing costs of having to "describe around" a well-known term).

Consider the example of "plexiglas." The next best alternative to this well-known descriptor might be: "unbreakable clear plastic sheets, or window material." That is not only a mouthful; it is more expensive to advertise (because it is longer), harder to remember, and more subject to mistakes and confusion. Thus it is not hard to see why "plexiglas" became the preferred shorthand for it. Consequently, although the originator of this term might have put substantial effort into creating it and encouraging its use, there is a good argument that it has become a standard name (or descriptor)— and hence generic. *But cf.* Rohm & Haas Co. v. Polycast Technology Corp., 172 U.S.P.Q. 167 (D. Del. 1971) (enjoining defendant's use of Plexiglas mark). As another example, consider "Yo-Yo"; how would you describe this kind of toy without using the word *yo-yo*? *Cf.* Donald F. Duncan, Inc. v. Royal Tops Mfg. Co., 343 F.2d 655 (7th Cir. 1965) (holding *yo-yo* generic, besides being descriptive in Tagalog).

The Role of Policing Costs. Folsom and Teply argue that policing costs (reflected in ads such as the one by Xerox, above) are always wasted and therefore should not be considered in determining whether a trademark has become generic. *See* Folsom & Teply, *supra*, at 1354. Do you agree? Can you defend expenditures to keep a mark from becoming generic on the basis that they are attempts to provide alternative "standards" that will thereby retain the source-indicating function of threatened trademarks? If consumers accept the premise of the ads and faithfully refer to the "copier" instead of the "Xerox," are consumers harmed? And do such expenditures show that the cost of informing the public about alternative product descriptors is worth it to the firm, given its investment in its trademark? *Cf.* E.I. duPont deNemours & Co. v. Yoshida Int'l, Inc., 393 F. Supp. 502, 523-24 (E.D.N.Y. 1975) ("Teflon" not generic, in part because of duPont's vigorous education and policing campaign). Of course, it may be impossible for a company to prevent genericide, for example, when a trademark achieves rapid and overwhelming acceptance. Then no amount of policing will work. *Cf.* Du Pont Cellophane Co. v. Waxed Prods. Co., 85 F.2d 75 (2d Cir.), *cert. denied*, 299 U.S. 601 (1936) ("Cellophane" generic despite vigorous policing efforts). Does such rapid acceptance indicate that the next best alternative descriptor is significantly less effective? *Cf.* Folsom & Teply, *supra*, at 1344 (noting that some alternative terms are better than others; comparing "lip balm" as alternative to "Chap Stick"; with "dextro-amphetamine sulphate" as alternative to "Dexadrine"); *Comment, Trademarks and Generic Words: An Effect-on-Competition Test*, 51 U. Chi. L. Rev. 868, 884-85 (1984) (advocating use of antitrust-like cross-elasticities of demand analysis to determine degree of substitutability between terms).

Can you see a less benign motive for expenditures to maintain the trademark status of a word that has become a widely used name for a product class? *See* Folsom & Teply, *supra*, at 1337 (suggesting two: (1) to maintain entry barriers to competition; and (2) to obtain "free advertising" every time someone uses the trademarked word to refer to a product class). This perspective certainly points away from a per se rule that significant policing expenditures alone can preserve the trademark status of a term. And, of course, to the extent that firms attempt to police the noncommercial use of marks, there may be a significant effect on the free flow of information and ideas. The First Amendment, discussed below in the Chapter 6 section on parody, comes into play in these situations.

PROBLEM

Problem 4-1. Google Inc. is the world's largest Internet search engine. Since the company's founding in 1998, it has grown to become one of the world's most famous brands. While Google faces competition in search today, and there were a number of Internet search engines before Google, a substantial portion of the public has come to associate searching the Internet with the term "Google," used as a verb. Internet users regularly speak of "Googling" something or someone. When they do so, however, they generally mean not just to search the Internet but to do so using the Google search engine. Following and documenting this popular usage, a number of dictionaries have now included the term "Google" as a verb.

Is Google generic?

B. DISTINCTIVENESS OF TRADE DRESS AND PRODUCT CONFIGURATION

Two Pesos, Inc. v. Taco Cabana, Inc.
505 U.S. 763 (1992)

Justice White delivered the opinion of the Court.

The issue in this case is whether the trade dress[1] of a restaurant may be protected under §43(a) of the Trademark Act of 1946 (Lanham Act), 60 Stat. 441, 15 U.S.C.

1. The District Court instructed the jury: "'Trade dress' is the total image of the business. Taco Cabana's trade dress may include the shape and general appearance of the exterior of the restaurant, the identifying sign, the interior kitchen floor plan, the decor, the menu, the equipment used to serve food, the

§1125(a) (1982 ed.), based on a finding of inherent distinctiveness, without proof that the trade dress has secondary meaning.

I

Respondent Taco Cabana, Inc., operates a chain of fast-food restaurants in Texas. The restaurants serve Mexican food. The first Taco Cabana restaurant was opened in San Antonio in September 1978, and five more restaurants had been opened in San Antonio by 1985. Taco Cabana describes its Mexican trade dress as "a festive eating atmosphere having interior dining and patio areas decorated with artifacts, bright colors, paintings and murals. The patio includes interior and exterior areas with the interior patio capable of being sealed off from the outside patio by overhead garage doors. The stepped exterior of the building is a festive and vivid color scheme using top border paint and neon stripes. Bright awnings and umbrellas continue the theme." 932 F.2d 1113, 1117 (CA5 1991).

In December 1985, a Two Pesos, Inc., restaurant was opened in Houston. Two Pesos adopted a motif very similar to the foregoing description of Taco Cabana's trade dress. Two Pesos restaurants expanded rapidly in Houston and other markets, but did not enter San Antonio. In 1986, Taco Cabana entered the Houston and Austin markets and expanded into other Texas cities, including Dallas and El Paso where Two Pesos was also doing business.

In 1987, Taco Cabana sued Two Pesos in the United States District Court for the Southern District of Texas for trade dress infringement under §43(a) of the Lanham Act, 15 U.S.C. §1125(a) (1982 ed.), and for theft of trade secrets under Texas common law. The case was tried to a jury, which was instructed to return its verdict in the form of answers to five questions propounded by the trial judge. The jury's answers were: Taco Cabana has a trade dress; taken as a whole, the trade dress is nonfunctional; the trade dress is inherently distinctive; the trade dress has not acquired a secondary meaning in the Texas market; and the alleged infringement creates a likelihood of confusion on the part of ordinary customers as to the source or association of the restaurant's goods or services. Because, as the jury was told, Taco Cabana's trade dress was protected if it either was inherently distinctive or had acquired a secondary meaning, judgment was entered awarding damages to Taco Cabana. In the course of calculating damages, the trial court held that Two Pesos had intentionally and deliberately infringed Taco Cabana's trade dress.

The Court of Appeals ruled that the instructions adequately stated the applicable law and that the evidence supported the jury's findings. In particular, the Court of Appeals rejected petitioner's argument that a finding of no secondary meaning contradicted a finding of inherent distinctiveness.

---

servers' uniforms and other features reflecting on the total image of the restaurant." The Court of Appeals accepted this definition and quoted from Blue Bell Bio-Medical v. Cin-Bad, Inc., 864 F.2d 1253, 1256 (CA5 1989): "The 'trade dress' of a product is essentially its total image and overall appearance." See 932 F.2d 1113, 1118 (CA5 1991). It "involves the total image of a product and may include features such as size, shape, color or color combinations, texture, graphics, or even particular sales techniques." John H. Harland Co. v. Clarke Checks, Inc., 711 F.2d 966, 980 (CA11 1983). RESTATEMENT (THIRD) OF UNFAIR COMPETITION §16, Comment a (Tent. Draft No. 2, Mar. 23, 1990).

II

The Lanham Act was intended to make "actionable the deceptive and misleading use of marks" and "to protect persons engaged in . . . commerce against unfair competition." § 45, 15 U.S.C. § 1127. Section 43(a) "prohibits a broader range of practices than does § 32," which applies to registered marks, Inwood Laboratories, Inc. v. Ives Laboratories, Inc., 456 U.S. 844, 858 (1982), but it is common ground that § 43(a) protects qualifying unregistered trademarks and that the general principles qualifying a mark for registration under § 2 of the Lanham Act are for the most part applicable in determining whether an unregistered mark is entitled to protection under § 43(a). See A. J. Canfield Co., v. Honickman, 808 F.2d 291, 299, n.9 (CA3 1986); Thompson Medical Co. v. Pfizer Inc., 753 F.2d 208, 215-216 (CA2 1985).

The Court of Appeals determined that the District Court's instructions were consistent with the foregoing principles and that the evidence supported the jury's verdict. Both courts thus ruled that Taco Cabana's trade dress was not descriptive but rather inherently distinctive, and that it was not functional. None of these rulings is before us in this case, and for present purposes we assume, without deciding, that each of them is correct. In going on to affirm the judgment for respondent, the Court of Appeals, following its prior decision in *Chevron,* held that Taco Cabana's inherently distinctive trade dress was entitled to protection despite the lack of proof of secondary meaning. It is this issue that is before us for decision, and we agree with its resolution by the Court of Appeals. There is no persuasive reason to apply to trade dress a general requirement of secondary meaning which is at odds with the principles generally applicable to infringement suits under § 43(a). Petitioner devotes much of its briefing to arguing issues that are not before us, and we address only its arguments relevant to whether proof of secondary meaning is essential to qualify an inherently distinctive trade dress for protection under § 43(a). Petitioner argues that the jury's finding that the trade dress has not acquired a secondary meaning shows conclusively that the trade dress is not inherently distinctive. The Court of Appeals' disposition of this issue was sound:

> Two Pesos' argument—that the jury finding of inherent distinctiveness contradicts its finding of no secondary meaning in the Texas market—ignores the law in this circuit. While the necessarily imperfect (and often prohibitively difficult) methods for assessing secondary meaning address the empirical question of current consumer association, the legal recognition of an inherently distinctive trademark or trade dress acknowledges the owner's legitimate proprietary interest in its unique and valuable informational device, regardless of whether substantial consumer association yet bestows the additional empirical protection of secondary meaning.

932 F.2d, at 1120, n.7.

This brings us to the line of decisions by the Court of Appeals for the Second Circuit that would find protection for trade dress unavailable absent proof of secondary meaning, a position that petitioner concedes would have to be modified if the temporary protection that it suggests is to be recognized. In Vibrant Sales, Inc. v. New Body Boutique, Inc., 652 F.2d 299 (1981), the plaintiff claimed protection under § 43(a) for a product whose features the defendant had allegedly copied. The Court of Appeals held that unregistered marks did not enjoy the "presumptive source association" enjoyed by registered marks and hence could not qualify for protection under §43(a) without proof of secondary meaning. Id. at 303, 304. The court's rationale seemingly denied protection for unregistered but inherently distinctive marks of all kinds, whether the claimed mark used distinctive words or symbols or distinctive product design. The court thus did not accept the arguments that an unregistered mark was capable of identifying a source and that copying such a mark could be making any kind of a false statement or representation under §43(a).

This holding is in considerable tension with the provisions of the Act. If a verbal or symbolic mark or the features of a product design may be registered under §2, it necessarily is a mark "by which the goods of the applicant may be distinguished from the goods of others," 60 Stat. 428, and must be registered unless otherwise disqualified. Since §2 requires secondary meaning only as a condition to registering descriptive marks, there are plainly marks that are registrable without showing secondary meaning. These same marks, even if not registered, remain inherently capable of distinguishing the goods of the users of these marks. Furthermore, the copier of such a mark may be seen as falsely claiming that his products may for some reason be thought of as originating from the plaintiff.

Some years after *Vibrant*, the Second Circuit announced in Thompson Medical Co. v. Pfizer Inc., 753 F.2d 208 (CA2 1985), that in deciding whether an unregistered mark is eligible for protection under §43(a), it would follow the classification of marks set out by Judge Friendly in *Abercrombie & Fitch*, 537 F.2d, at 9. Hence, if an unregistered mark is deemed merely descriptive, which the verbal mark before the court proved to be, proof of secondary meaning is required; however, "suggestive marks are eligible for protection without any proof of secondary meaning, since the connection between the mark and the source is presumed." 753 F.2d, at 216. The Second Circuit has nevertheless continued to deny protection for trade dress under §43(a) absent proof of secondary meaning, despite the fact that §43(a) provides no basis for distinguishing between trademark and trade dress. See, e.g., Stormy Clime Ltd. v. ProGroup, Inc., 809 F.2d, at 974; Union Mfg. Co. v. Han Baek Trading Co., 763 F.2d 42, 48 (1985); Le Sportsac, Inc. v. K Mart Corp., 754 F.2d 71, 75 (1985).

The Fifth Circuit was quite right in *Chevron,* and in this case, to follow the *Abercrombie* classifications consistently and to inquire whether trade dress for which protection is claimed under §43(a) is inherently distinctive. If it is, it is capable of identifying products or services as coming from a specific source and secondary meaning is not required. This is the rule generally applicable to trademark, and the protection of trademarks and trade dress under §43(a) serves the same statutory purpose of preventing deception and unfair competition. There is no persuasive reason to apply different analysis to the two. The "proposition that secondary meaning must be shown even if the trade dress is a distinctive, identifying mark, [is] wrong, for the reasons explained by Judge Rubin for the Fifth Circuit in *Chevron*." Blau Plumbing, Inc. v. S.O.S. Fix-it, Inc., 781 F.2d 604, 608 (CA7 1986). The Court of Appeals for the Eleventh Circuit also follows *Chevron,* Ambrit, Inc. v. Kraft, Inc., 805 F.2d 974, 979 (1986), and the Court of Appeals for the Ninth Circuit appears to think that proof of secondary meaning is superfluous if a trade dress is inherently distinctive. Fuddruckers, Inc. v. Doc's B.R. Others, Inc., 826 F.2d 837, 843 (1987).

It would be a different matter if there were textual basis in §43(a) for treating inherently distinctive verbal or symbolic trademarks differently from inherently distinctive trade dress. But there is none. The section does not mention trademarks or trade dress, whether they be called generic, descriptive, suggestive, arbitrary, fanciful, or functional. Nor does the concept of secondary meaning appear in the text of §43(a).

Where secondary meaning does appear in the statute, 15 U.S.C. § 1052 (1982 ed.), it is a requirement that applies only to merely descriptive marks and not to inherently distinctive ones. We see no basis for requiring secondary meaning for inherently distinctive trade dress protection under § 43(a) but not for other distinctive words, symbols, or devices capable of identifying a producer's product.

Engrafting onto § 43(a) a requirement of secondary meaning for inherently distinctive trade dress also would undermine the purposes of the Lanham Act. Protection of trade dress, no less than of trademarks, serves the Act's purpose to "secure to the owner of the mark the goodwill of his business and to protect the ability of consumers to distinguish among competing producers. National protection of trademarks is desirable, Congress concluded, because trademarks foster competition and the maintenance of quality by securing to the producer the benefits of good reputation." *Park 'N Fly*, 469 U.S., at 198, citing S. Rep. No. 1333, 79th Cong., 2d Sess., 3-5 (1946) (citations omitted). By making more difficult the identification of a producer with its product, a secondary meaning requirement for a nondescriptive trade dress would hinder improving or maintaining the producer's competitive position.

Suggestions that under the Fifth Circuit's law, the initial user of any shape or design would cut off competition from products of like design and shape are not persuasive. Only nonfunctional, distinctive trade dress is protected under § 43(a). The Fifth Circuit holds that a design is legally functional, and thus unprotectable, if it is one of a limited number of equally efficient options available to competitors and free competition would be unduly hindered by according the design trademark protection. See Sicilia Di R. Biebow & Co. v. Cox, 732 F.2d 417, 426 (CA5 1984). This serves to assure that competition will not be stifled by the exhaustion of a limited number of trade dresses.

On the other hand, adding a secondary meaning requirement could have anticompetitive effects, creating particular burdens on the start-up of small companies. It would present special difficulties for a business, such as respondent, that seeks to start a new product in a limited area and then expand into new markets. Denying protection for inherently distinctive nonfunctional trade dress until after secondary meaning has been established would allow a competitor, which has not adopted a distinctive trade dress of its own, to appropriate the originator's dress in other markets and to deter the originator from expanding into and competing in these areas.

As noted above, petitioner concedes that protecting an inherently distinctive trade dress from its inception may be critical to new entrants to the market and that withholding protection until secondary meaning has been established would be contrary to the goals of the Lanham Act. Petitioner specifically suggests, however, that the solution is to dispense with the requirement of secondary meaning for a reasonable, but brief period at the outset of the use of a trade dress. If § 43(a) does not require secondary meaning at the outset of a business' adoption of trade dress, there is no basis in the statute to support the suggestion that such a requirement comes into being after some unspecified time.

III

We agree with the Court of Appeals that proof of secondary meaning is not required to prevail on a claim under § 43(a) of the Lanham Act where the trade dress at issue is inherently distinctive, and accordingly the judgment of that court is affirmed.

COMMENTS AND QUESTIONS

1. *Two Pesos* reverses the prior rule of a number of circuit courts, which had held that secondary meaning was a required element of a Section 43(a) action for trade dress infringement, even if the trade dress was inherently distinctive. *See, e.g.*, Ferrari S.p.A. v. Roberts, 944 F.2d 1235, 1239 (6th Cir. 1991), *cert. denied*, 505 U.S. 1219 (1992). But see the case that follows these comments, throwing the issue into some doubt.

2. Focus for a moment on the policy justifications the Court offers in support of its ruling. Two such justifications appear: that protecting distinctive trade dress will enable companies to appropriate their own goodwill, and that small companies may be unable to protect their trade dress from larger infringers if they are required to establish secondary meaning. Are these justifications persuasive? Should the Court focus on the rights of the trademark holder to protect its goodwill, or on the rights of the public to accurate product information? Are these two goals likely to come into conflict here?

3. Does the Court adopt either the "incentive" or property-rights theory of trademark law? *See* Stephen L. Carter, *Does It Matter Whether Intellectual Property Is Property?*, 68 Chi.-Kent L. Rev. 715, 721-22 (1993) (arguing that *Two Pesos* is indicative of a trend to strengthen the "property" nature of intellectual property). Certainly, the Court expresses a concern that seems consistent with the incentive theory: "protecting an inherently distinctive trade dress from its inception may be critical to new entrants to the market." Early protection encourages the development of new marks, in the Court's view.

A moral argument can also be made in favor of protecting inherently distinctive trade dress, at least against intentional copying. Such an argument asserts that the infringer can make no valid moral claim to copy the trade dress, so a right to it ought to reside in its creator. This is different from saying that the originator of the trade dress has earned it; it says that he gets it by default, because no one else has a superior claim. *See* Lawrence Becker, Property Rights: Philosophic Foundations 41 (1977) ("[i]t is not so much that the producers *deserve* the produce of their labors. It is rather that no one else does. . . ."); *see also* Robert C. Denicola, *Institutional Publicity Rights: An Analysis of the Merchandising of Famous Trade Symbols*, 62 N.C. L. Rev. 603, 640-41 (1984) (arguing no one has better claim to trademark's commercial value than its producer). This moral view — that knock-offs are bad — appears to be behind the "New York rule" discussed above. Arguably, though, this approach misses the point. Isn't the question not *who* should own the right to a mark, but whether *anyone* should have exclusive rights to it?

Judge Posner gives an economic answer to this question; he says that in some situations we declare property rights merely to prevent wasteful dissipation of the value of the asset covered by the right. He explicitly applies this to the right of publicity. *See* Richard Posner, Economic Analysis of Law 43 (4th ed. 1992):

> [W]hatever information value a celebrity's endorsement has to consumers would be lost if every advertiser can use the celebrity's name and picture. . . . The existence of a congestion externality provides an argument that rights of publicity should be perpetual and thus

> inheritable (a matter of legal controversy today). We don't want this form of information or expression to be in the public domain, because it will be less valuable there, whether the celebrity is dead or alive.

Is this such a situation? What waste would occur if other restaurants were permitted to duplicate the Taco Cabana décor? For a contrary argument, that the copying of product design should be permitted in a market economy unless society needs to subsidize the creation of such designs, see Robert C. Denicola, *Freedom to Copy*, 108 YALE L.J. 1661 (1999); Mark A. Lemley, *Ex Ante Versus Ex Post Justifications for Intellectual Property*, 71 U. CHI. L. REV. 147 (2004).

4. Should trade dress protection extend to the décor of a restaurant? Does *Two Pesos* open the door to a wide variety of claims that a particular style of doing business is protectable "trade dress?" An extreme example of a trade dress claim allowed in the wake of *Two Pesos* is Toy Mfrs. of America v. Helmsley-Spear, Inc., 960 F. Supp. 673 (S.D.N.Y. 1997), where the court held that the plaintiff's "unique" registration process, forms, and location for a toy fair (taken together) constituted protectable trade dress which the defendants had infringed.

Wal-Mart Stores, Inc. v. Samara Brothers, Inc.

529 U.S. 205 (2000)

Justice SCALIA delivered the opinion of the Court.

In this case, we decide under what circumstances a product's design is distinctive, and therefore protectible, in an action for infringement of unregistered trade dress under § 43(a) of the Trademark Act of 1946 (Lanham Act), 60 Stat. 441, as amended, 15 U.S.C. § 1125(a).

I

Respondent Samara Brothers, Inc., designs and manufactures children's clothing. Its primary product is a line of spring/summer one-piece seersucker outfits decorated with appliques of hearts, flowers, fruits, and the like. A number of chain stores, including JCPenney, sell this line of clothing under contract with Samara.

Petitioner Wal-Mart Stores, Inc., is one of the nation's best known retailers, selling among other things children's clothing. In 1995, Wal-Mart contracted with one of its suppliers, Judy-Philippine, Inc., to manufacture a line of children's outfits for sale in the 1996 spring/summer season. Wal-Mart sent Judy-Philippine photographs of a number of garments from Samara's line, on which Judy-Philippine's garments were to be based; Judy-Philippine duly copied, with only minor modifications, 16 of Samara's garments, many of which contained copyrighted elements. In 1996, Wal-Mart briskly sold the so-called knockoffs, generating more than $1.15 million in gross profits. . . .

After sending cease-and-desist letters, Samara brought this action in the United States District Court for the Southern District of New York against Wal-Mart, Judy-Philippine, Kmart, Caldor, Hills, and Goody's for copyright infringement under federal law, consumer fraud and unfair competition under New York law, and—

most relevant for our purposes—infringement of unregistered trade dress under §43(a) of the Lanham Act, 15 U.S.C. §1125(a). . . .

After a weeklong trial, the jury found in favor of Samara on all of its claims. . . . The Second Circuit affirmed . . . , 165 F.3d 120 (1998), and we granted certiorari. . . .

II

The Lanham Act provides for the registration of trademarks, which it defines in §45 to include "any word, name, symbol, or device, or any combination thereof [used or intended to be used] to identify and distinguish [a producer's] goods . . . from those manufactured or sold by others and to indicate the source of the goods. . . ." 15 U.S.C. §1127. . . . In addition to protecting registered marks, the Lanham Act, in §43(a), gives a producer a cause of action for the use by any person of "any word, term, name, symbol, or device, or any combination thereof . . . which . . . is likely to cause confusion . . . as to the origin, sponsorship, or approval of his or her goods. . . ." 15 U.S.C. §1125(a). It is the latter provision that is at issue in this case.

The breadth of the definition of marks registrable under §2, and of the confusion-producing elements recited as actionable by §43(a), has been held to embrace not just word marks, such as "Nike," and symbol marks, such as Nike's "swoosh" symbol, but also "trade dress"—a category that originally included only the packaging, or "dressing," of a product, but in recent years has been expanded by many courts of appeals to encompass the design of a product. See, e.g., Ashley Furniture Industries, Inc. v. Sangiacomo N.A., Ltd., 187 F.3d 363 (C.A.4 1999) (bedroom furniture); Knitwaves, Inc. v. Lollytogs, Ltd., 71 F.3d 996 (C.A.2 1995) (sweaters); Stuart Hall Co., Inc. v. Ampad Corp., 51 F.3d 780 (C.A.8 1995) (notebooks). These courts have assumed, often without discussion, that trade dress constitutes a "symbol" or "device" for purposes of the relevant sections, and we conclude likewise. "Since human beings might use as a 'symbol' or 'device' almost anything at all that is capable of carrying meaning, this language, read literally, is not restrictive." Qualitex Co. v. Jacobson Products Co., 514 U.S. 159, 162 (1995). This reading of §2 and §43(a) is buttressed by a recently added subsection of §43(a), §43(a)(3), which refers specifically to "civil action[s] for trade dress infringement under this chapter for trade dress not registered on the principal register." 15 U.S.C.A. §1125(a)(3) (Oct. 1999 Supp.).

The text of §43(a) provides little guidance as to the circumstances under which unregistered trade dress may be protected. It does require that a producer show that the allegedly infringing feature is not "functional," see §43(a)(3), and is likely to cause confusion with the product for which protection is sought, see §43(a)(1)(A), 15 U.S.C. §1125(a)(1)(A). Nothing in §43(a) explicitly requires a producer to show that its trade dress is distinctive, but courts have universally imposed that requirement, since without distinctiveness the trade dress would not "cause confusion . . . as to the origin, sponsorship, or approval of [the] goods," as the section requires. Distinctiveness is, moreover, an explicit prerequisite for registration of trade dress under §2, and "the general principles qualifying a mark for registration under §2 of the Lanham Act are for the most part applicable in determining whether an unregistered mark is entitled to protection under §43(a)." Two Pesos, Inc. v. Taco Cabana, Inc., 505 U.S. 763, 768 (1992) (citations omitted).

In evaluating the distinctiveness of a mark under § 2 (and therefore, by analogy, under § 43(a)), courts have held that a mark can be distinctive in one of two ways. First, a mark is inherently distinctive if "[its] intrinsic nature serves to identify a particular source." Ibid. In the context of word marks, courts have applied the now-classic test originally formulated by Judge Friendly, in which word marks that are "arbitrary" ("Camel" cigarettes), "fanciful" ("Kodak" film), or "suggestive" ("Tide" laundry detergent) are held to be inherently distinctive. See Abercrombie & Fitch Co. v. Hunting World, Inc., 537 F.2d 4, 10-11 (C.A.2 1976). Second, a mark has acquired distinctiveness, even if it is not inherently distinctive, if it has developed secondary meaning, which occurs when, "in the minds of the public, the primary significance of a [mark] is to identify the source of the product rather than the product itself." Inwood Laboratories, Inc. v. Ives Laboratories, Inc., 456 U.S. 844, 851, n.11 (1982).

The judicial differentiation between marks that are inherently distinctive and those that have developed secondary meaning has solid foundation in the statute itself. Section 2 requires that registration be granted to any trademark "by which the goods of the applicant may be distinguished from the goods of others" — subject to various limited exceptions. 15 U.S.C. § 1052. It also provides, again with limited exceptions, that "nothing in this chapter shall prevent the registration of a mark used by the applicant which has become distinctive of the applicant's goods in commerce" — that is, which is not inherently distinctive but has become so only through secondary meaning. § 2(f), 15 U.S.C. § 1052(f). Nothing in § 2, however, demands the conclusion that *every* category of mark necessarily includes some marks "by which the goods of the applicant may be distinguished from the goods of others" *without* secondary meaning — that in every category some marks are inherently distinctive.

Indeed, with respect to at least one category of mark — colors — we have held that no mark can ever be inherently distinctive. See *Qualitex,* 514 U.S., at 162-163. In *Qualitex,* petitioner manufactured and sold green-gold dry-cleaning press pads. After respondent began selling pads of a similar color, petitioner brought suit under § 43(a), then added a claim under § 32 after obtaining registration for the color of its pads. We held that a color could be protected as a trademark, but only upon a showing of secondary meaning. Reasoning by analogy to the *Abercrombie & Fitch* test developed for word marks, we noted that a product's color is unlike a "fanciful," "arbitrary," or "suggestive" mark, since it does not "almost *automatically* tell a customer that [it] refer[s] to a brand," ibid., and does not "immediately . . . signal a brand or a product 'source,'" id., at 163. However, we noted that, "over time, customers may come to treat a particular color on a product or its packaging . . . as signifying a brand." Id., at 162-163. Because a color, like a "descriptive" word mark, could eventually "come to indicate a product's origin," we concluded that it could be protected *upon a showing of secondary meaning.* Ibid.

It seems to us that design, like color, is not inherently distinctive. The attribution of inherent distinctiveness to certain categories of word marks and product packaging derives from the fact that the very purpose of attaching a particular word to a product, or encasing it in a distinctive packaging, is most often to identify the source of the product. Although the words and packaging can serve subsidiary functions — a suggestive word mark (such as "Tide" for laundry detergent), for instance, may invoke positive connotations in the consumer's mind, and a garish form of packaging (such as Tide's squat, brightly decorated plastic bottles for its liquid laundry detergent) may attract an otherwise indifferent consumer's attention on a crowded store shelf — their predominant function remains source identification. Consumers are therefore predisposed to regard those symbols as indication of the producer, which is why such symbols "almost *automatically* tell a customer that they refer to a brand," id., at 162-163, and "immediately . . . signal a brand or a product 'source,'" id., at 163. And where it is not reasonable to assume consumer predisposition to take an affixed word or packaging as indication of source — where, for example, the affixed word is descriptive of the product ("Tasty" bread) or of a geographic origin ("Georgia" peaches) — inherent distinctiveness will not be found. That is why the statute generally excludes, from those word marks that can be registered as inherently distinctive, words that are "merely descriptive" of the goods, § 2(e)(1), 15 U.S.C. § 1052(e)(1), or "primarily geographically descriptive of them," see § 2(e)(2), 15 U.S.C. § 1052(e)(2). In the case of product design, as in the case of color, we think consumer predisposition to equate the feature with the source does not exist. Consumers are aware of the reality that, almost invariably, even the most unusual of product designs — such as a cocktail shaker shaped like a penguin — is intended not to identify the source, but to render the product itself more useful or more appealing.

The fact that product design almost invariably serves purposes other than source identification not only renders inherent distinctiveness problematic; it also renders application of an inherent-distinctiveness principle more harmful to other consumer interests. Consumers should not be deprived of the benefits of competition with regard to the utilitarian and esthetic purposes that product design ordinarily serves by a rule of law that facilitates plausible threats of suit against new entrants based upon alleged inherent distinctiveness. How easy it is to mount a plausible suit depends, of course, upon the clarity of the test for inherent distinctiveness, and where product design is concerned we have little confidence that a reasonably clear test can be devised. Respondent and the United States as *amicus curiae* urge us to adopt for product design relevant portions of the test formulated by the Court of Customs and Patent Appeals for product packaging in Seabrook Foods, Inc. v. Bar-Well Foods, Ltd., 568 F.2d 1342 (1977). That opinion, in determining the inherent distinctiveness of a product's packaging, considered, among other things, "whether it was a 'common' basic shape or design, whether it was unique or unusual in a particular field, [and] whether it was a mere refinement of a commonly-adopted and well-known form of ornamentation for a particular class of goods viewed by the public as a dress or ornamentation for the goods." Id., at 1344 (footnotes omitted). Such a test would rarely provide the basis for summary disposition of an anticompetitive strike suit. Indeed, at oral argument, counsel for the United States quite understandably would not give a definitive answer as to whether the test was met in this very case, saying only that "[t]his is a very difficult case for that purpose."

It is true, of course, that the person seeking to exclude new entrants would have to establish the nonfunctionality of the design feature, see § 43(a)(3), 15 U.S.C.A. § 1125(a)(3) (Oct. 1999 Supp.) — a showing that may involve consideration of its esthetic appeal, see *Qualitex,* 514 U.S., at 170. Competition is deterred, however, not merely by successful suit but by the plausible threat of successful suit, and given the unlikelihood of inherently source-identifying design, the game of allowing suit based upon alleged inherent distinctiveness seems to us not worth the candle. That is especially so since the producer can ordinarily obtain protection for a design that *is* inherently source identifying (if any such exists), but that does not yet have secondary meaning, by securing a design patent or a copyright for the design — as, indeed, respondent did for certain elements of the designs in this case. The availability of these other protections greatly reduces any harm to the producer that might ensue from our conclusion that a product design cannot be protected under § 43(a) without a showing of secondary meaning.

Respondent contends that our decision in *Two Pesos* forecloses a conclusion that product-design trade dress can never be inherently distinctive. In that case, we held that the trade dress of a chain of Mexican restaurants, which the plaintiff described as "a festive eating atmosphere having interior dining and patio areas decorated with artifacts, bright colors, paintings and murals," 505 U.S., at 765 (internal quotation marks and citation omitted), could be protected under § 43(a) without a showing of secondary meaning, see id., at 776. *Two Pesos* unquestionably establishes the legal principle that trade dress can be inherently distinctive, see, e.g., id., at 773, but it does not establish that *product-design* trade dress can be. *Two Pesos* is inapposite to our holding here because the trade dress at issue, the decor of a restaurant, seems to us not to constitute product *design*. It was either product packaging — which, as we have discussed, normally *is* taken by the consumer to indicate origin — or else some tertium quid that is akin to product packaging and has no bearing on the present case.

Respondent replies that this manner of distinguishing *Two Pesos* will force courts to draw difficult lines between product-design and product-packaging trade dress. There will indeed be some hard cases at the margin: a classic glass Coca-Cola bottle, for instance, may constitute packaging for those consumers who drink the Coke and then discard the bottle, but may constitute the product itself for those consumers who are bottle collectors, or part of the product itself for those consumers who buy Coke in the classic glass bottle, rather than a can, because they think it more stylish to drink from the former. We believe, however, that the frequency and the difficulty of having to distinguish between product design and product packaging will be much less than the frequency and the difficulty of having to decide when a product design is inherently distinctive. To the extent there are close cases, we believe that courts should err on the side of caution and classify ambiguous trade dress as product design, thereby requiring secondary meaning. The very closeness will suggest the existence of relatively small utility in adopting an inherent-distinctiveness principle, and relatively great consumer benefit in requiring a demonstration of secondary meaning. . . .

We hold that, in an action for infringement of unregistered trade dress under § 43(a) of the Lanham Act, a product's design is distinctive, and therefore protectible, only upon a showing of secondary meaning. The judgment of the Second Circuit is reversed, and the case is remanded for further proceedings consistent with this opinion.

It is so ordered.

COMMENTS AND QUESTIONS

1. *Trade Dress Classification.* The Supreme Court establishes three categories for determining whether a product's trade dress is protectable: (1) product packaging; (2) product design; and (3) a "tertium quid" (defined in the *Oxford English Dictionary* as "[s]omething (indefinite or left undefined) related in some way to two (definite or known) things, but distinct from both."). Product packaging can be inherently distinctive while product design cannot. But how is one to distinguish the two? Should close cases (such as the Coca-Cola bottle) be characterized as product design and hence subject to the higher threshold of secondary meaning? Did the Court introduce

needless confusion by not simply acknowledging that its finding in *Two Pesos* that the décor of a Mexican restaurant was inherently distinctive was ill-advised? Furthermore, the Court leaves unresolved who decides on the classification of trade dress. *Two Pesos* seems to suggest that this question is for the jury, whereas *Samara* emphasizes summary adjudication. Who should decide?

2. Does the classification scheme established for word marks help to distinguish descriptive from inherently distinctive trade dress? In Rock and Roll Hall of Fame and Museum, Inc. v. Gentile Productions, 134 F.3d 749 (6th Cir. 1998), the owner of the Rock and Roll Hall of Fame building in Cleveland, Ohio, sued a photographer who marketed pictures of the building set against the Cleveland skyline, alleging that the photographer was infringing the building's trade dress. The district court issued a preliminary injunction, but the Sixth Circuit reversed. The majority and the dissent battled over the proper classification of the museum. The majority agreed that the design of the museum was "fanciful" but denied that it was "fanciful in a trademark sense." It concluded that the design of the museum itself did not function as a trademark and that the public did not recognize it as such. Important to the court's determination was the trademark owner's inconsistent use of the museum's design as a source-identifying function:

> [A]lthough the Museum has used drawings or pictures of its building design on various goods, it has not done so with any consistency. As museum director Robert Bosak stated in his affidavit, "the Museum has used versions of the building shape trademark on . . . a wide variety of products." Several items marketed by the Museum display only the rear of the Museum's building, which looks dramatically different from the front. Drawings of the front of the Museum on the two T-shirts in the record are similar, but they are quite different from the photograph featured in the Museum's poster. And, although the photograph from the poster is also used on a postcard, another postcard displays various close-up photographs of the Museum which, individually and perhaps even collectively, are not even immediately recognizable as photographs of the Museum. In this regard, this case is similar to those in which a party has claimed trademark rights in a famous person's likeness. In Estate of Presley [v. Russen, 513 F. Supp. 1339, 1363-64 (D.N.J. 1981)], the court concluded that, although one particular image of [Elvis] Presley had been used consistently as a mark, "the available evidence [did] not support [the estate's] broad position" that all images of Presley served such a function.

134 F.3d 749, 754-55.

In another case, the Sixth Circuit had little difficulty in applying *Samara*'s classification scheme to furniture. *See* Herman Miller v. Palazzetti Imports and Exports, Inc., 270 F.3d 298 (6th Cir. 2001) (finding genuine issue of material fact as to whether lounge chair and ottoman had acquired secondary meaning). *But see* McNeil Nutrition v. Heartland Sweeteners, 566 F. Supp. 2d 378 (E.D. Pa. 2008) (finding that the yellow packaging of Splenda sugar substitute was arbitrary and thus inherently distinctive).

3. *Product Configurations and Overlapping Intellectual Property Rights.* An old rule of intellectual property law called the "principle of election" used to limit an author to one type of intellectual property protection. That doctrine was resoundingly rejected in In re Yardley, 493 F.2d 1389 (C.C.P.A. 1974). *Yardley* involved a design patent application for a watch which featured a caricature of Spiro Agnew. The patent examiner rejected the application on the ground that Yardley had already received several copyright registrations for the watch. The Court of Customs and Patent

Appeals reversed, concluding that the principle of election was in direct conflict with the patent, copyright, and trademark statutes. The court reasoned that because each statute strikes its own "coverage" balance, a work that qualifies for protection under more than one statute is entitled to the protection of each.

Nonetheless, where Congress has not expressly dictated the principles for channeling protection among the various modes of intellectual property, the courts have construed the scope of protection in order to effectuate the larger policies of federal intellectual property law. In general, utility patent protection trumps all other modes of intellectual property with regard to the functional features of products. The courts recognize that patent law imposes high thresholds for protection (novelty, nonobviousness, and disclosure) and an examination process and affords a relatively short duration of protection in order to balance the short-run hampering of free competition with the longer-term benefits of innovation. Were copyright law or trademark law to afford protection for utilitarian features of products, patent law would be unnecessary and competition would give way to monopolization by the first to design a product, regardless of the effort that went into the design. In order to minimize this threat, the Supreme Court in *Baker v. Selden* foreclosed competition under copyright law for accounting systems. (Congress reinforced this limitation in the 1976 Copyright Act, *see* 17 U.S.C. §102(b).) The Supreme Court acknowledged a similarly high burden for establishing that a product feature or configuration that has been the subject of a utility patent can ever qualify for trade dress protection. *See* TrafFix Devices, Inc. v. Marketing Displays, Inc., 532 U.S. 23 (2001), excerpted, *infra*, in section C.

How do dress designs fit into this framework? Copyright law denies protection for dress (as opposed to fabric) designs, *see* Whimsicality, Inc. v. Rubie's Costume Co., Inc., 891 F.2d 452 (2d Cir. 1989); Fashion Originators Guild v. FTC, 114 F.2d 80, 84 (2d Cir. 1940) (L. Hand, J.) (holding that clothes, as useful articles, are not copyrightable), *aff'd*, 312 U.S. 457 (1941); see also 1 Nimmer on Copyright, *supra*, §2.08[H]; H.R. Rep. No. 1476, 94th Cong., 2d Sess. 55 (1976), *reprinted in* 1976 U.S.C.C.A.N. 5659, 5668 (noting that the Copyright Act of 1976 did not affect the prior law in this regard), and design patent law affords protection for the ornamental features of articles of manufacture. Should trade dress law be permitted to enter this sphere? While not excluding trade dress protection for dress designs, the *Samara* decision reflects a concern for not unduly hindering free competition. The Court noted the fact that product design "almost invariably serves purposes other than source identification," such as making products more useful or appealing. The Court also stated that application of the inherently distinctive test in product design cases could deprive consumers of "the benefits of competition with regard to the utilitarian and esthetic purposes that product design ordinarily serves." *See also* Samara Bros., Inc. v. Wal-Mart Stores, Inc., 165 F.3d 120, 133 (2d Cir. 1999) (Newman, dissenting) (noting that "we must construe the Lanham Act 'in the light of a strong federal policy in favor of vigorously competitive markets' "; "courts are to 'exercise[ ] particular caution when extending [trademark] protection to product designs' "; " 'just as copyright law does not protect ideas but only their concrete expression, neither does trade dress law protect an idea, a concept, or a generalized type of appearance.' ").

The Supreme Court took a sharply different tack from *Yardley* in its most recent treatment of the issue. In Dastar Corp. v. Twentieth Century Fox Film Corp., 539 U.S. 23 (2003), defendant Dastar produced and sold its own copies of plaintiff's video series, in which the copyright had expired. Fox sued on the grounds that Dastar was misrepresenting the origin of the goods in violation of the Lanham Act. The Court rejected that argument, construing "origin" narrowly to mean only the physical source of the videotapes, not who had actually filmed or produced them. In so holding, the Court was expressly concerned to avoid reading the Lanham Act to conflict with copyright law, which would permit such copying. It warned "against misuse or over-extension of trademark and related protections into areas traditionally occupied by patent or copyright," and explained that "allowing a cause of action under §43(a) for that representation would create a species of mutant copyright law that limits the public's federal right to copy and to use expired copyrights." *Id.* at 34. The Court seems quite concerned with channeling protection between the copyright and trademark regimes and unwilling to permit much overlap between the two. For more on the *Dastar* opinion, including the opinion itself, see Chapter 9.F.4 *infra.*

4. Should "Tide's squat, brightly decorated plastic bottles for its liquid laundry detergent" be deemed inherently distinctive, as Justice Scalia seems to suggest? How would you analyze this example?

PROBLEM

Problem 4-2. Alice Richland, a gourmet chef world renowned for her chocolate desserts, designs a new line of chocolate products. Called "Chocolate Shells," these products are made of dark chocolate flavored in special ways with a combination of ingredients Alice hit upon after months of work in her kitchens. The use of the special ingredients imparts a unique flavor to the Shells, and has the additional property of making the usually soft chocolate feel sandy or grainy to the touch. The Shells are made in the shapes of different seashells native to the Florida coast, and each shell is colored in a different, unusual pattern. On the advice of her lawyer, Alice files a trademark application seeking to register each of her shell designs. What aspects of the Shells are entitled to registration? To Section 43(a) protection?

C. FUNCTIONALITY

Regardless of whether a trade dress feature is distinctive of source, it will not qualify for protection if it is "functional." Of course, all trade dress features that are source-distinctive are functional in the lay sense that they function to indicate the source of the product to which they are attached or of which they form a part. In trademark law, however, "functionality" is a term of art denoting a legal conclusion. As we saw above, in Qualitex Co. v. Jacobson Products Co., Inc., 514 U.S. 159 (1995), the Supreme Court explained the pro-competitive rationale underlying functionality doctrine:

> The functionality doctrine prevents trademark law, which seeks to promote competition by protecting a firm's reputation, from instead inhibiting legitimate competition by

> allowing a producer to control a useful product feature. It is the province of patent law, not trademark law, to encourage invention by granting inventors a monopoly over new product designs or functions for a limited time, 35 U.S.C. §§154, 173, after which competitors are free to use the innovation. If a product's functional features could be used as trademarks, however, a monopoly over such features could be obtained without regard to whether they qualify as patents and could be extended forever (because trademarks may be renewed in perpetuity). See Kellogg Co. v. National Biscuit Co., 305 U.S. 111, 119-120, 59 S. Ct. 109, 113-114 . . . (1938) (Brandeis, J.); *Inwood Laboratories, Inc.*, supra, 456 U.S., at 863, 102 S. Ct., at 2193 (White, J., concurring in result) ("A functional characteristic is 'an important ingredient in the commercial success of the product,' and, after expiration of a patent, it is no more the property of the originator than the product itself") (citation omitted). Functionality doctrine therefore would require, to take an imaginary example, that even if customers have come to identify the special illumination-enhancing shape of a new patented light bulb with a particular manufacturer, the manufacturer may not use that shape as a trademark, for doing so, after the patent had expired, would impede competition — not by protecting the reputation of the original bulb maker, but by frustrating competitors' legitimate efforts to produce an equivalent illumination-enhancing bulb. See, e.g., *Kellogg Co.*, supra, 305 U.S., at 119-120, 59 S. Ct., at 113-114 (trademark law cannot be used to extend monopoly over "pillow" shape of shredded wheat biscuit after the patent for that shape had expired). This Court consequently has explained that, "[i]n general terms, a product feature is functional," and cannot serve as a trademark, "if it is essential to the use or purpose of the article or if it affects the cost or quality of the article," that is, if exclusive use of the feature would put competitors at a significant non-reputation-related disadvantage. *Inwood Laboratories, Inc.*, 456 U.S., at 850, n.10, 102 S. Ct., at 2186, n.10.

Id. at 165.

The final sentence of this passage from the *Qualitex* opinion, which appears to suggest that the "significant non-reputation-related disadvantage" standard for functionality is simply a restatement of — and interchangeable with — the "essential to the use or purpose" standard, came back to haunt the Supreme Court. In the following opinion, the Court revisited the issue of trademark functionality and sought to clarify the meaning of *Qualitex*'s foray into functionality doctrine.

TrafFix Devices, Inc. v. Marketing Displays, Inc.
532 U.S. 23 (2001)

Justice Kennedy delivered the opinion of the Court.

Temporary road signs with warnings like "Road Work Ahead" or "Left Shoulder Closed" must withstand strong gusts of wind. An inventor named Robert Sarkisian obtained two utility patents for a mechanism built upon two springs (the dual-spring design) to keep these and other outdoor signs upright despite adverse wind conditions. The holder of the now-expired Sarkisian patents, respondent Marketing Displays, Inc. (MDI), established a successful business in the manufacture and sale of sign stands incorporating the patented feature. MDI's stands for road signs were recognizable to buyers and users (it says) because the dual-spring design was visible near the base of the sign.

This litigation followed after the patents expired and a competitor, TrafFix Devices, Inc., sold sign stands with a visible spring mechanism that looked like

MDI's. MDI and TrafFix products looked alike because they were. When TrafFix started in business, it sent an MDI product abroad to have it reverse engineered, that is to say copied. Complicating matters, TrafFix marketed its sign stands under a name similar to MDI's. MDI used the name "WindMaster," while TrafFix, its new competitor, used "WindBuster." . . .

I

We are concerned with the trade dress question. The District Court ruled against MDI on its trade dress claim. 971 F. Supp. 262 (E.D. Mich. 1997). After determining that the one element of MDI's trade dress at issue was the dual-spring design, id., at 265, it held that "no reasonable trier of fact could determine that MDI has established secondary meaning" in its alleged trade dress, id., at 269. In other words, consumers did not associate the look of the dual-spring design with MDI. As a second, independent reason to grant summary judgment in favor of TrafFix, the District Court determined the dual-spring design was functional. . . .

The Court of Appeals for the Sixth Circuit reversed the trade dress ruling. 200 F.3d 929 (1999). . . . In its criticism of the District Court's ruling on the trade dress question, the Court of Appeals took note of a split among Courts of Appeals in various other Circuits on the issue whether the existence of an expired utility patent forecloses the possibility of the patentee's claiming trade dress protection in the product's design. 200 F.3d, at 939. Compare Sunbeam Products, Inc. v. West Bend Co., 123 F.3d 246 (C.A.5 1997) (holding that trade dress protection is not foreclosed), Thomas & Betts Corp. v. Panduit Corp., 138 F.3d 277 (C.A.7 1998) (same), and Midwest Industries, Inc. v. Karavan Trailers, Inc., 175 F.3d 1356 (C.A.Fed. 1999) (same), with Vornado Air Circulation Systems, Inc. v. Duracraft Corp., 58 F.3d 1498, 1500 (C.A.10 1995) ("Where a product configuration is a significant inventive component of an invention covered by a utility patent . . . it cannot receive trade dress protection"). To resolve the conflict, we granted certiorari.

II

It is well established that trade dress can be protected under federal law. The design or packaging of a product may acquire a distinctiveness which serves to identify the product with its manufacturer or source; and a design or package which acquires this secondary meaning, assuming other requisites are met, is a trade dress which may not be used in a manner likely to cause confusion as to the origin, sponsorship, or approval of the goods. In these respects protection for trade dress exists to promote competition. . . . Congress confirmed this statutory protection for trade dress by amending the Lanham Act to recognize the concept. Title 15 U.S.C. §1125(a)(3) (1994 ed., Supp. V) provides: "In a civil action for trade dress infringement under this chapter for trade dress not registered on the principal register, the person who asserts trade dress protection has the burden of proving that the matter sought to be protected is not functional." This burden of proof gives force to the well-established rule that trade dress protection may not be claimed for product features that are functional. *Qualitex*, supra, at 164-165; Two Pesos, Inc. v. Taco Cabana, Inc., 505 U.S. 763, 775

(1992). And in *Wal-Mart*, supra, we were careful to caution against misuse or overextension of trade dress. We noted that "product design almost invariably serves purposes other than source identification." Id., at 213.

Trade dress protection must subsist with the recognition that in many instances there is no prohibition against copying goods and products. In general, unless an intellectual property right such as a patent or copyright protects an item, it will be subject to copying. As the Court has explained, copying is not always discouraged or disfavored by the laws which preserve our competitive economy. Bonito Boats, Inc. v. Thunder Craft Boats, Inc., 489 U.S. 141, 160 (1989). Allowing competitors to copy will have salutary effects in many instances. "Reverse engineering of chemical and mechanical articles in the public domain often leads to significant advances in technology." Ibid.

The principal question in this case is the effect of an expired patent on a claim of trade dress infringement. A prior patent, we conclude, has vital significance in resolving the trade dress claim. A utility patent is strong evidence that the features therein claimed are functional. If trade dress protection is sought for those features the strong evidence of functionality based on the previous patent adds great weight to the statutory presumption that features are deemed functional until proved otherwise by the party seeking trade dress protection. Where the expired patent claimed the features in question, one who seeks to establish trade dress protection must carry the heavy burden of showing that the feature is not functional, for instance by showing that it is merely an ornamental, incidental, or arbitrary aspect of the device.

In the case before us, the central advance claimed in the expired utility patents (the Sarkisian patents) is the dual-spring design; and the dual-spring design is the essential feature of the trade dress MDI now seeks to establish and to protect. The rule we have explained bars the trade dress claim, for MDI did not, and cannot, carry the burden of overcoming the strong evidentiary inference of functionality based on the disclosure of the dual-spring design in the claims of the expired patents.

The dual springs shown in the Sarkisian patents were well apart (at either end of a frame for holding a rectangular sign when one full side is the base) while the dual springs at issue here are close together (in a frame designed to hold a sign by one of its corners). As the District Court recognized, this makes little difference. The point is that the springs are necessary to the operation of the device. The fact that the springs in this very different-looking device fall within the claims of the patents is illustrated by MDI's own position in earlier litigation. In the late 1970's, MDI engaged in a long-running intellectual property battle with a company known as Winn-Proof. Although the precise claims of the Sarkisian patents cover sign stands with springs "spaced apart," U.S. Patent No. 3,646,696, col. 4; U.S. Patent No. 3,662,482, col. 4, the Winn-Proof sign stands (with springs much like the sign stands at issue here) were found to infringe the patents by the United States District Court for the District of Oregon, and the Court of Appeals for the Ninth Circuit affirmed the judgment. Sarkisian v. Winn-Proof Corp., 697 F.2d 1313 (1983). Although the Winn-Proof traffic sign stand (with dual springs close together) did not appear, then, to infringe the literal terms of the patent claims (which called for "spaced apart" springs), the Winn-Proof sign stand was found to infringe the patents under the doctrine of equivalents. . . . In light of this past ruling—a ruling procured at MDI's own insistence—it must be concluded the products here at issue would have been covered by the claims of the expired patents.

The rationale for the rule that the disclosure of a feature in the claims of a utility patent constitutes strong evidence of functionality is well illustrated in this case. The dual-spring design serves the important purpose of keeping the sign upright even in heavy wind conditions; and, as confirmed by the statements in the expired patents, it does so in a unique and useful manner. As the specification of one of the patents recites, prior art "devices, in practice, will topple under the force of a strong wind." U.S. Patent No. 3,662,482, col. 1. The dual-spring design allows sign stands to resist toppling in strong winds. Using a dual-spring design rather than a single spring achieves important operational advantages. For example, the specifications of the patents note that the "use of a pair of springs . . . as opposed to the use of a single spring to support the frame structure prevents canting or twisting of the sign around a vertical axis," and that, if not prevented, twisting "may cause damage to the spring structure and may result in tipping of the device." U.S. Patent No. 3,646,696, col. 3. In the course of patent prosecution, it was said that "[t]he use of a pair of spring connections as opposed to a single spring connection . . . forms an important part of this combination" because it "forc[es] the sign frame to tip along the longitudinal axis of the elongated ground-engaging members." The dual-spring design affects the cost of the device as well; it was acknowledged that the device "could use three springs but this would unnecessarily increase the cost of the device." These statements made in the patent applications and in the course of procuring the patents demonstrate the functionality of the design. MDI does not assert that any of these representations are mistaken or inaccurate, and this is further strong evidence of the functionality of the dual-spring design.

III

In finding for MDI on the trade dress issue the Court of Appeals gave insufficient recognition to the importance of the expired utility patents, and their evidentiary significance, in establishing the functionality of the device. The error likely was caused by its misinterpretation of trade dress principles in other respects. As we have noted, even if there has been no previous utility patent the party asserting trade dress has the burden to establish the nonfunctionality of alleged trade dress features. MDI could not meet this burden. Discussing trademarks, we have said " '[i]n general terms, a product feature is functional,' and cannot serve as a trademark, 'if it is essential to the use or purpose of the article or if it affects the cost or quality of the article.' " *Qualitex*, 514 U.S., at 165 (quoting Inwood Laboratories, Inc. v. Ives Laboratories, Inc., 456 U.S. 844, 850, n.10 (1982)). Expanding upon the meaning of this phrase, we have observed that a functional feature is one the "exclusive use of [which] would put competitors at a significant non-reputation-related disadvantage." 514 U.S. at 165. The Court of Appeals in the instant case seemed to interpret this language to mean that a necessary test for functionality is "whether the particular product configuration is a competitive necessity." 200 F.3d at 940. See also *Vornado*, 58 F.3d, at 1507 ("Functionality, by contrast, has been defined both by our circuit, and more recently by the Supreme Court, in terms of competitive need"). This was incorrect as a comprehensive definition. As explained in *Qualitex*, supra, and *Inwood*, supra, a feature is also functional when it is essential to the use or purpose of the device or when it affects the cost or quality of the device. The *Qualitex* decision did not purport to displace this traditional rule. Instead, it quoted the rule as *Inwood* had set it forth. It is proper to inquire into a "significant non-reputation-related disadvantage" in cases of aesthetic functionality, the question involved in *Qualitex*. Where the design is functional under the *Inwood* formulation there is no need to proceed further to consider if there is a competitive necessity for the feature. In *Qualitex*, by contrast, aesthetic functionality was the central question, there having been no indication that the green-gold color of the laundry press pad had any bearing on the use or purpose of the product or its cost or quality.

The Court has allowed trade dress protection to certain product features that are inherently distinctive. *Two Pesos*, 505 U.S., at 774. In *Two Pesos*, however, the Court at the outset made the explicit analytic assumption that the trade dress features in question (decorations and other features to evoke a Mexican theme in a restaurant) were not functional. Id., at 767, n.6. The trade dress in those cases did not bar competitors from copying functional product design features. In the instant case, beyond serving the purpose of informing consumers that the sign stands are made by MDI (assuming it does so), the dual-spring design provides a unique and useful mechanism to resist the force of the wind. Functionality having been established, whether MDI's dual-spring design has acquired secondary meaning need not be considered.

There is no need, furthermore, to engage, as did the Court of Appeals, in speculation about other design possibilities, such as using three or four springs which might serve the same purpose. 200 F.3d, at 940. Here, the functionality of the spring design means that competitors need not explore whether other spring juxtapositions might be used. The dual-spring design is not an arbitrary flourish in the configuration of MDI's product; it is the reason the device works. Other designs need not be attempted.

Because the dual-spring design is functional, it is unnecessary for competitors to explore designs to hide the springs, say by using a box or framework to cover them, as suggested by the Court of Appeals. Ibid. The dual-spring design assures the user the device will work. If buyers are assured the product serves its purpose by seeing the operative mechanism that in itself serves an important market need. It would be at cross-purposes to those objectives, and something of a paradox, were we to require the manufacturer to conceal the very item the user seeks.

In a case where a manufacturer seeks to protect arbitrary, incidental, or ornamental aspects of features of a product found in the patent claims, such as arbitrary curves in the legs or an ornamental pattern painted on the springs, a different result might obtain. There the manufacturer could perhaps prove that those aspects do not serve a purpose within the terms of the utility patent. The inquiry into whether such features, asserted to be trade dress, are functional by reason of their inclusion in the claims of an expired utility patent could be aided by going beyond the claims and examining the patent and its prosecution history to see if the feature in question is shown as a useful part of the invention. No such claim is made here, however. MDI in essence seeks protection for the dual-spring design alone. The asserted trade dress consists simply of the dual-spring design, four legs, a base, an upright, and a sign. MDI has pointed to nothing arbitrary about the components of its device or the way they are assembled. The Lanham Act does not exist to reward manufacturers for their innovation in creating a particular device; that is the purpose of the patent law and its period of exclusivity. The Lanham Act, furthermore, does not protect trade dress in a functional design simply because an investment has been made to encourage the public to associate a particular functional feature with a single manufacturer or seller. The

Court of Appeals erred in viewing MDI as possessing the right to exclude competitors from using a design identical to MDI's and to require those competitors to adopt a different design simply to avoid copying it. MDI cannot gain the exclusive right to produce sign stands using the dual-spring design by asserting that consumers associate it with the look of the invention itself. Whether a utility patent has expired or there has been no utility patent at all, a product design which has a particular appearance may be functional because it is "essential to the use or purpose of the article" or "affects the cost or quality of the article." *Inwood*, 456 U.S., at 850, n.10.

TrafFix and some of its *amici* argue that the Patent Clause of the Constitution, Art. I, § 8, cl. 8, of its own force, prohibits the holder of an expired utility patent from claiming trade dress protection. We need not resolve this question. If, despite the rule that functional features may not be the subject of trade dress protection, a case arises in which trade dress becomes the practical equivalent of an expired utility patent, that will be time enough to consider the matter. The judgment of the Court of Appeals is reversed, and the case is remanded for further proceedings consistent with this opinion.

It is so ordered.

Note on Lower Courts' Interpretation of *TrafFix Devices*

By establishing the "essential to the use or purpose" test as the dominant test for trademark functionality, the Supreme Court appears to have attempted to expand the scope of the functionality bar to protection and thus restrict the subject matter of trademark protection. For if a product feature is "essential to the use or purpose" of the product, then it is per se functional and unprotectable regardless of whether competitors could use an alternative product feature to accomplish the same purpose. But how do courts determine whether a product feature is "essential to the use or purpose" of the product? Can they take into account the existence of competitive alternatives to that product feature? In the wake of *TrafFix Devices*, the lower courts struggled with these questions and with what role, if any, the availability of competitive alternatives should play in the functionality analysis.

The Federal Circuit was the first appellate court to enter the fray. Its opinion two decades earlier in In re Morton-Norwich Products, Inc., 671 F.2d 1332 (C.C.P.A. 1982), was still highly influential on functionality analysis across the circuits. The case addressed the question of whether the configuration of a spray bottle was functional. Judge Rich began his analysis by inducing from previous case law four factors that bear on the functionality issue: (1) whether a previous utility patent disclosed any utilitarian advantages of the design sought to be registered as a trademark, (2) whether any advertising or promotion of the design touts its utilitarian advantages, (3) whether alternative designs will perform its function equally as well, and (4) whether the design results from a comparatively cheap, simple, or superior method of manufacturing. *Id.* at 1340-41. But in analyzing the functionality of the spray bottle configuration, Judge Rich focused only on the third of the "Morton-Norwich factors" going to competitive alternatives. In subsequent functionality cases not involving a preexisting utility patent, the competitive alternative factor emerged as by far the most influential. *See* McCarthy, McCarthy on Trademarks and Unfair Competition § 7:75.

With this background, the Federal Circuit sought to apply *TrafFix Devices* to the facts before it in Valu Engineering, Inc. v. Rexnord Corp., 278 F.3d 1268 (Fed. Cir. 2002), which involved an appeal of the Trademark Trial and Appeal Board's determination that certain guide rail configurations for conveyer belts were functional. After reviewing the holding of *TrafFix Devices*, the court stated:

> We do not understand the Supreme Court's decision in *TrafFix* to have altered the *Morton-Norwich* analysis. As noted above, the *Morton-Norwich* factors aid in the determination of whether a particular feature is functional, and the third factor focuses on the availability of "other alternatives." *Morton-Norwich*, 671 F.2d at 1341. We did not in the past under the third factor require that the opposing party establish that there was a "competitive necessity" for the product feature. Nothing in *TrafFix* suggests that consideration of alternative designs is not properly part of the overall mix, and we do not read the Court's observations in *TrafFix* as rendering the availability of alternative designs irrelevant. Rather, we conclude that the Court merely noted that once a product feature is found functional based on other considerations there is no need to consider the availability of alternative designs, because the feature cannot be given trade dress protection merely because there are alternative designs available. But that does not mean that the availability of alternative designs cannot be a legitimate source of evidence to determine whether a feature is functional in the first place. We find it significant that neither party argues that *TrafFix* changed the law of functionality, and that scholarly commentary has reached exactly the same conclusion that we have:
>
>> In the author's view, the observations by the Supreme Court in *TrafFix* do not mean that the availability of alternative designs cannot be a legitimate source of evidence to determine in the first instance if a particular feature is in fact "functional." Rather, the Court merely said that once a design is found to be functional, it cannot be given trade dress status merely because there are alternative designs available. . . .
>>
>> . . . The existence of actual or potential alternative designs that work equally well strongly suggests that the particular design used by plaintiff is not needed by competitors to effectively compete on the merits.
>
> J. Thomas McCarthy, 1 McCarthy on Trademarks and Unfair Competition, §7:75, 7-180-1 (4th ed. 2001). In sum, *TrafFix* does not render the Board's use of the *Morton-Norwich* factors erroneous.

Valu Engineering, Inc., *supra*, at 1276. Subsequent courts following *Valu Engineering*'s interpretation of *TrafFix Devices* have continued with the application of the *Morton-Norwich* factors. *See, e.g.*, Fuji Kogyo Co., Ltd. v. Pacific Bay Int'l, Inc., 461 F.3d 675, 685 (citing *TrafFix Devices* in passing but otherwise applying the *Morton-Norwich* factors).

The next year, the Fifth Circuit reviewed the import of *TrafFix Devices* in Eppendorf-Netheler-Hinz GmbH v. Ritter GmbH, 289 F.3d 351 (5th Cir. 2002), which involved the issue of whether certain design features of disposable pipette tips used for dispensing of liquids were functional:

> It is clear that functional product features do not qualify for trade dress protection. However, the definition of "functionality" has not enjoyed such clarity. . . . In *TrafFix*, the Supreme Court recognized two tests for functionality. First, the Court recognized the "traditional" definition of functionality: "a product feature is functional, and cannot serve as a trademark, 'if it is essential to the use or purpose of the article or if it affects the cost or quality of an article.'" *TrafFix*, 532 U.S. at 32 (citations omitted). Under this traditional definition, if a product feature is "the reason the device works," then the feature is functional. Id. at 34. The availability of alternative designs is irrelevant. Id. at 33-34.
>
> In addition to the traditional definition, *TrafFix* recognized a second test for functionality: "a functional feature is one the 'exclusive use of which would put competitors at a significant non-reputation-related disadvantage.'" Id. at 32 (quoting *Qualitex*, 514 U.S. at

165). This "competitive necessity" test for functionality is an expansion of the traditional test. Id. The Court emphasized, however, that the "competitive necessity" test is not "a comprehensive definition" of functionality. Id. at 33. The primary test for functionality is the traditional test, and there is no need to consider the "competitive necessity" test where a product feature is functional under the traditional definition. Id. at 33-35.

Eppendorf correctly argues that before *TrafFix*, this circuit had adopted a "utilitarian" test of functionality. Under this utilitarian test, "[t]he ultimate inquiry concerning functionality[ ] is whether characterizing a feature or configuration as protected 'will hinder competition or impinge upon the rights of others to compete effectively in the sale of goods.' " Sicilia Di R. Biebow & Co. v. Cox, 732 F.2d 417, 429 (5th Cir. 1984) (citation omitted); see also, Pebble Beach Co. v. Tour 18 I Ltd., 155 F.3d 526, 537-38 (5th Cir. 1998); Sunbeam Products, Inc. v. West Bend Co., 123 F.3d 246, 255 (5th Cir. 1997). This court's "utilitarian" test, with its focus on the ability of competitors to compete effectively in the marketplace, is virtually identical to the "competitive necessity" test discussed in *TrafFix*. Accordingly, *TrafFix* supersedes the definition of functionality previously adopted by this court. The "utilitarian" test, although still valid as a secondary test, is not a comprehensive definition of functionality. *TrafFix*, 532 U.S. at 32-33. In light of *TrafFix*, the primary test for determining whether a product feature is functional is whether the feature is essential to the use or purpose of the product or whether it affects the cost or quality of the product. Id. . . .

Eppendorf's theory of non-functionality focused on the existence of alternative designs. Eppendorf's design expert summarized Eppendorf's approach to functionality: "My conclusion was that to achieve the same functional purpose, [the design elements identified by Eppendorf] can be changed significantly, considerably without affecting the overall intended purpose." Although alternative designs are relevant to the utilitarian test of functionality, alternative designs are not germane to the traditional test for functionality. Each of the eight design elements identified by Eppendorf is essential to the use or purpose of the Combitips, and is not arbitrary or ornamental features. Therefore, no reasonable juror could conclude that Eppendorf carried its burden of proving non-functionality.

Eppendorf-Netheler-Hinz GmbH, *supra*, at 355-58.

Have *Valu Engineering* and *Eppendorf* correctly applied *TrafFix Devices*? Are the two circuit court cases consistent with each other?

COMMENTS AND QUESTIONS

1. *Channeling Principles of Intellectual Property Law. TrafFix Devices* addresses the interplay of the patent and trademark domains. *See generally* Kellogg Co. v. National Biscuit Co., 305 U.S. 111, 122 (1938) (suggesting that lapse of patent on shredded wheat cereal, together with lax policing of the mark and widespread use, obviate trademark status of term "Shredded Wheat"); *cf. Trade-Mark Cases*, 100 U.S. 82 (1879) (trademark statute cannot be predicated upon the Patent and Copyright Clause of the Constitution). These cases bolster the primacy of the patent system as the means for protecting exclusive rights for functional features of products. Had MDI been able to protect its spring design for road signs as trade dress, it would have the equivalent of a perpetual patent through the "back door" of trademark law. The social welfare loss of perpetual protection of functional features could be substantial indeed. In fact, the right to exclude others from making, using, selling, or importing a design during the patent term enables the patentee to build source identification in the marketplace for its distinctive (and functional) design. The rule

articulated in *TrafFix* ensures that the patent quid pro quo — disclosure in exchange for protection of *limited* duration — continues to operate. *Cf.* Theodore H. Davis, Jr., *Copying in the Shadow of the Constitution: The Rational Limits of Trade Dress Protection*, 80 MINN. L. REV. 595 (1996). But does this balance potentially come at cost in terms of consumer confusion? Should society's interest in free competition (after the expiration of a patent) trump some confusion as to the source of products?

2. Congress codified functionality as a basis to refuse registration, as well as a ground for opposition and cancellation and a defense to incontestability. Functional marks may not appear on the Supplemental Register. *See* 15 U.S.C. §§ 1052, 1064, 1091, 1115 (1998).

3. *Definition of "Functional."* Section 17 of the *Restatement (Third) of Unfair Competition* offers the following definition of "functional designs":

> A design is "functional" for purposes of the rule stated in § 16 if the design affords benefits in the manufacturing, marketing, or use of the goods or services with which the design is used, apart from any benefits attributable to the design's significance as an indication of source, that are important to effective competition by others and that are not practically available through the use of alternative designs.
>
> Comment:
>
> a. [I]n determining whether a particular design is "functional" and therefore ineligible for protection as a trademark, the ultimate inquiry is whether a prohibition against copying will significantly hinder competition by others. . . .
>
> b. Functionality. A packaging or product feature is not functional merely because the feature serves a utilitarian purpose. The recognition of trademark rights is precluded only when the particular design affords benefits that are not practically available through alternative designs. A bottle, for example, is a utilitarian element of the packaging for wine, but the design of a particular wine bottle is not functional under the rule of this Section unless the shape or other aspects of the bottle provide significant benefits that are not practically obtainable through the use of alternative bottle designs.
>
> In general, a functional design is one that is costly to do without. Thus, the benefits afforded by a particular design do not themselves determine whether that design is functional; a design is functional only if those benefits cannot practically be duplicated through the use of other designs. The availability of alternative designs that satisfy the utilitarian requirements or that otherwise afford similar advantages is therefore decisive in determining functionality. If a particular design affords benefits that are superior to those of any practical alternative design, it is functional if the benefits are important to effective competition. . . .
>
> The benefit conferred by a particular packaging or product design may take various forms. The benefit may lie, for example, in greater economy in manufacturing, shipping, or handling, in increased utility or durability, or in enhanced effectiveness or ease of use. (On aesthetic benefits, see Comment c.) If the benefit afforded by the design resides solely in its association with a particular source, however, the design is not functional; the extent to which others may use such a design is determined by the rules of this Chapter governing trademark infringement. See § 20.
>
> Any evidence that relates to the advantages inherent in a particular design is relevant to the issue of functionality. Functionality may thus be inferred from evidence of advertising or other promotional efforts by the plaintiff that emphasize the benefits of the design. Benefits claimed in pursuit of a utility patent may be particularly persuasive evidence of functionality. Discussions of the design in textbooks or trade literature and engineering analysis of its utilitarian aspects are also relevant. The fact that other manufacturers familiar with the design have rejected it in favor of other designs is evidence that the design is not functional. . . .

How does this definition compare with the Supreme Court's definition? Are either of these tests practical?

One might well wonder after these inquiries whether designs can be protected directly without undermining the balance between free competition and innovation reflected in the patent law. Are designs so expensive that they need a special incentive system to call forth the optimal number? Or do design and manufacturing processes provide enough built-in "lead time" to compensate the creators of innovative designs? The prevalence of piracy in many parts of the world suggests that the answer to the last question may be no. *See* J.H. Reichman, *Legal Hybrids Between the Patent and Copyright Paradigms*, 94 COLUM. L. REV. 2432 (1994) (arguing that natural lead time has diminished in recent years). Note in this regard the growing expansion of design protection through *sui generis* regimes. *See, e.g.*, 17 U.S.C. §§ 901-14 (semiconductors); 17 U.S.C. §§ 1301-32 (boat hull designs). Are these expansions of intellectual property protection merely power grabs by powerful industries or responses to gaps in the fabric of intellectual property law that hinder design innovation?

The Paris Convention for the Protection of Industrial Property obliges parties to grant protection to industrial designs and models, although this requirement can be met through copyright, trade dress, and unfair competition law protections. *See* GRAEME B. DINWOODIE, WILLIAM O. HENNESSEY & SHIRA PERLMUTTER, INTERNATIONAL INTELLECTUAL PROPERTY LAW AND POLICY 348-71 (2001) (surveying design protection in the European Union); *see also* Mattel, Inc. v. MCA Records, 296 F.3d 894, 907-08 (9th Cir. 2002) (stating that the Paris Convention does not define specific minimum requirements for design protection but rather ensures "national treatment" of foreign nationals.)

4. *Separability of Functional and Distinctive Elements.* The fact that a product or feature has been patented does not necessarily mean that all of its aspects are functional. Many patented products have distinctive features that can be separated from the functional elements. What should courts do about designs that are partially distinctive and partially functional (a category that includes most, if not all, designs)? Should there be a threshold (say, 80% functional) below which defendants are free to copy the design? Or must copiers attempt to parse the functional from the non-functional? (Compare in this regard the copyright rules, which allow the copying of ideas but not their expression.) Suppose the two cannot be separated? Ought there to be a "utilitarian function" exception in trademark law, along the lines of the useful article doctrine in copyright law?

Copyright law allows the manufacturer of useful articles to show that the expressive elements are physically or conceptually separable. As we saw, conceptual separability is not easily applied in particular cases. *See, e.g.*, Brandir Int'l, Inc. v. Cascade Pacific Lumber Co., 834 F.2d 1142 (2d Cir. 1987) (metal tubing sculpture used as a bike rack); Carol Barnhart Inc. v. Economy Cover Corp., 773 F.2d 411 (2d Cir. 1985) (upper torso sculpture sold as mannequins). The *TrafFix* case addresses the separability problem through the use of a legal presumption: "Where the expired patent claimed the features in question, one who seeks to establish trade dress protection must carry the heavy burden of showing that the feature is not functional, for instance by showing that it is merely an ornamental, incidental, or arbitrary aspect of the device." Is this standard any more determinative than the conceptual separability standard in copyright law?

5. *Aesthetic Functionality.* In *TrafFix*, the Supreme Court characterizes its prior decision in *Qualitex* (allowing protection of green-gold color for dry cleaning press pads) as centering on the question of "aesthetic functionality." In so doing, the Court

confined its references to "competitive need" and putting competitors at "significant non-reputation-related disadvantage" in that case to the "aesthetic functionality" inquiry. Such concepts have no relevance to the analysis of utilitarian functionality. If a feature is found to be utilitarian, then it can be freely copied regardless of whether competitors have alternative means of competing effectively.

The concept of "aesthetic functionality" has troubled courts and commentators from its earliest recognition. *See* A. Samuel Oddi, *The Functions of "Functionality" in Trademark Law*, 22 HOUS. L. REV. 925, 963 (1985) (commenting that "[f]rom the outset, 'aesthetic functionality' has proved to be a most controversial and ill-defined concept."). Section 742 of the *Restatement of Torts* (1938) captured the concept in the following manner: "[w]hen goods are bought largely for their aesthetic value, their features may be functional." The *Restatement* gave as an example a heart-shaped box for chocolates. *Id.* (comment *a*). Such a shape is no better at holding chocolates than a rectangular box (and hence cannot properly be characterized as functional in a utilitarian sense), but it is easy to see why the heart-shaped box would be particularly appealing to consumers, especially on Valentine's Day. The aesthetic functionality doctrine aims to ensure that such shapes are not monopolized (in the absence of patent or copyright protection).

The Ninth Circuit addressed this doctrine in the 1950s in a case involving china designs. By that time, the Wallace China Company had developed a reputation for "overall" patterns of china in the commercial (hotel and restaurant) marketplace. Unlike other manufacturers, which used artistic designs to decorate the rim of their plates, Wallace china contained bold print designs, such as leaves and woven images, covering the entirety of their eating surface. Tepco appropriated these designs and sold them on plates made of lower quality china. In an action for unfair competition, the Ninth Circuit held that Wallace could not enjoin Tepco's activities even though Wallace established secondary meaning. *See* Pagliero v. Wallace China Co., 198 F.2d 339 (9th Cir. 1952). The court concluded that the design constituted both an indication of sources and an aesthetically pleasing aspect of the product. "If the particular feature is an important ingredient in the commercial success of the product," to enjoin its use in the absence of a patent or copyright would undermine "the interest in free competition." *Id.* at 343.

Subsequent cases have criticized the *Pagliero* doctrine as unduly limiting the protection of trade dress. They have sought to balance the source identification benefit of trade dress protection for aesthetic features against the threat to free competition posed by such protection. They have relaxed the *Pagliero* standard (no trade dress protection if a design enhances the appeal of a product to consumers) by focusing on the extent to which trade dress protection forecloses alternative designs. *See* Wallace Int'l Silversmiths, Inc. v. Godinger Silver Art Co., Inc., 916 F.2d 76 (2d Cir. 1990), *cert. denied*, 499 U.S. 976 (1991); RESTATEMENT (THIRD) UNFAIR COMPETITION § 17, comment *c* (stating that a feature is aesthetically functional only if it "confers a significant benefit that cannot practically be duplicated by the use of alternative designs."); *see generally* Graeme B. Dinwoodie, *The Death of Ontology: A Teleological Approach to Trademark Law*, 84 IOWA L. REV. 611, 692-93 (1999). But in *TrafFix*, the Supreme Court took a broader view of aesthetic functionality, asking only whether the inability to copy the design would put the defendant at a significant disadvantage for reasons not related to reputation.

The retreat from the *Pagliero* standard and the emphasis on the utilitarian functionality doctrine (which prevents backdoor patents) overlooks an analogous concern with backdoor copyrights. Such controversies do not arise nearly as frequently as utilitarian functionality disputes for a number of reasons, including the more limited market power typically associated with copyright protection and the ease with which copyright claims can be asserted (relative to patent protection).[2] Now that copyright protection is not subject to forfeiture as a result of failure to observe formalities, as occurred in *Pagliero*, there is arguably no need for trademark law to protect aesthetic features. Relative to trademark concerns, the primacy of copyright law in the protection of creative expression rests on a comparable footing to the primacy of patent law in the protection of utilitarian features. Therefore, when a copyright has expired (or protection lost), the developer of an expressive work should not be able to gain protection for such expression through the backdoor of trademark law. Furthermore, engaging courts in the determination of whether copying an aesthetic design foreclosed competition may well be unworkable, *see* Kohler Co. v. Moen, Inc., 12 F.3d 632, 649 (7th Cir. 1993) (Cudahy, J. dissenting) (noting that "the attempt to categorize product features as 'essential' or 'nonessential' for competition is perplexing and ultimately vain"); *see also* McCarthy, McCarthy on Trademark and Unfair Competition ¶7.81, and improperly transmutes trademark law into design protection, *see* Krueger, Int'l Inc. v. Nightingale, 915 F. Supp. 595, 606 (S.D.N.Y. 1996) (criticizing aesthetic functionality doctrine on the grounds that it denied protection for design features "whose only sin was to delight the sense"); Keene Corp. v. Paraflex Indus., Inc., 653 F.2d 822, 825 (3d Cir. 1981) (observing that a narrow scope of trade dress protection "provides a disincentive for development of imaginative and attractive design" and that "[t]he more appealing the design, the less protection it would receive" under a broad conception of the aesthetic functionality doctrine); Mitchell M. Wong, *The Aesthetic Functionality Doctrine and the Law of Trade-Dress Protection*, 83 Cornell L. Rev. 1116, 1157 (1998).

Doesn't *Krueger* have it backwards? Shouldn't the question be whether there is a reputation-related reason to protect designs?

Should our intellectual property system tolerate backdoor copyrights through trademark law? Why might courts be inclined to the view that utilitarian functionality represents a higher hurdle to overcome than aesthetic functionality (requiring proof of a "significant non-reputation-related disadvantage")? Could the problem be solved through remedies — for example, allowing free competition in expressive designs so long as the copyist used reasonable indications of source (and possibly disclaimers) to minimize consumer confusion? Or should courts expressly balance trademark interests (avoiding consumer confusion) against the threat to free competition (where copyright does not afford protection)?

6. *Functional Marks.* While most functionality cases involve trade dress, the functionality doctrine also extends to word marks if they serve a function. Can you think of situations in which names, words, or other forms of traditional registered trademarks might be functional? How would a functional name differ from a generic name?

2. The *Pagliero* case, arising as it did prior to the effective elimination of the notice requirement under the 1976 Act, was undoubtedly brought as a trademark dispute because Wallace had failed to provide copyright notice upon the first publication of designs on its plates and hence forfeited copyright protection. Hence, trade dress protection served as an alternative potential theory for recovery. Had the plates been designed after 1978, Wallace would have been able to pursue a copyright cause of action even if notice had not been provided when the plates were "published."

PROBLEMS

Problem 4-3. Depicted below is the design of a folding chair for which the Patent and Trademark Office issued Registration No. 2,803,875 in 2004. A competitor to the registrant subsequently began selling a folding-chair of a very similar design. The registrant sued for trademark infringement and the competitor claimed that the registrant's design was functional. What result?

Problem 4-4. Ferrari is a world-famous maker of upscale sports cars. It limits the number of cars it produces, and each car costs approximately $200,000. Ferrari's cars have the same general features as normal cars — wheels, chassis, etc. — but they also have a distinctive look that is easily recognized. They are sleek and low to the ground, a fact that may make them accelerate more quickly and that makes them more attractive to look at.

Roberts sells a fiberglass kit that replicates the exterior features of a Ferrari, though not the engine or performance. When sued for trade dress infringement, Roberts defends on the grounds that the Ferrari design is functional. Is it?

Problem 4-5. Eighteen years ago, Spartan Laboratories invented and patented a new pain-relieving drug called asperol. During the term of the patent, Spartan retained the exclusive right to sell asperol, which it manufactured in bright orange capsules. After the Spartan patent expired, a number of other companies began making generic asperol. Each of these companies sells the generic asperol in the same bright orange capsules as Spartan. Although the orange capsules are not visible inside the manufacturers' boxes (which do not resemble each other), asperol is sold only by prescription, and pharmacists invariably remove the drug from its original packaging and repackage it in their own bottles. The result is that the consumer sees only the name "asperol" and the orange capsules, regardless of who makes the drug.

Spartan filed suit under Section 43(a) of the Lanham Act, alleging that the other manufacturers had infringed its trade dress protection by coloring the capsules orange. At trial, Spartan proves that the color orange is protectable because it is distinctive and because, over the 17 years of the patent, pharmacists and customers had come to equate orange with Spartan's asperol. The generic manufacturers defend the suit on the grounds that the color is functional. In support of this claim, they present survey evidence that patients, particularly elderly patients, may become upset if the color of the drug is changed, and may refuse to believe that the drug is in fact asperol. The generic manufacturers present further evidence that pharmacists rely in part on color in making sure that they have packaged and labeled drugs correctly. Is the color orange functional?

D. PRIORITY

Many trademark cases turn on issues of priority. Section 45(a) of the Lanham Act, which defines a trademark, requires that the mark either be (1) "used in commerce" or (2) registered with a bona fide intention to use it in commerce. Both at common law and under the traditional Lanham Act registration procedures, determining who owned a trademark meant determining who was first to use it to identify her goods.

The requirement of "use in commerce" is an historical result of the constitutional basis for the trademark laws, which (unlike the patent and copyright statutes) rely on the congressional power to regulate interstate commerce. This requirement also goes hand in hand with the basic trademark theory elaborated in the introduction to this chapter; recall that this theory emphasizes the protection of consumer associations of a brand with a particular product, which can arise only after a trademark is placed on goods sold in commerce.

But just what constitutes use of a trademark? And how much use is enough to secure legal protection for the mark? The case and notes that follow provide some guidance.

Zazu Designs v. L'Oreal, S.A.
979 F.2d 499 (7th Cir. 1992)

EASTERBROOK, Circuit Judge.

In 1985 Cosmair, Inc., concluded that young women craved pink and blue hair. To meet the anticipated demand, Cosmair developed a line of "hair cosmetics" — hair coloring that is easily washed out. These inexpensive products, under the name ZAZU, were sold in the cosmetic sections of mass merchandise stores. Apparently the teenagers of the late 1980s had better taste than Cosmair's marketing staff thought. The product flopped, but its name gave rise to this trademark suit. Cosmair is the United States licensee of L'Oreal, S.A., a French firm specializing in perfumes, beauty aids, and related products. Cosmair placed L'Oreal's marks on the bottles and ads. . . .

L'Oreal hired Wordmark, a consulting firm, to help it find a name for the new line of hair cosmetics. After checking the United States Trademark Register for conflicts, Wordmark suggested 250 names. L'Oreal narrowed this field to three, including ZAZU, and investigated their availability. This investigation turned up one federal registration of ZAZU as a mark for clothing and two state service mark registrations including that word. One of these is Zazu Hair Designs; the other was defunct.

Zazu Hair Designs is a hair salon in Hinsdale, Illinois, a suburb of Chicago. We call it "ZHD" to avoid confusion with the ZAZU mark. . . . The salon is a partnership between Raymond R. Koubek and Salvatore J. Segretto, hairstylists who joined forces in 1979. ZHD registered ZAZU with Illinois in 1980 as a trade name for its salon. L'Oreal called the salon to find out if ZHD was selling its own products. The employee who answered reported that the salon was not but added, "we're working on it." L'Oreal called again; this time it was told that ZHD had no products available under the name ZAZU.

L'Oreal took the sole federal registration, held by Riviera Slacks, Inc., as a serious obstacle. Some apparel makers have migrated to cosmetics, and if Riviera were about to follow Ralph Lauren (which makes perfumes in addition to shirts and skirts) it might have a legitimate complaint against a competing use of the mark. Sands, Taylor & Wood Co. v. Quaker Oats Co., 24 U.S.P.Q.2d 1001, 1011 (7th Cir. 1992). Riviera charged L'Oreal $125,000 for a covenant not to sue if L'Oreal used the ZAZU mark on cosmetics. In April 1986, covenant in hand and satisfied that ZHD's state trade name did not prevent the introduction of a national product, L'Oreal made a small interstate shipment of hair cosmetics under the ZAZU name. It used this shipment as the basis of an application for federal registration, filed on June 12, 1986. By August L'Oreal had advertised and sold its products nationally.

Unknown to L'Oreal, Koubek and Segretto had for some time aspired to emulate Vidal Sassoon by marketing shampoos and conditioners under their salon's trade name. In 1985 Koubek began meeting with chemists to develop ZHD's products. Early efforts were unsuccessful; no one offered a product that satisfied ZHD. Eventually ZHD received acceptable samples from Gift Cosmetics, some of which Segretto sold to customers of the salon in plain bottles to which he taped the salon's business card. Between November 1985 and February 1986 ZHD made a few other sales. Koubek shipped two bottles to a friend in Texas, who paid $13. He also made two shipments to a hair stylist friend in Florida — 40 bottles of shampoo for $78.58. These were designed to interest the Floridian in the future marketing of the product line. These bottles could not have been sold to the public, because they lacked labels listing the ingredients and weight. See 21 U.S.C. §362(b); 15 U.S.C. §§1452, 1453(a); 21 CFR §§701.3, 701.13(a). After L'Oreal's national marketing was under way, its representatives thrice visited ZHD and found that the salon still had no products for sale under the ZAZU name. Which is not to say that ZHD was supine. Late in 1985 ZHD had ordered 25,000 bottles silkscreened with the name ZAZU. Later it ordered stick-on labels listing the ingredients of its products. In September 1986 ZHD began to sell small quantities of shampoo in bottles filled (and labeled) by hand in the salon. After the turn of the year ZHD directed the supplier of the shampoo and conditioner to fill some bottles; the record does not reveal how many.

After a bench trial the district court held that ZHD's sales gave it an exclusive right to use the ZAZU name nationally for hair products. 9 U.S.P.Q.2d 1972 (N.D. Ill. 1988). The court enjoined L'Oreal from using the mark (a gesture, since the product had bombed and L'Oreal disclaimed any interest in using ZAZU again). It also awarded ZHD $100,000 in damages on account of lost profits and $1 million more to pay for corrective advertising to restore luster to the ZAZU mark. [The final judgment also included a $1 million punitive damage award for "oppressive and deceitful" tactics used in the litigation.]

Federal law permits the registration of trademarks and the enforcement of registered marks. Through §43(a) of the Lanham Act, 15 U.S.C. §1125(a), a provision addressed to deceit, it also indirectly allows the enforcement of unregistered marks. But until 1988 federal law did not specify how one acquired the rights that could be registered or enforced without registration. That subject fell into the domain of state law, plus federal common law elaborating on the word "use" in § 43(a). . . . At common law, "use" meant sales to the public of a product with the mark attached. *Trade-Mark Cases*, 100 U.S. 82, 94-95 (1879). See also Hanover Star Milling Co. v. Metcalf, 240 U.S. 403, 414 (1916); United Drug Co. v. Theodore Rectanus Co., 248 U.S. 90, 97 (1918).

"Use" is neither a glitch in the Lanham Act nor a historical relic. By insisting that firms use marks to obtain rights in them, the law prevents entrepreneurs from reserving brand names in order to make their rivals' marketing more costly. Public sales let others know that they should not invest resources to develop a mark similar to one already used in the trade. Blue Bell, Inc. v. Farah Manufacturing Co., 508 F.2d 1260, 1264-65 (5th Cir. 1975); see also William M. Landes and Richard A. Posner, *Trademark Law: An Economic Perspective*, 30 J.L. & Econ. 265, 281-84 (1987). Only active use allows consumers to associate a mark with particular goods and notifies other firms that the mark is so associated.

Under the common law, one must win the race to the marketplace to establish the exclusive right to a mark. Blue Bell v. Farah; La Societe Anonyme des Parfums LeGalion v. Jean Patou, Inc., 495 F.2d 1265, 1271-74 (2d Cir. 1974). Registration modifies this system slightly, allowing slight sales plus notice in the register to substitute for substantial sales without notice. 15 U.S.C. § 1051(a). (The legislation in 1988 modifies the use requirement further, but we disregard this.) ZHD's sales of its product are insufficient use to establish priority over L'Oreal. A few bottles sold over the counter in Hinsdale, and a few more mailed to friends in Texas and Florida, neither link the ZAZU mark with ZHD's product in the minds of consumers nor put other producers on notice. As a practical matter ZHD had no product, period, until months after L'Oreal had embarked on its doomed campaign.

In finding that ZHD's few sales secured rights against the world, the district court relied on cases such as Department of Justice v. Calspan Corp., 578 F.2d 295 (C.C.P.A. 1978), which hold that a single sale, combined with proof of intent to go on selling, permit the vendor to register the mark. See also Axton-Fisher Tobacco Co. v. Fortune Tobacco Co., 82 F.2d 295 (C.C.P.A. 1936); Maternally Yours, Inc. v. Your Maternity Shop, Inc., 234 F.2d 538, 542 (2d Cir. 1956). . . . But use sufficient to register a mark that soon is widely distributed is not necessarily enough to acquire rights in the absence of registration. The Lanham Act allows only trademarks "used in commerce" to be registered. 15 U.S.C. § 1051(a). Courts have read "used" in a way that allows firms to seek protection for a mark before investing substantial sums in promotion. See Fort Howard Paper Co. v. Kimberly-Clark Corp., 390 F.2d 1015 (C.C.P.A. 1968); cf. Jim Dandy Co. v. Martha White Foods, Inc., 458 F.2d 1397, 1399 (C.C.P.A. 1972) (party may rely on advertising to show superior registration rights); but see Weight Watchers International, Inc. v. I. Rokeach & Sons, Inc., 211 U.S.P.Q. 700, 709 (T.M.T.A.B. 1981) (more than minimal use is required to register because the statute allows only "owner[s]" to register, and ownership of a mark depends on commercial use). Liberality in registering marks is not problematic, because the registration gives notice to latecomers, which token use alone does not. Firms need only search the register before embarking on development. Had ZHD registered ZAZU, the parties could have negotiated before L'Oreal committed large sums to marketing.

ZHD applied for registration of ZAZU after L'Oreal not only had applied to register the mark but also had put its product on the market nationwide. Efforts to register came too late. At oral argument ZHD suggested that L'Oreal's knowledge of ZHD's plan to enter the hair care market using ZAZU establishes ZHD's superior right to the name. Such an argument is unavailing. Intent to use a mark, like a naked registration, establishes no rights at all. Hydro-Dynamics, Inc. v. George Putnam & Co., 811 F.2d 1470, 1472 (Fed. Cir. 1987). Even under the 1988 amendments (see note), which allow registration in advance of contemplated use, an unregistered plan to use a mark creates no rights. Just as an intent to buy a choice parcel of land does not prevent a rival from closing the deal first, so an intent to use a mark creates no rights a competitor is bound to respect. A statute granting no rights in bare registrations cannot plausibly be understood to grant rights in "intents" divorced from either sales or registrations. Registration itself establishes only a rebuttable presumption of use as of the filing date. Rolley, Inc. v. Younghusband, 204 F.2d 209, 211 (9th Cir. 1953). ZHD made first use of ZAZU in connection with hair services in Illinois, but this does not translate to a protectable right to market hair products nationally. The district court construed L'Oreal's knowledge of ZHD's use of ZAZU for salon services as knowledge "of [ZHD's] superior rights in the mark." 9 U.S.P.Q.2d at 1978. ZHD did not, however, have superior rights in the mark as applied to hair products, because it neither marketed such nor registered the mark before L'Oreal's use. Because the mark was not registered for use in conjunction with hair products, any knowledge L'Oreal may have had of ZHD's plans is irrelevant. Cf. Weiner King, Inc. v. Wiener King Corp., 615 F.2d 512 (C.C.P.A. 1980).

Imagine the consequences of ZHD's approach. Businesses that knew of an intended use would not be entitled to the mark even if they made the first significant use of it. Businesses with their heads in the sand, however, could stand on the actual date they introduced their products, and so would have priority over firms that intended to use a mark but had not done so. Ignorance would be rewarded—and knowledgeable firms might back off even though the rivals' "plans" or "intent" were unlikely to come to fruition. Yet investigations of the sort L'Oreal undertook prevent costly duplication in the development of trademarks and protect consumers from the confusion resulting from two products being sold under the same mark. See Natural Footwear Ltd. v. Hart, Shaffner & Marx, 760 F.2d 1383, 1395 (3d Cir. 1985). L'Oreal should not be worse off because it made inquiries and found that, although no one had yet used the mark for hair products, ZHD intended to do so. Nor should a potential user have to bide its time until it learns whether other firms are serious about marketing a product. The use requirement rewards those who act quickly in getting new products in the hands of consumers. Had L'Oreal discovered that ZHD had a product on the market under the ZAZU mark or that ZHD had registered ZAZU for hair products, L'Oreal could have chosen another mark before committing extensive marketing resources. Knowledge that ZHD planned to use the ZAZU mark in the future does not present an obstacle to L'Oreal's adopting it today. Selfway, Inc. v. Travelers Petroleum, Inc., 579 F.2d 75, 79 (C.C.P.A. 1978).

Occasionally courts suggest that "bad faith" adoption of a mark defeats a claim to priority. See California Cedar Products Co. v. Pine Mountain Corp., 724 F.2d 827, 830 (9th Cir. 1984); Stern Electronics, Inc. v. Kaufman, 669 F.2d 852, 857 (2d Cir. 1982); Blue Bell v. Farah, 508 F.2d at 1267. Although ZHD equates L'Oreal's knowledge of its impending use with "bad faith," the cases use the term differently. In each instance the court applied the label "bad faith" to transactions designed merely to reserve a mark, not to link the name to a product ready to be sold to the public. In *California Cedar Products*, for example, two firms sprinted to acquire the abandoned DURAFLAME mark. One shipped some of its goods in the abandoning company's wrapper with a new name pasted over it. Two days later the other commenced bona fide sales under the DURAFLAME mark. The court disregarded the first shipment, calling it "both premature and in bad faith," 724 F.2d at 830, and held that the first firm to make bona fide sales to customers was the prior user. "Bad faith" was no more than an epithet stapled to the basic conclusion: that reserving a mark is forbidden, so that the first producer to make genuine sales gets the rights. If these cases find a parallel in our dispute, ZHD occupies the place of the firm trying to reserve a mark for "intended" exploitation. ZHD doled out a few samples in bottles lacking labeling necessary for sale to the public. Such transactions are the sort of pre-marketing maneuvers that these cases hold insufficient to establish rights in a trademark.

The district court erred in equating a use sufficient to support registration with a use sufficient to generate nationwide rights in the absence of registration. Although whether ZHD's use is sufficient to grant it rights in the ZAZU mark is a question of fact on which appellate review is deferential, *California Cedar Products*, 724 F.2d at 830 . . . , the extent to which ZHD used the mark is not disputed. ZHD's sales of hair care products were insufficient as a matter of law to establish national trademark rights at the time L'Oreal put its electric hair colors on the market.

[In a forcefully stated section of the opinion, the court also reversed the punitive damages holding.]

Reversed and remanded.

CUDAHY, C.J., dissenting:

On the important issue of good faith, L'Oreal's conduct here merits a very hard look. In the case of Riviera, a men's clothing retailer, L'Oreal was careful to pay $125,000 for an agreement not to sue. Yet men's clothing and hair cosmetics marketed to women hardly seem related at all. On the other hand, a women's hair salon developing a line of hair care products is a purveyor of goods and services that seem closely related to hair cosmetics. Therefore, L'Oreal's knowledge of ZHD's use defeats any claim L'Oreal may have to priority.

One of the keys here seems to be the use of ZAZU as a service mark connected with the provision of salon services by ZHD. A service mark can be infringed by its use on a closely related product.[1] . . . [See] 2 J. THOMAS MCCARTHY, TRADEMARK AND UNFAIR COMPETITION §24:6, at 71 (2d ed. 1984 & Supp. 1991) (stating that "[w]here the services consist of retail sales services, likelihood of confusion is found when another mark is used on goods which are commonly sold through such a retail outlet"). A service and a product are related if buyers are likely to assume a common source or sponsorship. . . . The salon services and hair products at issue in this case,

1. Our recent opinion in Sands, Taylor & Wood Co. v. Quaker Oats Co., 24 U.S.P.Q.2d 1001 (7th Cir. 1992), states explicitly that modern trademark law prohibits the use of a senior user's mark on products that are closely related to the senior user's, as well as those products in direct competition. See 24 U.S.P.Q.2d at 1010; International Kennel Club, Inc. v. Mighty Star, Inc., 846 F.2d 1079, 1089 (7th Cir. 1988). This "protects the owner's ability to enter product markets . . . into which it might reasonably be expected to expand in the future." *Sands, Taylor & Wood*, 24 U.S.P.Q.2d at 1011; 2 J. THOMAS MCCARTHY, TRADEMARK AND UNFAIR COMPETITION §24:5, at 177 (2d ed. 1984).

which are nearly as kindred as a service and product can be, offer the paradigmatic illustration of things that are closely related. Thus the majority's disregard for ZHD's substantial use of ZAZU in connection with salon services is unfounded.

As the majority correctly notes, the standard for granting federal registration is somewhat less exacting than that for establishing common law trademark rights. . . . But that distinction is so slight as to be inconsequential here. While any bona fide transaction that is more than a "mere sham" will, when combined with intent to continue use, suffice to support federal registration, Avakoff v. Southern Pacific Co., 765 F.2d 1097, 1098 (Fed. Cir. 1985) . . . , any use greater than de minimis will still warrant trademark protection in the absence of registration. Thus, bona fide test marketing or small experimental sales — indeed, any use that is not nominal or token — can satisfy the test. . . .

In this case, ZHD's use of the ZAZU mark, both in its highly successful salon service business, which drew some out-of-state clients, and in its local and interstate product sales to customers and to a potential marketer, surely is more than de minimis. The extensive evidence of ZHD's intent to step up hair product sales — such as its order for 25,000 ZAZU-emblazoned bottles and its inquiry about advertising rates in a national magazine — bolsters this assessment. Even if ZHD did fail to demonstrate more than a de minimis market penetration nationally, at the very least it successfully established exclusive rights within its primary area of operation. The salon's substantial advertising, increasing revenue and staff and preliminary product sales indicate sufficient market penetration to afford trademark protection in that region. See Natural Footwear Ltd. v. Hart, Schaffner & Marx, 760 F.2d 1383 (3d Cir.) (senior user can establish common law rights in geographic areas where it achieved market penetration), *cert. denied*, 474 U.S. 920, 106 S. Ct. 249, 88 L. Ed. 2d 257 (1985). . . .

L'Oreal concedes that ZHD has exclusive rights to use ZAZU for salon services in the Hinsdale area. Those exclusive rights also preclude L'Oreal from using the mark on hair products in the local area because of the likelihood of confusion between those products and ZHD's salon services, even apart from any confusion between the two parties' products. Given the deferential standard of review on the factual question of use, therefore, I think it clear that ZHD has achieved market penetration and exclusive rights to the ZAZU mark at the very least in the Chicago area.

ZHD's contention that its rights in the ZAZU mark extend beyond the local area is enhanced by evidence that L'Oreal did not, as we have noted, act in good faith. The majority's consideration of the good faith issue minimizes the important role good faith plays in trademark disputes, particularly disputes involving unregistered marks. . . . See, e.g., A. J. Canfield Co. v. Honickman, 808 F.2d 291 (3d Cir. 1986) (stating the doctrine that a senior user "has enforceable rights against any junior user who adopted the mark with knowledge of its senior use"). . . . Contrary to the majority's narrow characterization of bad faith as a concept employed solely to deter attempts to reserve marks prior to genuine sales, courts have examined junior users' good faith in a variety of contexts. In fact, this court has held that a good faith in a variety of contexts. In fact, this court has held that a good faith junior user is simply one that begins using a mark without knowledge that another party already is using it. The Money Store v. Harriscorp Finance, Inc., 689 F.2d 666, 674 (7th Cir. 1982); see 2 McCarthy, supra, § 26:4 at 292 (equating good faith to "the junior user's lack of knowledge"). And while such knowledge may not automatically negate good faith, only the most unusual situations encompass both knowledge and good faith. . . .

COMMENTS AND QUESTIONS

1. The majority opinion mentions that Zazu Hair Design, "ZHD," had registered its "trade name" as a "service mark" in Illinois in 1980. But how does prior use of a trade name or "service mark" such as Zazu Hair Design, used on a hair salon, affect subsequent use of the same term for hair color products? *See* Malcolm Nicol & Co. v. Witco Corp., 881 F.2d 1063, 1065 (Fed. Cir. 1989) (a trade name, even one that lacks any independent trademark or service mark significance, may bar registration of a trademark or service mark that is confusingly similar to that trade name).

2. The *Zazu* case was decided under pre-1989 federal trademark law. As noted earlier, Congress in 1989 made several important changes in trademark law, including the adoption of "intent to use" registration under Section 1 of the Lanham Act. *See* Trademark Law Revision Act of 1989 (hereinafter "TLRA"), Pub. L. No. 100-667, 102 Stat. 3935, codified at 15 U.S.C. § 1051. Under pre-1989 law, *actual* use in commerce, prior to application for registration, was a requirement for registration. This requirement spurred prospective applicants to ship and/or sell a small batch of goods in order to secure trademark protection, a practice that came to be known as "token use."

Among other things, the TLRA amended Section 1 of the Lanham Act, 15 U.S.C. § 1051, to provide that "[a] person who has a bona fide intention, under circumstances showing the good faith of such person, to use a trademark in commerce may apply to register the trademark . . . on the principal register." Assuming an application based on an intention to use a mark is otherwise allowable, the Trademark Office will issue a "notice of allowance" to the trademark owner (rather than simply registering the mark on the Principal Register). 15 U.S.C. § 1063(b)(2). After the notice of allowance is granted, the trademark owner has six months (extendable to one year automatically and to three years for good cause shown) to submit a verified statement that the trademark has in fact been used in commerce, at which point it is entered on the Principal Register. If the trademark owner does not submit such a statement, the trademark is considered abandoned. 15 U.S.C. § 1051(d). Assuming that the intent-to-use registrant does eventually use the mark, however, the initial application will be considered "constructive use," entitling the registrant to nationwide priority from the date of the application. 15 U.S.C. § 1057(c).

The TLRA was passed largely to bring U.S. law into harmony with the law in the rest of the world. No country other than the United States required actual use before a mark could be registered. Because international treaties required the United States to give full credit to foreign applicants who had registered marks outside the United States, the United States use requirement in practice meant that *only* U.S. citizens were required to show use in commerce in order to register a mark in the United States.

Is the intent-to-use provision constitutional? Recall that the original U.S. trademark statute was struck down as unsupported by the Patent and Copyright Clause, and that subsequent trademark statutes (including the Lanham Act) were then enacted under the Commerce Clause. The old requirement in the Lanham Act that registered marks be used in interstate commerce was thought necessary to invoke federal jurisdiction under the Commerce Clause. Does an intent to use a product in interstate commerce confer federal jurisdiction? *Compare* Charles J. Vinicombe, *The Constitutionality of an Intent to Use Amendment to the Lanham Act*, 78 TRADEMARK

Rep. 361, 369-73 (1988) (courts likely to defer to Congress by assuming that an intention to use a mark means that it is part of the "flow of commerce") *with* Kenneth L. Port, *Foreword: Symposium on Intellectual Property Law Theory*, 68 Chi.-Kent L. Rev. 585, 595 n.63 (1993) (Trademark Law Revision Act "should fail constitutional review based on the Commerce Clause").

3. Is the "intent-to-use" registration process established by Lanham Act § 1(b) available to non-inherently distinctive marks? Stated differently, can a trademark owner register a descriptive mark through the intent-to-use process on the ground that the mark has acquired distinctiveness? In general, the answer is no. If a trademark owner intends to use a descriptive mark but has not yet done so, thus necessitating the 1(b) filing basis, then, logically, the trademark owner cannot reasonably assert that its descriptive mark has acquired secondary meaning through use. "[A] claim of acquired distinctiveness, by definition, requires prior use." TMEP § 1212.09(a). If the examining attorney determines that the mark sought to be registered under § 1(b) is merely descriptive, the application will be rejected. *See* McCarthy, McCarthy on Trademarks and Unfair Competition § 11:51.50.

There is, however, one rare exception to the general rule that acquired distinctiveness requires prior use. Where appropriate, the ITU applicant may claim that (1) its descriptive mark has acquired distinctiveness with respect to the goods or services referenced in the ITU application as a result of its use on goods or services other than those referenced in the application, and (2) this acquired distinctiveness will transfer to the goods referenced in the ITU application once use in commerce begins. *See* In re Rogers, 53 U.S.P.Q.2d 1741 (TTAB 1999); TMEP § 1212.09(a).

4. Imagine the following chain of events: (1) an applicant files an ITU application for a mark on specified goods; (2) a competitor makes an actual use of that mark on those goods; (3) the applicant then makes its own actual use of the mark on the same goods. Given these facts, can the competitor short-circuit the ITU process by seeking to enjoin the applicant from perfecting its application on the basis that the competitor is the first user in commerce? Faced with these facts, the Second Circuit held that the first actual user who begins its use after another's ITU filing date cannot obtain an injunction against the ITU applicant. *See* WarnerVision Entertainment, Inc. v. Empire of Carolina, 101 F.3d 259, 262 (2d Cir. 1996) ("To permit such an injunction would eviscerate the ITU provisions and defeat their very purpose.").

Can the ITU applicant seek in turn to enjoin the competitor from making an actual use of the mark before the ITU applicant has perfected its application? *See* Talk To Me Prods. v. Larami Corp., 804 F. Supp. 555, 559-60 (S.D.N.Y. 1992), *aff'd*, 992 F.2d 469 (2d Cir. 1993) ("An application may confer a right or priority, but this is only triggered by registration. [Plaintiff's] mark is not registered. Until it is, [plaintiff] cannot rely on the constructive use provision of the new Act."). The effect of this holding is that the competitor "is living on borrowed time." McCarthy, McCarthy on Trademarks and Unfair Competition § 19.30. Upon perfecting its application, the applicant will then be in a position to claim priority and may at that time seek to enjoin the competitor's intervening actual use.

5. It is widely believed that the TLRA has eliminated "token use" by raising the standard for determining when a mark has been "use[d] in commerce." Consider, for example, the case of Paramount Pictures Corp. v. White, 31 U.S.P.Q.2d 1768 (TTAB 1994), *aff'd*, 108 F.3d 1392 (Fed Cir. 1997) (unpub.), where Paramount opposed registration of "The Romulans" for a connect-the-dots game distributed by White, leader of a rock group called The Romulans. One ground for the opposition was that

the mark had not been used in commerce; in particular, that the distribution of connect-the-dots games on promotional fliers for the band was not a statutory use in commerce justifying registration. In commenting on the magnitude of use, the Trademark Trial and Appeal Board stated: "The legislative history of the Trademark Law Revision Act reveals that the purpose of the amendment was to eliminate 'token use' as a basis for registration, and that the new stricter standard contemplates instead commercial use of the type common to the particular industry in question." 31 U.S.P.Q.2d at 1774. Footnote 8 of the Board's opinion quotes from the Congressional Record of November 19, 1987, p. 196-97:

> Amendment of the definition of "use in commerce" is one of the most far-reaching changes the legislation contains. Revised to eliminate the commercially-transparent practice of token use, which becomes unnecessary with the legislation's provision for an intent-to-use application system, it will have a measurable effect on improving the accuracy of the register. . . . The committee intends that the revised definition of "use in commerce" be interpreted to mean commercial use which is typical in a particular industry.

Id. But cf. Allard Enters., Inc. v. Advanced Programming Resources, Inc., 146 F.3d 350 (6th Cir. 1998) (plaintiff's somewhat extensive "word-of-mouth" campaign to popularize "APR" mark for computer professional placement service established priority under post-TLRA law). For an example of the pre-1989 rule, see Fort Howard Paper v. Kimberly Clark Corp., 390 F.2d 1015 (C.C.P.A. 1968), *cert. denied*, 393 U.S. 831 (1968) (very limited use sufficient to establish priority). *But cf.* La Societe Anonyme des Parfums LeGalion v. Jean Patou, Inc., 495 F.2d 1265 (2d Cir. 1974) (token sales program not sufficient use to avoid abandonment); Procter and Gamble v. Johnson & Johnson, Inc., 485 F. Supp. 1185 (S.D.N.Y. 1979), *aff'd without opinion*, 636 F.2d 1203 (2d Cir. 1980) ("minor brands program" not sufficient use).

Could it be argued in the *Zazu* case that ZHD's shipments of hair products were only a "token use"? How might the TLRA have affected the dissent in *Zazu*? Would L'Oreal's good faith still be an issue under the TLRA?

6. Consider this passage from Judge Easterbrook's opinion: "Liberality in registering marks is not problematic, because the registration gives notice to latecomers, which token use alone does not. Firms need only search the register before embarking on development. Had ZHD registered ZAZU, the parties could have negotiated before L'Oreal committed large sums to marketing."

But ZHD *did* register Zazu—not as a federal trademark but as a business (trade name) in the State of Illinois. Why is this any different from the *national* registration contemplated by Easterbrook? Does it provide less opportunity for negotiating prior to large investments? Recall the evidence in the case, which established not only that L'Oreal did find the ZHD trade name in its pre-product introduction search, but also that L'Oreal did contact ZHD. Standard trademark search services generally find all state and federal registrations, together with many "common law" (i.e., nonregistered) uses. Given this evidence, why was state registration any less of a basis for negotiation than federal registration?

7. Judge Easterbrook says that through the use requirement, "the law prevents entrepreneurs from reserving brand names in order to make their rivals' marketing more costly." Could a rival reserve all the potential trademarks that would allow a firm

to identify its products? *Cf.* Stephen L. Carter, *The Trouble with Trademarks*, 99 YALE L.J. 759, 760 (1990):

> The traditional economic justification for trademark law rests on the premise that the set of available marks is virtually infinite and, in consequence, that the actual mark chosen by a firm to represent its goods is irrelevant. If that assumption turns out to be false—if even before the public comes to associate a mark with any particular goods or services, some marks are more desirable than others—then allowing protection of marks devoid of market significance may raise substantial barriers to entry by competitors. For this reason, I . . . argue, the theoretical case is clearer for the common law model than for the Federal scheme.

Note that another rationale for the use requirement stems not from rivals' costs, but from the desire not to encourage firms to specialize in identifying and registering potential trademarks. See the note below on "Priority and Trademark Theory."

8. Judge Easterbrook provides another explanation for the use requirement: "Public sales let others know that they should not invest resources to develop a mark similar to one already used in the trade." Is there a better and more accurate way to do this? After all, public sales may be quite limited. Does the new federal intent-to-use registration process serve this purpose more effectively?

9. An important case, Blue Bell, Inc. v. Farah Mfg. Co., 508 F.2d 1260 (5th Cir. 1975), teaches that although the race is to the swift in trademark law, the race must be run cleanly if a firm wants to prevail. In the case, Farah's management settled on the name "Time Out" for a new line of blue jeans on May 16. Sample tags using the new name were drawn up on June 27, and on July 3 Farah sent out 12 pair of jeans bearing the new mark to its regional sales managers. More extensive shipments occurred on July 11. Meanwhile, Blue Bell management decided on the name "Time Out" for *its* new line of jeans on June 18. Blue Bell commissioned several hundred sample tags (bearing the new logo) that were attached over the top of existing tags on a large shipment of jeans sent out on July 5. By October both firms had received substantial orders for their respective new lines of jeans. The court ruled (1) that Blue Bell's "secondary" use of the new logo was in "bad faith" and therefore its July 5 shipment did not establish priority and (2) that Farah's minimal shipments on July 3 also did not establish priority. This left Farah's July 11 shipment as the first substantial use of the new mark in commerce—so Farah won.

When Blue Bell slapped new labels on old jeans, the court condemned it as "a bad faith attempt to reserve a mark." What if, subsequent to the relabeling but before Farah's first shipments, Blue Bell had made actual sales to consumers; would their prior bad faith deprive them of priority? Should it? Why did the court not characterize Farah's sales of pants to employees as an attempt to "reserve a mark"? For more on the myriad roles that bad faith plays in trademark cases, see *infra*, Chapter 5.B, Likelihood of Consumer Confusion, and Chapter 6.A, Abandonment.

10. Both Blue Bell and Farah began advertising prior to their first sales to customers, yet ultimately the respective sales dates to consumers determined priority. Can advertising or other "promotional activities" ever form the basis for priority?

Maryland Stadium Authority v. Becker, 806 F. Supp. 1236 (D. Md. 1992), *aff'd*, 36 F.3d 1093 (4th Cir. 1994), is instructive on this point. As early as 1987, the Maryland Stadium Authority (MSA) used the name "Camden Yards" in promotional materials (widely distributed to the press and public) describing the new stadium for the Baltimore Orioles baseball team. A number of other names were under consideration at the time, however. In 1989, MSA distributed to the press and sold to the public photographic renditions of the proposed ballpark labeled with the name Camden Yards—again, before the name had been finalized. Defendant Becker, meanwhile, began selling baseball T-shirts under the "Camden Yards" mark in July 1991, shortly after the ballpark's name was made final and official but before the park opened. In an action by MSA against Becker for trademark infringement under Maryland law, the court found that Becker had intentionally adopted MSA's mark, creating a presumption of the likelihood of confusion that Becker could not overcome. The totality of MSA's activities constituted adoption and use of the mark, generated secondary meaning, and was sufficient to establish priority over Becker. *But cf.* Societe de Developpements et d'Innovations des Marches Agricoles et Alimentaires-Sodima Union de Cooperatives Agricoles v. International Yogurt, 662 F. Supp. 839, 847 (D. Ore. 1987) ("An axiom of trademark law is: no trade, no trademark."). Note the emphasis on "bad faith" in the *Maryland Stadium* case. Does this distinguish it from cases such as *Paramount*? Or is it another instance of Judge Easterbrook's observation in the *Zazu* opinion that bad faith can be merely "an epithet stapled to . . . [a] conclusion"?

Another use-based limitation on trademark rights is highlighted by Buti v. Impressa Perosa S.R.L., 139 F.3d 98 (2d Cir. 1998). In that case, a restaurant located in Milan, Italy, named "Fashion Café" advertised its business in the United States just before Buti began using the same mark for restaurants in the United States. The court held that the Italian restaurant could not obtain U.S. trademark rights through its advertising because the services it was providing were not themselves offered in commerce in the United States.

11. *Analogous Use.* In rare instances a trademark user may establish priority through "use analogous to trademark use," provided that the user makes actual use of the mark within a reasonable period of time following the analogous use. *See, e.g.*, Chance v. Pac-Tel Teletrac Inc., 242 F.3d 1151 (9th Cir. 2001) (finding that defendant's pre-launch marketing campaign, including distribution of press releases and presentations to prospective customers, soon followed by launch of service established analogous use priority). Qualifying analogous uses typically take the form of pre-sales activity, such as pre-sales publicity directed at potential purchasers, that is sufficient to "create an association in the minds of the purchasing public between the mark and the [analogous user]'s goods." Herbko Int'l, Inc. v. Kappa Books, Inc., 308 F.3d 1156, 1162 (Fed. Cir. 2002). Analogous use *vel non* will not support trademark protection or registration, typically because the analogous use does not satisfy the requirement that the mark be affixed to goods or services for it to qualify for protection. However, when analogous use is followed by actual use, the user may establish priority as of its first analogous use. *See* Shalom Children's Wear Inc. v. In-Wear A/S, 26 U.S.P.Q.2d 1516, 1519 (T.T.A.B. 1993) ("Use analogous to trademark use . . . is non-technical use of a trademark in connection with the promotion or sale of a product under circumstances which do not provide a basis for an application to register, usually because the statutory requirement for use on or in connection with the sale of goods in commerce has not been met. Although never considered an appropriate basis for an application to register, such use has consistently been held sufficient use to establish priority rights as against subsequent users of the same or similar marks.").

Note on Geographic Limitations on Trademark Use

At common law (and today for unregistered marks), ownership of a trademark does not necessarily confer nationwide protection. Rather, common law trademarks are protected only in the areas where the marked products are sold or advertised. This is known as the *Tea Rose-Rectanus* doctrine after the two landmark Supreme Court cases that established it. *See* Hanover Star Milling Co. v. Metcalf, 240 U.S. 403 (1916) (commonly known as the "Tea Rose case") and United Drug Co. v. Theodore Rectanus Co., 248 U.S. 90 (1918). In the latter of these cases, Justice Pitney declared in a still oft-cited passage:

> There is no such thing as property in a trade-mark except as a right appurtenant to an established business or trade in connection with which the mark is employed. The law of trade-marks is but a part of the broader law of unfair competition; the right to a particular mark grows out of its use, not its mere adoption; its function is simply to designate the goods as the product of a particular trader and to protect his good will against the sale of another's product as his; and it is not the subject of property except in connection with an existing business. . . .
>
> It results that the adoption of a trade-mark does not, at least in the absence of some valid legislation enacted for the purpose, project the right of protection in advance of the extension of the trade, or operate as a claim of territorial rights over areas into which it thereafter may be deemed desirable to extend the trade. And the expression, sometimes met with, that a trade-mark right is not limited in its enjoyment by territorial bounds, is true only in the sense that wherever the trade goes, attended by the use of the mark, the right of the trader to be protected against the sale by others of their wares in the place of his wares will be sustained.

Id. at 97-98. Thus the owner of an unregistered trademark for goods sold in Oregon and Washington, but not elsewhere, is entitled to prevent others from using that mark for similar goods only in Oregon and Washington. The rationale is that trademarks are not intended to confer a broad property right but merely to protect the goodwill the trademark owner has invested in the mark. Because no one outside Oregon or Washington could associate the mark with the owner, there is no reason to protect it elsewhere. Thus a seller of similar goods in New York can use the same name for the goods without conflict.

There are two exceptions to this common law rule, both based on concerns that the trademark owner's goodwill will be unfairly taken. First, a trademark owner is entitled to the exclusive use of her mark in any geographic area in which the mark's reputation has been established, even if the product is not sold in that geographic area. Such a broader geographic reputation might be established, for example, by national advertising or media coverage of a local business such as a restaurant. Further, the trademark owner is entitled to protect the mark in a territory that he is expected to reach in the normal expansion of his business, even if there is no current likelihood of confusion in that area. *See* Hanover Star Milling Co. v. Metcalf, 240 U.S. 403 (1916). Second, a trademark owner is entitled to prevent anyone from intentionally trading on her goodwill, even outside her established geographic area. Only innocent (or "good faith") use of the same mark is protected.

One of the principal advantages of trademark registration is that it automatically confers nationwide protection of the mark, retroactive to the date of the trademark application, even if the goods for which the mark is used are sold or advertised in only a small part of the country. Thus trademark registration is vital to protect businesses that plan to expand geographically, as well as those that fear a large national company might use the same name.

What happens, then, if two parties use the same mark for the same goods? If neither party registers its mark, then the common law rule applies. Each party is entitled to exclusive use of the mark in the areas where it has established goodwill. Should the two marks come into conflict in a particular geographic area, the conflict will be resolved in favor of the earliest user *in that area*. If one party registers her mark and the other does not, the registrant will generally be entitled to the exclusive right to use the mark throughout the country. However, the non-registering party may assert a "limited area" defense. This defense allows the non-registering party to claim priority in those geographic areas where he has made continuous use of the mark since *before* the registering party filed her application. The non-registering party is "frozen" in the use of his mark, however, and cannot expand it outside his existing territory or a natural "zone of expansion." See Weiner King, Inc. v. Wiener King Corp., 615 F.2d 512 (C.C.P.A. 1980).

Finally, if both parties file for registration of marks that were in use in different areas at the same time, the Trademark Office will generally declare an "interference" between the two applications. But if the parties agree, or if the Trademark Board determines that registration of both marks is unlikely to cause confusion, it is possible that both marks may be registered for "concurrent use."[8] If two or more marks are registered concurrently, however, the Trademark Office will impose whatever restrictions on the use of the marks are necessary to prevent confusion among consumers.

COMMENTS AND QUESTIONS

1. *The* Dawn Donut *Rule*. While federal registration entitles the registrant to nationwide constructive use priority under Lanham Act §7(c), 15 U.S.C. 1057(c), there remains an important limitation on the registrant's ability to enjoin competitors from using the mark. To obtain an injunction, the senior federal registrant must show more than mere priority. The registrant must also show that the competitor's use is likely to cause consumer confusion as to source. If the registrant has not yet entered and has no immediate plans to enter the competitor's geographic area, then the registrant may find it exceedingly difficult to make this showing—because consumers may not be aware of the registrant's use of the mark and so will not confuse the competitor's use with the registrant's. Because the court will not issue an injunction to prevent consumer confusion if there is, in fact, no confusion to prevent, the strange result is that the competitor may continue to use the mark until the registrant finally expands or shows reasonable plans to expand into the competitor's area. This rule was first set forth in Dawn Donut Co. v. Hart's Food Stores, Inc., 267 F.2d 358 (2d Cir. 1959), and continues to be applied by courts. *See, e.g.*, What-A-Burger of Virginia, Inc. v. Whataburger, Inc. of Corpus Christi, Texas, 357 F.3d 441 (4th Cir. 2004) (declining to find laches in the senior registrant's failure to bring an infringement action during 30-year "Dawn Donut" period because there was no infringing use during that period). *But see* Circuit City Stores, Inc. v. CarMax, Inc., 165 F.3d

8. Concurrent use applies only to two marks that are actually in use, not to applications based on an intent to use.

1047 (6th Cir. 1999) (Jones, J., concurring) ("The *Dawn Donut* Rule was enunciated in 1959. Entering the new millennium, our society is far more mobile than it was four decades ago. For this reason, and given that recent technological innovations such as the Internet are increasingly deconstructing geographical barriers for marketing purposes, it appears to me that a re-examination of precedents would be timely to determine whether the *Dawn Donut* Rule has outlived its usefulness.")

2. Compare the current U.S. trademark system to the various schemes for filing patent applications. The United States has long used a "first to invent" rule for determining who is entitled to own a patent, while the rest of the world awards a patent to the "first to file." Is there a similar distinction in trademark law, between "first to use" and "first to file"? If so, does the Trademark Law Revision Act turn the United States into a "first to file" system?

3. Why should the user of an arbitrary or suggestive, but unregistered, trademark be limited to protection in a particular geographic area? The asserted justification is that the trademark owner has established goodwill only in that limited area. But why should that matter? Distinctive marks, unlike descriptive marks, are entitled to automatic protection under trademark law without proof that the public associates them with a particular product. *See infra* section A.1. Isn't it inconsistent to limit the scope of that protection to geographic areas in which the public has formed such an association?

4. Priority disputes are often resolved by the Trademark Trial and Appeal Board through oppositions or interferences. Section 13 of the Lanham Act, 15 U.S.C. § 1063, provides that "[a]ny person who believes that he would be damaged by the registration of a mark upon the principal register may . . . file an opposition in the Patent and Trademark Office, stating the grounds therefor." Further, 15 U.S.C. § 1062(a) expressly provides that trademark applications be published before issuance, so that interested parties may have the opportunity to search for and oppose potentially damaging applications. Applications may be opposed by showing that the mark is not entitled to registration, for example, because others had made use of it before the applicant did.

Often the party objecting to an application will herself have filed an application for the same or a similar mark. In that circumstance, the Trademark Commissioner may declare an interference between the two applications. Under Section 16 of the Lanham Act, 15 U.S.C. § 1066, interferences may also be declared between pending applications and registered trademarks (unless they have become "incontestable"). Interferences are heard by the Trademark Trial and Appeal Board, which may register neither, either, or both marks, and may impose restrictions or conditions on the registration of the mark. 15 U.S.C. §§ 1067, 1068. Both oppositions and interference decisions may be appealed to the Court of Appeals for the Federal Circuit.

Note on Priority and Trademark Theory

Do any of the tests for priority discussed so far make sense in terms of lowering consumer search costs? Consider: If a second user can freely appropriate a mark, then consumers who have begun to rely on the association between the mark and the first user's product will be thwarted. This situation not only destroys that particular association with the first user's product, but it also may make consumers less likely to establish such associations in the future. The upshot is that unless we protect the rights of the first user, more consumers will spend more time searching for goods.

On the other hand, many priority cases involve very limited uses in commerce; these cases typically occur early in the life of a new product or marketing campaign. As a consequence, very few consumers will, at the time of the litigation, have come to associate the mark in question with any goods. Where this is so, we might consider issues other than absolute priority to be important. For example, we might ask whether the first or second user was better positioned to distribute the goods bearing the mark. If the second user was in a better position — for example, was larger, had more money to spend on advertising, etc. — why not let it use the mark? If consumer search costs are the key, why not take into account the interests of *future* consumers, who may be better served by allowing a search-cost-reducing trademark to fall into the hands of a large company that can make best use of it?

Then again, if the second user can really make better use of the mark, wouldn't it buy the trademark from the first user? When this is so, an award of priority to the first user will give it a share of the value of the market that will ultimately be served by the second user. Perhaps the payment to the first user will compensate it to some extent for the effort expended in coming up with a mark that, in the second user's hands, has real commercial value. (Notice that if this is so, it is a far cry from the consumer protection theory of trademark protection; it comes closer to the property theory described in the Introduction. No one is paying the consumers whose expectations are dashed.)

Priority by Contract: Covenants Not to Sue and the Like. Notice in this connection the $125,000 paid by L'Oreal to Riviera Slacks, Inc. in *Zazu*. Recall that Riviera was an early user of the Zazu mark on related goods (clothes). (Note also that the court characterizes this agreement as a "covenant not to sue." For an explanation of this characterization — as opposed to "trademark license agreement" — see *infra*, Chapter 6.A.1.) This payment is interesting for several reasons. First, it suggests that priority is not a once-and-for-all determination. Since the first user can license the trademark to the second-comer, an award of priority does not determine for all time who can use the mark. In some cases, it merely sets the scene for a subsequent contract. Where the second-comer is in a better position to exploit the mark, an award of priority to the first user may simply result in an exchange of money for the right to use the mark. On the other hand, where the first user can more efficiently exploit the mark, economic theory suggests that it will continue to do so.

Priority and the Prevention of Trademark Races. Why should the law grant rights to the first user of a mark? Consider the alternative: If two entities have to "race" to establish nationwide recognition for their mark, will they spend more money widely distributing their new product — and advertising it — than they would otherwise? Would such extensive, early promotional efforts be wasteful? Is the role of trademark priority to forestall such wasteful expenditures and instead promote a more rational product "rollout" nationwide? Should the parties ever be able to divide up the nation?

Some guidance may be gleaned from a prominent justification for secure title in real property holdings. It has been argued that without secure property rights, assigned in advance, those seeking use of a resource will make wasteful expenditures seeking to claim it. The idea is that the orderly, rational development of the resource will be distorted by the absence of property rights. For example, consider "land rushes," such as the famous Oklahoma Land Rush. *See* Terry L. Anderson & Peter J. Hill, *The Race for Property Rights*, 33 J.L. & ECON. 177 (1990); R. Taylor Dennen, *Some Efficiency Effects of Nineteenth-Century Federal Land Policy: A Dynamic Analysis*, 51 AGRIC. HIST. 718 (1977); David D. Haddock, *First Possession Versus Optimal Timing: Limiting the Dissipation of Economic Value*, 64 WASH. U. L.Q. 775 (1986). Economic historians have detected evidence of wasteful spending by prospective claimants to real property. *See generally* GARY D. LIBECAP, CONTRACTING FOR PROPERTY RIGHTS (1989). Instead of allocating early expenditures rationally — for example, some money for land, some for seeds, fertilizer, and building materials — people put all their money into the pursuit of land claims. The upshot was that the land was not utilized in an efficient manner.

If the analogy between land development and trademark investment makes sense, why not go all the way to a pure registration system, under which virtually no expenditures need be made to secure trademark rights?

As another branch of economic theory would predict, "pure" registration systems — those where broad rights can be acquired without actual use in commerce — have been known to give rise to the scattershot acquisition of numerous trademarks solely for their resale value to real prospective users. In short, pure registration also invites "rent seeking." *Cf.* William M. Landes & Richard A. Posner, *Trademark Law: An Economic Perspective*, 30 J.L. & ECON. 265, 275 (1987). Consider the case of Robert Aries, who in 1965 had the foresight to register over 100 valuable American trademarks, including Pan American, NBC, Texaco, Monsanto, and Goodrich, with the National Trademark Office of Monaco. After registering the trademarks, Mr. Aries forced the American companies to buy their own marks back from him. Gerald D. O'Brien, *The Madrid Agreement Adherence Question*, 56 TRADEMARK REP. 326, 328 (1966). Similar practices were well known under French trademark law until the 1960s. *See, e.g.*, Andre Armengaud, *The New French Law on Trademarks*, 56 TRADEMARK REP. 430, 435-36 (1966):

> In France, during the last few years before the enactment of the 1964 Act, trademark registrations were becoming more and more numerous. This was due to the fact that many persons to whom a fancy name would come to mind, would register the name with the ulterior motive of obtaining some financial return from a possible subsequent user should the occasion arise. As a result, the area of choice for marks for new products was becoming narrower every day. Another drawback was that a merchant, or a manufacturer engaged in a particular trade area like hosiery for instance, would register his mark in all thirty-four classes. The relatively low cost of trademark registration in France, negligible as compared to the high costs a large company usually bears for advertising, made such practices possible. . . . [T]hese two practices . . . were responsible for the tremendous volume of trademark registration.

On the end of these practices in France, see Gerard Dassas, *Survey of Experience Under the French Trademark Law*, 66 TRADEMARK REP. 485, 491 (1976).

A similar phenomenon occurred more recently with Internet domain names. The registration of domain names was initially handled by Network Solutions, Inc. (NSI) and is now overseen by a variety of domain name registries operating under the auspices of a nonprofit entity called the Internet Corporation for Assigned Names and Numbers (ICANN). These entities have allocated domain names on a first-come, first-served basis for a modest fee. During its initial period of operation, this system wreaked havoc among trademark holders as "cybersquatters" rushed in to register well-known trademarks held by others. These registrants would then offer to sell them to the trademark owners at exorbitant prices. Some companies even registered the marks of their competitors and used the sites to put up comparative product information. *See, e.g.*, Joshua Quittner, *Making a Name on the Internet*, NEWSDAY, Oct. 7, 1994, at A4 ("It['s] . . . like a gold rush: Two thousand requests a month are coming in to stake claim to a name on the Internet, nearly 10 times as many as a year ago."). As we discuss below, courts, ICANN, and legislatures developed rules and dispute resolution processes to curtail such extortionate rent seeking. The potential to profit from registering domain names closely related to the trademarks of others continues to occur, although the opportunities for extracting value from trademark owners have been greatly reduced and the penalties for crossing the line greatly enhanced. *See, e.g.*, Shields v. Zuccarini, 254 F.3d 476 (3d Cir. 2001) (enjoining "typosquatting"—registering misspelled versions of trademarks—and imposing a large fine under the Anticybersquatting Consumer Protection Act).

There seems to be good reason to allow some sort of early claiming system (i.e., registration with national effect after minimal use) without going all the way to "pure" registration (which invites equally wasteful rent seeking). An alternative would be to allow pure registration with lapse for nonuse after some period of time. Notice that this quite adequately describes the current system of "intent to use" registration.

Incentives to Create Trademarks. Recall the respective efforts of Zazu Hair Design (ZHD), the plaintiff in the case that begins this section, and Wordmark, the consulting firm that L'Oreal hired to help identify a catchy name for its new hair coloring products. Why should ZHD potentially receive rights to the trademark when it appears that Wordmark thought to use Zazu as a product name first? (ZHD had only been using it as a trade name.) In other words, why doesn't the law grant rights to firms that specialize in creating new trademarks? Why must a mark be "used in commerce," as the statute phrases it, to receive legal protection? An argument for abolishing this requirement was made by Stephen Carter in his article, *Does It Matter Whether Intellectual Property Is Property?*, 68 CHI.-KENT L. REV. 715, 721 (1993): "But perhaps we should say, So what? How simple and elegant it would be to conclude that secondary meaning is unnecessary because the first to appropriate the mark owns it; owns it not because of its representational nature, but because it is a product of the mind."

Consider some counterarguments. In a seminal article written more than 50 years ago, Ralph S. Brown, Jr. highlighted the dual nature of trademark as serving both private and public interests. *See* Ralph S. Brown, Jr., *Advertising and the Public Interest: Legal Protection of Trade Symbols*, 57 YALE L.J. 1165, 1167 (1948). Expanding on this theme, Professor Wendy Gordon observes that:

> Promotional value, good will, popularity, and similar elements of value are joint products of both the public and the creator to a greater extent than are intellectual products themselves. True, even standard intellectual products—collocations of words, music, scenes—will be beneficial only if someone appreciates them; labor is never the only source of value, even for Locke. But with standard intellectual products the active role of the producer and the comparatively passive role of the public makes it easier to assign the resulting value primarily to the laborer. By contrast, with products such as popularity and "commercial magnetism," the chain of causality and responsibility is much harder to

> trace. . . . Usually a trademark is not purposely created for its own sake; the "benefit" purposely created is the good will of the owning entity (such as its reputation for manufacturing high-quality products), which the trademark merely happens to represent.

Wendy J. Gordon, *A Property Right in Self-Expression: Equality and Individualism in the Natural Law of Intellectual Property*, 102 YALE L.J. 1533, 1588 n.277 (1993); *cf.* HAL MORGAN, SYMBOLS OF AMERICA (1987) (noting broad cultural impact of well-known trademarks). Note the skepticism Professor Gordon apparently feels regarding the claim that trademarks are brought about by legal incentives. This skepticism is shared by Rochelle Dreyfuss. *See* Rochelle C. Dreyfuss, *Expressive Genericity: Trademarks as Language in the Pepsi Generation*, 65 NOTRE DAME L. REV. 397, 399 (1990) ("[T]here is little need to create economic incentives to encourage businesses to develop a vocabulary with which to conduct commerce. . . .").

What do you think would happen if the law did give rights to firms such as Wordmark? Would it deplete the "stock" of potential trademarks available to actual manufacturers and sellers? Would it be burdensome if many firms who wanted to start a business had to go first to a firm like Wordmark to "shop for a trademark"? How would the parties agree on a fair price for a trademark?

Keep in mind when thinking about these issues that even though firms such as Wordmark are not granted a legal right under the Lanham Act, such firms exist anyway. Indeed, from published reports it would appear that the image/identity industry is thriving. Is this a good argument against a system that granted rights to these firms?

Do you suppose ZHD would have a cause of action against Wordmark? How about L'Oreal, on the grounds that Wordmark chose a trademark that wound up in costly litigation? Perhaps in the contract specifying Wordmark's services, Wordmark expressly disclaims liability for subsequent litigation.

COMMENTS AND QUESTIONS

1. The *Zazu* case and its ilk center on what constitutes "use" for trademark purposes. But what happens when the "use" asserted by a plaintiff originates not with the seller of goods itself, but with the common parlance of consumers? Consider, for example, Volkswagenwerk A.G. v. Advanced Welding & Mfg. Co., 193 U.S.P.Q. 673 (TTAB 1976), which concerned trademark rights in the word "Bug." To Volkswagen (VW), the official moniker for its classic economy car was "Type I," or, later, "Beetle." But in common parlance, this car was universally referred to as a "Bug." Importantly, it was the consuming public, and not VW, that originated this usage. Should trademark law protect the association between VW and "Bug," even though "Bug" originated with consumers themselves? If so, it is a reflection of the "consumer protection" rationale for trademarks, as opposed to the incentive/property rationale. (Do you see why? How much did VW invest in creating the "Bug" mark?) Courts tend toward the view that consumer associations should be protected in this context. *Id. See also* National Cable Television Ass'n v. American Cinema Editors, Inc., 937 F.2d 1572 (Fed. Cir. 1991) (ACE used in common parlance as an acronym for association of film (cinema) editors).

2. Difficult priority problems arise when a well-known trademark is abandoned by its original owner. The priority question involves a race among rivals to capture the mark. *See* California Cedar Products Co. v. Pine Mountain Corp., 724 F.2d 827, 830

(9th Cir. 1984) (bad faith of first rival to claim abandoned Duraflame mark for ersatz fireplace logs negates its claim, leaving second rival to claim the mark with priority). *See generally* Jerome Gilson & Anne Gilson LaLonde, *The Zombie Trademark: A Windfall and a Pitfall*, 98 TRADEMARK REP. 1280 (2008) (discussing the problem of "residual goodwill"). Are the issues the same as when firms race to obtain rights to a new mark? Under a strict consumer protection rationale for trademarks, is there an argument that abandoned marks should be off-limits to rival firms, at least for a number of years? Why would a firm abandon a mark when it has value to rivals—why not sell it? (See the discussion *infra* on Assignments in Gross in Chapter 6.A.2.)

Note on Secondary Meaning in the Making

Consider how the doctrine of priority interacts with the doctrine of secondary meaning. Under trademark priority rules, the trademark is presumptively owned by the first person to use it in commerce (barring a federal registration). But the secondary meaning doctrine provides that *descriptive* marks are not entitled to protection until their owner can prove secondary meaning in the minds of consumers. So when does a trademark owner obtain priority of use in a descriptive mark? When she first uses the mark? Or only after she can establish secondary meaning?

This issue has arisen in a number of cases where the defendant is accused of quickly adopting a plaintiff's descriptive mark before the plaintiff can establish secondary meaning. In Laureyssens v. Idea Group, Inc., 964 F.2d 131 (2d Cir. 1992), the court considered a trade dress infringement suit by the makers of "Happy Cube" 3-D puzzles against the makers of "Snafooz" puzzles:

> The district court found that there was no serious question whether actual secondary meaning exists in the HAPPY CUBE trade dress. We think this conclusion is sound given the weak sales of the HAPPY CUBE puzzles, low expenditures for advertising and promotion, minimal unsolicited media coverage, and the brief period of exclusive use of the HAPPY CUBE trade dress.[4] And, while there was evidence of intentional imitation as to the puzzles themselves, there was no evidence of copying of the trade dress.
>
> The district court concluded, however, that Laureyssens satisfied the requirement of secondary meaning by raising a serious question whether the flat-form, shrink-wrapped HAPPY CUBE trade dress should be protected under the doctrine of secondary meaning in the making.
>
> In Metro Kane Imports, Ltd. v. Federated Dept. Stores, Inc., 625 F. Supp. 313, 316 (S.D.N.Y. 1985), *aff'd*, 800 F.2d 1128 (2d Cir. 1986), Judge Sweet explained that a trade dress will be "protected against intentional, deliberate attempts to capitalize on a distinctive product" where "secondary meaning is 'in the making' but not yet fully developed." See also Jolly Good Industries, Inc. v. Elegra, Inc., 690 F. Supp. 227, 230-31 (S.D.N.Y. 1988) (indicating that the theory has been "well-received by commentators" and citing as an example, 3 R. CALLMAN, THE LAW OF UNFAIR COMPETITION, TRADEMARKS AND MONOPOLIES § 77.3, at 356 (3d ed. 1971)).[5] The supposed doctrine seeks to prevent pirates

4. The record indicates that the HAPPY CUBE trade dress was adopted in 1990, and for some of that time Idea Group was marketing its puzzles in the allegedly infringing trade dress.

5. The subsequent edition of Callman's treatise, however, contains no language expressing approval for the doctrine of secondary meaning in the making. See 3 R. CALLMAN, THE LAW OF UNFAIR COMPETITION, TRADEMARKS, AND MONOPOLIES § 19.27 (4th ed. 1989).

from intentionally siphoning off another's nascent consumer recognition and goodwill. See, e.g., *Jolly Good*, 690 F. Supp. at 230-31.

In this case, Judge Sweet found that although Idea Group offered evidence that the SNAFOOZ packaging was developed without prior knowledge of the HAPPY CUBE trade dress, "the evidence does not indicate when [Idea Group] developed its flat-form shrink wrapped package, and therefore Plaintiffs have barely established a serious question of [Idea Group's] 'intentional deliberate attempts' to copy their trade dress." 768 F. Supp. at 1048.

We are, then, squarely presented for the first time with the question whether the doctrine of secondary meaning in the making should be recognized under the Lanham Act. . . .

. . . "The doctrine, if taken literally, is inimical to the purpose of the secondary meaning requirement." Restatement, supra, § 13 reporter's note, comment *e* at 53. The secondary meaning requirement exists to insure that something worth protecting exists — an association that has developed in the purchasing public's mind between a distinctive trade dress and its producer — before trademark law applies to limit the freedom of a competitor to compete by copying. As the drafters of the *Restatement*, supra, § 17 comment b at 104-05, explain:

> The freedom to copy product and packaging features is limited by the law of trademarks only when the copying is likely to confuse prospective purchasers as to the source or sponsorship of the goods. The imitation or even complete duplication of another's product or packaging creates no risk of confusion unless some aspect of the duplicated appearance is identified with a particular source. Unless a design is distinctive . . . and thus distinguishes the goods of one producer from those of others, it is ineligible for protection as a trademark.

See also Norwich Pharmacal Co. v. Sterling Drug, Inc., 271 F.2d 569, 572 (2d Cir. 1959) ("Absent confusion, imitation of certain successful features in another's product is not unlawful and to that extent a 'free ride' is permitted."), *cert. denied*, 362 U.S. 919, 4 L. Ed. 2d 739, 80 S. Ct. 671 (1960); Perfect Fit Industries, Inc. v. Acme Quilting Co., 618 F.2d 950, 952-53 (2d Cir. 1980). The so-called doctrine of secondary meaning in the making, by affording protection before prospective purchasers are likely to associate the trade dress with a particular sponsor, constrains unnecessarily the freedom to copy and compete.

The Eighth Circuit previously recognized the improper focus of the concept of secondary meaning in the making in Black & Decker Mfg. v. Ever-Ready Appliance Mfg., 684 F.2d 546, 550 (8th Cir. 1982): "Such a theory focuses solely upon the intent and actions of the seller of the product to the exclusion of the consuming public; but the very essence of secondary meaning is the association in the mind of the public of particular aspects of trade dress with a particular product and producer." See also Scagnelli, *Dawn of a New Doctrine? — Trademark Protection for Incipient Secondary Meaning*, 71 Trademark Rep. 527, 542-43 (1981).

The argument in favor of permitting development of a doctrine of secondary meaning in the making, offered by Laureyssens, rests principally on the supposition that, without such a doctrine, there will be strong incentives for pirates to capitalize on products that have not yet developed secondary meaning. This argument, however, underestimates the level of protection afforded under existing law to prevent piracy in the early stages of product development. See Scagnelli, supra, at 543-49. For example, intentional copying is "persuasive evidence" of secondary meaning. *Coach Leatherware*, 933 F.2d at 169 (noting, however, that "conscious replication alone does not establish secondary meaning"); see also Restatement, supra, § 17 comment b at 106. Furthermore, secondary meaning can develop quickly to preclude knock-off artists from infringing. See Maternally Yours, Inc. v. Your Maternity Shop, Inc., 234 F.2d 538, 541 (2d Cir. 1956) (secondary meaning acquired in mark MATERNALLY YOURS for maternity apparel store in the 11 months preceding defendant's opening of store named YOUR MATERNITY SHOP). Finally, under New York's common law of unfair competition, a producer's trade dress is protected without proof of secondary meaning against practices imbued with an odor of bad faith. See Saratoga Vichy Spring Co. v. Lehman, 625 F.2d 1037, 1044 (2d Cir. 1980). These practices include palming off, actual deception, appropriation of another's property, see *Norwich Pharmacal*, 271 F.2d at 570-71; Upjohn Co. v. Schwartz, 246 F.2d 254, 261-62 (2d Cir. 1957), or deliberate copying. See Morex S.P.A. v. Design Inst. of Am., Inc., 779 F.2d 799, 801-02 (2d Cir. 1985); *Perfect Fit Indus.*, 618 F.2d at 952-54; RESTATEMENT, supra, § 16 reporter's note at 115. Therefore, true innovators, at least under New York law, have adequate means of recourse against free-riders.

For these reasons, we reject the doctrine of secondary meaning in the making under section 43(a) of the Lanham Act. Accordingly, we reverse the district court's decision to grant a preliminary injunction against Idea Group based on section 43(a) of the Lanham Act. Given our holding, we need not address the likelihood of confusion which may have been created by the SNAFOOZ trade dress.

COMMENTS AND QUESTIONS

1. Courts have been virtually unanimous in rejecting the idea of protecting "secondary meaning in the making" as inconsistent with the idea that descriptive marks are not protected. Indeed, many courts expressly require that a trademark plaintiff obtain secondary meaning before the defendant begins any use of the term. *See* MCCARTHY, MCCARTHY ON TRADEMARKS AND UNFAIR COMPETITION § 16.12, at 16-40 to 16-43 (collecting cases). *Cf.* Fuddruckers, Inc. v. Doc's B.R. Others, Inc., 826 F.2d 837 (9th Cir. 1987) (plaintiff was entitled to protect restaurant with trade dress nationally recognized among travelers against infringement by restaurant in Arizona, even though plaintiff had not established secondary meaning in Arizona directly).

What happens to trademarks that acquire secondary meaning too late? Are they wholly unprotectable? Or can they be asserted against a third party who uses the mark after secondary meaning is acquired? Note that the Trademark Office will register a descriptive mark that is first to acquire secondary meaning, regardless of when other users began use without secondary meaning. Presumably that registration confers some rights, at least against subsequent adopters. But does it make sense that earlier users are "grandfathered" into the market and can continue to use the mark in competition with its owner?

2. What is wrong with protecting secondary meaning "in the making"? Suppose that in *Laureyssens*, the plaintiff had proven that Idea Group copied its descriptive packaging exactly because it knew that Laureyssens was advertising its product heavily and that Idea Group intended to trade on Laureyssens's expected success in making its packaging distinctive. Is it really fair to permit Idea Group to borrow Laureyssens's future goodwill merely because Laureyssens hasn't yet succeeded in establishing that goodwill? The court acknowledges this argument but contends that the doctrine of secondary meaning adequately protects against "piracy in the early stages of product development." Is the court's argument persuasive?

PROBLEMS

Problem 4-6. Preco Industries began using the term "Porcelaincote" for its porcelain resurfacing material in 1966. Preco concedes that, at the time it began use, the "Porcelaincote" mark was unprotectable because it was descriptive. Preco continued to use the mark for a relatively minor product line. In 1977, Ceramco began to use the identical mark for identical goods. (Both companies sell their products on a nationwide basis.) In 1979, Ceramco began a nationwide advertising campaign using the "Porcelaincote" mark. Shortly thereafter, in 1980, Preco began a similar campaign. In 1981, the parties filed complaints against each other for trademark infringement. The court determined at trial that Ceramco established secondary meaning in 1979, and that Preco established it in 1980.

Assume that neither party ever registered its mark. Who should prevail in the lawsuits? Does either party have rights against a third company that began using the name in 1990? Does your answer to either of these questions change if one or both parties registered its mark on the Principal Register?

Problem 4-7. In May 1989, Shalom Children's Wear begins advertising and planning a line of clothes to be called "Body Gear." In November 1989, In-Wear Corp. files an intent-to-use application for the mark "Body Gear." Shalom files an intent-to-use application for the same mark in December 1989 and begins selling its products in February 1990. Is either party entitled to register the Body Gear mark? (Assume that the mark is otherwise protectable.) Does the result change if In-Wear fails to begin selling its clothes by November 1992?

E. TRADEMARK OFFICE PROCEDURES

Administrative proceedings concerning trademarks in the United States are among the most stringent in the world. Unlike most foreign registration systems, which review applications only for compliance with formal requirements, the U.S. Patent and Trademark Office (PTO) reviews applications to ensure that they meet both formal requirements (which are largely set forth in § 1 of the Lanham Act) and substantive requirements (largely found in § 2 of the Lanham Act). For marks already being used in commerce, the application process consists of five basic stages: (1) application, (2) examination, (3) publication in the PTO's Official Gazette, (4) opposition, and (5) registration. For marks that the applicant intends to use in commerce in the near future, the process consists of two additional stages following opposition and preceding registration: (4.a) the issuance by the PTO of a "Notice of Allowance" and (4.b) the filing by the applicant of a Statement of Use. We review each of these stages below. But first we consider why a trademark owner should federally register its mark.

1. Principal vs. Supplemental Register

Although registration is not a prerequisite to trademark protection, trademarks registered on the Principal Register enjoy a number of significant advantages. The primary advantages are: (1) nationwide constructive use and constructive notice, which cut off rights of other users of the same or similar marks, Lanham Act § 22

(15 U.S.C. § 1072) and Lanham Act § 7(c) (15 U.S.C. § 1057(c)), (2) the possibility of achieving incontestable status after five years, which greatly enhances rights by eliminating a number of defenses, Lanham Act § 15 (15 U.S.C. § 1065), and (3) a prima facie presumption of the validity of the mark and the registrant's ownership of the mark, Lanham Act § 33(a) (15 U.S.C. § 1115(a)).[3] In practice, however, it is not clear how much weight courts place on the § 33 presumption of validity. *See, e.g.*, Custom Vehicles, Inc. v. Forest River, Inc., 476 F.3d 481, 486 (7th Cir. 2007) ("[T]he presumption of validity that registration creates is easily rebuttable, since it merely shifts the burden of production to the alleged infringer."); Door Systems, Inc. v. Pro-Line Door Systems, Inc., 83 F.3d 169, 172 (7th Cir. 1996) ("The presumption of validity that federal registration confers evaporates as soon as evidence of invalidity is presented. Its only function is to incite such evidence and when the function has been performed the presumption drops out of the case.").

Trademark applications are maintained in an index at the PTO and made available for public scrutiny soon after filing. This procedure is different from patent applications, the contents of which are kept secret for 18 months after filing in most cases.

The Supplemental Register was established by the 1946 Lanham Act "to enable persons in this country to domestically register trademarks so that they might obtain registration under the laws of foreign countries." McCarthy, McCarthy on Trademarks and Unfair Competition, § 19.09[1] (1996), at 19-68. Under the Paris Convention, foreign registration could not be granted in the absence of domestic registration. Because there are countries where trademark registration is granted to marks that would not qualify for the U.S. Principal Register, the Supplemental Register was created. Thus, even if a U.S. mark cannot gain the advantages of registration on the Principal Register, it may obtain protection in foreign countries.

To be eligible for the Supplemental Register a mark need only be capable of distinguishing goods or services. There is no need to prove that it actually functions in that capacity. The Supplemental Register is not available for clearly generic names, but it is available for the registration of trade dress.

Unlike the Principal Register, registration on the Supplemental Register confers no substantive trademark rights "beyond common law." *See, e.g.*, Clairol, Inc. v. Gillette Co., 389 F.2d 264 (2d Cir. 1968). Registration on the Supplemental Register has no evidentiary effects, it does not provide constructive notice of ownership, the mark cannot become incontestable, and it cannot be used as a basis for the Treasury Department to prevent the importation of infringing goods. However, a mark on the Supplemental Register may be litigated in federal court, may be cited by the PTO against a later applicant, and may provide notice to others that the mark is in use. *See In re* Clorox Co., 578 F.2d 305 (C.C.P.A. 1978). Marks registered on the Supplemental Register are not subject to intent-to-use filings, interference proceedings, or opposition challenges, but may be canceled at any time by a court.

3. Other advantages include: (1) the right to request customs officials to bar the importation of goods bearing infringing trademarks, Lanham Act § 42 (15 U.S.C. § 1124), (2) provisions for treble damages, attorney fees, and certain other remedies in civil infringement actions, Lanham Act §§ 34-38 (15 U.S.C. §§ 1116-20), and (3) in the case of registered trade dress, owners do not bear the burden of establishing nonfunctionality (*see* Lanham Act § 43(a)(3) (15 U.S.C. § 1125(a)(3)), which imposes this burden on owners of unregistered trade dress).

2. Application

Trademark applications may be filed electronically or, at additional cost, in paper form. In 2009, 97.8 percent of trademark applications at the PTO were filed electronically.[4] The application is relatively simple. *See* Lanham Act §§ 1(a) & 1(b) (setting out the required contents of use-based and intent-to-use applications, respectively). The following are the most important elements of the application:

- *Filing Basis*: The Lanham Act establishes five bases for filing a trademark application: (1) actual use of the mark in commerce (Lanham Act § 1(a)); (2) bona fide intent to use the mark in commerce (Lanham Act § 1(b)); (3) a claim of priority based on an earlier-filed foreign application to register the mark (Lanham Act § 44(d)); (4) registration of the mark in a foreign applicant's country of origin (Lanham Act § 44(e)); and (5) extension of protection of an international registration under the Madrid System for the international registration of trademarks (Lanham Act § 66(a)), which is discussed in the following Note. Most trademark applications at the PTO are now filed under the Lanham Act § 1(b) intent to use basis.
- *Designation of Goods and Services*: The applicant must identify the particular goods or services on or in connection with which it uses or intends to use the mark. The applicant should also identify the international class number(s) of the identified goods or services. *See* Trademark Manual of Examining Procedure (TMEP) § 805. Importantly, this identification of goods or services does not limit the breadth of the applicant's exclusive rights. The sole purpose of the identification of goods and services is to aid the PTO in internal administration and review of applications.
- *Drawing*: The applicant must submit a drawing of the trademark. As of 2003, if the mark consists of colors, the drawing must as well. For word marks, a typed representation of the mark is sufficient. For nonvisual marks, such as sound or scent marks, the applicant need not submit a drawing. The PTO relies instead on the applicant's description of the mark given elsewhere in the application and on the applicant's specimen of use. TMEP § 807.09.
- *Specimen of Use*: Applicants filing a "1(a)" use-based application must submit a specimen showing use of the mark in commerce. For electronic applications, this specimen typically takes the form of digital photographs of the mark attached to goods or .pdf images of materials promoting services. Applicants filing a "1(b)" intent-to-use application need not (because they very likely cannot) submit a specimen of use with their application, but must do so instead when they file their Statement of Use. *See* Lanham Act § 1(d)(1) (15 U.S.C. 1051(d)(1)).

To give a sense of scale, the PTO received 352,051 trademark applications in 2009. There were a total of 1,547,168 active certificates of registration at the PTO at the end of its fiscal year in September 2009.[5] Average total pendency of trademark applications at the PTO in 2009 was approximately 11.2 months.[6]

4. *See* United States Patent and Trademark Office, Performance and Accountability Report, Fiscal Year 2009, at 21 (2009).
5. *See id.*, Table 15.
6. *Id.* at 19.

Note on the Madrid System of Trademark Registration

Despite the obvious desirability of international trademark registration, the United States did not join an international convention that goes beyond the rather minimal protections afforded by the Paris Union until 2002. The Madrid Trademark Agreement (MTA) is the main international trademark convention.[7] The MTA does not itself protect any trademark rights; it simply facilitates trademark prosecution in member states. Under the MTA, a trademark owner files a single registration with its domestic trademark office.[8] The owner may then extend this "basic registration" by filing, within six months of the original filing, an international application with the domestic trademark office designating other MTA member countries in which protection is sought.[9]

The United States recently joined the Madrid Protocol (MP), a corollary to the broader MTA. The MP considerably softens some of the harsher impacts of the MTA, especially on the United States.[10] Specifically, the MP (1) allows for filing in English or French, in the U.S. PTO or any other member country trademark office; (2) allows the filing of an international application based not only on a "basic" (or home country) registration but also on a basic *application*—a substantial advantage given the relatively stringent prosecution standards in the United States, which can lead to long gaps between applications and registrations, and especially now in light of intent-to-use registrations under the Lanham Act; and (3) substantially lessens the impact of a "central attack" provision, under which a trademark invalidated in its home country is invalid everywhere, by allowing an international registrant to convert a successfully attacked registration into a bundle of individual national registrations if the attack occurs during the first five years of the international registration.[11]

Although some problems remain,[12] the MP is a substantial step towards international harmonization. Under the "Madrid Union," which includes a combined

7. Madrid Agreement Concerning the International Registration of Marks, April 14, 1891, 175 Consol. T.S. 57. This is an agreement under the Paris Convention for the Protection of Industrial Property, Stockholm Revision, done July 14, 1967, art. 2(1), 21 U.S.T. 1629, 1631, 828 U.N.T.S. 305, 313. There are currently 56 members, including China and most of the European nations. *See* World Intellectual Property Org., Madrid System for the International Registration of Marks: Report for 2009 (2010). Various other international agreements exist, but for the most part they only cover relations between pairs of countries. *See, e.g.*, McCarthy, McCarthy on Trademarks and Unfair Competition § 29.26 (describing bilateral treaties signed by the U.S.).

8. Madrid Agreement, art. 1(2), 828 U.N.T.S. at 393.

9. *See* arts. 3(1), 3ter (1), 828 U.N.T.S. at 395, 397; Art. 4(2), 828 U.N.T.S. at 399; Paris Convention, *supra*, Art. 4(C), 21 U.S.T. at 1632, 828 U.N.T.S. at 315 (six-month priority "grace period" for trademark registration filings).

10. Technically, members of the MP join the Madrid Union without signing the MTA. See MTA art. 1, 828 U.N.T.S. at 391 (states adhering to the Madrid Agreement "constitute a Special Union for the international registration of marks," known as the "Madrid Union."); Madrid Agreement Protocol, art. 1, at 9 (states adhering to the Madrid Agreement Protocol are also members of the Madrid Union).

11. MP, art. 9, at 43-45.

12. *See, e.g.*, Allan Zelnick, *The Madrid Protocol—Some Reflections*, 82 Trademark Rep. 651 (1992). Zelnick argues that U.S. companies might still prefer to pursue foreign trademark rights by filing individual foreign applications because of the liberality of most foreign trademark systems regarding the classes of goods that can be identified with the mark in the application. (In many countries, a trademark application can specify *all* classes of goods — giving applicants substantially broader rights than under U.S. law.) According to Zelnick,

> [I]t seems likely that on the whole, most American trademark owners who file abroad today are unlikely to make use of the Madrid Protocol. The reason for this conclusion is that under our practice the specification of goods or services that will appear in domestic application, on which the international application will be based, must be narrowly drawn to the specific goods or services in respect of which

total of 84 member nations who have signed the MTA and/or the MP,[13] there are currently over 515,000 registrations in force.[14] Indeed, some degree of harmonization would seem to be necessary, if only to keep up with trading partners. In Europe, for example, 1995 saw the advent of the Community Trademark Convention, a treaty providing for a single Community Trade Mark (CTM) based on a single European trademark registration.[15] If further proof were needed, the CTC shows convincingly that the logic of trademark harmonization is compelling in this era of global trade and instantaneous communication.

3. Examination and Grounds for Refusing Registration

Initial examination of the application is conducted ex parte by a PTO examining attorney. If the examining attorney identifies a substantive problem with the application, she will typically issue an "Office Action" rejecting the application and explaining the basis for the rejection. The applicant is given six months to respond. *See* Lanham Act § 12(b) (15 U.S.C. 1062(b)). Upon the first or any subsequent examination, the examining attorney may issue a "final rejection." The applicant may then appeal the examining attorney's decision to the Trademark Trial and Appeal Board, an administrative body within the PTO, and finally to the federal courts.

Section 2 of the Lanham Act provides the basis for many of the grounds for refusing registration on the Principal Register:

> No trademark by which the goods of the applicant may be distinguished from the goods of others shall be refused registration on the principal register on account of its nature unless it—

> the mark shall have been used in interstate or foreign commerce of the United States (in the case of applications based on use) or restricted to the particular items or services identified by their common trade names in respect of which the applicant shall have a bona fide intention to use the mark. Since the international application under the Madrid Protocol will have the same specification of goods or services as the United States application upon which it is based, we will have, in effect, transferred our domestic practice in this regard to United States trademark owners' international filings.

Id. at 652.

13. *See* World Intellectual Property Org., Madrid System for the International Registration of Marks: Report for 2009 (2010)

14. *Id.*

15. Council Regulation (EC) no. 40/94 of 20 December 1993 on the Community Trademark, OJ L 11/1. The CTM Regulation built on a 1980 Directive that substantially harmonized the national trademark laws of the EC member states. Primary features of the recently added CTM are:

- Trademarks with renewable ten-year term, to be registered in the new European Trademark Office in Alicante, Spain.
- Marks valid in all member states but invalid everywhere if revoked.
- Substantive requirements for registration and grounds for opposition that would largely be familiar to American trademark practitioners, e.g., registration of nondistinctive marks upon proof of secondary meaning, and for a limited class of goods or services.
- The working languages are German, English, Spanish, French, and Italian. Applications can be filed in any Community language and are translated for free; opposition proceedings, however, are conducted in only one of the official languages, which must be selected at the time of filing.

See Eric P. Raciti, *The Harmonization of Trademarks in the European Community: The Harmonization Directive and the Community Trademark*, 78 J. PAT. & TRADEMARK OFF. SOC'Y 51 (1996).

> (a) Consists of or comprises immoral, deceptive, or scandalous matter; or matter which may disparage or falsely suggest a connection with persons, living or dead, institutions, beliefs, or national symbols, or bring them into contempt, or disrepute.
>
> (b) Consists of or comprises the flag or coat of arms or other insignia of the United States, or of any State or municipality, or of any foreign nation, or any simulation thereof.
>
> (c) Consists of or comprises a name, portrait, or signature identifying a particular living individual except by his written consent, or the name, signature, or portrait, of a deceased President of the United States during the life of his widow, if any, except by the written consent of the widow.
>
> (d) Consists of or comprises a mark which so resembles a mark registered in the Patent and Trademark Office, or a mark or trade name previously used in the United States by another and not abandoned, as to be likely, when used on or in connection with the goods of the applicant, to cause confusion, or to cause mistake, or to deceive: *Provided,* That, if the Commissioner determines [accordingly, concurrent registrations may be possible; *see* below].
>
> (e) Consists of a mark which, (1) when used on or in connection with the goods of the applicant is merely descriptive or deceptively misdescriptive of them, (2) when used on or in connection with the goods of the applicant is primarily geographically descriptive of them, except as indications of regional origin may be registrable under section 1054 of this title, (3) when used on or in connection with the goods of the applicant is primarily geographically deceptively misdescriptive of them, (4) is primarily merely a surname, or (5) comprises any matter that, as a whole, is functional.

Lanham Act § 2 (15 U.S.C. § 1052). Marks rejected under subsection (e)(1), (2), and (4) may be registered if the applicant can demonstrate secondary meaning, however. *See* Lanham Act § 2(f) (15 U.S.C. § 1052(f)).

a. Immoral, Scandalous, or Disparaging Marks

Section 2(a) forbids the registration of "immoral" or "scandalous" matter as well as matter that is "disparaging," even if it is otherwise eligible for trademark protection. At the PTO, the test for whether a mark is scandalous (the PTO has traditionally collapsed the category of the "immoral" into the "scandalous") is slightly different from the test for whether a mark is disparaging.

To determine whether a mark is scandalous, the PTO engages in a two-step process: First, it determines the likely meaning of the matter in question, typically by reference to dictionary definitions, media usages, and the nature of the good or service to which the mark is affixed; second, it determines whether the likely meaning of the matter in question would be perceived as scandalous by a "substantial composite of the general public" at the time the registration of the matter is sought. Harjo v. Pro-Football Inc. 50 U.S.P.Q.2d (BNA) 1705, 1735 (T.T.A.B. 1999). The standard for what constitutes scandalous matter has changed over time to reflect contemporary mores. *In re* Old Glory Condom Corp., 26 U.S.P.Q.2d 1216 (TTAB 1993), offers a good example. The applicant was attempting to register the following mark to denote its condom product:

FIGURE 4-2
Logo for old glory condom corp.

The Board reversed rejection of the application by the examining attorney. In the course of reviewing older cases finding scandalous marks such as "QUEEN MARY" for women's underwear and "BUBBY TRAP" for brassieres, the court said:

> What was once considered scandalous as a trademark or service mark twenty, thirty or fifty years ago may no longer be considered so. Marks one thought scandalous may now be thought merely humorous (or even quaint). The point to be made here is that, in deciding whether a mark is scandalous under Section 2(a), we must consider that mark in the context of contemporary attitudes. . . .

Id. at 1218-19.

To determine whether a mark is disparaging, the PTO engages in a different two-step process: First, it determines the likely meaning of the mark in essentially the same way that it does for scandalous marks; but second, if that likely meaning is found to refer to identifiable persons, institutions, beliefs, or national symbols, it determines whether this likely meaning would be perceived as disparaging by a substantial composite of the referenced group. *See* Harjo v. Pro-Football Inc. 50 U.S.P.Q.2d (BNA) 1705, 1737-40 (TTAB 1999); TMEP § 1203.03(c). *See also In re* Squaw Valley Development Co., 80 U.S.P.Q.2d 1264 (TTAB 2006) (finding that the terms Squaw and Squaw One when used in connection with clothing and retail sporting goods services were disparaging because they would be perceived as offensive by a substantial composite of Native Americans, but finding that the same terms when applied to ski equipment were not disparaging because the likely meaning of Squaw in relation to these goods is applicant's Squaw Valley Ski resort).

Because Section 2(a) applies only to registration, a cancellation or refusal to register would affect only the mark owner's ownership of federal registrations. What effect will it have on enforcement of the trademarks under Lanham Act § 43(a) or under state statutory and common law? Under federal anti-dilution protection? Later in this chapter we explain that a mark must be found to be famous to be protected against dilution under the federal statute. Can a mark be disparaging yet still famous? Is it consistent with trademark law to protect consumer associations even though a mark has been declared disparaging?

Who can challenge a mark as scandalous? The short answer appears to be: virtually anyone. In Ritchie v. Simpson, 170 F.3d 1092 (Fed. Cir. 1999), William B. Ritchie opposed registration of various trademarks associated with O.J. Simpson. Ritchie argued that the trademarks recited immoral or scandalous material given the well-known past of the registrant (i.e., spousal abuse, accusation of murder, etc.). The Federal Circuit upheld Ritchie's standing to oppose the marks, holding that he had shown a sufficiently real and personal interest in the outcome of the opposition proceeding (in the form of a deep personal belief in non-abusive relationships) to defeat a motion to dismiss for lack of standing.

PROBLEM

Problem 4-8. The Washington Redskins is a professional football team that has used that name for decades. Susan Harjo is a Native American who is offended by the use of the term "redskin," which she says is offensive to Native Americans. She petitions the PTO to cancel the Redskins mark.

In support, Harjo presents the testimony of her linguistics expert, Dr. Geoffrey Nunberg, regarding the usage of the word "redskin(s)." He contends that the primary denotation of "redskin(s)" is Native American people; that, only with the addition of the word "Washington," has "redskin(s)" acquired a secondary denotation in the sports world, denoting the NFL Football club; that the "offensive and disparaging qualities" of "redskin(s)" arise from its connotations; and that these negative connotations pertain to the word "redskin(s)" in the context of the team name "Washington Redskins." Regarding whether the negative connotations of "redskin(s)" are inherent or arise from the context of its usage, he argues that "redskin(s)" is inherently offensive and disparaging.

The NFL contends that the word "redskin(s) has throughout history, been a purely denotative term, used interchangeably with 'Indian.' " It argues that "redskin(s)" is "an entirely neutral and ordinary term of reference" from the relevant time period to the present; and that, as such, "redskin(s)" is "[synonymous] with ethnic identifiers such as 'American Indian,' 'Indian,' and 'Native American.' " It also states that, through its long and extensive use of "Redskins" in connection with professional football, the word has developed a meaning "separate and distinct from the core, ethnic meaning" of the word "redskin(s)," denoting the "Washington Redskins" football team; and that such use by respondent "has absolutely no negative effect on the word's neutrality—and, indeed, serves to enhance the word's already positive associations—as football is neither of questionable morality nor per se offensive to or prohibited by American Indian religious or cultural practices."

Petitioners conducted a survey of 301 people, which showed that 46.6 percent of all respondents, and 36.6 percent of Native Americans, found "redskin" offensive.

Should the PTO cancel the mark?

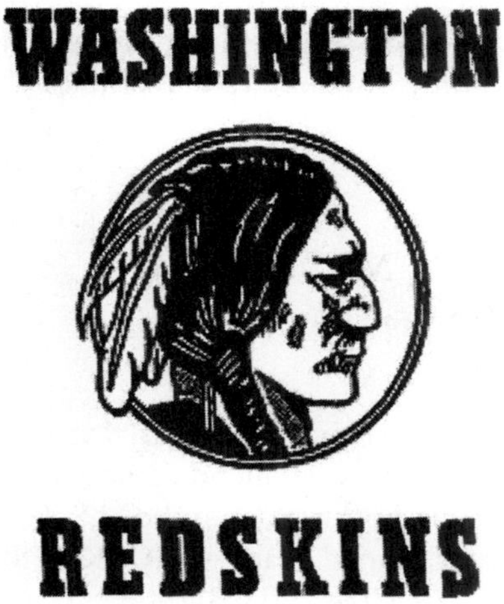

FIGURE 4-3
Trademark Registration Number 986,668

b. *Geographic Marks*

A complex body of doctrine has formed around the registrability and protectability of geographic terms attached to goods or services. Generally speaking, a "primarily geographically descriptive" term may be registered only upon a showing of secondary meaning. Lanham Act §§ 2(e)(2) & 2(f); 15 U.S.C. §§ 1052(e)(2) & (f). A term is geographically descriptive if (1) its primary significance is a generally known geographic location (rather than an obscure locale that happens to have as its name the term sought to be registered; (2) the goods or services originate in that geographic location; and (3) purchasers would be likely to believe that the goods originate from that location, i.e., that consumers perceive a "goods/place association" between the goods and the place from which they originate. *See, e.g.*, In re Spirits of New Merced, LLC, 85 U.S.P.Q.2d 1614 (T.T.A.B. 2007) (finding Yosemite Beer, which was advertised as brewed near Yosemite National Park, primarily geographically descriptive of applicant's beer); In re Brouwerij Nacional Balashi NV, 80 U.S.P.Q.2d 1820 (T.T.A.B. 2006) (finding Balashi Beer and Balashi for beer brewed in the Balashi area of Aruba not primarily geographically descriptive because the geographic term is so obscure that U.S. consumers of beer would not recognize it as indicating the geographical source of the goods); In re Nantucket, Inc., 677 F.2d 95 (C.C.P.A. 1982) (finding Nantucket for men's shirts manufactured elsewhere not geographically descriptive, but rather arbitrary, because consumers would not perceive a goods/place association).

By contrast, terms determined to be "primarily geographically deceptively misdescriptive" are unregistrable and unprotectable even upon a showing of secondary meaning. Lanham Act §§ 2(e)(3) & 2(f); 15 U.S.C. §§ 1052(e)(3) & 1052(f). (*Non-geographic* deceptively misdescriptive marks, however, are registrable upon a showing of secondary meaning, Lanham Act §§2(e)(1) & 2(f); 15 U.S.C. §§1052(e)(1) & 1052(f)). The following case discusses the rather more stringent test that courts have recently developed to determine whether a term is primarily geographically deceptively misdescriptive.

In re Spirits Int'l, N.V.

563 F.3d 1347 (Fed. Cir. 2009)

DYK, Circuit Judge.

Spirits International B.V. (formerly Spirits International N.V.) ("Spirits"), appeals a decision of the Trademark Trial and Appeal Board ("Board"). The Board affirmed a decision by an examining attorney at the U.S. Patent and Trademark Office ("PTO") refusing to register Spirits' mark—MOSKOVSKAYA—for vodka. *In re* Spirits Int'l N.V., 86 USPQ2d 1078 (TTAB 2008). The Board concluded that the mark was primarily geographically deceptively misdescriptive under 15 U.S.C. §1052(e)(3). Because the Board applied an incorrect test for materiality in determining that the mark was geographically deceptive, we vacate and remand.

Background

Spirits filed an application for use of the mark MOSKOVSKAYA for vodka on April 22, 1993, based on an allegation of bona fide intention to use the mark in commerce. Spirits admitted that the vodka "will not be manufactured, produced or sold in Moscow and will not have any other connection with Moscow." Id. at 1081. On August 31, 1993, the examining attorney refused registration. . . . On March 13, 2006 . . . , the Final Office Action issued, refusing registration on the ground that MOSKOVSKAYA is primarily geographically deceptively misdescriptive.

Applying the doctrine of foreign equivalents (discussed below), the examining attorney translated the mark from Russian and found that the primary significance of the mark thus translated was "of or from Moscow." The examining attorney then found that Moscow was a generally known geographic location and that the public would likely believe the goods were from Moscow because there was a goods/place association between vodka and Moscow. Finally, the examining attorney found that this belief would likely be material to consumers because Russian vodka is highly regarded.

On September 1, 2006, Spirits filed a response and motion for reconsideration. Spirits contended that the rejection was inappropriate. . . . On November 2, 2006, the examining attorney denied the motion for reconsideration. Spirits sought review by the Board, and on February 11, 2008, the Board affirmed.

The Board analyzed the mark under 15 U.S.C. §1052(e)(3), which prohibits the registration of marks that are primarily geographically deceptively misdescriptive of the goods. Citing our decision In re California Innovations, Inc., 329 F.3d 1334 (Fed. Cir. 2003), the Board noted that the analysis of whether a mark should be rejected under subsection (e)(3) had recently changed to include a requirement that the mark materially deceive the public. The Board stated the following requirements for establishing a prima facie case that a mark is primarily geographically deceptively misdescriptive of the goods:

> (1) the mark's primary significance is a generally known geographic location; (2) the relevant public would be likely to believe that the goods originate in the place named in the mark (i.e., that a goods/place association exists) when in fact the goods do not come from that place; and (3) the misrepresentation is a material factor in the consumer's decision.

Spirits, 86 USPQ2d at 1081. Like the examining attorney, the Board, under the doctrine of foreign equivalents, translated the mark into English and found that the primary significance of the mark was a generally known geographic location, establishing the first element of the prima facie case. The Board also found that Moscow is well known for vodka, and that this established the second element. Id. at 1086.

The Board also found that Moscow is reputed for high quality vodka, and thus that the public would likely be materially influenced by the mark in the purchasing decision. Id. In analyzing the materiality element, the Board stated that "an appreciable number of consumers for the goods or services at issue" must be deceived. Id. at 1085. But the Board concluded that "it is never necessary to show that all, or even most, of the relevant consumers would be deceived. All that is required is a showing that *some portion* of relevant consumers will be deceived." Id. at 1084 (emphasis added). The Board found that the mark met the materiality requirement because of its deception to Russian speakers.

The Board concluded that there is a "presum[ption] that a word in one of the common, modern languages of the world will be spoken or understood by an appreciable number of U.S. consumers for the product or service at issue." Id. at 1085. The Board also took judicial notice of the fact that, according to the 2000 U.S. Census, Russian is spoken by 706,000 people in the United States. Id. The Board then appears to have found that 706,000 people is an "appreciable number" in an absolute sense. The Board found that "[a]t least one significant group of 'ordinary American purchasers' is the purchaser who is knowledgeable in English as well as the pertinent foreign language." Id. The Board therefore concluded that this established a prima facie showing of deception under subsection (e)(3). Id. at 1086. . . .

Discussion

One aspect of the doctrine of foreign equivalents generally requires considering the meaning of a mark in a non-English language to the speakers of that language. As we stated in *Palm Bay*, "[u]nder the doctrine of foreign equivalents, foreign words from common languages are translated into English. . . ." Palm Bay Imps., Inc. v. Veuve Clicquot Ponsardin Maison Fondee en 1772, 396 F.3d 1369, 1377 (Fed. Cir. 2005); In re N. Paper Mills, 64 F.2d 998, 998-99, 20 C.C.P.A. 1109, 1933 Dec. Comm'r Pat. 452 (CCPA 1933). The doctrine has been summarized in a leading trademark treatise in the context of determining whether a mark is descriptive (or geographically descriptive) under subsections (e)(1) and (e)(2) of the statutory section governing registration:

> Under the "doctrine of foreign equivalents," foreign words are translated into English. . . . However, the "doctrine of foreign equivalents" is not an absolute rule,

> for it does not mean that words from dead or obscure languages are to be literally translated into English for descriptive purposes.

2 J. Thomas McCarthy, McCarthy on Trademarks and Unfair Competition § 11:34 (4th ed. 2009) (hereinafter "McCarthy") (footnotes omitted). The parties do not dispute this general requirement of translation under the doctrine of foreign equivalents. Nor do we. . . .

That is not, however, the end of the inquiry. Once the word or phrase is translated, its impact must be "material" under subsection (e)(3). The question here is the scope of the materiality requirement.

I

We begin with a brief description of the history of subsection (e)(3). As discussed at length in *California Innovations*, 329 F.3d at 1336-42, current subsection (e)(3) was added by the NAFTA Implementation Act in 1993. Prior to NAFTA, marks that were primarily geographically deceptively misdescriptive were treated together with marks that were primarily geographically descriptive under subsection (e)(2):

> [The PTO shall not register a mark that] when used on or in connection with the goods of the applicant is primarily geographically descriptive or deceptively misdescriptive of them.

15 U.S.C. § 1052(e)(2) (1988); see *Cal. Innovations*, 329 F.3d at 1336-41; Institut National Des Appellations D'Origine v. Vintners Int'l Co., 958 F.2d 1574, 1580 (Fed. Cir. 1992) (describing the law prior to NAFTA).

The NAFTA Act made two relevant changes to the law. First, the NAFTA Act amended subsection (e)(2) to remove any mention of primarily geographically deceptively misdescriptive marks. Subsection (e)(2) now reads "[the PTO shall not register a mark that] when used on or in connection with the goods of the applicant is primarily geographically descriptive of them. . . ." Second, the NAFTA Act created new subsection (e)(3) specifically dealing with primarily geographically deceptively misdescriptive marks. In doing so, Congress implicitly added a requirement that the PTO establish that the misdescription materially affect the public's decision to purchase the goods. *Cal. Innovations*, 329 F.3d at 1339-40.[1] Subsection (e)(3) now reads "[the PTO shall not register a mark that] when used on or in connection with the goods of the applicant is primarily geographically deceptively misdescriptive of them." 15 U.S.C. § 1052(e)(3).

Before the NAFTA Act, it was "quite easy for the PTO to deny registration on the principal register to geographically deceptively misdescriptive marks under § 1052(e)(2)." *Cal. Innovations*, 329 F.3d at 1337. There were two elements: (1) the primary significance of the mark was a generally known geographic location, and (2) a consumer would likely believe incorrectly that the mark is an accurate description

1. It should be noted that rejections under both the pre-NAFTA Act (e)(2) and the current (e)(2) are not permanent, but can be overcome upon a showing of acquired distinctiveness/secondary meaning. On the other hand, post-NAFTA Act (e)(3) rejections are permanent, and so cannot be overcome by acquired distinctiveness. *See Cal. Innovations*, 329 F.3d at 1336-39.

of the origin or other association of the goods with the geographic location. See *In re* Wada, 194 F.3d 1297, 1299-300 (Fed. Cir. 1999); *Cal. Innovations, Inc.*, 329 F.3d at 1340; TRADEMARK MANUAL OF EXAMINING PROCEDURE § 1210.01(a) (5th ed. 2007).

In contrast to this pre-existing approach under subsection (e)(2), "the PTO required a much more demanding finding to reject for geographical deception under § 1052(a)," which barred and continues to bar "immoral, deceptive, or scandalous" marks. *Cal. Innovations*, 329 F.3d at 1338. In order to deny a mark as deceptive under subsection (a), the PTO has been required to establish, in addition to the two elements listed above for geographic misdescriptiveness, a third element: that the misdescription would "materially affect the public's decision to purchase the goods." Id. at 1336-37.

The "addition of a materiality inquiry [to subsection (e)(3)] equates this test with the elevated standard applied under § 1052(a)." Id. at 1340. Since the NAFTA Act, the deceptiveness of the mark must be material under subsection (e)(3) just as it is under subsection (a).

However, *California Innovations* did not address the question of whether the materiality test of subsection (e)(3) embodies a requirement that a significant portion of the relevant consumers be deceived. We hold that subsection (e)(3) does incorporate such a requirement, and that the appropriate inquiry for materiality purposes is whether a substantial portion of the relevant consumers is likely to be deceived, not whether any absolute number or particular segment of the relevant consumers (such as foreign language speakers) is likely to be deceived.

In interpreting the materiality requirement of 15 U.S.C. § 1052 (e)(3), it is appropriate to look to the history of subsection (a), which includes the same materiality requirement as modern subsection (e)(3). *Cal. Innovations*, 329 F.3d at 1340. . . .

As the legislative history of the Lanham Act makes clear, subsection (a) was designed to codify common law standards for trademark infringement in the context of the registrability of trademarks under federal law. Although the Lanham Act departed from the common law in certain respects, the prohibition in § 1052(a) of deceptive marks was not a departure from the prior common law. The Lanham Act was designed to codify, not change, the common law in this area by prohibiting the registration of deceptive marks that were unenforceable at common law. The Supreme Court has recognized the appropriateness of construing the Lanham Act provisions dealing with federal trademark registration together with provisions codifying the law concerning the infringement of common law trademarks. See Wal-Mart Stores, Inc. v. Samara Bros., 529 U.S. 205, 209-10 (2000); Two Pesos, Inc. v. Taco Cabana, Inc., 505 U.S. 763, 767-68 (1992).

We thus must examine the common law to determine the scope of subsection (a). Before the Lanham Act, deceptive common law trademarks were unenforceable. This fell under the rubric of the doctrine of "unclean hands," an equitable defense under the common law. Worden & Co. v. Cal. Fig Syrup Co., 187 U.S. 516, 528 (1903). This meant that "if the plaintiff makes any material false statement in connection with . . . any symbol or label claimed as a trade-mark . . . no property can be claimed on it, or, in other words, the right to the exclusive use of it cannot be maintained." Id. But the common law doctrine did not apply in situations where a relatively small number of consumers was misled, as was made clear by Justice Holmes' opinion in Coca-Cola Co. v. Koke Co. of America, 254 U.S. 143, 144-47 (1920). There the Supreme Court held that the trademark "Coca-Cola" was not deceptive, and thus did not give rise to a defense of unclean hands to trademark infringement. Id. The Court first described the historical formulation of the beverage involving substantial quantities of the extract of the coca leaf (cocaine) and the extract of the cola nut. Id. The Court noted that the formulation of the beverage had changed over the years, and no longer contained significant quantities of coca or cola. Id. On this basis the defendant asserted that the mark was now deceptive. The Court stated that "[o]f course a man is not to be protected in the use of a device the very purpose and effect of which is to swindle the public" but that this defense was not "a very broad" one and "should be scrutinized with a critical eye." Id. Although the Court noted that there may be some people "here and there" who would drink the beverage because they thought it contained cocaine, this was insufficient to invoke the unclean hands doctrine because the mark "conveyed little or nothing [about the contents of the drink] to most who saw it." Id. (emphasis added).

The same common law requirement continues to this day. For example, the *Restatement (Third) of Unfair Competition* § 32 cmt. b discusses unclean hands and states that "a designation used as a trademark [that] . . . misdescribes the goods . . . in a manner likely to influence the purchasing decisions of a significant number of prospective purchasers . . . is deceptive" (emphasis added). See also id. § 14 cmt. c. . . .

Under the circumstances it is clear that section (e)(3)—like subsection (a) . . . and the common law—requires that a significant portion of the relevant consuming public be deceived. That population is often the entire U.S. population interested in purchasing the product or service. We note that, in some cases, the use of a non-English language mark can be evidence that the product in question is targeted at the community of those who understand that language. In such cases, the relevant consuming public will be composed of those who are members of that targeted community, and, as a result, people who speak the non-English language could comprise a substantial portion of the relevant consumers. See 2 McCarthy § 11:35 (discussing In re New Yorker Cheese Co., 130 USPQ 120 (TTAB 1961) (mark in Polish for canned ham marketed toward the Polish community)). There is no such contention here.

II

We turn then to this particular case. In this case, as in every case, in order to establish a prima facie case of materiality there must be some indication that a substantial portion of the relevant consumers would be materially influenced in the decision to purchase the product or service by the geographic meaning of the mark. Here the Board properly recognized that in order to be deceptive, foreign language marks must meet the requirement that "an appreciable number of consumers for the goods or services at issue will be deceived." In re Spirits, 86 USPQ2d at 1085. The problem with the Board's decision is that it elsewhere rejected a requirement of proportionality, and discussed instead the fact that Russian is a "common, modern language[ ] of the world [that] will be spoken or understood by an appreciable number of U.S. consumers for the product or service at issue," such number being in this case 706,000 people, according to the 2000 Census. Id. The Board, however, failed to consider whether Russian speakers were a "substantial portion of the intended audience." Because the Board applied an incorrect test, a remand is required.

We express no opinion on the ultimate question of whether a substantial portion of the intended audience would be materially deceived. We note that only 0.25% of the U.S. population speaks Russian. Appellant's Br. 26. If only one quarter of one percent of the relevant consumers was deceived, this would not be, by any measure, a substantial portion. However, it may be that Russian speakers are a greater percentage of the vodka-consuming public; that some number of non-Russian speakers would understand the mark to suggest that the vodka came from Moscow; and that these groups would together be a substantial portion of the intended audience.

We remand to the Board for a determination of whether there is a prima facie case of material deception under the correct legal test in the first instance. . . .

VACATED and REMANDED.

COMMENTS AND QUESTIONS

1. In light of *Spirits Int'l*, the PTO has updated the Trademark Manual of Examining Procedure to specify that the elements of a refusal to register under Section 2(e)(3) are the following: "(1) The primary significance of the mark is a generally known geographic location; (2) The goods or services do not originate in the place identified in the mark; (3) Purchasers would be likely to believe that the goods or services originate in the geographic place identified in the mark; and (4) The misrepresentation would be a material factor in a significant portion of the relevant consumers' decision to buy the goods or use the services." TMEP § 1210.05(b).

2. Consider the implications of the Federal Circuit's holding in In re California Innovations, Inc., 329 F.3d 1334, (Fed. Cir. 2003), which is described in *Spirits Int'l*. Before the NAFTA/TRIPS amendments in 1993, geographically deceptively misdescriptive marks could be registered upon a showing of secondary meaning. Certain U.S. trade partners, particularly European countries, objected to this apparently lax standard for the registration of geographically deceptively misdescriptive terms. In response, the United States changed its law to provide that any terms that qualify as geographically deceptively misdescriptive may not be registered. However, by adding a materiality requirement, *California Innovations* then made it much more difficult for terms to qualify as geographically deceptively misdescriptive. As a result, at least for certain marks, the United States has arguably adopted an even laxer standard for registration of geographically misdescriptive terms. If the misdescriptiveness of such terms is not material to the consumer's decision to purchase, then the term may be registrable, and now *without any need to show secondary meaning*. For if such terms are not geographically deceptively misdescriptive (because the materiality requirement is not satisfied), neither are they geographically descriptive, a status which would trigger the secondary meaning requirement. Instead, in the wake of *California Innovations*, it would appear that such terms are essentially suggestive or arbitrary, i.e., inherently distinctive. For a thorough discussion of this turn of events, see Robert Brauneis & Roger E. Schechter, *Geographic Trademarks and the Protection of Competitor Communication*, 96 TRADEMARK REP. 782 (2006).

3. In some cases prospective trademark registrants may be trying to seize on the descriptiveness of a term of geographic origin; "Napa" for wine would be an example. Another motivation is to seize on the good feelings engendered by a place name. *See, e.g.*, Singer Mfg. Co. v. Birginal-Bigsby Corp., 319 F.2d 273 (C.C.P.A. 1963)

(American Beauty is primarily geographically deceptively misdescriptive when applied to sewing machines of Japanese origin). For example, a trademark applicant might try to register "Cuban" for cigars made in New Hampshire; this would very likely lead to a finding of deceptiveness (Section 2(a)), and the application would be barred completely.

On the other hand, the use of a geographic term is not always forbidden. As the *Nantucket* case demonstrates, the question is whether the public connects the geographic indication with the source of goods. For a questionable application of the deceptive misdescriptiveness doctrine, see *In re* Broyhill Furn. Indus., 60 U.S.P.Q.2d 1511 (T.T.A.B. 2001) ("Toscana" primarily geographically deceptively misdescriptive for furniture).

If the public does not in fact associate the trademarked goods with the place, why would brand owners want to use that name? *See* Alan L. Durham, *Trademarks and the Landscape of Imagination*, 79 TEMPLE L. REV. 1181 (2006) (arguing that place names "evoke ideas with which the[] manufacturer would like to associate its brand" rather than the place of manufacture).

4. In many countries, geographic terms — usually for food or wine — serve also to certify composition, traditional preparation techniques, quality, and actual taste. In Europe, for example, so-called "appellations of origin" for wine — such as "Champagne," "Chablis," and "Chianti" — are protected by statute and administered by national authorities. *See* Institut National des Appellations d'Origine v. Vintners Int'l Co., 958 F.2d 1574 (Fed. Cir. 1992) (affirming denial of opposition by plaintiff, French national authority for establishing and policing appellations of origin, for registration of "Chablis with a Twist" for citrus-flavored wine drink that did not originate in France).

As part of the GATT amendments in 1994, Congress (as a concession to European interests) adopted limited recognition of the appellations of origin concept.

Lanham Act § 2(a) [15 U.S.C. § 1052(a)]

> No trademark . . . shall be refused registration on the principal register on account of its nature unless it —
>
> > (a) Consists of or comprises . . . a geographical indication which, when used on or in connection with wines or spirits, identifies a place other than the origin of the goods and is first used on or in connection with wines or spirits by the applicant on or after one year after the date on which the WTO [World Trade Organization] Agreement (as defined in section 3501(9) of Title 19) enters into force with respect to the United States.

Section 2(e) has also long provided that appellations of origin registered under the Lanham Act § 4 (15 U.S.C § 1054) (collective and certification marks) are an exception to the prohibition on geographically descriptive trademarks. A certification mark is a guarantee of authenticity — "Belgian chocolates" must come from Belgium, for example. Certification marks may be registered without proof of secondary meaning but must be made available in a nondiscriminatory fashion to anyone who complies with the terms of the certification. *See* Community of Roquefort v. William Faehndrich, Inc., 303 F.2d 494 (2d Cir. 1962) (French city of Roquefort was entitled to prevent use of the term "Roquefort" to describe cheese made in Hungary, based on U.S. certification mark). Note that group certification marks serve much the same quality assurance function as individual trademarks, but (assuming collective action problems are overcome) they may effectively protect small businesses who could not establish a well-known mark on their own.

For a spirited debate on appellations of origin, see Jim Chen, *A Sober Second Look at Appellations of Origin: How the United States Will Crash France's Wine and Cheese Party*, 5 MINN. J. GLOBAL TRADE 29 (1996) (arguing that appellations of origin are artificial market segmentation devices that detract from consumer welfare); Louis Lorvellec, *You've Got to Fight for Your Right to Party*, 5 MINN. J. GLOBAL TRADE 65 (1996) (begging to differ, from French perspective). *See also* Justin Hughes, *Champagne, Feta, and Bourbon: The Spirited Debate About Geographical Indications*, 58 HASTINGS L.J. 299 (2006).

Europe has a detailed set of rules regulating the use of geographically descriptive terms, particularly certification marks. Generally, these rules are more restrictive than U.S. law has been.

5. Marks that are "deceptively misdescriptive" cannot be registered even if they are not geographic in nature. *See, e.g.*, Glendale Int'l Corp. v. PTO, 374 F. Supp. 2d 479 (E.D. Va. 2005) (the mark "Titanium" was deceptively misdescriptive for a recreational vehicle that contained no titanium).

c. *Marks Which Are "Primarily Merely a Surname"*

In re Joint-Stock Company "Baik"

84 U.S.P.Q.2d 1921 (TTAB 2007)

Opinion by CATALDO, Administrative Trademark Judge:

On November 23, 2004, Joint-Stock Company Baik (applicant) filed an application to register the mark BAIK on the Principal Register in standard character form for "vodka" in International Class 33. Applicant asserts a bona fide intention to use the mark in commerce as its basis for registration.

The examining attorney refused registration on the ground that the mark is primarily merely a surname under Section 2(e)(4) of the Trademark Act, 15 U.S.C. § 1052(e)(4). When the refusal was made final, applicant appealed. Applicant and the examining attorney have filed main briefs on the case. In addition, applicant has filed a reply brief.

We reverse.

Section 2(e)(4) of Trademark Act precludes registration of a mark which is "primarily merely a surname" on the Principal Register without a showing of acquired distinctiveness under § 2(f) of the Act, 15 U.S.C. § 1052(f). We must decide on the facts of each case whether the mark at issue is "primarily merely a surname" under the Act. See In re Etablissements Darty et Fils, 759 F.2d 15, 225 USPQ 652, 653 (Fed. Cir. 1985). The examining attorney bears the initial burden to make a prima facie showing of surname significance. See id. If the examining attorney makes that showing, then we must weigh all of the evidence from the examining attorney and the applicant, to determine ultimately whether the mark is primarily merely a surname. See In re Sava Research Corp., 32 USPQ2d 1380, 1381 (TTAB 1994). If there is any doubt, we must resolve the doubt in favor of applicant. See In re Benthin Management GmbH, 37 USPQ2d 1332, 1334 (TTAB 1995).

In *Benthin*, the Board identified five factors, four of which are relevant here, to consider in determining whether a mark is primarily merely a surname: (1) the degree of the surname's "rareness"; (2) whether anyone connected with applicant has the mark as a surname; (3) whether the mark has any recognized meaning other than as a surname; and (4) whether the mark has the "look and feel" of a surname. Id. at 1332-33. Because BAIK is in standard character form, we need not consider the fifth *Benthin* factor here, that is, whether the manner in which the mark is displayed might negate any surname significance.

Rareness

With the first Office action, the examining attorney provided a summary and partial listing of 456 individuals having "Baik" as a surname, retrieved by a search of the Verizon superpages.com computer database. In that action, the examining attorney stated that "Baik appears to be a relatively rare surname. . . ." Based upon such evidence, however, Baik appears to be an extremely rare surname. With the final Office action, the examining attorney submitted four stories, one financial abstract and four "screenshots" from the Lexis/Nexis computer database concerning individuals with the surname Baik. In that action, the examining attorney stated that "the surname Baik commonly appears in newspapers and other media." We note, however, that three of the four "screenshots" are bankruptcy notices concerning individuals with the surname Baik while the fourth displays several listings of the same financial report, filed by an individual with the surname Baik. The report, from Nelson's Research Report Headlines, contains financial information regarding Isu Chemical Co. and lists an individual named Baik as the reporting analyst in the body thereof. Such bankruptcy notices and the financial report are not as widely read as articles for general circulation and do not support a finding that the public has been widely exposed to Baik as a surname. With regard to the articles, two are from trade papers (*New Jersey Law Journal* and *Pennsylvania Law Weekly*) that similarly would appear to have limited readership. The two remaining articles appear in general circulation newspapers (*The Indianapolis Star* (Indiana) and *Los Angeles Times*). However, in all cases the name Baik is buried in the text of the articles and would be likely to go unnoticed by most readers. Thus, while the Lexis/Nexis evidence suggests that Baik appears as a surname in printed media, these nine articles fall far short of supporting the examining attorney's contention that "the surname Baik commonly appears in newspapers and other media," or a finding that Baik is well recognized as a surname. Nor does such evidence support a finding that the number of individuals with Baik as a surname is any higher than was suggested by the evidence submitted with the first Office action.

As a result, on this record, we conclude that Baik is an extremely rare surname. In concluding so, we rely on the fact that only 456 examples of the Baik surname were located from a comprehensive directory of the entire United States. See In re Sava Research Corp., supra at 1381; and In re Garan Inc., 3 USPQ2d 1537, 1540 (TTAB 1987).

Applicant's Surname Use

The examining attorney acknowledges that "the record does not reveal any connection" (brief, p. 6) between the surname Baik and anyone associated with applicant.

Applicant confirms in its reply brief (p. 4) that Baik "is not the surname of anyone connected with the applicant." As a result, this point is neutral, and does not support either applicant or the examining attorney.

Other Meanings

The examining attorney argues that BAIK has no meaning other than as a surname and offers with the final Office action dictionary evidence from Dictionary.com, Microsoft Encarta, and Merriam-Webster OnLine in support of this position. Applicant asserts that BAIK is "an arbitrary Russian sounding word mark that has no meaning to consumers of the Applicant's goods." However, applicant goes on to argue that the "term sounds similar to Baikal, a Russian lake in Siberia" and the Baikal mountain range in Siberia. Applicant further argues that BAIK "is promoted along with the words 'Vodka Siberia' " and that, as a result, the "primary significance of the mark to the purchasing pubic is as a fanciful Russian term used in a trademark sense. . . ." In support of its contention, applicant submits with its reply brief an entry for Baikal Lake, from the printed reference work *Encyclopedia International* (1979), which describes it as the deepest body of fresh water in the world, located in Siberia.

We accept applicant's representation that BAIK is a coined term, particularly because there is no evidence that the term has any recognized meaning. Furthermore, we agree with applicant that BAIK, even though a coined term, sounds like a word in the Russian language. We also agree that the mark evokes or sounds similar to the word "Baikal," which has a recognized geographic significance, denoting a lake and mountain range in the Siberian region of Russia. Thus, while this is unlike cases where the mark is a recognized foreign term, or a mark derived from allegedly recognized foreign terms, the evidence of record nonetheless supports applicant's contention that BAIK sounds like a Russian language term.

Further, we note the absence of evidence that any person with the Baik surname has achieved any notoriety. Cf. In re Gregory, 70 USPQ2d 1792, 1795 (TTAB 2004) (evidence of public figures with surname Rogan found supported conclusion that public would perceive Rogan as a surname).

Look and Feel

Lastly we must consider whether BAIK has the "look and feel" of a surname. As to this factor, the examining attorney argues that BAIK has the look and feel of a surname because the evidence of record "established that the proposed mark does not have any primary recognition other than that of a surname." Applicant argues, instead, that "BAIK has the appearance and sound of an acronym or made-up Russian-sounding nonsense word."

We reject the examining attorney's argument that the mere fact that a mark may not have any recognized meaning other than that of a surname imbues the mark with the "look and feel" of a surname. As discussed above, BAIK may not have a defined meaning; nonetheless the term gives the appearance of a word in the Russian language and evokes the Baikal region of Siberian Russia. In addition, in a case such as this involving a very rare surname, we cannot assume that the purchasing public will view the mark as a surname based on exposure to the surname use. See In re Garan Inc., supra at 1540. It is in the case of a rare surname that we need to weigh "look and feel" carefully. For example, certain surnames, though rare, resemble common surnames "in their structure and pronunciation." See In re Industrie Pirelli Societa per Azioni, 9 USPQ2d 1564, 1566 (TTAB 1988). However, we see no evidence that such is the case with BAIK. In this case, there is no evidence that relevant purchasers would perceive BAIK as a surname.

In further support of the refusal to register, the examining attorney introduced evidence with the final Office action from the Yahoo People Search computer database to show that "more common" surnames, such as "Paik" and "Bak," are similar in appearance and sound to BAIK. We note, however, that such evidence reveals approximately 800 individuals with the surname "Paik," less than 900 with the surname "Naik," and 1100 with the surname "Bak." As such, the examining attorney's own evidence only suggests that the extremely rare surname Baik is similar to surnames that are almost as rare, i.e., fewer than 3,000 other people in this country. Thus, we are not convinced that the similarity of Baik to other obscure surnames somehow results in Baik having the "look and feel" of a surname.

In sum, based on the record in this case, we conclude that the examining attorney has failed to meet the burden of establishing a prima facie case that BAIK is primarily merely a surname. Accordingly, we conclude that BAIK is not primarily merely a surname. Furthermore, and as noted above, we must resolve any doubt in favor of applicant. See In re Benthin Management GmbH, 37 USPQ2d at 1334.

Decision: The refusal to register applicant's mark on the ground that it is primarily merely a surname is reversed.

CONCURRING OPINION

SEEHERMAN, Administrative Trademark Judge:

I add this concurring opinion to express my views about the way the "look and feel" factor should be interpreted in assessing whether a mark is primarily merely a surname. The statute provides that a mark should be refused registration not if it is a surname, but if it is primarily merely a surname. As a result, a mark such as HILL, which can be a surname, is registrable without resort to Section 2(f) because it has another meaning. I believe the "look and feel" factor should have the same effect. That is, if a term does not have the "look and feel" of a surname, it should not be refused registration even if there is evidence to show that it is, in fact, a surname.

However, I do not think that, in the converse situation, registration should be refused simply because the mark at issue is similar in sound or appearance to other surnames. The purpose behind prohibiting the registration of marks that are primarily merely surnames is not to protect the public from exposure to surnames, as though there were something offensive in viewing a surname. Rather, the purpose behind Section 2(e)(4) is to keep surnames available for people who wish to use their own surnames in their businesses, in the same manner that merely descriptive terms are prohibited from registration because competitors should be able to use a descriptive term to describe their own goods or services.

Because the purpose of Section 2(e)(4) is not to protect the public from being exposed to surname marks, the fact that the public may view a mark as a surname because it has the "look and feel" of a surname should not be the basis for refusing registration of rare surnames. If a surname is extremely rare, it is also extremely unlikely that someone other than the applicant will want to use the surname for the same or related goods or services as that of the applicant. Therefore, if the Office is not able to muster sufficient evidence to show that the mark is the surname of a reasonable number of people, and must instead resort to finding other surnames which rhyme with the mark or differ from the mark by one or two letters, I believe that it is not proper to refuse registration. Interpreting the "look and feel" factor to refuse registration of marks simply because they are similar to recognized surnames does not serve the intention of the statute.

COMMENTS AND QUESTIONS

1. As Judge Seeherman's concurrence emphasizes, the statutory hesitance to register surnames springs in part from an old common law policy in favor of the right to use one's name, a policy that still has some life. Basile, S.p.A. v. Basile, 899 F.2d 35 (D.C. Cir. 1990), for example, is a case where an Italian watchmaker by the name of Basile sought to use that name on watches in the United States — against the wishes of an established company, well known for its watches sold under the same name. In his opinion reviewing the scope of the injunction granted by the district court in the case, Judge Williams of the D.C. Circuit summarized the common law rule and its more recent interpretation:

> A seller's right to use his family name might have carried the day against a risk of buyer confusion in an era when the role of personal and localized reputation gave the right a more exalted status. In Burgess v. Burgess, 3 De G.M. & G. 896, 903-904, 43 Eng. Rep. 351, 354 (1853), the plaintiff's son had followed him into the trade of making anchovy paste; Lord Justice Bruce said:
>
> > All the Queen's subjects have a right, if they will, to manufacture and sell pickles and sauces, and not the less that their fathers have done so before them. All the Queen's subjects have a right to sell these articles in their own names, and not the less so that they bear the same name as their fathers.
>
> See also Brown Chemical Co. v. Meyer, 139 U.S. 540, 544, 11 S. Ct. 625, 627, 35 L. Ed. 247 (1891) ("[a] man's name is his own property, and he has the same right to its use and enjoyment as he has to that of any other species of property"); Stix, Baer & Fuller Dry Goods Co. v. American Piano Co., 211 F. 271, 274 (8th Cir. 1913). But even quite old decisions have enjoined a second comer's use of his name where necessary to prevent confusion. See, e.g., Thaddeus Davids Co. v. Davids Manufacturing Co., 233 U.S. 461, 472, 34 S. Ct. 648, 652, 58 L. Ed. 1046 (1914); Hat Corp. of America v. D.L. Davis Corp., 4 F. Supp. 613, 623 (D. Conn. 1933). The commentators, moreover, have been scornful of protecting the second comer's right to use his name at the expense of customer confusion, anathematizing it as the "sacred rights" theory. See Milton Handler & Charles Pickett, *Trade-Marks and Trade Names — An Analysis and Synthesis*, 30 Colum. L. Rev. 168, 197-200 (1930). . . . *Case Note*, 38 Harv. L. Rev. 405, 406 (1925).
>
> True, even recent decisions have invoked the right to use one's name, at least as an interest against which the senior user's are balanced. See Taylor Wine [Co., Inc. v. Bully Hill Vineyards, Inc., 569 F.2d 731, 734 (2d Cir. 1978)], . . . at 735. . . . But its weight has decidedly diminished. The courts are now consistent in imposing tighter restrictions on the second comer in the face of possible confusion . . . ; any residual protection of the second comer's use of his own name seems amply explained by the more general principle

> that an equitable remedy should be no broader than necessary to correct the wrong. . . . Where the second comer had established no reputation under his own name, one court did not even purport to "balance."
>
> This trend in the law unsurprisingly reflects trends in the marketplace. In a world of primarily local trade, the goodwill of an anchovy paste seller may well have depended on his individual reputation within the community. Indeed, one elderly decision tells us that an entrepreneur's failure to use his family name once risked "the reproach of doing business under false colors." *Hat Corp.*, 4 F. Supp. at 623. By contrast, the court went on, "[i]n an age when by corporate activity, mass production, and national distribution, the truly personal element has been so largely squeezed out of business, there is naturally less legitimate pecuniary value in a family name." Id.; see also Handler & Pickett, 30 COLUM. L. REV. at 199. That was in 1933 and the point is more obvious today. Other than understandable pride and sense of identity, the modern businessman loses nothing by losing the name. A junior user's right to use his name thus must yield to the extent its exercise causes confusion with the senior user's mark. . . .
>
> Here Francesco Basile's interest in the use of his name is peculiarly weak. He has no reputation in the United States as a watchmaker. . . . There is no suggestion that the watch industry is one where an individual proprietor's personal presentation of his wares plays a key commercial role, as may still be true of high fashion designers such as Yves St. Laurent and Christian Dior. Nor is it a business that has remained largely local in scope. Although none of these conditions would allow a second comer to use his own name at a serious cost of customer confusion, their absence means that Francesco's interest in his own name here is scarcely greater than his interest in the name Bulova. . . . [W]e think the only plausible motivation for his fight here is a wish to free-ride on Basile's goodwill, precisely what the law means to suppress.

Id. at 39-40.

2. The scope of injunctions shows the remnants of the common law concern with the right to use one's name. Courts are more likely to permit the junior use if the user disclaims any connection with the more famous senior user. See Taylor Wine Co. v. Bully Hill Vineyards, 569 F.2d 731 (2d Cir. 1978).

3. Should the nature of the defendant's use matter? One court has held that the restrictions applied to registering personal names should not apply where the name in question ("Niles") was used for a plush toy camel, since unlike personal names there was no strong business interest in using one's own name for a camel. Peaceable Planet, Inc. v. Ty, Inc., 362 F.3d 986 (7th Cir. 2004).

PROBLEM

Problem 4-9. Ernest and Julio Gallo are the nation's largest seller of wine. They sell their wine under the "Gallo" label and have advertised that trademark heavily. Ernest and Julio's younger brother Joseph Gallo runs a company called Gallo Cattle Co. Gallo Cattle begins selling cheese and salami under the name "Gallo Cheese" and "Gallo Salami." If Ernest and Julio Gallo wish to stop their brother from marketing meat and cheese under the Gallo name, what must they be able to show at trial? If they win, how should a court craft the injunction granting relief? What should it forbid and permit?

4. Publication

If the examining attorney determines that the trademark is entitled to registration on the Principal Register, the mark is published for opposition in the PTO's *Official Gazette*. Any notice of opposition (or request for extension of time to oppose) must be filed within 30 days after the date of the mark's publication. *See* Lanham Act §§ 12 & 13(a) (15 U.S.C. §§ 1062 & 1063(a)). Marks entitled to registration on the Supplemental Register are registered upon publication in the *Official Gazette*. Such marks cannot be opposed, but they are subject to cancellation under Lanham Act § 14 (15 U.S.C. § 1064). *See also* TMEP § 1502.

5. Opposition

Section 13(a) of the Lanham Act reads in part:

> (a) Any person who believes that he would be damaged by the registration of a mark upon the principal register may, upon payment of the prescribed fee, file an opposition in the Patent and Trademark Office, stating the grounds therefor, within thirty days after the publication . . . of the mark sought to be registered.

Because potential opposers must become aware of the contested mark's future registration, opposition is meaningful protection only for firms possessing the resources to conduct frequent searches of the *Official Gazette*, where prospective trademarks are published.

An opposer must plead and prove that: (1) it is likely to be damaged by registration of the applicant's mark (this is the standing requirement); and (2) that there are valid legal grounds why the applicant is not entitled to register its claimed mark. The opposer is in the plaintiff position, and the applicant is in the defendant position. The opposer has the burden of proving that the applicant has no right to register the contested mark. In general, there has been a trend toward liberalization of the standing requirement. *See* McCarthy § 20.7. "To establish standing to oppose, the opposer need only be something more than a gratuitous interloper or a vicarious avenger of someone else's rights." *Id.*

Once the standing threshold has been crossed, the opposer may rely on any legal ground that negates the applicant's right to registration. *See, e.g.*, Estate of Biro v. Bic Corp., 18 U.S.P.Q.2d 1382 (TTAB 1991). For example, an opposer might argue that the applicant did not make sufficient use of the mark in interstate commerce to receive a use-based registration. Generally, opposers rely on one of the bars to registration described in Lanham Act § 2, with Section 2(d) being the most common. Section 2(d) prohibits registration where the applicant's mark so resembles either (1) opposer's registered mark or (2) opposer's prior common law mark or trade name, as to be likely to cause confusion. The test for likelihood of confusion is generally the same as that used in general litigation, which we describe in detail *infra* in Chapter 5.B.

6. Registration

With respect to use-based applications, if no opposition is filed within 30 days or if the opposition fails, then the PTO issues a certificate of registration and notice of the registration is published in the *Official Gazette*. With respect to intent-to-use applications that are either unopposed or unsuccessfully opposed, the PTO issues a Notice of Allowance. The applicant then has six months (extendable for a total of three years) to file a Statement of Use showing that it is making use of the mark in commerce. *See* Lanham Act § 2(d) (15 U.S.C. § 1052(d)). *See also* TMEP § 1106.

7. Post-Registration Actions

Maintenance and Renewal. The term of registration is ten years. Lanham Act § 8 (15 U.S.C. § 1058). The registration may be renewed indefinitely provided that the registrant complies with the requirements of Lanham Act §§ 8 & 9 (15 U.S.C. §§ 1058 & 1059). Section 8 requires the registrant to file an Affidavit of Continuing Use during the sixth year and every tenth year following the date of registration (thus, the registrant must file a "Section 8 affidavit" in the sixth year, the tenth year, the twentieth year, etc.). Section 9 requires the registrant to file a Renewal Application every tenth year following the date of registration.[16] Registrants typically file the Affidavit of Continuing Use and the Renewal Application as a single document.

For reasons which will become clear in a moment, registrants are also strongly advised to file an Affidavit of Incontestability under Lanham Act § 15 (15 U.S.C. § 1065) within one year after any five-year period of continuous use of the mark. In practice, sophisticated trademark owners typically combine their first Section 8 Affidavit of Continuing Use (filed in the sixth year following registration) with a Section 15 Affidavit of Incontestability. A Section 15 affidavit may be filed at any time during the duration of the registration of the mark, however, provided that it is filed within the year following five years' continuous use of the mark. *See* TMEP § 1605.03.

Cancellation. If opposition is the first "backstop" to ex parte examination of trademarks, cancellation may be thought of as the second. Even after a trademark examiner is satisfied that a mark meets the requirements for registration and the mark is in fact registered, it may still be challenged in an inter partes proceeding. The Lanham Act allows one who "believes that he is or will be damaged by registration" to petition for cancellation of marks on either the Principal or Supplemental Register. Lanham Act § 18. Cancellation petitions are heard by the Trademark Trial and Appeal Board (TTAB). In civil suits where a federally registered mark is at issue, such as suits under Lanham Act § 2, the court may order cancellation of the registration.

The standing requirement for cancellation proceedings is quite similar to that for opposition. In both cases the statute speaks in terms of the plaintiff's belief that he or she will be damaged.

Even after cancellation of the registration, a mark may still enjoy common law rights. *See, e.g.*, National Trailways Bus System v. Trailway Van Lines, 269 F. Supp. 352 (E.D.N.Y. 1965).

16. Note that Sections 8 and 9 add a six-month grace period to these deadlines. *See* Lanham Act §§ 8(c) & 9(a) (15 U.S.C. §§ 1058(c) & 1059(a)). Thus, for example, the first Section 8 affidavit must be filed, strictly speaking, during the sixth year following registration or the six-month grace period following that year.

Note on Concurrent Registration

Concurrent use registration is provided for in Lanham Act §2(d):

> No trademark . . . shall be refused registration on the principal register . . . unless it— . . .
>
> (d) Consists of or comprises a mark which so resembles a mark . . . as to be likely . . . to cause confusion . . . : *Provided,* That if the Commissioner determines that confusion, mistake, or deception is not likely to result from the continued use by more than one person of the same or similar marks under conditions and limitations as to the mode or place of use of the marks or the goods on or in connection with which such marks are used, concurrent registrations may be issued to such persons when they have become entitled to use such marks as a result of their concurrent lawful use in commerce prior to (1) the earliest of the filing dates of the applications pending or of any registration issued under this Act. . . .

Lanham Act §2(d), 15 U.S.C. §1052(d). Section 2(d) goes on to say that prior use may be waived by agreement of the parties seeking concurrent registration, and that the commissioner may also issue concurrent use registrations when ordered to do so by a court. *Id.*

The most important condition for approval of concurrent use registration is that such registration cannot be likely to cause confusion of buyers or others. Application of Beatrice Foods Co., 429 F.2d 466 (C.C.P.A. 1970). In *Beatrice,* the senior user (Beatrice) had used a mark in 23 states and the junior user (Fairway) had used a mark in five states by the time the registration hearing commenced. Both had filed registration applications, and a concurrent use proceeding was instituted. The court established the general rule that the senior user can be awarded registration covering all parts of the United States except those regions where the subsequent (junior) user can establish existing rights in its actual area of use or zones of natural expansion. The junior user must show that confusion is not likely to result from the concurrent registration. The court then recognized three exceptions to this general rule: (1) the PTO is not required to grant registration contrary to an agreement between the parties that leaves some territory open; (2) where the junior user is the first to obtain federal registration, the junior user obtains nationwide rights subject only to the territorial limitations of the senior user (*see, e.g.,* Weiner King, Inc. v. Wiener King Corp., 615 F.2d 512 (C.C.P.A. 1980) (junior user who registered first and expanded after discovering the senior user was entitled to registration covering the entire United States with the exception of a small enclave encompassing the senior user's territory)); (3) areas of mutual nonuse may be maintained if the mark, goods, and territories are such that this is the only way to avoid the likelihood of confusion.

COMMENTS AND QUESTIONS

Should an agreement settling a dispute between parties seeking concurrent registration—hence carving up the nation into exclusive territories—be scrutinized for antitrust issues? *See* VMG Enterprises Inc. v. F. Quesada & Franco Inc., 788 F. Supp. 648 (D.P.R. 1992).

F. INCONTESTABILITY

Park 'N Fly, Inc. v. Dollar Park and Fly, Inc.
469 U.S. 189 (1985)

Justice O'CONNOR delivered the opinion of the Court.

In this case we consider whether an action to enjoin the infringement of an incontestable trade or service mark may be defended on the grounds that the mark is merely descriptive. We conclude that neither the language of the relevant statutes nor the legislative history supports such a defense.

I

Petitioner operates long-term parking lots near airports. After starting business in St. Louis in 1967, petitioner subsequently opened facilities in Cleveland, Houston, Boston, Memphis, and San Francisco. Petitioner applied in 1969 to the United States Patent and Trademark Office (Patent Office) to register a service mark consisting of the logo of an airplane and the words "Park 'N Fly." The registration issued in August 1971. Nearly six years later, petitioner filed an affidavit with the Patent Office to establish the incontestable status of the mark. As required by § 15 of the Trademark Act of 1946 (Lanham Act), 60 Stat. 433, as amended, 15 U.S.C. § 1065, the affidavit stated that the mark had been registered and in continuous use for five consecutive years, that there had been no final adverse decision to petitioner's claim of ownership or right to registration, and that no proceedings involving such rights were pending. Incontestable status provides, subject to the provisions of § 15 and § 33(b) of the Lanham Act, "conclusive evidence of the registrant's exclusive right to use the registered mark. . . ." § 33(b), 15 U.S.C. § 1115(b).

Respondent also provides long-term airport parking services, but only has operations in Portland, Oregon. Respondent calls its business "Dollar Park and Fly." Petitioner filed this infringement action in 1978 in the United States District Court for the District of Oregon and requested the court permanently to enjoin respondent from using the words "Park and Fly" in connection with its business. Respondent counterclaimed and sought cancellation of petitioner's mark on the grounds that it is a generic term. See § 14(c), 15 U.S.C. § 1064(c). Respondent also argued that petitioner's mark is unenforceable because it is merely descriptive. See § 2(e), 15 U.S.C. § 1052(e). As two additional defenses, respondent maintained that it is in privity with a Seattle corporation that has used the expression "Park and Fly" since a date prior to the registration of petitioner's mark, see § 33(b)(5), 15 U.S.C. § 1115(b)(5), and that it has not infringed because there is no likelihood of confusion. See § 32(1), 15 U.S.C. § 1114(1). . . .

II . . .

This case requires us to consider the effect of the incontestability provisions of the Lanham Act in the context of an infringement action defended on the grounds that the mark is merely descriptive. Statutory construction must begin with the language employed by Congress and the assumption that the ordinary meaning of that language accurately expresses the legislative purpose. See American Tobacco Co. v. Patterson, 456 U.S. 63, 68 (1982). With respect to incontestable trade or service marks, § 33(b) of the Lanham Act states that "registration shall be conclusive evidence of the registrant's exclusive right to use the registered mark" subject to the conditions of § 15 and certain enumerated defenses. Section 15 incorporates by reference subsections (c) and (e) of § 14, 15 U.S.C. § 1064. An incontestable mark that becomes generic may be canceled at any time pursuant to § 14(c). That section also allows cancellation of an incontestable mark at any time if it has been abandoned, if it is being used to misrepresent the source of the goods or services in connection with which it is used, or if it was obtained fraudulently or contrary to the provisions of § 4, 15 U.S.C. § 1054, or §§ 2(a)-(c), 15 U.S.C. §§ 1052(a)-(c). . . .

The language of the Lanham Act also refutes any conclusion that an incontestable mark may be challenged as merely descriptive. A mark that is merely descriptive of an applicant's goods or services is not registrable unless the mark has secondary meaning. Before a mark achieves incontestable status, registration provides prima facie evidence of the registrant's exclusive right to use the mark in commerce. § 33(a), 15 U.S.C. § 1115(a). The Lanham Act expressly provides that before a mark becomes incontestable an opposing party may prove any legal or equitable defense which might have been asserted if the mark had not been registered. Ibid. Thus, § 33(a) would have allowed respondent to challenge petitioner's mark as merely descriptive if the mark had not become incontestable. With respect to incontestable marks, however, § 33(b) provides that registration is conclusive evidence of the registrant's exclusive right to use the mark, subject to the conditions of § 15 and the seven defenses enumerated in § 33(b) itself. Mere descriptiveness is not recognized by either § 15 or § 33(b) as a basis for challenging an incontestable mark.

The statutory provisions that prohibit registration of a merely descriptive mark but do not allow an incontestable mark to be challenged on this ground cannot be attributed to inadvertence by Congress. The Conference Committee rejected an amendment that would have denied registration to any descriptive mark, and instead retained the provisions allowing registration of a merely descriptive mark that has acquired secondary meaning. See H.R. Conf. Rep. No. 2322, 79th Cong., 2d Sess., 4 (1946) (explanatory statement of House managers). The Conference Committee agreed to an amendment providing that no incontestable right can be acquired in a mark that is a common descriptive, i.e., generic, term. Id., at 5. Congress could easily have denied incontestability to merely descriptive marks as well as to generic marks had that been its intention.

The Court of Appeals in discussing the offensive/defensive distinction observed that incontestability protects a registrant against cancellation of his mark. 718 F.2d, at 331. This observation is incorrect with respect to marks that become generic or which otherwise may be canceled at any time pursuant to §§ 14(c) and (e). Moreover, as applied to marks that are merely descriptive, the approach of the Court of Appeals makes incontestable status superfluous. Without regard to its incontestable status, a mark that has been registered five years is protected from cancellation except on the grounds stated in §§ 14(c) and (e). Pursuant to § 14, a mark may be canceled on the grounds that it is merely descriptive only if the petition to cancel is filed within five years of the date of registration. § 14(a), 15 U.S.C. § 1064(a). The approach adopted by the Court of Appeals implies that incontestability adds nothing to the protections against cancellation already provided in § 14. The decision below not only lacks support in the words of the statute; it effectively emasculates § 33(b) under the circumstances of this case.

III

Nothing in the legislative history of the Lanham Act supports a departure from the plain language of the statutory provisions concerning incontestability. Indeed, a conclusion that incontestable status can provide the basis for enforcement of the registrant's exclusive right to use a trade or service mark promotes the goals of the statute. The Lanham Act provides national protection of trademarks in order to secure to the owner of the mark the goodwill of his business and to protect the ability of consumers to distinguish among competing producers. See S. Rep. No. 1333, at 3, 5. National protection of trademarks is desirable, Congress concluded, because trademarks foster competition and the maintenance of quality by securing to the producer the benefits of good reputation. Id., at 4. The incontestability provisions, as the proponents of the Lanham Act emphasized, provide a means for the registrant to quiet title in the ownership of his mark. See Hearings on H.R. 82 before the Subcommittee of the Senate Committee on Patents, 78th Cong., 2d Sess., 21 (1944) (remarks of Rep. Lanham); id., at 21, 113 (testimony of Daphne Robert, ABA Committee on Trade Mark Legislation); Hearings on H.R. 102 et al. before the Subcommittee on Trade-Marks of the House Committee on Patents, 77th Cong., 1st Sess., 73 (1941) (remarks of Rep. Lanham). The opportunity to obtain incontestable status by satisfying the requirements of § 15 thus encourages producers to cultivate the goodwill associated with a particular mark. This function of the incontestability provisions would be utterly frustrated if the holder of an incontestable mark could not enjoin infringement by others so long as they established that the mark would not be registrable but for its incontestable status.

Respondent argues, however, that enforcing petitioner's mark would conflict with the goals of the Lanham Act because the mark is merely descriptive and should never have been registered in the first place. . . .

The alternative of refusing to provide incontestable status for descriptive marks with secondary meaning was expressly noted in the hearings on the Lanham Act. Id., at 64, 69 (testimony of Robert Byerley, New York Patent Law Assn.); Hearings on S.895 before the Subcommittee of the Senate Committee on Patents, 77th Cong., 2d Sess., 42 (1942) (testimony of Elliot Moyer, Special Assistant to the Attorney General). Also mentioned was the possibility of including as a defense to infringement of an incontestable mark the "fact that a mark is a descriptive, generic, or geographical term or device." Id., at 45, 47. Congress, however, did not adopt either of these alternatives. Instead, Congress expressly provided in §§ 33(b) and 15 that an incontestable mark could be challenged on specified grounds, and the grounds identified by Congress do not include mere descriptiveness.

The dissent echoes arguments made by opponents of the Lanham Act that the incontestable status of a descriptive mark might take from the public domain language that is merely descriptive. As we have explained, Congress has already addressed concerns to prevent the "commercial monopolization" of descriptive language. The Lanham Act allows a mark to be challenged at any time if it becomes generic, and, under certain circumstances, permits the nontrademark use of descriptive terms contained in an incontestable mark. Finally, if "monopolization" of an incontestable mark threatens economic competition, § 33(b)(7), 15 U.S.C. § 1115(b)(7), provides a defense on the grounds that the mark is being used to violate federal antitrust laws. At bottom, the dissent simply disagrees with the balance struck by Congress in determining the protection to be given to incontestable marks. . . .

VI

We conclude that the holder of a registered mark may rely on incontestability to enjoin infringement and that such an action may not be defended on the grounds that the mark is merely descriptive. Respondent urges that we nevertheless affirm the decision below based on the "prior use" defense recognized by § 33(b)(5) of the Lanham Act. Alternatively, respondent argues that there is no likelihood of confusion and therefore no infringement justifying injunctive relief. The District Court rejected each of these arguments, but they were not addressed by the Court of Appeals. 718 F.2d, at 331-332, n.4. That court may consider them on remand. The judgment of the Court of Appeals is reversed, and the case is remanded for further proceedings consistent with this opinion. It is so ordered.

Justice STEVENS, dissenting.

In trademark law, the term "incontestable" is itself somewhat confusing and misleading because the Lanham Act expressly identifies over 20 situations in which infringement of an allegedly incontestable mark is permitted.[1] Moreover, in § 37 of the Act, Congress unambiguously authorized judicial review of the validity of the registration "in any action involving a registered mark."[2] The problem in this case arises because of petitioner's attempt to enforce as "incontestable" a mark that Congress has plainly stated is inherently unregistrable.

The mark "Park 'N Fly" is at best merely descriptive in the context of airport parking.[3] Section 2 of the Lanham Act plainly prohibits the registration of such a mark unless the applicant proves to the Commissioner of the Patent and Trademark

1. Section 33(b) enumerates seven categories of defenses to an action to enforce an incontestable mark. See 15 U.S.C. § 1115(b), quoted ante, at 3, n.1. In addition, a defendant is free to argue that a mark should never have become incontestable for any of the four reasons enumerated in § 15. 15 U.S.C. § 1065. Moreover, § 15 expressly provides that an incontestable mark may be challenged on any of the grounds set forth in subsections (c) and (e) of § 14, 15 U.S.C. § 1064, and those sections, in turn, incorporate the objections to registrability that are defined in §§ 2(a), 2(b), and 2(c) of the Act. 15 U.S.C. §§ 1052(a), (b), and (c).

2. Section 37, in pertinent part, provides: "In any action involving a registered mark the court may determine the right to registration, order the cancellation of registrations in whole or in part, restore canceled registrations, and otherwise rectify the register with respect to registrations of any party to the action." 15 U.S.C. § 1119.

3. In the Court of Appeals petitioner argued that its mark was suggestive with respect to airport parking lots. The Court of Appeals responded: "We are unpersuaded. Given the clarity of its first word, Park 'N Fly's mark seen in context can be understood readily by consumers as an offering of airport parking—imagination, thought, or perception is not needed. Simply understood, 'park and fly' is a clear and concise description of a characteristic or ingredient of the service offered—the customer parks his car and flies from the airport. We conclude that Park 'N Fly's mark used in the context of airport parking is, at best, a merely descriptive mark." 718 F.2d 327, 331 (CA9 1983).

Although the Court appears to speculate that even though the mark is now merely descriptive it might not have been merely descriptive in 1971 when it was first registered. . . . I find such speculation totally unpersuasive. But even if the Court's speculation were valid, the entire rationale of its opinion is based on the assumption that the mark is in the "merely descriptive" category.

Office that the mark "has become distinctive of the applicant's goods in commerce," or to use the accepted shorthand, that it has acquired a "secondary meaning." See 15 U.S.C. §§ 1052(e), (f). Petitioner never submitted any such proof to the Commissioner, or indeed to the District Court in this case. Thus, the registration plainly violated the Act.

The violation of the literal wording of the Act also contravened the central purpose of the entire legislative scheme. Statutory protection for trademarks was granted in order to safeguard the goodwill that is associated with particular enterprises. A mark must perform the function of distinguishing the producer or provider of a good or service in order to have any legitimate claim to protection. A merely descriptive mark that has not acquired secondary meaning does not perform that function because it simply "describes the qualities or characteristics of a good or service." No legislative purpose is served by granting anyone a monopoly in the use of such a mark. . . .

The word "incontestable" is not defined in the Act. Nor, surprisingly, is the concept explained in the Committee Reports on the bill that was enacted in 1946. The word itself implies that it was intended to resolve potential contests between rival claimants to a particular mark. And, indeed, the testimony of the proponents of the concept in the Committee hearings that occurred from time to time during the period when this legislation was being considered reveals that they were primarily concerned with the problem that potential contests over the ownership of registrable marks might present. No one ever suggested that any public purpose would be served by granting incontestable status to a mark that should never have been accepted for registration in the first instance.

In those hearings the witnesses frequently referred to incontestability as comparable to a decree quieting title to real property. Such a decree forecloses any further contest over ownership of the property, but it cannot create the property itself. Similarly the incontestability of a trademark precludes any competitor from contesting the registrant's ownership, but cannot convert unregistrable subject matter into a valid mark. Such a claim would be clearly unenforceable. . . .

. . . In light of this legislative history, it is apparent that Congress could not have intended that incontestability should preserve a merely descriptive trademark from challenge when the statutory procedure for establishing secondary meaning was not followed and when the record still contains no evidence that the mark has ever acquired a secondary meaning. . . .

In sum, if petitioner had complied with § 2(f) at the time of its initial registration, or if it had been able to prove secondary meaning in this case, I would agree with the Court's disposition. I cannot, however, subscribe to its conclusion that the holder of a mark which was registered in violation of an unambiguous statutory command "may rely on incontestability to enjoin infringement." . . . Accordingly, I respectfully dissent.

COMMENTS AND QUESTIONS

1. Why should marks be allowed to become incontestable? Does this privilege reflect a judgment that judicial review of trademarks is unnecessary after a certain time? That the Trademark Office can be trusted to make the right decision in an ex parte

proceeding? Certainly, no similar right is afforded the holders of patents, even though they are in some sense a "stronger" intellectual property right. At least one commentator has suggested that incontestability ought to be abolished. Kenneth L. Port, *The Illegitimacy of Trademark Incontestability*, 26 IND. L. REV. 519 (1993). Port reasons that trademark incontestability creates what is in effect a property right in trademarks, since 15 U.S.C. §1115(b) speaks of a conclusive presumption of the trademark holder's "ownership of the mark." (Certainly, the Court's "quiet title" rationale smacks of real property law.) This property right, he asserts, is inconsistent with general principles of trademark law. He explains:

> Patent and copyright owners enjoy the "bundle of rights" notion of property. Their rights are divisible, freely alienable, and exclusive for the duration of statutory protection.
>
> Trademarks, on the other hand, enjoy none of the "bundle of rights" that other forms of property enjoy. Trademark holders possess only the right to exclude others from using that specific trademark on similar goods. Holders of marks possess the right to protect the sphere of interest in which they are using the mark by excluding others, but nothing more. Mark holders do not possess a property right in the mark itself, because trademarks are nothing when devoid of the goodwill they have come to represent or the product on which they are used.

Id. Read Section 1115(b) carefully. Is this a fair criticism?

2. How does the dissent in *Park 'N Fly* deal with the majority's argument that "incontestability" would be worthless if a trademark holder could not use it to enforce his rights against an infringer? Is Justice Stevens's argument persuasive? If the owner of a descriptive mark improperly registered is not entitled to judicial enforcement of his "incontestable" trademark, why should he be entitled to Customs assistance in stopping the importation of goods? To registration of the invalid trademark in other countries? Further, why have incontestability at all? Wouldn't the legal system be better served by a rule that improperly issued trademarks could be cancelled at any time?

This debate was resurrected in Shakespeare Co. v. Silstar Corp., 9 F.3d 1091 (4th Cir. 1993). There, the District Court cancelled plaintiff's registration for a color scheme on a fishing rod on the grounds that it was functional (apparently because it helped to catch fish). The Fourth Circuit reversed, noting that the mark had become incontestable and holding that incontestable marks cannot be cancelled for functionality because functionality was not specifically enumerated in Section 1064. The dissent argued that federal courts should not enforce the mark, even if they could not cancel it.

The functionality problem raises an interesting question about incontestability. What happens when trade dress which is initially not functional *becomes* functional over time? (This may happen because of widespread adoption of the owner's trade dress. For example, a computer graphical user interface (GUI) may become so familiar to so many users that it becomes a "standard" in the industry, and it is a commercial advantage to use the standard product.) Would trademark defendants lose *any* opportunity to defeat the mark on functionality grounds? Apparently concerned by the result in *Shakespeare*, Congress revised the Lanham Act in 1998 to provide that functionality may be asserted even against an "incontestable" mark. 15 U.S.C. §1064(3).

3. Note that the presumptions afforded registered trademarks differ in several ways from those given to issued patents. Registered trademarks, while entitled to

a presumption of validity, are not entitled to the benefit of the "clear and convincing evidence" rule applied in patent cases. At the same time, there is no provision for incontestability of patents after a certain number of years. Is there any reason for these differing presumptions?

4. Patent law gives inventors no rights at all unless the Patent Office issues them a patent. By contrast, copyright law gives full protection to unregistered works as soon as they are created, and there are current legislative efforts to abolish the Copyright Office entirely. Trademark law appears to fall somewhere in between. Trademark owners are entitled to protection without registration, but there are still substantial benefits to registering a trademark. Can you think of any reason for the different administrative schemes? Which is preferable?

5 *Infringement*

We now turn to the circumstances in which a defendant is liable for the use of a mark similar or identical to the plaintiff's mark. We begin with the threshold question of whether the defendant has "used" the mark at all.

A. USE AS A TRADEMARK

Rescuecom Corp. v. Google Inc.
562 F.3d 123 (2d Cir. 2009)

LEVAL, Circuit Judge:

Background

As this appeal follows the grant of a motion to dismiss, we must take as true the facts alleged in the Complaint and draw all reasonable inferences in favor of Rescuecom. Rescuecom is a national computer service franchising company that offers on-site computer services and sales. Rescuecom conducts a substantial amount of business over the Internet and receives between 17,000 to 30,000 visitors to its website each month. It also advertises over the Internet, using many web-based services, including those offered by Google. Since 1998, "Rescuecom" has been a registered federal trademark, and there is no dispute as to its validity.

Google operates a popular Internet search engine, which users access by visiting www.google.com. Using Google's website, a person searching for the website of a particular entity in trade (or simply for information about it) can enter that entity's name or trademark into Google's search engine and launch a search. Google's proprietary system responds to such a search request in two ways. First, Google provides a list of links to websites, ordered in what Google deems to be of descending relevance to the user's search terms based on its proprietary algorithms. Google's search engine assists the public not only in obtaining information about a provider, but also in purchasing products and services. If a prospective purchaser, looking for goods or services of a particular provider, enters the provider's trademark as a search term on Google's website and clicks to activate a search, within seconds, the Google search engine will provide on the searcher's computer screen a link to the webpage maintained by that provider (as well as a host of other links to sites that Google's program determines to be relevant to the search term entered). By clicking on the link of the provider, the searcher will be directed to the provider's website, where the searcher can obtain information supplied by the provider about its products and services and can perhaps also make purchases from the provider by placing orders.

The second way Google responds to a search request is by showing context-based advertising. When a searcher uses Google's search engine by submitting a search term, Google may place advertisements on the user's screen. Google will do so if an advertiser, having determined that its ad is likely to be of interest to a searcher who enters the particular term, has purchased from Google the placement of its ad on the screen of the searcher who entered that search term. What Google places on the searcher's screen is more than simply an advertisement. It is also a link to the advertiser's website, so that in response to such an ad, if the searcher clicks on the link, he will open the advertiser's website, which offers not only additional information about the advertiser, but also perhaps the option to purchase the goods and services of the advertiser over the Internet. Google uses at least two programs to offer such context-based links: AdWords and Keyword Suggestion Tool.

AdWords is Google's program through which advertisers purchase terms (or keywords). When entered as a search term, the keyword triggers the appearance of the advertiser's ad and link. An advertiser's purchase of a particular term causes the advertiser's ad and link to be displayed on the user's screen whenever a searcher launches a Google search based on the purchased search term. Advertisers pay Google based on the number of times Internet users "click" on the advertisement, so as to link to the advertiser's website. For example, using Google's AdWords, Company Y, a company engaged in the business of furnace repair, can cause Google to display its advertisement and link whenever a user of Google launches a search based on the search term, "furnace repair." Company Y can also cause its ad and link to appear whenever a user searches for the term "Company X," a competitor of Company Y in the furnace repair business. Thus, whenever a searcher interested in purchasing furnace repair services from Company X launches a search of the term X (Company X's trademark), an ad and link would appear on the searcher's screen, inviting the searcher to the furnace repair services of X's competitor, Company Y. And if the searcher clicked on Company Y's link, Company Y's website would open on the searcher's screen, and the searcher might be able to order or purchase Company Y's furnace repair services.

In addition to Adwords, Google also employs Keyword Suggestion Tool, a program that recommends keywords to advertisers to be purchased. The program is designed to improve the effectiveness of advertising by helping advertisers identify keywords related to their area of commerce, resulting in the placement of their ads before users who are likely to be responsive to it. Thus, continuing the example given above, if Company Y employed Google's Keyword Suggestion Tool, the Tool might suggest to Company Y that it purchase not only the term "furnace repair" but also the term "X," its competitor's brand name and trademark, so that Y's ad would appear on the screen of a searcher who searched Company X's trademark, seeking Company X's website.

Once an advertiser buys a particular keyword, Google links the keyword to that advertiser's advertisement. The advertisements consist of a combination of content and a link to the advertiser's webpage. Google displays these advertisements on the search result page either in the right margin or in a horizontal band immediately above the column of relevance-based search results. These advertisements are generally associated with a label, which says "sponsored link." Rescuecom alleges, however, that a user might easily be misled to believe that the advertisements which appear on the screen are in fact part of the relevance-based search result and that the appearance of a competitor's ad and link in response to a searcher's search for Rescuecom is likely to cause trademark confusion as to affiliation, origin, sponsorship, or approval of service. This can occur, according to the Complaint, because Google fails to label the ads in a manner which would clearly identify them as purchased ads rather than search results. The Complaint alleges that when the sponsored links appear in a horizontal bar at the top of the search results, they may appear to the searcher to be the first, and therefore the most relevant, entries responding to the search, as opposed to paid advertisements.

Google's objective in its AdWords and Keyword Suggestion Tool programs is to sell keywords to advertisers. Rescuecom alleges that Google makes 97% of its revenue from selling advertisements through its AdWords program. Google therefore has an economic incentive to increase the number of advertisements and links that appear for every term entered into its search engine.

Many of Rescuecom's competitors advertise on the Internet. Through its Keyword Suggestion Tool, Google has recommended the Rescuecom trademark to Rescuecom's competitors as a search term to be purchased. Rescuecom's competitors, some responding to Google's recommendation, have purchased Rescuecom's trademark as a keyword in Google's AdWords program, so that whenever a user launches a search for the term "Rescuecom," seeking to be connected to Rescuecom's website, the competitors' advertisement and link will appear on the searcher's screen. This practice allegedly allows Rescuecom's competitors to deceive and divert users searching for Rescuecom's website. According to Rescuecom's allegations, when a Google user launches a search for the term "Rescuecom" because the searcher wishes to purchase Rescuecom's services, links to websites of its competitors will appear on the searcher's screen in a manner likely to cause the searcher to believe mistakenly that a competitor's advertisement (and website link) is sponsored by, endorsed by, approved by, or affiliated with Rescuecom.

The District Court granted Google's 12(b)(6) motion and dismissed Rescuecom's claims. The court believed that our 1-800 [Contacts, Inc. v. WhenU.com, Inc., 414 F.3d 400 (2d Cir. 2005)] decision compels the conclusion that Google's allegedly infringing activity does not involve use of Rescuecom's mark in commerce, which is an essential element of an action under the Lanham Act. The district court explained its decision saying that even if Google employed Rescuecom's mark in a manner likely to cause confusion or deceive searchers into believing that competitors are affiliated with Rescuecom and its mark, so that they believe the services of Rescuecom's competitors are those of Rescuecom, Google's actions are not a "use in commerce" under the Lanham Act because the competitor's advertisements triggered by Google's programs did not exhibit Rescuecom's trademark. The court rejected the argument that Google "used" Rescuecom's mark in recommending and selling it as a keyword to trigger competitor's advertisements because the court read *1-800* to compel the conclusion that this was an internal use and therefore cannot be a "use in commerce" under the Lanham Act.

Discussion

I. Google's Use of Rescuecom's Mark Was a "Use in Commerce"

Our court ruled in *1-800* that a complaint fails to state a claim under the Lanham Act unless it alleges that the defendant has made "use in commerce" of the plaintiff's trademark as the term "use in commerce" is defined in 15 U.S.C. § 1127. The district court believed that this case was on all fours with *1-800*, and that its dismissal was required for the same reasons as given in *1-800*. We believe the cases are materially different. The allegations of Rescuecom's complaint adequately plead a use in commerce.

In *1-800*, the plaintiff alleged that the defendant infringed the plaintiff's trademark through its proprietary software, which the defendant freely distributed to computer users who would download and install the program on their computer. The program provided contextually relevant advertising to the user by generating pop-up advertisements to the user depending on the website or search term the user entered in his browser. Id. at 404-05. For example, if a user typed "eye care" into his browser, the defendant's program would randomly display a pop-up advertisement of a company engaged in the field of eye care. Similarly, if the searcher launched a search for a particular company engaged in eye care, the defendant's program would display the pop-up ad of a company associated with eye care. See id. at 412. The pop-up ad appeared in a separate browser window from the website the user accessed, and the defendant's brand was displayed in the window frame surrounding the ad, so that there was no confusion as to the nature of the pop-up as an advertisement, nor as to the fact that the defendant, not the trademark owner, was responsible for displaying the ad, in response to the particular term searched. Id. at 405.

Sections 32 and 43 of the Act, which we also refer to by their codified designations, 15 U.S.C. §§ 1114 & 1125, inter alia, impose liability for unpermitted "use in commerce" of another's mark which is "likely to cause confusion, or to cause mistake, or to deceive," § 1114, "as to the affiliation . . . or as to the origin, sponsorship or approval of his or her goods [or] services . . . by another person." § 1125(a)(1)(A). The *1-800* opinion looked to the definition of the term "use in commerce" provided in § 45 of the Act, 15 U.S.C. § 1127. That definition provides in part that "a mark shall be deemed to be in use in commerce . . . (2) on services when it is used or displayed in the sale or advertising of services and the services are rendered in commerce." 15 U.S.C. § 1127. Our court found that the plaintiff failed to show that the defendant made a "use in commerce" of the plaintiff's mark, within that definition.

At the outset, we note two significant aspects of our holding in *1-800*, which distinguish it from the present case. A key element of our court's decision in *1-800* was that under the plaintiff's allegations, the defendant did not use, reproduce, or display the plaintiff's mark *at all*. The search term that was alleged to trigger the pop-up ad was the plaintiff's *website address*. *1-800* noted, notwithstanding the similarities between the website address and the mark, that the website address was not used or claimed by the plaintiff as a trademark.[1] Thus, the transactions alleged to be infringing were not transactions involving use of the plaintiff's trademark. Id. at 408-09. 1-800 suggested in dictum that is highly relevant to our case that had the defendant used the plaintiff's trademark as the trigger to pop-up an advertisement, such conduct might, depending on other elements, have been actionable. 414 F.3d at 409 & n.11.

Second, as an alternate basis for its decision, *1-800* explained why the defendant's program, which might randomly trigger pop-up advertisements upon a searcher's input of the plaintiff's website address, did not constitute a "use in commerce," as defined in § 1127. Id. at 408-09. In explaining why the plaintiff's mark was not "used or displayed in the sale or advertising of services," *1-800* pointed out that, under the defendant's program, advertisers could not request or purchase keywords to trigger their ads. Id. at 409, 412. Even if an advertiser wanted to display its advertisement to a searcher using the plaintiff's trademark as a search term, the defendant's program did not offer this possibility. In fact, the defendant "did not disclose the proprietary contents of [its] directory to its advertising clients. . . ." Id. at 409. In addition to not selling trademarks of others to its customers to trigger these ads, the defendant did not "otherwise manipulate which category-related advertisement will pop up in response to any particular terms on the internal directory." Id. at 411. The display of a particular advertisement was controlled by the category associated with the website or keyword, rather than the website or keyword itself. The defendant's program relied upon categorical associations such as "eye care" to select a pop-up ad randomly from a predefined list of ads appropriate to that category. To the extent that an advertisement for a competitor of the plaintiff was displayed when a user opened the plaintiff's website, the trigger to display the ad was not based on the defendant's sale or recommendation of a particular trademark.

The present case contrasts starkly with those important aspects of the *1-800* decision. First, in contrast to *1-800*, where we emphasized that the defendant made no use whatsoever of the plaintiff's trademark, here what Google is recommending and selling to its advertisers is Rescuecom's trademark. Second, in contrast with the facts of *1-800* where the defendant did not "use or display," much less sell, trademarks as search terms to its advertisers, here Google displays, offers, and sells Rescuecom's mark to Google's advertising customers when selling its advertising services. In addition, Google encourages the purchase of Rescuecom's mark through its Keyword Suggestion Tool. Google's utilization of Rescuecom's mark fits literally within the terms specified by 15 U.S.C. § 1127. According to the Complaint, Google uses and sells Rescuecom's mark "in the sale . . . of [Google's advertising] services . . . rendered in commerce." § 1127.

Google, supported by amici, argues that *1-800* suggests that the inclusion of a trademark in an internal computer directory cannot constitute trademark use. Several district court decisions in this Circuit appear to have reached this conclusion. See e.g., S&L Vitamins, Inc. v. Australian Gold, Inc., 521 F. Supp. 2d 188, 199-202 (E.D.N.Y. 2007) (holding that use of a trademark in metadata did not constitute trademark use within the meaning of the Lanham Act because the use "is strictly internal and not communicated to the public"); Merck & Co., Inc. v. Mediplan Health Consulting,

1. We did not imply in *1-800* that a website can never be a trademark. In fact, the opposite is true. *See* Trademark Manual of Examining Procedures § 1209.03(m) (5th ed. 2007) ("A mark comprised of an Internet domain name is registrable as a trademark or service mark only if it functions as an identifier of the source of goods or services."). . . .

Inc., 425 F. Supp. 2d 402, 415 (S.D.N.Y. 2006) (holding that the internal use of a keyword to trigger advertisements did not qualify as trademark use). This over-reads the *1-800* decision. First, regardless of whether Google's use of Rescuecom's mark in its internal search algorithm could constitute an actionable trademark use, Google's recommendation and sale of Rescuecom's mark to its advertising customers are not internal uses. Furthermore, *1-800* did not imply that use of a trademark in a software program's internal directory precludes a finding of trademark use. Rather, influenced by the fact that the defendant was not using the plaintiff's trademark at all, much less using it as the basis of a commercial transaction, the court asserted that the particular use before it did not constitute a use in commerce. See *1-800*, 414 F.3d at 409-12. We did not imply in *1-800* that an alleged infringer's use of a trademark in an internal software program insulates the alleged infringer from a charge of infringement, no matter how likely the use is to cause confusion in the marketplace. If we were to adopt Google and its amici's argument, the operators of search engines would be free to use trademarks in ways designed to deceive and cause consumer confusion.[2] This is surely neither within the intention nor the letter of the Lanham Act.

Google and its amici contend further that its use of the Rescuecom trademark is no different from that of a retail vendor who uses "product placement" to allow one vender to benefit from a competitors' name recognition. An example of product placement occurs when a store-brand generic product is placed next to a trademarked product to induce a customer who specifically sought out the trademarked product to consider the typically less expensive, generic brand as an alternative. See *1-800*, 414 F.3d at 411. Google's argument misses the point. From the fact that proper, non-deceptive product placement does not result in liability under the Lanham Act, it does not follow that the label "product placement" is a magic shield against liability, so that even a deceptive plan of product placement designed to confuse consumers would similarly escape liability. It is not by reason of absence of a use of a mark in commerce that benign product placement escapes liability; it escapes liability because it is a benign practice which does not cause a likelihood of consumer confusion. In contrast, if a retail seller were to be paid by an off-brand purveyor to arrange product display and delivery in such a way that customers seeking to purchase a famous brand would receive the off-brand, believing they had gotten the brand they were seeking, we see no reason to believe the practice would escape liability merely because it could claim the mantle of "product placement." The practices attributed to Google by the Complaint, which at this stage we must accept as true, are significantly different from benign product placement that does not violate the Act.

Unlike the practices discussed in *1-800*, the practices here attributed to Google by Rescuecom's complaint are that Google has made use in commerce of Rescuecom's mark. Needless to say, a defendant must do more than use another's mark in commerce to violate the Lanham Act. The gist of a Lanham Act violation is an unauthorized use, which "is likely to cause confusion, or to cause mistake, or to deceive as to the affiliation, . . . or as to the origin, sponsorship, or approval of . . . goods [or] services."

2. For example, instead of having a separate "sponsored links" or paid advertisement section, search engines could allow advertisers to pay to appear at the top of the "relevance" list based on a user entering a competitor's trademark-a functionality that would be highly likely to cause consumer confusion. Alternatively, sellers of products or services could pay to have the operators of search engines automatically divert users to their website when the users enter a competitor's trademark as a search term. Such conduct is surely not beyond judicial review merely because it is engineered through the internal workings of a computer program.

See 15 U.S.C. § 1125(a); Estee Lauder Inc. v. The Gap, Inc., 108 F.3d 1503, 1508-09 (2d Cir. 1997). We have no idea whether Rescuecom can prove that Google's use of Rescuecom's trademark in its AdWords program causes likelihood of confusion or mistake. Rescuecom has alleged that it does, in that would-be purchasers (or explorers) of its services who search for its website on Google are misleadingly directed to the ads and websites of its competitors in a manner which leads them to believe mistakenly that these ads or websites are sponsored by, or affiliated with Rescuecom. This is particularly so, Rescuecom alleges, when the advertiser's link appears in a horizontal band at the top of the list of search results in a manner which makes it appear to be the most relevant search result and not an advertisement. What Rescuecom alleges is that by the manner of Google's display of sponsored links of competing brands in response to a search for Rescuecom's brand name (which fails adequately to identify the sponsored link as an advertisement, rather than a relevant search result), Google creates a likelihood of consumer confusion as to trademarks. If the searcher sees a different brand name as the top entry in response to the search for "Rescuecom," the searcher is likely to believe mistakenly that the different name which appears is affiliated with the brand name sought in the search and will not suspect, because the fact is not adequately signaled by Google's presentation, that this is not the most relevant response to the search. Whether Google's actual practice is in fact benign or confusing is not for us to judge at this time. We consider at the 12(b)(6) stage only what is alleged in the Complaint.

We conclude that the district court was mistaken in believing that our precedent in *1-800* requires dismissal.

Conclusion

The judgment of the district court is vacated and the case is remanded for further proceedings.

COMMENTS AND QUESTIONS

1. Does the court's effort to distinguish *1-800 Contacts* succeed? Should the law make actionable the placement of ads based on the search term "800-contacts" but not the term "800-contacts.com"?

2. Despite its rejection in *Rescuecom*, the trademark use doctrine has been recognized and applied by a number of courts. *See, e.g.*, North American Medical Corp. v. Axiom Worldwide, Inc., 522 F.3d 1211 (11th Cir. 2008) (distinguishing and criticizing *1-800 Contacts* and finding that the defendant's use of the plaintiff's mark in meta tags qualified as a use actionable under the Lanham Act); DaimlerChrysler AG v. Bloom, 315 F.3d 932 (8th Cir. 2003) (holding that a telecommunications company did not use the term "Mercedes" in a trademark sense merely by licensing a vanity phone number that spelled "1-800-MERCEDES" to Mercedes dealers); Interactive Prods. Corp. v. A2Z Mobile Office Solutions, Inc., 326 F.3d 687, 695 (6th Cir. 2003) ("If defendants are only using [plaintiff's] trademark in a 'non-trademark' way — that is, in a way that does not identify the source of a product — then trademark infringement and false designation of origin laws do not apply."); Lockheed Martin Corp. v. Network Solutions, Inc., 141 F. Supp. 2d 648, 656 (N.D. Tex. 2001) (holding that

Network Solutions' "acceptance of registrations for domain names is not a use of a mark; nor does it reflect an intent to profit from the mark"); Acad. of Motion Picture Arts & Scis. v. Network Solutions, Inc., 989 F. Supp. 1276, 1280 (C.D. Cal. 1997) (concluding that Network Solutions' registering and cataloging of domain names did not constitute "commercial use" of the marks and thus is not liable as a direct trademark infringement); Lockheed Martin Corp. v. Network Solutions, Inc., 985 F. Supp. 949, 957 (C.D. Cal. 1997) ("[Network Solutions] merely uses domain names to designate host computers on the Internet. This is the type of purely 'nominative' function that is not prohibited by trademark law.").

But other courts have refused to apply the doctrine, often by simply ignoring it, *see* Playboy Enters., Inc. v. Netscape Communications Corp., 354 F.3d 1020, 1024 (9th Cir. 2004), but sometimes by concluding that the doctrine is coterminous with the jurisdictional requirement of "use in commerce" and therefore satisfied whenever interstate commerce is present. *See, e.g.*, Planned Parenthood Federation of America Inc. v. Bucci, 42 U.S.P.Q.2d 1430, 1434-37 (S.D.N.Y. 1997).

The cases applying trademark use are relatively recent, prompting some of the leading commentators to suggest that the doctrine is a post-hoc creation rather than an actual requirement of the statute. See 4 J. Thomas McCarthy, McCarthy on Trademarks and Unfair Competition § 23:11:50 (arguing that the doctrine does not exist, and that likelihood of confusion is the only requirement for infringement); Mark P. McKenna, *Trademark Use and the Problem of Source*, 2009 U. Ill. L. Rev. 773 (2009); Graeme Dinwoodie & Mark D. Janis, *Confusion Over Use: Contexualism in Trademark Law*, 92 Iowa L. Rev. (2007); *but see* Stacey L. Dogan & Mark A. Lemley, *Grounding Trademark Law Through the Doctrine of Trademark Use*, 92 Iowa L. Rev. (2007); Margreth Barrett, *Internet Trademark Suits and the Demise of Trademark Use*, 39 U.C. Davis L. Rev. 371 (2006).

2. Dogan and Lemley argue that the trademark use doctrine serves an important limiting function. They explain:

> The speech-oriented objectives of the trademark use doctrine protect more than just intermediaries; they prevent trademark holders from asserting a generalized right to control language, an interest that applies equally—and sometimes especially—when the speaker competes directly with the trademark holder. The trademark use doctrine has broad application—because of it, newspapers aren't liable for using a trademarked term in a headline, even if the use is confusing or misleading. Writers of movies and books aren't liable for using trademarked goods in their stories. Makers of telephone directories aren't liable for putting all the ads for taxi services together on the same page. Marketing surveyors aren't liable for asking people what they think of a competitor's brand-name product. Magazines aren't liable for selling advertisements that relates to the content of their special issues, even when that content involves trademark owners. Gas stations and restaurants aren't liable for locating across the street from an established competitor, trading on the attraction the established company has created or benefiting from the size of the sign the established company has put up. Individuals aren't liable for their use of a trademark in conversation, even in an inaccurate or misleading way (referring to a Puffs brand facial tissue as a "Kleenex," or a competing cola as a "Coke," for example). Generic drug manufacturers aren't liable for placing their drugs near their brand-name equivalents on drug store shelves, and the stores aren't liable for accepting the placement. They may be making money from their "uses" of the trademark, and the uses may be ones the trademark owner objects to, but they are not *trademark* uses and therefore are not within the ambit of the statute.

Stacey L. Dogan & Mark A. Lemley, *Trademarks and Consumer Search Costs on the Internet*, 41 Hous. L. Rev. 777 (2004).

The statute speaks only of a defendant's use "on or in connection with" the sale of goods and services. 15 U.S.C. § 1127. Does it make sense to interpret this as a requirement that the defendant use the plaintiff's mark as a trademark? Can the statutory language do the work the authors require of it?

3. Should it matter that Google is making money by selling ads that appear when a user searches for "rescuecom"? Should it matter what the content of those ads is? Is "trading on the goodwill" associated with a trademark always illegal?

B. LIKELIHOOD OF CONSUMER CONFUSION

Virgin Enterprises Ltd. v. Nawab

335 F.3d 141 (2d Cir. 2003)

Leval, Circuit Judge.

Plaintiff Virgin Enterprises Limited ("VEL" or "plaintiff") appeals from the denial of its motion for a preliminary injunction. This suit, brought under § 32 of the Lanham Act, 15 U.S.C. § 1114(1), alleges that defendants infringed plaintiff's rights in the registered mark VIRGIN by operating retail stores selling wireless telephones and related accessories and services under the trade name VIRGIN WIRELESS. The United States District Court for the Eastern District of New York (Sifton, *J.*) denied plaintiff's motion for a preliminary injunction, based upon its finding that plaintiff's registration did not cover the retail sale of wireless telephones and related products, and that plaintiff failed to show a likelihood of consumer confusion.

Background

Plaintiff VEL, a corporation with its principal place of business in London, owns U.S. Registration No. 1,851,817 ("the 817 Registration"), filed on May 5, 1991, and registered on August 30, 1994, for the VIRGIN mark as applied to "*retail store services* in the fields of . . . computers and *electronic apparatus*" (emphasis added). . . . Plaintiff also owns U.S. Registration No. 1,852,776 ("the 776 Registration"), filed on May 9, 1991, and registered on September 6, 1994, for a stylized version of the VIRGIN mark for use in connection with "retail store services in the fields of . . . computers and electronic apparatus," and U.S. Registration No. 1,863,353 ("the 353 Registration"), filed on May 19, 1992, and registered on November 15, 1994, for the VIRGIN MEGASTORE mark. It is undisputed that these three registrations have become incontestable pursuant to 15 U.S.C. § 1065.

VEL, either directly or through corporate affiliates, operates various businesses worldwide under the trade name VIRGIN, including an airline, large-scale record stores called Virgin Megastores, and an internet information service. Plaintiff or its affiliates also market a variety of goods branded with the VIRGIN name, including music recordings, computer games, books, and luggage. Three of plaintiff's megastores are located in the New York area. According to an affidavit submitted to the district court in support of plaintiff's application for preliminary injunction, Virgin Megastores sell a variety of electronic apparatus, including video game systems, portable CD players, disposable cameras, and DVD players. These stores advertise in a variety of media, including radio.

Defendants Simon Blitz and Daniel Gazal are the sole shareholders of defendants Cel-Net Communications, Inc. ("Cel-Net"); The Cellular Network Communications, Inc., doing business as CNCG ("CNCG"); and SD Telecommunications, Inc. ("SD Telecom"). Blitz and Gazal formed Cel-Net in 1993 to sell retail wireless telephones and services in the New York area. Later, they formed CNCG to sell wireless phones and services on the wholesale level. CNCG now sells wireless phones and services to more than 400 independent wireless retailers. In 1998, Cel-Net received permission from New York State regulators to resell telephone services within the state.

Around 1999, Andrew Kastein, a vice-president of CNCG, began to develop a Cel-Net brand of wireless telecommunications products. In early 1999, Cel-Net entered into negotiations with the Sprint PCS network to provide telecommunications services for resale by Cel-Net. In August 1999, Cel-Net retained the law firm Pennie & Edmonds to determine the availability of possible service marks for Cel-Net. Pennie & Edmonds associate Elizabeth Langston researched for Kastein a list of possible service marks; among the marks Cel-Net asked to have researched was VIRGIN. Defendants claim that Langston told Cel-Net officer Simon Corney that VIRGIN was available for use in the telecommunications field. Plaintiff disputed this, offering an affidavit from Langston that she informed defendants that she would not search the VIRGIN mark because her firm represented plaintiff.

According to defendants, in December 1999, Cel-Net retained Corporate Solutions, LLC and its principals Nathan Erlich and Tahir Nawab as joint venture partners to help raise capital to launch Cel-Net's wireless telephone service. On December 2, 1999, Erlich and Nawab filed four intent-to-use applications with the U.S. Patent and Trademark Office ("PTO") to register the marks VIRGIN WIRELESS, VIRGIN MOBILE, VIRGIN COMMUNICATIONS, and VIRGIN NET in the field of telecommunications services, class 38. On December 24, 1999, Corporate Solutions incorporated defendant Virgin Wireless, Inc. ("VWI") and licensed to VWI the right to use the marks VIRGIN WIRELESS and VIRGIN MOBILE. Meanwhile, one of plaintiff's affiliates had begun to offer wireless telecommunication services bearing the VIRGIN mark in the United Kingdom. A press release dated November 19, 1999, found on plaintiff's website, stated that its Virgin Mobile wireless services were operable in the United States.

On June 23, 2000, defendant Blitz signed a lease under the name Virgin Wireless for a kiosk location in South Shore Mall in Long Island from which to re-sell AT & T wireless services, telephones, and accessories under the retail name Virgin Wireless. Defendants Cel-Net and VWI later expanded their telecommunications re-sale operations to include two retail stores and four additional retail kiosks in malls in the New York area and in Pennsylvania. All of these stores have been run by VWI under the trade name VIRGIN WIRELESS. VWI also has leases and bank accounts in its name, and has shown evidence of actual retail transactions and newspaper advertisements.

In August 2000, plaintiff licensed Virgin Mobile USA, LLC, to use the VIRGIN mark for wireless telecommunications services in the United States. On August 10,

2000, plaintiff filed an intent-to-use application with the PTO for use of the VIRGIN mark in the United States on telecommunications services and mobile telephones. On October 11, 2001, the PTO suspended this mark's registration in international class 9, which covers wireless telephones, and class 38, which covers telecommunications services, because the VIRGIN mark was already reserved by a prior filing, presumably defendants'. On August 16, 2001, plaintiff filed another intent-to-use application for the mark VIRGIN MOBILE to brand telecommunications services. The PTO issued a non-final action letter for both of plaintiff's pending new registrations on October 31, 2001, which stated that defendant Corporation Solutions' pending applications for similar marks in the same class could give rise to "a likelihood of confusion." The PTO suspended action on plaintiff's application pending the processing of Corporation Solutions' applications.

In October 2001, plaintiff issued a press release announcing that it was offering wireless telecommunications services and mobile telephones in the United States.

Plaintiff became aware of Corporation Solutions' application for registration of the VIRGIN WIRELESS and VIRGIN MOBILE marks by May 2000. In October 2001 and December 2001, defendant VWI filed suits against plaintiff in the federal district courts in Arizona and Delaware, alleging that plaintiff was using VWI's mark. Plaintiff maintains (and the district court found) that it learned in January 2002 that VWI and Cel-Net were operating kiosks under the VIRGIN WIRELESS name and two days later filed the present suit seeking to enjoin defendants from selling mobile phones in VIRGIN-branded retail stores.

On May 2, 2002, the district court considered plaintiff's application for a preliminary injunction. It found that no essential facts were in dispute, and therefore no evidentiary hearing was required. It was uncontested (and the district court accordingly found) that plaintiff sold "electronic apparatus" in its stores, including "various video game systems, portable cassette tape, compact disc, mp3, and mini disc players, portable radios, and disposable cameras," but not including telephones or telephone service, and that the only products the defendants sold in their stores were wireless telephones, telephone accessories, and wireless telephone services.

. . . Arguing against plaintiff's likelihood of success, the court noted that plaintiff's registrations did not claim use of the VIRGIN mark "in telecommunications services or in the associated retail sale of wireless telephones and accessories." While plaintiff's 817 and 776 Registrations covered the retail sale of "computers and electronic apparatus," they did not extend to telecommunications services and wireless phones.

The court noted that the defendants were the first to use the VIRGIN mark in telecommunications, and the first to attempt to register VIRGIN for telecommunications and retail telephone sales. . . .

Discussion

II.

A claim of trademark infringement, whether brought under 15 U.S.C. §1114(1) (for infringement of a registered mark) or 15 U.S.C. §1125(a) (for infringement of rights in a mark acquired by use), is analyzed under the familiar two-prong test described in Gruner + Jahr USA Publ'g v. Meredith Corp., 991 F.2d 1072 (2d

Cir. 1993). See Time, Inc. v. Petersen Publ'g Co. L.L.C., 173 F.3d 113, 117 (2d Cir. 1999) (noting that *Gruner* test is applicable to claims brought under § 1114(1) and § 1125(a)). The test looks first to whether the plaintiff's mark is entitled to protection, and second to whether defendant's use of the mark is likely to cause consumers confusion as to the origin or sponsorship of the defendant's goods. *Gruner*, 991 F.2d at 1074. Examining the question as the test dictates, we have no doubt that plaintiff was entitled to a preliminary injunction.

We believe the district court accorded plaintiff too narrow a scope of protection for its famous, arbitrary, and distinctive mark. There could be no dispute that plaintiff prevailed as to the first prong of the test-prior use and ownership. For years, plaintiff had used the VIRGIN mark on huge, famous stores selling, in addition to music recordings, a variety of consumer electronic equipment. At the time the defendants began using VIRGIN, plaintiff owned rights in the mark. The focus of inquiry thus turns to the second prong of the test-whether defendants' use of VIRGIN as a mark for stores selling wireless telephone services and phones was likely to cause confusion. There can be little doubt that such confusion was likely.

The landmark case of Polaroid Corp. v. Polarad Electronics Corp., 287 F.2d 492 (2d Cir. 1961) (Friendly, J.), outlined a series of nonexclusive factors likely to be pertinent in addressing the issue of likelihood of confusion, which are routinely followed in such cases. . . .

Six of the *Polaroid* factors relate directly to the likelihood of consumer confusion. These are the strength of the plaintiff's mark; the similarity of defendants' mark to plaintiff's; the proximity of the products sold under defendants' mark to those sold under plaintiff's; where the products are different, the likelihood that plaintiff will-bridge the gap by selling the products being sold by defendants; the existence of actual confusion among consumers; and the sophistication of consumers. Of these six, all but the last (which was found by the district court to be neutral) strongly favor the plaintiff. The remaining two *Polaroid* factors, defendants' good or bad faith and the quality of defendants' products, are more pertinent to issues other than likelihood of confusion, such as harm to plaintiff's reputation and choice of remedy. We conclude that the *Polaroid* factors powerfully support plaintiff's position.

Strength of the Mark. The strength of a trademark encompasses two different concepts, both of which relate significantly to likelihood of consumer confusion. The first and most important is inherent strength, also called "inherent distinctiveness." This inquiry distinguishes between, on the one hand, inherently distinctive marks — marks that are arbitrary or fanciful in relation to the products (or services) on which they are used — and, on the other hand, marks that are generic, descriptive or suggestive as to those goods. The former are the strong marks. Abercrombie & Fitch Co. v. Hunting World, Inc., 537 F.2d 4, 9 (2d Cir. 1976). The second sense of the concept of strength of a mark is "acquired distinctiveness," i.e., fame, or the extent to which prominent use of the mark in commerce has resulted in a high degree of consumer recognition. See TCPIP Holding Co. v. Haar Communications Inc., 244 F.3d 88, 100 (2d Cir. 2001) (describing these two concepts of strength); *Streetwise Maps*, 159 F.3d at 743.

Considering first *inherent distinctiveness*, the law accords broad, muscular protection to marks that are arbitrary or fanciful in relation to the products on which they are used, and lesser protection, or no protection at all, to marks consisting of words that identify or describe the goods or their attributes. The reasons for the distinction arise from two aspects of market efficiency. The paramount objective of the trademark law is to avoid confusion in the marketplace. The purpose for which the trademark law accords merchants the exclusive right to the use of a name or symbol in their area or commerce is ***identification***, so that the merchants can establish goodwill for their goods based on past satisfactory performance, and the consuming public can rely on a mark as a guarantee that the goods or services so marked come from the merchant who has been found to be satisfactory in the past. See Estee Lauder Inc. v. The Gap, Inc., 108 F.3d 1503, 1510 (2d Cir. 1997) (quoting RESTATEMENT (THIRD) OF UNFAIR COMPETITION § 21 comment i (1995)); Power Test Petroleum Distribs., Inc. v. Calcu Gas, Inc., 754 F.2d 91, 97 (2d Cir. 1985); McGregor-Doniger Inc. v. Drizzle Inc., 599 F.2d 1126, 1131 (2d Cir. 1979). At the same time, efficiency and the public interest require that every merchant trading in a class of goods be permitted to refer to the goods by their name, and to make claims about their quality. Thus, a merchant who sells pencils under the trademark *Pencil* or *Clear Mark*, for example, and seeks to exclude other sellers of pencils from using those words in their trade, is seeking an advantage the trademark law does not intend to offer. To grant such exclusivity would deprive the consuming public of the useful market information it receives where every seller of pencils is free to call them pencils. *Abercrombie*, 537 F.2d at 9; CES Publ'g Corp. v. St. Regis Publ'ns, Inc., 531 F.2d 11, 13 (2d Cir. 1975). The trademark right does not protect the exclusive right to an advertising message — only the exclusive right to an identifier, to protect against confusion in the marketplace. Thus, as a matter of policy, the trademark law accords broader protection to marks that serve exclusively as identifiers and lesser protection where a grant of exclusiveness would tend to diminish the access of others to the full range of discourse relating to their goods. See *TCPIP*, 244 F.3d at 100; Nabisco, Inc. v. PF Brands, Inc., 191 F.3d 208, 215 (2d Cir. 1999); Otokoyama Co. Ltd. v. Wine of Japan Import, Inc., 175 F.3d 266, 270 (2d Cir. 1999).

The second aspect of efficiency that justifies according broader protection to marks that are inherently distinctive relates directly to the likelihood of confusion. If a mark is arbitrary or fanciful, and makes no reference to the nature of the goods it designates, consumers who see the mark on different objects offered in the marketplace will be likely to assume, because of the arbitrariness of the choice of mark, that they all come from the same source. For example, if consumers become familiar with a toothpaste sold under an unusual, arbitrary brand name, such as *ZzaaqQ*, and later see that same inherently distinctive brand name appearing on a different product, they are likely to assume, notwithstanding the product difference, that the second product comes from the same producer as the first. The more unusual, arbitrary, and fanciful a trade name, the more unlikely it is that two independent entities would have chosen it. In contrast, every seller of foods has an interest in calling its product "delicious." Consumers who see the word ***delicious*** used on two or more different food products are less likely to draw the inference that they must all come from the same producer. Cf. *Streetwise Maps*, 159 F.3d at 744 (noting that several map producers use "street" in product names; thus plaintiff's mark using "street" was not particularly distinctive); *W. Publ'g*, 910 F.2d at 61 (noting numerous registrations of marks using word "golden"). In short, the more distinctive the mark, the greater the likelihood that the public, seeing it used a second time, will assume that the second use comes from the same source as the first. The goal of avoiding consumer confusion thus dictates that the inherently distinctive, arbitrary, or fanciful marks, i.e., strong marks, receive broader protection than weak marks, those that are descriptive or suggestive of the products on which they are used. See *Abercrombie*, 537 F.2d at 9-11; *TCPIP*, 244 F.3d at 100-01.

The second sense of trademark strength, fame, or "acquired distinctiveness," also bears on consumer confusion. See *TCPIP*, 244 F.3d at 100-01; *Streetwise Maps*, 159 F.3d at 744. If a mark has been long, prominently and notoriously used in commerce, there is a high likelihood that consumers will recognize it from its prior use. Widespread consumer recognition of a mark previously used in commerce increases the likelihood that consumers will assume it identifies the previously familiar user, and therefore increases the likelihood of consumer confusion if the new user is in fact not related to the first. See *Nabisco*, 191 F.3d at 216-17. A mark's fame also gives unscrupulous traders an incentive to seek to create consumer confusion by associating themselves in consumers' minds with a famous mark. The added likelihood of consumer confusion resulting from a second user's use of a famous mark gives reason for according such a famous mark a broader scope of protection, at least when it is also inherently distinctive. See *McGregor*, 599 F.2d at 1132 (noting that secondary meaning may further enlarge the scope of protection accorded to inherently distinctive marks).

Plaintiff's VIRGIN mark undoubtedly scored high on both concepts of strength. In relation to the sale of consumer electronic equipment, the VIRGIN mark is inherently distinctive, in that it is arbitrary and fanciful; the word "virgin" has no intrinsic relationship whatsoever to selling such equipment. Because there is no intrinsic reason for a merchant to use the word "virgin" in the sale of consumer electronic equipment, a consumer seeing VIRGIN used in two different stores selling such equipment will likely assume that the stores are related.

Plaintiff's VIRGIN mark was also famous. The mark had been employed with world-wide recognition as the mark of an airline and as the mark for megastores selling music recordings and consumer electronic equipment. The fame of the mark increased the likelihood that consumers seeing defendants' shops selling telephones under the mark VIRGIN would assume incorrectly that defendants' shops were a part of plaintiff's organization. See Lois Sportswear, U.S.A., Inc. v. Levi Strauss & Co., 799 F.2d 867, 873 (2d Cir.1986).

There can be no doubt that plaintiff's VIRGIN mark, as used on consumer electronic equipment, is a strong mark, as the district court found. It is entitled as such to a broad scope of protection, precisely because the use of the mark by others in connection with stores selling reasonably closely related merchandise would inevitably have a high likelihood of causing consumer confusion.

Similarity of Marks. When the secondary user's mark is not identical but merely similar to the plaintiff's mark, it is important to assess the degree of similarity between them in assessing the likelihood that consumers will be confused. See *McGregor*, 599 F.2d at 1133. Plaintiff's and defendants' marks were not merely similar; they were identical to the extent that both consisted of the same word, "virgin."

The district court believed this factor did not favor plaintiff because it found some differences in appearance. Defendants' logo used a difference typeface and different colors from plaintiff's. While those are indeed differences, they are quite minor in relation to the fact that the name being used as a trademark was the same in each case.

Advertisement and consumer experience of a mark do not necessarily transmit all of the mark's features. Plaintiff, for example, advertised its Virgin Megastores on the radio. A consumer who heard those advertisements and then saw the defendants' installation using the name VIRGIN would have no way of knowing that the two trademarks looked different. See Sports Auth., Inc. v. Prime Hospitality Corp., 89 F.3d 955, 962 (2d Cir.1996). A consumer who had visited one of plaintiff's Virgin Megastores and remembered the name would not necessarily remember the typeface and color of plaintiff's mark. The reputation of a mark also spreads by word of mouth among consumers. One consumer who hears from others about their experience with Virgin stores and then encounters defendants' Virgin store will have no way knowing of the differences in typeface. See Hills Bros. Coffee, Inc. v. Hills Supermarkets, Inc., 428 F.2d 379, 381 (2d Cir. 1970) (per curiam).

In view of the fact that defendants used the same name as plaintiff, we conclude the defendants' mark was sufficiently similar to plaintiff's to increase the likelihood of confusion. This factor favored the plaintiff as a matter of law. We conclude that the district court erred in concluding otherwise on the basis of comparatively trivial and often irrelevant differences.

Proximity of the Products and Likelihood of Bridging the Gap. The next factor is the proximity of the products being sold by plaintiff and defendant under identical (or similar) marks. See *Arrow Fastener*, 59 F.3d at 396. This factor has an obvious bearing on the likelihood of confusion. When the two users of a mark are operating in completely different areas of commerce, consumers are less likely to assume that their similarly branded products come from the same source. In contrast, the closer the secondary user's goods are to those the consumer has seen marketed under the prior user's brand, the more likely that the consumer will mistakenly assume a common source. See Cadbury Beverages, Inc. v. Cott Corp., 73 F.3d 474, 480-81 (2d Cir. 1996).

While plaintiff had not sold telephones or telephone service prior to defendant's registration evincing intent to sell those items, plaintiff had sold quite similar items of consumer electronic equipment. These included computer video game systems, portable cassette-tape players, compact disc players, MP3 players, mini-disc players, and disposable cameras. Like telephones, many of these are small consumer electronic gadgets making use of computerized audio communication. They are sold in the same channels of commerce. Consumers would have a high expectation of finding telephones, portable CD players, and computerized video game systems in the same stores. We think the proximity in commerce of telephones to CD players substantially advanced the risk that consumer confusion would occur when both were sold by different merchants under the same trade name, VIRGIN.

Our classic *Polaroid* test further protects a trademark owner by examining the likelihood that, even if the plaintiff's products were not so close to the defendants' when the defendant began to market them, there was already a likelihood that plaintiff would in the reasonably near future begin selling those products. See *Cadbury Beverages*, 73 F.3d at 482. VEL's claim of proximity was further strengthened in this regard because, as the district court expressly found, "plans had been formulated [for VEL] to enter [the market for telecommunications products and services] shortly in the future." VEL had already begun marketing telephone service in England which would operate in the United States, and, as the district court found, had made plans to sell telephones and wireless telephone service under the VIRGIN name from its retail stores.

The district court, nonetheless, found in favor of the defendants with respect to the proximity of products and services. We would ordinarily give considerable deference to a factual finding on this issue. Here, however, we cannot do so because it appears the district court applied the wrong test. The court did not assess the *proximity* of defendants' VIRGIN-branded retail stores selling telephone products to plaintiff's VIRGIN-branded retail stores selling other consumer electronic products. It simply concluded that, because defendants were selling exclusively telephone products and services, and plaintiff's electronic products did not include telephones or related services, the defendants must prevail as to the proximity factor.

This represents a considerable misunderstanding of the *Polaroid* test. The famous list of factors of likely pertinence in assessing likelihood of confusion in *Polaroid* was specially designed for a case like this one, in which the secondary user is not in direct competition with the prior user, but is selling a somewhat different product or service. In *Polaroid*, the plaintiff sold optical and camera equipment, while the defendant sold electronic apparatus. The test the court discussed was expressly addressed to the problem "how far a valid trademark shall be protected with respect to goods *other than those to which its owner has applied it.*" 287 F.2d at 495 (emphasis added); see also *Arrow Fastener*, 59 F.3d at 396 (noting that products need not actually compete with each other). The very fact that the test includes the "proximity" between the defendant's products and the plaintiff's and the likelihood that the plaintiff will "bridge the gap" makes clear that the trademark owner does not lose, as the district court concluded, merely because it has not previously sold the precise good or service sold by the secondary user.

In our view, had the district court employed the proper test of proximity, it could not have failed to find a high degree of proximity as between plaintiff VEL's prior sales of consumer electronic audio equipment and defendants' subsequent sales of telephones and telephone services, which proximity would certainly contribute to likelihood of consumer confusion. And plaintiff was all the more entitled to a finding in its favor in respect of these matters by virtue of the fact, which the district court *did* find, that at the time defendants began using the VIRGIN mark in the retail sale of telephones and telephone services, plaintiff already had plans to bridge the gap by expanding its sales of consumer electronic equipment to include sales of those very goods and services in the near future. Consumer confusion was more than likely; it was virtually inevitable.

Actual Confusion. It is self-evident that the existence of actual consumer confusion indicates a likelihood of consumer confusion. *Nabisco*, 191 F.3d at 228. We have therefore deemed evidence of actual confusion "particularly relevant" to the inquiry. *Streetwise Maps*, 159 F.3d at 745.

Plaintiff submitted to the district court an affidavit of a former employee of defendant Cel-Net, who worked at a mall kiosk branded as Virgin Wireless, which stated that individuals used to ask him if the kiosk was affiliated with plaintiff's VIRGIN stores. The district court correctly concluded that this evidence weighed in plaintiff's favor.

Sophistication of Consumers. The degree of sophistication of consumers can have an important bearing on likelihood of confusion. Where the purchasers of a products are highly trained professionals, they know the market and are less likely than untrained consumers to be misled or confused by the similarity of different marks. The district court recognized that "[r]etail customers, such as the ones catered to by both the defendants and [plaintiff], are not expected to exercise the same degree of care as professional buyers, who are expected to have greater powers of discrimination." On the other hand, it observed that purchasers of cellular telephones and the service plans were likely to give greater care than self-service customers in a supermarket. Noting that neither side had submitted evidence on the sophistication of consumers, the court made no finding favoring either side. We agree that the sophistication factor is neutral in this case.

Bad Faith and the Quality of the Defendants' Services or Products. Two factors remain of the conventional *Polaroid* test: the existence of bad faith on the part of the secondary user and the quality of the secondary user's products or services. *Polaroid*, 287 F.2d at 495. Neither factor is of high relevance to the issue of likelihood of confusion. A finding that a party acted in bad faith can affect the court's choice of remedy or can tip the balance where questions are close. It does not bear directly on whether consumers are likely to be confused. See *TCPIP*, 244 F.3d at 102. The district court noted some evidence of bad faith on the defendants' part, but because the evidence on the issue was scant and equivocal, the court concluded that such a finding "at this stage [would be] speculative." The court therefore found that this factor favored neither party.

The issue of the quality of the secondary user's product goes more to the harm that confusion can cause the plaintiff's mark and reputation than to the likelihood of confusion. See *Arrow Fastener*, 59 F.3d at 398 (noting that first user's reputation may be harmed if secondary user's goods are of poor quality). In any event, the district court found this factor to be "neutral" with respect to likelihood of confusion.

* * *

In summary we conclude that of the six *Polaroid* factors that pertain directly to the likelihood of consumer confusion, all but one favor the plaintiff, and that one — sophistication of consumers — is neutral. The plaintiff is strongly favored by the strength of its mark, both inherent and acquired; the similarity of the marks; the proximity of the products and services; the likelihood that plaintiff would bridge the gap; and the existence of actual confusion. None of the factors favors the defendant. The remaining factors were found to be neutral. Although we do not suggest that likelihood of confusion may be properly determined simply by the number of factors in one party's favor, the overall assessment in this case in our view admits only of a finding in plaintiff's favor that defendants' sale of telephones and telephone-related services under the VIRGIN mark was likely to cause substantial consumer confusion.

One issue remains. Defendants argue that plaintiff should be barred by laches from seeking injunctive relief. They contend that because of plaintiff's delay after learning of the defendants' applications to register the VIRGIN marks, they expended considerable sums and developed goodwill in their use of the VIRGIN marks before plaintiff brought suit. Because the district court ruled in the defendants' favor it made no express finding on the issue of laches. But the district court explicitly found that plaintiff first learned of defendants' use of the name VIRGIN in commerce only two days before plaintiff instituted this suit. Given that finding, plaintiff could not be chargeable with laches.

We conclude that, as a matter of law, plaintiff demonstrated irreparable harm and likelihood of success on the merits and was entitled to a preliminary injunction.

Conclusion

REVERSED and REMANDED.

COMMENTS AND QUESTIONS

1. *The Likelihood of Confusion Multifactor Test Across the Circuits.* Each circuit applies its own multifactor test for the likelihood of consumer confusion. *See, e.g.*, Interpace Corp. v. Lapp, Inc., 721 F.2d 460, 463 (3d Cir. 1983) (establishing the ten "*Lapp* factors"); Pizzeria Uno Corp. v. Temple, 747 F.2d 1522, 1527 (4th Cir. 1984) (establishing the seven "*Pizzeria Uno* factors"); Frisch's Restaurants, Inc. v. Elby's Big Boy of Steubenville, Inc., 670 F.2d 642, 648 (6th Cir. 1982) (establishing the eight "*Frisch* factors"); Squirtco v. Seven-Up Co., 628 F.2d 1086, 1091, 207 U.S.P.Q. 897 (8th Cir. 1980) (establishing the six "*Squirtco* factors"); AMF Inc. v. Sleekcraft Boats, 599 F.2d 341, 348-49 (9th Cir. 1979) (establishing the eight "*Sleekcraft* factors"); In re E.I. duPont deNemours & Co., 476 F.2d 1357, 1361 (C.C.P.A. 1973) (establishing the 13 "duPont factors"). In general, the circuits' various multifactor tests are closely related. *See* GILSON ON TRADEMARKS § 5.02.

2. *The* Abercrombie *Spectrum.* In its discussion of inherent distinctiveness, the court divides the *Abercrombie* spectrum into inherently and non-inherently distinctive marks: "This inquiry distinguishes between, on the one hand, inherently distinctive marks — marks that are arbitrary or fanciful in relation to the products (or services) on which they are used — and, on the other hand, marks that are generic, descriptive or suggestive as to those goods." Do you detect an error in this division?

Later in the opinion, the court refers to the Virgin mark as "arbitrary and fanciful." Should we treat these two *Abercrombie* categories as indistinguishable for purposes of the inherent distinctiveness analysis? Why might we seek to accord a greater scope of protection to fanciful marks than to arbitrary marks?

3. *Are All Factors Equally Important?* In order to prevail in the overall likelihood of confusion multifactor test, must a plaintiff win all of the factors, a majority of them, some of them? Is the outcome of any particular factor necessary or sufficient to trigger a particular overall test outcome?

Empirical work offers some insight into these questions. *See* Barton Beebe, *An Empirical Study of the Multifactor Tests for Trademark Infringement*, 94 CAL. L. REV. 1581 (2006). Beebe's evidence suggests that the plaintiff must win the similarity factor in order to win the overall test. Of the 192 preliminary injunction and bench trial opinions studied by Beebe, 65 opinions found that the marks were not similar, and each of these 65 opinions found in favor of the defendant in the overall likelihood of confusion test. Notwithstanding the *Virgin* court's assertion that the intent factor is not "of high relevance" and may only "tip the balance where the questions are close," Beebe's study also suggests that the outcome of the intent factor correlates very strongly with the outcome of the overall test. Sixty-seven of the 192 preliminary injunction and bench trial opinions found that the intent factor favored the plaintiff. Of these 67 opinions, 65 found in favor of the plaintiff in the overall test (and in the two outlying opinions, the court found that the similarity factor favored the defendant). Overall, across the circuits, five core factors appear to drive the outcome of the likelihood of confusion test. In order of importance, these factors are the similarity of the marks, the defendant's intent, the proximity of the goods, evidence of actual confusion, and the strength of the plaintiff's mark. The remaining factors appear, in practice, to be largely irrelevant to the outcome of the test.

4. *Similarity.* Courts generally consider three kinds of similarity — sight, sound, and meaning. (Note that the second, and possibly the third, kind of similarity have little or no relevance to trade dress.) Similarity is generally tested by comparing the marks as a whole, rather than by dissecting them. *See* Brennan's, Inc. v. Brennan's Restaurant, L.L.C., 360 F.3d 125, 133 (2d Cir. 2004) ("Each mark must be compared against the other as a whole; juxtaposing fragments of each mark does not aid in deciding whether the compared marks are confusingly similar."). This approach makes sense because consumers are likely to pay attention to the whole mark in context. *See* Reno Air Racing Ass'n, Inc. v. McCord, 452 F.3d 1126, 1137 (9th Cir. 2006) (holding that "a court does not consider the similarity of the marks in the abstract, but rather in light of the way the marks are encountered in the marketplace and the circumstances surrounding the purchase") (citation omitted). On the other hand, dissection is appropriate if the aim is to prevent trademark owners from exercising control over generic, functional, or disclaimed portions of a trademark or trade dress. The trademark owner shouldn't be able to point to similarities between parts of a composite mark that are generic. *See* Dixi-Cola Laboratories, Inc. v. Coca-Cola Co., 117 F.2d 352 (4th Cir. 1941) (in finding that the mark Dixi-Cola does not infringe Coca-Cola, according no weight to the two marks' shared usage of the generic or descriptive term "cola").

Because the perception of the consumer when exposed to the whole mark in context is the linchpin of trademark infringement, a defendant's use of a similar or even identical trademark on similar products may be ameliorated by other differences between the mark and the packaging. For example, similarities in trade dress may not confuse consumers if the packages contain very different product names in large, obvious letters on the front. *See* Nabisco, Inc. v. Warner-Lambert Co., 220 F.3d 43 (2d Cir. 2000) (finding that the mark Dentyne Ice for breath-freshening chewing gum does not infringe the mark Ice Breakers for the same product in light of the prominence of the house mark Dentyne on the defendant's packaging). Disclaimers may also be effective in reducing confusion, if consumers notice them. If consumers would nonetheless be confused, however, efforts to ameliorate the effects of similar marks will not avoid trademark infringement.

5. *Intent.* What does the defendant's intent have to do with the likelihood that consumers will be confused by the two marks? Certainly, intentional copying is likely to be closer than accidental similarity, and therefore quite possibly more confusing, but isn't that adequately tested by the other factors that the court employs? Has the court slipped in a "fairness" factor to create what is in effect a presumption that counterfeiting (that is, intentional copying of a trademark) is illegal? Is such a presumption appropriate?

6. *Proximity.* An interesting case on proximity of goods (factor 2) is Death Tobacco, Inc. v. Black Death USA, 31 U.S.P.Q.2d 1899, 1903 (C.D. Cal. 1993):

> In this case, defendant's ["Black Death"] vodka and plaintiff's ["Death"] cigarettes are related products. They are, to some extent, complementary in that smoking and drinking are related vices that are often undertaken together. They are also somewhat similar in use and function. Cigarettes and vodka both have a mood altering effect and both are used for recreation and relaxation. . . .

> The most important factor in the determination of relatedness, here, is that the two items are sold to the same class of purchasers. Defendant introduced evidence that Black Death vodka and Death cigarettes are sold in the same package stores in both San Francisco and Los Angeles. Several store owners display the two products adjacent to one another on the shelf.

7. *Bridge the Gap*. Should it matter that the plaintiff is likely to enter the defendant's market in the near future? A minority of circuits include the bridge the gap factor as part of their likelihood of confusion test, and even then, they appear to accord it little weight. *See* Beebe, *supra*, at 1644. Why are plaintiff's plans to "bridge the gap" relevant to a court's analysis of the likelihood of consumer confusion? Do such plans have any bearing on consumers' perception of the plaintiff's or the defendant's marks?

8. *Actual Confusion*. Courts generally accept two kinds of evidence of actual confusion: anecdotal evidence such as what the Second Circuit considered in *Virgin* and survey evidence. As in *Virgin*, courts routinely rely on remarkably sparse anecdotal evidence in their analysis of the actual confusion factor. *See, e.g.*, Coca-Cola Co. v. Purdy, 382 F.3d 774, 784 (8th Cir. 2004) (relying on an e-mail from "one Internet user" mistakenly attributing the defendant's Web site to Coca-Cola and "[s]everal" other Internet users who mistakenly attributed his Web site to the *Washington Post* as evidence of actual confusion). *See also* GILSON ON TRADEMARKS, § 5.04.

As will be discussed in the Note that follows, courts also rely on survey evidence.

9. *Why Should Strong Marks Receive More Protection?* The conventional rationale for according a greater scope of protection to strong marks is that, due to their notoriety, they are more easily called to mind by similar marks. *See* Jacob Jacoby, *The Psychological Foundations of Trademark Law: Secondary Meaning, Genericism, Fame, Confusion and Dilution*, 91 TRADEMARK REP. 1013, 1038-42 (2001). But shouldn't strong marks actually require less protection? Consider the example of Coke. Having been exposed to the Coke mark countless times through their lives, are American consumers more or less likely to detect slight differences between the Coke mark and other similar marks?

10. *Sophistication of the Relevant Consumer Population*. The consumer who is tested is the "reasonable purchaser" of the products at issue. This standard allows for a great deal of flexibility in testing marks used with different products. For example, the "reasonable purchaser" of fleets of commercial airplanes may be expected both to be more sophisticated and to pay more attention to the decision than the reasonable purchaser of pencils for home use. Similarly, purchasers of expensive goods are assumed to take more care in their purchasing decisions. *See* Heartsprings, Inc. v. Heartspring, Inc., 143 F.3d 550, 557 (10th Cir. 1998) (finding that consumers would not likely confuse defendant's mark Heartspring for a residential school for physically disabled children with plaintiff's mark Heartsprings for printed materials teaching children to resolve conflicts non-violently where tuition for defendant's school ranged from $90,000 to $150,000 per year).

A related question is how many consumers must be likely to be confused. The fact that the "reasonable consumer" is at issue might suggest that at least half of the consuming public must be confused in order to constitute trademark infringement. After all, if the median consumer is not "reasonable," who is? But courts have not been willing to require such a showing from plaintiffs. Instead, likelihood of confusion is regularly found if as few as 10 to 15 percent of the consumers surveyed were confused. Is it reasonable to test infringement on the basis of the reactions of a small minority of the population? If not, how much confusion should be required? *See* Mushroom Makers, Inc. v. R. G. Barry Corp., 580 F.2d 44, 47 (2d Cir. 1978) (testing the "likelihood that *an appreciable number of ordinarily prudent purchasers* will be misled, or indeed simply confused, as to the source of the goods in question.") (emphasis added).

A recent Canadian case captured consumer sophistication doctrine quite memorably. In Atomic Energy of Canada Limited v. Areva NP Canada Ltd., 2009 FC 980 (2009), the plaintiff used a stylized "A" as its trademark for services relating to the design and construction of nuclear reactors while the defendant also used a stylized "A" in connection with the sale of nuclear reactor parts and components. The court noted: "All of [the plaintiff's] experts acknowledged in cross-examination that the relevant consumers would not be confused into purchasing the wrong nuclear reactor." *Id.* at ¶19. Citing English case law, the court recognized that "[I]t is not sufficient that the only confusion would be to a very small, unobservant section of society; or as Foster J. put it recently, if the only person who would be misled was a 'moron in a hurry.'" *Id.* at ¶28. Mr. Justice Zinn added: "In this industry, the fact that Homer Simpson may be confused is insufficient to find confusion." *Id.*

11. The fact that a trademark has been made incontestable precludes a defendant from challenging it on the basis of descriptiveness. *See Park 'N Fly v. Dollar Park and Fly*, discussed *supra*. An incontestable mark is not necessarily a *strong* mark for purposes of determining likelihood of confusion, however. In Petro Stopping Centers v. James River Petroleum Inc., 130 F.3d 88 (4th Cir. 1997), the Fourth Circuit affirmed a district court conclusion that plaintiff's Petro mark was merely descriptive and therefore weak, despite the fact that it was incontestable. The court noted that validity and infringement are separate inquiries and that incontestability applies only to the validity of a trademark. *Accord* Sports Authority Inc. v. Abercrombie & Fitch, 965 F. Supp. 925 (E.D. Mich. 1997).

12. How does the Internet affect the analysis of "marketing channels"? Are two goods marketed in the same channels because they are both available on the Internet? Early cases suggested the answer was yes. *See, e.g.*, Brookfield Communications v. West Coast Entertainment Corp., 174 F.3d 1036 (9th Cir. 1999). But other courts disagree. *See* Volkswagen AG v. Dorling Kindersley Publishing Inc., 2009 WL 909573 (E.D. Mich. Mar. 31, 2009) (Volkswagen car accessories and a book about cars weren't marketed in the same channels, even though both were available on different sections of amazon.com).

13. *Is It Necessary for Courts Explicitly to Consider Each Factor?* District courts are generally required explicitly to address each of the factors listed in their circuit's multifactor test. If a factor is irrelevant, the court must explain why. Failure to do so can result in remand. *See, e.g.*, Sabinsa Corp. v. Creative Compounds, 609 F.3d 175 (3d Cir. 2010), which reviewed a district court opinion that addressed only three of the ten *Lapp* factors used by the Third Circuit. The Third Circuit explained: "[W]hile it is true that a district court may find that certain of the *Lapp* factors are inapplicable or unhelpful in a particular case, the court must still explain its choice not to employ those factors. Here, the District Court failed to explain whether it viewed these remaining factors as neutral or irrelevant or how it weighed and balanced the combined factors." *Id.* at *3. Finding that the facts were "largely undisputed," *id.*, the Third Circuit declined to remand. Instead, it considered each of the ten *Lapp* factors and reversed.

Note on Survey Evidence

It is widely believed that survey evidence is routinely submitted in trademark litigation. In a statement before Congress, the American Bar Association offered a typical expression of this view: "survey evidence is traditionally one of the most classic and most persuasive and most informative forms of trial evidence that trademark lawyers utilize in both prosecuting and defending against trademark claims of various sorts." *Committee Print to Amend the Federal Trademark Dilution Act: Hearing Before the Subcomm. on Courts, the Internet, and Intellectual Property of the Comm. on the Judiciary*, 108th Cong. 14 (2004) (statement of Robert W. Sacoff, Chair, Section of Intellectual Property Law, American Bar Association). In fact, empirical work suggests that survey evidence plays a surprisingly small role in deciding actual cases. *See* Barton Beebe, *An Empirical Study of the Multifactor Tests for Trademark Infringement*, 94 CAL. L. REV. 1581, 1641-42 (2006). Beebe studied all federal court opinions applying a likelihood of confusion multifactor test over a five-year period from 2000 to 2004 and found that only 65 (20%) of the 331 opinions addressed survey evidence, 34 (10%) credited the survey evidence, and 24 (7%) ultimately ruled in favor of the outcome that the credited survey evidence itself favored. Eleven (24%) of the 46 bench trial opinions addressed survey evidence (with eight crediting it), while 24 (16%) of the 146 preliminary injunction opinions addressed survey evidence (with 12 crediting it). *Id.* These data do not support the proposition that survey evidence is routine in trademark litigation.

Nevertheless, in the small subset of cases involving high-stakes litigation between well-funded parties, survey evidence is customary, so much so that courts will sometimes draw an "adverse inference" against a party for failing to present it. *See, e.g.*, Eagle Snacks, Inc. v. Nabisco Brands, Inc., 625 F. Supp. 571, 583 (D.N.J. 1985) ("Failure of a trademark owner to run a survey to support its claims of brand significance and/or likelihood of confusion, where it has the financial means of doing so, may give rise to the inference that the contents of the survey would be unfavorable, and may result in the court denying relief."); *but see, e.g.*, Tools USA and Equipment Co. v. Champ Frame Straightening Equipment Inc., 87 F.3d 654, 661 (4th Cir. 1996) ("Actual confusion can be demonstrated by survey evidence, but contrary to [defendant's] suggestion, survey evidence is not necessarily the best evidence of actual confusion and surveys are not required to prove likelihood of confusion.").

When litigants do present survey evidence, courts' analysis of this evidence can be painstaking, especially when the litigants present dueling survey experts. A characteristic example of this situation appeared in the following case.

Quality Inns Int'l, Inc. v. McDonald's Corp.
695 F. Supp. 198 (D. Md. 1988)

NIEMEYER, District Judge:

[In 1987, Quality Inns International announced a new chain of economy hotels to be marketed under the name "McSleep Inn." McDonald's cease and desist letter prompted Quality Inns International to seek a declaratory judgment of no infringement. In its recitation of the facts, the court described the survey evidence before it as follows.]

It is undisputed that appropriate survey evidence is meaningful to establish the likelihood of confusion, and at trial each party presented survey evidence of its own and offered a critique of the survey evidence presented by the other.

A mall intercept survey was conducted on behalf of Quality International by Dr. Jacob Jacoby, a professor at New York University. This type of survey is conducted at randomly selected shopping malls by showing participants a visual stimulus and obtaining responses to questions.

Dr. Jacoby's survey was actually four separate surveys, each conducted in connection with a different visual stimulus. About 160 respondents were interviewed in each of the surveys. The first of the four stimuli used in the mall intercept survey by Dr. Jacoby was an advertisement for Quality International as it would appear in an airline magazine. The text of the advertisement contained a reference to McSleep Inn along with other products of Quality International, and the four chain logo was included at the bottom. That advertisement did not advertise McSleep Inn specifically. The second stimulus was a mock up of a yellow page display advertisement in which a McSleep Inn was advertised with the McSleep Inn logo and the four chain logo which included the name Quality International. The third stimulus was an artist rendering of a proposed McSleep Inn in front of which was a sign on a pylon that included the McSleep Inn logo and under which there was a smaller sign with the words "by Quality International." Finally, a control survey was conducted by showing the respondents a picture of an Egg McMuffin sandwich with the words Egg McMuffin written underneath it.

In connection with the survey involving the airline advertisement, despite the fact that arrows were added to the advertisement pointing to McSleep Inn, only 57 percent of those surveyed were aware that McSleep Inn was being advertised. Of those 57 percent, in response to the question "Who or what company, or companies, is that [that owns or operates this motel]?" only 7.5 percent responded "McDonald's."

In connection with the yellow page stimulus, of 164 respondents, 83 percent (or 136 respondents) knew that the advertisement was advertising McSleep Inn. Of those, 10.3 percent identified McDonald's as the name of the company that owns or operates McSleep Inn.

With respect to the artist's rendering of a McSleep Inn, 163 respondents were shown the picture and 147 indicated they knew that McSleep Inn was being advertised. Of those 16.3 percent said that McDonald's was the company that owns or operates the hotel. If the responses are limited to those who had made decisions during the previous year about staying in hotels or motels, 21.4 percent of those responding identified McDonald's as the owner or operator of the McSleep Inn.

Finally, with respect to the picture of an Egg McMuffin, 87 percent of those shown the picture identified it as a product of McDonald's.

Dr. Jacoby concluded that these figures reflected "a low level of likelihood of confusion." He went on to point out that one would predict that as McSleep Inns were advertised and became more widely known to the public "even the current low level of likely confusion would be substantially reduced."

McDonald's offered two surveys conducted by Dr. Hans Zeisel, a professor at the University of Chicago. His first survey was a telephone survey conducted of a statistical sample of the population consisting of 400 persons randomly selected. The first two questions asked of the respondents were:

> If you were driving along the highway and you saw a sign for a hotel called McSleep Inn [the name is spelled out], what would you expect this hotel to be like?

and

> And who or what company do you believe owns or operates this hotel called McSleep Inn?

Dr. Zeisel testified that the first question was a warmup that introduces the respondent to the subject of the inquiry, i.e. McSleep Inn, and that the second question was the critical one. In response to the second question, 31 percent of the people surveyed answered, "McDonald's." If only the respondents who stayed in a hotel at least once during the past 12 months are included, 33 percent answered "McDonald's"; and if only respondents who stayed in hotels at least 12 times during the past year are counted, 39 percent responded "McDonald's." He concluded that naming a hotel "McSleep Inn" would likely cause confusion among "a substantial proportion of the population by leading them to believe that this hotel is somehow related to McDonald's."

Dr. Jacoby, Quality International's expert, criticized the survey by Dr. Zeisel, arguing that the warmup question was merely a free association question which was leading and prompted the answer to the second question. It was also contended that the survey only tested auditory response to McSleep Inn and provided no visual stimulus, which was unlike the real world. He urged that a "mall intercept" survey would be superior.

Although Dr. Zeisel was not in favor of mall intercept surveys because such surveys cannot as a practical matter be performed on a valid statistical sample, in response to the criticism of Dr. Jacoby he conducted a second survey using a visual stimulus. In the second survey, Dr. Zeisel also eliminated the first question of his first survey to prove, as he testified, that the first question did not materially alter the results.

The mall intercept survey conducted by Dr. Zeisel interviewed 401 persons at randomly selected shopping malls across the country. After two unrelated warmup questions, the respondent was asked the following question:

> Please take a look at this. Here is a photograph of a sign for a hotel you might see if you were driving along the highway. [The witness was then shown the McSleep Inn logo that is the subject of registration before the Patent and Trademark Office.] Who or what company do you believe owns or operates this hotel?

Over 31 percent (31.9%) of all the respondents expressed the belief that McDonald's owns or operates the hotel. If only respondents who stayed in a hotel at least once during the last 12 months are included, 34.5 percent believed that McDonald's owns or operates McSleep Inn; and if only respondents who stayed in hotels 12 or more times during the past year are included, 38.5 percent believed that McDonald's owns or operates McSleep Inn.

The results obtained by Dr. Zeisel in his two surveys are not materially different, producing results within a percentage point or two of each other.

Dr. Zeisel criticized Dr. Jacoby's surveys in several respects. The principal criticisms were in three areas. With respect to the airline magazine advertisement and the yellow page advertisement, the McSleep Inn trademark was so diluted by the Quality Inns logo that a significant number of people did not even know that McSleep Inn was being advertised. In that context, he did not believe that any meaningful results were obtained. With respect to the artist's rendering of the McSleep Inn, he agreed that the concept was appropriate, but criticized the fact that the respondent was shown a logo that included the phrase "by Quality International" underneath it. Not only did he consider that to be nothing more than a reading exercise for the respondent, but he observed that the respondent was allowed to retain the picture in front of him when answering the questions.

McDonald's presented evidence that showed that of the 70 persons in Dr. Jacoby's survey who correctly identified the hotel with Quality International, 50 said they did so because they read it on the sign. When asked why they identified McSleep Inn with Quality International, typical responses were: "It says so on the ad," "The ad tells you that it's operated by Quality Inns International," "Because it says so," or "Because it says so on the sign I just read." McDonald's offered similar evidence on the yellow page advertisement and the airline advertisement where the respondents indicated they simply read Quality International in the advertisement.

Quality International justified its inclusion of "by Quality International" with the reason that it had made the decision to include that on the sign and wanted to test real life circumstances.

[Later in its opinion, the court analyzed this evidence as follows:]

The question whether a "likelihood of confusion" exists is, however, answered most persuasively by the survey evidence presented at trial. Although none of the surveys was perfect, they all spoke consistently that an appreciable number of consumers would be confused.

In Dr. Zeisel's telephonic survey, the responses were closest to a statistical sample. Its greatest shortcoming was that perhaps the first question, which allowed the respondent to associate, brought McDonald's to mind and therefore provided fuel for the next question as to who owns or sponsors McSleep Inn. The fear of any poison from that methodology, however, was allayed by his second survey which produced almost the same results. It is also noted that Dr. Zeisel conducted surveys, which he used as control for the research here, with the names "McTravel" and a concocted name "McTavish." With respect to McTravel (using "Mc" plus a generic word), confusion with McDonald's resulted, but with respect to McTavish (using what appears to be a proper name), there was virtually no confusion. In both Dr. Zeisel used the same warm-up question as he did in the telephone survey.

Because the telephonic survey could not present visual depictions of the mark, Dr. Zeisel did a mall intercept survey. That type of survey traditionally does not have a statistical probability because as a practical matter it is focused on randomly sampled shopping malls which are inherently biased. Both experts used this method, however, and the testimony received indicated that it was a popular method for use in the marketing industry. This survey by Dr. Zeisel revealed the same level of confusion as did the telephone survey. Over 30 percent confused the name McSleep Inn with McDonald's, a level which the Court concludes is substantial.

Projecting 30 percent to the 144 million people, which Dr. Zeisel concluded was the potential audience for McSleep Inn, over 40 million people would be expected to be confused if his surveys were statistically correct.

Dr. Jacoby, Quality International's expert, criticized Dr. Zeisel's leading question and the absence of visual stimuli. As the Court has noted, it concludes that at least the leading question criticism may have been theoretically correct, but it did not as a practical matter materially alter the data.

Dr. Jacoby conducted his own survey using as stimuli: an airline travel magazine advertisement for Quality International, a mock up yellow pages advertisement, and an artist's rendering showing McSleep Inn with a clarifying sign underneath it which reads, "by Quality International." The magazine advertisement was so diluted in its presentation, focusing principally on the Quality Inns range of products, that the Court concludes that it was not useful data to consider. Likewise, there was significant confusion relating to the yellow page advertising. In addition, the yellow page advertisement was under a display advertisement for Hilton Hotels leaving a significant number of respondents to relate the advertisement to Hilton Hotels. The Court does not consider the results of the surveys on these two stimuli as relevant.

The response to the question of who owns or sponsors McSleep Inn as shown in the artist's rendering was relevant. This was a depiction of what a McSleep Inn would look like to a consumer and measures at least that response.

The Court accepts that data, however, with some reservations in view of the inclusion of the sign "by Quality International" prominently added under the McSleep Inn logo. The issues in this lawsuit were framed around the use of the name McSleep Inn and perhaps the use of McSleep Inn's logo that is subject to registration in the Patent and Trademark Office. In none of those usages is the qualifying language "by Quality International" included. Quality International contends, however, that since it will be using the qualifying words, they should be included in any inquiry. Nothing requires that "by Quality International" be included in every use of McSleep Inn. The evidence showed that in fact individual franchisees of Quality International did not advertise the association with Quality International. Thus, a Comfort Inn franchisee would only advertise in brochures its own inn and the amenities offered there. Also, interstate and limited access highways that have signs advertising inns do not allow the qualifying language "by Quality International" on them. They would only allow the McSleep Inn logo. The spoken or written use of McSleep Inn would not always be able to include the limiting phrase.

The most troubling aspect of the survey using the limiting phrase, however, was the fact that over 70 percent of the respondents who correctly associated McSleep Inn with Quality International did so because they were reading the qualifying language "by Quality International." While that response may measure the particular stimulus which includes the logo with the qualifying language, it does not measure the confusion that is caused by the name McSleep Inn or by the McSleep Inn logo.

Notwithstanding these concerns with the Jacoby survey, it did measure the extent of confusion in response to that limited stimulus. Twenty-four of the 147 persons who understood that McSleep Inn was being advertised, or 16.3 percent, said that McDonald's was the owner or operator of the hotel, and if the survey is limited to persons who make the decision about where to stay when traveling, 21.4 percent believed that McSleep Inn, even with the clarifying language, was owned or sponsored by McDonald's. This is, in the Court's judgment, the most indicting evidence on the likelihood of confusion. In the absence of the clarifying language, the evidence shows that the extent of confusion jumps significantly. Even the 16.3 percent is an appreciable number that cannot be dismissed.

Both experts acknowledged that there are inherent distortions in surveys which they call "noise." But none estimated that the extent of this noise would ever rise above a few percentage points. Thus, the Court concludes that with the 16.3 percent minimum shown by the evidence, an appreciable number of consumers are likely to be confused by the use of the name McSleep Inn, even with the qualifying language "by Quality International."

[The Court ultimately found, inter alia, that "the name McSleep Inn is likely to cause an appreciable number of the public to be confused by believing that

McSleep Inn is sponsored, associated, affiliated, connected, or endorsed by McDonald's."]

The so-called *Ever-Ready* format has become the most common survey format used by survey experts. In Union-Carbide Corp. v. Ever-Ready, Inc., 531 F.2d 366 (7th Cir. 1976), the plaintiff introduced the results of two surveys as evidence to show that consumers were likely to confuse the source of the defendant's Ever-Ready lamps and mini-bulbs with the source of the plaintiff's Everready batteries, flashlights, and bulbs. Each survey consisted in part of the following questions asked of approximately 1,000 interviewees:

1. Who do you think puts out the lamp/mini-bulbs shown here?
2. What makes you think so?
3. Please name any other products put out by the same concern which you think puts out the lamps/mini-bulbs shown here.

Id. at 385. More recently, survey experts have developed a variation on the *Ever-Ready* format consisting of additional questions. In Starbucks U.S. Brands LLC v. Ruben, 78 U.S.P.Q.2d (BNA) 1741 (TTAB 2006), the Trademark Trial and Appeal Board analyzed such a survey. The defendant Ruben applied to register the mark Lessbucks in connection with a planned nationwide chain of discount coffee stores. Starbucks successfully opposed. The TTAB reviewed Starbucks' survey evidence approvingly:

> Starbucks retained Mr. Reitter, a recognized expert in the field of marketing and market research. Mr. Reitter designed a mall intercept survey involving interviews with two hundred respondents at shopping malls in eight geographically dispersed metropolitan areas.
>
> Mr. Ruben challenges Starbucks' survey results by criticizing the survey's format. He argues that several of the survey's key questions are leading—guiding respondents to think that another company might own or be associated with LESSBUCKS COFFEE. However, we find that the survey questions are consistent with those accepted in our established precedent on trademark surveys.
>
> This Board has had occasion to review the so-called *Ever-Ready* survey format. . . . See Carl Karcher Enterprises Inc. v. Stars Restaurants Corp., 35 USPQ2d 1125, 1132 (TTAB 1995); and Miles Laboratories, Inc. v. Naturally Vitamin Supplements, Inc., 1 USPQ2d 1445 (TTAB 1986). We agree with opposers that Questions 1a and 1b of Starbucks' survey[31] parallel the precise formats approved in *Ever-Ready* and *Carl Karcher*. Next, we note that consistent with *Ever-Ready*, Starbucks' Question 2a[32] and Question 3a[33] were designed to elicit responses concerning sponsorship, affiliation, permission and

31. (Question 1a): "This is the name of a retail establishment that serves coffee, tea, and other beverages. Just from knowing this, have you formed an opinion about the name of a company that owns this retail establishment?"

[Respondents answering Question 1a "yes" were then asked:]

(Question 1b): "What is the name of the company?"

32. (Question 2a): "Do you think the company that owns this retail establishment is connected or affiliated with any other company?"

[Respondents answering Question 2a "yes" were then asked:]

(Question 2b): "What other company?"

33. (Question 3a): "Do you think the company that owns this retail establishment has authorization, permission or approval from another company to use this name?"

[Respondents answering Question 3a "yes" were then asked:]

(Question 3b): "From what other company?"

> approval. While these types of questions were not expressly addressed in *Ever-Ready*, a leading commentator[34] suggests, and court opinions[35] have found, that affiliation and connection queries are appropriate in light of the specific language of the Lanham Act. Additionally, all these survey questions contain the follow-up question: "What makes you think so?" The answers given to these follow-up questions persuade us that the respondents were not merely guessing.
>
> Rather, given the way in which this survey format carefully follows the Ever-Ready likelihood of confusion survey format, we find that it is reliable and therefore of probative value on the issue of likelihood of confusion herein. Turning to the results of the survey, almost half of the ordinary consumer participants who encountered the term LESSBUCKS COFFEE believed that the products offered under the LESS-BUCKS designation were in some way connected to STARBUCKS. When the interviewer asked what made them believe that there was a connection or association between LESSBUCKS COFFEE and STARBUCKS, substantially all of the respondents referred to the similarity of the marks.

Starbucks U.S. Brands, supra, id. at 1753.

COMMENTS AND QUESTIONS

1. Do you have confidence in these survey formats, either those used in the *Quality Inns International* litigation or the *Ever-Ready* format? Is it reasonable to test infringement on the basis of the reactions of a small minority of the population? Is it appropriate to ask survey respondents questions going to connection, affiliation, authorization, or approval as Starbucks' survey expert did?

2. If you do find such survey evidence persuasive, then what proportion of survey respondents should be shown to be confused for the evidence to favor the plaintiff? Courts generally require a showing that a "substantial" or "appreciable" number of reasonably prudent consumers are likely to be confused. *See, e.g.*, International Ass'n of Machinists & Aero. Workers v. Winship Green Nursing Ctr., 103 F.3d 196, 201 (1st Cir. 1996) ("the law has long demanded a showing that the allegedly infringing conduct carries with it a likelihood of confounding an appreciable number of reasonably prudent purchasers exercising ordinary care"). As in *Quality Inns International*, courts have found survey results showing confusion among as little as 10 to 20 percent of survey respondents to be persuasive evidence of confusion. *See* McCarthy, McCarthy on Trademarks and Unfair Competition § 32:185.

Note on Other Types of Confusion

The traditional case for consumer confusion is that consumers will believe the infringer's product is the same as the trademark owner's product because of the

34. *See, e.g.*, 5 J. Thomas McCarthy, McCarthy on Trademarks and Unfair Competition, § 32:175 (4th ed. 2004).

35. *See, e.g.*, McDonald's Corp. v. McBagel's, Inc., 649 F. Supp. 1268 (S.D.N.Y. 1986); James Burrough Limited v. Sign of the Beefeater, Inc., 540 F.2d 266 (7th Cir. 1976); National Football League Properties, Inc. v. Wichita Falls Sportswear, Inc., 532 F. Supp. 651 (W.D. Wash. 1982); Pebble Beach Co. v. Tour 18 I. Ltd., 155 F.3d 526 (5th Cir. 1998); Indianapolis Colts, Inc. v. Metropolitan Baltimore Football Club Ltd. Partnership, 34 F.3d 410 (7th Cir. 1994); and Anheuser-Busch. Inc. v. Balducci Publications, 28 F.3d 769 (8th Cir. 1994).

similarity between the marks. Presumably, this confusion will allow the infringer to take sales away from the trademark owner by trading on the latter's goodwill. Although such confusion is the central problem at which trademark law is aimed, it is only one of many different ways in which consumers may be confused by different marks. Consider the following types of consumer confusion actionable under the Lanham Act.

Confusion as to Source. Two products bearing similar trademarks are likely to be confused only if both companies actually sell the same or similar products. Suppose, however, that an accused infringer uses a trademark on a group of products that the trademark owner does not sell. In that case, presumably, consumers cannot buy the infringer's products *instead of* the trademark owner's, because the trademark owner does not sell the products at all. For this reason, early courts sometimes found no infringement in situations where the plaintiff's and defendant's products did not directly compete. *See, e.g.*, Borden Ice Cream v. Borden's Condensed Milk Co., 201 F. 510 (7th Cir. 1912) (use of identical trademark for different milk products does not constitute trademark infringement).

But courts have gradually come to recognize that identical trademarks can sometimes cause confusion *as to the source of the products* even in the absence of direct product competition. For example, "Prell" is a trademark for a brand of shampoo and conditioner. If another company uses the term "Prell" for its hair coloring product, consumers may well believe that they are buying a product sold by the same company that sells Prell shampoo, particularly given the proximity of the two goods. *Cf.* Zazu Designs v. L'Oreal S.A., 979 F.2d 499 (7th Cir. 1992) (involving entry from one market into the other). While the infringer will not take sales of hair colors away from the trademark owner in this instance, the trademark owner may be hurt by this confusion in at least two ways. First, if the quality of the hair color is inferior, consumers may blame the maker of shampoo and stop buying Prell products altogether.[1] Second, it is possible that the trademark owner may wish to expand into the market for hair colors. If it does, confusion between the products will almost certainly result if both parties use the Prell mark.

Confusion as to Sponsorship. Even in situations in which consumers will not believe that the trademark owner is the one selling the product, the use of a similar trademark may still confuse them by causing them to believe that the trademark owner is affiliated with or sponsors the infringer's products. For example, suppose that a company that sells soup uses the trade symbol of the United States Olympic Committee on its soup cans. Presumably, the USOC does not sell soup, and no reasonable consumer would be likely to conclude that she was in fact buying USOC soup. But consumers might well conclude that the infringer was somehow affiliated with the USOC, or that one group had agreed to sponsor the other. This confusion as to affiliation or sponsorship is actionable under the Lanham Act, assuming the other requirements for protecting a mark are met.[2]

1. In fact, however, marketing scholarship suggests that this sort of harm is surprisingly rare. *See* Mark McKenna, *Testing Modern Trademark Law's Theory of Harm*, 95 Iowa L. Rev. 63 (2009).

2. Confusion as to affiliation or sponsorship is only expressly addressed in Section 43(a) of the Lanham Act, which applies to unregistered marks. But at least one commentator has quite reasonably suggested that the protections afforded to unregistered marks under Section 43(a) also apply to registered marks, whether under Section 32 of the Lanham Act or under Section 43(a). *See* Jay Dratler, Jr., Intellectual Property Law: Commercial, Creative, and Industrial Property § 10.01[1][i], at 10-5–10-6.

In cases of confusion either as to source or as to sponsorship, the essential question remains whether consumers are likely to be confused by the similarity of the marks. Because of this, many of the same factors listed in *AMF* apply with equal force to these inquiries. For example, proximity between the products sold by the parties, while not required, does tend to increase both the likelihood of confusion as to source and the chance that the parties will eventually be in direct competition. A similar analysis of infringement can be conducted to determine whether any of these types of confusion is likely.

Should it matter whether consumers are confused about the relationship between two unrelated companies, if that confusion doesn't affect their purchasing decisions? Why or why not? *See* Mark A. Lemley & Mark McKenna, *Irrelevant Confusion*, 62 STAN. L. REV. 413 (2009).

Initial Interest Confusion. What happens when confusion is dispelled before a product is ever purchased? For example, suppose that a competing fast-food restaurant put a large McDonald's sign by a highway exit. There is no McDonald's at the exit, so consumers won't end up thinking they are buying from one. However, they might be lured into the competitor's establishment once they have left the highway. Should this sort of deliberate effort to confuse consumers, but not at the point of purchase, be actionable? At least some courts have said yes. *See, e.g.*, Malletier v. Burlington Coat Factory Warehouse Corp., 426 F.3d 532, 537 n.2 (2d Cir. 2005); Checkpoint Sys., Inc. v. Check Point Software Techs., Inc., 269 F.3d 270, 292 (3d Cir. 2001) (suggesting that whether the parties compete and the level of care exercised by consumers are relevant factors in determining initial interest confusion); Elvis Presley Enters., Inc. v. Capece, 141 F.3d 188, 204 (5th Cir. 1998); Australian Gold, Inc. v. Hatfield, 436 F.3d 1228, 1238 (10th Cir. 2006); GILSON ON TRADEMARKS § 5:14. *See also* Jennifer Rothman, *Initial Interest Confusion: Standing at the Crossroads of Trademark Law*, 27 CARDOZO L. REV. 105 (2005).

Claims of initial interest confusion arise most frequently on the Internet. Early search engines categorized results in part by the site's use of "metatags," which are words on the page invisible to the user but which are read by computer search engines. Some companies began putting the names of their competitors' products (or even just popular trademarks such as "Playboy") into their metatags in an effort to draw unsuspecting consumers to their site. Is the use of a competitor's trademark in a metatag infringement? The cases seem to turn on whether there was a legitimate reason to make reference to the trademark on the Web page. *Compare* Brookfield Communications v. West Coast Entertainment Corp., 174 F.3d 1036 (9th Cir. 1999) (use of plaintiff's trademark in a Web site "metatag" was trademark infringement where it contributed to customer confusion) and People for the Ethical Treatment of Animals v. Doughney, 263 F.3d 359 (4th Cir. 2001) *with* Playboy Enterprises v. Welles, 279 F.3d 796 (9th Cir. 2002) (use of "Playmate of the Year" in a metatag to accurately describe defendant's resume was not illegal).

Doughney is a particularly interesting application of the idea of initial interest confusion. The plaintiff, People for the Ethical Treatment of Animals (PETA), is an advocacy group opposed to eating meat, wearing fur, and conducting research on animals. The defendant registered the Internet domain name peta.org, where he set up a page entitled "People Eating Tasty Animals" that was a parody of PETA and its goals. The Fourth Circuit found that using the domain name peta.org impermissibly caused initial interest confusion, even though visitors to the site discovered almost immediately that it had no affiliation with PETA and even though Doughney was not competing with PETA in any commercial sense. Is this result correct? Or should initial interest confusion be limited to cases in which the parties are direct competitors, as the Third Circuit held in *Checkpoint*? *See* Stacey L. Dogan & Mark A. Lemley, *Trademarks and Search Costs on the Internet*, 41 Hous. L. Rev. 777 (2004) (making the latter argument).

Commentators have been quite critical of the expansion of the doctrine, particularly in the Internet. *See, e.g.*, Eric Goldman, *Deregulating Relevancy in Internet Trademark Law*, 54 Emory L.J. 507 (2005). They argue that attraction of initial interest is easy to reverse in the Internet context—the confused surfer simply clicks the "back" button on their Internet browser.

In Playboy Enters. v. Netscape Comms., 354 F.3d 1020 (9th Cir. 2004), the Ninth Circuit extended the doctrine of initial interest confusion to hold that a search engine was liable for either direct or contributory infringement (the court didn't specify which) when it encouraged competing pornography companies to run ads that appeared when users searched on the term "playboy." Concurring, Judge Berzon expressed significant concerns about the doctrine:

> I do not think it is reasonable to find initial interest confusion when a consumer is never confused as to source or affiliation, but instead knows, or should know, from the outset that a product or web link is not related to that of the trademark holder because the list produced by the search engine so informs him.
>
> There is a big difference between hijacking a customer to another website by making the customer think he or she is visiting the trademark holder's website (even if only briefly), which is what may be happening in this case when the banner advertisements are not labeled, and just distracting a potential customer with another *choice*, when it is clear that it is a choice. True, when the search engine list generated by the search for the trademark ensconced in a metatag comes up, an internet user might *choose* to visit westcoastvideo.com, the defendant's website in *Brookfield*, instead of the plaintiff's moviebuff.com website, but such choices do not constitute trademark infringement off the internet, and I cannot understand why they should on the internet.

Playboy Enters. v. Netscape Commc'ns, 354 F.3d 1020, 1034-35 (9th Cir. 2004) (Berzon, J., concurring). While *Playboy* applied the doctrine, even in the Fourth and Ninth Circuits courts have started to back away from broad application of initial interest confusion. *See, e.g.*, Lamparello v. Falwell, 420 F.3d 309 (4th Cir. 2005); Bosley Med. Inst. v. Kremer, 403 F.3d 672 (9th Cir. 2005); Gibson Guitar Corp. v. Paul Reed Smith Guitars, 423 F.3d 539 (6th Cir. 2005) (all criticizing the broad reach of the doctrine and refusing to apply it).

Search engines no longer use metatags, perhaps because of the potential for manipulation. Instead, the issue of initial interest confusion comes up in the context of search results and ads which may attract Internet users to sites other than the one they are searching for. Should the same analysis apply to ad text that attracts consumer attention away from their "intended" search result?

Post-Sale Confusion. Suppose that consumers do not confuse two products but that, because of similarities in design, third parties who see the product from a distance (or stripped of identifying trademarks) will assume that the products are the same. This was the situation in Lois Sportswear v. Levi Strauss & Co., 799 F.2d 867 (2d Cir. 1986). There, Levi Strauss had registered not only its trade name and its jean labels, but also the pattern of stitching on the back pockets of its jeans. Lois Sportswear sold jeans with clearly different labels, but with an identical stitching pattern. The trial court found that there was no evidence of actual confusion by purchasers but that nonpurchasers, seeing the jeans "worn by a passer-by," would likely be confused. Should such "post-sale confusion" be actionable? The Second Circuit held that post-sale confusion constituted trademark infringement: "The confusion the Act seeks to prevent in this context is that a consumer seeing the familiar stitching pattern will associate the jeans with [Levi's] and that association will influence his buying decisions."

The district court also concluded that the Lois jeans were not of inferior quality. Given that, how is Levi Strauss & Co. hurt by any confusion that does arise? It will not lose sales, since customers themselves are not confused. Further, any confusion inures to the company's benefit, doesn't it? Whose interests are being protected by this decision? *See also* Levi Strauss & Co. v. Blue Bell, Inc., 632 F.2d 817, 822 (9th Cir. 1980) ("Wrangler's use of [Levi Strauss's] projecting label is likely to cause confusion among prospective purchasers who carry even an imperfect recollection of Strauss's mark and who observe Wrangler's projecting label after the point of sale.").

Although some courts still require point of sale confusion, *see, e.g.*, Gibson Guitar Corp. v. Paul Reed Smith Guitars, 423 F.3d 539 (6th Cir. 2005); Beneficial Corp. v. Beneficial Capital Corp., 529 F. Supp. 445 (S.D.N.Y. 1982) (holding that trademark law protects only against mistaken purchasing decisions); Nike, Inc. v. "Just Did It" Enterprises, 6 F.3d 1225 (7th Cir. 1993), many also recognize confusion after the sale of a product as actionable. *See, e.g.*, Au-Tomotive Gold, Inc. v. Volkswagen of Am., Inc., 457 F.3d 1062, 1078 (9th Cir. 2006) (finding that the declaratory plaintiff's key chains and license plate covers incorporating defendants' trademarks caused "post-purchase confusion."). In Mastercrafters Clock & Radio Co. v. Vacheron & Constantin-Le Coultre Watches, Inc., 221 F.2d 464 (2d Cir. 1955), the junior user copied the distinctive appearance of the senior user's expensive "Atmos" clock. Judge Frank held that

> at least some customers would buy [the copier's] cheaper clock for the purpose of acquiring the prestige gained by displaying what many visitors at the customers' homes would regard as a prestigious article. [The copier's] wrong thus consisted of the fact that such a visitor would be likely to assume that the clock was an Atmos clock. . . . [T]he likelihood of such confusion suffices to render [the copier's] conduct actionable.

Id. at 466. This same problem arises in the sale of "knockoff" versions of high-quality goods on street corners and flea markets. The purchaser of a "Rolex" branded watch for $25 appreciates that he or she is not purchasing an authentic product. *See* Rolex Watch U.S.A., Inc. v. Canner, 645 F. Supp. 484 (S.D. Fla. 1986); United States v. Torkington, 812 F.2d 1347 (11th Cir. 1987). The Second Circuit has recognized, however, that

> [t]he creation of confusion in the post-sale context can be harmful in that if there are too many knockoffs in the market, sales of the originals may decline because the public is fearful that what they are purchasing may not be an original. Furthermore, the public may be deceived in the resale market if it requires expertise to distinguish between an original and a knockoff. Finally, the purchaser of an original is harmed by the widespread existence of knockoffs because the high value of originals, which derives in part from their scarcity, is lessened.

See Hermes Int'l v. Lederer de Paris Fifth Ave., Inc., 219 F.3d 104, 108 (2d Cir. 2000). *See generally* McCarthy, McCarthy on Trademarks and Unfair Competition § 23:7. *See also* Alex Kozinski, *Trademarks Unplugged*, 68 NYU L. Rev. 960 (1993) (discussing the issue of "third-party confusion").

How would one prove post-sale confusion? Who are the relevant "consumers"? *See* General Motors Corp. v. Urban Gorilla LLC, 500 F.3d 1222 (10th Cir. 2007) (denying injunction against company that made "body kits" that made another truck look like a Hummer; court found insufficient evidence of post-sale confusion).

Reverse Confusion. Ordinary trademark confusion occurs when the junior user trades on the reputation of the trademark owner, confusing the public into thinking that his goods are associated with those of the senior trademark owner. At times, however, a large company will adopt the mark of a smaller trademark owner. In this case, the danger is presumably not that the junior user will trade on the smaller company's goodwill. The risk is, instead, that the public will come to associate the mark not with its true owner but with the infringer (who has spent a great deal of money to advertise it). Several courts have made it clear that reverse confusion is trademark infringement, and that the relative size of the companies doesn't matter. Indeed, companies have periodically been forced to halt or even retract major advertising campaigns because of reverse confusion problems. *See, e.g.*, Big O Tire Dealers, Inc. v. Goodyear Tire & Rubber Co., 561 F.2d 1365 (10th Cir. 1977); Sands, Taylor & Wood v. Quaker Oaks Co., 34 F.3d 1340 (7th Cir. 1994).

In Illinois High School Ass'n v. GTE Vantage, 99 F.3d 244 (7th Cir. 1996) (Posner, J.), the Seventh Circuit took a remarkably different approach. The plaintiffs were the owners of the trademark "March Madness" for their annual high school basketball tournament. After the media began using the term to describe the NCAA *college* basketball tournament, the NCAA and its various licensees adopted the term and used it in advertising their own products and services. The Illinois High School Association sued, alleging reverse confusion — that their mark had been appropriated by the NCAA. The Seventh Circuit rejected this claim, creating a new trademark classification: the "dual use trademark." The court reasoned that where *the public*, not the defendant, had appropriated a trademark for use to describe another product or service, trademark law should not stand in the way.

Does this result make sense? Why isn't this an ordinary case of reverse confusion? Under the Seventh Circuit's opinion, presumably *both* IHSA and NCAA now have rights to the mark. Does this comport with the rationales for trademark protection? Who now has the right to sue infringers? To license the use of the mark?

A number of reverse confusion cases have come up in the context of plagiarism of works of authorship, where the author claims that the copier has engaged in "reverse passing off" — that is, selling the plaintiff's work as her own rather than vice versa. In Dastar Corp. v. Twentieth Century Fox Film Corp., 539 U.S. 23 (2003), however, the Supreme Court made it clear that Lanham Act § 43(a) does not prevent the unaccredited copying of a work of authorship; any such rights must come from copyright law. For discussion, see Jane C. Ginsburg, *The Right to Claim Authorship in U.S. Copyright and Trademark Laws*, 41 Hous. L. Rev. 263 (2004) and David Nimmer, *The Moral Imperative Against Academic Plagiarism (Without a Moral Right Against Reverse Passing Off)*, 54 DePaul L. Rev. 1 (2004). For more on *Dastar*, including the opinion itself, see Chapter 9.F.4 *infra*.

PROBLEMS

Problem 5-1. Bristol-Myers (B-M), a major pharmaceutical company, markets "Excedrin" pain reliever. Since 1968, B-M has marketed "Excedrin PM," which is a pain reliever that does not interfere with sleep. Excedrin PM tablets are sold in a solid blue box whose color fades from dark at the top to light at the bottom. The box contains the words "Excedrin PM" in large white letters across the top third of the box. In the bottom right-hand corner of the box is a depiction of two tablets labeled "PM." B-M also sells Excedrin PM capsules, which are packaged identically except that the background is green and the two capsules in the picture read "Excedrin PM." Both the mark Excedrin PM and the dress of both boxes are registered with the Trademark Office.

In 1991, McNeil Pharmaceuticals introduced "Tylenol PM," a pain reliever chemically identical to Excedrin PM. Tylenol PM tablets are sold in a solid blue box whose color fades from dark at the top to light at the bottom. The box contains the words "Tylenol PM" in large white and yellow letters across the top third of the box. In the bottom right-hand corner of the box is a depiction of two tablets, one labeled "Tylenol" and the other labeled "PM." McNeil also sells Tylenol PM capsules, which are packaged identically except that the background is blue and the two capsules in the picture both read "Tylenol PM."

B-M sues McNeil, alleging that both its use of the term PM and its trade dress are likely to confuse consumers. Who should prevail?

Problem 5-2. Ivory Soap is sold for approximately $1.00 a bar. It is a heavily advertised brand name, which identifies itself as "99.44% pure." Whitewash Soap Co. makes and sells counterfeit Ivory Soap bars, which are packaged identically to Ivory (using the Ivory name and trade dress) and which contain chemically identical bars of soap. These counterfeit "Ivory" bars are sold for $.50 each. If a consumer buys the Whitewash soap thinking it is Ivory, how has he been injured? Hasn't he benefited? Is there any reason to protect Ivory's trademark against infringement at the expense of consumer welfare?

C. DILUTION

Trademark law has traditionally focused on preventing consumer confusion as to source. It has focused on preventing the defendant from using a trademark (e.g., Microsaft) sufficiently similar to the plaintiff's trademark (e.g., Microsoft) as to cause consumers to believe that defendant's goods originate in the plaintiff. But what if the defendant uses a trademark similar or identical to the plaintiff's trademark on goods entirely unrelated to the plaintiff's goods? For example, what if the defendant uses the trademark Microsaft—or Microsoft, for that matter—as a trademark for apple juice or bed linens? In these instances, consumers are unlikely to be confused as to the true source of the defendant's goods. Nevertheless, trademark law has long held that the plaintiff may be harmed. The canonical case in this regard involved Kodak bicycles. Despite the fact — well recognized by the court — that consumers were not likely to assume a connection between Kodak, the famous maker of film and cameras, and the seller of bicycles, the court issued an injunction. It did so because it found that the use of the Kodak name on bicycles would harm Kodak, Inc., even in the absence of confusion as to source. *See* Eastman Photographic Materials Co. v. Kodak Cycle Co., 15 [British] R.P.C. 105 (1898). *See generally* Beverly W. Pattishall, *Dawning Acceptance of the Dilution Rationale for Trademark–Trade Identity Protection*, 74 TRADEMARK REP. 289, 289 n.2 (1984) (citing early trademark "dilution" cases).

What is the nature of this harm? The legislative history of the Federal Trademark Dilution Act of 1995 (FTDA), Pub. L. 104-98, which added a new Section 43(c) to the Lanham Act, contained this instructive summary:

> [This bill would] create a federal cause of action to protect famous marks from unauthorized users that attempt to trade upon the goodwill and established renown of such marks and, thereby, dilute their distinctive quality. The provision is intended to protect famous marks where the subsequent, unauthorized commercial use of such marks by others dilutes the distinctiveness of the mark. The bill defines the term "dilution" to mean "the lessening of the capacity of a famous mark to identify and distinguish goods or services regardless of the presence or absence of (a) competition between the parties, or (b) likelihood of confusion, mistakes, or deception." Thus, for example, the use of DUPONT shoes, BUICK aspirin, and KODAK pianos would be actionable under this legislation. The protection of marks from dilution differs from the protection accorded marks from trademark infringement. Dilution does not rely upon the standard test of infringement, that is, likelihood of confusion, deception or mistake. Rather, it applies when the unauthorized use of a famous mark reduces the public's perception that the mark signifies something unique, singular, or particular. As summarized in one decision:
>
> > Dilution is an injury that differs materially from that arising out of the orthodox confusion. Even in the absence of confusion, the potency of a mark may be debilitated by another's use. This is the essence of dilution. Confusion leads to immediate injury, while dilution is an infection, which if allowed to spread, will inevitably destroy the advertising value of the mark.
>
> Mortellito v. Nina of California, Inc., 335 F. Supp. 1288, 1296 (S.D.N.Y. 1972).

The Federal Trademark Dilution Act was passed in 1996. It proved to be a remarkably unsuccessful statute. Courts struggled to apply its definition of dilution. *See, e.g.*, Ringling Bros.-Barnum & Bailey Combined Shows, Inc. v. Utah Division of Travel Development, 170 F.3d 449 (4th Cir.). The Second Circuit took advantage of the statute's imprecise language to find that only inherently distinctive marks could qualify for anti-dilution protection. *See, e.g.*, Nabisco, Inc. v. PF Brands, Inc., 191 F.3d 208 (2d Cir. 1999). Other courts developed the concept of "niche fame" to work around the statute's requirement that marks be "famous" in order to qualify for anti-dilution protection. *See, e.g.*, Times Mirror Magazines, Inc. v. Las Vegas Sports News, L.L.C., 212 F.3d 157 (3d Cir. 2000) (finding that the plaintiff's trademark "The Sporting News" qualified for anti-dilution protection under the FTDA because it was famous in its "niche market" of sports news periodicals). To make matters worse, in 2003, the Supreme Court interpreted the statute to require that the plaintiff show actual dilution rather than a likelihood of dilution to qualify for relief. Moseley v. V Secret Catalogue, 537 U.S. 418 (2003). All of these applications of the statute were likely contrary to its drafters' intent.

Congress intervened in late 2006 with the Trademark Dilution Revision Act of 2006 (TDRA), Pub. L. 109-312, which substantially amended Section 43(c) of the Lanham Act. Section 43(c) now provides in part:

> (c) Dilution by blurring; dilution by tarnishment
>
> (1) Injunctive relief. Subject to the principles of equity, the owner of a famous mark that is distinctive, inherently or through acquired distinctiveness, shall be entitled to an injunction against another person who, at any time after the owner's mark has become famous, commences use of a mark or trade name in commerce that is likely to cause dilution by blurring or dilution by tarnishment of the famous mark, regardless of the presence or absence of actual or likely confusion, of competition, or of actual economic injury.
>
> (2) Definitions
>
> (A) For purposes of paragraph (1), a mark is famous if it is widely recognized by the general consuming public of the United States as a designation of source of the goods or services of the mark's owner. In determining whether a mark possesses the requisite degree of recognition, the court may consider all relevant factors, including the following:
>
> (i) The duration, extent, and geographic reach of advertising and publicity of the mark, whether advertised or publicized by the owner or third parties.
>
> (ii) The amount, volume, and geographic extent of sales of goods or services offered under the mark.
>
> (iii) The extent of actual recognition of the mark.
>
> (iv) Whether the mark was registered under the Act of March 3, 1881, or the Act of February 20, 1905, or on the principal register.
>
> (B) For purposes of paragraph (1), "dilution by blurring" is association arising from the similarity between a mark or trade name and a famous mark that impairs the distinctiveness of the famous mark. In determining whether a mark or trade name is likely to cause dilution by blurring, the court may consider all relevant factors, including the following:
>
> (i) The degree of similarity between the mark or trade name and the famous mark.
>
> (ii) The degree of inherent or acquired distinctiveness of the famous mark.
>
> (iii) The extent to which the owner of the famous mark is engaging in substantially exclusive use of the mark.
>
> (iv) The degree of recognition of the famous mark.
>
> (v) Whether the user of the mark or trade name intended to create an association with the famous mark.
>
> (vi) Any actual association between the mark or trade name and the famous mark.
>
> (C) For purposes of paragraph (1), "dilution by tarnishment" is association arising from the similarity between a mark or trade name and a famous mark that harms the reputation of the famous mark.
>
> (3) Exclusions. The following shall not be actionable as dilution by blurring or dilution by tarnishment under this subsection:
>
> (A) Any fair use, including a nominative or descriptive fair use, or facilitation of such fair use, of a famous mark by another person other than as a

designation of source for the person's own goods or services, including use in connection with—

(i) advertising or promotion that permits consumers to compare goods or services; or

(ii) identifying and parodying, criticizing, or commenting upon the famous mark owner or the goods or services of the famous mark owner.

(B) All forms of news reporting and news commentary.

(C) Any noncommercial use of a mark.

15 U.S.C. § 1125(c).

COMMENTS AND QUESTIONS

1. *Frank Schechter's Original Proposal.* The early-twentieth-century trademark lawyer Frank Schechter first articulated the rationale for protection against trademark dilution in his article *The Rational Basis of Trademark Protection*, 40 HARV. L. REV. 813 (1927). Schechter proposed that anti-dilution protection be available only when (1) the senior user's mark was fanciful or arbitrary, (2) the mark was "unique," i.e., no other company made significant use of it, (3) the junior user's mark was identical to the senior user's mark, and (4) the junior user used this mark on goods that did not compete with the senior user's goods. Courts and lawmakers have since expanded the scope of the doctrine far beyond what Schechter originally envisioned. For example, the TDRA explicitly provides for the protection of marks that are distinctive "through acquired distinctiveness," 43(c)(1), and instructs courts to consider the "similarity" of the plaintiff's and defendant's marks as only one factor—albeit it a very important one—in determining dilution by blurring, 43(c)(2)(B)(i). The TDRA nowhere calls for any consideration of whether the parties' goods compete. What concerns might have motivated Schechter to attempt to limit the scope of the doctrine he proposed?

2. At least some commentators believe that anti-dilution law does not go far enough in protecting trademark owners. *See* Jerre B. Swann, *Dilution Redefined for the Year 2002*, 92 TRADEMARK REP. 585 (2002); Jerre B. Swann, *Dilution Redefined for the Year 2000*, 37 HOUSTON L. REV. 729 (2000); Jerre B. Swann &Theodore H. Davis, Jr., *Dilution, An Idea Whose Time Has Gone: Brand Equity as Protectable Property, The New/Old Paradigm*, 1 J. INTELL. PROP. L. 219 (1994) (arguing for explicit property rights in brand equity, going beyond anti-dilution law). On the other hand, some commentators suggest the opposite. *See* Kenneth L. Port, *The "Unnatural" Expansion of Trademark Rights: Is a Federal Dilution Statute Necessary?*, 85 TRADEMARK REP. 525 (1995); Megan Gray, *Defending Against a Dilution Claim: A Practitioner's Guide*, 4 TEX. INTELL. PROP. L.J. 205 (1996).

3. *"Blurring" and "Tarnishment."* Note that the new TDRA does not offer a general definition of "dilution," as did the old FTDA. Instead, the TDRA more precisely defines "dilution by blurring" as "association arising from the similarity between a mark or trade name and a famous mark that impairs the distinctiveness of the famous mark," and "dilution by tarnishment" as "association arising from the similarity between a mark or trade name and a famous mark that harms the reputation of the famous mark." Trademark "blurring" and trademark "tarnishment" are two very different species of dilution. How, if at all, are they related? Can a defendant logically

both blur and tarnish a plaintiff's mark? In the cases that follow, the first addresses a claim for blurring, while the second address a claim for both blurring and tarnishment.

Nike, Inc. v. Nikepal International, Inc.
84 U.S.P.Q.2d 1820 (E.D. Cal. 2007)

BURRELL, JR., J.:

Nike seeks an injunction preventing Nikepal from using the term "Nike" (or any term confusingly similar thereto) alone or as part of any trademark, domain name or business name under which Nikepal offers goods or services in commerce. Nike also seeks a reversal of the TTAB's ruling allowing Nikepal to register the NIKEPAL mark. Nikepal seeks an affirmation of the TTAB's April 21, 2005 order. (TTAB's April 21, 2005 Order ("TTAB Decision").)

Findings of Fact

I. The Parties and Their Businesses

A. Nike

. . . Nike is the largest seller of athletic footwear and apparel in the world. Nike sells around 180 million pairs of shoes annually in the United States alone. . . .

B. Nikepal

Nikepal was incorporated on May 18, 1998 by the company's founder and president, Palminder Sandhu . . . who then began using the NIKEPAL mark in commerce. Nikepal provides services and products to analytical, environmental, and scientific laboratories. Nikepal's trademark application to the PTO requested registration for: "import and export agencies and wholesale distributorships featuring scientific, chemical, pharmaceutical, biotechnology testing instruments and glassware for laboratory use, electrical instruments, paper products and household products and cooking appliances." Nikepal distributes glass syringes in varying volumes and other laboratory products to testing and power companies and also distributes paper boxes (syringe carrying cases) and nylon valves and caps for use with the syringes. Nikepal only distributes its products to laboratories, not to individuals.

II. The Parties' Marks

B. Nikepal

Mr. Sandhu testified that he conceived of the term Nikepal when he wanted to create a vanity license plate for his car. He testified that he selected the word "Nike" by opening a dictionary to a random page and choosing the first word he saw, and then combined it with the first three letters of his first name "Pal." "Pal" means friend or benefactor. Mr. Sandhu admits he knew of the existence of the company Nike and its use of the NIKE mark at the time he devised the term NIKEPAL. Despite Mr. Sandhu's trial testimony concerning the manner in which he conceived of the term NIKEPAL, the court does not find it to be credible.

The "Nike" portion of the NIKEPAL mark is pronounced the same way as the NIKE mark is pronounced: with a hard "i" (like bike) in the first syllable and a hard "e" (like in "key") in the second syllable. The articles of incorporation signed by Mr. Sandhu for Nikepal in 1998 display the company name as "NikePal International, Inc.," with the first word of the company name spelled "NikePal," with a capital "N" and a capital "P."

In addition to using Nikepal as the company name, NIKEPAL appears directly on some of Nikepal's products, including on its syringe products, and on its marketing materials. Nikepal also places www.nikepal.com on its syringes to identify the source of the syringe. Nikepal also uses the NIKEPAL mark in a vanity phone number (1-877-N-I-K-E-P-A-L), on its website, and in its domain names, including nikepal.com, nikepal.biz, nikepal.us, nikepal.tv, nikepal.info, and nikepal.net.

III. Nike's Sales

By the late 1980s, United States sales of NIKE branded products were over one billion dollars per year. Starting in 1991 and through the mid 1990s, sales of NIKE products in the United States were approximately two billion dollars per year, and were above five billion dollars per year by 1997. By 1997, Nike was the largest seller of athletic footwear and apparel in the world. The geographic area of Nike's sales includes the United States and 140 countries throughout the world. Since 1997, Nike has sold over 100,000,000 pairs of NIKE shoes each year.

IV. Advertising and Promotion of the NIKE Mark

Nike has undertaken significant expense to promote the NIKE mark. Nike advertises in various types of media, including traditional print advertising, such as magazines (of both special and general interest), newspapers (of general circulation), leaflets, and billboards. Nike also advertises in electronic media, including radio, television, cable and internet, on sides of buildings, on taxi cabs, and through direct mailings. Nike's television advertisements have run on network channels and have reached national audiences. Nike has also promoted its mark by associating with athletes through endorsement arrangements. By 1991, Nike was spending in excess of one hundred million dollars per year in the United States alone to advertise products bearing the NIKE mark. By 1997, Nike had spent at least $1,567,900,000.00 to promote the NIKE mark in the United States.

V. Notoriety of NIKE

The NIKE mark has been consistently ranked as a top brand in publications that survey the top brands each year. Since at least 1990, Nike has been named one of the top forty (40) brands in the United States based on the EquiTrend and other studies published in BrandWeek and Financial World Magazine. . . . One story printed in Forbes magazine, reported a survey conducted by Young & Rubicam that ranked the NIKE brand among the top ten (10) in the United States in 1996 with COKE, DISNEY, and HALLMARK.

VI. Evidence of Actual Association

A survey conducted by Phillip Johnson . . . determined that a significant number of Nikepal's potential laboratory customers actually associated NIKE with NIKEPAL. . . .

In designing his study, Mr. Johnson used a universe of survey participants randomly selected from lists of companies that Mr. Sandhu's deposition testimony identified as the sources for Nikepal's current and prospective customers. Mr. Johnson conducted the survey by phone and asked respondents about their perception of a website called nikepal.com. In designing his survey, Mr. Johnson chose one of the ways that the NIKEPAL mark is used in commerce which allowed him to reasonably recreate a purchasing context while obtaining a controlled and accurate measurement. . . .

Once survey respondents were screened to confirm that they were the persons most responsible for ordering laboratory equipment at their business, they were asked: "What if anything, came to your mind when I first said the word Nikepal?" Many survey respondents who were not actually confused about the source of the Nikepal website nonetheless identified Nike. Mr. Johnson testified that his survey revealed that the vast majority of respondents, 87%, associated Nikepal with Nike; that is, when they encounter the mark NIKEPAL, they think of Nike and/or its offerings. . . .

Conclusions of Law

I. Dilution

. . . To prevail on its dilution claim, Nike must prove 1) that its mark was famous as of a date prior to the first use of the NIKEPAL mark and 2) that Nikepal's use of its allegedly diluting mark creates a likelihood of dilution by blurring or tarnishment.

A. Whether NIKE Was Famous Prior to the First Use of NIKEPAL

A "famous" mark is one that "is widely recognized by the general consuming public of the United States as a designation of source of the goods or services of the mark's owner." 15 U.S.C. §1125(c)(2)(A).

In determining whether a mark possesses the requisite degree of recognition, the court may consider all relevant factors, including the following:

(i) The duration, extent, and geographic reach of advertising and publicity of the mark, whether advertised or publicized by the owner or third parties.
(ii) The amount, volume, and geographic extent of sales of goods or services offered under the mark.

(iii) The extent of actual recognition of the mark.
(iv) Whether the mark was registered under the Act of March 3, 1881, or the Act of February 20, 1905, or on the principal register.

Id. Since Nikepal's first use of NIKEPAL commenced in May 1998, Nike must show that NIKE was famous before that date.

With regard to the first factor, the evidence clearly establishes that through various combinations of athlete endorsements, television, radio, print media, and billboard placements, NIKE was promoted nationally for more than two decades before 1998. By the 1990s, Nike was had spent in excess of a billion dollars for promotion of NIKE products in the United States.

With regard to the second factor, Nike's sales of NIKE products reached the billion dollar per year level in the United States well before May 1998. By 1997, Nike had spent in excess of one billion dollars to promote the NIKE mark in the United States.

Nike also satisfies the third factor, since recognition of the success of NIKE has been recorded by various publications in surveys and articles written prior to May 1998. Since the early 1990s, NIKE has been consistently ranked as a top brand in brand surveys in the United States and the world. . . . Nikepal counters that only Nike's Swoosh design mark, and not the NIKE mark itself, is famous. However, Mr. Johnson's survey revealed that when participants were exposed solely to the word "Nike" without the Swoosh, the response overwhelmingly indicated recognition of the NIKE mark.

Finally, with regard to the fourth factor, the NIKE mark is registered on the PTO's principal register. Nike owns ten (10) federal registrations for NIKE covering uses prior to 1998 which include retail services, bags, footwear, apparel, heart monitors, electrical items and paper products. Accordingly, the court concludes that NIKE was famous under 15 U.S.C. § 1125(c)(2)(A), prior to Nikepal's first use of the NIKEPAL mark.

B. Likelihood of Dilution by Blurring

The TDRA defines dilution by blurring as an "association arising from the similarity between a mark or trade name and a famous mark that impairs the distinctiveness of the famous mark." 15 U.S.C. § 1125(c)(2)(A).

In determining whether a mark or trade name is likely to cause dilution by blurring, the court may consider all relevant factors, including the following:

(i) The degree of similarity between the mark or trade name and the famous mark.
(ii) The degree of inherent or acquired distinctiveness of the famous mark.
(iii) The extent to which the owner of the famous mark is engaging in substantially exclusive use of the mark.
(iv) The degree of recognition of the famous mark.
(v) Whether the user of the mark or trade name intended to create an association with the famous mark.
(vi) Any actual association between the mark or trade name and the famous mark.

Id.

(i) The Degree of Similarity

Marks in a dilution analysis must be "identical" or "nearly identical." Thane Int'l, Inc. v. Trek Bicycle Corp., 305 F.3d 894, 906 (9th Cir. 2002). "For marks to be nearly identical to one another, they 'must be similar enough that a significant segment of the target group of customers sees the two marks as essentially the same.'" Playboy Enters., Inc. v. Welles, 279 F.3d 796, 806 n.41 (9th Cir. 2002) (internal citation omitted).

The parties' marks are nearly identical. The NIKEPAL mark is a composite of the word "Nike" with the term of affinity, "pal." The composite nature of the NIKEPAL mark is evident in the logo selected by the company which clearly features an "N" and a "P." In each case the dominant feature of the mark is the term "Nike." In addition, the term "Nike" in both marks is pronounced identically with an "i" like in "bike" and an "e" like in "key." See *Porsche Cars N. Am., Inc.*, 2000 WL 641209, at *3, (finding that the trademark PORSCHE was diluted by PORCHESOURCE.-COM); see also *Jada Toys, Inc.*, 496 F.3d 974, 2007 WL 2199286, at *4 (concluding "that a reasonable trier of fact could find that the HOT WHEELS and HOT RIGZ marks are nearly identical.").

Further, as shown by Mr. Johnson's survey, the vast majority of the survey respondents, representing a significant segment of Nikepal's target customer group, associate Nike and/or its products and services when they encounter the mark NIKEPAL, thus perceiving the two marks as essentially the same. See *Thane Int'l, Inc.*, 305 F.3d at 906 ("The marks must be of sufficient similarity so that, in the mind of the consumer, the junior mark will conjure an association with the senior.") (citing Nabisco, Inc. v. PF Brands, 191 F.3d 208 (2d Cir. 1999)). Accordingly, this factor favors Nike.

(ii) Distinctiveness

. . . Nikepal does not dispute that NIKE is, at the very least, suggestive. Accordingly, NIKE is inherently distinctive and this factor favors Nike.

(iii) Substantially Exclusive Use

The law does not require that use of the famous mark be absolutely exclusive, but merely "substantially exclusive." See L.D.Kichler Co. v. Davoil Inc., 192 F.3d 1349, 1352 (Fed. Cir. 1999) (holding that in the trademark context, "substantially exclusive" use does not mean totally exclusive use). Therefore, a limited amount of third party use is insufficient to defeat a showing of substantially exclusive use. . . .

. . . Nikepal introduced evidence of use of the term "Nike" in the company name "Nike Hydraulics, Inc.," through a bottle jack purchased from the company and a 1958 trademark registration for "Nike" owned by Nike Hydraulics. However, this evidence is insufficient to disprove Nike's claim that its use of NIKE is substantially exclusive. Even Nikepal's witness, Roger Smith, admitted that he had not encountered Nike Hydraulics before hearing that name in connection with this action. Accordingly, the court finds that Nike's use of the NIKE mark is substantially exclusive and this factor therefore favors Nike.

(iv) Degree of Recognition

The degree of recognition of NIKE is quite strong. Millions of NIKE products are sold in the United States annually and the evidence demonstrates that NIKE is readily recognized. This factor therefore favors Nike.

(v) Intent to Create Association

Mr. Sandhu admitted that he was aware of the existence of the NIKE mark before he adopted the company name. Although he testified at trial that he came up with the term Nikepal by opening the dictionary to a random page and essentially finding that word by "fate," his testimony was not credible. Therefore, this factor favors Nike.

(vi) Actual Association

Nikepal registered the domain names nikepal.biz, nikepal.net, nikepal.us, nikepal.info and nikepal.tv. The evidence shows that the domain registrar assigned the domain names an "under construction" page and then associated with that page promotions and advertisement links to a number of web pages that offered NIKE products (or products of Nike's competitors in the shoe and apparel field). Thus, in the internet context, there is actual association between NIKEPAL and NIKE.

Further, Mr. Johnson's survey also evinced that there is a strong degree of association between NIKEPAL and NIKE. Mr. Johnson's survey showed over 87% of the people in Nikepal's own customer pool associated the stimulus "Nikepal" with NIKE. The survey presents ample proof of association between the marks to support a finding that such exists in the general public. Accordingly, the court finds that there is actual association between the NIKEPAL and NIKE marks and this factor favors Nike.

In conclusion, since the six factors considered in the likelihood of dilution analysis favor Nike, there is a likelihood that NIKE will suffer dilution if Nikepal is allowed to continue its use of NIKEPAL. Accordingly, Nike prevails on its federal and state dilution claims.

III. Reversal of TTAB Decision

Finally, Nike seeks reversal of the TTAB's decision denying its opposition to the registration of the NIKEPAL mark. Specifically, the TTAB held there was no likelihood of dilution based on its finding that the parties' marks were not sufficiently similar.

. . . Here, Nike presented new evidence in the form of, inter alia, Mr. Johnson's survey showing that the vast majority of the survey respondents, representing a significant segment of Nikepal's target customer group, associate Nike and/or its products and services when they encounter NIKEPAL, thus perceiving the two marks as essentially the same. See *Thane Int'l, Inc.*, 305 F.3d at 906 ("The marks must be of sufficient similarity so that, in the mind of the consumer, the junior mark will conjure an association with the senior.") (citing *Nabisco, Inc.*, 191 F.3d at 208); see also *Playboy Enters., Inc.*, 279 F.3d at 806 n.41 (holding that "[f]or marks to be nearly identical to one another, they 'must be similar enough that a significant segment of the target group of customers sees the two marks as essentially the same.' "). The new evidence submitted by Nike therefore compels a contrary finding on the similarity of the parties' marks.

. . . Accordingly, although the court gives deference to TTAB's fact-finding, the evidence presented by Nike in this action compels reversal of the TTAB's decision dismissing Nike's opposition to the registration of Nikepal's mark.

Therefore, the TTAB ruling is reversed and Nike's request for an order sustaining the opposition to Nikepal's registration for the NIKEPAL mark is granted.

Conclusion

For the reasons stated, Nike prevails on its federal and state dilution claims, the decision of the TTAB is reversed, and the opposition to Nikepal's registration of the NIKEPAL mark is sustained. Further, Nikepal is permanently enjoined from using NIKEPAL in connection with the offering of goods or services in commerce, including its use in domain names, on web pages, in printed matter, and on products, and shall cease any such uses of NIKEPAL within sixty (60) days of the date on which this order is filed. Nikepal may continue to use its numeric telephone number, but may not advertise or associate it with the designation "1-877-NIKEPAL."

COMMENTS AND QUESTIONS

1. *How Similar Must the Parties Marks Be to Show Dilution?* Following Thane Int'l, Inc. v. Trek Bicycle Corp., 305 F.3d 894 (9th Cir. 2002), the *Nikepal* court applied an identical or nearly identical standard of similarity in its blurring analysis. Other circuits also apply a heightened standard of similarity in this context. *See, e.g.*, AutoZone, Inc. v. Tandy Corp., 373 F.3d 786 (6th Cir. 2004) ("Powerzone" not similar enough to dilute "AutoZone"). The Second Circuit, however, has rejected this approach. In Starbucks Corp. v. Wolfe's Borough Coffee, Inc., 588 F.3d 97 (2d Cir. 2009), it emphasized that the new statute "does not use the words 'very' or 'substantial' in connection with the similarity factor," *id.* at 108, and reasoned that if courts were to impose a heightened similarity standard, this would give undue weight to the similarity factor — by turning the heightened similarity requirement into a threshold requirement that would short-circuit the six-factor multifactor balancing test for blurring. (The Second Circuit found that New York state anti-dilution law, by contrast, does impose a requirement that the marks be " 'substantially' similar," *id.* at 114.) Do you find the Second Circuit's reasoning persuasive? As a matter of sound policy, should courts require a heightened standard of similarity when analyzing a blurring claim? And in any case, are you persuaded that Nike and Nikepal are nearly identical?

2. *Association or Association that Impairs Distinctiveness?* Recall that the TDRA defines dilution by blurring as "association . . . that impairs the distinctiveness of the famous mark." The *Nikepal* court found evidence of association, but it never addressed the question of whether this association "impairs the distinctiveness of the famous mark." Can we assume, as the *Nikepal* court appears to do, that any association

necessarily impairs the distinctiveness of the plaintiff's mark? Consider what the Supreme Court said in *Moseley*:

> We do agree, however, with [the] conclusion that, at least where the marks at issue are not identical, the mere fact that consumers mentally associate the junior user's mark with a famous mark is not sufficient to establish actionable dilution. [S]uch mental association will not necessarily reduce the capacity of the famous mark to identify the goods of its owner, the statutory requirement for dilution under the FTDA. For even though Utah drivers may be reminded of the circus when they see a license plate referring to the "greatest *snow* on earth," it by no means follows that they will associate "the greatest show on earth" with skiing or snow sports, or associate it less strongly or exclusively with the circus. "Blurring" is not a necessary consequence of mental association. (Nor, for that matter, is "tarnishing.")

Moseley v. V Secret Catalogue, 537 U.S. 418 (2003). On remand, the *Moseley* district court took the Supreme Court's teaching very much to heart. *See* V Secret Catalogue, Inc. v. Moseley, 558 F. Supp. 2d 734 (W.D. Ky. 2008). It found all six blurring factors to favor the plaintiff, but nevertheless found no blurring: "The choice of name and presentation by the Moseleys being just slightly different from the VICTORIA'S SECRET mark, conjured the association with the famous mark, but fell short of blurring its distinctiveness in this instance." *Id.* at 748. How can the plaintiff prove that association impairs the distinctiveness of its mark? (Note that the *Moseley* district court found tarnishment instead, *id.* at 750).

3. *Fame.* The requirement of fame is designed as an important limitation on the reach of federal anti-dilution protection. The drafters of the 1995 FTDA intended that its extraordinary scope of protection be available only to truly famous marks. *See* TCPIP Holding Co., Inc. v. Haar Communications, Inc., 244 F.3d 88 (2d Cir. 2001) ("It seems most unlikely that Congress intended to confer on marks that have enjoyed only brief fame in a small part of the country or among a small segment of the population, the power to enjoin all other users throughout the nation in all realms of commerce."); *see generally* McCarthy, McCarthy on Trademarks and Unfair Competition § 24:104. Yet soon after the FTDA's passage, numerous courts uncritically applied its "fame" requirement in an effort to snare cyber-pirates. Thus courts found a host of obscure marks to be famous. *See, e.g.*, Intermatic, Inc. v. Toeppen, 947 F. Supp. 1227 (N.D. Ill. 1996); Teletech Customer Care Management, Inc. v. Tele-Tech Company, Inc., 977 F. Supp. 1407 (C.D. Cal. 1997); Panavision International v. Toeppen, 141 F. 3d 1316 (9th Cir. 1998). Outside the domain name context, others courts significantly reduced the FTDA's standard for fame by finding that a mark can be "famous" in a narrow product market. *See* Times Mirror Magazines v. Las Vegas Sporting News, 212 F.3d 157 (3d Cir. 2000), *cert. denied*, 531 U.S. 1071 (2001) (holding that "The Sporting News" is a famous mark); *see also* Syndicate Sales, Inc. v. Hampshire Paper Corp., 192 F.3d 633 (7th Cir. 1999) (noting that § 43(c)(1)(F) "indicates that fame may be constricted to a particular market"); Washington Speakers Bureau, Inc. v. Leading Authorities, Inc., 33 F. Supp. 2d 488 (E.D. Va. 1999) (same).

When Congress revised the dilution statute in 2006, it tightened up the requirements to prove fame, in part by abolishing the concept of niche fame. The statute now requires that a mark be "widely recognized by the general consuming public of the United States." As Representative Howard Berman explained in hearings on the

FTDA, "[d]ilution should once again be used sparingly as an 'extraordinary' remedy, one that requires a significant showing of fame. . . . [I]t is our hope that the dilution remedy will be used in the rare circumstance and not as the alternative pleading." *Trademark Dilution Revision Act of 2005: Hearing on H.R. 683 Before the Subcomm. on Courts, the Internet and Intellectual Property of the H. Comm. on the Judiciary*, 109th Cong. (2005) (statement of Rep. Howard L. Berman, California, ranking member, Subcommittee on Courts, the Internet and Intellectual Property), *reprinted in* H.R. Rep. No. 109-23, at 25 (2005). Some courts appear to be applying this new fame standard as Congress intended. *See, e.g.*, Board of Regents, the University of Texas System v. KST Electric, Ltd., 550 F. Supp. 2d 657 (W.D. Tex. 2008) (finding that the longhorn silhouette associated with the University of Texas at Austin was not famous outside the "niche" of college sporting events); Milbank Tweed Hadley & McCloy LLP v. Milbank Holding Corp., 82 U.S.P.Q.2d 1583 (C.D. Cal. 2007) (New York law firm Milbank not famous outside niche market). Other courts, however, appear to be unaware of the new standard. *See, e.g.*, Rain Bird Corp. v. Taylor, 665 F. Supp. 2d 1258, 1270 (N.D. Fla. Sept. 10, 2009) (finding that the trademark RAIN BIRD qualifies for TDRA protection because "the Rain Bird Marks are famous in the State of Florida"); Shreveport La. Hayride Co., L.L.C. v. Kent, 2009 U.S. Dist. LEXIS 41411 (W.D. La. May 14, 2009) (finding that LOUISIANA HAYRIDE qualifies for TDRA protection); Rhino Membranes & Coatings Inc. v. Rhino Seamless, 2008 U.S. Dist. LEXIS 79491 (S.D. Tex. Sept. 30, 2008) (finding that RHINO qualifies for TDRA protection).

4. *Are Some Trademarks So Strong as to Be Immune to Blurring?* In 2000, Professors Maureen Morrin and Jacob Jacoby, the latter of whom is a highly regarded trademark survey expert, reported the results of two studies they conducted to detect the effects of diluting stimuli on brand recognition and recall in test subjects. *See* Maureen Morrin & Jacob Jacoby, *Trademark Dilution: Empirical Measures for an Elusive Concept*, 19 J. Pub. Pol. & Marketing 265 (2000). Among other findings, they reported: "It appears that very strong brands are immune to dilution because their memory connections are so strong that it is difficult for consumers to alter them or create new ones with the same brand name." *Id.* at 274. Does this make sense to you? What are the implications of such a finding for anti-dilution protection, a form of protection granted only to brands "widely recognized by the general consuming public of the United States"?

Louis Vuitton Malletier S.A. v. Haute Diggity Dog, LLC

507 F.3d 252 (4th Cir. 2007)

Niemeyer, Circuit Judge:

Louis Vuitton Malletier S.A., a French corporation located in Paris, that manufactures luxury luggage, handbags, and accessories, commenced this action against Haute Diggity Dog, LLC, a Nevada corporation that manufactures and sells pet products nationally, alleging trademark infringement under 15 U.S.C. § 1114(1)(a), trademark dilution under 15 U.S.C. § 1125(c), copyright infringement under 17 U.S.C. § 501, and related statutory and common law violations. Haute Diggity Dog manufactures, among other things, plush toys on which dogs can chew, which, it claims, parody famous trademarks on luxury products, including those of Louis Vuitton Malletier. The particular Haute Diggity Dog chew toys in question here are small imitations of handbags that are labeled "Chewy Vuiton" and that mimic Louis Vuitton Malletier's LOUIS VUITTON handbags.

On cross-motions for summary judgment, the district court concluded that Haute Diggity Dog's "Chewy Vuiton" dog toys were successful parodies of Louis Vuitton Malletier's trademarks, designs, and products, and on that basis, entered judgment in favor of Haute Diggity Dog on all of Louis Vuitton Malletier's claims.

On appeal, we agree with the district court that Haute Diggity Dog's products are not likely to cause confusion with those of Louis Vuitton Malletier and that Louis Vuitton Malletier's copyright was not infringed. On the trademark dilution claim, however, we reject the district court's reasoning but reach the same conclusion through a different analysis. Accordingly, we affirm.

I

Louis Vuitton Malletier S.A. ("LVM") is a well known manufacturer of luxury luggage, leather goods, handbags, and accessories, which it markets and sells worldwide. In connection with the sale of its products, LVM has adopted trademarks and trade dress that are well recognized and have become famous and distinct. Indeed, in 2006, *BusinessWeek* ranked LOUIS VUITTON as the 17th "best brand" of all corporations in the world and the first "best brand" for any fashion business.

LVM has registered trademarks for "LOUIS VUITTON," in connection with luggage and ladies' handbags (the "LOUIS VUITTON mark"); for a stylized monogram of "LV," in connection with traveling bags and other goods (the "LV mark"); and for a monogram canvas design consisting of a canvas with repetitions of the LV mark along with four-pointed stars, four-pointed stars inset in curved diamonds, and four-pointed flowers inset in circles, in connection with traveling bags and other products (the "Monogram Canvas mark"). In 2002, LVM adopted a brightly-colored version of the Monogram Canvas mark in which the LV mark and the designs were of various colors and the background was white (the "Multicolor design"), created in collaboration with Japanese artist Takashi Murakami. For the Multicolor design, LVM obtained a copyright in 2004. In 2005, LVM adopted another design consisting of a canvas with repetitions of the LV mark and smiling cherries on a brown background (the "Cherry design").

As LVM points out, the Multicolor design and the Cherry design attracted immediate and extraordinary media attention and publicity in magazines such as *Vogue, W, Elle, Harper's Bazaar, Us Weekly, Life and Style, Travel & Leisure, People, In Style*, and *Jane*. The press published photographs showing celebrities carrying these handbags, including Jennifer Lopez, Madonna, Eve, Elizabeth Hurley, Carmen Electra, and Anna Kournikova, among others. When the Multicolor design first appeared in 2003, the magazines typically reported, "The Murakami designs for Louis Vuitton, which were the hit of the summer, came with hefty price tags and a long waiting list." *People Magazine* said, "the wait list is in the thousands." The handbags retailed in the range of $995 for a medium handbag to $4500 for a large travel bag. The medium size handbag that appears to be the model for the "Chewy Vuiton" dog toy retailed for $1190. The Cherry design appeared in 2005, and the handbags including that design were priced similarly—in the range of $995 to $2740. LVM does not currently market products using the Cherry design.

The original LOUIS VUITTON, LV, and Monogram Canvas marks, however, have been used as identifiers of LVM products continuously since 1896.

During the period 2003-2005, LVM spent more than $48 million advertising products using its marks and designs, including more than $4 million for the Multicolor design. It sells its products exclusively in LVM stores and in its own in-store boutiques that are contained within department stores such as Saks Fifth Avenue, Bloomingdale's, Neiman Marcus, and Macy's. LVM also advertises its products on the Internet through the specific websites www.louisvuitton.com and www.eluxury.com.

Although better known for its handbags and luggage, LVM also markets a limited selection of luxury pet accessories—collars, leashes, and dog carriers—which bear the Monogram Canvas mark and the Multicolor design. These items range in price from approximately $200 to $1600. LVM does not make dog toys.

Haute Diggity Dog, LLC, which is a relatively small and relatively new business located in Nevada, manufactures and sells nationally—primarily through pet stores—a line of pet chew toys and beds whose names parody elegant high-end brands of products such as perfume, cars, shoes, sparkling wine, and handbags. These include—in addition to Chewy Vuiton (LOUIS VUITTON)—Chewnel No. 5 (Chanel No. 5), Furcedes (Mercedes), Jimmy Chew (Jimmy Choo), Dog Perignonn (Dom Perignon), Sniffany & Co. (Tiffany & Co.), and Dogior (Dior). The chew toys and pet beds are plush, made of polyester, and have a shape and design that loosely imitate the signature product of the targeted brand. They are mostly distributed and sold through pet stores, although one or two Macy's stores carries Haute Diggity Dog's products. The dog toys are generally sold for less than $20, although larger versions of some of Haute Diggity Dog's plush dog beds sell for more than $100.

Haute Diggity Dog's "Chewy Vuiton" dog toys, in particular, loosely resemble miniature handbags and undisputedly evoke LVM handbags of similar shape, design, and color. In lieu of the LOUIS VUITTON mark, the dog toy uses "Chewy Vuiton"; in lieu of the LV mark, it uses "CV"; and the other symbols and colors employed are imitations, but not exact ones, of those used in the LVM Multicolor and Cherry designs. . . .

[The Court found that the Chewy Vuiton toys were successful parodies that were not likely to confuse consumers].

III

LVM also contends that Haute Diggity Dog's advertising, sale, and distribution of the "Chewy Vuiton" dog toys dilutes its LOUIS VUITTON, LV, and Monogram Canvas marks, which are famous and distinctive, in violation of the Trademark Dilution Revision Act of 2006 ("TDRA"), 15 U.S.C.A. § 1125(c) (West Supp. 2007). It argues, "Before the district court's decision, Vuitton's famous marks were unblurred by any third party trademark use." "Allowing defendants to become the first to use similar marks will obviously blur and dilute the Vuitton Marks." It also contends that "Chewy Vuiton" dog toys are likely to tarnish LVM's marks because they "pose a choking hazard for some dogs."

Haute Diggity Dog urges that, in applying the TDRA to the circumstances before us, we reject LVM's suggestion that a parody "automatically" gives rise to "actionable dilution." Haute Diggity Dog contends that only marks that are "identical or substantially similar" can give rise to actionable dilution, and its "Chewy Vuiton" marks are not identical or sufficiently similar to LVM's marks. It also argues that "[its] spoof, like other obvious parodies," " 'tends to increase public identification' of [LVM's] mark with [LVM]," quoting *Jordache*, 828 F.2d at 1490, rather than impairing its distinctiveness, as the TDRA requires. As for LVM's tarnishment claim, Haute Diggity Dog argues that LVM's position is at best based on speculation and that LVM has made no showing of a likelihood of dilution by tarnishment. . . .

[T]o state a dilution claim under the TDRA, a plaintiff must show:

(1) that the plaintiff owns a famous mark that is distinctive;
(2) that the defendant has commenced using a mark in commerce that allegedly is diluting the famous mark;
(3) that a similarity between the defendant's mark and the famous mark gives rise to an association between the marks; and
(4) that the association is likely to impair the distinctiveness of the famous mark or likely to harm the reputation of the famous mark.

In the context of blurring, distinctiveness refers to the ability of the famous mark uniquely to identify a single source and thus maintain its selling power. See N.Y. Stock Exch. v. N.Y., N.Y. Hotel LLC, 293 F.3d 550, 558 (2d Cir. 2002) (observing that blurring occurs where the defendant's use creates "the possibility that the [famous] mark will lose its ability to serve as a unique identifier of the plaintiff's product"). In proving a dilution claim under the TDRA, the plaintiff need not show actual or likely confusion, the presence of competition, or actual economic injury. See 15 U.S.C.A. §1125(c)(1).

The TDRA creates three defenses based on the defendant's (1) "fair use" (with exceptions); (2) "news reporting and news commentary"; and (3) "noncommercial use." Id. §1125(c)(3).

A

We address first LVM's claim for dilution by blurring.

The first three elements of a trademark dilution claim are not at issue in this case. LVM owns famous marks that are distinctive; Haute Diggity Dog has commenced using "Chewy Vuiton," "CV," and designs and colors that are allegedly diluting LVM's marks; and the similarity between Haute Diggity Dog's marks and LVM's marks gives rise to an association between the marks, albeit a parody. The issue for resolution is whether the association between Haute Diggity Dog's marks and LVM's marks is likely to impair the distinctiveness of LVM's famous marks.

In deciding this issue, the district court correctly outlined the six factors to be considered in determining whether dilution by blurring has been shown. See 15 U.S.C.A. §1125(c)(2)(B). But in evaluating the facts of the case, the court did not directly apply those factors it enumerated. It held simply:

> [The famous mark's] strength is not likely to be blurred by a parody dog toy product. Instead of blurring Plaintiff's mark, the success of the parodic use depends upon the continued association with LOUIS VUITTON.

Louis Vuitton Malletier, 464 F. Supp. 2d at 505. The amicus supporting LVM's position in this case contends that the district court, by not applying the statutory factors, misapplied the TDRA to conclude that simply because Haute Diggity Dog's product was a parody meant that "there can be no association with the famous mark as a matter of law." Moreover, the amicus points out correctly that to rule in favor of Haute Diggity Dog, the district court was required to find that the "association" did not impair the distinctiveness of LVM's famous mark.

LVM goes further in its own brief, however, and . . . suggests that any use by a third person of an imitation of its famous marks dilutes the famous marks as a matter of law. This contention misconstrues the TDRA.

The TDRA prohibits a person from using a junior mark that is likely to dilute (by blurring) the famous mark, and blurring is defined to be an impairment to the famous mark's distinctiveness. "Distinctiveness" in turn refers to the public's recognition that the famous mark identifies a single source of the product using the famous mark.

To determine whether a junior mark is likely to dilute a famous mark through blurring, the TDRA directs the court to consider all factors relevant to the issue, including six factors that are enumerated in the statute:

(i) The degree of similarity between the mark or trade name and the famous mark.
(ii) The degree of inherent or acquired distinctiveness of the famous mark.
(iii) The extent to which the owner of the famous mark is engaging in substantially exclusive use of the mark.
(iv) The degree of recognition of the famous mark.
(v) Whether the user of the mark or trade name intended to create an association with the famous mark.
(vi) Any actual association between the mark or trade name and the famous mark.

15 U.S.C.A. § 1125(c)(2)(B). Not every factor will be relevant in every case, and not every blurring claim will require extensive discussion of the factors. But a trial court must offer a sufficient indication of which factors it has found persuasive and explain why they are persuasive so that the court's decision can be reviewed. The district court did not do this adequately in this case. Nonetheless, after we apply the factors as a matter of law, we reach the same conclusion reached by the district court.

We begin by noting that parody is not automatically a complete defense to a claim of dilution by blurring where the defendant uses the parody as its own designation of source, i.e., as a trademark. Although the TDRA does provide that fair use is a complete defense and allows that a parody can be considered fair use, it does not extend the fair use defense to parodies used as a trademark. As the statute provides:

> The following shall not be actionable as dilution by blurring or dilution by tarnishment under this subsection:
>
> > (A) Any fair use . . . other than as a designation of source for the person's own goods or services, including use in connection with . . . parodying. . . .

15 U.S.C.A. § 1125(c)(3)(A)(ii) (emphasis added). Under the statute's plain language, parodying a famous mark is protected by the fair use defense only if the parody is not "a designation of source for the person's own goods or services."

The TDRA, however, does not require a court to ignore the existence of a parody that is used as a trademark, and it does not preclude a court from considering parody as part of the circumstances to be considered for determining whether the plaintiff has made out a claim for dilution by blurring. Indeed, the statute permits a court to consider "all relevant factors," including the six factors supplied in § 1125(c)(2)(B).

Thus, it would appear that a defendant's use of a mark as a parody is relevant to the overall question of whether the defendant's use is likely to impair the famous mark's distinctiveness. Moreover, the fact that the defendant uses its marks as a parody is specifically relevant to several of the listed factors. For example, factor (v) (whether the defendant intended to create an association with the famous mark) and factor (vi) (whether there exists an actual association between the defendant's mark and the famous mark) directly invite inquiries into the defendant's intent in using the parody, the defendant's actual use of the parody, and the effect that its use has on the famous mark. While a parody intentionally creates an association with the famous mark in order to be a parody, it also intentionally communicates, if it is successful, that it is not the famous mark, but rather a satire of the famous mark. See *PETA*, 263 F.3d at 366. That the defendant is using its mark as a parody is therefore relevant in the consideration of these statutory factors.

Similarly, factors (i), (ii), and (iv) — the degree of similarity between the two marks, the degree of distinctiveness of the famous mark, and its recognizability — are directly implicated by consideration of the fact that the defendant's mark is a successful parody. Indeed, by making the famous mark an object of the parody, a successful parody might actually enhance the famous mark's distinctiveness by making it an icon. The brunt of the joke becomes yet more famous. See *Hormel Foods*, 73 F.3d at 506 (observing that a successful parody "tends to increase public identification" of the famous mark with its source); see also Yankee Publ'g Inc. v. News Am. Publ'g Inc., 809 F. Supp. 267, 272-82 (S.D.N.Y. 1992) (suggesting that a sufficiently obvious parody is unlikely to blur the targeted famous mark).

In sum, while a defendant's use of a parody as a mark does not support a "fair use" defense, it may be considered in determining whether the plaintiff-owner of a famous mark has proved its claim that the defendant's use of a parody mark is likely to impair the distinctiveness of the famous mark.

In the case before us, when considering factors (ii), (iii), and (iv), it is readily apparent, indeed conceded by Haute Diggity Dog, that LVM's marks are distinctive, famous, and strong. The LOUIS VUITTON mark is well known and is commonly identified as a brand of the great Parisian fashion house, Louis Vuitton Malletier. So too are its other marks and designs, which are invariably used with the LOUIS VUITTON mark. It may not be too strong to refer to these famous marks as icons of high fashion.

While the establishment of these facts satisfies essential elements of LVM's dilution claim, see 15 U.S.C.A. § 1125(c)(1), the facts impose on LVM an increased burden to demonstrate that the distinctiveness of its famous marks is likely to be impaired by a successful parody. Even as Haute Diggity Dog's parody mimics the famous mark, it communicates simultaneously that it is not the famous mark, but is only satirizing it. See *PETA*, 263 F.3d at 366. And because the famous mark is particularly strong and distinctive, it becomes more likely that a parody will not impair the distinctiveness of the mark. In short, as Haute Diggity Dog's "Chewy Vuiton" marks are a successful parody, we conclude that they will not blur the distinctiveness of the famous mark as a unique identifier of its source.

It is important to note, however, that this might not be true if the parody is so similar to the famous mark that it likely could be construed as actual use of the famous mark itself. Factor (i) directs an inquiry into the "degree of similarity between the junior mark and the famous mark." If Haute Diggity Dog used the actual marks of LVM (as a parody or otherwise), it could dilute LVM's marks by blurring, regardless of whether Haute Diggity Dog's use was confusingly similar, whether it was in competition with LVM, or whether LVM sustained actual injury. See 15 U.S.C.A. § 1125(c)(1). Thus, "the use of DUPONT shoes, BUICK aspirin, and KODAK pianos would be actionable" under the TDRA because the unauthorized use of the famous marks themselves on unrelated goods might diminish the capacity of these trademarks to distinctively identify a single source. *Moseley*, 537 U.S. at 431 (quoting H.R. Rep. No. 104-374, at 3 (1995), as reprinted in 1995 U.S.C.C.A.N. 1029, 1030). This is true even though a consumer would be unlikely to confuse the manufacturer of KODAK film with the hypothetical producer of KODAK pianos.

But in this case, Haute Diggity Dog mimicked the famous marks; it did not come so close to them as to destroy the success of its parody and, more importantly, to diminish the LVM marks' capacity to identify a single source. Haute Diggity Dog designed a pet chew toy to imitate and suggest, but not use, the marks of a high-fashion LOUIS VUITTON handbag. It used "Chewy Vuiton" to mimic "LOUIS VUITTON"; it used "CV" to mimic "LV"; and it adopted imperfectly the items of LVM's designs. We conclude that these uses by Haute Diggity Dog were not so similar as to be likely to impair the distinctiveness of LVM's famous marks.

In a similar vein, when considering factors (v) and (vi), it becomes apparent that Haute Diggity Dog intentionally associated its marks, but only partially and certainly imperfectly, so as to convey the simultaneous message that it was not in fact a source of LVM products. Rather, as a parody, it separated itself from the LVM marks in order to make fun of them.

In sum, when considering the relevant factors to determine whether blurring is likely to occur in this case, we readily come to the conclusion, as did the district court, that LVM has failed to make out a case of trademark dilution by blurring by failing to establish that the distinctiveness of its marks was likely to be impaired by Haute Diggity Dog's marketing and sale of its "Chewy Vuiton" products.

B

LVM's claim for dilution by tarnishment does not require an extended discussion. To establish its claim for dilution by tarnishment, LVM must show, in lieu of blurring, that Haute Diggity Dog's use of the "Chewy Vuiton" mark on dog toys harms the reputation of the LOUIS VUITTON mark and LVM's other marks. LVM argues that the possibility that a dog could choke on a "Chewy Vuiton" toy causes this harm. LVM has, however, provided no record support for its assertion. It relies only on speculation about whether a dog could choke on the chew toys and a logical concession that a $10 dog toy made in China was of "inferior quality" to the $1190 LOUIS VUITTON handbag. The speculation begins with LVM's assertion in its brief that "defendant Woofie's admitted that 'Chewy Vuiton' products pose a choking hazard for some dogs. Having prejudged the defendant's mark to be a parody, the district court made light of this admission in its opinion, and utterly failed to give it the weight it deserved," citing to a page in the district court's opinion where the court states:

> At oral argument, plaintiff provided only a flimsy theory that a pet may some day choke on a Chewy Vuiton squeak toy and incite the wrath of a confused consumer against LOUIS VUITTON.

Louis Vuitton Malletier, 464 F. Supp. 2d at 505. The court was referring to counsel's statement during oral argument that the owner of Woofie's stated that "she would not sell this product to certain types of dogs because there is a danger they would tear it open and choke on it." There is no record support, however, that any dog has choked on a pet chew toy, such as a "Chewy Vuiton" toy, or that there is any basis from which to conclude that a dog would likely choke on such a toy.

We agree with the district court that LVM failed to demonstrate a claim for dilution by tarnishment. See *Hormel Foods*, 73 F.3d at 507. . . .

The judgment of the district court is

AFFIRMED.

COMMENTS AND QUESTIONS

1. Are consumers likely to be confused by the defendant's use of Chewy Vuiton for dog toys? If not, why doesn't that fact also dispose of the dilution case? Are you persuaded that dilution should apply to marks in the same market, even if they are not confusingly similar? If so, what role is there left for a trademark infringement claim in such a case? Is dilution a form of "super-trademark law"? In Moseley v. V Secret Catalogue, 537 U.S. 418 (2003), the court said:

> Unlike traditional infringement law, the prohibitions against trademark dilution are not the product of common-law development, and are not motivated by an interest in protecting consumers.

Is that right? If not protecting consumers, what purpose does dilution law serve?

2. *Does Dilution Protection Make Any Difference in Practice?* Commentators have long asserted that the very marks that qualify for dilution protection rarely need it. This is because such marks will likely win the conventional likelihood of confusion cause of action both because of their enormous fame and because the scope of the likelihood of confusion cause of action has expanded dramatically in the past few decades. *See, e.g.*, Mark P. McKenna, *The Normative Foundations of Trademark Law*, 82 Notre Dame L. Rev. 1839, 1913-14 (2007). For example, if a defendant were to begin to sell Coca-Cola brand bicycles, how likely is it that Coca-Cola's lawyers would be able to prove some degree of confusion?

Empirical evidence suggests that when courts consider both confusion and dilution, their dilution determinations are usually redundant of their confusion determinations. One study found that in the year following the October 6, 2006, effective date of the TDRA, no reported federal court opinion that considered both confusion and dilution found the latter but not the former. *See* Barton Beebe, *The Continuing Debacle of U.S. Antidilution Law: Evidence from the First Year of Trademark Dilution Revision Act Case Law*, 24 Santa Clara Computer & High Tech. L.J. 449 (2008). This trend appears to have continued. In the three and a half years following the effective date of the TDRA, two reported federal court opinions have analyzed both confusion and dilution and found the latter but not the former, and one of these opinions was a dissent. *See* Hershey Co. v. Art Van Furniture, Inc., No. 08 Civ. 14463, 2008 WL 4724756 (E.D. Mich. Oct. 24, 2008); American Century Proprietary Holdings, Inc. v. American Century Casualty Co., 295 Fed. Appx. 630 (5th Cir. Oct. 3, 2008) (Garwood, J., dissenting).

This is not to say that the dilution case of action never provides relief not already provided by a confusion cause of action. As in *Nikepal*, courts may decline to consider confusion at all in their opinions and move directly to a finding of dilution.

3. *Nature of Harm Flowing from Tarnishment.* Tarnishment arises where a junior user undermines the image that consumers hold of a famous mark by using the mark to advertise unsavory products. For example, the marketing of posters printed with the words "Enjoy Cocaine" featuring the same typeface and red and white color scheme as Coca-Cola's "Enjoy Coca-Cola" advertisements was found to tarnish Coca-Cola's famous mark. *See* Coca-Cola Co. v. Gemini Rising, Inc., 346 F. Supp. 1183 (E.D.N.Y. 1972); *see also* Dallas Cowboys Cheerleaders, Inc. v. Pussycat Cinema, Ltd., 604 F.2d 200 (2d Cir. 1979) (dilution to promote a pornographic movie by suggesting that Dallas Cowboys Cheerleaders were participants and to use actresses whose costumes resembled those of the Dallas Cowboys cheerleaders).

By contrast, using a mark to criticize the mark's owner is not tarnishment under the statute. Nor is it illegal to use the mark to display or refer to the plaintiff's own product, even if it is in a context the plaintiff might find repugnant. For example, in Wham-O, Inc. v. Paramount Pictures Corp., 286 F. Supp. 2d 1254 (C.D. Cal. 2003), the owner of the Slip 'N Slide trademark sued the makers of the film "Dickie Roberts: Former Child Star" over a scene in which the fictional Roberts injured himself by misusing a Slip 'N Slide water slide. The court held that the film's depiction of the product was "silly" but could not tarnish the plaintiff's mark. *See also* Caterpillar Inc. v. Walt Disney Co., 287 F. Supp. 2d 913 (N.D. Ill. 2003) (depicting plaintiff's bulldozers being used by a villain in a children's movie did not tarnish plaintiff's marks). Rather, tarnishment occurs only when the famous mark is used on the *defendant's* unsavory goods, causing the public to draw a connection between the plaintiff's goods and the defendant's.

4. *Dilution by "Genericization"?* Some argue that dilution can occur through genericization of a famous mark, *see* Elliott Staffin, *The Dilution Doctrine: Towards Reconciliation with the Lanham Act*, 6 Fordham Intell. Prop. Media & Ent. L.J. 105, 139-42 (1995), though no court has endorsed such a theory. It is likely foreclosed by the 2006 statutory revisions, since such a use is by definition use "otherwise than as a designation of source" and so subject to an exception under Section 1125(c)(3). *See also* Freecycle Network v. Oey, 505 F.3d 898, 906 (9th Cir. 2007) ("[t]he Lanham Act itself, however, contains no provision preventing the use of a trademarked term in its generic sense.").

Which claim was at issue in *Louis Vuitton*?

5. *Dual Requirements of Distinctiveness and Fame?* In Nabisco, Inc. v. PF Brands, 191 F.3d 208 (2d Cir. 1999), the court suggested that the FTDA required proof of both distinctiveness of the plaintiff's mark and fame in order to receive federal protection. The practical effect of this interpretation was to exclude descriptive marks from dilution protection. McDonald's, United Airlines, Ace Hardware, National Semiconductor, and American Airlines were not eligible for federal dilution protection under the Second Circuit approach because they are not inherently distinctive marks (even though they could well meet the "fame" requirement).

The 2006 revisions to the dilution statute reversed this decision, making it clear in subsection (c)(1) that famous marks can be either inherently distinctive or have acquired distinctiveness.

Should the law extend dilution protection to descriptive marks? Is there a greater need for companies in other fields to use those marks than there is to use an inherently distinctive mark? *Consider* Visa Int'l Serv. Ass'n v. JSL Corp., 2010 WL 2559003, ____ F.3d ____ (9th Cir. June 28, 2010) (affirming the district courts' finding that eVisa for an English language school in Japan diluted the famous Visa credit card mark). Can the use of an English language term ("visa") dilute the brand significance of a mark even if the term is used in its descriptive sense? Could Apple Computer sue a seller of fruit that used the term "apple" prominently?

6. *Should Anti-dilution Protection Be Provided to Trade Dress?* In Nabisco, Inc. v. PF Brands, 191 F.3d 208 (2d Cir. 1999), the declaratory defendant Pepperidge Farm claimed that its goldfish-shaped "Goldfish" crackers were diluted by Nabisco's "Cat-Dog" crackers, which included goldfish-shaped crackers. The Second Circuit affirmed the district court's finding of dilution.

7. *Noncommercial and Non-trademark Uses.* The dilution statute requires that the defendant's use be use as a "mark or trade name," not simply use "otherwise than as a designation of source." Whatever the merits of a general trademark use requirement (discussed above), therefore, it seems that the defendant must engage in trademark use to be liable under the dilution statute. *See* Stacey L. Dogan & Mark A. Lemley, *The Trademark Use Requirement in Dilution Cases*, 24 SANTA CLARA COMPUTER & HIGH TECH. L.J. 571 (2008). Thus, mere registration of a trademark as a domain name does not constitute commercial use. As explained by one court,

> [w]hen a domain name is used only to indicate an address on the Internet, the domain name is not functioning as a trademark. . . . NSI's acceptance of domain name registrations is connected only with the names' technical function on the Internet to designate a set of computers. . . . Something more than the registration of the name is required before the use of a domain name is infringing.

Lockheed Martin Corp. v. Network Solutions, Inc., 985 F. Supp. 949, 956-57 (C.D. Cal. 1997), *aff'd*, 141 F.3d 1316 (9th Cir. 1998).

8. *Referential Uses; Comparative Advertising.* It is a defense to a dilution claim that the famous mark was used in lawful comparative advertising. In Ty, Inc. v. Perryman, 306 F.3d 509 (7th Cir. 2002), the court held that it also could not dilute a mark to use it to refer to the trademark owner. Ty, the maker of Beanie Babies, sued an individual who accurately advertised second-hand Beanie Babies for resale. Judge Posner's opinion explained that there was no blurring or tarnishment of the Beanie Baby mark here, since the use of the mark was only to refer accurately to the plaintiff's own goods. The court acknowledged Ty's argument that Perryman was free-riding on the fame of its mark, but said that "in that attenuated sense of free riding, almost everyone in business is free riding." [We discuss this issue further in the section on nominative use, *infra.*]

Subsection (3) of the statute creates a broad list of things exempt from the reach of the dilution statute, including all noncommercial uses, fair uses, non-trademark uses, comparative advertising, news reporting, parody, commentary, and criticism. Given these defenses, was there any need for Judge Posner to decide that there was no blurring or tarnishment in *Ty*? Could he simply have relied on the exemption for non-trademark use?

9. *International Scope of Dilution Protection.* The Paris Convention, including Article 6*bis*, is silent on the protection of trademarks against dilution. GATT-TRIPs signatory countries, however, must now provide some form of protection against dilution of a mark, at least if it is famous.

> Article 6*bis* of the Paris Convention (1967) shall apply, mutatis mutandis, to goods or services which are not similar to those in respect of which a trademark is registered, provided that use of that trademark in relation to those goods or services would indicate a connection between those goods and services and the owner of the registered trademark and provided that the interests of the owner of the registered trademark are likely to be damaged by such use.

Final Act Embodying the Results of the Uruguay Round of Multilateral Trade Negotiations, done at Marrakech, Morocco, April 15, 1994, Annex 1C: Agreement on Trade-Related Aspects of Intellectual Property Rights ("TRIPs"), at Article 16(3). For congressional approval, see Uruguay Rounds Agreements Act, Pub. L. No. 103-465, Dec. 8, 1994. Why can a mark not currently used in a country be protected against dilution in another country? Does it matter whether the mark is registered? Should foreign marks be protected against dilution in anticipation of their possible entry into the market? This provision has been used to target "trademark pirates": individuals who identify famous trademarks not yet used in their country and register those marks in anticipation of the famous trademark owner's expansion abroad.

Note on Dilution and "Search Theory"

How would you define the harm that comes with dilution in terms of the consumer search rationale described earlier in this chapter? As a consumer, is locating Kodak film in the store or picking out the Kodak film ad in a magazine more difficult if there are many unassociated products or ads that use the Kodak name? As an experiment, try walking down the "generic" aisle in a supermarket, where all the boxes are plain black and white, trying to pick out the macaroni among the spaghetti, rigatoni, and so on. Would distinctive labels — all brightly colored, with striking designs — make a difference? From a certain distance, to take a different example, it is difficult to pick out a single marathon runner from the crowd of other runners, even though — or because — each runner is dressed in day-glo warmups, running shoes, and so on. The point is simply this: If many products share a similar label, the fact that the label is striking when viewed in isolation is irrelevant. It is as difficult to discern a single blazing orange poppy in a field full of them as it is to identify a lone grey pebble out of a rock pile.

If, as suggested earlier, attention spans are truly taxed in the current era, with its barrage of information and images, dilution may be an even more important adjunct to traditional "consumer confusion" rationales for trademarks. Indeed, the harm that dilution seeks to address might best be described as a loss of consumer *attention* due to the proliferation of similar or identical symbols of trade. Rebecca Tushnet documents this loss of attention, pointing to studies that show that it takes consumers longer to recognize dilute marks than unique ones. Rebecca Tushnet, *Gone in Sixty Milliseconds: Trademark Law and Cognitive Science*, 86 Tex. L. Rev. 507 (2008). The difference is measured in milliseconds, though.

Trademark owners thus seek to protect the distinctiveness of their marks — first, to ensure a moment of unfettered attention, and then to indicate a unique connection between the mark and the seller's product. For an argument that prohibiting trademark dilution is consistent with the law's general focus on reducing consumer search costs, see Stacey L. Dogan & Mark A. Lemley, *The Merchandising Right: Fragile Theory or Fait Accompli?*, 54 EMORY L.J. 461 (2005). *But see* Tushnet, *supra* (arguing that if this attention deficit was indeed a problem dilution law would have to prevent far more uses than in fact it does).

PROBLEMS

Problem 5-3. Mead Data Central is the owner of the registered trademark LEXIS for a legal and business-related electronic database. The service is extremely well known among lawyers, but not among the general public.

A decade after the first use of the Lexis mark, Toyota names its new luxury car the "Lexus." Mead sues for dilution of its Lexis mark. What result? On what facts does your decision depend?

Problem 5-4. The National Pork Producers Council has registered as a trademark the phrase "The Other White Meat" in connection with its promotion of the consumption of pork. Through over $500 million worth of advertising, the phrase has become well known in the United States. Supreme Lobster and Seafood Company subsequently begins to use the phrase "The Other Red Meat" in connection with its sale in various parts of the country of fresh and frozen salmon. The National Pork Producers Council sues for dilution. What result?

Note on Trademark Preemption

There has been surprisingly little litigation over the preemptive effect of the Lanham Act. Because the Lanham Act was passed under the aegis of the Commerce Clause of the Constitution, rather than the Patent and Copyright Clause, other IP preemption cases are not directly relevant to the problem of trademark preemption. Instead, courts turn to Commerce Clause cases, which focus on whether Congress intended to "preempt the field" of trademark law and on whether there is an actual or potential conflict between the state and federal statutes.

Two early cases held that the Lanham Act preempted all state trademark laws. Sargen & Co. v. Welco Feed Mfg., 195 F.2d 929 (8th Cir. 1952); Time, Inc. v. T.I.M.E. Inc., 123 F. Supp. 446 (S.D. Cal. 1954). But commentators are skeptical of these broad preemptive holdings, largely because Congress clearly intended in passing the Lanham Act to allow it to coexist with some state trademark laws. *See* 15 U.S.C. §§1065, 1115(b)(5) (both referring to the continued effect of state law). *See* Richard A. De Sevo, *Antidilution Laws: The Unresolved Dilemma of Preemption Under the Lanham Act*, 84 TRADEMARK REP. 300, 301-04 (1994). However, at least some courts continue to hold that state statutes which are directed at the same types of conduct as the Lanham Act are preempted. *See* Three Blind Mice Designs Co. v. Cyrk Inc., 892 F. Supp. 303 (D. Mass. 1995) (state anti-dilution statute "wholly preempted" to the extent that it seeks to regulate directly competitive goods).

A more difficult question is presented where state trademark statutes may conflict with the general federal rule. Sometimes such conflicts are clear. For example, state laws that attempt to grant priority to a party other than the earliest federal registrant are surely preempted under 15 U.S.C. §1127, since the laws "interfere" with the rights granted federal registrants under the Act.

Preemption will also occur if the state law is at odds with the "purpose of Congress" in passing the Lanham Act. Before the passage into law of the 1995 FTDA, state anti-dilution laws might very well have failed this test, since they did not require a likelihood of consumer confusion. *See* De Sevo, *supra*, at 312-20. Courts and commentators split on this issue. *See* David S. Welkowitz, *Preemption, Extraterritoriality and the Problem of State Antidilution Laws*, 67 TUL. L. REV. 1, 4 (1992) (arguing that "injunctions like the one issued in Mead Data Central, Inc. v. Toyota Motor Sales, U.S.A., 702 F. Supp. 1031 (S.D.N.Y. 1988), *rev'd on other grounds*, 875 F.2d 1026 (2d Cir. 1989) exceed [constitutional] limits" under the Commerce Clause, though state anti-dilution statutes are not wholly preempted, and in many cases injunctions based on state intellectual property law are enforceable under the Full Faith and Credit Clause). *Cf.* Milton W. Handler, *Are the State Antidilution Laws Compatible with the National Protection of Trademarks?*, 75 TRADEMARK REP. 269 (1985); Joseph P. Bauer, *A Federal Law of Unfair Competition: What Should Be the Reach of Section 43(a) of the Lanham Act?*, 31 UCLA L. REV. 671 (1984); Charles Bunn, *The National Law of Unfair Competition*, 62 HARV. L. REV. 987 (1949); Paul Heald, *Comment, Unfair Competition and Federal Law: Constitutional Restraints on the Scope of State Law*, 54 U. CHI. L. REV. 1411 (1987).

The creation of a federal anti-dilution law in 1995 changed the preemption analysis, of course. Many people expected that such a law would preempt state anti-dilution statutes, replacing the patchwork of inconsistent protections with uniform national protection.[3] Instead, Section 43(c)(3) of the 1995 FTDA charted a narrow course around state anti-dilution laws by allowing them to continue in force but granting owners of federally registered marks immunity from suit under such state laws. Unregistered marks, as well as those registered under state law, received no such immunity. The legislative history explains:

> Under section 3 of the bill, a new Section 43(c)(3) of the Lanham Act would provide that ownership of a valid federal trademark registration is a complete bar to an action brought against the registrant under state dilution law. This section provides a further incentive for the federal registration of marks and recognizes that to permit a state to regulate the use of federally registered marks is inconsistent with the intent of the Lanham Act "to protect registered marks used in such commerce from interference by state, or territorial legislation." It is important to note that *the proposed federal dilution statute would not preempt state dilution laws.* Unlike patent and copyright laws, federal trademark law coexists with state trademark law, and it is to be expected that the federal dilution statute should similarly coexist with state dilution statutes.

3. Indeed, some saw little purpose for the federal law otherwise. *See* Kenneth L. Port, *The "Unnatural" Expansion of Trademark Rights: Is a Federal Dilution Statute Necessary?*, 18 SETON HALL LEGIS. J. 433 (1994).

Federal Trademark Dilution Act of 1995, H.R. REP. No. 104-374 at 7 (1995) (accompanying H.R. 1295) (emphasis added).

The situation after the 2006 TDRA is even more complicated. Because of a (likely inadvertent) change to the numbering of statutory sections, Lanham Act §43(c)(6)(B) can now be read to preempt any trademark-like claim to the extent it is asserted against a federally registered mark. *See* MCCARTHY, MCCARTHY ON TRADEMARKS AND UNFAIR COMPETITION, §24:129. *But see* Jada Toys, Inc. v. Mattel, Inc., 518 F.3d 628, 635 n.4 (2008) (finding that the bar to state unfair competition actions established by §43(c)(6)(B) is inapplicable where the state law claimant seeks cancellation of the federally registered mark).

Thus parallel state anti-dilution claims will not wither away completely. Indeed, depending on whether state law affords more attractive remedies (note the "injunction only" rule for most cases under the federal dilution provision, §43(c)(2)), parties may well continue to bring at least some anti-dilution cases under state law, particularly because state anti-dilution laws typically do not establish as high a standard for the famousness of the mark as federal anti-dilution law does. *See* MCCARTHY, MCCARTHY ON TRADEMARKS AND UNFAIR COMPETITION, §24:87. Note that for the most part, however, nationwide injunctions are more difficult to acquire under state anti-dilution statutes, making federal claims more likely if such an injunction is the trademark owner's major goal.

COMMENTS AND QUESTIONS

Is the lack of preemption troubling? Consider the following possibilities:

- A federal anti-dilution claim fails because the use is found to be a "fair" one (say, for news reporting purposes). A parallel action is brought under a state statute that contains no such limitation, and the court grants a nationwide injunction against dilution on the basis of the state statute.
- A nationally famous but unregistered product configuration is found to dilute a locally known product configuration under a state statute.

Do the state statutes at issue in these cases interfere with federal trademark policy?

D. EXTENSION BY CONTRACT: FRANCHISING AND MERCHANDISING

Trademarks and Organizational Forms: The Growth of Franchising. From its modern founding, trademark law has been at the service of emerging patterns in the organization of industry. In the beginning, that meant protecting emerging channels of trade in relatively local settings. Next came the great nationalization of the economy with the growth of large retail empires in the late nineteenth and early twentieth centuries. Today, trademarks form an integral part of the variegated economic landscape of the industrialized world.

Business historian Mira Wilkins has written:

> The legally-backed trade marks . . . became essential intangible assets, providing the basis for the rise of the modern enterprise. . . . The trade mark's fundamental contribution to the modern corporation was that it generated efficiency gains by creating for the firm the opportunity for large sales over long periods. . . . Without the trade mark, the introduction and acceptance by buyers of modern products, produced with economies of scale or scope, and marketed over long distances, would have been impossible. . . . The trade mark by reducing the costs of information led to efficiencies in production and distribution.

Mira Wilkins, *The Neglected Intangible Asset: The Influence of the Trademark on the Rise of the Modern Corporation*, 34 Bus. & Hist. 66, 87-88 (1992). Interestingly, Wilkins also points out the role that trademarks play in facilitating organizational diversity, or making possible various alternative forms of production. The clearest and most important recent example is franchising.

Trademarks are the "cornerstone of a franchise system." Susser v. Carvel Corp., 206 F. Supp. 636, 640 (S.D.N.Y. 1962), *aff'd*, 332 F.2d 505, *cert. granted*, 379 U.S. 885, *cert. dismissed*, 381 U.S. 125 (1965). The trademark of the franchisor is the identifiable symbol of continuity; it indicates the presence of the national brand at each location. Thus, whatever the precise nature of the franchise, the franchisor and franchisee are very likely to be parties to a trademark license agreement.

Here again we see the stretching of traditional theory. The individual source from which the national brand emanates is the franchisor. This is often a remote corporate entity, whereas one could argue that the franchisee is the real "source" (at the local level) of the goods. To maintain uniformity (and stay on the good side of the abandonment issue; see below), the franchisor almost invariably imposes certain contractual requirements on the franchisee. Yet it is still the franchisee, in the last instance, who actually runs the establishment where the goods are sold. *See* James M. Treece, *Trademark Licensing and Vertical Restraints in Franchising Arrangements*, 116 U. Pa. L. Rev. 435 (1968); Lynn M. LoPucki, *Toward a Trademark-Based Liability System*, 49 UCLA L. Rev. 1099 (2002) (suggesting that tort liability should follow the trademark rather than the franchisee).

In economic terms, franchising is an interesting mix of contractual and integrated governance characteristics — a kind of hybrid organization in which the franchisee is neither an employee of the franchisor nor an arm's-length buyer of the franchisor's goods. *See* James A. Brickley & Frederick H. Dark, *The Choice of Organizational Form: The Case of Franchising*, 18 J. Fin. Econ. 401, 403-07 (1987); Gillian K. Hadfield, *Problematic Relations: Franchising and the Law of Incomplete Contracts*, 42 Stan. L. Rev. 927 (1990). The franchise trademark plays an interesting role in this relationship. It is one of the franchisor's great assets, one of the things it can sell to franchisees. Yet once a franchisee begins to use the trademark, he or she is in a position to harm the franchise's reputation by selling inferior quality goods. (Note that doing so hurts other franchisees as well.) Indeed, if many of the franchise's customers are travelers who come from afar and do not pass through often, a franchisee might be tempted to "free-ride" off the quality investments of the franchisor and other franchisees by selling inferior goods. Many of the provisions in franchise agreements are directed at preventing such an outcome, for example, agreements to purchase ingredients and other inputs from the franchisor, stipulations to frequent inspections, and profit-sharing arrangements. *See* Paul H. Rubin, *The Theory of the Firm and the Structure of the Franchise Contract*, 21 J.L. & ECON. 223 (1978). *Cf.* Patrick J. Kaufman & Francine Lafontaine, *Costs of Control: The Source of Economic Rents for McDonald's Franchisees*, 37 J.L. & ECON. 417 (1994) (finding substantial "rents" or profits left to the franchisee after the franchisor's "cut," indicating that incentive system in franchise contracts was working). In this complicated relationship, trademarks are a key strategic asset. Note also that in many states various aspects of franchise contracts — especially termination provisions — are closely regulated. *See, e.g.*, Thomas M. Pitegoff, *Franchise Relationship Laws: A Minefield for Franchisors*, 45 BUS. LAW. 289 (1989).

What significance does the growth of franchising have for trademark doctrine? Should we be concerned about the disaggregation of trademarks from the goods they represent? See the discussion in the previous section on trademarks sold as valuable items in and of themselves. Does the selling of trademarks without goods attached to them make trademark owners less able to use the mark as a guarantee of quality? Alternatively, does it suggest that the trademark owner will invest even more in quality assurance, since the value of the mark is all it has to offer? *See* Mark A. Lemley & Mark P. McKenna, *Owning Mark(et)s*, 109 MICH. L. REV. 137 (2010) (casting doubt on the social value of protecting marks as goods in and of themselves).

"Turning Logos into Profit Centers." Evidence is everywhere that a boom is under way in the licensing of trademarks. From sports team logos to university names to designer symbols, badges of affiliation and prestige are ever more common on products of all kinds. And, importantly, these badges come at a premium. As Robert Denicola has written,

> [a]t any sporting goods store one can find plain, unadorned shirts, shorts, and jackets in assorted styles and colors. They are usually near the rear. Closer to the front are items apparently similar in all respects except one — they are prominently decorated with a variety of words and symbols. Some bear the names of athletic equipment manufacturers. Others display the names or insignia of professional sports teams, the name and seal of the state university, or the nickname and mascot of the local high school. They frequently cost significantly more than the items in the rear, yet they sell.

Robert C. Denicola, *Institutional Publicity Rights: An Analysis of the Merchandising of Famous Trade Symbols*, 62 N.C. L. REV. 603 (1983).

Turning logos into profit centers may make sense as a business strategy, but it poses problems for the legal system. The cases in this chapter highlight the fundamental problem: Traditionally, trademarks were thought of as symbols representing products, rather than as products in and of themselves. Thus traditional trademark law protects a trademark only because, and only insofar as, it is emblematic of the goodwill behind a product. The mark itself is not the point; it is simply a vehicle to convey useful information regarding a product's quality, prestige, and so on. The trademark guides the consumer to the transaction; sale of the underlying product is the "profit center."

All this changes when the trademark becomes the *subject* of the transaction rather than an adjunct to it. In such a transaction, the mark does not represent the product: It *is* the product.

Consider, for example, the licensing of a sports team logo for use on a T-shirt or hat. The logo does not summarize information about the quality of the hat; it demonstrates loyalty to a team. Indeed, many if not most sports logos are licensed to a broad array of products, many of differing degrees of quality. The "high end" Red Sox cap ("just like the pros wear!") is a far different product — qua hat — than the cheap synthetic cap costing a few dollars and sold in discount stores. The same is true for sweatshirts and T-shirts emblazoned with the logos of college and professional teams. Similar examples can be drawn from other avenues of commerce. Thus, outdoor equipment companies with a certain consumer cachet have been known to lend their logos for application to sport-utility vehicles. Yet no one, or very few, can suppose that companies specializing in backpacks, long underwear, and hiking boots have suddenly taken up truck production.

In these cases, the consumer is buying an image. The trademark owner possesses rights in a symbol associated with certain qualities. Lending that symbol to diverse products connects those products to the feelings the symbol evokes. (The same thing happens outside commerce as well; consider the difference when the "stars and stripes" image is added to a plain object such as a flag or a tombstone.)

Trademark law has begun to recognize the importance of the logo as a product. For instance, a 1975 case held that unauthorized sales of team emblems violated the Lanham Act:

> The certain knowledge of the buyer that the source and origin of the trademark symbols were the plaintiffs satisfies the requirements of the Act. The argument that confusion must be as to source of the manufacture of the emblem itself is unpersuasive, where the trademark, originated by the team, is the triggering mechanism for the sale of the emblem.

Boston Professional Hockey Ass'n v. Dallas Cap & Emblem Mfg., Inc., 510 F.2d 1004, 1012 (5th Cir. 1975) (permanent injunction).

This holding seems to follow a felt sense that it would be improper to permit an anonymous third party to profit from the plaintiff's logo. However equitable it may appear, though, such a holding is arguably at odds with traditional trademark theory. How does the logo lower consumer search costs? If the logo does not summarize product attributes such as quality, why protect it? Tribunals such as the *Boston Professional Hockey* court have ignored these anomalies and protected logos against use by another. Indeed, one court has gone so far as to prevent the sale of T-shirts in university colors even if they don't include any trademarks from those universities. Board of Supervisors for Louisiana State University v. Smack Apparel Co., 550 F.3d 465 (5th Cir. 2008).

Not all courts do so, however. Stacey Dogan and Mark Lemley review the cases and conclude that the majority refuse to protect trademarks on merchandise absent a showing of consumer confusion. Further, they point out that the Supreme Court has never recognized a merchandising right, and argue that the current Court is unlikely to do so given its many recent decisions limiting trademark protection. Stacey L. Dogan & Mark A. Lemley, *The Merchandising Right: Fragile Theory or Fait Accompli?*, 54 Emory L.J. 461 (2005).

Assuming that Dogan and Lemley are right that a merchandising right doesn't fit well within existing trademark doctrine, what should happen if people have come to believe that only the Dallas Cowboys are permitted to sell Dallas Cowboys merchandise? Should the law expand over time to take account of changing consumer norms, or should it set the rules according to trademark principles and force consumer norms to adapt to those rules?

PROBLEM

Problem 5-5. A popular "cult" movie includes characters who have tattooed famous brand logos on various parts of their bodies. The practice quickly catches on, first among "avant-garde" artists, and then among college and high school students.

Post-Modern Concepts, Inc. (PMC), seeing an opportunity, opens a storefront tattoo parlor in a popular retail mall in the Midwest. Here PMC applies popular logos as tattoos. At first, customers are primarily interested in the ironic use of logos, as in the film; the logos are primarily used as a spoof or commentary on consumerism. One popular tattoo, for instance, includes the famous "Calvin Klein" word mark and logo, drawn inside a red circle with a slash. Soon, however — perhaps predictably — the ironic intent of the original practice is lost as it becomes very chic to have a logo tattoo. Thus many people begin to request tattoos without the red slash and circle. The most popular trademark logo tattoos are "Rolls Royce," "Nike," the original "Calvin Klein," and "Harley-Davidson."

Success is instantaneous. In response to torrid demand, PMC sets up franchises all over the country.

Owners of the trademarks begin to notice PMC. They are concerned primarily about lost revenues, because PMC has never taken out any trademark licenses. But some trademark owners are also concerned that pictures of people with logo tattoos are beginning to appear in the press. Even some famous celebrities, such as popular musicians and sports stars, have tattoos in prominent places. When their picture appears in the newspaper, the logo — or part of it — does too. Other trademark owners are concerned that logo tattoos are being applied on parts of the body traditionally covered by clothing. These owners fear that when pictures of people with logo tattoos in these places appear — sometimes in press outlets not fit for family viewing — the trademarks are denigrated.

What hurdles will the trademark owners have to clear to enforce their rights? (Are these marks attached to a product? Also, PMC will undoubtedly argue that sports team fanatics have long painted their faces in team colors, or drawn the team logo on their faces; and that even before PMC, some permanent tattoos consisting of corporate logos were popular, such as "Chevy," "Red Sox Forever," or, perhaps most common, "Harley Davidson.") Are there any risks to letting the practice continue without any enforcement efforts? Does PMC, or its customers, have a defense not based in trademark law?

E. DOMAIN NAMES AND CYBERSQUATTING

Since the early days of the Internet, people have communicated with each other using domain names, mnemonic devices that map to a particular Internet Protocol address. Individuals, organizations, and companies have registered domain names that correspond to their names, to their trademarks, or to their products. Thus, Microsoft can be found at www.microsoft.com. Internet domain names are registered on a first-come, first-served basis by a variety of registrars for a low price (less than $30 per domain name per year).

In the mid-1990s, a number of individuals registered domain names that corresponded to the name or trademark of someone else, often a large corporation. Many of these individuals registered the domain name not in order to use it themselves, but in order to sell the valuable domain name to the trademark owner for a price well in excess of $30. This practice is known as "cybersquatting." Others registered generic terms like business.com and resold them for a substantial profit. Still others may register a company's name for legitimate reasons: to criticize the company, or to advertise the availability of that company's products at a Web site.

Trademark owners have been trying for years to stop cybersquatting. Existing trademark law has not adapted terribly well to cybersquatting, and in recent years trademark owners have turned to new statutes and rules to help them in their fight. Courts have struggled to stop cybersquatting without punishing legitimate uses of domain names. In this section, we consider Internet domain name cases decided under two new legal regimes.

1. Anticybersquatting Consumer Protection Act

Trademark infringement and dilution are not well suited to preventing cybersquatting. While some uses of a domain name are infringing, most are not. Dilution reaches classic cases of cybersquatting — the registration of a domain name corresponding to someone else's trademark in order to extort money from the trademark owner — but only in the small number of cases in which the trademark in question is famous. This led to two problems. First, some instances of cybersquatting can't be punished under existing trademark laws. Second, courts sometimes stretched the requirements of the law in order to stop cybersquatting. For instance, many courts ignored or reduced the requirement of fame in order to apply dilution law against clear cases of cybersquatting.

In 1999, Congress sought to address both of these problems by passing a law directed specifically at cybersquatting. The Anticybersquatting Consumer Protection Act makes it illegal to register or use a domain name that corresponds to a trademark where the domain name registrant has no legitimate interest in using the name and acts in bad faith to deprive the trademark owner of the use of the name. 15 U.S.C. § 1125(d). Since the end of 1999, over a hundred cases have been decided under the ACPA. The critical parts of the statute are the definitions of bad faith and legitimate interest, which are discussed in the cases that follow.

People for the Ethical Treatment of Animals v. Doughney
263 F.3d 359 (4th Cir. 2001)

Gregory, Circuit Judge:

[The plaintiff, People for the Ethical Treatment of Animals (PETA), is an advocacy group opposed to eating meat, wearing fur, and conducting research on animals. The defendant registered the Internet domain name peta.org, where he set up a page entitled "People Eating Tasty Animals" that was a parody of PETA and its goals. In a portion of the opinion omitted here, the Fourth Circuit found that using the domain name peta.org impermissibly caused initial interest confusion, and therefore found Doughney liable for trademark infringement.]

B. *Anticybersquatting Consumer Protection Act*

The district court found Doughney liable under the Anticybersquatting Consumer Protection Act ("ACPA"), 15 U.S.C. § 1125(d)(1)(A). To establish an ACPA violation, PETA was required to (1) prove that Doughney had a bad faith intent to profit from using the *peta.org* domain name, and (2) that the *peta.org* domain name is identical or confusingly similar to, or dilutive of, the distinctive and famous PETA Mark. 15 U.S.C. § 1125(d)(1)(A).

Doughney makes several arguments relating to the district court's ACPA holding: (1) that PETA did not plead an ACPA claim, but raised it for the first time in its motion for summary judgment; (2) that the ACPA, which became effective in 1999, cannot be applied retroactively to events that occurred in 1995 and 1996; (3) that Doughney did not seek to financially profit from his use of PETA's Mark; and (4) that Doughney acted in good faith.

None of Doughney's arguments are availing . . . we reject Doughney's first contention.

Doughney's second argument—that the ACPA may not be applied retroactively—also is unavailing. The ACPA expressly states that it "shall apply to all domain names registered before, on, or after the date of the enactment of this Act[.]" Pub. L. No. 106-113, § 3010, 113 Stat. 1536. See also Sporty's Farm L.L.C. v. Sportsman's Market, Inc., 202 F.3d 489, 496 (2d Cir. 2000) (same). Moreover, while the ACPA precludes the imposition of *damages* in cases in which domain names were registered, trafficked, or used before its enactment, Pub. L. No. 106-113, § 3010, 113 Stat. 1536 ("damages under subsection (a) or (d) of section 35 of the Trademark Act of 1946 (15 U.S.C. 1117), . . . shall not be available with respect to the registration, trafficking, or use of a domain name that occurs before the date of the enactment of this Act"), it does not preclude the imposition of *equitable remedies.* See also Virtual Works, Inc. v. Volkswagen of America, Inc., 238 F.3d 264, 268 (4th Cir. 2001). Here, the district court did not award PETA damages (nor did PETA request damages), but ordered Doughney to relinquish the domain name, transfer its registration to PETA, and limit his use of domain names to those that do not use PETA's Mark. *Doughney*, 113 F. Supp. 2d at 922. Thus, the district court properly applied the ACPA to this case.

Doughney's third argument—that he did not seek to financially profit from registering a domain name using PETA's Mark—also offers him no relief. It is undisputed that Doughney made statements to the press and on his website recommending that PETA attempt to "settle" with him and "make him an offer." The undisputed evidence belies Doughney's argument.

Doughney's fourth argument—that he did not act in bad faith—also is unavailing. [The court recited the statutory factors listed in *Shields*]. In addition to listing these nine factors, the ACPA contains a safe harbor provision stating that bad faith intent "shall not be found in any case in which the court determines that the person believed and had reasonable grounds to believe that the use of the domain name was fair use or otherwise lawful." 15 U.S.C. § 1225(d)(1)(B)(ii).

The district court reviewed the factors listed in the statute and properly concluded that Doughney (I) had no intellectual property right in *peta.org;* (II) *peta.org* is not Doughney's name or a name otherwise used to identify Doughney; (III) Doughney had no prior use of *peta.org* in connection with the bona fide offering of any goods or services; (IV) Doughney used the PETA Mark in a commercial manner; (V) Doughney "clearly intended to confuse, mislead and divert internet users into accessing his web site which contained information antithetical and therefore harmful to the goodwill represented by the PETA Mark"; (VI) Doughney made statements on his web site and in the press recommending that PETA attempt to "settle" with him and "make him an offer"; (VII) Doughney made false statements when registering the domain name; and (VIII) Doughney registered other domain names that are identical or similar to the marks or names of other famous people and organizations. *People for the Ethical Treatment of Animals*, 113 F. Supp. 2d at 920.

Doughney claims that the district court's later ruling denying PETA's motion for attorney fees triggers application of the ACPA's safe harbor provision. In that ruling, the district court stated that

> Doughney registered the domain name because he thought that he had a legitimate First Amendment right to express himself this way. The Court must consider Doughney's state of mind at the time he took the actions in question. Doughney thought he was within his First Amendment rights to create a parody of the plaintiff's organization.

People for the Ethical Treatment of Animals, Inc. v. Doughney, Civil Action No. 99-1336-A, Order at 4 (E.D. Va. Aug. 31, 2000). With its attorney's fee ruling, the district court did not find that Doughney "had reasonable grounds to believe" that his use of PETA's Mark was lawful. It held only that Doughney *thought* it to be lawful.

Moreover, a defendant "who acts even partially in bad faith in registering a domain name is not, as a matter of law, entitled to benefit from [the ACPA's] safe harbor provision." *Virtual Works, Inc.*, 238 F.3d at 270. Doughney knowingly provided false information to NSI upon registering the domain name, knew he was registering a domain name identical to PETA's Mark, and clearly intended to confuse Internet users into accessing his website, instead of PETA's official website. Considering the evidence of Doughney's bad faith, the safe harbor provision can provide him no relief.

IV

For the foregoing reasons, the judgment of the district court is affirmed.

Lamparello v. Falwell

420 F.3d 309 (4th Cir. 2005)

Motz, Circuit Judge.

Christopher Lamparello appeals the district court's order enjoining him from maintaining a gripe website critical of Reverend Jerry Falwell. For the reasons stated below, we reverse.

I.

Reverend Falwell is "a nationally known minister who has been active as a commentator on politics and public affairs." Hustler Magazine v. Falwell, 485 U.S. 46, 47 (1988). He holds the common law trademarks "Jerry Falwell" and "Falwell," and the registered trademark "Listen America with Jerry Falwell." Jerry Falwell Ministries can be found online at "www.falwell.com," a website which receives 9,000 hits (or visits) per day.

Lamparello registered the domain name "www.fallwell.com" on February 11, 1999, after hearing Reverend Falwell give an interview "in which he expressed opinions about gay people and homosexuality that [Lamparello] considered . . . offensive." Lamparello created a website at that domain name to respond to what he believed were "untruths about gay people." Lamparello's website included headlines such as "Bible verses that Dr. Falwell chooses to ignore" and "Jerry Falwell has been bearing false witness (*Exodus* 20:16) against his gay and lesbian neighbors for a long time." The site also contained in-depth criticism of Reverend Falwell's views. For example, the website stated:

> Dr. Falwell says that he is on the side of truth. He says that he will preach that homosexuality is a sin until the day he dies. But we believe that if the reverend were to take another thoughtful look at the scriptures, he would discover that they have been twisted around to support an anti-gay political agenda . . . at the expense of the gospel.

Although the interior pages of Lamparello's website did not contain a disclaimer, the homepage prominently stated, "This website is NOT affiliated with Jerry Falwell or his ministry"; advised, "If you would like to visit Rev. Falwell's website, you may click here"; and provided a hyperlink to Reverend Falwell's website.

At one point, Lamparello's website included a link to the Amazon.com webpage for a book that offered interpretations of the Bible that Lamparello favored, but the parties agree that Lamparello has never sold goods or services on his website. The parties also agree that "Lamparello's domain name and web site at www.fallwell.com," which received only 200 hits per day, "had no measurable impact on the quantity of visits to [Reverend Falwell's] web site at www.falwell.com."

Nonetheless, Reverend Falwell sent Lamparello letters in October 2001 and June 2003 demanding that he cease and desist from using www.fallwell.com or any variation of Reverend Falwell's name as a domain name. Ultimately, Lamparello filed this action against Reverend Falwell and his ministries (collectively referred to hereinafter as "Reverend Falwell"), seeking a declaratory judgment of noninfringement. Reverend Falwell counter-claimed [under the Lanham Act].

The parties stipulated to all relevant facts and filed cross-motions for summary judgment. The district court granted summary judgment to Reverend Falwell, enjoined Lamparello from using Reverend Falwell's mark at www.fallwell.com, and required Lamparello to transfer the domain name to Reverend Falwell. *Lamparello*, 360 F. Supp. 2d at 773, 775. . . .

II.

We first consider Reverend Falwell's claims of trademark infringement and false designation of origin.

A.

. . . Trademark law serves the important functions of protecting product identification, providing consumer information, and encouraging the production of quality goods and services. *See* Qualitex Co. v. Jacobson Prods. Co., 514 U.S. 159, 164 (1995). But protections "'against unfair competition'" cannot be transformed into "'rights to control language.'" CPC Int'l, Inc. v. Skippy Inc., 214 F.3d 456, 462 (4th Cir. 2000) (quoting Mark A. Lemley, *The Modern Lanham Act and the Death of Common Sense*, 108 YALE L.J. 1687, 1710-11 (1999)). "Such a transformation" would raise serious First Amendment concerns because it would limit the ability to discuss the products or criticize the conduct of companies that may be of widespread public concern and importance. Much useful social and commercial discourse would be all but impossible if speakers were under threat of an infringement lawsuit every time they made reference to a person, company or product by using its trademark. *Id.* (internal quotation marks and citations omitted).

Lamparello and his amici argue at length that application of the Lanham Act must be restricted to "commercial speech" to assure that trademark law does not become a tool for unconstitutional censorship. The Sixth Circuit has endorsed this view, see Taubman Co. v. Webfeats, 319 F.3d 770, 774 (6th Cir. 2003), and the Ninth Circuit recently has done so as well, see Bosley Med. Inst., Inc. v. Kremer, 403 F.3d 672, 674 (9th Cir. 2005).

In its two most significant recent amendments to the Lanham Act, the Federal Trademark Dilution Act of 1995 ("FTDA") and the Anticybersquatting Consumer Protection Act of 1999 ("ACPA"), Congress left little doubt that it did not intend for trademark laws to impinge the First Amendment rights of critics and commentators. The dilution statute applies to only a "commercial use in commerce of a mark," 15 U.S.C. § 1125(c)(1), and explicitly states that the "[n]oncommercial use of a mark" is not actionable. Id. § 1125(c)(4). Congress explained that this language was added to "adequately address [ ] legitimate First Amendment concerns," H.R. REP. No. 104-374, at 4 (1995), *reprinted in* 1995 U.S.C.C.A.N. 1029, 1031, and "incorporate[d] the concept of 'commercial' speech from the 'commercial speech' doctrine." *Id.* at 8, reprinted in 1995 U.S.C.C.A.N. at 1035; cf. Lorillard Tobacco Co. v. Reilly, 533 U.S. 525, 554 (2001) (defining commercial speech as "speech proposing a commercial transaction") (internal quotation marks and citation omitted). Similarly, Congress directed that in determining whether an individual has engaged in cybersquatting, the courts may consider whether the person's use of the mark is a "bona fide noncommercial or fair use." 15 U.S.C. § 1125(d)(1)(B)(i)(IV). The legislature believed this provision necessary to "protect[ ] the rights of Internet users and the interests of all Americans in free speech and protected uses of trademarked names for such things as parody, comment, criticism, comparative advertising, news reporting, etc." S. REP. No. 106-140 (1999), 1999 WL 594571, at *8.

In contrast, the trademark infringement and false designation of origin provisions of the Lanham Act (Sections 32 and 43(a), respectively) do not employ the term "noncommercial." They do state, however, that they pertain only to the use of a mark "in connection with the sale, offering for sale, distribution, or advertising of any goods or services," 15 U.S.C. § 1114(1)(a), or "in connection with any goods or services," *id.* § 1125(a)(1). But courts have been reluctant to define those terms narrowly. Rather, as the Second Circuit has explained, "[t]he term 'services' has been interpreted broadly" and so "[t]he Lanham Act has . . . been applied to defendants furnishing a wide variety of non-commercial public and civic benefits." United We Stand Am., Inc. v. United We Stand, Am. N.Y., Inc., 128 F.3d 86, 89-90 (2d Cir. 1997). Similarly, in *PETA* we noted that a website need not actually sell goods or services for the use of a mark in that site's domain name to constitute a use " 'in connection with' goods or services." *PETA*, 263 F.3d at 365; see also *Taubman Co.*, 319 F.3d at 775 (concluding that website with *two* links to websites of for-profit entities violated the Lanham Act).

Thus, even if we accepted Lamparello's contention that Sections 32 and 43(a) of the Lanham Act apply only to commercial speech, we would still face the difficult question of what constitutes such speech under those provisions. In the case at hand, we need not resolve that question or determine whether Sections 32 and 43(a) apply exclusively to commercial speech because Reverend Falwell's claims of trademark infringement and false designation fail for a more obvious reason. The hallmark of such claims is a likelihood of confusion — and there is no likelihood of confusion here.

B.

[The court reviewed the likelihood of confusion factors and found that] those viewing the content of Lamparello's website probably were unlikely to confuse Reverend Falwell with the source of that material.

2.

Nevertheless, Reverend Falwell argues that he is entitled to prevail under the "initial interest confusion" doctrine. This relatively new and sporadically applied doctrine holds that "the Lanham Act forbids a competitor from luring potential customers away from a producer by initially passing off its goods as those of the producer's, even if confusion as to the source of the goods is dispelled by the time any sales are consummated." *Dorr-Oliver*, 94 F.3d at 382. According to Reverend Falwell, this doctrine requires us to compare his mark with Lamparello's website domain name, www.fallwell.com, *without* considering the content of Lamparello's website. Reverend Falwell argues that some people who misspell his name may go to www.fallwell.com assuming it is his site, thus giving Lamparello an unearned audience — albeit one that quickly disappears when it realizes it has not reached Reverend Falwell's site. This argument fails for two reasons.

First, we have never adopted the initial interest confusion theory; rather, we have followed a very different mode of analysis, requiring courts to determine whether a likelihood of confusion exists by "examin[ing] the allegedly infringing use *in the context in which it is seen by the ordinary consumer.*" Anheuser-Busch, Inc. v. L & L Wings, Inc., 962 F.2d 316, 319 (4th Cir. 1992) (emphasis added) (citing cases); see also What-A-Burger of Va., Inc. v. Whataburger, Inc., 357 F.3d 441, 450 (4th Cir. 2004).

Contrary to Reverend Falwell's arguments, we did not abandon this approach in *PETA*. Our inquiry in *PETA* was limited to whether Doughney's use of the domain name "www.peta.org" constituted a successful enough parody of People for the Ethical Treatment of Animals that no one was likely to believe www.peta.org was sponsored or endorsed by that organization. For a parody to be successful, it "must convey two simultaneous — and contradictory — messages: that it is the original, but also that it is *not* the original and is instead a parody." *PETA*, 263 F.3d at 366 (internal quotation marks and citation omitted). Doughney argued that his domain name conveyed the first message (that it was PETA's website) and that the content of his website conveyed the requisite second message (that it was not PETA's site). *Id.* Although "[t]he website's content ma[de] it clear that it [wa]s not related to PETA," *id.*, we concluded that the website's content could not convey the requisite second message because the site's content "[wa]s not conveyed *simultaneously* with the first message, [i.e., the domain name itself,] as required to be considered a parody." *Id.* at 366. Accordingly, we found the "district court properly rejected Doughney's parody defense." *Id.* at 367.

PETA simply outlines the parameters of the parody defense; it does not adopt the initial interest confusion theory or otherwise diminish the necessity of examining context when determining whether a likelihood of confusion exists. Indeed, in *PETA* itself, rather than embracing a new approach, we reiterated that [t]o determine whether a likelihood of confusion exists, a court should not consider how closely a *fragment* of a given use duplicates the trademark, but must instead consider *whether the use in its entirety creates a likelihood of confusion. Id.* at 366 (emphasis added). When dealing with domain names, this means a court must evaluate an allegedly infringing domain name in conjunction with the content of the website identified by the domain name.

Moreover, even if we did endorse the initial interest confusion theory, that theory would not assist Reverend Falwell here because it provides no basis for liability in circumstances such as these. The few appellate courts that have followed the Ninth Circuit and imposed liability under this theory for using marks on the Internet have done so only in cases involving a factor utterly absent here — one business's use of another's mark for its own financial gain. See, e.g., PACCAR Inc. v. TeleScan Techs., L.L.C., 319 F.3d 243, 253 (6th Cir. 2003); Promatek Indus., Ltd. v. Equitrac Corp., 300 F.3d 808, 812 (7th Cir. 2002); Brookfield Communications, Inc. v. West Coast Entm't Corp., 174 F.3d 1036, 1055-56 (9th Cir. 1999).

Profiting financially from initial interest confusion is thus a key element for imposition of liability under this theory. When an alleged infringer does not compete with the markholder for sales, "some initial confusion will not likely facilitate free riding on the goodwill of another mark, or otherwise harm the user claiming infringement. Where confusion has little or no meaningful effect in the marketplace, it is of little or no consequence in our analysis." *Checkpoint Sys.*, 269 F.3d at 296-97. For this reason, even the Ninth Circuit has stated that a firm is not liable for using another's mark in its domain name if it "could not financially capitalize on [a] misdirected consumer [looking for the markholder's site] even if it so desired." Interstellar Starship Servs., Ltd. v. Epix, Inc., 304 F.3d 936, 946 (9th Cir. 2002).

This critical element — use of another firm's mark to capture the markholder's customers and profits — simply does not exist when the alleged infringer establishes a gripe site that criticizes the markholder. *See* Hannibal Travis, *The Battle For Mindshare: The Emerging Consensus that the First Amendment Protects Corporate Criticism and Parody on the Internet*, 10 Va. J.L. & Tech. 3, 85 (Winter 2005) ("The premise of the 'initial interest' confusion cases is that by using the plaintiff's trademark to divert its customers, the defendant is engaging in the old 'bait and switch.' But because . . . Internet users who find [gripe sites] are not sold anything, the mark may be the 'bait,' but there is simply no 'switch.'") (citations omitted). Applying the initial interest confusion theory to gripe sites like Lamparello's would enable the markholder to insulate himself from criticism — or at least to minimize access to it. We have already condemned such uses of the Lanham Act, stating that a markholder cannot "'shield itself from criticism by forbidding the use of its name in commentaries critical of its conduct.'" *CPC Int'l*, 214 F.3d at 462 (quoting L.L. Bean, Inc. v. Drake Publishers, Inc., 811 F.2d 26, 33 (1st Cir. 1987)). "[J]ust because speech is critical of a corporation and its business practices is not a sufficient reason to enjoin the speech." *Id.*

In sum, even if we were to accept the initial interest confusion theory, that theory would not apply in the case at hand. Rather, to determine whether a likelihood of confusion exists as to the source of a gripe site like that at issue in this case, a court must look not only to the allegedly infringing domain name, but also to the underlying content of the website. When we do so here, it is clear, as explained above, that no likelihood of confusion exists. Therefore, the district court erred in granting Reverend Falwell summary judgment on his infringement, false designation, and unfair competition claims.

III

We evaluate Reverend Falwell's cybersquatting claim separately because the elements of a cybersquatting violation differ from those of traditional Lanham Act violations. To prevail on a cybersquatting claim, Reverend Falwell must show that Lamparello: (1) "had a bad faith intent to profit from using the [www.fallwell.com] domain name," and (2) the domain name www.fallwell.com "is identical or confusingly similar to, or dilutive of, the distinctive and famous [Falwell] mark." *PETA*, 263 F.3d at 367 (citing 15 U.S.C. § 1125(d)(1)(A)).

"The paradigmatic harm that the ACPA was enacted to eradicate" is "the practice of cybersquatters registering several hundred domain names in an effort to sell them to the legitimate owners of the mark." Lucas Nursery & Landscaping, Inc. v. Grosse, 359 F.3d 806, 810 (6th Cir. 2004). The Act was also intended to stop the registration of multiple marks with the hope of selling them to the highest bidder, "distinctive marks to defraud consumers" or "to engage in counterfeiting activities," and "well-known marks to prey on consumer confusion by misusing the domain name to divert customers from the mark owner's site to the cybersquatter's own site, many of which are pornography sites that derive advertising revenue based on the number of visits, or 'hits,' the site receives." S. Rep. No. 106-140, 1999 WL 594571, at *5-6. The Act was not intended to prevent "noncommercial uses of a mark, such as for comment, criticism, parody, news reporting, etc.," and thus they "are beyond the scope" of the ACPA. Id. at *9. . . .

After close examination of the undisputed facts involved in this case, we can only conclude that Reverend Falwell cannot demonstrate that Lamparello "had a bad faith intent to profit from using the [www.fallwell.com] domain name." *PETA*, 263 F.3d at 367. Lamparello clearly employed www.fallwell.com simply to criticize Reverend Falwell's views. Factor IV of the ACPA, 15 U.S.C. § 1125(d)(1)(B)(i)(IV), counsels against finding a bad faith intent to profit in such circumstances because "use of a domain name for purposes of . . . comment, [and] criticism," H.R. Rep. No. 106-412, 1999 WL 970519, at *11, constitutes a "bona fide noncommercial or fair use" under the statute, 15 U.S.C. § 1125(d)(1)(B)(i)(IV). That Lamparello provided a link to an Amazon.com webpage selling a book he favored does not diminish the communicative function of his website. The use of a domain name to engage in criticism or commentary "even where done for profit" does not alone evidence a bad faith intent to profit,

H.R. Rep. No. 106-412, 1999 WL 970519, at *11, and Lamparello did not even stand to gain financially from sales of the book at Amazon.com. Thus factor IV weighs heavily in favor of finding Lamparello lacked a bad faith intent to profit from the use of the domain name.

Equally important, Lamparello has not engaged in the type of conduct described in the statutory factors as typifying the bad faith intent to profit essential to a successful cybersquatting claim. First, we have already held, *supra* Part II.B, that Lamparello's domain name does not create a likelihood of confusion as to source or affiliation. Accordingly, Lamparello has not engaged in the type of conduct — "creating a likelihood of confusion as to the source, sponsorship, affiliation, or endorsement of the site," 15 U.S.C. §1125(d)(1)(B)(i)(V) — described as an indicator of a bad faith intent to profit in factor V of the statute.

Factors VI and VIII also counsel against finding a bad faith intent to profit here. Lamparello has made no attempt — or even indicated a willingness — "to transfer, sell, or otherwise assign the domain name to [Reverend Falwell] or any third party for financial gain." 15 U.S.C. §1125(d)(1)(B)(i)(VI). Similarly, Lamparello has not registered "multiple domain names," 15 U.S.C. §1125(d)(1)(B)(i)(VIII); rather, the record indicates he has registered only one. Thus, Lamparello's conduct is not of the suspect variety described in factors VI and VIII of the Act.

Notably, the case at hand differs markedly from those in which the courts have found a bad faith intent to profit from domain names used for websites engaged in political commentary or parody. For example, in *PETA* we found the registrant of www.peta.org engaged in cybersquatting because www.peta.org was one of *fifty* to *sixty* domain names Doughney had registered, *PETA*, 263 F.3d at 362, and because Doughney had evidenced a clear intent to sell www.peta.org to PETA, stating that PETA should try to " 'settle' with him and 'make him an offer.' " *Id.* at 368. *See also Virtual Works*, 238 F.3d at 269-70. Similarly, in Coca-Cola Co. v. Purdy, 382 F.3d 774 (8th Cir. 2004), the Eighth Circuit found an anti-abortion activist who had registered domain names incorporating famous marks such as "Washington Post" liable for cybersquatting because he had registered almost *seventy* domain names, had offered to stop using the Washington Post mark if the newspaper published an opinion piece by him on its editorial page, and posted content that created a likelihood of confusion as to whether the famous markholders sponsored the anti-abortion sites and "ha[d] taken positions on hotly contested issues." *Id.* at 786. In contrast, Lamparello did not register multiple domain names, he did not offer to transfer them for valuable consideration, and he did not create a likelihood of confusion.

Instead, Lamparello, like the plaintiffs in two cases recently decided by the Fifth and Sixth Circuits, created a gripe site. Both courts expressly refused to find that gripe sites located at domain names nearly identical to the marks at issue violated the ACPA. In TMI, Inc. v. Maxwell, 368 F.3d 433, 434-35 (5th Cir. 2004), Joseph Maxwell, a customer of homebuilder TMI, registered the domain name "www.trendmakerhome.com," which differed by only one letter from TMI's mark, TrendMaker Homes, and its domain name, "www.trendmakerhomes.com." Maxwell used the site to complain about his experience with TMI and to list the name of a contractor whose work pleased him. After his registration expired, Maxwell registered "www.trendmakerhome.info." TMI then sued, alleging cybersquatting. The Fifth Circuit reversed the district court's finding that Maxwell violated the ACPA, reasoning that his site was noncommercial and designed only "to inform potential customers about a negative experience with the company." Id. at 438-39.

Similarly, in *Lucas Nursery & Landscaping*, a customer of Lucas Nursery registered the domain name "www.lucasnursery.com" and posted her dissatisfaction with the company's landscaping services. Because the registrant, Grosse, like Lamparello, registered a single domain name, the Sixth Circuit concluded that her conduct did not constitute that which Congress intended to proscribe—i.e., the registration of multiple domain names. *Lucas Nursery & Landscaping*, 359 F.3d at 810. Noting that Grosse's gripe site did not create any confusion as to sponsorship and that she had never attempted to sell the domain name to the markholder, the court found that Grosse's conduct was not actionable under the ACPA. The court explained: "One of the ACPA's main objectives is the protection of consumers from slick internet peddlers who trade on the names and reputations of established brands. The practice of informing fellow consumers of one's experience with a particular service provider is surely not inconsistent with this ideal." *Id.* at 811.

Like Maxwell and Grosse before him, Lamparello has not evidenced a bad faith intent to profit under the ACPA. To the contrary, he has used www.fallwell.com to engage in the type of "comment[ ] [and] criticism" that Congress specifically stated militates against a finding of bad faith intent to profit. *See* S. Rep. No. 106-140, 1999 WL 594571, at *14. And he has neither registered multiple domain names nor attempted to transfer www.fallwell.com for valuable consideration. We agree with the Fifth and Sixth Circuits that, given these circumstances, the use of a mark in a domain name for a gripe site criticizing the markholder does not constitute cybersquatting.

COMMENTS AND QUESTIONS

1. A number of courts have rejected the *Doughney* court's conclusion (omitted here) that visitors to the peta.org site were confused, even briefly. In addition to *Lamparello, see* Bosley Med. Inst. v. Kremer, 403 F.3d 672 (9th Cir. 2005). Does it make sense to find a violation of the ACPA if there is no confusion? Does the ACPA do away with the requirement of proving infringement or dilution?

The statute applies only to domain names that are confusingly similar to ordinary trademarks, or that are likely to dilute a famous trademark. This is because trademark owners must demonstrate that they are entitled to control the domain names in question. But the infringement and dilution inquiries under the ACPA focus on the domain name itself, not how it is used. Does the fact that the ACPA imposes this requirement limit its effectiveness?

2. Is it fair to apply the ACPA retroactively, as *Shields v. Zuccarini*, 254 F.3d 476 (3d Cir. 2001), does, to anyone who registered a domain name before the effective date of the Act but who continues to use the name after 1999? What is the point of making injunctive relief retroactive and damages prospective if continued use of an existing domain name can justify a "prospective" claim for damages?

3. What constitutes a legitimate interest in a domain name? Consider the following possible uses:

- *The defendant has its own trademark that corresponds to the domain name.* Identical trademarks often coexist in different industries. Consider Delta, a well-known trademark for an airline, but also for other companies that make faucets, that provide dental insurance, and that even deal with telecommunications. If more than one company has a legitimate claim to a trademark, any of those companies can register the domain name. The ACPA does not require that the domain name be assigned to the "best" or largest trademark owner. Nonetheless, some courts have ruled for plaintiffs in cases in which they apparently concluded that a defendant's bad faith outweighed its legitimate rights in the name. For example, in Virtual Works, Inc. v. Volkswagen of America, 238 F.3d 264 (4th Cir. 2001), the court found Virtual Works (a legitimate trademark owner in its own right) to have violated the ACPA by registering vw.net. It concluded that Virtual's knowledge of likely confusion with Volkswagen's mark, and its discussion of the possibility of selling the domain name to Volkswagen, meant that it did not have a legitimate interest in the name despite its corporate name. Why does bad faith matter under the statute if the defendant is in fact a legitimate trademark owner?

- *The defendant is a legal reseller of the plaintiff's product.* A number of independent businesses sell trademarked products. They may be retailers who sell consumer products, independent service organizations who service or resell used cars, or the like. Can a company that services Porsche's register "porscheservice.com"? *See* General Motors v. E-Publications, Inc., 2001 WL 1798648 (E.D. Mich. 2001) (legitimate parts seller can't refer to "GM" in a domain name); Toma's LLC v. Florida Hi Performance, AF 00968 (eResolution Sept. 10, 2001) (collecting decisions on both sides of the issue and ruling that advertising lawful resale is a legitimate use of a domain name).
- *The defendant wants to criticize or make fun of the plaintiff.* A number of cybersquatting cases involve suits against disaffected customers who set up criticism sites. For example, it is relatively common for an irate consumer to register [company name]sucks.com. It seems ludicrous to think that consumers viewing the site would be confused into thinking that it was owned or sponsored by the company. Nonetheless, while some cases have held that "sucks" sites are non-infringing, other decisions have granted the trademark owner the right to prevent the registration of such sites. *Compare* Ohio Art Co. v. Watts, No. 98 CV 7338, slip op. at 4 (N.D. Ohio June 23, 1998); BellSouth Corp. v. Internet Classified of Ohio, 1997 WL 33107251, No. 1:96-CV-0769-CC, slip op. at 29-30 (N.D. Ga. Nov. 12, 1997) (both finding infringement from the use of a "sucks" domain name) *with* Bally Total Fitness v. Faber, 29 F. Supp. 2d 1161 (C.D. Cal. 1998) (Web page that used "ballysucks" in the URL was not dilution). Other defendants use the plaintiff's trademark in order to make fun of it. Consider the *PETA* case, above.

Should a bona fide desire to criticize a trademark owner be a legitimate reason to register a domain name? Should it matter whether the name consists merely of the trademark itself, or whether it contains an appendage like "sucks.com" that makes it unlikely anyone could confuse the site with the official trademark owner's site? If trademark owners can prevent the use of their mark in criticism, how can anyone criticize or make fun of the mark or its owner?

4. If a domain name is confusingly similar to a trademark, and the registrant has no legitimate interest in using the name, shouldn't that be enough? Why require proof that the defendant registered the domain name in bad faith? The answer seems to be that the ACPA is not intended to allocate all domain names to the proper owner. Rather, it is designed to single out a smaller class of cases in which the defendant's registration is clearly problematic.

How should a court decide whether a defendant has acted in bad faith? The statute provides a number of factors for the court to consider. Those factors are based on the characteristics of traditional "serial cybersquatters," many of whom have registered hundreds of different trademarks as domain names. Congress concluded that the registration of many different names, the use of false contact information, and demands for payment from trademark owners were all evidence of classic cybersquatting of the sort that the act was intended to prevent.

Was Doughney acting in bad faith? Suppose that he had come to you in 1998, before the ACPA was even adopted, to ask whether it was legal to register peta.org in order to parody PETA. Would you have told him he had a legitimate argument?

5. A variant on cybersquatting is "typosquatting." Typosquatters register common misspellings or variants on trademarked terms, hoping to draw consumers who type the wrong domain name into the URL. Should typosquatting be treated just as any other form of cybersquatting, because typosquatters can divert consumers away from their intended destination? Or is typosquatting different because the typosquatter is not creating confusion, but rather merely capitalizing on preexisting confusion? Courts have generally treated typosquatters just as they have cybersquatters. *Shields* is an obvious example. On the other hand, courts in other contexts have refused to hold a defendant liable for capitalizing on confusion it did not create. *See* Holiday Inns, Inc. v. 800 Reservation, Inc., 86 F.3d 619 (6th Cir. 1996) (finding that a company who registered a phone number that was a commonly misdialed variant of the Holiday Inns phone number and used it to sell hotel reservations wasn't liable for trademark infringement, since it explained to customers that it wasn't affiliated with Holiday Inns)

6. The ACPA is designed to protect trademarks against cybersquatters. But cybersquatters have also registered domain names that correspond to terms other than trademarks. In particular, cybersquatters have registered the names of various celebrities, such as Julia Roberts. Does the ACPA protect celebrities, just as it does trademark owners? Generally speaking, the answer is no. Personal names are generally not trademarks, and so not entitled to protection. There are exceptions, however — some celebrities, like O.J. Simpson, have registered their name as a trademark, and they are entitled to the same protection as any corporate trademark owner under the statute. 15 U.S.C. § 1125(d)(1)(A). And some UDRP decisions have ordered the transfer of personal names, despite the absence of any clear authorization to do so in the UDRP. *See* Roberts v. Boyd, No. D2000-0210 (WIPO May 29, 2000) (ordering transfer of juliaroberts.com). *But see* Turner v. Fahmi, No. D2002-0251 (WIPO July 4, 2002) (refusing to transfer tedturner.com); Springsteen v. Burgar, No. D2000-1532 (WIPO Jan. 25, 2001) (refusing to transfer brucespringsteen.com).

7. Cybersquatting is an international phenomenon, and one of the problems trademark owners face is how to find cybersquatters in order to sue them. The ACPA includes two ways for plaintiffs to get jurisdiction over cybersquatters. First, a trademark owner who finds a cybersquatter in the United States can sue him in any district with which the cybersquatter has minimum contacts. Second, the ACPA provides that if a trademark owner cannot find the cybersquatter, it can obtain in rem jurisdiction in the jurisdiction where the domain name "resides" by publishing legal notice of the suit and then filing suit "against" the domain name itself. 15 U.S.C. § 1125(d)(2).

In rem jurisdiction has traditionally been used against real property, which of course doesn't move. But a number of courts have held that domain names themselves aren't property. *See, e.g.*, Network Solutions, Inc. v. Umbro Int'l, 529 S.E.2d 80 (Va.

2000). Is proceeding in rem against an intangible thing like a domain name consistent with due process? Or is it fundamentally unfair to the owner of the domain name, who is likely to receive no notice of the suit and be unable to defend the domain name? *See* Harrods Ltd. v. Sixty Internet Domain Names, 302 F.3d 214 (4th Cir. 2002); Porsche Cars North America v. Porsche.net, 302 F.3d 248 (4th Cir. 2002) (both upholding the constitutionality of the ACPA in rem provisions on the basis that domain names are property).

8. Because the ACPA — like other trademark doctrines — is designed to protect trademark owners, it does not create rights in generic terms. Nonetheless, generic domain names were very popular at the end of the twentieth century, and — because a domain name is necessarily exclusive in the sense that an ordinary trademark isn't — names like pets.com and toys.com gained widespread recognition. Some courts have given protection to generic domain names on a theory of unfair competition. *Cf.* E-Cards v. King, No. C-99-3726 SC (N.D. Cal. Dec. 13, 1999) (denying preliminary injunction to E-Cards in suit against ecards.com; the plaintiff later won a jury verdict at trial). Interestingly, a German court has held that the very act of registering a generic domain name constitutes unfair competition, on the theory that the name will give the registrant an unfair advantage over those who cannot use the name. *See* Epson v. Engelke, 340 O 191/96 (District Court Dusseldorf, 4 April 1997).

2. The Uniform Dispute Resolution Procedure

Congress and the courts were not the only ones concerned with cybersquatting. In the latter half of the 1990s, Network Solutions Inc., the company that registered domain names in the global top-level domains (gTLDs), faced a series of lawsuits by trademark owners that sought to hold NSI liable for permitting cybersquatters to register their trademarks as domain names. To solve this problem, NSI drafted a series of dispute resolution policies to help it determine when to turn a domain name over to a trademark owner or to put the name "on hold." NSI's policies have generally provided that domain name registrants agreed to arbitrate disputes with NSI. They have not, however, mandated arbitration between trademark owners and domain name registrants.

When the Internet Corporation for Assigned Names and Numbers (ICANN) was formed in 1999, it sought to deal with the problem of cybersquatting in a comprehensive way outside the judicial system. ICANN established a compulsory private dispute resolution process for dealing with cases of cybersquatting and required all Internet registrars to require their customers to subscribe to the process. Under this process, known as the Uniform Dispute Resolution Procedure (UDRP), a trademark owner can file a complaint online with an approved dispute resolution provider for a small fee. The domain name owner is notified and has a short time to file a responsive pleading. Then the dispute panelist or panelists rule on the case. Unlike arbitration or other forms of private dispute resolution, there is no discovery, no oral presentation, and the process is quick and relatively informal. However, the panelist's powers are limited to deciding whether or not to transfer the domain name in question to the complainant. If the loser objects to the decision, he or she has ten days to file suit in court challenging the result.

The UDRP is international in scope. The substantive rules governing UDRP cases do not rely expressly on any nation's trademark law. Rather, they are designed to cover only true cases of cybersquatting, leaving doubtful cases for resolution by the courts. The standard for proving cybersquatting under the UDRP is quite similar to the standard under the ACPA:

> This Paragraph sets forth the type of disputes for which you are required to submit to a mandatory administrative proceeding. These proceedings will be conducted before one of the administrative-dispute-resolution service providers listed at www.icann.org/udrp/approved-providers.htm (each, a "Provider").
>
> a. Applicable Disputes. You are required to submit to a mandatory administrative proceeding in the event that a third party (a "complainant") asserts to the applicable Provider, in compliance with the Rules of Procedure, that
>
> (i) your domain name is identical or confusingly similar to a trademark or service mark in which the complainant has rights; and
>
> (ii) you have no rights or legitimate interests in respect of the domain name; and
>
> (iii) your domain name has been registered and is being used in bad faith.
>
> In the administrative proceeding, the complainant must prove that each of these three elements are present.
>
> b. Evidence of Registration and Use in Bad Faith. For the purposes of Paragraph 4(a)(iii), the following circumstances, in particular but without limitation, if found by the Panel to be present, shall be evidence of the registration and use of a domain name in bad faith:
>
> (i) circumstances indicating that you have registered or you have acquired the domain name primarily for the purpose of selling, renting, or otherwise transferring the domain name registration to the complainant who is the owner of the trademark or service mark or to a competitor of that complainant, for valuable consideration in excess of your documented out-of-pocket costs directly related to the domain name; or
>
> (ii) you have registered the domain name in order to prevent the owner of the trademark or service mark from reflecting the mark in a corresponding domain name, provided that you have engaged in a pattern of such conduct; or
>
> (iii) you have registered the domain name primarily for the purpose of disrupting the business of a competitor; or
>
> (iv) by using the domain name, you have intentionally attempted to attract, for commercial gain, Internet users to your web site or other on-line location, by creating a likelihood of confusion with the complainant's mark as to the source, sponsorship, affiliation, or endorsement of your web site or location or of a product or service on your web site or location.
>
> c. How to Demonstrate Your Rights to and Legitimate Interests in the Domain Name in Responding to a Complaint. When you receive a complaint, you should refer to Paragraph 5 of the Rules of Procedure in determining how your response should be prepared. Any of the following circumstances, in particular but without limitation, if found by the Panel to be proved based on its evaluation of all evidence presented, shall demonstrate your rights or legitimate interests to the domain name for purposes of Paragraph 4(a)(ii):
>
> (i) before any notice to you of the dispute, your use of, or demonstrable preparations to use, the domain name or a name corresponding to the domain name in connection with a bona fide offering of goods or services; or

(ii) you (as an individual, business, or other organization) have been commonly known by the domain name, even if you have acquired no trademark or service mark rights; or

(iii) you are making a legitimate noncommercial or fair use of the domain name, without intent for commercial gain to misleadingly divert consumers or to tarnish the trademark or service mark at issue.

The fast and cheap nature of the UDRP process—and arguably the pro-trademark slant of its decisions during the initial years of the program—has attracted hordes of trademark owners. The UDRP went into effect at the end of 1999, around the same time as the ACPA. But while the ACPA had produced just over 50 reported decisions by the middle of 2002, there were UDRP decisions in cases involving over 7,000 domain names. By the end of 2009, UDRP panelists produced 16,770 decisions involving 30,947 domain names, with over 80 perecent of these decisions favoring the trademark owner. *See* WIPO Domain Name Dispute Resolution Statistics, ***available at*** http://www.wipo.int/amc/en/domains/statistics/.

The typical UDRP case is straightforward, and involves a classic case of cybersquatting: a defendant who registers many different domain names corresponding to trademarks in the hopes of either selling those domains to the trademark owner or diverting traffic and therefore generating advertising revenue. Not surprisingly, these cases tend to be resolved in the trademark owner's favor.

But individual UDRP decisions have garnered their share of controversy. Those controversies have centered on each of the four basic elements of a UDRP claim:

A Legitimate Trademark Right. Ordinarily this is not a problem; almost all of the complainants in UDRP proceedings are trademark owners. But sometimes a complainant will not have a trademark in the name it seeks to control. When that happens, the proper result under the UDRP is to dismiss the case. But panelists and even courts have occasionally been persuaded to grant the complainant rights in words that it simply doesn't own as a trademark. For example, panelists have transferred the domain name sex.biz to a company claiming to have trademarked the term "sex," *see* Schatte v. Personal, FA0209000124756 (NAF Nov. 4, 2002); transferred the common French term merci.com to a company that claimed to own it as a trademark, August Storck KG v. Unimetal Sanayi ve Tic A.S., No. D2001-1125 (WIPO November 23, 2001); and transferred paint.biz to a company that claims to own a trademark in the word "paint," Valspar Sourcing, Inc. v. TIGRE, FA0204000112596 (NAF June 4, 2002). *Cf.* Archdiocese of St. Louis v. Internet Entertainment Group, 34 F. Supp. 2d 1145 (E.D. Mo. 1999) (concluding that "Papal Visit 1999" was a famous trademark entitled to dilution protection). By contrast, other panels have refused to transfer generic terms on the ground that they were not trademarks. For example, one panel refused to transfer the munich.biz domain name on the grounds that the city did not own the exclusive right to its name. Landeshauptstadt Muenchen v. Beanmills, Inc., Case No. DBIZ2002-00147 (WIPO July 1, 2002). *See also* X/Open Company Limited v. Expeditious Investments, Case No. D2002-0294 (WIPO 2002) (refusing to transfer unix.com; a different panel decided the opposite way in a case involving unix.net).

An Identical or Confusingly Similar Domain Name. Trademark owners are entitled to prevent the registration only of names that are identical to or confusingly similar to their trademarks. But some panelists have ordered the transfer of domain names that seem unlikely to meet this standard. For example, a significant number of the cases involving domains of the type [trademark]sucks.com have been transferred to the trademark owner, even though it is highly doubtful any consumer would think that Wal-Mart sponsored the domain name "walmartsucks.com." [Many other cases come to the opposite conclusion, however. For a discussion of the panel decisions on both sides, see Homer TLC v. GreenPeople, FA0508000550345 (NAF Oct. 25, 2005) (refusing to transfer homedepotsucks.com)]. And one panelist even held that the trademark "Tata," the name of a large Indian conglomerate, was infringed by the domain name "bodacioustatas.com." Tata Sons Limited v. D & V Enterprises, Case No. D2000-0479 (WIPO Aug. 18, 2000).

Absence of a Legitimate Right. Cybersquatting under the UDRP requires proof that the domain name registrant lacks any legitimate right to use the domain name. Trademark owners cannot use the UDRP to oust other trademark owners from the use of a mark; if both have a legitimate claim to use the name in commerce, the UDRP will not step in to decide who is "best" entitled to use the mark. But other claims to legitimate use are more controversial. Several panelists have considered whether a legitimate dealer in the plaintiff's products is entitled to use the plaintiff's trademark to advertise the presence of those products. *See* Toma's LLC v. Florida Hi-Performance, AF 0968 (eResolution Sept. 10, 2001):

> Florida appears to be using Toma's trademarked domain name to sell Toma's products. The question is whether this is a legitimate use.
>
> A number of prior panel decisions have considered whether a distributor of a trademark owner's goods who uses the trademark as its domain name has made a bona fide use of the trademark. Unfortunately, the decisions are not in agreement. Compare Kabushiki Kaisha Toshiba v. Distribution Purchasing and Logistics Corp., WIPO D2000-0464 (July 27, 2000); Hydraroll Ltd. v. Morgan Corp., NAF FA2000094108 (April 14, 2000); Mariah Boats, Inc. v. Shoreline Marina, NAF FA4000094392 (May 5, 2000) (all concluding that a distributor has no right to use the trademark of the distributed goods as a domain name) with Freni Brembo S.p.A. v. Webs We Weave, WIPO D2000-1717 (March 19, 2001); K&N Engineering v. Kinnor Servs., WIPO D2000-1077 (January 19, 2001); Weber-Stephen Prods. v. Armitage Hardware, WIPO D2000-0187 (May 11, 2000); Koninklijke Philips Electronics v. Cun Siang Wang, WIPO D2000-1778 (March 15, 2001); Hewlett-Packard Co. v. Napier, NAF FA3000094368 (April 28, 2000) (all concluding that a distributor *is* entitled to use the trademark of the distributed goods as a domain name). See also *Philips*, supra (noting three additional decisions on each side of the issue).
>
> It is clear as a matter of trademark law that the purchaser of bona fide goods is entitled to resell those goods, and to truthfully advertise the goods bearing the trademark. Once the goods are sold into commerce, a trademark owner's rights in those goods are exhausted. See *Philips*, supra (citing authority).[3] Were it not so, distributors could not advertise their goods, car owners could not advertise their used cars, and so on. Since Toma's has not alleged that the "Fake Bake" goods sold on Florida's Web page are counterfeit or altered in any way, Florida is free to truthfully advertise that it is selling those products by using the trademark "Fake Bake." See generally Prestonettes, Inc. v. Coty, 264 U.S. 359, 368 (1924) ("When the mark is used in a way that does not deceive the public we see no such sanctity in the word as to prevent its being used to tell the truth.").

3. The "gray market" importation of bona fide goods from another country presents a more contentious issue, but there is no evidence of importation here.

> Here, though, Florida has done somewhat more than truthfully advertise the availability of bona fide "Fake Bake" products on its Web site. By using the domain name "fakebake.com," Toma's alleges that Florida has confused consumers into thinking that Toma's runs or sponsors the Web page. Toma's is particularly concerned about this because Florida also sells competing products on its page. Whether this exceeds Florida's rights as a reseller of legitimate goods is a difficult question under trademark law. In *Mariah Boats*, supra, the panel concluded that because Shoreline sold both Mariah's boats and other, competing boats, its use of the domain name mariahboats.net was likely to confuse consumers. By contrast, in both *Freni Brembo*, supra and *Weber-Stephens*, supra, the panels concluded that such a use was legitimate notwithstanding the fact that the respondent also sold other goods on its site. And in *Philips*, the panel concluded as follows:
>
>> The Panel accepts that it is possible for a trader in branded goods to advertise and sell goods under the brand without using a domain name incorporating the brand name. Nevertheless such a domain name is of considerable assistance to a business selling the branded goods. The Panel considers that a person can have a legitimate interest in using a particular domain name even if it is not an essential requirement for him to do so.
>
> Whether a bona fide reseller of trademarked goods is always entitled to use a domain name incorporating the trademark is an unsettled legal question. It depends in part on the detailed factual circumstances of the case — how the name is being used, what evidence of confusion there is, whether there is an agreement between the parties, and so on. None of that evidence has been presented to me in this case, other than Toma's allegation (unsupported by evidence) that consumers are being confused. Such a case is not appropriate for resolution under the UDRP, which was designed to deal only with a narrow class of abusive registrations by cybersquatters. The difficult and uncertain allocation of rights in this case should be decided by a court, not by a UDRP panel. *Accord Freni-Brembo*; *Weber-Stephen*. Thus, I cannot conclude that Florida's use here was necessarily illegitimate.

Compare Educational Testing Service v. TOEFL USA, Case No. D2002-0380 (WIPO July 11, 2002) (ordering transfer of toeflusa.com, a domain name owned by TOEFL USA as a trademark for services related to the TOEFL test).

As a general matter in trademark law, "nominative" or non-trademark use — the use by a defendant of the plaintiff's mark to refer to the plaintiff's own products — is not infringement. But in the context of domain names, the defendant's registration of the plaintiff's mark as a domain name may be more likely to confuse consumers into thinking that the defendant is the actual source of the product. This depends on the nature of the name, though. A domain name like microsoft.com might suggest to consumers that the owner is Microsoft, not just an authorized dealer. By contrast, a name like porscheservice.com is more likely to accurately convey that the owner services Porsches, not that the owner is Porsche itself. *But see* Academy of Motion Picture Arts and Sciences v. Khan, FA0109000100142 (NAF Nov. 14, 2001) (ordering cancellation of the domain name oscarbetexchange.com for an online service in which people could bet on the outcome of the Oscars). Some trademark owners have even sued "fan sites" that register domain names in order to praise their subject. *See, e.g.*, 2001 White Castle Way, Inc. v. Glyn O. Jacobs D2004-0001 (Mar. 26, 2004) (declining to order the transfer of patbenetar.com); David Gilmour, David Gilmour Music Limited and David Gilmour Music Overseas Limited v. Ermanno Cenicolla D2000-1459 (Dec. 15, 2000) (ordering the transfer of davidgilmour.com).

Other disputed issues of legitimate use involve noncommercial uses of a name. For instance, a personal name or nickname may be a legitimate reason to register a domain name. An infamous case in this regard involves pokey.org, in which a 12-year-old nicknamed "Pokey" was threatened with suit by the owners of the "Gumby and Pokey" marks. *See also* Strick Corp. v. Strickland, No. FA #94801 (NAF July 3, 2000) (refusing to transfer strick.com, owned by an individual whose nickname was "Strick"). Proof of a legitimate nickname presumably provides a legitimate reason to register a domain name.[4] At the same time, nickname arguments are particularly susceptible to abuse. For example, one panelist held that the registrant of the domain oxforduniversity.com could not show a legitimate interest in the mark by changing his legal name to Oxford University. *See* University of Oxford v. Seagle, No. D2001-7046 (WIPO Aug. 14, 2001).

A final category of possible legitimate interests involves criticism of the trademark owner. Frustrated customers and others who want to criticize a company naturally want to post their criticisms at a domain name that includes the trademark of the company in question. Where the domain name in question is one — like walmartsucks.com — that is unlikely to confuse consumers, the defendant has a legitimate interest in using the mark. The question is more difficult if the critic registers only the trademark — say, walmart.com. Consumers may well be confused, at least initially, if walmart.com isn't run by Wal-Mart. *See Doughney, supra.* But even if the use will draw customers to the site because they are confused, arguably the critic has a legitimate interest in registering the domain name in order to attract the attention of those consumers. *See* Lucas Nursery & Landscaping Inc. v. Grosse, 359 F.3d 806 (6th Cir. 2004) (rejecting ACPA claim against dissatisfied customer who registered "lucasnursery.com"); TMI, Inc. v. Maxwell, 368 F.3d 433 (5th Cir. 2004); Northland Ins. Co. v. Blaylock, 115 F. Supp. 2d 1108 (D. Minn. 2000) (registration of company's trademark as a domain name in order to criticize the company was not infringing).

Bad Faith. Like the ACPA, the UDRP identifies a number of factors evidentiary of bad faith. Registration of multiple names, demanding money to relinquish them, and providing false address information are all considered evidence of bad faith. Some panelists have gone farther, however, holding that a desire to criticize a trademark owner can itself be evidence of bad faith. *See* Reg Vardy Plc v. Wilkinson, Case No. D2001-0593 (WIPO July 3, 2001). *Compare* Savannah College of Art & Design v. Houeix, No. CPR 0206 (CPR Feb. 19, 2002) (former employee could register scad.info in order to criticize the college).

On the other hand, at least one panelist has held that the mere registration of domain names does not constitute bad faith, leaving open the possibility that cybersquatters who do not ask for money may be entitled to keep the domain names they have registered even if they cannot show any legitimate interest in the name. *See* Ingram Micro v. Ingredients Among Modern Microwaves, No. D2002-0301 (WIPO May 15, 2002). *But see* Telstra Corporation Limited v. Nuclear Marshmallows, Case No. D2000-0003 (WIPO Feb. 18, 2000) (finding bad faith absent any "positive action" by registrant).

---

4. It does not necessarily provide the registrant with the right to compete. For example, someone with the last name McDonald will be prevented from opening a hamburger stand using the name "McDonald's," because of the likelihood that consumers will be confused. *See* E. & J. Gallo Winery v. Gallo Cattle Co., 967 F.2d 1280 (9th Cir. 1992) (brother of Ernest & Julio Gallo could not use Gallo name to sell meat because of the possibility of confusion).

UDRP decisions have been criticized as unduly favorable to trademark owners, particularly in the first two years of operation. *See, e.g.*, Michael Geist, *Fair.com?: An Examination of the Allegations of Systematic Unfairness in the ICANN UDRP*, 27 Brook. J. Int'l L. 903 (2002); Elizabeth G. Thornburg, *Fast, Cheap and Out of Control: Lessons from the ICANN Dispute Resolution Process*, 6 J. Small & Emerging Bus. L. 191 (2002). These critics focus both on the outcomes of the early cases, which overwhelmingly ordered transfers of domain names, and on deficiencies in the process by which the cases are decided. Because only the trademark owner gets to choose which dispute resolution company will decide the case, dispute resolution providers sometimes seem to compete for the approval of trademark owners. NAF and WIPO seem to assign cases to favored panelists, rather than randomly distributing them among eligible panelists. And NAF in particular has advertised its pro-trademark decisions in an effort to drum up more business. Notwithstanding these problems, panel opinions decided after 2003 have been substantially less skewed in favor of trademark owners than the earlier opinions.

Other concerns center on the short deadlines and the sketchy nature of the process required. Registrants have only a short time to respond to a UDRP complaint, and if they lose have only ten days to go to court to stop the transfer of their domain name. Many registrants are not represented by counsel, and so may have difficulty understanding the process and their obligations. As a result, a large percentage of registrants fail to answer a complaint, and relatively few registrants challenge the transfer of their domain names in court.

Michael Froomkin has proposed a series of procedural reforms to improve the UDRP. A. Michael Froomkin, *ICANN's "Uniform Dispute Resolution Policy": Causes and (Partial) Cures*, 67 Brook. L. Rev. 605 (2002). Among other things, Froomkin suggests procedures for removing biased arbitrators; the creation of a substantive doctrine of "reverse domain name hijacking," in which domain name owners who are subject to abusive claims could recover money; and making it easier for respondents to meet the deadlines for filing a response and selecting an arbitration panel. Others have argued that an administrative appeal process would be a good idea. And it also seems reasonable to allow registrants to respond online, as eResolution once did.

Because of the limited nature of the UDRP process, courts to consider the issue have unanimously concluded that it is not "arbitration" subject to judicial deference under the Federal Arbitration Act. Rather, UDRP decisions are reviewed de novo in the courts. *See, e.g.*, Sallen v. Corinthians Licenciamentos Ltd., 273 F.3d 14 (1st Cir. 2001); Parisi v. Netlearning, Inc., 139 F. Supp. 2d 745 (E.D. Va. 2001).

F. INDIRECT INFRINGEMENT

Tiffany (NJ) Inc. v. eBay Inc.
600 F.3d 93 (2d Cir. 2010)

Sack, Circuit Judge:

eBay, Inc. ("eBay"), through its eponymous online marketplace, has revolutionized the online sale of goods, especially used goods. It has facilitated the buying and selling by hundreds of millions of people and entities, to their benefit and eBay's profit. But that marketplace is sometimes employed by users as a means to perpetrate fraud by selling counterfeit goods.

Plaintiffs Tiffany (NJ) Inc. and Tiffany and Company (together, "Tiffany") have created and cultivated a brand of jewelry bespeaking high-end quality and style. Based on Tiffany's concern that some use eBay's website to sell counterfeit Tiffany merchandise, Tiffany has instituted this action against eBay, asserting various causes of action — sounding in trademark infringement, trademark dilution and false advertising — arising from eBay's advertising and listing practices. . . .

Background

By opinion dated July 14, 2008, following a week-long bench trial, the United States District Court for the Southern District of New York (Richard J. Sullivan, Judge) set forth its findings of fact and conclusions of law. Tiffany (NJ) Inc. v. eBay, Inc., 576 F. Supp. 2d 463 (S.D.N.Y. 2008) ("*Tiffany*"). . . . Except where noted otherwise, we conclude that the district court's findings of fact are not clearly erroneous. We therefore rely upon those non-erroneous findings in setting forth the facts of, and considering, this dispute.

eBay

eBay is the proprietor of www.ebay.com, an Internet-based marketplace that allows those who register with it to purchase goods from and sell goods to one another. It "connect[s] buyers and sellers and [ ] enable[s] transactions, which are carried out directly between eBay members." *Tiffany*, 576 F. Supp. 2d at 475. In its auction and listing services, it "provides the venue for the sale [of goods] and support for the transaction[s], [but] it does not itself sell the items" listed for sale on the site, id. at 475, nor does it ever take physical possession of them, id. Thus, "eBay generally does not know whether or when an item is delivered to the buyer." Id.

eBay has been enormously successful. More than six million new listings are posted on its site daily. At any given time it contains some 100 million listings.

eBay generates revenue by charging sellers to use its listing services. For any listing, it charges an "insertion fee" based on the auction's starting price for the goods being sold and ranges from $0.20 to $4.80. For any completed sale, it charges a "final value fee" that ranges from 5.25% to 10% of the final sale price of the item. . . .

eBay also generates revenue through a company named PayPal, which it owns and which allows users to process their purchases. PayPal deducts, as a fee for each transaction that it processes, 1.9% to 2.9% of the transaction amount, plus $0.30. This gives eBay an added incentive to increase both the volume and the price of the goods sold on its website.

Tiffany

Tiffany is a world-famous purveyor of, among other things, branded jewelry. Since 2000, all new Tiffany jewelry sold in the United States has been available exclusively through Tiffany's retail stores, catalogs, and website, and through its Corporate Sales Department. It does not use liquidators, sell overstock merchandise, or put its goods on sale at discounted prices. It does not — nor can it, for that matter — control the "legitimate secondary market in authentic Tiffany silvery jewelry," i.e., the market for second-hand Tiffany wares. The record developed at trial "offere[d] little basis from which to discern the actual availability of authentic Tiffany silver jewelry in the secondary market."

Sometime before 2004, Tiffany became aware that counterfeit Tiffany merchandise was being sold on eBay's site. Prior to and during the course of this litigation, Tiffany conducted two surveys known as "Buying Programs," one in 2004 and another in 2005, in an attempt to assess the extent of this practice. Under those programs, Tiffany bought various items on eBay and then inspected and evaluated them to determine how many were counterfeit. Tiffany found that 73.1% of the purported Tiffany goods purchased in the 2004 Buying Program and 75.5% of those purchased in the 2005 Buying Program were counterfeit. The district court concluded, however, that the Buying Programs were "methodologically flawed and of questionable value," id. at 512, and "provide[d] limited evidence as to the total percentage of counterfeit goods available on eBay at any given time," id. at 486. The court nonetheless decided that during the period in which the Buying Programs were in effect, a "significant portion of the 'Tiffany' sterling silver jewelry listed on the eBay website . . . was counterfeit," and that eBay knew "that some portion of the Tiffany goods sold on its website might be counterfeit," id. at 507. The court found, however, that "a substantial number of authentic Tiffany goods are [also] sold on eBay." Id. at 509.

Reducing or eliminating the sale of all second-hand Tiffany goods, including genuine Tiffany pieces, through eBay's website would benefit Tiffany in at least one sense: It would diminish the competition in the market for genuine Tiffany merchandise. . . . The immediate effect would be loss of revenue to eBay, even though there might be a countervailing gain by eBay resulting from increased consumer confidence about the bona fides of other goods sold through its website.

Anti-Counterfeiting Measures

Because eBay facilitates many sales of Tiffany goods, genuine and otherwise, and obtains revenue on every transaction, it generates substantial revenues from the sale of purported Tiffany goods, some of which are counterfeit. "eBay's Jewelry & Watches category manager estimated that, between April 2000 and June 2004, eBay earned $4.1 million in revenue from completed listings with 'Tiffany' in the listing title in the Jewelry & Watches category." Id. at 481. Although eBay was generating revenue from all sales of goods on its site, including counterfeit goods, the district court found eBay to have "an interest in eliminating counterfeit Tiffany merchandise from eBay . . . to preserve the reputation of its website as a safe place to do business." Id. at 469. The buyer of fake Tiffany goods might, if and when the forgery was detected, fault eBay. Indeed, the district court found that "buyers . . . complain[ed] to eBay" about the sale of counterfeit Tiffany goods. Id. at 487. "[D]uring the last six weeks of 2004, 125 consumers complained to eBay about purchasing 'Tiffany' items through the eBay website that they believed to be counterfeit." Id.

Because eBay "never saw or inspected the merchandise in the listings," its ability to determine whether a particular listing was for counterfeit goods was limited. Id. at 477-78. Even had it been able to inspect the goods, moreover, in many instances it likely would not have had the expertise to determine whether they were counterfeit. . . .

Notwithstanding these limitations, eBay spent "as much as $20 million each year on tools to promote trust and safety on its website." Id. at 476. For example, eBay and PayPal set up "buyer protection programs," under which, in certain circumstances, the buyer would be reimbursed for the cost of items purchased on eBay that were discovered not to be genuine. eBay also established a "Trust and Safety" department, with some 4,000 employees "devoted to trust and safety" issues, including over 200 who "focus exclusively on combating infringement" and 70 who "work exclusively with law enforcement." Id. at 476.

By May 2002, eBay had implemented a "fraud engine," "which is principally dedicated to ferreting out illegal listings, including counterfeit listings." Id. at 477. eBay had theretofore employed manual searches for keywords in listings in an effort to "identify blatant instances of potentially infringing . . . activity." Id. "The fraud engine uses rules and complex models that automatically search for activity that violates eBay policies." Id. In addition to identifying items actually advertised as counterfeit, the engine also incorporates various filters designed to screen out less-obvious instances of counterfeiting using "data elements designed to evaluate listings based on, for example, the seller's Internet protocol address, any issues associated with the seller's account on eBay, and the feedback the seller has received from other eBay users." Id. In addition to general filters, the fraud engine incorporates "Tiffany-specific filters," including "approximately 90 different keywords" designed to help distinguish between genuine and counterfeit Tiffany goods. Id. at 491. During the period in dispute, eBay also "periodically conducted [manual] reviews of listings in an effort to remove those that might be selling counterfeit goods, including Tiffany goods." Id.

For nearly a decade, including the period at issue, eBay has also maintained and administered the "Verified Rights Owner ('VeRO') Program"—a " 'notice-and-takedown' system" allowing owners of intellectual property rights, including Tiffany, to "report to eBay any listing offering potentially infringing items, so that eBay could remove such reported listings." Id. at 478. Any such rights-holder with a "good-faith belief that [a particular listed] item infringed on a copyright or a trademark" could report the item to eBay, using a "Notice Of Claimed Infringement form or NOCI form." Id. During the period under consideration, eBay's practice was to remove reported listings within twenty-four hours of receiving a NOCI, but eBay in fact deleted seventy to eighty percent of them within twelve hours of notification.

On receipt of a NOCI, if the auction or sale had not ended, eBay would, in addition to removing the listing, cancel the bids and inform the seller of the reason for the cancellation. If bidding had ended, eBay would retroactively cancel the transaction. In the event of a cancelled auction, eBay would refund the fees it had been paid in connection with the auction.

In some circumstances, eBay would reimburse the buyer for the cost of a purchased item, provided the buyer presented evidence that the purchased item was counterfeit. During the relevant time period, the district court found, eBay "never refused to remove a reported Tiffany listing, acted in good faith in responding to Tiffany's NOCIs, and always provided Tiffany with the seller's contact information." Id. at 488.

In addition, eBay has allowed rights owners such as Tiffany to create an "About Me" webpage on eBay's website "to inform eBay users about their products, intellectual property rights, and legal positions." Id. at 479. eBay does not exercise control over the content of those pages in a manner material to the issues before us.

Tiffany, not eBay, maintains the Tiffany "About Me" page. With the headline "**BUYER BEWARE**," the page begins: "**Most of the purported TIFFANY & CO. silver jewelry and packaging available on eBay is counterfeit.**" (bold face type in original). It also says, inter alia:

> The only way you can be certain that you are purchasing a genuine TIFFANY & CO. product is to purchase it from a Tiffany & Co. retail store, via our website (www.tiffany.com) or through a Tiffany & Co. catalogue. Tiffany & Co. stores do not authenticate merchandise. A good jeweler or appraiser may be able to do this for you.

In 2003 or early 2004, eBay began to use "special warning messages when a seller attempted to list a Tiffany item." *Tiffany*, 576 F. Supp. 2d at 491. These messages "instructed the seller to make sure that the item was authentic Tiffany merchandise and informed the seller that eBay 'does not tolerate the listing of replica, counterfeit, or otherwise unauthorized items' and that violation of this policy 'could result in suspension of [the seller's] account.'" Id. (alteration in original). The messages also provided a link to Tiffany's "About Me" page with its "buyer beware" disclaimer. If the seller "continued to list an item despite the warning, the listing was flagged for review." Id.

In addition to cancelling particular suspicious transactions, eBay has also suspended from its website " 'hundreds of thousands of sellers every year,' tens of thousands of whom were suspected [of] having engaged in infringing conduct." Id. at 489. eBay primarily employed a " 'three strikes rule' " for suspensions, but would suspend sellers after the first violation if it was clear that "the seller 'listed a number of infringing items,' and '[selling counterfeit merchandise] appears to be the only thing they've come to eBay to do.' " Id. But if "a seller listed a potentially infringing item but appeared overall to be a legitimate seller, the 'infringing items [were] taken down, and the seller [would] be sent a warning on the first offense and given the educational information, [and] told that . . . if they do this again, they will be suspended from eBay.' " Id. (alterations in original).[5]

By late 2006, eBay had implemented additional anti-fraud measures: delaying the ability of buyers to view listings of certain brand names, including Tiffany's, for 6 to 12 hours so as to give rights-holders such as Tiffany more time to review those listings; developing the ability to assess the number of items listed in a given listing; and restricting one-day and three-day auctions and cross-border trading for some brand-name items.

5. According to the district court, "eBay took appropriate steps to warn and then to suspend sellers when eBay learned of potential trademark infringement under that seller's account." *Tiffany*, 576 F. Supp. 2d at 489. The district court concluded that it was understandable that eBay did not have a "hard-and-fast, one-strike rule" of suspending sellers because a NOCI "did not constitute a definitive finding that the listed item was counterfeit" and because "suspension was a very serious matter, particularly to those sellers who relied on eBay for their livelihoods." Id. The district court ultimately found eBay's policy to be "appropriate and effective in preventing sellers from returning to eBay and re-listing potentially counterfeit merchandise." Id.

The district court concluded that "eBay consistently took steps to improve its technology and develop anti-fraud measures as such measures became technologically feasible and reasonably available." Id. at 493.

Discussion

I. Direct Trademark Infringement

[The court found that eBay's use of the Tiffany trademark on the eBay Web site and in sponsored links appearing on Google and Yahoo! was non-infringing nominative fair use.]

II. Contributory Trademark Infringement

The more difficult issue, and the one that the parties have properly focused our attention on, is whether eBay is liable for contributory trademark infringement—i.e., for culpably facilitating the infringing conduct of the counterfeiting vendors. Acknowledging the paucity of case law to guide us, we conclude that the district court correctly granted judgment on this issue in favor of eBay.

A. Principles

Contributory trademark infringement is a judicially created doctrine that derives from the common law of torts. See, e.g., Hard Rock Cafe Licensing Corp. v. Concession Servs., Inc., 955 F.2d 1143, 1148 (7th Cir.1992); cf. Metro-Goldwyn-Mayer Studios Inc. v. Grokster, Ltd., 545 U.S. 913, 930 (2005) ("[T]hese doctrines of secondary liability emerged from common law principles and are well established in the law.") (citations omitted). The Supreme Court most recently dealt with the subject in Inwood Laboratories, Inc. v. Ives Laboratories, Inc., 456 U.S. 844 (1982). There, the plaintiff, Ives, asserted that several drug manufacturers had induced pharmacists to mislabel a drug the defendants produced to pass it off as Ives'. See id. at 847-50. According to the Court, "if a manufacturer or distributor intentionally induces another to infringe a trademark, or if it continues to supply its product to one whom it knows or has reason to know is engaging in trademark infringement, the manufacturer or distributor is contributorially responsible for any harm done as a result of the deceit." Id. at 854. . . .

Inwood's test for contributory trademark infringement applies on its face to manufacturers and distributors of goods. Courts have, however, extended the test to providers of services.

The Seventh Circuit applied *Inwood* to a lawsuit against the owner of a swap meet, or "flea market," whose vendors were alleged to have sold infringing Hard Rock Cafe T-shirts. See *Hard Rock Cafe*, 955 F.2d at 1148-49. The court "treated trademark infringement as a species of tort," id. at 1148, and analogized the swap meet owner to a landlord or licensor, on whom the common law "imposes the same duty . . . [as *Inwood*] impose[s] on manufacturers and distributors," id. at 1149; see also Fonovisa,

Inc. v. Cherry Auction, Inc., 76 F.3d 259 (9th Cir. 1996) (adopting *Hard Rock Café*'s reasoning and applying *Inwood* to a swap meet owner).

Speaking more generally, the Ninth Circuit concluded that *Inwood*'s test for contributory trademark infringement applies to a service provider if he or she exercises sufficient control over the infringing conduct. Lockheed Martin Corp. v. Network Solutions, Inc., 194 F.3d 980, 984 (9th Cir. 1999); see also id. ("Direct control and monitoring of the instrumentality used by a third party to infringe the plaintiff's mark permits the expansion of *Inwood Lab.*'s 'supplies a product' requirement for contributory infringement.").

We have apparently addressed contributory trademark infringement in only two related decisions, see Polymer Tech. Corp. v. Mimran, 975 F.2d 58, 64 (2d Cir. 1992) ("*Polymer I*"); Polymer Tech. Corp. v. Mimran, 37 F.3d 74, 81 (2d Cir. 1994) ("*Polymer II*"), and even then in little detail. Citing *Inwood*, we said that "[a] distributor who intentionally induces another to infringe a trademark, or continues to supply its product to one whom it knows or has reason to know is engaging in trademark infringement, is contributorially liable for any injury." *Polymer I*, 975 F.2d at 64.

The limited case law leaves the law of contributory trademark infringement ill-defined. Although we are not the first court to consider the application of *Inwood* to the Internet, see, e.g., *Lockheed*, 194 F.3d 980, supra (Internet domain name registrar), we are apparently the first to consider its application to an online marketplace.[9]

B. Discussion

1. Does *Inwood* Apply?

In the district court, the parties disputed whether eBay was subject to the *Inwood* test. See *Tiffany*, 576 F. Supp. 2d at 504. eBay argued that it was not because it supplies a service while *Inwood* governs only manufacturers and distributors of products. Id. The district court rejected that distinction. It adopted instead the reasoning of the Ninth Circuit in *Lockheed* to conclude that *Inwood* applies to a service provider who exercises sufficient control over the means of the infringing conduct. Id. at 505-06. Looking "to the extent of the control exercised by eBay over its sellers' means of infringement," the district court concluded that *Inwood* applied in light of the "significant control" eBay retained over the transactions and listings facilitated by and conducted through its website. Id. at 505-07.

9. European courts have done so. A Belgian court declined to hold eBay liable for counterfeit cosmetic products sold through its website. See Lancôme v. eBay, Brussels Commercial Court (Aug. 12, 2008), Docket No. A/07/06032. French courts, by contrast, have concluded that eBay violated applicable trademark laws. See, e.g., S.A. Louis Vuitton Malletier v. eBay, Inc., Tribunal de Commerce de Paris, Premiere Chambre B. (Paris Commercial Court), Case No. 200677799 (June 30, 2008); Hermes v. eBay, Troyes High Court (June 4, 2008), Docket No. 06/0264; see also Max Colchester, "EBay to Pay Damages To Unit of LVMH," The Wall Street Journal, Feb. 12, 2010, http://online.wsj.com/article_email/SB10001424052748704337004575059523018541764-lMyQjAxMTAwMDEwMjExNDIyWj.html (last visited Mar. 1, 2010) ("A Paris court Thursday ordered eBay to pay Louis Vuitton Q200,000 ($275,000) in damages and to stop paying search engines to direct certain key words to the eBay site."); see generally, Valerie Walsh Johnson & Laura P. Merritt, TIFFANY v. EBAY: *A Case of Genuine Disparity in International Court Rulings on Counterfeit Products*, 1 No. 2 Landslide 22 (2008) (surveying decisions by European courts in trademark infringement cases brought against eBay).

On appeal, eBay no longer maintains that it is not subject to *Inwood*. We therefore assume without deciding that *Inwood*'s test for contributory trademark infringement governs.

2. Is eBay Liable Under *Inwood*?

The question that remains, then, is whether eBay is liable under the *Inwood* test on the basis of the services it provided to those who used its website to sell counterfeit Tiffany products. As noted, when applying *Inwood* to service providers, there are two ways in which a defendant may become contributorially liable for the infringing conduct of another: first, if the service provider "intentionally induces another to infringe a trademark," and second, if the service provider "continues to supply its [service] to one whom it knows or has reason to know is engaging in trademark infringement." *Inwood*, 456 U.S. at 854. Tiffany does not argue that eBay induced the sale of counterfeit Tiffany goods on its website—the circumstances addressed by the first part of the *Inwood* test. It argues instead, under the second part of the *Inwood* test, that eBay continued to supply its services to the sellers of counterfeit Tiffany goods while knowing or having reason to know that such sellers were infringing Tiffany's mark. . . .

On appeal, Tiffany argues that the distinction drawn by the district court between eBay's general knowledge of the sale of counterfeit Tiffany goods through its website, and its specific knowledge as to which particular sellers were making such sales, is a "false" one not required by the law. Tiffany posits that the only relevant question is "whether all of the knowledge, when taken together, puts [eBay] on notice that there is a substantial problem of trademark infringement. If so and if it fails to act, [eBay] is liable for contributory trademark infringement."

We agree with the district court. For contributory trademark infringement liability to lie, a service provider must have more than a general knowledge or reason to know that its service is being used to sell counterfeit goods. Some contemporary knowledge of which particular listings are infringing or will infringe in the future is necessary.

We are not persuaded by Tiffany's proposed interpretation of *Inwood*. Tiffany understands the "lesson of *Inwood*" to be that an action for contributory trademark infringement lies where "the evidence [of infringing activity]—direct or circumstantial, taken as a whole— . . . provide[s] a basis for finding that the defendant knew or should have known that its product or service was being used to further illegal counterfeiting activity." Appellants' Br. 30. We think that Tiffany reads *Inwood* too broadly. Although the *Inwood* Court articulated a "knows or has reason to know" prong in setting out its contributory liability test, the Court explicitly declined to apply that prong to the facts then before it. See *Inwood*, 456 U.S. at 852 n.12 ("The District Court also found that the petitioners did not continue to provide drugs to retailers whom they knew or should have known were engaging in trademark infringement. The Court of Appeals did not discuss that finding, and we do not address it.") (internal citation omitted). The Court applied only the inducement prong of the test. *See* id. at 852-59.

We therefore do not think that *Inwood* establishes the contours of the "knows or has reason to know" prong. Insofar as it speaks to the issue, though, the particular phrasing that the Court used—that a defendant will be liable if it "continues to supply its product to *one* whom it knows or has reason to know is engaging in trademark infringement," id. at 854 (emphasis added)—supports the district court's interpretation of *Inwood*, not Tiffany's.

We find helpful the Supreme Court's discussion of *Inwood* in a subsequent *copyright* case, Sony Corp. of America v. Universal City Studios, Inc., 464 U.S. 417 (1984). There, defendant Sony manufactured and sold home video tape recorders. Id. at 419. Plaintiffs Universal Studios and Walt Disney Productions held copyrights on various television programs that individual television-viewers had taped using the defendant's recorders. Id. at 419-20. The plaintiffs contended that this use of the recorders constituted copyright infringement for which the defendants should be held contributorily liable. Id. In ruling for the defendants, the Court discussed *Inwood* and the differences between contributory liability in trademark versus copyright law.

> If *Inwood*'s *narrow standard* for contributory trademark infringement governed here, [the plaintiffs'] claim of contributory infringement would merit little discussion. Sony certainly does not 'intentionally induce[ ]' its customers to make infringing uses of [the plaintiffs'] copyrights, nor does it supply its products to *identified individuals known by it* to be engaging in continuing infringement of [the plaintiffs'] copyrights.

Id. at 439 n.19 (quoting *Inwood*, 456 U.S. at 855, 102 S. Ct. 2182; emphases added).

Thus, the Court suggested, had the *Inwood* standard applied in *Sony*, the fact that Sony might have known that some portion of the purchasers of its product used it to violate the copyrights of others would not have provided a sufficient basis for contributory liability. *Inwood*'s "narrow standard" would have required knowledge by Sony of "identified individuals" engaging in infringing conduct. Tiffany's reading of *Inwood* is therefore contrary to the interpretation of that case set forth in *Sony*.

Although the Supreme Court's observations in *Sony*, a copyright case, about the "knows or has reason to know" prong of the contributory trademark infringement test set forth in *Inwood* were dicta, they constitute the only discussion of that prong by the Supreme Court of which we are aware. We think them to be persuasive authority here.

Applying *Sony*'s interpretation of *Inwood*, we agree with the district court that "Tiffany's general allegations of counterfeiting failed to provide eBay with the knowledge required under *Inwood*." *Tiffany*, 576 F. Supp. 2d at 511. Tiffany's demand letters and Buying Programs did not identify particular sellers who Tiffany thought were then offering or would offer counterfeit goods. Id. at 511-13.[13] And although the NOCIs and buyer complaints gave eBay reason to know that certain sellers had been selling counterfeits, those sellers' listings were removed and repeat offenders were suspended from the eBay site. Thus Tiffany failed to demonstrate that eBay was supplying its service to individuals who it knew or had reason to know were selling counterfeit Tiffany goods.

Accordingly, we affirm the judgment of the district court insofar as it holds that eBay is not contributorially liable for trademark infringement.

3. Willful Blindness

Tiffany and its amici express their concern that if eBay is not held liable except when specific counterfeit listings are brought to its attention, eBay will have no incentive to root out such listings from its website. They argue that this will effectively

13. The demand letters did say that eBay should presume that sellers offering five or more Tiffany goods were selling counterfeits, id. at 511, but we agree with the district court that this presumption was factually unfounded, id. at 511-12.

require Tiffany and similarly situated retailers to police eBay's website — and many others like it — "24 hours a day, and 365 days a year." Council of Fashion Designers of America, Inc. Amicus Br. 5. They urge that this is a burden that most mark holders cannot afford to bear.

First, and most obviously, we are interpreting the law and applying it to the facts of this case. We could not, even if we thought it wise, revise the existing law in order to better serve one party's interests at the expense of the other's.

But we are also disposed to think, and the record suggests, that private market forces give eBay and those operating similar businesses a strong incentive to minimize the counterfeit goods sold on their websites. eBay received many complaints from users claiming to have been duped into buying counterfeit Tiffany products sold on eBay. *Tiffany*, 576 F. Supp. 2d at 487. The risk of alienating these users gives eBay a reason to identify and remove counterfeit listings.[14] Indeed, it has spent millions of dollars in that effort.

Moreover, we agree with the district court that if eBay had reason to suspect that counterfeit Tiffany goods were being sold through its website, and intentionally shielded itself from discovering the offending listings or the identity of the sellers behind them, eBay might very well have been charged with knowledge of those sales sufficient to satisfy *Inwood*'s "knows or has reason to know" prong. *Tiffany*, 576 F. Supp. 2d at 513-14. A service provider is not, we think, permitted willful blindness. When it has reason to suspect that users of its service are infringing a protected mark, it may not shield itself from learning of the particular infringing transactions by looking the other way. See, e.g., *Hard Rock Cafe*, 955 F.2d at 1149 ("To be willfully blind, a person must suspect wrongdoing and deliberately fail to investigate."); *Fonovisa*, 76 F.3d at 265 (applying *Hard Rock Cafe*'s reasoning to conclude that "a swap meet can not disregard its vendors' blatant trademark infringements with impunity").[15] In the words of the Seventh Circuit, "willful blindness is equivalent to actual knowledge for purposes of the Lanham Act." *Hard Rock Cafe*, 955 F.2d at 1149.

eBay appears to concede that it knew as a general matter that counterfeit Tiffany products were listed and sold through its website. *Tiffany*, 576 F. Supp. 2d at 514. Without more, however, this knowledge is insufficient to trigger liability under *Inwood*. The district court found, after careful consideration, that eBay was not willfully blind to the counterfeit sales. Id. at 513. That finding is not clearly erroneous.[17] eBay did not ignore the information it was given about counterfeit sales on its website.

14. At the same time, we appreciate the argument that insofar as eBay receives revenue from undetected counterfeit listings and sales through the fees it charges, it has an incentive to permit such listings and sales to continue.

15. To be clear, a service provider is not contributorially liable under *Inwood* merely for failing to anticipate that others would use its service to infringe a protected mark. *Inwood*, 456 U.S. at 854 n.13, 102 S. Ct. 2182 (stating that for contributory liability to lie, a defendant must do more than "reasonably anticipate" a third party's infringing conduct (internal quotation marks omitted)). But contributory liability may arise where a defendant is (as was eBay here) made aware that there was infringement on its site but (unlike eBay here) ignored that fact.

17. Tiffany's reliance on the "flea market" cases, *Hard Rock Cafe* and *Fonovisa*, is unavailing. eBay's efforts to combat counterfeiting far exceeded the efforts made by the defendants in those cases. *See Hard Rock Cafe*, 955 F.2d at 1146 (defendant did not investigate any of the seizures of counterfeit products at its swap meet, even though it knew they had occurred); *Fonovisa*, 76 F.3d at 265 (concluding that plaintiff stated a claim for contributory trademark infringement based on allegation that swap meet "disregard[ed] its vendors' blatant trademark infringements with impunity"). Moreover, neither case concluded that the

COMMENTS AND QUESTIONS

1. *Who Is the Lowest-Cost Avoider of Infringement?* Has the Second Circuit reached the correct result? In its discussion of willful blindness, the Second Circuit followed the lead of the district court, which stated early in its opinion that "under the law as it currently stands, it does not matter whether eBay or Tiffany could more efficiently bear the burden of policing the eBay website for Tiffany counterfeits—an open question left unresolved by this trial." Tiffany (NJ) Inc. v. eBay Inc., 576 F. Supp. 2d 463, 470 (S.D.N.Y. 2008). Should indirect infringement doctrine take into account who can more efficiently bear the burden of policing for counterfeits? In other areas of trademark law, we have seen courts justify outcomes based on their effects on consumer search costs. Why shouldn't courts apply economic analysis in the indirect infringement context as well? eBay's technology and business model very powerfully reduce consumer search costs. Could that be influencing the courts' thinking?

2. *The Implications of Perfect Copies.* In the *eBay* district court's recitation of the facts, it noted that Tiffany's own expert could not be sure if nearly one-quarter of the merchandise he purchased from various eBay sellers was authentic or counterfeit. *See* Tiffany (NJ) Inc. v. eBay, Inc., 576 F. Supp. 2d 463, 485 (S.D.N.Y. 2008). How can eBay be expected effectively to police for counterfeiting when Tiffany itself may not be able to do so? For further consideration of the legal and social implications of perfect counterfeits, see Barton Beebe, *Intellectual Property Law and the Sumptuary Code*, 123 HARV. L. REV. 809 (2010).

3. *Bricks-and-Mortar Merchants.* What are the implications of the *eBay* decision for practices in the non-virtual world? In Hard Rock Cafe Licensing Corp. v. Concession Services, Inc., 955 F.2d 1143, 1149 (7th Cir. 1992), the Seventh Circuit applied the *Inwood* test for contributory trademark liability to the operator of a flea market, and found that the operator would be liable for the copyright infringement of vendors it permits on its premises if it knows or has reason to know that the vendor "is acting or will act tortiously." However, the operator still "has no affirmative duty to take precautions against the sale of counterfeits." *Id.* In *eBay*, the Second Circuit distinguished *Hard Rock Cafe* and *Fonovisa* on the ground that "eBay's efforts to combat counterfeiting far exceeded the efforts made by the defendants in those cases." How much control should we expect the proprietor of a market to exert to avoid the charge of "willful blindness"?

4. *Domain Name Registries.* A related problem has arisen in the context of domain name registries. Should they be liable for registering domain names that infringe the trademarks of others? In Lockheed Martin Corp. v. Network Solutions, Inc., 194 F.3d 980 (9th Cir. 1999), the court held that Network Solutions, Inc., the exclusive domain name registry from 1991 to 1999, had no responsibility to screen domain names and bore "no affirmative duty to police the Internet in search of potentially infringing uses of domain names." The Anticybersquatting Consumer Protection Act in 1999 immunizes domain name registrars from monetary relief for registering a domain name that infringes trademark rights. *See* 15 U.S.C. §1114(2)(D); Lanham

---

defendant was willfully blind. The court in *Hard Rock Cafe* remanded so that the district court could apply the correct definition of "willful blindness," 955 F.2d at 1149, and the court in *Fonovisa* merely sustained the plaintiff's complaint against a motion to dismiss, 76 F.3d at 260-61, 265.

Act § 32(2)(D). This section also provides a safe harbor for domain registries from liability for refusing to register, canceling, or transferring a domain name in furtherance of its dispute resolution policy.

5. *Google Adwords.* We saw earlier that Rescuecom v. Google, 562 F.3d 123 (2d Cir. 2009), merely established that Google is making a "use in commerce" of the various trademarks it recommends to its Adwords program clients. The Second Circuit explicitly stated that it had "no idea" whether Google's use of others' trademarks confuses consumers. *Id.* at 130. In GEICO v. Google, 2005 WL 1903128 (E.D. Va. Aug. 8, 2005), the district court rejected such a claim, ruling that the plaintiff could not demonstrate that the mere sale of a keyword confused consumers. The court left open the possibility that the advertisers themselves might be liable for infringement if the text of the ads were confusing, and that Google might be liable for contributory infringement if it encouraged such confusion. *See* Stacey L. Dogan & Mark A. Lemley, *Trademarks and Consumer Search Costs on the Internet*, 41 Hous. L. Rev. 777 (2004) (arguing for this approach); *see also* Google France and Google Inc. et al. v. Louis Vuitton Malletier et al., Case Nos. C-236/08 to C-238/08 (Mar. 23, 2010 ECJ) (generally adopting this approach). Does it make sense to distinguish between ads that are likely to confuse consumers and those that aren't? Or is the mere use of a trademark as a keyword problematic even if no one will be confused by the resulting ad? Even if an advertiser is liable for running a confusing ad, is Google contributing to that infringement? How? What could Google do to avoid liability, short of terminating its entire advertising program?

6 Defenses

Even when the plaintiff is able to show a likelihood of consumer confusion or trademark dilution, the defendant may still escape liability if it succeeds in establishing one of various affirmative defenses to trademark infringement. In what follows we consider the most important of these defenses. We begin with the defense that the plaintiff has "abandoned" its mark.

A. ABANDONMENT

Major League Baseball Properties, Inc. v. Sed Non Olet Denarius, Ltd.
817 F. Supp. 1103 (S.D.N.Y. 1993)

MOTLEY, District Judge.

I. Introduction

Plaintiffs, Major League Baseball Properties, Inc. ("Properties") and Los Angeles Dodgers, Inc. ("Los Angeles"), allege in their Amended Complaint that the conduct of the . . . defendants [corporate operators of three restaurants, and their principals] (hereinafter collectively "The Brooklyn Dodger") . . . constitute: a) an infringement upon the rights of plaintiffs' trademarks in violation of 15 U.S.C. §§ 1114 and 1117; b) a wrongful appropriation of plaintiffs' trademarks in violation of 15 U.S.C. § 1125; c) a violation of plaintiffs' common law trademark and property rights; d) a violation of plaintiffs' rights under the New York General Business Law § 368-d; e) unfair competition; and f) the intentional use by defendants of a counterfeit mark in violation of 15 U.S.C. § 1117(b).

Each of these six causes of action is alleged to flow from defendants' use of the words "The Brooklyn Dodger" as the name and servicemark of the restaurants which defendants have operated in Brooklyn, New York, beginning in March 1988. Plaintiffs initially sought permanent injunctive relief, an accounting of profits, the destruction of physical items containing the allegedly infringing marks, monetary damages, and attorneys' fees.

By their Answer and Amended Answer defendants denied any infringement of plaintiffs' alleged right to use a "Brooklyn Dodger" trademark. Defendants also pleaded the defenses of abandonment by plaintiffs of any "Brooklyn Dodgers" mark which plaintiffs may have owned at one time, as well as laches. The abandonment defense was premised upon the plaintiffs' failure to make any commercial or trademark use of the "Brooklyn Dodgers" name for at least 25 years after Los Angeles left Brooklyn in 1958. The laches defense was premised upon the fact that plaintiffs waited for more than a year and a half after learning of defendants' use of the allegedly infringing trademark before advising defendants of any alleged infringement. During this period defendants expended substantial resources and monies in establishing their restaurants in Brooklyn, New York. . . .

Finally, in their Amended Answer, defendants counterclaimed for the cancellation of various trademark registrations for "Brooklyn Dodgers" filed by plaintiffs after defendants' application to register the "Brooklyn Dodger" servicemark was filed on April 28, 1988. . . .

II. Findings of Facts . . .

Plaintiff Los Angeles is a corporation with offices and its principal place of business in Los Angeles, California. It is the owner of the Los Angeles Dodgers, a professional baseball team which, since 1958, has played baseball in Los Angeles, California under the name the "Los Angeles Dodgers." . . . Prior to 1958 the same professional baseball team played baseball in Brooklyn, New York and were known as the "Brooklyn Dodgers" or the "Dodgers."

In 1958, the team moved the site of its home games from Brooklyn to Los Angeles. . . . It pointedly changed its name to Los Angeles Dodgers, Inc. . . .

By agreement with the Major League Clubs, Properties has been granted the exclusive right to market, license, publish, publicize, promote nationally, and protect the trademarks owned by the Major League Clubs, including those owned by the Los Angeles Dodgers. . . .

. . . By 1991, retail sales of licensed Major League Baseball merchandise were in excess of $2 billion. [Plaintiffs estimate that of the total Dodgers merchandising revenue, only $9 million of 1991 sales carried the *Brooklyn* Dodgers name.]

. . . On March 17, 1988 SNOD began doing business as a restaurant under the name "The Brooklyn Dodger Sports Bar and Restaurant." . . .

It was the individual defendants' decision that their restaurants would emphasize the multiple themes of fun, sports and Brooklyn. Their intention was to create a nostalgic setting where Brooklynites could relax and reminisce about times gone by. . . .

They initially chose to name their establishment "Ebbets Field" after the former baseball park located in Brooklyn, New York in which a baseball team known as the "Brooklyn Dodgers" played baseball until October, 1957. . . .

[Defendants rejected the name "Ebbets Field" because of a conflict with a small restaurant elsewhere in New York.]

The defendants knew that the departure of the "Brooklyn Dodgers" in 1958 had been accompanied by monumental hard feelings in the Borough of Brooklyn. In fact the relocation was one of the most notorious abandonments in the history of sports. . . . At the time defendants selected their logo, they were aware that Los Angeles owned federal trademark registrations for the word "Dodgers." . . . However, at no time during their consideration of the "Brooklyn Dodger" name did the individual defendants have any reason to believe that "The Brooklyn Dodger" mark was being used by Los Angeles, and certainly not for restaurant or tavern services. . . . When considering the use of the "Brooklyn Dodger" mark, at no time was there any discussion among the individual defendants and Brian Boyle about trading on the goodwill of Los Angeles in Brooklyn. . . . Indeed, non-party witness Brian Boyle, a life-long Brooklyn resident, testified that, given the acrimonious abandonment of Brooklyn by Los Angeles, the idea of trading on Los Angeles' "goodwill" in Brooklyn is almost "laughable."

C. Defendants' Use of the Trademark

In connection with each of defendants' [three] "The Brooklyn Dodger" restaurants, defendants make and/or made prominent use of the "Dodger" name and the "Brooklyn Dodger" name, with the word "Dodger" in stylized script, in the color blue, and in blue script.

The defendants' composite design mark consisted of three words: "The," "Brooklyn" and "Dodger" are entwined with one another and with an impish character, . . . which was styled after the Charles Dickens' character, the "Artful Dodger" from the novel Oliver Twist, leaning against the "r" in "Dodger." . . . Defendants, however, make significant use of their logo without the cartoon character to promote their business, including on merchandise such as apparel, in advertisements, on their letterhead and as part of their servicemark.

Defendants' logo is similar to Los Angeles' trademarks. The name "Brooklyn Dodger" is similar to the name "Brooklyn Dodgers" as used by plaintiffs. The script used by the defendants in their logo is similar to that used in Los Angeles' trademarks. The color blue used by defendants is similar to the color blue used by and associated with Los Angeles' [team] in Brooklyn. The swash or tail of the word "Dodger" used by defendants is similar to that used in Los Angeles' trademarks in terms of style and length. . . .

In selecting their logo, defendants intentionally sought to reproduce the Brooklyn Dodgers' trademarks. Indeed, the script for the defendants' logo was intentionally chosen by defendants to track the script used by the Brooklyn Dodgers. . . .

D. Plaintiffs' Use of the Trademark . . .

Plaintiffs' use of the "Brooklyn Dodgers" mark was based upon its physical location, until October 1957, in Brooklyn, New York. However, in 1959, Los Angeles made prominent commercial use and reference to their Brooklyn heritage and trademarks in connection with the promotion of Roy Campanella Night, honoring the former Brooklyn Dodgers player and present employee. . . . Los Angeles made prominent use of their trademarks incorporating the word "Brooklyn" at their annual oldtimers games. . . . Oldtimers games are commercial baseball exhibitions at which former players are honored and perform so that older fans can recall the past and younger fans can learn about the history of the Club.

[The court describes extensive licensing and use of the Los Angeles Dodgers trademarks, including for food services and restaurants.]

While plaintiffs have from time to time made use of their former "Brooklyn Dodgers" mark occasionally and sporadically for historical retrospective[s] such as "Old Timer's Day" festivities, the documentary proof establishes that, following its departure from Brooklyn, Los Angeles' earliest licensing of the "Brooklyn Dodgers" mark occurred on April 6, 1981.

Between 1981 and March 17, 1988, the date of defendants' first use of their mark for restaurant and tavern services, plaintiffs used their "Brooklyn Dodgers" mark for a variety of purposes. Those uses were almost exclusively in the context of T-shirts, jackets, sportswear, sports paraphernalia and on various types of novelty items (i.e. on drinking mugs, cigarette lighters, pens, Christmas tree ornaments, wristbands, etc.). . . . However, none of these uses competes with defendants' use of the mark for restaurant and tavern services.

[The court describes several instances between 1981 and 1988 where businesses sought and received permission to use the "Brooklyn Dodgers" name and logo, including several that were restaurant-related.]

III. Conclusions of Law

[The court concluded that plaintiffs had failed to prove a likelihood of confusion; for completeness, it then considered defenses.]

C. Defendants' Affirmative Defenses

1. Abandonment

Under the Lanham Act a federally registered trademark is considered abandoned if its "use has been discontinued with intent not to resume." Cerveceria Centroamericana, S.A. v. Cerveceria India, Inc., 892 F.2d 1021, 1023 (Fed. Cir. 1989) (quoting Lanham Act, 15 U.S.C. §1127 (1988)).

Abandonment is defined in the Lanham Act: "A mark shall be deemed 'abandoned' — (a) When its use has been discontinued with intent not to resume. Intent not to resume may be inferred from circumstances." 15 U.S.C. §1127 (1988).

. . . The burden of proving abandonment falls upon the party seeking cancellation of a registered mark because a certificate of registration is "'prima facie evidence of the validity of the registration' and continued use." *Cerveceria India*, 892 F.2d at 1023 . . . ; Exxon Corp. v. Humble Exploration Co., 695 F.2d 96, 99 (5th Cir.), *reh'g denied*, 701 F.2d 173 (5th Cir. 1983). . . . The party seeking cancellation must establish abandonment by a preponderance of the evidence. See *Cerveceria India*, 892 F.2d at 1023-24.

The Lanham Act provides that "[n]onuse for two consecutive years shall be prima facie abandonment." 15 U.S.C. §1127. . . . Prima facie abandonment establishes a rebuttable presumption of abandonment. . . . The evidence presented at trial established that between 1958 and 1981 plaintiffs made no commercial trademark use whatsoever of any "Brooklyn Dodgers" mark. Minor changes in a trademark that do not affect the overall commercial impression of the mark do not constitute abandonment. . . . However, Los Angeles' change, in this case, from "Brooklyn Dodgers" to "Los Angeles Dodgers" was not minor; it involved an essential element affecting the public's perception of the mark and the team.[19] . . .

Plaintiffs argue that their "Dodgers" mark without a geographical reference— that is, "Dodgers" alone—is a protected use infringed by defendants actions. However, in this context, "Brooklyn" is more than a geographic designation or appendage to the word "Dodgers." The "Brooklyn Dodgers" was a non-transportable cultural institution separate from the "Los Angeles Dodgers" or the "Dodgers" who play in Los Angeles. It is not simply the "Dodgers," (and certainly not the "Los Angeles Dodgers"), that defendants seek to invoke in their restaurant; rather defendants specifically seek to recall the nostalgia of the cultural institution that was the "Brooklyn Dodgers." It was the "Brooklyn Dodgers" name that had acquired secondary meaning in New York in the early part of this century, prior to 1958. It was that cultural institution that Los Angeles abandoned.

. . . In this case, in order to maintain use of the mark, Los Angeles would have had to continue to use "Brooklyn Dodgers" as the name of its baseball team. Only in this way would the public continue to identify the name with the team. Defiance Button Mach. Co. v. C & C Metal Products Corp., 759 F.2d 1053, 1059 (2d Cir.), *cert. denied*, 474 U.S. 844 . . . (1985). . . .[20]

Rather than using the "Brooklyn Dodgers" mark in the ordinary course of trade, a more accurate description of Los Angeles' use of the mark, at least between 1958 and 1981, was given by its General Counsel in a 1985 letter to someone seeking to use it on a novelty item:

19. While Los Angeles ceased commercial use of the trademark because of its relocation from Brooklyn to Los Angeles, its motive, justifiable or not, is irrelevant. *Stetson*, 955 F.2d at 851. Nevertheless, Los Angeles' nonuse in this case was voluntary. Courts have been more reluctant to find an absence of intent to resume where the trademark owner had an excusable reason for nonuse—that is, where nonuse was involuntary. See, e.g., Defiance Button Machine Co. v. C & C Metal Products Corp., 759 F.2d 1053, 1059 (2d Cir.), *cert. denied*, 474 U.S. 844, 106 S. Ct. 131, 88 L. Ed. 2d 108 (1985) (no abandonment where cessation of business was involuntary); American International Group, Inc. v. American International Airways, Inc., 726 F. Supp. 1470 (E.D. Pa. 1989) (where airline declared bankruptcy, remaining goodwill and lack of intent to abandon precluded finding abandonment).

20. The outcome in *Defiance*, finding no abandonment, is distinguishable from the case at hand because the court in *Defiance* held that the continued goodwill toward the button company after it stopped producing goods and the fact that the company intended to retain its trademark for some commercial use precluded a finding of abandonment. Similarly, the court in *Schenley Industries*, 441 F.2d 675, held that continued goodwill and lack of intent to abandon precluded finding of abandonment. In the unique facts of this case, however, plaintiffs have not succeeded in demonstrating that much goodwill in Brooklyn survived Los Angeles' move in 1957. But more importantly, while plaintiff in *Defiance* was at least able to demonstrate an intent not to abandon, plaintiffs here have not even demonstrated an intent not to abandon, much less the statutory requirement of intent to resume. A mark retains "residual" goodwill "if the proponent of a mark stops using it but demonstrates an intent to keep the mark alive for use in resumed business." Pan American World Airways, Inc. v. Panamerican School of Travel, Inc., 648 F. Supp. 1026, 1031 (S.D.N.Y.), *aff'd without op.*, 810 F.2d 1160 (2d Cir. 1986) (citing *Defiance*, supra). The claim to residual goodwill will not preclude a finding of abandonment where, as in this case, the owner unequivocally declares its intention to discontinue use.

> Since the Dodgers moved to Los Angeles in 1958 the name "Brooklyn Dodgers" has been reserved strictly for use in conjunction with items of historical interest.

. . . Under the law, such warehousing is not permitted. . . . Rights in a trademark are lost when trademarks are "warehoused" as plaintiffs attempted to "warehouse" the "Brooklyn Dodgers" mark for more than two (2) decades. . . . Plaintiffs' failure to use the "Brooklyn Dodgers" trademark between 1958, when Los Angeles left Brooklyn, and 1981 constitutes abandonment of the trademark. . . .

Abandonment under the Lanham Act, however, requires both nonuse and intent not to resume use. . . .

Once prima facie abandonment has been proven, the trademark registrants — in this case plaintiffs — must carry their burden of producing evidence that there was an intent to resume use of the trademark. *Cerveceria India*, 892 F.2d at 1025-26. . . .

Rather than merely proving that it did not intend to abandon its trademark, the trademark registrant must demonstrate that it intended to use or resume use. See *Exxon*, 695 F.2d at 99, 102-03 ("Stopping at an 'intent not to abandon' [rather than 'intent to resume'] tolerates an owner's protecting a mark with neither commercial use nor plans to resume commercial use. Such a license is not permitted by the Lanham Act"). . . .

Plaintiffs have in no way demonstrated their intent to resume commercial use of the "Brooklyn Dodgers" mark within two years after Los Angeles left Brooklyn in 1958 or at anytime within the ensuing quarter century. . . .

2. Resumption

Having determined that plaintiffs abandoned the "Brooklyn Dodgers" mark, the next inquiry is to determine the effect of that abandonment, given that plaintiffs have recently resumed limited use of the trademark. . . .

[I]f plaintiffs have any interest in a "Brooklyn Dodgers" mark, that interest arose in 1981 when commercial use of the mark resumed after a twenty-three (23) year hiatus. Plaintiffs' preemptive rights in the "Brooklyn Dodgers" mark would extend only to the precise goods on or in connection with which the trademark was used since its resumption (i.e. clothing, jewelry, novelty items).

In other words, the fact that plaintiffs resumed use prior to defendants' use does not mean that plaintiffs may preclude defendants' use of the mark in their restaurant business in Brooklyn. . . .

Accordingly, the court declines to enjoin defendants' very limited use of the "Brooklyn Dodger" mark by defendants for use in connection with its local restaurants directed toward older Brooklyn Dodgers fans in the Brooklyn community in the city of New York. . . .

COMMENTS AND QUESTIONS

1. Would the result change if "The Brooklyn Dodger" restaurant began selling Brooklyn Dodger T-shirts? Other memorabilia?

2. Section 45 of the Lanham Act, on abandonment, was amended in 1994 (effective Jan. 1, 1996) to change the presumptive abandonment period from two

to three years, in accordance with the Uruguay Round amendments. *See* GATT TRIPs, art. 19(1). This provision of the Act was the U.S. version of article 19(1) of The Agreement on Trade-Related Aspects of Intellectual Property Rights, Including Trade in Counterfeit Goods, opened for signature Apr. 15, 1994, 33 I.L.M. 81.

Thus Section 45 now reads in part:

> A mark shall be deemed to be "abandoned" when either of the following occurs:
>
> (1) When its use has been discontinued with intent not to resume such use. Intent not to resume may be inferred from circumstances. Nonuse for three consecutive years shall be prima facie evidence of abandonment. "Use" of a mark means the bona fide use of such mark made in the ordinary course of trade, and not made merely to reserve a right in a mark.
>
> (2) When any course of conduct of the owner, including acts of omission as commission, causes the mark to . . . lose its significance as a mark. . . .

Lanham Act §45, 15 U.S.C. §1127. The *Dawn Donut* case and notes, below, deal with the §45(2) type of abandonment.

3. *How Soon Must the Trademark Owner Intend to Resume Use?* The trademark owner cannot overcome the presumption of abandonment triggered by three years of non-use by asserting that it intends to resume use at some indefinite point in the future. In Silverman v. CBS, Inc., 870 F.2d 40 (2d Cir. 1989), CBS asserted that it intended to resume use of the Amos 'n Andy mark at some point in the future when the mark would no longer be perceived as being demeaning of African Americans (the mark had been used in the 1940s in connection with a radio show whose performers appeared in promotional materials in blackface). The Second Circuit found abandonment on the ground that the trademark owner must show that it intends to resume use "in the reasonably foreseeable future." *Id.* at 47. "A bare assertion of possible future use is not enough." *Id.*

4. If trademark rights are essentially about protecting consumers from confusion, why does the legal standard require anything other than a showing that the mark's meaning has faded sufficiently so that it can now be "reclaimed" by another? Why does the statute settle for a presumption; why not a per se rule, perhaps based on a longer period — say ten years? *Cf. Note, The Song Is Over But the Melody Lingers On: Persistence of Goodwill and the Intent Factor in Trademark Abandonment*, 56 FORDHAM L. REV. 1003, 1006-07 (1988) ("[W]hen a trademark has persisting or residual goodwill, even after a period of nonuse, doubts should be resolved in favor of the trademark owner and against the competitor charging abandonment. . . . [Courts] should . . . make it as difficult as possible to find a trademark abandoned whenever goodwill in the mark persists."). What arguments can you think of in favor of this liberal rule? Against? Should there be an incentive to aggressively "recycle" marks that have shown some usefulness?

Do you think the association between the name "Brooklyn Dodgers" and the major league baseball team now located in Los Angeles had faded sufficiently for someone else to reclaim the name? What if the defendant had set up a baseball team rather than a restaurant? Do the unusual facts in this case — especially the animosity between ex-Brooklyn Dodger fans and the Los Angeles Dodgers — suggest why a per se rule might not make sense in every case? Is the court right to assume the absence of "goodwill" here, where consumers recognize the Dodger mark but simply have bad associations with it? Or does the continual connection in the public's mind suggest an ongoing role for trademark law? Dogan and Lemley argue that companies should not be permitted to race to grab up abandoned marks that still carry goodwill in the minds of consumers, because those consumers will be injured when a new company starts selling different products under the same mark. Stacey L. Dogan & Mark A. Lemley, *A Search-Costs Theory of Limiting Doctrines in Trademark*, 97 TRADEMARK RPTR. 1223 (2007).

5. Are there reasons to limit the abandonment doctrine where it may affect names that clearly seem to "belong" to the trademark owner? In Kareem Abdul-Jabbar v. General Motors, 85 F.3d 407, 411 (9th Cir. 1996), the court rejected defendant's claim that basketball star Abdul-Jabbar had abandoned his birth name, Lew Alcindor. The court established a per se rule: "A proper name thus cannot be deemed abandoned throughout its possessor's life, despite his failure to use it. . . ."

6. *Securing Teams Names in Advance of Use.* Whereas *Major League Baseball Properties, Inc. v. Sed Non Olet Denarius, Ltd.* deals with rights in a team name after the team has left a city, a dispute involving the move of the Los Angeles Rams to St. Louis highlights some of the issues accompanying the birth of a mark following the relocation of an existing team to a new locale. On January 17, 1995, St. Louis Mayor Freeman Bosley and Georgia Frontiere, owner of the Los Angeles Rams Football Company, announced that the Los Angeles Rams football franchise intended to relocate to St. Louis, Missouri. By early February of 1995, the Rams organization had received over 72,000 personal seat license applications for the St. Louis stadium where the Rams would play. On February 22, 1995, Johnny Blastoff, a corporation in the business of creating and marketing cartoon characters, filed a trademark application in Wisconsin for the name of a fictional cartoon sports team named the "St. Louis Rams." On March 10, 1995, Blastoff filed two federal intent-to-use trademark applications for the "St. Louis Rams" mark. One month later, the Rams' move to St. Louis was approved by the National Football League. Although a number of vendors began selling unlicensed merchandise bearing the mark "St. Louis Rams" in January of 1995, officially licensed vendors began using the "St. Louis Rams" mark in a wide variety of merchandise sales in April of 1995. In March 1997, Blastoff filed a declaratory judgment against the Rams football organization, the NFL, and others, alleging that he did not infringe the NFL defendants' trademark rights. In determining that the Rams first appropriated the mark through use as a designation of origin, the court placed emphasis on the nature of franchise relocations, *see* Indianapolis Colts, Inc. v. Metropolitan Baltimore Football Club Ltd., 34 F.3d 410, 413 (7th Cir. 1994) (finding a strong presumption of franchise owner priority in a team mark when a franchise relocates to a new city), and the role of "advertising brochures, catalogs, newspaper ads, and articles in newspapers and trade publications" and use on television and radio in establishing public identification of a mark with a product or service, *see* T.A.B. Systems v. Pactel Teletrac, 77 F.3d 1372, 1375 (Fed. Cir. 1996); *In re* Owens-Corning Fiberglas Corp., 774 F.2d 1116, 1125 (Fed. Cir. 1985). *See* Johnny Blastoff, Inc. v. Los Angeles Rams Football Co., 188 F.3d 427 (7th Cir. 1999).

Note on the Defense of Laches

The Lanham Act repeatedly invokes "the principles of equity" as limiting courts' powers to grant injunctive relief, damages, or other remedies under the Act. *See, e.g.*, Lanham Act §§ 34 & 35; 15 U.S.C. §§ 1116 & 1117. *See also* Lanham Act §§ 19,

33(a), and 33(b)(9); 15 U.S.C. 1069, 1115(a), and 1115(b)(9) (invoking equity). Once such principle of equity is laches, which "is founded on the notion that equity aids the vigilant and not those who slumber on their rights." NAACP v. NAACP Legal Def. & Educ. Fund, Inc., 753 F.2d 131, 137 (D.C. Cir. 1985). In trademark law as elsewhere, the defense of laches "requires proof of (1) lack of diligence by the party against whom the defense is asserted, and (2) prejudice to the party asserting the defense." Nat'l R.R. Passenger Corp. v. Morgan, 536 U.S. 101, 121-22 (2002). Because the Lanham Act itself includes no statute of limitations provision, defendants who might otherwise seek to take advantage of such a provision often turn to the defense of laches. *See* MCCARTHY, MCCARTHY ON TRADEMARKS AND UNFAIR COMPETITION §§ 31.1–31.43.

To meet its burden of proving that it has been prejudiced by the plaintiff's delay, the defendant typically must do more than merely show that it has continued to use its infringing mark during the delay period. *See, e.g.*, Tap Publications, Inc. v. Chinese Yellow Pages (New York) Inc., 925 F. Supp. 212, 223-224 (S.D.N.Y. 1996) (mere continuing use of infringing mark without expansion does not satisfy laches requirement of prejudice). Courts generally require some showing that defendant has expanded its activities under the mark during the delay period or otherwise substantially increased its level of investment in the promotion of the mark. *See, e.g.*, Grupo Gigante S.A. De C.V. v. Dallo & Co., Inc., 391 F.3d 1088, 1105 (9th Cir. 2004) ("[A] defendant can make the required showing of prejudice by proving that it has continued to build a valuable business around its trademark during the time that the plaintiff delayed the exercise of its legal rights."); Chattanoga Mfg., Inc. v. Nike, Inc., 301 F.3d 789, 795 (7th Cir. 2002) (finding laches where, during the delay period "[defendant] Nike spent millions of dollars annually promoting its Michael Jordan-endorsed products and has acquired a position as a market leader").

One significant exception to the laches defense is available under the doctrine of "progressive encroachment." This doctrine typically comes into play in situations where the defendant formerly used the plaintiff's mark on goods unrelated to the plaintiff's, but has since expanded its use of the mark to goods related to the plaintiff's. Given these facts, courts will not find laches for the plaintiff's failure to sue on the former use. *See, e.g.*, Westchester Media v. PRL USA Holdings, Inc., 214 F.3d 658 (5th Cir. 2000) (finding plaintiff's obligation to sue was triggered only when defendant Polo Magazine expanded its content beyond news of the sport of polo and began to feature mainstream fashion and travel news closer to plaintiff's market). *See also* Copy Cop v. Task Printing, 908 F. Supp. 37, 47 (D. Mass. 1995) ("That [plaintiff] waited until some viable impact on its business is excusable delay.").

PROBLEMS

Problem 6-1. Until 1972 the Humble Oil & Refining Co. was one of the largest producers and sellers of gasoline in the world. In that year, after a merger with Esso, Humble decided to change its name to Exxon, an arbitrary mark it had selected for the purpose. The company invested an enormous amount of money advertising the new name and placing its new brand on all its products, services, and correspondence. However, the new Exxon also started a "brand maintenance program," under which it continued to make a few sales every year under the Humble name. It sent certain invoices on Humble letterhead, and bulk oil was sometimes sold in Humble barrels. Exxon continued this program throughout the 1970s.

In 1975, a new oil exploration company decided to call itself the Humble Oil Exploration Co. The new company picked the Humble name because they hoped to trade on residual goodwill left in the name, and because they believed Exxon had abandoned its old name. Can the new company use the Humble name?

Problem 6-2. International Business Machines is a world-famous company. For decades, people have informally referred to IBM as "Big Blue," both in conversation and in published articles and papers about the company. However, IBM does not itself use or claim the name "Big Blue." It has never registered the name Big Blue, its employees are forbidden by company policy to use the name in referring to the company, and at one point an exasperated company spokesperson is reported to have said "We're not Big Blue—please don't call us that. We want nothing to do with the name." Nonetheless, the nickname persists.

In 1994, a small repair shop that specializes in fixing IBM computers decided to call itself the "Big Blue Repair Shop." After BBRS started using the name, IBM sent it a cease-and-desist letter alleging that IBM owned the rights to the name Big Blue, since people used it to refer to IBM. Who has priority in use of the Big Blue mark?

1. Unsupervised Licenses

Dawn Donut Company, Inc. v. Hart's Food Stores, Inc.

267 F.2d 358 (2d Cir. 1959)

[Dawn Donut, a Michigan wholesaler of doughnut mix, owned federally registered trademarks Dawn and Dawn Donut. Dawn brought a trademark infringement suit against defendant Hart's Food Stores (Hart), which used the mark "Dawn" in connection with its sale of doughnuts and baked goods in stores in and around Rochester, New York. Hart filed a counterclaim to cancel plaintiff's registrations, on the ground that plaintiff had abandoned its trademarks due to inadequate quality control and supervision on the part of its licensees—the retail bakeries that sold doughnuts made from Dawn's mix. The district court denied Dawn's request for an injunction and dismissed Hart's counterclaim. This appeal followed. In an omitted (and oft-cited) portion of this opinion, Circuit Judge Lumbard held that plaintiff was not entitled to any relief under the Lanham Act because there was no present likelihood that plaintiff would expand its retail use of its trademarks into defendant's market area. See our discussion of this part of the opinion, *supra*, following the Note on Geographical Limitations on Trademark Use. A majority of the panel also found that there was no abandonment by plaintiff of its registrations, and that therefore defendant was not entitled to have plaintiff's registrations of trademarks cancelled.]

LUMBARD, Circuit Judge [dissenting in part]. . . .

The final issue presented is raised by defendant's appeal from the dismissal of its counterclaim for cancellation of plaintiff's registration on the ground that the plaintiff failed to exercise the control required by the Lanham Act over the nature and quality of the goods sold by its licensees.

We are all agreed that the Lanham Act places an affirmative duty upon a licensor of a registered trademark to take reasonable measures to detect and prevent misleading uses of his mark by his licensees or suffer cancellation of his federal registration. The Act, 15 U.S.C.A. § 1064, provides that a trademark registration may be cancelled because the trademark has been "abandoned." And "abandoned" is defined in 15 U.S.C.A. § 1127 to include any act or omission by the registrant which causes the trademark to lose its significance as an indication of origin.

Prior to the passage of the Lanham Act many courts took the position that the licensing of a trademark separately from the business in connection with which it had been used worked an abandonment. Reddy Kilowatt, Inc. v. MidCarolina Electric Cooperative, Inc., 4 Cir., 1957, 240 F.2d 282, 289; American Broadcasting Co. v. Wahl Co., 2 Cir., 1941, 121 F.2d 412, 413; Everett O. Fisk & Co. v. Fisk Teachers' Agency, Inc., 8 Cir., 1924, 3 F.2d 7, 9. The theory of these cases was that:

> A trade-mark is intended to identify the goods of the owner and to safeguard his good will. The designation if employed by a person other than the one whose business it serves to identify would be misleading. Consequently, "a right to the use of a trade-mark or a trade-name cannot be transferred in gross."

American Broadcasting Co. v. Wahl Co., supra, 121 F.2d at page 413.

Other courts were somewhat more liberal and held that a trademark could be licensed separately from the business in connection with which it had been used provided that the licensor retained control over the quality of the goods produced by the licensee. E.I. DuPont de Nemours & Co. v. Celanese Corporation of America, 1948, 167 F.2d 484, 35 CCPA 1061. . . . But even in the DuPont case the court was careful to point out that naked licensing, viz. the grant of licenses without the retention of control, was invalid. E.I. DuPont de Nemours & Co. v. Celanese Corporation of America, supra, 167 F.2d at page 489.

The Lanham Act clearly carries forward the view of these latter cases that controlled licensing does not work an abandonment of the licensor's registration, while a system of naked licensing does. 15 U.S.C.A. § 1055 provides:

> Where a registered mark or a mark sought to be registered is or may be used legitimately by related companies, such use shall inure to the benefit of the registrant or applicant for registration, and such use shall not affect the validity of such mark or of its registration, provided such mark is not used in such manner as to deceive the public. . . .*

* [Lanham Act § 45 now reads in relevant part: "The term 'related company' means any person whose use of a mark is controlled by the owner of the mark with respect to the nature and quality of the goods or services on or in connection with which the mark is used." 15 U.S.C. § 1127. The portion of 15 U.S.C. § 1055 (Lanham Act § 5) quoted just above in the case has not changed. — EDS.]

Without the requirement of control, the right of a trademark owner to license his mark separately from the business in connection with which it has been used would create the danger that products bearing the same trademark might be of diverse qualities. See *American Broadcasting Co. v. Wahl Co.*, supra; *Everett O. Fisk & Co. v. Fisk Teachers' Agency, Inc.*, supra. If the licensor is not compelled to take some reasonable steps to prevent misuses of his trademark in the hands of others the public will be deprived of its most effective protection against misleading uses of a trademark. The public is hardly in a position to uncover deceptive uses of a trademark before they occur and will be at best slow to detect them after they happen. Thus, unless the licensor exercises supervision and control over the operations of its licensees the risk that the public will be unwittingly deceived will be increased and this is precisely what the Act is in part designed to prevent. See SEN. REPORT No. 1333, 79th Cong., 2d Sess. (1946). Clearly the only effective way to protect the public where a trademark is used by licensees is to place on the licensor the affirmative duty of policing in a reasonable manner the activities of his licensees.

The critical question on these facts therefore is whether the plaintiff sufficiently policed and inspected its licensees' operations to guarantee the quality of the products they sold under its trademarks to the public. The trial court found that: "By reason of its contacts with its licensees, plaintiff exercised legitimate control over the nature and quality of the food products on which plaintiff's licensees used the trademark 'Dawn.' Plaintiff and its licensees are related companies within the meaning of Section 45 of the Trademark Act of 1946." It is the position of the majority of this court that the trial judge has the same leeway in determining what constitutes a reasonable degree of supervision and control over licensees under the facts and circumstances of the particular case as he has on other questions of fact; and particularly because it is the defendant who has the burden of proof on this issue they hold the lower court's finding not clearly erroneous.

I dissent from the conclusion of the majority that the district court's findings are not clearly erroneous because while it is true that the trial judge must be given some discretion in determining what constitutes reasonable supervision of licensees under the Lanham Act, it is also true that an appellate court ought not to accept the conclusions of the district court unless they are supported by findings of sufficient facts. It seems to me that the only findings of the district judge regarding supervision are in such general and conclusory terms as to be meaningless. In the absence of supporting findings or of undisputed evidence in the record indicating the kind of supervision and inspection the plaintiff actually made of its licensees, it is impossible for us to pass upon whether there was such supervision as to satisfy the statute. There was evidence before the district court in the matter of supervision, and more detailed findings thereon should have been made.

Plaintiff's licensees fall into two classes: (1) those bakers with whom it made written contracts providing that the baker purchase exclusively plaintiff's mixes and requiring him to adhere to plaintiff's directions in using the mixes; and (2) those bakers whom plaintiff permitted to sell at retail under the "Dawn" label doughnuts and other baked goods made from its mixes although there was no written agreement governing the quality of the food sold under the Dawn mark.[6]

6. On cross-examination plaintiff's president conceded that during 1949 and 1950 the company in some instances, the number of which is not made clear by his testimony, distributed its advertising and packaging material to bakers with whom it had not reached any agreement relating to the quality of the

The contracts that plaintiff did conclude, although they provided that the purchaser use the mix as directed and without adulteration, failed to provide for any system of inspection and control. Without such a system plaintiff could not know whether these bakers were adhering to its standards in using the mix or indeed whether they were selling only products made from Dawn mixes under the trademark "Dawn."

The absence, however, of an express contract right to inspect and supervise a licensee's operations does not mean that the plaintiff's method of licensing failed to comply with the requirements of the Lanham Act. Plaintiff may in fact have exercised control in spite of the absence of any express grant by licensees of the right to inspect and supervise.

The question then, with respect to both plaintiff's contract and non-contract licensees, is whether the plaintiff in fact exercised sufficient control.

Here the only evidence in the record relating to the actual supervision of licensees by plaintiff consists of the testimony of two of plaintiff's local sales representatives that they regularly visited their particular customers and the further testimony of one of them, Jesse Cohn, the plaintiff's New York representative, that "in many cases" he did have an opportunity to inspect and observe the operations of his customers. The record does not indicate whether plaintiff's other sales representatives made any similar efforts to observe the operations of licensees.

Moreover, Cohn's testimony fails to make clear the nature of the inspection he made or how often he made one. His testimony indicates that his opportunity to observe a licensee's operations was limited to "those cases where I am able to get into the shop" and even casts some doubt on whether he actually had sufficient technical knowledge in the use of plaintiff's mix to make an adequate inspection of a licensee's operations.

The fact that it was Cohn who failed to report the defendant's use of the mark "Dawn" to the plaintiff casts still further doubt about the extent of the supervision Cohn exercised over the operations of plaintiff's New York licensees.

Thus I do not believe that we can fairly determine on this record whether plaintiff subjected its licensees to periodic and thorough inspections by trained personnel or whether its policing consisted only of chance, cursory examinations of licensees' operations by technically untrained salesmen. The latter system of inspection hardly constitutes a sufficient program of supervision to satisfy the requirements of the Act.

. . . I would direct the district court to order the cancellation of plaintiff's registrations if it should find that the plaintiff did not adequately police the operations of its licensees. . . .

The district court's denial of an injunction restraining defendant's use of the mark "Dawn" on baked and fried goods and its dismissal of defendant's [abandonment] counterclaim are affirmed.

---

goods sold in packages bearing the name "Dawn." It also appears from plaintiff's list of the 16 bakers who were operating as exclusive Dawn shops at the time of the trial that plaintiff's contract with 3 of these shops had expired and had not been renewed and that in the case of 2 other such shops the contract had been renewed only after a substantial period of time had elapsed since the expiration of the original agreement. The record indicates that these latter 2 bakers continued to operate under the name "Dawn" and purchase "Dawn" mixes during the period following the expiration of their respective franchise agreements with the plaintiff. Particularly damaging to plaintiff is the fact that one of the 2 bakers whose franchise contracts plaintiff allowed to lapse for a substantial period of time has also been permitted by plaintiff to sell doughnuts made from a mix other than plaintiff's in packaging labeled with plaintiff's trademark.

COMMENTS AND QUESTIONS

1. Despite its age and the fact that it was a dissent, Judge Lumbard's discussion in *Dawn Donut* regarding licensee supervision and abandonment is still the standard in the area. *See* McCarthy, McCarthy on Trademarks and Unfair Competition § 18:42.

2. Trademark rights are regularly lost because of unsupervised licensing. *See, e.g.*, Stanfield v. Osborne Indus., Inc., 52 F.3d 867 (10th Cir. 1995) (denying plaintiff's advertising-related trademark claim because rights were lost due to unsupervised license); Barcamerica Int'l USA Trust v. Tyfield Importers, Inc., 289 F. 2d 589 (9th Cir. 2002) (finding lack of express contractual right to inspect and supervise licensee's operation as well as no actual supervision).

3. The *Celanese* case cited in *Dawn Donut*, E.I. du Pont de Nemours & Co. v. Celanese Corporation, 167 F.2d 484 (C.C.P.A. 1948), was one of the first cases to establish the legitimacy of trademark licensing over the objection that licensing necessarily entailed an abandonment. Obviously, the growth of franchising, character merchandising, and related practices depended on such a holding. Much modern business would be impossible if corporations could not expand their brand names in these ways. *Cf.* "Extension by Contract: Franchising and Merchandising," Chapter 5.D, *supra*.

4. If a trademark owner wants to spend its own goodwill by licensing those who sell lower quality products, why not let it? The company would surely be permitted to reduce the quality of the products it makes itself. For criticism of the requirement that a trademark owner control the quality of a licensee's products, see Irene Calboli, *The Sunset of "Quality Control" in Modern Trademark Licensing*, 57 Am. U. L. Rev. 341 (2007).

2. The Rule Against Assignments in Gross

The rule that unsupervised or "naked" licenses can amount to abandonment has a logical corollary: that outright assignments of trademarks are invalid. This common law rule was codified in Section 10 of the Lanham Act: "A registered mark or a mark for which application to register has been filed shall be assignable with the goodwill of the business in which the mark is used, or with that part of the goodwill of the business connected with the use of and symbolized by the mark." Lanham Act § 10, 15 U.S.C. § 1060.

Assignments of trademarks alone, without any underlying assets or "goodwill," are called "assignments in gross." They are invalid, *see* McCarthy, McCarthy on Trademarks and Unfair Competition § 18.01 (3d ed. 1992 & Supp. 1996), a result said to follow from the fact that trademarks are only repositories and symbols of goodwill, rather than true property rights. *See* American Steel Foundries v. Robertson, 269 U.S. 372, 380 (1926). That case reasoned that consumers, having come to rely on a trademark to identify the characteristics of a product as manufactured and sold by Firm *A*, would be harmed if *A* simply sold the mark outright to Firm *B* without transferring any of the employees or production machinery that Firm *A* had used to make its product. *Id.* By the same reasoning, courts invalidated trademarks when sold to another firm for use on a different product. *See* Filkins v. Blackman, 9 Fed. Cas. 50, 51 (No. 4786) (C.C.D. Conn. 1876) ("The right to the use of a trademark cannot be so enjoyed by an assignee that he shall have the right to affix the mark to goods differing in character or species from the article to which it was originally attached.").

As originally applied, the rule against assignments in gross was quite strict; in general, a firm was required to assign tangible assets along with the trademark. *See, e.g.*, PepsiCo, Inc. v. Grapette Co., 416 F.2d 285 (8th Cir. 1969) (assignment of trademark Peppy without underlying assets invalid). More recently, however, the traditional rule has been relaxed, partly in recognition of the increased frequency and importance of trademark-related transactions. The contemporary rule can be seen operating in cases involving assignment of "soft" trademark-related assets, such as customer lists, production formulas (as opposed to machinery), and even amorphous "goodwill." *See, e.g.*, In re Roman Cleanser Co., 802 F.2d 207 (6th Cir. 1986) (validating transfer of trademark in satisfaction of security interest in it, together with formulas and customer lists); Money Store v. Harriscorp Finance, Inc., 689 F.2d 666 (7th Cir. 1982) (assignment of Money Store trademark by senior user for $1 not invalid; nominal recitation of "goodwill" in assignment contract, without transfer of any other assets, was enough). *Cf.* William M. Landes & Richard A. Posner, *Trademark Law: An Economic Perspective*, 30 J.L. & ECON. 265, 274-75 (1987) (arguing that the "assignment in gross" doctrine makes sense only in "final period" cases, where sellers of goods are leaving the market and hence do not care if consumers are disappointed by the low quality of the assignee's goods).

By contrast, Japan, for example, recognizes private property rights in the trademark itself. Therefore, assignments in gross are valid even if totally divorced from any goodwill. Trademark rights are also severable; they may be assigned by class, providing the goods of the remaining classification would not cause confusion with the goods of the class assigned. *See generally* Kazuko Matsuo, *Trademarks*, *in* 4 DOING BUSINESS IN JAPAN (Zentaro Kitagawa ed., 1991).

The rule against assignments in gross makes sense from the point of view of protecting consumer associations between a mark and an underlying product. If the symbol changes hands, and is now used to "refer to" a different product, consumers might be confused. (Imagine if language experts decided to change the meaning of a common word, without telling anyone.) As Landes and Posner, *supra*, argue, the risk of confusion is greatest when the trademark assignor is leaving the market.

This rationale for the doctrine assumes that consumers cannot see the lower quality of the assignee's product when they look at the product. Moreover, the doctrine seems highly questionable as applied to cases where the assignee uses the mark on a completely different type of product altogether. In such a case, any consumers who retain an association between the mark and the old product will quickly grasp the changed circumstances when they see the new product.

With these points in mind, why not encourage the transfer of trademarks that have proven effective? Why restrict transfers to those accompanied by underlying assets? For cogent criticism of the rule against assignments in gross, see Irene Calboli, *Trademark Assignment "With Goodwill": A Concept Whose Time Has Gone*, 57 FLA. L. REV. 771 (2005); Allison Sell McDade, *Note, Trading in Trademarks — Why the Anti-Assignment in Gross Doctrine Should Be Abolished When Trademarks Are Used as Collateral*, 77 TEX. L. REV. 465 (1998) (focusing on the use of trademarks as security interests); *but see* Mark A. Lemley, *The Modern Lanham Act and the Death of Common Sense*, 108 YALE L.J. 1687 (1999) (supporting the doctrine as consistent with the consumer-oriented focus of trademark law). What would happen to consumer expectations if a lending company foreclosed on a trademark?

Does (or should) the law similarly prohibit the original trademark owner from significantly decreasing the quality of his or her goods, or from changing the type of product to which the mark is attached? *See* McCarthy, McCarthy on Trademarks and Unfair Competition § 17:24 (citing cases and arguing that this would amount to deceit under the Lanham Act). The latter may be an issue for registered marks, where the classification of goods is important.

COMMENTS AND QUESTIONS

Article 21 of the General Agreements on Tariffs and Trade, which entered into force in the United States in 1995, provides that "the owner of a registered trademark shall have the right to assign his trademark with or without the transfer of the business to which the trademark belongs." Does this article require the United States to abolish the rule against assignment in gross?

B. FAIR USE

We addressed the fair use doctrine when we considered the *Zatarains* case, *supra*. But properly understood, fair use is a defense to a trademark infringement claim. We consider the consequences of that fact here.

KP Permanent Make-Up, Inc. v. Lasting Impression I, Inc., et al.
543 U.S. 111 (2004)

Justice Souter delivered the opinion of the Court.

The question here is whether a party raising the statutory affirmative defense of fair use to a claim of trademark infringement, 15 U.S.C. § 1115(b)(4), has a burden to negate any likelihood that the practice complained of will confuse consumers about the origin of the goods or services affected. We hold it does not.

I

Each party to this case sells permanent makeup, a mixture of pigment and liquid for injection under the skin to camouflage injuries and modify nature's dispensations, and each has used some version of the term "micro color" (as one word or two, singular or plural) in marketing and selling its product. Petitioner KP Permanent Make-Up, Inc., claims to have used the single-word version since 1990 or 1991 on advertising flyers and since 1991 on pigment bottles. Respondents Lasting Impression I, Inc., and its licensee, MCN International, Inc. (Lasting, for simplicity), deny that KP began using the term that early, but we accept KP's allegation as true for present purposes. . . . The PTO registered the mark to Lasting in 1993, and in 1999 the registration became incontestable. § 1065.

It was also in 1999 that KP produced a 10-page advertising brochure using "microcolor" in a large, stylized typeface, provoking Lasting to demand that KP stop using the term. Instead, KP sued Lasting in the Central District of California, seeking, on more than one ground, a declaratory judgment that its language infringed no such exclusive right as Lasting claimed. Lasting counterclaimed, alleging, among other things, that KP had infringed Lasting's "Micro Colors" trademark.

KP sought summary judgment on the infringement counterclaim, based on the statutory affirmative defense of fair use, 15 U.S.C. § 1115(b)(4). After finding that Lasting had conceded that KP used the term only to describe its goods and not as a mark, the District Court held that KP was acting fairly and in good faith because undisputed facts showed that KP had employed the term "microcolor" continuously from a time before Lasting adopted the two-word, plural variant as a mark. Without inquiring whether the practice was likely to cause confusion, the court concluded that KP had made out its affirmative defense under § 1115(b)(4) and entered summary judgment for KP on Lasting's infringement claim. See Case No. SA CV 00-276-GLT (EEx) (May 16, 2001), pp. 8-9, App. to Pet. for Cert. 29a-30a.

On appeal, 328 F.3d 1061 (2003), the Court of Appeals for the Ninth Circuit thought it was error for the District Court to have addressed the fair use defense without delving into the matter of possible confusion on the part of consumers about the origin of KP's goods. The reviewing court took the view that no use could be recognized as fair where any consumer confusion was probable, and although the court did not pointedly address the burden of proof, it appears to have placed it on KP to show absence of consumer confusion. Id., at 1072 ("Therefore, KP can only benefit from the fair use defense if there is no likelihood of confusion between KP's use of the term 'micro color' and Lasting's mark"). Since it found there were disputed material facts relevant under the Circuit's eight-factor test for assessing the likelihood of confusion, it reversed the summary judgment and remanded the case.

We granted KP's petition for certiorari, 540 U.S. 1099, 124 S. Ct. 981, 157 L. Ed. 2d 811 (2004), to address a disagreement among the Courts of Appeals on the significance of likely confusion for a fair use defense to a trademark infringement claim, and the obligation of a party defending on that ground to show that its use is unlikely to cause consumer confusion. Compare 328 F.3d, at 1072 (likelihood of confusion bars the fair use defense); PACCAR Inc. v. TeleScan Technologies, L.L.C., 319 F.3d 243, 256 (C.A.6 2003) ("[A] finding of a likelihood of confusion forecloses a fair use defense"); and Zatarains, Inc. v. Oak Grove Smokehouse, Inc., 698 F.2d 786, 796 (C.A.5 1983) (alleged infringers were free to use words contained in a trademark "in their ordinary, descriptive sense, so long as such use [did] not tend to confuse customers as to the source of the goods"), with Cosmetically Sealed Industries, Inc. v. Chesebrough-Pond's USA Co., 125 F.3d 28, 30-31 (C.A.2 1997) (the fair use defense may succeed even if there is likelihood of confusion); Shakespeare Co. v. Silstar Corp. of Am., Inc., 110 F.3d 234, 243 (C.A.4 1997) ("[A] determination of likely confusion [does not] preclud[e] considering the fairness of use"); Sunmark, Inc. v. Ocean Spray Cranberries, Inc., 64 F.3d 1055, 1059 (C.A.7 1995) (finding that likelihood of confusion did not preclude the fair use defense). We now vacate the judgment of the Court of Appeals.

II

A

. . . The holder of a registered mark (incontestable or not) has a civil action against anyone employing an imitation of it in commerce when "such use is likely to cause confusion, or to cause mistake, or to deceive." § 1114(1)(a). Although an incontestable registration is "conclusive evidence . . . of the registrant's exclusive right to use the . . . mark in commerce," § 1115(b), the plaintiff's success is still subject to "proof of infringement as defined in section 1114," ibid. And that, as just noted, requires a showing that the defendant's actual practice is likely to produce confusion in the minds of consumers about the origin of the goods or services in question. See Two Pesos, Inc. v. Taco Cabana, Inc., 505 U.S. 763, 780, 112 S. Ct. 2753, 120 L. Ed. 2d 615 (1992) (STEVENS, J., concurring); Lone Star Steakhouse & Saloon, Inc. v. Alpha of Virginia, Inc., 43 F.3d 922, 935 (C.A.4 1995); RESTATEMENT (THIRD) OF UNFAIR COMPETITION § 21, Comment a (1995) (hereinafter RESTATEMENT). This plaintiff's burden has to be kept in mind when reading the relevant portion of the further provision for an affirmative defense of fair use, available to a party whose

> "use of the name, term, or device charged to be an infringement is a use, otherwise than as a mark, . . . of a term or device which is descriptive of and used fairly and in good faith only to describe the goods or services of such party, or their geographic origin. . . ." § 1115(b)(4).

Two points are evident. Section 1115(b) places a burden of proving likelihood of confusion (that is, infringement) on the party charging infringement even when relying on an incontestable registration. And Congress said nothing about likelihood of confusion in setting out the elements of the fair use defense in § 1115(b)(4).

Starting from these textual fixed points, it takes a long stretch to claim that a defense of fair use entails any burden to negate confusion. It is just not plausible that Congress would have used the descriptive phrase "likely to cause confusion, or to cause mistake, or to deceive" in § 1114 to describe the requirement that a markholder show likelihood of consumer confusion, but would have relied on the phrase "used fairly" in § 1115(b)(4) in a fit of terse drafting meant to place a defendant under a burden to negate confusion. . . .[4]

Finally, a look at the typical course of litigation in an infringement action points up the incoherence of placing a burden to show nonconfusion on a defendant. If a plaintiff succeeds in making out a prima facie case of trademark infringement, including the element of likelihood of consumer confusion, the defendant may offer rebutting evidence to undercut the force of the plaintiff's evidence on this (or any) element, or raise an affirmative defense to bar relief even if the prima facie case is sound, or do both. But it would make no sense to give the defendant a defense of showing affirmatively that the plaintiff cannot succeed in proving some element (like confusion); all the defendant needs to do is to leave the factfinder unpersuaded that the plaintiff has

4. Not only that, but the failure to say anything about a defendant's burden on this point was almost certainly not an oversight, not after the House Subcommittee on Trademarks declined to forward a proposal to provide expressly as an element of the defense that a descriptive use be "'[un]likely to deceive the public.'" Hearings on H.R. 102 et al. before the Subcommittee on Trade-Marks of the House Committee on Patents, 77th Cong., 1st Sess., 167-168 (1941) (hereinafter Hearings) (testimony of Prof. Milton Handler).

carried its own burden on that point. A defendant has no need of a court's true belief when agnosticism will do. Put another way, it is only when a plaintiff has shown likely confusion by a preponderance of the evidence that a defendant could have any need of an affirmative defense, but under Lasting's theory the defense would be foreclosed in such a case. "[I]t defies logic to argue that a defense may not be asserted in the only situation where it even becomes relevant." Shakespeare Co. v. Silstar Corp., 110 F.3d, at 243. Nor would it make sense to provide an affirmative defense of no confusion plus good faith, when merely rebutting the plaintiff's case on confusion would entitle the defendant to judgment, good faith or not. . . .

B

Since the burden of proving likelihood of confusion rests with the plaintiff, and the fair use defendant has no free-standing need to show confusion unlikely, it follows (contrary to the Court of Appeals's view) that some possibility of consumer confusion must be compatible with fair use, and so it is. The common law's tolerance of a certain degree of confusion on the part of consumers followed from the very fact that in cases like this one an originally descriptive term was selected to be used as a mark, not to mention the undesirability of allowing anyone to obtain a complete monopoly on use of a descriptive term simply by grabbing it first. Canal Co. v. Clark, 13 Wall., at 323-324, 327. The Lanham Act adopts a similar leniency, there being no indication that the statute was meant to deprive commercial speakers of the ordinary utility of descriptive words. "If any confusion results, that is a risk the plaintiff accepted when it decided to identify its product with a mark that uses a well known descriptive phrase." Cosmetically Sealed Industries, Inc. v. Chesebrough-Pond's USA Co., 125 F.3d, at 30. See also Park 'N Fly, Inc. v. Dollar Park and Fly, Inc., 469 U.S. 189, 201, 105 S. Ct. 658, 83 L. Ed. 2d 582 (1985) (noting safeguards in Lanham Act to prevent commercial monopolization of language); Car-Freshner Corp. v. S.C. Johnson & Son, Inc., 70 F.3d 267, 269 (C.A.2 1995) (noting importance of "protect[ing] the right of society at large to use words or images in their primary descriptive sense"). This right to describe is the reason that descriptive terms qualify for registration as trademarks only after taking on secondary meaning as "distinctive of the applicant's goods," 15 U.S.C. § 1052(f), with the registrant getting an exclusive right not in the original, descriptive sense, but only in the secondary one associated with the markholder's goods, 2 McCarthy, *supra*, § 11:45, p. 11-90 ("The only aspect of the mark which is given legal protection is that penumbra or fringe of secondary meaning which surrounds the old descriptive word").

While we thus recognize that mere risk of confusion will not rule out fair use, we think it would be improvident to go further in this case, for deciding anything more would take us beyond the Ninth Circuit's consideration of the subject. It suffices to realize that our holding that fair use can occur along with some degree of confusion does not foreclose the relevance of the extent of any likely consumer confusion in assessing whether a defendant's use is objectively fair. Two Courts of Appeals have found it relevant to consider such scope, and commentators and amici here have urged us to say that the degree of likely consumer confusion bears not only on the fairness of using a term, but even on the further question whether an originally descriptive term has become so identified as a mark that a defendant's use of it cannot realistically be called descriptive. See Shakespeare Co. v. Silstar Corp., 110 F.3d, at 243 ("[T]o the degree that confusion is likely, a use is less likely to be found fair . . ." (emphasis deleted)); Sunmark, Inc. v. Ocean Spray Cranberries, Inc., 64 F.3d, at 1059; RESTATEMENT § 28.

Since we do not rule out the pertinence of the degree of consumer confusion under the fair use defense, we likewise do not pass upon the position of the United States, as amicus, that the "used fairly" requirement in § 1115(b)(4) demands only that the descriptive term describe the goods accurately. Accuracy of course has to be a consideration in assessing fair use, but the proceedings in this case so far raise no occasion to evaluate some other concerns that courts might pick as relevant, quite apart from attention to confusion. The Restatement raises possibilities like commercial justification and the strength of the plaintiff's mark. RESTATEMENT § 28. As to them, it is enough to say here that the door is not closed.

III

In sum, a plaintiff claiming infringement of an incontestable mark must show likelihood of consumer confusion as part of the prima facie case, 15 U.S.C. § 1115(b), while the defendant has no independent burden to negate the likelihood of any confusion in raising the affirmative defense that a term is used descriptively, not as a mark, fairly, and in good faith, § 1115(b)(4).

Because we read the Court of Appeals as requiring KP to shoulder a burden on the issue of confusion, we vacate the judgment and remand the case for further proceedings consistent with this opinion.

It is so ordered.

COMMENTS AND QUESTIONS

1. On remand, the Ninth Circuit held that while no longer determinative, consumer confusion was still relevant in deciding whether a use was fair:

> Among the relevant factors for consideration by the jury in determining the fairness of the use are the degree of likely confusion, the strength of the trademark, the descriptive nature of the term for the product or service being offered by KP and the availability of alternate descriptive terms, the extent of the use of the term prior to the registration of the trademark, and any differences among the times and contexts in which KP has used the term.

KP Permanent Make-Up, Inc. v. Lasting Impression I, Inc., 408 F.3d 596, 609 (9th Cir. 2005).

2. While many argue that "fair use" applies only to descriptive marks that have acquired secondary meaning, the leading trademark commentator has argued for a broader role for the doctrine. MCCARTHY, MCCARTHY ON TRADEMARKS AND UNFAIR COMPETITION § 11.45. Professor McCarthy's position was endorsed by the Second Circuit in Car-Freshner Corp. v. S.C. Johnson & Son, 70 F.3d 267, 269 (2d Cir. 1995) ("[I]t should make no difference whether the plaintiff's mark is to be classed on the descriptive tier of the trademark ladder. . . . What matters is whether the defendant is using the protected word or image descriptively, and not as a mark."). How can inherently distinctive marks be used in a descriptive sense?

3. An example of the application of trademark's fair use doctrine can be found in Cosmetically Sealed Industries, Inc. v. Chesebrough-Pond's USA, 125 F.3d 28 (2d Cir. 1997). There the plaintiff registered the trademark "Sealed With a Kiss" for a brand of long-lasting lipstick. Plaintiff sued after the defendant began an advertising campaign for its own brand of lipstick that encouraged users to place a lipstick "kiss" on a postcard and mail it to someone. The defendant's campaign used the phrase "Seal it with a Kiss!!" The court held that the phrase "sealed with a kiss" was in common use and that the defendant was not liable because it merely used that common phrase in its descriptive (rather than its trademark) sense.

C. NON-TRADEMARK (OR NOMINATIVE) USE, PARODY, AND THE FIRST AMENDMENT

Mattel, Inc. v. MCA Records

296 F.3d 894 (9th Cir. 2002)

KOZINSKI, Circuit Judge:

If this were a sci-fi melodrama, it might be called Speech-Zilla meets Trademark Kong.

I

Barbie was born in Germany in the 1950s as an adult collector's item. Over the years, Mattel transformed her from a doll that resembled a "German street walker," as she originally appeared, into a glamorous, long-legged blonde. Barbie has been labeled both the ideal American woman and a bimbo. She has survived attacks both psychic (from feminists critical of her fictitious figure) and physical (more than 500 professional makeovers). She remains a symbol of American girlhood, a public figure who graces the aisles of toy stores throughout the country and beyond. With Barbie, Mattel created not just a toy but a cultural icon.

With fame often comes unwanted attention. Aqua is a Danish band that has, as yet, only dreamed of attaining Barbie-like status. In 1997, Aqua produced the song Barbie Girl on the album *Aquarium*. In the song, one bandmember impersonates Barbie, singing in a high-pitched, doll-like voice; another bandmember, calling himself Ken, entices Barbie to "go party." (The lyrics are in the Appendix.) Barbie Girl singles sold well and, to Mattel's dismay, the song made it onto Top 40 music charts.

Mattel brought this lawsuit against the music companies who produced, marketed and sold Barbie Girl: MCA Records, Inc., Universal Music International Ltd. . . .

Mattel appeals the district court's ruling that Barbie Girl is a parody of Barbie and a nominative fair use [and] that MCA's use of the term Barbie is not likely to confuse consumers as to Mattel's affiliation with Barbie Girl or dilute the Barbie mark. . . .

III

A.

A trademark is a word, phrase or symbol that is used to identify a manufacturer or sponsor of a good or the provider of a service. See New Kids on the Block v. News Am. Publ'g, Inc., 971 F.2d 302, 305 (9th Cir. 1992). It's the owner's way of preventing others from duping consumers into buying a product they mistakenly believe is sponsored by the trademark owner. A trademark "inform[s] people that trademarked products come from the same source." Id. at 305 n.2. Limited to this core purpose — avoiding confusion in the marketplace — a trademark owner's property rights play well with the First Amendment. "Whatever first amendment rights you may have in calling the brew you make in your bathtub 'Pepsi' are easily outweighed by the buyer's interest in not being fooled into buying it." [Alex Kozinski,] *Trademarks Unplugged*, 68 N.Y.U. L. Rev. 960, 973 (1993).

The problem arises when trademarks transcend their identifying purpose. Some trademarks enter our public discourse and become an integral part of our vocabulary. How else do you say that something's "the Rolls Royce of its class"? What else is a quick fix, but a Band-Aid? Does the average consumer know to ask for aspirin as "acetyl salicylic acid"? See Bayer Co. v. United Drug Co., 272 F. 505, 510 (S.D.N.Y. 1921). Trademarks often fill in gaps in our vocabulary and add a contemporary flavor to our expressions. Once imbued with such expressive value, the trademark becomes a word in our language and assumes a role outside the bounds of trademark law.

Our likelihood-of-confusion test, see AMF Inc. v. Sleekcraft Boats, 599 F.2d 341, 348-49 (9th Cir. 1979), generally strikes a comfortable balance between the trademark owner's property rights and the public's expressive interests. But when a trademark owner asserts a right to control how we express ourselves — when we'd find it difficult to describe the product any other way (as in the case of aspirin), or when the mark (like Rolls Royce) has taken on an expressive meaning apart from its source-identifying function — applying the traditional test fails to account for the full weight of the public's interest in free expression.

The First Amendment may offer little protection for a competitor who labels its commercial good with a confusingly similar mark, but "[t]rademark rights do not entitle the owner to quash an unauthorized use of the mark by another who is communicating ideas or expressing points of view." L.L. Bean, Inc. v. Drake Publishers, Inc., 811 F.2d 26, 29 (1st Cir. 1987). Were we to ignore the expressive value that some marks assume, trademark rights would grow to encroach upon the zone protected by the First Amendment. See Yankee Publ'g, Inc. v. News Am. Publ'g, Inc., 809 F. Supp. 267, 276 (S.D.N.Y. 1992) ("[W]hen unauthorized use of another's mark is part of a communicative message and not a source identifier, the First Amendment is implicated in opposition to the trademark right."). Simply put, the trademark owner does not have the right to control public discourse whenever the public imbues his mark with a meaning beyond its source-identifying function. See Anti-Monopoly, Inc. v. Gen. Mills Fun Group, 611 F.2d 296, 301 (9th Cir. 1979) ("It is the source-denoting function which trademark laws protect, and nothing more.").

B.

There is no doubt that MCA uses Mattel's mark: Barbie is one half of Barbie Girl. But Barbie Girl is the title of a song about Barbie and Ken, a reference that — at least today — can only be to Mattel's famous couple. We expect a title to describe the underlying work, not to identify the producer, and Barbie Girl does just that.

The Barbie Girl title presages a song about Barbie, or at least a girl like Barbie. The title conveys a message to consumers about what they can expect to discover in the song itself; it's a quick glimpse of Aqua's take on their own song. The lyrics confirm this: The female singer, who calls herself Barbie, is "a Barbie girl, in [her] Barbie world." She tells her male counterpart (named Ken), "Life in plastic, it's fantastic. You can brush my hair, undress me everywhere/Imagination, life is your creation." And off they go to "party." The song pokes fun at Barbie and the values that Aqua contends she represents. See Cliffs Notes, Inc. v. Bantam Doubleday Dell Publ'g Group, 886 F.2d 490, 495-96 (2d Cir. 1989). The female singer explains, "I'm a blond bimbo girl, in a fantasy world/Dress me up, make it tight, I'm your dolly."

The song does not rely on the Barbie mark to poke fun at another subject but targets Barbie herself. See Campbell v. Acuff-Rose Music, Inc., 510 U.S. 569 (1994); see also Dr. Seuss Ents., L.P. v. Penguin Books USA, Inc., 109 F.3d 1394, 1400 (9th Cir. 1997). This case is therefore distinguishable from *Dr. Seuss*, where we held that the book *The Cat NOT in the Hat!* borrowed Dr. Seuss's trademarks and lyrics to get attention rather than to mock *The Cat in the Hat!* The defendant's use of the Dr. Seuss trademarks and copyrighted works had "no critical bearing on the substance or style of" *The Cat in the Hat!*, and therefore could not claim First Amendment protection. Id. at 1401. *Dr. Seuss* recognized that, where an artistic work targets the original and does not merely borrow another's property to get attention, First Amendment interests weigh more heavily in the balance. See id. at 1400-02; see also Harley-Davidson, Inc. v. Grottanelli, 164 F.3d 806, 812-13 (2d Cir. 1999) (a parodist whose expressive work aims its parodic commentary at a trademark is given considerable leeway, but a claimed parodic use that makes no comment on the mark is not a permitted trademark parody use).

The Second Circuit has held that "in general the [Lanham] Act should be construed to apply to artistic works only where the public interest in avoiding consumer confusion outweighs the public interest in free expression." Rogers v. Grimaldi, 875 F.2d 994, 999 (2d Cir. 1989); see also *Cliffs Notes*, 886 F.2d at 494 (quoting *Rogers*, 875 F.2d at 999). *Rogers* considered a challenge by the actress Ginger Rogers to the film *Ginger and Fred*. The movie told the story of two Italian cabaret performers who made a living by imitating Ginger Rogers and Fred Astaire. Rogers argued that the film's title created the false impression that she was associated with it.

At first glance, Rogers certainly had a point. Ginger was her name, and Fred was her dancing partner. If a pair of dancing shoes had been labeled Ginger and Fred, a dancer might have suspected that Rogers was associated with the shoes (or at least one of them), just as Michael Jordan has endorsed Nike sneakers that claim to make you fly through the air. But Ginger and Fred was not a brand of shoe; it was the title of a movie and, for the reasons explained by the Second Circuit, deserved to be treated differently.

A title is designed to catch the eye and to promote the value of the underlying work. Consumers expect a title to communicate a message about the book or movie, but they do not expect it to identify the publisher or producer. See Application of Cooper, 254 F.2d 611, 615-16 (C.C.P.A. 1958) (A "title . . . identifies a specific literary work, . . . and is not associated in the public mind with the . . . manufacturer." (internal quotation marks omitted)). If we see a painting titled "Campbell's Chicken Noodle Soup," we're unlikely to believe that Campbell's has branched into the art business. Nor, upon hearing Janis Joplin croon "Oh Lord, won't you buy me a Mercedes-Benz?," would we suspect that she and the carmaker had entered into a joint venture. A title tells us something about the underlying work but seldom speaks to its origin: Though consumers frequently look to the title of a work to determine what it is about, they do not regard titles of artistic works in the same way as the names of ordinary commercial products. Since consumers expect an ordinary product to be what the name says it is, we apply the Lanham Act with some rigor to prohibit names that misdescribe such goods. But most consumers are well aware that they cannot judge a book solely by its title any more than by its cover. *Rogers*, 875 F.2d at 1000 (citations omitted).

Rogers concluded that literary titles do not violate the Lanham Act "unless the title has no artistic relevance to the underlying work whatsoever, or, if it has some artistic relevance, unless the title explicitly misleads as to the source or the content of the work." Id. at 999 (footnote omitted). We agree with the Second Circuit's analysis and adopt the *Rogers* standard as our own.

Applying *Rogers* to our case, we conclude that MCA's use of Barbie is not an infringement of Mattel's trademark. Under the first prong of *Rogers*, the use of Barbie in the song title clearly is relevant to the underlying work, namely, the song itself. As noted, the song is about Barbie and the values Aqua claims she represents. The song title does not explicitly mislead as to the source of the work; it does not, explicitly or otherwise, suggest that it was produced by Mattel.

The only indication that Mattel might be associated with the song is the use of Barbie in the title; if this were enough to satisfy this prong of the *Rogers* test, it would render *Rogers* a nullity. We therefore agree with the district court that MCA was entitled to summary judgment on this ground. We need not consider whether the district court was correct in holding that MCA was also entitled to summary judgment because its use of Barbie was a nominative fair use.

IV

Mattel separately argues that, under the Federal Trademark Dilution Act ("FTDA"), MCA's song dilutes the Barbie mark in two ways: It diminishes the mark's capacity to identify and distinguish Mattel products, and tarnishes the mark because the song is inappropriate for young girls. See 15 U.S.C. § 1125(c). . . .

Originally a creature of state law, dilution received nationwide recognition in 1996 when Congress amended the Lanham Act by enacting the FTDA. The statute protects "[t]he owner of a famous mark . . . against another person's commercial use in commerce of a mark or trade name, if such use begins after the mark has become famous and causes dilution of the distinctive quality of the mark." 15 U.S.C. § 1125(c). Dilutive uses are prohibited unless they fall within one of the three statutory exemptions discussed below. . . . Barbie easily qualifies under the FTDA as a famous and distinctive mark, and reached this status long before MCA began to market the Barbie Girl song. The commercial success of Barbie Girl establishes beyond dispute that the Barbie mark satisfies each of these elements.

We are also satisfied that the song amounts to a "commercial use in commerce." Although this statutory language is ungainly, its meaning seems clear: It refers to a use of a famous and distinctive mark to sell goods other than those produced or authorized by the mark's owner. *Panavision*, 141 F.3d at 1324-25. That is precisely what MCA did with the Barbie mark: It created and sold to consumers in the marketplace commercial products (the Barbie Girl single and the *Aquarium* album) that bear the Barbie mark.

MCA's use of the mark is dilutive. MCA does not dispute that, while a reference to Barbie would previously have brought to mind only Mattel's doll, after the song's popular success, some consumers hearing Barbie's name will think of both the doll and the song, or perhaps of the song only. This is a classic blurring injury and is in no way diminished by the fact that the song itself refers back to Barbie the doll. To be dilutive, use of the mark need not bring to mind the junior user alone. The distinctiveness of the mark is diminished if the mark no longer brings to mind the senior user alone.[4]

We consider next the applicability of the FTDA's three statutory exemptions. These are uses that, though potentially dilutive, are nevertheless permitted: comparative advertising; news reporting and commentary; and noncommercial use. 15 U.S.C. § 1125(c)(4)(B). The first two exemptions clearly do not apply; only the exemption for noncommercial use need detain us.

A "noncommercial use" exemption, on its face, presents a bit of a conundrum because it seems at odds with the earlier requirement that the junior use be a "commercial use in commerce." If a use has to be commercial in order to be dilutive, how then can it also be noncommercial so as to satisfy the exception of section 1125(c)(4)(B)? If the term "commercial use" had the same meaning in both provisions, this would eliminate one of the three statutory exemptions defined by this subsection, because any use found to be dilutive would, of necessity, not be noncommercial.

Such a reading of the statute would also create a constitutional problem, because it would leave the FTDA with no First Amendment protection for dilutive speech other than comparative advertising and news reporting. This would be a serious problem because the primary (usually exclusive) remedy for dilution is an injunction.[5] As noted above, tension with the First Amendment also exists in the trademark context, especially where the mark has assumed an expressive function beyond mere identification of a product or service. See supra; *New Kids on the Block*, 971 F.2d at 306-08. These concerns apply with greater force in the dilution context because dilution lacks two very significant limitations that reduce the tension between trademark law and the First Amendment.

First, depending on the strength and distinctiveness of the mark, trademark law grants relief only against uses that are likely to confuse. See 5 McCarthy § 30:3, at 30-8 to 30-11; Restatement § 35 cmt. c at 370. A trademark injunction is usually limited to uses within one industry or several related industries. Dilution law is the antithesis of trademark law in this respect, because it seeks to protect the mark from association in

4. Because we find blurring, we need not consider whether the song also tarnished the Barbie mark.

5. The FTDA provides for both injunctive relief and damages, but the latter is only available if plaintiff can prove a willful intent to dilute. 15 U.S.C. § 1125(c)(2).

the public's mind with wholly unrelated goods and services. The more remote the good or service associated with the junior use, the more likely it is to cause dilution rather than trademark infringement. A dilution injunction, by contrast to a trademark injunction, will generally sweep across broad vistas of the economy.

Second, a trademark injunction, even a very broad one, is premised on the need to prevent consumer confusion. This consumer protection rationale—averting what is essentially a fraud on the consuming public—is wholly consistent with the theory of the First Amendment, which does not protect commercial fraud. Cent. Hudson Gas & Elec. v. Pub. Serv. Comm'n, 447 U.S. 557, 566 (1980); see Thompson v. W. States Med. Ctr., 122 S. Ct. 1497 (2002) (applying *Central Hudson*). Moreover, avoiding harm to consumers is an important interest that is independent of the senior user's interest in protecting its business.

Dilution, by contrast, does not require a showing of consumer confusion, 15 U.S.C. § 1127, and dilution injunctions therefore lack the built-in First Amendment compass of trademark injunctions. In addition, dilution law protects only the distinctiveness of the mark, which is inherently less weighty than the dual interest of protecting trademark owners and avoiding harm to consumers that is at the heart of every trademark claim.

Fortunately, the legislative history of the FTDA suggests an interpretation of the "noncommercial use" exemption that both solves our interpretive dilemma and diminishes some First Amendment concerns: "Noncommercial use" refers to a use that consists entirely of noncommercial, or fully constitutionally protected, speech. See 2 Jerome Gilson et al., Trademark Protection and Practice § 5.12[1][c][vi], at 5-240 (this exemption "is intended to prevent the courts from enjoining speech that has been recognized to be [fully] constitutionally protected," "such as parodies"). Where, as here, a statute's plain meaning "produces an absurd, and perhaps unconstitutional, result[, it is] entirely appropriate to consult all public materials, including the background of [the statute] and the legislative history of its adoption." Green v. Bock Laundry Mach. Co., 490 U.S. 504, 527 (1989) (Scalia, J., concurring).

The legislative history bearing on this issue is particularly persuasive. First, the FTDA's sponsors in both the House and the Senate were aware of the potential collision with the First Amendment if the statute authorized injunctions against protected speech. Upon introducing the counterpart bills, sponsors in each house explained that the proposed law "will not prohibit or threaten noncommercial expression, such as parody, satire, editorial and other forms of expression that are not a part of a commercial transaction." 141 Cong. Rec. S1930610, S19310 (daily ed. Dec. 29, 1995) (statement of Sen. Hatch); 141 Cong. Rec. H14317-01, H14318 (daily ed. Dec. 12, 1995) (statement of Rep. Moorhead). The House Judiciary Committee agreed in its report on the FTDA. H.R. Rep. No. 104-374, at 4 (1995), reprinted in 1995 U.S.C.C.A.N. 1029, 1031 ("The bill will not prohibit or threaten, noncommercial expression, as that term has been defined by the courts.").[6]

6. Our interpretation of the noncommercial use exemption does not eliminate all tension between the FTDA and the First Amendment because the exemption does not apply to commercial speech, which enjoys "qualified but nonetheless substantial protection." Bolger, 463 U.S. 60, 68 (applying Central Hudson Gas & Electric Corp. v. Pub. Serv. Comm'n, 447 U.S. 557 (1980)). See also Thompson, 122 S. Ct. at 1503-04 (same). It is entirely possible that a dilution injunction against purely commercial speech would run afoul of the First Amendment. Because that question is not presented here, we do not address it.

The FTDA's section-by-section analysis presented in the House and Senate suggests that the bill's sponsors relied on the "noncommercial use" exemption to allay First Amendment concerns. H.R. REP. No. 104-374, at 8, reprinted in 1995 U.S.C.C.A.N. 1029, 1035 (the exemption "expressly incorporates the concept of 'commercial' speech from the 'commercial speech' doctrine, and proscribes dilution actions that seek to enjoin use of famous marks in 'non-commercial' uses (such as consumer product reviews)"); 141 CONG. REC. S19306-10, S19311 (daily ed. Dec. 29, 1995) (the exemption "is consistent with existing case law[, which] recognize[s] that the use of marks in certain forms of artistic and expressive speech is protected by the First Amendment"). At the request of one of the bill's sponsors, the section-by-section analysis was printed in the Congressional Record. 141 CONG. REC. S19306-10, S19311 (daily ed. Dec. 29, 1995). Thus, we know that this interpretation of the exemption was before the Senate when the FTDA was passed, and that no senator rose to dispute it.

To determine whether Barbie Girl falls within this exemption, we look to our definition of commercial speech under our First Amendment caselaw. See H.R. REP. No. 104-374, at 8, reprinted in 1995 U.S.C.C.A.N. 1029, 1035 (the exemption "expressly incorporates the concept of 'commercial' speech from the 'commercial speech' doctrine"); 141 CONG. REC. S19306-10, S19311 (daily ed. Dec. 29, 1995) (the exemption "is consistent with existing [First Amendment] case law").

"Although the boundary between commercial and noncommercial speech has yet to be clearly delineated, the 'core notion of commercial speech' is that it 'does no more than propose a commercial transaction.'" Hoffman v. Capital Cities/ABC, Inc., 255 F.3d 1180, 1184 (9th Cir. 2001) (quoting Bolger v. Youngs Drug Prods Corp., 463 U.S. 60, 66 (1983)). If speech is not "purely commercial" — that is, if it does more than propose a commercial transaction — then it is entitled to full First Amendment protection. Id. at 1185-86 (internal quotation marks omitted).

In *Hoffman*, a magazine published an article featuring digitally altered images from famous films. Computer artists modified shots of Dustin Hoffman, Cary Grant, Marilyn Monroe and others to put the actors in famous designers' spring fashions; a still of Hoffman from the movie "Tootsie" was altered so that he appeared to be wearing a Richard Tyler evening gown and Ralph Lauren heels. Hoffman, who had not given permission, sued under the Lanham Act and for violation of his right to publicity. Id. at 1183.

The article featuring the altered image clearly served a commercial purpose: "to draw attention to the for-profit magazine in which it appear[ed]" and to sell more copies. Id. at 1186. Nevertheless, we held that the article was fully protected under the First Amendment because it included protected expression: "humor" and "visual and verbal editorial comment on classic films and famous actors." Id. at 1185 (internal quotation marks omitted). Because its commercial purpose was "inextricably entwined with [these] expressive elements," the article and accompanying photographs enjoyed full First Amendment protection. Id.

Hoffman controls: Barbie Girl is not purely commercial speech, and is therefore fully protected. To be sure, MCA used Barbie's name to sell copies of the song. However, as we've already observed, see pp. 1189-90 supra, the song also lampoons the Barbie image and comments humorously on the cultural values Aqua claims she represents. Use of the Barbie mark in the song Barbie Girl therefore falls within the noncommercial use exemption to the FTDA. For precisely the same reasons, use of the mark in the song's title is also exempted. . . .

VI

After Mattel filed suit, Mattel and MCA employees traded barbs in the press. When an MCA spokeswoman noted that each album included a disclaimer saying that Barbie Girl was a "social commentary [that was] not created or approved by the makers of the doll," a Mattel representative responded by saying, "That's unacceptable. . . . It's akin to a bank robber handing a note of apology to a teller during a heist. [It n]either diminishes the severity of the crime, nor does it make it legal." He later characterized the song as a "theft" of "another company's property."

MCA filed a counterclaim for defamation based on the Mattel representative's use of the words "bank robber," "heist," "crime" and "theft." But all of these are variants of the invective most often hurled at accused infringers, namely "piracy." No one hearing this accusation understands intellectual property owners to be saying that infringers are nautical cutthroats with eyepatches and peg legs who board galleons to plunder cargo. In context, all these terms are nonactionable "rhetorical hyperbole," Gilbrook v. City of Westminster, 177 F.3d 839, 863 (9th Cir.1999). The parties are advised to chill.

Affirmed.

Appendix

"Barbie Girl" by Aqua
- Hiya Barbie!
- Hi Ken!
- You wanna go for a ride?
- Sure, Ken!
- Jump in!
- Ha ha ha ha!
(CHORUS)
I'm a Barbie girl, in my Barbie world
Life in plastic, it's fantastic
You can brush my hair, undress me everywhere
Imagination, life is your creation
Come on Barbie, let's go party!
(CHORUS)
I'm a blonde bimbo girl, in a fantasy world
Dress me up, make it tight, I'm your dolly
You're my doll, rock and roll, feel the glamour in pink
Kiss me here, touch me there, hanky-panky
You can touch, you can play
If you say "I'm always yours," ooh ooh
(CHORUS)
(BRIDGE)
Come on, Barbie, let's go party, ah ah ah yeah
Come on, Barbie, let's go party, ooh ooh, ooh ooh
Come on, Barbie, let's go party, ah ah ah yeah
Come on, Barbie, let's go party, ooh ooh, ooh ooh

Make me walk, make me talk, do whatever you please
I can act like a star, I can beg on my knees
Come jump in, be my friend, let us do it again
Hit the town, fool around, let's go party
You can touch, you can play
You can say "I'm always yours"
You can touch, you can play
You can say "I'm always yours"
(BRIDGE)
(CHORUS ×2)
(BRIDGE)
- Oh, I'm having so much fun!
- Well, Barbie, we're just getting started!
- Oh, I love you Ken!

COMMENTS AND QUESTIONS

1. To similar effect is Mattel v. Walking Mountain Prods., 353 F.3d 792 (9th Cir. 2003), where the court held that an artist who posed Barbie dolls nude in photographs in which they were attacked by vintage household appliances was not liable for trademark infringement or dilution, since his use of the term Barbie accurately stated the content of his works, he was criticizing or parodying Barbie, and his use was not commercial use.

2. *Non-trademark or "Nominative" Use.* In New Kids on the Block v. News Am. Publ'g, Inc., 971 F.2d 302 (9th Cir. 1992), *USA Today* asked its readers: "Who's the best on the block?" This feature commented that "New Kids on the Block are pop's hottest group. Which of the five is your fave? Or are they a turn off? . . . Each call [to a 900 number] costs 50 cents. Results in Friday's Life Section." In finding that this use of the band's name did not infringe its trademark rights, Judge Kozinski articulated the contours and elements of the nominative use (sometimes called "nominative fair use") doctrine:

> [W]e may generalize a class of cases where the use of the trademark does not attempt to capitalize on consumer confusion or to appropriate the cachet of one product for a different one. Such *nominative use* of a mark—where the only word reasonably available to describe a particular thing is pressed into service—lies outside the strictures of trademark law: Because it does not implicate the source-identification function that is the purpose of trademark, it does not constitute unfair competition; such use is fair because it does not imply sponsorship or endorsement by the trademark holder. "When the mark is used in a way that does not deceive the public we see no such sanctity in the word as to prevent its being used to tell the truth." Prestonettes, Inc. v. Coty, 264 U.S. 359, 368 (1924) (Holmes, J.).
>
> To be sure, this is not the classic fair use case where the defendant has used the plaintiff's mark to describe the defendant's *own* product. Here, the New Kids trademark is used to refer to the New Kids themselves. We therefore do not purport to alter the test applicable in the paradigmatic fair use case. If the defendant's use of the plaintiff's trademark refers to something other than the plaintiff's product, the traditional fair use inquiry will continue to govern. But, where the defendant uses a trademark to describe the plaintiff's product, rather than its own, we hold that a commercial user is entitled to a nominative fair use defense

> provided he meets the following three requirements: First, the product or service in question must be one not readily identifiable without use of the trademark; second, only so much of the mark or marks may be used as is reasonably necessary to identify the product or service; and third, the user must do nothing that would, in conjunction with the mark, suggest sponsorship or endorsement by the trademark holder.

New Kids on the Block v. News Am. Publ'g, Inc., 971 F.2d at 307-08.

How would the court rule if *USA Today* had used the band's logo in the feature? How would the court in *Mattel* have responded if MCA used the Barbie logo on the Aqua album cover? What if the Barbie logo had a red circle with a slash symbol ("no") through it? What if it merely had a Barbie look-alike on the cover? Does the 2006 Trademark Dilution Revision Act, which explicitly protects "identifying and parodying, criticizing, or commenting upon the famous mark owner or the goods," change the court's analysis?

Is nominative use a defense to a trademark infringement case, or is it simply a different way of analyzing the basic question of consumer confusion? As with the fair use doctrine, the practical effect of the characterization can be substantial: A defense must apply even if consumers are confused.

The Third Circuit has rejected the *New Kids on the Block* formulation of nominative use, concluding that as a defense, nominative use should not depend on whether the use confuses some consumers. *See* Century 21 Real Estate Corp. v. LendingTree, Inc., 425 F.3d 211 (3d Cir. 2006). Who is right? Does *KP Permanent* shed any light on the question?

3. How does the non-trademark use doctrine square with the merchandising rights in logos and university names that some courts have granted to trademark owners?

4. Terri Welles, *Playboy Magazine*'s Playmate of the Year in 1981, created a Web site offering photographs of Welles (some for free, others for sale), membership in her photo club, and links to other commercial sites. Her Web site contained "playboy" and "playmate" in metatags, the phrase "Playmate of the Year 1981" on the masthead of the Web site and in banner advertisements, and the repeated use of the abbreviation "PMOY'81" as a watermark on the Web pages. How should each of these uses be evaluated under the *New Kids on the Block* test? *See* Playboy Enterprises, Inc. v. Welles, 279 F.3d 796 (9th Cir. 2002) (Welles was free to use Playboy's trademarks to accurately advertise her affiliation with the magazine, but could not go beyond that to trade on those marks).

5. *Non-Dilution Parody Analysis.* Parody has been an effective defense not only against claims grounded in state dilution laws, but also against trademark infringement per se. But a parody that confuses consumers will not be immune from trademark infringement. Cliffs Notes, Inc. v. Bantam Doubleday Dell Publishing Group, Inc., 886 F.2d 490 (2d Cir. 1989). In Mutual of Omaha Ins. Co. v. Novak, 836 F.2d 397 (8th Cir. 1987), the court observed that

> [a] parody must convey two simultaneous—and contradictory—messages: that it is the original, but also that it is not the original and is instead a parody. To the extent that it does only the former but not the latter, it is not only a poor parody but also vulnerable under trademark law, since the customer will be confused.

Id. at 494 (affirming district court's finding of likelihood of confusion between plaintiff's famous "Mutual of Omaha" mark and defendant's anti-nuclear T-shirts, bearing funny picture and "Mutant of Omaha" legend).

Another case demonstrates the application of the likelihood of confusion to parody cases. In Hormel Foods Corp. v. Jim Henson Prods., Inc., 73 F.3d 497 (2d Cir. 1996), the court held that defendant's use of a character named "SPA'AM" in a movie was an acceptable parody of the plaintiff's famous registered mark "SPAM" for meat-related products. The opinion treats the case strictly under "likelihood of confusion" principles. Although no confusion is found to be likely, and the parody is permitted, the First Amendment is never mentioned. Should the First Amendment protect even confusing parodies? *See* Steven M. Perez, *Confronting Biased Treatment of Trademark Parody Under the Lanham Act*, 44 Emory L.J. 1451 (1995) (arguing that trademark-based "likelihood of confusion" analysis makes parody cases too unpredictable and inconsistent with free speech interests).

6. *Parody/Satire Distinction.* Courts distinguish between parody and satire in applying copyright's fair use doctrine, finding parody of a copyrighted work much more likely to fall within the scope of the doctrine than satirical treatment. The court in *Mattel* suggests that Congress intended to exclude "parody, satire, editorial and other forms of expression that are not a part of a commercial transaction" from the scope of the dilution cause of action. Should this clearer and broader exemption also apply to traditional (likelihood of confusion) trademark claims?

In Elvis Presley Enterprises v. Capece, 141 F.3d 188 (5th Cir. 1998), the Fifth Circuit imported the parody/satire distinction from copyright law into traditional trademark analysis. The court held that defendant's 1960s theme bar could not use the name "Velvet Elvis" because it infringed on the rights of Elvis Presley's estate. The owner of the bar claimed that he was engaged in a legitimate parody of the kitsch associated with certain aspects of the 1960s. The Fifth Circuit concluded that "parody is not a defense to trademark infringement," and that in any event the "Velvet Elvis" was engaged in satire and not parody because its statement did not require the use of the Elvis trademark.

Does it make sense to import the parody/satire distinction into trademark law? Aren't the purposes of the laws different? In any event, how likely is it that consumers will be confused by the use of the "Velvet Elvis" name? Contrast this case with E.S.S. Entertainment 2000 v. Rock Star Videos, 547 F.3d 1095 (9th Cir. 2008), which held that the First Amendment protected the depiction of a strip club with a name and likeness similar to plaintiff's "Play Pen" in the video game Grand Theft Auto: San Andreas so long as the use had at least "some artistic relevance" and was not "expressly misleading."

PROBLEMS

Problem 6-3. Toho, Inc. is the owner of the copyrights in several Japanese "Godzilla" movies as well as the registered U.S. trademark "Godzilla." Toho granted a license to a major American movie company to use the name and the monster in its recent high-budget film and various related products and promotional efforts.

Capitalizing on the hype surrounding the new Godzilla film, Edgar publishes a book cataloguing the history of Godzilla in film and print. He titles his book "Godzilla" and places a picture of the monster on the cover. Toho sues for trademark infringement.

How should the court rule? Would it matter if Toho had licensed a different writer to produce an "authorized" history?

Problem 6-4. Anheuser-Busch sells beer under a variety of brand names, including Michelob. As part of a general trend of brand proliferation in the beer industry, Busch has recently produced sub-brands of Michelob, including Michelob Dry, Michelob Lite, and Michelob Ice.

After the waters near a Busch plant are polluted in an oil spill, Balducci runs the accompanying advertisement [Figure 6-1] for "Michelob Oily" on the back of a humor magazine. The ad identifies itself as a parody in micro-print along the side. The pictures in the ad are takeoffs from those in real Michelob commercials.

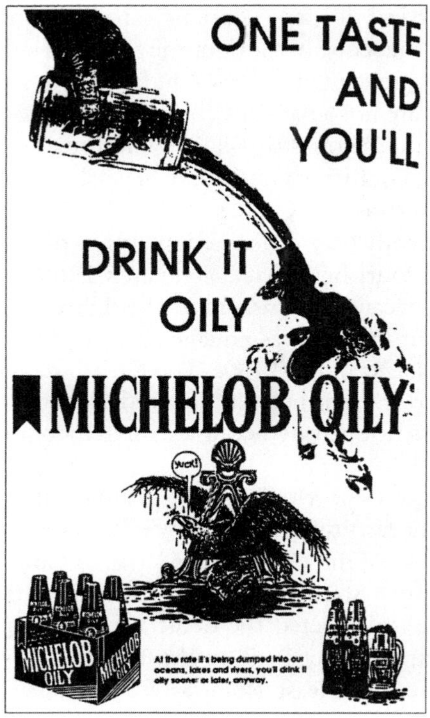

FIGURE 6-1
Parody of Michelob advertisement.

Anheuser-Busch sues Balducci for trademark infringement. At trial, Busch can show only a tiny percentage of consumers who thought Michelob Oily was a real product, but it proves that half the people surveyed believed Balducci should have to get permission from Busch to run the ad. Who should prevail?

Problem 6-5. The Coca-Cola Co. maintains an extremely strong and well-recognized trademark in the word "Coke" for its soft drink, and in the phrase "Enjoy Coke," particularly when used in connection with its red and white patterned logo. Gemini Rising, Inc., which distributes commercial posters, designs a poster with font and colors identical to Coca-Cola's, which reads "Enjoy Cocaine." After passersby who saw the poster complain to the local press, Coca-Cola brings suit against Gemini Rising. At trial, Coca-Cola offers evidence from a few members of the public who apparently believed that Coca-Cola had sponsored the posters, including one woman who threatened to organize a boycott of Coca-Cola products. What result?

Does your result change if Gemini Rising is a nonprofit political organization devoted to drug legalization? If it agrees to include a statement in medium-sized print at the bottom of the poster disclaiming any affiliation with the Coca-Cola Co.?

7 International Issues in Trademark

National borders are less of a barrier to economic exchange now than at almost any time in history. As economic activity continues its relentless drive toward worldwide scope, trademarks become even more important.[1] Just as the growth of the national economy in the United States set the stage for trademark law of national scope, the growth of the worldwide economy shows the importance of some sort of international trademark system. In Chapter 3 we discussed the "Madrid System" for the international registration of trademarks. Here, we briefly consider other aspects of the international registration and use of trademarks.

Foreign Trademarks in the United States: Limited Internationalization. Even before U.S. adherence to an international trademark treaty, certain provisions of U.S. law made some slight concessions to the need for foreign trademark owners to register their marks in the United States. Primarily, §44 of the Lanham Act allows foreign trademark owners to register their marks in the United States. Lanham Act §44, 15 U.S.C. §1126.

Although §44(d)(2) requires a statement of bona fide intent to use,[2] no subsequent proof of actual use in commerce in the United States is required. This allows foreign trademark owners to register their marks in the United States on terms somewhat more favorable than those extended to domestic applicants under the Lanham Act. Even so, foreign trademark owners are subject to the same rules regarding abandonment as domestic trademark owners, with the result that a foreign trademark owner may be deemed to have abandoned its registered mark if it does not meet the requirements of U.S. abandonment doctrine. *See, e.g.*, Imperial Tobacco, Ltd., Assignee of Imperial Group PLC v. Philip Morris, Inc., 899 F.2d 1575 (Fed. Cir.

1. Shari Caudron, *Strike Up the Brand*, Indus. Wk., Mar. 7, 1994, at 64 ("[I]n a world ruled by mass production and product standardization, the brand is the only remaining distinction among many products and services.").

2. This provision was added in 1988 (effective 1989) in response to the decision of Trademark Trial and Appeal Board's decision in Crocker National Bank v. Canadian Imperial Bank of Commerce, 223 U.S.P.Q. (BNA) 909 (TTAB 1984), which held valid a trademark registration application filed by a Canadian bank, despite the absence of an allegation of use anywhere in the world.

1990) (finding that foreign registrant failed to overcome presumption that it had abandoned its mark).

Some courts have held that § 44 incorporates the substantive provisions of the Paris Convention governing trademarks and unfair competition, providing a cause of action for violation of those provisions. *See, e.g.*, General Motors Corp. v. Lopez, 948 F. Supp. 684 (E.D. Mich. 1996). *See also* McCarthy, McCarthy on Trademarks and Unfair Competition § 29:33.

For further discussion of § 44, see Chapter 9.H *infra*.

Note on the "Gray Market"

United States law prohibits the importation of any goods bearing a registered U.S. trademark without the consent of the domestic trademark owner, even if the goods are genuine and even if they are imported by a licensed manufacturer (or the original trademark owner itself). 19 U.S.C. § 1526. The so-called gray market or "parallel imports" problem is a troubling one for courts and commentators alike. The Supreme Court has described the problem as follows:

> The gray market arises in any of three general contexts. The prototypical gray-market victim (case 1) is a domestic firm that purchases from an independent foreign firm the rights to register and use the latter's trademark as a United States trademark and to sell its foreign-manufactured products here. Especially where the foreign firm has already registered the trademark in the United States or where the product has already earned a reputation for quality, the right to use that trademark can be very valuable. If the foreign manufacturer could import the trademarked goods and distribute them here, despite having sold the trademark to a domestic firm, the domestic firm would be forced into sharp intrabrand competition involving the very trademark it purchased. Similar intrabrand competition could arise if the foreign manufacturer markets its wares outside the United States, as is often the case, and a third party who purchases them abroad could legally import them. In either event, the parallel importation, if permitted to proceed, would create a gray market that could jeopardize the trademark holder's investment.
>
> The second context (case 2) is a situation in which a domestic firm registers the United States trademark for goods that are manufactured abroad by an affiliated manufacturer. In its most common variation (case 2a), a foreign firm wishes to control distribution of its wares in this country by incorporating a subsidiary here. The subsidiary then registers under its own name (or the manufacturer assigns to the subsidiary's name) a United States trademark that is identical to its parent's foreign trademark. The parallel importation by a third party who buys the goods abroad (or conceivably even by the affiliated foreign manufacturer itself) creates a gray market. Two other variations on this theme occur when an American-based firm establishes abroad a manufacturing subsidiary corporation (case 2b) or its own unincorporated manufacturing division (case 2c) to produce its United States trademarked goods, and then imports them for domestic distribution. If the trademark holder or its foreign subsidiary sells the trademarked goods abroad, the parallel importation of the goods competes on the gray market with the holder's domestic sales.
>
> In the third context (case 3), the domestic holder of a United States trademark authorizes an independent foreign manufacturer to use it. Usually the holder sells to the foreign manufacturer an exclusive right to use the trademark in a particular foreign location, but conditions the right on the foreign manufacturer's promise not to import its trademarked goods into the United States. Once again, if the foreign manufacturer or a

> third party imports into the United States, the foreign-manufactured goods will compete on the gray market with the holder's domestic goods.

K-Mart Corp. v. Cartier, Inc., 486 U.S. 281, 286-87 (1988).

What is wrong with importing gray market goods? In this case, unlike the typical trademark dispute, there is no question that the goods are genuine and are being sold as precisely what they are. Further, there is no question that they originated with the trademark owner (at least at some point). If a gray market transaction occurred entirely within the United States, would it constitute trademark infringement? If not, is there any reason to treat importation differently?

One obvious rationale for prohibiting gray market imports is that the U.S. trademark owner is losing the benefit of what it thought was an "exclusive" right to sell the trademarked goods in the United States. But does it really have such an exclusive right? Certainly, the right to use the Ford trademark on cars in the United States does not prevent bona fide purchasers of Ford cars from identifying them as such upon resale. And even if the U.S. trademark owner did obtain the exclusive rights to the first sale of goods in the United States from the manufacturer, isn't the problem here really one of breach of contract?

Another justification for prohibiting gray market goods is if they are of different quality than the goods normally sold in the United States. If so, consumers may be confused. Significantly, in certain factual scenarios, courts have held that gray market importation is legal unless the imported goods differ in some relevant way from the goods the trademark owner sold in the United States. American Circuit Breaker Corp. v. Oregon Breakers Inc., 406 F.3d 577 (9th Cir. 2005) (circuit breakers that differed only in color from those sold in the United States could legally be imported after first sale abroad); SKF USA v. International Trade Comm'n, 2005 WL 2218460 (Fed. Cir. Sept. 14, 2005) (variation in goods could include variation in technical support provided, but in this case plaintiff did not uniformly provide support for its U.S. sales, and so could not complain of gray market imports without technical support). *But cf.* Beltronics USA v. Midwest Inventory Distrib. LLC, 562 F.3d 1067 (10th Cir. 2009) (first sale doctrine does not protect resellers who don't provide the same warranty as the original manufacturer).

Section 1526 of 19 U.S.C., which regulates gray market goods, may violate Article 2 of the Paris Convention because it treats U.S. trademark holders differently from foreign trademark holders, and U.S. infringers differently from foreign infringers. *See* Raimund Steiner & Robert Sabath, *Intellectual Property and Trade Law Approaches to Gray Market Importation, and the Restructuring of Transnational Entities to Permit Blockage of Gray Goods in the United States*, 15 Wm. Mitchell L. Rev. 433, 441 (1989) (after *K-Mart*, to obtain benefits of Section 526 of the Tariff Act of 1930 and the Lanham Act, companies must separate ownership of foreign and domestic trademarks); *see generally Note, The Use of Copyright Law to Block the Importation of Gray-Market Goods: The Black and White of It All*, 23 Loy. L.A. L. Rev. 645 (1990).

There is a debate in the economics literature about the wisdom of permitting gray market imports. The argument generally runs along these lines: Those favoring restrictions on the gray market cite the importance of encouraging investments in brand quality by retailers, coupled with differing international product quality standards. In essence, the argument is that retailers will not engage in optimal expenditures to promote the product (advertising, clean showrooms, knowledgeable sales staff, etc.) if gray market imports will undercut the retailers' prices. On the opposite side, those who support the gray market say it undercuts blatant price discrimination. *See* Robert J. Staaf, *International Price Discrimination and the Gray Market*, 4 INTELL. PROP. J. 301 (1989) (gray market presents an opportunity for arbitrage, allowing competitors to circumvent attempted price discrimination and therefore benefiting consumers).

The Problem of Worldwide Famous Marks. Worldwide trademark protection is based on proof of either registration or use in each country in which protection is sought. In theory this creates a significant burden for companies with marks that are famous worldwide: They must register their mark in every country in the world or risk losing rights to that mark to a competing registrant. In fact a number of opportunistic individuals have registered famous marks such as "Coke" in countries where Coca-Cola does not yet do business.

In an effort to deal with this problem, courts around the world have increasingly been willing to recognize goodwill in a world-famous mark even if the mark is not actually used in the country. *See* Paris Convention art. 6*bis*. Courts have held that K-Mart was entitled to prevent a competing use in Jamaica (*see* Kmart Corp. v. Kay Mart Ltd., Suit No. C.L. 1993, K066) and that McDonald's was permitted to "take back" rights in South Africa to marks it had ceased using there during the world embargo of that country. The United States seems less willing than other nations to act against domestic citizens who trade on the goodwill of foreign marks; courts are split on the question of whether a mark famous abroad can be protected despite lack of use in the United States. *Compare* ITC Ltd. v. Punchgini, Inc., 482 F.3d 135 (2d Cir. 2007); Buti v. Impressa Perosa S.R.L., 139 F.3d 98 (2d Cir. 1998); Person's Co. v. Christman, 900 F.2d 1565 (Fed. Cir. 1990) (all saying no) *with* Grupo Gigante S.A. v. Dallo & Co., 391 F.3d 1088 (9th Cir. 2004) (yes).

8 Remedies

A. INJUNCTIONS

Like patent law and much of copyright law, trademark remedies are organized around a property rule. This means that infringers have no "right" to use the trademark upon payment of damages; trademark owners are entitled to injunctions against infringement as a matter of course. The application of a property rule makes sense in the trademark context because trademarks serve to protect a unique good — the plaintiff's business goodwill. Infringers who trade on or dilute (and thus appropriate or destroy) a plaintiff's goodwill cannot simply "buy back" that goodwill with money. Once it is dissipated, it is gone forever. And paying the plaintiff damages doesn't undo the harm to consumers.

As is normal with property rule regimes, the principal remedy for trademark infringement is an injunction. Section 34(a) of the Lanham Act, 15 U.S.C. § 1116(a), gives courts the power to grant injunctions "to prevent the violation of any right of the registrant of a mark . . . or to prevent a violation under section 1125(a) of this title [Lanham Act § 43(a)]." Plaintiffs are entitled to injunctions as a matter of course once infringement is proven. *See* Champion Spark Plug Co. v. Sanders, 331 U.S. 125, 130-31 (1947). Injunctions may include prohibitions against the sale of goods or the use of a mark on goods or in advertising, or they may be affirmative injunctions requiring corrective advertising or the inclusion of disclaimers on products or advertising.

Trademark law is not a typical property rule, however. Owners of real property are entitled to sell it to whomever they wish. They may also let other people rent it for a fee. Trademark owners have no such unfettered rights to sell or license their trademarks. As discussed in Chapter 6.A *supra*, both the sale and the licensing of trademarks are subject to significant legal restrictions. Having given trademark owners a property right to enable them to protect their goodwill, the government appears unwilling to allow trademark owners to do what they see fit with that right. Instead, restrictions on alienation of trademarks are designed to make sure that the trademark is in fact used to promote the goodwill of the associated business.

At the same time, the consumer stake in avoiding confusion means that the public interest will weigh more heavily in favor of injunctive relief in trademark cases than in other kinds of IP cases. Consumers, after all, don't benefit from damage awards to trademark plaintiffs, and it would seem odd for a court to conclude that the defendant was confusing consumers, but permit it to continue doing so.

B. DAMAGES

1. Infringer's Gain and Mark Owner's Loss

While injunctions are the fundamental Lanham Act remedy, they are not the only one. Damages are also sometimes available in trademark infringement cases. Section 35(a) of the Lanham Act, 15 U.S.C. § 1117(a), provides that plaintiffs are entitled:

> to recover (1) defendant's profits, (2) any damages sustained by the plaintiff, and (3) the costs of the action. . . . In assessing profits the plaintiff shall be required to prove defendant's sales only; defendant must prove all elements of cost or deduction claimed. In assessing damages the court may enter judgment . . . for any sum above the amount found as actual damages, not exceeding three times such amount.

Lindy Pen Company, Inc. v. Bic Pen Corporation
982 F.2d 1400 (9th Cir. 1993)

Roll, District Judge:

This trademark infringement case brought by Lindy Pen Company, Inc. against Bic Pen Corporation returns to this court for the third time seeking review of the district court's damages order upon remand. For the reasons set forth below, we affirm the decision of the district court and deny Bic's cross-appeal.

Introduction

The origins of this case go back to the mid-1960s when Appellant Lindy Pen Company (Lindy) and Appellee Bic Pen Corporation (Bic) were competitors in the production and manufacture of ball point pens. Each marketed a fine-point tip for use by accountants and auditors. In 1965, before Lindy's trademark was perfected and registration issued, Bic used the mark "Auditor's" on its pen barrels. Lindy contacted Bic, making a claim to the mark, and Bic voluntarily agreed to stop using it. On September 20, 1966, United States Trademark Registration No. 815,488 was issued to Lindy for the word "Auditor's." Lindy Pen Co., Inc. v. Bic Pen Corp., 550 F. Supp. 1056, 1059 (C.D. Cal. 1982). Lindy perfected the registration by filing the appropriate documents pursuant to federal statute. Id.

Fourteen years later, Bic adopted the legend "Auditor's Fine Point" to describe a certain pen model. Prior to this use, Bic researched the term "Auditor's" and found that at least three other manufacturers employed a variation of the word "Auditor's" in their marketing materials. This investigation revealed that Lindy also used the term, but that Lindy exerted no proprietary interest over it in its advertising.

Lindy learned of Bic's renewed use of the mark and filed suit in 1980 alleging trademark infringement, unfair competition, breach of contract, and trademark dilution. The district court entered judgment in favor of Bic on all claims. The circuit court upheld the district court's ruling that Bic did not infringe in the major retail markets, but remanded the case to determine whether there was a likelihood of confusion in telephone order sales. Lindy Pen Co., Inc. v. Bic Pen Corp., 725 F.2d 1240 (9th Cir. 1984), *cert. denied*, 469 U.S. 1188, 105 S. Ct. 955, 83 L. Ed. 2d 962 (1985) (*Lindy I*). The court specifically found that "there is no evidence of actual confusion [and] that Bic adopted the designation 'Auditor's fine point' without intent to capitalize on Lindy's goodwill. . . ." Id. at 1246.

Upon remand, the district court determined that there was a likelihood of confusion in the telephone order market because the purchaser did not have the opportunity to view the pens at the time of purchase. The court went on to find, however, that the confusion could be cured upon receipt of the goods because the purchaser could return the product. The circuit court again disagreed and found that Lindy had established a likelihood of confusion in the telephone order market which post-sale inspection could not cure. Lindy Pen Co., Inc. v. Bic Pen Corp., 796 F.2d 254 (9th Cir. 1986) (*Lindy II*). In words which now comprise the nub of the current appeal, this court ordered that the case be remanded to district court "with instructions to enter an order enjoining Bic from using the word 'Auditor's' on or in connection with its pens. We additionally instruct the district court to order an accounting and to award damages and other relief as appropriate." Id. . . .

Accounting of Profits

Following the damages proceeding, the district court held that an accounting of profits was inappropriate because Bic's infringement was innocent and accomplished without intent to capitalize on Lindy's trade name. Section 35 of the Lanham Act, 15 U.S.C. § 1117(a), governs the award of monetary remedies in trademark infringement cases and provides for an award of defendant's profits, any damages sustained by the plaintiff, and the costs of the action.

The Supreme Court has indicated that an accounting of profits follows as a matter of course after infringement is found by a competitor. Hamilton-Brown Shoe Co. v. Wolf Bros. & Co., 240 U.S. 251, 259, 36 S. Ct. 269, 271, 60 L. Ed. 629, 634 (1916). Nonetheless, an accounting of profits is not automatic and must be granted in light of equitable considerations. Champion Spark Plug Co. v. Sanders, 331 U.S. 125, 131, 67 S. Ct. 1136, 1139, 91 L. Ed. 1386, 1391 (1947). Where trademark infringement is deliberate and willful, this court has found that a remedy no greater than an injunction "slights" the public. Playboy Enterprises, Inc. v. Baccarat Clothing Co., Inc., 692 F.2d 1272, 1274 (9th Cir. 1982). This standard applies, however, only in those cases where the infringement is "willfully calculated to exploit the advantage of an established mark." Id. The intent of the infringer is relevant evidence on the issue of awarding profits and damages and the amount. *Maier Brewing Co.*, 390 F.2d at 123. When awarding profits, the court is cautioned that the "Plaintiff is not . . . entitled to a windfall." *Bandag, Inc.*, 750 F.2d at 918.

Lindy posits that Bic's actions require an accounting as a remedy for willful infringement. The parties agree that as early as 1965, Bic had knowledge of Lindy's claim to trademark rights in the term "Auditor's" when Bic published a catalog advertising pens with the mark stamped on their barrels. Bic voluntarily suspended use of the mark after Lindy informed Bic of its claim to the term. Fourteen years after this exchange, Bic began using the legend "Auditor's Fine Point" on its extra-fine point pens, the subject of the current litigation.

Willful infringement carries a connotation of deliberate intent to deceive. Courts generally apply forceful labels such as "deliberate," "false," "misleading," or "fraudulent" to conduct that meets this standard. . . .

Indeed, this court has cautioned that an accounting is proper only where the defendant is "attempting to gain the value of an established name of another." *Maier Brewing Co.*, 390 F.2d at 123.

The present case simply does not involve willful infringement. Evidence taken at the damages proceeding shows that Lindy in general, and its Auditor's line in particular, was experiencing an overall business decline. The trial court also found that any knowledge that Bic may have had of Lindy's mark stemming from the 1965 interchange was conducted by outside counsel, thereby implying that Bic's knowledge of Lindy's interest was attenuated at best. *Lindy Pen*, 550 F. Supp. at 1059. The district court also determined that Lindy's mark was weak and that there was no evidence of actual confusion. Id. at 1058-60. Based on these facts, it was reasonable for the district court to conclude that Bic's actions were not "willfully calculated to exploit the advantage of an established mark," *Bandag, Inc.*, 750 F.2d at 921, and that Bic's conduct did not rise to the level of willfulness which would have mandated an award.[4]

This circuit has announced a deterrence policy in response to trademark infringement and will grant an accounting of profits in those cases where infringement yields financial rewards. Playboy Enterprises, Inc. v. Baccarat Clothing Co., Inc., 692 F.2d 1272, 1274 (9th Cir. 1982) (plaintiff damaged through defendant's intentional use of counterfeit product labels). However, the policy considerations which clearly justified an award in *Playboy Enterprises* are not present in this case. Unlike the *Playboy Enterprises* plaintiff, Lindy's trademark was weak and Bic's infringement was unintentional. Moreover, Bic's major position in the pen industry makes it clear that it was not trading on Lindy's relatively obscure name. Accordingly, the policy considerations announced by *Playboy Enterprises* would be trivialized by insisting on an accounting in this case. See *ALPO Petfoods Inc.*, 913 F.2d at 969 ("deterrence is too weak and too easily invoked a justification for the severe and often cumbersome remedy of a profits award. . . ."). To award profits in this situation would amount to a punishment in violation of the Lanham Act which clearly stipulates that a remedy "shall constitute compensation not a penalty." 15 U.S.C. § 1117(a).

4. Even assuming that Bic could be termed a willful infringer, "willful infringement may support an award of profits to the plaintiff, but does not require one." Faberge, Inc. v. Saxony Products, Inc., 605 F.2d 426, 429 (9th Cir. 1979) (citing *Maier Brewing Co.*, 390 F.2d at 121).

Award of Damages

15 U.S.C. § 1117(a) further provides for an award, subject to equitable principles, of "any damages sustained by the plaintiff. . . ." A plaintiff must prove both the fact and the amount of damage. 2 J. THOMAS MCCARTHY, TRADEMARKS AND UNFAIR COMPETITION § 30:27, at 511 (2d ed. 1984). Damages are typically measured by any direct injury which a plaintiff can prove, as well as any lost profits which the plaintiff would have earned but for the infringement. Id. at 509. Because proof of actual damage is often difficult, a court may award damages based on defendant's profits on the theory of unjust enrichment. Id. at 511. See also *Bandag, Inc.*, 750 F.2d at 918.

The district court gave Lindy the opportunity to prove its damages under both methods: actual damages in the form of its lost profits, or if that proved too difficult, through proof of Bic's unjust enrichment in the form of Bic's profits. . . .

After final briefing, the court concluded that Lindy had failed to show any actual damage because it did not put forth sufficient proof of its lost profits. To establish damages under the lost profits method, a plaintiff must make a "prima facie showing of reasonably forecast profits." 2 J.T. MCCARTHY, TRADEMARKS AND UNFAIR COMPETITION § 30:27, at 511 (2d ed. 1984). The court found Lindy's calculations to be irreparably flawed because Lindy did not isolate its own telephone order sales from total pen sales. Consequently, Lindy's calculations contained items in which no likelihood of confusion existed and therefore were inappropriately included. The district court reasoned that it had no rational basis upon which to estimate an award as to the infringing items and accordingly denied Lindy's request.

Trademark remedies are guided by tort law principles. Id. at 509 ("Plaintiff's damages should be measured by the tort standard under which the infringer-tortfeasor is liable for all injuries caused to plaintiff by the wrongful act. . . ."). As a general rule, damages which result from a tort must be established with reasonable certainty. DAN B. DOBBS, REMEDIES § 3.3, at 151 (1973). The Supreme Court has held that "damages are not rendered uncertain because they cannot be calculated with absolute exactness," yet, a reasonable basis for computation must exist. Eastman Kodak Co. v. Southern Photo Materials Co., 273 U.S. 359, 379, 47 S. Ct. 400, 405, 71 L. Ed. 684, 691 (1927). . . .

Lindy produced evidence of its total pen sales, as available, for the designated time period. Although it divided its sales into total sales and specific sales of Auditor's, it failed to further subdivide its data into the category of telephone order sales. Lindy was in the best position to identify its own sales, but declined to provide the court with any evidence of its loss caused by Bic's wrongdoing. Although Lindy offers excuses for this deficiency, its explanations do not negate the fact that Lindy never furnished the court any reasonable estimate of its own sales. It would have been error for the district court to select an arbitrary percentage of total sales to represent the more narrow submarket of telephone sales. The court was correct, therefore, in finding that Lindy failed to sustain its burden of proving reasonably forecast profits.

Lindy also sought an accounting of Bic's profits based on a theory of unjust enrichment. Lindy assesses as error the district court's requirement that Lindy separate Bic's telephone order sales from total sales of goods. Lindy maintains that this requirement had the effect of shifting the burden of proving infringing sales from the infringer to the trademark holder. However, an accounting is intended to award profits only on sales that are attributable to the infringing conduct. The plaintiff has only the burden of establishing the defendant's gross profits from the infringing activity with reasonable certainty. Once the plaintiff demonstrates gross profits, they are presumed to be the result of the infringing activity. Mishawaka Rubber & Woolen Mfg. Co. v. S.S. Kresge Co., 316 U.S. 203, 206-07, 62 S. Ct. 1022, 1024-25, 86 L. Ed. 1381, 1385-86 (1942). The defendant thereafter bears the burden of showing which, if any, of its total sales are not attributable to the infringing activity, and, additionally, any permissible deductions for overhead. 15 U.S.C. §1117(a).

Lindy failed to come forward with any evidence of sales of the Bic "Auditor's Fine Point" in the infringing market. Lindy instead brought forth proof of Bic's total sales. Lindy averred to the court that a division of Bic's sales into the telephone submarket "is impossible from Bic's records since Bic never separated its pens according to telephone sales. . . ." To the contrary, Lindy had access through discovery to Bic's records from which a reasonable estimate could have been accomplished.

We find that Lindy's appeal on the question of actual damages fails due to a lack of proof at the damages proceeding. . . .

Award of . . . Attorneys' Fees

Nor can we agree that the district court's refusal to award attorneys' fees pursuant to §1117(a) was in error. While the term "exceptional" is not defined in the statute, generally a trademark case is exceptional for purposes of an award of attorneys' fees when the infringement is malicious, fraudulent, deliberate or willful. Sealy, Inc. v. Easy Living, Inc., 743 F.2d 1378, 1384 (9th Cir.1984). See also Playboy Enterprises, 692 F.2d at 1276 (failure to award attorneys' fees was abuse of discretion where defendant "deliberately arranged to obtain counterfeit goods and to sell such goods as genuine PEI products."). An award is within the discretion of the trial court and will not be disturbed absent abuse of that discretion. Transgo, Inc. v. Ajac Transmission Parts Corp., 768 F.2d 1001, 1026 (9th Cir.1985). Other than its longevity, there is nothing exceptional about this case. We therefore find that the trial court did not abuse its discretion in ruling that there are no exceptional circumstances requiring an award of Lindy's attorneys' fees.

COMMENTS AND QUESTIONS

1. How is the *public* "slighted" by a court's failure to award damages for willful infringement? Does it matter to the public whether an infringer pays damages to the trademark owner or not? Surely, any confusion that the public has suffered is not ameliorated because the trademark owner receives compensation. Why isn't an injunction, which the courts agree is a sufficient remedy in the case of "innocent infringement," sufficient in cases of intentional infringement as well?

2. Is an accounting for profits ever possible in a dilution case? If so, why? If the plaintiff is compensated for her losses caused by the dilution, does it make any sense to take away the defendant's profits in an unrelated market as well? 15 U.S.C. §1125(c) makes damages available in dilution cases only upon a showing of willful infringement.

3. Who should bear the burden of proof in determining profits? *See* Mishawaka Rubber & Woolen Mfg. Co. v. S.S. Kresge Co., 316 U.S. 203, 206-07 (1942) (defendant bears the burden of proving that not all profits associated with a sale should

be awarded to plaintiff). The Court reasoned: "There may well be a windfall to the trade-mark owner where it is impossible to isolate the profits which are attributable to the use of the infringing mark. But to hold otherwise would give the windfall to the wrongdoer."

Suppose that a defendant has established significant goodwill of its own between the time it adopted a mark and the time it is found to have infringed. If the plaintiff is entitled to an injunction, does the defendant have any way of recovering the value of its investment in goodwill? Is it at least entitled to a setoff against damages for its monetary losses as a result of the injunction? Does it matter if the case is a dilution case and the defendant is in a separate market?

4. *Disgorgement.* For many years, courts have followed the holding in Champion Spark Plug v. Sanders, 331 U.S. 125, 130-31 (1947), that an accounting is appropriate only when fraud or palming off is present, and will grant an accounting of defendant's profits only if the defendant acted in bad faith. *See, e.g.*, W. Diversified Servs. v. Hyundai Motor Am., Inc., 427 F.3d 1269 (10th Cir. 2005). Some recent decisions have questioned this limitation on the disgorgement remedy, however. The Third Circuit's decision in Banjo Buddies, Inc. v. Renosky, 399 F.3d 168 (3d Cir. 2005), for example, concludes that a "bright-line willfulness requirement has been superseded by" a 1999 amendment to the Lanham Act:

> In August 1999 . . . Congress amended § 35. Prior to the amendment, that section provided as follows:
>
> > When a violation of any right of the registrant of a mark registered in the Patent and Trademark Office, or a violation under section 43(a) [15 U.S.C. § 1125(a)], shall have been established . . . the plaintiff shall be entitled . . . , subject to the principles of equity, to recover (1) defendant's defendant's profits, (2) any damages sustained by the plaintiff, and (3) the costs of the action.
>
> . . . The 1999 amendment replaced "or a violation under section 43(a)" with "a violation under section 43(a), or a willful violation under section 43(c)," see Pub. L. No. 106-43, § 3(b), 113 Stat. 219 (Aug. 5, 1999) (emphasis added). The plain language of the amendment indicates that Congress intended to condition monetary awards for § 43(c) violations, but not § 43(a) violations, on a showing of willfulness. . . .
>
> This conclusion is supported by *Quick Technologies*, 313 F.3d at 349, the only other appellate decision to reach the issue. The Fifth Circuit in Quick Technologies considered the effect of the 1999 amendment and held that, based on earlier decisions of that court as well as "the plain language of [§ 43(a)]," willful infringement was not a prerequisite to an accounting of the infringer's infringer's profits. *Id.* The court noted the wealth of contrary authority . . . but pointed out that all of those cases preceded the statutory change. *Id.* at 347-48. The *Quick Technologies* court reaffirmed the factor-based approach elaborated in prior Fifth Circuit cases . . . explaining that the infringer's infringer's intent was an important — but not indispensable — factor in evaluating whether equity supports disgorging the infringer's profits. *Quick Techs.*, 313 F.3d at 349. These factors "include, but are not limited to (1) whether the defendant had the intent to confuse or deceive, (2) whether sales have been diverted, (3) the adequacy of other remedies, (4) any unreasonable delay by the plaintiff in asserting his rights, (5) the public interest in making the misconduct unprofitable, and (6) whether it is a case of palming off." *Id.* (internal citations omitted).

Id. at 174-75 (some internal citations omitted). *Cf.* George Basch Co., Inc. v. Blue Coral, Inc., 968 F.2d 1532, 1540 (2d Cir. 1992) ("[I]n the absence of . . . a showing [of willfulness], a plaintiff is not foreclosed from receiving monetary relief. Upon proof of actual consumer confusion, a plaintiff may still obtain damages—which, in turn, may be inclusive of plaintiff's own lost profits.").

Not all courts agree that the 1999 amendment referenced in *Banjo Buddies* was intended to alter the rule that the disgorgement remedy is conditional upon proof of willfulness. *See* Louis Vuitton Malletier v. Dooney & Bourke, Inc., 500 F. Supp. 2d 276, 280-82 & n.22 (S.D.N.Y. 2007) (agreeing with *McCarthy on Trademarks* that *Banjo Buddies* places too much weight on the 1999 amendment, and concluding that willfulness remains a requirement for disgorgement). Which interpretation is more persuasive? Should the defendant's state of mind be a relevant consideration in award disgorgement of the defendant's profits? Should it be the sole consideration? Or does disgorgement serve an important deterrent purpose even in the absence of willful deception?

5. For an interesting case that explores what constitutes "bad faith" for enhanced damages purposes, see Int'l Star Class Yacht Racing Ass'n v. Tommy Hilfiger U.S.A., Inc., 1999 WL 108739 (S.D.N.Y., Mar. 3, 1999) (on remand from Second Circuit, adhering to earlier opinion finding no bad faith in adoption of plaintiff's mark, despite very limited search of trademark databases). *See also* Roger D. Blair & Thomas F. Cotter, *An Economic Analysis of Damage Rules in Intellectual Property Law*, 39 Wm. & Mary L. Rev. 1585, 1691 (1998) (arguing that the law should require "some level of search activity" for a trademark defendant to escape a damage award). *Cf.* Banff, Ltd. v. Colberts, Inc., 996 F.2d 33, 35 (2d Cir.), *cert. denied*, 510 U.S. 1010 (1993).

6. On the availability of defendant's profits, see Minnesota Pet-Breeders, Inc. v. Schell & Kampeter, Inc., 843 F. Supp. 506, 512-13 (D. Minn. 1993), *aff'd on other grounds*, 41 F.3d 1242 (8th Cir. 1994):

> A number of courts have held that an accounting of defendant's profits in cases of trademark infringement or unfair competition is warranted if (1) the plaintiff sustained damage from the infringement, (2) the infringer is unjustly enriched, and (3) [it is] necessary to deter a willful infringer from doing so again. At least one court has held that "deterrence alone cannot justify such an award [of infringing defendant's profits]." [Alpo Petfoods, Inc. v. Ralston Purina Co., 913 F.2d 958, 969 (D.C. Cir. 1990).]

Note that in affirming the decision below, the Eighth Circuit added these qualifications: "[I]n this case, in which there was no actual competition between the trademarked and the infringing products, it is most likely that MPB would be entitled to injunctive but not monetary relief, and virtually inconceivable that only monetary relief would be appropriate." *Id.* at 1247-48.

7. For a detailed exposition of how to calculate the infringer's profits in an accounting, see Dennis S. Corgill, *Measuring the Gains from Trademark Infringement*, 65 Fordham L. Rev. 1909 (1997).

8. *Enhancements.* In an appropriate case a court may award enhanced damages for trademark infringement. *See* Lanham Act § 35(a) (15 U.S.C. § 1117(a)) (stating that "the court may enter judgment, according to the circumstances of the case, for any sum above the amount found as actual damages, not exceeding three times such amount," and that if the court instead awards defendant's profits, if it finds the amount "either inadequate or excessive the court may in its discretion enter judgment for such sum as the court shall find to be just, according to the circumstances of the case," but that in either instance the award "shall constitute compensation and not a penalty").

In determining whether to increase damages or adjust profits, courts may consider a variety of factors. For example, in ALPO Petfoods, Inc. v. Ralston Purina Co., 778 F. Supp. 555, 564 (D.D.C. 1991), the district court listed three factors relevant to determining whether a damages award is inadequate (and hence a candidate for enhancement): "the impact of the unlawful conduct directly upon the plaintiff competitor, the systemic distortion which the wrongdoer's wrongdoer's conduct has upon the particular product market in which the plaintiff must compete in the future, and the costs incurred by the competitor in its efforts to mitigate its damages." Applying these factors, the district court awarded a 50 percent enhancement to compensate ALPO for unquantifiable lost profits, market distortion, costs incurred in discovering the defendant's misconduct, and inflation and interest. *Id.* at 564-66. The Court of Appeals affirmed in part, stating that "lost profits and market distortion are . . . appropriate bases for the catch-all enhancement contemplated by § 35(a)," but that "interest and inflation are not such elusive quanta. . . . We thus remand . . . to compute the precise amounts to be awarded for interest and the effect of inflation, and to reconsider such enhancement as may be appropriate solely in order to compensate ALPO for its lost profits . . . and the continuing distortion of the market. . . ." ALPO Petfoods, Inc. v. Ralston Purina Co., 997 F.2d 949, 955 (D.C. Cir. 1993). (We return to *ALPO* case *supra* in our discussion of false advertising remedies).

9. *Attorney fees.* In "exceptional cases," a court may award "reasonable attorney fees to the prevailing party" for either trademark infringement or false advertising. 15 U.S.C. § 1117(a). As noted in *Lindy Pen*, courts generally interpret this to mean that courts may award prevailing plaintiffs their attorneys fees only for willful or bad faith conduct by the defendant. Standards for determining what constitutes exceptional circumstances resulting in fee awards to prevailing *defendants* differ somewhat from one circuit to another. *See* McCarthy, *supra*, § 30:101 (providing for an overview of various approaches).

10. *Prejudgment interest.* In some circuits, the prevailing plaintiff in a Lanham Act case is generally entitled to prejudgment interest absent exceptional circumstances. *See, e.g.*, Pioneer Hi-Bred Int'l v. Holden Foundation Seeds, Inc., 35 F.3d 1226, 1246 (8th Cir. 1994) (noting, however, that while prevailing plaintiffs are normally entitled to prejudgment interest, "[o]ne of the major goals thought to be served by prejudgment interest — promoting settlement — is far less compelling in a case such as this where the issue of liability is highly challenged and the damages are quite large but virtually impossible to ascertain prior to trial"). In other circuits, prejudgment interest itself is *available* only in exceptional cases. *See* Am. Honda Motor Co. v. Two Wheel Corp., 918 F.2d 1060, 1064 (2d Cir. 1990). *See generally* McCarthy, *supra*, § 30:93. When state law provides more generous entitlements to prejudgment interest (or other remedies) than does the law of the regional federal circuit, plaintiffs may be well advised to plead corresponding pendent claims under state Little FTC Acts.

Note on Trademark Remedies

In a recent article Professor Mark Thurmon argues that, prior to enactment of the Lanham Act, courts had reached a rough consensus on several points relating to trademark remedies. First, in actions at common law, prevailing trademark owners could recover their lost profits — assuming that any such profits were provable, which they often were not. Second, in actions at equity, courts would award injunctive relief and, as a monetary award, either the plaintiff's lost profit or (more commonly) the defendant's profit attributable to the infringement. Typically, however, awards of defendants' profits required proof of willful infringement—a vestige of trademark law's origins in the law of deceit. Third, in actions in equity, courts retained discretion to raise or lower monetary awards to reflect the equities of the case, but not to award "penalties." Fourth, by the mid-twentieth century a few courts had begun to entertain the possibility of awarding punitive damages in trademark cases, though arguably only when the plaintiff sought its own actual damages (and not defendant's profits). *See* Mark A. Thurmon, *Confusion Codified: Why Trademark Remedies Make No Sense*, 17 J. INTELL. PROP. L. 245 (2010). Thurmon argues that Congress blundered when it attempted to codify these rules in enacting the Lanham Act in 1946—and that the courts have done no better—because the codification was in some respects ill-advised and in other respects ambiguous. What does it mean, for example, to say that courts may award enhancements as "compensation and not a penalty"? By what authority (and for what purpose) have the majority of courts continued to apply the common-law rule that awards of defendant's profits require proof of willful infringement? Where exactly does the statute say that courts may not award punitive damages?

Roger Blair and Thomas Cotter have argued that the standards courts apply in awarding damages and profits to trademark plaintiffs nevertheless may embody a (largely) coherent economic rationale. Blair and Cotter argue that, as a general matter, in cases involving any of the four major branches of intellectual property law (patents, copyrights, trademarks, and trade secrets), as a first approximation courts should award the prevailing plaintiff the greater of (1) its own lost profit or (2) the defendant's profit attributable to the infringement. *See* ROGER D. BLAIR & THOMAS F. COTTER, INTELLECTUAL PROPERTY: ECONOMIC AND LEGAL DIMENSIONS OF RIGHTS AND REMEDIES (2005). This standard would encourage the defendant to avoid infringing when it is more efficient for the plaintiff exclusively to make, use, or sell the product covered by its IP right, because in such a case the plaintiff's lost profit should exceed the defendant's profit attributable to the infringement. When, on the other hand, the defendant is the more efficient manufacturer, user, or seller of the product at issue, the defendant's profit attributable to the infringement should exceed the plaintiff's lost profit. Awarding the plaintiff the defendant's profit when that profit exceeds the plaintiff's own lost profit therefore encourages the defendant to negotiate, ex ante, for a license to use the IP in exchange for a royalty. (As an alternative to awarding the plaintiff the defendant's profit, a court could instead award the royalty it believes the parties voluntarily would have negotiated ex ante. If courts can estimate this amount with reasonable accuracy, a reasonable royalty award may avoid potential overdeterrence and holdup problems associated with restitutionary recoveries.) As a further refinement to their theory, Blair and Cotter argue that awarding enhanced damages above this baseline recovery makes sense in cases in which the infringement is of a type that might have gone undetected; awards of attorney's fees might also help in this regard.

Blair and Cotter then argue that the Lanham Act's remedial provisions, as applied by the courts, appear roughly consistent with what their model would predict. First, the act permits courts to award plaintiffs their provable lost profits. Awarding lost profits makes sense when the plaintiff is the more efficient user of the mark (meaning, in this context, that the plaintiff can make, use, or sell products the goodwill of which is symbolized by the trademark at lower cost than can the defendant). Proving lost profits can be difficult, however, because the harm to the trademark owner may be largely reputational and thus hard to quantify. Moreover, the liability standard for trademark infringement, likelihood of confusion, is prospective in nature; liability sufficient to sustain an injunction therefore may exist absent any actual, consummated harm. Perhaps, as Thurmon also argues, a system that entitled prevailing trademark owners to some form of presumed or statutory damages (as in copyright law) would be an improvement.[1] Second, the act as interpreted by the courts parallels patent law by permitting awards of enhanced damages only for willful infringement, and again this arguably makes rough economic sense in the present context. When the infringement is willful there is a greater risk of actual, albeit difficult to quantify, harm—though a rule that conditioned enhanced or punitive damages on proof of a low probability of detection might be better yet. Third, conditioning awards of defendant's profits on proof of willful infringement also might make sense, given the unique characteristics of trademark infringement. Strictly speaking, in trademark cases the defendant's profit attributable to the infringement should be only the amount above what the defendant would have made had it used the next-best available trademark. In cases of innocent infringement, it may be fair to assume that the defendant would have made about the same profit had it chosen a different mark. When the infringement was willful, by contrast, it may be reasonable to assume that a good portion (maybe all, in the case of outright counterfeiting) of the defendant's profit was attributable to consumers' incorrect association of the defendant's products with the plaintiff's. To avoid the risk of overdeterrence, courts therefore may be wise to limit restitutionary awards to cases of willful trademark infringement, at least if they are willing to award reasonable royalties in lieu of defendant's profits in cases involving non-willful infringement.

2. Corrective Advertising

Big O Tire Dealers, Inc. v. The Goodyear Tire & Rubber Company
561 F.2d 1365 (10th Cir. 1977)

LEWIS, Chief Judge.

This civil action was brought by Big O Tire Dealers, Inc. ("Big O") asserting claims of unfair competition against The Goodyear Tire & Rubber Co. ("Goodyear") based upon false designation of origin under 15 U.S.C. § 1125(a) and common law trademark infringement. After a ten-day trial and three days of deliberation, the jury returned the following verdict:

> We the jury in the above entitled cause, upon our oath do say that we find the following as our verdict herein:
>
> Upon the claim of liability for trademark infringement we find for Big O Inc.
>
> Upon the claim of liability for false designation of origin we find for Goodyear.
>
> Upon the claim for trademark disparagement we find for Big O Inc.
>
> We find that plaintiff has proven special compensatory damages in the amount of $None.

1. The Lanham Act does permit statutory damages for use of counterfeit marks and for cybersquatting. *See* 15 U.S.C. § 1117(c), (d).

> We find that plaintiff has proven general compensatory damages in the amount of $2,800,000.
>
> We assess punitive or exemplary damages in the amount of $16,800,000.
>
> Dated September 4, 1975.

Filing a comprehensive post-trial opinion the United States District Court for the District of Colorado entered judgment on the jury's verdict, permanently enjoined Goodyear from infringing on Big O's trademark, and dismissed Goodyear's counterclaim for equitable relief. 408 F. Supp. 1219. Goodyear appeals that judgment.

Big O is a tire-buying organization which provides merchandising techniques, advertising concepts, operating systems, and other aids to approximately 200 independent retail tire dealers in 14 states who identify themselves to the public as Big O dealers. These dealers sell replacement tires using the Big O label on "private brand" tires. They also sell other companies' brands such as B. F. Goodrich and Michelin Tires. At the time of trial Big O's total net worth was approximately $200,000.

Goodyear is the world's largest tire manufacturer. In 1974 Goodyear's net sales totaled more than $5.25 billion and its net income after taxes surpassed $157 million. In the replacement market Goodyear sells through a nationwide network of company-owned stores, franchise dealers, and independent retailers.

In the fall of 1973 Big O decided to identify two of its lines of private brand tires as "Big O Big Foot 60" and "Big O Big Foot 70." These names were placed on the sidewall of the respective tires in raised white letters. The first interstate shipment of these tires occurred in February 1974. Big O dealers began selling these tires to the public in April 1974. Big O did not succeed in registering "Big Foot" as a trademark with the United States Patent and Trademark Office. . . .

In July 1974 Goodyear decided to use the term "Bigfoot" in a nationwide advertising campaign to promote the sale of its new "Custom Polysteel Radial" tire. The name "Custom Polysteel Radial" was molded into the tire's sidewall. Goodyear employed a trademark search firm to conduct a search for "Bigfoot" in connection with tires and related products. This search did not uncover any conflicting trademarks. After this suit was filed Goodyear filed an application to register "Bigfoot" as a trademark for tires but withdrew it in 1975. Goodyear planned to launch its massive, nationwide "Bigfoot" advertising campaign on September 16, 1974.

On August 24, 1974, Goodyear first learned of Big O's "Big Foot" tires. Goodyear informed Big O's president, Norman Affleck, on August 26 of Goodyear's impending "Bigfoot" advertising campaign. Affleck was asked to give Goodyear a letter indicating Big O had no objection to this use of "Bigfoot." When Affleck replied he could not make this decision alone, it was suggested Affleck talk with John Kelley, Goodyear's vice-president for advertising.

Affleck called Kelley and requested more information on Goodyear's impending advertising campaign. A Goodyear employee visited Affleck on August 30 and showed him rough versions of the planned Goodyear "Bigfoot" commercials and other promotional materials. On September 10, Affleck and two Big O directors met in New Orleans, with Kelley and Goodyear's manager of consumer market planning to discuss the problem further. At this time the Big O representatives objected to Goodyear using "Bigfoot" in connection with tires because they believed any such use would severely damage Big O. They made it clear they were not interested in money in exchange for granting Goodyear the right to use the "Bigfoot" trademark, and asked Goodyear to wind down the campaign as soon as possible. Goodyear's response to this request was indefinite and uncertain.

During the trial several Goodyear employees conceded it was technically possible for Goodyear to have deleted the term "Bigfoot" from its television advertising as late as early September. However, on September 16, 1974, Goodyear launched its nationwide "Bigfoot" promotion on ABC's Monday Night Football telecast. By August 31, 1975, Goodyear had spent $9,690,029 on its massive, saturation campaign.

On September 17 [1974] Affleck wrote Kelley a letter setting forth his understanding of the New Orleans meeting that Goodyear would wind up its "Bigfoot" campaign as soon as possible. Kelley replied on September 20, denying any commitment to discontinue use of "Bigfoot" and declaring Goodyear intended to use "Bigfoot" as long as it continued to be a helpful advertising device.

On October 9 Kelley told Affleck he did not have the authority to make the final decision for Goodyear and suggested that Affleck call Charles Eaves, Goodyear's executive vice-president. On October 10 Affleck called Eaves and Eaves indicated the possibility of paying Big O for the use of the term "Bigfoot." When Affleck stated no interest in the possibility Eaves told him Goodyear wished to avoid litigation but that if Big O did sue, the case would be in litigation long enough that Goodyear might obtain all the benefits it desired from the term "Bigfoot."

This was the final communication between the parties until Big O filed suit on November 27, 1974. The district court denied Big O's request for a temporary restraining order and a preliminary injunction. After judgment was entered on the jury's verdict for Big O, Goodyear appealed to this court. Goodyear's allegations of error are discussed below. . . .

IV

. . . Big O does not claim nor was any evidence presented showing Goodyear intended to trade on the goodwill of Big O or to palm off Goodyear products as being those of Big O. Instead, Big O contends Goodyear's use of Big O's trademark created a likelihood of confusion concerning the source of Big O's "Big Foot" tires.

The facts of this case are different from the usual trademark infringement case. As the trial judge stated, the usual trademark infringement case involves a claim by a plaintiff with a substantial investment in a well established trademark. The plaintiff would seek recovery for the loss of income resulting from a second user attempting to trade on the goodwill associated with that established mark by suggesting to the consuming public that his product comes from the same origin as the plaintiff's product. The instant case, however, involves reverse confusion wherein the infringer's use of plaintiff's mark results in confusion as to the origin of plaintiff's product. Only one reported decision involves the issue of reverse confusion. In Westward Coach Mfg. Co. v. Ford Motor Co., 7 Cir., 388 F.2d 627, *cert. denied*, 392 U.S. 927, 88 S. Ct. 2286, 20 L. Ed. 2d 1386, the court held reverse confusion is not actionable as a trademark infringement under Indiana law.

Consequently, Goodyear argues the second use of a trademark is not actionable if it merely creates a likelihood of confusion concerning the source of the first user's product. Since both parties agree Colorado law is controlling in this case, we must decide whether this so-called reverse confusion is actionable under Colorado law. To our knowledge, the Colorado courts have never considered whether a second use creating the likelihood of confusion about the source of the first user's products is actionable. However, the Colorado Court of Appeals in deciding a trade name infringement case involving an issue of first impression, cogently pointed out that the Colorado Supreme Court "has consistently recognized and followed a policy of protecting established trade names and preventing public confusion and the tendency has been to widen the scope of that protection." Wood v. Wood's Homes Inc., 33 Colo. App. 285, 519 P.2d 1212, 1215-16.

Using that language as a guiding light in divining what Colorado law is on this issue of first impression, we hold that the Colorado courts, if given the opportunity, would extend its common law trademark infringement actions to include reverse confusion situations. Such a rule would further Colorado's "policy of protecting trade names and preventing public confusion" as well as having "the tendency [of widening] the scope of that protection."

The district court very persuasively answered Goodyear's argument that liability for trademark infringement cannot be imposed without a showing that Goodyear intended to trade on the goodwill of Big O or to palm off Goodyear products as being those of Big O's when it said

> The logical consequence of accepting Goodyear's position would be the immunization from unfair competition liability of a company with a well established trade name and with the economic power to advertise extensively for a product name taken from a competitor. If the law is to limit recovery to passing off, anyone with adequate size and resources can adopt any trademark and develop a new meaning for that trademark as identification of the second user's products. The activities of Goodyear in this case are unquestionably unfair competition through an improper use of a trademark and that must be actionable.

408 F. Supp. at 1236.

Goodyear further argues there was no credible evidence from which the jury could have found a likelihood of reverse confusion. A review of the record demonstrates the lack of merit in this argument. Big O presented more than a dozen witnesses who testified to actual confusion as to the source of Big O's "Big Foot" tires after watching a Goodyear "Bigfoot" commercial. The jury could have reasonably inferred a likelihood of confusion from these witnesses' testimony of actual confusion. Moreover, two of Goodyear's executive officers, Kelley and Eaves, testified confusion was likely or even inevitable. . . .

VII

Finally, Goodyear challenges the jury's verdict awarding Big O $2.8 million in compensatory damages and $16.8 million in punitive damages. . . .

Big O also asserts the evidence provided the jury with a reasonable basis for determining the amount of damages. Big O claims the only way it can be restored to the position it was in before Goodyear infringed its trademark is to conduct a corrective advertising campaign. Big O insists it should be compensated for the advertising expenses necessary to dispel the public confusion caused by Goodyear's infringement. Goodyear spent approximately $10 million on its "Bigfoot" advertising campaign. Thus, Big O advances two rationales in support of the $2.8 million award: (1) there were Big O Tire Dealers in 28 percent of the states (14 of 50) and 28 percent of $10 million equals the amount of the award; and (2) the Federal Trade Commission generally orders businesses who engage in misleading advertising to spend approximately 25 percent of their advertising budget on corrective advertising and this award is roughly 25 percent of the amount Goodyear spent infringing on Big O's trademark. The district court used the first rationale in denying Goodyear's motion to set the verdict aside. The second rationale was presented by Big O at oral argument. . . .

There is precedent for the recovery of corrective advertising expenses incurred by a plaintiff to counteract the public confusion resulting from a defendant's wrongful conduct. . . . Unlike the wronged parties in those cases Big O did not spend any money prior to trial in advertising to counteract the confusion from the Goodyear advertising. It is clear from the record Big O did not have the economic resources to conduct an advertising campaign sufficient to counteract Goodyear's $9,690,029 saturation advertising campaign. We are thus confronted with the question whether the law should apply differently to those who have the economic power to help themselves concurrently with the wrong than to those who must seek redress through the courts. Under the facts of this case we are convinced the answer must be no. Goodyear contends the recovery of advertising expenses should be limited to those actually incurred prior to trial. In this case the effect of such a rule would be to recognize that Big O has a right to the exclusive use of its trademark but has no remedy to be put in the position it was in prior to September 16, 1974, before Goodyear effectively usurped Big O's trademark. The impact of Goodyear's "Bigfoot" campaign was devastating. The infringing mark was seen repeatedly by millions of consumers. It is clear from the record that Goodyear deeply penetrated the public consciousness. Thus, Big O is entitled to recover a reasonable amount equivalent to that of a concurrent corrective advertising campaign.

As the district court pointed out, the jury's verdict of $2.8 million corresponds to 28 percent of the approximately $10 million Goodyear spent infringing Big O's mark. Big O has dealers in 14 states which equals 28 percent of the 50 states. Big O also points out the jury's award is close to 25 percent of the amount Goodyear spent infringing on Big O's mark. Big O emphasizes that the Federal Trade Commission often requires businesses who engage in misleading advertising to spend 25 percent of their advertising budget on corrective advertising.

Taking cognizance of these two alternative rationales for the jury's award for compensatory damages we are convinced the award is not capable of support as to any amount in excess of $678,302. As the district court implied in attempting to explain the jury's verdict, Big O is not entitled to the total amount Goodyear spent on its nationwide campaign since Big O only has dealers in 14 states, thus making it unnecessary for Big O to run a nationwide advertising campaign. Furthermore, implicit in the FTC's 25 percent rule in corrective advertising cases is the fact that dispelling confusion and deception in the consuming public's mind does not require a dollar-for-dollar expenditure. In keeping with " '(t)he constant tendency of the courts . . . to find some way in which damages can be awarded where a wrong has been done,' " we hold that the maximum amount which a jury could reasonably find necessary to place Big O in the position it was in before September 16, 1974, vis-à-vis its "Big Foot" trademark, is $678,302. We arrive at this amount by taking 28 percent of the $9,690,029 it was stipulated Goodyear spent on its "Bigfoot" campaign, and then reducing that figure by 75 percent in accordance with the FTC rule, since we agree with that agency's determination that a dollar-for-dollar expenditure for corrective advertising is unnecessary to dispel the effects of confusing and misleading advertising.

[The court also awarded $4 million in punitive damages.]

COMMENTS AND QUESTIONS

1. How was Big O hurt by Goodyear's massive advertising campaign? If the products have the same name, and if Goodyear spends much more on advertising than Big O does, shouldn't sales of Big O Tires increase? One possible answer is that Big O feared that Goodyear's tires would be of lower quality than its own and that its public image would suffer as a result of being associated with Goodyear. But that doesn't seem to be the case here, since Goodyear was selling premium tires and Big O was selling off-brands. Can you envision any way in which Goodyear's advertising of the brand would reduce Big O's sales?

Is the public hurt by thinking that Big O is affiliated with Goodyear? How? Is Big O hurt? Should that matter?

2. In the *Big O Tires* case, the court ordered as a remedy that Goodyear pay $4 million in punitive damages plus $678,302 — what it would cost in corrective advertising to "undo" the "damage" Goodyear had done in connecting itself with the Big O name.

This punitive damage award raises an interesting point. Is the court justified in ordering compensation — whether in the form of corrective advertising or a cash payment — beyond the point where advertising would have benefited Big O? If Goodyear benefits more from the advertising than Big O would have — as is perhaps shown by the fact that it costs more to restore the status quo for Big O — does this establish that the trademark is better left in Goodyear's hands? What if Goodyear realizes that it can make better use of a trademark currently held by a competitor; should we allow Goodyear to appropriate the mark by paying damages as set by the court? (Note that this is an example of a "liability rule"; see the discussion on patent remedies in Chapter 3.) What would be the effects of such a rule?

Further, consider that *any* spending is really a windfall to Big O, since it did not have the resources to shell out anything like $4 million in advertising. Is there any consumer interest served by corrective advertising in a reverse confusion case? Won't it just confuse consumers more?

The idea of punitive damages for trademark infringement seems to deny the possibility of "efficient" trademark infringement. This in turn suggests that trademarks are property and that courts are willing to grant "specific performance" remedies in infringement cases. Does this view make sense?

3. How should damages be measured in cases of reverse confusion? Presumably, a company like Big O Tires might be able to prove that it lost sales (rather than gained them) as a result of Goodyear's use of its "Bigfoot" trademark. But is Big O also entitled to Goodyear's profits from infringement? Its "unjust enrichment"? Most courts would say yes, at least where Big O can prove intentional or willful infringement. But doing so can provide a significant windfall to Big O, which would never have made such profits in the absence of infringement.

What unjust profits has Goodyear gained *through infringement*? Must it turn over all its profits from the sale of "Bigfoot" tires, even though it is Goodyear and not Big O that has built a national reputation for the "Bigfoot" name? How about the increase in sales attributable to the use of the name "Bigfoot"? Or are Goodyear's profits from infringement limited to whatever sales it took away from Big O (presumably the same measure as Big O's lost profits)?

PROBLEM

Problem 8-1. A small Vermont company named STW (and its predecessors) has used the mark "Thirst-Aid" for soft drinks since 1921. STW has never sold its products widely, however, and in fact its sales are declining. In 1983, Quaker Oats adopted the slogan "Gatorade is Thirst Aid" for its popular Gatorade beverage. STW sued for trademark infringement. At trial, STW proves that Quaker Oats knew of STW's trademark, but its lawyers advised it that the Gatorade slogan made "fair use" of STW's "descriptive" mark. The trial court disagreed, finding that Quaker Oats had infringed STW's mark in bad faith.

During the period that the "Thirst-Aid" campaign ran, pretax profits on the sale of Gatorade came to $247 million on sales of $2.6 billion. Quaker Oats proves that Gatorade had approximately $475 million in sales before the ad campaign. It also demonstrates that STW had previously offered to license the "Thirst-Aid" mark to another company for one-third of 1 percent of sales, and that STW's total goodwill in 1984 was less than $100,000 and declining. What damages should be awarded in this case?

Note on the Trademark Counterfeiting Act of 1984

In 1984, Congress substantially increased the penalties for intentional copying of a trademark (called "counterfeiting").[2] 18 U.S.C. § 2320 makes it a felony to knowingly use a counterfeit mark in connection with the sale of goods or services. It provides for fines and imprisonment of the offenders, and it permits the destruction of goods bearing counterfeit marks (rather than simply the removal of the marks themselves). The Act also added

- Section 34(d) of the Lanham Act, 15 U.S.C. § 1116(d), which provides for the seizure of counterfeit goods and records of sale before trial upon an ex parte application;
- Section 35(b) of the Lanham Act, 15 U.S.C. § 1117(b), which provides for the award of treble damages plus attorney fees and prejudgment interest against counterfeiters unless the court finds "extenuating circumstances";

2. Section 45 of the Lanham Act, 15 U.S.C. § 1127, defines a "counterfeit" as "a spurious mark which is identical with, or substantially indistinguishable from, a registered mark." While this definition does not contain an explicit intent requirement, courts are generally unwilling to find good faith use of an infringing mark to be "spurious."

- language in Section 36 of the Lanham Act, 15 U.S.C. § 1118, concerning the right of the court to destroy counterfeit goods after trial.

An exception to the broad reach of the act applies to those who are authorized to use a trademark "at the time of the manufacture or production" of the goods. *See* United States v. Bohai Trading Co., Inc., 45 F.3d 577 (1st Cir. 1995) (upholding the constitutionality of this provision in the face of a challenge on the grounds of vagueness). Although the ex parte nature of the remedies has brought the 1984 Act under constitutional scrutiny, courts have generally upheld the legality of its remedies and procedures. *See, e.g.*, United States v. McEvoy, 820 F.2d 1170 (11th Cir.). *But cf.* Time Warner Entertainment Co., L.P. v. Does Nos. 1-2, 876 F. Supp. 407 (E.D.N.Y. 1994) (overturning on Fourth Amendment grounds proposed seizure order drafted by owners of copyrights and trademarks; court cited role of private investigator in conducting seizure and impoundment, failure to provide sufficient particularity for premises to be searched or articles to be seized, inclusion of private residence as site to be searched, and failure to sufficiently describe infringing materials).

With the Anti-Counterfeiting Consumer Protection Act of 1996, Pub. L. No. 104-153, 110 Stat. 1386, Congress amended Section 35(c) to provide statutory damages as an alternative to actual damages in civil counterfeiting cases. In 2008, Congress doubled the range of statutory damages provided for by the 1996 amendment, so that a court may now award statutory damages of "not less than $1,000 or more than $200,000 per counterfeit mark per type of goods or services sold" and may award up to $2 million if the violation is "willful."

COMMENTS AND QUESTIONS

1. The Trademark Counterfeiting Act of 1984 is clearly punitive in nature, providing for both criminal sanctions and treble damages. Is such a punitive approach warranted? If so, why not apply these remedies to all trademark infringements?

2. Are consumers hurt by counterfeiting, or is it only trademark owners who are being protected by the Lanham Act? Where the counterfeit goods are inferior, the problems can extend beyond mere consumer confusion. Counterfeit medicines or aerospace parts can create a health and safety hazard. But what if the counterfeit goods were not in fact inferior to genuine goods with the same trademark? Have consumers suffered any injury if they mistakenly buy counterfeit goods equal in quality to the trademark owner's goods? Is the mere prospect that goods might be inferior itself a relevant injury.

3. Should it be a defense to a counterfeiting claim that the reasonable consumer was aware that the goods were not genuine (for example, because they were purchased from a street vendor without a certificate of authenticity for approximately 10 percent of the retail price of the genuine goods in stores)? Are consumers likely to be "confused" by such sales?

4. Judge Posner suggests one good reason for multiple damages in counterfeiting cases: deterrence. In holding that treble damages were an appropriate remedy even for innocent infringement, he argued:

> [T]he sale of counterfeit merchandise has become endemic—perhaps pandemic. Most of the infringing sellers are small retailers, such as K-Econo. Obtaining an injunction against

> each and every one of them would be infeasible. Trademark owners cannot hire investigators to shop every retail store in the nation. And even if they could and did, and obtained injunctions against all present violators, this would not stop the counterfeiting. Other infringers would spring up, and would continue infringing until enjoined. . . . Treble damages are a particularly suitable remedy in cases where surreptitious violations are possible, for in such cases simple damages (or profits) will underdeter; the violator will know that he won't be caught every time, and merely confiscating his profits in the cases in which he is caught will leave him with a net profit from infringement. . . . [T]he smaller the violator, the less likely he is to be caught, and the more needful, therefore, is a heavy punishment if he is caught.

Louis Vuitton S.A. v. Lee, 875 F.2d 584 (7th Cir. 1989). Is this rationale persuasive?

Part II

UNFAIR COMPETITION AND BUSINESS TORTS

9 False Advertising, Product Disparagement, and Related Claims

The first half of this casebook focused mostly on the law of trademarks. The second half will focus on a variety of other claims that are sometimes grouped together under the heading "unfair competition," as well as some related business torts. Sometimes plaintiffs assert the types of claims we will be discussing here along with claims for trademark infringement or dilution (recall that the law of trademarks itself is sometimes viewed as a species of unfair competition law). Alternatively, sometimes plaintiffs assert the types of claims we will be discussing in this half of the casebook in connection with copyright, patent, antitrust, consumer protection, or common-law breach of contract claims. In yet other circumstances, these claims stand alone, filling gaps that these other bodies of law leave untouched. Whether all of these gaps need to be filled, and if so whether the law of unfair competition and business torts provide the optimal remedies for the asserted harms, is often a hotly contested issue. As we will see, courts, legislatures, and commentators have expressed widely varying opinions on the optimal scope and structure of these types of claims, both historically and in the present day.

A. THE ECONOMICS OF ADVERTISING

The present chapter covers the law of false advertising (as well as related claims involving product disparagement and false designations of origin.) A good place to begin the discussion is to focus on the *why*: Why do we need a body of law that penalizes firms or individuals for engaging in false advertising? Many people sense, intuitively, that having such a body of law in place is desirable; but it may help to understand the various ways in which the law has responded to false advertising by explicitly considering, first, the possible social benefits and costs of advertising *generally*; and second, whether (or how) a body of law that penalizes *false* advertising might increase the surplus of benefits over costs, in light of other alternatives.

Opinion over time has varied widely in its assessment of the social benefits and costs of advertising. One perspective, which gained force in the early to middle part of the twentieth century and is sometimes associated with the economic theory of monopolistic competition, emphasizes the role that advertising can play in enabling sellers to differentiate their products from one another. To the extent that much of this product differentiation is more apparent than real, advertising may enable sellers to discourage new entry into the market, and also to charge higher prices than they would in a more perfectly competitive system. *See* Kyle Bagwell, *The Economic Analysis of Advertising, in* 3 HANDBOOK OF INDUSTRIAL ORGANIZATION 1701, 1705-06 (Mark Armstrong & Robert Porter eds., 2007) (discussing this view); JOHN KENNETH GALBRAITH, THE AFFLUENT SOCIETY 156 (1958) (arguing that advertising "creates the wants it seeks to satisfy"). This view, in other words, stresses the social costs of advertising in artificially raising costs to consumers by preventing competition among products that are in fact equal. Ralph Sharp Brown Jr., *Advertising and the Public Interest: Legal Protection of Trade Symbols*, 57 YALE L.J. 1165 (1948), *reprinted in* 108 YALE L.J. 1619 (1999). All other things being equal, it might suggest that legal policymakers should strictly regulate advertising in order to minimize those costs.

An alternative perspective, rooted in the Chicago School economics that came to prominence in the 1960s and thereafter, argues that advertising provides a social benefit by providing consumers with valuable information (about product availability, cost, quality, durability, and the like) which they often would have difficulty obtaining prior to the point of purchase. *See* Bagwell, *supra*, at 1706. On this view, advertising (like trademarks) can help to reduce consumer search costs and is generally pro- rather than anti-competitive. To be sure, the magnitude of the social benefits provided by advertising may vary from one product market to another. Consumers may care more about product quality and durability, for example, when the product under consideration is an expensive, infrequent purchase item such as an automobile than when the product is a low-cost, repeat purchase item such as chewing gum. In addition, as discussed in Chapter 2, information that reduces search costs (whether in the form of a trademark or in the form of advertising) is likely to be more valuable if the product characteristic at issue is an "experience" or "credence" characteristic such as taste or durability, as opposed to a "search" characteristic such as product availability, appearance, or price.[1] *See* Michael R. Darby & Edi Karni, *Free Competition and the Optimal Amount of Fraud*, 16 J.L. & ECON. 67, 68-69 (1973); Philip Nelson, *Information and Consumer Behavior*, 78 J. POL. ECON. 311 (1970). All other things being equal, if the informational view of advertising is correct, policymakers should be careful not to discourage truthful advertising. For reasons we elaborate on below, however, they might want to discourage false advertising, which threatens to reduce advertising's social benefits (though how strictly false advertising should be policed remains a matter of debate, as we shall see).

A common objection to the informational view of advertising is that a good deal of the advertising we encounter in everyday life seems to make very few *direct*

1. Even some ostensibly search characteristics such as product availability or price, however, may turn out on closer inspection to be experience characteristics. Under the right circumstances, a firm might be tempted to lie about product availability in order to lure customers who will then buy a different product—or to deter competitors from entering a new market (e.g., the "vaporware" phenomenon). Firms also may sometimes make deceptive statements about price, such as how much a product will cost in the long run when factoring in the cost of borrowing, repairs, and the like, or how much an allegedly discounted price has been reduced.

statements about product characteristics such as price, quality, or durability.[2] When a famous athlete appears on a box of WHEATIES cereal, for example, you might draw the inference that the athlete endorses the product; but does the fact of the athlete's endorsement necessarily tell you anything about whether you will like the product too? Surely the average consumer realizes that his or her tastes may be different from the athlete's; that (although proper nutrition is important) the consumption of WHEATIES probably has a negligible effect on athletic skill; and that the athlete's compensation for the endorsement may have played some role in forming his opinion about the product.[3] Nevertheless, economists such as Philip Nelson, Benjamin Klein, and Keith Leffler have developed Chicago-influenced rationales for this type of advertising as well.[4] Although the details of their analyses differ in some respects, the thrust of the theory is that, independent of the actual *content* of its advertising, the mere *fact* that a firm has invested heavily in advertising indirectly communicates valuable information about the firm's products (especially products with significant "experience" characteristics). Heavy investment in advertising may signal, for example, that the firm anticipates substantial consumer demand for its products into the foreseeable future, on the theory that advertising generally correlates with expected future sales. Such indirect information about the product's expected popularity among the targeted audience might be especially valuable to members of that target audience who have yet to try the product. Relatedly, firms that have invested heavily in the sunk costs of advertising can be viewed as signaling that they expect to retain (at least) their present market share. Such firms, in contrast to more fly-by-night operations, may be more likely to have invested resources in developing and maintaining a reputation for producing quality products.[5] Finally, consumers suffering from information overload and limited attention spans may be more likely to make repeat purchases of products they have enjoyed, if those products are the subject of memorable advertising; once again, the firms that have the most to gain from investing in such advertising will be those that market satisfying products.

The theory that advertising is often less relevant for what it actually asserts than for the mere fact that it exists remains the subject of lively debate. Some critics dispute the premise that intense advertising supports the inference of product popularity or quality. Anecdotally, some students may remember the lavish commercials that

2. Or, as Robert Gordon once put it, "an economist is a person who believes that advertising is a means of conveying information." *See* James Boyle, *A Theory of Law and Information: Copyright, Spleens, Blackmail, and Insider Trading*, 80 CAL. L. REV. 1413, 1456 n.107 (1992). We think Gordon was being facetious.

3. To be sure, one can imagine some situations in which a celebrity endorsement might lead consumers to believe, rationally, that the endorsed product has desirable characteristics. An endorsement on the part of someone who enjoys a widespread reputation for deep personal integrity (think, for example, of the Dalai Lama's appearance in an ad for APPLE computers in the 1990s) might rationally lead consumers to lend the endorsement more weight than an endorsement from a typical celebrity. Such ads appear to be relatively uncommon, however; and even icons of integrity like the Dalai Lama (or Mother Teresa) have their critics, so perhaps any such endorsement should be taken with a grain of salt in any event. A better example might be a celebrity endorsement of a product the use of which is perceived to be embarrassing (such as a cure for baldness or erectile dysfunction), on the theory that anyone willing to go public with the use of such a product must have a high opinion of its properties. But even these examples (though distressingly common, in the views of some arbiters of taste) are not the norm of celebrity endorsements.

4. *See* Benjamin Klein & Keith B. Leffler, *The Role of Market Forces in Assuring Contractual Performance*, 89 J. POL. ECON. 615, 629-33 (1981); Phillip Nelson, *Advertising as Information*, 82 J. POL. ECON. 729 (1974); Phillip Nelson, *The Economic Consequences of Advertising*, 48 J. BUS. 213 (1975). *See also* Bagwell, *supra*, at 1718-20.

5. They are also more likely to attract attention from government regulators, if their ads are deceptive. *See* Nelson, *The Economic Consequences of Advertising*, at 215.

aired during the January 2000 Super Bowl for firms such as Pets.com that never turned a profit. More significantly, perhaps, Bagwell reports that the empirical studies thus far "do not offer strong support for the hypothesis of a systematic positive relationship between advertising and product quality," though "a positive relationship is more likely when advertising conveys direct information (broadly defined) to consumers." Bagwell, *supra*, at 1748. Other research, while not directly responding to the informational theory, may suggest reasons to doubt that celebrity endorsement and other "fluff" ads facilitate rational decisionmaking. Marketing guru Martin Lindstrom, for instance, contends that evidence from neurobiology shows that people respond positively to certain ads more than others because the successful ads do a better job of tapping into consumers' unconscious desires for status, security, ritual, or other perceived wants. *See* MARTIN LINDSTROM, BUY-OLOGY: TRUTHS AND LIES ABOUT WHY WE BUY (2008). On this view, firms may use celebrity endorsements (for example) to craft a subliminal message that its products are glamorous (young, chic, sexy, etc.) and that some of that glamour will rub off on the consumer. Finally, the "advertising as quality investment" claim is inherently self-limiting. If it works, it works because consumers see advertisements and therefore pay more for the advertised product because they believe it must be of higher quality. But if that is true, makers of low-quality products will advertise as well, hoping to free-ride on that assumption. (And they do; watch daytime television sometime.) And that in turn will undermine the consumer assumption that advertising is an indicator of quality.

A third possible rationale for advertising is what Bagwell refers to as the "complementary" theory of advertising: namely, that "consumers may value 'social prestige,' and the consumption of a product may generate greater social prestige when the product is (appropriately) advertised." Bagwell, *supra*, at 1706. This theory is identical to one of the rationales sometimes put forward in support of trademark anti-dilution laws (*see* Chapter 5.C *supra*): that these laws better enable consumers to gratify their desires for signaling information about themselves (for example, their social status, taste, income, or sex appeal). Indeed, some evolutionary psychologists argue (albeit controversially) that consumer purchasing decisions often reflect evolutionary pressures to signal characteristics such as agreeability and intelligence that correlate with reproductive and social success. *See* GEOFFREY MILLER, SPENT: SEX, EVOLUTION AND CONSUMER BEHAVIOR (2009). As we discussed above, however, even if these theories are correct, opinions strongly differ over the normative question of whether the law *should* gratify people's desires to engage in status competition; Miller himself argues that the signaling effects of our purchases are often socially wasteful.

These differing views of advertising lead to different policy implications. On the one hand, if advertising serves principally to manipulate consumers' desires and emotions in normatively troubling ways, while generating few if any social benefits, legal policymakers may want to strictly regulate even *truthful* advertising — though regulation itself can be costly, and (as we will see) the First Amendment presents some substantial obstacles to the regulation of truthful advertising. On the other hand, if truthful advertising is generally beneficial, policymakers might be well-advised to target only *false* advertising, which (it might seem) can only undermine advertising's social benefits (and exacerbate its social costs). Indeed, if firms could falsely advertise with impunity, both consumers and the false advertiser's competitors would stand to suffer a variety of harms. Most obviously, a consumer who relies on a false statement about some product characteristic may forgo the purchase of a competing product that genuinely possesses that characteristic. In such a case, the consumer is worse off for having been deceived into buying the wrong product, and so is the firm that would have sold the consumer the alternative product. But other, more subtle harms may result as well. A consumer who buys a product falsely advertised as "genuine mahogany wood," for example, may draw the (incorrect) inference that mahogany is a substandard type of wood if the product falls apart after a short time. In this scenario, not only has the consumer been deceived, to her detriment, but firms that market genuine mahogany wood products also may suffer a loss of future business. *See* RESTATEMENT OF TORTS § 761, cmt. a.[6] Moreover, if false advertising is both rampant and difficult to distinguish *ex ante* from truthful advertising, consumers may become less likely to rely on advertising at all, thus forgoing the potential benefits of even truthful advertising. In the extreme, false advertising might tend to drive out truthful advertising, because firms would be unable to signal truthful private information about their products in ways that consumers could trust. *See* George Akerlof, *The Market for "Lemons": Quality Uncertainty and the Market Mechanism*, 84 Q.J. ECON. 488 (1970).

Even so, there may be a variety of reasons to be skeptical about possible legal responses to false advertising. First, one might question the value of false advertising law if other laws or social institutions work to reduce the incidence of false advertising independently of laws specifically targeting false advertising. As noted above, consumers might have common-law claims against deceptive sellers for breach of contract or for fraud; and while these claims individually often may be too insignificant to induce consumers to file suit, in theory modern legal reforms such as small claims courts, class actions, and the availability of punitive damages could enhance consumers' incentives to protect themselves through litigation. Or perhaps consumers could find other ways to protect themselves from false advertising, at relatively little cost to themselves. *Ex ante*, consumers can sample search goods (and thus one might expect relatively less false advertising with respect to such goods). In addition, consumers usually can be confident that goods bearing trademarks are genuine (due to trademark owners' incentives to protect and police the use of their marks), and if they do not like the way the branded good performs they can retaliate by not purchasing that brand again. Of course, resolving never to buy a particular product again might seem like cold comfort to the consumer who has already been defrauded once by the seller of that product. A firm that can predict that its deceptive advertising will lead to consumer retaliation nevertheless will have less of an incentive to engage in deceptive advertising in the first instance. Firms acting in their own self-interest therefore may have a market incentive to avoid engaging in false advertising, at least with respect to repeat-purchase branded goods. Whether this market effect is adequate may depend on whether one buys into the informational view of advertising (which sees most advertising as a social good) or the persuasive view (which, if anything, would err on the side of regulation).

Finally, industry itself could (and often does) engage in its own self-regulation of advertising, thus potentially reducing the need for formal legal intervention. *Consider, e.g., The Advertising Industry's Process of Voluntary Self-Regulation: Policies and Procedures by the National Advertising Review Council (NARC)* (Aug. 30, 2007) ("Policies and Procedures"), *available at* http://www.nadreview.org/07_Procedures.pdf. These policies and procedures govern three entities, the National Advertising Division (NAD), the Children's Advertising Review Unit (CARU), and the National Advertising Review Board (NARB), and are administered by the Council of Better Business Bureaus

6. What if a firm falsely advertises a product feature that neither it nor any of its competitors actually has?

(CBBB). NAD and CARU are "responsible for receiving or initiating, evaluating, investigating, analyzing . . . and holding negotiations with an advertiser, and resolving complaints or questions from any source involving the truth or accuracy of national advertising, or consistency with CARU's *Self-Regulatory Program for Children's Advertising*." *Id.* § 2.1.A. NAD and CARU also "are charged with independent responsibility for monitoring and reviewing national advertising for truthfulness, accuracy and, in the case of CARU, consistency with CARU's *Self-Regulatory Program for Children's Advertising*." *Id.* § 2.1.B. "Any person or legal entity, including NAD/CARU as part of their monitoring responsibility . . . may submit to NAD/CARU any complaint regarding national advertising." *Id.* § 2.2. The NAD describes the ensuing proceeding as "a unique, hybrid form of alternative dispute resolution" which provides "a written decision within 60 business days." *See About NAD, available at* http://www.bbb.org/us/About-National-Advertising-Division/. Proceedings are confidential, but the CBBB publishes press releases announcing its decisions. It also publishes case reports of its final decisions that are available to subscribers. *See id.*; *see also* Policies and Procedures, §§ 2.1.C, E. An advertiser that "does not agree to comply with NAD/CARU's decision on one or more issues . . . shall be entitled to panel review by the NARB." Policies and Procedures, § 3.1.A. If an advertiser does not agree to comply with NAD, CARU, or NARB recommendations, "NAD/CARU may refer the file to the appropriate government agency." *Id.* § 4.1.B.[7] For further discussion of the NAD, see Ross D. Petty, *Supplanting Government Regulation with Competitor Lawsuits: The Case of Controlling False Advertising*, 25 Ind. L. Rev. 351 (1991). And independent product evaluation entities such as Consumer Reports may also reduce any harm from false advertising, at least for large purchases for which they are more widely used.

Two caveats nevertheless must be made with respect to industry self-regulation of this sort. The first is that, but for the possibility of legal action, industry might have less of an incentive to develop dispute resolution systems such as the NAD Policies and Procedures as an alternative to litigation. The existence of such alternative systems, in other words, does not necessarily dispel the need for formal legal regulation. The second is that, in some instances, the social costs of self-regulation can themselves be very high. Anytime industry groups band together to develop advertising codes of conduct, the possibility of anti-competitive behavior cannot be ignored. *See* Richard A. Posner, Antitrust Law 30 (2d ed. 2001).

Following up from this last point, a criticism sometimes made in response to false advertising laws is that, in practice, they may lead to anti-competitive results or otherwise increase social costs. Like other laws, false advertising laws can be abused in ways that subvert their underlying purpose. Some scholars have argued, for example, that competitor suits under the Lanham Act (see section B *infra*) often involve relatively trivial misstatements and serve, in practice, as a means of keeping aggressive competitors at bay. *See* Lillian R. BeVier, *Competitor Suits for False Advertising Under*

7. For media discussion of some recent disputes, see Ann Zimmerman, *Wal-Mart Rapped on Ad Claim*, Wall St. J. (June 23, 2009), at B5 (discussing an NAD ruling that disclaimers in a Wal-Mart ad would not "temper the message that viewers, regardless of where they live, can expect to obtain" annual savings of $700 by shopping at Wal-Mart); Jessica E. Vascellaro, *Will eHarmony Restore Romance to Web Dating*, Wall St. J. (Sept. 17, 2007) (discussing an NAD ruling that Chemistry.com failed to defend certain claims relating to its Internet dating service technology). NAD does not address concerns over the good taste of advertising, however. *About NAD, available at* http://www.bbb.org/us/About-National-Advertising-Division/. Counterpart organizations in other countries sometimes do. *See, e.g.*, Aaron O. Patrick, *Ryanair Discounts U.K.'s Ad Rulings*, Wall St. J. (Mar. 14, 2008), at B4.

Section 43(a) of the Lanham Act: A Puzzle in the Law of Deception, 78 VA. L. REV. 1 (1992); Ellen R. Jordan & Paul H. Rubin, *An Economic Analysis of the law of False Advertising*, 8 J. LEGAL STUD. 527 (1979). Others have argued that state-law reforms to the common law of false advertising have overcorrected for the perceived flaws of the common-law scheme, to the extent that these laws now overdeter beneficial conduct. *See* Henry N. Butler & Jason S. Johnson, *Consumer Harm Acts? An Economic Analysis of State Consumer Protection Acts* (Apr. 8, 2009), *available at* http://ssrn.com/abstract=1125305. Yet others have expressed concern over the possible impact of false advertising law on freedom of speech. Although current First Amendment law permits government to ban false commercial speech altogether, some scholars have argued that, as with political and other forms of "core" First Amendment speech, some false speech is the inevitable by-product of any system that encourages speech generally; too much concern with banning all false commercial speech, in other words, might have a "chilling effect" with respect to the production of truthful commercial speech as well. We discuss these matters in some detail in section G *infra*. In general, though, once again the optimal regulation of advertising depends in large part on whether one views advertising as for the most part a social good (in which case less regulation might avoid the risks of overdeterrence) or at best a necessary evil (in which case stricter regulation might be worth the risk of overdeterrence).

B. THE COMMON LAW APPROACH TO FALSE ADVERTISING

Ely-Norris Safe Co. v. Mosler Safe Co.

7 F.2d 603 (2d Cir. 1925)

The jurisdiction of the District Court depended upon diverse citizenship and the suit was for unfair competition. The bill alleged that the plaintiff manufactured and sold safes under certain letters patent, which had as their distinctive feature an explosion chamber, designed for protection against burglars. Before the acts complained of, no one but the plaintiff had ever made or sold safes with such chambers, and, except for the defendant's infringement, the plaintiff has remained the only manufacturer and seller of such safes. By reason of the plaintiff's efforts the public has come to recognize the value of the explosion chamber and to wish to purchase safes containing them. Besides infringing the patent, the defendant has manufactured and sold safes without a chamber, but with a metal bank around the door, in the same place where the plaintiff put the chamber, and has falsely told its customers that this bank was employed to cover and close an explosion chamber. Customers have been thus led to buy safes upon the faith of the representation, who in fact wished to buy safes with explosion chambers, and would have done so, but for the deceit.

The bill prayed an injunction against selling safes with such metal bands, and against representing that any of its safes contained an explosion chamber. From the plaintiff's answers to interrogatories it appeared that all the defendant's safes bore the defendant's name and address, and were sold as its own. Furthermore, that the defendant never gave a customer reason to suppose that any safe sold by it was made by the plaintiff.

HAND, Circuit Judge (after stating the facts as above).

. . . We must concede, therefore, that on the cases as they stand the law is with the defendant, and the especially high authority of the court which decided *American Washboard Co. v. Saginaw Mfg. Co., supra*, makes us hesitate to differ from their conclusion. Yet there is no part of the law which is more plastic than unfair competition, and what was not reckoned an actionable wrong 25 years ago may have become such today. We find it impossible to deny the strength of the plaintiff's case on the allegations of its bill. As we view it, the question is, as it always is in such cases, one of fact. While a competitor may, generally speaking, take away all the customers of another that he can, there are means which he must not use. One of these is deceit. The false use of another's name as maker or source of his own goods is deceit, of which the false use of geographical or descriptive terms is only one example. But we conceive that in the end the questions which arise are always two: Has the plaintiff in fact lost customers? And has he lost them by means which the law forbids? The false use of the plaintiff's name is only an instance in which each element is clearly shown.

In the case at bar the means are as plainly unlawful as in the usual case of palming off. It is as unlawful to lie about the quality of one's wares as about their maker; it equally subjects the seller to action by the buyer. . . . The reason, as we think, why such deceits have not been regarded as actionable by a competitor, depends only upon his inability to show any injury for which there is a known remedy. In an open market it is generally impossible to prove that a customer, whom the defendant has secured by falsely describing his goods, would have bought of the plaintiff, if the defendant had been truthful. Without that, the plaintiff, though aggrieved in company with other honest traders, cannot show any ascertainable loss. He may not recover at law, and the equitable remedy is concurrent. The law does not allow him to sue as a vicarious avenger of the defendant's customers.

But, if it be true that the plaintiff has a monopoly of the kind of wares concerned, and if to secure a customer the defendant must represent his own as of that kind, it is a fair inference that the customer wants those and those only. Had he not supposed that the defendant could supply him, presumably he would have gone to the plaintiff, who alone could. At least, if the plaintiff can prove that in fact he would, he shows a direct loss, measured by his profits on the putative sale. If a tradesman falsely foists on a customer a substitute for what the plaintiff alone can supply, it can scarcely be that the plaintiff is without remedy, if he can show that the customer would certainly have come to him, had the truth been told.

Yet that is in substance the situation which this bill presents. It says that the plaintiff alone could lawfully make such safes, and that the defendant has sold others to customers who asked for the patented kind. It can make no difference that the defendant sold them as its own. The sale by hypothesis depended upon the structure of the safes, not on their maker. To be satisfied, the customer must in fact have gone to the plaintiff, or the defendant must have infringed. Had he infringed, the plaintiff could have recovered his profit on the sale; had the customer gone to him, he would have made that profit. Any possibilities that the customers might not have gone to the plaintiff, had they been told the truth, are foreclosed by the allegation that the plaintiff in fact lost the sales. It seems to us merely a corollary of *Federal Trade Commission v. Winsted Hosiery Co., supra*, that, if this can be proved, a private suit will lie.

Decree reversed.

Mosler Safe Co. v. Ely-Norris Safe Co.

273 U.S. 132 (1927)

Mr. Justice HOLMES delivered the opinion of the Court.

This is a bill in equity brought by a corporation of New Jersey against a corporation of New York alleging unfair competition. It was treated below as a suit by the only manufacturer of safes containing an explosion chamber for protection against burglars. It seeks an injunction against selling safes with a metal band around the door in the place where the plaintiff put the chamber, or falsely representing that the defendant's safes contain an explosion chamber. The plaintiff admitted that the defendant's safes bore the defendant's name and address and that the defendant never gave any customer reason to believe that its safes were of the plaintiff's make. The District Court, following American Washboard Co. v. Saginaw Manufacturing Co. (C. C. A.) 103 F. 281, 50 L. R. A. 609, held that representations such as were sought to be enjoined did not give a private cause of action. The Circuit Court of Appeals held that if, as it took it to be alleged, the plaintiff had the monopoly of explosion chambers and the defendant falsely represented that its safes had such chambers, the plaintiff had a good case, and that since the decision above cited the law had grown more liberal in granting relief. It therefore reversed the decree below. . . .

It is consistent with every allegation in the bill and the defendant in argument asserted it to be a fact, that there are other safes with explosion chambers beside that for which the plaintiff has a patent. The defendant is charged only with representing that its safes had 'an explosion chamber,' which, so far as appears, it had a perfect right to do if the representation was true. If on the other hand the representation was false as it is alleged sometimes to have been, there is nothing to show that customers had they known the facts would have gone to the plaintiff rather than to other competitors in the market, or to lay a foundation for the claim for a loss of sales. The bill is so framed as to seem to invite the decision that was obtained from the Circuit Court of Appeals, but when scrutinized is seen to have so limited its statements as to exclude the right to complain.

Decree reversed.

COMMENTS AND QUESTIONS

1. Both the Court of Appeals and the Supreme Court decisions in *Ely-Mosler* cite to American Washboard Co. v. Saginaw Mfg. Co., 103 F. 281 (6th Cir. 1904). In that case, the plaintiff alleged that it was the sole producer of washboards that included an aluminum rubbing face, and that the defendant induced consumers to buy the defendant's zinc-faced washboards by falsely advertising that its washboards contained aluminum. The Sixth Circuit held that, absent proof that the defendant was deceiving consumers into thinking that the source of the defendant's products was the plaintiff (that is, absent proof that the defendant was "passing off" its goods as those of the plaintiff), the plaintiff had no viable cause of action:

> [T]he private right of action in such cases is not based upon fraud or imposition upon the public, but is maintained solely for the protection of the property rights of a complainant. It is true that in these cases it is an important factor that the public are deceived,

> but it is only where this deception induces the public to buy the goods as those of complainant that a private right of action arises. . . .
>
> It is doubtless morally wrong and improper to impose upon the public by the sale of spurious goods, but this does not give rise to a private right of action unless the property rights of the plaintiff are thereby invaded. There are many wrongs which can only be righted through public prosecution, and for which the legislature, and not the courts, must provide a remedy. . . .
>
> If the doctrine contended for by complainant in this case was to be carried to its legitimate results, we should, as suggested by Mr. Justice Bradley in the case of New York & R. Cement Co. v. Coplay Cement Co. (C.C.) 44 Fed. 277, open a Pandora's box of litigation. A person who undertook to manufacture a genuine article could suppress the business of all untruthful dealers, although they were in no wise undertaking to pirate his trade. . . .
>
> Take the metal which is the subject-matter of the controversy in this case. Many articles are now being put upon the market under the name of aluminum, because of the attractive qualities of that metal, which are not made of pure aluminum, yet they answer the purpose for which they are made and are useful. Can it be that the courts have the power to suppress such trade at the instance of others starting in the same business who use only pure aluminum, yet they answer the purpose for which they are made and are useful. Can it be that the courts have the power to suppress such trade at the instance of others starting in the same business who use only pure aluminum? There is a wide-spread suspicion that many articles sold as being manufactured of wool are not entirely made of that material. Can it be that a dealer who should make such articles only of pure wool could invoke the equitable jurisdiction of the courts to suppress the trade and business of all persons whose goods may deceive the public? We find no such authority in the books, and are clear in the opinion that, if the doctrine is to be thus extended, and all persons compelled to deal solely in goods which are exactly what they are represented to be, the remedy must come from the legislature, and not from the courts.

Id. at 285-86. Are the Sixth Circuit's concerns about vexatious litigation and judicial competence sound?

2. Under the common law rule announced in *American Washboard*, would there be *any* circumstances in which Competitor A could successfully sue Competitor B for false advertising? In a few cases, courts permitted competitor suits to proceed when the alleged misstatement related to the geographic origin of the defendant's products and the plaintiffs consisted of firms that actually produced goods within that geographic market. *See* RESTATEMENT (THIRD) OF UNFAIR COMPETITION § 2 cmt. b (1995); Richard F. Dole, Jr., *The Emergence of Deceptive Advertising as a Group Tort: A Possible Consequence of the 1966 Federal Rule Amendment with Respect to Class Actions*, 62 NW. U. L. REV. 661, 666-67 (1966). What if only one competitor within the group that competed within the geographical market at issue filed suit?

3. *Ely-Norris* presents something of a "clash of the titans." Two of the leading jurists in American history, Learned Hand and Oliver Wendell Holmes, reach different conclusions as to whether Ely-Norris alleged sufficient facts to state a claim for common-law false advertising. Judge Hand appears willing to depart from *American Washboard* by (1) permitting Competitor A to state a claim against Competitor B where Competitor A alleges that Competitor B's deceptive advertising caused Competitor A to suffer actual harm (e.g., to lose profits on sales made by Competitor B that Competitor A would have made, but for the deception); and (2) permitting the trier of fact to infer that, where Competitor A is the *single source* of the product feature that was the subject of Competitor B's false statement, Competitor A has suffered resulting

harm. Does Justice Holmes reject Judge Hand's invitation to recognize (what has come to be called) a "single source" exception to the *American Washboard* principle, or does he conclude only that the exception does not apply here? Wasn't Ely-Norris the single source of the patented explosion chamber that Mosler claimed to be selling? Does Justice Holmes's understanding of the relationship of patents to discrete product markets prefigure (much) later developments in the law? *See* Illinois Tool Works Inc. v. Independent Ink, Inc., 547 U.S. 28 (2006) (holding that, in antitrust tying cases, courts should not presume that patents confer market power).

4. Notice that there was no federal statutory claim at issue in *Ely-Norris*. Instead, the case wound up in federal court due to diversity of citizenship between the parties. Prior to *Erie R.R. Co. v. Tompkins*, 304 U.S. 64 (1938), federal courts developed and applied federal common law, rather than state law, in such cases. Following *Erie*, a federal court hearing a common-law claim for false advertising would be obligated to apply state law; *which* state's law would depend on the conflict of laws rules of the state in which the federal district court is located. *See* Klaxon Co. v. Stentor Elec. Mfg. Co., 313 U.S. 487 (1941).

5. Subsequent cases, as well as the 1939 *Restatement of Torts*, seemed to accept, in principle, the single source exception advocated by Judge Hand, under which Competitor A could state a claim where Competitor A was the single source of the product feature that formed the subject matter of Competitor B's alleged false advertising. *See* Restatement of Torts § 761 (1939) (stating that "[o]ne who diverts trade from a competitor by fraudulently representing that the goods which he markets have ingredients or qualities which in fact they do not have but which the goods of the competitor do have is liable to the competitor for the harm so caused, if (a) when making the representation he intends that it should, or knows or should know that it is likely to, divert trade from the competitor, and (b) the competitor is not marketing his goods with material fraudulent misrepresentations about them"). Proving that Competitor A was the single source nevertheless remained difficult in practice, as you can imagine; monopolies tend to be the exception, not the rule, in most product markets. Even with a single source exception, then, won't a good deal of false advertising go unremedied? If the answer to this question is "yes," reforms could proceed along any of three different paths.

First, one could empower the government to pursue claims for false advertising. As evidenced by Judge Hand's citation of Federal Trade Commission v. Winsted Hosiery Co., 258 U.S. 483 (1922), this method was already in existence at the time of *Ely-Norris*: In *Winsted Hosiery*, the Supreme Court affirmed an FTC order enjoining a defendant from engaging in false advertising that affected interstate commerce.[8] In addition, other federal (and state) entities, such as the Food and Drug Administration and the United States Department of Agriculture, also to some extent regulate advertising as it relates to products or services within the agency's jurisdiction. We discuss the FTC's false advertising jurisprudence in section D *infra*. There is no private right of action under the FTC Act, however, and like any agency the FTC must

8. In Federal Trade Comm'n v. Raladam Co., 283 U.S. 643, 649 (1931), however, the Supreme Court limited the reach of *Winsted Hosiery* by holding that the FTC's jurisdiction over false advertising extended only to cases in which "the trader whose methods are assailed as unfair [has] present or potential rivals in trade whose business will be, or is likely to be, lessened or otherwise injured." In 1938, Congress expressly conferred upon the FTC broader authority to combat deceptive advertising and unfair trade practices in interstate commerce. *See* section D.1 *infra*.

exercise prosecutorial discretion in deciding which cases are important enough to merit its attention.

Second, one could empower defrauded consumers to pursue claims for false advertising, for example, by offering the prospect of recovering enhanced damages and attorneys' fees, or by making it procedurally easier to aggregate consumer claims by means of class actions. Reforms like these have been implemented in many states over the last 30 years, pursuant to laws sometimes referred to as "Little FTC Acts" or "Baby FTC Acts." Many of these acts also empower state attorneys general to pursue false advertising claims as well. We discuss these acts in section E *infra*.

Third, one could empower competitors (like Ely-Norris) to file suit by modifying or eliminating the requirement that they prove actual harm — perhaps by adopting a "likelihood of injury" standard similar to the standard that applies in trademark infringement actions. At first blush, a reform of this nature might seem ideal. Unlike FTC actions, competitor suits conserve governmental resources by delegating prosecutorial responsibility to private parties. And unlike consumers, whose aggregate losses may be high but whose individual losses may be insufficient to motivate them to file suit, competitors often have a strong motivation to police one another's behavior. Though acting in their own self-interest, competitors asserting claims for false advertising therefore might also incidentally serve (in Judge Hand's words) as "vicarious avengers" of the public interest.

Before we sign off on competitor suits as the ideal solution to the underdeterrence problem, though, it might be worthwhile to consider whether there are any possible unintended consequences of making it easier for competitors to file suit. An initial problem involves defining who a competitor is: Should courts undertake an antitrust-like inquiry to define the relative product market in false advertising cases, or can they rely more on common sense notions of market definition? Note too that in a large industry (such as, say, the business of preparing annual income tax returns), there might be thousands of potential competitors. Should each one of them have a claim against any tax preparer that engages in false advertising? Are there any risks that competitors will abuse their power to sue another? And is the trademark analogy apt? If Firm B infringes Firm A's trademark, after all, consumers who are displeased with a product they (erroneously) think emanates from Firm A may vow never to buy even genuine goods from Firm A. Firm A's future reputation will be compromised, and so to prevent this from happening in the first place it might make sense to allow Firm A to sue before any actual consumer confusion has occurred (i.e., on a showing of likelihood of confusion). If Firm B falsely advertises the merits of its own product, however, consumers who are displeased with that product might cease doing business with Firm B while continuing to do business with Firm A (though not if the false representation concerns a characteristic that consumers believe is common to both Firm A and Firm B's products, as in the mahogany wood example above).

If the competitor were able to sue without a showing of harm, would it be desirable to substitute a requirement of consumer harm? If a defendant makes a false statement that doesn't injure anyone, should it be illegal? For an argument that trademark law as well as false advertising law should pay more attention to evidence of consumer harm from representations, see Mark A. Lemley & Mark McKenna, *Irrelevant Confusion*, 62 STAN. L. REV. 311 (2010).

Finally, even if elimination of the actual harm requirement is desirable, is this reform constitutional? In other words, is actual harm an Article III requirement, or could the common law standard be replaced with a likelihood of harm standard as in trademark law?

C. FALSE ADVERTISING UNDER THE LANHAM ACT

Over time, cases such as *Ely-Norris* prompted criticism from some commentators that the common law approach to false advertising claims (even with a single source exception) was indeed too grudging. *See* RESTATEMENT (THIRD) OF UNFAIR COMPETITION § 2 cmt. b (noting critical commentary); EDMUND W. KITCH & HARVEY S. PERLMAN, INTELLECTUAL PROPERTY AND UNFAIR COMPETITION 69-70 (5th ed. 1998) (same). The movement to discard an actual harm standard in favor of a "likelihood of injury" standard had gained steam by 1946 when Congress enacted the Lanham Act. As discussed in earlier chapters of this casebook, the Lanham Act for the most part deals with trademarks, for example, by creating a more expansive federal registration system for marks used in interstate commerce. In crafting Lanham Act § 43(a), however, Congress ventured beyond the federal trademark registration scheme and (filling a gap left by *Erie R.R. Co. v. Tompkins*) created a federal *statutory* law of unfair competition.[9] As originally enacted in 1946, § 43(a) read as follows:

> Any person who shall affix, apply, or annex, or use in connection with any goods or services, or any container or containers for goods, a false designation of origin, or any false description or representation, including words or other symbols tending falsely to describe or represent the same, and shall cause such goods or services to enter into commerce, and any person who shall with knowledge of the falsity of such designation of origin or description or representation cause or procure the same to be transported or used in commerce or deliver the same to any carrier to be transported or used, shall be liable in a civil action by any person doing business in the locality falsely indicated as that of origin or the region in which said locality is situated, or by any person who believes that he is or is likely to be damaged by the use of such false description or representation.

On one reading, this language seems broad enough to cover trademark infringement, which could be viewed as a sort of "false designation of origin" or as involving the use of "words of other symbols tending falsely to . . . represent" goods or services. This reading may not be the only plausible one, however. *See* 5 J. THOMAS MCCARTHY, MCCARTHY ON TRADEMARKS AND UNFAIR COMPETITION, § 27:14, at 27-28 (4th ed. 2009) (stating that initially the term "false description or representation" was understood to refer only to false advertising, and "false designation of origin" to refer only to false advertising of geographic origin). Nevertheless, as we have seen in earlier

9. Whether the "original intent" behind § 43(a) was to create a general federal law of unfair competition, however, is dubious. According to Professor McCarthy, "[a]t the time the Lanham Act was enacted, its supporters apparently viewed § 43(a) as a minor, but useful section, which would ease the restrictive requirements of proof in the common law false advertising cases." 5 J. THOMAS MCCARTHY, MCCARTHY ON TRADEMARKS AND UNFAIR COMPETITION § 27:7, at 27-14 (4th ed. 2009) (citing DAPHNE ROBERT, THE NEW TRADEMARK MANUAL 183-86 (1947)). Some early promoters of the Lanham Act viewed Lanham Act § 44, 15 U.S.C. § 1126, as providing a firmer basis for a general federal law of unfair competition. *See id.* (citing Edward S. Rogers, *Introduction, in* ROBERT, *supra*, at xv-xx, and ROBERT, *supra* at 170-77, 178-80); Walter J. Derenberg, *Federal Unfair Competition Law at the End of the First decade of the Lanham Act: Prologue or Epilogue?*, 32 N.Y.U. L. REV. 1029, 1030-31 (1957). In relevant part, § 44(h) extends to qualifying foreign nationals "effective protection against unfair competition," and § 44(i) states that "[c]itizens or residents of the United States shall have the same benefits. . . ." As discussed in section H *infra*, however, courts have interpreted §§ 44(h) and (i) very narrowly, leaving § 43(a) to play the more important role in creating a federal law of unfair competition — albeit one limited to the type of conduct specified therein.

chapters, for many years now courts have interpreted § 43(a) as providing a federal statutory cause of action for the infringement of even unregistered, common-law trademarks, where the infringement affects interstate commerce. *See supra* Chapters 3 and 4.

Of greater significance for present purposes, the language also is broad enough—and was probably intended—to cover some types of false advertising, assuming the requisite connection with interstate commerce, if the false advertising involves the use of a "false description or representation" in connection with goods or services. Moreover, the language referring to "any person who believes that he is *or is likely to be* damaged by the use of such false description or representation," might seem to overturn the common law actual harm requirement. One early decision nevertheless interpreted § 43(a) as not pertaining to false advertising at all, *see* Samson Crane Co. v. Union Nat'l Sales, Inc., 87 F. Supp. 218, 221-22 (D. Mass. 1950), *aff'd*, 180 F.2d 896 (1st Cir. 1950) (per curiam), while another suggested that it merely codified the common law as reflected in *Ely-Norris, see* Chamberlain v. Columbia Pictures Corp., 186 F.2d 923, 924-25 (9th Cir. 1951). In 1954, however, the Third Circuit held that § 43(a) addressed false advertising, and that the last clause did indeed repudiate the actual harm requirement. *See* L'Aiglon Apparel, Inc. v. Lana Lobell, Inc., 214 F.2d 649, 650-51 (3d Cir. 1954). Thereafter a consensus slowly emerged in favor of the Third Circuit's interpretation, and neither the First nor the Ninth Circuit today relies upon the two early cases to the contrary. Courts do not appear to have read the original version of § 43(a), however, as creating a federal cause of action for commercial disparagement (i.e., the defendant's making false representations about the *plaintiff's* goods or services). *See* Ethan Horwitz & Benjamin Levi, *Fifty Years of the Lanham Act: A Retrospective of Section 43(a)*, 7 FORDHAM INTELL. PROP. MEDIA & ENT. L.J. 59, 71 & n.66 (1996).[10]

In passing the Trademark Revision Act of 1988, Congress expanded § 43(a) (later relabeled as § 43(a)(1)) and divided it into two subparts. In relevant part, the statute now reads:

> (a) Civil action
>
> (1) Any person who, on or in connection with any goods or services, or any container for goods, uses in commerce any word, term, name, symbol, or device, or any combination thereof, or any false designation of origin, false or misleading description of fact, or false or misleading representation of fact, which—
>
> (A) is likely to cause confusion, or to cause mistake, or to deceive as to the affiliation, connection, or association of such person with another person, or as to the origin, sponsorship, or approval of his or her goods, services, or commercial activities by another person, or
>
> (B) in commercial advertising or promotion, misrepresents the nature, characteristics, qualities, or geographic origin of his or her or another person's goods, services, or commercial activities,
>
> shall be liable in a civil action by any person who believes that he or she is or is likely to be damaged by such act.

10. Note also that federal and state courts have concurrent subject matter jurisdiction over Lanham Act claims. Thus, it is permissible for the plaintiff to file a Lanham Act claim in state court if the plaintiff so wishes. In such a case, however, the defendant has the option of removing the case to federal court. As a practical matter, the vast majority of Lanham Act claims are litigated in federal court.

Under the current version, then, §43(a)(1)(A) deals with trademark infringement ("uses in commerce any word, term, name, symbol, or device . . . which . . . is likely to cause confusion"), as well as analogous claims for false designations of origin (*see* section F *infra*) and false endorsement (*see* Chapter 10 *infra*). Section 43(a)(1)(B) addresses false advertising. Further, by adding the words "his or her or another person's goods, services, or commercial activities," Congress not only expanded the statute to encompass false statements relating to "commercial activities," but also created a federal cause of action for commercial disparagement (insofar as the defendant's false statement relates to "another person's", i.e., the plaintiff's, goods, services, or commercial activities).

The following two cases discuss some of the elements plaintiffs must prove in order to prevail on a Lanham Act false advertising claim.

1. The Elements of a Lanham Act False Advertising Claim

Time Warner Cable, Inc. v. DIRECTV, Inc.
497 F.3d 144 (2d Cir. 2007)

STRAUB, Circuit Judge:

Defendant-Appellant DIRECTV, Inc. ("DIRECTV") appeals from the February 5, 2007 opinion and order of the United States District Court for the Southern District of New York . . . preliminarily enjoining it from disseminating, in any market in which Plaintiff-Appellee Time Warner Cable, Inc. ("TWC") provides cable service, certain television commercials and Internet advertisements found likely to violate the Lanham Act on literal falsity grounds. . . .

Factual Background

A. *The Parties*

TWC and DIRECTV are major players in the multichannel video service industry. TWC is the second-largest cable company in the United States, serving more than 13.4 million subscribers. Like all cable providers, TWC must operate through franchises let by local government entities; it is currently the franchisee in the greater part of New York City. DIRECTV is one of the country's largest satellite service providers, with more than 15.6 million customers nationwide. Because DIRECTV broadcasts directly via satellite, it is not subject to the same franchise limitations as cable companies. As a result, in the markets where TWC is the franchisee, DIRECTV and other satellite providers pose the greatest threat to its market share. The competition in these markets for new customers is extremely fierce, a fact to which the advertisements challenged in this case attest.

TWC offers both analog and digital television services to its customers. DIRECTV, on the other hand, delivers 100% of its programming digitally. Both companies, however, offer high-definition ("HD") service on a limited number of their respective channels. Transmitted at a higher resolution than analog or traditional digital programming, HD provides the home viewer with theater-like picture quality on a wider screen. . . .

There is no dispute, at least on the present record, that the HD programming provided by TWC and DIRECTV is equivalent in picture quality. In terms of non-HD programming, digital service generally yields better picture quality than analog service, because a digital signal is more resistant to interference. . . .

B. DIRECTV's "Source Matters" Campaign

In the fall of 2006, DIRECTV launched a multimedia advertising campaign based on the theme of "SOURCE MATTERS." The concept of the campaign was to educate consumers that to obtain HD-standard picture quality, it is not enough to buy an HD television set; consumers must also receive HD programming from the "source," i.e., the television service provider.

1. Jessica Simpson Commercial

As part of its new campaign, DIRECTV began running a television commercial in October 2006 featuring celebrity Jessica Simpson. In the commercial, Simpson, portraying her character of Daisy Duke from the movie *The Dukes of Hazzard*, says to some of her customers at the local diner:

> Simpson: Y'all ready to order?
> Hey, 253 straight days at the gym to get this body and you're not gonna watch me on DIRECTV HD?
> You're just not gonna get the best picture out of some fancy big screen TV without DIRECTV.
> It's broadcast in 1080i. I totally don't know what that means, but I want it.

The original version of the commercial concluded with a narrator saying, "For picture quality that beats cable, you've got to get DIRECTV."

In response to objections by TWC, and pursuant to agreements entered into by the parties, DIRECTV pulled the original version of the commercial and replaced it with a revised one ("Revised Simpson Commercial"), which began airing in early December 2006. The Revised Simpson Commercial is identical to the original, except that it ends with a different tag line: "For an HD picture that can't be beat, get DIRECTV."

2. William Shatner Commercial

DIRECTV debuted another commercial in October 2006, featuring actor William Shatner as Captain James T. Kirk, his character from the popular *Star Trek* television show and film series. The following conversation takes place on the Starship Enterprise:

> Mr. Chekov: Should we raise our shields, Captain?
> Captain Kirk: At ease, Mr. Chekov.

> Again with the shields. I wish he'd just relax and enjoy the amazing picture clarity of the DIRECTV HD we just hooked up.
> With what Starfleet just ponied up for this big screen TV, settling for cable would be illogical.
> Mr. Spock: [Clearing throat.]
> Captain Kirk: What, I can't use that line?

The original version ended with the announcer saying, "For picture quality that beats cable, you've got to get DIRECTV."

DIRECTV agreed to stop running the Shatner commercial in November 2006. In January 2007, DIRECTV released a revised version of the commercial ("Revised Shatner Commercial") with the revamped tag line, "For an HD picture that can't be beat, get DIRECTV."

3. Internet Advertisements

DIRECTV also waged its campaign in cyberspace, placing banner advertisements on various websites to promote the message that when it comes to picture quality, "source matters." The banner ads have the same basic structure. They open by showing an image that is so highly pixelated that it is impossible to discern what is being depicted. On top of this indistinct image is superimposed the slogan, "SOURCE MATTERS." After about a second, a vertical line splits the screen into two parts, one labeled "OTHER TV" and the other "DIRECTV." On the OTHER TV side of the line, the picture is extremely pixelated and distorted, like the opening image. By contrast, the picture on the DIRECTV side is exceptionally sharp and clear. The DIRECTV screen reveals that what we have been looking at all along is an image of New York Giants quarterback Eli Manning; in another ad, it is a picture of two women snorkeling in tropical waters. The advertisements then invite browsers to "FIND OUT WHY DIRECTV'S picture beats cable" and to "LEARN MORE" about a special offer. In the original design, users who clicked on the "LEARN MORE" icon were automatically directed to the HDTV section of DIRECTV's website.

In addition to the banner advertisements, DIRECTV created a demonstrative advertisement that it featured on its own website. Like the banner ads, the website demonstrative uses the split-screen technique to compare the picture quality of "DIRECTV" to that of "OTHER TV," which the ad later identifies as representing "basic cable," i.e., analog cable. The DIRECTV side of the screen depicts, in high resolution, an image of football player Kevin Dyson making a touchdown at the Super Bowl. The portion of the image on the OTHER TV side is noticeably pixelated and blurry. . . .

. . . TWC filed a motion for a preliminary injunction against the Revised Simpson Commercial, as well as the banner advertisements and website demonstrative (collectively, "Internet Advertisements"). . . . TWC claimed that each of these advertisements was literally false, obviating the need for extrinsic evidence of consumer confusion. TWC further argued that as DIRECTV's direct competitor, it was entitled to a presumption of irreparable injury. On January 4, 2007, after discovering that DIRECTV had started running the Revised Shatner Commercial, TWC filed supplemental papers requesting that this commercial also be preliminarily enjoined on literal falsity grounds. . . .

[The district court granted the preliminary injunction, and DIRECTV appealed.]

Discussion

A. *Likelihood of Success on the Merits*

1. Television Commercials

. . . Two different theories of recovery are available to a plaintiff who brings a false advertising action under § 43(a) of the Lanham Act. First, the plaintiff can demonstrate that the challenged advertisement is literally false, i.e., false on its face. *See* [Johnson & Johnson v. GAC Int'l, Inc. 862 F.2d 975, 977 (2d Cir. 1988)]. When an advertisement is shown to be literally or facially false, consumer deception is presumed, and "the court may grant relief without reference to the advertisement's [actual] impact on the buying public." [Coca-Cola Co. v. Tropicana Prods., Inc., 690 F.2d 312, 317 (2d Cir. 1982)]. "This is because plaintiffs alleging a literal falsehood are claiming that a statement, on its face, conflicts with reality, a claim that is best supported by comparing the statement itself with the reality it purports to describe." Schering Corp. v. Pfizer Inc., 189 F.3d 218, 229 (2d Cir. 1999).

Alternatively, a plaintiff can show that the advertisement, while not literally false, is nevertheless likely to mislead or confuse consumers. *See Coca-Cola Co.*, 690 F.2d at 317. "[P]laintiffs alleging an implied falsehood are claiming that a statement, whatever its literal truth, has left an impression on the listener [or viewer] that conflicts with reality"—a claim that "invites a comparison of the impression, rather than the statement, with the truth." *Schering Corp.*, 189 F.3d at 229. Therefore, whereas "plaintiffs seeking to establish a literal falsehood must generally show the substance of what is conveyed, . . . a district court must rely on extrinsic evidence [of consumer deception or confusion] to support a finding of an implicitly false message." *Id.* (internal quotation marks omitted).[3]

Here, TWC chose to pursue only the first path of literal falsity, and the District Court granted the preliminary injunction against the television commercials on that basis. In this appeal, DIRECTV does not dispute that it would be a misrepresentation to claim that the picture quality of DIRECTV HD is superior to that of cable HD. Rather, it argues that neither commercial explicitly makes such a claim and therefore cannot be literally false.

a. Revised Simpson Commercial

DIRECTV's argument is easily dismissed with respect to the Revised Simpson Commercial. In the critical lines, Simpson tells audiences, "You're just not gonna get the best picture out of some fancy big screen TV without DIRECTV. It's broadcast in 1080i." These statements make the explicit assertion that it is impossible to obtain "the best picture"—i.e., a "1080i"-resolution picture—from any source other than DIRECTV. This claim is flatly untrue; the uncontroverted factual record establishes that viewers can, in fact, get the same "best picture" by ordering HD programming

3. Under either theory, the plaintiff must also demonstrate that the false or misleading representation involved an inherent or material quality of the product. *See* S.C. Johnson & Son, Inc., 241 F.3d at 238; Nat'l Basketball Ass'n v. Motorola, Inc., 105 F.3d 841, 855 (2d Cir. 1997). TWC has met this requirement, as it is undisputed that picture quality is an inherent and material characteristic of multichannel video service.

from their cable service provider. We therefore affirm the District Court's determination that the Revised Simpson Commercial's contention "that a viewer cannot 'get the best picture' without DIRECTV is . . . likely to be proven literally false." *Time Warner Cable, Inc.*, 475 F. Supp. 2d at 306.

b. Revised Shatner Commercial

The issue of whether the Revised Shatner Commercial is likely to be proven literally false requires more analysis. When interpreting the controversial statement, "With what Starfleet just ponied up for this big screen TV, settling for cable would be illogical," the District Court looked not only at that particular text, but also at the surrounding context. In light of Shatner's opening comment extolling the "amazing picture quality of[ ] DIRECTV HD" and the announcer's closing remark highlighting the unbeatable "HD picture" provided by DIRECTV, the District Court found that the line in the middle — "settling for cable would be illogical" — clearly referred to cable's HD picture quality. Since it would only be "illogical" to "settle" for cable's HD picture if it was materially inferior to DIRECTV's HD picture, the District Court concluded that TWC was likely to establish that the statement was literally false.

DIRECTV argues that the District Court's ruling was clearly erroneous because the actual statement at issue, "settling for cable would be illogical," does not explicitly compare the picture quality of DIRECTV HD with that of cable HD, and indeed, does not mention HD at all. In DIRECTV's view, the District Court based its determination of literal falsity not on the words actually used, but on what it subjectively perceived to be the general message conveyed by the commercial as a whole. DIRECTV contends that this was plainly improper under this Court's decision in American Home Products Corp. v. Johnson & Johnson, 577 F.2d 160 (2d Cir. 1978).

TWC, on the other hand, maintains that the District Court properly took context into account in interpreting the commercial, as directed by this Court in Avis Rent A Car System, Inc. v. Hertz Corp., 782 F.2d 381 (2d Cir. 1986). . . .

These two cases, read together, compel us to now formally adopt what is known in other circuits as the "false by necessary implication" doctrine. Under this doctrine, a district court evaluating whether an advertisement is literally false "must analyze the message conveyed in full context," [Castrol v. Pennzoil Co., 987 F.2d 939, 946 (3d Cir. 1993)], i.e., it "must consider the advertisement in its entirety and not . . . engage in disputatious dissection," *Avis Rent A Car*, 782 F.2d at 385 (internal quotation marks omitted). If the words or images, considered in context, necessarily imply a false message, the advertisement is literally false and no extrinsic evidence of consumer confusion is required. *See* Novartis Consumer Health, Inc. v. Johnson & Johnson-Merck Pharm. Co., 290 F.3d 578, 586-87 (3d Cir. 2002) ("A 'literally false' message may be either explicit or 'conveyed by necessary implication when, considering the advertisement in its entirety, the audience would recognize the claim as readily as if it had been explicitly stated.'" (quoting Clorox Co. P.R. v. Procter & Gamble Commercial Co., 228 F.3d 24, 35 (1st Cir. 2000)). However, "only an unambiguous message can be literally false." *Id.* at 587. Therefore, if the language or graphic is susceptible to more than one reasonable interpretation, the advertisement cannot be literally false. *See Scotts Co.*, 315 F.3d at 275 (stating that a literal falsity argument fails if the statement or image "can reasonably be understood as conveying different messages"); *Clorox Co. Puerto Rico*, 228 F.3d at 35 ("[A] factfinder might conclude that the message conveyed by a particular advertisement remains so balanced between several plausible meanings that the claim made by the advertisement is too uncertain to serve as the basis of a literal falsity claim. . . ."). There may still be a "basis for a claim that the advertisement is misleading," *Clorox Co. Puerto Rico*, 228 F.3d at 35, but to resolve such a claim, the district court must look to consumer data to determine what "the person to whom the advertisement is addressed find[s] to be the message," *Am. Home Prods.*, 577 F.2d at 166 (citation omitted). In short, where the advertisement does not unambiguously make a claim, "the court's reaction is at best not determinative and at worst irrelevant." *Id.*

Here, the District Court found that Shatner's assertion that "settling for cable would be illogical," considered in light of the advertisement as a whole, unambiguously made the false claim that cable's HD picture quality is inferior to that of DIRECTV's. We cannot say that this finding was clearly erroneous, especially given that in the immediately preceding line, Shatner praises the "amazing picture clarity of DIRECTV HD." We accordingly affirm the District Court's conclusion that TWC established a likelihood of success on its claim that the Revised Shatner Commercial is literally false.

2. Internet Advertisements

We have made clear that a district court must examine not only the words, but also the "visual images . . . to assess whether [the advertisement] is literally false." *S.C. Johnson & Son, Inc.*, 241 F.3d at 238. It is uncontroverted that the images used in the Internet Advertisements to represent cable are inaccurate depictions of the picture quality provided by cable's digital or analog service. The Internet Advertisements are therefore explicitly and literally false.

DIRECTV does not contest this point. Rather, it asserts that the images are so grossly distorted and exaggerated that no reasonable buyer would take them to be accurate depictions "of how a consumer's television picture would look when connected to cable." Consequently, DIRECTV argues, the images are obviously just puffery, which cannot form the basis of a Lanham Act violation. Notably, TWC agrees that no Lanham Act action would lie against an advertisement that was so exaggerated that no reasonable consumer would rely on it in making his or her purchasing decisions. TWC contends, however, that DIRECTV's own evidence—which indicates that consumers are highly confused about HD technology—shows that the Internet Advertisements pose a real danger of consumer reliance.

This Court has had little occasion to explore the concept of puffery in the false advertising context. In Lipton v. Nature Co., 71 F.3d 464 (2d Cir. 1995), the one case where we discussed the subject in some depth, we characterized puffery as "[s]ubjective claims about products, which cannot be proven either true or false." *Id.* at 474 (internal quotation marks omitted). We also cited to the Third Circuit's description of puffery in *Pennzoil Co.*: "Puffery is an exaggeration or overstatement expressed in broad, vague, and commendatory language. 'Such sales talk, or puffing, as it is commonly called, is considered to be offered and understood as an expression of the seller's opinion only, which is to be discounted as such by the buyer. . . . The 'puffing' rule amounts to a seller's privilege to lie his head off, so long as he says nothing specific.'" *Pennzoil Co.*, 987 F.2d at 945 (quoting W. Page Keeton et al., Prosser and Keeton on the Law of Torts § 109, at 756-57 (5th ed. 1984)). Applying this definition, we concluded that the defendant's contention that he had conducted "thorough" research was just puffery, which was not actionable under the Lanham Act. *See Lipton*, 71 F.3d at 474.

Lipton's and *Pennzoil Co.*'s definition of puffery does not translate well into the world of images. Unlike words, images cannot be vague or broad. *Cf. Pennzoil Co.*, 987 F.2d at 945. To the contrary, visual depictions of a product are generally "specific and measurable," *id.* at 946, and can therefore "be proven either true or false," *Lipton*, 71 F.3d at 474 (internal quotation marks omitted), as this case demonstrates. Yet, if a visual representation is so grossly exaggerated that no reasonable buyer would take it at face value, there is no danger of consumer deception and hence, no basis for a false advertising claim. *Cf.* Johnson & Johnson–Merck Consumer Pharm. Co. v. Smithkline Beecham Corp., 960 F.3d 294, 298 (2d Cir. 1992) ("[T]he injuries redressed in false advertising cases are the result of public deception. Thus, where the plaintiff cannot demonstrate that a statistically significant part of the commercial audience holds the false belief allegedly communicated by the challenged advertisement, the plaintiff cannot establish that it suffered any injury as a result of the advertisement's message. Without injury there can be no claim, regardless of commercial context, prior advertising history, or audience sophistication."); *see also* U.S. Healthcare, Inc. v. Blue Cross of Greater Philadelphia, 898 F.2d 914, 922 (3d Cir. 1990) ("Mere puffery, advertising that is not deceptive for no one would rely on its exaggerated claims, is not actionable under §43(a)." (internal quotation marks omitted)).

Other circuits have recognized that puffery can come in at least two different forms. *See, e.g.*, Pizza Hut, Inc. v. Papa John's Int'l, Inc., 227 F.3d 489, 497 (5th Cir. 2000). The first form we identified in Lipton — "a general claim of superiority over comparable products that is so vague that it can be understood as nothing more than a mere expression of opinion." *Id.*; *see Lipton*, 71 F.3d at 474. The second form of puffery, which we did not address in *Lipton*, is "an exaggerated, blustering, and boasting statement upon which no reasonable buyer would be justified in relying." *Pizza Hut, Inc.*, 227 F.3d at 497; *accord* United Indus. Corp. v. Clorox Co., 140 F.3d 1175, 1180 (8th Cir. 1998) ("Puffery is exaggerated advertising, blustering, and boasting upon which no reasonable buyer would rely and is not actionable under §43(a)." (internal quotation marks omitted)). We believe that this second conception of puffery is a better fit where, as here, the "statement" at issue is expressed not in words, but through images. . . .

Our review of the record persuades us that the District Court clearly erred in rejecting DIRECTV's puffery defense. The "OTHER TV" images in the Internet Advertisements are — to borrow the words of Ronald Boyer, TWC's Senior Network Engineer — "unwatchably blurry, distorted, and pixelated, and . . . nothing like the images a customer would ordinarily see using Time Warner Cable's cable service." . . .

As Boyer's declaration establishes, the Internet Advertisements' depictions of cable are not just inaccurate; they are not even remotely realistic. It is difficult to imagine that any consumer, whatever the level of sophistication, would actually be fooled by the Internet Advertisements into thinking that cable's picture quality is so poor that the image is "nearly entirely obscure[d]." As DIRECTV states in its brief, "even a person not acquainted with cable would realize TWC could not realistically supply an unwatchably blurry image and survive in the marketplace."

In reaching the contrary conclusion, the District Court relied heavily on the declaration of Jon Gieselman, DIRECTV's Senior Vice-President of Advertising and Public Relations. However, Gieselman merely stated that the common misconception amongst first-time purchasers of HD televisions is that "they will automatically get exceptional clarity on every channel" just by plugging their new television sets into the wall. Nothing in Gieselman's declaration indicates that consumers mistakenly believe that hooking up their HD televisions to an analog cable feed will produce an unwatchably distorted picture. More importantly, the Internet Advertisements do not claim that the "OTHER TV" is an HD television set, or that the corresponding images represent what happens when an HD television is connected to basic cable. The Internet Advertisements simply purport to compare the picture quality of DIRECTV's programming to that of basic cable programming, and as discussed above, the comparison is so obviously hyperbolic that "no reasonable buyer would be justified in relying" on it in navigating the marketplace. *Pizza Hut, Inc.*, 227 F.3d at 497.

For these reasons, we conclude that the District Court exceeded its permissible discretion in preliminarily enjoining DIRECTV from disseminating the Internet Advertisements.

[The remainder of the opinion addresses the elements of likelihood of injury and causation. We present this portion of the case in section C.2 *infra.*]

Pizza Hut, Inc. v. Papa John's Int'l, Inc.
227 F.3d 489 (5th Cir. 2000)

E. Grady Jolly, Circuit Judge:

This appeal presents a false advertising claim under section 43(a) of the Lanham Act, resulting in a jury verdict for the plaintiff, Pizza Hut. At the center of this appeal is Papa John's four word slogan "Better Ingredients. Better Pizza."

The appellant, Papa John's International Inc. ("Papa John's"), argues that the slogan "cannot and does not violate the Lanham Act" because it is "not a misrepresentation of fact." The appellee, Pizza Hut, Inc., argues that the slogan, when viewed in the context of Papa John's overall advertising campaign, conveys a false statement of fact actionable under section 43(a) of the Lanham Act. The district court, after evaluating the jury's responses to a series of special interrogatories and denying Papa John's motion for judgment as a matter of law, entered judgment for Pizza Hut stating:

> When the "Better Ingredients. Better Pizza." slogan is considered in light of the entirety of Papa John's post-May 1997 advertising which violated provisions of the Lanham Act and in the context in which it was juxtaposed with the false and misleading statements contained in Papa John's print and broadcast media advertising, the slogan itself became tainted to the extent that its continued use should be enjoined.

We conclude that (1) the slogan, standing alone, is not an objectifiable statement of fact upon which consumers would be justified in relying, and thus not actionable under section 43(a); and (2) while the slogan, when utilized in connection with some of the post-May 1997 comparative advertising—specifically, the sauce and dough campaigns—conveyed objectifiable and misleading facts, Pizza Hut has failed to adduce any evidence demonstrating that the facts conveyed by the slogan were material to the purchasing decisions of the consumers to which the slogan was directed. Thus, the district court erred in denying Papa John's motion for judgment as a matter of law. We therefore reverse the judgment of the district court denying Papa John's motion for judgment as a matter of law, vacate its final judgment, and remand the case to the district court for entry of judgment for Papa John's.

I

A

Pizza Hut is a wholly owned subsidiary of Tricon Global Restaurants. With over 7000 restaurants (both company and franchisee-owned), Pizza Hut is the largest pizza chain in the United States. In 1984, John Schnatter founded Papa John's Pizza in the back of his father's tavern. Papa John's has grown to over 2050 locations, making it the third largest pizza chain in the United States.

In May 1995, Papa John's adopted a new slogan: "Better Ingredients. Better Pizza." In 1996, Papa John's filed for a federal trademark registration for this slogan with the United States Patent & Trademark Office ("PTO"). Its application for registration was ultimately granted by the PTO. Since 1995, Papa John's has invested over $300 million building customer goodwill in its trademark "Better Ingredients. Better Pizza." The slogan has appeared on millions of signs, shirts, menus, pizza boxes, napkins and other items, and has regularly appeared as the "tag line" at the end of Papa John's radio and television ads, or with the company logo in printed advertising. . . .

. . . Papa John's ran a series of ads comparing specific ingredients used in its pizzas with those used by its "competitors." During the course of these ads, Papa John's touted the superiority of its sauce and its dough. During the sauce campaign, Papa John's asserted that its sauce was made from "fresh, vine-ripened tomatoes," which were canned through a process called "fresh pack," while its competitors — including Pizza Hut — make their sauce from remanufactured tomato paste. During the dough campaign, Papa John's stated that it used "clear filtered water" to make its pizza dough, while the "biggest chain" uses "whatever comes out of the tap." Additionally, Papa John's asserted that it gives its yeast "several days to work its magic," while "some folks" use "frozen dough or dough made the same day." At or near the close of each of these ads, Papa John's punctuated its ingredient comparisons with the slogan "Better Ingredients. Better Pizza."

Pizza Hut does not appear to contest the truthfulness of the underlying factual assertions made by Papa John's in the course of these ads. Pizza Hut argues, however, that its own independent taste tests and other "scientific evidence" establishes that filtered water makes no difference in pizza dough, that there is no "taste" difference between Papa John's "fresh-pack" sauce and Pizza Hut's "remanufactured" sauce, and that fresh dough is not superior to frozen dough. In response to Pizza Hut's "scientific evidence," Papa John's asserts that "each of these 'claims' involves a matter of common sense choice (fresh versus frozen, canned vegetables and fruit versus remanufactured paste, and filtered versus unfiltered water) about which individual consumers can and do form preferences every day without 'scientific' or 'expert' assistance."

In November 1997, Pizza Hut filed a complaint regarding Papa John's "Better Ingredients. Better Pizza." advertising campaign with the National Advertising Division of the Better Business Bureau, an industry self-regulatory body. This complaint, however, did not produce satisfactory results for Pizza Hut.

B

On August 12, 1998, Pizza Hut filed a civil action in the United States District Court for the Northern District of Texas charging Papa John's with false advertising in violation of Section 43(a)(1)(B) of the Lanham Act. . . . Papa John's asserted a counterclaim, charging Pizza Hut with engaging in false advertising [based on a Pizza Hut ad campaign touting the "better taste" of Pizza Hut's pizza and daring anyone to find a "better pizza"]. . . .

The trial began on October 26, 1999, and continued for over three weeks. At the close of Pizza Hut's case, and at the close of all evidence, Papa John's moved for a judgment as a matter of law. The motions were denied each time. The district court, without objection, submitted the liability issue to the jury through special interrogatories. The special issues submitted to the jury related to (1) the slogan and (2) over Papa John's objection, certain classes of groups of advertisements referred to as "sauce claims," "dough claims," "taste test claims," and "ingredients claims."

On November 17, 1999, the jury returned its responses to the special issues finding that Papa John's slogan, and its "sauce claims" and "dough claims" were false or misleading and deceptive or likely to deceive consumers. The jury also determined that Papa John's "taste test" ads were not deceptive or likely to deceive consumers, and that Papa John's "ingredients claims" were not false or misleading. . . .

On January 3, 2000, the trial court, based upon the jury's verdict and the evidence presented by the parties in support of injunctive relief and on the issue of damages, entered a Final Judgment and issued a Memorandum Opinion and Order. The court concluded that the "Better Ingredients. Better Pizza." slogan was "consistent with the legal definition of non-actionable puffery" from its introduction in 1995 until May 1997. However, the slogan "became tainted . . . in light of the entirety of Papa John's post-May 1997 advertising." Based on this conclusion, the magistrate judge permanently enjoined Papa John's from "using any slogan in the future that constitutes a recognizable variation of the phrase 'Better Ingredients. Better Pizza.' or which uses the adjective 'Better' to modify the terms 'ingredients' and/or 'pizza'." . . . The court also awarded Pizza Hut $467,619.75 in damages for having to run corrective ads. . . .

II

***

The law governing false advertising claims under section 43(a) of the Lanham Act is well settled. In order to obtain monetary damages or equitable relief in the form of an injunction, "a plaintiff must demonstrate that the commercial advertisement or promotion is either literally false, or that [if the advertisement is not literally false,] it is likely to mislead and confuse consumers." . . .

Essential to any claim under section 43(a) of the Lanham Act is a determination of whether the challenged statement is one of fact — actionable under section 43(a) — or one of general opinion-not actionable under section 43(a). Bald assertions of superiority or general statements of opinion cannot form the basis of Lanham Act liability. Rather the statements at issue must be a "specific and measurable claim, capable of being proved false or of being reasonably interpreted as a statement of objective fact." Coastal Abstract Serv., Inc. v. First Am. Title Ins. Co., 173 F.3d 725, 731 (9th Cir. 1999); *see also American Council*, 185 F.3d at 614 (stating that "a Lanham Act claim must be based upon a statement of fact, not of opinion"). As noted by our court in *Presidio*:

"[A] statement of fact is one that (1) admits of being adjudged true or false in a way that (2) admits of empirical verification." *Presidio*, 784 F.2d at 679; *see also* Southland Sod Farms v. Stover Seed Co., 108 F.3d 1134, 1145 (9th Cir. 1997) (stating that in order to constitute a statement of fact, a statement must make "a specific and measurable advertisement claim of product superiority").

[The court goes on to define "puffery" along the lines discussed above in *Time-Warner*, i.e., as "(1) an exaggerated, blustering, and boasting statement upon which no reasonable buyer would be justified in relying; or (2) a general claim of superiority over comparable products that is so vague that it can be understood as nothing more than a mere expression of opinion."]

With respect to materiality, when the statements of fact at issue are shown to be literally false, the plaintiff need not introduce evidence on the issue of the impact the statements had on consumers. *See* Castrol, Inc. v. Quaker State Corp., 977 F.2d 57, 62 (2d Cir. 1992); Avila v. Rubin, 84 F.3d 222, 227 (7th Cir. 1996). In such a circumstance, the court will assume that the statements actually misled consumers. *See American Council*, 185 F.3d at 614; Johnson & Johnson, Inc. v. GAC Int'l, Inc., 862 F.2d 975, 977 (2d Cir. 1988); U-Haul Int'l, Inc. v. Jartran, Inc., 793 F.2d 1034, 1040 (9th Cir. 1986). On the other hand, if the statements at issue are either ambiguous or true but misleading, the plaintiff must present evidence of actual deception. *See American Council*, 185 F.3d at 616. The plaintiff may not rely on the judge or the jury to determine, "based solely upon his or her own intuitive reaction, whether the advertisement is deceptive." *Smithkline*, 960 F.2d at 297. Instead, proof of actual deception requires proof that "consumers were actually deceived by the defendant's ambiguous or true-but-misleading statements." *American Council*, 185 F.3d at 616; *see also* Avis Rent A Car Sys., Inc. v. Hertz Corp., 782 F.2d 381, 386 (2d Cir. 1986) (stating that the plaintiff's claim fails due to its failure to introduce evidence establishing that the public was actually deceived by the statements at issue).

The type of evidence needed to prove materiality also varies depending on what type of recovery the plaintiff seeks. Plaintiffs looking to recover monetary damages for false or misleading advertising that is not literally false must prove actual deception. *See* Balance Dynamics Corp. v. Schmitt Ind., 204 F.3d 683, 690 (6th Cir. 2000); *Resource Developers*, 926 F.2d at 139. Plaintiffs attempting to prove actual deception have to produce evidence of actual consumer reaction to the challenged advertising or surveys showing that a substantial number of consumers were actually misled by the advertisements. *See, e.g.*, PPX Enters., Inc. v. Audiofidelity Enters., *Inc.*, 818 F.2d 266, 271 (2d Cir. 1987) ("Actual consumer confusion often is demonstrated through the use of direct evidence, e.g., testimony from members of the buying public, as well as through circumstantial evidence, e.g., consumer surveys or consumer reaction tests.").

Plaintiffs seeking injunctive relief must prove that defendant's representations "have a tendency to deceive consumers." *Balance Dynamics*, 204 F.3d 690. Although this standard requires less proof than actual deception, plaintiffs must still produce evidence that the advertisement tends to deceive consumers. *See* Coca-Cola Co. v. Tropicana Prod., Inc., 690 F.2d 312, 317 (2d Cir. 1982) (noting that when seeking a preliminary injunction barring an advertisement that is implicitly false, "its tendency to violate the Lanham Act by misleading, confusing or deceiving should be tested by public reaction"). To prove a tendency to deceive, plaintiffs need to show that at least some consumers were confused by the advertisements. *See, e.g., American Council*, 185 F.3d at 618 ("Although plaintiff need not present consumer surveys or testimony demonstrating actual deception, it must present evidence of some sort demonstrating that consumers were misled.")

IV

We turn now to consider the case before us. Reduced to its essence, the question is whether the evidence, viewed in the most favorable light to Pizza Hut, established that Papa John's slogan "Better Ingredients. Better Pizza." Is misleading and violative of section 43(a) of the Lanham Act. In making this determination, we will first consider the slogan "Better Ingredients. Better Pizza." Standing alone to determine if it is a statement of fact capable of deceiving a substantial segment of the consuming public to which it was directed. Second, we will determine whether the evidence supports the district court's conclusion that after May 1997, the slogan was tainted, and therefore actionable, as a result of its use in a series of ads comparing specific ingredients used by Papa John's with the ingredients used by its "competitors."

A

The jury concluded that the slogan itself was a "false or misleading" statement of fact, and the district court enjoined its further use. Papa John's argues, however, that this statement "quite simply is not a statement of fact, [but] rather, a statement of belief or opinion, and an argumentative one at that." Papa John's asserts that because "a statement of fact is either true or false, it is susceptible to being proved or disproved. A statement of opinion or belief, on the other hand, conveys the speaker's state of mind, and even though it may be used to attempt to persuade the listener, it is a subjective communication that may be accepted or rejected, but not proven true or false." Papa John's contends that its slogan "Better Ingredients. Better Pizza." falls into the latter category, and because the phrases "better ingredients" and "better pizza" are not subject to quantifiable measures, the slogan is non-actionable puffery.

We will therefore consider whether the slogan standing alone constitutes a statement of fact under the Lanham Act. Bisecting the slogan "Better Ingredients. Better Pizza.," it is clear that the assertion by Papa John's that it makes a "Better Pizza." Is a general statement of opinion regarding the superiority of its product over all others. This simple statement, "Better Pizza.," epitomizes the exaggerated advertising, blustering, and boasting by a manufacturer upon which no consumer would reasonably rely. *See, e.g., In re Boston Beer Co.*, 198 F.3d 1370, 1372 (Fed. Cir. 1999) (stating that the phrase "The Best Beer in America" was "trade puffery" and that such a general claim of superiority "should be freely available to all competitors in any given field to refer to their products or services"); Atari Corp. v. 3D0 Co., 1994 WL 723601, *2 (N.D. Cal. 1994) (stating that a manufacturer's slogan that its product was "the most advanced home gaming system in the universe" was non-actionable puffery); Nikkal Indus., Ltd. v. Salton, Inc., 735 F. Supp. 1227, 1234 n.3 (S.D.N.Y. 1990) (stating that a manufacturers claim that its ice cream maker was "better" than competition ice cream makers is non-actionable puffery). Consequently, it appears indisputable that Papa John's assertion "Better Pizza." Is non-actionable puffery.[8]

8. It should be noted that Pizza Hut uses the slogan "The Best Pizza Under One Roof." Similarly, other nationwide pizza chains employ slogans touting their pizza as the "best": (1) Domino's Pizza uses the slogan "Nobody Delivers Better."; (2) Danato's uses the slogan "Best Pizza on the Block."; (3) Mr. Gatti's uses the slogan "Best Pizza in Town: Honest!"; and (4) Pizza Inn uses the slogans "Best Pizza Ever." and "The Best Tasting Pizza."

Moving next to consider separately the phrase "Better Ingredients.," the same conclusion holds true. Like "Better Pizza.," it is typical puffery. The word "better," when used in this context is unquantifiable. What makes one food ingredient "better" than another comparable ingredient, without further description, is wholly a matter of individual taste or preference not subject to scientific quantification. Indeed, it is difficult to think of any product, or any component of any product, to which the term "better," without more, is quantifiable. . . .

Finally, turning to the combination of the two non-actionable phrases as the slogan "Better Ingredients. Better Pizza.," we fail to see how the mere joining of these two statements of opinion could create an actionable statement of fact. . . . Consequently, the slogan as a whole is a statement of non-actionable opinion. Thus, there is no legally sufficient basis to support the jury's finding that the slogan standing alone is a "false or misleading" statement of fact.

B

We next will consider whether the use of the slogan "Better Ingredients. Better Pizza." in connection with a series of comparative ads found by the jury to be misleading—specifically, ads comparing Papa John's sauce and dough with the sauce and dough of its competitors—"tainted" the statement of opinion and made it misleading under section 43(a) of the Lanham Act. Before reaching the ultimate question of whether the slogan is actionable under the Lanham Act, we will first examine the sufficiency of the evidence supporting the jury's conclusion that the comparison ads were misleading.

(1)

[T]he district court, while apparently recognizing that the slogan "Better Ingredients. Better Pizza." standing alone is non-actionable puffery under the Lanham Act, concluded that after May 1997, the slogan was transformed as a result of its use in connection with a series of ads that the jury found misleading. These ads had compared specific ingredients used by Papa John's with the ingredients used by its competitors. In essence, the district court held that the comparison ads in which the slogan appeared as the tag line gave objective, quantifiable, and fact-specific meaning to the slogan. Consequently, the court concluded that the slogan was misleading and actionable under section 43(a) of the Lanham Act and enjoined its further use. . . .

Turning first to the sauce ads, the evidence establishes that despite the differences in the methods used to produce their competing sauces: (1) the primary ingredient in both Pizza Hut and Papa John's sauce is vine-ripened tomatoes; (2) at the point that the competing sauces are placed on the pizza, just prior to putting the pies into the oven for cooking, the consistency and water content of the sauces are essentially identical; and (3) as noted by the district court, at no time "prior to the close of the liability phase of trial was any credible evidence presented [by Papa John's] to demonstrate the existence of demonstrable differences" in the competing sauces. Consequently, the district court was correct in concluding that: "Without any scientific support or properly conducted taste preference test, by the written and/or oral negative connotations conveyed that pizza made from tomato paste concentrate is inferior to the 'fresh pack' method used by Papa John's, its sauce advertisements conveyed an impression which is misleading. . . ." Turning our focus to the dough ads, while the evidence clearly established that Papa John's and Pizza Hut employ different methods in making their pizza dough, again, the evidence established that there is no quantifiable difference between pizza dough produced through the "cold or slow-fermentation method" (used by Papa John's), or the "frozen dough method" (used by Pizza Hut).[10] Further, although there is some evidence indicating that the texture of the dough used by Papa John's and Pizza Hut is slightly different, this difference is not related to the manufacturing process used to produce the dough. Instead, it is due to a difference in the wheat used to make the dough. Finally, with respect to the differences in the pizza dough resulting from the use of filtered water as opposed to tap water, the evidence was sufficient for the jury to conclude that there is no quantifiable difference between dough produced with tap water, as opposed to dough produced with filtered water.

We should note again that Pizza Hut does not contest the truthfulness of the underlying factual assertions made by Papa John's in the course of the sauce and dough ads. Pizza Hut concedes that it uses "remanufactured" tomato sauce to make its pizza sauce, while Papa John's uses "fresh-pack." Further, in regard to the dough, Pizza Hut concedes the truth of the assertion that it uses tap water in making its pizza dough, which is often frozen, while Papa John's uses filtered water to make its dough, which is fresh — never frozen. Consequently, because Pizza Hut does not contest the factual basis of Papa John's factual assertions, such assertions cannot be found to be factually false, but only impliedly false or misleading.

Thus, we conclude by saying that although the ads were true about the ingredients Papa John's used, it is clear that there was sufficient evidence in the record to support the jury's conclusion that Papa John's sauce and dough ads were misleading — but not false — in their suggestion that Papa John's ingredients were superior.

(3)

Thus, having concluded that the record supports a finding that the sauce and dough ads are misleading statements of fact, we must now determine whether the district court was correct in concluding that the use of the slogan "Better Ingredients. Better Pizza." in conjunction with these misleading ads gave quantifiable meaning to the slogan making a general statement of opinion misleading within the meaning of the Lanham Act.

In support of the district court's conclusion that the slogan was transformed, Pizza Hut argues that "in construing any advertising statement, the statement must be considered in the overall context in which it appears." . . . Pizza Hut argues, that because Papa John's gave consumers specific facts supporting its assertion that its sauce and dough are "better" — specific facts that the evidence, when viewed in the light most favorable to the verdict, are irrelevant in making a better pizza — Papa John's

10. The testimony of Pizza Hut's expert, Dr. Faubion, established that although consumers stated a preference for fresh dough rather than frozen dough, when taste tests were conducted, respondents were unable to distinguish between pizza made on fresh as opposed to frozen dough.

statement of opinion that it made a "Better Pizza" became misleading. In essence, Pizza Hut argues, that by using the slogan "Better Ingredients. Better Pizza." in combination with the ads comparing Papa John's sauce and dough with the sauce and dough of its competitions, Papa John's gave quantifiable meaning to the word "Better" rendering it actionable under section 43(a) of the Lanham Act.

We agree that the message communicated by the slogan "Better Ingredients. Better Pizza." is expanded and given additional meaning when it is used as the tag line in the misleading sauce and dough ads. The slogan, when used in combination with the comparison ads, gives consumers two fact-specific reasons why Papa John's ingredients are "better." Consequently, a reasonable consumer would understand the slogan, when considered in the context of the comparison ads, as conveying the following message: Papa John's uses "better ingredients," which produces a "better pizza" because Papa John's uses "fresh-pack" tomatoes, fresh dough, and filtered water. In short, Papa John's has given definition to the word "better." Thus, when the slogan is used in this context, it is no longer mere opinion, but rather takes on the characteristics of a statement of fact. When used in the context of the sauce and dough ads, the slogan is misleading for the same reasons we have earlier discussed in connection with the sauce and dough ads.[11]

(4)

Concluding that when the slogan was used as the tag line in the sauce and dough ads it became misleading, we must now determine whether reasonable consumers would have a tendency to rely on this misleading statement of fact in making their purchasing decisions. We conclude that Pizza Hut has failed to adduce evidence establishing that the misleading statement of fact conveyed by the ads and the slogan was material to the consumers to which the slogan was directed. Consequently, because such evidence of materiality is necessary to establish liability under the Lanham Act, the district court erred in denying Papa John's motion for judgment as a matter of law.

As previously discussed, none of the underlying facts supporting Papa John's claims of ingredient superiority made in connection with the slogan were literally false. Consequently, in order to satisfy its prima facie case, Pizza Hut was required to submit evidence establishing that the impliedly false or misleading statements were

11. The judgment of the district court enjoining the future use by Papa John's of the slogan "Better Ingredients. Better Pizza." did not simply bar Papa John's use of the slogan in future ads comparing its sauce and dough with that of its competitors. Rather, the injunction permanently enjoined any future use of the slogan "in association with the sale, promotion and/or identification of pizza products sold under the Papa John's name." Further, the injunction precluded Papa John's from using the "adjective 'better' to modify the terms 'ingredients' and/or 'pizza.' " While it is clear that the jury did not make any finding to support such a broad injunction, and Pizza Hut offered no survey evidence indicating how potential consumers viewed the slogan, the district court concluded that the evidence established that

> Papa John's deliberately and intentionally exploited its slogan as a centerpiece of its subsequent advertising campaign after May 1997 which falsely portrayed Papa John's tomato sauce and pizza dough as being superior to the sauce and dough components used in Pizza Hut's products. . . . [Thus,] the slogan itself became tainted to the extent that its continued use should be enjoined.

Our review of the record convinces us that there is simply no evidence to support the district court's conclusion that the slogan was irreparably tainted as a result of its use in the misleading comparison sauce and dough ads. At issue in this case were some 249 print ads and 29 television commercials. . . .

material to, that is, they had a tendency to influence the purchasing decisions of, the consumers to which they were directed.[12] *See American Council*, 185 F.3d at 614 (stating that "a plaintiff relying upon statements that are literally true yet misleading cannot obtain relief by arguing how consumers could react; it must show how consumers actually do react"); *Smithkline*, 960 F.2d at 298; Sandoz Pharm. Corp. v. Richardson-Vicks, Inc., 902 F.2d 222, 228-29 (3d Cir. 1990); *Avis*, 782 F.2d at 386; *see also* 4 J. THOMAS MCCARTHY, MCCARTHY ON TRADEMARKS AND UNFAIR COMPETITION, § 27:35 (4th ed. 1997) (stating that the "[p]laintiff must make some showing that the defendant's misrepresentation was 'material' in the sense that it would have some effect on consumers' purchasing decision"). We conclude that the evidence proffered by Pizza Hut fails to make an adequate showing.

In its appellate brief and during the course of oral argument, Pizza Hut directs our attention to three items of evidence in the record that it asserts establishes materiality to consumers. First, Pizza Hut points to the results of a survey conducted by an "independent expert" (Dr. DuPont) regarding the use of the slogan "Better Ingredients. Better Pizza." as written on Papa John's pizza box (the box survey). The results of the box survey, however, were excluded by the district court. Consequently, these survey results provide no basis for the jury's finding.

Second, Pizza Hut points to two additional surveys conducted by Dr. DuPont that attempted to measure consumer perception of Papa John's "taste test" ads. This survey evidence, however, fails to address Pizza Hut's claim of materiality with respect to the slogan. Moreover, the jury rejected Pizza Hut's claims of deception with regard to Papa John's "taste test" ads—the very ads at issue in these surveys.

Finally, Pizza Hut attempts to rely on Papa John's own tracking studies and on the alleged subjective intent of Papa John's executives "to create a perception that Papa John's in fact uses better ingredients" to demonstrate materiality. Although Papa John's 1998 Awareness, Usage & Attitude Tracking Study showed that 48% of the respondents believe that "Papa John's has better ingredients than other national pizza chains," the study failed to indicate whether the conclusions resulted from the advertisements at issue, or from personal eating experiences, or from a combination of both. Consequently, the results of this study are not reliable or probative to test whether the slogan was material. Further, Pizza Hut provides no precedent, and we are aware of none, that stands for the proposition that the subjective intent of the defendant's corporate executives to convey a particular message is evidence of the fact that consumers in fact relied on the message to make their purchases. Thus, this evidence does not address the ultimate issue of materiality.

In short, Pizza Hut has failed to offer probative evidence on whether the misleading facts conveyed by Papa John's through its slogan were material to consumers: that is to say, there is no evidence demonstrating that the slogan had the tendency to deceive consumers so as to affect their purchasing decisions. Thus, the district court erred in denying Papa John's motion for judgment as a matter of law. . . .

In sum, we hold that the slogan "Better Ingredients. Better Pizza." standing alone is not an objectifiable statement of fact upon which consumers would be justified

12. Since Pizza Hut sought only equitable relief and no monetary damages, it was required to offer evidence sufficient to establish that the claims made by Papa John's had the "tendency to deceive consumers," rather than evidence indicating that the claims made by Papa John's actually deceived consumers. *American Council*, 185 F.3d at 606; *see also Balance Dynamics*, 204 F.3d at 690 (emphasis added).

in relying. Thus, it does not constitute a false or misleading statement of fact actionable under section 43(a) of the Lanham Act.

Additionally, while the slogan, when appearing in the context of some of the post-May 1997 comparative advertising—specifically, the sauce and dough campaigns—was given objectifiable meaning and thus became misleading and actionable, Pizza Hut has failed to adduce sufficient evidence establishing that the misleading facts conveyed by the slogan were material to the consumers to which it was directed. Thus, Pizza Hut failed to produce evidence of a Lanham Act violation, and the district court erred in denying Papa John's motion for judgment as a matter of law.

Therefore, the judgment of the district court denying Papa John's motion for judgment as a matter of law is REVERSED; the final judgment of the district court is VACATED; and the case is REMANDED for entry of judgment for Papa John's. . . .

COMMENTS AND QUESTIONS

1. *Elements.* A complete listing of the elements of a Lanham Act claim under §43(a)(1)(B), as articulated and elaborated upon by the courts, would be as follows: (1) a false or misleading (2) description or representation of fact (3) regarding the nature, characteristics, qualities, or geographic origin (4) of the plaintiff's or defendant's goods, services, or commercial activities (5) in commercial advertising or promotion, which (6) either actually deceives or has a tendency to deceive a substantial segment of the intended audience, (7) is material, and (8) is used in interstate commerce, such that (9) the plaintiff has been or likely to be injured as a result. Except for the portion of element (6) that refers to "a substantial segment of the intended audience," a concept shared with the law of trademark infringement, and element (7) (materiality), all of these elements come directly from the language of the statute. In practical terms, then, the only difference between the elements of a Lanham Act false advertising claim and of a Lanham Act commercial disparagement claim relate to element (4): As mentioned above, in a false advertising case the plaintiff must prove that the statement concerns the defendant's own goods, services, or commercial activities, whereas in a commercial disparagement case the statement concerns the plaintiff's goods, services, or commercial activities. The fact that the elements are otherwise identical means that case law interpreting the elements in the context of a Lanham Act false advertising case should be equally valid precedent in the context of a Lanham Act commercial disparagement case, and vice versa. Our discussion in this section, however, will focus exclusively on false advertising; commercial disparagement is discussed in section F *infra.*

Recall that "intent to deceive" was an element of a common law false advertising claim. *See, e.g.*, Restatement of Torts §761 (1939). It is not one of the elements of a Lanham Act false advertising claim, although proof that the defendant intended to deceive may be relevant evidence in support of one of those elements, *see* comment 6 *infra.* In general, then, the Lanham Act appears to depart from the common law of false advertising by rendering false advertising a strict liability offense.[11] By making it more difficult for firms to evade liability for false advertising, does this change effect good public policy? Or does even commercial speech need some "breathing space"?

11. Printers and news media, however, are generally exempt from damages liability for innocently printing or publishing false advertising. *See* Lanham Act §32(2), 15 U.S.C. §1114(2).

Courts disagree on whether false advertising claims are subject to the general pleading requirements of Federal Rule of Civil Procedure 8(a)(2) (stating that a complaint must contain "a short and plain statement of the claim showing that the pleader is entitled to relief"), or the heightened pleading requirements of Rule 9(b) (stating that, "[i]n alleging fraud . . . a party must state with particularity the circumstances constituting fraud"). *Compare* Conditioned Ocular Enhancement, Inc. v. Bonaventura, 458 F. Supp. 2d 704, 709 (N.D. Ill. 2006) ("Claims that allege false representation or false advertising under the Lanham Act are subject to the heightened pleading requirements of" Rule 9(b)), *with* Advanstar Communications Inc. v. Dirt Motosports, Inc., No. 1:05-CV-1291, 2006 WL 2739700, at *4 (Sept. 25, 2006) (stating that "while it is arguable that a specific false advertising claim which includes all elements of a fraud claim would be subject to Rule 9(b)'s particularity requirement . . . there is no basis to require particularity of pleading in every claim of false advertising"). Does the choice between Rule 8(a) and Rule 9(b) matter so much under the Supreme Court's current interpretation Rule 8(a)? *See* Bell Atlantic Corp. v. Twombly, 550 U.S. 544, 555 (2007) (stating that, "[w]hile a complaint . . . does not need to detailed factual allegations . . . a plaintiff's obligation to provide the 'grounds' of his 'entitle[ment] to relief' requires more than labels and conclusions, and a formulaic recitation of the elements of a cause of action will not do. . . . Factual allegations must be enough to raise a right to relief above the speculative level"); *see also* Ashcroft v. Iqbal, 129 S. Ct. 1937, 1953-54 (2009) (confirming that *Twombly*'s interpretation of Rule 8(a) applies in non-antitrust cases).

2. *False or Misleading*. As *Time Warner* and *Pizza Hut* both discuss, there are three different ways in which a statement may be actionably false or misleading. First, it may be literally false (false on its face). In *Time Warner*, the court held that Jessica Simpson's statements "You're just not gonna get the best picture out of some fancy big screen TV without DIRECTV. It's broadcast in 1080i" were literally false, where "the uncontroverted factual record establishes that viewers can, in fact, get the same 'best picture' by ordering HD programming from their cable service providers." *See also* Surdyk's Liquor, Inc. v. MGM Liquor Stores, Inc., 83 F. Supp. 2d 1016, 1022 (D. Minn. 2000) (stating that the test for literal falsity is "(1) whether the challenged advertisement conveys an explicit factual message and (2) whether that explicit message is false"; that the message must be evaluated in the full context of the advertisement; and that the more suggestive the message is, the less likely there is to be literal falsity).

Second, a statement may be literally false by necessary implication. In *Time Warner*, the court appears to have held that William Shatner's statement that "settling for cable would be illogical" was literally false by necessary implication, because when "considered in light of the advertisement as a whole, [it] unambiguously made the false claim that cable's HD picture quality is inferior to that of DIRECTV's." The distinction between statements that are literally false and statements that are literally false by necessary implication is not always easy to discern, however. *See* Clorox Co. P.R. v. Procter & Gamble Commercial Co., 228 F.3d 24, 35 (1st Cir. 2000):

> A claim is conveyed by necessary implication when, considering the advertisement in its entirety, the audience would recognize the claim as readily as if it had been explicitly stated. For instance, a factfinder found that an advertisement that claimed a motor oil provided "longer engine life and better engine protection" without explicitly mentioning competitors nonetheless drew a comparison by necessary implication vis à vis those

competitors. *See* Castrol [Inc. v. Pennzoil Co., 987 F.2d 939, 941, 946 (3d Cir. 1992)]. This is not to say, however, that all messages implied by an advertisement will support a finding of literal falsity by a factfinder:

> The greater the degree to which a message relies upon the viewer or consumer to integrate its components and draw the apparent conclusion, however, the less likely it is that a finding of literal falsity will be supported. Commercial claims that are implicit, attenuated, or merely suggestive usually cannot fairly be characterized as literally false.

United Indus. Corp. [v. Clorox Co., 140 F.3d 1175, 1181 (8th Cir. 1998)]. Similarly, a factfinder might conclude that the message conveyed by a particular advertisement remains so balanced between several plausible meanings that the claim made by the advertisement is too uncertain to serve as the basis of a literal falsity claim, though even in that case it could still form the basis for a claim that the advertisement is misleading. *See id.* at 1182; Abbott Labs. [v. Mead Johnson & Co., 971 F.2d 6, 14 (7th Cir. 1992)].

A third possibility is that a statement may be literally true or ambiguous but misleading. The distinction between statements that are literally false and statements that are literally true or ambiguous but misleading can have considerable practical importance. Most courts agree that the trier of fact may conclude that a statement is literally false without resort to extrinsic evidence. (Determining whether a statement is literally false by necessary implication may depend on *contextual* evidence, as discussed above, but it generally does not require *extrinsic* evidence such as consumer surveys.) Proving that a literally true or ambiguous statement is misleading, on the other hand, usually requires extrinsic evidence in the form of a consumer survey. *See, e.g.*, Johnson & Johnson Vision Care, Inc. v. 1-800 Contacts, Inc., 299 F.3d 1242, 1247 (11th Cir. 2002); *Clorox*, 228 F.3d at 36; *see also* comment 4 *infra*. Tying in with element (6) (actual or likely deception), the overarching question is whether a "substantial portion of the audience" for whom the advertisement was intended would likely be deceived by the statement. *See Clorox*, 228 F.3d at 33 n.6, 36; *Pizza Hut*, 227 F.3d at 493 n.2.

The distinction between statements that are literally false and statements that are literally true or ambiguous but misleading can be important for another reason as well: According to some courts, a determination that a statement is literally false may give rise to a presumption that some of the other elements are satisfied too. *See* comments 9 and 11 *infra*. Relieving the plaintiff of the burden of having to prove some of these other elements obviously gives the plaintiff a leg up in negotiating a settlement. From a policy standpoint, does it make sense to accord so much practical weight to the distinction between statements that are literally false and statements that are only misleading? Alternatively, should the trier of fact be permitted to infer that a literally true or ambiguous statement is misleading, without resort to extrinsic evidence? As we will see, courts generally allow the FTC to make such an inference, even in the absence of extrinsic evidence, out of deference to the FTC's expertise with regard to false advertising. Does such deference make sense?

3. Can a literally true statement be rendered actionably misleading because consumers misinterpret the meaning of the words? In Mead Johnson & Co. v. Abbott Laboratories, 201 F.3d 883 (7th Cir. 2000), the maker of ENFAMIL infant formula sued the maker of SIMILAC infant formula over the latter's use of the slogan "First Choice of Doctors" on its packaging. The evidence showed that pediatricians preferred SIMILAC to ENFAMIL (the second-place formula), often by a two-to-one margin,

but none of the surveys the district court admitted disclosed that a majority of pediatricians preferred SIMILAC to other brands. (SIMILAC was the first choice of between 25 and 48%, depending on the survey; ENFAMIL was the first choice of between 10 and 40%; and in none of the surveys did ENFAMIL beat SIMILAC.) The plaintiff offered a consumer survey, however, in which over 80 percent of survey participants stated that for the statement "1st Choice of Doctors" to be true a *majority* of doctors would have to prefer the product. The district court granted the plaintiff's motion for a preliminary injunction, but the Seventh Circuit, in an opinion by Judge Easterbrook, reversed on the ground that "1st Choice of Doctors" implies only an ordinal ranking (as in "Who came in first in the race?"), whereas the survey question "was bound to produce a misleading if not meaningless answer" by treating the word "first" as cardinal. More generally, the court expressed misgivings about the use of survey evidence to determine the meaning of words, reasoning that "interpreting 'misleading' to include factual propositions that are susceptible to misunderstanding would make consumers as a whole worse off by suppressing truthful statements that will help many of them find superior products." *Id.* at 886. On petition for rehearing, however, the court amended its opinion to clarify that (1) literally true statements are misleading when they imply "something that is false"; (2) whether a claim is false or misleading is a question of fact, not law; and (3) on the facts presented, the plaintiff's evidence "would not support a conclusion by a reasonable person that [defendant's] claim either was false or implied a falsehood." Mead Johnson & Co. v. Abbott Laboratories, 209 F.3d 1032, 1034 (7th Cir. 2000) (per curiam).

Is Judge Easterbrook correct that surveys cannot change the meaning of words? What if survey evidence shows that a substantial segment of consumers misunderstand the meaning of some term used by an advertiser? On the other hand, if advertisers must conform their ads to the understanding of even small numbers of easily misled consumers, will they be forced (in Judge Easterbrook's words) to reduce "ads and packaging to meaningless puffery"? *See also* Richard Craswell, *Interpreting Deceptive Advertising*, 65 B.U. L. Rev. 657, 688-92 (1985).

4. Alternatively, can a literally false statement ever be rendered true when taken in its appropriate context? Consider the following excerpt from the opinion by Judge Easterbrook's Seventh Circuit colleague, Judge Posner, in Schering-Plough Health Care Products, Inc. v. Schwarz Pharma, Inc., 586 F.3d 500 (7th Cir. 2009). The plaintiff, Schering, sold an oral laxative, polyethylene glycol 3350, under the trademark MiraLAX. The defendants sold generic versions of the same laxative. Schering originally sold the laxative by prescription only, but later obtained FDA permission to sell it over-the-counter; the defendants remained authorized to sell it by prescription only. In accordance with FDA policy, however, the defendants' labels had to be the same as Schering's original label, which included the notice "Rx only." Schering filed suit for false advertising, claiming that the generic companies' labels were literally false: Not *all* polyethylene glycol 3350 is by prescription only (Schering's isn't). In rejecting Schering's claim, the court focused in part on the potential conflict with FDA law that might result if the court were to require the generic companies to change their labels in the manner Schering urged. (See *infra* at pp. 424-25, for further discussion of FDA/Lanham Act conflicts.) In addition, however, the court addressed Schering's claim that the literal falsity of the defendants' labels entitled Schering to prevail:

> . . . Schering has made no attempt to prove that anyone was misled, because it thinks that all it needs to show is "literal falsity."

This is an unfortunately common example of a litigant misled by general language in judicial opinions. Opinions would be even longer than they are if judges couldn't use short phrases to denote what may be complex legal doctrines. When those phrases are taken to be exhaustive statements of entire doctrines with all necessary qualifications, the result is likely to be a misapprehension of the law. William Blake declared that "to Generalize is to be an Idiot. To Particularize is the Alone Distinction of Merit." That is a bit extreme; but uncritical generalization is a path to error. One form of uncritical generalization, ironically in view of Schering's invocation of the doctrine of "literal falsity," is reading general language literally.

The purpose of the false-advertising provisions of the Lanham Act is to protect sellers from having their customers lured away from them by deceptive ads (or labels, or other promotional materials). Many literally false statements are not deceptive. When the Soviet Union in the 1930s declared that "2 + 2 = 5," it was not deceiving anyone; it was announcing a slogan designed to spur workers to complete the Five-Year Plan in four years. If one opened the New York Times "literally" at random one might find an ad that calls Graff Diamonds "The Most Fabulous Jewels in the World." That is literally false because the jewels sold by Graff are no more fabulous than, say, the Crown Jewels of England, or the Hope Diamond. But no one is deceived, so there is no injury, and a suit by a competitor of Graff would fail. See Time Warner Cable, Inc. v. DIRECTV, Inc., supra, 497 F.3d at 159-61; Johnson & Johnson–Merck Consumer Pharmaceuticals Co. v. Smithkline Beecham Corp., 960 F.2d 294, 298 (2d Cir. 1992); Castrol Inc. v. Pennzoil Co., 987 F.2d 939, 945 (3d Cir. 1993); Pizza Hut, Inc. v. Papa John's International, Inc., 227 F.3d 489, 496-97 (5th Cir. 2000); United Industries Corp. v. Clorox Co., 140 F.3d 1175, 1180 (8th Cir. 1998); cf. Muha v. Encore Receivable Management, Inc., 558 F.3d 623, 627 (7th Cir. 2009). The cases that reject liability do so in the name of "puffery"— meaningless superlatives — but the principle cuts deeper; if no one is or could be fooled, no one is or could be hurt. Cf. Hahn v. Triumph Partnerships LLC, 557 F.3d 755, 757-58 (2009); Wahl v. Midland Credit Management, Inc., 556 F.3d 643, 645-46 (7th Cir. 2009).

The other side of this coin is that a representation may be so obviously misleading that there is no need to gather evidence that anyone was confused. See, e.g., Abbott Laboratories v. Mead Johnson & Co., supra, 971 F.2d at 13-14; PPX Enterprises, Inc. v. Audiofidelity Enterprises, Inc., 818 F.2d 266, 271-73 (2d Cir. 1987). And it is often clearer that a claim is misleading than that it is literally false, because what is "literally" false is often a semantic question.

What the cases mean when they say that proof of literal falsity allows the plaintiff to dispense with evidence that anyone was misled or likely to be misled is that the seller who places an indisputably false statement in his advertising or labeling probably did so for a malign purpose, namely to sell his product by lies, and if the statement is false probably at least some people were misled, and since it was a lie why waste time on costly consumer surveys? See PPX Enterprises, Inc. v. Audiofidelity Enterprises, Inc., supra, 818 F.2d at 272-73; Castrol Inc. v. Pennzoil Co., supra, 987 F.2d at 951 (dissenting opinion). When this is stated as the doctrine of "literal falsity," "literal" must be understood in the common colloquial sense in which Americans (not realizing, or perhaps not caring, that they are making Fowler turn in his grave) say things like "I am literally out of my mind." A "literal" falsehood is bald-faced, egregious, undeniable, over the top.

We know this is what the cases are driving at because they add to "literal falsity" such qualifiers as that the meaning of the alleged literal falsehood must be considered in context and with reference to the audience to which the statement is addressed. Avis Rent A Car System, Inc. v. Hertz Corp., 782 F.2d 381, 385-86 (2d Cir. 1986) (Friendly, J.) ("fundamental to any task of interpretation is the principle that text must yield to context"); see also Castrol Inc. v. Pennzoil Co., supra, 987 F.2d at 946-47; Pizza Hut, Inc. v. Papa John's International, Inc., supra, 227 F.3d at 495 n.5; Southland Sod Farms v.

> Stover Seed Co., 108 F.3d 1134, 1139 (9th Cir. 1997). That is how one obtains an understanding of the real meaning of "2 + 2 = 5" in Soviet propaganda.
>
> The proper domain of "literal falsity" as a doctrine that dispenses with proof that anyone was misled or likely to be misled is the patently false statement that means what it says to any linguistically competent person, unlike the examples we have given. So suppose the labels on the defendants' products stated: "All polyethylene glycol 3350, by whomever made, can be sold only by prescription; there is no over-the-counter version of this drug." That would be false and misleading per se; there would be no need to consider context or audience.
>
> But that is not what the labels say. There is no statement in the ordinary sense, because there is no verb. There is the manufacturer's name at the top, the name of the active ingredient, the symbol "Rx only," and some other information. Obviously this product, the product of the named manufacturer, is prescription only, but it is not obvious, as Schering contends, either from the labels or from the package inserts (which say "Polyethylene Glycol 3350 NF Powder for Oral Solution is a prescription only laxative which has been prescribed by your physician to treat constipation"), that every other product containing polyethylene glycol 3350 is prescription only. Schering cannot just intone "literal falsity" and by doing so prove a violation of the Lanham Act. . . .

Is Judge Posner's analysis of literally false claims correct? Would it eliminate the category of "literally false by necessary implication" on the theory that such claims are not sufficiently "bald-faced, egregious, undeniable, over the top"? How, if at all, might it affect establishment claims or comparative claims of the type discussed below (*see infra* "A Note on Establishment Claims and Substantition")? Compare also Judge Posner's discussion of puffery with comment 11 *infra*.

5. Can we even be sure whether a statement is true? Consider representations that a food product is "organic" or "dolphin-safe." Can we assess the truth of these claims without knowing what consumers understand them to mean? What if consumers are not of one mind, so that the claim is considered accurate by some but inaccurate by others? For an exploration of these issues, see Rebecca Tushnet, *It Depends on What the Meaning of "False" Is: Falsity and Misleadingness in Commercial Speech Doctrine*, 41 Loy. L.A. L. Rev. 227 (2007).

6. *Proving That a Literally True or Ambiguous Statement Is Misleading.* As noted above, plaintiffs usually must offer extrinsic evidence in the form of a properly conducted consumer survey in order to prove that a literally true or ambiguous statement is misleading. To be admissible, such surveys must satisfy the applicable evidentiary rules relating to expert and scientific evidence. *See, e.g.*, Scott's Co. v. United Indus., 315 F.3d 264, 276-81 (3d Cir. 2000); Southland Seed Farms v. Stover Seed Co., 108 F.3d 1134, 1143 & n.8 (9th Cir. 1997). In the context of false advertising litigation, surveys are more likely to be admissible if they pose questions in a nonleading manner (that is, if they do not suggest the answer the researcher is trying to obtain) and if they compare the reactions of consumers who have been exposed to the advertisement in question to a control group of consumers who have not been so exposed. *See, e.g.*, Novartis Consumer Health, Inc. v. Johnson & Johnson-Merck Consumer Pharms. Co., 290 F.3d 578, 590-94 (3d Cir. 2002); Johnson & Johnson–Merck Consumer Pharms. Co. v. Smithkline Beecham Corp., 960 F.2d 294, 300-01 (2d Cir. 1992).

Although courts usually expect plaintiffs to offer survey evidence to back up an allegation that a statement is literally true or ambiguous but misleading, there are some possible exceptions. In *Pizza Hut*, for example, the court affirmed a finding that the sauce and dough claims, both in isolation and in combination with the slogan "Better

Ingredients, Better Pizza," were misleading, based on expert testimony that use of fresh ingredients did not affect the taste of Papa John's pizza. Even so, the lack of survey evidence impacted Pizza Hut's ability to prove that the statements were material to consumers' purchasing decisions. *See Pizza Hut*, 227 F.3d at 500-03 & nn.11, 13. In addition, "in some circuits, if the defendant 'intentionally set out to deceive the public,' using 'deliberate conduct' of an 'egregious nature' in light of the advertising culture of the marketplace in which the defendant competes, a presumption arises that customers were, in fact, deceived, dispensing with the need for the plaintiff to commission a consumer survey." *Clorox*, 228 F.3d at 36 n.9 (citations omitted); *cf.* Johnson & Johnson-Merck Consumer Pharms. Co v. Rhone-Poulenc Rorer Pharms., 19 F.3d 125, 131-32 (3d Cir. 1994) (holding that an "intent to mislead" of a kind that was "unfortunately common in the antacid industry" did not amount to the sort of "deliberate conduct" of an "egregious nature" that might warrant the presumption). Evidence that the defendant intended to deceive the public might consist of the defendant's persistence in communicating the allegedly deceptive statement despite warnings that it would be misconstrued, or other incriminating evidence turned up in the course of discovery. Does a burden-shifting rule make sense in this context? If so, how should a defendant go about rebutting the presumption that the statement is misleading?

7. *Description or Representation of Fact.* An actionable statement must be a false or misleading "description or representation of fact." Opinions and omissions are not descriptions or representations of fact, and thus generally are not actionable. *See Pizza Hut*, 227 F.3d at 495-96; *see also* Insignia Sys., Inc. v. News Am. Marketing In-Store, Inc., Civil No. 04-4213 (JRT/AJB), 2007 WL 2893374, at *3 (D. Minn. Sept. 28, 2007) (stating that "[c]ourts are to look at four factors to distinguish statements of fact from those of opinion: (a) a statement's precision and specificity, (b) a statement's verifiability, (c) the social and literary context in which the statement was made, and (d) the statement's public context," and that some courts have "highlighted the importance of the second factor"). As the cases above discuss, one form of nonactionable "puffery" is a statement of opinion that one's products are, for example, the "best."

Opinions can be actionable, however, if they reasonably can be interpreted as stating or implying some provable fact. *See* Boule v. Hutton, 328 F.3d 84, 92 (2d Cir. 2003); Groden v. Random House, Inc., 61 F.3d 1045, 1051-52 (2d Cir. 1995); RESTATEMENT (THIRD) OF UNFAIR COMPETITION § 3 cmt. d. Similarly, omissions can be actionable if, for example, an omission in the form of a half-truth is reasonably understood as communicating a "fact" that is untrue. *See* Register.com v. Domain Registry of Am., Inc., No. 02 Civ. 6915(NRB), 2002 WL 31894625, at *14 (S.D.N.Y. Dec. 27, 2002); RESTATEMENT (THIRD) OF UNFAIR COMPETITION § 2 cmts. d, e.

8. *Nature, Characteristics, Qualities, or Geographic Origin.* An actionable representation or description of fact also must relate to the "nature, characteristics, qualities, or geographic origin" of goods, services, or commercial activities. Some Second Circuit cases have stated that an actionable statement must relate to an "inherent quality or characteristic" of the product. *See, e.g.*, Nat'l Ass'n of Pharm. Mfrs., Inc. v. Ayerst Labs., 850 F.2d 904, 917 (2d Cir. 1988). On this view, false statements that a product is the subject of an "exclusive TV offer," for example), might not be actionable. *See, e.g.*, Abernathy & Closther, Ltd. v. E & M Advertising, Inc., 553 F. Supp. 834, 837-38 (E.D.N.Y. 1982). More recent decisions from that Circuit, however, have either construed the term "inherent quality or characteristic" broadly, *see* Project Strategies Corp. v. Nat'l Commc'ns Corp., 38 U.S.P.Q.2d 1053, 1056 (E.D.N.Y. Oct. 27, 1995) (false statement "as seen on TV" related to inherent quality or characteristic

if it would mislead consumers into believing that defendant's product was plaintiff's); Telebrands Corp. v. Wilton Indus., 983 F. Supp. 471, 475-76 (S.D.N.Y. 1997) (similar), or to equate "inherent qualities or characteristics" with any qualities or characteristics that would influence consumer purchasing decisions (i.e., that are "material"), *see Time Warner*, 497 F.3d at 153 n.3 (stating that "the plaintiff must also demonstrate that the false or misleading representation involved an inherent or material quality of the product"); Nat'l Basketball Ass'n v. Motorola, Inc., 105 F.3d 841, 855 (2d Cir. 1997) (stating that the requirement of "inherent quality or characteristic" is "essentially one of materiality, a term explicitly used in other circuits"). In general, most courts construe this element broadly.

In addition, a statement must concern the defendant's (or, in the case of commercial disparagement, the plaintiff's) "goods, services, or commercial activities"; and must be made in the context of "commercial advertising or promotion." We discuss these two elements in greater depth in section F.3 *infra*.

Some courts have held or suggested that falsely representing that one's goods are covered by a patent, copyright, or trademark rights (or that such rights are pending) may constitute false advertising under the Lanham Act. For citations, see RESTATEMENT (THIRD) OF UNFAIR COMPETITION § 3, Reporter's Note to cmt. c, illus.3; 5 MCCARTHY, *supra*, § 27:78. Other claims may be viable as well. *See, e.g.*, 35 U.S.C. § 292 (patent law false marking statute); 17 U.S.C. § 506(c) (fraudulent copyright notice); *id.* § 1202(a) (false copyright management information); Forest Group v. Bon Tool Co., 590 F.3d 1295 (Fed. Cir. 2009) (holding that a § 292 false patent marking claim has two elements: (1) marking an unpatented article, and (2) intent to deceive the public; and that the statute "requires the penalty to be imposed on a per article basis," that is, "each article that is falsely marked with intent to deceive constitutes an offense under 35 U.S.C. § 292."); Paul J. Heald, *Payment Demands for Spurious Copyrights: Four Causes of Action*, 1 J. INTELL. PROP. 259 (1994). Falsely accusing another of patent infringement also may constitute commercial disparagement under some circumstances. *See infra* section F.

9. *Actual Deception or Tendency to Deceive a Substantial Segment of the Targeted Audience.* If the statement at issue is literally false, most courts will presume this element. *See, e.g., Pizza Hut*, 227 F.3d at 497; Porous Media Corp. v. Pall Corp., 110 F.3d 1329, 1332-33 (8th Cir. 1997). *But see* B. Sanfield, Inc. v. Finlay Fine Jewelry Corp., 258 F.3d 578, 581 (7th Cir. 2001) (Easterbrook, J.) (requiring proof of actual or likely injury resulting from actual or likely consumer deception, even if the statement at issue is literally false). If the statement is not literally false, but is instead literally true or ambiguous but misleading, then the plaintiff must offer some evidence of actual deception/tendency to deceive. Often the same survey or other evidence that is offered in support of the allegation that the statement is misleading will also be relevant to prove actual or likely deception. *See, e.g.*, Novartis Consumer Health, Inc. v. Johnson & Johnson-Merck Consumer Pharm. Co., 290 F.3d 578, 594-95 (3d Cir. 2002). As with that element, the focus is on whether a substantial portion of the relevant audience is likely to be deceived. *See* RESTATEMENT (THIRD) OF UNFAIR COMPETITION § 2 cmt. d:

> In many instances a representation may be likely to deceive or mislead only some of the prospective purchasers to whom it is directed. A person is subject to liability under this Section only if the representation is likely to deceive or mislead a significant portion of the audience. As a general matter, if the representation would deceive a reasonably prudent

> purchaser of the goods or services, it is likely to deceive or mislead under the rule in this Section. If a reasonably prudent purchaser would not be deceived or misled by the representation, the actor is not subject to liability in the absence of other evidence indicating that the representation is nevertheless likely to deceive or mislead a significant portion of its audience.
>
> Imposition of liability in connection with a representation likely to deceive only a portion of the audience necessarily interferes with the communication of non-deceptive speech between the actor and that portion of the audience not likely to be misled. In determining whether the portion of the audience likely to be deceived is "significant," the potential harm to such persons and to the interests of competitors must be weighed against the harm that the imposition of liability and contemplated relief would cause to the actor and the remainder of the audience. It is thus not possible to analyze the issue solely in terms of absolute numbers or percentages. Among the relevant factors are the seriousness of the threatened injury to deceived purchasers and the extent to which the representation could be easily recast to convey the information in a form less likely to deceive or mislead.

If the statement at issue is not literally false (so no presumption of deception arises), should plaintiffs be required to submit evidence that some consumers have been *actually* misled? If the Lanham Act is intended to overrule the single source rule, one might expect the answer to this question to be "no." In the analogous trademark infringement context, after all, proof of actual confusion, while helpful in proving likelihood of confusion, is not required. The *Restatement (Third) of Unfair Competition* § 2 cmt. d (1995) agrees, stating:

> When the representation is literally false, a court may conclude in the absence of credible evidence to the contrary that the representation is likely to deceive or mislead. When the tendency to deceive or mislead turns instead upon the inferences to be drawn from the representation or upon a choice among several possible interpretations, direct evidence of the meaning attached to the representation by the relevant audience may be necessary to establish a likelihood of deception. Surveys, when properly structured and conducted, can be helpful in ascertaining the meaning likely to be attributed to a representation and hence the likelihood that it will deceive or mislead. Evidence of actual deception, misunderstanding, or confusion, although not required under the rule in this Section, is relevant in determining whether the audience is likely to be deceived or misled.

See also 5 McCarthy, *supra*, § 27:36 (stating that "[w]hen plaintiff seeks only an injunction, there is no requirement that it be proven that purchasers were actually deceived, only that the advertisement has a tendency to deceive") (citations omitted). Note, however, what the court in *Pizza Hut* says about this element: "To prove a tendency to deceive, plaintiffs need to show that at least some consumers were confused by the advertisements." *Pizza Hut*, 227 F.3d at 497.[12] Following this precedent, some courts have quoted the *Pizza Hut* language as requiring proof of at least some actual deception, when the statement at issue is not literally false. Can that be right? Or do the courts simply mean that a survey demonstrating that a substantial portion of survey respondents were deceived will suffice?

12. *But see Pizza Hut*, 227 F.3d at 502 n.12 ("since Pizza Hut sought only equitable relief and no monetary damages, it was required to offer evidence sufficient to establish that the claims made by Papa John's had the '*tendency to deceive consumers*,' rather than evidence indicating that the claims made by Papa John's *actually deceived consumers*") (quotations omitted). *Cf.* Ralph Waldo Emerson, Self-Reliance ("A foolish consistency is the hobgoblin of little minds . . .").

10. As the preceding comment indicates, there is some overlap between element (1) (false or misleading) and element (6) (actual deception/tendency to deceive). Does element (6) overlap with any of the other elements? In the *Pizza Hut* case, the court appears to conflate this element with materiality, *see Pizza Hut*, 227 F.3d at 497; while in *B. Sanfield*, the court arguably combines it with injury to the plaintiff, by requiring proof that even a literally false statement actually or potentially deceived consumers into forgoing purchases from the plaintiff. Logically, though, couldn't a statement be actually or potentially deceptive and yet immaterial to consumers' purchasing decisions? Similarly, isn't the question of whether consumers have been or might be deceived logically distinct from the question of whether the plaintiff itself has suffered or stands to suffer injury as a result of the deception? See Lemley & McKenna, *supra* (making this point).

11. *Materiality.* Although the Lanham Act does not expressly mention this element, courts have held that for a statement to be actionable false advertising it must be material, in the sense that it would likely affect consumer purchasing decisions. *See, e.g.*, Cashmere & Camel Hair Mfrs. Inst. v. Saks Fifth Ave., 284 F.3d 302, 311 (1st Cir. 2002); *see also* RESTATEMENT (THIRD) OF UNFAIR COMPETITION § 3 cmt. b (stating that "[i]t is not necessary that the representation be the sole or predominant factor influencing the conduct of prospective purchasers," or "to demonstrate that purchasers would have acted differently in the absence of the representation," but only that "the representation is likely to influence prospective purchasers to some substantial degree").[13] In *Pizza Hut*, the district court granted JMOL in favor of Papa John's on the ground that the slogan "Better Ingredients, Better Pizza," in combination with the "sauce" and "dough" claims, though misleading, was immaterial. 227 F.3d at 501-02. The court also suggested, however, that if the statement at issue had been literally false, the plaintiff would have been entitled to a rebuttable presumption of materiality. *See id.* at 497. Other courts have rejected the rule that literally false statements are presumptively material. *See* Johnson & Johnson Vision Care, Inc. v. 1-800 Contacts, Inc., 299 F.3d 1242, 1250-51 (11th Cir. 2002) (citing cases, and disapproving of the *Pizza Hut* presumption). Does it make sense to presume that all literally false statements are material? For criticism, see BeVier, 78 VA. L. REV. at 27-39. If the presumption applies, how would a defendant go about rebutting it?

According to the *Time Warner* and *Pizza Hut* cases (and many others), one type of nonactionable "puffery" is a statement so obviously boastful and exaggerated that consumers are *unlikely* to rely upon it. Does it make sense to apply this definition of puffery, in preference to the "opinion" definition of puffery, to visual ads (as in *Time Warner*)?

Courts have not always spoken clearly on the question of whether materiality is a question of fact, a question of law, or a mixed question of law and fact. At least two commentators, however, read the cases as (more or less) standing for the proposition

13. Further, "[i]f a reasonably prudent purchaser of the goods or services would not rely on the representation, the actor is not subject to liability in the absence of evidence establishing that the representation is nevertheless likely to be relied upon by a significant number of prospective purchasers." RESTATEMENT (THIRD) OF UNFAIR COMPETITION § 3 cmt. d.

In the context of trademark infringement, courts generally do *not* require proof that the likelihood of confusion arising from the defendant's conduct is material, in the sense of influencing consumers to buy the wrong product. Rather, they presume that representations as to source are sufficiently material that they will affect consumer purchasing decisions. Some commentators have argued, however, that courts should apply a materiality requirement to at least some forms of alleged trademark infringement as well. *See* Mark A. Lemley & Mark P. McKenna, *Irrelevant Confusion*, 62 STAN. L. REV. 311 (2010); Glynn S. Lunney, Jr., *Trademark Monopolies*, 48 EMORY L.J. 367, 482-83 (1999). Should they?

that materiality is a mixed question of law and fact. *See* Jean Wegman Burns, *Confused Jurisprudence: False Advertising Under the Lanham Act*, 79 B.U. L. Rev. 807, 882 (1999) (citing cases); Richard J. Leighton, *Materiality and Puffing in Lanham Act False Advertising Cases: The Proofs, Presumptions, and Pretexts*, 94 Trademark Rptr. 585, 604 (2004) (similar). Which characterization is preferable from a policy standpoint?

12. *Interstate commerce.* The interstate commerce element is usually easy to satisfy. For example, in Highmark, Inc. v. UMPC Health Plan, Inc., 276 F.3d 160 (3d Cir. 2001), the court rejected the defendant's argument that its allegedly false advertisements did not affect interstate commerce:

> First, we address the jurisdictional issues with respect to Highmark's Lanham Act claim. This is essentially a legal issue and our standard of review is plenary.
>
> UPMC argues that the Lanham Act's interstate commerce requirement is not met because it directed its Ad to employees of Allegheny County, Pennsylvania, and the advertised health plans are sold only in Pennsylvania. Thus, it maintains that there is no substantial effect on interstate commerce. The District Court rejected this argument, holding that the Ad does indeed substantially affect interstate commerce. . . .
>
> The Lanham Act provides civil liability for any person who "uses in commerce" any false or misleading description or representation of fact which in commercial advertising misrepresents the nature, characteristics, or qualities of any person's services or commercial activities. 15 U.S.C. § 1125(a)(1)(B). The term "commerce," as used in the Act, refers to "all commerce which may lawfully be regulated by Congress." 15 U.S.C. § 1127. It has long been acknowledged that the Act "confers broad jurisdictional powers upon the courts of the United States." Steele v. Bulova Watch Co., 344 U.S. 280, 283 (1952). Congress's authority under the interstate commerce clause extends even to purely intrastate activity if that activity substantially affects interstate commerce. United States v. Lopez, 514 U.S. 549, 558-59 (1995).
>
> The District Court held that five nexi substantially affect interstate commerce. First, the *Pittsburgh Post-Gazette* is distributed interstate and, therefore, the Ad appeared outside Pennsylvania. Second, the health plans referred to in the advertisements offer emergency care to patients outside of Pennsylvania. Third, the Highmark plan applies to subscribers residing outside of Pennsylvania, and services may be provided to a subscriber's dependents who reside outside of Pennsylvania. Fourth, subscribers may be referred to a hospital or medical facility outside of Pennsylvania. Finally, the Ad might have an impact on the parties outside of Pennsylvania. UPMC does not challenge the Court's factual findings, appealing only the Court's holding that these facts are sufficient to give the Court Lanham Act jurisdiction.
>
> The District Court's findings relating to the health plan services offered outside of Pennsylvania support its conclusion with respect to interstate commerce. Cynthia Dellecker, Highmark's vice president of product management and development, testified that CommunityBlue Direct covers subscribers' dependents residing outside of Pennsylvania, and that CommunityBlue Direct offers emergency care outside of the state and country. She also testified that CommunityBlue Direct subscribers have access to out-of-state hospitals such as Sloan-Kettering, the Cleveland Clinic, Massachusetts General Hospitals, and the Mayo Clinic. Dr. Kenneth Melani, the executive vice president of Highmark for strategic business development and health services, testified that Highmark has approved care for subscribers at Sloan-Kettering. Melani further noted that Joslin Clinic, a CommunityBlue Direct network hospital situated in Boston, Massachusetts, is an internationally recognized diabetes treatment center.
>
> John DeGruttola, the chief marketing officer for UPMC, acknowledged that Highmark has arrangements with the Cleveland Clinic and Johns Hopkins University, situated in Baltimore, Maryland. Moreover, UPMC covers medical emergency care outside

> Pennsylvania, and, according to DeGruttola, he's "never had a complaint come across . . . that said th[e UPMC] card wasn't recognized across the United States or in the world." The record testimony amply supports the District Court's conclusion with respect to the substantial effect on interstate commerce.

Id. at 165-66.

A Note on Establishment Claims and Substantiation

Companies often advertise their products by making claims such as "Tests prove," "Studies show," or "4/5 doctors surveyed agree." In false advertising case law, these types of claims are referred to as "establishment" claims. Such claims are literally false if the firm has not substantiated the claim by conducting the appropriate tests (studies, surveys, etc.) before making the claim. In Castrol Inc. v. Quaker State Corp., 977 F.2d 57, 63 (2d Cir. 1992), for example, the Second Circuit affirmed a judgment that the defendant's commercial, stating that "Tests prove" its motor oil provided better protection against engine wear, was literally false. "Where a plaintiff challenges a test-proven superiority advertisement, the defendant must identify the cited tests. Plaintiff must then prove that these tests did not establish the proposition for which they were cited." The court explained:

> Where, as in the current case, defendant's ad explicitly or implicitly represents that tests or studies prove its product superior, plaintiff satisfies its burden by showing that the tests did not establish the proposition for which they were cited. We have held that a plaintiff can meet this burden by demonstrating that the tests were not sufficiently reliable to permit a conclusion that the product is superior. The . . . "sufficiently reliable" standard of course assumes that the tests in question, if reliable, would prove the proposition for which they are cited. If the plaintiff can show that the tests, even if reliable, do not establish the proposition asserted by the defendant, the plaintiff has obviously met its burden. In such a case, tests which may or may not be "sufficiently reliable," are simply irrelevant.

Suppose, however, that the statement at issue neither expressly nor implicitly claims any substantiation. In other words, suppose there is neither an explicit nor an implicit claim to the effect that "tests prove" the defendant's product is superior to the plaintiff's or performs in a certain manner; there is simply a bald assertion that the product is superior or performs in a certain manner. This type of claim (a "nonestablishment" claim) is literally false if the relevant tests that one would use to substantiate such a claim do not support the claim. *See* Castrol Inc. v. Pennzoil Co., 987 F.2d 939, 943-44 (3d Cir. 1993) (affirming judgment that the slogan "Outperforms any leading motor oil against viscosity breakdown" was literally false, in light of evidence that the relevant tests for determining viscosity breakdown did not support the claim). Not surprisingly, the parties may differ over what those relevant tests are. *See id.* at 945 & n.5 (stating that the defendant's proposed test was "not a credible test upon which Pennzoil could reasonably rely for its advertisements," because it did "not measure viscosity breakdown" but rather "percent viscosity loss," but conceding that in an appropriate case a test that is not an industry standard could "yield accurate results").

But what if the relevant tests *do* support the nonestablishment claim? In other words, suppose that the defendant failed adequately to substantiate its claim of product superiority before making that claim; but that, after the fact, the relevant tests show that the product *really is* superior? According to some authorities, proof that the advertiser had no support for the statement does not necessarily prove falsity. *See* United Indus. Corp. v. Clorox Co., 140 F.3d 1175, 1182 (8th Cir. 1998); BASF Corp. v. Old World Trading Co., Inc, 41 F.3d 1081, 1090-91 (7th Cir. 1994); 5 McCarthy, *supra*, § 27:61; Restatement (Third) of Unfair Competition § 2 cmt. d. At least one court, however, has held that where a nonestablishment claim lacks any substantiation whatsoever it is literally false, "without any additional evidence from the plaintiff to that effect." *See* Novartis Consumer Health, Inc. v. Johnson & Johnson-Merck Consumer Pharm. Co., 290 F.3d 578, 590 (3d Cir. 2002); *accord* Restatement (Third) of Unfair Competition § 2 Reporters' Note on cmt. d. Do these rules make sense? Or does the fact that a claim was unsubstantiated when first made render the statement literally false? Misleading? Are nonestablishment claims an empty set, because consumers necessarily infer that firms have substantiation for the claims they make, even when those claims do not expressly refer to tests or studies? The FTC appears to take this latter position, as we shall see in section D *infra*, but the FTC's approach is not binding in the Lanham Act context. In a case in which substantiation supports the claim ex post, would the false impression that substantiation was performed ex ante be material? If not, would firms be tempted to make too many unsubstantiated statements?

PROBLEMS

Problem 9-1. Cotco markets in interstate commerce a nonprescription pain reliever, COTTER'S HEADACHE PILLS, which it markets under the slogan "COTTER'S HEADACHE PILLS: THEY'RE THE BEST." In truth, COTTER'S HEADACHE PILLS, while safe and effective, relieve pain no faster than other nonprescription pain relievers such as aspirin, ibuprofen, and acetaminophen. Is this actionable false advertising? What if the slogan reads "COTTER'S HEADACHE PILLS relieve headache pain twice as fast"? Alternatively, what if the slogan "COTTER'S HEADACHE PILLS relieve pain twice as fast" turns out to be true, after appropriate testing is performed, but Cotco only got around to performing that testing after suit was filed?

Problem 9-2. Suppose that the slogan from Problem 9-1 reads instead "Four out five doctors surveyed recommend COTTER'S HEADACHE PILLS to their patients who suffer headache pain." What sort of substantiation must Cotco have before it can make this sort of statement? Suppose instead that the slogan reads "COTTER'S HEADACHE PILLS meet all industry specifications for pain relief." Is this an establishment or a nonestablishment claim?

Problem 9-3. Merisant Co. markets EQUAL, an artificial sweetener made from aspartame, as well as SWEET 'N LOW, an artificial sweetener made from saccharin. McNeil Nutritionals, LLC markets SPLENDA, an artificial sweetener made from sucralose. Unlike aspartame and saccharin, sucralose is made from sugar. More precisely, sucralose is a chemical compound formed by the addition of three atoms of chlorine to a molecule of sugar. The resulting compound is chemically *not* a sugar, though many people believe that it tastes like sugar and is superior in taste to other artificial sweeteners. Since being introduced to the market in the early 2000s, sucralose steadily gained market share in the market for artificial sweeteners, to the point at which it commanded more than 60 percent of that market. In marketing SPLENDA artificial sweetener, McNeil used the slogan "Made from sugar, so it tastes like sugar." Merisant files suit against McNeil for false advertising in violation of § 43(a)(1)(B). What result? Is the slogan literally false? Is it literally true or ambiguous but misleading? Is it not false advertising at all? What significance, if any, would you ascribe to the words "so it" in the slogan? What significance, if any, would you ascribe to the fact that the slogan initially read "Made from sugar, so it tastes like sugar, but it isn't sugar," but that McNeil management decided to delete the words "but it isn't sugar"?

Problem 9-4. In October 2009, Verizon Wireless launched an ad campaign that compared its 3G wireless network to AT&T's. In particular, Verizon aired commercials titled "There's a Map for That" that used the following graphic:

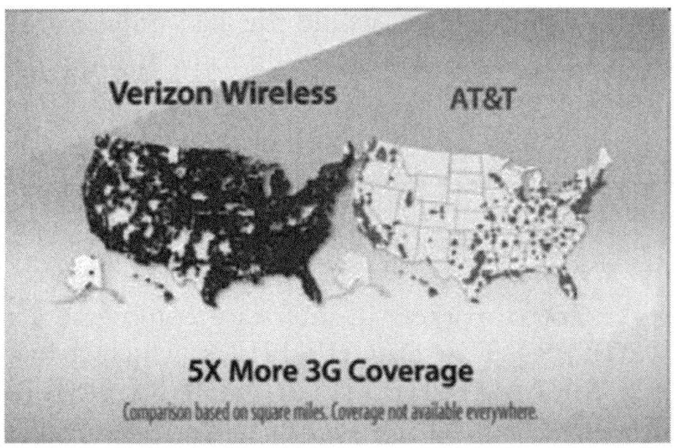

At the time the ads aired, the maps featured in the graphic were accurate: Verizon did indeed have more thorough wireless 3G coverage than AT&T. AT&T claims, however, that the graphic suggests not only that AT&T lacks 3G coverage in the "white spaces" depicted on the right-hand map, but also that it provides no wireless coverage at all in those areas. What result?

Problem 9-5. For many years the Keebler Company advertised its cookies with a jingle the lyrics to which stated "Man, you never would believe where the Keebler Cookies come from. They're baked by little elves in a hollow tree. And what do you think makes these cookies so uncommon? They're baked in magic ovens, and there's no factory. Hey!" Assuming that the cookies are not really "baked by little elves in a hollow tree" with the use of "magic ovens," did the jingle constitute actionable false advertising? If not, why not?

Suppose instead that a firm markets its dry pasta to consumers under the slogan "America's Favorite Pasta." A competitor argues that the slogan violates § 43(a)(1)(B), because it communicates the false message that the defendant's pasta is the nation's number one selling pasta, when in fact (1) it is merely a regional (not a national) brand, and (2) dried pasta sold by another firm (not a party to the litigation) occupies the number one position nationally. Actionable false advertising?

2. Standing

In relevant part, § 43(a)(1)(B) states that "[a]ny person who, on or in connection with any goods or services . . . uses in commerce . . . any . . . false or misleading description of fact, or false or misleading representation of fact, which . . . in commercial advertising or promotion, misrepresents the nature, characteristics, qualities, or geographic origin of his or her or another person's goods, services, or commercial activities, shall be liable in a civil action *by any person who believes that he or she is or is likely to be damaged by such act*" [emphasis added]. On its face, the statute seems to confer standing to sue upon "any person" — a competitor, a trade association, even a consumer — who "believes" (subjectively?) that he (or she or it) is likely to suffer injury as a result of the defendant's false advertising. If one believes that false advertising is rampant, and that a strong deterrent is needed to reduce its harms, such an expansive standing rule might make sense. Nevertheless, the vast majority of courts have interpreted the statute much more narrowly. (Does that make the Lanham Act itself literally false?)

First, almost all of the courts that have addressed the issue have concluded that *consumers* do not have standing to sue for violations of § 43(a)(1)(B). *See, e.g.*, Serbin v. Ziebart Int'l Corp., 11 F.3d 1163 (3d Cir. 1993); Colligan v. Activities Club, Ltd., 442 F.2d 686 (2d Cir. 1971). From both a textual and a policy perspective, this interpretation might seem curious, insofar as defrauded consumers are the ultimate victims of false advertising. As the scholarly opinions of Judge Moore in *Colligan* and of Judge Pollak in *Serbin* point out, however, there are a variety of reasons for construing the statute more narrowly. For one thing, even if it is fair to interpret § 43(a) as expressing a policy choice in favor of expanding the common law of false advertising — by eliminating the single source rule in preference to a likelihood of injury standard, and by eliminating the element of intent — interpreting the statute as conferring standing upon consumers would constitute an even more radical departure from the common law of false advertising. (It would also depart from the trademark law analogy, insofar as consumers also lack standing to sue for trademark infringement, but rather must depend on trademark owners to vindicate consumer interests by protecting the trademark owners' own self-interest in the integrity of their marks.) Furthermore, nothing in the legislative history arising from the passage of the Lanham Act suggests that Congress intended to confer standing upon consumers; and while arguments from congressional silence are always somewhat precarious, it might seem odd that Congress would have intended to open the proverbial "floodgates" to consumer false advertising suits in federal court without any discussion whatsoever reflected in the legislative history or contemporaneous debates. In addition, when Congress amended the Lanham Act in 1988, it specifically rejected a proposed amendment that would have expressly conferred standing upon consumers. *See Serbin*, 11 F.3d at 1177-78.

Interpreting statutory standing provisions in a somewhat less than literal fashion also is not without precedent. The federal antitrust laws, for example, contain a similarly expansively worded standing provision. *See* Clayton Act § 4, 15 U.S.C. § 15 (stating that "any person who shall be injured in his business or property by reason of anything forbidden in the antitrust laws may sue therefor . . ."). The Supreme Court nevertheless has (in effect) narrowed the scope of this provision by holding that a party asserting an antitrust claim must be able to prove injury "of the type the antitrust laws were intended to prevent," Brunswick Corp. v. Pueblo Bowl-O-Mat, Inc., 429 U.S. 477, 489 (1977), and must survive a variety of prudential standing requirements as well, *see* Associated General Contractors v. California State Council of Carpenters, 459 U.S. 519 (1983). The end result is that, in the antitrust realm, it is often easier for consumers to assert antitrust claims than it is for competitors; courts are often skeptical of competitor suits out of concern that interests of competitors frequently would be served by less, rather than more, competition. This creates a seeming paradox, however, inasmuch as the similarly worded standing provision of Lanham Act §43(a) is interpreted in precisely the opposite manner, that is, as preferring competitor suits to suits by consumers. The paradox resolves itself only if we accept the view that words take their meaning in part from the underlying policy considerations. For further discussion of the differences between the antitrust and Lanham Act standards for determining standing, see Jean Wegman Burns, *The Paradox of Antitrust and Lanham Act Standing*, 42 UCLA L. Rev. 47 (1994).

Second, as the preceding discussion suggests, competitors generally do have standing to assert claims for false advertising (though subject to certain prudential considerations discussed below). Indeed, as the *Phoenix of Broward* case excerpted below indicates, some circuits appear to limit standing to competitors, though others have permitted claims by somewhat less directly impacted plaintiffs. The Second Circuit, for example, follows the rule that a false advertising plaintiff must have a "reasonable interest" to be protected, and a "reasonable basis" for believing that interest is likely to be harmed. A "reasonable interest" may be a commercial interest, or a direct pecuniary interest, or a future potential for commercial or competitive injury; a "reasonable basis" rests on proof of likely injury and a causal nexus between the defendant's conduct and the injury. *See* ITC Ltd. v. Punchgini, Inc., 482 F.3d 135, 169-70 (2d Cir. 2007).

Third, some courts may presume both likely injury and the requisite causal nexus when the advertisement is literally false, is comparative, and mentions the plaintiff's product by name. N. Am. Med. Corp. v. Axiom Worldwide, Inc., 522 F.3d 1211, 1227 (11th Cir. 2008); Time Warner Cable, Inc. v. DIRECTV, Inc., 497 F.3d 144, 161-62 (2d Cir. 2007); *see also* Porous Media Corp. v. Pall Corp., 110 F.3d 1329, 1333-36 (8th Cir. 1997) (stating that a presumption of injury and causation may be appropriate if the deception was willful and the advertisements refer to the plaintiff's product, but that when the defendant merely misrepresents its own product without referring to the plaintiff's, on the other hand, such a presumption may be inappropriate, at least where money damages are sought).

So far we have considered only the standing of competitors to complain of false statements made by a defendant about either the plaintiff's or the defendant's product. What about false statements made about a third-party product? About the market in general? Should a competitor be able to assert an interest in preventing such false speech? How might such speech injure them? If the products are not directly competitive or the ads do not directly refer to plaintiff's products, however, the plaintiff normally must prove harm and causation — typically through (once again) surveys, or testimony, or at least a logical connection between the ad and some loss suffered by plaintiff. *See* Ortho Pharm. Corp. v. Cosprophar, Inc., 32 F.3d 690, 696-97 (2d Cir. 1994); Johnson & Johnson v. Carter-Wallace Inc., 631 F.2d 186, 190-91 (2d Cir. 1980). The *Time Warner* case presents an interesting take on how this presumption operates:

> In general, "[t]he likelihood of injury and causation will not be presumed, but must be demonstrated in some manner." [Citation omitted] We have held, however, that these elements may be presumed "where [the] plaintiff demonstrates a likelihood of success in

> showing literally false [the] defendant's comparative advertisement which mentions [the] plaintiff's product by name." *Castrol, Inc.*, 977 F.2d at 62. We explained the reason for the presumption in McNeilab, Inc. v. American Home Products Corp., 848 F.2d 34 (2d Cir. 1988). . . . There, we observed that in the case of a "misleading, non-comparative commercial[ ] which tout[s] the benefits of the product advertised but ma[kes] no direct reference to any competitor's product," the injury "accrues equally to all competitors; none is more likely to suffer from the offending broadcasts than any other." *Id.* at 38 Thus, "some indication of actual injury and causation" is necessary "to satisfy Lanham Act standing requirements and to ensure [the] plaintiff's injury [is] not speculative." *Id.* By contrast, where the case presents a false comparative advertising claim, "the concerns . . . regarding speculative injury do not arise." *Id.* This is because a false "comparison to a specific competing product necessarily diminishes that product's value in the minds of the consumer." *Id.* Accordingly, no proof of likely injury is necessary.
>
> Although neither of the television commercials identifies TWC by name, the rationale for a presumption of irreparable harm applies with equal force to this case. The Revised Shatner Commercial explicitly disparages the picture quality of "cable." As the District Court found, TWC *is* "cable" in the areas where it is the franchisee. Thus, even though Shatner does not identify TWC by name, consumers in the markets covered by the preliminary injunction would undoubtedly understand his derogatory statement, "settling for cable would be illogical," as referring to TWC. Because the Revised Shatner Commercial "necessarily diminishes" TWC's value "in the minds of the consumer," the District Court properly accorded TWC a presumption of irreparable harm.
>
> The Revised Simpson Commercial, unlike the original version pulled in December 2006, does not explicitly refer to "cable." However, the fact that the commercial does not name plaintiff's product is not necessarily dispositive. As we said in Ortho Pharmaceutical Corp. v. Cosprophar, Inc., 32 F.3d 690 (2d Cir. 1994), the application of the presumption is disfavored "where the products are not obviously in competition *or* where the defendant's advertisements make no direct reference to any competitor's products." *Id.* at 696 (emphasis added); *see also* Hutchinson v. Pfeil, 211 F.3d 515, 522 (10th Cir. 2000) ("[T]he presumption [of irreparable injury] is properly limited to circumstances in which injury would indeed likely flow from the defendant's objectionable statements, i.e., when the defendant has explicitly compared its product to the plaintiff's or the plaintiff is an obvious competitor with respect to the misrepresented product." (citing *Ortho Pharm. Corp.*, 32 F.3d at 694)). According to a survey in the record, approximately 90% of households have either cable or satellite service. Given the nearly binary structure of the television services market, it would be obvious to consumers that DIRECTV's claims of superiority are aimed at diminishing the value of cable—which, as discussed above, is synonymous with TWC in the areas covered by the preliminary injunction. Therefore, although the Revised Simpson Commercial does not explicitly mention TWC or cable, it "necessarily diminishes" the value of TWC's product. *McNeilab, Inc.*, 848 F.2d at 38. The District Court thus did not err in presuming that TWC has "a reasonable basis" for believing that the advertisement will likely cause it injury.

Time Warner, 497 F.3d at 161-62. In other cases, some courts have found standing to sue when the plaintiff was a trade association representing firms within the defendant's industry, *see, e.g.*, Nat'l Ass'n of Pharm. Mfrs., Inc. v. Ayerst Labs., 850 F.2d 904, 914 (2d Cir. 1988); a 45 percent shareholder in a corporation in competition with the defendant, *see* Thorn v. Reliance Van Co., 736 F.2d 929 (3d Cir. 1984); or a firm that sells an ingredient that defendant emphasizes as having been incorporated into its product, *see Johnson & Johnson*, 631 F.2d at 930-31.

As in antitrust law, standing doctrine in false advertising law might be viewed as a tool for screening out claims that have a high probability of being more anti-competitive than pro-competitive in nature. *Cf.* RESTATEMENT (THIRD) OF UNFAIR COMPETITION § 3 cmt. f ("an important factor is the presence or absence of harm to a less remote party whose self-interest would normally motivate the party to vindicate the public interest in exposing the actor's deceptive representation"). Returning once again to our discussion of the pros and cons of advertising, if most advertising serves a socially valuable purpose of providing useful information to consumers, one might suspect that firms sometimes would resort to false advertising law as a means of keeping aggressive competitors at bay by making it more difficult for them to communicate information about their products. *Cf.* Wal-Mart Stores, Inc. v. Samara Bros., 529 U.S. 205 (2000) (citing the anti-competitive risks of an overly expansive regime of trademark rights). If, on the other hand, one believes that false advertising is rampant and harmful to consumer interests, a strict standing requirement might not provide adequate deterrence (though the slack could, in theory, be taken up by expanding government efforts to combat false advertising or enhancing consumers' ability to protect their own interests directly). Based on your limited exposure thus far to the law of false advertising, which perspective do you find more persuasive? If you think that standing in false advertising cases should be limited to competitors, is the analytical framework as set forth in cases like *Time Warner* adequate to pinpoint which firms are (directly or indirectly) competitive with one another, or should courts employ a more rigorous approach — for example, by first defining the market using the tools of antitrust analysis? *See* U.S. DEP'T OF JUSTICE & FED. TRADE COMM'N, HORIZONTAL MERGER GUIDELINES § 1.0, at 4 (1992) (rev. Apr. 8, 1997) (defining a market as "a product or group of products and a geographic area in which it is produced or sold such that a hypothetical profit-maximizing firm . . . that was the only present and future producer or seller of those products in that area likely would impose at least a 'small but significant and nontransitory' increase in price"). Would the costs of such an approach outweigh the benefits?

Fourth, according to some courts, just because the plaintiff is in some sense a competitor with the defendant does not necessarily ensure that the plaintiff has standing, as the next case demonstrates.

Phoenix of Broward, Inc. v. McDonald's Corp.
489 F.3d 1156 (11th Cir. 2007)

KRAVITCH, Circuit Judge:

The primary issue in this appeal is the proper test for determining whether a party has prudential standing to bring a false advertising claim under § 43(a) of the Lanham Act, 15 U.S.C. § 1125(a). Phoenix of Broward, Inc. ("Phoenix") appeals the district court's dismissal of its false advertising claim against McDonald's Corporation ("McDonald's") for lack of prudential standing. For the reasons that follow, we adopt the test for prudential standing set forth in Conte Bros. Automotive, Inc. v. Quaker State-Slick 50, Inc., 165 F.3d 221, 225 (3d Cir. 1998), and affirm the district court's dismissal.

I. Background

Burger King Corporation ("Burger King") owns, operates, and franchises fast food restaurants throughout the world. Today, there are approximately 11,000

Burger King restaurants worldwide. Appellant Phoenix is a licensed Burger King franchisee that owns and operates a Burger King franchise in Fort Lauderdale, Florida. McDonald's, like Burger King, owns, operates, and franchises fast food restaurants throughout the world, and there are approximately 30,000 McDonald's restaurants worldwide. As competitors in the fast food industry, both McDonald's and Burger King have employed a variety of marketing and promotional strategies to attract customers, generate sales, and ensure customer loyalty.

From 1995 to August 2001, McDonald's offered customers the opportunity to participate in various promotional games such as "Monopoly Games at McDonald's," "The Deluxe Monopoly Game," "Who Wants to be a Millionaire," and "Hatch, Match and Win." Each of the promotional games featured low-value, mid-value, and high-value prizes. The low-value prizes included low-dollar cash awards and food and beverage items, while the high-value prizes included automobiles and cash awards of up to $1 million dollars. In general, customers could win the $1 million grand prize in one of two ways-by obtaining one of the rare $1 million, instant-winner game pieces or by collecting and matching a combination of certain other game pieces.

McDonald's conducted an extensive advertising and marketing campaign for each of the games it offered. In these advertisements, McDonald's represented that all customers who participated in the games had a fair and equal opportunity to win the offered prizes. The advertisements also represented the specific odds of winning certain prizes, including the high-value prizes.

In approximately April 2000, the Federal Bureau of Investigation ("FBI") began investigating the promotional games. While the games were still underway, the FBI informed McDonald's that there were problems with the random distribution of its game pieces. In spite of this alleged knowledge, McDonald's continued to advertise that customers had a fair and equal opportunity to win the offered prizes, including the high-value prizes.

On August 21, 2001, the United States Department of Justice ("DOJ") and the FBI announced that between 1995 and August 2001, certain of McDonald's promotional games had been compromised by a criminal ring led by an employee of Simon Marketing, Inc. ("Simon"), the company McDonald's engaged to operate the promotional games. From approximately 1995 to August 2001, Simon's Director of Security, Jerome Jacobson, diverted at least $20 million in high-value prizes by embezzling winning, high-value game pieces and distributing them to a network of "winners" who claimed (or recruited others to claim) the prizes from McDonald's. The DOJ and FBI announced that eight individuals, including Jacobson, had been arrested in connection with the scheme. In announcing the arrests, the U.S. Attorney General stated that the "fraud scheme denied McDonald's customers a fair and equal chance of winning." In a corporate press release issued after the arrests, McDonald's Chairman and Chief Executive Officer described the scheme as "a highly sophisticated inside game of fraud and deception."

On or about April 5, 2002, Jacobson pleaded guilty to charges of conspiracy and mail fraud. Approximately 50 other persons either pleaded guilty or were convicted in connection with the conspiracy.

Following the disclosure of the scheme, McDonald's created an independent task force to review all of its promotional practices, and it introduced additional security procedures to ensure the integrity of future promotional games. Nonetheless, consumers throughout the U.S. filed several class actions against McDonald's, alleging consumer fraud, negligence, and unjust enrichment. On April 19, 2002, McDonald's settled these class actions by, inter alia, agreeing to implement a $15 million "Instant Giveaway," providing class members and the general public an opportunity to win fifteen $1 million prizes.

On February 22, 2006, Phoenix filed the instant action against McDonald's on behalf of itself and all similarly situated Burger King franchisees (a proposed class of approximately 1,100 franchisees), alleging false advertising in violation of §43(a) of the Lanham Act. Specifically, Phoenix alleged that McDonald's misrepresented that each player in its promotional games had a fair and equal chance of winning high-value prizes and misrepresented the specific odds of winning high-value prizes. According to Phoenix, McDonald's promotional games were "rigged from approximately 1995-2001," those games lured customers away from Burger King and yielded an "unnatural" spike in profits for McDonald's, the high-value prizes (including the $1 million prizes) were diverted from McDonald's customers, and the "advertising campaigns that touted million dollar prizes were literally false." Phoenix also alleged that after learning that the games had been compromised, McDonald's knowingly and deliberately continued to advertise the games as though customers had a fair and equal chance of winning.

McDonald's moved to dismiss Phoenix's complaint on the grounds that Phoenix lacked prudential standing under the Lanham Act. . . . On August 1, 2006, the district court issued a written order granting McDonald's motion and dismissing the action with prejudice. . . .

II. Discussion

. . . "In every federal case, the party bringing the suit must establish standing to prosecute the action." Elk Grove Unified Sch. Dist. v. Newdow, 542 U.S. 1, 11 (2004). As the Supreme Court has explained, standing jurisprudence is comprised of "two strands: Article III standing, which enforces the Constitution's case-or-controversy requirement, and prudential standing, which embodies judicially self-imposed limits on the exercise of federal jurisdiction." Id. at 11-12 (internal quotation marks and citation omitted).

To demonstrate Article III standing, a plaintiff must allege that (1) he has suffered an actual or threatened injury, (2) the injury is fairly traceable to the challenged conduct of the defendant, and (3) the injury is likely to be redressed by a favorable ruling. Primera Iglesia Bautista Hispana of Boca Raton, Inc. v. Broward County, 450 F.3d 1295, 1304 (11th Cir. 2006).

McDonald's does not dispute that the allegations in Phoenix's complaint satisfy these constitutional standing requirements. . . .

Even where constitutional standing exists, however, prudential considerations may preclude standing. Wooden v. Bd. of Regents of Univ. Sys. of Ga., 247 F.3d 1262, 1273 n.12 (11th Cir. 2001). We therefore turn to the issue of prudential standing.

A. *Whether Prudential Standing Doctrine Applies to the Lanham Act*

We must first determine whether Congress intended to abrogate prudential standing doctrine in passing §43(a) of the Lanham Act. [The court quoted §43(a).]

The issue of whether prudential standing doctrine applies to § 43(a) of the Lanham Act is one of first impression in this circuit. The Third and Fifth Circuits have addressed this question, and both have held that Congress did not abrogate prudential limitations on the standing of plaintiffs to bring suit under § 43(a). *See Conte Bros.*, 165 F.3d at 227-30; Procter & Gamble Co. v. Amway Corp., 242 F.3d 539, 561-62 (5th Cir. 2001). We agree.

Congress is presumed to incorporate background prudential standing limitations unless the statute expressly negates such principles. Bennett v. Spear, 520 U.S. 154, 163 (1997). Although § 43(a)'s use of the term "any person" might lead to the conclusion that Congress intended to negate the background of prudential standing by allowing "any person" who could achieve Article III standing to bring suit, "the Supreme Court has twice held that Congress has not expressly abrogated prudential standing doctrine merely by passing a statute the text of which admits a broad interpretation." *Conte Bros.*, 165 F.3d at 227. For example, in *Associated General Contractors of California, Inc. v. California State Council of Carpenters*, the Supreme Court held that Congress did not abrogate prudential standing principles when it enacted the Clayton Act, despite statutory language allowing "[a]ny person who shall be injured in his business or property" to bring suit under that act. 459 U.S. 519, 535 & n.31 (1983). And as noted by the courts in *Conte Bros.* and *Procter & Gamble*, language contained in § 45 of the Lanham Act "makes clear that the focus of the [Lanham Act] is on anti-competitive conduct in a commercial context," so that conferring standing to the full extent implied by the plain language of § 43(a) would give standing to parties that have not had their competitive or commercial interests affected by the defendant's conduct. *Conte Bros.*, 165 F.3d at 229; *Procter & Gamble*, 242 F.3d at 561. Rather, "[t]he congressionally-stated purpose of the Lanham Act" evinces a congressional "intent to limit standing to a narrow class of potential plaintiffs possessing interests the protection of which furthers" that congressionally stated purpose. *Conte Bros.*, 165 F.3d at 229.

Accordingly, in light of the text of § 43(a) and the purpose of the Lanham Act as expressed in § 45, we join the Third and the Fifth Circuits and hold that Congress did not intend to abrogate prudential standing limitations when it enacted the Lanham Act.

B. *The Appropriate Test for Prudential Standing Under § 43(a)*

Phoenix argues that the district court applied the wrong test to determine whether Phoenix had prudential standing to bring its false advertising claim against McDonald's. According to Phoenix, the district court erred in applying the five-factor test articulated by the Third Circuit in *Conte Bros.*, and instead, the court should have applied the "categorical approach" that, according to Phoenix, "controls in most" of the circuit courts of appeals.

This court has not addressed the appropriate test for determining whether a plaintiff has prudential standing to bring a false advertising claim under § 43(a) of the Lanham Act. After surveying the caselaw from other circuits and examining the parties' arguments, we join the Third and Fifth Circuits and adopt the test for prudential standing articulated in *Conte Bros.* We therefore hold that to determine whether a party has prudential standing to bring a false advertising claim under § 43(a) of the Lanham Act, a court should consider and weigh the following factors:

(1) The nature of the plaintiff's alleged injury: Is the injury of a type that Congress sought to redress in providing a private remedy for violations of the [Lanham Act]?
(2) The directness or indirectness of the asserted injury.
(3) The proximity or remoteness of the party to the alleged injurious conduct.
(4) The speculativeness of the damages claim.
(5) The risk of duplicative damages or complexity in apportioning damages.

Conte Bros., 165 F.3d at 233 (internal quotation marks and citations omitted); *Procter & Gamble*, 242 F.3d at 562 (adopting the *Conte Bros.* test for determining prudential standing under the Lanham Act). We believe that this test "provides appropriate flexibility in application to address factually disparate scenarios that may arise in the future, while at the same time supplying a principled means for addressing standing under . . . § 43(a)." . . .

Phoenix argues that this court should adopt the so-called "categorical approach" that is applied in the majority of the circuits, as under that approach, "actual" or "direct" competition is the "exclusive requirement" for determining prudential standing. To that end, Phoenix argues that the *Conte Bros.* test was formulated in order to extend prudential standing under the Lanham Act to parties who are not in "actual" or "direct" competition. Thus, according to Phoenix, the *Conte Bros.* factors "inevitably collapse" into the categorical approach when applied to a "direct competitor" alleging a "competitive injury," and therefore, direct competitors "invariably satisfy" the *Conte Bros.* requirements. We address each argument in turn.

Of the circuits that have not adopted the *Conte Bros.* test, the Seventh, Ninth, and Tenth Circuits have come the closest to "categorically" holding that the plaintiff must be in "actual" or "direct" competition with the defendant and assert a "competitive injury to establish prudential standing under § 43(a)."

In contrast to the Seventh, Ninth, and Tenth Circuits, the First and Second Circuits have applied a less categorical approach to determine standing, wherein the dispositive issue is not the degree of "competition," but whether the plaintiff has a "reasonable interest" to be protected against the type of harm that the Lanham Act is intended to prevent. . . .

In the Second Circuit, a plaintiff bringing a false advertising claim under the Lanham Act "must demonstrate both (1) a reasonable interest to be protected against the advertiser's false or misleading claims, and (2) a reasonable basis for believing that this interest is likely to be damaged by the false or misleading advertising." *ITC Ltd. v. Punchgini, Inc.*, 482 F.3d 135, 169 (2d Cir. 2007) (internal quotation marks omitted). "The reasonable interest prong of this test includes commercial interests, direct pecuniary interests, and even a future potential for a commercial or competitive injury[,]" while "the reasonable basis prong requires the plaintiff to show both likely injury and a causal nexus to the false advertising." *ITC*, 482 F.3d at 169-70 (internal quotation marks omitted) (emphasis added). And under the Second Circuit's approach, a plaintiff asserting a false advertising claim under § 43(a) need not be a "competitor." See *PDK Labs.*, 103 F.3d at 1111; *Ortho*, 32 F.3d at 694; Berni v. Int'l Gourmet Rests. of Am., Inc., 838 F.2d 642, 648 (2d Cir. 1988). Instead, "where the plaintiff's products are not obviously in competition with [the] defendant's products," the "plaintiff must make a more substantial showing of injury and causation." *PDK Labs.*, 103 F.3d at 1111 (quotation marks omitted).

Thus, contrary to Phoenix's assertions, the majority of the circuits do not hold "categorically" that actual or direct competition is the exclusive requirement for standing to bring a false advertising claim under the Lanham Act. . . .

Finally, we disagree with Phoenix's contention that "direct competitors" alleging a "competitive" injury "invariably satisfy" the *Conte Bros.* requirements. Rather than blindly accept a plaintiff's allegation that it is a "competitor" that has suffered a "competitive injury," the *Conte Bros.* test is designed to determine whether the injury alleged is the type of injury that the Lanham Act was designed to redress — harm to the plaintiff's "ability to compete" in the marketplace and erosion of the plaintiff's "good will and reputation" that has been directly and proximately caused by the defendant's false advertising. *Id.* at 234-36. . . .

In summary, we hold that to determine whether a plaintiff has prudential standing to bring a false advertising claim under §43(a) of the Lanham Act, a court must consider and weigh the five factors articulated in the *Conte Bros.* opinion.

C. *Applying the* Conte Bros. *Test for Prudential Standing*

Phoenix argues that it satisfied the requirements of prudential standing under the *Conte Bros.* test. After examining and weighing the *Conte Bros.* factors, we conclude otherwise.

1. Type of Injury Alleged

The first factor directs us to determine "whether the alleged injury is of a type Congress sought to redress in providing a private remedy for violations of the Lanham Act." *Procter & Gamble*, 242 F.3d at 563. As the *Conte Bros.* court noted, the focus of §43(a) is on protecting "commercial interests [that] have been harmed by a competitor's false advertising, and in secur[ing] to the business community the advantages of reputation and good will by preventing their diversion from those who have created them to those who have not." *Conte Bros.*, 165 F.3d at 234 (alterations in original) (citation omitted).

In its complaint, Phoenix alleges that (1) McDonald's falsely advertised that customers who purchased its products had a fair and equal chance to win any of the prizes offered, including the high-value prizes; (2) during the run of the games, McDonald's experienced an "unnatural spike" in its sales while Burger King experienced a decrease in its sales; and (3) Burger King franchisees incurred counter-promotion costs in an effort to "lure back customers who frequented McDonald's while the fraudulent games were running." In our view, these allegations amount to an assertion by Phoenix that its "commercial interests" were "harmed by a competitor's false advertising," and this is the type of harm the Lanham Act was intended to redress. *See id.*

McDonald's argues that its "conduct was in no way anti-competitive" because it "was the victim of a criminal fraud scheme" perpetrated by a third party. According to McDonald's, "to the extent any of its advertising was 'false,' it was false solely because of the intervening criminal conduct of Jacobson and his coconspirators." We find this argument unavailing, however, because Phoenix alleges that McDonald's "knowingly and deliberately continued to advertise" that its customers had a "fair and equal chance" to win high-value prizes even after learning that the integrity of its promotional games had been compromised. Moreover, "[s]ection 43(a) provides a strict liability tort cause of action." Vector Prods., Inc. v. Hartford Fire Ins. Co., 397 F.3d 1316, 1319 (11th Cir. 2005) ("It is well-settled that no proof of intent or willfulness is required to establish a violation of Lanham Act § 43(a) for false advertising.").

McDonald's also contends that Phoenix's alleged injuries are not competitive in nature because the challenged advertisements "did not tout the products and services of McDonald's or disparage the products and services of Burger King." We cannot agree. Although the advertisements did not disparage Burger King or tout some intrinsic quality of McDonald's goods and services, the advertisements nonetheless asserted that customers who patronized McDonald's restaurants had an opportunity to win prizes, including the high-value prizes that had been stolen. Moreover, Phoenix alleges that the promotional games were sometimes "physically attached to McDonald's products."

McDonald's further contends that because Phoenix "has neither alleged nor suggested that its reputation was adversely affected by McDonald's advertising," this lack of "reputational injury" counsels against prudential standing. Although McDonald's is correct in asserting that Phoenix does not allege that its reputation was harmed by McDonald's conduct, we cannot say that the lack of alleged "reputational injury," in and of itself, directs us to conclude that Phoenix has failed to allege the type of injury that the Lanham Act was intended to redress. . . . We therefore conclude that the first factor weighs in favor of prudential standing.

2. Directness of the Asserted Injury

The second factor requires us to examine the "directness" with which the defendant's conduct affected the plaintiff. Phoenix alleges that by falsely advertising that customers had a fair and equal opportunity to win high-value prizes, McDonald's lured customers to its restaurants and away from Burger King restaurants. According to Phoenix, as a direct result of these false advertisements, it lost sales and incurred additional promotional expenses in its attempts to lure back the customers it lost to McDonald's during the fraudulent promotion.

On one hand, the causal chain Phoenix alleges is similar to that of the typical false advertising claim in which a plaintiff alleges that it lost sales and/or market share as a result of the defendant's false or misleading representations about some characteristic of the defendant's product or services. . . .

On the other hand, the causal chain Phoenix alleges is more attenuated than that alleged in cases like Logan [v. Burgers Ozark Country Cured Hams Inc., 263 F.3d 447 (5th Cir. 2001)]. Phoenix essentially alleges that (1) McDonald's advertisements falsely represented that customers had a fair and equal chance to win one of the "rare" high-value prizes if those customers patronized McDonald's restaurants and played its games; (2) as a direct result of the misrepresentation regarding the high-value prizes, McDonald's lured customers who would have eaten at Burger King (as opposed to one of numerous other fast food competitors), causing Burger King to lose sales; and (3) but for this misrepresentation, these customers would have eaten at Burger King, even though the chances of winning one of the "rare" high-value prizes would have been minute had there been no theft, even though only "certain" high-value prizes were stolen, and even though these customers still had a fair and equal opportunity to win all of the other prizes. Accepting Phoenix's allegations as true, the causal chain linking McDonald's alleged misrepresentations about one aspect of its promotional games to a decrease in Burger King's sales is tenuous, to say the least.

Taking care not to conflate the prudential standing inquiry with the "materiality" element Phoenix must establish to succeed on the merits of its claim, we conclude that the second factor counsels against prudential standing.

3. Proximity to the Allegedly Harmful Conduct

The third factor requires us to examine the proximity of the plaintiff to the allegedly harmful conduct. In examining this factor, we must determine whether there is an "identifiable class" of persons "whose self-interest would normally motivate them to vindicate the public interest" by bringing a suit. *Conte Bros.*, 165 F.3d at 234. "The existence of such a class diminishes the justification for allowing a more remote party . . . to perform the office of a private attorney general." Joint Stock Soc'y v. UDV N. Am., Inc., 266 F.3d 164, 182 (3d Cir. 2001) (internal quotation marks omitted).

Here, the district court held, and McDonald's asserts on appeal, that the consumers who were denied a fair and equal opportunity to win the high-value prizes as advertised constitute an "identifiable class" of persons whose self-interest would normally motivate them to sue McDonald's regarding its false advertising. But this can be said about any false advertising claim, as the consumers who were diverted from the plaintiff's product to the defendant's product in reliance on the defendant's allegedly false advertisements would always have a natural self-interest in suing for fraud. As such, if we accept the district court's and McDonald's reasoning, this factor would never counsel in favor of prudential standing. Moreover, consumers would not be able to vindicate the public interest via the Lanham Act, as "the several circuits that have dealt with the question are uniform in their categorical denial of Lanham Act standing to consumers." Made in the USA Found. v. Phillips Foods, Inc., 365 F.3d 278, 281 (4th Cir. 2004).

Furthermore, courts applying the Conte Bros. test have generally considered whether other commercial entities were the more appropriate parties to vindicate the competitive harm wrought by the defendant's alleged misconduct. As such, consumers "should be irrelevant to this analysis." Ford v. NYLCare Health Plans of Gulf Coast, Inc., 301 F.3d 329, 338 (5th Cir. 2002) (Benavides, J., concurring).

Again, Phoenix alleges that as a direct result of McDonald's false and misleading representations regarding the high-value prizes, McDonald's lured customers away from Phoenix and its affiliated franchisees, which, in turn, lost sales and market share. Accepting these allegations as true, we can think of no "identifiable class" of persons that is more proximate to the claimed injury than fast food franchisees such as Phoenix and the putative class it seeks to represent. As such, the third factor weighs in favor of prudential standing.

4. Speculative Nature of the Alleged Damages

Under the fourth factor of the *Conte Bros.* test, we examine the speculative nature of the plaintiff's alleged damages. According to Phoenix, its damages are not "speculative" because it would be "relatively straightforward" to calculate its damages as "an appropriate share of all profits associated with sales generated by the fixed promotional games" based on market share. We disagree.

As the district court noted, only "certain" high-value prizes were stolen, and customers still had a fair and equal opportunity to win one of the relatively numerous low- and mid-value prizes McDonald's offered, because those prizes were unaffected by the theft. Moreover, the fast food market consists of many competitors, only two of which are McDonald's and Burger King. In our view, it requires too much speculation to conclude that an ascertainable percentage of both the increase in McDonald's sales and the concomitant decrease in Burger King's sales during the several-year run of the games is directly attributable to McDonald's alleged misrepresentations about the chances of winning high-value prizes.

Phoenix also argues that at the pleading stage, the focus should be on what the complaint alleges, not on whether Phoenix may be able to prove the exact number of customers lured to McDonald's, because this is a matter for discovery and expert testimony. Although "general factual allegations of injury resulting from the defendant's conduct may suffice" to support standing "[a]t the pleading stage," Lujan v. Defenders of Wildlife, 504 U.S. 555, 561 (1992) (emphasis added), to "presume" that Phoenix's allegations "embrace those specific facts that are necessary to support" its claim to an appropriate share of McDonald's profits from the compromised games requires too much conjecture. See id. Even accepting Phoenix's allegations as true, the speculative nature of the damages it allegedly incurred as a result of McDonald's representations regarding the high-value prizes is inescapable.

Phoenix also contends that disgorgement of the profits McDonald's made during the "fixed" promotion would be an appropriate remedy "if the district court's premature fears [regarding the incalculable nature of Phoenix's damages] were substantiated." Disgorgement of "wrongful" profits "initially developed as a remedy to provide a plaintiff relief in equity, to serve as a proxy for damages, or to deter the wrongdoer from continuing his violations" and "is most appropriate if damages are otherwise nominal." BASF Corp. v. Old World Trading Co., 41 F.3d 1081, 1095-96 (7th Cir. 1994). But as the Third Circuit stated in *Joint Stock Soc'y*, "[i]f a request for relief that may be sought by any party sufficed under the fourth factor of the *Conte Bros.* test, that factor would be essentially meaningless, and we refuse to undermine the fourth factor in this way." *Joint Stock Soc'y*, 266 F.3d at 185. "The aim of [prudential standing] is to determine whether the plaintiff is 'a proper party to invoke judicial resolution of the dispute and the exercise of the court's remedial powers.'" *Conte Bros.*, 165 F.3d at 225 (quoting Bender v. Williamsport Area Sch. Dist., 475 U.S. 534, 546 n.8 (1986)). Accordingly, Phoenix may not bolster its "case for prudential standing by relying on forms of monetary relief that [it] would receive as a vicarious avenger of the general public's right to be protected against . . . false advertisements." *Joint Stock Soc'y*, 266 F.3d at 185 (internal quotation marks omitted).

We thus conclude that the fourth factor weighs against prudential standing.

5. Risk of Duplicative Damages

The fifth and final factor under the *Conte Bros.* test requires us to assess the risk of duplicative damages or the complexity of apportioning damages. The district court concluded that this factor weighs against standing. We agree.

If we were to hold that Phoenix has prudential standing to bring the instant claim, then every fast food competitor of McDonald's asserting that its sales had fallen by any amount during the relevant time period would also have prudential standing to bring such a claim. And if every fast food competitor had standing to bring such a claim, regardless of the amount in controversy, regardless of the amount of lost sales or market share directly attributable to the falsity of the advertisement, and regardless of the impact on the competitor's goodwill or reputation (as the advertisements made no mention of any competitor), the impact on the federal courts would be substantial. Furthermore, apportioning damages among these competitors would be a highly complex endeavor. . . .

6. Weighing The Totality of the Factors

To summarize, the first and third *Conte Bros.* factors weigh in favor of prudential standing, while the second, fourth, and fifth factors weigh against prudential standing. Admittedly it is a close question, but we conclude that on balance, Phoenix does not have prudential standing to bring its claim against McDonald's. Although Phoenix and the class it seeks to represent are McDonald's "direct competitors," Phoenix has alleged a competitive harm to their commercial interests, and there is no identifiable class of persons that is more proximate to the claimed injury, because of the attenuated link between the alleged injury and McDonald's alleged misrepresentations, the speculative nature of the claimed damages, the potential complexity in apportioning damages, and the significant risk of duplicative damages, we hold that Phoenix does not have prudential standing to bring a false advertising claim under the Lanham Act against McDonald's.

In so holding, we say nothing about the outcome of this analysis if, for example, the facts were such that McDonald's had falsely advertised the odds of winning all of its prizes (low-, mid-, and high-value), or if McDonald's were only giving away a single prize and falsely represented the odds of winning, as these hypotheticals present factual scenarios materially different from the facts of this case. Indeed, as stated above, a salient virtue of the *Conte Bros.* test is that it provides a flexible yet principled means of determining the existence of prudential standing for disparate factual scenarios, thereby allowing courts to foreclose standing on one set of facts while recognizing standing when presented with a slightly (but materially) different set of facts. . . .

COMMENTS AND QUESTIONS

1. Some commentators have argued that the Eleventh Circuit's application of the prudential standing factors in *Phoenix of Broward* creates an unacceptably high risk of underdeterring false advertising. *See* Gregory Apgar, Note, *Prudential Standing Limitations on Lanham Act False Advertising Claims*, 76 Fordham L. Rev. 2389 (2008) (generally favoring the *Conte Bros.* approach, but arguing that "direct" competitors such as Phoenix of Broward invariably should *satisfy* that approach); Gerald P. Meyer, Note, *Standing Out: A Commonsense Approach to Standing for False Advertising Suits Under Lanham Act Section 43(a)*, 2009 U. Ill. L. Rev. 295, 324 (arguing that the court's reasoning "would prevent any party from having standing to sue another party for false advertising whenever those parties compete in a large market or whenever the

defendant's false advertisements affect a large number of similarly situated parties," and advocating in its place a three-pronged approach that combines *Conte Bros.* factors (2), (4), and (5) into one factor only). Apgar quotes Professor Rebecca Tushnet, who wrote about *Phoenix of Broward* on her blog "43(b)log: False Advertising and More," as arguing that "*Conte Bros.* depends on a background assumption that *competitors* enjoy standing and the only question is how much further that extends"; and that the Eleventh Circuit's reasons for denying standing relate more to materiality and consumer effect, two issues that "should have been addressed at a later stage of the litigation where evidence could be considered, not at the pleadings stage where judges rely solely on their 'hunches.'" Apgar, *supra*, at 2420. Are these critiques persuasive? If *Phoenix of Broward* had come out the other way, would every fast food restaurant in America have had a viable claim against McDonald's? Concerns about "vexatious" litigation motivated the common law single source rule. Is *Phoenix of Broward* a throwback to the common law approach?

2. *Conte Bros.* factors (2) and (4), referring respectively to the "directness or indirectness of the asserted injury" and to the "speculativeness of the damages claim," would almost always point in the same direction, wouldn't they? *See* Meyer, *supra*, at 320-21 (arguing that "the fourth factor compels courts to weigh causation at least twice in the balance"). Factors (4) and (5) refer, respectively, to the "speculativeness of the damages claim" and the "risk of duplicative damages or complexity in apportioning damages." What if the plaintiff seeks only injunctive relief?

3. Should the fact that other parties have already challenged the defendant's alleged false advertising (as was the case in *Phoenix of Broward*, where the Department of Justice had filed criminal charges against Jerome Jacobson and seven others, and consumers had filed civil actions against McDonald's) play a role in deciding whether to permit a specific private plaintiff to proceed? Or should courts ignore such evidence of other possible deterrents? If the plaintiff's injury differs from that of other litigants, shouldn't it have a right to sue?

PROBLEMS

Problem 9-6. A nationwide chain that markets individual income tax preparation services to consumers advertises that consumers who used its service during the preceding year had an average refund of $500 more than the average IRS refund. Suppose that that statement is materially false. Would a sole practitioner accountant, who prepares about 200 individual tax returns every year from her home office, have standing to sue the chain for false advertising? How about a midsize law firm whose tax department prepares about 2,000 individual returns every year? Or would the only likely plaintiff be another major tax preparation chain?

Problem 9-7. The American Association of Orthodontists (AAO) files suit against Yellow Book USA, a publisher of Yellow Pages directories, alleging that Yellow Book violates §43(a)(1)(B) by listing general dentists under the category "Dentists-Orthodontists." According to AAO, orthodontics is a dental specialty that involves straightening the teeth. The American Dental Association's ethical rules describe as "improper" a general dentist's holding himself out as a specialist when he "has not completed the requisite education relative to such specialty," but there appears to be no state law expressly forbidding general dentists from holding themselves out as orthodontists. Yellow Book moves to dismiss on the ground that AAO lacks standing. What result? Does the case present a standing issue or something else?

D. FALSE ADVERTISING UNDER THE FEDERAL TRADE COMMISSION ACT

1. Overview

In 1914, Congress enacted both the Clayton Antitrust Act and the Federal Trade Commission (FTC) Act, in part to remedy perceived flaws in antitrust enforcement under the Sherman Act. In 1912, for example, the Supreme Court had held that tying arrangements did not constitute "contracts, combinations, or conspiracies" in violation of the Sherman Act. *See* Henry v. A.B. Dick & Co., 224 U.S. 1 (1912). In response, Congress included a provision in the Clayton Act specifically rendering some tying arrangements illegal. *See* Clayton Act, ch. 323, § 3, 38 Stat. 731 (1914) (codified as amended at 15 U.S.C. § 14). In enacting the FTC Act, Congress created a new federal agency, the Federal Trade Commission, whose responsibilities would include the investigation and prosecution of anti-competitive trade practices affecting interstate commerce. Initially, some advocates of creating such an agency hoped that Congress would spell out in detail the sorts of practices that the agency would challenge. The alternative position was that it would be preferable to define those practices in very general terms and leave the agency with broad discretion to interpret their specific meaning. *See* Marc Winerman, *The Origins of the FTC: Concentration, Cooperation, Control, and Competition*, 71 ANTITRUST L.J. 1, 67-68 (2003). The latter view ultimately prevailed, and as a result § 5 of the FTC Act as originally enacted stated merely that "[u]nfair methods of competition in or affecting commerce are hereby declared unlawful." From the beginning, the FTC interpreted this grant of authority as investing it with authority to challenge anti-competitive practices, including (but not necessarily limited to) practices that violated the Sherman and Clayton Acts. The FTC also interpreted its authority as extending to at least some cases involving false advertising, but (as noted in a preceding section) the Supreme Court in 1931 held that the FTC's authority to challenge false advertising applied only to cases in which the false advertising at issue harmed competition. *See* FTC v. Raladam Co., 283 U.S. 643, 649 (1931).

In a somewhat belated response to *Raladam*, Congress in 1938 amended the FTC Act to confer authority upon the agency to challenge practices in addition to "unfair methods of competition." As amended, § 5(a)(1) now states that "[u]nfair methods of competition in or affecting commerce, *and unfair or deceptive acts or practices in or affecting commerce*, are hereby declared unlawful." 15 U.S.C.

§ 45(a)(1) (emphasis added). *See also id.* § 45(b) (authorizing the FTC to commence an action whenever the Commission has "reason to believe that any . . . person, partnership, or corporation has been or is using any unfair method of competition or unfair or deceptive act or practice in or affecting commerce, and . . . it shall appear to the Commission that a proceeding by it in respect thereof would be to the interest of the public"). In addition, Congress added a new provision, § 12, which states:

> (a) Unlawfulness
>
> It shall be unlawful for any person, partnership, or corporation to disseminate, or cause to be disseminated, any false advertisement—
>
> (1) By United States mails, or in or having an effect upon commerce, by any means, for the purpose of inducing, or which is likely to induce, directly or indirectly the purchase of food, drugs, devices, services, or cosmetics; or
>
> (2) By any means, for the purpose of inducing, or which is likely to induce, directly or indirectly, the purchase in or having an effect upon commerce, of food, drugs, devices, services, or cosmetics.
>
> (b) Unfair or deceptive act or practice
>
> The dissemination or the causing to be disseminated of any false advertisement within the provisions of subsection (a) of this section shall be an unfair or deceptive act or practice in or affecting commerce within the meaning of section 45 of this title.

15 U.S.C. § 52.

Under the statutory regime as revised in 1938, the FTC's authority can be seen as falling into three broad categories. First, the FTC continues to have authority (which it shares with the Antitrust Division of the United States Department of Justice) to challenge anti-competitive practices as "unfair methods of competition." As before, these practices largely coincide with practices that would violate the Sherman or Clayton Acts. Thus, when the FTC challenges a practice as an "unfair method of competition," courts usually apply the same standards that would apply had the practice been challenged as a "contract, combination, or conspiracy" or other practice in violation of the Sherman or Clayton Acts. Nevertheless, the FTC retains some authority to define as "unfair methods of competition" certain practices that do not violate the other antitrust laws. *See* FTC v. Sperry & Hutchinson Co., 405 U.S. 233 (1972); Negotiated Data Solutions LLC, Analysis of Proposed Consent Order to Aid Public Comment, 73 Fed. Reg. 5846–01, at 5848-49 (Jan. 31, 2008).

Second, the statute grants authority to the FTC to challenge "unfair trade practices" and "deceptive trade practices" that affect interstate commerce. Responsibility for investigating both unfair and deceptive trade practices falls to the FTC's Bureau of Consumer Protection (as opposed to unfair methods of competition, responsibility for which lies with the FTC's Competition Bureau). "Unfair" and "deceptive" trade practices are not necessarily synonymous, however. The term "unfair trade practices" encompasses a wide variety of practices that harm consumers, such as (for example) abusive telemarketing practices, violations of data privacy policies, and certain types of abusive lending practices. The term "deceptive trade practices" refers more narrowly to false advertising. Nevertheless, there is some overlap between the two categories, and cases involving false advertising are often brought under both clauses.

At this point, it may be helpful to understand a bit about the structure and powers of the FTC. By statute, the FTC has five commissioners, each of whom is appointed to a seven-year term by the president with the advice and consent of the Senate, and no more than three of whom may belong to the same political party. FTC staff includes, as noted above, both a Competition Bureau and the Consumer Protection Bureau.

The FTC may investigate matters falling within its jurisdiction *sua sponte* or pursuant to complaints lodged by private parties. In pursuing investigations, the FTC may issue formal Civil Investigative Demands that are in the nature of subpoenas. If the FTC believe that a party is in violation of § 5 or 12, it may issue a proposed consent order to the party. The party may either agree to the terms of the order (in which case the order will be entered, subject to a period for public commentary) or reject them. In the latter case, the FTC will then vote on whether to file a formal complaint. If the FTC decides to file a complaint, the case is assigned to an administrative law judge (ALJ), with the FTC's Complaint Counsel representing the FTC.[14] Normally the remedy the FTC seeks is a cease and desist order, though sometimes it seeks other injunctive relief such as an order compelling a firm to provide consumers with refunds. In an appropriate case, the FTC also may request that a firm take out corrective advertising or be assessed civil penalties for rule violations (see below on FTC rule-making authority). Following trial and decision by the ALJ, the losing party may appeal to the full Commission. An appeal from the Commission's decision would go to any U.S. Court of Appeals that has personal jurisdiction and venue over the defendant. Occasionally, the losing party on appeal may pursue further review before the U.S. Supreme Court.

In addition to serving as both investigator and prosecutor, the FTC, like other federal agencies, engages in both formal and informal rulemaking. Formal rules, promulgated pursuant to the Administrative Procedure Act, have the force of law and are included in the Code of Federal Regulations. Examples include certain rules relating to telemarketing practices. *See* 16 C.F.R. §§ 310.1 et seq. Informal rulemaking (which does not have the force of law) may be embodied in FTC Guides or Policy Statements, some of which are excerpted below. These reflect the FTC's current views of what sorts of practices are permissible or impermissible and often serve as persuasive authority in court. It also sometimes is possible for a firm to obtain an advisory opinion from the FTC to help determine if the firm is in compliance with a cease and desist order. *See* 16 C.R.F. § 2.41(d).

Over the years, courts have shown considerable deference to the FTC's interpretation of its authority under § 5. The FTC itself has interpreted that authority in different ways at different times. Importantly, however, there is no private right of action under the FTC Act. Thus, if the FTC overlooks a particular practice, or decides that challenging the practice is not worth the investment of its own investigatory and prosecutorial resources, challenge must come, if at all, from private parties or other governmental agencies such as state attorneys general.

14. In an appropriate case, the FTC may proceed initially into federal district court for a temporary restraining order or preliminary injunction pending trial before the ALJ. *See* FTC Act § 13(b), 15 U.S.C. § 53(b).

2. FTC Regulation of False Advertising

a. The "Wayfaring Fools" Test

Charles of the Ritz Distributors Corp. v. FTC
143 F.2d 676 (2d Cir. 1944)

CLARK, Circuit Judge.

This is a petition to review and set aside a cease and desist order issued by the Federal Trade Commission, pursuant to a complaint charging petitioner with having violated the Federal Trade Commission Act, 15 U.S.C.A. §§41 et seq., by falsely advertising its cosmetic preparation "Charles of the Ritz Rejuvenescence Cream." Petitioner is a New York corporation engaged in the sale and distribution in interstate commerce of various cosmetics, one of which is the cream, in issue. This is a preparation of the type commonly known to the trade as a powder base or foundation cream for make-up. During the years from 1934 until December, 1939, when sales were "temporarily discontinued" because of the issuance of the present complaint, petitioner's Rejuvenescence Cream enjoyed a vast popularity, with total sales amounting to approximately $1,000,000. The extensive advertising campaign which accompanied this business placed emphasis upon the rejuvenating proclivities of the product. The advertisements typically referred to "a vital organic ingredient" and certain "essence and compounds" which Rejuvenescence Cream allegedly contained, and stated that the preparation brings to the user's "skin quickly the clear radiance . . . the petal-like quality and texture of youth," that it "restores natural moisture necessary for a live, healthy skin," with the result that "Your face need know no drought years," and that it gives to the skin "a bloom which is wonderfully rejuvenating," and is "constantly active in keeping your skin clear, radiant, and young looking."

After a hearing, the Commission found that such advertising falsely represented that Rejuvenescence Cream will rejuvenate and restore youth or the appearance of youth to the skin, regardless of the condition of the skin or the age of the user, since external applications of cosmetics cannot overcome skin condition which result from systemic causes or from physiological changes occurring with the passage of time and since there is no treatment known to medical science by which changes in the condition of the skin of an individual can be prevented or by which an aged skin can be rejuvenated or restored to a youthful condition. It, therefore, ordered petitioner to cease and desist disseminating in commerce any advertisement of Charles of the Ritz Rejuvenescence Cream: "(a) In which the word 'Rejuvenescence,' or any other word or term of similar import or meaning, is used to designate, describe, or refer to respondent's (petitioner's) said cosmetic preparation; or (b) which represents, directly or by inference, that respondent's said cosmetic preparation will rejuvenate the skin of the user thereof or restore youth or the appearance of youth to the skin of the user."

***

On the merits, petitioner first attacks the finding of fact that its preparation does not act as a rejuvenating agent and preserve or restore the youthful appearance of the skin. Two medical experts, one a leading dermatologist, testified for the Commission; and both affirmatively stated that there was nothing known to medical science which could bring about such results. There was no testimony to the contrary. . . . Further, petitioner was not privileged, under the circumstances, to stand upon its refusal to disclose the true formula of its preparation as a trade secret, and its failure to introduce evidence thus within its immediate knowledge and control, if existing anywhere, of the rejuvenating constituents and therapeutic effect of its preparation is strong confirmation of the Commission's charges.

Next, and as the crux of its appeal, petitioner attacks the propriety of the finding that by use of the trade-mark "Rejuvenescence" it has represented that is preparation will rejuvenate and restore the appearance of youth to the skin. In view of the finding which we have just held supported on the evidence, that in fact there are no rejuvenating qualities in petitioner's cream, the question is then simply whether or not the trade-mark is deceptive and misleading within the meaning of the Federal Trade Commission Act. But the dictionaries treat "rejuvenescence" as a common word with a plain meaning of "a renewing of youth" or the perhaps more usual "rejuvenation"; cf. WEBSTER'S NEW INTERNATIONAL DICTIONARY, 2d Ed., Unabridged, 1939. Nor does the record show any other special meaning to have developed in the trade. On the contrary, the Commission's expert and practicing dermatologist testified directly that rejuvenescence still meant not only to him, but also, as far as he knew, to his female patients, the restoration of youth. In the light of this plain meaning, petitioner's contention can hardly be sustained that "rejuvenescence" is a nondeceptive "boastful and fanciful word," utilized solely for its attractiveness as a trade-mark. . . .

There is no merit to petitioner's argument that, since no straight-thinking person could believe that its cream would actually rejuvenate, there could be no deception. Such a view results from a grave misconception of the purposes of the Federal Trade Commission Act. That law was not "made for the protection of experts, but for the public- that vast multitude which includes the ignorant, the unthinking and the credulous," Florence Mfg. Co. v. J. C. Dowd & Co., 2 Cir., 178 F. 73, 75; and the "fact that a false statement may be obviously false to those who are trained and experienced does not change its character, nor take away its power to deceive others less experienced." Federal Trade Commission v. Standard Education Soc., 302 U.S. 112, 116. See, also, Stanley Laboratories, Inc. v. Federal Trade Commission, 9 Cir., 138 F.2d 388, 392, 393; Aronberg v. Federal Trade Commission, 7 Cir., 132 F.2d 165, 167; D. D. D. Corporation v. Federal Trade Commission, 7 Cir., 125 F.2d 679, 682. The important criterion is the net impression which the advertisement is likely to make upon the general populace. *Stanley Laboratories, Inc. v. Federal Trade Commission*, supra; *Aronberg v. Federal Trade Commission*, supra; *Federal Trade Commission v. Standard Education Soc.*, supra; Ford Motor Co. v. Federal Trade Commission, 6 Cir., 120 F.2d 175, 182, *certiorari denied* 314 U.S. 668; Newton Tea & Spice Co. v. United States, 6 Cir., 288 F. 475, 479. And, while the wise and the worldly may well realize the falsity of any representations that the present product can roll back the years, there remains "that vast multitude" of others who, like Ponce deLeon, still seek a perpetual fountain of youth. As the Commission's expert further testified, the average woman, conditioned by talk in magazines and over the radio of "vitamins, hormones, and God knows what," might take "rejuvenescence" to mean that this "is one of the modern miracles" and is "something which would actually cause her youth to be restored." It is for this reason that the Commission may "insist upon the most literal truthfulness" in advertisements, Moretrench Corp. v. Federal Trade Commission, 2 Cir., 127 F.2d 792, 795, and should have the discretion, undisturbed by the courts, to insist if it chooses "upon a form of advertising clear enough so that, in the words of the prophet Isaiah, 'wayfaring men, though fools, shall not err therein.' "

General Motors Corp. v. Federal Trade Commission, 2 Cir., 114 F.2d 33, 36, *certiorari denied*, 312 U.S. 682.

That the Commission did not produce consumers to testify to their deception does not make the order improper, since actual deception of the public need not be shown in Federal Trade Commission proceedings. Representations merely having a "capacity to deceive" are unlawful; and, as we have seen, the facts here more than warrant a conclusion of such capacity. Likewise it is not material that there was no consumer testimony as to the meaning of petitioner's representations. The testimony of the dermatologist, a person whose occupation took him among the buyers of Rejuvenescence Cream, is a qualified source of information "as to the buyers' understanding of the words they hear and use."

Petitioner contends finally that, even if the Commission's findings of fact be upheld, that part of the order is inappropriate which bars use of the word "rejuvenescence." To delete this part of the order, however, would be not merely to create a patent ambiguity as to the meaning and effect of the broad prohibition of the remaining part of the order, but also to a large extent to frustrate the purposes of the whole proceeding to insure truth telling in the cosmetic trade. Certainly courts should be reluctant to emasculate a remedial order by striking out its more dynamic and practically effective parts while they affirm the Commission's proceedings as a whole. In any event, as we recently pointed out in *Herzfeld v. Federal Trade Commission*, supra, 140 F.2d at page 209, the Supreme Court in recent cases "has as much circumscribed our powers to review the decisions of administrative tribunals in point of remedy, as they have always been circumscribed in the review of facts"; and the present order seems peculiarly one wherein the special competence of the Commission in deciding "how far the chance of deception outweighs the inconvenience, or worse, to the merchant inevitable in compelling him to change his mark, his name, or his package" makes it "for all practical purposes supreme."

The order if affirmed and an enforcement decree will be entered.

COMMENTS AND QUESTIONS

1. The standard applied in *Charles of the Ritz* is sometimes referred to as the "wayfaring fools" test. Does it make sense to apply a standard that seeks to prevent even a small minority of consumers from being misled? (There are, reputedly, people who write letters to soap opera characters advising them about their love lives.) Are there any social costs in doing so? On the other hand, there surely is nothing honorable about misleading the gullible, is there? Note that trademark law clearly endeavors to protect "the ignorant, the unthinking, and the credulous"; while trademark law asks whether actual consumers are likely to be confused, it is willing to find liability even if as few as 10 percent of them are. Should the standard for false advertising be different? Why or why not?

2. In the face of uncertainty concerning which standard best serves the public interest, does it make sense to defer to the FTC's expertise? Or should courts take a more active, independent role?

3. As the following excerpt suggests, in the years following *Charles of the Ritz* the FTC did not always apply such a broad definition of deceptive practices. Moreover, in a 1984 law review article, for example, two FTC commissioners argued that (until the changes reflected in the Policy Statement on Deception excerpted below, from which

these two commissioners dissented) the FTC's "definition of the term 'deceptive,' . . . provide[d] that an act or practice is deceptive if (1) it has the tendency or capacity to mislead (2) a substantial number of consumers (3) in a material way." Patricia P. Bailey & Michael Pertschuk, *The Law of Deception: The Past as Prologue*, 33 AM. U. L. REV. 849, 850 (1984). The term "substantial number of consumers" might suggest a more rigorous test than "wayfaring fools," or perhaps a standard to identical to the one courts employ in Lanham Act cases. On the other hand, the term "tendency or capacity to mislead" arguably could permit the FTC to challenge practices that (as in *Charles of the Ritz*) present only a small probability of misleading a substantial number of consumers. *See id.* at 886 & n.167 (stating that the FTC does not "hold a company to the literal meaning of its words when such an interpretation is bizarre or idiosyncratic," but also noting that "[e]arly court decisions," such as *Charles of the Ritz*, "suggest . . . that the Commission does have power under § 5 to hold companies to literal interpretations of their advertisements"). *See also* Ernest Gellhorn, *Proof of Consumer Deception Before the Federal Trade Commission*, 17 U. KAN. L. REV. 559, 562-64 (1969) (stating that, while the FTC "has banned ads which seemingly could be misunderstood only by the 'credulous' or 'fools,'" "most of these cases can be explained on other grounds or can be justified by looking at the particular group to whom the ad is directed," or "can be explained simply as time-worn cases of another day"; in addition, that "judicial reluctance to interfere with an administrative agency's fact determination" may explain "[t]he emphasis in judicial opinions . . . on protecting the credulous, the trusting, and even wayfaring fools"); Ivan L. Preston, *The Definition of Deceptiveness in Advertising and Other Commercial Speech*, 39 CATH. U. L. REV. 1035, 1044-46, 1055-56 (1990) (citing Bailey & Pertschuk for the proposition that, even before the FTC shifted course in the 1980s, it generally did not find deception if survey evidence showed less than 20-25% of consumers were likely to be deceived). Nevertheless, the Policy Statement excerpted below clearly seems to eliminate any possibility that the FTC today would find deceptiveness in a case with as weak an evidentiary basis as *Charles of the Ritz.*

b. The "Reasonable Consumer" Standard

By the 1970s, some commentators (influenced in part by Chicago School arguments over the social value of advertising) had begun to question whether too stringent a standard was apt to inhibit advertisers from providing useful information to consumers. Recall, for example, Judge Easterbrook's comment (in the context of the Lanham Act) that if advertisers must conform their ads to the understanding of even small numbers of easily misled consumers, they will be forced to reduce "ads and packaging to meaningless puffery," Mead Johnson & Co. v. Abbott Laboratories, 201 F.3d 883, 886 (7th Cir. 2000), and similar sentiments expressed in RESTATEMENT (THIRD) OF UNFAIR COMPETITION § 2 cmt. d. Change eventually came with a change in administrations.

In 1981, President Reagan nominated James B. Miller III as chair of the FTC. Chairman Miller (who shared a Chicago School perspective with President Reagan's choice to head the Department of Justice's Antitrust Division, Stanford Law Professor William Baxter) thereafter seized the opportunity to assert a new standard for assessing deceptive advertising. In *Cliffdale Assocs., Inc.*, 103 F.T.C. 110 (1984), the FTC adopted the following Policy Statement on Deception, appended in the form of a letter from Chairman Miller to Congressman John Dingell. The FTC (and federal courts reviewing FTC decisions) have followed this Policy Statement ever since.

FTC Policy Statement on Deception

Appended to Cliffdale Associates, Inc., 103 F.T.C. 110, 174 (1984)

. . . Section 5 of the FTC Act declares unfair or deceptive acts or practices unlawful. Section 12 specifically prohibits false ads likely to induce the purchase of food, drugs, devices or cosmetics. Section 15 defines a false ad for purposes of Section 12 as one which is "misleading in a material respect."[2] Numerous Commission and judicial decisions have defined and elaborated on the phrase "deceptive acts or practices" under both Sections 5 and 12. Nowhere, however, is there a single definitive statement of the Commission's view of its authority. The Commission believes that such a statement would be useful to the public, as well as the Committee in its continuing review of our jurisdiction.

We have therefore reviewed the decided cases to synthesize the most important principles of general applicability. We have attempted to provide a concrete indication of the manner in which the Commission will enforce its deception mandate. In so doing, we intend to address the concerns that have been raised about the meaning of deception, and thereby attempt to provide a greater sense of certainty as to how the concept will be applied.

I. Summary

Certain elements undergird all deception cases. First, there must be a representation, omission or practice that is likely to mislead the consumer.[4] Practices that have been found misleading or deceptive in specific cases include false oral or written

2. In determining whether an ad is misleading, Section 15 requires that the Commission take into account "representations made or suggested" as well as "the extent to which the advertisement fails to reveal facts material in light of such representations or material with respect to consequences which may result from the use of the commodity to which the advertisement relates under the conditions prescribed in said advertisement, or under such conditions as are customary or usual." 15 U.S.C. 55. If an act or practice violates Section 12, it also violates Section 5. *Simeon Management Corp.*, 87 F.T.C. 1184, 1219 (1976), *aff'd*, 579 F.2d 1137 (9th Cir. 1978); *Porter & Dietsch*, 90 F.T.C. 770, 873-74 (1977), *aff'd*, 605 P.2d 294 (7th Cir. 1979), *cert. denied*, 445 U.S. 950 (1980).

4. A misrepresentation is an express or implied statement contrary to fact. A misleading omission occurs when qualifying information necessary to prevent a practice, claim, representation, or reasonable expectation or belief from being misleading is not disclosed. Not all omissions are deceptive, even if providing the information would benefit consumers. . . . In determining whether an omission is deceptive, the Commission will examine the overall impression created by a practice, claim, or representation. For example, the practice of offering a product for sale creates an implied representation that it is fit for the purposes for which it is sold. Failure to disclose that the product is not fit constitutes a deceptive omission. [See discussion below at 5-6.] Omissions may also be deceptive where the representations made are not literally misleading, if those representations create a reasonable expectation or belief among consumers which is misleading, absent the omitted disclosure.

Non-deceptive emissions may still violate Section 5 if they are unfair. For instance, the R-Value Rule, 16 C.F.R. 460.5 (1983), establishes a specific method for testing insulation ability, and requires disclosure of the figure in advertising. The Statement of Basis and Purpose, 44 FR 50,242 (1979), refers to a deception theory to support disclosure requirements when certain misleading claims are made, but the rule's general disclosure requirement is based on an unfairness theory. Consumers could not reasonably avoid injury in selecting insulation because no standard method of measurement existed.

representations, misleading price claims, sales of hazardous or systematically defective products or services without adequate disclosures, failure to disclose information regarding pyramid sales, use of bait and switch techniques, failure to perform promised services, and failure to meet warranty obligations.[5]

Second, we examine the practice from the perspective of a consumer acting reasonably in the circumstances. If the representation or practice affects or is directed primarily to a particular group, the Commission examines reasonableness from the perspective of that group.

Third, the representation, omission, or practice must be a "material" one. The basic question is whether the act or practice is likely to affect the consumer's conduct or decision with regard to a product or service. If so, the practice is material, and consumer injury is likely, because consumers are likely to have chosen differently but for the deception. In many instances, materiality, and hence injury, can be presumed from the nature of the practice. In other instances, evidence of materiality may be necessary.

Thus, the Commission will find deception if there is a representation, omission or practice that is likely to mislead the consumer acting reasonably in the circumstances, to the consumer's detriment. We discuss each of these elements below.

II. There must be a Representation, Omission, or Practice that is Likely to Mislead the Consumer.

Most deception involves written or oral misrepresentations, or omissions of material information. Deception may also occur in other forms of conduct associated with a sales transaction. The entire advertisement, transaction or course of dealing will be considered. The issue is whether the act or practice is likely to mislead, rather than whether it causes actual deceptions.

Of course, the Commission must find that a representation, omission, or practice occurred in cases of express claims, the representation itself establishes the meaning. In cases of implied claims, the Commission will often be able to determine meaning through an examination of the representation itself, including an evaluation of such factors as the entire document, the juxtaposition of various phrases in the document, the nature of the claim, and the nature of the transactions. In other situations, the Commission will require extrinsic evidence that reasonable consumers reach the implied claims. In all instances, the Commission will carefully consider any extrinsic evidence that is introduced.

Some cases involve omission of material information, the disclosure of which is necessary to prevent the claim, practice, or sale from being misleading. Information

5. Advertising that lacks a reasonable basis is also deceptive. *Firestone*, 81 F.T.C. 398, 451-52 (1972), *aff'd*, 481 F.2d 246 (6th Cir.), *cert. denied*, 414 U.S. 1112 (1973). *National Dynamics*, 82 F.T.C. 488, 549-50 (1973); *aff'd and remanded on other grounds*, 492 F.2d 1333 (2d Cir.), *cert. denied*, 419 U.S. 993 (1974), *reissued*, 85 F.T.C. 391 (1976). *National Comm'n on Egg Nutrition*, 88 F.T.C. 89, 191 (1976), *aff'd*, 570 P.2d 157 (7th Cir.), *cert. denied*, 439 U.S. 821, *reissued*, 92 F.T.C. 848 (1978). The deception theory is based on the fact that most ads making objective claims imply, and many expressly state, that an advertiser has certain specific grounds for the claims. If the advertiser does not, the consumer is acting under a false impression. The consumer might have perceived the advertising differently had he or she known the advertiser had no basis for the claim. This letter does not address the nuances of the reasonable basis doctrine, which the Commission is currently reviewing. 48 FR 10,471 (March 11, 1983).

may be omitted from written or oral representations or from the commercial transaction.

In some circumstances, the Commission can presume that consumers are likely to reach false beliefs about the product or service because of an omission. At other times, however, the Commission may require evidence on consumers' expectations.

Marketing and point-of-sales practices that are likely to mislead consumers are also deceptive. For instance, in bait and switch cases, a violation occurs when the offer to sell the product is not a bona fide offer. The Commission has also found deception where a sales representative misrepresented the purpose of the initial contact with customers. When a product is sold, there is an implied representation that the product is fit for the purposes for which it is sold. When it is not, deception occurs. There may be a concern about the way a product or service is marketed, such as where inaccurate or incomplete information is provided. A failure to perform services promised under a warranty or by contract can also be deceptive.

III. The Act or Practice must be Considered from the Perspective of the Reasonable Consumer

The Commission believes that to be deceptive the representation, omission or practice must be likely to mislead reasonable consumers under the circumstances. The test is whether the consumer's interpretation or reaction is reasonable. When representations or sales practices are targeted to a specific audience, the Commission determines the effect of the practice on a reasonable member of that group. In evaluating a particular practice, the Commission considers the totality of the practice in determining how reasonable consumers are likely to respond.

A company is not liable for every interpretation or action by a consumer. In an advertising context, this principle has been well-stated:

> An advertiser cannot be charged with liability with respect to every conceivable misconception, however outlandish, to which his representations might be subject among the foolish or feeble-minded. Some people, because of ignorance or incomprehension, may be misled by even a scrupulously honest claim. Perhaps a few misguided souls believe, for example, that all "Danish pastry" is made in Denmark. Is it therefore an actionable deception to advertise "Danish pastry" when it is made in this country? Of course not, A representation does not become "false and deceptive" merely because it will be unreasonably misunderstood by an insignificant and unrepresentative segment of the class of persons to whom the representation is addressed. *Heinz W. Kirchner*, 63 F.T.C. 1282, 1290 (1963).

To be considered reasonable, the interpretation or reaction does not have to be the only one. When a seller's representation conveys more than one meaning to reasonable consumers, one of which is false, the seller is liable for the misleading interpretation. An interpretation will be presumed reasonable if it is the one the respondent intended to convey.

The Commission has used this standard in its past decisions. The test applied by the Commission is whether the interpretation is reasonable in light of the claim. In the Listerine case, the Commission evaluated the claim from the perspective of the "average listener." In a case involving the sale of encyclopedias, the Commission observed "[i]n determining the meaning of an advertisement, a piece of promotional material or a sales presentation, the important criterion is the net impression that it is likely to make on the general populace." The decisions in American Home Products, Bristol Myers, and Sterling Drug are replete with references to reasonable consumer interpretations. In a land sales case, the Commission evaluated the oral statements and written representations "in light of the sophistication and understanding of the persons to whom they were directed." Omission cases are no different: the Commission examines the failure to disclose in light of expectations and understandings of the typical buyer regarding the claims made.

When representations or sales practices are targeted to a specific audience, such as children, the elderly, or the terminally ill, the Commission determines the effect of the practice on a reasonable member of that group. For instance, if a company markets a cure to the terminally ill, the practice will be evaluated from the perspective of how it affects the ordinary member of that group. Thus, terminally ill consumers might be particularly susceptible to exaggerated cure claims. By the same token, a practice or representation directed to a well-educated group, such as a prescription drug advertisement to doctors, would be judged in light of the knowledge and sophistication of that group.

As it has in the past, the Commission will evaluate the entire advertisement, transaction, or course of dealing in determining how reasonable consumers are likely to respond. . . .

Commission cases reveal specific guidelines. Depending on the circumstances, accurate information in the text may not remedy a false headline because reasonable consumers may glance only at the headline. Written disclosures or fine print may be insufficient to correct a misleading representations. Other practices of the company may direct consumers' attention away from the qualifying disclosures. Oral statements, label disclosures or point-of-sale material will not necessarily correct a deceptive representation or omission. Thus, when the first contact between a seller and a buyer occurs through a deceptive practice, the law may be violated even if the truth is subsequently made known to the purchaser. Pro forma statements or disclaimers may not cure otherwise deceptive messages or practices.

Qualifying disclosures must be legible and understandable. In evaluating such disclosures, the Commission recognizes that in many circumstances, reasonable consumers do not read the entirety of an ad or are directed away from the importance of the qualifying phrase by the acts or statements of the seller. Disclosures that conform to the Commission's Statement of Enforcement Policy regarding clear and conspicuous disclosures, which applies to television advertising, are generally adequate, CCH Trade Regulation Reporter, ¶7569.09 (Oct. 21, 1970). Less elaborate disclosures may also suffice.

Certain practices, however, are unlikely to deceive consumers acting reasonably. Thus, the Commission generally will not bring advertising cases based on subjective claims (taste, feel, appearance, smell) or on correctly stated opinion claims if consumers understand the source and limitations of the opinion. Claims phrased as opinions are actionable, however, if they are not honestly held, if they misrepresent the qualifications of the holder or the basis of his opinion or if the recipient reasonably interprets them as implied statements of fact.

The Commission generally will not pursue cases involving obviously exaggerated or puffing representations, *i.e.*, those that the ordinary consumers do not take seriously. Some exaggerated claims, however, may be taken seriously by consumers and are actionable. For instance, in rejecting a respondent's argument that use of the words "electronic miracle" to describe a television antenna was puffery, the Commission stated:

> Although not insensitive to respondent's concern that the term miracle is commonly used in situations short of changing water into wine, we must conclude that the use of "electronic miracle" in the context of respondent's grossly exaggerated claims would lead consumers to give added credence to the overall suggestion that this device is superior to other types of antennae. *Jay Norris*, 91 F.T.C. 751, 847 n.20 (1978), *aff'd*, 598 F.2d 1244 (2d Cir.), *cert. denied*, 444 U.S. 980 (1979).

Finally, as a matter of policy, when consumers can easily evaluate the product or service, it is inexpensive, and it is frequently purchased, the Commission will examine the practice closely before issuing a complaint based on deception. There is little incentive for sellers to misrepresent (either by an explicit false statement or a deliberate false implied statement) in these circumstances since they normally would seek to encourage repeat purchases. Where, as here, market incentives place strong constraints on the likelihood of deception, the Commission will examine a practice closely before proceeding.

In sum, the Commission will consider many factors in determining the reaction of the ordinary consumer to a claim or practice. As would any trier of fact, the Commission will evaluate the totality of the ad or the practice and ask questions such as: how clear is the representation? How conspicuous is any qualifying information? How important is the omitted information? Do other sources for the omitted information exist? How familiar is the public with the product or service?

IV. The Representation, Omission or Practice must be Material

The third element of deception is materiality. That is, a representation, omission or practice must be a material one for deception to occur. A "material" misrepresentation or practice is one which is likely to affect a consumer's choice of or conduct regarding a product. In other words, it is information that is important to consumers. If inaccurate or omitted information is material, injury is likely.

The Commission considers certain categories of information presumptively material. First, the Commission presumes that express claims are material. As the Supreme Court stated recently, "[i]n the absence of factors that would distort the decision to advertise, we may assume that the willingness of a business to promote its products reflects a belief that consumers are interested in the advertising." Where the seller knew, or should have known, that an ordinary consumer would need omitted information to evaluate the product or service, or that the claim was false, materiality will be presumed because the manufacturer intended the information or omission to have an effect. Similarly, when evidence exists that a seller intended to make an implied claim, the Commission will infer materiality.

The Commission also considers claims or omissions material if they significantly involve health, safety, or other areas with which the reasonable consumer would be concerned. Depending on the facts, information pertaining to the central characteristics of the product or service will be presumed material. Information has been found material where it concerns the purpose, safety, efficacy, or cost, of the product or service. Information is also likely to be material if it concerns durability, performance, warranties or quality. Information pertaining to a finding by another agency regarding the product may also be material.

Where the Commission cannot find materiality based on the above analysis, the Commission may require evidence that the claim or omission is likely to be considered important by consumers. This evidence can be the fact that the product or service with the feature represented costs more than an otherwise comparable product without the feature, a reliable survey of consumers, or credible testimony.[57]

A finding of materiality is also a finding that injury is likely to exist because of the representation, omission, sales practice, or marketing technique. Injury to consumers can take many forms. Injury exists if consumers would have chosen differently but for the deception. If different choices are likely, the claim is material, and injury is likely as well. Thus, injury and materiality are different names for the same concept.

V. Conclusion

The Commission will find an act or practice deceptive if there is a misrepresentation, omission, or other practice, that misleads the consumer acting reasonably in the circumstances, to the consumer's detriment. The Commission will not generally require extrinsic evidence concerning the representations understood by reasonable consumers or the materiality of a challenged claim, but in some instances extrinsic evidence will be necessary.

The Commission intends to enforce the FTC Act vigorously. We will investigate, and prosecute where appropriate, acts or practices that are deceptive. We hope this letter will help provide you and the public with a greater sense of certainty concerning how the Commission will exercise its jurisdiction over deception. We hope this letter will help provide you and the public with a greater sense of certainty concerning how the Commission will exercise its jurisdiction over deception. Please do not hesitate to call if we can be of any further assistance.

By direction of the Commission, Commissioners Pertschuk and Bailey dissenting, with separate statements attached and with separate response to the Committee's request for a legal analysis to follow.

Kraft, Inc. v. Federal Trade Commission

970 F.2d 311 (7th Cir. 1992)

FLAUM, Circuit Judge.

Kraft, Inc. ("Kraft") asks us to review an order of the Federal Trade Commission ("FTC" or "Commission") finding that it violated §§ 5 and 12 of the Federal Trade Commission Act ("Act"), 15 U.S.C. §§ 45, 52. The FTC determined that Kraft, in an

57. In *American Home Products*, the Commission approved the ALJ's finding of materiality from an economic perspective:

> If the record contained evidence of a significant disparity between the prices of Anacin and plain aspirin, it would form a further basis for a finding of materiality. That is, there is a reason to believe consumers are willing to pay a premium for a product believed to contain a special analgesic ingredient but not for a product whose analgesic is ordinary aspirin. *American Home Products*, 98 F.T.C. 136, 369 (1981), *aff'd*, 695 F.2d 681 (3d Cir. 1982).

advertising campaign, had misrepresented information regarding the amount of calcium contained in Kraft Singles American Pasteurized Process Cheese Food ("Singles") relative to the calcium content in five ounces of milk and in imitation cheese slices. The FTC ordered Kraft to cease and desist from making these misrepresentations and Kraft filed this petition for review. We enforce the Commission's order.

I.

Three categories of cheese compete in the individually wrapped process slice market: process cheese food slices, imitation slices, and substitute slices. Process cheese food slices, also known as "dairy slices," must contain at least 51% natural cheese by federal regulation. 21 C.F.R. § 133.173(a)(5). Imitation cheese slices, by contrast, contain little or no natural cheese and consist primarily of water, vegetable oil, flavoring agents, and fortifying agents. While imitation slices are as healthy as process cheese food slices in some nutrient categories, they are as a whole considered "nutritionally inferior" and must carry the label "imitation." *Id.* at § 101.3(e)(4). Substitute slices fit somewhere in between; they fall short of the natural cheese content of process cheese food slices yet are nutritionally superior to imitation slices. *Id.* at § 101.3(e)(2). Consistent with FTC usage, we refer to both imitation and substitute slices as "imitation" slices.

Kraft Singles are process cheese food slices. In the early 1980s, Kraft began losing market share to an increasing number of imitation slices that were advertised as both less expense and equally nutritious as dairy slices like Singles. Kraft responded with a series of advertisements, collectively known as the "Five Ounces of Milk" campaign, designed to inform consumers that Kraft Singles cost more than imitation slices because they are made from five ounces of milk rather than less expensive ingredients. The ads also focused on the calcium content of Kraft Singles in an effort to capitalize on growing consumer interest in adequate calcium consumption.

The FTC filed a complaint against Kraft charging that this advertising campaign materially misrepresented the calcium content and relative calcium benefit of Kraft Singles. The FTC Act makes it unlawful to engage in unfair or deceptive commercial practices, 15 U.S.C. § 45, or to induce consumers to purchase certain products through advertising that is misleading in a material respect. *Id.* at §§ 52, 55. Thus, an advertisement is deceptive under the Act if it is likely to mislead consumers, acting reasonably under the circumstances, in a material respect. *Thompson Medical Co.*, 104 F.T.C. 648, 788 (1984), *aff'd*, 791 F.2d 189 (D.C. Cir. 1986), *cert. denied*, 479 U.S. 1086 (1987), *Cliffdale Assocs., Inc.*, 103 F.T.C. 110, 164-66 (1984); Federal Trade Commission Policy Statement on Deception, 103 F.T.C. 174 (1984) (appended to *Cliffdale Assocs.*) [hereinafter "FTC Policy Statement"]. In implementing this standard, the Commission examines the overall net impression of an ad and engages in a three-part inquiry: (1) what claims are conveyed in the ad; (2) are those claims false or misleading; and (3) are those claims material to prospective consumers.

Two facts are critical to understanding the allegations against Kraft. First, although Kraft does use five ounces of milk in making each Kraft Single, roughly 30% of the calcium contained in the milk is lost during processing. Second, the vast majority of imitation slices sold in the United States contain 15% of the U.S. Recommended Daily Allowance (RDA) of calcium per ounce, roughly the same amount contained in Kraft Singles. Specifically then, the FTC complaint alleged that the challenged advertisements made two implied claims, neither of which was true: (1) that a slice of Kraft Singles contains the same amount of calcium as five ounces of milk (the "milk equivalency" claim); and (2) that Kraft Singles contain more calcium than do most imitation cheese slices (the "imitation superiority" claim).[1]

The two sets of ads at issue in this case, referred to as the "Skimp" ads and the "Class Picture" ads, ran nationally in print and broadcast media between 1985 and 1987. The Skimp ads were designed to communicate the nutritional benefit of Kraft Singles by referring expressly to their milk and calcium content. The broadcast version of this ad on which the FTC focused contained the following audio copy:

Lady (voice over): I admit it. I thought of skimping. Could you look into those big blue eyes and skimp on her? So I buy Kraft Singles. Imitation slices use hardly any milk. But Kraft has five ounces per slice. Five ounces. So her little bones get calcium they need to grow. No, she doesn't know what that big Kraft means. Good thing I do.
Singers: Kraft Singles. More milk makes 'em . . . more milk makes 'em good.
Lady (voice over): Skimp on her? No way.

The visual image corresponding to this copy shows, among other things, milk pouring into a glass until it reaches a mark on the glass denoted "five ounces." The commercial also shows milk pouring into a glass which bears the phrase "5 oz. milk slice" and which gradually becomes part of the label on a package of Singles. In January 1986, Kraft revised this ad, changing "Kraft has five ounces per slice" to "Kraft is made from five ounces per slice," and in March 1987, Kraft added the disclosure, "one 3/4 ounce slice has 70% of the calcium of five ounces of milk" as a subscript in the television commercial and as a footnote in the print ads.

The Class Picture ads also emphasized the milk and calcium content of Kraft Singles but, unlike the Skimp ads, did not make an express comparison to imitation slices. The version of this ad examined by the FTC depicts a group of school children having their class picture taken, and contains the following audio copy:

Announcer (voice over): Can you see what's missing in this picture? Well, a government study says that half the school kids in America don't get all the calcium recommended for growing kids. That's why Kraft Singles are important. Kraft is made from five ounces of milk per slice. So they're concentrated with calcium. Calcium the government recommends for strong bones and healthy teeth!
Photographer: Say Cheese!
Kids: Cheese!
Announcer (voice over): Say Kraft Singles. 'Cause kids love Kraft Singles, right down to their bones.

The Class Picture ads also included the subscript disclaimer mentioned above.

. . . As to the Skimp ads, the Commission found that four elements conveyed the milk equivalency claim: (1) the use of the word "has" in the phrase "Kraft has five

1. Because Kraft concedes that these claims, if made, are false, the second step of the aforementioned inquiry—whether the alleged claims are false—is not before us on appeal.

ounces per slice"; (2) repetition of the precise amount of milk in a Kraft Single (five ounces); (3) the use of the word "so" to link the reference to milk with the reference to calcium; and (4) the visual image of milk being poured into a glass up to a five-ounce mark, and the superimposition of that image onto a package of Singles. It also found two additional elements that conveyed the imitation superiority claim: (1) the express reference to imitation slices combined with the use of comparative language ("hardly any," "but"); and (2) the image of a glass containing very little milk during the reference to imitation slices, followed by the image of a glass being filled to the five-ounce mark during the reference to Kraft Singles. The Commission based all of these findings on its own impression of the advertisements and found it unnecessary to resort to extrinsic evidence; it did note, however, that the available extrinsic evidence was consistent with its determinations.

The Commission then examined the Class Picture ads — once again, without resorting to extrinsic evidence — and found that they contained copy substantially similar to the copy in the Skimp ads that conveyed the impression of milk equivalency. It rejected, however, the ALJ's finding that the Class Picture ads made an imitation superiority claim, determining that the ads neither expressly compared Singles to imitation slices, nor contained any visual images to prompt such a comparison, and that available extrinsic evidence did not support the ALJ's finding.

The FTC next found that the claims were material to consumers. It concluded that the milk equivalency claim is a health-related claim that reasonable consumers would find important and that Kraft believed that the claim induced consumers to purchase Singles. The FTC presumed that the imitation superiority claim was material because it found that Kraft intended to make that claim. It also found that the materiality of that claim was demonstrated by evidence that the challenged ads led to increased sales despite a substantially higher price for Singles than for imitation slices.

Finally, the FTC modified the ALJ's cease and desist order by extending its coverage from "individually wrapped slices of cheese, imitation cheese, and substitute cheese" to "any product that is a cheese, related cheese product, imitation cheese, or substitute cheese." The Commission found that the serious, deliberate nature of the violation, combined with the transferability of the violations to other cheese products, justified a broader order. Kraft filed this petition to set-aside the Commission's order or, alternatively, to modify its scope.

II.

Our standard for reviewing FTC findings has been traditionally limited to the highly deferential, substantial evidence test. . . . [The court rejects Kraft's argument that the First Amendment compels *de novo* review of the FTC's factual findings.]

III.

Kraft makes numerous arguments on appeal, but its principal claim is that the FTC erred as a matter of law in not requiring extrinsic evidence of consumer deception. Without such evidence, Kraft claims (1) that the FTC had no objective basis for determining if its ads actually contained the implied claims alleged, and (2) that the

FTC's order chills constitutionally protected commercial speech. Alternatively, Kraft contends that substantial evidence does not support the FTC's finding that the Class Picture ads contain the milk equivalency claim. Finally, Kraft maintains that even if it did make the alleged milk equivalency and imitation superiority claims, substantial evidence does not support the FTC's finding that these claims were material to consumers. We address each contention in turn.

A.

1.

In determining what claims are conveyed by a challenged advertisement, the Commission relies on two sources of information: its own viewing of the ad and extrinsic evidence. Its practice is to view the ad first and, if it is unable on its own to determine with confidence what claims are conveyed in a challenged ad, to turn to extrinsic evidence. *Thompson Medical*, 104 F.T.C. at 788-89; *Cliffdale Assocs.*, 103 F.T.C. 110, 164-66 (1984); FTC Policy Statement, 103 F.T.C. at 176. The most convincing extrinsic evidence is a survey "of what consumers thought upon reading the advertisement in question," *Thompson Medical*, 104 F.T.C. at 788-89, but the Commission also relies on other forms of extrinsic evidence including consumer testimony, expert opinion, and copy tests of ads. FTC Policy Statement, 103 F.T.C. at 176 n.8.

Kraft has no quarrel with this approach when it comes to determining whether an ad conveys express claims, but contends that the FTC should be required, as a matter of law, to rely on extrinsic evidence rather than its own subjective analysis in all cases involving allegedly implied claims. The basis for this argument is that implied claims, by definition, are not self-evident from the face of an ad. This, combined with the fact that consumer perceptions are shaped by a host of external variables — including their social and educational backgrounds, the environment in which they view the ad, and prior experiences with the product advertised, *see* Richard Craswell, *Interpreting Deceptive Advertising*, 65 B.U. L. Rev. 658, 672-74, 717 (1985); Richard Pollay, *Deceptive Advertising and Consumer Behavior: A Case for Legislative and Judicial Reform*, 17 U. Kan. L. Rev. 625, 629-31 (1969), makes review of implied claims by a five-member commission inherently unreliable. The Commissioners, Kraft argues, are simply incapable of determining what implicit messages consumers are likely to perceive in an ad.

Kraft buttresses its argument by pointing to the use of extrinsic evidence in an analogous context: cases brought under §43(a) of the Lanham Act. 15 U.S.C. §1125(a). Courts hearing deceptive advertising claims under that Act, which provides a private right of action for deceptive advertising, generally require extrinsic proof that an advertisement conveys an implied claim. Were this a Lanham Act case, a reviewing court in all likelihood would have relied on extrinsic evidence of consumer perceptions. While this disparity is sometimes justified on grounds of advertising "expertise" — the FTC presumably possesses more of it than courts, *see* American Home Prods. Corp. v. Johnson & Johnson, 577 F.2d 160, 172 n.27 (2d Cir. 1978) — Kraft maintains this justification is an illusory one in that the FTC has no special expertise in discerning consumer perceptions. *See* Robert Pitofsky, *Beyond Nader: Consumer Protection and the Regulation of Advertising*, 90 HARV. L. REV. 661, 678 (1977); Ernest Gellhorn, *Proof of Consumer Deception Before the Federal Trade Commission*, 17 U. KAN. L. REV. 559, 564-65 (1969). Indeed, proof of the FTC's inexpertise abounds: false advertising cases makes up a small part of the Commission's workload, most commissioners have little prior experience in advertising, and the average tenure of commissioners is very brief. That evidence aside, no amount of expertise in Kraft's view can replace the myriad of external variables affecting consumer perceptions. Here, the Commission found implied claims based solely on its own intuitive reading of the ads (although it did reinforce that conclusion by examining the proffered extrinsic evidence). Had the Commission fully and properly relied on available extrinsic evidence, Kraft argues it would have conclusively found that consumers do not perceive the milk equivalency and imitation superiority claims in the ads.

While Kraft's arguments may have some force as a matter of policy, they are unavailing as a matter of law. Courts, including the Supreme Court, have uniformly rejected imposing such a requirement on the FTC, *see Colgate-Palmolive*, 380 U.S. at 391-92 (FTC not required to conduct consumer surveys before determining that a commercial has a tendency to mislead), and we decline to do so as well. We hold that the Commission may rely on its own reasoned analysis to determine what claims, including implied ones, are conveyed in a challenged advertisement, so long as those claims are reasonably clear from the face of the advertisement.

Kraft's case for a per se rule has two flaws. First, it rests on the faulty premise that implied claims are inescapably subjective and unpredictable. In fact, implied claims fall on a continuum, ranging from the obvious to the barely discernible. *Thompson Medical*, 104 F.T.C. at 788-89. The Commission does not have license to go on a fishing expedition to pin liability on advertisers for barely imaginable claims falling at the end of this spectrum. However, when confronted with claims that are implied, yet conspicuous, extrinsic evidence is unnecessary because common sense and administrative experience provide the Commission with adequate tools to makes its findings. *See Colgate-Palmolive*, 380 U.S. at 391-92 (FTC need not conduct a consumer survey in finding commercial misleading). . . . The implied claims Kraft made are reasonably clear from the face of the advertisements, and hence the Commission was not required to utilize consumer surveys in reaching its decision.

Second, Kraft's reliance on Lanham Act decisions is misplaced. For one, not all courts applying the Lanham Act rely on extrinsic evidence when confronted with implied claims, *see, e.g.*, Better Business Bureau, Inc. v. Medical Directors, Inc., 681 F.2d 397, 403 (5th Cir. 1982); American Home Prods. v. Johnson & Johnson, 654 F. Supp. 568, 583 (S.D.N.Y. 1987), but more importantly, when they do, it is because they are ill equipped — unlike the Commission — to detect deceptive advertising. *See, e.g.*, Sandoz Pharmaceuticals Corp. v. Richardson-Vicks, Inc., 902 F.2d 222, 228 (3d Cir. 1990); Procter & Gamble Co. v. Chesebrough-Pond's Inc., 588 F. Supp. 1082, 1094 (S.D.N.Y.), *aff'd*, 747 F.2d 114 (2d Cir. 1984). And the Commission's expertise in deceptive advertising cases, Kraft's protestations notwithstanding, undoubtedly exceeds that of courts as a general matter. That false advertising cases constitute a small percentage of the FTC's overall workload does not negate the fact that significant resources are devoted to such cases in absolute terms, nor does it account for the institutional expertise the FTC gains through investigations, rulemakings, and consent orders. The Commissioners' personal experiences quite obviously affect their perceptions, but it does not follow that they are incapable of predicting whether a particular claim is likely to be perceived by a reasonable number of consumers.

2.

[The court next rejects Kraft's First Amendment argument "that the FTC's current subjective approach chills some truthful commercial speech." We discuss First Amendment issues in section G *infra.*]

B.

Alternatively, Kraft argues that substantial evidence does not support the FTC's finding that the Class Picture ads convey a milk equivalency claim. (Recall that the FTC, unlike the ALJ, concluded that the Class Picture ads did not contain the imitation superiority claim, leaving only the milk equivalency finding on appeal.) Kraft claims that the Commission merely extrapolated its analysis from the Skimp ads to the Class Picture ads without considering significant differences between the two. The Commission stated, for example, that the Class Picture ads "contain copy elements substantially similar to the 'Skimp' ad elements that convey the impression of milk equivalency." *In re Kraft, Inc.*, FTC No. 9208, slip op. at 22. Kraft points out that the Class Picture ads contain only one of the four elements of the Skimp ads — the reference to five ounces of milk juxtaposed with a reference to calcium content — that contributed to the FTC's milk equivalence finding. And Kraft adds that the reference to five ounces of milk per slice and to calcium merely states that each slice has a large amount of calcium because of its milk content, a completely true inference. The ads do not state or imply that each slice actually contains five ounces of milk or its calcium equivalent. Indeed, Kraft asserts that no reasonable consumer could think that a 3/4 ounce of slice of cheese contains five ounces of milk.

We find substantial evidence in the record to support the FTC's finding. Although Kraft downplays the nexus in the ads between milk and calcium, the ads emphasize visually and verbally that five ounces of milk go into a slice of Kraft Singles; this image is linked to calcium content, strongly implying that the consumer gets the calcium found in five ounces of milk. The fact that the Commission listed four elements in finding an implied claim in the Skimp ads does not mean that those same elements must all be present in the Class Picture ad to reach that same conclusion. Furthermore, the Class Picture ads contained one other element reinforcing the milk equivalency claim, the phrase "5 oz. milk slice" inside the image of a glass superimposed on the Singles package, and it was reasonable for the Commission to conclude that there were important similarities between these two ads. Finally, to support its own interpretation of the ads, the Commission examined available extrinsic evidence and this evidence, in the Commission's view, bolstered its findings.

Kraft asserts that the literal truth of the Class Picture ads-they are made from five ounces of milk and they do have a high concentration of calcium-makes it illogical to render a finding of consumer deception. The difficulty with this argument is that even literally true statements can have misleading implications. *See Zauderer*, 471 U.S. at 652; *see also Thompson Medical*, 791 F.2d at 197; *Removatron Int'l Corp.*, 111 F.T.C. 206, 292-95 (1988), *aff'd*, 884 F.2d 1489 (1st Cir. 1989); *American Home Prods.*, 695 F.2d at 687. Here, the average consumer is not likely to know that much of the calcium in five ounces of milk (30%) is lost in processing, which leaves consumers with a misleading impression about calcium content. The critical fact is not that reasonable consumers might believe that a 3/4 ounce slice of cheese actually contains five ounces of milk, but that reasonable consumers might believe that a 3/4 ounce slice actually contains the calcium in five ounces of milk.

C.

Kraft next asserts that the milk equivalency and imitation superiority claims, even if made, are not material to consumers. A claim is considered material if it "involves information that is important to consumers and, hence, likely to affect their choice of, or conduct regarding a product." *Cliffdale Assocs.*, 103 F.T.C. at 165; FTC Policy Statement, 103 F.T.C. at 175, 182. The Commission is entitled to apply, within reason, a presumption of materiality, *Colgate-Palmolive*, 380 U.S. at 392, and it does so with three types of claims: (1) express claims; (2) implied claims where there is evidence that the seller intended to make the claim; and (3) claims that significantly involve health, safety, or other areas with which reasonable consumers would be concerned. *Thompson Medical*, 104 F.T.C. at 816-17; FTC Policy Statement, 103 F.T.C. at 182-83. Absent one of these situations, the Commission examines the record and makes a finding of materiality or immateriality. *Id.*

Here, the ALJ concluded that both claims were presumptively material because calcium is a significant health concern to consumers. The Commission upheld this conclusion, although it applied a presumption of materiality only to the imitation superiority claim. Kraft asserts the Commission's determination is not supported by substantial evidence. We disagree.

In determining that the milk equivalency claim was material to consumers, the FTC cited Kraft surveys showing that 71% of respondents rated calcium content an extremely or very important factor in their decision to buy Kraft Singles, and that 52% of female, and 40% of all respondents, reported significant personal concerns about adequate calcium consumption. The FTC further noted that the ads were targeted to female homemakers with children and that the 60 milligram difference between the calcium contained in five ounces of milk and that contained in a Kraft Single would make up for most of the RDA calcium deficiency shown in girls aged 9-11. Finally, the FTC found evidence in the record that Kraft designed the ads with the intent to capitalize on consumer calcium deficiency concerns.

Significantly, the FTC found further evidence of materiality in Kraft's conduct: despite repeated warnings, Kraft persisted in running the challenged ads. [The court notes that Kraft received warnings from ABC television, Kraft's ad agency, a consumer group, the FTC, and the California Attorney General's Office.] From this, the FTC inferred—we believe, reasonably—that Kraft thought the challenged milk equivalency claim induced consumers to purchase Singles and hence that the claim was material to consumers. *See Cliffdale Associates*, 103 F.T.C. at 165; FTC Policy Statement, 103 F.T.C. at 175, 182.

With regard to the imitation superiority claim, the Commission applied a presumption of materiality after finding evidence that Kraft intended the challenged ads to convey this message. (Recall that intent to convey a claim is one of three categories qualifying for a presumption of materiality. *See, e.g., Thompson Medical*, 104 F.T.C. at 816-17.) It found this presumption buttressed by the fact that the challenged ad copy led to increased sales of Singles, even though they cost 40 percent more than imitation slices. Finally, the FTC determined that Kraft's consumer surveys were insufficient to rebut this inference and in particular criticized Kraft's survey methodology because it offered limited response options to consumers.

Kraft asserts that neither materiality finding is supported by substantial evidence. It contends that the survey evidence on which the Commission relied shows only that calcium, not milk equivalency, is important to consumers. Materiality, Kraft maintains, turns on whether the claim itself, rather than the subject matter of the claim, affects consumer decision-making; accordingly, the Commission had to show that consumers would have acted differently with knowledge that Singles contain 70% rather than 100% of the calcium in five ounces of milk. See FTC Policy Statement, 103 F.T.C. at 175 (claim is material if it is "likely to affect the consumer's conduct or decision with regard to a product"). With the inquiry defined in this manner, the only relevant evidence on point — a Kraft consumer survey showing that 1.7% of respondents would stop buying Singles if informed of the effect of processing on calcium content — definitively disproves materiality. With regard to its conduct, Kraft argues it persisted in running the ads because it thought the ads as a whole, not the milk equivalency claim per se, contributed to increased sales and that, in any event, it responded to warnings by making a good faith attempt to modify the ads. Kraft repeats these arguments in attacking the FTC's finding that imitation superiority claim was material to consumers, claiming the evidence adduced showed only that Kraft intended to use the ads to differentiate Singles from imitation slices based on milk content, and not on calcium content, and that sales increased as a result of this general theme; inferring that the imitation superiority claim contributed to increased sales is pure conjecture.

Kraft's arguments lack merit. The FTC found solid evidence that consumers placed great importance on calcium consumption and from this reasonably inferred that a claim quantifying the calcium in Kraft Singles would be material to consumers. It rationally concluded that a 30% exaggeration of calcium content was a nutritionally significant claim that would affect consumer purchasing decisions. This finding was supported by expert witnesses who agreed that consumers would prefer a slice of cheese with 100% of the calcium in five ounces of milk over one with only 70%. See Tr. 1176-78 (Stewart); Tr. 3663-64 (Jacoby). Likewise, the materiality presumption applied to the imitation superiority claim was supported by substantial evidence. This finding rested on internal company documents showing that Kraft designed the ads to deliver an imitation superiority message. Although Kraft produced a study refuting this finding, the Commission discounted that study after finding its methodology flawed. Kraft concedes that the Skimp ads increased sales of Singles, but contends that the Commission cannot carry its burden of demonstrating a linkage between the ads and the imitation superiority claim per se. However, this increase in sales corresponded directly with the ad campaign and indisputably reversed that sagging sales and market share of Kraft Singles that had been attributed to competition from imitation slices. Moreover, Kraft's increase in market share came at a time when Singles were priced roughly 40% higher than imitation slices. Thus, the Commission reasonably inferred that the imitation superiority message, as a central theme in the ads, contributed to increased sales and market share. . . .

For the foregoing reasons, Kraft's petition to set-aside the order is Denied and the Commission's order is Enforced.

Manion, concurring.

While I concur with the opinion of the court, I am concerned that the FTC can avoid extrinsic evidence by simply concluding that a deceptive, implied claim is facially apparent. While the FTC has expertise, consumer surveys provide at least some objective determination of what the purchaser thinks and should be considered since, after all, the consumer is among those we are trying to protect. . . .

. . . Rather than leaving judges to hew the contours of this issue, the FTC would be well-advised to take this court's suggestion-apply its expertise and develop a consumer survey methodology that advertisers can use to ascertain whether their ads contain implied, deceptive messages.

COMMENTS AND QUESTIONS

1. Is the three-part "reasonable consumer" test promulgated in *Cliffdale Associates* and applied in *Kraft* an improvement over the "wayfaring fools" test? Does it screen out a sufficient quantity of misleading advertising? How many reasonable consumers must be misled for an advertisement to be false?

2. Whether the FTC's approach is stricter or more lenient than the standards applied under the Lanham Act may depend on which aspects of the approach one focuses on. Recall that the *Restatement (Third) of Unfair Competition*, § 2 cmt. d states that "[i]f a reasonably prudent purchaser would not be deceived or misled by the representation, the actor is not subject to liability in the absence of other evidence indicating that the representation is nevertheless likely to deceive or mislead a significant portion of its audience." Under this approach, some statements that would not mislead reasonably prudent purchasers could nevertheless be actionable. Is this outcome possible under the FTC's Policy Statement on Deception?

On the other hand, in *Kraft* the court explains why the FTC, unlike a private plaintiff in a Lanham Act case, is not necessarily required to present extrinsic evidence that a claim is misleading. The court also upholds the FTC's authority to presume materiality in a wide range of circumstances—again, in contrast to the Lanham Act, where materiality is presumed (if at all) only when a claim is literally false. Does it make sense to defer to the FTC's expertise, or does Kraft have a valid point that FTC commissioners may be no less knowledgeable about advertising than their judicial peers?

3. In *Kraft*, the Seventh Circuit states that "not all courts applying the Lanham Act rely on extrinsic evidence when confronted with implied claims, *see, e.g.*, Better Business Bureau, Inc. v. Medical Directors, Inc., 681 F.2d 397, 403 (5th Cir. 1982); American Home Prods. v. Johnson & Johnson, 654 F. Supp. 568, 583 (S.D.N.Y. 1987)." The court is technically correct—the two cited cases both involved courts making a finding that a statement was literally false by necessary implication. Neither case, however, stands for the proposition that a literally true or ambiguous claim may be found misleading without extrinsic evidence.

c. *Substantiation*

FTC Policy Statement Regarding Advertising Substantiation

Appended to Thompson Medical Co., 104 F.T.C. 648, 839 (1984), aff'd, 791 F.2d 189 (D.C. Cir. 1986)

. . . This statement articulates the Commission's policy with respect to advertising substantiation.

The Reasonable Basis Requirement

First, we reaffirm our commitment to the underlying legal requirement of advertising substantiation — that advertisers and ad agencies have a reasonable basis for advertising claims before they are disseminated.

The Commission intends to continue vigorous enforcement of this existing legal requirement that advertisers substantiate express and implied claims, however conveyed, that make objective assertions about the item or service advertised. Objective claims for products or services represent explicitly or by implication that the advertiser has a reasonable basis supporting these claims. These representations of substantiation are material to consumers. That is, consumers would be less likely to rely on claims for products and services if they knew the advertiser did not have a reasonable basis for believing them to be true. Therefore, a firm's failure to possess and rely upon a reasonable basis for objective claims constitutes an unfair and deceptive act or practice in violation of Section 5 of the Federal Trade Commission Act.

Standards for Prior Substantiation

Many ads contain express or implied statements regarding the amount of support the advertiser has for the product claim. When the substantiation claim is express (e.g., "tests prove," "doctors recommend," and "studies show"), the Commission expects the firm to have at least the advertised level of substantiation. Of course, an ad may imply more substantiation than it expressly claims or may imply to consumers that the firm has a certain type of support; in such cases, the advertiser must possess the amount and type of substantiation the ad actually communicates to consumers.

Absent an express or implied reference to a certain level of support, and absent other evidence indicating what consumer expectations would be, the Commission assumes that consumers expect a "reasonable basis" for claims. The Commission's determination of what constitutes a reasonable basis depends, as it does in an unfairness analysis, on a number of factors relevant to the benefits and costs of substantiating a particular claim. These factors include: the type of claim, the product, the consequences of a false claim, the benefits of a truthful claim, the cost of developing substantiation for the claim, and the amount of substantiation experts in the field believe is reasonable. Extrinsic evidence, such as expert testimony or consumer surveys, is useful to determine what level of substantiation consumers expect to support a particular product claim and the adequacy of evidence an advertiser possesses.

One issue the Commission examined was substantiation for implied claims. Although firms are unlikely to possess substantiation for implied claims they do not believe the ad makes, they should generally be aware of reasonable interpretations and will be expected to have prior substantiation for such claims. The Commission will take care to assure that it only challenges reasonable interpretations of advertising claims.

Procedures for Obtaining Substantiation

. . . [T]he Commission has determined that in the future it will rely on nonpublic requests for substantiation directed to individual companies via an informal access letter or, if necessary, a formal civil investigative demand. The Commission believes that tailored, firm-specific requests, whether directed to one firm or to several firms within the same industry, are a more efficient law enforcement technique. The Commission cannot presently foresee circumstances under which the past approach of industry-wide rounds would be appropriate in the ad substantiation area.

Relevance of Post-Claim Evidence in Substantiation Cases

The reasonable basis doctrine requires that firms have substantiation before disseminating a claim. The Commission has on occasion exercised its discretion, however, to consider supporting materials developed after disseminations The Commission has not previously identified in one document the circumstances in which it may, in its discretion, consider post-claim evidence in substantiation cases. Such guidance can serve to clarify the program's actual operation as well as focus consideration of post-claim evidence on cases in which it is appropriate.

The Commission emphasizes that as a matter of law, firms lacking a reasonable basis before an ad is disseminated violate Section 5 of the FTC Act and are subject to prosecution. The goal of the advertising substantiation requirement is to assure that advertising is truthful, however, and the truth or falsity of a claim is always relevant to the Commission's deliberations. Therefore, it is important that the agency retain the discretion and flexibility to consider additional substantiating evidence, not as a substitute for an advertiser's prior substantiation, but rather in the following circumstances:

- When deciding, before issuance of a complaint, whether there is a public interest in proceeding against a firm;
- When assessing the adequacy of the substantiation an advertiser possessed before a claim was made; and
- When deciding the need for or appropriate scope of an order to enter against a firm that lacked a reasonable basis prior to disseminating an advertisement.

First, using post-claim evidence to evaluate the truth of a claim, or otherwise using such evidence in deciding whether there is a public interest in continuing an investigation or issuing a complaint, is appropriate policy. This does not mean that the Commission will postpone action while firms create post-claim substantiation to prove the truthfulness of claims, nor does it mean that subsequent evidence of truthfulness absolves a firm of liability for failing to possess prior substantiation for a claim. The Commission focuses instead on whether existing evidence that claims are true should lead us in the exercise of our prosecutorial discretion to decline to initiate a law enforcement proceeding. If available post-claim evidence proves that the claim is true, issuing a complaint against a firm that may have violated the prior substantiation requirement is often inappropriate, particularly in light of competing demands on the Commission's resources.

Second, post-claim evidence may indicate that apparent deficiencies in the pre-claim substantiation materials have no practical significance. In evaluating the adequacy of prior substantiation, the Commission will consider only post-claim substantiation that sheds light on pre-existing substantiation. Thus, advertisers will not be allowed to create entirely new substantiation simply because their prior substantiation was inadequate.

Finally, the Commission may use post-claim evidence in determining the need for or appropriate scope of an order to be entered against a firm that lacked a reasonable basis. Thus, when additional evidence offered for the first time at trial suggests that the claim is true, the Commission may frame a narrower order than if there had been no post-claim evidence.

The Commission remains committed to the prior substantiation requirement and further believes that these discretionary factors will provide necessary flexibility. The Commission will consider post-claim evidence only in the circumstances listed above. But, whether it will do so in any particular case remains within its discretion.

Self-Regulation Groups and Government Agencies

The Commission traditionally has enjoyed a close working relationship with self-regulation groups and government agencies whose regulatory policies have some bearing on our law enforcement initiatives. The Commission will not necessarily defer, however, to a finding by a self-regulation group. An imprimatur from a self-regulation group will not automatically shield a firm from Commission prosecution, and an unfavorable determination will not mean the Commission will automatically take issue, or find liability if it does. Rather the Commission will make its judgment independently, evaluating each case on its merits. We intend to continue our useful relationships with self-regulation groups and to rely on the expertise and findings of other government agencies in our proceedings to the greatest extent possible.

Thompson Medical Co. v. Federal Trade Commission

791 F.2d 189 (D.C. Cir. 1986)

MIKVA, Circuit Judge:

This case concerns a complaint brought by the Federal Trade Commission ("FTC" or "Commission") against petitioner Thompson Medical Company under §§ 5 and 12 of the FTC Act. The complaint alleged and the Commission found that Thompson's advertising for Aspercreme, a topical analgesic, was false and misleading, and constituted an unfair and deceptive practice. The Commission ordered Thompson to refrain from making unsubstantiated claims that Aspercreme is effective and to disclose in the product's labeling and advertising that it does not contain aspirin. Thompson challenges the FTC's order as arbitrary and capricious, contrary to public policy, unsupported by substantial evidence, and discordant with applicable Commission precedent. We find that the Commission's order and decision are supported by the law and the facts, and therefore affirm the FTC.

Background

Petitioner sells an over-the-counter ("OTC") analgesic (pain reliever) known as Aspercreme. Aspercreme is supposed to help arthritis victims and others who seek relief from minor aches and pains. As the name suggests, Aspercreme is a cream meant to be rubbed on the area where an analgesic effect is desired. Despite its name, however, Aspercreme contains no aspirin (acetyl salicylic acid). Rather, Aspercreme's active ingredient is trolamine salicylate (sometimes referred to as TEA/S or TEAS), a chemical relation of aspirin.

Even though Aspercreme contains no aspirin, Thompson's advertising strongly suggested that Aspercreme and aspirin were somehow related. One television advertisement used by Thompson, for example, contained the following monologue:

> When you suffer from arthritis, imagine putting the strong relief of aspirin right where you hurt. Aspercreme is an odorless rub which concentrates the relief of aspirin. When you take regular aspirin, it goes throughout your body like this. But, in seconds, Aspercreme starts concentrating all the temporary relief of two aspirin directly at the point of minor arthritis pain. . . . [Voice over:] Aspercreme. The strong relief of aspirin right where you hurt.

In this and similar ads, the announcer is shown holding aspirin tablets at the beginning of her monologue; as she speaks the aspirin is replaced by a tube of Aspercreme.

In February of 1981, the FTC issued an administrative complaint against Thompson. Thompson was charged with having violated sections 5 and 12 of the FTC Act. . . . Specifically, Thompson was charged with having made unsupported claims that Aspercreme was effective for the relief of arthritic pain, having falsely represented that this efficacy had been scientifically established, and having falsely represented that Aspercreme contained aspirin. The FTC complaint was heard before an administrative law judge (ALJ). After compiling a record in excess of 6500 pages, he issued a 127-page opinion finding Thompson liable. . . .

The FTC affirmed the ALJ's finding "that Thompson lacked reliable and credible information constituting a reasonable basis for the efficacy claims it made for Aspercreme." *Thompson* Opinion at 787-88, 821-28. The Commission found that Thompson had represented that Aspercreme was more effective than aspirin, and that Thompson had represented that Aspercreme's effectiveness had been scientifically substantiated. The Commission also found that Thompson had falsely represented that Aspercreme contained aspirin. It found that the alleged misrepresentations were material, and that they were likely to mislead consumers. The Commission also determined that Thompson's false and deceptive advertising had been deliberate. *Id.* at 791-839.

The FTC issued a final order against Thompson that prohibited the company from using the name Aspercreme unless its advertising and packaging made clear that Aspercreme does not contain aspirin. *See* Order, 104 F.T.C. 842, part I.A. The Commission also prohibited Thompson from representing that Aspercreme "involves a new scientific principle" when it has "been available for purchase in the United States as an [OTC] drug for more than one year," *id.*, part I.B., and from misrepresenting either the ingredients of Aspercreme or the results of any tests or studies of Aspercreme. *Id.*, parts I.C. & D. In the part of its order that has engendered the most controversy, the FTC ordered Thompson to refrain from

> A. Representing that [Aspercreme] is effective for the relief of minor pain and other symptoms of any musculoskeletal disorder. . . .
> B. Representing that [Aspercreme] is as fast or faster than, or is as effective as, or more effective than any other drug or device in the relief of minor pain and other symptoms of

> any musculoskeletal disorder . . . ; unless at the time of . . . such representation, [Thompson] possesses and relies upon a reasonable basis for such representation consisting of competent and reliable scientific or medical evidence.

Order, part II.

The FTC's Order went on to provide that "competent and reliable scientific evidence shall include at least two adequate and well-controlled, double-blinded clinical studies. . . ." *Id.*

Discussion

Thompson mounts a tripartite attack on the Commission's decision and order. Thompson first argues that the Commission was not acting in the public interest when it undertook to review Thompson's advertising. Thompson supports this contention by asserting that the Food and Drug Administration's ongoing review of OTC drugs preempts the FTC's jurisdiction here. Thompson next argues that the "reasonable basis" standard imposed by the Commission was improper. Thompson insists that requiring two clinical studies before Aspercreme can be advertised as effective is onerous and unwarranted. Finally, Thompson attacks the Commission's decision to require the company to make clear to consumers that Aspercreme does not contain aspirin. We take up these challenges in turn.

A. The Public Interest

[The court first rejects an argument that the Food and Drug Administration "has exclusive regulatory authority over the marketing and labelling of OTC drugs while its review is pending." We discuss the interplay of FDA law with false advertising law *infra* at pp. 424-25.]

B. Reasonable Basis

Thompson contends that the FTC erred in requiring two clinical studies as a prerequisite for any future representation that Aspercreme is an effective analgesic. Thompson correctly acknowledges that in general an advertisement is considered deceptive if the advertiser lacks a "reasonable basis" to support the claims made in it. *See In re Pfizer*, 81 F.T.C. 23 (1972); Porter & Dietsch, Inc. v. Federal Trade Commission, 605 F.2d 294, 302 (7th Cir. 1979). The controversy here concerns what constitutes such a basis. Thompson is unhappy with the Commission's requirement of two clinical studies. Thompson asserts that neither case law nor scientific wisdom justifies the imposition of this requirement, and that it has never before been imposed.

The Commission's opinion contains a thorough discussion of the framework traditionally used by the FTC in deciding when ads are properly supported by a reasonable basis, *Thompson* Opinion at 821-29, and why the order issued here contained the term it did. *Id.* at 829-39. We think the Commission has properly employed the framework established by its precedents in concluding that there was no reasonable basis shown here and in requiring two clinical studies before any representations can be made about Aspercreme's efficacy.

In evaluating the reasonable basis arguments, it is important to distinguish between two types of advertising claims. Some advertisements contain express representations about the level of support for a particular claim. Such advertisements are said to contain establishment claims. *See Thompson* Opinion at 813. The FTC has traditionally required that if an advertisement contains an establishment claim (*e.g.*, if it states that a product has been found to be superior by scientific tests) "the advertiser must possess the level of proof claimed in the ad." Bristol-Myers Co. v. Federal Trade Commission, 102 F.T.C. 21, 321, *aff'd*, 738 F.2d 554 (2d Cir. 1984), *cert. denied*, 469 U.S. 1189 (1985). If the claim is more general, but nevertheless constitutes an establishment claim, the FTC will specify the nature and extent of substantiation that will support the claim. *See, e.g.*, Sterling Drug, Inc. v. Federal Trade Commission, 741 F.2d 1146, 1152-53 (9th Cir. 1984); *American Home Products, supra*, 695 F.2d at 691-93; *Bristol-Myers, supra*, 102 F.T.C. at 351-52, 738 F.2d at 558-59. The FTC has usually required two well-controlled clinical tests before such a non-specific establishment claim may be made. (It should be noted that whether a claim of establishment is in fact made is a question of fact the evaluation of which is within the FTC's peculiar expertise. *See* Chrysler Corp. v. Federal Trade Commission, 561 F.2d 357, 363 (D.C. Cir. 1977).)

In the case of a simple claim of efficacy — a "non-establishment" claim — the reasonable basis required has been defined more flexibly. In *In re Pfizer Inc.*, 81 F.T.C. 23 (1972), the Commission established guidelines for the level of substantiation needed to support non-establishment claims. "*Pfizer* holds that the Commission itself may identify the appropriate level of substantiation for ads that do not expressly or impliedly claim a particular level of substantiation." *Thompson* Opinion at 822 n.59. In particular cases, however, the Commission has not always explained what would constitute "the appropriate level of substantiation" with great specificity. . . .

. . . Here, the FTC's requirement of clinical testing before an efficacy claim can be made extends to both establishment and non-establishment claims. *See Thompson* Opinion at 813-14 (discussing Thompson's representations that it had a particular level of support for its efficacy claims), 821-22 & n.58 (discussing reasonable basis requirements for establishment and non-establishment claims). Indeed, the FTC downplays the significance of the distinction between establishment and non-establishment claims. The FTC states that

> There is no conceptual or practical reason to single out such [establishment] claims for special treatment. They are but one example of an express or implied claim that an advertiser possesses a particular level of substantiation. . . . [T]he Commission itself may identify the appropriate level of substantiation for ads that do not expressly or impliedly claim a particular level of substantiation. . . . We do not have to perform such an evaluation where an advertisement itself makes . . . substantiation claims.

Id. at 822 n.59.

Despite the continuum that various sorts of claims lie along, it does not appear that the FTC has ever before required clinical testing to support a non-establishment claim. This forms the crux of Thompson's challenge to the FTC's Order. We think Thompson's attack is inadequate to overturn the FTC's decision. Despite the FTC's departure from its usual result, its reasoning in arriving at the requirement of clinical testing *is* well-founded in precedent. That is, the Commission carefully reviewed the factors laid out in its precedents before concluding that a two-clinical-test standard was appropriate here. *See Thompson* Opinion at 821-29; FTC Policy Statement Regarding Advertising Substantiation, Appendix to *Thompson* Opinion, 104 F.T.C. 839. The controversy thus turns on whether the FTC has properly applied the law to the facts.

Thompson rests its argument in large part on *In re Pfizer, supra*. Thompson argues that the reasonable basis standard for non-establishment claims articulated there and in subsequent FTC cases would have been satisfied here without the imposition of a clinical testing requirement. In essence, Thompson argues that the FTC has unreasonably and without explanation imposed a more severe standard here than it ever has in the past. Thompson's argument is unconvincing because in this case the Commission did not categorically impose a requirement of clinical testing for non-establishment claims. Rather, the Commission employed the multi-factorial analysis first expounded in *Pfizer* that Thompson acknowledges is appropriate, exercised its remedial discretion, and determined that the particular facts here warranted the imposition of a clinical testing requirement. The Commission's catalog and analysis of the factors deemed relevant in fashioning a remedy was extensive and painstaking. *See Thompson* Opinion at 821-29.

The cases cited by Thompson for the proposition that non-establishment claims need not be substantiated by clinical testing do not support that conclusion. Rather, as noted above, they simply constitute instances in which the Commission has not imposed such a requirement or has rejected its categoric imposition. . . .

Thompson is really arguing that non-establishment claims can never support a clinical testing requirement. Because the FTC did not impose a scientific testing requirement in some previous OTC drug cases, Thompson asserts that clinical testing should never be required in an OTC case. Thompson does not offer convincing support for this rather extreme position. Merely citing cases that are arguably similar to this one and observing that a less stringent standard was applied in them does not amount to proof that the FTC acted contrary to law in imposing a higher standard in this case.

It is worth noting that the Commission would be placed in a difficult position should we decide that a clinical testing requirement was inappropriate here. The Commission has had some difficulty with orders governing non-establishment claims that have been attacked on vagueness grounds. In *American Home Products Corp., supra*, 695 F.2d at 710, the court struck down on vagueness grounds part of an FTC order requiring "competent and reliable scientific evidence" as a reasonable basis for non-establishment claims. The court rested its holding in part on the large range of products covered by the order. In *Bristol-Myers Co., supra*, 738 F.2d at 560-61, by contrast, the court upheld an FTC order against a vagueness challenge. In *Bristol-Myers* the order's language was substantially similar to that in *American Home Products*, but it did not extend to as wide a range of products. The court distinguished *American Home Products* by noting that *AHP* depended not only on the allegedly vague language in the order, but also on the order's breadth. Despite the court's ultimate approval of the FTC's order in *Bristol-Myers*, however, the FTC had to go through a lengthy and uncertain appellate process before enforcing the order. *See also Sterling Drug, Inc. v. FTC*, 741 F.2d at 1156-57.

Obviously, both courts and the FTC would prefer that the FTC's orders were unequivocally legal. If we were to conclude that the two-clinical-test standard was unjustified under the *Pfizer* reasonable basis framework, it would be difficult for the FTC to fashion an acceptable set of requirements for non-establishment claims. The Commission has special expertise in determining what sort of substantiation is necessary to assure that advertising is not deceptive. We decline to interfere with its exercise of that discretion in the circumstances of this case. . . .

C. Aspirin Content

Thompson also challenges the portion of the FTC order requiring it to disclose in all advertising and labelling that Aspercreme does not contain aspirin. This part of Thompson's argument borders on the frivolous. Thompson argues that no misrepresentation occurred, that it is not material to consumers whether Aspercreme contains aspirin or not, that Aspercreme is merely a trademark and does not convey any information about the product's content, and that in any event Aspercreme labelling has always indicated that Aspercreme does not contain aspirin. (One wonders why Thompson is upset about being ordered to disclose that its product does not contain aspirin if no one cares and everyone has always known anyway.)

The issue of what message was reasonably likely to be conveyed to consumers by Aspercreme's advertising was extensively addressed by expert testimony. *See Thompson* Opinion at 788-816. The FTC's summation of the law in this area is accurate and succinct.

> Advertising representations will be condemned if they are likely to deceive; actual deception need not be shown. The tendency of a particular advertisement to deceive is determined by the net impression it is likely to make upon the viewing public. Consequently, literally true statements may nonetheless be found deceptive, and advertisements reasonably capable of being interpreted in a misleading way are unlawful even though other, non-misleading interpretations may also be possible.
>
> In determining the meaning likely to be conveyed by advertisements, the Commission is engaged in fact-finding, and its findings are to be regarded as conclusive if supported by substantial evidence. Moreover, in interpreting advertisements, the Commission may rely on its own reasoned analysis of the advertisements themselves, without resorting to surveys or consumer testimony. Although the meaning of the statutory phrase "deceptive acts or practices" is ultimately a matter for judicial construction, the Commission's conclusion that acts or practices are likely to deceive is due special deference owing to the nature of the inquiry and the Commission's expertise in evaluating deception.

Brief for the FTC at 49-50 (footnotes omitted). The factual nature of the FTC's findings with respect to the aspirin claims and the FTC's expertise and experience in this area make its opinion very difficult to challenge.

Conclusion

The FTC adequately considered a large mass of technical evidence and concluded that Thompson had engaged in deceptive advertising with respect to Aspercreme. We cannot find fault in the Commission's conclusions or in the remedial measures it imposed. Indeed, in all respects, we find the FTC Order and Opinion clear and logical. If and when Thompson comes up with evidence that Aspercreme is effective, it will be free to again make efficacy claims in its advertising. Until that time, it should not say what it cannot prove. The FTC's requirement of aspirin-content disclaimers also is entirely appropriate; Aspercreme does not contain any aspirin, and its makers should not imply that it does. Accordingly, Thompson's petition for review of the FTC's order is

Denied.

COMMENTS AND QUESTIONS

1. Notice the following language from the Policy Statement on Advertising Substantiation: "The Commission's determination of what constitutes a reasonable basis depends, *as it does in an unfairness analysis*, on a number of factors relevant to the benefits and costs of substantiating a particular claim" (emphasis added). FTC cases involving questions of advertising substantiation often are litigated as "unfair trade practices," rather than (exclusively) as "deceptive trade practice" cases, because the Commission's "unfairness" analysis contemplates the sort of cost-benefit analysis that the Commission refers to in the Policy Statement. Section 5(n) of the FTC Act, 15 U.S.C. §45(n), states that

> The Commission shall have no authority under this section or section 57(a) of this title to declare unlawful an act or practice on the grounds that such act or practice is unfair unless the act or practice causes or is likely to cause substantial injury to consumers which is not reasonably avoidable by consumers themselves and not outweighed by countervailing benefits to consumers or to competition. In determining whether an act or practice is unfair, the Commission may consider established public policies as evidence to be considered with all other evidence. Such public policy considerations may not serve as a primary basis for such determination.

See also FTC Policy Statement on Unfairness (Dec. 17, 1980), *available at* http://www.ftc.gov/bcp/policystmt/ad-unfair.htm:

> By 1964 enough cases had been decided to enable the Commission to identify three factors that it considered when applying the prohibition against consumer unfairness. These were: (1) whether the practice injures consumers; (2) whether it violates established public policy; (3) whether it is unethical or unscrupulous. These factors were later quoted with apparent approval by the Supreme Court in the 1972 case of *Sperry & Hutchinson.* Since then the Commission has continued to refine the standard of unfairness in its cases and rules, and it has now reached a more detailed sense of both the definition and the limits of these criteria.[10]
>
> *Consumer injury*
>
> Unjustified consumer injury is the primary focus of the FTC Act, and the most important of the three *S&H* criteria. By itself it can be sufficient to warrant a finding of unfairness. The Commission's ability to rely on an independent criterion of consumer injury is consistent with the intent of the statute, which was to "[make] the consumer who

10. These standards for unfairness are generally applicable to both advertising and non-advertising cases.

may be injured by an unfair trade practice of equal concern before the law with the merchant injured by the unfair methods of a dishonest competitor."

The independent nature of the consumer injury criterion does not mean that every consumer injury is legally "unfair," however. To justify a finding of unfairness the injury must satisfy three tests. It must be substantial; it must not be outweighed by any countervailing benefits to consumers or competition that the practice produces; and it must be an injury that consumers themselves could not reasonably have avoided.

First of all, the injury must be substantial. The Commission is not concerned with trivial or merely speculative harms.[12] In most cases a substantial injury involves monetary harm, as when sellers coerce consumers into purchasing unwanted goods or services. . . . Emotional impact and other more subjective types of harm, on the other hand, will not ordinarily make a practice unfair. Thus, for example, the Commission will not seek to ban an advertisement merely because it offends the tastes or social beliefs of some viewers, as has been suggested in some of the comments.

Second, the injury must not be outweighed by any offsetting consumer or competitive benefits that the sales practice also produces. Most business practices entail a mixture of economic and other costs and benefits for purchasers. A seller's failure to present complex technical data on his product may lessen a consumer's ability to choose, for example, but may also reduce the initial price he must pay for the article. The Commission is aware of these tradeoffs and will not find that a practice unfairly injures consumers unless it is injurious in its net effects. The Commission also takes account of the various costs that a remedy would entail. These include not only the costs to the parties directly before the agency, but also the burdens on society in general in the form of increased paperwork, increased regulatory burdens on the flow of information, reduced incentives to innovation and capital formation, and similar matters. Finally, the injury must be one which consumers could not reasonably have avoided. Normally we expect the marketplace to be self-correcting, and we rely on consumer choice — the ability of individual consumers to make their own private purchasing decisions without regulatory intervention — to govern the market. We anticipate that consumers will survey the available alternatives, choose those that are most desirable, and avoid those that are inadequate or unsatisfactory. However, it has long been recognized that certain types of sales techniques may prevent consumers from effectively making their own decisions, and that corrective action may then become necessary. . . .

Violation of public policy

The second *S&H* standard asks whether the conduct violates public policy as it has been established by statute, common law, industry practice, or otherwise. This criterion may be applied in two different ways. It may be used to test the validity and strength of the evidence of consumer injury, or, less often, it may be cited for a dispositive legislative or judicial determination that such injury is present.

Although public policy was listed by the *S&H* Court as a separate consideration, it is used most frequently by the Commission as a means of providing additional evidence on the degree of consumer injury caused by specific practices. To be sure, most Commission actions are brought to redress relatively clear-cut injuries, and those determinations are based, in large part, on objective economic analysis. As we have indicated before, the Commission believes that considerable attention should be devoted to the analysis of whether substantial net harm has occurred, not only because that is part of the unfairness

12. An injury may be sufficiently substantial, however, if it does a small harm to a large number of people, or if it raises a significant risk of concrete harm.

test, but also because the focus on injury is the best way to ensure that the Commission acts responsibly and uses its resources wisely. Nonetheless, the Commission wishes to emphasize the importance of examining outside statutory policies and established judicial principles for assistance in helping the agency ascertain whether a particular form of conduct does in fact tend to harm consumers. Thus the agency has referred to First Amendment decisions upholding consumers' rights to receive information, for example, to confirm that restrictions on advertising tend unfairly to hinder the informed exercise of consumer choice. . . .

Unethical or unscrupulous conduct

Finally, the third *S&H* standard asks whether the conduct was immoral, unethical, oppressive, or unscrupulous. This test was presumably included in order to be sure of reaching all the purposes of the underlying statute, which forbids "unfair" acts or practices. It would therefore allow the Commission to reach conduct that violates generally recognized standards of business ethics. The test has proven, however, to be largely duplicative. Conduct that is truly unethical or unscrupulous will almost always injure consumers or violate public policy as well. The Commission has therefore never relied on the third element of *S&H* as an independent basis for a finding of unfairness, and it will act in the future only on the basis of the first two.

2. The FTC's views on advertising substantiation contrasts with the rules followed in Lanham Act cases. As we have seen, in the Lanham Act context courts do not view unsubstantiated claims as false unless the claim expressly or implicitly communicates a message that the speaker has substantiated the claim before making it (although some authorities disapprove of completely unsubstantiated claims). By contrast, the FTC Policy Statement Regarding Advertising Substantiation states that the FTC generally requires substantiation (a "reasonable basis for advertising claims before they are disseminated") even for "nonestablishment" claims (although adequate substantiation after the fact may indicate that any deficiencies in the *ex ante* substantiation have little if any practical significance). Which rule is preferable? Do the rules necessarily conflict in practice? What advice would you give a client that is considering making unsubstantiated product claims?

d. Endorsements and Testimonials

Another common practice in advertising is the use of endorsements and testimonials from consumers or celebrities. There are a variety of ways in which endorsements may run afoul of the law, however. First, suppose that in advertising its weight-loss program XYZ Company claims that Myron, a well-known actor, lost 30 pounds by using the company's system; but that Myron neither used the program nor consented to the use of his name in the ad. In such a case, the false claim about Myron's weight loss surely would be actionable false advertising under both the Lanham and the FTC Acts. In addition, as we discuss in Chapter 10, Myron himself probably would have a claim for false endorsement under Lanham Act §43(a)(1)(A) and for violation of his right of publicity under state law.

Alternatively, suppose that Myron really did lose 30 pounds by using XYZ's system, but that he never agreed to having his name used in the company's ads. Even though the claim about Myron's weight loss is true, Myron still would have a claim for violation of his right of publicity—and probably for false endorsement as well—because of his lack of consent. *See infra* Chapter 10.

Now suppose that Myron *agrees* to endorse XYZ's weight-loss product. There should be no problems now in including his endorsement in the ads, right? Wrong. Although Myron himself would not have a cause of action for false endorsement, in this example (and, *a fortiori*, in the examples described above) XYZ still could be engaging in actionable false advertising if, for example, the ad falsely conveys the message that the product is effective, or that Myron's experience with the product was typical of what other consumers could expect. Consider other possibilities too. What if Myron's endorsement of the product does not reflect his honest opinion about its merits? What if neither Myron nor XYZ disclose that Myron was paid to provide the endorsement? Should such conduct be deemed false advertising (or, in FTC parlance, an unfair or deceptive practice)? Should Myron himself be subject to liability under any or all of these variations? Should a disclaimer ever suffice to avoid liability?

The FTC has played a role in regulating the use of endorsements and testimonials since at least the 1970s, when it first published guides for this type of advertising. The FTC amended these guides in 1980 and then again in late 2009. The newly revised guides are excerpted below. The new guides create somewhat stricter standards for endorsements and testimonials in several respects. Some advertisers, for example, read the 1980 guides as providing a "safe harbor" under which a clear and conspicuous disclaimer stating that "Results may vary" or "Results not typical" would immunize advertisers from liability for falsely claiming that an endorser's experience was representative or typical of what consumers could expect to achieve from using a given product. In recent years, however, the FTC had come to doubt the efficacy of such "disclaimers of typicality" even when (as was not always the case in practice) they truly were "clear and conspicuous." In one study conducted by FTC staff, for instance, "despite the presence of strongly worded, highly prominent disclaimers of typicality, between 44.1% and 70.5% of respondents indicated that the dietary supplement in question would reduce breathing problems, increase energy levels, and relieve pain in at least half of the people who try it." In light of findings such as these, § 255.2(b) of the new guides (excerpted below) eliminates the safe harbor of disclaimers of typicality provided under the old guides. (In response, some critics have argued that the new guides will harm consumers by inhibiting firms from using "aspirational" testimonials that serve a valid purpose in motivating consumers (for example, to achieve their own fitness goals); and that the new guides will impose substantial burdens on advertisers to ascertain what generally representative results would be. Persuasive?)

Other portions of the new guides also address potential liability on the part of bloggers who fail to disclose material connections with persons whose products they promote; these provisions have proven controversial in some quarters. Should bloggers be required to disclose such information? Is a firm's effort to stir up "buzz marketing" by providing free products to bloggers and other consumers an unfair or deceptive trade practice?

Read through the following excerpts from the new guides, and then consider whether the *Garvey* case would come out the same way or differently under the new guides.

FTC Guides Concerning Use of Endorsements and Testimonials in Advertising

http://www.ftc.gov/os/2009/10/091005revisedendorsementguides.pdf

§ 255.0 Purpose and Definitions.

(a) The Guides in this part represent administrative interpretations of laws enforced by the Federal Trade Commission for the guidance of the public in conducting its affairs in conformity with legal requirements. Specifically, the Guides address the application of Section 5 of the FTC Act (15 U.S.C. 45) to the use of endorsements and testimonials in advertising. The Guides provide the basis for voluntary compliance with the law by advertisers and endorsers. Practices inconsistent with these Guides may result in corrective action by the Commission under Section 5 if, after investigation, the Commission has reason to believe that the practices fall within the scope of conduct declared unlawful by the statute. The Guides set forth the general principles that the Commission will use in evaluating endorsements and testimonials, together with examples illustrating the application of those principles. The Guides do not purport to cover every possible use of endorsements in advertising. Whether a particular endorsement or testimonial is deceptive will depend on the specific factual circumstances of the advertisement at issue.

(b) For purposes of this part, an endorsement means any advertising message (including verbal statements, demonstrations, or depictions of the name, signature, likeness or other identifying personal characteristics of an individual or the name or seal of an organization) that consumers are likely to believe reflects the opinions, beliefs, findings, or experiences of a party other than the sponsoring advertiser, even if the views expressed by that party are identical to those of the sponsoring advertiser. The party whose opinions, beliefs, findings, or experience the message appears to reflect will be called the endorser and may be an individual, group, or institution.

(c) The Commission intends to treat endorsements and testimonials identically in the context of its enforcement of the Federal Trade Commission Act and for purposes of this part. The term endorsements is therefore generally used hereinafter to cover both terms and situations.

(d) For purposes of this part, the term product includes any product, service, company or industry. . . .

> Example 1: A film critic's review of a movie is excerpted in an advertisement. When so used, the review meets the definition of an endorsement because it is viewed by readers as a statement of the critic's own opinions and not those of the film producer, distributor, or exhibitor. Any alteration in or quotation from the text of the review that does not fairly reflect its substance would be a violation of the standards set by this part because it would distort the endorser's opinion. [*See* § 255.1(b).]
>
> Example 2: A TV commercial depicts two women in a supermarket buying a laundry detergent. The women are not identified outside the context of the advertisement. One comments to the other how clean her brand makes her family's clothes, and the other then comments that she will try it because she has not been fully satisfied with her own brand. This obvious fictional dramatization of a real life situation would not be an endorsement.

Example 3: In an advertisement for a pain remedy, an announcer who is not familiar to consumers except as a spokesman for the advertising drug company praises the drug's ability to deliver fast and lasting pain relief. He purports to speak, not on the basis of his own opinions, but rather in the place of and on behalf of the drug company. The announcer's statements would not be considered an endorsement.

Example 4: A manufacturer of automobile tires hires a well-known professional automobile racing driver to deliver its advertising message in television commercials. In these commercials, the driver speaks of the smooth ride, strength, and long life of the tires. Even though the message is not expressly declared to be the personal opinion of the driver, it may nevertheless constitute an endorsement of the tires. Many consumers will recognize this individual as being primarily a racing driver and not merely a spokesperson or announcer for the advertiser. Accordingly, they may well believe the driver would not speak for an automotive product unless he actually believed in what he was saying and had personal knowledge sufficient to form that belief. Hence, they would think that the advertising message reflects the driver's personal views. This attribution of the underlying views to the driver brings the advertisement within the definition of an endorsement for purposes of this part.

Example 5: A television advertisement for a particular brand of golf balls shows a prominent and well-recognized professional golfer practicing numerous drives off the tee. This would be an endorsement by the golfer even though she makes no verbal statement in the advertisement.

Example 6: An infomercial for a home fitness system is hosted by a well-known entertainer. During the infomercial, the entertainer demonstrates the machine and states that it is the most effective and easy-to-use home exercise machine that she has ever tried. Even if she is reading from a script, this statement would be an endorsement, because consumers are likely to believe it reflects the entertainer's views.

Example 7: A television advertisement for a housewares store features a well-known female comedian and a well-known male baseball player engaging in light-hearted banter about products each one intends to purchase for the other. The comedian says that she will buy him a Brand X, portable, high-definition television so he can finally see the strike zone. He says that he will get her a Brand Y juicer so she can make juice with all the fruit and vegetables thrown at her during her performances. The comedian and baseball player are not likely to be deemed endorsers because consumers will likely realize that the individuals are not expressing their own views.

Example 8: A consumer who regularly purchases a particular brand of dog food decides one day to purchase a new, more expensive brand made by the same manufacturer. She writes in her personal blog that the change in diet has made her dog's fur noticeably softer and shinier, and that in her opinion, the new food definitely is worth the extra money. This posting would not be deemed an endorsement under the Guides.

Assume that rather than purchase the dog food with her own money, the consumer gets it for free because the store routinely tracks her purchases and its computer has generated a coupon for a free trial bag of this new brand. Again, her posting would not be deemed an endorsement under the Guides.

Assume now that the consumer joins a network marketing program under which she periodically receives various products about which she can write reviews if she wants to do so. If she receives a free bag of the new dog food through this program, her positive review would be considered an endorsement under the Guides.

§ 255.1 General Considerations.

(a) Endorsements must reflect the honest opinions, findings, beliefs, or experience of the endorser. Furthermore, an endorsement may not convey any express or implied representation that would be deceptive if made directly by the advertiser. [*See* §§ 255.2(a) and (b) regarding substantiation of representations conveyed by consumer endorsements.]

(b) The endorsement message need not be phrased in the exact words of the endorser, unless the advertisement affirmatively so represents. However, the endorsement may not be presented out of context or reworded so as to distort in any way the endorser's opinion or experience with the product. An advertiser may use an endorsement of an expert or celebrity only so long as it has good reason to believe that the endorser continues to subscribe to the views presented. An advertiser may satisfy this obligation by securing the endorser's views at reasonable intervals where reasonableness will be determined by such factors as new information on the performance or effectiveness of the product, a material alteration in the product, changes in the performance of competitors' products, and the advertiser's contract commitments.

(c) When the advertisement represents that the endorser uses the endorsed product, the endorser must have been a bona fide user of it at the time the endorsement was given. Additionally, the advertiser may continue to run the advertisement only so long as it has good reason to believe that the endorser remains a bona fide user of the product. [*See* § 255.1(b) regarding the "good reason to believe" requirement.]

(d) Advertisers are subject to liability for false or unsubstantiated statements made through endorsements, or for failing to disclose material connections between themselves and their endorsers [*see* § 255.5]. Endorsers also may be liable for statements made in the course of their endorsements.

Example 1: A building contractor states in an advertisement that he uses the advertiser's exterior house paint because of its remarkable quick drying properties and durability. This endorsement must comply with the pertinent requirements of Section 255.3 (Expert Endorsements). Subsequently, the advertiser reformulates its paint to enable it to cover exterior surfaces with only one coat. Prior to continued use of the contractor's endorsement, the advertiser must contact the contractor in order to determine whether the contractor would continue to specify the paint and to subscribe to the views presented previously.

Example 2: A television advertisement portrays a woman seated at a desk on which rest five unmarked computer keyboards. An announcer says, "We asked X, an administrative assistant for over ten years, to try these five unmarked keyboards and tell us which one she liked best." The advertisement portrays X typing on each keyboard and then picking the advertiser's brand. The announcer asks her why, and X gives her reasons. This endorsement would probably not represent that X actually uses the advertiser's keyboard at work. In addition, the endorsement also may be required to meet the standards of Section 255.3 (expert endorsements). . . .

Example 4: A well-known celebrity appears in an infomercial for an oven roasting bag that purportedly cooks every chicken perfectly in thirty minutes. During the shooting of the infomercial, the celebrity watches five attempts to cook chickens using the bag. In each attempt, the chicken is undercooked after thirty minutes and requires sixty minutes of cooking time. In the commercial, the celebrity places an uncooked chicken in the oven roasting bag and places the bag in one oven. He then takes a chicken roasting bag from a second oven, removes from the bag what appears to be a perfectly cooked chicken, tastes the chicken, and says that if you want perfect chicken every time, in just thirty minutes, this is the product you need. A significant percentage of consumers are likely to believe the celebrity's statements represent his own views even though he is reading from a script. The celebrity is subject to liability for his statement about the product. The advertiser is also liable for misrepresentations made through the endorsement.

Example 5: A skin care products advertiser participates in a blog advertising service. The service matches up advertisers with bloggers who will promote the advertiser's products on their personal blogs. The advertiser requests that a blogger try a new body lotion and write a review of the product on her blog. Although the advertiser does not make any specific claims about the lotion's ability to cure skin conditions and the blogger does not ask the advertiser whether there is substantiation for the claim, in her review the blogger writes that the lotion cures eczema and recommends the product to her blog readers who suffer from this condition. The advertiser is subject to liability for misleading or unsubstantiated representations made through the blogger's endorsement. The blogger also is subject to liability for misleading or unsubstantiated representations made in the course of her endorsement. The blogger is also liable if she fails to disclose clearly and conspicuously that she is being paid for her services. [*See* § 255.5.]

In order to limit its potential liability, the advertiser should ensure that the advertising service provides guidance and training to its bloggers concerning the need to ensure that statements they make are truthful and substantiated. The advertiser should also monitor bloggers who are being paid to promote its products and take steps necessary to halt the continued publication of deceptive representations when they are discovered.

§ 255.2 Consumer Endorsements.

(a) An advertisement employing endorsements by one or more consumers about the performance of an advertised product or service will be interpreted as representing that the product or service is effective for the purpose depicted in the advertisement. Therefore, the advertiser must possess and rely upon adequate substantiation, including, when appropriate, competent and reliable scientific evidence, to support such claims made through endorsements in the same manner the advertiser would be required to do if it had made the representation directly, i.e., without using endorsements. Consumer endorsements themselves are not competent and reliable scientific evidence.

(b) An advertisement containing an endorsement relating the experience of one or more consumers on a central or key attribute of the product or service also will likely be interpreted as representing that the endorser's experience is representative of what consumers will generally achieve with the advertised product or service in actual, albeit variable, conditions of use. Therefore, an advertiser should possess and rely upon adequate substantiation for this representation. If the advertiser does not have substantiation that the endorser's experience is representative of what consumers will generally achieve, the advertisement should clearly and conspicuously disclose the generally expected performance in the depicted circumstances, and the advertiser must possess and rely on adequate substantiation for that representation.[1]

(c) Advertisements presenting endorsements by what are represented, directly or by implication, to be "actual consumers" should utilize actual consumers in both the audio and video, or clearly and conspicuously disclose that the persons in such advertisements are not actual consumers of the advertised product.

Example 1: A brochure for a baldness treatment consists entirely of testimonials from satisfied customers who say that after using the product, they had amazing hair growth and their hair is as thick and strong as it was when they were teenagers. The advertiser must have competent and reliable scientific evidence that its product is effective in producing new hair growth.

The ad will also likely communicate that the endorsers' experiences are representative of what new users of the product can generally expect. Therefore, even if the advertiser includes a disclaimer such as, "Notice: These testimonials do not prove our product works. You should not expect to have similar results," the ad is likely to be deceptive unless the advertiser has adequate substantiation that new users typically will experience results similar to those experienced by the testimonialists.

Example 2: An advertisement disseminated by a company that sells heat pumps presents endorsements from three individuals who state that after installing the company's heat pump in their homes, their monthly utility bills went down by $100, $125, and $150, respectively. The ad will likely be interpreted as conveying that such savings are representative of what consumers who buy the company's heat pump can generally expect. The advertiser does not have substantiation for that representation because, in fact, less than 20% of purchasers will save $100 or more. A disclosure such as, "Results not typical" or, "These testimonials are based on the experiences of a few people and you are not likely to have similar results" is insufficient to prevent this ad from being deceptive because consumers will still interpret the ad as conveying that the specified savings are representative of what consumers can generally expect. The ad is less likely to be deceptive if it clearly and conspicuously discloses the generally expected savings and the advertiser has adequate substantiation that homeowners can achieve those results. There are multiple ways that such a disclosure could be phrased, e.g., "the average homeowner saves $35 per month," "the

1. The Commission tested the communication of advertisements containing testimonials that clearly and prominently disclosed either "Results not typical" or the stronger "These testimonials are based on the experiences of a few people and you are not likely to have similar results." Neither disclosure adequately reduced the communication that the experiences depicted are generally representative. Based upon this research, the Commission believes that similar disclaimers regarding the limited applicability of an endorser's experience to what consumers may generally expect to achieve are unlikely to be effective.

typical family saves $50 per month during cold months and $20 per month in warm months," or "most families save 10% on their utility bills."

Example 3: An advertisement for a cholesterol-lowering product features an individual who claims that his serum cholesterol went down by 120 points and does not mention having made any lifestyle changes. A well-conducted clinical study shows that the product reduces the cholesterol levels of individuals with elevated cholesterol by an average of 15% and the advertisement clearly and conspicuously discloses this fact. Despite the presence of this disclosure, the advertisement would be deceptive if the advertiser does not have adequate substantiation that the product can produce the specific results claimed by the endorser (i.e., a 120-point drop in serum cholesterol without any lifestyle changes).

Example 4: An advertisement for a weight-loss product features a formerly obese woman. She says in the ad, "Every day, I drank 2 WeightAway shakes, ate only raw vegetables, and exercised vigorously for six hours at the gym. By the end of six months, I had gone from 250 pounds to 140 pounds." The advertisement accurately describes the woman's experience, and such a result is within the range that would be generally experienced by an extremely overweight individual who consumed WeightAway shakes, only ate raw vegetables, and exercised as the endorser did. Because the endorser clearly describes the limited and truly exceptional circumstances under which she achieved her results, the ad is not likely to convey that consumers who weigh substantially less or use WeightAway under less extreme circumstances will lose 110 pounds in six months. (If the advertisement simply says that the endorser lost 110 pounds in six months using WeightAway together with diet and exercise, however, this description would not adequately alert consumers to the truly remarkable circumstances leading to her weight loss.) The advertiser must have substantiation, however, for any performance claims conveyed by the endorsement (e.g., that WeightAway is an effective weight loss product).

If, in the alternative, the advertisement simply features "before" and "after" pictures of a woman who says "I lost 50 pounds in 6 months with WeightAway," the ad is likely to convey that her experience is representative of what consumers will generally achieve. Therefore, if consumers cannot generally expect to achieve such results, the ad should clearly and conspicuously disclose what they can expect to lose in the depicted circumstances (e.g., "most women who use WeightAway for six months lose at least 15 pounds").

If the ad features the same pictures but the testimonialist simply says, "I lost 50 pounds with WeightAway," and WeightAway users generally do not lose 50 pounds, the ad should disclose what results they do generally achieve (e.g., "most women who use WeightAway lose 15 pounds").

Example 5: An advertisement presents the results of a poll of consumers who have used the advertiser's cake mixes as well as their own recipes. The results purport to show that the majority believed that their families could not tell the difference between the advertised mix and their own cakes baked from scratch. Many of the consumers are actually pictured in the advertisement along with relevant, quoted portions of their statements endorsing the product. This use of the results of a poll or survey of consumers represents that this is the typical result that ordinary consumers can expect from the advertiser's cake mix.

Example 6: An advertisement purports to portray a "hidden camera" situation in a crowded cafeteria at breakfast time. A spokesperson for the advertiser asks a series of actual patrons of the cafeteria for their spontaneous, honest opinions of the advertiser's recently introduced breakfast cereal. Even though the words "hidden camera" are not displayed on the screen, and even though none of the actual patrons is specifically identified during the advertisement, the net impression conveyed to consumers may well be that these are actual customers, and not actors. If actors have been employed, this fact should be clearly and conspicuously disclosed.

Example 7: An advertisement for a recently released motion picture shows three individuals coming out of a theater, each of whom gives a positive statement about the movie. These individuals are actual consumers expressing their personal views about the movie. The advertiser does not need to have substantiation that their views are representative of the opinions that most consumers will have about the movie. Because the consumers' statements would be understood to be the subjective opinions of only three people, this advertisement is not likely to convey a typicality message.

If the motion picture studio had approached these individuals outside the theater and offered them free tickets if they would talk about the movie on camera afterwards, that arrangement should be clearly and conspicuously disclosed. [*See* § 255.5.]

***

§ 255.5 Disclosure of Material Connections.

When there exists a connection between the endorser and the seller of the advertised product that might materially affect the weight or credibility of the endorsement (i.e., the connection is not reasonably expected by the audience), such connection must be fully disclosed. For example, when an endorser who appears in a television commercial is neither represented in the advertisement as an expert nor is known to a significant portion of the viewing public, then the advertiser should clearly and conspicuously disclose either the payment or promise of compensation prior to and in exchange for the endorsement or the fact that the endorser knew or had reason to know or to believe that if the endorsement favored the advertised product some benefit, such as an appearance on television, would be extended to the endorser. Additional guidance, including guidance concerning endorsements made through other media, is provided by the examples below.

Example 1: A drug company commissions research on its product by an outside organization. The drug company determines the overall subject of the research (e.g., to test the efficacy of a newly developed product) and pays a substantial share of the expenses of the research project, but the research organization determines the protocol for the study and is responsible for conducting it. A subsequent advertisement by the drug company mentions the research results as the "findings" of that research organization. Although the design and conduct of the research project are controlled by the outside research organization, the weight consumers place on the reported results could be materially affected by knowing that the advertiser had funded the project. Therefore, the advertiser's payment of expenses to the research organization should be disclosed in this advertisement.

Example 2: A film star endorses a particular food product. The endorsement regards only points of taste and individual preference. This endorsement must, of course, comply with § 255.1; but regardless of whether the star's compensation for the commercial is a $1 million cash payment or a royalty for each product sold by the advertiser during the next year, no disclosure is required because such payments likely are ordinarily expected by viewers.

Example 3: During an appearance by a well-known professional tennis player on a television talk show, the host comments that the past few months have been the best of her career and during this time she has risen to her highest level ever in the rankings. She responds by attributing the improvement in her game to the fact that she is seeing the ball better than she used to, ever since having laser vision correction surgery at a clinic that she identifies by name. She continues talking about the ease of the procedure, the kindness of the clinic's doctors, her speedy recovery, and how she can now engage in a variety of activities without glasses, including driving at night. The athlete does not disclose that, even though she does not appear in commercials for the clinic, she has a contractual relationship with it, and her contract pays her for speaking publicly about her surgery when she can do so. Consumers might not realize that a celebrity discussing a medical procedure in a television interview has been paid for doing so, and knowledge of such payments would likely affect the weight or credibility consumers give to the celebrity's endorsement. Without a clear and conspicuous disclosure that the athlete has been engaged as a spokesperson for the clinic, this endorsement is likely to be deceptive. Furthermore, if consumers are likely to take away from her story that her experience was typical of those who undergo the same procedure at the clinic, the advertiser must have substantiation for that claim.

Assume that instead of speaking about the clinic in a television interview, the tennis player touts the results of her surgery — mentioning the clinic by name — on a social networking site that allows her fans to read in real time what is happening in her life. Given the nature of the medium in which her endorsement is disseminated, consumers might not realize that she is a paid endorser. Because that information might affect the weight consumers give to her endorsement, her relationship with the clinic should be disclosed.

Assume that during that same television interview, the tennis player is wearing clothes bearing the insignia of an athletic wear company with whom she also has an endorsement contract. Although this contract requires that she wear the company's clothes not only on the court but also in public appearances, when possible, she does not mention them or the company during her appearance on the show. No disclosure is required because no representation is being made about the clothes in this context.

Example 4: An ad for an anti-snoring product features a physician who says that he has seen dozens of products come on the market over the years and, in his opinion, this is the best ever. Consumers would expect the physician to be reasonably compensated for his appearance in the ad. Consumers are unlikely, however, to expect that the physician receives a percentage of gross product sales or that he owns part of the company, and either of these facts would likely materially affect the credibility that consumers attach to the endorsement. Accordingly, the advertisement should clearly and conspicuously disclose such a connection between the company and the physician.

Example 5: An actual patron of a restaurant, who is neither known to the public nor presented as an expert, is shown seated at the counter. He is asked for his "spontaneous" opinion of a new food product served in the restaurant. Assume, first, that the advertiser had posted a sign on the door of the restaurant informing all who entered that day that patrons would be interviewed by the advertiser as part of its TV promotion of its new soy protein "steak." This notification would materially affect the weight or credibility of the patron's endorsement, and, therefore, viewers of the advertisement should be clearly and conspicuously informed of the circumstances under which the endorsement was obtained.

Assume, in the alternative, that the advertiser had not posted a sign on the door of the restaurant, but had informed all interviewed customers of the "hidden camera" only after interviews were completed and the customers had no reason to know or believe that their response was being recorded for use in an advertisement. Even if patrons were also told that they would be paid for allowing the use of their opinions in advertising, these facts need not be disclosed.

Example 6: An infomercial producer wants to include consumer endorsements for an automotive additive product featured in her commercial, but because the product has not yet been sold, there are no consumer users. The producer's staff reviews the profiles of individuals interested in working as "extras" in commercials and identifies several who are interested in automobiles. The extras are asked to use the product for several weeks and then report back to the producer. They are told that if they are selected to endorse the product in the producer's infomercial, they will receive a small payment. Viewers would not expect that these "consumer endorsers" are actors who were asked to use the product so that they could appear in the commercial or that they were compensated. Because the advertisement fails to disclose these facts, it is deceptive.

Example 7: A college student who has earned a reputation as a video game expert maintains a personal weblog or "blog" where he posts entries about his gaming experiences. Readers of his blog frequently seek his opinions about video game hardware and software. As it has done in the past, the manufacturer of a newly released video game system sends the student a free copy of the system and asks him to write about it on his blog. He tests the new gaming system and writes a favorable review. Because his review is disseminated via a form of consumer-generated media in which his relationship to the advertiser is not inherently obvious, readers are unlikely to know that he has received the video game system free of charge in exchange for his review of the product, and given the value of the video game system, this fact likely would materially affect the credibility they attach to his endorsement. Accordingly, the blogger should clearly and conspicuously disclose that he received the gaming system free of charge. The manufacturer should advise him at the time it provides the gaming system that this connection should be disclosed, and it should have procedures in place to try to monitor his postings for compliance.

Example 8: An online message board designated for discussions of new music download technology is frequented by MP3 player enthusiasts. They exchange information about new products, utilities, and the functionality of numerous playback devices. Unbeknownst to the message board community, an employee of a leading playback device manufacturer has been posting messages on the discussion board promoting the manufacturer's product.

Knowledge of this poster's employment likely would affect the weight or credibility of her endorsement. Therefore, the poster should clearly and conspicuously disclose her relationship to the manufacturer to members and readers of the message board.

Example 9: A young man signs up to be part of a "street team" program in which points are awarded each time a team member talks to his or her friends about a particular advertiser's products. Team members can then exchange their points for prizes, such as concert tickets or electronics. These incentives would materially affect the weight or credibility of the team member's endorsements. They should be clearly and conspicuously disclosed, and the advertiser should take steps to ensure that these disclosures are being provided.

FTC v. Garvey

383 F.3d 891 (9th Cir. 2004)

PREGERSON, Circuit Judge:

. . . The FTC . . . appeals the ruling . . . that Steven Patrick Garvey and Garvey Management Group, Inc. (collectively, the "Garvey defendants") relied on adequate substantiation and therefore are not liable for Garvey's advertising claims for the weight loss product at issue in this case.

For the reasons discussed below, we reverse in part and affirm in part.

Background

A. *The Enforma System and Its Marketing*

This lawsuit arises out of the marketing of a weight loss system sold by Enforma Natural Products, Inc. ("Enforma").[1] Enforma created and marketed two dietary supplements, "Fat Trapper" (or "Fat Trapper Plus") and "Exercise in a Bottle." Together, these two products constitute the "Enforma System." The Fat Trapper product contains chitosan and is a mixture of the shells of certain seafood. It allegedly "surrounds the fat in the food you eat and entraps it," preventing fat absorption. Exercise in a Bottle contains pyruvate, which is found naturally in the body, and allegedly helps enhance one's metabolism.

Modern Interactive Technology, Inc., is a video production company that specializes in producing television infomercials. . . . In conjunction with the marketing of its products, Enforma retained Modern Media, a subsidiary of Media Interactive Technology, Inc., to prepare two thirty-minute infomercials.

Following the advice of Modern Media, Enforma hired Steven Patrick Garvey to star in the infomercials and to be a spokesperson for the Enforma System. Garvey is a retired first baseman for the Los Angeles Dodgers. . . .

Three or four weeks before the filming of the first infomercial, Enforma's Executive Director of Marketing, Michael Ehrman, gave Garvey and his wife a supply

1. As discussed further below, Enforma is not a party to this action. The FTC, Enforma, and two of Enforma's principals entered into a stipulated judgment in another case in May 2000.

of the Enforma System. Between that time and the time of filming, Garvey used the Enforma System and lost approximately eight pounds. Between the filming of the first infomercial and the date the infomercial was broadcast, Garvey's wife used the Enforma System and lost approximately twenty-seven pounds. At some point, Garvey also received two booklets produced by Enforma, which provided information about Fat Trapper and Exercise In A Bottle. . . .

Two or three days before the filming of the first infomercial, Garvey received a draft script. There had been as many as fifteen prior drafts that Garvey never saw. Garvey did not see a final version of the script until Grey rewrote it on the infomercial soundstage. Before filming began, Garvey made minor, non-substantive edits to the script to ensure that it matched his own speech patterns and vocabulary preferences.

The process leading up to the second infomercial was similar, although the second infomercial was less scripted than the first. Garvey did not receive the script until two days before filming; there were at least three versions of the script that Garvey did not see. Garvey made similar, non-substantive edits to the script for the second infomercial.

During both infomercials Garvey largely read from the prepared scripts. He and his co-host, Lark Kendall, ad libbed when conducting a demonstration of the Fat Trapper product[, but even then, Levine, Richmond, and Grey provided them with a framework for their dialogue.] In the infomercials, Garvey made a number of statements regarding the Enforma System, including:

- "Now, if you're tired of trying every new fad diet, if you're tired of trying to work a rigid exercise regime into your busy schedule, if you want to be able to enjoy all those delicious foods that you crave without the guilt while losing weight and keeping it off, call us now. . . ."
- "If you're having trouble losing weight, if you're tired of depriving yourself of all those wonderful and delicious foods that you love, if you find that you don't have the time to exercise as much as you'd like, the Enforma System is the miracle you've been waiting for. It's all natural, it's safe and it works."
- "I love this. So, you can enjoy all these delicious foods like fried chicken, pizza, cheeseburgers, even butter and sour cream, and stop worrying about the weight."
- "The Enforma System has inspired so many to embrace a healthier, more active lifestyle, making good food choices, exercising more and everyone is here to celebrate a system that can end binge dieting forever, because with Enforma you trap the fat from food before it can go to your waistline."
- "[L]ook at all these delicious supposedly forbidden foods; barbecued chicken and ribs, buttered biscuits. Foods you can eat when you crave them without guilt, and it's all because of a few little capsules."
- "Forget all those complicated, expensive diets that deprive you. With all natural Fat Trapper and Exercise in a Bottle — the Enforma System — you simply take Exercise in a Bottle twice a day and Fat Trapper before any meal that contains fat. Then go ahead and enjoy the foods that you love without the fear of fat. It's that easy."

. . . Together, the two infomercials were aired almost 48,000 times throughout the United States from December 1998 through May 2000.

After filming the two infomercials, Garvey made several radio and television appearances to promote the Enforma System. His statements at these appearances were based on script points and guidelines provided by Enforma.

From December 1998 to December 2000, Enforma's sales of Fat Trapper, Fat Trapper Plus, and Exercise in a Bottle exceeded $100 million. . . .

The FTC began investigating claims made regarding the Enforma System in 1999. . . . On April 25, 2000, the FTC filed suit against Enforma. . . .

A proposed Stipulated Final Order settling the *Enforma* action as to Enforma . . . was filed along with the complaint, and it was entered by Judge J. Spencer Letts on May 11, 2000. This settlement prohibited Enforma . . . from undertaking specific conduct, such as making certain representations about Enforma's products without reliable scientific support. The settlement also required Enforma . . . to pay $10 million to the FTC.

C. *The Instant Case*

. . . The FTC filed a complaint against the Garvey defendants . . . on August 31, 2000. This complaint was similar to that filed in the *Enforma* action; it alleged that the defendants, in marketing the Enforma System, violated Sections 5(a) and 12 of the FTCA. . . .

The district court held a three-day bench trial on the FTC's claims against the Garvey defendants. On November 25, 2002, the district court issued its findings of fact and conclusions of law and entered judgment in favor of the Garvey defendants. The court concluded that Garvey could not be held liable under a "participant" theory of liability. The court found that Garvey did not have actual knowledge of any material misrepresentations, that he was not recklessly indifferent to the truth or falsity of any representations he made, and that he was neither aware of a high probability that he was making fraudulent representations nor intentionally avoiding the truth with respect to the qualities of the Enforma System. *Cf.* FTC v. Publ'g Clearing House, Inc., 104 F.3d 1168, 1171 (9th Cir. 1997). The district court also found that Garvey could not be held liable as an "endorser" because there was no evidence showing that his statements did not reflect his good faith belief and opinions and there was reasonable substantiation for the statements he made.

The FTC appeals the summary judgment order, the order denying the motion for reconsideration, and the order and judgment issued after the bench trial. . . .

a. "Direct Participant" Liability

In FTC v. Publishing Clearing House, Inc., 104 F.3d 1168 (9th Cir. 1997), an action brought pursuant to Sections 5 and 13(b) of the FTCA, we held that an individual may be subject to injunctive relief if the FTC can prove that an individual "participated directly" in the acts in question or "had authority to control them." *Id.* at 1170 (citation omitted). We concluded that, to hold an individual liable for restitution, the FTC must also show that the individual had actual knowledge of the material misrepresentations, was recklessly indifferent to the truth or falsity of a misrepresentation, or had an awareness of a high probability of fraud along with an intentional avoidance of the truth. *Id.* at 1171 (citation omitted). The district court employed these standards here but did not distinguish between injunctive relief and restitution.[10]

i. "Participant"

The Garvey defendants do not seriously dispute that Garvey was a "participant." Instead, they attempt to short-circuit the FTC's appeal on this issue by arguing that the FTC has failed in meeting its burden of proving the falsity of the claims at issue. They point out that nothing in this case or in the *Enforma* action established that the claims made were false or unsubstantiated. The FTC does not argue that it proved the claims at issue were false and unsubstantiated. Instead, the FTC contends that "settled Commission law" imposes an obligation on an active participant in an advertising campaign to ascertain the existence of substantiation for the claims that the participant makes.

In *Publishing Clearing House*, we put the burden of proving falsity or deception on the FTC. We held that an individual "may be held individually liable for injunctive relief under the [Federal Trade Commission Act] for corporate practices *if the FTC can prove* [among other things] that the corporation committed misrepresentations or omissions of a kind usually relied on by a reasonably prudent person, resulting in consumer injury. . . ." 104 F.3d at 1170 (citing *Am. Standard Credit Sys.*, 874 F. Supp. at 1087) (emphasis added). But in FTC v. Pantron I Corp., 33 F.3d 1088 (9th Cir.1994), a Section 12 case, we presented a somewhat more nuanced picture:

> [T]he Commission has identified two theories on which the government can and often does rely in section 12 cases involving objective product claims. First, the government can assert a so-called "falsity" theory. To prevail on such a theory, the government must carry the burden of proving that the express or implied message conveyed by the ad is false. Alternatively, the government can rely on a so-called "reasonable basis" theory. To prevail on this theory, the government must show that the advertiser lacked a reasonable basis for asserting that the message was true.

Id. at 1096 (quotation marks and citations omitted). The "reasonable basis" theory supports the FTC's argument because it does not require the FTC to prove that the message was false in order to prevail. "In determining whether an advertiser has satisfied the reasonable basis requirement, the Commission or court must first determine what level of substantiation the advertiser is required to have for his advertising claims. Then, the adjudicator must determine whether the advertiser possessed that level of substantiation." *Pantron I*, 33 F.3d at 1096. In this case, the "reasonable basis" theory essentially collapses into the knowledge requirement for restitution. The relevant inquiry in both contexts is, essentially: what did the individual know when making the claims at issue?

ii. The Knowledge Requirement

The district court concluded that Garvey had no actual knowledge of any material misrepresentations regarding the Enforma System. The FTC does not claim that this

10. Given the broad language of the Stipulated Final Order, it apparently applies to the Garvey defendants and likely provides the FTC all of the injunctive relief it could get against the Garvey defendants in this case. Therefore, as a practical matter, all the FTC stands to gain from the Garvey defendants here is restitution; the issue of injunctive relief is moot.

finding was erroneous. The district court also found the following evidence that provides substantiation for Garvey's advertising claims. First, Garvey himself used the system and lost approximately eight pounds during a three- or four-week period. Second, Garvey's wife, while using the Enforma System, lost approximately twenty-seven pounds between the filming of the first infomercial and the date the program was broadcast to the public. Third, Garvey received and reviewed two booklets containing substantiation materials for Fat Trapper and Exercise In A Bottle. These booklets were produced by Enforma Natural. Fourth, prior to the filming of the second infomercial, Garvey met and spoke with several individuals who had experienced "positive results" using the Enforma System. Fifth, Garvey learned of a pyruvate study published in the American Journal of Clinical Nutrition.

The FTC attempts, unconvincingly, to undercut the significance of this evidence. The FTC argues that Garvey's weight loss was less than the amount by which his weight normally fluctuated during the course of a year. But Garvey clearly stated that his weight had been relatively stable and that, "once I started taking the Enforma System, I saw noticeable weight loss." The FTC also points out that Garvey's wife's weight loss followed childbirth, and she had lost weight after childbirth before. But the relevant testimony provides no indication as to how much she had lost at other times following childbirth or whether the weight loss occurred in a similar time span.

The FTC is also unpersuasive when pointing out flaws in the two booklets that Garvey reviewed. Although they may not conclusively establish the efficacy of the Enforma System, both booklets contain significant, relevant information. In its attack on the Fat Trapper booklet, the FTC states that the booklet does not even mention chitosan. But the Fat Trapper booklet relates information regarding scientific studies and clearly indicates that fiber intake has been found to decrease fat digestibility. Chitosan either is a dietary fiber or is akin to dietary fiber. Even though the booklet may not explicitly mention chitosan, the booklet provides some relevant substantiation for the advertising claims made.

In its attack on the Exercise In A Bottle booklet, the FTC argues that the booklet does not support the contention that pyruvate use has been linked to an increased metabolic rate in humans. But the Exercise In A Bottle booklet points to findings that pyruvate supplementation significantly reduced fat accumulation in rats and pigs and states that pyruvate may cause fat and weight loss through increasing metabolism and fat utilization. It is reasonable for Garvey to have found that this information supported the representations he made.

In sum, we find that the FTC has failed to show that Garvey was recklessly indifferent to the truth of his statements or was aware that fraud was highly probable and intentionally avoided the truth. *See Publ'g Clearing House*, 104 F.3d at 1170-71. Garvey had first-hand anecdotal evidence of the efficacy of the Enforma System and had information that purported to present scientific bases for his claims. *Cf.* Simeon Mgmt. Corp. v. FTC, 579 F.2d 1137, 1143 (9th Cir. 1978) (noting that, alone, anecdoctal evidence where individuals state that they "believe" a drug is effective cannot provide "substantial evidence of effectiveness"). We find that the substantiation he had was sufficient—at least for someone in Garvey's position[12] to avoid participant liability.

12. The Garvey defendants note that there is no settled standard for the level of inquiry to which a commercial spokesperson is held when he or she is hired to participate in a television advertisement. In the context of the knowledge requirement, we find that the fact that the individual is merely a spokesperson is

b. "Endorser" Liability

The FTC premises its "endorser" theory of liability on the FTC Guides Concerning Use of Endorsements and Testimonials in Advertising (the "Guides"). According to the Guides, an "endorsement" is "any advertising message . . . which message consumers are likely to believe reflects the opinions, beliefs, findings, or experience of a party other than the sponsoring advertiser." 16 C.F.R. §255.0(b). Among other things, the Guides state that "[e]ndorsements must always reflect the honest opinions, findings, beliefs, or experience of the endorser. Furthermore, they may not contain any representations which would be deceptive, or could not be substantiated if made directly by the advertiser." 16 C.F.R. §255.1(a).

The FTC acknowledges that the Guides lack the force of law but contends that they are entitled to deference because of their persuasiveness.[13] Indeed, the Supreme Court has made clear that where, as here, an agency pronouncement is not necessarily entitled to deference under Chevron, U.S.A., Inc. v. Natural Resources Defense Council, Inc., 467 U.S. 837 (1984), the pronouncement's persuasiveness may nevertheless entitle it to respect.

But we decline to decide to what degree of deference the Guides may be entitled or whether the Guides can form an independent basis for spokesperson liability.[14] . . . Even if the Guides had the full force of law, we would find that Garvey is not liable under them.

The district court found that Garvey did not provide an endorsement as defined in the Guides. Specifically, the district court found that "[t]he Commission has failed to present . . . any facts establishing that consumers are likely to believe that Garvey's statements with respect to the Enforma System reflect the opinions, beliefs, findings and experiences of a party other than Enforma Natural." The district court was presented with evidence from both sides on this issue. For example, the FTC pointed to statements made by Garvey in the infomercials that the Enforma System "works," that he "truly believe[s that it] is the greatest weight loss program in history," that he is "convinced," that he "love[s] this," and that "this is the most amazing system that [he has] ever seen." Further, the FTC offered a rebuttal expert, Dr. Mazis, who testified that Garvey provided an endorsement. The Garvey defendants offered the expert testimony of Dr. Thomas Hollihan, who concluded that Garvey was not an endorser under the Guides.

Under the highly deferential standard of review for findings of fact, we affirm, with the narrow exception described below, the district court's conclusion that Garvey did not provide an endorsement. Because of the conflicting expert testimony and the fact that the statements in the infomercials do not necessarily reflect Garvey's, rather

---

relevant. For instance, the requirement that she be "aware that fraud was highly probable and intentionally avoided the truth" clearly turns on subjective knowledge. Likewise, the "reckless indifference" standard implies that an individual's subjective understanding should be taken into account. . . . Indeed, the FTC points out that, in assessing scientific material, Garvey was only required to examine the material from the perspective of a reasonable layperson. *See In re Am. Home Prods. Corp.*, 98 F.T.C. 136, 397-98 (1981).

13. 16 C.F.R. Part 17 states that the "[i]ndustry guides are administrative interpretations of laws administered by the Commission for the guidance of the public in conducting its affairs in conformity with legal requirements. . . . Failure to comply with the guides may result in corrective action by the commission under applicable statutory provisions." *Id.*

14. Given the tenor of the Guides, they in fact seem aimed at controlling the behavior of the advertisers rather than the endorsers themselves. *See* 16 C.F.R. §§255.0-255.5. In any case, this is an area of law that would benefit from clarification by Congress or the FTC.

than Enforma's, beliefs, we are not "left with the definite and firm conviction that a mistake has been committed."

But Garvey did make at least a few statements during one appearance on a television show called "Night Talk" (not one of the infomercials) that appear to be clearly an endorsement under the Guides. On that show, the following exchange took place:

MONICA: And I was wondering if you use the product and have you had success with it? . . .

STEVE GARVEY: Yeah. I've endorsed products through the years and we have a family philosophy and that is either we have to take the product or it has to be a product that we would be willing to give ou[r] children. . . .

I took the product. I was about 195. . . . My normal weight is about 190 and I got down to about 186, so I lost 9 pounds. My wife had just had our second son, Sean Fitzpatrick, and she ended up losing about 28, 29 pounds on the product.

So it worked for both of us and that's why I ended up doing the infomercial because it worked.

As to these particular statements, the district court's findings of fact may have been clearly erroneous.

Nevertheless, we find that the FTC has still failed to meet its burden of proving liability under the Guides. As noted above, the Guides state that "[e]ndorsements must always reflect the honest opinions, findings, beliefs, or experience of the endorser." 16 C.F.R. § 255.1(a). This part of the test for liability is not at issue; Garvey has asserted that all of his statements regarding the Enforma System were statements of his actual beliefs and experiences, and the FTC does not dispute this contention. The next element of endorser liability concerns substantiation. *See* 16 C.F.R. § 255.1 (stating that endorsements "may not contain any representations which would be deceptive, or could not be substantiated if made directly by the advertiser."). On the Night Talk program, Garvey's only statements of endorsement related to his and his wife's weight loss. The Garveys' weight loss is undisputed, and Garvey undoubtedly has first-hand knowledge of those facts. The endorsement claims — that he and his wife lost a certain number of pounds — clearly pass any substantiation requirement for celebrity endorsers.

Therefore, we find that, even if the Guides provided an alternative basis for liability, Garvey would not be liable as an "endorser" under the Guides.

COMMENTS AND QUESTIONS

1. In *Garvey*, Enforma — the firm that marketed "Fat Trapper" and "Exercise in a Bottle" — had already settled the FTC's claims against it, in part by agreeing not to make certain representations about these products in the absence of reliable scientific support. The FTC proceeded against the Garvey defendants only to obtain restitution (presumably, of the fees that Garvey was paid to endorse the products). The court held, however, that Garvey was not liable because he had sufficient reason to believe that the statements he made were true. The court also deferred to the district court's determination that Garvey was not an "endorser," except for the one occasion on which he endorsed the product outside the context of an infomercial. Should persons who agree to appear in product commercials be held to a higher standard than this?

2. The FTC has published other guides setting forth its views of various types of advertising. Although these do not have the force of law, they may provide guidance regarding "safe harbors" within which firms may operate. Some of the more important guides include the FTC Enforcement Policy Statement on Food Advertising (May 1994), *available at* http://www.ftc.gov/bcp/policystmt/ad-food.shtm; the FTC Enforcement Policy Statement on U.S. Origin Claims (Dec. 1997), *available at* http://www.ftc.gov/os/1997/12/epsmadeusa.htm; the FTC Guides Against Deceptive Pricing, *available at* http://www.ftc.gov/bcp/guides/decptprc.htm; and the Guides for the Use of Environmental Marketing Claims, *available at* http://www.ftc.gov/bcp/grnrule/guides980427.htm. *See also* FTC Staff Report: Self-Regulatory Principles for Online Behavioral Advertising (Feb. 2009), *available at* http://www.ftc.gov/os/2009/02/P085400behavadreport.pdf; Statement of Policy Regarding Comparative Advertising (Aug. 13, 1979), *available at* http://www.ftc.gov/bcp/policystmt/ad-compare.htm.

PROBLEM

Problem 9-8. In January 2010, TC, Inc., a corporation organized under the laws of, and having its principal place of business in, Chicago, Illinois, began marketing a product known as the "T-Ray Ionized Bracelet" through a series of televised "infomercials" aired primarily in Illinois, Wisconsin, and Indiana. (Prior to that date, the product had been on sale through the Internet and at a few selected stores in Chicago for approximately one year.) The bracelet, which comes in four sizes and six styles, is a C-shaped bracelet with screw caps; it appears to consist of 85 percent copper and 15 percent zinc. The principal message the infomercials convey is that use of the T-Ray bracelet can provide immediate, significant relief from chronic pain due to its "ionization" effect. (The infomercials never explain what the word "ionized" means in this context, however, or how the bracelet promotes ionization or why ionization would reduce pain.[15]) Each infomercial presents apparently satisfied users of the T-Ray bracelet. To illustrate, the first infomercial includes an unidentified male speaker stating that "I got tingly all over and the pain is gone." Following a narrator's introduction of the bracelet, an unidentified female states "And I felt this tingly throughout my body and all of a sudden—I didn't feel the pain anymore." This is immediately followed by another male, identified as "Peter Dole," stating on camera "I came up here, put the bracelet on my wrist, and immediately my shoulder—I have movement—the pain just went away." Dole's testimonial is accompanied by the onscreen written statement "the pain just went away." The message that the bracelet provides immediate relief from pain is repeatedly reinforced by the infomercial through additional testimonials and onscreen written statements, and by the host, who at one point states "Time and time again people are telling us their T-Ray bracelet works wonders to relieve the aches and pains they live with every day. Not just from

15. According to a standard definition found on Wikipedia, "ionization is the physical process of converting an atom or molecule into an ion by adding or removing charged particles such as electrons or other ions," while "an ion is an atom or molecule which has lost or gained one or more electrons, giving it a positive or negative electrical charge."

persistent headaches, but joint stiffness, injuries, even back pain." During the testimonials, however, a brief message stating "Results may vary" in small print flashes across the screen for approximately two seconds.

At the time TC aired the infomercials, it had no valid scientific evidence to support its claims that the bracelet was effective in relieving pain, that it was ionized, or that ionization was the cause of the alleged pain relief. In August 2010, however, TC received the results of a double-blind test of the T-Ray bracelet versus a placebo, conducted pursuant to standard scientific and statistical methods by the Mayo Clinic in Rochester, Minnesota, which appears to show that the T-Ray bracelet was twice as effective as the placebo in relieving self-reported chronic pain among a group of 200 patients studied. The results are statistically significant at the 5 percent level, meaning that one would expect such results to be the result of random chance only 5 percent of the time.

Since the infomercials started airing in January 2010, TC has sold approximately 200,000 of its T-Ray bracelets at an average price of $49.99 plus shipping and handling. TC has earned approximately $1 million in net profits from these sales. The FTC would like to commence an action against TC (but not against any of the individuals appearing in the infomercials).

Does the FTC have a viable claim against TC under the FTC Act? What defense or defenses is TC likely to assert under the FTC Guides Concerning Use of Endorsements and Testimonials in Advertising?

E. "LITTLE" OR "BABY" FTC ACTS

Beginning in the 1960s, many states enacted statutes that, like the FTC Act, target unfair and deceptive trade practices. These statutes, sometimes referred to as "Little" or "Baby" FTC Acts, come in many varieties. Like the federal FTC Act, most of them provide for public enforcement, often by the state attorney general. Like the Lanham Act, many (though not all) of them also provide for private enforcement by competitors or other business entities. Unlike the Lanham Act and the FTC Act, however, these state laws typically also confer upon consumers the right to sue for a variety of practices including false advertising. Sometimes they enhance the remedies or otherwise make it easier for consumers to proceed than if consumers were relegated to their common-law claims; sometimes too they provide consumer claims based upon violations of state administrative regulations.

Although a comprehensive discussion of Little FTC Acts would go beyond the scope of this casebook, lawyers practicing in the field of unfair competition law should be familiar with these laws and how they differ from the common law, the Lanham Act, and the federal FTC Act. The following excerpt from Peter S. Menell, *Regulating "Spyware": The Limitations of State "Laboratories" and the Case for Federal Preemption of State Unfair Competition Laws*, 20 Berkeley Tech. L.J. 1363, 1385-94 (2005), provides a good overview of the evolution of the Little FTC Acts:

> During the heyday of the civil rights, environmental, and consumer movements of the 1960s, the FTC led an effort to expand the effectiveness of consumer protection

regulation by encouraging states to adopt what have come to be known as "little" FTC Acts. In order to guide states in the development of such laws, the FTC drafted a model act in the late 1960s — the Unfair Trade Practices and Consumer Protection Law (UTPCPL). Like the FTC Act, the model state law authorized the creation of state agencies to promulgate standards to combat unfair and deceptive practices and expand enforcement. Of comparable significance, the model law, reflecting the spirit of the times, proposed the establishment of a private right of action against those who engage in unfair or deceptive selling practices. This provision — focusing on persons who suffer ascertainable losses from the purchase or lease of goods or services primarily for personal, family, or household purposes — envisioned consumer and consumer class action suits against unscrupulous sellers.

Mindful of the need for harmonization among jurisdictions (and with the federal regime), the FTC model state unfair competition law tethered interpretation to the FTC's evolving definitions and standards. . . .

State unfair competition law has expanded most significantly through several waves of legislation. Although the impetus for the first wave of state unfair competition legislation was to unify this field of law, the effects have tended in the opposite direction. Even the FTC's encouragement of state consumer protection regimes tethered to federal standards has resulted in centrifugal rather than centripetal results. The landscape of unfair competition law today can best be characterized as fragmented, uncoordinated, and amorphous. The proliferation of state statutes aimed at controlling deceptive advertising, including many authorizing treble or punitive damages, has broadened the field, expanded the tools available, and promoted recourse to state unfair competition law. . . .

. . . In its 1958 report, a special committee [of the American Bar Association's Section of Patents, Trademark and Copyright Law] concluded that with the exception of California unfair competition law, which was codified in statute, all state unfair competition laws were "ambiguous," "archaic," and inadequate to cope with current conditions of commerce. The Committee passed a resolution which stated that "there should be uniformity in the law of unfair competition among the respective states." Efforts to achieve a new federal law, however, stalled in Congress. Meanwhile, the ABA Committee drafted the Uniform Deceptive Trade Practices Act (UDTPA), which the National Conference of Commissioners on Uniform State Laws adopted in 1964.

The Uniform Act sought to update state law to provide businesses with a direct cause of action against competitors for deceptive trade practices. In so doing, it removed traditional common law restrictions, such as the single source rule. The uniform law was modeled roughly after California law. The Act incorporated the following principles: likelihood of confusion is sufficient to establish liability; actual competition between the parties is not a prerequisite to relief; and a defendant need not be an intentional wrongdoer to incur liability. [Section 2 of t]he statute avoids a restrictive or exclusive definition of unfair competition, providing instead a list of a dozen specific and broad prohibited practices ranging from passing off to various forms of false advertising. [Section 3 of t]he UDTPA provides solely for injunctive relief, although it permits damages to be awarded for the same conduct where actionable under the common law or other statutes.

The UDTPA affords business enterprises a cause of action against other businesses which obtain a competitive advantage by deceiving consumers. After being adopted by fourteen states [Colorado, Delaware, Georgia, Hawaii, Illinois, Kansas, Minnesota, Nebraska, Nevada, New Mexico, Ohio, Oklahoma, Oregon, and Utah] relatively soon after its promulgation, the UDTPA lost momentum and has declined in significance. The 1988 amendments to the Lanham Act fully extended the coverage of federal law into this field. The UDTPA was withdrawn from recommendation for enactment by the National Conference of Commissioners on Uniform State Laws in 2000 on the grounds that it had become obsolete. The NCCUSL website no longer maintains information about this uniform statute. Nonetheless, the dozen or so state statutes modeled after the UDPTA remain in effect and they have assumed a life of their own within the particular states in which they were enacted. The ABA's goal of creating "uniformity in the law of unfair competition among the respective states" through adoption of a uniform state law has not come to pass. Even in states with such statutes, common law remedies have remained viable. Hence, unfair competition law continues to be amorphous and variable across state jurisdictions. . . .

In theory, state common law doctrines of deceit and fraud afforded remedies against unscrupulous sellers, although neither proved particularly effective in practice. These causes of action impose relatively high burdens of proof upon plaintiffs. Since most consumers suffer relatively small harms, common law remedies were rarely utilized to combat practices that collectively imposed significant consumer harm. In recognition of these limitations, the limited effective reach of the FTC Act (due to resource and information constraints), and the growing public support for stronger consumer protection laws, every state had passed its own consumer protection statute by the mid 1970s. Most of these statutes trace their specific provisions to one of the alternatives recommended by the FTC in the Unfair Trade Practices and Consumer Protection Law. Fourteen states[114] adopted some variation on Alternative 1 of the FTC model act. Kentucky and Texas adopted Alternative 2, which omits reference to the FTC's standard of "unfair methods of competition" and focuses on "false, misleading, or deceptive acts or practices." Ten states[116] adopted some version of Alternative 3, which enumerates twelve (and in some cases more) specific unlawful trade practices. Twenty other states and the District of Columbia have an itemized list of unlawful acts or practices.[117]

By creating a private right of action and the opportunity to obtain treble and/or punitive damages in many states, these statutes expanded the role of courts in regulating unfair and deceptive practices. These statutes provide a much broader assault on unfair and deceptive trade practices than the UDTPA and have come to dominate the field, at least with regard to consumer-related harms. Variation in the substantive provisions of these statutes as well as the role of the courts in interpreting them have resulted in a rather complex legal landscape for companies operating nationally. As noted by two commentators, "[t]he process of judicial interpretation followed by legislative clarification or adjustment has further eroded the uniformity of the [FTC's] original proposal." Furthermore, some states have enacted both deceptive practices statutes focused on business competition as well as FTC-like consumer protection statutes. Over time, the courts have tended to blur the distinctions between the two regimes.

From a practical standpoint, the state regimes differ along three critical dimensions: (1) standing to sue; (2) scope and extent to which they look to applicable federal law (under either the Lanham Act or the FTC Act); and (3) remedies. With regard to standing, the FTC's model act (the UTPCPL) limited the private right of action to consumers purchasing goods for personal use. Many states, however, adopted a modified version of this provision omitting the limitations on the type of injured party. Furthermore, some state courts have interpreted standing under such statutes broadly. With regard to scope, the UTPCPL provided for states to look to federal interpretations of unfair competition in construing their acts. State commissions and courts have varied in the extent to which they

114. Connecticut, Florida, Hawaii, Louisiana, Illinois, Massachusetts, Maine, Montana, Nebraska, North Carolina, Vermont, South Carolina, Washington, and West Virginia. California, Wisconsin, and Utah have statutes patterned directly upon the FTC Act, including the Act's emphasis on "unfair methods of competition."

116. Alabama, Alaska, Georgia, Idaho, Maryland, Mississippi, New Hampshire, Pennsylvania, Rhode Island, and Tennessee.

117. Indiana, Michigan, New York, South Dakota, Virginia, and Wyoming have crafted their own consumer protection statutes blending elements of the different model acts with distinctive language and procedures.

> have followed the evolution of federal standards, producing divergent standards. Most states do not require that private litigants meet a "public interest" standard, as required under the FTC Act.[122] States also vary in terms of whether they follow the pre- or post-*Cliffdale Associates* test for deception and the remedies available, with some states allowing plaintiffs to recover treble or punitive damages and fees.

Professor Menell is correct in pointing to the diversity of Little FTC Acts from one state to another.[16] Is this diversity of approaches desirable? Menell thinks not, arguing that

> From the standpoint of businesses operating in many or all states, the patchwork of unfair competition and consumer protection regimes creates significant confusion, increases the costs of assessing legal standards, and may inhibit some forms of innovation. Due to the relative ease of hauling Internet businesses into court in just about any state, such businesses are particularly exposed to the constraints of the most restrictive state unfair competition laws.

Id. at 1394-95. For a similarly critical perspective, see Henry N. Butler & Jason S. Johnson, *Consumer Harm Acts? An Economic Analysis of State Consumer Protection Acts* (Apr. 8, 2009), at 5, 70 (arguing that "the cumulative effect of these CPA [Consumer Protection Act] provisions is to encourage an inefficiently large amount of litigation," that "the traditional common law protection of requiring reasonable reliance, causation, and injury should be restored to consumer class actions," and that "[s]tatutory damages, damage multipliers, and punitive damages are not necessary for consumer class actions to solve the basic economic problem addressed by CPAs"), *available at* http://ssrn.com/abstract=1125305; Henry N. Butler & Joshua D. Wright, *Are State Consumer Protection Acts Really Little FTC Acts?*, 63 FLA. L. REV. 163 (2011). For a more favorable assessment of the effect of Little FTC Acts and other consumer protection laws both in the United States and the European Union, see Luisa Antoniolli, *Consumer Law as an Instance of the Law of Diversity*, 30 VT. L. REV. 855 (2006).

In states whose Little FTC Acts allow business entities, as well as consumers, to file suits for false advertising, why would they? Isn't the Lanham Act sufficient? The answer is, not always. First, standing may be easier to satisfy under a Little FTC Act than under the Lanham Act. Second, a Lanham Act claim must involve actionable conduct in interstate commerce. Third, some remedies may be easier to obtain under state law than under the Lanham Act. Punitive damages, for example, are not available under the Lanham Act (though enhanced damages sometimes are); given the right set of facts, however, punitive damages might be a possibility under state law. *See* Wildlife Research Center, Inc. v. Robinson Outdoors, Inc., 409 F. Supp. 2d 1131, 1137-38 (D. Minn. 2005) (suggesting that prejudgment interest would be more readily available under state law than under the Lanham Act). Thus, even when a firm files a

122. Of the 42 states that afford a private cause of action under statutes derived from the UTPCPL, only six have imposed a showing of a "public interest" by a private plaintiff. *See* Marshall A. Leaffer & Michael H. Lipson, *Consumer Actions Against Unfair or Deceptive Acts or Practices: The Private Uses of Federal Trade Commission Jurisprudence*, 48 GEO. WASH. L. REV. 521 (1980).

16. Even *within* a given state, there may be multiple statutes all targeting (for example) false advertising. *See, e.g.*, Minnesota Unlawful Trade Practices Act, MINN. STAT. § 325D.13; Minnesota Uniform Deceptive Trade Practices Act, MINN. STAT. § 325D.44; Minnesota False Statement in Advertisement Act, MINN. STAT. § 325F.67; and Minnesota Prevention of Consumer Fraud Act, MINN. STAT. § 325F.69(1).

Lanham Act claim in federal court, it often appends supplemental state law claims, where available, under the relevant Little FTC Act.

A Note on Federal Displacement of State (and Federal) False Advertising Claims

Neither the Lanham Act nor the FTC Act preempts Little FTC claims. Sometimes defendants argue, however, that other federal laws, such as the Food, Drug and Cosmetic Act (FDCA), preempt state (or even other federal) false advertising laws in certain types of cases.[17] Courts often have rejected these arguments, subject to some qualifications. *See, e.g.*, Altria Group, Inc. v. Good, 129 S. Ct. 538 (2009) (holding that Federal Cigarette Labeling and Advertising Act did not preempt claim under Maine Unfair Trade Practices Act that advertising cigarettes as "light" and having "lowered tar and nicotine" was deceptive); Photomedix, Inc. v. Irwin, 601 F.3d 919, 924-25 (9th Cir. 2010) (stating that "a private action brought under the Lanham Act may not pursued when, as here, the claim would require litigation of the alleged underlying FDCA violation in a circumstance where the FDA has not itself concluded that there was such a violation," but that if "it was clear that an affirmative statement of approval by the FDA was required before a given product could be marketed and that no such FDA approval had been granted, a Lanham Act claim could be pursued"); Mylan Labs., Inc. v. Matkari, 7 F.3d 1130, 1137-30 (4th Cir. 1993) (holding that a Lanham Act claim premised on an alleged false statement that the FDA had approved defendant's product was preempted, because otherwise the Lanham Act would become a vehicle for attempting to enforce the FDCA; but that a claim relating to alleged false statements concerning generic equivalence and bioequivalence were not preempted); *Thompson Medical Co.*, 791 F.2d 189, 192 (D.C. Cir. 1986) (finding "no evidence in the regulatory scheme that Congress has fashioned for over-the-counter medications that the FTC is indefinitely barred from all regulatory authority over drug advertising while the FDA conducts its comprehensive review of drug safety"); Mutual Pharm. Co. v. Ivax Pharm., Inc., 459 F. Supp. 2d 925, 934-35 (C.D. Cal. 2006) (stating that "courts have refused to allow a Lanham Act claim to proceed where, in order to determine the falsity or misleading nature of the representation at issue, the court would be required to interpret and then apply FDCA statutory or regulatory provisions," but that "once the FDA has taken a position on a particular matter, courts have consistently allowed the Lanham Act claim to proceed even if in determining the falsity of the alleged representation the court must make reference to the FDA action"); *cf.* Sandoz Pharm. Corp. v. Richardson-Vicks, Inc., 902 F.2d 222, 227, 232 (3d Cir. 1990) (noting that the FDA and FTC have reached an understanding that "the FDA regulates the labeling of OTC [over-the-counter] drugs while the FTC monitors the advertising for these drugs," but that "the issue of whether an ingredient is properly labeled 'active' or 'inactive' under FDA standards is not properly decided as an original matter by a district court in a Lanham Act case"); Schwarz Pharm., Inc. v. Breckenridge Pharm., Inc., 388 F. Supp. 2d 967, 974 (E.D.

17. In other contexts, defendants sometimes argue that federal patent or copyright law preempts state unfair competition laws such as right of publicity laws. We discuss these types of preemption issues in greater depth in Chapter 10.

Wis. 2005) ("the mere FDA regulation of a term does not necessarily bar all Lanham Act claims that pertain to that term").

In general, a Lanham Act claim should not be precluded on the basis of FDCA law as long as the Lanham Act claim can be resolved without reference to that body of law. This can create a problem if, for example, the FDA sets a minimum requirement for what must be displayed on a label, and a Lanham Act defendant complies with this minimum requirement while adding other elements to a label that could create consumer confusion. To resolve cases such as these, a court might have to consider to what extent Congress intended the FDCA to prevent consumer confusion or deception (in addition to its goal of improving consumer safety), as well as whether the Lanham Act was intended to impose additional requirements in an area already under FDA purview.

F. CLAIMS RELATED TO FALSE ADVERTISING: COMMERCIAL DISPARAGEMENT AND FALSE ATTRIBUTION

1. Introduction to Commercial Disparagement

> *Iago*: Good name in man and woman, dear my lord,
> Is the immediate jewel of their souls.
> Who steals my purse steals trash; 'tis something, nothing;
> 'Twas mine, 'tis his, and has been slave to thousands;
> But he that filches from me my good name
> Robs me of that which not enriches him,
> And makes me poor indeed.
>
> William Shakespeare, Othello, act III, sc. 3.

The tort we refer to in this casebook as "commercial disparagement" goes by a number of different names: Product disparagement, business disparagement, injurious falsehood, slander on title, and trade libel are all terms that are used more or less synonymously to refer, roughly, to the publication of false statements about another person's property or business. Today, the tort of commercial disparagement has two different branches: an older, common law branch, which the courts developed by analogy to the law of defamation, and a more recent branch that has arisen as an offshoot of the law of false advertising.

The common law tort is said to date to about the year 1600, when courts in England began to recognize the tort of "slander on title." The gist of this cause of action was the defendant's false assertion that the plaintiff did not own land that the plaintiff did, in fact, own. Courts thereafter extended the cause of action to cover false statements concerning the ownership or quality of the plaintiff's personal, as well as real, property. Early on, the courts made an analogy to the law of defamation: Whereas a defamatory statement disparages a *person*, a "slander on title" or "trade libel" disparages a person's *property*. Indeed, in some cases the same statement might give rise to claims for both defamation and trade libel. Imagine, for example, a false statement to the effect that "Podunk Law School graduates students who can't pass the bar." In addition to possibly defaming the students, the statement also (arguably) defames Podunk Law School insofar as it casts aspersions on the school's professional competence. (Like natural persons, businesses and other organizations can state claims for defamation.) Beyond this, however, the statement also (arguably) defames or disparages Podunk's "product," namely its graduates. The resulting harm is, in a sense, distinct from the reputational or dignitary harm that the law of defamation protects; by disparaging its "products," the false statement may cause quantifiable financial harm to the extent Podunk loses sales (e.g., it can no longer attract as many tuition-paying students).

If we take the analogy to defamation seriously, the question arises how, if at all, the elements of a claim for commercial disparagement (as we will resume calling it) should differ from the elements of a defamation claim. Although the elements of a defamation claim differed to some extent from one common law jurisdiction to another, and were sometimes beset by enormous complexity, the *Restatement (Second) of Torts* listed the following three elements as being common to most American jurisdictions: (1) the defendant published (2) a defamatory statement (3) of and concerning the plaintiff. Moreover, at common law, defamation was a strict liability offense; truth was a defense, meaning that the defendant shouldered the burden of proving that the statement was true; and damages could be presumed for a statement that was defamatory on its face (per se) (such as a statement attributing to the plaintiff a character for dishonesty, fraud, unchastity, reprehensible personal characteristics, or professional incompetence.) The common law, in other words, took Iago's view to heart: Injurious statements about a person's reputation or character were serious indeed (people fought duels over this sort of thing, after all), and the law made it relatively easy to plead and prove a cause of action for defamation. Any analogy between defamation and commercial disparagement therefore gives rise to two important questions: First, should a commercial disparagement claim be easier or more difficult to prove than a claim for defamation; and second, if the law of defamation changes over time, should the law of commercial disparagement change accordingly?

In answer to the first question, the common law emphatically came down on the side of making it more difficult to prove a claim for commercial disparagement. In one sense, this distinction is easy to understand. If personal honor and reputation are paramount, the law should (and did) make it relatively easy for plaintiffs to plead and prove claims for defamation by, for example, making defamation a strict liability tort, requiring the defendant to prove truth, and in some cases by presuming damages (meaning that the plaintiff would not have to prove quantifiable financial harm). By contrast, commercial disparagement involves statements about *things*: important things, sometimes, like land or other valuable property, but things nonetheless. Moreover, one might expect competing business entities occasionally to say bad things about one another's products, and if every such statement was potentially actionable the risk of vexatious litigation might become substantial. On this view, it might make sense for the common law to hold plaintiffs asserting claims for commercial disparagement to a somewhat higher standard than the standard that applied in defamation actions—and this is exactly what the common law did, by (as we discuss in greater detail below) requiring the plaintiff to prove intent, falsity, and special damages.

The answer to the second question (whether the law of commercial disparagement should change as the law of defamation changes) remains, as of this writing, somewhat indeterminate. What is clear is that the law of defamation *has* changed greatly, at least in this country. (The United Kingdom still retains many of the common law attributes of the law of defamation, including the characterization of truth as a defense, with the result that the United Kingdom has become something of a magnet for defamation actions.) As discussed in section H *infra*, beginning in the 1960s, the U.S. Supreme Court decided a series of cases premised on the assumption that the enforcement of defamation claims in court involved state action, and thus implicated the First Amendment.[18] As a result, the law of defamation now carries with it a substantial *constitutional* overlay. The upshot is that a defamation claim is now considerably more difficult to prove than it would have been at common law; it may even be more difficult to prove a defamation claim today than it would have been to prove a commercial disparagement claim at common law. The common law, after all, never required commercial disparagement plaintiffs to prove their cases by clear and convincing evidence, or subjected trial court findings of fact to de novo review. (The common law's treatment of "actual malice," as we shall see, varied from one jurisdiction to another.) The question today, then, is whether the First Amendment (or sound policy) requires that some or all of these modifications be incorporated into the law of commercial disparagement. As we shall see in the next section, the answer to this question remains unresolved.

Another way of thinking about commercial disparagement might forgo the analogy to defamation altogether. If commercial disparagement concerns itself with commercial harm, after all, rather than with personal honor or reputation, why should defamation law provide a closer analogy than any other body of law? Indeed, if we're looking for analogies, perhaps the law of false advertising provides a better fit. False advertising, strictly speaking, involves false statements about one's *own* products that threaten harm to competitors by deceiving consumers; but it doesn't take much imagination to consider expanding false advertising law to cover false statements about one's *competitors'* products that threaten to harm competitors by deceiving consumers. On this view, commercial disparagement might be characterized as just another type of false advertising, subject to the same rules that apply in false advertising cases and (perhaps) no others.

This latter view is embodied in the current (1989) version of Lanham Act §43(a), which as we have already seen now refers to depictions or representations concerning "his or her or another's goods, services, or commercial activities." The addition of the words "or another's" makes §43(a) broad enough to cover commercial disparagement—as long as all of the other elements of a §43(a) claim are met.

18. *See* N.Y. Times Co. v. Sullivan, 376 U.S. 254, 265 (1964) (holding that when a litigant invokes the courts to intervene regarding speech, it is sufficient to qualify as state action implicating the First Amendment); *see also* Cohen v. Cowles Media Co., 501 U.S. 663, 668 (1991). In most contexts, the enforcement of private rights in court is not viewed as implicating the state action doctrine, because if it did then private actors would be required to adhere to all of the personal liberty protections afforded by the U.S. Constitution. Enforcement of defamation law and intellectual property rights nevertheless is viewed as involving state action and thus provides a basis for defendants' assertions of countervailing First Amendment rights. The only other context in which the Supreme Court has characterized judicial enforcement as a type of state action implicating constitutional protections is with respect to racially restrictive covenants. *See* Shelley v. Kraemer, 334 U.S. 1 (1948).

This qualification is important, however, because not every materially false statement about another person's goods, services, or commercial activities will necessarily be actionable under § 43(a). For example, to be actionable under § 43(a) the statement must not only have some impact on interstate commerce (which is often fairly easy to prove) but also must be made in the context of "commercial advertising or promotion." False statements not made in the context of commercial advertising or promotion therefore will be actionable, if at all, only under the common law of product disparagement (which, for that reason, remains important). On the other hand, it might be easier to prove a Lanham Act violation than a common law violation, depending on the facts. As we have seen, the Lanham Act imposes liability on a strict liability basis and does not (on its face, at any rate) incorporate any First Amendment safeguards borrowed from the constitutional law of defamation. Whether it should remains, once again, a matter of dispute.

2. Common Law Commercial Disparagement

A comprehensive listing of the elements a plaintiff would have to prove to prevail on a claim for common law commercial disparagement would include the following: (1) publication by the defendant of (2) disparaging words (3) of and concerning the ownership, quality, or other characteristics of the plaintiff's goods, services, or property; (4) falsity; (5) intent; and (6) special damages. *See, e.g.*, Paidar v. Hughes, 615 N.W.2d 276, 279-80 (Minn. 2000); Hurlbut v. Gulf Atl. Life Ins. Co., 749 S.W.2d 762, 766 (Tex. 1987); Restatement (Second) of Torts § 623A (1977) (stating that "[o]ne who publishes a false statement harmful to the interests of another is subject to liability for pecuniary loss resulting to the other if (a) he intends for publication of the statement to result in harm to interest of the other having a pecuniary value, or either recognizes or should recognize that it is likely to do so, and (b) he knows that the statement is false or acts in reckless disregard of its truth or falsity").[19] In this context, as in the context of defamation law, the term "publication" means any "communication intentionally or negligently made." Restatement (Second) of Torts § 630. "A statement is disparaging if it is understood to cast doubt upon the quality of another's land, chattels or intangible things, or upon the existence or extent of his property in them, and (a) the publisher intends the statement to cast doubt, or (b) the recipient's understanding of it as casting the doubt was reasonable." *Id.* § 629. As for "intent," according to the *Restatement* the plaintiff must show that the defendant "intends for publication of the statement to result in harm to interest of the other having a pecuniary value, or either recognizes or should recognize that it is likely to do so." *Id.* § 623A.

Difficulties sometimes arise in connection with element (6), special damages. As a general rule, the plaintiff must prove special damages in the form of "pecuniary loss that results directly and immediately from the effect of the conduct of third persons . . . and . . . the expense of measures reasonably necessary to counteract the publication." *Id.* § 633(1). At common law, the plaintiff needed to prove specific lost sales attributable to the disparaging statement. Some modern-day courts have

19. The *Restatement* discusses slander on title and trade libel as two specific applications of the general principles relating to injurious falsehood. *See* Restatement (Second) of Torts §§ 624, 627.

softened this rule a bit. Although speculative damages are precluded, evidence that reasonably demonstrates that plaintiff lost specific sales or growth opportunities can support a damages award. *See* Porous Media Corp. v. Pall Corp., 110 F.3d 1329, 1339 (8th Cir. 1997). The plaintiff must exclude other causes of its loss. *See id.* (citing Advanced Training Sys. v. Caswell Equip. Co., 352 N.W. 2d at 8). Further, "[i]f the plaintiff cannot show a loss of specific sales, it may still satisfy this burden by proving a general decline of business, provided that the decline can be shown to have resulted from the defendant's disparaging statements, and not because of other possible causes." Lenscrafters, Inc. v. Vision World, Inc., 943 F. Supp. 1481, 1490 (D. Minn. 1996) (citing *Advanced Training Sys.*, 352 N.W.2d at 7-8). *See generally* RESTATEMENT (SECOND) OF TORTS § 633 cmt. h & illus. 1.

Further difficulties arise with respect to a possible *seventh* element, "malice." The law of different states shows considerable variety with respect to this element. In some, malice is presumed upon proof of the above elements. *See, e.g.*, Cont'l Dev. Corp. of Fla. v. Duval Title & Abstract Co., 356 So. 2d 925, 927 (Fla. App. 1978). Practically speaking, this means that the burden shifts to the defendant to prove the existence of a privilege (see below), and that plaintiff wins unless defendant carries this burden. In other states, malice is an element the plaintiff must prove. The *Restatement* favors this approach. *See* RESTATEMENT (SECOND) OF TORTS, § 623A. In some of this latter category of states, the plaintiff can prove malice by showing that (1) the defendant knew the statement was false or acted with reckless disregard of its falsity; or (2) the defendant was motivated by ill will towards plaintiff; or (3) the defendant intended to interfere with the economic interest of the plaintiff in an unprivileged fashion. *See* Hurlbut v. Gulf Atl. Life Ins. Co., 749 S.W.2d 762, 766 (Tex. 1987).[20] In other states falling into this latter category, courts require proof that the defendant knowingly made a false statement or acted with reckless disregard for the truth or falsity of the statement. *See, e.g.*, State ex rel. BP Prods. N. Am. v. Ross, 163 S.W.3d 922, 928 (Mo. 2005).

20. The *Restatement* takes no position on "[w]hether, instead of showing the publisher's knowledge or reckless disregard of the falsity of the statement . . . [plaintiff] may recover by showing that the publisher had either (a) a motive of ill will toward him, or (b) an intent to interfere in an unprivileged manner with his interests;" or "[w]hether either of these alternative bases, if not alone sufficient, would be made sufficient by being combined with a showing of negligence regarding the truth or falsity of the statement." RESTATEMENT (SECOND) OF TORTS, § 623A. For examples of malice as ill will or an intent to interfere, see RESTATEMENT (SECOND) OF TORTS § 623A illus. 7-10:

> 7. A, advertising his cigarettes, broadcasts over television a listing and rating of the ten most popular tunes of the week. In doing so he omits songs published by B, which are in fact among the ten most popular. As a result B loses customers for his songs. A believes that his rating is correct and that he has made a sufficient investigation to justify it, although a reasonably diligent investigation would have disclosed the facts. A is not liable to B.
> 8. The same facts as in Illustration 7, except that A, although he believes that his rating is correct and that he has a sufficient basis for it, broadcasts it out of motives of ill will toward B, and a desire to injure B's business. The Institute expresses no opinion on whether A can constitutionally be held subject to liability to B.
> 9. The same facts as in Illustration 7, except that A, although he believes that his rating is correct and that he has a sufficient basis for it, and has no personal ill will toward B, broadcasts for the purpose of creating a public impression that B's music business is unsuccessful, so that he can buy stock in B's company at a lower price. A knows and intends that the publication will damage B's sales. The Institute expresses no opinion on whether A can constitutionally be held subject to liability to B.
> 10. The same facts as in Illustration 7, except that A has either ill will toward B as in Illustration 8 or an intent to affect his interests as in Illustration 9, and he knows that he has not made a sufficient investigation to justify his rating. The Institute expresses no opinion on whether A is subject to liability to B.

If plaintiff proves all of the necessary elements, whatever they are, the burden shifts to the defendant to prove the existence of a privilege. The plaintiff wins unless defendant carries this burden. Some statements, such as statements made in court, are absolutely privileged from becoming the basis of a product disparagement claim. *See* RESTATEMENT (SECOND) OF TORTS § 635. Others are only subject to a conditional (qualified) privilege. *See id.* § 646A. These include the following:

1. *Product comparisons.* Speaker makes unduly unfavorable comparisons of his own products with another's (e.g., "My products are better than the other leading brand."). Arguably, such statements are not disparaging at all; they merely assert the superiority of the speaker's product without suggesting that the other's products are bad. But *just in case*, there is a privilege to make these types of statements, even if the speaker knows the statement is false. Why does this privilege exist? For one thing, some such statements are just puffery and therefore immaterial. Others might, conceivably, be actionable as false advertising, but they are not actionable as product disparagement unless the speaker makes false assertions of specific unfavorable facts. *See generally* RESTATEMENT (SECOND) OF TORTS § 649.
2. *Rival claimant.* Speaker asserts that he, not the plaintiff, owns title to property (assertion of an inconsistent legal interest); statement is privileged, even if unreasonable, as long as it is subjectively honest and in good faith. *See id.* § 647. Why? Courts don't want to chill people from asserting what they believe are their legal rights.
3. *Common interest.* Speaker and recipient have a common interest; the speaker reasonably believes that publication protects or furthers that interest; and the publication is reasonable and in good faith. *See* Kemart Corp. v. Printing Arts Research Labs., Inc., 269 F.2d 375, 391-92 (9th Cir. 1959).
4. *Speaker's interest.* Speaker has a sufficiently important interest (such as a legitimate business interest); and he or she reasonably believes that publication protects or furthers that interest. *See* Flotech, Inc. v. E.I. duPont deNemours & Co., 814 F.2d 775, 778 (1st Cir. 1987). For a more recent variation on this privilege, in the Lanham Act context, see below at pp. 446-50.
5. *Recipient's interest.* Speaker reasonably believes that information affects a sufficiently important interest of recipient; and the speaker has an obligation to inform recipient. *See Flotech*, 814 F.2d at 779.
6. *Fair comment.* At common law, the majority rule was that this privilege was limited to statements of opinion. Because statements of opinion today are viewed as absolutely privileged, unless they imply specific facts, this privilege has little applicability *except* in states that have transformed it into a tool for factual statements relating to matters of public concern. *See* Dairy Stores, Inc. v. Sentinel Publ'g Co., 516 A.2d 220 (N.J. 1986), *infra* section G.

If the defendant establishes a conditional privilege, plaintiff can try to prove that defendant abused the privilege. *See* RESTATEMENT (SECOND) OF TORTS § 650A. Proof of malice negates all of the conditional privileges, except for the product comparison privilege. Alternatively, the plaintiff could prove that the defendant abused the privilege by engaging in excessive (more than reasonably necessary) publication.

PROBLEM

Problem 9-9. The United States Triple Crown of Thoroughbred Racing is a series of three horse races, featuring three-year-old thoroughbred horses, that takes place every spring. The event begins with the Kentucky Derby on the first Saturday in May; continues with the Preakness two weeks later; and concludes with the Belmont Stakes three weeks after the Preakness. For a horse to win all three races (a phenomenon known as the "Triple Crown") is rare; it last happened in 1978.

Silly Side Ventures LLC owns a horse, Silly Side, that wins the Kentucky Derby in 2011. Four days after that race is run, the *Chicago Centurion* (a nationally circulated newspaper) publishes a story falsely claiming that Silly Side's jockey, Sanders, admitted carrying an object in his hand during the Derby; and falsely implying that Sanders cheated by using an illegal battery-operated device. The newspaper retracts the story and admits its error, but not until three months later. Meanwhile, Sanders rides Silly Side to victory in the Preakness but comes in third in the Belmont Stakes. Silly Side Ventures files suit against the *Centurion* for commercial disparagement, claiming that publication of the false report caused Sanders to "override" the horse in the Preakness in an effort to vindicate himself and the horse, thus using up too much of the horse's strength and leading to the third-place in the Belmont Stakes. Silly Sides Ventures seeks monetary damages in the form of the winner's purse for the Belmont Stakes and an additional bonus that would have been earned from winning the Triple Crown. The *Centurion* moves for summary judgment. What result? Suppose instead that Sanders's significant other filed suit against the *Centurion*, claiming that the stress caused by publication of the false report has irredeemably damaged the couple's relationship. What result?

3. Lanham Act Commercial Disparagement

As was noted above, the elements of a Lanham Act commercial disparagement claim are identical to the elements of a Lanham Act false advertising claim, except for the requirement that the false statement relate to the plaintiff's, as opposed to the defendant's, goods, services, or commercial activities. The following two cases, however, shed some light on two elements (common to both types of Lanham Act claims) that we have not discussed at any length until now: "commercial activities" and "commercial advertising and promotion."

*Proctor & Gamble Co. v. Haugen**
222 F.3d 1262 (10th Cir. 2000)

LUCERO, Circuit Judge.

The Proctor & Gamble Company and Proctor & Gamble Distributing Company ("P & G") appeal from a final judgment dismissing their lawsuit against parties who

* [Although the court titles the opinion, and refers to the plaintiff, as "Proctor & Gamble Co.," the correct spelling is "Procter & Gamble Co." — EDS.]

disseminated the rumor that P & G is a corporate agent of Satan. We decide whether the district court erred in granting summary judgment on P & G's Lanham Act claim on the ground that the message — associating P & G with Lucifer — does not relate to qualities or characteristics of P & G's products and hence falls outside the ambit of the Lanham Act. . . .

I

The corporate butt of the Beelzebub canard in this case, P & G, is the manufacturer and distributor of numerous products for personal care, household use, and consumption. Defendant-appellee Amway Corporation ("Amway") likewise sells numerous consumer products, including detergents, cosmetics, nutrition supplements, housewares, and cleaning agents — some in direct competition with P & G's products — as well as the brand-name products of third-party companies. Amway sells through a network of distributors, who in turn sell the products to other distributors and consumers.

The relationships between Amway and its distributors and between the distributors themselves bear some explanation. Amway's distribution system consists of more than a million distributors around the world. It sells its products to distributors who, in addition to selling directly to consumers, sell to and recruit further distributors, who in turn follow suit-in a cycle that replicates itself. There is record evidence that Amway distributors are responsible for inspiring and encouraging distributors to whom they sell, who in turn are encouraged to emulate those above them in the Amway distribution hierarchy. Although Amway distributors are strongly encouraged to purchase, distribute, and consume Amway products, they may also purchase and consume P & G products.

To facilitate communication between its distributors, Amway sells them a communication system known as AmVox. Using AmVox, Amway and its distributors have the ability to send messages to, and receive messages from, other Amway distributors who subscribe to AmVox.

Defendant-appellee Randy L. Haugen is a distributor of Amway products and a developer of Amway business in the Amway distribution chain. At the time this action was commenced, Haugen had established a network of an estimated 100,000 distributors of Amway products throughout Utah, Nevada, Texas, Mexico, and Canada and served on the Amway Distributors Association Council — an advisory and consultative body for Amway. Freedom Associates, Inc., Freedom Tools Inc., Roger D. Patton, Steven E. Brady, Stephen L. Bybee, Eagle Business Development, Inc., Ted Randall Walker, and Walker International Network (hereinafter "the distributor appellees") are Amway distributors in Haugen's distribution network. Using AmVox, Haugen is capable of distributing any message to 25,000-30,000 of the distributors beneath him in the Amway hierarchy.

In April 1995, defendant-appellee Haugen posted the following message ("the subject message") on AmVox after receiving the message from other Amway distributors:

> I wanna run something by you real quick that I think you will find pretty interesting. Just talking to a guy the other night about this very subject and it just so happens that a guy brings information in and lays it on my desk this morning, so here it goes.

> It says the president of Procter & Gamble appeared on the Phil Donahue Show on March 1, '95. He announced that due to the openness of our society, he was coming out of the closet about his association with the church of satan. He stated that a large portion of the profits from [P & G] products go to support his satanic church. When asked by Donahue if stating this on television would hurt his business, his reply was, "There are not enough Christians in the United States to make a difference." And below it has a list of the [P & G] products which I'll read: [the subject message then lists 43 P & G products].
>
> It says if you are not sure about a product, look for the symbol of the ram's horn that will appear on each product beginning in April. The ram's horn will form the 666 which is known as satan's number. I'll tell you it really makes you count your blessings to have available to all of us a business that allows us to buy all the products that we want from our own shelf and I guess my real question is, if people aren't being loyal to themselves and buying from their own business, then whose business are they supporting and who are they buying from. Love you. Talk to you later. Bye.

Although it is unclear from the record how many distributors the subject message reached it was spread via AmVox among at least two groups of distributors. The record is replete with evidence that P & G received complaints and inquiries from a large number of individuals regarding similar allegations of affiliation with Satan that were disseminated by leaflet and otherwise, but not primarily through the subject message.

After learning of the subject message, an Amway representative called Haugen, suggesting he post a retraction of the message designed to reach those distributors who had received it. Amway also delivered to Haugen a copy of a P & G information package explaining the falsity of rumors of P & G's conspiracy with Satan. Prior to his conversation with Amway, Haugen had posted a tentative retraction on AmVox describing the subject message as unsubstantiated. On April 26, 1995, after his conversation with Amway, Haugen again posted a retraction on AmVox. . . . Haugen's retraction went on to categorically deny the allegation of an affiliation between P & G and the Evil One. One or both of the retractions were sent to Haugen's entire distribution network, though the number of people receiving the retraction is unclear from the record. The subject message continued to circulate on Amvox after the retractions.

The subject message was not the first such missive regarding the Lucifer-P & G connection circulated by Amway distributors. Rumors of such a fiendish relation — some spread by Amway distributors — have been prevalent for nearly twenty years, dogging P & G despite its attempts to eliminate them through both public relations and litigation.

On August 28, 1995, P & G filed suit in United States District Court for the District of Utah against Haugen, the distributor appellees, and Amway, claiming that as a result of the subject message and other similar missives disseminated by defendants, P & G lost customers concerned about supporting Satan through their purchase of P & G's products. . . .

The district court granted defendants-appellees' motion for summary judgment on P & G's Lanham Act claim because it found the subject message, although "identif[ying] . . . [P & G] products," did not "contain false representations about the qualities or characteristics of those products," and so did "not relate to a product within the meaning of the Lanham Act." P & G v. Haugen, No. 1:95 CV 0094K, at 3 (D. Utah Sept. 4, 1998) (order). We agree with the district court that the subject message did not implicate the nature, characteristics, or qualities of P & G's products because it impugned no feature of the products themselves, such as price . . . or substitutability for another product.

However, in addition to challenging on appeal the district court's conclusion that there was no genuine issue as to misrepresentation of the qualities or characteristics of its goods or services, P & G argues that the district court erred in granting summary judgment because the subject message's representations regarding the infernal affiliation of P & G and the use of its profits misrepresented "the nature, characteristics, [or] qualities . . . of . . . [its] commercial activities." 15 U.S.C. § 1125(a)(1)(B) (emphasis added). While P & G properly raised the bulk of its Lanham Act arguments below, appellees correctly point out that P & G did not timely raise the instant argument before the district court. It made a passing reference to a "commercial activities" claim during oral argument, but admitted in its motion for reconsideration that it had directed the court to focus on the Lanham Act terms "goods" or "services" rather than the term "commercial activities." It did not explicitly make the argument until its motion for reconsideration of the district court's grant of summary judgment under Fed. R. Civ. P. 60(b), a motion the court denied as not presenting any of the "exceptional circumstances" warranting relief under that Rule. *See* Bud Brooks Trucking, Inc. v. Bill Hodges Trucking Co., 909 F.2d 1437, 1440 (10th Cir. 1990) (noting that "[r]elief under Rule 60(b) is extraordinary and may only be granted in exceptional circumstances").

When an issue has not been properly raised below, "to preserve the integrity of the appellate structure, we should not be considered a 'second-shot' forum . . . where secondary, back-up theories may be mounted for the first time." "We will consider matters not raised or argued in the trial court only in 'the most unusual circumstances,'" as when "public interest is implicated, . . . or manifest injustice would result." Where the issue "is purely a matter of law . . . and . . . its proper resolution is certain," however, we may consider it.

In the present case, we are faced with just such an exceptional situation involving a "pure[ ] matter of law" the "proper resolution" of which is certain. *See Ross*, 168 F.3d at 1195 n.5. . . . We thus elect to consider the issue on the merits.

We begin our analysis of the meaning of statutes by examining the relevant statutory language. . . . Although Congress did not define the term "commercial activities" in the Act, the plain language meaning of that term encompasses "commercial transactions" or all activities surrounding the peculiar "commerce" of a company, defined as "the exchange or buying and selling of commodities." WEBSTER'S THIRD NEW INTERNATIONAL DICTIONARY (Unabridged) 456 (1993).

The subject message linking P & G to Beelzebub clearly concerned the "nature, characteristics, [or] qualities . . . of . . . [P & G's] commercial activities," under the plain meaning of that phrase. In particular, the subject message asserted that "a large portion of the profits from [P & G] products go to support [the church of Satan]." Given the common association of Satan and immorality, a direct affiliation with the church of Satan could certainly undermine a corporation's reputation and goodwill by suggesting the corporation conducts its commercial activities in an unethical or immoral manner.[7] There can be little doubt that products are often marketed and

7. *See* National Artists Management Co. v. Weaving, 769 F. Supp. 1224, 1229-36 (S.D.N.Y. 1991) (holding actionable under a Lanham Act false advertising claim a defendant's allegations that a competing theater booking agency engaged in improper and unethical practices); *cf.* Coastal Abstract Serv., Inc. v. First Am. Tit. Ins. Co., 173 F.3d 725, 732 (9th Cir. 1999) (holding actionable under § 43(a)(1)(B) a statement that an escrow agent was not paying his bills); Fuente Cigar, Ltd. v. Opus One, 985 F. Supp. 1448, 1454 (M.D. Fla. 1997) (holding a defendant's statements about the plaintiff's misuse of the defendant's reputation were "plainly statements . . . about . . . commercial activities," even though they were not statements

purchased not only on the basis of their inherent utility, but also for the images they project and the values they promote. In that regard, the subject message itself implies that recipients should question the values promoted by the businesses from whom they purchase goods. In light of the foregoing reality of the marketplace, corporations cultivate their images and values through a wide array of activities, including celebrity endorsements, sponsorships, and charitable giving. See Faith Stevelman Kahn, *Pandora's Box: Managerial Discretion and the Problem of Corporate Philanthropy*, 44 UCLA L. Rev. 579, 665 (1997) ("There is considerable empirical evidence that charitable contributions have been assimilated into corporate marketing and advertising functions, either as a complement to or as a substitute therefor." (footnotes omitted)). Allegations that P & G tithes the church of Satan concern just such commercial activities.

That conclusion is reinforced by an examination of the Act's "object and policy," as evidenced by its language and legislative history. *Aulston*, 915 F.2d at 589. As a general matter, the drafters and promoters of the original Lanham Trademark Act of 1946, ch. 540, 60 Stat. 427 (1946), sought to create a general federal law of unfair competition to protect competing companies in the wake of the Supreme Court's decision in Erie R. Co. v. Tompkins, 304 U.S. 64, (1938), which was thought to have eliminated the existing body of federal unfair competition law.

In 1988 Congress amended the Act. See Trademark Law Revision Act of 1988, Pub. L. No. 100-667, tit. I, § 132, 102 Stat. 3935. Of greatest relevance to our present inquiry is the amendment's addition of "commercial activities" to the original coverage of the provision, which until then had been applicable exclusively to "goods or services." *Id.* The legislative history of the 1988 amendments is scant, *see* Jean Wegman Burns, *Confused Jurisprudence: False Advertising Under the Lanham Act*, 79 B.U. L. Rev. 807, 820-21 (1999), though as a general matter they were intended to codify existing case law, *see* Vornado Air Circulation Sys. Inc. v. Duracraft Corp., 58 F.3d 1498, 1505-06 (10th Cir. 1995). However, the amendments also overruled aspects of existing law, most significantly by covering trade libel or product disparagement (i.e., misrepresentations about the plaintiff's goods and services) and by permitting actions based on misrepresentations about commercial activities as well as goods and services. *See* Burns, 79 B.U. L. Rev. at 821. The latter addition indicates that the term "commercial activities" was intended to denote something other than mere "goods or services." *See* Bridger Coal Co./Pac. Minerals, Inc. v. Director, Office of Workers' Compensation Programs, 927 F.2d 1150, 1153 (10th Cir. 1991) ("We will not construe a statute in a way that renders words or phrases meaningless, redundant, or superfluous.").

It is therefore apparent, in the context of the Act's broad purpose of proscribing unfair competition and the 1988 amendment of § 43(a), that Congress did not intend to narrowly limit the term "commercial activities," but rather intended to encompass those activities which do not solely involve the provision of services or the production of goods. Properly construed, the term "commercial activities" in § 43(a) encompasses P & G's use of the profits from the sale of its goods. The district court's grant of summary judgment to defendants-appellees on the ground that the subject message

---

about "goods or services," and therefore were actionable under § 43(a)(1)(B)); H & R. Indus., Inc. v. Kirshner, 899 F. Supp. 995, 1005-06 (E.D.N.Y. 1995) (holding actionable under § 43(a)(1)(B) a representation that the plaintiff used improper methods of soliciting customers).

did not directly implicate "goods" or "services" was improvident because P & G has shown a genuine issue of material fact exists as to whether the subject message is actionable under the "commercial activities" prong of §43(a)(1)(B).

In addition to the grounds on which the district court relied in granting summary judgment, appellees, in support of their motion for summary judgment and in their appellate brief, raise the argument that the subject message is not "commercial advertising or promotion" for purposes of §43(a)(1)(B) liability; specifically, appellees argue that whatever advertising or promotion there was in this case was not "commercial speech" and therefore was not actionable under the Lanham Act. Although the district court did not rely on that ground for granting summary judgment to defendants-appellees, we must address any alternative ground for affirmance that appellees have properly preserved below and raised on appeal and for which there is a sufficient record. *See* Tinkler v. United States, 982 F.2d 1456, 1461 n.4 (10th Cir. 1992). We therefore turn now to that alternative ground.

We find Gordon & Breach Science Publishers, S.A. v. American Institute of Physics, 859 F. Supp. 1521, 1535-36 (S.D.N.Y. 1994), helpful in framing the question of whether the representations constitute "commercial advertising or promotion" under §43(a)(1)(B). In Gordon & Breach, the court set out the following four-part test, which we adopt:

> In order for representations to constitute "commercial advertising or promotion" under Section 43(a)(1)(B), they must be: (1) commercial speech; (2) by a defendant who is in commercial competition with plaintiff; (3) for the purpose of influencing consumers to buy defendant's goods or services. While the representations need not be made in a "classic advertising campaign," but may consist instead of more informal types of "promotion," the representations (4) must be disseminated sufficiently to the relevant purchasing public to constitute "advertising" or "promotion" within that industry.

859 F. Supp. at 1535-36; *see also* Coastal Abstract Serv., Inc. v. First Am. Tit. Ins. Co., 173 F.3d 725, 734 (9th Cir. 1999) (adopting the same test); Seven-Up Co. v. Coca-Cola Co., 86 F.3d 1379, 1384 (5th Cir. 1996) (same). In the present case, appellees effectively raise only P & G's failure to fulfill the first element of the four-prong test as grounds for affirmance, and it is that element which we examine here.[9] In so doing, we hold-as the parties implicitly assumed in their briefs on appeal-that the meaning of "commercial speech" in the context of §43(a)(1)(B) of the Lanham Act tracks the First Amendment "commercial speech" doctrine. *See* Porous Media Corp. v. Pall Corp., 173 F.3d 1109, 1120-21 (8th Cir. 1999); *Seven-Up Co.*, 86 F.3d at 1383

9. On appeal, defendants-appellees raise an argument they did not raise in the summary judgment motion before the district court. They argue, with respect to the fourth element of the test for "commercial advertising or promotion" under §43(a)(1)(B), that the subject message was "circulated informally among a few distributors on a private voicemail system" and cite case law for the proposition that it therefore was not disseminated sufficiently "within the consumer goods industry." (Appellees' Br. at 37 (citing Synygy, Inc. v. Scott-Levin, Inc., 51 F. Supp. 2d 570, 577 (1999); Fashion Boutique of Short Hills v. Fendi USA, Inc., 942 F. Supp. 209, 216 (S.D.N.Y. 1996)).) This argument is not a pure matter of law the resolution of which is certain, *see Ross*, 168 F.3d at 1195 n.8, but rather involves a difficult factual determination as to the number and identity of those individuals reached by the subject message. Thus, unlike the "commercial activities" claim that we reached despite waiver below, the instant claim is not one that we may properly reach. See id. Furthermore, there is a genuine issue of material fact as to the fourth element of a showing of "commercial advertisement or promotion" due to the uncertainty as to the number of Amway distributors—part of the "relevant purchasing public" in this case—actually reached by the subject message. *Gordon & Breach*, 859 F. Supp. at 1536.

n.6; Oxycal Labs., Inc. v. Jeffers, 909 F. Supp. 719, 722-723 (S.D. Cal. 1995); *Gordon & Breach*, 859 F. Supp. at 1536 ("Congress intended Section 43(a) to extend only to false and misleading speech that is encompassed within the 'commercial speech' doctrine developed by the United States Supreme Court." (internal quotations omitted)); *cf.* Semco, Inc. v. Amcast, Inc., 52 F.3d 108, 111 (6th Cir. 1995) (finding the legislative history of § 43(a)(1)(B) ambiguous with regard to the meaning of "commercial speech").

While commercial speech jurisprudence is not remarkable for its clarity, the Supreme Court has enunciated certain principles with some consistency in drawing "the 'common-sense' distinction between speech proposing a commercial transaction . . . and other varieties of speech." Ohralik v. Ohio State Bar Ass'n, 436 U.S. 447, 455-56 (1978) (quoting Virginia State Bd. of Pharmacy v. Virginia Citizens Consumer Council, Inc., 425 U.S. 748, 771 n.24 (1976)). To begin with, a representation is not necessarily commercial speech merely because — by way of example — it is contained in an advertisement, made with an economic motive, or refers to a specific product, although the combination of those characteristics strongly supports classification as commercial speech. *See* Bolger v. Youngs Drug Products Corp., 463 U.S. 60, 66 (1983); *see also* City of Cincinnati v. Discovery Network, Inc., 507 U.S. 410, 420-21 (1993) (noting the fact that a representation is contained in an advertisement is insufficient to strip that representation of the protections of the First Amendment). Rather, the difference between commercial speech and noncommercial speech "is a matter of degree." *Discovery Network*, 507 U.S. at 423. . . .

In the present case, we are . . . dealing with a message containing both a non-commercial, "theological" component and a commercial component. As *Bolger* and *Fox* indicate, however, the bare fact that the subject message contains a "theological" component is insufficient to transform it into noncommercial speech. If appellees had argued that a significant theological, political, or other noncommercial purpose underlay the subject message, the message might be accorded the substantially greater First Amendment protections enjoyed by "core" religious speech and the other varieties of noncommercial First Amendment speech such as political speech. *See, e.g.*, Pleasant v. Lovell, 876 F.2d 787, 795 (10th Cir. 1989) (holding "that the presence of some commercial activity does not change the standard of first amendment review" where the organization engaged in such activity had a clear political purpose (citing In re Grand Jury Proceeding, 842 F.2d 1229, 1235 (11th Cir. 1988))). Significantly, appellees in the instant case have made no such claim. At no time have they argued there is any theological purpose underlying the subject message or its dissemination via their AmVox system.

Furthermore, we reject appellees' assertion that the subject message does not promote "commercial transactions." On the contrary, the message unambiguously urges recipients to eschew purchasing P & G products in favor of Amway products. While economic motivation or reference to a specific brand name and products, when viewed in isolation, might not render a message commercial speech, we conclude that those factors taken together with the instant message's promotion of Amway products at the expense of P & G products support the characterization of the subject message as commercial speech. *See Bolger*, 463 U.S. at 67; *Porous Media Corp.*, 173 F.3d at 1120-21 & n.8 (holding that a communication alleging health risks associated with a competitor's product was commercial speech under the Lanham Act, notwithstanding the fact that the communication concerned an issue of public importance); *cf.* U.S. West, Inc. v. FCC, 182 F.3d 1224, 1232-33 (10th Cir. 1999) (holding that a telecommunications company's use of speech "for the purpose of soliciting . . . customers to purchase more or different telecommunications services" was "commercial speech"). Nor are we faced with a situation in which the "theological" component of the subject message is "inextricably intertwined" with its commercial nature, as in the charitable contribution context. *See, e.g.*, Riley v. National Fed'n of the Blind, Inc., 487 U.S. 781, 796 (1988) (concluding that mandated disclosure of administrative costs was "inextricably intertwined" with noncommercial charitable solicitation and therefore subject to heightened First Amendment scrutiny); Village of Schaumburg v. Citizens for a Better Env't, 444 U.S. 620, 631-37 (1980) (same). In the absence of a genuine issue as to the subject message's "theological" content, and in light of the message's exhortation to eschew purchasing P & G's products in favor of Amway products, the conclusion that the subject message constitutes commercial speech for purposes of liability under the Lanham Act is unavoidable.

In classifying the patently fallacious message in the present case as commercial speech, we are acting in the spirit of the policy underlying the First Amendment protections accorded such speech, namely, to ensure that the "numerous private economic decisions" of our market economy are "in the aggregate, . . . intelligent and well informed." *Virginia State Bd. of Pharmacy*, 425 U.S. at 765. As in *Ohralik*, 436 U.S. at 457 (quoting Bates v. State Bar, 433 U.S. 350, 364, (1977)), the subject message "actually may disserve the individual and societal interest . . . in facilitating 'informed and reliable decisionmaking.'" We conclude that the district court improvidently granted summary judgment to defendants-appellees on P & G's Lanham Act claim.[10]

[In the remainder of the opinion, the court affirmed the judgment in favor of defendant Amway on the ground that Amway was not vicariously liable for the conduct of its independent contractors. It also addressed state law claims with respect to the individual defendants.]

Fashion Boutique of Short Hills, Inc. v. Fendi USA, Inc.

314 F.3d 48 (2d Cir. 2002)

John M. WALKER, JR., Chief Judge.

Plaintiff-appellant Fashion Boutique of Short Hills, Inc. ("Fashion Boutique"), challenges a host of rulings by the United States District Court for the Southern District of New York (Miriam Goldman Cedarbaum, District Judge) during this lengthy litigation arising from the demise of its business. Fashion Boutique, formerly a seller of Fendi products, claims that its business was ruined by a campaign of disparagement conducted by a competing boutique, defendant-appellee Fendi Stores, Inc. ("Fendi Stores") and its parent company, defendant-appellee Fendi USA, Inc. ("Fendi USA") (collectively, "Fendi").

Fashion Boutique contends principally that the district court erred . . . by granting the motion for partial summary judgment in favor of Fendi, dismissing plaintiff's claims under the Lanham Act, *see* Fashion Boutique of Short Hills, Inc. v. Fendi USA, Inc., 942 F. Supp. 209 (S.D.N.Y. 1996) ("Fashion Boutique I"). . . .

For the following reasons, we affirm.

10. We leave it to the district court to consider whether P & G has met those elements of a §43(a) Lanham Act claim not before us in this appeal. . . .

Background

I. Overview

Between 1983 and July 1991, Fashion Boutique sold products bearing the internationally-renowned Fendi trademark in an upscale mall in Short Hills, New Jersey. Fashion Boutique was the only freestanding Fendi boutique in the greater New York metropolitan area until Fendi Stores opened on Fifth Avenue in New York City in October 1989. Both Fashion Boutique and Fendi Stores carried only the international line of Fendi products. This "exclusive" line is considered superior in quality to the domestic line sold in American department stores.

Two months after Fendi opened its Fifth Avenue Store, Fashion Boutique experienced a sharp decline in its sales and, by July 1991, Fashion Boutique closed its retail operations. Fashion Boutique alleged in its complaint that the precipitous fall in its sales was caused by a corporate policy carried out by Fendi to misrepresent the quality and authenticity of the products sold at Fashion Boutique.

Fashion Boutique conceded in the district court that it could not show that many of its customers heard disparaging statements first-hand at the Fifth Avenue store. Rather, its theory was and is that Fendi employees made misrepresentations to some customers at the Fifth Avenue store, those customers relayed the comments to others, and the false rumors were thus spread throughout Fashion Boutique's customer base. Prior to the close of its business, Fashion Boutique maintained a mailing list of over 8,000 customers.

Fashion Boutique claims that the actions by Fendi led to the destruction of its retail business, violated Section 43(a)(1)(B) of the Lanham Act, 15 U.S.C. § 1125(a) (1994), which prohibits misrepresentation of another person's goods or services in "commercial advertising or promotion," and violated New York law on product disparagement and slander.

II. Motion for Summary Judgment on the Lanham Act Claim

After the close of discovery, Fendi moved for summary judgment on Fashion Boutique's Lanham Act claim. Following certain pre-trial evidentiary rulings, the district court granted defendants' motion. *See Fashion Boutique I,* 942 F. Supp. at 217.

In challenging the district court's grant of partial summary judgment, Fashion Boutique relies primarily on reported conversations between Fendi personnel and nine undercover investigators hired to pose as shoppers and on declarations by forty Fashion Boutique customers. In none of the proffered interactions did employees at the Fifth Avenue store initiate conversations about Fashion Boutique. They commented on Fashion Boutique only after the customers mentioned plaintiff. For example, several customers who reported their conversations with Fendi employees went to the Fifth Avenue store seeking to repair or exchange products or were wearing Fendi products as they shopped at that store. After the customer informed Fendi personnel that the item had been bought at Fashion Boutique, the employee reacted by making critical comments about the quality of Fashion Boutique's merchandise and, on several occasions, refused to exchange or repair the product.

(1) Incidents Prior to the Close of Fashion Boutique

Prior to Fashion Boutique's demise, Fendi personnel told a total of eleven customers that Fashion Boutique carried an inferior, "department store" line of products or that Fashion Boutique sold "fake" or "bogus" merchandise. During four visits to Fendi's Fifth Avenue store, undercover investigators were told that Fashion Boutique's merchandise was of inferior quality. Five shoppers and several undercover investigators related incidents in which Fendi employees described Fashion Boutique's goods as a "different line" from that sold at the Fifth Avenue store. In addition, Fendi employees made critical comments about the customer service at Fashion Boutique to six investigators and one customer.

Sixteen Fashion Boutique customers reported having "heard rumors" that Fashion Boutique sold fake Fendi merchandise "[d]uring the period 1990-1991." One shopper heard similar rumors but could not remember when she heard them.

(2) Statements Made After the Close of Fashion Boutique

Eight customers identified statements made after Fashion Boutique's demise in July 1991. Fendi employees told four of them that Fashion Boutique sold a "different line" of products, three others that Fashion Boutique sold inferior or fake Fendi goods, and one other that Fashion Boutique closed because it caused trouble or was too costly to maintain. In addition, a Fendi employee told one investigator that the owners of Fashion Boutique were filing for bankruptcy.

(3) Caroline Clarke Deposition

As evidence of the alleged policy of disparagement, plaintiff presented the deposition of Caroline Clarke, a former employee of Fendi USA. Although Clarke's superiors never explicitly told her of a policy to disparage Fashion Boutique, she learned from speaking to managers and salespersons at Fendi Stores that salespersons followed a practice of disparaging the customer service at Fashion Boutique.

(4) The District Court's Decisions

After carefully reviewing the evidence, Judge Cedarbaum determined that most of the evidence submitted by Fashion Boutique failed to support the Lanham Act claim. Specifically, the district court found that (1) the statements suggesting that Fashion Boutique sold a "different" line were not disparaging because "different" does not impugn the quality of the product; (2) the declarations by customers alleging to have "heard rumors" that Fashion Boutique sold fake items was inadmissable hearsay and thus could not be considered on a motion for summary judgment; and (3) disparaging remarks made after Fashion Boutique closed were not actionable under the Lanham Act and, because plaintiff and defendants were no longer competitors, were not relevant. *See id.* at 215.

Judge Cedarbaum concluded that the remaining evidence was insufficient to withstand a motion for summary judgment because it did not fall within the meaning of "commercial advertising or promotion" as set forth in the Lanham Act. The district court held that the Lanham Act is violated when the defendants proactively pursue customer contacts and disparage the plaintiff's goods or services. *See id.* at 215-16 (listing cases). Because each disparaging comment was made only after the customer initiated a discussion about Fashion Boutique, the district court concluded that the communications were reactive and not proactive. *See id.* at 216.

Moreover, relying on the four-part test announced in Gordon & Breach Sci. Publishers S.A. v. Am. Inst. of Physics, 859 F. Supp. 1521, 1535-36 (S.D.N.Y. 1994) ("*Gordon & Breach I*"), the district court held that to constitute "commercial advertising or promotion" the statements must be sufficiently disseminated to the relevant purchasing public. *See Fashion Boutique I*, 942 F. Supp. at 216. The district court concluded that plaintiff had failed to prove sufficient dissemination because it presented only a dozen admissible comments within a purchasing public universe consisting of thousands of customers. . . .

Discussion

I. Section 43(a) of the Lanham Act

Fashion Boutique contends that the district court abused its discretion when it decided the summary judgment motion by not considering the rumor evidence, "different line" statements, and comments made after the close of the store. Fashion Boutique also argues that the district court erred in finding that Fendi's actions did not constitute "commercial advertising or promotion" under the Lanham Act. Specifically, Fashion Boutique maintains that its proof of several disparaging comments by defendants, together with evidence of rumors that plaintiff sold fake or inferior merchandise, falls into the category "commercial advertising or promotion." . . .

B. "Commercial Advertising or Promotion"

. . . An important issue in this case is whether the allegedly disparaging statements by salespersons at the Fendi Fifth Avenue store constituted "commercial advertising or promotion" within the meaning of Section 43(a).

The statute does not define the phrase "commercial advertising or promotion." In determining whether representations qualify as "commercial advertising or promotion," most courts have adopted the four-part test set forth in *Gordon & Breach I.* Under the test, in order to qualify as "commercial advertising or promotion," the contested representations must be "(1) commercial speech; (2) by a defendant who is in commercial competition with plaintiff; (3) for the purpose of influencing consumers to buy defendant's goods or services"; and (4) although representations less formal than those made as part of a classic advertising campaign may suffice, they must be disseminated sufficiently to the relevant purchasing public. *See Gordon & Breach I*, 859 F. Supp. at 1535-36; *see also* Proctor & Gamble Co. v. Haugen, 222 F.3d 1262, 1273-74 (10th Cir. 2000) (adopting four-part test); Coastal Abstract Serv., Inc. v.

First Am. Title Ins. Co., 173 F.3d 725, 735 (9th Cir. 1999) (same); Seven-Up Co. v. Coca-Cola Co., 86 F.3d 1379, 1384 (5th Cir. 1996) (same); *see also* Porous Media Corp. v. Pall Corp., 173 F.3d 1109, 1121 (8th Cir. 1999) (although defining advertising as communication that "propose[s] a commercial transaction," analyzing whether dissemination was sufficient to satisfy fourth element of *Gordon & Breach* test).

. . . [W]e easily accept the first and third elements of the *Gordon & Breach* test that define the term "commercial" as referring to "commercial speech" that is made for the purpose of influencing the purchasing decisions of the consuming public. *See Gordon & Breach I*, 859 F. Supp. at 1536.

The precise meaning of "advertising or promotion" has been subject to various interpretations. *Compare* Gordon & Breach Sci. Publishers S.A. v. Am. Inst. of Physics, 905 F. Supp. 169, 182 (S.D.N.Y. 1995) (holding that "any promotional statement directed at actual or potential purchasers falls within the reach" of the Lanham Act), and Mobius Mgmt. Sys., Inc. v. Fourth Dimension Software, Inc., 880 F. Supp. 1005, 1020-21 (S.D.N.Y. 1994) (holding that single letter addressed to one purchaser constitutes "advertising or promotion"); *with* Garland Co. v. Ecology Roof Sys., Corp., 895 F. Supp. 274, 279 (D. Kan. 1995) (rejecting *Mobius* and holding that the Lanham Act is violated only where the misrepresentations are widely disseminated within the relevant purchasing public), and Med. Graphics Corp. v. SensorMedics Corp., 872 F. Supp. 643, 650-51 (D. Minn. 1994). The statute's disjunctive wording compels us to give meanings to both "advertising" and "promotion" that do not render either term superfluous. *See* Connecticut ex rel. Blumenthal v. United States Dep't of the Interior, 228 F.3d 82, 88 (2d Cir. 2000). We conclude that the distinction between advertising and promotion lies in the form of the representation. Although advertising is generally understood to consist of widespread communication through print or broadcast media, "promotion" may take other forms of publicity used in the relevant industry, such as displays at trade shows and sales presentations to buyers. *See, e.g., Seven-Up*, 86 F.3d at 1386 (finding sales presentation to a significant percentage of industry customers constitutes advertising under the Lanham Act).

The Seventh Circuit has recently limited the scope of the Lanham Act to advertising defined as "a form of promotion to anonymous recipients, as distinguished from face-to-face communication . . . [and] a subset of persuasion [that relies on] dissemination of prefabricated promotional material." *See* First Health Group Corp. v. BCE Emergis Corp., 269 F.3d 800, 803 (7th Cir. 2001) (internal quotations omitted). The problem with the Seventh Circuit's focus on the term "advertising" is that it fails to define the term "promotion" in any meaningful way.

Although the Lanham Act encompasses more than the traditional advertising campaign, the language of the Act cannot be stretched so broadly as to encompass all commercial speech. *See, e.g.*, Sports Unlimited, Inc. v. Lankford Enters., Inc., 275 F.3d 996, 1005 (10th Cir. 2002); *First Health Group*, 269 F.3d at 803. The ordinary understanding of both "advertising" and "promotion" connotes activity designed to disseminate information to the public. *Cf. Garland*, 895 F. Supp. at 276. Thus, the touchstone of whether a defendant's actions may be considered "commercial advertising or promotion" under the Lanham Act is that the contested representations are part of an organized campaign to penetrate the relevant market. Proof of widespread dissemination within the relevant industry is a normal concomitant of meeting this requirement. Thus, businesses harmed by isolated disparaging statements do not have redress under the Lanham Act; they must seek redress under state-law causes of action.

See, e.g., id. at 279; Am. Needle & Novelty, Inc. v. Drew Pearson Mktg., Inc., 820 F. Supp. 1072, 1078 n.2 (N.D. Ill. 1993).

In determining whether a defendant's misrepresentations are designed to reach the public, we find the district court's proactive-reactive distinction instructive, but not necessarily dispositive. Although most reactive statements will doubtless consist of off-the-cuff comments that do not violate the Lanham Act because no broad dissemination is intended or effected, we leave open the possibility that a cause of action might exist where a defendant maintains a well-enforced policy to disparage its competitor each time it is mentioned by a customer, if such a policy of reactive disparagement successfully reaches a substantial number of the competitor's potential customers.

In sum, we adopt the first, third and fourth elements of the *Gordon & Breach* test. To decide this appeal, we need not decide whether the second element-that defendant and plaintiff be competitors. We note that the requirement is not set forth in the text of Section 43(a) and express no view on its soundness.

C. Fashion Boutique's Lanham Act Claim

Based on the foregoing principles, we easily conclude that Fashion Boutique failed to put forward sufficient evidence that defendants' actions constituted "commercial advertising or promotion" under the Lanham Act.

Turning first to plaintiff's evidentiary claims, we believe that the district court did not abuse its discretion in excluding the evidence of rumors. *See* Nora Beverages, Inc. v. Perrier Group of Am., Inc., 164 F.3d 736, 746 (2d Cir. 1998) (stating that evidentiary rulings, even those made at the summary judgment stage, are reviewed for "manifest error"). Regardless of whether the rumor evidence was properly rejected as hearsay, the district court later decided, in any event, that its prejudicial effect outweighed its minimal probative value. We find no "manifest error" in this decision given the absence of proof connecting defendants to the rumors.

There is no evidence to suggest that the remaining statements were part of an organized campaign to penetrate the marketplace. Even including the "different line" statements, post-closing statements, and comments made to undercover investigators, Fashion Boutique has presented a total of twenty-seven oral statements regarding plaintiff's products in a marketplace of thousands of customers. Such evidence is insufficient to satisfy the requirement that representations be disseminated widely in order to constitute "commercial advertising or promotion" under the Lanham Act. The Clark deposition was specifically limited to disparagement of the customer service at Fashion Boutique, as distinct from the products sold there, and there is nothing to suggest that the comments were anything more than individual reactions to particular customers' mention of Fashion Boutique.

COMMENTS AND QUESTIONS

1. The court in *Procter & Gamble* adopts a broad reading of the phrase "goods, services or commercial activities." Just how far can this definition be stretched? In Freecycle Network, Inc. v. Oey, 505 F.3d 898 (9th Cir. 2007), plaintiff The Freecycle Network (TFN) was a nonprofit corporation dedicated to the "reusing,

recycling, and gifting of goods." At the urging of network member Oey, TFN began actively policing others' use of the term "freecycle" and sought a federal trademark registration. Oey thereafter had a change of heart about trademarking the word "freecycle," and he began posting messages on a Web site to the effect that TFN lacked trademark rights because "freecycle" was a generic term. While the federal registration was still pending, TFN sued Oey for a variety of claims, including contributory trademark infringement and "trademark disparagement," allegedly in violation of the Lanham Act, and for injurious falsehood under state law. The district court granted an injunction on the Lanham Act claims, but the Ninth Circuit reversed. The court concluded, first, that the facts alleged did not make out a claim for trademark infringement because Oey himself was not using the word "freecycle" to promote any competing product or service, and also because there was no basis for concluding that consumers would be confused by his use of the term. The court also concluded that the facts alleged did not state a claim under Lanham Act §43(a)(1)(B) because Oey's statements were neither made in the context of "commercial advertising or promotion," nor did they refer to TFN's goods, services, or commercial activities. *See id.* In particular, the court rejected the argument that disparaging TFN's mark constituted disparagement of the services symbolized by that mark. *See id.* at 903 n.8. Relatedly, the court held that there is no Lanham Act cause of action for "trademark disparagement" and that, even if there were, Oey's statements that TFN lacked trademark rights constituted nonactionable opinion. *See id.* The court remanded for further consideration of the state law claims.

2. Both sides in *Procter & Gamble* neglected some serious arguments when the matter first came before the district court. In the district court, P & G asserted that Haugen's message pertained to P & G's goods or services; it did not raise the argument that the message pertained to P & G's "commercial activities" until after the district court had granted summary judgment in favor of the defendants. Normally an issue not properly raised at trial is waived, but in this instance the Court of Appeals was willing to consider the matter nonetheless because it involved a "pure matter of law" and its "proper resolution" was certain, and because the matter implicated the public interest. The defendants, however, were not so lucky. As the court discusses in footnote 44 (footnote 9 in the original opinion), defense counsel failed to raise the issue of whether the statements constituted "commercial advertising or promotion," and the Court of Appeals was unwilling to consider that issue for the first time on appeal because of the factual issues inherent to its resolution. (Presumably, though, defendants were allowed to raise this issue on remand.) Under the Second Circuit's standard as reflected in *Fashion Boutique*, were the statements part of "an organized campaign to penetrate the relevant market"? Under the Seventh Circuit's approach (rejected in *Fashion Boutique*), were the statements "advertising and promotion" in the sense of being "promotion to anonymous recipients, as distinguished from face-to-face communication"?

3. After the Tenth Circuit remanded P & G, the case went to trial and ultimately resulted in a $19.25 million damages award in favor of P & G. *See* Procter & Gamble Co. v. Haugen, 627 F. Supp. 2d 1287, 1290-93 (D. Utah 2008). Do you think that Haugen's message actually caused P & G to suffer $19 million in harm?

4. No doubt when Shakespeare wrote "Who steals my purse steals trash," he didn't have Fendi's upscale merchandise in mind. But did Fendi U.S.A. filch Fashion Boutique's good name? More to the point, did the Second Circuit reach the right result in construing "commercial advertising and promotion" to include even oral

communications that are part of an "organized campaign to penetrate the relevant market"? Or are the terms (for Lanham Act purposes) synonymous, and limited to communications made to anonymous recipients, as the Seventh Circuit seemed to think? Are there any risks in permitting cases to go forward based on false statements that are communicated orally? What about flyers handed out on the street? Sales presentations? Letters to a customer? For other cases addressing the meaning of the term "commercial advertising and promotion," *see, e.g*, Sports Unlimited v. Lankford Enters., 275 F.3d 996 (10th Cir. 2002) (concluding that the distribution of defamatory information to between two and seven people did not constitute "commercial advertising"); Seven-Up Co. v. Coca-Cola Co., 86 F.3d 1379 (5th Cir. 1996) (concluding that a series of sales presentations made to bottlers qualified as advertising for purposes of the Lanham Act); Champion Labs. v. Parker-Hannifin, 2009 WL 1266924 (E.D. Mich. Apr. 30, 2009) (presentation to General Motors could be "commercial promotion" where GM was the only market for the product).

5. False statements about possible health risks arising from eating certain foods have sometimes caused huge losses for the affected industries as consumers, at least temporarily, shy away from consuming those foods. In 1959, for example, U.S. Secretary of Health, Education, and Welfare Arthur Flemming announced that some cranberries produced in the northwest United States had been contaminated with a weed killer that caused cancer in rats. The market for cranberries dropped precipitously and took several years to recover, even after Secretary Flemming and Agriculture Secretary Ezra Taft Benson announced that the contaminated cranberries had been destroyed (and probably didn't present a serious health risk, in any event). Similarly, after a 1989 broadcast of the TV news program "60 Minutes" presented interviews from an EPA administrator and others to the effect that the chemical Alar posed a cancer risk, the demand for apples (some of which, at the time, were sprayed with Alar) dropped dramatically. Members of the Washington apple industry sued "60 Minutes" for product disparagement. The Court of Appeals affirmed a grant of summary judgment for the defendants, however, on the ground that the plaintiffs had not proven that the statements made during the broadcast were false. *See* Auvil v. CBS "60 Minutes," 67 F.3d 816 (9th Cir. 1995) (per curiam).

In the wake of the Alar scare, some states began passing statutes (sometimes referred to as "food disparagement" or "veggie libel laws") aimed at making it easier to assert claims for false and disparaging statements about food products. In the most high profile case to date, the Texas Beef Growers Association filed suit against talk show host Oprah Winfrey after Winfrey broadcast a show that, in the opinion of the plaintiffs, falsely implied that beef products for sale in the United States were at risk for "mad cow" disease. Following the broadcast, the market for "fed cattle" in the Texas Panhandle dropped precipitously. The case went to trial, but the district court granted JMOL on the plaintiffs' claims under Texas's False Disparagment of Perishable Food Products Act,[21] reasoning that (1) the statute might not apply to "fed cattle," (2) the cattle did not "perish" or "decay beyond marketability," and (3) the plaintiffs had not

21. The Act states that a person may be liable for damages sustained by the producer of a perishable food product if that person knowingly disseminates false information to the public stating or implying that the producer's product is not safe for public consumption. Tex. Civ. Prac. & Rem. §96.002. It defines a "perishable food product" as "a food product of agriculture or aquaculture that is sold or distributed in a form that will perish or decay beyond marketability within a limited period of time," *id.* §96.001, and states that in determining truth or falsity the trier of fact should determine "whether the information was based on reasonable and reliable scientific inquiry, facts, or data." *Id.* §96.003.

proven that the defendants knowingly disseminated false information. The court submitted the plaintiffs' claim for common law commercial disparagement to the jury, but with a special interrogatory asking whether the plaintiffs had proven that the defendants' alleged disparaging statements were "of and concerning" the plaintiffs in this civil action. To this question, the jury responded "no," and the court entered judgment for the defendants. The Court of Appeals affirmed the JMOL on the ground that the defendants had not knowingly disseminated false information; it reserved judgment on whether the Texas statute applied to fed cattle and as to the meaning of "perishable food product."[22] The court also affirmed the judgment for the defendants on the commercial disparagement claim, reasoning that the plaintiffs had not preserved their objection to the instruction requiring the jury to determine if the alleged disparaging statements disparaged *their specific cattle*. *See* Texas Beef Group v. Winfrey, 201 F.3d 680 (5th Cir. 2000) (per curiam). Once again, raising issues at the proper time can be crucial.

With regard to the common law commercial disparagement claim, should the plaintiffs be required to prove that the alleged false statements concern their specific cattle? Should the Texas statute apply to false statements about cattle, as long as cattle *can* decay beyond marketability? Why couldn't the plaintiffs in *Winfrey* assert a Lanham Act product disparagement claim?

A Note on Commercial Disparagement (and Other Business Tort) Claims Premised on False Accusations of Infringement

A common type of commercial disparagement claim is premised on the defendant's allegedly having falsely accused the plaintiff of infringing a patent or other intellectual property right. The accusation may take the form of a communication directed at the plaintiff itself (such as a "cease and desist" letter that threatens legal action) or a communication warning others against using or buying allegedly infringing products made by the plaintiff. At common law, many of these claims would be privileged, and hence nonactionable, if made in good faith. *See* Kemart Corp. v. Printing Arts Research Labs., 269 F.2d 375, 391 (9th Cir. 1959) (holding that "a qualified privilege is recognized in cases where the publisher and the recipient of the publication have a common inerest which might be reasonably believed to be protected or furthered by the publication and the publication is made reasonably and in good faith," and that this privilege protected the defendant against a claim of common law disparagement, absent proof of actual malice, despite the fact that its patents turned out to be non-infringed). Nevertheless, in recent years some courts have seen fit to resolve such cases on the basis of a legal framework that draws on two different strands of analysis, one rooted in federal patent policy and the other in the First Amendment.

First, as a matter of federal patent policy, at least two provisions of the Patent Act might be read as having some bearing on the viability of disparagement claims premised on the invalid assertion of patent rights. One is 35 U.S.C. § 282, which states that, once issued, patents are presumed valid. Case law holds that this presumption can

22. Judge Edith Jones, concurring in the judgment, argued that the statute applies to food products that "*could* decay beyond marketability," and that the question of whether the food products at issue *did* decay beyond marketability goes only to the issue of damages. *See Winfrey*, 201 F.3d at 690-92 (Jones, J., concurring).

be overcome only by proof of invalidity by clear and convincing evidence. *See, e.g.*, Ariad Pharm. v. Eli Lilly & Co., 560 F.3d 1366, 1371 (Fed. Cir. 2009). Some courts have found this provision to be relevant in the context of antitrust challenges to patent settlements, among other things. *See* Asahi Glass Co. v. Pentec Pharm. Co., 289 F. Supp. 2d 986, 992-93 (N.D. Ill. 2003) (Posner, J.). The other is 25 U.S.C. §287(a), which states that patentees "may give notice to the public that [an article] is patented, either by fixing thereon the word 'patent' or the abbreviation 'pat.,' together with the number of the patent, or when, from the character of the article, this can not be done, by fixing to it, or to the package wherein one or more of them is contained, a label containing a like notice." This provision might be undermined if the mere act of publicizing one's patent could result in liability for commercial disparagement, though of course the plaintiff would have to prove all of the elements of a commercial disparagement claim, including falsity, in order to prevail.

Second, a First Amendment strand arises from a series of cases addressing the impact on federal *antitrust* law of the First Amendment right to petition the government. Because the Sherman Antitrust Act condemns contracts, combinations, or conspiracies in restraint in trade, *see* 15 U.S.C. §1, one might assume that it would be illegal for competitors to agree among themselves to petition public officials for legislative or other favors to shield them from competition (for example, for laws that would work to the disadvantage of other potential competitors). In a series of cases beginning in the 1960s, however, the U.S. Supreme Court has held that the First Amendment right to petition the government generally shields competitors from antitrust liability under these circumstances. *See* E. R.R. Presidents Conf. v. Noerr Motor Freight Inc., 365 U.S. 127 (1961); United Mine Workers v. Pennington, 381 U.S. 657 (1965). Subsequent cases extended the so-called *Noerr-Pennington* doctrine to petitions directed at administrative agencies and courts in addition to the legislative and executive branches. *See* Cal. Motor Transp. Co. v. Trucking Unltd., 404 U.S. 508, 510 (1972). As a general matter, then, it is not an antitrust violation to procure a patent (even though the end result may be that the patent confers monopoly power) or to assert (or threaten to assert) a claim for patent infringement. An exception to this rule applies, however, where the petitioning entity or entities engage in so-called "sham petitioning," that is, where "persons use the governmental *process*— as opposed to the *outcome* of that process — as an anticompetitive weapon," City of Columbia v. Omni Outdoor Adver., Inc., 499 U.S. 365, 380 (1991). For example, if the owner of an intellectual property right asserts a baseless claim of infringement against a competitor merely to raise the competitor's costs of doing business (and perhaps to discourage others from entering the market), such "sham litigation" may violate the antitrust laws, if all of the other elements of an antitrust claim (e.g., market power) are satisfied. *See* Professional Real Estate Investors, Inc. v. Columbia Pictures Indus., 508 U.S. 49 (1993); Handgards, Inc. v. Ethicon, Inc., 601 F.2d 986 (9th Cir. 1979).[23] Sham litigation claims nevertheless are very difficult to prove. A plaintiff asserting a sham litigation claim must prove (by clear and convincing evidence, *see*

23. Similarly, where the plaintiff can prove that the defendant obtained its patent by making knowing and willful misrepresentations to the Patent Office, the defendant may be liable for monopolization or attempted monopolization, again assuming that all of the other elements of an antitrust claim are met. *See* Walker Process Equip., Inc. v. Food Mach. & Chem. Corp., 382 U.S. 172 (1965). The Federal Circuit views such *Walker Process* claims as an alternative ground for antitrust liability rather than as an exception to *Noerr-Pennington* immunity. *See* Nobelpharma AB v. Implant Innovations, Inc., 141 F.3d 1059, 1071 (Fed. Cir. 1998). Like sham litigation claims, however, *Walker Process* claims rarely succeed.

Loctite Corp. v. Ultraseal Ltd., 781 F.2d 861, 876-77 (Fed. Cir. 1985), *overruled in part on other grounds*, 141 F.3d 1059, 1068 (Fed. Cir. 1998) (en banc)), that the patentee's assertion of a claim of infringement was both "objectively baseless in the sense that no reasonable litigant could realistically expect success on the merits," and subjectively baseless in the sense that the "lawsuit conceals 'an attempt to interfere *directly* with the business relationships of a competitor,' through the 'use [of] the governmental *process*—as opposed to the *outcome* of that process—as an anticompetitive weapon.'" *Professional Real Estate Investors*, 508 F.3d at 60-61 (citations omitted); Nobelpharma AB v. Implant Innovations, Inc., 141 F.3d 1059, 1071-72 (Fed. Cir. 1998). As a result, very few sham litigation claims succeed.

From these intersections of antitrust, patent, and First Amendment law, the Federal Circuit (and some other courts as well) have developed a body of law that imposes substantial obstacles for unfair competition claims premised on the alleged false assertion of patent or other intellectual property rights. For example, in Hunter Douglas, Inc. v. Harmonic Design, 153 F.3d 1318, 1335-37 (Fed. Cir. 1998), the Federal Circuit cited all of the above sources in concluding that federal patent law preempted[24] a state law commercial disparagement claim absent proof of bad faith:

> [I]n a case involving a patentholder's conduct in obtaining or publicizing its patent, if the plaintiff were to fail to allege that the defendant patentholder was guilty of fraudulent conduct before the PTO or bad faith in the publication of a patent, then the complaint would be dismissed for failure to state a claim upon which relief can be granted because of federal preemption. If the complaint were sufficient but the proof were not to show such conduct, then the claim would fail on the merits. Of course, neither fraud nor bad faith need be a required element of a state law tort for that cause of action to stave off preemption by federal patent law, because a plaintiff could prove fraud or bad faith for a tort that not only would be met by such a showing of proof, but also would be satisfied by less. Although to state and maintain a claim under a state law tort, a plaintiff may not be required to allege or prove that the patentholder perpetrated fraud before the PTO or acted in bad faith in the marketplace, to escape preemption, the plaintiff would need to allege and prove ultimately such conduct. To require less would impermissibly alter the balance between the competing purposes of federal patent law that Congress has prescribed.

The Federal Circuit has extended this "bad faith" requirement to claims for tortious interference with contract and tortious interference with prospective contractual relations, when such claims are premised on false allegations of patent infringement. *See* 800 Adept, Inc. v. Murex Sec., Ltd., 539 F.3d 1354, 1369 (Fed. Cir. 2008) (stating that "[s]tate tort claims against a patent holder, including tortious interference claims, based on enforcing a patent in the marketplace, are 'preempted' by federal patent laws, unless the claimant can show that the patent holder acted in 'bad faith' in the publication or enforcement of its patent"); Dow Chem. Co. v. Exxon Corp., 139 F.3d 1470 (Fed. Cir. 1998).

A preemption rationale, however, wouldn't apply if the claim at issue is another federal claim, such as a Lanham Act-based commercial disparagement claim. The Federal Circuit nevertheless has extended the "bad faith" requirement to Lanham Act disparagement claims too. In Zenith Elecs. Corp. v. Exzec, Inc., 182 F.3d 1340, 1352-55 (Fed. Cir. 1999), for example, the court concluded that requiring

24. Preemption is a topic we cover in greater depth in Chapter 15.

plaintiffs asserting Lanham Act disparagement claims to prove bad faith would reconcile the competing interests of federal unfair competition law with those of federal patent law. In other cases, the court has cited the First Amendment right to petition the government, as reflected in the *Noerr-Pennington* doctrine, as providing a rationale for requiring plaintiffs to prove bad faith with respect to both federal and state unfair competition and business tort claims premised on allegedly false prelitigation communications of patent infringement (for example, cease and desist letters). *See* Globetrotter Software, Inc. v. Elan Computer Group, Inc., 362 F.3d 1367, 1376-77 (Fed. Cir. 2004) (holding that, for the prelitigation communication of infringement of patent rights to constitute actionable disparagement under state law, both the First Amendment and principles of patent preemption require that the communication be both objectively and subjectively baseless); Golan v. Pingel Enters., 310 F.3d 1360, 1371 (Fed. Cir. 2002); *see also* IGEN Int'l, Inc. v. Roche Diagnostics GmbH, 335 F.3d 303, 310 (4th Cir. 2003) (citing Cheminor Drugs, Ltd. v. Ethyl Corp., 168 F.3d 119, 128-29 (3d Cir. 1999) for the proposition that the *Noerr-Pennington* doctrine "applies to common law claims of malicious prosecution, tortious interference with contract, tortious interference with prospective economic advantage, and unfair competition").[25]

The Federal Circuit initially reserved decision on whether unfair competition and business tort claims based merely on publicizing of a patent in the marketplace requires proof of both objective and subjective bad faith, *see Globetrotter Software*, 362 F.3d at 1377 n.9. More recently, however, the court has held that in this context as well plaintiffs must prove, by clear and convincing evidence, both objective and subjective bad faith. *See 800 Adept*, 539 F.3d at 1370 (stating that plaintiff asserting tortious interference claims arising out of alleged false claim of patent infringement must prove both objective and subjective bad faith); Dominant Semiconductors SDN BHD v. Osram GmbH, 524 F.3d 1254, 1260 n.5 (Fed. Cir. 2008). This is an interesting development, insofar as these types of claims are not necessarily based on *Noerr-Pennington* petitioning immunity but rather, as noted above, on patent preemption principles. Nevertheless, the standards the plaintiffs must satisfy now appear to be identical, whether the unfair competition or business tort claim at issue arises under federal or state law, and whether it arises in the context of prelitigation communications such as a cease and desist letter or merely in the context of publicizing a patent in the marketplace.

In the context of disparagement and other business tort claims, was the application of *Noerr-Pennington* immunity (or federal preemption) a necessary step, in light

25. The requirement that the plaintiff prove objective and subjective bad faith by clear and convincing evidence appears in other patent law contexts as well. *See* In re Seagate Tech., Inc., 497 F.3d 1360 (Fed. Cir. 2007) (en banc) (requiring proof of objective and subjective bad faith, by clear and convincing evidence, in order to sustain a judgment of "willful" infringement necessary for the imposition of enhanced damages); In re Tamoxifen Citrate Antitrust Litig., 466 F.3d 187, 213 (2d Cir. 2006) (holding that party challenging patent settlement on antitrust grounds must prove that the patent was procured by fraud, that the underlying patent litigation was objectively baseless, or that the patentee sough to extend the patent beyond its scope); Brooks Furniture Mfg., Inc. v. Dutailier Int'l, Inc., 393 F.3d 1378, 1381 (Fed. Cir. 2005) (stating that a patent infringement "case may be deemed exceptional," and thus meriting an award of attorney's fees to the prevailing party, "when there has been some material inappropriate conduct related to the matter in litigation, such as willful infringement, fraud or inequitable conduct in procuring the patent, misconduct during litigation, vexatious or unjustified litigation, conduct that violates FED. R. CIV. P. 11, or like infractions," and that "[a]bsent misconduct in conduct of the litigation or in securing the patent, sanctions may be imposed against the patentee only if both (1) the litigation is brought in subjective bad faith, and (2) the litigation is objectively baseless").

of the common law privileges such as the one applied in *Kemart*? (Common law privileges similar to the ones that traditionally have applied to common law disparagement claims also apply to tortious interference claims. *See* Chapter 14 *infra*.) Should the standard be the same for prelitigation communications and for publicizing one's patent in the marketplace? Note that one practical consequence of the Federal Circuit's approach is that it might be marginally more difficult than it would have been at common law for plaintiffs to prove business torts premised on the defendant's false assertions of patent rights. To the extent the common law was ambiguous with respect to the question of whether plaintiffs had to prove both objective and subjective bad faith, and to the extent common law courts would have been satisfied with proof of bad faith by a preponderance of the evidence, plaintiffs are clearly in a tighter spot in light of the Federal Circuit case law cited above. Even so, one commentator has argued that even a remote possibility of being hauled into court for spreading word that someone is infringing your patent can have substantial chilling effects on the assertion of patent rights. *See* Greg A. McAllister, *Publicizing Your Patent Rights May Land You in Court*, BNA PATENT, TRADEMARK, AND COPYRIGHT LAW DAILY, Dec. 17, 2008. Given the risk not only of provoking an unfair competition claim (even if it lacks merit), as well as (after *MedImmune*) a declaratory judgment action for invalidity or non-infringement, has it become unduly costly to assert patent rights in some instances? In combination, what effects, if any, might these developments in the law have on the market for patent licenses?

4. False Attribution

Many authors and other creative artists place a high value on proper attribution — that is, on being accurately credited for their creations. In recognition of this interest, copyright laws in many countries confer upon authors a "moral right" of attribution. French and German law, for example, recognize inalienable rights (1) against misattribution (being attributed as the author of another's work, or having another attributed as the author of one's own work); (2) against nonattribution (the omission of one's name from one's own work); (3) to publish anonymously or pseudonymously; and (4) (in some circumstances) a right to void a promise to publish anonymously or pseudonymously. *See* Thomas F. Cotter, *Pragmatism, Economics, and the* Droit Moral, 96 N.C. L. REV. 1, 12 (1997); *see also* Berne Convention for the Protection of Literary and Artistic Works, art. 6bis (1), July 24, 1971, 1161 U.N.T.S. 31 ("Independently of the author's economic rights, and even after the transfer of said rights, the author shall have the right to claim authorship of the work"). These laws also typically confer upon authors a right of integrity, which though subject to different formulations generally permits the author "to object to any distortion, mutilation or other modification of, or other derogatory action in relation to the said work, which would be prejudicial to his honor or reputation." *Id.*

For many years these rights did not appear to exist under U.S. copyright law. Efforts to craft something in the nature of authors' moral rights through creative applications of copyright, unfair competition, or miscellaneous common law doctrines were generally unsuccessful. *See* Cotter, *supra*, at 15-16. Matters began to change to some extent in the 1970s, in the wake of (1) cases such as *Gilliam* (excerpted below), which seemed more favorable to some of these creative extensions of existing law; (2) state laws, such as laws enacted in California and New York, which created limited moral rights protection in certain qualifying works of visual art, *see* CAL. CIV. CODE

§987; N.Y. Arts & Cult. Aff. Law §14.03; and (3) the Visual Artists Rights Act (VARA), Pub. L. No. 101-650, §§601-610, 104 Stat. 5089, 5128-33 (codified as amended in scattered sections of 17 U.S.C.), a federal statute enacted two years after the United States acceded to the Berne Convention. VARA expressly confers upon authors of qualifying "works of visual art" rights of attribution and integrity.[26] *See* 17 U.S.C. §106A(a). VARA's reach is limited, however, because the term "work of visual art" includes only (1) paintings, drawings, prints, or sculptures existing in a single copy or in specified limited edition copies, and (2) still photographic images produced for exhibition purposes only, existing in a single copy signed by the author or in certain limited edition copies. *See* 17 U.S.C. §101. All other works (including motion pictures, literary works, and all "works made for hire") are outside the scope of the Act, as are reproductions of works of visual art other than the specified limited edition copies and any work created before the Act's effective date (June 1, 1991) if the author had transferred title prior to that date.

Authors who wish to preserve their interest in attribution and whose works do not qualify for moral rights protection under VARA or corresponding state laws therefore must continue to seek legal protection from other sources. One possibility is for authors (or performers) to seek such protection through contractual or licensing arrangements with the purchasers or licensees of the works to which they contribute. For example, an artist could attempt to obtain from his purchaser a binding promise to properly attribute and to avoid mutilating the artists' painting or sculpture. Possible disparities of bargaining power between artists and purchasers, however, as well as courts' reluctance to enforce covenants running with chattels (so that any such promise granted by the initial purchaser would not be binding upon subsequent owners of the work), are seen by some as reasons why contractual solutions are not a good substitute for moral rights laws. Even so, at least in some contexts negotiated solutions might be feasible. Many authors today take advantage of a "Creative Commons" license that conditions the use of their copyrighted works of authorship upon the licensee's agreement to accord the author proper attribution. *See* http://creativecommons.org/about/licenses/. And with respect to films, the Directors Guild of America's collective bargaining agreements with the movie studios give directors the option of having their names removed from the credits (and having the fictitious name "Allen Smithee" inserted instead) in the event that the director is displeased with the studio's editing of her work. *See* Directed by Allan Smithee (Jeremy Braddock & Stephen Hock eds., 2001).

Other possibilities for authors are suggested by the following case.

Gilliam v. American Broadcasting Cos.

538 F.2d 14 (2d Cir. 1976)

Lumbard, Circuit Judge:

Plaintiffs, a group of British writers and performers known as "Monty Python,"[1] appeal from a denial by Judge Lasker in the Southern District of a preliminary

26. VARA does not explicitly endow authors with a right to publish anonymously or pseudonymously. Other provisions of U.S. copyright law, however, have expressly permitted the registration of anonymous and pseudonymous works for over 100 years.

1. Appellant Gilliam is an American citizen residing in England.

injunction to restrain the American Broadcasting Company (ABC) from broadcasting edited versions of three separate programs originally written and performed by Monty Python for broadcast by the British Broadcasting Corporation (BBC). We agree with Judge Lasker that the appellants have demonstrated that the excising done for ABC impairs the integrity of the original work. We further find that the countervailing injuries that Judge Lasker found might have accrued to ABC as a result of an injunction at a prior date no longer exist. We therefore direct the issuance of a preliminary injunction by the district court.

Since its formation in 1969, the Monty Python group has gained popularity primarily through its thirty-minute television programs created for BBC as part of a comedy series entitled "Monty Python's Flying Circus." In accordance with an agreement between Monty Python and BBC, the group writes and delivers to BBC scripts for use in the television series. This scriptwriters' agreement recites in great detail the procedure to be followed when any alterations are to be made in the script prior to recording of the program. The essence of this section of the agreement is that, while BBC retains final authority to make changes, appellants or their representatives exercise optimum control over the scripts consistent with BBC's authority and only minor changes may be made without prior consultation with the writers. Nothing in the scriptwriters' agreement entitles BBC to alter a program once it has been recorded. The agreement further provides that, subject to the terms therein, the group retains all rights in the script.

Under the agreement, BBC may license the transmission of recordings of the television programs in any overseas territory. The series has been broadcast in this country primarily on non-commercial public broadcasting television stations. . . . In each instance, the thirty-minute programs have been broadcast as originally recorded and broadcast in England in their entirety and without commercial interruption.

In October 1973, Time-Life Films acquired the right to distribute in the United States certain BBC television programs, including the Monty Python series. Time-Life was permitted to edit the programs only "for insertion of commercials, applicable censorship or governmental . . . rules and regulations, and National Association of Broadcasters and time segment requirements." No similar clause was included in the scriptwriters' agreement between appellants and BBC. Prior to this time, ABC had sought to acquire the right to broadcast excerpts from various Monty Python programs in the spring of 1975, but the group rejected the proposal for such a disjoined format. Thereafter, in July 1975, ABC agreed with Time-Life to broadcast two ninety-minute specials each comprising three thirty-minute Monty Python programs that had not previously been shown in this country. . . .

ABC broadcast the first of the specials on October 3, 1975. Appellants did not see a tape of the program until late November and were allegedly "appalled" at the discontinuity and "mutilation" that had resulted from the editing done by Time-Life for ABC. Twenty-four minutes of the original 90 minutes of recording had been omitted. Some of the editing had been done in order to make time for commercials; other material had been edited, according to ABC, because the original programs contained offensive or obscene matter.

In early December, Monty Python learned that ABC planned to broadcast the second special on December 26, 1975. . . . [O]n December 15 the group filed this action to enjoin the broadcast and for damages. Following an evidentiary hearing, Judge Lasker found that "the plaintiffs have established an impairment of the integrity of their work" which "caused the film or program . . . to lose its iconoclastic verve." According to Judge Lasker, "the damage that has been caused to the plaintiffs is irreparable by its nature." Nevertheless, the judge denied the motion for the preliminary injunction on the grounds that it was unclear who owned the copyright in the programs produced by BBC from the scripts written by Monty Python; that there was a question of whether Time-Life and BBC were indispensable parties to the litigation; that ABC would suffer significant financial loss if it were enjoined a week before the scheduled broadcast; and that Monty Python had displayed a "somewhat disturbing casualness" in their pursuance of the matter.

Judge Lasker granted Monty Python's request for more limited relief by requiring ABC to broadcast a disclaimer during the December 26 special to the effect that the group dissociated itself from the program because of the editing. A panel of this court, however, granted a stay of that order until this appeal could be heard and permitted ABC to broadcast, at the beginning of the special, only the legend that the program had been edited by ABC. We heard argument on April 13 and, at that time, enjoined ABC from any further broadcast of edited Monty Python programs pending the decision of the court.

I

In determining the availability of injunctive relief at this early stage of the proceedings, Judge Lasker properly considered the harm that would inure to the plaintiffs if the injunction were denied, the harm that defendant would suffer if the injunction were granted, and the likelihood that plaintiffs would ultimately succeed on the merits. *See* Hamilton Watch Co. v. Benrus Watch Co., 206 F.2d 738 (2d Cir. 1953). We direct the issuance of a preliminary injunction because we find that all these factors weigh in favor of appellants.

There is nothing clearly erroneous in Judge Lasker's conclusion that any injury suffered by appellants as a result of the broadcast of edited versions of their programs was irreparable by its nature. ABC presented the appellants with their first opportunity for broadcast to a nationwide network audience in this country. If ABC adversely misrepresented the quality of Monty Python's work, it is likely that many members of the audience, many of whom, by defendant's admission, were previously unfamiliar with appellants, would not become loyal followers of Monty Python productions. The subsequent injury to appellants' theatrical reputation would imperil their ability to attract the large audience necessary to the success of their venture. Such an injury to professional reputation cannot be measured in monetary terms or recompensed by other relief. *See* Coca-Cola Co. v. Gemini Rising, Inc., 346 F. Supp. 1183, 1189 (E.D.N.Y. 1972); Estee Lauder, Inc. v. Watsky, 323 F. Supp. 1064, 1067 (S.D.N.Y. 1970).

In contrast to the harm that Monty Python would suffer by a denial of the preliminary injunction, Judge Lasker found that ABC's relationship with its affiliates would be impaired by a grant of an injunction within a week of the scheduled December 26 broadcast. The court also found that ABC and its affiliates had advertised the program and had included it in listings of forthcoming television programs that were distributed to the public. Thus a last minute cancellation of the December 26 program, Judge Lasker concluded, would injure defendant financially and in its reputation with the public and its advertisers.

However valid these considerations may have been when the issue before the court was whether a preliminary injunction should immediately precede the broadcast, any injury to ABC is presently more speculative. No rebroadcast of the edited specials has been scheduled and no advertising costs have been incurred for the immediate future. Thus there is no danger that defendant's relations with affiliates or the public will suffer irreparably if subsequent broadcasts of the programs are enjoined pending a disposition of the issues.

We then reach the question whether there is a likelihood that appellants will succeed on the merits. In concluding that there is a likelihood of infringement here, we rely especially on the fact that the editing was substantial, i.e., approximately 27 per cent of the original program was omitted, and the editing contravened contractual provisions that limited the right to edit Monty Python material. It should be emphasized that our discussion of these matters refers only to such facts as have been developed upon the hearing for a preliminary injunction. Modified or contrary findings may become appropriate after a plenary trial.

Judge Lasker denied the preliminary injunction in part because he was unsure of the ownership of the copyright in the recorded program. Appellants first contend that the question of ownership is irrelevant because the recorded program was merely a derivative work taken from the script in which they hold the uncontested copyright. Thus, even if BBC owned the copyright in the recorded program, its use of that work would be limited by the license granted to BBC by Monty Python for use of the underlying script. We agree.

Section 7 of the Copyright Law, 17 U.S.C. s7, provides in part that "adaptations, arrangements, dramatizations . . . or other versions of . . . copyrighted works when produced with the consent of the proprietor of the copyright in such works . . . shall be regarded as new works subject to copyright. . . ." Manifestly, the recorded program falls into this category as a dramatization of the script, and thus the program was itself entitled to copyright protection. However, section 7 limits the copyright protection of the derivative work, as works adapted from previously existing scripts have become known, to the novel additions made to the underlying work, Reyher v. Children's Television Workshop, 533 F.2d 87 (2d Cir. 1976), and the derivative work does not affect the "force or validity" of the copyright in the matter from which it is derived. *See* Grove Press, Inc. v. Greenleaf Publishing Co., 247 F. Supp. 518 (S.D.N.Y. 1965). Thus, any ownership by BBC of the copyright in the recorded program would not affect the scope or ownership of the copyright in the underlying script.

Since the copyright in the underlying script survives intact despite the incorporation of that work into a derivative work, one who uses the script, even with the permission of the proprietor of the derivative work, may infringe the underlying copyright.

If the proprietor of the derivative work is licensed by the proprietor of the copyright in the underlying work to vend or distribute the derivative work to third parties, those parties will, of course, suffer no liability for their use of the underlying work consistent with the license to the proprietor of the derivative work. Obviously, it was just this type of arrangement that was contemplated in this instance. The scriptwriters' agreement between Monty Python and BBC specifically permitted the latter to license the transmission of the recordings made by BBC to distributors such as Time-Life for broadcast in overseas territories.

One who obtains permission to use a copyrighted script in the production of a derivative work, however, may not exceed the specific purpose for which permission was granted. . . . Appellants herein do not claim that the broadcast by ABC violated media or time restrictions contained in the license of the script to BBC. Rather, they claim that revisions in the script, and ultimately in the program, could be made only after consultation with Monty Python, and that ABC's broadcast of a program edited after recording and without consultation with Monty Python exceeded the scope of any license that BBC was entitled to grant.

The rationale for finding infringement when a licensee exceeds time or media restrictions on his license the need to allow the proprietor of the underlying copyright to control the method in which his work is presented to the public applies equally to the situation in which a licensee makes an unauthorized use of the underlying work by publishing it in a truncated version. Whether intended to allow greater economic exploitation of the work, as in the media and time cases, or to ensure that the copyright proprietor retains a veto power over revisions desired for the derivative work, the ability of the copyright holder to control his work remains paramount in our copyright law. We find, therefore, that unauthorized editing of the underlying work, if proven, would constitute an infringement of the copyright in that work similar to any other use of a work that exceeded the license granted by the proprietor of the copyright.

If the broadcast of an edited version of the Monty Python program infringed the group's copyright in the script, ABC may obtain no solace from the fact that editing was permitted in the agreements between BBC and Time-Life or Time-Life and ABC. BBC was not entitled to make unilateral changes in the script and was not specifically empowered to alter the recordings once made; Monty Python, moreover, had reserved to itself any rights not granted to BBC. Since a grantor may not convey greater rights than it owns, BBC's permission to allow Time-Life, and hence ABC, to edit appears to have been a nullity. *See* Hampton v. Paramount Pictures Corp., 279 F.2d 100 (9th Cir.), *cert. denied*, 364 U.S. 882 (1970); Ilyin v. Avon Publications, 144 F. Supp. 368, 372 (S.D.N.Y. 1956). . . .

Several of the deletions made for ABC, such as elimination of the words "hell" and "damn," seem inexplicable given today's standard television fare. If, however, ABC honestly determined that the programs were obscene in substantial part, it could have decided not to broadcast the specials at all, or it could have attempted to reconcile its differences with appellants. The network could not, however, free from a claim of infringement, broadcast in a substantially altered form a program incorporating the script over which the group had retained control.

Our resolution of these technical arguments serves to reinforce our initial inclination that the copyright law should be used to recognize the important role of the artist in our society and the need to encourage production and dissemination of artistic works by providing adequate legal protection for one who submits his work to the public. *See* Mazer v. Stein, 347 U.S. 201 (1954). We therefore conclude that there is a substantial likelihood that, after a full trial, appellants will succeed in proving infringement of their copyright by ABC's broadcast of edited versions of Monty Python programs. In reaching this conclusion, however, we need not accept appellants' assertion that any editing whatsoever would constitute infringement. Courts have recognized that licensees are entitled to some small degree of latitude in arranging the licensed work for presentation to the public in a manner consistent with the licensee's style or standards. That privilege, however, does not extend to the degree of editing that occurred here especially in light of contractual provisions that limited the right to edit Monty Python material.

II

It also seems likely that appellants will succeed on the theory that, regardless of the right ABC had to broadcast an edited program, the cuts made constituted an actionable mutilation of Monty Python's work. This cause of action, which seeks redress for deformation of an artist's work, finds its roots in the continental concept of droit moral, or moral right, which may generally be summarized as including the right of the artist to have his work attributed to him in the form in which he created it. *See* 1 M. Nimmer, *supra*, at § 110.1.

American copyright law, as presently written, does not recognize moral rights or provide a cause of action for their violation, since the law seeks to vindicate the economic, rather than the personal, rights of authors. Nevertheless, the economic incentive for artistic and intellectual creation that serves as the foundation for American copyright law, Goldstein v. California, 412 U.S. 546 (1973); Mazer v. Stein, 347 U.S. 201 (1954), cannot be reconciled with the inability of artists to obtain relief for mutilation or misrepresentation of their work to the public on which the artists are financially dependent. Thus courts have long granted relief for misrepresentation of an artist's work by relying on theories outside the statutory law of copyright, such as contract law, Granz v. Harris, 198 F.2d 585 (2d Cir. 1952) (substantial cutting of original work constitutes misrepresentation), or the tort of unfair competition, Prouty v. National Broadcasting Co., 26 F. Supp. 265 (D. Mass. 1939). *See* Strauss, *The Moral Right of the Author* 128-138, *in* Studies on Copyright (1963). Although such decisions are clothed in terms of proprietary right in one's creation, they also properly vindicate the author's personal right to prevent the presentation of his work to the public in a distorted form. *See* Gardella v. Log Cabin Products Co., 89 F.2d 891, 895-96 (2d Cir. 1937); Roeder, *The Doctrine of Moral Right*, 53 Harv. L. Rev. 554, 568 (1940).

Here, the appellants claim that the editing done for ABC mutilated the original work and that consequently the broadcast of those programs as the creation of Monty Python violated the Lanham Act § 43(a), 15 U.S.C. § 1125(a).[10] This statute, the federal counterpart to state unfair competition laws, has been invoked to prevent misrepresentations that may injure plaintiff's business or personal reputation, even where no registered trademark is concerned. *See* Mortellito v. Nina of California, 335 F. Supp. 1288, 1294 (S.D.N.Y. 1972). It is sufficient to violate the Act that a representation of a product, although technically true, creates a false impression of the product's origin. *See* Rich v. RCA Corp., 390 F. Supp. 530 (S.D.N.Y. 1975) (recent picture of plaintiff on cover of album containing songs recorded in distant past held to be a false representation that the songs were new); Geisel v. Poynter Products, Inc., 283 F. Supp. 261, 267 (S.D.N.Y. 1968).

These cases cannot be distinguished from the situation in which a television network broadcasts a program properly designated as having been written and performed by a group, but which has been edited, without the writer's consent, into a

10. That statute provides in part:

> Any person who shall affix, apply, or annex, or use in connection with any goods or services, . . . a false designation of origin, or any false description or representation . . . and shall cause such goods or services to enter into commerce . . . shall be liable to a civil action by any person . . . who believes that he is or is likely to be damaged by the use of any such false description or representation.

form that departs substantially from the original work. "To deform his work is to present him to the public as the creator of a work not his own, and thus makes him subject to criticism for work he has not done." Roeder, *supra*, at 569. In such a case, it is the writer or performer, rather than the network, who suffers the consequences of the mutilation, for the public will have only the final product by which to evaluate the work. Thus, an allegation that a defendant has presented to the public a "garbled," *Granz v. Harris, supra* (Frank, J., concurring), distorted version of plaintiff's work seeks to redress the very rights sought to be protected by the Lanham Act, 15 U.S.C. § 1125(a), and should be recognized as stating a cause of action under that statute. *See* Autry v. Republic Productions, Inc., 213 F.2d 667 (9th Cir. 1954); Jaeger v. American Int'l Pictures, Inc., 330 F. Supp. 274 (S.D.N.Y. 1971), which suggest the violation of such a right if mutilation could be proven.

During the hearing on the preliminary injunction, Judge Lasker viewed the edited version of the Monty Python program broadcast on December 26 and the original, unedited version. After hearing argument of this appeal, this panel also viewed and compared the two versions. We find that the truncated version at times omitted the climax of the skits to which appellants' rare brand of humor was leading and at other times deleted essential elements in the schematic development of a story line.[12] We therefore agree with Judge Lasker's conclusion that the edited version broadcast by ABC impaired the integrity of appellants' work and represented to the public as the product of appellants what was actually a mere caricature of their talents. We believe that a valid cause of action for such distortion exists and that therefore a preliminary injunction may issue to prevent repetition of the broadcast prior to final determination of the issues.[13] . . .

For these reasons we direct that the district court issue the preliminary injunction sought by the appellants.

GURFEIN, Circuit Judge (concurring):

I concur in my brother Lumbard's scholarly opinion, but I wish to comment on the application of Section 43(a) of the Lanham Act, 15 U.S.C. § 1125(a).

I believe that this is the first case in which a federal appellate court has held that there may be a violation of Section 43(a) of the Lanham Act with respect to a common-law copyright. The Lanham Act is a trademark statute, not a copyright statute. Nevertheless, we must recognize that the language of Section 43(a) is broad. It speaks of the affixation or use of false designations of origin or false descriptions or

12. A single example will illustrate the extent of distortion engendered by the editing. In one skit, an upper class English family is engaged in a discussion of the tonal quality of certain words as "woody" or "tinny." The father soon begins to suggest certain words with sexual connotations as either "woody" or "tinny," whereupon the mother fetches a bucket of water and pours it over his head. The skit continues from this point. The ABC edit eliminates this middle sequence so that the father is comfortably dressed at one moment and, in the next moment, is shown in a soaked condition without any explanation for the change in his appearance.

13. Judge Gurfein's concurring opinion suggests that since the gravamen of a complaint under the Lanham Act is that the origin of goods has been falsely described, a legend disclaiming Monty Python's approval of the edited version would preclude violation of that Act. We are doubtful that a few words could erase the indelible impression that is made by a television broadcast, especially since the viewer has no means of comparing the truncated version with the complete work in order to determine for himself the talents of plaintiffs. Furthermore, a disclaimer such as the one originally suggested by Judge Lasker in the exigencies of an impending broadcast last December would go unnoticed by viewers who tuned into the broadcast a few minutes after it began. We therefore conclude that Judge Gurfein's proposal that the district court could find some form of disclaimer would be sufficient might not provide appropriate relief.

representations, but proscribes such use "in connection with any goods or services." It is easy enough to incorporate trade names as well as trademarks into Section 43(a) and the statute specifically applies to common law trademarks, as well as registered trademarks. Lanham Act §45, 15 U.S.C. §1127.

In the present case, we are holding that the deletion of portions of the recorded tape constitutes a breach of contract, as well as an infringement of a common-law copyright of the original work. There is literally no need to discuss whether plaintiffs also have a claim for relief under the Lanham Act or for unfair competition under New York law. I agree with Judge Lumbard, however, that it may be an exercise of judicial economy to express our view on the Lanham Act claim, and I do not dissent therefrom. I simply wish to leave it open for the District Court to fashion the remedy.

The Copyright Act provides no recognition of the so-called droit moral, or moral right of authors. Nor are such rights recognized in the field of copyright law in the United States. *See* 1 Nimmer on Copyright, §110.2 (1975 ed.). If a distortion or truncation in connection with a use constitutes an infringement of copyright, there is no need for an additional cause of action beyond copyright infringement. *Id.* at §110.3. An obligation to mention the name of the author carries the implied duty, however, as a matter of contract, not to make such changes in the work as would render the credit line a false attribution of authorship, Granz v. Harris, 198 F.2d 585 (2 Cir. 1952).

So far as the Lanham Act is concerned, it is not a substitute for droit moral which authors in Europe enjoy. If the licensee may, by contract, distort the recorded work, the Lanham Act does not come into play. If the licensee has no such right by contract, there will be a violation in breach of contract. The Lanham Act can hardly apply literally when the credit line correctly states the work to be that of the plaintiffs which, indeed it is, so far as it goes. The vice complained of is that the truncated version is not what the plaintiffs wrote. But the Lanham Act does not deal with artistic integrity. It only goes to misdescription of origin and the like. *See* Societe Comptoir De L'Industrie Cotonniere Etablissements Boussac v. Alexander's Dept. Stores, Inc., 299 F.2d 33, 36 (2 Cir. 1962).

The misdescription of origin can be dealt with, as Judge Lasker did below, by devising an appropriate legend to indicate that the plaintiffs had not approved the editing of the ABC version. With such a legend, there is no conceivable violation of the Lanham Act. If plaintiffs complain that their artistic integrity is still compromised by the distorted version, their claim does not lie under the Lanham Act, which does not protect the copyrighted work itself but protects only against the misdescription or mislabelling.

So long as it is made clear that the ABC version is not approved by the Monty Python group, there is no misdescription of origin. So far as the content of the broadcast itself is concerned, that is not within the proscription of the Lanham Act when there is no misdescription of the authorship.

I add this brief explanation because I do not believe that the Lanham Act claim necessarily requires the drastic remedy of permanent injunction. That form of ultimate relief must be found in some other fountainhead of equity jurisprudence.

COMMENTS AND QUESTIONS

1. *Gilliam* recognizes what might be referred to as quasi-moral rights in literary works (the scripts of the Monty Python programs) using existing tools of copyright and unfair competition law. Copyright law (independently of VARA, which did not

exist in 1976) confers upon authors an exclusive right to prepare derivative works. *See* 17 U.S.C. § 106(2).[27] A derivative work is defined as "a work based upon one or more preexisting works, such as a translation, musical arrangement, dramatization, fictionalization, motion picture version, sound recoding, art reproduction, abridgment, condensation, or any other form in which a work may be recast, transformed, or adapted. A work consisting of editorial revision, annotations, elaborations, or other modifications which, as a whole, represent an original work of authorship, is a 'derivative work.'" 17 U.S.C. § 101. An author who has retained his or her right to prepare derivative works therefore may be able to prevent others from making unauthorized revisions or modifications to the original work. In *Gilliam*, the court concluded that the plaintiffs had never assigned to BBC the right to make derivative works based on their scripts. BBC therefore had no right or ability to convey such an interest to anyone else, and so ABC's preparation of a heavily edited version of the Monty Python programs constituted an unauthorized derivative of the underlying scripts. In this way, Monty Python was able to enjoy something like a moral right of integrity in its scripts. Note, however, that if the authors had assigned to BBC their right to prepare derivative works based upon the scripts, U.S. copyright law would have provided them no recourse. (If the case arose today, VARA would be no help either, because literary works and motion pictures are excluded from the definition of qualifying works of visual art.) The author's right to prepare derivative works, therefore, while helpful to Monty Python in the *Gilliam* litigation, is not quite the same as the inalienable moral right of integrity that authors enjoy in some other countries.

The second rationale, which the court also endorsed in *Gilliam*, was that the programs ABC actually broadcast were so distorted from the original that ABC's representation that it was broadcasting "Monty Python" programs was false, in violation of § 43(a) of the Lanham Act. The case is somewhat ambiguous, however, in indicating precisely which language of § 43(a) was at issue. At the time the case was decided, the relevant text of § 43(a), as set forth in footnote 53 (footnote 10 of the original opinion), stated "Any person who shall affix, apply, or annex, or use in connection with any goods or services, . . . a false designation of origin, or any false description or representation . . . and shall cause such goods or services to enter into commerce . . . shall be liable to a civil action by any person . . . who believes that he is or is likely to be damaged by the use of any such false description or representation." So was misrepresentation of the edited program as the work of Monty Python a "false designation of origin" or a "false description or representation"? Was it both? *See Gilliam*, 538 F.2d at 27 (Gurfein, J., concurring) (referring to "[t]he misdescription of origin").

In theory—and subject to qualifications raised in the next case excerpted below—there are a few different ways in which a misrepresentation concerning authorship might amount to a type of unfair competition. One would be to equate such misrepresentations to a type of "passing off" or "reverse passing off." As summarized by the *Restatement of Unfair Competition*, a person is subject to liability for passing off "if, in connection with the marketing of goods or services, the actor makes a representation likely to deceive or mislead prospective purchasers by causing the mistaken belief that the actor's business is the business of the other, or that the actor is the

27. The court in *Gilliam* cites to the 1909 Copyright Act, which was in effect at the time the case was decided, but the relevant principles relating to derivative works would be the same under the version of the Copyright Act in effect today.

agent, affiliate, or associate of the other, or that the goods or services that the actor markets are produced, sponsored, or approved by the other." RESTATEMENT (THIRD) OF UNFAIR COMPETITION § 4. For example, if A puts B's trademark or other distinctive indicia on A's products, or makes false statements about A's products such that consumers are likely to be confused into thinking that B is the source or sponsor of A's goods, A would be liable for passing off. (Much commonplace trademark infringement therefore involves passing off, but the theory is broad enough to encompass other conduct that confuses consumers into thinking that B is the source of A's products.) The harm caused by passing off is obvious: Consumers are misled into buying the wrong product, and B gets the benefit of A's goodwill. Alternatively, a person is liable for reverse passing off "if in marketing goods or services manufactured, produced, or supplied by the other, the actor makes a representation likely to deceive or mislead prospective purchasers by causing the mistaken belief that the actor or a third person is the manufacturer, producer, or supplier of the goods or services if the representation is to the likely commercial detriment of the other. . . ." *Id.* § 5. The paradigm example of reverse passing off would be for A to put A's own trademark or other distinctive indicia on B's goods, such that consumers are misled into thinking that A is the source of B's goods. The harm here is a little less obvious, because A's conduct doesn't threaten B's reputation directly (as with passing off). But A's conduct might divert future business from B to A, and it might mislead consumers into thinking that A produces better goods than A is in fact capable of producing. False representations of authorship could be analogized to either passing off or reverse passing off, depending on the circumstances. "Passing off" might be said to occur when, as in *Gilliam*, the defendant puts the plaintiff's name on a work that (in some sense) is not really the plaintiff's. "Reverse passing off" might occur when the defendant puts its own name on someone else's work. The common word for this latter sort of misattribution is plagiarism.

Relatedly, in a case like *Gilliam* where the name "Monty Python" probably qualifies as a trademark, the unauthorized use of that name in connection with goods or services (here, entertainment services) might amount to trademark infringement and false endorsement. Consumers viewing the program ABC aired might be likely to be confused into thinking that the program comes from, or is endorsed by, members of the Monty Python troupe. Reverse passing off claims, by contrast, are less likely to dovetail with trademark infringement or false endorsement claims, insofar as they involve removal of the source-identifying characteristics from the original.

Yet another possibility is that a misrepresentation as to authorship might amount to false advertising, if all of the other elements of a false advertising claim are present. Thus, when ABC advertised that it would be airing a Monty Python special, that claim arguably involved a false representation of fact in connection with commercial advertising.

Distinguishing among these different theories arguably made no difference in 1976, given the wording of the statute at that time. As discussed above, however, in 1989 Congress amended § 43(a) by rewording it and splitting it into two sections. Under the current text, § 43(a)(1)(A) covers the use of "any word, term, name, symbol, or device, or any combination thereof, or any false designation of origin, false or misleading description of fact, or false or misleading representation of fact, which . . . is likely to cause confusion. . . ." Section 43(a)(1)(B) covers such uses "in commercial advertising or promotion" which "misrepresent[ ] the nature, charactertistics, qualities, or geographic origin of his or her or another person's goods, services, or commercial activities." After *Dastar*, pleading the proper theory might be more important today than it was 30 years ago.

Dastar Corp. v. Twentieth Century Fox Film Corp.
539 U.S. 23 (2003)

Justice SCALIA delivered the opinion of the Court.

In this case, we are asked to decide whether § 43(a) of the Lanham Act, 15 U.S.C. § 1125(a), prevents the unaccredited copying of a work. . . .

I

In 1948, three and a half years after the German surrender at Reims, General Dwight D. Eisenhower completed Crusade in Europe, his written account of the allied campaign in Europe during World War II. Doubleday published the book, registered it with the Copyright Office in 1948, and granted exclusive television rights to an affiliate of respondent Twentieth Century Fox Film Corporation (Fox). Fox, in turn, arranged for Time, Inc., to produce a television series, also called Crusade in Europe, based on the book, and Time assigned its copyright in the series to Fox. The television series, consisting of 26 episodes, was first broadcast in 1949. It combined a soundtrack based on a narration of the book with film footage from the United States Army, Navy, and Coast Guard, the British Ministry of Information and War Office, the National Film Board of Canada, and unidentified "Newsreel Pool Cameramen." In 1975, Doubleday renewed the copyright on the book as the "'proprietor of copyright in a work made for hire.'" App. to Pet. for Cert. 9a. Fox, however, did not renew the copyright on the Crusade television series, which expired in 1977, leaving the television series in the public domain.

In 1988, Fox reacquired the television rights in General Eisenhower's book, including the exclusive right to distribute the Crusade television series on video and to sublicense others to do so. Respondents SFM Entertainment and New Line Home Video, Inc., in turn, acquired from Fox the exclusive rights to distribute Crusade on video. SFM obtained the negatives of the original television series, restored them, and repackaged the series on videotape; New Line distributed the videotapes.

Enter petitioner Dastar. In 1995, Dastar decided to expand its product line from music compact discs to videos. Anticipating renewed interest in World War II on the 50th anniversary of the war's end, Dastar released a video set entitled World War II Campaigns in Europe. To make Campaigns, Dastar purchased eight beta cam tapes of the *original* version of the Crusade television series, which is in the public domain, copied them, and then edited the series. Dastar's Campaigns series is slightly more than half as long as the original Crusade television series. Dastar substituted a new opening sequence, credit page, and final closing for those of the Crusade television series; inserted new chapter-title sequences and narrated chapter introductions; moved the "recap" in the Crusade television series to the beginning and retitled it as a "preview"; and removed references to and images of the book. Dastar created new packaging for its Campaigns series and (as already noted) a new title.

Dastar manufactured and sold the Campaigns video set as its own product. The advertising states: "Produced and Distributed by: *Entertainment Distributing*" (which is owned by Dastar), and makes no reference to the Crusade television series. Similarly, the screen credits state "DASTAR CORP presents" and "an ENTERTAINMENT DISTRIBUTING Production," and list as executive producer, producer, and associate producer employees of Dastar. Supp. App. 2-3, 30. The Campaigns videos themselves also make no reference to the Crusade television series, New Line's Crusade videotapes, or the book. Dastar sells its Campaigns videos to Sam's Club, Costco, Best Buy, and other retailers and mail-order companies for $25 per set, substantially less than New Line's video set.

In 1998, respondents Fox, SFM, and New Line brought this action alleging that Dastar's sale of its Campaigns video set infringes Doubleday's copyright in General Eisenhower's book and, thus, their exclusive television rights in the book. Respondents later amended their complaint to add claims that Dastar's sale of Campaigns "without proper credit" to the Crusade television series constitutes "reverse passing off"[1] in violation of §43(a) of the Lanham Act, 60 Stat. 441, 15 U.S.C. §1125(a). . . . On cross-motions for summary judgment, the District Court found for respondents on all three counts. . . .

The Court of Appeals for the Ninth Circuit affirmed the judgment for respondents on the Lanham Act claim, but reversed as to the copyright claim and remanded. . . . With respect to the Lanham Act claim, the Court of Appeals reasoned that "Dastar copied substantially the entire *Crusade in Europe* series created by Twentieth Century Fox, labeled the resulting product with a different name and marketed it without attribution to Fox[, and] therefore committed a 'bodily appropriation' of Fox's series." *Id.*, at 314. It concluded that "Dastar's 'bodily appropriation' of Fox's original [television] series is sufficient to establish the reverse passing off."[2] . . .

II

The Lanham Act was intended to make "actionable the deceptive and misleading use of marks," and "to protect persons engaged in . . . commerce against unfair competition." 15 U.S.C. §1127. While much of the Lanham Act addresses the registration, use, and infringement of trademarks and related marks, §43(a), 15 U.S.C. §1125(a) is one of the few provisions that goes beyond trademark protection. As originally enacted, §43(a) created a federal remedy against a person who used in commerce either "a false designation of origin, or any false description or representation" in connection with "any goods or services." 60 Stat. 441. As the Second Circuit accurately observed with regard to the original enactment, however—and as remains true after the 1988 revision—§43(a) "does not have boundless application as a remedy for unfair trade practices," Alfred Dunhill, Ltd. v. Interstate Cigar Co., 499 F.2d 232, 237 (C.A.2 1974). "[B]ecause of its inherently limited wording, §43(a) can never be a federal 'codification' of the overall law of 'unfair competition,'" 4 J. McCarthy, Trademarks and Unfair Competition §27:7, p. 27-14 (4th ed. 2002) (McCarthy), but can apply only to certain unfair trade practices prohibited by its text.

1. Passing off (or palming off, as it is sometimes called) occurs when a producer misrepresents his own goods or services as someone else's. "Reverse passing off," as its name implies, is the opposite: The producer misrepresents someone else's goods or services as his own.

2. As for the copyright claim, the Ninth Circuit held that the tax treatment General Eisenhower sought for his manuscript of the book created a triable issue as to whether he intended the book to be a work for hire, and thus as to whether Doubleday properly renewed the copyright in 1976. See 34 Fed. Appx., at 314. The copyright issue is still the subject of litigation, but is not before us. We express no opinion as to whether petitioner's product would infringe a valid copyright in General Eisenhower's book.

. . . [T]he gravamen of respondents' claim is that, in marketing and selling Campaigns as its own product without acknowledging its nearly wholesale reliance on the Crusade television series, Dastar has made a "false designation of origin, false or misleading description of fact, or false or misleading representation of fact, which . . . is likely to cause confusion . . . as to the origin . . . of his or her goods." § 43(a). See, *e.g.*, Brief for Respondents 8, 11. That claim would undoubtedly be sustained if Dastar had bought some of New Line's Crusade videotapes and merely repackaged them as its own. Dastar's alleged wrongdoing, however, is vastly different: It took a creative work in the public domain — the Crusade television series — copied it, made modifications (arguably minor), and produced its very own series of videotapes. If "origin" refers only to the manufacturer or producer of the physical "goods" that are made available to the public (in this case the videotapes), Dastar was the origin. If, however, "origin" includes the creator of the underlying work that Dastar copied, then someone else (perhaps Fox) was the origin of Dastar's product. At bottom, we must decide what § 43(a)(1)(A) of the Lanham Act means by the "origin" of "goods."

III

The dictionary definition of "origin" is "[t]he fact or process of coming into being from a source," and "[t]hat from which anything primarily proceeds; source." WEBSTER'S NEW INTERNATIONAL DICTIONARY 1720-1721 (2d ed. 1949). And the dictionary definition of "goods" (as relevant here) is "[w]ares; merchandise." *Id.*, at 1079. We think the most natural understanding of the "origin" of "goods" — the source of wares — is the producer of the tangible product sold in the marketplace, in this case the physical Campaigns videotape sold by Dastar. The concept might be stretched . . . to include not only the actual producer, but also the trademark owner who commissioned or assumed responsibility for ("stood behind") production of the physical product. But as used in the Lanham Act, the phrase "origin of goods" is in our view incapable of connoting the person or entity that originated the ideas or communications that "goods" embody or contain. Such an extension would not only stretch the text, but it would be out of accord with the history and purpose of the Lanham Act and inconsistent with precedent.

Section 43(a) of the Lanham Act prohibits actions like trademark infringement that deceive consumers and impair a producer's goodwill. It forbids, for example, the Coca-Cola Company's passing off its product as Pepsi-Cola or reverse passing off Pepsi-Cola as its product. But the brand-loyal consumer who prefers the drink that the Coca-Cola Company or PepsiCo sells, while he believes that that company produced (or at least stands behind the production of) that product, surely does not necessarily believe that that company was the "origin" of the drink in the sense that it was the very first to devise the formula. The consumer who buys a branded product does not automatically assume that the brand-name company is the same entity that came up with the idea for the product, or designed the product-and typically does not care whether it is. The words of the Lanham Act should not be stretched to cover matters that are typically of no consequence to purchasers.

It could be argued, perhaps, that the reality of purchaser concern is different for what might be called a communicative product — one that is valued not primarily for its physical qualities, such as a hammer, but for the intellectual content that it conveys, such as a book or, as here, a video. The purchaser of a novel is interested not merely, if at all, in the identity of the producer of the physical tome (the publisher), but also, and indeed primarily, in the identity of the creator of the story it conveys (the author). And the author, of course, has at least as much interest in avoiding passing off (or reverse passing off) of his creation as does the publisher. For such a communicative product (the argument goes) "origin of goods" in §43(a) must be deemed to include not merely the producer of the physical item (the publishing house Farrar, Straus and Giroux, or the video producer Dastar) but also the creator of the content that the physical item conveys (the author Tom Wolfe, or—assertedly—respondents).

The problem with this argument according special treatment to communicative products is that it causes the Lanham Act to conflict with the law of copyright, which addresses that subject specifically. The right to copy, and to copy without attribution, once a copyright has expired, like "the right to make [an article whose patent has expired]—including the right to make it in precisely the shape it carried when patented—passes to the public." Sears, Roebuck & Co. v. Stiffel Co., 376 U.S. 225, 230, 84 S.Ct. 784, 11 L. Ed. 2d 661 (1964); see also Kellogg Co. v. National Biscuit Co., 305 U.S. 111, 121-122, 59 S. Ct. 109, 83 L. Ed. 73 (1938). "In general, unless an intellectual property right such as a patent or copyright protects an item, it will be subject to copying." TrafFix Devices, Inc. v. Marketing Displays, Inc., 532 U.S. 23, 29, 121 S. Ct. 1255, 149 L. Ed. 2d 164 (2001). The rights of a patentee or copyright holder are part of a "carefully crafted bargain," Bonito Boats, Inc. v. Thunder Craft Boats, Inc., 489 U.S. 141, 150-151, 109 S. Ct. 971, 103 L. Ed. 2d 118 (1989), under which, once the patent or copyright monopoly has expired, the public may use the invention or work at will and without attribution. Thus, in construing the Lanham Act, we have been "careful to caution against misuse or over-extension" of trademark and related protections into areas traditionally occupied by patent or copyright. *TrafFix*, 532 U.S., at 29, 121 S. Ct. 1255. "The Lanham Act," we have said, "does not exist to reward manufacturers for their innovation in creating a particular device; that is the purpose of the patent law and its period of exclusivity." *Id.*, at 34, 121 S. Ct. 1255. Federal trademark law "has no necessary relation to invention or discovery," *In re Trade-Mark Cases*, 100 U.S. 82, 94, 25 L. Ed. 550 (1879), but rather, by preventing competitors from copying "a source-identifying mark," "reduce[s] the customer's costs of shopping and making purchasing decisions," and "helps assure a producer that it (and not an imitating competitor) will reap the financial, reputation-related rewards associated with a desirable product," Qualitex Co. v. Jacobson Products Co., 514 U.S. 159, 163-164, 115 S. Ct. 1300, 131 L. Ed. 2d 248 (1995) (internal quotation marks and citation omitted). Assuming for the sake of argument that Dastar's representation of itself as the "Producer" of its videos amounted to a representation that it originated the creative work conveyed by the videos, allowing a cause of action under §43(a) for that representation would create a species of mutant copyright law that limits the public's "federal right to 'copy and to use' " expired copyrights, *Bonito Boats, supra*, at 165, 109 S. Ct. 971.

When Congress has wished to create such an addition to the law of copyright, it has done so with much more specificity than the Lanham Act's ambiguous use of "origin." The Visual Artists Rights Act of 1990, §603(a), 104 Stat. 5128, provides that the author of an artistic work "shall have the right . . . to claim authorship of that work." 17 U.S.C. §106A(a)(1)(A). That express right of attribution is carefully limited and focused: It attaches only to specified "work[s] of visual art," §101, is personal to the artist, §§106A(b) and (e), and endures only for "the life of the author," §106A(d)(1). Recognizing in §43(a) a cause of action for misrepresentation of authorship of noncopyrighted works (visual or otherwise) would render these limitations superfluous. . . .

Reading "origin" in §43(a) to require attribution of uncopyrighted materials would pose serious practical problems. Without a copyrighted work as the basepoint, the word "origin" has no discernable limits. A video of the MGM film Carmen Jones, after its copyright has expired, would presumably require attribution not just to MGM, but to Oscar Hammerstein II (who wrote the musical on which the film was based), to Georges Bizet (who wrote the opera on which the musical was based), and to Prosper Merimee (who wrote the novel on which the opera was based). In many cases, figuring out who is in the line of "origin" would be no simple task. Indeed, in the present case it is far from clear that respondents have that status. Neither SFM nor New Line had anything to do with the production of the Crusade television series — they merely were licensed to distribute the video version. While Fox might have a claim to being in the line of origin, its involvement with the creation of the television series was limited at best. Time, Inc., was the principal, if not the exclusive, creator, albeit under arrangement with Fox. And of course it was neither Fox nor Time, Inc., that shot the film used in the Crusade television series. Rather, that footage came from the United States Army, Navy, and Coast Guard, the British Ministry of Information and War Office, the National Film Board of Canada, and unidentified "Newsreel Pool Cameramen." If anyone has a claim to being the *original* creator of the material used in both the Crusade television series and the Campaigns videotapes, it would be those groups, rather than Fox. We do not think the Lanham Act requires this search for the source of the Nile and all its tributaries.

Another practical difficulty of adopting a special definition of "origin" for communicative products is that it places the manufacturers of those products in a difficult position. On the one hand, they would face Lanham Act liability for *failing* to credit the creator of a work on which their lawful copies are based; and on the other hand they could face Lanham Act liability for *crediting* the creator if that should be regarded as implying the creator's "sponsorship or approval" of the copy, 15 U.S.C. §1125(a)(1)(A). In this case, for example, if Dastar had simply "copied [the television series] as Crusade in Europe and sold it as Crusade in Europe," without changing the title or packaging (including the original credits to Fox), it is hard to have confidence in respondents' assurance that they "would not be here on a Lanham Act cause of action," Tr. of Oral Arg. 35.

Finally, reading §43(a) of the Lanham Act as creating a cause of action for, in effect, plagiarism — the use of otherwise unprotected works and inventions without attribution — would be hard to reconcile with our previous decisions. For example, in Wal-Mart Stores, Inc. v. Samara Brothers, Inc., 529 U.S. 205, 120 S. Ct. 1339, 146 L. Ed. 2d 182 (2000), we considered whether product-design trade dress can ever be inherently distinctive. Wal-Mart produced "knockoffs" of children's clothes designed and manufactured by Samara Brothers, containing only "minor modifications" of the original designs. *Id.*, at 208, 120 S. Ct. 1339. We concluded that the designs could not be protected under §43(a) without a showing that they had acquired "secondary meaning," *id.*, at 214, 120 S. Ct. 1339, so that they "'identify the source of the product rather than the product itself,'" *id.*, at 211, 120 S. Ct. 1339 (quoting Inwood Laboratories, Inc. v. Ives Laboratories, Inc., 456 U.S. 844, 851, n.11, 102 S. Ct. 2182, 72 L. Ed. 2d 606 (1982)). This carefully considered limitation would be entirely pointless if the "original" producer could turn around and pursue a reverse-passing-off claim under exactly the same provision of the Lanham Act. Samara would merely have had to argue that it was the "origin" of the designs that Wal-Mart was selling as its own line. It was not, because "origin of goods" in the Lanham Act referred to the producer of the clothes, and not the producer of the (potentially) copyrightable or patentable designs that the clothes embodied.

Similarly under respondents' theory, the "origin of goods" provision of § 43(a) would have supported the suit that we rejected in *Bonito Boats*, 489 U.S. 141, 109 S. Ct. 971, where the defendants had used molds to duplicate the plaintiff's unpatented boat hulls (apparently without crediting the plaintiff). And it would have supported the suit we rejected in *TrafFix*, 532 U.S. 23, 121 S. Ct. 1255: The plaintiff, whose patents on flexible road signs had expired, and who could not prevail on a trade-dress claim under § 43(a) because the features of the signs were functional, would have had a reverse-passing-off claim for unattributed copying of his design.

In sum, reading the phrase "origin of goods" in the Lanham Act in accordance with the Act's common-law foundations (which were *not* designed to protect originality or creativity), and in light of the copyright and patent laws (which *were*), we conclude that the phrase refers to the producer of the tangible goods that are offered for sale, and not to the author of any idea, concept, or communication embodied in those goods. Cf. 17 U.S.C. § 202 (distinguishing between a copyrighted work and "any material object in which the work is embodied"). To hold otherwise would be akin to finding that § 43(a) created a species of perpetual patent and copyright, which Congress may not do. See Eldred v. Ashcroft, 537 U.S. 186, 208, 123 S. Ct. 769, 154 L. Ed. 2d 683 (2003).

The creative talent of the sort that lay behind the Campaigns videos is not left without protection. The original film footage used in the Crusade television series could have been copyrighted, see 17 U.S.C. § 102(a)(6), as was copyrighted (as a compilation) the Crusade television series, even though it included material from the public domain, see § 103(a). Had Fox renewed the copyright in the Crusade television series, it would have had an easy claim of copyright infringement. And respondents' contention that Campaigns infringes Doubleday's copyright in General Eisenhower's book is still a live question on remand. If, moreover, the producer of a video that substantially copied the Crusade series were, in advertising or promotion, to give purchasers the impression that the video was quite different from that series, then one or more of the respondents might have a cause of action — not for reverse passing off under the "confusion . . . as to the origin" provision of § 43(a)(1)(A), but for misrepresentation under the "misrepresents the nature, characteristics [or] qualities" provision of § 43(a)(1)(B). For merely saying it is the producer of the video, however, no Lanham Act liability attaches to Dastar. . . .

Justice Breyer took no part in the consideration or decision of this case.

COMMENTS AND QUESTIONS

1. *Dastar* appears to stand for the proposition that, for purposes of the Lanham Act, the term "false designations of origin" refers to the physical origin of goods or services, and not to their "intellectual" origin. *See Dastar*, 539 U.S. at 31 ("We think the most natural understanding of the 'origin' of 'goods' — the source of wares — is the producer of the tangible product sold in the marketplace, in this case the physical Campaigns videotape sold by Dastar"). Thus, if the *Gilliam* case arose today and the plaintiffs argued that ABC's misrepresentation of the programs as works of Monty Python constituted a false designation of origin, they would lose. Of course, the fact

pattern of *Gilliam* is not precisely the same as in *Dastar*. The plaintiff's theory in *Dastar* was that the defendants were engaged in "reverse passing off," that is, in putting their own name on the plaintiff's work. In the hypothetical relitigation of *Gilliam*, the plaintiffs' theory would be that the defendant was engaged in "passing off," that is, in putting Monty Python's name on a work that is no longer genuine Monty Python. Nevertheless, the Court's holding that "false designation of origin" refers only to physical origin would appear to render the false designation of origin theory inapplicable to *Gilliam*, notwithstanding the distinction between passing off and reverse passing off.

2. At the same time, the Court in *Dastar* stated that it was not basing its decision on the false advertising provision of §43(a):

> If, moreover, the producer of a video that substantially copied the Crusade series were, in advertising or promotion, to give purchasers the impression that the video was quite different from that series, then one or more of the respondents might have a cause of action-not for reverse passing off under the "confusion . . . as to the origin" provision of §43(a)(1)(A), but for misrepresentation under the "misrepresents the nature, characteristics [or] qualities" provision of §43(a)(1)(B). For merely saying it is the producer of the video, however, no Lanham Act liability attaches to Dastar.

Dastar, 539 U.S. at 38. And, although the Court briefly mentioned the topic of trademark infringement in passing, *see id.* at 32-33 & n.5, it had no occasion to express an opinion about the interplay of trademark infringement and misattribution because the defendants in *Dastar* weren't using Dastar's trademark; the case involved alleged *reverse* passing off, after all. Would *Gilliam* therefore come out the same way today, as long as the plaintiffs pleaded a false advertising claim or a trademark infringement (or false endorsement) claim? A narrow interpretation of *Dastar*, focused on the Court's holding that the word "origin" refers to physical origin, would not preclude this result. *See* 5 McCarthy, *supra*, §27:83, at 27-196 (arguing that "[c]ases like Monty Python probably fit within the §43(a)(1)(B) 'false advertising' prong," notwithstanding *Dastar*, but not the §43(a)(1)(A) "trademark" prong); Jane C. Ginsburg, *The Right to Claim Authorship in U.S. Copyright and Trademarks Law*, 41 Hous. L. Rev. 263, 274-79 (2004) (suggesting that this reading might be feasible in cases in which a misattribution is materially false, but noting the Lanham Act's requirements that the use by in "commercial advertising or promotion" and its limitations on standing). On the other hand, the Court also expressed concern about reading §43(a) in such a way as to conflict with federal copyright law (for example, by conferring attribution rights with respect to works whose copyrights have expired); and that last sentence in the portion quoted above ("For merely saying it is the producer of the video . . . no Lanham Act liability attaches to Dastar"), if construed broadly, might preclude any §43(a) claim based on misattribution of authorship. *See* Greg Lastowka, *The Trademark Function of Authorship*, 85 B.U. L. Rev. 1171, 1208-09 (2005) ("[S]ome very erudite commentators have held out the possibility that the issues presented by *Dastar* might be resolved by looking to the niceties of pleading. Fox should have claimed misattribution under the false advertising provisions of the trademark law, §43(a)(1)(B), instead of section §43(a)(1)(A), which addresses confusion over the origin of goods. While it is possible that some subsequent district court interpreting *Dastar* might take this approach, it hasn't happened yet. Instead, courts have spoken broadly about §43(a) and *Dastar*'s tangibility limitations.").

3. Prior to *Dastar*, authors and performers occasionally succeeded in asserting §43(a) false advertising claims premised on the defendant's falsely advertising the plaintiff's authorship of, performance in, or substantial involvement with, a creative work. For example, in King v. Innovation Books, 976 F.2d 824 (2d Cir. 1992), author Stephen King assigned a producer the motion picture rights to his short story "Lawnmower Man." The resulting film was billed as "Stephen King's The Lawnmower Man" (a so-called "possessory credit") and as being "based upon" a short story by King. King filed suit under §43(a), claiming that the film departed from his story in so many particulars that both the possessory credit and the "based upon" credit were literally false. The Second Circuit concluded that King was likely to succeed with respect to his claim that the possessory credit was literally false; but that he was unlikely to succeed with regard to his objection to the "based upon" credit, for which the law affords more "leeway." *See also* PPX Enters. v. Audiofidelity Enters., 818 F.2d 266 (2d Cir. 1987) (holding that misattribution of Jimi Hendrix as the feature performer in certain sound recording with respect to which Hendrix either did not participate at all, or participated only as a background or session player, violated §43(a)); Follett v. Arbor House Publishing Co., 208 U.S.P.Q. 597 (S.D.N.Y. 1980) (holding that defendant's representation that best-selling author Ken Follett was the principal author of a book that he only had revised constituted false advertising); CBS Inc. v. Springboard Int'l Records, 429 F. Supp. 563 (S.D.N.Y. 1976) (holding that defendant violated §43(a) by selling recordings of outdated Charlie Rich and LaBelle performances with recent photos of Rich and LaBelle on the album covers). In other cases, however, courts concluded that the editing was not substantial enough to make the representation of authorship actionable. Two cases in particular seem to stand for the proposition that *de minimis non curat lex*. In Choe v. Fordham University School of Law, 920 F. Supp. 44 (S.D.N.Y. 1995) (Mukasey, J.), the court dismissed a former law student's §43(a) claim based on the Fordham International Law Journal's publication of his student comment with "numerous alleged substantive and typographical errors." Similarly, in Stratta v. George Duke Enterprises Inc., 43 U.S.P.Q.2d 1628 (S.D.N.Y. 1997) (Sotomayor, J.), the court dismissed a conductor's §43(a) claim premised on the defendant's release of a CD the cover of which misspelled his name as "Strata." *See also* Lish v. Harper's Magazine Found., 807 F. Supp. 1090 (S.D.N.Y. 1992) (dismissing writer's claim based on magazine's editing of his letter to the editor); Considine v. Penguin U.S.A., 24 U.S.P.Q.2d 1947 (S.D.N.Y. 1992) (dismissing writer's claim based on magazine's editing of excerpt from his book). Would any of these cases go forward after *Dastar*?

Even in cases in which the editing is substantial, though, isn't there something odd about authors and performers asserting false advertising claims against publishers under these circumstances? Consider the following thought experiment. Suppose that Company X falsely represents that its candy bar contains milk chocolate, when in fact it contains some inferior chocolate substitute. Surely this sort of misrepresentation, concerning a key ingredient, is material and should be actionable. A publisher who falsely claims that the new novel it is publishing was written by Ken Follett is engaging in a similar sort of wrongdoing; it is misrepresenting that Follett's talent and imagination are among the "ingredients" of the novel. In the candy example, however, the most likely plaintiff would be a rival candy maker, wouldn't it? In the authorship cases cited above, however, the plaintiff is usually the author, not a rival publisher. Isn't that a little like chocolate (the ingredient) suing Company X (an odd concept, to be sure)? Or is it more like a *supplier* of chocolate suing Company X? A supplier might have standing to assert a Lanham Act false advertising claim in a circuit that does not require a directly competitive relationship between plaintiff and defendant. So does Follett have standing on the analogy that Follett is a supplier of a crucial ingredient (Follett's talent and imagination)?

PROBLEMS

Problem 9-10. Liz Chavez is an aspiring, but so far largely unknown, author of short stories. In fact, she has yet to sell any of her stories to a publisher and so far has resisted the impulse to self-publish. One day, she decides to submit one of her stories to the *New Yorker* magazine under the name "Stephen King," with a request that the magazine consider publishing the piece. Has Chavez violated the Lanham Act?

Alternatively, what if Chavez submits her story for consideration under the pseudonym "Joe Abbottsford"? The use of pseudonyms (Moliére, Voltaire, Stendhal, Mark Twain, George Eliot, and George Sand, to name just a few) has a long pedigree in literature. Has Chavez nevertheless violated the Lanham Act? What if someone whose real name happens to be Joe Abbottsford complains? Should it matter whether Chavez's use of the name is coincidental (she simply made up the name) or intentional?

Problem 9-11. Following from the facts of Problem 9-10, suppose that Chavez puts her own name on a Stephen King story and begins selling copies of the story from her Web site. Does King have a Lanham Act claim against Chavez? Aren't consumers *less* likely to buy a story authored by an unknown writer than by Stephen King?

Alternatively, what if King were to get hold of one of Chavez's stories, put his name on it, and begin selling copies from his Web site?

Problem 9-12. Peter Politician hires one of his speech writers, Ted Larson, to "ghostwrite" a book, *Profiles in Bravery*, under Politician's name. Larson agrees that he will not receive credit as the book's author; he will instead be credited (in the book's preface) as a "research assistant." Larson then writes the book, with input from Politician, and the book becomes a best seller. Assuming that someone (perhaps a rival publishing house) has standing to sue, would it have a viable Lanham Act claim against Politician? Against Larson? Against the publisher of *Profiles in Bravery*?

Problem 9-13. Bergen Movie Studios of Burbank, California, produces low-budget action and comedy films. Bergen hires as the leading man in its new film, *Burbank Buddies*, a little-known actor by the name of Roger Fraser. After a contractual dispute with Fraser, Bergen releases the film and credits "Ralph Graham" (a fictitious name) as the leading man. Fraser files suit against Bergen for violating the Lanham Act. Does Fraser have a viable claim?

Alternatively, suppose that Bergen substitutes for Roger Fraser the name "Brad Pitt." Would Fraser have a Lanham Act claim? Would the real Brad Pitt have a Lanham Act claim? Would Pitt have any additional claims if *Burbank Buddies* were a porno film?

Problem 9-14. Bergen Recording Studios releases a CD of the band *Spaghetti Western* performing ten songs. The CD lists all of the composers of each song, except for the song *Loafin'*, for which two of the four composers (Bevacqua and Chouillard) are omitted. Bevacqua and Chouillard file suit against Bergen. Lanham Act violation?

Problem 9-15. Every Sunday, the *Fredonia Times-Dispatch* publishes a weekly list purporting to rank best-selling books based on national sales during the preceding week. Inclusion of an author's hardback book on the list is believed to benefit the author by increasing consumer demand for his or her work and by increasing the value of paperback and film rights. Alec Blaine, author of the novel *Trumpet Call*, discovers that the *Times-Dispatch* erroneously left his novel off of the list for several weeks in 2009 when (according to his publisher's research) it should have been listed as one of the top-ten best sellers nationally. Blaine files suit alleging violation of Lanham Act §43(a). Result?

The same week Blaine files his suit, Bergen Movie Studios begins running ads in the *Times-Dispatch* and other nationally circulated newspapers for its film *Burbank Buddies*. The ads quote movie critic Dolores Mandrake referring to the film as "One of the year's ten best! A laugh-out-loud, action-filled summer adventure!" Three weeks later, Bergen admits that there is no "Dolores Manning" and that it made up the quotes itself. Has Bergen violated the Lanham Act? The FTC Act? State Baby FTC Acts? What about the *Times-Dispatch*?

G. FIRST AMENDMENT CONSTRAINTS ON FALSE ADVERTISING AND COMMERCIAL DISPARAGEMENT CLAIMS

An issue lurking in some of the preceding cases is whether the First Amendment constrains the way in which courts may apply false advertising or commercial disparagement law in specific cases. As we noted above, state action probably is implicit in the courts' application and enforcement of these laws. To what extent, then, does the First Amendment have an impact in these types of cases? To map out the relevant legal landscape requires a brief disquisition into First Amendment case law; note that much of this discussion will also be relevant to the materials in later chapters addressing the right of publicity, trade secret law, and even certain business torts.

A good place to begin is by dividing state regulation of speech into content-based and content-neutral regulations.[28] A regulation is content-based if it regulates on the

28. Contemporary law construes the word "speech" broadly, to include not only written and oral communications but also music, pictures, motion pictures, paintings, drawings, and dramatic works, *see* Nat'l Endowment for Arts v. Finley, 524 U.S. 569, 602 (1998), and even expressive conduct, *see* United States v. Eichman, 496 U.S. 310, 315 (1990); Texas v. Johnson, 491 U.S. 397, 406 (1989). As for the meaning of "content," according to one commentator "it typically is deemed to include at least viewpoint and subject matter, and sometimes also to include any elements — such as the use of communicative symbols — relating to speech's 'communicative impact.' " Heidi Kitrosser, *Containing Unprotected Speech*, 57 FLA. L. REV. 843, 846 n.10 (2005).

basis of content, whereas content-neutral regulations are "justified without reference to the content of the regulated speech."[29] Content-based regulations of noncommercial speech generally are subject to strict scrutiny, meaning that such restrictions survive First Amendment challenge only if they serve a compelling state interest and are narrowly tailored to achieve that end.[30] Content-neutral regulations, by contrast, are subject to some form of intermediate scrutiny. Content-neutral time, place, and manner restrictions, for example, satisfy intermediate scrutiny "so long as they are designed to serve a substantial governmental interest and do not unreasonably limit alternative avenues of communication." *See* City of Renton v. Playtime Theatres, Inc., 475 U.S. 41, 47 (1986). Alternatively, a content-neutral regulation that imposes incidental burdens on speech satisfies intermediate scrutiny if "it furthers an important or substantial governmental interest; if the governmental interest is unrelated to the suppression of free expression; and if the incidental restriction on alleged First Amendment freedoms is no greater than is essential to the furtherance of that interest." Turner Broad. Co. v. FCC, 512 U.S. 622, 662 (1994) (quoting O'Brien v. United States, 391 U.S. 367, 377 (1968)).

The preceding framework is subject to several qualifications, however. For example, the enforcement of laws of general applicability, such as the enforcement of a fire code that results in the shutting down of a newspaper office, are subject at most only to rational basis review. *See* Leathers v. Medlock, 499 U.S. 439 (1991); LYRISSA BARNETT LIDSKY & R. GEORGE WRIGHT, FREEDOM OF THE PRESS: A REFERENCE GUIDE TO THE UNITED STATES CONSTITUTION 33 (2004). In addition, the Supreme Court has held that certain forms of what in everyday discourse would appear to be "speech" are of such low social value that they fall outside the scope of First Amendment law altogether. Obscenity, fighting words, "true threats," the incitement of imminent lawless action, and child pornography all fall within these categories of unprotected speech.[31] *See, e.g.*, Virginia v. Black, 538 U.S. 343, 358-59 (2003); Ashcroft v. Free Speech Coalition, 535 U.S. 234, 239 (2002); Miller v. California, 413 U.S. 15, 23-24 (1973). Finally, certain other regulations of (what would appear to be) speech have almost never elicited First Amendment scrutiny, despite appearing to be content-based and not falling within one of the categorical exceptions. According to one

29. Bartnicki v. Vopper, 532 U.S. 514, 526 (2001) (quoting Ward v. Rock Against Racism, 491 U.S. 781, 791 (1989) (quoting Clark v. Community for Creative Non-Violence, 468 U.S. 288, 293 (1984) (emphasis added))). *See also* City of Los Angeles v. Alameda Books, Inc., 535 U.S. 425, 433-34 (2002) (plurality opinion) (stating that a zoning ordinance designed to decrease "secondary effects" of adult-themed businesses and not speech is content neutral, and thus subject to intermediate scrutiny) (citing City of Renton v. Playtime Theatres, Inc., 475 U.S. 41, 47-49 (1986)); *id.* at 448 (Kennedy, J., concurring) (stating that "if the statute describes speech by content then it is content based," but that the zoning ordinance at issue nevertheless was subject to intermediate scrutiny).

30. *See* United States v. Playboy Entertainment Group, Inc., 529 U.S. 803, 813 (2000).

31. There are other exceptions to this principle. A regulation that discriminates among classes of unprotected speech on the basis of viewpoint is presumptively invalid, *see R.A.V. v. City of St. Paul*, but a regulation may discriminate among unprotected speech on the basis of content if the content discrimination "consists entirely of the very reason the entire class of speech at issue is proscribable." Virginia v. Black, 538 U.S. 343, 361 (2003) (quoting *R.A.V.*, 505 U.S. 377, 388 (1992)). Based on these distinctions, the Court invalidated an ordinance that prohibited cross burnings intended to communicate a message of bias against racial and other minorities, but upheld a state law that prohibited cross burnings intended to communicate a more general message of intimidation. Strict scrutiny also is not warranted when government acts in a capacity other than as a regulator, such as when government itself subsidizes speech or excludes speakers from a nonpublic forum on viewpoint-neutral subject matter grounds, *see* Davenport v. Washington Educ. Ass'n, 551 U.S. 177, 189 (2008); or when the government is regulating students' speech, *see* Morse v. Frederick, 551 U.S. 393 (2008); or when the government itself is speaking, *see* Pleasant Grove City v. Summum, 129 S. Ct. 1125 (2009).

commentator, these include laws criminalizing conspiracy and solicitation, as well as speech regulation "in the context of securities, antitrust, labor organizing, copyrights, trademarks, sexual harassment, the regulation of doctors, lawyers, and other professionals, and vast amounts of evidence and torts law."[32]

Further complicating matters is the Supreme Court's treatment of commercial speech and of defamation. Although defamatory content, in and of itself, falls within the class of unprotected speech, *see Ashcroft*, 535 U.S. at 236, as noted above the Supreme Court in a series of cases beginning with *New York Times Co. v. Sullivan* has held that the First Amendment requires a variety of limitations upon common law claims for defamation in order to avoid potential "chilling effects" with respect to the publication of nondefamatory speech. Recall from above that, under the common law, defamation was a strict liability offense; truth was a defense (rather than falsity being an element of the plaintiff's case-in-chief); and damages could sometimes be presumed. Contemporary First Amendment law modifies these requirements by requiring public official or public figure plaintiffs to prove falsity and, by clear and convincing evidence, "actual malice" (in the sense of *knowing* falsity or reckless disregard for the truth), *see New York Times*, 376 U.S. 254; Curtis Publ'g Co. v. Butts, 388 U.S. 130 (1967) (extending *New York Times* to public figures). Current law also requires even private plaintiffs to prove actual malice as a prerequisite to recovering presumed or punitive damages, *see* Gertz v. Robert Welch, Inc., 418 U.S. 323 (1974), and to prove falsity with respect to a media defendant's publication relating to a matter of public concern, *see* Philadelphia Newspapers, Inc. v. Hepps, 475 U.S. 761 (1986); *cf.* Dun & Bradstreet, Inc. v. Greenmoss Builders, Inc., 472 U.S. 749 (1985) (holding that false statements in a credit report did not involve matters of public concern and therefore did not require proof of actual malice as prerequisite to recovery of presumed or punitive damages). In economic terms, one might say that, at least in cases involving public figures and matters of public concern, the Court views the common law of defamation as generating such high error and adjudication costs as to discourage the production of too much high-value speech. Of course, not everyone agrees with the balance the Court has struck in these cases. *See, e.g.*, David Anderson, *Tortious Speech*, 47 WASH. & LEE L. REV. 71, 79 (1990) (arguing that *New York Times* and its progeny raises adjudication costs while failing to protect plaintiffs' reputations).

Like defamation, commercial speech at one time was understood as falling outside the scope of First Amendment protection altogether. *See* Valentine v. Chrestensen, 316 U.S. 52 (1942). The Supreme Court changed direction, however, in Virginia State Board of Pharmacy v. Virginia Citizens Consumer Council, 425 U.S. 748 (1976), in which the Court struck down a Virginia law forbidding the truthful advertising of retail prescription drug prices. In support of its holding that commercial speech falls within the protection for the First Amendment, the Court noted, among other things, a strong public interest in the "free flow of commercial information." Further case law, however, was necessary to develop a workable definition of "commercial speech" and to develop an appropriate standard of constitutional scrutiny.

32. Neil M. Richards, *Reconciling Data Privacy and the First Amendment*, 52 UCLA L. REV. 1149, 1171 (2005). Richards's classification of copyright and trademark laws as meriting at most only rational basis scrutiny is not necessarily accurate, however. *See, e.g.*, Golan v. Holder, 611 F. Supp. 2d 1165 (D. Colo. 2009) (applying intermediate scrutiny to strike down law restoring terminated copyrights to qualifying foreign authors); William McGeveran, *Rethinking Trademark Fair Use*, 94 IOWA L. REV. 49, 100-03 (2008) (discussing cases applying First Amendment law as a constraint on trademark rights).

As for the definition, the Court in *Virginia Pharmacy* referred to commercial speech as speech that "does no more than propose a commercial transaction." 425 U.S. at 762.[33] As in *Virginia Pharmacy* itself, the most common example of commercial speech is probably product advertisements. *See, e.g.*, 44 Liquormart v. Rhode Island, 517 U.S. 484 (1996) (liquor price advertisements); Posadas de Puerto Rico Assocs. v. Tourism Co. of P.R., 478 U.S. 328 (1986) (casino advertisements); Zauderer v. Office of Disciplinary Counsel, 471 U.S. 626 (1985) (lawyer advertisements). Other cases have further elaborated on the term, though without providing a comprehensive definition. In Bolger v. Young Drug Products Corp., 463 U.S. 60 (1983), for example, the Court held that informational pamphlets discussing contraceptives in general and the defendant's products in particular constituted purely commercial speech, based on a combination of three factors: (1) the pamphlets were conceded to be advertisements; (2) they referred to a specific product; and (3) the defendant manufacturer had an economic motivation for distributing them. Although none of these factors alone was sufficient to render the pamphlets pure commercial speech, "the combination of *all* these characteristics" did, even though the pamphlets discussed important public issues such as family planning. *See also* Bd. of Trustees of State Univ. of N.Y. v. Fox, 492 U.S. 469 (1989) (holding that product demonstrations in campus dormitory rooms constituted purely commercial speech, even though they also touched on other subjects such as how to be financially responsible and how to run an efficient home); Riley v. Nat'l Fed'n of Blind of N.C., 487 U.S. 781 (1988) (invalidating a state law requiring professional solicitors to disclose to potential donors the percentage of charitable collections during the previous 12 months that were actually turned over to charity, on the ground that charitable solicitation does not retain its commercial character if "it is inextricably intertwined with otherwise fully protected speech"); Schamburg v. Citizens for a Better Environment, 444 U.S. 620, 630 (1980) (invalidating an ordinance requiring charitable solicitors to apply 75% of all funds solicited for charitable purposes, on the ground that charitable solicitation is "characteristically intertwined with information and perhaps persuasive speech seeking support for particular causes or for particular views on economic, political, or social issues" and thus does not constitute purely commercial speech).

As for the appropriate level of scrutiny, the Court has stated that commercial speech is entitled only to a lesser (albeit "substantial") degree of First Amendment protection than is noncommercial speech, because the very reason underlying constitutional protection of commercial speech is to provide accurate information to consumers about proposed commercial transactions. *See Virginia Pharmacy*, 425 U.S. at 760. Hence, to the extent a regulation seeks to either prevent misleading or deceptive commercial speech, or to provide more information, it is likely to pass a constitutional muster. Moreover, commercial speech can be more heavily regulated than other kinds of speech because it is "objective" and "more easily verified," and it is more "hardy" than other types of speech in that it is less likely to be chilled by regulation. *Id.* at 777. To balance the First Amendment interests in the context of commercial speech, the Supreme Court in Central Hudson Gas & Elec. Corp. v.

33. *Id.* at 762. In *Central Hudson*, 447 U.S. at 561, the Court cited *Virginia Pharmacy* for the proposition that commercial speech is "expression related solely to the economic interests of the speaker and its audience." The Court arguably has shied away from this overly broad definition, however. *See* City of Cincinnati v. Discovery Network, Inc., 507 U.S. 410, 422-23 (1993) (suggesting that the *Central Hudson* definition is too broad); Gary Williams, *Can Government Limit Tenant Blacklisting?*, 24 Sw. U. L. Rev. 1077, 1106 (1995).

Public Serv. Comm'n, 447 U.S. 557, 565 (1980), developed a four-part test that inquires: (1) whether the speech is misleading (or promotes illegal transactions); (2) whether the regulation serves an important government interest; (3) whether the regulation directly advances the government interest; and (4) whether the regulation is narrowly tailored to achieve its goals and does not restrict more speech than necessary. In relation to the first factor, if the speech at issue is false or misleading (or concerns illegal transactions), the state can ban it altogether.[34] If, on the other hand, the speech at issue is truthful commercial speech, inquiry then proceeds to the other three factors. With respect to the second factor, courts consider a wide array of government interests to be sufficiently important to warrant restrictions on purely commercial speech. In *Fox*, for example, the Court held that the state interests in promoting education, safety, and security, and in preventing the commercial exploitation of students, were sufficiently important to support the university's ban against holding "Tupperware parties" in campus dormitories. *See Fox*, 492 U.S. at 475. On the other hand, one of the few government interests the Court has held to be insufficient in this context is the interest in forbidding speech that some listeners may perceive as offensive. Thus in *Bolger*, the Court invalidated a statute that barred the distribution of pamphlets about contraceptive use, characterizing the government's interest in preventing dissemination of potentially offensive information as plainly insufficient. *See Bolger*, 463 U.S. at 75. As for the third and fourth factors, the Court has explained that *Central Hudson* does not require that a government regulation be the least-restrictive means of serving the government's interest at issue; rather, all that is required is "a reasonable fit" between the regulation and the government interest involved. *See Fox*, 492 U.S. at 480; *see also* City of Cincinnati v. Discovery Network, Inc., 507 U.S. 410, 416 (1993) (striking down city's ban on newsracks, where city failed "to establish a 'reasonable fit' between its legitimate interests in safety and esthetics" and its selective prohibition of newsracks as the means to serve those interests). In connection with this inquiry, courts likely will consider whether enjoining the allegedly improper use would keep ample alternative means of communicating a speaker's message. *See* Lorillard Tobacco Co. v. Reilly, 533 U.S. 525, 562 (2001) (striking down state regulations of outdoors advertising of tobacco, because they would constitute "a nearly complete ban" on truthful communication of information about smokeless tobacco to adult consumers).

The Court's current commercial speech doctrine has its share of critics from both sides of the aisle. On the one hand, some commentators have questioned the wisdom of according constitutional protection to commercial speech. *See, e.g.*, Richards, *supra*, at 1219-20 (arguing that the extension "opened the door to the resuscitation of *Lochner*-style economic rights," but that nevertheless "[t]he line between economic and political rights has persisted"). Others, however, including some Supreme Court justices, have argued that the distinction is untenable, both because commercial speech is (for many people) just as or more important than noncommercial speech and because the distinction between commercial and noncommercial speech can be difficult to discern in specific cases. *See, e.g., Lorillard*, 533 U.S. at 574-75 & n.2 (Thomas, J., concurring) (referring to the "malleability" of the four-step test and doubting the coherence of the distinction between commercial and noncommercial speech); Alex Kozinski & Stuart Banner, *Who's Afraid of Commercial Speech?*, 76 Va. L. Rev. 627

34. *See* In re R.M.J., 455 U.S. 191, 203 (1982) ("Misleading advertising may be prohibited entirely").

(1990). And although a majority of the Supreme Court has yet to overrule the commercial speech doctrine, recent cases arguably have reflected much less deference to state regulations that curtail commercial speech.[35]

For now, however, the distinction between commercial and noncommercial speech remains, and it continues to play an important role in the regulation of false advertising and other bodies of unfair competition law. The following two cases raise the question of whether the Supreme Court's defamation jurisprudence applies to commercial disparagement cases. The second of the two cases also raises the question of how the commercial speech doctrine relates to this tort, and the Comments and Questions following the excerpts raise additional questions relating to the applicability of the First Amendment to the regulation of false advertising.

Bose Corp. v. Consumers Union of U.S., Inc.

692 F.2d 189 (1st Cir. 1982), aff'd, 466 U.S. 485 (1984)

BOWNES, Circuit Judge.

This product disparagement case arises from an article evaluating the Bose 901 Series I stereo loudspeaker system by *Consumer Reports*, the monthly magazine of defendant-appellant, Consumers Union (CU). The district court found, in a bench trial limited to liability, that one statement in the article was false and was published with knowledge that it was false or with reckless disregard of its falsity. In a subsequent trial, damages were assessed in the amount of $115,296.00 plus interest and costs of $95,609.64. CU appeals both the finding of liability and the assessment of damages. We reverse on the issue of liability.

The Facts

Dr. Amar Bose founded the Bose Corporation in 1964 and is the corporation's principal owner and chief executive officer. CU conceded that he is an expert in the field of loudspeaker design. Dr. Bose designed the Bose 901 in 1967, and it was first marketed late in that year or early in 1968. . . .

Consumer Reports provides information about consumer products to mail subscribers and newsstand customers. At the time the article in question was published the magazine enjoyed "a very favorable reputation for independence, integrity, accuracy, and freedom from bias." *Id.* at 1252. In the article, entitled "Loudspeakers," CU evaluated the quality and performance of twenty-four loudspeakers based on tests it had conducted. In a section boxed off from the main portion of the article and entitled

35. *See, e.g.*, *Lorillard*, 533 U.S. at 556-67 (holding that state law prohibiting the advertising of tobacco products within 1,000 feet of schools and playgrounds was more extensive than necessary to attain the goal of limiting underage use, in violation of *Central Hudson*'s fourth step, and that regulation requiring indoor point of sale ads to be placed at least five feet from the floor failed both the third and fourth steps); 44 Liquormart, Inc. v. Rhode Island, 517 U.S. 484 (1996) (holding that a state law prohibiting the truthful advertising of retail liquor prices was unconstitutional); Lyrissa Barnett Lidsky, *Nobody's Fools: The Rational Audience as First Amendment Ideal*, Univ. of Fla. Legal Studies Research Paper No. 2009-19 (Jan. 2009), *available at* http://ssrn.com/abstract=1365979, at 29-31 (stating that "the modern trend, even in commercial speech cases, is to give more credit to the targets of commercial speech").

"Some speakers of special interest," seven paragraphs of the eight-page article discussed the Bose 901. . . .

The article explained the novel design of the Bose 901 as an attempt to simulate the sound patterns in a live concert hall, where listeners hear most of the sound after reflection off the walls and not directly from the orchestra. After describing the various components of the Bose system, the article next explained a test in which CU engineers compared the Bose 901 to another speaker by using a special recording "of a cricket-like noisemaker moving from extreme left to extreme right." CU played the recording through the speakers in a listening room and "asked a panel to judge the direction from which the sound appeared to come." CU concluded from this test that, "at least for pinpointing sharp noises, there appeared to be no difference between the speaker systems."

The next two paragraphs of the article described the results of a second test that CU performed on the Bose 901:

> We repeated the experiment using a variety of stereo sounds. When it came to music, the panelists immediately noted a remarkable difference between the systems. The Bose 901 seemed considerably more spacious and reverberant, actually to the point of giving the impression that the wall of the listening room had dropped away. The effect was rather dramatic and was felt from any listening position.
>
> But after listening to a number of recordings, it became clear that the panelists could pinpoint the location of various instruments much more easily with a standard speaker than with the Bose system. Worse, individual instruments heard through the Bose system seemed to grow to gigantic proportions and tended to wander about the room. For instance, a violin appeared to be 10 feet wide and a piano stretched from wall to wall. With orchestral music, such effects seemed inconsequential. But we think they might become annoying when listening to soloists. On an impulse, we also played some monophonic records through the Bose. To our surprise, they too acquired the same spacial openness and size distortions as the stereo records.

The article then discussed the sound quality of the Bose 901 and stated that if the speaker had been tested with the main group of speakers "it would have fallen between the high- and medium-accuracy groups. The overall sound was of good quality . . . [but] the speakers tended to overemphasize the middle bass, giving it a somewhat overly full, heavy sound." The article concluded that because the Bose 901 "is so unusual . . . a prospective buyer must listen to it and judge it for himself." It noted that the Bose 901 "requires a gigantic amount of power" and recommended "an amplifier of 50 watts per channel for the deepest base response."

The Findings of the District Court

The court determined that under the applicable law of product disparagement,[6] it was the plaintiff's burden to prove that the statements made by CU were of a disparaging or defamatory nature and that the statements were false. After concluding that "the Article, when read as a whole is disparaging," the court proceeded to analyze in detail each alleged factual error in the article to determine if it was false and if it was

6. The parties had agreed that the law of their respective states, Massachusetts and New York, was identical with respect to the elements of this tort. Thus, choice of law was not an issue.

disparaging. It found that although the use of the words "panel and panelists" was misleading because there were only two persons doing the testing, it was not disparaging. Bose's attack on the "sound quality" critique was rejected on the grounds that "it is nothing more than an opinion and, as such, it cannot be proved to be true or false," citing to Gertz v. Robert Welch, Inc., 418 U.S. 323, 339 (1974). The court found that Bose had not sustained its burden of proof that the statement as to the power requirements of the system was false.

The district court's finding of liability was based on part of one sentence in the article which reads: "Worse, individual instruments heard through the Bose system seemed to grow to gigantic proportions and tended to wander about the room." The court, in its analysis, divided the sentence into two parts. It found that the description "seemed to grow to gigantic proportions" had not been proven false but found the statement that the instruments "tended to wander about the room" was both false and disparaging. The evidence on which this finding was based is summarized as follows. CU's two employees who conducted the listening test "testified that the wandering sounds they heard were confined to an area within a few feet of the wall near which the Bose 901 loudspeakers were placed." CU conceded that the words "about the room" might not have described the wandering with precise accuracy, but argued that the *wandering* of sound was important to consumers, not *where* it wandered. CU maintained that the statement was substantially true because it accurately described the important observation. The district court referred to testimony that an amount of movement is expected with all stereo speakers and concluded that the location of the sounds' movement was as important to a consumer as the fact of movement. Thus, the court found the statement not to be substantially true. After rejecting CU's argument that the statements in the article about "a violin appear[ing] to be 10 feet wide and a piano stretch[ing] from wall to wall" modified the statements about wandering sounds to imply that the wandering occurred along the wall between the speakers, the court stated that the ordinary meaning of "about" the room was "around" the room. The court found the statement to be disparaging: "A statement that attributes such grotesque qualities as instruments wandering about the room to the plaintiff's product could have no effect other than to harm the reputation of the product." The use of the word "worse" to introduce the statement in the article showed that CU intended it to have a harmful effect.

Having determined that Bose had proved by a preponderance of the evidence that the statement about individual instruments tending to wander about the room was false and disparaging, the district court proceeded to analyze the impact of the first amendment on the standard of care required of CU. It cited several lower court decisions and discussed the first amendment balance between the need for an uninhibited press and the legitimate state interest in compensating victims of defamation in concluding that the actual malice standard of New York Times v. Sullivan, 376 U.S. 254 (1964), applies to product disparagement cases. It then applied the analysis of Bruno & Stillman, Inc. v. Globe Newspaper Co., 633 F.2d 583 (1st Cir. 1980), to conclude that "Bose is a public figure, at least with respect to the limited issues of the characteristics and quality of the Bose," and was required to show by clear and convincing proof that CU's false statement was published with knowledge that it was false or with reckless disregard of its truth of falsity. CU's project engineer, Arnold Seligson, conducted the listening test and wrote the words upon which the statements in the article were based. Due in part to his demeanor at trial, the court found that Seligson's testimony as to what the words "about the room" meant was not credible. Seligson maintained that he perceived that the wandering sounds were confined to an area near the wall behind the loudspeakers. The court found that Seligson was too intelligent to not be aware of the ordinary meaning of "about" and thus concluded that Seligson knew at the time of publication that the article did not accurately describe the effects he had perceived during the test. In the court's view, this was clear and convincing proof that CU "published a false statement of material fact with the knowledge that it was false or with reckless disregard of its truth or falsity."

Our Review

As the parties acknowledge, the first amendment permeates our review. The question of the truth or falsity of the statement that individual instruments tended to wander about the room is intertwined with the question of whether that statement is one of opinion or fact; both questions are difficult to answer. CU argues that if the statement is considered in its full context it becomes clear that the statement is merely the opinion of the panelists who conducted the listening test. This full context includes the tentative language that "instruments . . . *seemed* to grow" and "*tended* to wander," that "[w]ith orchestral music, such effects *seemed* inconsequential [although] we *think* they *might* become annoying when listening to soloists," and finally that "the Bose system is so unusual that a prospective buyer must listen to it and judge for himself." CU cites numerous cases to support the proposition that a reviewer's published description of what he or she observed in a public performance, book, or restaurant is protected by the first amendment. Also, the Supreme Court has stated that "[u]nder the First Amendment there is no such thing as a false idea. However pernicious an opinion may seem, we depend for its correction not on the conscience of judges and juries but on the competition of other ideas." Gertz v. Robert Welch, Inc., 418 U.S. 323, 339-40, 94 S. Ct. 2997, 3006-07, 41 L. Ed. 2d 789 (1974) (dictum) (footnote omitted). This statement of the Court implies that an opinion can be neither true nor false as a matter of constitutional law. The proposition that an opinion can be neither true nor false also is reasonable as a matter of common sense. The determination of whether a statement is one of opinion or fact, however, is difficult to make and perhaps unreliable as a basis for decision. Although CU's argument that the statement is an opinion is plausible, the seeming scientific nature of the article—indicated by quantitative ratings, a description in the beginning of the article of the laboratory testing performed, and the use of such terms as "panelists" and "engineers" to describe the CU employees who performed the tests—would support the position that the statements are factual. *See* Hotchner v. Castillo-Puche, 551 F.2d 910, 913 (2nd Cir.), *cert. denied sub nom.* Hotchner v. Doubleday, 434 U.S. 834 (1977) (An expression of an opinion may become as damaging as an assertion of fact, and liability for libel thus attach, if the writer indicates that "he has private, firsthand knowledge which substantiates the opinions he expresses. . . ."). Similarly, and stemming at least in part from the uncertain nature of the statement as one of fact or opinion, it is difficult to determine with confidence whether it is true or false. As the district court noted, at trial the CU panelists, Seligson and Lefkow, "testified that the wandering sounds that they heard were confined to an area within a few feet of the wall near which the Bose 901 loudspeakers were placed." Given the subjective nature of a listener's perceptions and the imprecise language employed in the CU article, we are not sure that the statement that instruments tended to wander about the room is false.

Due to our ultimate conclusion that Bose has failed to meet its burden of proof with respect to actual malice, however, we will assume that the statement was both factual and false and not explore further the intricacies of these concepts. Before analyzing actual malice, we should first briefly note our agreement with the district court that the statement in question disparaged Bose 901 speakers. CU concedes that the statement told readers that the "movement of individual instruments is more pronounced and localization therefore more difficult with the Bose than with conventional speakers." The tenor of the paragraph that contained the statement was clearly that of criticism; this is highlighted by the use of the word "worse" to introduce the statement. There can be little question that the statement was disparaging.

At oral argument Bose acknowledged that it does not dispute the finding of the district court that the corporation is a public figure with respect to the subject matter of the CU article. Bose also conceded that the rule of *New York Times v. Sullivan* applies in this case, and thus accepted the district court's conclusion that the actual malice standard applies to product disparagement cases. As we have indicated earlier, the district court analyzed both of these issues at length and we accept its conclusions for the purposes of this case.

We focus, therefore, on the district court's holding that Bose proved by clear and convincing evidence that CU published the words "individual instruments . . . tended to wander about the room" with knowledge that they were false or with reckless disregard of their truth or falsity. In performing this review we are not limited to the clearly erroneous standard of FED. R. CIV. P. 52(a); instead, we must perform a de novo review, independently examining the record to ensure that the district court has applied properly the governing constitutional law and that the plaintiff has indeed satisfied its burden of proof. *See, e.g.*, New York Times v. Sullivan, 376 U.S. at 285 & n.26; Time, Inc. v. Pape, 401 U.S. 279, 284 (1971). At the same time, we recognize that we are in no position to consider the credibility of witnesses and must leave questions of demeanor to the trier of fact. . . .

A plaintiff required to prove actual malice under the *New York Times v. Sullivan* standard must do so with "convincing clarity." 376 U.S. at 285-86. This requirement, now the "clear and convincing proof" test, Gertz v. Robert Welch, Inc., 323 U.S. at 342, *see* Bruno & Stillman, 633 F.2d at 586 n.2, calls for the plaintiff to prove more than would be necessary under the preponderance of the evidence standard but something less than what the beyond a reasonable doubt standard requires. . . .

It is important to point out that in conducting the listening test CU used experts, Seligson and Lefkow, who brought their expertise and experience to bear in evaluating the Bose speakers. In Reliance Insurance Co. v. Barron's, 442 F. Supp. 1341 (S.D.N.Y. 1977), the court noted the expertise of the author and granted a motion for summary judgment because there was no triable issue of fact that the article was published with actual malice. *Id.* at 1350-51. The Second Circuit found lack of expertise to be evidence of malice in Goldwater v. Ginzburg, 414 F.2d 324 (2d Cir. 1969). The court affirmed a jury finding of actual malice in an article stating that Senator Goldwater suffered from the mental disease of paranoia. The court noted that this conclusion "was reached only upon his [the author's] own non-expert evaluation of Senator Goldwater's life and political career." *Id.* at 331.

Some evidence of actual malice may be found "if there is a complete departure from the standards of investigation and reporting ordinarily adhered to by responsible publishers." *Reliance Insurance*, 442 F. Supp. at 1341. CU's editorial procedures reveal no evidence of actual malice. As in *Reliance Insurance*, the testimony in this case indicated that normal editorial procedures were followed; there was no evidence of CU knowingly departing from these procedures in order to publish the article regardless of its truth or falsity. . . .

Even though we accord relatively little weight to CU's claims of good faith and lack of any motivation to disparage the Bose 901, we are unable to find clear and convincing evidence that CU published the statement that individual instruments tended to wander about the room with knowledge that it was false or with reckless disregard of whether it was false or not. The evidence presented merely shows that the words in the article may not have described precisely what the two panelists heard during the listening test. CU was guilty of using imprecise language in the article—perhaps resulting from an attempt to produce a readable article for its mass audience. Certainly this does not support an inference of actual malice. . . .

Reversed.

Levin H. CAMPBELL, Circuit Judge (concurring).

In joining as I do in the court's opinion, I wish merely to emphasize my understanding that this court is in no way passing upon the actual merits of the district court's finding that Bose Corporation was a public figure.

U.S. Healthcare, Inc. v. Blue Cross of Greater Philadelphia

898 F.2d 914 (3d Cir. 1990)

SCIRICA, Circuit Judge.

U.S. Healthcare, Inc. and its subsidiaries . . . (collectively, "U.S. Healthcare"), appeal from the district court's post-trial entry of judgment in favor of Blue Cross of Philadelphia, its president David Markson, and Pennsylvania Blue Shield (collectively, "Blue Cross/Blue Shield"), directed under FED. R. CIV. P. 50(b) on U.S. Healthcare's federal and pendent state law claims alleging violations of § 43(a) of the Lanham Act, 15 U.S.C. § 1125(a) (1982), commercial disparagement, defamation and tortious interference with contractual relations. Blue Cross/Blue Shield, in turn, appeals from the entry of judgment on the verdict in favor of U.S. Healthcare on Blue Cross/Blue Shield's counterclaims alleging the same causes of action brought by U.S. Healthcare. . . . We will reverse the grant of the Rule 50(b) motions. . . .

I. Facts and Procedural History

[In the 1970s, Blue Cross/Blue Shield, a health insurer providing traditional medical insurance coverage, began to face competition from U.S. Healthcare, an HMO. In 1985, Blue Cross/Blue Shield introduced a product called "Personal Choice," known generically as a preferred provider organization or "PPO." Blue Cross/Blue Shield then launched a comparative advertising campaign touting its PPO against HMOs. U.S. Healthcare responded with its own comparative advertising campaign and with a civil action against Blue Cross/Blue Shield for commercial disparagement, defamation, and tortious interference; Blue Cross/Blue Shield filed counterclaims alleging that U.S. Healthcare had committed the very same torts against Blue Cross/Blue Shield. The jury returned a verdict for U.S. Healthcare on Blue

Cross/Blue Shield's counterclaims but could not reach a verdict on U.S. Healthcare's claims against Blue Cross. The district court then granted Blue Cross/Blue Shield's motion for judgment as a matter of law on U.S. Healthcare's claims, "on the grounds that the advertisements were entitled to heightened constitutional protection under the First Amendment, and that U.S. Healthcare had not met the applicable standard of proof, set forth in New York Times Co. v. Sullivan, 376 U.S. 254 (1964), *et seq*. The district court granted the motion. The court held that because the objects of the advertisements are 'public figures,' and because the matters in the advertisements are 'community health issues of public concern,' heightened constitutional protections attach to this speech. The court reasoned that the First Amendment limited the power of the state and of Congress to award damages resulting from the allegedly false and misleading advertisements. Accordingly, the district court held that in order to prevail on their respective claims of Lanham Act violation, commercial disparagement, defamation and tortious interference with contract, both parties were required to prove each claim by clear and convincing evidence: (1) that the other side published the advertisements with knowledge or with reckless disregard of their falsity, and (2) that the advertisements were false. Applying this standard of proof, the court concluded that '[a]lthough the jury could reasonably have concluded that both sides had proven falsity and actual malice by a preponderance of the evidence, neither side has presented clear and convincing evidence [of this].' "] . . .

III. First Amendment Principles and the Standard of Proof in Claims Arising from a Comparative Advertising Campaign

Having determined that some of the advertisements may be actionable under federal and state law, we must now consider whether the First Amendment affects the standard of proof. As we have already noted, the district court held that under *New York Times Co. v. Sullivan et seq.* each party must prove as to each claim, by clear and convincing evidence, that the other party acted with actual malice — that is, with knowledge that the advertisement was false or with reckless disregard of whether it was false or not. 376 U.S. 254, 279-80 (1964). In so holding, the court rejected U.S. Healthcare's argument that the advertisements were commercial speech and thereby entitled to less constitutional protection. The district court viewed the comparative advertising campaign giving rise to this litigation as a "dispute . . . about how best to deal with spiraling medical costs," and concluded that, "[t]o characterize the advertisements in this case as mere commercial speech ignores the fact that, at their core, they are instruments in a debate between two providers of public health care 'intimately involved in the resolution of important public questions.' "

In arguing that the district court erred in applying heightened evidentiary standards to any of its claims, U.S. Healthcare maintains that the *New York Times* standard is "not mandated where, as here, false commercial speech is at issue." In response, Blue Cross/Blue Shield contends that the principles set forth in the commercial speech doctrine are inapplicable to this case because the United States Supreme Court "views damage claims [brought by private citizens] and government restrictions of speech as requiring distinctly different analysis for First Amendment purposes." . . .

. . . [W]e do not limit our consideration of the applicability of the *New York Times* standard to the parties' claims for defamation alone. The Supreme Court has already applied a similar analysis to other torts, such as intentional infliction of emotional distress, Hustler Magazine, Inc. v. Falwell, 485 U.S. 46, 56 (1988), and "false light," Time, Inc. v. Hill, 385 U.S. 374, 390-91 (1967). *Cf.* Bose Corp. v. Consumers Union of U.S., Inc., 466 U.S. 485, 513 (1984) (in case involving district court conclusion that "the *New York Times* rule should be applied to a claim of product disparagement," the Supreme Court "express[ed] no view on that ruling, but . . . accepted it for purposes of deciding th[e] case"). *But see* Zacchini v. Scripps-Howard Broadcasting Co., 433 U.S. 562, 578-79 (1977) (First Amendment does not limit state's ability to protect performer's commercial stake in act by allowing damage action for violations of common law "right to publicity").

. . . [T]raditional defamation analysis would have us consider the public or private nature of the speech in assessing the weight of the First Amendment interests. We believe, however, that the novel facts here require a different approach. Our appraisal of these interests depends on whether the speech at issue can properly be characterized as commercial speech. "There is no longer any room to doubt that what has come to be known as 'commercial speech' is entitled to the protection of the First Amendment, albeit to protection somewhat less extensive than that afforded 'noncommercial speech.'" Zauderer v. Office of Disciplinary Counsel, 471 U.S. 626, 637 (1985). If the speech here is commercial speech, then it likely does not mandate heightened constitutional protection.

We recognize that the Supreme Court cases creating the commercial speech doctrine all involve some form of government regulation of speech and that none involve defamation actions. Further, the focus in the commercial speech cases is on First Amendment protection itself, not the heightened protection afforded by the actual malice standard. However, we believe the subordinate valuation of commercial speech is not confined to the government regulation line of cases.

In *Dun & Bradstreet*, the Court held that speech on matters of private concern, such as a credit report for business, receives less First Amendment protection than speech on matters of public concern. 472 U.S. at 757-59. More significantly for our purposes, the Court justified its decision to allow less protection for speech of private concern by drawing an analogy to the reduced First Amendment protection afforded commercial speech. . . .

The Court has elaborated on the reasons why commercial speech receives less than heightened protection. First, commercial speech generally makes a different contribution to the exposition of ideas. *Compare Dun & Bradstreet*, 472 U.S. at 762 (holding private speech of reduced constitutional dimension partly because it was "solely in the individual interest of the speaker and its specific business audience") (citing *Central Hudson*, 447 U.S. at 561) *with Central Hudson*, 447 U.S. at 561 (defining commercial speech as "expression related solely to the economic interests of the speaker and its audience"). In short, "[t]he First Amendment's concern for commercial speech is based on the informational function of advertising. . . ." *Central Hudson*, 447 U.S. at 563.

Second, commercial speech tends to be more durable than other types of speech. As the commercial speaker has an economic self-interest in dissemination, there is little likelihood of the speech being chilled by proper regulation. *Id.* at 564 n.6; Bates v. State Bar, 433 U.S. 350, 381 (1977). This attribute, the Court concluded, "may make it less necessary to tolerate inaccurate statements for fear of silencing the speaker." *Virginia Pharmacy Bd.*, 425 U.S. at 772 n.24; *see Dun & Bradstreet*, 472 U.S. at 758 n.5, 762 & n.8 (discussing durability "to show how many of the same concerns that argue in favor of reduced constitutional protection" in regulation of commercial speech actions apply to defamation actions involving private speech).

Third, commercial speakers have extensive knowledge of both their market and their own products. Consequently, they are uniquely situated to evaluate the truthfulness of their speech. *Central Hudson*, 447 U.S. at 564 n.6; *Bates*, 433 U.S. at 381; *see Virginia Pharmacy Bd.*, 425 U.S. at 772 n.24; *see also Dun & Bradstreet*, 472 U.S. at 758 n.5, 762 & n.8 (discussing objective verifiability "to show how many of the same concerns that argue in favor of reduced constitutional protection" in regulation of commercial speech actions apply to defamation actions involving private speech).

The fourth reason is extrinsic. "To require a parity of constitutional protection for commercial and noncommercial speech alike could invite dilution, simply by a leveling process, of the force of the [First] Amendment's guarantee with respect to the latter kind of speech." *Ohralik*, 436 U.S. at 456.

In this case . . . the statements here are commercial in nature. First, there is no question that they are advertisements; they were disseminated as part of an expensive, professionally run promotional campaign. Second, the speech specifically refers to a product; it touts the relative merits of Personal Choice (or U.S. Healthcare's HMO) over competing products. Third, the desire for revenue motivated the speech; the record contains abundant evidence that Blue Cross/Blue Shield launched the promotional campaign in order to recoup its share of the health insurance market. The trial testimony of Blue Cross/Blue Shield's president plainly states that the aggressive Personal Choice promotional campaign was developed for the express purpose of competing with HMOs. Moreover, Blue Cross/Blue Shield concedes that it developed a series of advertisements to introduce and increase the attractiveness of its products. Similarly, protection of its new market share motivated U.S. Healthcare's speech. In short, "common sense" informs us that the statements here propose a commercial transaction, and thus differ from other types of speech.

Even more importantly, we find it significant that the advertisements have all of the characteristics that the Supreme Court has identified in the commercial speech cases as making speech durable, not susceptible to "chill." Consequently, they do not require the heightened protection we extend to our most valuable forms of speech. Because the thrust of all of the advertisements is to convince the consuming public to bring its business to one of these health care giants rather than the other, there is no doubt that the advertisements were motivated by economic self-interest. Furthermore, given the size of the health care market in the Delaware Valley — Blue Shield virtually shouts about the hundreds of millions of dollars at stake — we believe it would have to be a cold day before these corporations would be chilled from speaking about the comparative merits of their products. *Cf. Dun & Bradstreet*, 472 U.S. at 762-63 (because credit report was solely motivated by profit "any incremental 'chilling' effect of libel suits would be of decreased significance").

In addition, these are advertisements for products and services in markets in which U.S. Healthcare and Blue Cross/Blue Shield deal — and, presumably, know more about than anyone else. *Virginia Pharmacy Bd.*, 425 U.S. at 772 n.24. The facts upon which the advertisements are based — comparative price, procedures, and services offered — are readily objectifiable. These advertisements were precisely calculated, developed over time and published only when the corporate speakers were ready. Consequently, the advertisements were unusually verifiable.

Finally, while the speech here does discuss costs and consequences of competing health insurance and health care delivery programs, some of the advertisements capable of defamatory meaning here add little information and even fewer ideas to the marketplace of health care thought. The expression in these advertisements "differs markedly from ideological expression because it is confined to the promotion of specific . . . services." *Virginia Pharmacy Bd.*, 425 U.S. at 780. *Cf. Zauderer*, 471 U.S. at 637 & n.7 (advertisement containing information that, in another context would be fully protected, nonetheless commercial speech, as it proposed commercial transaction in advertiser's self-interest). And to the extent that the advertisements are false statements of fact, of course, the speech has no constitutional value at all. *Central Hudson*, 447 U.S. at 563.

It is important to note that we do not have a situation in which a corporation addresses an issue of public concern involving a competitor, but does so with speech that is neither commercial nor chill resistant. We simply recognize here, as the Court has in a similar context, that "[a] company has the full panoply of protections available to its direct comments on public issues, so there is no reason for providing similar protection when such statements are made in the context of commercial transactions." *Bolger*, 463 U.S. at 68 (footnote omitted).

Despite these conclusive indications that the speech here is commercial in nature, Blue Cross/Blue Shield argues that the speech should be accorded heightened constitutional protection. Relying on Bigelow v. Virginia, 421 U.S. 809 (1975), it argues that speech which does more than "simply propose a commercial transaction" constitutes something more than commercial speech. Furthermore, it maintains that the "*Bigelow* standard" is applicable when the products are not merely linked to a public debate but are themselves "at the center of the public debate." Blue Cross/ Blue Shield concludes that its own advertisements "educate[d] the public about the substantial differences among the[ ] available means for financing and delivering health care, thereby ensuring informed purchasing decisions" and rendering the advertisements non-commercial.

Notwithstanding Blue Cross/Blue Shields's call for application of the "*Bigelow* standard," we believe the *Central Hudson* decision, in which the Supreme Court expressly rejected such attempts to "blur further the line the Court has sought to draw in commercial speech cases," 447 U.S. at 563 n.5, represents the proper approach. *Central Hudson* prevents an advertiser from immunizing, in effect, otherwise defamatory speech — behind the actual malice standard afforded to core speech by the First Amendment — simply by reference to an issue of public concern. . . .

We find no principled distinction between the products in *Central Hudson* and those at issue here. Like the energy products advertised in *Central Hudson*, the products advertised here — health care insurance and delivery — are at the center of public debate. Consequently, while we agree that the quality, availability, and cost of health care are among the most important and debated issues of our time, these particular advertisements for specific health care products do not escape the commercial speech category. We conclude, as did the *Zauderer* Court, that whatever the precise boundaries of the "category of expression that may be termed commercial speech, . . . it is clear enough that the speech at issue in this case — advertising pure and simple — falls within those bounds." 471 U.S. at 637.

Therefore, while the speech here is protected by the First Amendment, we hold that the First Amendment requires no higher standard of liability than that mandated by the substantive law for each claim. The heightened protection of the actual malice standard is not "necessary to give adequate 'breathing space' to the freedoms protected by the First Amendment." Hustler Magazine, Inc. v. Falwell, 485 U.S. 46, 56 (1988).

Having concluded that the speech here is commercial speech that does not warrant heightened constitutional protection, we nonetheless proceed to consideration of the nature and weight of the state's interest in compensating individuals for injuries resulting from each of the distinct torts alleged. We have previously discussed the state and federal interests implicated. As we shall see in this case, however, traditional defamation analysis is not well suited to strike the proper balance between the state and federal interests and First Amendment values in the context of commercial speech.

In weighing the state interest, we must look to the status of the claimants. *See Gertz*, 418 U.S. at 342-45; *see also Dun & Bradstreet*, 472 U.S. at 756. As we have noted, the Court has determined that the state has only a "limited" interest in compensating public persons for injury to reputation but has a "strong and legitimate" interest in compensating private persons for the same injury. *See Gertz*, 418 U.S. at 343 & 348-49. Contending that the actual malice standard applies because a public figure is implicated, Blue Cross/Blue Shield argues that the following factors render U.S. Healthcare a "public figure": it has voluntarily exposed itself to public comment on the issues involved in this dispute; it is a contributor to the ongoing debate concerning health care insurance; it is among the nation's largest providers of HMO-type insurance coverage; it markets its products extensively and aggressively, and has a substantial annual advertising budget; and it frequently and consistently asserts the advantages of its method of health care financing and delivery, and has done so in advertisements, press releases, professional journals, newspapers, magazines and speeches before public assemblies. These activities, Blue Cross/Blue Shield submits, "constitute a voluntary effort to influence the consuming public." Similar statements can be made regarding Blue Cross/Blue Shield.

Gertz identified three classes of public figures: those who achieve such stature or notoriety that they are considered public figures in all contexts; those who become public figures involuntarily, but these are "exceedingly rare"; and those who are deemed public figures only within the context of a particular public dispute. *Id.* at 345. The Court defined the last group, limited purpose public figures, as individuals who voluntarily "thrust themselves to the forefront of particular public controversies in order to influence the resolution of the issues involved." *Id.*

At the outset, we note that "the classification of a [claimant] as a public or private figure is a question of law to be determined initially by the trial court and then carefully scrutinized by an appellate court." Marcone v. Penthouse Int'l Magazine for Men, 754 F.2d 1072, 1081 n.4 (3d Cir.) (citations omitted), *cert. denied*, 474 U.S. 864 (1985). Because neither claimant explicitly classified the other as a full purpose or involuntary public figure, the issue is whether either constitutes a limited purpose public figure.

Generally, two factors inform this determination. The first factor indicative of a claimant's status is his relative access to the media. Clearly, both parties have access to the media. Moreover, the magnitude of the advertising campaigns shows their ability to utilize it on a vast scale. While access to the media does not always make one a public figure for purposes of First Amendment analysis, the tremendous ability of these parties to advertise, indicating their lack of vulnerability, would support a finding that both are public figures.

The second factor is the manner in which the risk of defamation came upon them. Both companies, attempting to influence consumers' decisions, have thrust themselves into the controversy of who provides better value in health care delivery and insurance. Blue Cross/Blue Shield began the comparative advertising war with its pointed attacks on HMO. U.S. Healthcare, even before responding with its own comparative advertising, had used advertising to help establish itself as a leading provider of health care in the Delaware Valley. Consequently, by inviting comment and assuming the risk of unfair comment, both claimants resemble public figures. *See* Steaks Unlimited, Inc. v. Deaner, 623 F.2d 264, 274 (3d Cir. 1980) ("In short, through its advertising blitz, [the plaintiff corporation] invited public attention, comment and criticism.").

Under traditional defamation analysis, the parties' considerable access to the media and their voluntary entry into a controversy are strong indicia that they are limited purpose public figures. Indeed, inflexible application of these factors would warrant a finding of public figure status and facilitate a finding of heightened constitutional protection. Nonetheless, we hold that these corporations are not public figures for the limited purpose of commenting on health care in this case.

As noted, *Gertz* defines the limited purpose public figure as one who has "thrust [himself] to the forefront of particular public controversies in order to influence the resolution of the issues involved." 418 U.S. at 345. Although some of the advertisements touch on matters of public concern, their central thrust is commercial. Thus, the parties have acted primarily to generate revenue by influencing customers, not to resolve "the issues involved."

While discerning motivations of the speaker is often difficult, we have a more fundamental reason for declining to find limited purpose public figure status in this case. The express analysis in *Gertz* is not helpful in the context of a comparative advertising war. Most products can be linked to a public issue. *See Central Hudson*, 447 U.S. at 563 n.5. And most advertisers — including both claimants here — seek out the media. Thus, it will always be true that such advertisers have voluntarily placed themselves in the public eye. It will be equally true that such advertisers have access to the media. Therefore, under the *Gertz* rationale, speech of public concern that implicates corporate advertisers — i.e., typical comparative advertising — will always be insulated behind the actual malice standard. *Cf.* Curtis Publishing Co. v. Butts, 388 U.S 134-35 (1967) (Warren, C.J., concurring). We believe a corporation must do more than the claimants have done here to become a limited purpose public figure under *Gertz.*

In summary, we conclude that the speech at issue does not receive heightened protection under the First Amendment. Because this speech is chill-resistant, the *New York Times* standard is not, as we have noted, "necessary to give adequate 'breathing space' to the freedoms protected by the First Amendment." Hustler Magazine, Inc. v. Falwell, 485 U.S. 46, 56 (1988). Therefore, the standard of proof needed to establish the substantive claims is that applicable under federal and state law.

For these reasons, we hold that the district court erred in applying the *New York Times* standard to the claims in this case and in directing entry of judgment under FED. R. CIV. P. 50(b). Accordingly, we will reverse the judgment of the district court and remand for proceedings consistent with this opinion. . . .

COMMENTS AND QUESTIONS

1. *Follow-up to the* Bose *decision.* The Supreme Court granted certiorari in *Bose* to decide what standard of appellate review applies to "a District Court's determination that a false statement was made with the kind of 'actual malice' described in New York

Times Co. v. Sullivan, 376 U.S. 254, 279-280 (1964)." Bose Corp. v. Consumers Union, Inc., 466 U.S. 485, 487 (1984). According to Rule 52 of the Federal Rules of Civil Procedure, a Court of Appeals should not set aside findings of fact unless those findings are "clearly erroneous." Nevertheless, the Supreme Court concluded that, where the First Amendment requires plaintiffs to prove actual malice by clear and convincing evidence, the First Amendment also requires independent (de novo) appellate review of that finding. *See Bose*, 466 U.S. at 510-11. The Court also noted, however, as had the First Circuit, that Bose itself had not contested "the conclusion that it was a public figure, or the applicability of the *New York Times* standard." *Id.* at 492. The Court therefore did not address whether the *New York Times* standard necessarily *does* apply to commercial disparagement cases. Although many courts since *Bose* have applied the *New York Times* analysis to common law commercial disparagement claims, *see* 5 McCarthy, *supra*, § 27:106, at 27-245 n.2 (listing cases), the Supreme Court has yet to decide this important issue. Had Bose chosen to contest this point, what do you think the correct result would have been?

2. In *U.S. Healthcare*, the Third Circuit concluded that the *New York Times* standard does not apply to commercial disparagement claims arising out of commercial speech. Common law disparagement claims sometimes do, and sometimes do not, involve commercial speech. Lanham Act disparagement claims, on the other hand, necessarily involve commercial speech if courts apply the *Gordon & Breach* definition of "commercial advertising and promotion." Thus, under the *U.S. Healthcare* approach, plaintiffs asserting Lanham Act commercial disparagement claims (or common law disparagement claims involving commercial speech) would not be required to prove actual malice. Some commentators nevertheless have argued that, even in disparagement cases involving commercial speech, the risk of "chilling effects" necessitates some level of First Amendment scrutiny. *See* 5 McCarthy, *supra*, § 27:107, at 27-249 (arguing that *New York Times* should apply if the challenged statement is of public concern, notwithstanding that it appears in commercial speech); Arlen W. Langvardt, *Section 43(a), Commercial Falsehood, and the First Amendment: A Proposed Framework*, 78 Minn. L. Rev. 309, 391-99 (1993) (arguing for First Amendment scrutiny, but not the actual malice standard). Others disagree. *See* Michael A. Albert & Robert L. Bocchino Jr., *Trade Libel: Theory and Practice Under the Common Law, the Lanham Act, and the First Amendment*, 89 Trademark Rep. 826, 866-68 (1999) (arguing against application of the *New York Times* standard). Which position is more persuasive? Is commercial speech less chill-proof than noncommercial speech? If defendants typically have a more difficult time verifying statements about their competitors' products, as opposed to their own products, should the law make it easier or more difficult (in comparison with false advertising claims) for plaintiffs to prove disparagement claims? Should the analysis hinge on whether the plaintiff (often a corporation) is a public figure and/or the matter at issue is of public concern? Won't those latter conditions be present in a large number of cases?

3. An alternative to constitutionalizing the law of commercial disparagement would be to incorporate speech-protective standards into the common law or statutory elements. One possible advantage of such an approach is its flexibility and adaptability. Different courts might experiment with different approaches to the problem, evaluate the relative merits of these approaches over time, and modify them as they see fit. A corresponding disadvantage of the constitutional approach is that, once a constitutional standard is adopted, it is usually very difficult to amend it (either

formally, through constitutional amendment, or informally through judicial reinterpretation). In any event, in some states the common law of commercial disparagement already does incorporate something very similar to the *New York Times* standard insofar as it requires all disparagement plaintiffs to prove actual malice (though in some of these states, proving that the defendant made the statement knowing it to be false or with reckless disregard for its truth or falsity is only one way of proving actual malice). *See supra* at p. 429. In other states, however, actual malice is still presumed upon proof of the other elements of a commercial disparagement claim, and it is the defendant's burden to rebut actual malice by demonstrating the applicability of a privilege. *See id.* Observers who worry about the effects of disparagement claims on freedom of speech might not be satisfied with this latter approach.

Yet another alternative is suggested by the New Jersey Supreme Court's decision in Dairy Stores, Inc. v. Sentinel Publishing Co., 516 A.2d 220 (N.J. 1986). In *Dairy Stores*, the plaintiff claimed that the defendant newspaper had disparaged the plaintiff's business by falsely claiming that the plaintiff's bottled water contained chlorine. Rather than modifying New Jersey common law so as to require proof of actual malice in every case—an approach that might underprotect sellers of disparaged products—the court adapted the old common law privilege of "fair comment" on matters of "legitimate public interest." In some ways, the court's doctrinal choice was curious. At common law, "[t]he majority view is that fair comment extends to opinion only," while under contemporary First Amendment law "[s]tatements of opinion . . . enjoy absolute immunity." *Id.* at 231. In its classic formulation, then, the fair comment privilege would seem to be something of a dead letter. The court nevertheless was able to resurrect the doctrine by extending it "beyond opinion to statements of fact" relating to matters of "legitimate public concern." *Id.* at 229, 232. Matters of public concern, in turn, might include "such essentials of life as food and water," products that have "widespread effects," and products characterized by "substantial government regulation." *Id.* at 230. Once a defendant establishes the fair comment privilege applies, the burden shifts back to the plaintiff to show that the statement at issue "was made with malice," meaning that the "plaintiff must establish that the publisher knew the statement to be false or acted in reckless disregard of its truth or falsity." *Id.* at 233. Does a modified fair comment privilege best accommodate the competing reputational and free speech interests? Or would it be preferable, whether as a matter of constitutional or common law, to require plaintiffs to prove actual malice in all cases? Note that, in a subsequent case, the New Jersey Supreme Court interpreted the *Dairy Stores* fair comment privilege somewhat narrowly. *See* Turf Lawnmower Repair, Inc. v. Bergen Record Corp., 655 A.2d 417, 427 (N.J. 1995) (stating that "we do not find the actual-malice standard appropriate or necessary with regard to businesses like the sale and repair of lawn mowers, the repair of shoes, the cleaning of clothes, and numerous other local businesses that involve everyday products or services that do not intrinsically involve a legitimate public interest").

Yet another subconstitutional device for fending off some chilling effects are "anti-SLAPP" statutes. The term "SLAPP" (an acronym for "strategic lawsuit against public participation") is sometimes used to refer to lawsuits, often defamation suits, "brought by plaintiffs solely to harass and to silence their critics." Lyrissa Barnett Lidsky, *Silencing John Doe: Defamation and Discourse in Cyberspace*, 49 DUKE L.J. 855, 865 (2000). Anti-SLAPP statutes typically enable the defendant to move to dismiss a nonmeritorious claim early in the litigation and, if successful, to recover his or her attorney fees from the plaintiff. *See, e.g.*, CAL. CIV. PROC. CODE § 25.16

(West Supp. 2007). By itself, however, an anti-SLAPP statute would not protect a defendant who falsely, but without malice, disparaged the plaintiff's products.

4. As noted above, some commentators (and some members of the current Supreme Court) have argued that commercial speech should be afforded the same degree of protection as is afforded to noncommercial speech. Should the Supreme Court ever adopt this standard, how would it affect the law of false advertising and commercial disparagement? Would the Court require proof of actual malice in some false advertising and disparagement cases? Would it apply strict scrutiny to content-based regulations of truthful commercial speech? Would the Court provide some "breathing space" for false commercial speech, in order to avoid chilling the production of truthful commercial speech?

A case in which the Supreme Court might have addressed (but ultimately did not address) issues like these was Kasky v. Nike, Inc., 45 P.3d 243 (Cal. 2002), *cert. dismissed as improvidently granted*, 539 U.S. 654 (2003) (per curiam). Kasky, purportedly acting on behalf of the public,[36] filed suit against Nike under a California false advertising statute, claiming that Nike had engaged in false advertising in connection with a public relations campaign it conducted to rebut charges that its overseas suppliers used sweatshop labor. In a 4-3 opinion, the California Supreme Court concluded that the statements at issue comprised commercial speech and that the matter should proceed to trial on the issue of whether the statements were false. The U.S. Supreme Court then granted certiorari, but later decided to dismiss the writ as improvidently granted. Justices O'Connor, Kennedy, and Breyer dissented from the dismissal, and Justice Breyer (joined by Justice O'Connor) wrote separately to explain, among other things, why he thought "true reversal [was] a highly realistic possibility":

> To understand how I reach this conclusion, the reader must recall the nature of the holding under review. The California Supreme Court held that certain specific communications, exemplified by the nine documents upon which Kasky rests his case, fall within that aspect of the Court's commercial speech doctrine that says the First Amendment protects only *truthful* commercial speech; hence, to the extent commercial speech is false or misleading, it is unprotected.
>
> The Court, however, has added, in commercial speech cases, that the First Amendment "'embraces at the least the liberty to discuss publicly and truthfully all matters of public concern.'" Consolidated Edison Co. of N.Y. v. Public Serv. Comm'n of N.Y., 447 U.S. 530, 534 (1980); accord, *Central Hudson*, 447 U.S., at 562-563, n.5. And in other contexts the Court has held that speech on matters of public concern needs "'breathing space'"—potentially incorporating certain false or misleading speech—in order to survive. *New York Times*, 376 U.S., at 272; *see also, e.g.*, Gertz v. Robert Welch, Inc., 418 U.S. 323, 340 (1974); Time, Inc. v. Hill, 385 U.S. 374, 388-389 (1967).
>
> This case requires us to reconcile these potentially conflicting principles. In my view, a proper resolution here favors application of the last mentioned public-speech principle, rather than the first mentioned commercial-speech principle. Consequently, I would apply a form of heightened scrutiny to the speech regulations in question, and I believe that those regulations cannot survive that scrutiny.
>
> First, the communications at issue are not purely commercial in nature. They are better characterized as involving a mixture of commercial and noncommercial (public-issue-oriented) elements. . . .

36. In 2004, California voters approved Proposition 64, which limits private plaintiffs from asserting state law claims for false advertising absent proof of injury.

At the same time, the regulatory regime at issue here differs from traditional speech regulation in its use of private attorneys general authorized to impose "false advertising" liability even though they themselves have suffered no harm. See CAL. BUS. & PROF. CODE ANN. §§ 17204, 17535 (West 1997). In this respect, the regulatory context is unlike most traditional false advertising regulation. And the "false advertising" context differs from other regulatory contexts — say, securities regulation — where a different balance of concerns calls for different applications of First Amendment principles. *Cf.* Ohralik v. Ohio State Bar Assn., 436 U.S. 447, 456-457 (1978).

These three sets of circumstances taken together — circumstances of format, content, and regulatory context — warrant treating the regulations of speech at issue differently from regulations of purer forms of commercial speech, such as simple product advertisements, that we have reviewed in the past. And, where all three are present, I believe the First Amendment demands heightened scrutiny.

Second, I doubt that this particular instance of regulation (through use of private attorneys general) can survive heightened scrutiny, for there is no reasonable "fit" between the burden it imposes upon speech and the important governmental "'interest served,'" *Fox, supra*, at 480. Rather, the burden imposed is disproportionate.

I do not deny that California's system of false advertising regulation — including its provision for private causes of action — furthers legitimate, traditional, and important public objectives. It helps to maintain an honest commercial marketplace. It thereby helps that marketplace better allocate private goods and services. See Virginia Bd. of Pharmacy v. Virginia Citizens Consumer Council, Inc., 425 U.S. 748, 765, 96 S.Ct. 1817, 48 L. Ed. 2d 346 (1976). It also helps citizens form "intelligent opinions as to how [the marketplace] ought to be regulated or altered." *Ibid.*

But a private "false advertising" action brought on behalf of the State, by one who has suffered no injury, threatens to impose a serious burden upon speech — at least if extended to encompass the type of speech at issue under the standards of liability that California law provides, see CAL. BUS. & PROF. CODE ANN. §§ 17200, 17500 (West 1997) (establishing regimes of strict liability, as well as liability for negligence); Cortez v. Purolator Air Filtration Products Co., 23 Cal. 4th 163, 181 (2000) (stating that California's unfair competition law imposes strict liability). The delegation of state authority to private individuals authorizes a purely ideological plaintiff, convinced that his opponent is not telling the truth, to bring into the courtroom the kind of political battle better waged in other forums. Where that political battle is hard fought, such plaintiffs potentially constitute a large and hostile crowd freely able to bring prosecutions designed to vindicate their beliefs, and to do so unencumbered by the legal and practical checks that tend to keep the energies of public enforcement agencies focused upon more purely economic harm. *Cf.* Forsyth County v. Nationalist Movement, 505 U.S. 123, 134-135 (1992); Bantam Books, Inc. v. Sullivan, 372 U.S. 58, 67-71 (1963).

That threat means a commercial speaker must take particular care — considerably more care than the speaker's noncommercial opponents — when speaking on public matters. A large organization's unqualified claim about the adequacy of working conditions, for example, could lead to liability, should a court conclude after hearing the evidence that enough exceptions exist to warrant qualification — even if those exceptions were unknown (but perhaps should have been known) to the speaker. Uncertainty about how a court will view these, or other, statements, can easily chill a speaker's efforts to engage in public debate — particularly where a "false advertising" law, like California's law, imposes liability based upon negligence or without fault. See *Gertz*, 418 U.S., at 340; *Time*, 385 U.S., at 389. At the least, they create concern that the commercial speaker engaging in public debate suffers a handicap that noncommercial opponents do not. See *First Nat. Bank*, 435 U.S., at 785-786; *see also* Rosenberger v. Rector and Visitors of Univ. of Va., 515 U.S. 819, 828 (1995).

> At the same time, it is difficult to see why California needs to permit such actions by private attorneys general — at least with respect to speech that is not "core" commercial speech but is entwined with, and directed toward, a more general public debate. The Federal Government regulates unfair competition and false advertising in the absence of such suits. 15 U.S.C. § 41 *et seq.* As far as I can tell, California's delegation of the government's enforcement authority to private individuals is not traditional, and may be unique. I do not see how "false advertising" regulation could suffer serious impediment if the Constitution limited the scope of private attorney general actions to circumstances where more purely commercial and less public-debate-oriented elements predominate. . . .
>
> These reasons convince me that it is likely, if not highly probable, that, if this Court were to reach the merits, it would hold that heightened scrutiny applies; that, under the circumstances here, California's delegation of enforcement authority to private attorneys general disproportionately burdens speech; and that the First Amendment consequently forbids it.

Nike, Inc. v. Kasky, 539 U.S. 654, 675-81, 683 (2003) (Breyer, J., dissenting). Do you agree with Justice Breyer's conclusion that the speech at issue was sufficiently different from "simple product advertisements" such that greater scrutiny was warranted than in the typical commercial speech context? How would you classify Nike's speech? Should courts recognize the need for some "breathing space"?

5. First Amendment issues also can arise in the context of the FTC's regulation of false advertising. Recall *Kraft, Inc. v. FTC* (excerpted above at pp. 381-90), in which the Seventh Circuit affirmed a judgment that certain claims Kraft made about its processed cheese slices were false and misleading. In another portion of the opinion, the court rejected Kraft's argument that the First Amendment required de novo review of the FTC's findings:

> Our standard for reviewing FTC findings has been traditionally limited to the highly deferential, substantial evidence test. FTC v. Indiana Fed'n of Dentists, 476 U.S. 447, 454 (1976); Hospital Corp. of Am. v. FTC, 807 F.2d 1381, 1384 (7th Cir. 1986), *cert. denied*, 481 U.S. 1038 (1987). However, Kraft argues as a threshold matter that two recent Supreme Court decisions, Bose Corp. v. Consumers Union, 466 U.S. 485, 510-11 (1984), and Peel v. Attorney Registration and Disciplinary Comm'n, 496 U.S. 91 (1990), compel us to review the FTC's factual findings *de novo* because they implicate Kraft's first amendment commercial speech rights.
>
> A deferential standard in reviewing FTC findings long predates *Bose* and *Peel.* In FTC v. Colgate-Palmolive Co., 380 U.S. 374, 385 (1965), the Supreme Court held that while the words "deceptive advertising" set forth a legal standard that derives its final meaning from judicial construction, an FTC finding is "to be given great weight by reviewing courts" because it "rests so heavily on inference and pragmatic judgment" and in light of the frequency with which the Commission handles these cases. *Id.* at 385. However, *Colgate-Palmolive* preceded the extension of first amendment protection to commercial speech, *see, e.g.*, Virginia Pharmacy Bd. v. Virginia Citizens Consumer Council, Inc., 425 U.S. 748, 770 (1976), and subsequent cases examining the contours of that right.
>
> *Bose* was a libel case holding that appellate courts have a constitutional responsibility to review *de novo* a lower court finding of fact that a defamatory statement was made with actual malice. *Bose*, 466 U.S. at 510-11. The Court declared that judges, as expositors of the Constitution, must independently decide whether evidence in the record is sufficient to strip allegedly libelous speech of first amendment protection. The Court, however, explicitly left unresolved the question of whether this higher standard of review extended to commercial speech cases. *Id.* at 504 n.22. Kraft asserts that the Court has since

answered that question. *Peel* held that a state regulation prohibiting attorneys from advertising a specialty or certification violated the first amendment and, significantly, a plurality of four Justices reviewed this issue *de novo, Peel*, 496 U.S. at 108 (citing *Bose)*, while Justice Marshall, writing separately, and providing a fifth vote, apparently did so as well. *Id.* at 111-117 (concurring opinion). Thus, *Peel* arguably extended *de novo* review to another subcategory of constitutionally protected speech, commercial advertising.

Nonetheless, we decline to apply *de novo* review in this context. For one, the implications of *Bose* are not as clear as Kraft suggests, *see* FTC v. Brown & Williamson Tobacco Corp., 778 F.2d 35, 41 n.3 (D.C. Cir. 1985) (refusing to extend *Bose* to the commercial speech context); *see also* Henry P. Monaghan, *Constitutional Fact Review*, 85 Colum. L. Rev. 229, 244-247 (1985), and *Bose* itself suggests that commercial speech might not warrant the higher standard of review established for libel cases. *Bose*, 466 U.S. at 504 n.22 (commercial speech generally considered less susceptible to the chilling effect of state regulation than other forms of speech). Although one might argue that *Bose* and *Peel* operating in tandem effectively overrule *Colgate-Palmolive*, we do not think that the Court intended that result. *See* Rodriquez de Quijas v. Shearson/American Express, Inc., 490 U.S. 477, 484 (1989) ("If a precedent of this Court has a direct application in a case, yet appears to rest on reasons rejected in some other line of decisions, [Courts] of Appeals should follow the case which directly controls, leaving to [the Supreme] Court the prerogative of overruling its own decisions."). Moreover, there are important distinctions between the sort of appellate review conducted in *Bose* and *Peel* and that done in *Colgate-Palmolive* and this case. The former involved review of court decisions, and courts generally lack the Commission's expertise in the field of deceptive advertising. . . .

Most important, the restriction challenged in *Peel* is a completely different animal than the one challenged here. In *Peel*, the issue was whether a prophylactic regulation applicable to all lawyers, completely prohibiting an entire category of potentially misleading commercial speech, passed constitutional muster. *Peel*, 496 U.S. at 108-09 (plurality); *id.* at 111 (concurrence). Here, by contrast, the issue is whether an individualized FTC cease and desist order, prohibiting a particular set of deceptive ads, passes constitutional muster. We find the restriction at issue in *Peel* and the one here sufficiently distinct to justify differing levels of appellate review. Accordingly, we decline to review *de novo* the FTC's findings and, with the substantial evidence test in mind, turn to the facts of this case.

H. INTERNATIONAL AND COMPARATIVE LAW CONSIDERATIONS

The Paris Convention, one of the international treaties discussed in the trademark portion of this casebook, requires member nations to recognize claims for false advertising and disparagement. In relevant part, Paris Convention article 10bis (titled "Unfair Competition") states:

> (1) The countries of the Union are bound to assure to nationals of such countries effective protection against unfair competition.
> (2) Any act of competition contrary to honest practices in industrial or commercial matters constitutes an act of unfair competition.
> (3) The following in particular shall be prohibited:
>
> > (i) all acts of such a nature as to create confusion by any means whatever with the establishment, the goods, or the industrial or commercial activities, of a competitor;

> (ii) false allegations in the course of trade of such a nature as to discredit the establishment, the goods, or the industrial or commercial activities, of a competitor;
> (iii) indications or allegations the use of which in the course of trade is liable to mislead the public as to the nature, the manufacturing process, the characteristics, the suitability for their purpose, or the quantity, of the goods.

Article 10ter goes on to provide that member states "undertake to assure to nationals of the other countries of the Union appropriate legal remedies effectively to repress all the acts referred to in" article 10bis, and "to provide measures to permit federations and associations representing interested industrialists, producers, or merchants, provided that the existence of such federations and associations is not contrary to the laws of their countries, to take action in the courts or before the administrative authorities, with a view to the repression of the acts referred to in [article 10bis] in so far as the law of the country in which protection is claimed allows such action by federations and associations of that country."

Although some nations view the Paris Convention provisions as being self-executing, until fairly recently there was no practical way for one member state (or for WIPO) to compel compliance on the part of another member state. Since 1995, however, the TRIPs Agreement has required members of the WTO to comply with, among other things, articles 1-12 of the Paris Convention, *see* TRIPs art. 2(1), and as we have seen, TRIPs backs up its requirements with the possibility of trade sanctions. Nevertheless, TRIPs itself says nothing specific about the content of member nations' false advertising or commercial disparagement laws, although it elaborates upon the meaning of "a manner contrary to honest commercial practices" in an article addressing trade secrets. *See* TRIPs art. 39(2) n.10 (defining the term as meaning "at least practices such as breach of contract, breach of confidence and inducement to breach, and includes the acquisition of undisclosed information by third parties who knew, or were grossly negligent in failing to know, that such practices were involved in the acquisition"). Moreover, while Paris Convention article 10bis appears to require member states to have in place some type of false advertising and commercial disparagement law, it leaves most of the details up to each member state to decide for itself. *See* Jane C. Ginsburg, *Four Reasons and a Paradox: The Manifest Superiority of Copyright over Sui Generis Protection of Computer Software*, 94 COLUM. L. REV. 2559, 2563 (1994) (stating that article 10bis "has not afforded a meaningful guarantee, for the treaty's definition of unfair competition leaves too much room for inconsistent and uncertain application"). The manner in which false advertising and commercial disparagement are regulated therefore can differ greatly from one country to another.

As we saw in the trademark portion of this casebook, the United States has implemented the trademark provisions of the Paris Convention principally through Lanham Act § 44. With respect to unfair competition in particular, Lanham Act § 44 (15 U.S.C. § 1126) includes the following relevant provisions:

> (b) Benefits of section to persons whose country of origin is party to convention or treaty
> Any person whose country of origin is a party to any convention or treaty relating to trademarks, trade or commercial names, or the repression of unfair competition, to which the United States is also a party, or extends reciprocal rights to nationals of the United States by law, shall be entitled to the benefits of this section under the conditions expressed herein to the extent necessary to give effect to any provision of such convention,

> treaty or reciprocal law, in addition to the rights to which any owner of a mark is otherwise entitled by this chapter. . . .
>
> (h) Protection of foreign nationals against unfair competition
>
> Any person designated in subsection (b) of this section as entitled to the benefits and subject to the provisions of this chapter shall be entitled to effective protection against unfair competition, and the remedies provided in this chapter for infringement of marks shall be available so far as they may be appropriate in repressing acts of unfair competition.
>
> (i) Citizens or residents of United States entitled to benefits of section
>
> Citizens or residents of the United States shall have the same benefits as are granted by this section to persons described in subsection (b) of this section.

An initial question of statutory interpretation is whether §§ 44(h) and (i) extend to U.S. citizens and residents (and to qualifying foreign nationals) any rights against unfair competition in addition to the rights set out in other portions of the Lanham Act itself. As discussed above in connection with the history of § 43(a), there is some reason to believe that the drafters of the Lanham Act expected just that — that courts would make use of §§ 44(h) and (i) to craft a general federal law of unfair competition. *See supra* p. 323 n.9. Some early cases read § 44(i) as providing federal jurisdiction over any claim involving unfair competition in interstate commerce, even if all of the parties were U.S. citizens or residents. *See, e.g.*, Stauffer v. Exley, 184 F.2d 962 (9th Cir. 1950). More recently, however, the Ninth Circuit repudiated this interpretation, *see* Toho Co. v. Sears, Roebuck & Co., 645 F.2d 788 (9th Cir. 1981), as have all other federal courts that have addressed it. *See* 6 McCarthy, §§ 32:15, 32:16 (collecting cases). As for suits between domestic parties, then, § 44(i) as currently understood does not create any substantive rights beyond those found in § 43(a).

As for § 44(h), the majority view is that this provision too does not confer any substantive rights (other than national treatment). *See, e.g.*, Int'l Café, S.A.L. v. Hard Rock Café Int'l (U.S.A.), Inc., 252 F.3d 1274, 1277-78 (11th Cir. 2001) (per curiam):

> Plaintiff argues that Section 44 of the Lanham Act incorporates the provisions governing unfair competition in the Paris Convention. The Paris Convention ensures that "foreign nationals should be given the same treatment in each of the member countries as that country makes available to its own citizens" as to trademark and related rights. Vanity Fair Mills, Inc. v. T. Eaton Co., 234 F.2d 633, 640 (2nd Cir. 1956). The Convention also sought to create uniformity by obligating each member nation "to assure to nationals of countries of the Union an effective protection against unfair competition." 53 Stat. 1780, art. 10(1).
>
> Subject-matter jurisdiction may arise under an international treaty like the Paris Convention if domestic law incorporates the treaty.[5] *See* United States v. Postal, 589

5. A treaty can also be self-executing if it "directly accords enforceable rights to persons without the benefit of Congressional implementation." Haitian Refugee Ctr., Inc. v. Baker, 949 F.2d 1109, 1110 (11th Cir. 1991). The Paris Convention is not self-executing because, on its face, the Convention provides that it will become effective only through domestic legislation. See 53 Stat. 1780, art. 17 ("It is understood that at the time an instrument of ratification or accession is deposited on behalf of a country, such country will be in a position under its domestic law to give effect to the provisions of this Convention."); *see also* Mannington Mills, Inc. v. Congoleum Corp., 595 F.2d 1287, 1298 (3rd Cir. 1979); Ortman v. Stanray Corp., 371 F.2d 154, 157 (7th Cir. 1967). *But see Vanity Fair*, 234 F.2d at 640 (noting, without discussion, that plaintiff "would appear to be correct" in asserting that Paris Convention is self-executing).

> F.2d 862, 878 (5th Cir. 1979). Section 44 of the Lanham Act provides that "[a]ny person whose country of origin is a party to the convention . . . shall be entitled to benefits [under § 1126] to the extent necessary to give effect to any provision of such convention. . . ." 15 U.S.C. § 1126(b). Also, any person covered by § 1126(b) "shall be entitled to effective protection against unfair competition, and the remedies . . . shall be available so far as they may be appropriate in repressing acts of unfair competition." 15 U.S.C. § 1126(h).
>
> We agree that section 44 of the Lanham Act incorporated, to some degree, the Paris Convention. But we disagree that the Paris Convention creates substantive rights beyond those independently provided in the Lanham Act. As other courts of appeals have noted, the rights articulated in the Paris Convention do not exceed the rights conferred by the Lanham Act. *See* Scotch Whisky Assoc. v. Majestic Distilling Co., Inc., 958 F.2d 594, 597 (4th Cir. 1992); *Vanity Fair*, 234 F.2d at 644; *see also* L'Aiglon Apparel v. Lana Lobell, Inc., 214 F.2d 649, 652-54 (3rd Cir. 1954). Instead, we conclude that the Paris Convention, as incorporated by the Lanham Act, only requires "national treatment."
>
> National treatment means that "foreign nationals should be given the same treatment in each of the member countries as that country makes available to its own citizens." *Vanity Fair*, 234 F.2d at 640. So, section 44 of the Lanham Act gives foreign nationals the same rights and protections provided to United States citizens by the Lanham Act. As such, foreign nationals like Plaintiff may seek protection in United States courts for violations of the Lanham Act. But the Paris Convention, as incorporated by section 44 of the Lanham Act, creates no new cause of action for unfair competition. Any cause of action based on unfair competition must be grounded in the substantive provisions of the Lanham Act.

On the facts presented, the court concluded that national treatment did not require a U.S. court to entertain a dispute involving competing uses of the name "Hard Rock Café" in Lebanon. Although national treatment would call for the extraterritorial application of the Lanham Act under some limited circumstances, those circumstances were not met in the present case. *See id.* at 1278-79. *See also* Empresa Cubana del Tabaco v. Culbro, Ltd., 399 F.3d 462, 484-85 (2d Cir. 2005) (stating that plaintiffs "cannot maintain a separate claim for unfair competition under Article 10bis and Sections 44(b) and (h). Rather, a claim for unfair competition must be brought under Section 43(a) or state law"); Mattel Inc. v. MCA Records, Inc., 296 F.3d 894, 907-08 (9th Cir. 2002) (same).

A few courts have reached the opposite conclusion. *See, e.g.*, General Motors Corp. v. Ignacio Lopez de Arriortua, 948 F. Supp. 684, 689 (E.D. Mich. 1996) (holding that § 44(h) "incorporates the substantive provisions of the Paris Convention and thus creates a federal law of unfair competition applicable in international disputes"); Maison Lazard et Cie. v. Manfra, Tordella & Brooks, Inc., 585 F. Supp. 1286, 1289 (S.D.N.Y. 1984) (same); *see also* Lanham Act § 45, 15 U.S.C. § 1127 (stating that the Lanham Act is intended, among other things, "to provide rights and remedies stipulated by treaties and conventions respecting trademarks, trade names, and unfair competition entered into between the United States and foreign nations"). The expansive reading of § 44(h) nevertheless remains the minority view. Moreover, even if the expansive reading might provide some additional substantive rights with respect to certain matters relating to trademarks, would it make any difference as to false advertising and commercial disparagement claims, given the vague language of article 10bis?

I. REMEDIES FOR FALSE ADVERTISING

1. Damages

ALPO Petfoods, Inc. v. Ralston Purina Co.
913 F.2d 958 (D.C. Cir. 1990)

Clarence THOMAS, Circuit Judge:

In this case, Ralston Purina Co. and ALPO Petfoods, Inc., two of the leading dog food producers in the United States, have sued each other under section 43(a) of the Lanham Act, 15 U.S.C. § 1125(a) (1982) (amended 1988), alleging false advertising. ALPO asserts that Ralston has violated section 43(a) by claiming that its Puppy Chow products can lessen the severity of canine hip dysplasia (CHD), a crippling joint condition. Ralston, for its part, attacks ALPO's claims that ALPO Puppy Food contains "the formula preferred by responding vets two to one over the leading puppy food."

After a sixty-one-day bench trial, the district court decided that Ralston's CHD-related advertising and ALPO's veterinarian preference advertising both violated section 43(a). ALPO Petfoods, Inc. v. Ralston Purina Co., 720 F. Supp. 194, 209-11 (D.D.C. 1989). The court permanently enjoined both companies from making "advertising or other related claims" similar to those held false, and ordered both parties to disseminate corrective statements. Id. at 216-17. Applying section 35(a) of the Lanham Act, 15 U.S.C. § 1117(a) (1982 & Supp. V 1987) (amended 1988), the court also awarded ALPO $10.4 million (plus costs and attorneys' fees). The court reached this figure by determining the amount that Ralston spent on its CHD-related advertising, using that amount as a measure of Ralston's benefit from the advertising, and then doubling the amount to capture the full harm that the advertising caused ALPO. *ALPO*, 720 F. Supp. at 215 (citing U-Haul Int'l, Inc. v. Jartran, Inc., 793 F.2d 1034, 1037 (9th Cir. 1986)). Ralston, in contrast, was awarded only its costs and attorneys' fees. Id. at 215, 216.

... Convinced that the court properly applied section 43(a) and found facts that are not clearly erroneous, we affirm the court's conclusion that both Ralston and ALPO have violated section 43(a). On several issues concerning remedies, however, we vacate and remand. The monetary award to ALPO is an award of Ralston's profits, rather than ALPO's actual damages, yet we do not see in Ralston's conduct willful, targeted wrongdoing, which is what an award of profits requires. See Foxtrap, Inc. v. Foxtrap, Inc., 671 F.2d 636, 641-42 (D.C. Cir. 1982) (per curiam). ALPO is entitled to its actual damages, however, and we try below to clarify what an award of actual damages under section 35(a) can include. Because ALPO, too, has violated section 43(a), Ralston is entitled to any actual damages that it can prove; in a case involving a meritorious claim and a meritorious counterclaim, section 35(a) does not authorize a court to compensate only the party considered less blameworthy. Attorneys' fees, in contrast, are available under section 35(a) only "in exceptional cases," which this court has defined as cases involving willful or bad-faith conduct. Lanham Act § 35(a), 15 U.S.C. § 1117(a); see Reader's Digest Ass'n v. Conservative Digest, Inc., 821 F.2d 800, 808 (D.C. Cir. 1987). This case does not fall into that category, so we reverse the district court's decision to grant attorneys' fees. Finally, we instruct the district court to enter an injunction more closely tailored to the harm posed by any repeat of Ralston's false advertising.

... Ralston attacks the ... $10.4 million judgment in favor of ALPO under section 35(a) of the Lanham Act, 15 U.S.C. § 1117(a) (1982 & Supp. V 1987).

Ralston concentrates its attack on the court's decision to use Ralston's advertising costs as a measure of monetary relief, a method derived from U-Haul Int'l, Inc. v. Jartran, Inc., 793 F.2d 1034, 1042 (9th Cir. 1986). Ralston argues that the court made an error of law in adopting *U-Haul*, and that the court incorporated clearly erroneous findings of fact into its *U-Haul* analysis. Reviewing the court's decision on monetary relief for abuse of discretion, see *Conservative Digest*, 821 F.2d at 807, we agree that the award against Ralston must be vacated.

The district court's opinion states that Ralston's false advertising caused ALPO financial harm, and describes the $10.4 million award to ALPO as damages. See, e.g., *ALPO*, 720 F. Supp. at 212 ("The court finds that ALPO was damaged by Ralston's misconduct. . . . A particularly effective way to measure the damages sustained would be to look to the sums Ralston expended in its CHD advertising campaign."). But cf. id. at 215 ("The measure of damages and profits may be assessed on a number of different bases where necessary to effectuate the purposes of the Act. . . ."). The two-part analysis supporting the amount of the monetary relief, however, shows that the court actually awarded Ralston's profits to ALPO. In deciding the amount of relief, the district court first adopted the reasoning in *U-Haul*, 793 F.2d at 1042. See *ALPO*, 720 F. Supp. at 215. In that case, the Ninth Circuit affirmed an unprecedented $40 million award to a competitor injured by a section 43(a) violation. See *U-Haul*, 793 F.2d at 1037, 1041-42 (explaining district court's alternative justifications for monetary award and deciding to affirm award based on one of those justifications). Of the award as affirmed, $12 million constituted the defendant's profits, calculated on the assumption that "the financial benefit [to the defendant] was at least equal to [its] advertising expenditures" and adjusted upward 100% under section 35(a). Id. at 1042; see also id. (repeatedly calling this part of award an award of profits). The district court here, after using the *U-Haul* approach to calculate Ralston's profits at $10.4 million, confirmed that figure by comparing it with "the 11 million dollar adjusted net profits Ralston earned from the sales of its Puppy Chow products during the period of its CHD advertising program." *ALPO*, 720 F. Supp. at 215; see id. at 212, 215 ("adjusted net profits" figure equals Ralston's nationwide pre-tax profits, multiplied by ALPO's percentage share of non-Ralston puppy food market).

Leaving aside whether the *U-Haul* standard[9] or the district court's alternative calculation[10] accurately measures the profits that Ralston derived from its false advertising, we hold that this case does not justify an award of profits. Section 35(a) authorizes courts to award to an aggrieved plaintiff both plaintiff's damages and defendant's profits, but, as this court noted in *Foxtrap*, 671 F.2d at 641, courts' discretion to award these remedies has limits. Just as "any award based on plaintiff's damages

9. The Ninth Circuit has already noted the limitations of the *U-Haul* rule. See *Harper House*, 889 F.2d at 209 n.8 (justification for *U-Haul* rule weakens in cases that do not involve passing off or direct comparative advertising). Commentators, too, have criticized the decision. See, e.g., Comment, *Money Damages and Corrective Advertising: An Economic Analysis*, 55 U. Chi. L. Rev. 629, 638-42 (1988) (refuting premise that defendants' advertising costs reflect value of plaintiffs' lost reputation and good will); Comment, *Monetary Relief for False Advertising Claims Arising Under Section 43(a) of the Lanham Act*, 34 UCLA L. Rev. 953, 955 n.6, 973-74 (1987) (large awards under *U-Haul* give firms incentives to attack rivals, particularly new entrants, with false-advertising suits). But cf. Best, *Monetary Damages for False Advertising*, 49 U. Pitt. L. Rev. 1, 18-22 (1987) (praising *U-Haul* for easing plaintiffs' burden of proving actual damages, but noting that the *U-Haul* surrogate measure itself can lead to overcompensation).

10. As Ralston points out, the alternative calculation "assumes that (1) all of Ralston's Puppy Chow profits were attributable solely to its advertising and (2) all the profits attributable to advertising were due to the CHD claims." Brief of Appellant at 47 (emphasis deleted).

requires some showing of actual loss," id. at 642; see also infra p. 969 (discussing actual damages under section 35(a)), an award based on a defendant's profits requires proof that the defendant acted willfully or in bad faith, see *Foxtrap*, 671 F.2d at 641; Frisch's Restaurants, Inc. v. Elby's Big Boy, 849 F.2d 1012, 1015 (6th Cir. 1988). Proof of this sort is lacking. Ralston's decision to run CHD-related advertising that lacked solid empirical support does not, without more, reflect willfulness or bad faith. See supra pp. 965-66; cf. U-Haul Int'l, Inc. v. Jartran, Inc., 601 F. Supp. 1140, 1147-48 (D. Ariz. 1984) (describing U-Haul defendant's targeted comparative advertising, which misrepresented plaintiff's and defendant's prices), aff'd in part and rev'd in part, 793 F.2d 1034 (9th Cir. 1986).

In *Conservative Digest* we "left open the possibility that a court could properly award damages to a plaintiff when the defendant has been unjustly enriched." 821 F.2d at 807-08 (citing *Foxtrap*, 671 F.2d at 641 & n.9). The unjust-enrichment theory, which emerged in trademark cases in which the infringer and the infringed were not competitors, holds that courts should divest an infringer of his profits, regardless of whether the infringer's actions have harmed the owner of the infringed trademark. Awards of profits are justified under the theory because they deter infringement in general and thereby vindicate consumers' interests. See, e.g., Monsanto Chemical Co. v. Perfect Fit Prods. Mfg. Co., 349 F.2d 389, 392, 395-97 (2d Cir. 1965), cert. denied, 383 U.S. 942, 86 S. Ct. 1195, 16 L. Ed. 2d 206 (1966); see also 2 J.T. McCarthy, supra p. 14, § 30:25(B) (citing cases). As we state below, however, we doubt the wisdom of an approach to damages that permits courts to award profits for their sheer deterrent effect.

Relying on *W.E. Bassett*, 435 F.2d at 664, and *Monsanto Chemical*, 349 F.2d at 396, ALPO proposes such an approach. See Brief of Appellee at 40-43. Indeed, at oral argument, counsel for ALPO claimed that because *Foxtrap*, 671 F.2d at 641, cites *W.E. Bassett*, this circuit has "adopted the *Bassett* theory for [profits awards based solely on] deterrence in an egregious case." Transcript of Oral Argument at 25 (Apr. 13, 1990). *Foxtrap*, however, cites *W.E. Bassett* to suggest that courts can award profits only when they find "a relatively egregious display of bad faith." *Foxtrap*, 671 F.2d at 641. Indeed, this court in *Foxtrap* advised a district court to make an award that would "deter the defendant, yet not be a windfall to plaintiff nor amount to punitive damages." Id. at 642 n.11 (emphasis added). Based on *Foxtrap*, as well as our concern that deterrence is too weak and too easily invoked a justification for the severe and often cumbersome remedy of a profits award, see Koelemay, *Monetary Relief for Trademark Infringement Under the Lanham Act*, 72 Trademark Rep. 458, 493-94, 536-37 (1982), we hold that deterrence alone cannot justify such an award.

Since this case lacks the elements required to support the court's award of Ralston's profits, we vacate the $10.4 million judgment in favor of ALPO. We do not mean, however, to deny ALPO all monetary relief for Ralston's false advertising. Because the district court has so far focused on awarding Ralston's profits, it has not yet decided what actual damages ALPO has proved. On remand, the court should award ALPO its actual damages, bearing in mind the requirement that any amount awarded have support in the record, see *Foxtrap*, 671 F.2d at 642; *Gold Seal*, 129 F. Supp. at 940, as well as the following points about the governing law.

In a false-advertising case such as this one, actual damages under section 35(a) can include:

> profits lost by the plaintiff on sales actually diverted to the false advertiser, see, e.g., *Foxtrap*, 671 F.2d at 642 (trademark case);

> profits lost by the plaintiff on sales made at prices reduced as a demonstrated result of the false advertising, see, e.g., Burndy Corp. v. Teledyne Indus., 748 F.2d 767, 773 (2d Cir. 1984);
>
> the costs of any completed advertising that actually and reasonably responds to the defendant's offending ads, see, e.g., Cuisinarts, Inc. v. Robot-Coupe Int'l Corp., 580 F. Supp. 634, 640-41 (S.D.N.Y. 1984); and
>
> quantifiable harm to the plaintiff's good will, to the extent that completed corrective advertising has not repaired that harm, see, e.g., Engineered Mech. Servs., Inc. v. Applied Mech. Technology, Inc., 591 F. Supp. 962, 966 (M.D. La. 1984); see also Comment, 55 U. CHI. L. REV. at 650-57 (discussing how courts might directly measure good will).

See generally Koelemay, 72 TRADEMARK REP. at 505-07.

When assessing these actual damages, the district court may take into account the difficulty of proving an exact amount of damages from false advertising, as well as the maxim that "'the wrongdoer shall bear the risk of the uncertainty which his own wrong has created.'" Otis Clapp & Son v. Filmore Vitamin Co., 754 F.2d 738, 745 (7th Cir. 1985) (quoting Bigelow v. RKO Radio Pictures, Inc., 327 U.S. 251, 265, 66 S. Ct. 574, 580, 90 L. Ed. 652 (1946)). At the same time, the court must ensure that the record adequately supports all items of damages claimed and establishes a causal link between the damages and the defendant's conduct, lest the award become speculative or violate section 35(a)'s prohibition against punishment. See, e.g., *Bigelow*, 327 U.S. at 264, 66 S. Ct. at 580 (stating, in antitrust case, that "speculation or guesswork" cannot sustain an award of damages); *Burndy Corp.*, 748 F.2d at 773 (asserted causal connection between defendant's conduct and plaintiff's reduced-price sales lacked support in record; denial of reduced-price-sales damages affirmed); *Foxtrap*, 671 F.2d at 642 (same problem with respect to lost sales; damages award vacated and case remanded for detailed findings).

Section 35(a) also authorizes the court to "enter judgment, according to the circumstances of the case, for any sum above the amount found as actual damages, not exceeding three times such amount." Lanham Act § 35(a), 15 U.S.C. § 1117(a) (1982 & Supp. V 1987) (amended 1988). This provision gives the court discretion to enhance damages, as long as the ultimate award qualifies as "compensation and not [as] a penalty." Id.; see Koelemay, 72 TRADEMARK REP. at 516-19, 521-25 (discussing interplay of damages enhancement provision and antipenalty clause); see also Getty Petroleum Corp. v. Bartco Petroleum Corp., 858 F.2d 103, 112-13 (2d Cir. 1988) (in trademark infringement case, interpreting section 35(a) to ban any awards of punitive damages), cert. denied, 490 U.S. 1006, 109 S. Ct. 1642, 104 L. Ed. 2d 158 (1989). Given this express statutory restriction, if the district court decides to enhance damages under section 35(a), it should explain why the enhanced award is compensatory and not punitive.

C. Denial of Monetary Relief in Favor of Ralston

The foregoing comments on actual damages apply as well to the monetary remedy for ALPO's false advertising. As noted above, the district court held that ALPO's veterinarian preference advertising violated section 43(a). *ALPO*, 720 F. Supp. at

209-11. Despite this decision, the court did not award Ralston any damages or profits under section 35(a) because "[t]he magnitude of the wrongdoing by Ralston in comparison to that of ALPO is so much greater that a damage award would not be justified," because ALPO, but not Ralston, had shown remorse, and because the court considered Ralston's counterclaim "an afterthought." Id. at 216; see also id. at 212 (finding an injunction the most appropriate redress for ALPO's false advertising).

The Lanham Act does not authorize courts to deny monetary relief for these reasons. Once a party establishes a violation of section 43(a), section 35(a) "entitle[s]" that party to monetary relief, subject only to the statutes referred to in the section and to the principles of equity. Lanham Act § 35(a), 15 U.S.C. § 1117(a); cf. *ALPO*, 720 F. Supp. at 214 (rejecting both parties' "unclean hands" defenses, a ruling that neither party appeals). Since section 35(a) expressly provides for compensation, rather than punishment, courts dealing with offsetting meritorious claims must let the degree of injury that each party proves, rather than the degree of opprobrium that the court attaches to each party's conduct, determine the monetary relief.

At more than one point in this case, Ralston came close to admitting that it cannot prove lost profits. See Brief of Appellee at 47 & app. B (citing Ralston's statement, in a proposed finding of fact, that none of its regression analyses proved diverted sales); Reply Brief of Appellant at 18-19 ("Ralston's position . . . is that under a proper construction of the Lanham Act, neither party can quantify lost profits sufficiently to recover damages."). In this appeal, however, Ralston has shown that it still considers its lost profits a live issue. See id. at 18 & n.40 (citing evidence, other than regressions, of lost sales). Since Ralston has some evidence of lost sales, and since, more importantly, section 35(a) entitles Ralston to damages other than lost profits, see supra p. 969, the district court should on remand award Ralston whatever actual damages it has proved. In this connection, as with A'PO's damages, the court should decide whether the parties have already had a sufficient opportunity to prove the types of damages outlined above, or whether further hearings are necessary.

D. Attorneys' Fees

The court awarded each company the attorneys' fees associated with its successful false-advertising claim. *ALPO*, 720 F. Supp. at 216. Only Ralston has appealed.

Section 35(a) entitles prevailing parties to attorneys' fees "in exceptional cases." This court's decision in *Conservative Digest*, 821 F.2d at 808, establishes an abuse-of-discretion standard for review of attorneys' fees awards. That same decision, however, holds that a court can award a plaintiff her attorneys' fees only in cases involving willful or bad-faith conduct by the defendant; applying that standard, the *Conservative Digest* court affirmed a denial of fees to a plaintiff who had proved trade dress infringement, but not willfulness or bad faith on the part of the infringer. Id. Seeing no relevant distinction between fee awards in trade dress infringement actions and fee awards in false-advertising actions, we apply *Conservative Digest* here. See id. at 803 (section 43(a) covers trade dress infringement).

In announcing its fee awards, the district court did not expressly find that Ralston had acted willfully or in bad faith. Indeed, it made no finding that this case is "exceptional" in any respect. See *ALPO*, 720 F. Supp. at 215, 216; supra p. 963. During a postjudgment hearing, the court explained that since, in its view, federal agencies are not sufficiently enforcing the laws against false advertising, it had awarded fees "to encourage private attorneys general in this case." Transcript of Motions Hearing at 7 (Sept. 18, 1989). Since neither the court's opinion nor its later statements support the award with a finding of willfulness or bad faith, and since we have decided that any such finding would be clearly erroneous, see supra pp. 965-66, we reverse the district court's decision to award attorneys' fees to ALPO.

Balance Dynamics Corp. v. Schmitt Industries
204 F.3d 683 (6th Cir. 2000)

Dowd, District Judge.

I. Introduction

The false advertising litigation before us has continued for six years, largely due to the paucity of legal rulings available to the trial court on some of the unique issues presented in this case. These issues pertain to the standards for establishing a violation of the Lanham Trade-Mark Act, the relief available once a violation is established, and the method of proofs necessary to establish entitlement to such relief. In particular, this case presents several issues of first impression: (1) whether, upon establishing a violation of the Lanham Act, a plaintiff can recover damage control costs without showing that the false advertising created actual confusion in the marketplace or actual damages in the marketplace; [and] (2) whether a plaintiff can recover damages to goodwill or disgorgement of profits upon showing that an advertisement is literally false or deliberately false, where the plaintiff has no other proof of damages to its business . . .

For the reasons set forth below, we hold: that a plaintiff seeking to recover damage control costs under the Lanham Act for a defendant's false advertising is not required to show that the false advertising created actual confusion or damages in the marketplace; [and] that in order to recover damage to goodwill or disgorgement of profits, a plaintiff must show at least some damage in the marketplace and cannot rely solely on the literal falsehood of an advertisement. . . .

II. Facts and History

Plaintiff-Appellant Balance Dynamics Corporation ("Balance Dynamics"), based in Ann Arbor, Michigan, and Defendant-Appellee Schmitt Industries ("Schmitt"), based in Portland, Oregon, manufacture products that balance industrial grinders and other machines that have a spinning shaft. In a process unique in the industry, Balance Dynamics' product uses a gas called Halon 1202 which is heated and vaporized in one chamber and allowed to condense back to liquid form in another. Schmitt's products accomplish the same result by balancing the spinning shafts with motor driven metal weights.

During the late summer of 1992, prior to Chicago's International Machine Tool Show in September, Schmitt mailed and distributed a postcard cartoon to 2,500 customers or potential customers depicting a "freon balancer" at the top of a "dead wheel balancer bone pile."

In late 1992 or early 1993, Schmitt received queries regarding its possible use of halons, freons, or other ozone-depleting materials. On March 16, 1993, Schmitt sent a letter to approximately 3,200 customers and prospective customers stating that

> Effective May 15, 1993, all products which contain or have been processed with ozone depleting substances (ODS) must have warning labels affixed. Subsequently, these substances will be banned from general use. Canada has already banned the substances. The ultimate financial responsibility for environmentally sound disposal of products containing ODS materials will rest with the end user.

After stating that Schmitt's balancing system did not use ozone depleting substances, the letter continued:

> Perhaps because one manufacturer of automatic grinding wheel balancers uses halon, this type of device has come under close scrutiny. . . . Should your company operate any halon balancers, and wish to dispose of them prior to May 15, Schmitt Industries can supply an SBS Balance System as an easy replacement.

The letter was signed by defendants Wayne A. Case, Schmitt's president, and James Morgan, Schmitt's sales manager.

In April of 1993, one of Balance Dynamics' largest customers faxed the letter to Thomas Schulte, Balance Dynamics' then-vice president of sales. Schulte consequently spoke with approximately 40 individuals from 12 different corporate customers with regard to the letter. Some of these customer contacts were initiated by Schulte, others by the customers themselves. After investigation, Balance Dynamics confirmed that its halon balancer was not subject to regulation, did not require labeling, and was not slated to be banned. It then responded by making visits to customers and sending a "fact sheet" to those customers who expressed concern.

Schmitt disagreed with certain items in the "fact sheet" and hired an environmental chemist to write an opinion, which stated that Halon 1202 had "managed to slip through the regulatory net" but that it is "quite certain the EPA would regulate its production and use." It also suggested that if the EPA failed to act, a private person could obtain a court order requiring the EPA to list Halon 1202 as a regulated substance, and that "it is almost certain that in the relatively near future Halon 1202 will become very difficult to obtain." The paper was provided to approximately 12 Schmitt customers or prospective customers.

In February of 1994, Balance Dynamics brought suit against Schmitt, Wayne A. Case, and James Morgan, seeking compensatory damages, treble damages, attorney fees, disgorgement of Schmitt's profits, and an injunction restraining Schmitt from similar mailings. Balance Dynamics claimed the defendants had violated various state laws as well as the false advertising language of the Lanham Trade-Mark Act, 15 U.S.C. § 1051 et seq. . . .

Balance Dynamics dropped its claim for injunctive relief on August 21, 1994. Balance Dynamics also stipulated that it experienced no lost sales, no lost profits, and no increased cost of seeking capital investments. However, Balance Dynamics reserved the right to seek treble damages, Schmitt's profits, damage control costs, and compensation for harm to goodwill. Schmitt then brought a supplemental motion for summary judgment on Balance Dynamics' damages claims. In August of 1995, Judge LaPlata adopted an R & R granting Schmitt's motion as to lost profits and costs but denying it as to Balance Dynamics' claim for damage control activities.

[The district granted judgment for the defendant Schmitt on the ground that Balance Dynamics had failed to prove actual confusion. The Sixth Circuit reversed, noting that "a communication that has a 'tendency to deceive' can be the subject of a Lanham Act violation if all other elements of the test are met." It then proceeded to consider what relief, if any, Balance Dynamics would be entitled to on remand.]

A. *Damage Control Costs*

The first form of relief to which Balance Dynamics stakes a claim is that of damage control — the costs of responding to Schmitt's false advertising.[2] Balance Dynamics argues that it can receive compensation for its damage control activities without showing actual confusion or what are commonly called "actual" damages. In other words, Balance Dynamics argues that Magistrate Judge Pepe was correct as a matter of law when he recommended denying Schmitt's motion for summary judgment on the issue of loss control. The R & R that Judge LaPlata adopted states:

> In light of the inquiries made by customers and other business contacts, a factfinder could conclude that plaintiff's actions in response to Schmitt's letter were reasonable attempts to nullify any potential damage to the corporation. A factfinder could also conclude that the letter caused serious risk to plaintiff's future sales and reputation. . . . Unlike plaintiff's claim for lost profits and costs, for purposes of this issue it is irrelevant whether plaintiff actually suffered damage through lost or potential sales. . . . Contrary to defendants' assertion, plaintiff's "damage control activities" are recoverable under the Lanham Act, which authorizes an award for any damages plaintiff sustains. 15 U.S.C. § 1117(a)(2). But for Schmitt's letter, plaintiff would not have incurred any expenses because it would not have had to take any corrective action. Therefore, the cost of plaintiff's response activities, if found reasonable and necessary by a jury, constitute 'damage' under the Lanham Act." (emphases in original).

On the other hand, Schmitt relies on Electronics Corp. of America v. Honeywell, 358 F. Supp. 1230 (D. Mass. 1973), to suggest that damage control costs are not recoverable in the absence of actual confusion or "actual" damages. In *Electronics Corp. of America*, plaintiff had waived any attempt to show so-called "actual business harm" in dollars and cents but nevertheless pressed its case for damages, punitive damages, costs, and attorney fees. Id. at 1233. The court held that the plaintiff could not recover in the absence of "actual business harm." Id. at 1234.

Like many other circuits, we have held that where plaintiffs seek to recover monetary damages for false or misleading advertising that is not literally false, "a violation can only be established by proof of actual deception (i.e., evidence that individual consumers perceived the advertisement in a way that misled them about the plaintiff's product)." *Podiatric Physicians*, 185 F.3d at 614 (quoting Sandoz Pharm. Corp. v. Richardson-Vicks, Inc., 902 F.2d 222, 229 (3d Cir. 1990)) (citations omitted). In *Podiatric Physicians*, we also set forth a more lenient standard for obtaining injunctive relief under the Lanham Act: "injunctive relief may be obtained by showing only that the defendant's representations about its product have a tendency to deceive

2. . . . There is some question as to whether all of Balance Dynamics' claimed damage control losses really related to an effort to mitigate damages from Schmitt's false advertising, or whether Balance Dynamics was simply overreaching and seeking a windfall for activities in which it would have engaged anyway.

consumers. . . ." Id. at 618 (quoting Max Daetwyler Corp. v. Input Graphics, Inc., 608 F. Supp. 1549, 1551 (E.D. Pa. 1985)). "This lower standard has arisen because when an injunction is sought, courts may protect the consumer without fear of bestowing an undeserved windfall on the plaintiff." Id.

Although *Podiatric Physicians* held that recovery of monetary damages is only available upon a showing of actual confusion, the question of the standard upon which damage control costs may be recovered is one of first impression. None of the courts requiring actual confusion as a prerequisite to monetary recovery have applied that rule to limit recovery for damage control activities; their opinions simply were not written to take account of that kind of damages. Rather, when courts have held that actual confusion must be demonstrated before monetary damages are recoverable, they have referred to plaintiffs who were seeking damages that would have been suffered in the marketplace, i.e., lost sales, lost profits, or loss of goodwill. See, e.g., *Web Printing Controls, Inc.*, 906 F.2d at 1204-05 (plaintiff wishing to recover damages for a violation of the Lanham Act must prove "actual injury, i.e., a loss of sales, profits, or present value (goodwill)."); *Podiatric Physicians*, supra; *PPX Enterprises, Inc. v. Audiofidelity Enterprises, Inc.*, 818 F.2d 266 (2d Cir. 1987); Electronics Corp. of America v. Honeywell, supra.

Actual confusion is a prerequisite to an award of such "marketplace damages" because actual confusion tends to show that these hard-to-prove damages probably exist. Yet there is no need to use such proxies with regard to damage control expenses, for the proof of such expenses is in the possession of the plaintiff and is therefore easily produced. Hence, there seems little reason to require "actual confusion" before awarding compensation for damage control expenses, even though such an award is "monetary." As Magistrate Judge Pepe noted, the plain language of the Lanham Act permits recovery of "any damages sustained by the plaintiff" upon a showing that the plaintiff is or is likely to be damaged by misrepresentative advertising. 15 U.S.C. §§ 1125(a), 1117. Magistrate Judge Pepe's view is reinforced by *Podiatric Physicians*, which allows a plaintiff to establish liability under the Lanham Act by showing that a false advertisement has a tendency to deceive a substantial portion of the audience, and that it has caused harm to the plaintiff. 185 F.3d at 613.

Damage control expenses must be treated differently from marketplace damages because, like an injunction, damage control is undertaken precisely to prevent such things as lost sales, lost profits, and lost goodwill. As is the case with plaintiffs seeking injunctive relief, plaintiffs engaging in damage control are still at a stage where substantial uncertainty exists as to the extent of "business harm" being inflicted by the false advertising. Cf. ALPO Petfoods, Inc. v. Ralston Purina Co., 997 F.2d 949, 952 (D.C. Cir. 1993). In the present case, Balance Dynamics first heard about Schmitt's March 16, 1993 letter when a customer faxed it to Mr. Schulte. The letter contained disparaging remarks which, if true, would ruin Balance Dynamics' business. Not yet knowing whether the letter was true or false, Schulte called his most important customers and found that most of them had received the letter and were concerned about the regulations pertaining to the halon balancer. Meanwhile, other customers initiated contact with Mr. Schulte or other officers of Balance Dynamics, and also expressed serious reservations about the continued use of the halon balancer. Balance Dynamics then investigated the veracity of the claims made in the letter and found they were false.

At this point, with 3,200 letters in circulation, must Balance Dynamics wait to take action until a customer actually tells someone at Balance Dynamics that she will not buy the halon balancer? Is Balance Dynamics limited to seeking injunctive relief to stop future letters being mailed out, when 3,200 people are reading statements about the halon balancer that, if believed, will be fatal to Balance Dynamics' business? At such a juncture, an injunction may be a mere palliative. We think it appropriate that Balance Dynamics, upon recognizing the reasonable likelihood of confusion, would undertake to protect its business. Cf. ALPO Petfoods, Inc. v. Ralston Purina Co., 997 F.2d at 952. We also think it appropriate that Schmitt, having violated the Lanham Act and thereby being responsible for "any damages" caused by such violation, should compensate Balance Dynamics for any reasonable and necessary expenses incurred in mitigating the detrimental effects of that transgression. Id.

Consequently, similar standards as apply to injunctive relief should also apply to recovery of damage control expenses. That is, damage control expenses should be recoverable upon a showing of the likelihood of actual confusion, rather than upon a showing of actual confusion itself. This rule recognizes that it is unreasonable to expect a businessperson faced with a Lanham Act violation to sit idly by until a customer manifests actual confusion. The law should encourage quick responses and the mitigation of damage, and should not require parties to suffer an injury before trying to prevent it. Moreover, a rule allowing recovery for damage control costs upon the likelihood of actual confusion does not risk an "undeserved windfall" to the plaintiff since such an award would not speak to the underlying marketplace damages. Cf. *Podiatric Physicians*, 185 F.3d at 618.

Distinct from Schmitt's argument that damage control costs are not recoverable without a showing of actual confusion is its assertion that damage control costs are not recoverable in the absence of "actual damages" or, we assume, marketplace damages. But we find that argument similarly unacceptable. No court has excluded damage control costs from its definition of damages that are considered "actual." And several courts have awarded damages for the expense of responsive or reparative advertising quite apart from an award of marketplace damages. See, e.g., *ALPO Petfoods, Inc. v. Ralston Purina Co.*, supra; U-Haul Int'l, Inc. v. Jartran, Inc., 793 F.2d 1034, 1041 (9th Cir. 1986); Otis Clapp & Son, Inc. v. Filmore Vitamin Co., 754 F.2d 738, 745 (7th Cir. 1985). Although none of these courts have awarded damage control costs in the absence of marketplace damages, none have treated marketplace injury as a prerequisite to recovery of damage control costs either. Moreover, a rule that predicated recovery of damage control expenses on a showing of marketplace damages would penalize successful efforts at mitigating damages. That is, under such a rule, a plaintiff who is successful in preventing marketplace damages would not be able to recover under the Lanham Act, but a plaintiff who is unsuccessful would be permitted to recover. That would be an anomaly.

We also note that the practical realities of business litigation favor a rule that damage control costs should be recoverable even where plaintiffs do not demonstrate actual confusion or marketplace injury. For one, marketplace damages and actual confusion are notoriously difficult and expensive to prove. See PPX Enterprises, Inc. v. Audiofidelity Enterprises, Inc., 818 F.2d at 272-73; U-Haul Int'l, Inc. v. Jartran, Inc., 793 F.2d at 1041. More importantly, however, even where marketplace damages or actual confusion are provable in theory, such proof often requires that a plaintiff solicit its own customers for affidavits, which puts the customers at risk of being subpoenaed by the defendant. Plaintiffs are justifiably hesitant to alienate or upset their customers in this way. In addition, plaintiffs may hesitate to put marketplace damages at issue because that would entitle a defendant to discover information about plaintiff's business. As may have been the case here, oftentimes the rational business decision is for a plaintiff to embark on a campaign of damage control and forego a demonstration of injury in the marketplace or actual confusion of their customers. Such a plaintiff should not be required to give up compensation for its damage control expenses when the defendant's wrongful action necessitated those expenses in the first place.

Nor should plaintiffs who are unwilling or unable to prove marketplace damages or actual confusion be limited to seeking injunctive relief. An injunction can halt a wrongful activity but it will not correct its effects. Responsive advertising may be the quickest, most effective way to mitigate damages or prevent them altogether. Further, limiting a plaintiff to injunctive relief is especially unfair where a plaintiff's inability to prove marketplace damages or actual confusion may merely reflect an understandable unwillingness to irk customers as the plaintiff pursues proof of harm.

Therefore, because a company may justifiably act before it actually sustains injury, standards similar to those applicable to injunctive relief are appropriate where plaintiffs seek to recover damage control expenses. Hence, to recover loss control damages, plaintiffs must show that a violation of the Lanham Act occurred, and that (1) there was a likelihood of confusion or damages to sales, profits, or goodwill; (2) its damage control expenses are attributable to the violation (i.e., caused by the violation); and (3) that its damage control efforts were reasonable under the circumstances and proportionate to the damage that was likely to occur.

B. Damage to Goodwill

Although Balance Dynamics stipulated that it suffered no lost sales or change in financial condition, it reserved the right to seek, inter alia, damages to its goodwill. To recover for damage to goodwill, the plaintiff bears the burden of proof. Web Printing Controls Co., Inc. v. Oxy-Dry Corp., 906 F.2d at 1204-05; Lithuanian Commerce Corp. v. Sara Lee Hosiery, 47 F. Supp. 2d 523, 533 (D.N.J. 1999). Schmitt contends that Balance Dynamics offered no evidence that its goodwill or reputation within the industry was actually damaged by Schmitt's communications. But Balance Dynamics presented evidence of the literal falsity of the Schmitt advertisements and also contended that Schmitt violated the Lanham Act with deliberate intent and bad faith. Though the "actual confusion" rule would ordinarily preclude Balance Dynamics' claim for goodwill, in certain circumstances the literal falsity of an advertisement or evidence of deliberate intent or bad faith has sufficed to entitle a plaintiff to certain forms of relief or to create a presumption of damages in the marketplace. The trial court seems to have acknowledged this in stating that literal falsity could prove the existence of actual confusion. However, we hold that in the present case, evidence of literal falsity and deliberate intent or bad faith does not entitle Balance Dynamics to recover money for damages to goodwill.

1. Literal Falsity

Because proof of "actual confusion" can be difficult to obtain, Lindy Pen Co. Inc. v. Bic Pen Corp., 982 F.2d 1400, 1407 (9th Cir. 1993), most of the circuits have ruled that when a statement is literally false, a plaintiff need not demonstrate actual customer deception in order to obtain relief under the Lanham Act. However, the "literal falsity" rule has never permitted a plaintiff to recover marketplace damages without other proof that such damages occurred. Rather, this rule has been stated in suits in which the plaintiff sought injunctive relief . . . ; or marketplace damages were not awarded under the Lanham Act; or literal falsity was accompanied by other proof of marketplace damages.

At trial, Balance Dynamics attempted to show that Schmitt's advertisements were literally false. But the above cases demonstrate that literal falsity, without more, is insufficient to support an award of money damages to compensate for marketplace injury such as harm to goodwill. A contrary rule would risk conferring an undue windfall on Balance Dynamics. Balance Dynamics presented no evidence that its goodwill was harmed, or that customers were actually deceived by its advertisement. To the contrary, the evidence indicated that Balance Dynamics' business was not harmed by Schmitt's letters. Balance Dynamics' sales increased after the period in question, and there was no decrease in the price of its product. Further, Balance Dynamics admitted that no customers had ever informed it that it was losing a sale due to the Schmitt communications. While literal falsehood or the likelihood of deception may be sufficient to entitle Balance Dynamics to injunctive relief or reimbursement for responsive advertising, it should not permit Balance Dynamics to recover for injuries to goodwill in the absence of some more substantial indication that these injuries actually occurred. Cf. BASF Corp. v. Old World Trading Co., 41 F.3d at 1085-88 (finding literal falsity but requiring further proof of marketplace damages); Castrol, Inc. v. Pennzoil, 987 F.2d 939, 941-43 (3d Cir. 1993) (affirming trial court decision granting injunctive relief but denying monetary damages despite finding of literal falsity).

2. Deliberate Intent or Bad Faith

Though literal falsity alone does not raise an inference of damage to goodwill, some courts have created a presumption of damages when literal falsity is accompanied by deliberate intent or bad faith. The Ninth Circuit reasons that

> the expenditure by a competitor of substantial funds in an effort to deceive consumers and influence their purchasing decisions justifies the existence of a presumption that consumers are, in fact, being deceived. He who has attempted to deceive should not complain when required to bear the burden of rebutting a presumption that he has succeeded.

U-Haul Int'l, Inc. v. Jartran, Inc., 793 F.2d at 1040-41; see also Southland Sod Farms v. Stover Seed Co., 108 F.3d 1134, 1146 (9th Cir. 1997); Resource Developers, Inc. v. Statue of Liberty-Ellis Island Foundation, Inc., 926 F.2d 134, 140 (2d Cir. 1991).

In Porous Media Corp. v. Pall Corp., 110 F.3d 1329 (8th Cir. 1997), the court followed the Ninth Circuit's reasoning and permitted a presumption of money damages where there existed proof of willful deception. Id. at 1336. However, acknowledging that a plaintiff seeking monetary relief under the Lanham Act generally must meet a higher level of proof than those seeking injunctive relief, the court clarified the presumptive damages rule as extending only to cases of comparative advertising where the plaintiff's product was specifically targeted. Id. at 1334-35. Otherwise, stated the *Porous Media* court, "a plaintiff might enjoy a windfall from a speculative award of damages by simply being a competitor in the same market." Id.; see also Harper House, Inc. v. Thomas Nelson, Inc., 889 F.2d 197, 209 fn. 8 (9th Cir. 1989).

The reasoning of *Porous Media* is applicable to the present case since Schmitt specifically targeted Balance Dynamics' balancer, which was the only product of its kind in the market. However, as stated above, the evidence shows that Balance Dynamics did not suffer marketplace injury as a result of Schmitt's advertisements. Therefore, even if the advertisements were found literally false and Balance Dynamics presented evidence of willfulness or bad faith, the evidence defeats any presumption of damage to goodwill in the present case.

C. *Disgorgement*

. . . Balance Dynamics argued that because it could show that Schmitt knowingly and willfully made false statements, it was entitled to disgorgement of profits. In a closely reasoned R & R, Magistrate Judge Pepe rejected this contention and found that Balance Dynamics was only entitled to disgorgement if it could show that defendant gained additional sales due to the advertisement, or that plaintiff lost sales, or was forced to see its product at a lower price. As Magistrate Judge Pepe pointed out, § 35(a) of the Lanham Act makes clear that an award of damages shall be "subject to the principles of equity" but also states that the award is to "constitute compensation and not a penalty." Reviewing the legislative history and case law concerning disgorgement of profits, Magistrate Judge Pepe concluded that unless there is some proof that plaintiff lost sales or profits, or that defendant gained them, the principles of equity do not warrant an award of defendant's profits. We agree with and adopt Magistrate Judge Pepe's reasoning.[6]

VI. Trial Court's Findings of Fact

. . . Balance Dynamics contests the trial court's finding that its damage control activities were an over-reaction to the problem. The trial court made the following factual determinations:

> the evidence really taken as a whole shows what happened here. Plaintiff got a copy of this letter just as Mr. Schulte testified, called a few of his partners together and began to over-react something horrible, and ran out and tried to, quote, put out the fire, when no fire was ever testified to. I don't know what fire the plaintiff is talking about. There was just no fire produced for this Court. . . . That damage that you called loss control is an over-reaction by the Plaintiff that I think the evidence on liability makes it very clear, you didn't

6. We do not believe that the "deterrence theory," in which one of the trial court's primary functions is to make violations of the Lanham Act unprofitable to the infringing party, See Wynn Oil Co. v. American Way Service Corp., 943 F.2d 595, 606-07 (6th Cir. 1991) (citing Roulo v. Russ Berrie & Co., 886 F.2d 931, 941 (7th Cir. 1989)), supports disgorgement in this case. As Magistrate Judge Pepe noted, the cases awarding profits under the deterrence theory upon a finding of willfulness or bad faith have been infringement cases "where defendant benefits directly from its wrongful conduct." See, e.g., International Star Class Yacht Racing Ass'n v. Tommy Hilfiger, U.S.A., Inc., 80 F.3d 749, 753 (2d Cir. 1996); Roulo v. Russ Berrie & Co., Inc., 886 F.2d at 941. Even in false advertising cases, disgorgement has not been awarded in the absence of harm to the plaintiff or benefit to the defendant. See, e.g., U-Haul Int'l v. Jartran, Inc., 793 F.2d at 1036.

> even have to do it. You could have handled half of these customers on the telephone, but more importantly his customers included sophisticated engineers at Ford Motor Car Company, the other auto manufacturers and big companies. Engineers know just exactly what those standards are, just exactly what . . . the EPA rulings are . . . frankly I have no idea why this case has been hanging around the court for three and a half years.

Balance Dynamics protests this finding on the grounds that Mr. Schulte had testified that, after the letter was disseminated, some of his customers contacted him in reference to its claims. Schulte further stated that of those companies with whom he had initiated contact, most had received the letter. Schulte testified that his customers told him "they didn't want to necessarily have anything to do with a product that had these stipulations associated with it." He also testified that many customers were concerned about the regulation and disposal of the Balance Dynamics products.

Obviously, the trial court did not have the benefit of an articulated standard for recovery of damage control costs. Under that standard, the testimony above contradicts the trial court's conclusion that Balance Dynamics failed to put on evidence showing the existence of a "fire" to put out. The customer inquiries Balance Dynamics received could be taken as proof of the likelihood of damage, cf. Harper House, Inc. v. Thomas Nelson, Inc., 889 F.2d at 210; PPX Enterprises, Inc. v. Audiofidelity Enterprises, Inc., 818 F.2d at 272, and may suffice to show that the deception was material and likely to influence a purchasing decision. Further, the customer inquiries belie the proposition that Balance Dynamics' customers are so familiar with EPA regulations that Schmitt's communications would not be off-putting. Therefore, this evidence creates a material issue of fact and the trial court should have let the matter go to a jury for determination. Jackson v. Quanex, 191 F.3d at 647. . . .

COMMENTS AND QUESTIONS

1. *Lost Profits.* Proving that the defendant's false advertising diverted sales from plaintiff to defendant is not easy, as the common law single source rule reminds us. Nevertheless, plaintiffs sometimes do succeed on this theory. *See, e.g.*, Porous Media Corp. v. Pall Corp., 110 F.3d 1329, 1335 (8th Cir. 1997) (stating that "[a] plaintiff suing to enjoin conduct that violates the Lanham Act need not prove specific damage," but that "courts require a heightened level of proof of injury in order to recover money damages"; nevertheless affirming judgment for plaintiff in the amount of $1.5 million resulting from willfully false comparative advertising). Alternatively, in BASF Corp. v. Old World Trading Co., 41 F.3d 1081, 1092-95 (7th Cir. 1994), the Seventh Circuit approved the use of a market-share approach:

> . . . Since the parties' all-or-nothing theories of damages were inconsistent with the district court's finding that BASF proved that it would have made some of the sales absent Old World, the district court was required to adopt a different method of calculating damages. The district court's choice of market share analysis logically follows from its finding that although prices drove some customers away from BASF, ordinary market forces would have pulled some sales back had Old World competed fairly in the market. We cannot conclude that the court erred by determining lost profits according to market shares.

2. Lost profits sometimes may arise from consequences other than loss of sales. In the *ALPO* case on remand, the district court awarded ALPO lost profits damages resulting from ALPO's having deferred its national expansion in reaction to Ralston's CHD campaign. On appeal once again, the D.C. Circuit affirmed the lost profits award but warned against double counting for prejudgment interest (why would this be a concern?). *See* ALPO Petfoods, Inc. v. Ralston Purina Co., 997 F.2d 949, 953-54 (D.C. Cir. 1993) (D.H. Ginsburg, J.). The court also approved the use of regression analysis to estimate each side's lost profits from diverted sales, as well as the district court's conclusion that Ralston nevertheless failed to prove "the magnitude of the effect that ALPO's advertisements had upon Ralston's profits." *Id.* at 955.

3. Where the defendant engaged in commercial disparagement, as opposed to false advertising, it sometimes may be easier to prove lost profits. (As you may recall, special damages are an element of common law commercial disparagement, though not of the corresponding Lanham Act claim for commercial disparagement. *See supra* for discussion of the "special damages" element in common law disparagement.) When *Procter & Gamble Co. v. Haugen* returned to the district court, for example, the jury returned a verdict for the plaintiff in the amount of $19.25 million. The district judge denied the defendants' post-trial motion for judgment as a matter of law, reasoning that (1) the literally false nature of the "Church of Satan" rumor gave rise to a presumption of actual consumer confusion, which the defendants did not rebut; (2) the evidence of proximate cause and damages consisted of more than just "chronology," including expert testimony comparing P & G's sales of targeted and nontargeted products. *See* Procter & Gamble Co. v. Haugen, 627 F. Supp. 2d 1287, 1290-93 (D. Utah 2008).

4. *Loss of Goodwill.* In *Balance Dynamics*, the court agrees with the Eighth and Ninth Circuits that injury can be presumed when the defendant engaged in willful deception, though only in "cases of comparative advertising where the plaintiff's product was specifically targeted." *Balance Dynamics*, 204 F.3d at 694. Because the defendant in *Balance Dynamics* had engaged in willfully deceptive comparative advertising, the presumption of injury to the plaintiff's goodwill came into play. Nevertheless, the defendant successfully rebutted the presumption by showing that "Balance Dynamics did not suffer marketplace injury as a result of Schmitt's advertisements." *Id.* *Compare* Porous Media Corp. v. Pall Corp., 173 F.3d 1109, 1122-23 (8th Cir. 1999) (affirming an award of $1.6 million for loss of goodwill, citing testimony and documentary evidence on fact and amount of injury.

5. *Responsive Advertising and Other Damage Control Costs.* As in trademark cases, damages for responsive advertising may be an appropriate remedy in false advertising cases. Both *ALPO* and *Balance Dynamics* hold that courts may award damages for responsive advertising expenses or other damage control costs already incurred by the plaintiff, but only to the extent these expenses were reasonably necessary to counter the defendant's false advertising. *See ALPO*, 913 F.2d at 969; *Balance Dynamics*, 204 F.3d at 692-93. When the *ALPO* case returned to the D.C. Circuit after remand, that court largely rejected Ralston's challenge to a $3.6 million award entered by the district court against Ralston for the cost of ALPO's responsive advertising. *See ALPO*, 997 F.2d at 951-53. Courts sometimes award damages to fund the plaintiff's *future* corrective advertising campaign as well. *See* Big O Tire Dealers, Inc. v. Goodyear Tire & Rubber Co., 561 F.2d 1365, 1375-76 (10th Cir. 1977) (trademark case); Callaway Golf Co. v. Slazenger, 384 F. Supp. 2d 735, 740-41 (D. Del. 2005) (noting the potential availability of such damages in false advertising cases, but denying them

where the products at issue had "long since been off the market").[37] Courts need to be careful, however, that awards for future advertising are reasonably necessary to restore the status quo ante and are not merely a windfall. *See* Zazu Designs v. L'Oreal S.A., 979 F.2d 499, 506-07 (7th Cir. 1992).

6. *Disgorgement.* The *ALPO* case states the traditional rule that plaintiffs may not obtain an award of the defendant's profits in false advertising (or trademark infringement) actions absent proof that the defendant's conduct was willful. *See ALPO*, 913 F.2d at 968 (limiting such damages to cases in which defendant acted willfully or in bad faith). As noted in Chapter 8 *supra*, however, some courts no longer view willfulness as a precondition to an award of defendant's profits, and may consider a variety of factors in deciding whether to order such an award. *See, e.g.*, Logan v. Burgers Ozark Country Cured Hams, 263 F.3d 447, 464-65 (5th Cir. 2001) (holding that where the plaintiff fails "to present evidence that the defendant benefitted from the alleged false advertising, the plaintiff will not be permitted to recover any of the defendant's profits"); *Balance Dynamics*, 204 F.3d at 695 (agreeing that "unless there is some proof that plaintiff lost sales or profits, or that defendant gained them, the principles of equity do not warrant an award of defendant's profits"); *BASF Corp.*, 41 F.3d at 1096 ("[D]isgorgement is most appropriate if damages are otherwise nominal. . . .").

2. Injunctions

ALPO Petfoods, Inc. v. Ralston Purina Co.
913 F.2d 958 (D.C. Cir. 1990)

[The facts and the portion of the case discussing damages are excerpted in section I.1 above]

E. Scope of Injunction Against Ralston

In addition to awarding monetary relief, the district court enjoined both parties to prepare, secure court approval of, and disseminate corrective releases, and it enjoined both parties from renewing their false advertising. In the only challenge leveled at these injunctions, Ralston asserts that the prohibitory injunction against it is overbroad, both on its face and as implemented by the district court. We agree, and remand the relevant orders for entry and implementation of a narrower injunction.

The injunction at issue permanently bars Ralston and its associates "from making any advertising or other related claims that are false, misleading, deceptive or made without substantiation in fact concerning the effects of Ralston Dog food products on hip joint formation, hip joint laxity, Canine Hip Dysplasia, Degenerative Joint Disease and similar conditions." *ALPO*, 720 F. Supp. at 216. The court also ordered Ralston and ALPO to adopt procedures for ensuring compliance with the injunction. Id. at 217. Ralston and ALPO have complied, and an October 11, 1989 district court order formalizes the procedures, which are themselves a subject of appeal. See supra note 2.

37. In other cases, an injunction may require the defendant to engage in corrective advertising. *See* Rhone-Poulenc Rorer Pharms., Inc. v. Marion Merrell Dow, Inc., 93 F.3d 511, 516 (8th Cir. 1996); *see also* the excerpt below from the *ALPO* court's discussion of injunctive relief.

The relevant section of these procedures subjects "any advertising or other related claim concerning the effects of Ralston dog or puppy food products or low anion gap diets on hip joint formation, hip joint laxity, canine hip dysplasia, degenerative joint disease, and similar conditions" to a pre-clearance process. Procedures for Assuring Compliance with Injunctive Provisions of July 28, 1989 Order para. 5(b) (Oct. 11, 1989); see id. paras. 6-8. Before releasing any statement in this category, Ralston must have a court-approved "outside attorney" write an opinion on whether the proposed statement violates the injunctions. Id. paras. 6-7. Ralston must submit the statement and the attorney's opinion letter to ALPO and the court, which then have fifteen days to object before Ralston can make its statement. Id. para. 8.

Since the district court originally entered its injunctions, it has decided that the prohibitory injunction applies to Ralston and non-Ralston scientists' scholarly articles on the anion gap theory, even when those articles do not refer to Ralston products. See Transcript of Motions Hearing at 20-22 (Sept. 18, 1989) (scientists who publish any such articles without getting court's advance approval "do it at their risk," id. at 22); see also id. at 22, 25-26 (suggesting that scientists could secure court's approval by referring in article to court's fact findings). In addition, a few weeks before the court approved the compliance procedures, it threatened Ralston with contempt for stating, in response to a veterinary journal's inquiry, that Ralston disagreed with the district court's ruling and planned to appeal. See Transcript of Status Call at 19-21 (Sept. 22, 1989); see also Reotutar, *Pet Food Makers Found Guilty of False Advertising Claims*, 195 J. AM. VETERINARY MED. ASS'N 873 (1989) (reporting Ralston's statement, which Ralston unsuccessfully tried to retract after court demanded immediate retraction).

The law requires that courts closely tailor injunctions to the harm that they address. Gulf Oil Corp. v. Brock, 778 F.2d 834, 842 (D.C. Cir. 1985); see also *Foxtrap*, 671 F.2d at 640 ("[T]he scope of an injunction should be determined by balancing [the] harm to the plaintiff, other means of avoiding such harm, and the relative inconvenience to the defendant."); FED. R. CIV. P. 65(d) (injunctive orders "shall be specific in terms"). In enjoining Ralston, the district court identified the harm redressed by the injunctions as deception of puppy food buyers and erosion of ALPO's business. See *ALPO*, 720 F. Supp. at 214-15. Yet the prohibitory injunction, both as entered and, particularly, as implemented, suppresses more speech than protecting these interests requires. ALPO's false-advertising claim against Ralston involves a dispute over whether Ralston may commercially claim that Puppy Chow confers certain unproved health benefits. Redressing the harm that these claims have caused in the puppy food market does not require that a court supervise all future debate on the anion gap theory. Moreover, we see little prospect that readers of a veterinary magazine who encounter a report on the false-advertising judgment against Ralston will conclude, simply because Ralston has had an opportunity to proclaim its innocence, that Puppy Chow actually ameliorates CHD. Especially given the prior restraint involved in the procedures described above, we think it important that the injunction and procedures cover only the speech most likely to deceive consumers and harm ALPO in the ways described in the district court's opinion: CHD-related advertising. See Better Business Bureau v. Medical Directors, Inc., 681 F.2d 397, 404-05 (5th Cir. 1982) (narrowing injunction to remove ban on noncommercial statements).

We remand the prohibitory injunction against Ralston, 720 F. Supp. at 216, for removal of the words "or other related," and remand the October 11, 1989 order for removal of the words "or other related" from paragraphs 5(b) and 8 and the words "or related" from paragraph 6. These changes, which limit the injunction and procedures to advertising, will tailor the injunction to the harms attacked by ALPO's section 43(a) claim.

COMMENTS AND QUESTIONS

1. Not surprisingly, plaintiffs in false advertising cases typically seek injunctive relief, namely in the form of an order that the defendant cease its alleged false advertising. *See* Lanham Act § 34(a), 15 U.S.C. § 1116(a) (authorizing courts to grant injunctions to prevent violations of § 43(a)). Since false advertising threatens to harm both the plaintiff and consumers, courts almost always accede to a request for injunctive relief if the plaintiff succeeds in proving its case. As in *ALPO*, however, difficult issues sometimes may arise in deciding how broadly to craft an injunction: Should the injunction forbid only the precise advertising at issue, or other similar advertising? If the latter, how similar must the forbidden advertising be? Are there any First Amendment issues (such as overbreadth) lurking here? For other Lanham Act decisions expressing concern over overly broad injunctions, see Osmose, Inc. v. Viance, LLC, 612 F.3d 1298, 1322-23 (11th Cir. 2010); U'Haul Int'l, Inc. v. Jartran, Inc., 793 F.2d 1034, 1042-43 (9th Cir. 1986).

2. Overbreadth issues also can arise in the context of FTC cease-and-desist orders. In the *Kraft* case discussed above in section D, however, the Seventh Circuit did not find the defendant's overbreadth argument persuasive:

> The Commission's cease and desist order prohibits Kraft from running the Skimp and Class Picture ads, as well as from advertising any calcium or nutritional claims not supported by reliable scientific evidence. This order extends not only to the product contained in the deceptive advertisements (Kraft Singles), but to all Kraft cheeses and cheese-related products, which include Cracker Barrel, Velveeta, and Philadelphia Brand Cream Cheese. Kraft contends this order is too broad and must be set-aside or modified because it (1) bans constitutionally protected commercial speech, and (2) is not rationally related to Kraft's violation of the Act. . . .
>
> First amendment infirmities arise, according to Kraft, from the sweep of the order: by banning commercial speech that is only *potentially* misleading, the order chills some non-deceptive advertising deserving of constitutional protection. Kraft acknowledges that sweeping bans of this variety comport with traditional FTC practice, *see, e.g., Cliffdale Assocs.*, 103 F.T.C. at 165, and have been repeatedly upheld against first amendment challenges in the past. It nonetheless again relies on the Supreme Court's recent decision in *Peel*, 496 U.S. 91 (plurality); *id.* at 111 (concurrence), in attacking the FTC's order. . . .
>
> Kraft asserts that its advertisements are only potentially misleading, like the letterhead statement in *Peel*, because the milk equivalency and imitation superiority claims are true and verifiable, there is no evidence that these claims actually misled consumers, and the advertising medium is not inherently conducive to deception. Alternative remedial measures were readily available to the Commission, such as modifications to the ads or prominent disclosures, and thus, Kraft contends, the order is broader than reasonably necessary to prevent deception. Moreover, Kraft asserts the order put the onus on it to come up with nonmisleading alternatives in contravention of *Peel.*
>
> We reject Kraft's argument. To begin with, the Commission determined that the ads were *actually* misleading, not *potentially* misleading, thus justifying a total ban on the challenged ads. Moreover, even if we were to assume the order bans some potentially misleading speech, it is only constitutionally defective if it is no "broader than reasonably

necessary to prevent the [deception]." We conclude that it is sufficiently narrow to pass constitutional muster. . . .

To reiterate, the FTC's order does two things: it prohibits the Skimp ads and the Class Picture ads (as *currently* designed) and it requires Kraft to base future nutrient and calcium claims on reliable scientific evidence. Kraft mischaracterizes the decision as a categorical ban on commercial speech when in fact it identifies with particularity two nutrient claims that the Commission found actually misleading and prohibits only those claims. It further places on Kraft the (minor) burden of supporting future nutrient claims with reliable data. This leaves Kraft free to use any advertisement it chooses, including the Skimp and Class Picture ads, so long as it either eliminates the elements specifically identified by the FTC as contributing to consumer deception or corrects this inaccurate impression by adding prominent, unambiguous disclosures. *See, e.g., Removatron*, 884 F.2d at 1497. We note one additional consideration further alleviating first amendment concerns; Kraft, like any party to an FTC order, may seek an advisory opinion from the Commission as to whether any future advertisements comply with its order, 16 C.F.R. §2.41(d), and this procedure has been specifically cited by courts as one method of reducing advertiser uncertainty. . . .

Alternatively, Kraft argues that the scope of the order is not "reasonably related" to Kraft's violation of the Act because it extends to products that were not the subject of the challenged advertisements. The FTC has discretion to issue multi-product orders, so-called "fencing-in" orders, that extend beyond violations of the Act to prevent violators from engaging in similar deceptive practices in the future. Such an order must be sufficiently clear that it is comprehensible to the violator, and must be "reasonably relat[ed]" to a violation of the Act. *Colgate-Palmolive*, 380 U.S. at 394-95. Kraft does not challenge the order's clarity or precision but only its reasonableness.

In determining whether a broad fencing-in order bears a "reasonable relationship" to a violation of the Act, the Commission considers (1) the deliberateness and seriousness of the violation, (2) the degree of transferability of the violation to other products, and (3) any history of prior violations. . . .

We find substantial evidence to support the scope of the order. The Commission based its finding of seriousness on the size ($15 million annually) and duration (two and one-half years) of the ad campaign and on the difficulty most consumers would face in judging the truth or falsity of the implied calcium claims. . . .

The Commission further found that the violations were readily transferable to other Kraft cheese products given the general similarity between Singles and other Kraft cheeses. . . . We conclude that the FTC's finding of transferability was also reasonable. . . .

. . . [T]he FTC reasonably concluded that the seriousness, deliberateness, and transferability of the violations took precedence over the absence of any prior Kraft violations.

Kraft, Inc. v. FTC, 970 F.2d 311, 324-27 (7th Cir. 1992) (some internal citations and section letters omitted).

10 The Right of Publicity

A. OVERVIEW

1. History and Rationales

The right of publicity protects an individual's marketable image or persona. The right developed in response to the rise of mass advertising and the growing recognition that a celebrity's imprimatur on a product or even association of a product with a celebrity's persona enhances its appeal to consumers. This right affords individuals a property-type interest in the use of their name, likeness, photograph, portrait, voice, and other personal characteristics in connection with the marketing of products and services. Jurisdictions approach publicity rights in a variety of ways.

The modern right of publicity reflects two distinct rationales — one grounded in privacy and the other in economic exploitation. The privacy branch can be traced back to an influential law review article published in the late nineteenth century. *See* Samuel D. Warren & Louis D. Brandeis, *The Right to Privacy*, 4 HARV. L. REV. 193 (1890). Lamenting technological and cultural developments invading the private sphere, Warren and Brandeis advocated a right of privacy to forbid the publication of idle gossip and restore "propriety and dignity" to the press. Legislatures and courts gradually came to recognize this interest. New York led the way with its privacy law, enacted in 1903, banning the unauthorized use of "the name, portrait or picture of any living persons" for "advertising purposes, or for purposes of trade."[1] The privacy right was quite limited in practice. Courts tended to view celebrities as inviting exploitation of their image and

1. The New York statute was enacted in response to a New York Court of Appeals decision holding that a plaintiff had failed to state a claim for emotional distress, based upon the unauthorized use of his photograph in a commercial advertisement. *See* Roberson v. Rochester Folding Box Co., 64 N.E.2d 442, 447-48 (N.Y. 1902). The first major case recognizing a cause of action on similar facts was the Georgia Supreme Court's 1905 decision in Pavesich v. New England Life Insurance Co., 50 S.E. 68 (Ga. 1905).

were reluctant to find the mere use of their image, even in advertising, to suggest endorsement. For example, in O'Brien v. Pabst Sales Co., 124 F.2d 167, 170 (5th Cir. 1941), the court held that a nationally famous football player who disapproved of alcohol consumption had no claim against a beer distributor that used his picture on a calendar advertising its product, because the player had actively sought publicity in other contexts. And even when liability was found in some cases, recovery was limited to the personal injury suffered, as opposed to the economic value to the advertiser.

As a result, celebrities pushed for stronger protection for the economic value of their image. In 1953, the Second Circuit found such a right in New York's common law, which it dubbed the "right of publicity." *See* Haelen Laboratories, Inc. v. Topps Chewing Gum, 202 F.2d 866 (2d Cir. 1953). In that case, Haelan had negotiated exclusive licenses from several Major League Baseball players authorizing the use of their images on baseball cards that it included with packs of gum. Topps sold its own gum with photographs of the same players. Although ruling that New York's statutory privacy law did not extend to such uses, the court ruled that "a man has a right in the publicity value of his photograph, i.e., the right to grant the exclusive privilege of publishing the picture, and that such a grant may validly be made 'in gross,' i.e., without an accompanying transfer of a business or of anything else" under New York's common law.[2] The concept was refined in a subsequent law review article by Melville Nimmer, *The Right of Publicity*, 19 Law & Contemp. Probs. 203 (1954). Beginning in the 1970s, a number of states enacted "publicity" statutes, which continue to evolve today. Today, 16 states recognize common law rights of publicity, and another 15 states have codified the right of publicity in statute. Some states, like California, recognize both statutory and common law sources for this form of protection. New York's statutory privacy and publicity protections are embodied in a single statute. For a discussion of this history, see Stacey L. Dogan & Mark A. Lemley, *What the Right of Publicity Can Learn from Trademark Law*, 58 Stan. L. Rev. 1161 (2006).

Why might a state wish to gratify an individual's interest in protecting the commercial value of her name and likeness, as a type of property right? Courts and commentators have suggested (and critiqued) the following possible rationales for extending the right of publicity beyond merely the protection of personal privacy interests:

Labor. Some theorists have proposed that publicity rights may be justified on the basis of a Lockean labor rationale. *See* Michael Madow, *Private Ownership of Public Image*, 81 Cal. L. Rev. 127, 175 (1993) (discussing, but not supporting, this rationale). You may recall from other intellectual property (or real property) courses John Locke's argument that mixing one's labor with the "commons" gives rise to a moral entitlement to the "fruit" of that labor, on the ground that one who appropriates that "fruit" without consent takes the labor that went creating into. *See* John Locke, An Essay Concerning the Original Extent and End of Civil Government 26-27 (Boston, Edes & Gill 1773).

Locke himself never extended the theory to intellectual products, however; and philosophers and property theorists have been debating its applicability to real, personal, and intellectual property for centuries. Critics have noted, for example, that an entitlement to the fruit of our intellectual labor, if taken to its logical

2. Ironically, Stephano v. News Group Publications, Inc., 64 N.Y.2d 174 (1984), held that *Haelan* had misinterpreted New York law, and that there was no right of publicity independent of the privacy protections in §§ 50 and 51 of the New York Civil Rights Law.

conclusion, would curtail practically *all* free-riding, including the free-riding on facts and ideas that intellectual property law generally views as a social good. For general discussion of the Lockean rationale and its critics, see William W. Fisher III, *Theories of Intellectual Property*, *in* NEW ESSAYS IN THE LEGAL AND POLITICAL THEORY OF PROPERTY (Stephen Munzer ed., 2001).

Even assuming that Locke's theory has some purchase with respect to some forms of intellectual property, however, does it make sense to apply the theory to personal names and other such indicia of identity? To be sure, people sometimes do invest considerable labor (and other effort) into creating a memorable "persona"; but that consideration seems more relevant to the value of the right than to its justification. Moreover, even with respect to celebrities, don't lots of other entities (fans, managers, agents) have a good deal to do with creating the value of the persona?

Autonomy. Professor Mark McKenna argues that publicity rights protect the individual's interest in preserving his or her ability to exercise autonomous self-definition. *See* Mark McKenna, *The Right of Publicity and Autonomous Self-Definition*, 57 U. PITT. L. REV. 225, 279-93 (2005). McKenna argues that the unauthorized use of a person's name or image so as to associate that person with a product or service against his will compromises the individual's ability to define who he is. McKenna cites as one example of such a compromising use a situation involving the elderly (noncelebrity) grandfather of a friend, who was surprised to see his image being used in an advertisement for an erectile dysfunction drug. McKenna argues further that this autonomy rationale provides a basis for extending publicity rights to celebrities and others who generally seek out publicity. The unauthorized use of football player Davy O'Brien's picture in connection with beer may not have invaded O'Brien's privacy, but (particularly given his stand against drinking) it did compromise his autonomy. *See id.* at 284-85 (discussing O'Brien v. Pabst Sales Co., 124 F.2d 167 (5th Cir. 1941)).

A variation on this rationale derives from the Kantian/Hegelian view of private property as being invested with the owner's inalienable will or personality. This perspective has influenced much of European copyright law, in particular the doctrine of "moral rights." Some theorists have argued that the "personality" theory provides a justification for publicity rights as well, reasoning that a person's public persona, like her works of authorship, manifest an investment of inalienable personality. See Alice Haemmerli, *Whose Who? The Case for a Kantian Right of Publicity*, 49 DUKE L.J. 383 (1999).[3] One possible problem with this theory as providing a general rationale for publicity rights is that moral rights have made only limited headway in American law; another is that, to the extent the personality rationale explains publicity rights, it might suggest that these rights are (like moral rights in copyright) not transferrable (though they might be descendible). And is it any more true, as a general matter, that a person's name or other indicia of identity reflect her unique personality than it is true, as a general matter, that these indicia reflect her labor?

Incentives. Another possibility is that the right of publicity, like some other types of intellectual property, serves a utilitarian purpose of providing an incentive for

3. Haemmerli's theory in some respects anticipates McKenna's, by characterizing publicity rights as serving an autonomy interest. The theories differ in that Haemmerli stresses the investment of personality as a ground for characterizing the right as a property right, whereas McKenna focuses more on emotional harms.

people to invest in creating and publicizing some sort of public good. In Zacchini v. Scripps-Howard Broadcasting Co., 433 U.S. 562, 575 (1977) (excerpted below at pp. 518 and 523 n.6), for example, the Supreme Court commented that "protecting the proprietary interest of the individual in his act" serves in part "to encourage such entertainment," which is "closely analogous to the goals of patent and copyright law." Although it seems unlikely that failure to protect uses of a celebrity's image would discourage the pursuit of fame generally, *see* Diane Leenheer Zimmerman, *Fitting Publicity Rights into Intellectual Property and Free Speech Theory: Sam, You Made the Pants Too Long!*, 10 DePaul-LCA J. Art & Ent. L. & Pol'y 283, 306 (2000) (observing that "not a shred of empirical data exists to show that [celebrities] would invest less energy and talent in becoming famous" without a publicity right), the absence of protection could discourage some performers and interfere with licensing deals that might fund particular creative projects. As you read through the cases below, ask yourself whether these are likely to be such cases. What would such a rationale say about the proper scope of the right of publicity doctrine?

A second utilitarian theory holds that failure to protect a celebrity's image could produce a congestion externality. Under this theory, the value of an image can be inefficiently depleted by oversaturation of the marketplace, which an exclusive right to exploit can prevent. *See* William M. Landes & Richard A. Posner, The Economic Structure of Intellectual Property Law 222-28 (2003); Mark Grady, *A Positive Economic Theory of the Right of Publicity*, 1 UCLA Ent. L. Rev. 97 (1994). Landes and Posner point to the Disney Corporation's self-imposed restraint on commercialization as a response to this problem: "To avoid overkill, Disney manages its character portfolio with care. It has hundreds of characters on its books, many of them just waiting to be called out of retirement. . . . Disney practices good husbandry of its characters and extends the life of its brands by not overexposing them. . . . They avoid debasing the currency." *See* B. Britt, *International Marketing: Disney's Global Goals*, Marketing 22-26 (May 17, 1990). Landes and Posner suggest that a similar oversaturation can arise with regard to some rights of publicity (use of persona in advertising) and trademarks (justifying protection against dilution by blurring). Do you find this argument persuasive? Does this theory apply to all celebrity images? If so, how do we account for nearly ubiquitous images, such as Mickey Mouse, Britney Spears, and the Coca-Cola logo? For images that survive without any protection, such as Uncle Sam or the Statue of Liberty? Is it possible that for at least some images, more exposure means *higher* value? Should the law try to distinguish between such images and those for which overexposure is more clearly a problem — for instance, the Rolls Royce logo? *See* Mark A. Lemley, *Ex Ante Versus Ex Post Justifications for Intellectual Property*, 71 U. Chi. L. Rev. 129, 145 (2004) (arguing that the congestion externality may be limited to a narrow subset of images or works that become cultural icons).

If we think congestion needs to be managed, how far should the law extend in constraining uses of another's image? Should celebrities be able to prevent the publication of unflattering photographs of themselves by papparazzi? What about parodies? Satire? *See* Stacey L. Dogan & Mark A. Lemley, *What the Right of Publicity Can Learn from Trademark Law*, 58 Stan. L. Rev. 1161 (2006) (disputing the congestion externality rationale on the grounds that it distorts the market by preventing the dissemination of truthful information about celebrities); *see also* Dennis S. Karjala, *Congestion Externalities and Extended Copyright Protection*, 94 Geo. L.J. 1065 (2006).

False Endorsement. In some instances, the right of publicity may prevent the unauthorized use of a person's name or other indicia of identity in connection with products or services, where the use would generate among consumers the false impression that the plaintiff endorses the product or service at issue. *See* RESTATEMENT (THIRD) OF UNFAIR COMPETITION § 46 cmt. c (noting that the right of publicity at least indirectly serves this interest); Stacey L. Dogan & Mark A. Lemley, *What the Right of Publicity Can Learn from Trademark Law*, 58 STAN. L. REV. 1161, 1190-1220 (2006). This interest, however, is also served by other provisions of the Lanham Act and counterpart state trademark and false advertising laws. *See infra* at pp. 538-39. To the extent the right of publicity also serves this interest, it largely duplicates these other legal protections. Moreover, as we shall see, the question whether laws should protect against mistaken perceptions of endorsement is a matter on which scholars disagree.

2. Variations Among the States

There is no federal right of publicity; neither is there a Uniform Law like the Uniform Trade Secrets Act or the Uniform Commercial Code. Details surrounding the right of publicity therefore can vary in some important ways from one state to another. Because of their relationship to the entertainment and publishing industries, New York and California have played particularly important roles in the development of publicity rights. The principal statutory provision in New York remains § 51 of the Civil Rights Act, the current version of which reads as follows:

N.Y. Civil Rights Law § 51. Action for Injunction and for Damages

Any person whose name, portrait, picture or voice is used within this state for advertising purposes or for the purposes of trade without the written consent first obtained [as provided in § 50] may maintain an equitable action in the supreme court of this state against the person, firm or corporation so using his name, portrait, picture or voice, to prevent and restrain the use thereof; and may also sue and recover damages for any injuries sustained by reason of such use and if the defendant shall have knowingly used such person's name, portrait, picture or voice in such manner as is forbidden or declared to be unlawful by section fifty of this article, the jury, in its discretion, may award exemplary damages. But nothing contained in this article shall be so construed as to prevent any person, firm or corporation from selling or otherwise transferring any material containing such name, portrait, picture or voice in whatever medium to any user of such name, portrait, picture or voice, or to any third party for sale or transfer directly or indirectly to such a user, for use in a manner lawful under this article; nothing contained in this article shall be so construed as to prevent any person, firm or corporation, practicing the profession of photography, from exhibiting in or about his or its establishment specimens of the work of such establishment, unless the same is continued by such person, firm or corporation after written notice objecting thereto has been given by the person portrayed; and nothing contained in this article shall be so construed as to prevent any person, firm or corporation from using the name, portrait, picture or voice of any manufacturer or dealer in connection with the goods, wares and merchandise manufactured, produced or dealt in by him which he has sold or disposed of with such name, portrait, picture or voice used in connection therewith; or from using the name, portrait, picture or voice of any author, composer or artist in connection with his literary, musical or artistic productions which he has sold or disposed of with such name, portrait, picture or voice used in connection therewith. Nothing contained in this section shall be construed to prohibit the copyright owner of a sound recording from disposing of, dealing in, licensing or selling that sound recording to any party, if the right to dispose of, deal in, license or sell such sound recording has been conferred by contract or other written document by such living person or the holder of such right. Nothing contained in the foregoing sentence shall be deemed to abrogate or otherwise limit any rights or remedies otherwise conferred by federal law or state law.

Unlike New York, California recognizes both a common law right of publicity and a statutory right, the latter dating to 1971. The California statute provides as follows.

Cal. Civ. Code § 3344. Unauthorized Commercial Use of Name, Voice, Signature, Photograph or Likeness

(a) Any person who knowingly uses another's name, voice, signature, photograph, or likeness, in any manner, on or in products, merchandise, or goods, or for purposes of advertising or selling, or soliciting purchases of, products, merchandise, goods or services, without such person's prior consent, or, in the case of a minor, the prior consent of his parent or legal guardian, shall be liable for any damages sustained by the person or persons injured as a result thereof. In addition, in any action brought under this section, the person who violated the section shall be liable to the injured party or parties in an amount equal to the greater of seven hundred fifty dollars ($750) or the actual damages suffered by him or her as a result of the unauthorized use, and any profits from the unauthorized use that are attributable to the use and are not taken into account in computing the actual damages. In establishing such profits, the injured party or parties are required to present proof only of the gross revenue attributable to such use, and the person who violated this section is required to prove his or her deductible expenses. Punitive damages may also be awarded to the injured party or parties. The prevailing party in any action under this section shall also be entitled to attorney's fees and costs.

(b) As used in this section, "photograph" means any photograph or photographic reproduction, still or moving, or any videotape or live television transmission, of any person, such that the person is readily identifiable. . . .

(c) Where a photograph or likeness of an employee of the person using the photograph or likeness appearing in the advertisement or other publication prepared by or in behalf of the user is only incidental, and not essential, to the purpose of the publication in which it appears, there shall arise a rebuttable presumption affecting the burden of producing evidence that the failure to obtain the consent of the employee was not a knowing use of the employee's photograph or likeness.

(d) For purposes of this section, a use of a name, voice, signature, photograph, or likeness in connection with any news, public affairs, or sports broadcast or account, or any political campaign, shall not constitute a use for which consent is required under subdivision (a).

(e) The use of a name, voice, signature, photograph, or likeness in a commercial medium shall not constitute a use for which consent is required under subdivision (a) solely because the material containing such use is commercially sponsored or contains paid advertising. Rather it shall be a question of fact whether or not the use of the person's name, voice, signature, photograph, or likeness was so directly connected with the commercial sponsorship or with the paid advertising as to constitute a use for which consent is required under subdivision (a).

(f) Nothing in this section shall apply to the owners or employees of any medium used for advertising, including, but not limited to, newspapers, magazines, radio and television networks and stations, cable television systems, billboards, and transit ads, by whom any advertisement or solicitation in violation of this section is published or disseminated, unless it is established that such owners or employees had knowledge of the unauthorized use of the person's name, voice, signature, photograph, or likeness as prohibited by this section.

(g) The remedies provided for in this section are cumulative and shall be in addition to any others provided for by law.[4]

Other states that recognize a right of publicity, either by statute or at common law, tend to follow either New York's approach (under which publicity rights are viewed as a type of privacy right) or the California approach (under which publicity rights are viewed more as a property interest). Many states also find persuasive the American Law Institute's pronouncements on publicity rights, as reflected in the *Restatement (Second) of Torts* and the more recent *Restatement (Third) of Unfair Competition*. The *Restatement (Second) of Torts* classifies the right of publicity under the heading of privacy rights, and states in § 652C that "[o]ne who appropriates to his own use or benefit the name or likeness of another is subject to liability to the other for invasion of his privacy."[5] Comment b states that this principle applies whether the defendant's use is commercial or noncommercial. By contrast, *Restatement (Third) of Unfair Competition* § 46 states that "[o]ne who appropriates *the commercial value* of a person's identity by using without consent the person's name, likeness, or other indicia of identify for purpose of trade is subject to liability" (emphasis added); and in comment g refers to the interest protected by the right of publicity as being in the nature of a property interest.

3. Who Is Entitled to a Right of Publicity?

In some early cases, the emphasis on privacy (protecting persons from unwanted publicity) meant that noncelebrities could bring claims for, for example, the unauthorized use of their photos in advertising. *See, e.g.*, Eick v. Perk Dog Food Co., 106 N.E.2d 742 (Ill. App. 1952) (recognizing claim for unauthorized use of noncelebrity's photo in dog food ad); Pavesich v. New England Life Ins. Co., 50 S.E. 68 (Ga. 1905) (recognizing claim for unauthorized use of noncelebrity plaintiff's photo in life insurance ad). As the above discussion of O'Brien v. Pabst Sales Co., 124 F.2d 167 (5th Cir. 1941), suggests, however, this emphasis on unwanted publicity led some courts to conclude that celebrities could not assert claims for violation of the right of publicity. More recently, the acceptance on the part of some courts of publicity rights as protecting a commercial interest might suggest precisely the opposite: that the right should be limited to persons whose names and likenesses are commercially valuable, that is, celebrities. *See, e.g.*, Allison v. Vintage Sports Plaques, 136 F.3d 1443, 1446-47 (11th Cir. 1998) (discussing Alabama law); Worthy v. Carroll, Civil Action No. 02-6882, 2003 WL 25706359, at *4 (E.D. Pa. 2003). The *Restatement of Unfair Competition*, however, and most courts that have addressed the issue, disapprove of this

4. California has a separate (and somewhat more limited) statute that extends the right of publicity after the death of the celebrity. CAL. CIV. CODE § 3344.1.

5. In this and many other respects, the *Restatement of Torts* reflects the influence of Dean William Prosser, who divided invasions of privacy into four distinct torts: public disclosure of private facts, intrusion on seclusion, false light, and "appropriation for the defendant's advantage of the plaintiff's name or likeness." William Prosser, *Privacy*, 48 CAL L. REV. 383 (1960).

approach. RESTATEMENT (THIRD) OF UNFAIR COMPETITION §§46 cmt. d, 49 cmt. d (1995) (stating that "evaluation of the relative fame of the plaintiff is more properly relevant to the determination of appropriate relief," and that "[p]rivate persons may . . . recover damages measured by the value of the use by establishing the market price that the defendant would have been required to pay in order to secure similar services from other private persons or from professional models"). Moreover, the strand of the tort rooted exclusively in privacy concerns still survives and is occasionally litigated by noncelebrities. *See, e.g.*, Lake v. Wal-Mart Stores, Inc., 582 N.W.2d 231, 236 (Minn. 1998). Nevertheless, even though right of privacy claims are theoretically available to any individual in many states, in practice these cases rarely arise outside of the celebrity realm. *See, e.g.*, William McGeveran, *Disclosure, Endorsement, and Identity in Social Marketing*, 2009 U. ILL. L. REV. 1105, 1151-55 (discussing the viability of consumer right of publicity claims in the context of unauthorized "social marketing messages" enabled by social networking sites, but noting that to date no such claims have been brought).

Another important distinction that arises out of the privacy/property divide, and that relates to the question of who can sue, is that when viewed as a property right a celebrity's interest in publicity is both assignable and descendible. In "privacy" regimes like New York, on the other hand, the right is not descendible. (The case law does not clearly indicate whether it is assignable.) In jurisdictions in which the right is descendible, the term of protection can vary substantially. In some states, postmortem publicity rights subsist for only 20 or 30 years, while in others they may last for 50, 70, or even 100 years after a person's death. *See* 1 J. THOMAS MCCARTHY, THE RIGHTS OF PUBLICITY AND PRIVACY § 9:18 (2009). Most states today do not condition the exercise of postmortem rights on the decedent's exercise of her right of publicity during her lifetime, though in the past some have.

Differences among the states relating to descendibility and terms of protection can give rise to complex problems. Courts deciding publicity cases may need to apply conflict of laws principles to determine which state's law governs an assertion of publicity rights. Sometimes questions concerning retroactivity can arise as well, as illustrated in recent litigation over claims to Marilyn Monroe's right of publicity. Monroe (née Norma Jean Baker) was a glamorous actress who starred in several popular motion pictures in the 1950s and 1960s. She was married at one time to baseball star Joe DiMaggio and at another to playwright Arthur Miller. At the time of her death in 1962, however, she was divorced, and she left no children or other close relatives. Her will left the bulk of her estate (including various unspecified assets, referred to in trusts and estates law as the "residue") to her acting coach, actor Lee Strasberg. In the late 1960s, Strasberg married an actress named Anna Mizrahi; when Strasberg died in 1982, the bulk of his estate went to Ms. Mizrahi. Mizrahi later formed a corporation, Marilyn Monroe LLC (MMLLC), to license Monroe's publicity rights (for example, her photographic image for merchandise such as posters and T-shirts). In recent years, the owners of copyright in some of these photographs have challenged MMLLC's assertion of publicity rights in court. (Can you imagine why the copyright owners might wish to mount such a challenge?)

An initial question in these disputes involves conflict of laws problem: Although Monroe died at her home in California, she also owned substantial property in New York and her will was probated in New York. Under applicable conflicts of laws rules, if Monroe was domiciled in New York at the time of the death, then New York's privacy-based law applies, and Monroe's right of publicity expired at her death in 1962. If, on the other hand, Monroe was domiciled in California, the issue becomes more complicated due to questions over the retroactivity of California's recognition of postmortem publicity rights. At the time of Monroe's death, California recognized only a common law right of publicity; statutory protection, as noted above, was enacted in 1971. In 1979, the California Supreme Court held that both common law and statutory publicity rights under California law terminated at death. *See* Lugosi v. Universal Pictures, 25 Cal. 3d 813 (1979); Guglielmi v. Spelling-Goldberg Prods., 25 Cal. 3d 860 (1979) (per curiam). In response, the California legislature enacted a new statute in 1984 to confer publicity rights upon deceased personalities in addition to living ones. Those provisions, which have been amended since, and are now codified as Civil Code § 3344.1.[6] If applicable, this statute would confer publicity rights in Monroe's name and other indicia of identity through the end of the year 2033.[7] The statute as enacted in 1984 and amended in 1999, however, was silent on the question of whether it applies retroactively.

After some initial setbacks, MMLLC and others successfully petitioned the California legislature to amend the California right of publicity statute to clarify that postmortem publicity rights *are* retroactive in that state. *See* CAL. CIV. CODE § 3344.1(p) ("The rights recognized by this section are expressly made retroactive, including to those deceased personalities who died before January 1, 1985"). (California State Senator Sheila Kuehl, herself a former television actress, sponsored the legislation, and it was signed into law by Governor Arnold Schwarzenegger in 2007.) Ultimately, however, a federal district court in California concluded that MMLLC was estopped from arguing that Monroe was a California domiciliary at the time of her death, in light of representations to the contrary made by the executor of Monroe's estate in connection with California estate tax proceedings in the 1960s

6. Like the right of publicity held by a living person, § 3344.1(a) declares broadly that "[a]ny person who uses a deceased personality's name, voice, signature, photograph, or likeness, in any manner, on or in products, merchandise, or goods, or for purposes of advertising or selling, or soliciting purchases of, products, merchandise, goods, or services, without prior consent from the person or persons specified in subdivision (c), shall be liable for any damages sustained by the person or persons injured as a result thereof." The amount recoverable includes the greater of $750 or actual damages and any profits, as well as punitive damages, attorney fees, and costs. The statute provides that the postmortem publicity right is freely transferable before or after the personality dies, by contract or by trust or will. § 3344.1(b). Consent to use the deceased personality's name, voice, photograph, etc., must be obtained from such a transferee or, if there is none, from certain described survivors of the personality. § 3344.1(c), (d). Any person claiming to be such a transferee or survivor must register the claim with the Secretary of State before recovering damages. § 3344.1(f). The statute contains exemptions for "news, public affairs, or sports broadcast or account, or any political campaign," § 3344.1(j), as well as for "a play, book, magazine, newspaper, musical composition, audiovisual work, radio or television program, single and original work of art, work of political or newsworthy value, or any advertisement or commercial announcement for any of these works . . . if it is fictional or nonfictional entertainment, or a dramatic, literary, or musical work," § 3344.1(a)(2). This latter list of exemptions is much broader than the exemptions listed in the provision addressing uses during the life of the celebrity (though First Amendment considerations may require some or all of these exemptions, for the use of both living and deceased celebrities' personae, regardless of what the statute expressly provides; *see infra* section C).

7. Under the original 1984 enactment, the postmortem term of protection was 50 years. In 1999, in response to a case holding that the unauthorized use of dancer Fred Astaire's image in a dance instructional video did not violate Astaire's right of publicity, *see* Astaire v. Best Film & Video Corp., 116 F.3d 1297 (9th Cir. 1997), *as amended*, 136 F.3d 1208 (9th Cir. 1998), California enacted the Astaire Celebrity Image Protection Act. The act retained the list of exempted uses from the earlier statute but included a provision stating that the exemptions relating to certain types of expressive works would not apply to uses that are "so directly connected with a product, article of merchandise, good, or service as to constitute an act of advertising, selling, or soliciting purchases of that product, article of merchandise, good, or service by the deceased personality without prior consent." CAL. CIV. CODE § 3344.1(a)(3). The act also extended the term of postmortem rights from 50 to 70 years. *See id.* § 3344.1(g).

and 1970s. New York law therefore applied, and Monroe's right of publicity terminated at her death, notwithstanding the 2007 amendment to California's statute. *See* Milton H. Greene Archives, Inc. v. CMG Worldwide, Inc., 568 F. Supp. 2d 1152 (C.D. Cal. 2008). A federal district court in New York that was hearing similar claims on the part of other copyright owners against an MMLLC-related entity thereafter deferred to this judgment. *See* Shaw Family Archives, Ltd. v. CMG Worldwide, Inc., 589 F. Supp. 2d 331 (S.D.N.Y. 2008).

COMMENTS AND QUESTIONS

1. From time to time, some commentators have argued in favor of a uniform federal right of publicity that would displace the patchwork of competing state approaches. *See, e.g.*, Natalie Grano, Note, *Million Dollar Baby: Celebrity Baby Pictures and the Right of Publicity*, 20 Fordham Intell. Prop. Media & Ent. L.J. 609, 659-65 (2010); Alicia M. Hunt, Comment, *Everyone Wants to Be a Star: Extensive Publicity Rights for Noncelebrities Unduly Restrict Commercial Speech*, 95 Nw. U. L. Rev. 1605, 1608 (2001) (citing numerous sources arguing in favor of a federal or state law). (Alternatively, a federal right could coexist with state rights, as is the case with respect to trademark law; whatever the merits of this approach might be, however, it would not put an end to problems arising from conflicting laws.) Does the Marilyn Monroe saga suggest the wisdom of this approach, or is it preferable to let the states operate as "laboratories of democracy" by testing out different approaches to publicity rights? (Consider this question again after reading *White v. Samsung Electronics* below.) Would a federal right solidify a body of legal doctrine that is of dubious merit to begin with? To the extent a federal law were to displace vested publicity rights under state law, would it give rise to a taking for which just compensation would be due under the Fifth Amendment?

2. Whatever the merits may be of extending publicity rights to deceased persons, does it make sense to accord such protection retroactively? In an earlier proceeding in the Marilyn Monroe litigation, the federal district court in California had concluded that California's law (at that time) did not apply with respect to persons who had died prior to 1985. Recognizing, however, that certain charities had been deriving revenue from their exercise of deceased celebrities' publicity interests and thus stood to be adversely affected by the court's decision, the court "noted that its ruling in no way prevented the California . . . legislature from enacting a right of publicity statute that vested the right directly in the residuary beneficiaries of a deceased personality's estate, or in the successors-in-interest of those residuary beneficiaries." *See* Milton H. Greene Archives, Inc. v. CMG Worldwide, Inc., No. CV 05-02200 MMM (MCx), 2008 WL 655604, at *2 (C.D. Cal. Jan. 7, 2008) (recounting earlier proceeding). The California legislature's response presumably worked to the benefit of these charities, even if not to the benefit of MMLLC. But is such retroactive legislation good public policy? Is it constitutional?

3. As a matter of policy, *should* the right of publicity be freely assignable to others? Should it be descendible to one's heirs? The answer may depend on precisely what policy or policies the right of publicity is understood to serve.

As noted above, the right of publicity originally arose as an aspect of the right of privacy, and at least some cases continue to be litigated on this theory. To the extent the right of publicity protects only a privacy interest, however, this may not bode well for the descendibility of the right; as the discussion above indicates, privacy interests normally are viewed as terminating at death. Are the states nevertheless free to extend privacy protection to deceased persons, if they wish to do so? Might there be any negative consequences? Alternatively, could a deceased person's family sometimes assert a claim based on the invasion of the family's own relational or familial privacy? *See, e.g.*, Nat'l Archives & Records Adm. v. Favish, 541 U.S. 157 (2003) (holding that FOIA did not require the federal government to release photographs of Vincent Foster's suicide in light of the family's interest in its own privacy); Clay Calvert, *The Privacy of Death: An Emergent Jurisprudence and Legal Rebuke to Media Exploitation and a Voyeuristic Culture*, 26 LOYOLA L.A. ENT. L. REV. 133 (2005).

To the extent the right of publicity protects only a privacy interest, and that interest is not descendible, can it nevertheless be assigned or licensed during one's lifetime? Why or why not? Even before the California statute was amended in 1984, however, cases in that state recognized the right of publicity as being transferrable inter vivos; New York law, as noted above, is unclear on the point.

If the right of publicity protects property interest instead of (or in addition to) a privacy interest, the rationale for conferring property rights in one's name or likeness might be important in determining whether such rights should be enforceable postmortem. Would McKenna's autonomy rationale, for example, provide a firmer basis for New York's extension of publicity rights to celebrities? For allowing the transfer of publicity rights? Would the autonomy rationale, by itself, provide any basis for the descendibility of publicity rights, or is autonomy (like privacy) a personal interest that terminates at death? What about the labor rationale? The incentive rationales? Would the false endorsement rationale provide any basis for conferring postmortem rights? For transferability of rights? For recognizing publicity rights in noncelebrities?

4. Another possible consequence of characterizing the right of publicity as a protecting a privacy, as opposed to a property, interest, is that § 230 of the Communications Decency Act immunizes providers of interactive computer services from liability based on user conduct, unless that conduct involves the infringement of intellectual property rights (in which case liability depends on principles of secondary liability such as contributory infringement). Courts are split on the question of whether right of publicity claims are subject to immunity under this provision. *See, e.g.*, Doe v. Friendfinder Network, Inc., 540 F. Supp. 2d 288, 302-04 (D.N.H. 2008) (holding that right of publicity claims pertain to intellectual property, but that privacy-based claims such as intrusion upon seclusion do not); *cf.* Perfect 10, Inc. v. CCBill LLC, 488 F.3d 1102, 1119 (9th Cir. 2007) (holding that § 230(e) excludes from immunity only federal intellectual property rights).

B. INDICIA OF IDENTITY

Midler v. Ford Motor Co.

849 F.2d 460 (9th Cir. 1988)

NOONAN, Circuit Judge:

This case centers on the protectibility of the voice of a celebrated chanteuse from commercial exploitation without her consent. Ford Motor Company and its advertising agency, Young & Rubicam, Inc., in 1985 advertised the Ford Lincoln Mercury with a series of nineteen 30 or 60 second television commercials in what the agency called "The Yuppie Campaign." The aim was to make an emotional connection with

Yuppies, bringing back memories of when they were in college. Different popular songs of the seventies were sung on each commercial. The agency tried to get "the original people," that is, the singers who had popularized the songs, to sing them. Failing in that endeavor in ten cases the agency had the songs sung by "sound alikes." Bette Midler, the plaintiff and appellant here, was done by a sound alike.

Midler is a nationally known actress and singer. She won a Grammy as early as 1973 as the Best New Artist of that year. Records made by her since then have gone Platinum and Gold. She was nominated in 1979 for an Academy award for Best Female Actress in *The Rose*, in which she portrayed a pop singer. *Newsweek* in its June 30, 1986 issue described her as an "outrageously original singer/comedian." Time hailed her in its March 2, 1987 issue as "a legend" and "the most dynamic and poignant singer-actress of her time."

When Young & Rubicam was preparing the Yuppie Campaign it presented the commercial to its client by playing an edited version of Midler singing "Do You Want To Dance," taken from the 1973 Midler album, "The Divine Miss M." After the client accepted the idea and form of the commercial, the agency contacted Midler's manager, Jerry Edelstein. The conversation went as follows: "Hello, I am Craig Hazen from Young and Rubicam. I am calling you to find out if Bette Midler would be interested in doing . . . ?" Edelstein: "Is it a commercial?" "Yes." "We are not interested."

Undeterred, Young & Rubicam sought out Ula Hedwig, whom it knew to have been one of "the Harlettes," a backup singer for Midler for ten years. Hedwig was told by Young & Rubicam that "they wanted someone who could sound like Bette Midler's recording of ['Do You Want To Dance']." She was asked to make a "demo" tape of the song if she was interested. She made an a capella demo and got the job.

At the direction of Young & Rubicam, Hedwig then made a record for the commercial. The Midler record of "Do You Want To Dance" was first played to her. She was told to "sound as much as possible like the Bette Midler record," leaving out only a few "aahs" unsuitable for the commercial. Hedwig imitated Midler to the best of her ability.

After the commercial was aired Midler was told by "a number of people" that it "sounded exactly" like her record of "Do You Want To Dance." Hedwig was told by "many personal friends" that they thought it was Midler singing the commercial. Ken Fritz, a personal manager in the entertainment business not associated with Midler, declares by affidavit that he heard the commercial on more than one occasion and thought Midler was doing the singing.

Neither the name nor the picture of Midler was used in the commercial; Young & Rubicam had a license from the copyright holder to use the song. At issue in this case is only the protection of Midler's voice. The district court described the defendants' conduct as that "of the average thief." They decided, "If we can't buy it, we'll take it." The court nonetheless believed there was no legal principle preventing imitation of Midler's voice and so gave summary judgment for the defendants. Midler appeals.

The First Amendment protects much of what the media do in the reproduction of likenesses or sounds. A primary value is freedom of speech and press. Time, Inc. v. Hill, 385 U.S. 374, 388, 17 L. Ed. 2d 456, 87 S. Ct. 534 (1967). The purpose of the media's use of a person's identity is central. If the purpose is "informative or cultural" the use is immune; "if it serves no such function but merely exploits the individual portrayed, immunity will not be granted." Felcher and Rubin, *"Privacy, Publicity and the Portrayal of Real People by the Media,"* 88 YALE L.J. 1577, 1596 (1979). Moreover, federal copyright law preempts much of the area. "Mere imitation of a recorded performance would not constitute a copyright infringement even where one performer deliberately sets out to simulate another's performance as exactly as possible." Notes of Committee on the Judiciary, 17 U.S.C.A. § 114(b). It is in the context of these First Amendment and federal copyright distinctions that we address the present appeal.

Nancy Sinatra once sued Goodyear Tire and Rubber Company on the basis of an advertising campaign by Young & Rubicam featuring "These Boots Are Made For Walkin'," a song closely identified with her; the female singers of the commercial were alleged to have imitated her voice and style and to have dressed and looked like her. The basis of Nancy Sinatra's complaint was unfair competition; she claimed that the song and the arrangement had acquired "a secondary meaning" which, under California law, was protectible. This court noted that the defendants "had paid a very substantial sum to the copyright proprietor to obtain the license for the use of the song and all of its arrangements." To give Sinatra damages for their use of the song would clash with federal copyright law. Summary judgment for the defendants was affirmed. Sinatra v. Goodyear Tire & Rubber Co., 435 F.2d 711, 717-718 (9th Cir. 1970), *cert. denied*, 402 U.S. 906, 28 L. Ed. 2d 646, 91 S. Ct. 1376 (1971). If Midler were claiming a secondary meaning to "Do You Want To Dance" or seeking to prevent the defendants from using that song, she would fail like Sinatra. But that is not this case. Midler does not seek damages for Ford's use of "Do You Want To Dance," and thus her claim is not preempted by federal copyright law. Copyright protects "original works of authorship fixed in any tangible medium of expression." 17 U.S.C. at 102(a). A voice is not copyrightable. The sounds are not "fixed." What is put forward as protectible here is more personal than any work of authorship.

Bert Lahr once sued Adell Chemical Co. for selling Lestoil by means of a commercial in which an imitation of Lahr's voice accompanied a cartoon of a duck. Lahr alleged that his style of vocal delivery was distinctive in pitch, accent, inflection, and sounds. The First Circuit held that Lahr had stated a cause of action for unfair competition, that it could be found "that defendant's conduct saturated plaintiff's audience, curtailing his market." Lahr v. Adell Chemical Co., 300 F.2d 256, 259 (1st Cir. 1962). That case is more like this one. But we do not find unfair competition here. One-minute commercials of the sort the defendants put on would not have saturated Midler's audience and curtailed her market. Midler did not do television commercials. The defendants were not in competition with her. See Halicki v. United Artists Communications, Inc., 812 F.2d 1213 (9th Cir. 1987).

California Civil Code section 3344 is also of no aid to Midler. The statute affords damages to a person injured by another who uses the person's "name, voice, signature, photograph or likeness, in any manner." The defendants did not use Midler's name or anything else whose use is prohibited by the statute. The voice they used was Hedwig's, not hers. The term "likeness" refers to a visual image not a vocal imitation. The statute, however, does not preclude Midler from pursuing any cause of action she may have at common law; the statute itself implies that such common law causes of action do exist because it says its remedies are merely "cumulative." Id. § 3344(g).

The companion statute protecting the use of a deceased person's name, voice, signature, photograph or likeness states that the rights it recognizes are "property rights." Id. § 990(b). By analogy the common law rights are also property rights. Appropriation of such common law rights is a tort in California. Motschenbacher v. R. J. Reynolds Tobacco Co., 498 F.2d 821 (9th Cir. 1974). In that case what the defendants used in their television commercial for Winston cigarettes was a photograph of a famous professional racing driver's racing car. The number of the car was changed and a wing-like device known as a "spoiler" was attached to the car; the car's features of white pinpointing, an oval medallion, and solid red coloring were retained. The driver, Lothar Motschenbacher, was in the car but his features were not visible. Some persons, viewing the commercial, correctly inferred that the car was his and that he was in the car and was therefore endorsing the product. The defendants were held to have invaded a "proprietary interest" of Motschenbacher in his own identity. Id. at 825.

Midler's case is different from Motschenbacher's. He and his car were physically used by the tobacco company's ad; he made part of his living out of giving commercial endorsements. But, as Judge Koelsch expressed it in *Motschenbacher*, California will recognize an injury from "an appropriation of the attributes of one's identity." Id. at 824. It was irrelevant that Motschenbacher could not be identified in the ad. The ad suggested that it was he. The ad did so by emphasizing signs or symbols associated with him. In the same way the defendants here used an imitation to convey the impression that Midler was singing for them.

Why did the defendants ask Midler to sing if her voice was not of value to them? Why did they studiously acquire the services of a sound-alike and instruct her to imitate Midler if Midler's voice was not of value to them? What they sought was an attribute of Midler's identity. Its value was what the market would have paid for Midler to have sung the commercial in person.

A voice is more distinctive and more personal than the automobile accouterments protected in *Motschenbacher*. A voice is as distinctive and personal as a face. The human voice is one of the most palpable ways identity is manifested. We are all aware that a friend is at once known by a few words on the phone. At a philosophical level it has been observed that with the sound of a voice, "the other stands before me." D. IHDE, LISTENING AND VOICE 77 (1976). A fortiori, these observations hold true of singing, especially singing by a singer of renown. The singer manifests herself in the song. To impersonate her voice is to pirate her identity. See W. KEETON, D. DOBBS, R. KEETON & D. OWEN, PROSSER & KEETON ON TORTS 852 (5th ed. 1984).

We need not and do not go so far as to hold that every imitation of a voice to advertise merchandise is actionable. We hold only that when a distinctive voice of a professional singer is widely known and is deliberately imitated in order to sell a product, the sellers have appropriated what is not theirs and have committed a tort in California. Midler has made a showing, sufficient to defeat summary judgment, that the defendants here for their own profit in selling their product did appropriate part of her identity.

Reversed and remanded for trial.

COMMENTS AND QUESTIONS

1. Young & Rubicam licensed the right to record the song "Do You Want to Dance" from the owner of the copyright in the musical composition. Why wasn't that enough? Should Midler have the additional right to prevent imitation of her voice? Note that the owner of the copyright in sound recordings is often the producer or the studio, rather than the singer who made the original recording. Does it matter whether Young & Rubicam could have purchased the rights to the recording of Midler herself singing "Do You Want to Dance" from the studio? If an artist doesn't control the rights to her own recording, why should she be able to prevent imitations of that recording?

A related question is whether the right of publicity is subject to an implicit first sale defense. In Allison v. Vintage Sports Plaques, 136 F.3d 1443 (11th Cir. 1998), the

Eleventh Circuit held that it was. The defendant had purchased authorized sports trading cards and framed them for resale. The court held that the defendant could lawfully resell the images of celebrities that he had lawfully purchased and that he was not impermissibly using the sports trading cards to sell the associated frames.

2. More generally, the question whether federal copyright law preempts the exercise of publicity rights arises in many right of publicity cases. We cover this issue, along with other preemption issues, in greater depth *infra* at Chapter 15.

3. Midler, the imitator, and independent third parties all provided evidence that people hearing the Ford commercial were confused — they thought that Midler was the one singing. Is likelihood of confusion (the test for trademark infringement) the relevant question here? Could Midler prevail even if the attempt to imitate her was not very good, so that most people could tell the difference? If a disclaimer at the beginning of the ad had indicated that the song was an impersonation, rather than Midler herself? *See* Stacey L. Dogan & Mark A. Lemley, *What the Right of Publicity Can Learn from Trademark Law*, 58 STAN. L. REV. 1161 (2006) (arguing that *Midler* is a case about consumer confusion over Midler's purported endorsement).

White v. Samsung Electronics America, Inc.
989 F.2d 1512 (9th Cir. 1993)

Before GOODWIN, PREGERSON and ALARCON, Circuit Judges.

The panel has voted unanimously to deny the petition for rehearing. . . .

KOZINSKI, Circuit Judge, with whom Circuit Judges O'SCANNLAIN and KLEINFELD join, dissenting from the order rejecting the suggestion for rehearing en banc.

I

Saddam Hussein wants to keep advertisers from using his picture in unflattering contexts. Clint Eastwood doesn't want tabloids to write about him. Rudolf Valentino's heirs want to control his film biography. The Girl Scouts don't want their image soiled by association with certain activities. George Lucas wants to keep Strategic Defense Initiative fans from calling it "Star Wars." Pepsico doesn't want singers to use the word "Pepsi" in their songs. Guy Lombardo wants an exclusive property right to ads that show big bands playing on New Year's Eve. Uri Geller thinks he should be paid for ads showing psychics bending metal through telekinesis. Paul Prudhomme, that household name, thinks the same about ads featuring corpulent bearded chefs. And scads of copyright holders see purple when their creations are made fun of.

Something very dangerous is going on here. Private property, including intellectual property, is essential to our way of life. It provides an incentive for investment and innovation; it stimulates the flourishing of our culture; it protects the moral entitlements of people to the fruits of their labors. But reducing too much to private property can be bad medicine. Private land, for instance, is far more useful if separated from other private land by public streets, roads and highways. Public parks, utility rights-of-way and sewers reduce the amount of land in private hands, but vastly enhance the value of the property that remains.

So too it is with intellectual property. Overprotecting intellectual property is as harmful as underprotecting it. Creativity is impossible without a rich public domain.

Nothing today, likely nothing since we tamed fire, is genuinely new: Culture, like science and technology, grows by accretion, each new creator building on the works of those who came before. Overprotection stifles the very creative forces it's supposed to nurture.

The panel's opinion is a classic case of overprotection. Concerned about what it sees as a wrong done to Vanna White, the panel majority erects a property right of remarkable and dangerous breadth: Under the majority's opinion, it's now a tort for advertisers to remind the public of a celebrity. Not to use a celebrity's name, voice, signature or likeness; not to imply the celebrity endorses a product; but simply to evoke the celebrity's image in the public's mind. This Orwellian notion withdraws far more from the public domain than prudence and common sense allow. It conflicts with the Copyright Act and the Copyright Clause. It raises serious First Amendment problems. It's bad law, and it deserves a long, hard second look.

II

Samsung ran an ad campaign promoting its consumer electronics. Each ad depicted a Samsung product and a humorous prediction: One showed a raw steak with the caption "Revealed to be health food. 2010 A.D." Another showed [talk show host] Morton Downey, Jr. in front of an American flag with the caption "Presidential candidate. 2008 A.D." The ads were meant to convey — humorously — that Samsung products would still be in use twenty years from now.

The ad that spawned this litigation starred a robot dressed in a wig, gown and jewelry reminiscent of Vanna White's hair and dress; the robot was posed next to a Wheel-of-Fortune-like game board [*see* Figure 10-1]. The caption read "Longest-running game show. 2012 A.D." The gag here, I take it, was that Samsung would still be around when White had been replaced by a robot.

FIGURE 10-1
Samsung's robot of a game show hostess

Perhaps failing to see the humor, White sued, alleging Samsung infringed her right of publicity by "appropriating" her "identity." Under California law, White has the exclusive right to use her name, likeness, signature and voice for commercial purposes. CAL. CIV. CODE § 3344(a); Eastwood v. Superior Court, 149 Cal. App. 3d 409, 417, 198 Cal. Rptr. 342, 347 (1983). But Samsung didn't use her name, voice or signature, and it certainly didn't use her likeness. The ad just wouldn't have been funny had it depicted White or someone who resembled her — the whole joke was that the game show host(ess) was a robot, not a real person. No one seeing the ad could have thought this was supposed to be White in 2012.

The district judge quite reasonably held that, because Samsung didn't use White's name, likeness, voice or signature, it didn't violate her right of publicity. 971 F.2d at 1396-97. Not so, says the panel majority: The California right of publicity can't possibly be limited to name and likeness. If it were, the majority reasons, a "clever advertising strategist" could avoid using White's name or likeness but nevertheless remind people of her with impunity, "effectively eviscerat[ing]" her rights. To prevent this "evisceration," the panel majority holds that the right of publicity must extend beyond name and likeness, to any "appropriation" of White's "identity" — anything that "evoke[s]" her personality. Id. at 1398-99.

III

But what does "evisceration" mean in intellectual property law? Intellectual property rights aren't like some constitutional rights, absolute guarantees protected against all kinds of interference, subtle as well as blatant. They cast no penumbras, emit no emanations: The very point of intellectual property laws is that they protect only against certain specific kinds of appropriation. I can't publish unauthorized copies of, say, *Presumed Innocent*; I can't make a movie out of it. But I'm perfectly free to write a book about an idealistic young prosecutor on trial for a crime he didn't commit. So what if I got the idea from *Presumed Innocent*? So what if it reminds readers of the original? Have I "eviscerated" Scott Turow's intellectual property rights? Certainly not. All creators draw in part on the work of those who came before, referring to it, building on it, poking fun at it; we call this creativity, not piracy.

The majority isn't, in fact, preventing the "evisceration" of Vanna White's existing rights; it's creating a new and much broader property right, a right unknown in California law.[16] It's replacing the existing balance between the interests of the celebrity and those of the public by a different balance, one substantially more favorable to the

16. In fact, in the one California case raising the issue, the three state Supreme Court Justices who discussed this theory expressed serious doubts about it. Guglielmi v. Spelling-Goldberg Prods., 25 Cal. 3d 860, 864 n.5, 160 Cal. Rptr. 352, 355 n.5, 603 P.2d 454, 457 n.5 (1979) (Bird, C. J., concurring) (expressing skepticism about finding a property right to a celebrity's "personality" because it is "difficult to discern any easily applied definition for this amorphous term"). Neither have we previously interpreted California law to cover pure "identity." Midler v. Ford Motor Co., 849 F.2d 460 (9th Cir. 1988), and Waits v. Frito-Lay, Inc., 978 F.2d 1093 (9th Cir. 1992), dealt with appropriation of a celebrity's voice. See id. at 1100-01 (imitation of singing style, rather than voice, doesn't violate the right of publicity). Motschenbacher v. R. J. Reynolds Tobacco Co., 498 F.2d 821 (9th Cir. 1974), stressed that, though the plaintiff's likeness wasn't directly recognizable by itself, the surrounding circumstances would have made viewers think the likeness was the plaintiff's. Id. at 827; see also Moore v. Regents of the Univ. of Cal., 51 Cal. 3d 120, 138, 271 Cal. Rptr. 146, 157, 793 P.2d 479, 490 (1990) (construing *Motschenbacher* as "hold[ing] that every person has a proprietary interest in his own likeness").

celebrity. Instead of having an exclusive right in her name, likeness, signature or voice, every famous person now has an exclusive right to anything that reminds the viewer of her. After all, that's all Samsung did: It used an inanimate object to remind people of White, to "evoke [her identity]." 971 F.2d at 1399.[17]

Consider how sweeping this new right is. What is it about the ad that makes people think of White? It's not the robot's wig, clothes or jewelry; there must be ten million blond women (many of them quasi-famous) who wear dresses and jewelry like White's. It's that the robot is posed near the "Wheel of Fortune" game board. Remove the game board from the ad, and no one would think of Vanna White. But once you include the game board, anybody standing beside it — a brunette woman, a man wearing women's clothes, a monkey in a wig and gown — would evoke White's image, precisely the way the robot did. It's the "Wheel of Fortune" set, not the robot's face or dress or jewelry that evokes White's image. The panel is giving White an exclusive right not in what she looks like or who she is, but in what she does for a living.[18]

This is entirely the wrong place to strike the balance. Intellectual property rights aren't free: They're imposed at the expense of future creators and of the public at large. Where would we be if Charles Lindbergh had an exclusive right in the concept of a heroic solo aviator? If Arthur Conan Doyle had gotten a copyright in the idea of the detective story, or Albert Einstein had patented the theory of relativity? If every author and celebrity had been given the right to keep people from mocking them or their work? Surely this would have made the world poorer, not richer, culturally as well as economically.

This is why intellectual property law is full of careful balances between what's set aside for the owner and what's left in the public domain for the rest of us: The relatively short life of patents; the longer, but finite, life of copyrights; copyright's idea-expression dichotomy; the fair use doctrine; the prohibition on copyrighting facts; the compulsory license of television broadcasts and musical compositions; federal preemption of overbroad state intellectual property laws; the nominative use doctrine in trademark law; the right to make soundalike recordings. All of these diminish an intellectual property owner's rights. All let the public use something created by

17. Some viewers might have inferred White was endorsing the product, but that's a different story. The right of publicity isn't aimed at or limited to false endorsements, Eastwood v. Superior Court, 149 Cal. App. 3d 409, 419-20, 198 Cal. Rptr. 342, 348 (1983); that's what the Lanham Act is for. Note also that the majority's rule applies even to advertisements that unintentionally remind people of someone. California law is crystal clear that the common-law right of publicity may be violated even by unintentional appropriations. Id. at 417 n.6, 198 Cal. Rptr. at 346 n.6; Fairfield v. American Photocopy Equipment Co., 138 Cal. App. 2d 82, 87, 291 P.2d 194 (1955).

18. Once the right of publicity is extended beyond specific physical characteristics, this will become a recurring problem: Outside name, likeness and voice, the things that most reliably remind the public of celebrities are the actions or roles they're famous for. A commercial with an astronaut setting foot on the moon would evoke the image of Neil Armstrong. Any masked man on horseback would remind people (over a certain age) of Clayton Moore. And any number of songs — "My Way," "Yellow Submarine," "Like a Virgin," "Beat It," "Michael, Row the Boat Ashore," to name only a few — instantly evoke an image of the person or group who made them famous, regardless of who is singing. See also Carlos V. Lozano, *West Loses Lawsuit over Batman TV Commercial*, L.A. TIMES, Jan. 18, 1990, at B3 (Adam West sues over Batman-like character in commercial); Nurmi v. Peterson, 10 U.S.P.Q.2d 1775, 1989 WL 407484 (C.D. Cal. 1989) (1950s TV movie hostess "Vampira" sues 1980s TV hostess "Elvira"); text accompanying notes 7-8 (lawsuits brought by Guy Lombardo, claiming big bands playing at New Year's Eve parties remind people of him, and by Uri Geller, claiming psychics who can bend metal remind people of him). Cf. *Motschenbacher*, where the claim was that viewers would think plaintiff was actually in the commercial, and not merely that the commercial reminded people of him.

someone else. But all are necessary to maintain a free environment in which creative genius can flourish.

The intellectual property right created by the panel here has none of these essential limitations: No fair use exception; no right to parody; no idea-expression dichotomy. It impoverishes the public domain, to the detriment of future creators and the public at large. Instead of well-defined, limited characteristics such as name, likeness or voice, advertisers will now have to cope with vague claims of "appropriation of identity," claims often made by people with a wholly exaggerated sense of their own fame and significance. . . . Future Vanna Whites might not get the chance to create their personae, because their employers may fear some celebrity will claim the persona is too similar to her own. The public will be robbed of parodies of celebrities, and our culture will be deprived of the valuable safety valve that parody and mockery create.

Moreover, consider the moral dimension, about which the panel majority seems to have gotten so exercised. Saying Samsung "appropriated" something of White's begs the question: Should White have the exclusive right to something as broad and amorphous as her "identity"? Samsung's ad didn't simply copy White's schtick—like all parody, it created something new. True, Samsung did it to make money, but White does whatever she does to make money, too; the majority talks of "the difference between fun and profit," 971 F.2d at 1401, but in the entertainment industry fun is profit. Why is Vanna White's right to exclusive for-profit use of her persona—a persona that might not even be her own creation, but that of a writer, director or producer—superior to Samsung's right to profit by creating its own inventions? Why should she have such absolute rights to control the conduct of others, unlimited by the idea-expression dichotomy or by the fair use doctrine?

To paraphrase only slightly Feist Publications, Inc. v. Rural Telephone Service Co., 111 S. Ct. 1282, 1289-90 (1991), it may seem unfair that much of the fruit of a creator's labor may be used by others without compensation. But this is not some unforeseen byproduct of our intellectual property system; it is the system's very essence. Intellectual property law assures authors the right to their original expression, but encourages others to build freely on the ideas that underlie it. This result is neither unfair nor unfortunate: It is the means by which intellectual property law advances the progress of science and art. We give authors certain exclusive rights, but in exchange we get a richer public domain. The majority ignores this wise teaching, and all of us are the poorer for it.

IV

The panel, however, does more than misinterpret California law: By refusing to recognize a parody exception to the right of publicity, the panel directly contradicts the federal Copyright Act. Samsung didn't merely parody Vanna White. It parodied Vanna White appearing in "Wheel of Fortune," a copyrighted television show, and parodies of copyrighted works are governed by federal copyright law.

Copyright law specifically gives the world at large the right to make "fair use" parodies, parodies that don't borrow too much of the original. Fisher v. Dees, 794 F.2d 432, 435 (9th Cir. 1986). . . .

The majority's decision decimates this federal scheme. It's impossible to parody a movie or a TV show without at the same time "evok[ing]" the "identit[ies]" of the actors. You can't have a mock *Star Wars* without a mock Luke Skywalker, Han Solo and Princess Leia, which in turn means a mock Mark Hamill, Harrison Ford and Carrie Fisher. You can't have a mock Batman commercial without a mock Batman, which means someone emulating the mannerisms of Adam West or Michael Keaton. See Carlos V. Lozano, *West Loses Lawsuit over Batman TV Commercial,* L.A. TIMES, Jan. 18, 1990, at B3 (describing Adam West's right of publicity lawsuit over a commercial produced under license from DC Comics, owner of the Batman copyright). The public's right to make a fair use parody and the copyright owner's right to license a derivative work are useless if the parodist is held hostage by every actor whose "identity" he might need to "appropriate."

Our court is in a unique position here. State courts are unlikely to be particularly sensitive to federal preemption, which, after all, is a matter of first concern to the federal courts. The Supreme Court is unlikely to consider the issue because the right of publicity seems so much a matter of state law. That leaves us. It's our responsibility to keep the right of publicity from taking away federally granted rights, either from the public at large or from a copyright owner. We must make sure state law doesn't give the Vanna Whites and Adam Wests of the world a veto over fair use parodies of the shows in which they appear, or over copyright holders' exclusive right to license derivative works of those shows. In a case where the copyright owner isn't even a party—where no one has the interests of copyright owners at heart—the majority creates a rule that greatly diminishes the rights of copyright holders in this circuit.

V

The majority's decision also conflicts with the federal copyright system in another, more insidious way. Under the dormant Copyright Clause, state intellectual property laws can stand only so long as they don't "prejudice the interests of other States." Goldstein v. California, 412 U.S. 546, 558, 93 S. Ct. 2303, 2310, 37 L. Ed. 2d 163 (1973). A state law criminalizing record piracy, for instance, is permissible because citizens of other states would "remain free to copy within their borders those works which may be protected elsewhere." Id. But the right of publicity isn't geographically limited. A right of publicity created by one state applies to conduct everywhere, so long as it involves a celebrity domiciled in that state. If a Wyoming resident creates an ad that features a California domiciliary's name or likeness, he'll be subject to California right of publicity law even if he's careful to keep the ad from being shown in California. See Acme Circus Operating Co. v. Kuperstock, 711 F.2d 1538, 1540 (11th Cir. 1983); Groucho Marx Prods. v. Day and Night Co., 689 F.2d 317, 320 (2d Cir. 1982); see also Factors Etc. v. Pro Arts, 652 F.2d 278, 281 (2d Cir. 1981).

The broader and more ill-defined one state's right of publicity, the more it interferes with the legitimate interests of other states. A limited right that applies to unauthorized use of name and likeness probably does not run afoul of the Copyright Clause, but the majority's protection of "identity" is quite another story. Under the majority's approach, any time anybody in the United States—even somebody who lives in a state with a very narrow right of publicity—creates an ad, he takes the risk that it might remind some segment of the public of somebody, perhaps somebody with only a local reputation, somebody the advertiser has never heard of. See note 17 supra (right of publicity is infringed by unintentional appropriations). So you made a commercial in Florida and one of the characters reminds Reno residents of their favorite local TV anchor (a California domiciliary)? Pay up.

This is an intolerable result, as it gives each state far too much control over artists in other states. No California statute, no California court has actually tried to reach this far. It is ironic that it is we who plant this kudzu in the fertile soil of our federal system.

VI

Finally, I can't see how giving White the power to keep others from evoking her image in the public's mind can be squared with the First Amendment. Where does White get this right to control our thoughts? The majority's creation goes way beyond the protection given a trademark or a copyrighted work, or a person's name or likeness. All those things control one particular way of expressing an idea, one way of referring to an object or a person. But not allowing any means of reminding people of someone? That's a speech restriction unparalleled in First Amendment law.

What's more, I doubt even a name-and-likeness-only right of publicity can stand without a parody exception. The First Amendment isn't just about religion or politics — it's also about protecting the free development of our national culture. Parody, humor, irreverence are all vital components of the marketplace of ideas. The last thing we need, the last thing the First Amendment will tolerate, is a law that lets public figures keep people from mocking them, or from "evok[ing]" their images in the mind of the public. 971 F.2d at 1399.

The majority dismisses the First Amendment issue out of hand because Samsung's ad was commercial speech. Id. at 1401 & n.3. So what? Commercial speech may be less protected by the First Amendment than noncommercial speech, but less protected means protected nonetheless. Central Hudson Gas & Elec. Corp. v. Public Serv. Comm'n, 447 U.S. 557 (1980). And there are very good reasons for this. Commercial speech has a profound effect on our culture and our attitudes. Neutral-seeming ads influence people's social and political attitudes, and themselves arouse political controversy. . . .

In our pop culture, where salesmanship must be entertaining and entertainment must sell, the line between the commercial and noncommercial has not merely blurred; it has disappeared. Is the Samsung parody any different from a parody on *Saturday Night Live* or in *Spy Magazine*? Both are equally profit-motivated. Both use a celebrity's identity to sell things — one to sell VCRs, the other to sell advertising. Both mock their subjects. Both try to make people laugh. Both add something, perhaps something worthwhile and memorable, perhaps not, to our culture. Both are things that the people being portrayed might dearly want to suppress. . . .

Commercial speech is a significant, valuable part of our national discourse. The Supreme Court has recognized as much, and has insisted that lower courts carefully scrutinize commercial speech restrictions, but the panel totally fails to do this. The panel majority doesn't even purport to apply the *Central Hudson* test, which the Supreme Court devised specifically for determining whether a commercial speech restriction is valid. The majority doesn't ask, as *Central Hudson* requires, whether the speech restriction is justified by a substantial state interest. It doesn't ask whether the restriction directly advances the interest. It doesn't ask whether the restriction is narrowly tailored to the interest. *See* id. at 566, 100 S. Ct. at 2351. These are all things the Supreme Court told us-in no uncertain terms-we must consider; the majority opinion doesn't even mention them.

Process matters. The Supreme Court didn't set out the *Central Hudson* test for its health. It devised the test because it saw lower courts were giving the First Amendment short shrift when confronted with commercial speech. *See Central Hudson*, 447 U.S. at 561-62, 567-68, 100 S. Ct. at 2348-49, 2352. The *Central Hudson* test was an attempt to constrain lower courts' discretion, to focus judges' thinking on the important issues-how strong the state interest is, how broad the regulation is, whether a narrower regulation would work just as well. If the Court wanted to leave these matters to judges' gut feelings, to nifty lines about "the difference between fun and profit," 971 F.2d at 1401, it could have done so with much less effort.

Maybe applying the test would have convinced the majority to change its mind; maybe going through the factors would have shown that its rule was too broad, or the reasons for protecting White's "identity" too tenuous. Maybe not. But we shouldn't thumb our nose at the Supreme Court by just refusing to apply its test.

VII

For better or worse, we are the Court of Appeals for the Hollywood Circuit. Millions of people toil in the shadow of the law we make, and much of their livelihood is made possible by the existence of intellectual property rights. But much of their livelihood—and much of the vibrancy of our culture—also depends on the existence of other intangible rights: The right to draw ideas from a rich and varied public domain, and the right to mock, for profit as well as fun, the cultural icons of our time.

In the name of avoiding the "evisceration" of a celebrity's rights in her image, the majority diminishes the rights of copyright holders and the public at large. In the name of fostering creativity, the majority suppresses it. Vanna White and those like her have been given something they never had before, and they've been given it at our expense. I cannot agree.

COMMENTS AND QUESTIONS

1. The Ninth Circuit at least partially reaffirmed its *White* decision in Wendt v. Host Int'l, 125 F.3d 806 (9th Cir. 1997). That case also involved animatronic robots. These were representative of characters from the television show "Cheers" and were placed in licensed airport Cheers bars. The bars had obtained rights from the producers of the television show but not from the actors themselves. The court held that the actors retained publicity rights in their portrayal of the fictional characters under California law and remanded the case for an analysis of the similarities between the plaintiffs and the robots.

If the actors had brought a claim under California law based on the use of their images from the TV show itself, they would have lost. *See* Fleet v. CBS, 50 Cal. App. 4th 1911 (1996) (California publicity law preempted to the extent it imposes controls on the exploitation of name or likeness through distribution of a motion picture in which actor appeared); Page v. Something Weird Video, 960 F. Supp. 1438 (C.D. Cal. 1996) (First Amendment allows use of drawing of character in film to promote that film). Should the result be any different where a spin-off product is licensed?

2. Cases other than *White* discuss "celebrity attributes" besides appearance and voice. *See, e.g.*, McFarland v. Miller, 14 F.3d 912 (3d Cir. 1994) (granting damages for use of appearance and name of "Our Gang" member Spanky McFarland in restaurant decor). Is there any natural boundary to the right of publicity? If mere "evocation of a celebrity" is required, which of the following could be protected by a right of publicity: (1) a characteristic walk or even running style; (2) a characteristic gesture, such as Clint Eastwood's sneer, or Johnny Carson's musically accompanied golf swing, or Michael Jackson's "moonwalking" dance steps; (3) a "signature" joke, such as Henny Youngman's "take my wife—please," or Joan Rivers's "can we talk?"—notwithstanding that both jokes were well known when they were adopted as "signatures"; (4) a style of chess opening that has become associated with a particular grand master; (5) a shot, move, or technique in sports that is closely identified with a particular athlete—for example, Tiger Woods's fist pump. Do cases that take too generous an approach to determining what may constitute protectable indicia of identity risk conferring protection over ideas? To the extent this is so, might there be a conflict with copyright law?

On the other hand, is there any natural limit to Judge Kozinski's reasoning? Or does it suggest that the entire concept of a right of publicity is ill-considered? Is there some identifiable reason that Bette Midler's claim seems more plausible than Vanna White's? Should it matter that a consumer might be confused by the Midler imitation, but won't be by the robot?

3. The *Restatement (Third) of Unfair Competition* takes the following position on what constitutes protectable indicia of identity:

> The right of publicity is infringed by an appropriation of another's identity for purposes of trade. The use must therefore be sufficient to identify the person whose identity the defendant is alleged to have appropriated. If the appropriation consists of the use of a name, for example, the name as used by the defendant must be understood by the audience as referring to the plaintiff. Similarly, in the case of an alleged visual likeness, the plaintiff must be reasonably identifiable from the photograph or other depiction. Whether the plaintiff is identified by the defendant's use is a question of fact. Relevant evidence includes the nature and extent of the identifying characteristics used by the defendant, the defendant's intent, the fame of the plaintiff, evidence of actual identification made by third persons, and surveys or other evidence indicating the perceptions of the audience.
>
> In most cases an appropriation of identity is accomplished through the use of a person's name or likeness. The person can be identified by a real name, nickname, or professional name, or by a likeness embodied in a photograph, drawing, film, or physical look-alike.

RESTATEMENT (THIRD) OF UNFAIR COMPETITION, § 46 cmt. d. These factors are similar to the factors courts use in trademark cases to determine whether a non-inherently distinctive word or symbol has acquired secondary meaning. *See id.* § 13 cmt. e.

4. Judge Kozinski emphasizes throughout his opinion that the right of publicity adds extra burdens to the creators of works that draw on celebrity attributes. For example, he states: "We must make sure state law doesn't give the Vanna Whites and Adam Wests of the world a veto over fair use parodies of the shows in which they appear, or over copyright holders' exclusive right to license derivative works of those shows." Judge Kozinski's point is that the right of publicity creates the need for an entirely new "layer" of transactions *on top of* the traditional copyright license. For example, in many of the "voice-alike" cases such as *Midler*, the defendant in the

publicity action is a legitimate licensee of the copyright holder in the song that the defendant used. The right of publicity cases thus implicitly hold that the copyright license does not shield the licensee from liability for using the work, at least under some circumstances. It also means that, at least for copyrighted works assigned prior to the rapid growth of the right of publicity, creators of works can use the new right to extract some extra value. *See* Eben Shapiro, *Rising Caution on Using Celebrity Images*, N.Y. Times, Nov. 4, 1992, at D20. For further discussion of copyright preemption issues as they relate to right of publicity claims, see *infra* Chapter 15.

Judge Kozinski's last argument, that the First Amendment limits the right of publicity, is the subject of section C below.

A Note on False Endorsement

Right of publicity claims are sometimes coupled with claims alleging false endorsement in violation of the Lanham Act. A false claim that a person (usually a celebrity) endorses a product may violate the Lanham Act in two ways. First, the claim may amount to false advertising if all of the elements of a false advertising claim are present. *See* Chapter 9 *supra*. Second, the claim may violate Lanham Act §43(a)(1)(A), which in relevant part states:

> Any person who, on or in connection with any goods or services, or any container for goods, uses in commerce any word, term, name, symbol, or device, or any combination thereof . . . which . . . is likely to cause confusion, or to cause mistake, or to deceive as to the affiliation, connection, or association of such person, or as to the origin, sponsorship, or approval of his or her goods, services, or commercial activities by another person . . . shall be liable in a civil action by any person who believes that he or she is or is likely to be damaged by such act.

This is the same language that is at issue in many cases involving allegations of trademark infringement. The elements the plaintiff must prove in a false endorsement case therefore are similar to the elements the plaintiff must prove in a trademark infringement case. In the case of false endorsement, these elements are: (1) imitation of a distinctive attribute of a celebrity's[8] identity (2) in connection with goods or services, or any container for goods, (3) defendant's use is in interstate commerce, and (4) is likely to cause confusion, among a substantial portion of the relevant class of purchasers, regarding the celebrity's endorsement of the goods or services. (Standards for determining whether the defendant imitated "a distinctive attribute of a celebrity's identity" would overlap with the standards for determining whether the defendant has appropriated distinctive indicia of identity, in the right of publicity context.) The factors relevant to likelihood of confusion, in the context of false endorsement, are: (1) the level of recognition that the plaintiff has among the segment of the society for whom the defendant's product is intended; (2) the relatedness of the fame or success of the plaintiff to the defendant's product; (3) the similarity of the likeness used by the defendant to the actual plaintiff; (4) evidence of actual confusion; (5) marketing

8. *But see* Stayart v. Yahoo! Inc., 651 F. Supp. 2d 873, 881 (E.D. Wis. 2009) (noting that, although many false endorsement cases "arise in the context of a popular celebrity, some cases hold that popularity or celebrity status is not a necessary prerequisite for a successful false endorsement claim under the Lanham Act"), *aff'd on other grounds*, 623 F.3d 436 (7th Cir. 2010).

channels used; (6) likely degree of purchase care; (7) defendant's intent on selecting the plaintiff; and (8) likelihood of expansion of the product lines. Downing v. Abercrombie & Fitch, 265 F.3d 994, 1007-08 (9th Cir. 2003).

In the *Downing* case the plaintiffs, professional surfers, asserted both right of publicity and false endorsement claims against A & F for including their pictures in an A & F catalogue, without their consent. The court held that there was a genuine issue of material fact on the issue of likelihood of confusion, noting among other things the plaintiffs' fame among the class of purchasers of A & F products; the relatedness of surfing and surfing-themed clothing; the use by the defendant of actual photographs of the plaintiffs; declarations demonstrating consumers' belief that the plaintiffs had endorsed the products; lack of care among the purchasers of A & F clothing; and the possibility that A & F intended to profit from indicating to consumers that the surfers at issue were endorsing A & F clothing. *See id.* at 1008-09. On the other hand, the " 'mere possibility' that consumers may be misled is insufficient to prevail on an endorsement claim." Kournikova v. General Media Commc'ns, 278 F. Supp. 2d 1111, 1128 (C.D. Cal. 2003) (citations omitted). As in right of publicity cases, if the use has artistic relevance, some courts may require a heightened showing of confusion or consider the "nominative use" defense. *See infra* section C n.26.

Do false claims of endorsement threaten consumers with serious harm? For a skeptical view, see Mark A. Lemley & Mark P. McKenna, *Irrelevant Confusion*, 62 Stan. L. Rev. 311 (2010) (doubting whether confusion as to sponsorship or affiliation often results in confusion that impairs consumer decisionmaking).

PROBLEMS

Problem 10-1. On March 1, 2009, Sam, a seller in Minnesota, posts on Internet classified advertising Web site craigslist.com an offer to sell his used car, a 1990 LeBaron. The advertisement states that the vehicle was "once owned by Jon Voight," without any further explanation of what this means. In fact, the person who owned the car from 1990 to 1994 was named Jon Voight, but this person was not the actor Jon Voight but a dentist living in New York City. Within a few days of the Internet posting, a potential buyer in Wisconsin, George, reads the Internet advertisement using his home computer. Within another few days, George agrees to buy the car, incorrectly believing the previous owner to be the actor Jon Voight. When Sam and George meet in mid-March 2009 to complete the transaction and transfer title to the vehicle to George, Sam again states that a previous owner of the car was Jon Voight. Sam never explicitly states, however, and George never explicitly asks, whether the previous owner was the *actor* Jon Voight. Nevertheless, in late April 2009, George discovers that the previous owner was a New York dentist named Jon Voight, not the actor Jon Voight. George then manages to get in touch with the actor Jon Voight and apprises him of the situation.

In a state that follows the *Restatement (Third) of Unfair Competition* approach to the right of publicity, would the actor Jon Voight have a claim for violation of his right of publicity? Would anyone have a viable claim for false advertising under Lanham Act §43(a)(1)(B)? For false endorsement? For false designation of origin?

Problem 10-2. During the 2010 Super Bowl, E*Trade (a firm that provides online brokerage services) aired a commercial featuring a baby boy and a baby girl having a videocam conversation. The baby boy says that he didn't call the previous night because he was checking his portfolio on E*Trade. The baby girl says "And that milk-a-holic Lindsay wasn't over?" Another baby girl then enters the room where the baby boy is, and says "Milk-a-what?" After the commercial aired, actress Lindsay Lohan—who has been in rehab for alcoholism—filed suit for violation of her right of publicity. Does the commercial appropriate Lindsay Lohan's indicia of identity? Is Lindsay Lohan one of those celebrities (like Cher and Prince) who is known by her first name alone? Should it matter that the names Lindsay and Lindsey were both among the 50 most popular baby girl names in the United States during the mid-1980s (Lindsay Lohan was born in 1986), but by 2009 had fallen to 524 and 326, respectively?

C. THE RIGHT OF PUBLICITY AND THE FIRST AMENDMENT

Zacchini v. Scripps-Howard Brodcasting Co.
433 U.S. 562 (1977)

Mr. Justice WHITE delivered the opinion of the Court.

Petitioner, Hugo Zacchini, is an entertainer. He performs a 'human cannonball' act in which he is shot from a cannon into a net some 200 feet away. Each performance occupies some 15 seconds. In August and September 1972, petitioner was engaged to perform his act on a regular basis at the Geauga County Fair in Burton, Ohio. He performed in a fenced area, surrounded by grandstands, at the fair grounds. Members of the public attending the fair were not charged a separate admission fee to observe his act.

On August 30, a freelance reporter for Scripps-Howard Broadcasting Co., the operator of a television broadcasting station and respondent in this case, attended the fair. He carried a small movie camera. Petitioner noticed the reporter and asked him not to film the performance. The reporter did not do so on that day; but on the instructions of the producer of respondent's daily newscast, he returned the following day and videotaped the entire act. This film clip approximately 15 seconds in length, was shown on the 11 o'clock news program that night, together with favorable commentary.

Petitioner then brought this action for damages, alleging that he is "engaged in the entertainment business," that the act he performs is one "invented by his father and . . . performed only by his family for the last fifty years," that respondent "showed and commercialized the film of his act without his consent," and that such conduct was an "unlawful appropriation of plaintiff's professional property." App. 4-5. Respondent answered and moved for summary judgment, which was granted by the trial court. . . .

We granted certiorari, 429 U.S. 1037, 97 S. Ct. 730, 50 L. Ed. 2d 747 (1977), to consider an issue unresolved by this Court: whether the First and Fourteenth Amendments immunized respondent from damages for its alleged infringement of petitioner's statelaw "right of publicity." Pet. for Cert. 2. Insofar as the Ohio Supreme Court held that the First and Fourteenth Amendments of the United States Constitution required judgment for respondent, we reverse the judgment of that court. . . .

II

The Ohio Supreme Court held that respondent is constitutionally privileged to include in its newscasts matters of public interest that would otherwise be protected by the right of publicity, absent an intent to injure or to appropriate for some nonprivileged purpose. If under this standard respondent had merely reported that petitioner was performing at the fair and described or commented on his act, with or without showing his picture on television, we would have a very different case. But petitioner is not contending that his appearance at the fair and his performance could not be reported by the press as newsworthy items. His complaint is that respondent filmed his entire act and displayed that film on television for the public to see and enjoy. This, he claimed, was an appropriation of his professional property. The Ohio Supreme Court agreed that petitioner had "a right of publicity" that gave him "personal control over commercial display and exploitation of his personality and the exercise of his talents." This right of "exclusive control over the publicity given to his performances" was said to be such a "valuable part of the benefit which may be attained by his talents and efforts" that it was entitled to legal protection. It was also observed, or at least expressly assumed, that petitioner had not abandoned his rights by performing under the circumstances present at the Geauga County Fair Grounds.

The Ohio Supreme Court nevertheless held that the challenged invasion was privileged, saying that the press "must be accorded broad latitude in its choice of how much it presents of each story or incident, and of the emphasis to be given to such presentation. No fixed standard which would bar the press from reporting or depicting either an entire occurrence or an entire discrete part of a public performance can be formulated which would not unduly restrict the 'breathing room' in reporting which freedom of the press requires." 47 Ohio St. 2d, at 235, 351 N.E.2d, at 461. Under this view, respondent was thus constitutionally free to film and display petitioner's entire act.[5]

The Ohio Supreme Court relied heavily on Time, Inc. v. Hill, 385 U.S. 374, 87 S. Ct. 534, 17 L. Ed. 2d 456 (1967), but that case does not mandate a media privilege to televise a performer's entire act without his consent. Involved in *Time, Inc. v. Hill* was a claim under the New York "Right of Privacy" statute that *Life Magazine*, in the course of reviewing a new play, had connected the play with a long-past incident involving petitioner and his family and had falsely described their experience and conduct at that time. The complaint sought damages for humiliation and suffering flowing from these

5. The court's explication was as follows:

> The proper standard must necessarily be whether the matters reported were of public interest, and if so, the press will be liable for appropriation of a performer's right of publicity only if its actual intent was not to report the performance, but, rather, to appropriate the performance for some other private use, or if the actual intent was to injure the performer. It might also be the case that the press would be liable if it recklessly disregarded contract rights existing between the plaintiff and a third person to present the performance to the public, but that question is not presented here.

nondefamatory falsehoods that allegedly invaded Hill's privacy. The Court held, however, that the opening of a new play linked to an actual incident was a matter of public interest and that Hill could not recover without showing that the *Life* report was knowingly false or was published with reckless disregard for the truth the same rigorous standard that had been applied in New York Times Co. v. Sullivan, 376 U.S. 254, 84 S. Ct. 710, 11 L. Ed. 2d 686 (1964).

Time, Inc. v. Hill, which was hotly contested and decided by a divided Court, involved an entirely different tort from the "right of publicity" recognized by the Ohio Supreme Court. As the opinion reveals in *Time, Inc. v. Hill*, the Court was steeped in the literature of privacy law and was aware of the developing distinctions and nuances in this branch of the law. The Court, for example, cited W. PROSSER, LAW OF TORTS 831-832 (3d ed. 1964), and the same author's well-known article, *Privacy*, 48 CALIF. L. REV. 383 (1960), both of which divided privacy into four distinct branches. The Court was aware that it was adjudicating a "false light" privacy case involving a matter of public interest, not a case involving "intrusion," 385 U.S., at 384-385, n.9, 87 S. Ct., at 540, "appropriation" of a name or likeness for the purposes of trade, id., at 381, 87 S. Ct., at 538, or "private details" about a non-newsworthy person or event, id., at 383 n.7, 87 S. Ct., at 539. It is also abundantly clear that *Time, Inc. v. Hill* did not involve a performer, a person with a name having commercial value, or any claim to a "right of publicity." This discrete kind of "appropriation" case was plainly identified in the literature cited by the Court and had been adjudicated in the reported cases.

The differences between these two torts are important. First, the State's interests in providing a cause of action in each instance are different. "The interest protected" in permitting recovery for placing the plaintiff in a false light "is clearly that of reputation, with the same overtones of mental distress as in defamation." Prosser, supra, 48 CALIF. L. REV., at 400. By contrast, the State's interest in permitting a "right of publicity" is in protecting the proprietary interest of the individual in his act in part to encourage such entertainment.[10] As we later note, the State's interest is closely analogous to the goals of patent and copyright law, focusing on the right of the individual to reap the reward of his endeavors and having little to do with protecting feelings or reputation. Second, the two torts differ in the degree to which they intrude on dissemination of information to the public. In "false light" cases the only way to protect the interests involved is to attempt to minimize publication of the damaging matter, while in "right of publicity" cases the only question is who gets to do the publishing. An entertainer such as petitioner usually has no objection to the widespread publication of his act as long as the gets the commercial benefit of such publication. Indeed, in the present case petitioner did not seek to enjoin the broadcast of his act; he simply sought compensation for the broadcast in the form of damages. . . .

Moreover, *Time, Inc. v. Hill*, *New York Times*, *Metromedia*, *Gertz*, and *Firestone* all involved the reporting of events; in none of them was there an attempt to broadcast or publish an entire act for which the performer ordinarily gets paid. It is evident, and there is no claim here to the contrary, that petitioner's state-law right of publicity would not serve to prevent respondent from reporting the newsworthy facts about

10. The Ohio Supreme Court expressed the view "that plaintiff's claim is one for invasion of the right of privacy by appropriation, and should be considered as such." 47 Ohio St. 2d, at 226, 351 N.E.2d, at 456. It should be noted, however, that the case before us is more limited than the broad category of lawsuits that may arise under the heading of "appropriation." Petitioner does not merely assert that some general use, such as advertising, was made of his name or likeness; he relies on the much narrower claim that respondent televised an entire act that he ordinarily gets paid to perform.

petitioner's act.[11] Wherever the line in particular situations is to be drawn between media reports that are protected and those that are not, we are quite sure that the First and Fourteenth Amendments do not immunize the media when they broadcast a performer's entire act without his consent. The Constitution no more prevents a State from requiring respondent to compensate petitioner for broadcasting his act on television than it would privilege respondent to film and broadcast a copyrighted dramatic work without liability to the copyright owner. Copyrights Act, 17 U.S.C. App. § 101 et seq. (1976 ed.); cf. Kalem Co. v. Harper Bros., 222 U.S. 55, 32 S. Ct. 20, 56 L. Ed. 92 (1911); Manners v. Morosco, 252 U.S. 317, 40 S. Ct. 335, 64 L. Ed. 590 (1920), or to film and broadcast a prize fight, Ettore v. Philco Television Broadcasting Corp., 229 F.2d 481 (CA3), cert. denied, 351 U.S. 926, 76 S. Ct. 783, 100 L. Ed. 1456 (1956); or a baseball game, Pittsburgh Athletic Co. v. KQV Broadcasting Co., 24 F. Supp. 490 (WD Pa. 1938), where the promoters or the participants had other plans for publicizing the event. There are ample reasons for reaching this conclusion.

The broadcast of a film of petitioner's entire act poses a substantial threat to the economic value of that performance. As the Ohio court recognized, this act is the product of petitioner's own talents and energy, the end result of much time, effort, and expense. Much of its economic value lies in the "right of exclusive control over the publicity given to his performance"; if the public can see the act free on television, it will be less willing to pay to see it at the fair.[12] The effect of a public broadcast of the performance is similar to preventing petitioner from charging an admission fee. "The rationale for (protecting the right of publicity) is the straightforward one of preventing unjust enrichment by the theft of good will. No social purpose is served by having the defendant get free some aspect of the plaintiff that would have market value and for which he would normally pay." Kalven, *Privacy in Tort Law: Were Warren and Brandeis Wrong?*, 31 LAW & CONTEMP. PROB. 326, 331 (1966). Moreover, the broadcast of petitioner's entire performance, unlike the unauthorized use of another's name for purposes of trade or the incidental use of a name or picture by the press, goes to the heart of petitioner's ability to earn a living as an entertainer. Thus, in this case, Ohio has recognized what may be the strongest case for a "right of publicity" involving, not the appropriation of an entertainer's reputation to enhance the attractiveness of a

11. W. PROSSER, LAW OF TORTS 806-807 (4th ed. 1971), generalizes on the cases:

> The New York courts were faced very early with the obvious fact that newspapers and magazines, to say nothing of radio, television and motion pictures, are by no means philanthropic institutions, but are operated for profit. As against the contention that everything published by these agencies must necessarily be 'for purposes of trade,' they were compelled to hold that there must be some closer and more direct connection, beyond the mere fact that the newspaper itself is sold; and that the presence of advertising matter in adjacent columns, or even the duplication of a news item for the purpose of advertising the publication itself, does not make any difference. Any other conclusion would in all probability have been an unconstitutional interference with the freedom of the press. Accordingly, it has been held that the mere incidental mention of the plaintiff's name in a book or a motion picture is not an invasion of his privacy; nor is the publication of a photograph or a newsreel in which he incidentally appears. (Footnotes omitted.)

Cf. RESTATEMENT (SECOND) OF TORTS § 652C, Comment d (Tent. Draft No. 22, 1976).

12. It is possible, of course, that respondent's news broadcast increased the value of petitioner's performance by stimulating the public's interest in seeing the act live. In these circumstances, petitioner would not be able to prove damages and thus would not recover. But petitioner has alleged that the broadcast injured him to the extent of $25,000, App. 5, and we think the State should be allowed to authorize compensation of this injury if proved.

commercial product, but the appropriation of the very activity by which the entertainer acquired his reputation in the first place.

Of course, Ohio's decision to protect petitioner's right of publicity here rests on more than a desire to compensate the performer for the time and effort invested in his act; the protection provides an economic incentive for him to make the investment required to produce a performance of interest to the public. This same consideration underlies the patent and copyright laws long enforced by this Court. As the Court stated in Mazer v. Stein, 347 U.S. 201, 219, 74 S. Ct. 460, 471, 98 L. Ed. 630 (1954):

> The economic philosophy behind the clause empowering Congress to grant patents and copyrights is the conviction that encouragement of individual effort by personal gain is the best way to advance public welfare through the talents of authors and inventors in "Science and useful Arts." Sacrificial days devoted to such creative activities deserve rewards commensurate with the services rendered.

These laws perhaps regard the "reward to the owner (as) a secondary consideration," United States v. Paramount Pictures, 334 U.S. 131, 158, 68 S. Ct. 915, 929, 92 L. Ed. 1260 (1948), but they were "intended definitely to grant valuable, enforceable rights" in order to afford greater encouragement to the production of works of benefit to the public. Washingtonian Publishing Co. v. Pearson, 306 U.S. 30, 36, 59 S. Ct. 397, 400, 83 L. Ed. 470 (1939). The Constitution does not prevent Ohio from making a similar choice here in deciding to protect the entertainer's incentive in order to encourage the production of this type of work. Cf. Goldstein v. California, 412 U.S. 546, 93 S. Ct. 2303, 37 L. Ed. 2d 163 (1973); Kewanee Oil Co. v. Bicron Corp., 416 U.S. 470, 94 S. Ct. 1879, 40 L. Ed. 2d 315 (1974).

There is no doubt that entertainment, as well as news, enjoys First Amendment protection. It is also true that entertainment itself can be important news. *Time, Inc. v. Hill.* But it is important to note that neither the public nor respondent will be deprived of the benefit of petitioner's performance as long as his commercial stake in his act is appropriately recognized. Petitioner does not seek to enjoin the broadcast of his performance; he simply wants to be paid for it. Nor do we think that a state-law damages remedy against respondent would represent a species of liability without fault contrary to the letter or spirit of Gertz v. Robert Welch, Inc., 418 U.S. 323, 94 S. Ct. 2997, 41 L. Ed. 2d 789 (1974). Respondent knew that petitioner objected to televising his act, but nevertheless displayed the entire film.

We conclude that although the State of Ohio may as a matter of its own law privilege the press in the circumstances of this case, the First and Fourteenth Amendments do not require it to do so.

Reversed.

Mr. Justice POWELL, with whom Mr. Justice BRENNAN and Mr. Justice MARSHALL join, dissenting.

Disclaiming any attempt to do more than decide the narrow case before us, the Court reverses the decision of the Supreme Court of Ohio based on repeated incantation of a single formula: "a performer's entire act." The holding today is summed up in one sentence:

> Wherever the line in particular situations is to be drawn between media reports that are protected and those that are not, we are quite sure that the First and Fourteenth

> Amendments do not immunize the media when they broadcast a performer's entire act without his consent. . . .

I doubt that this formula provides a standard clear enough even for resolution of this case.[1] In any event, I am not persuaded that the Court's opinion is appropriately sensitive to the First Amendment values at stake, and I therefore dissent.

Although the Court would draw no distinction, ante, at 2857, I do not view respondent's action as comparable to unauthorized commercial broadcasts of sporting events, theatrical performances, and the like where the broadcaster keeps the profits. There is no suggestion here that respondent made any such use of the film. Instead, it simply reported on what petitioner concedes to be a newsworthy event, in a way hardly surprising for a television station by means of film coverage. The report was part of an ordinary daily news program, consuming a total of 15 seconds. It is a routine example of the press' fulfilling the informing function so vital to our system.

The Court's holding that the station's ordinary news report may give rise to substantial liability has disturbing implications, for the decision could lead to a degree of media self-censorship. Cf. Smith v. California, 361 U.S. 147, 150-154, 80 S. Ct. 215, 217-219, 4 L. Ed. 2d 205 (1959). Hereafter, whenever a television news editor is unsure whether certain film footage received from a camera crew might be held to portray an "entire act," he may decline coverage even of clearly newsworthy events or confine the broadcast to watered-down verbal reporting, perhaps with an occasional still picture. The public is then the loser. This is hardly the kind of news reportage that the First Amendment is meant to foster. See generally Miami Herald Publishing Co. v. Tornillo, 418 U.S. 241, 257-258, 94 S. Ct. 2831, 2839, 41 L. Ed. 2d 730 (1974); Time, Inc. v. Hill, 385 U.S. 374, 389, 87 S. Ct. 534, 542, 17 L. Ed. 2d 456 (1967); New York Times Co. v. Sullivan, 376 U.S. 254, 270-272, 279, 84 S. Ct. 710, 720-721, 725, 11 L. Ed. 2d 686 (1964).

In my view the First Amendment commands a different analytical starting point from the one selected by the Court. Rather than begin with a quantitative analysis of the performer's behavior — is this or is this not his entire act? — we should direct initial attention to the actions of the news media: what use did the station make of the film footage? When a film is used, as here, for a routine portion of a regular news program, I would hold that the First Amendment protects the station from a "right of publicity" or "appropriation" suit, absent a strong showing by the plaintiff that the news broadcast was a subterfuge or cover for private or commercial exploitation.

I emphasize that this is a "reappropriation" suit, rather than one of the other varieties of "right of privacy" tort suits identified by Dean Prosser in his classic article. Prosser, *Privacy*, 48 CALIF. L. REV. 383 (1960). In those other causes of action the competing interests are considerably different. The plaintiff generally seeks to avoid any sort of public exposure, and the existence of constitutional privilege is therefore

1. Although the record is not explicit, it is unlikely that the "act" commenced abruptly with the explosion that launched petitioner on his way, ending with the landing in the net a few seconds later. One may assume that the actual firing was preceded by some fanfare, possibly stretching over several minutes, to heighten the audience's anticipation: introduction of the performer, description of the uniqueness and danger, last-minute checking of the apparatus, and entry into the cannon, all accompanied by suitably ominous commentary from the master of ceremonies. If this is found to be the case on remand, then respondent could not be said to have appropriated the "entire act" in its 15-second newsclip and the Court's opinion then would afford no guidance for resolution of the case. Moreover, in future cases involving different performances, similar difficulties in determining just what constitutes the "entire act" are inevitable.

less likely to turn on whether the publication occurred in a news broadcast or in some other fashion. In a suit like the one before us, however, the plaintiff does not complain about the fact of exposure to the public, but rather about its timing or manner. He welcomes some publicity, but seeks to retain control over means and manner as a way to maximize for himself the monetary benefits that flow from such publication. But having made the matter public having chosen, in essence, to make it newsworthy he cannot, consistent with the First Amendment, complain of routine news reportage. Cf. Gertz v. Robert Welch, Inc., 418 U.S. 323, 339-348, 351-352, 94 S. Ct. 2997, 3006-3011, 3012-3013, 41 L. Ed. 2d 789 (1974) (clarifying the different liability standards appropriate in defamation suits, depending on whether or not the plaintiff is a public figure).

Since the film clip here was undeniably treated as news and since there is no claim that the use was subterfuge, respondent's actions were constitutionally privileged. I would affirm.

[The dissenting opinion of Justice STEVENS is omitted.]

COMMENTS AND QUESTIONS

1. It seems reasonably clear that the right of publicity regulates speech (words, visual images, sounds, and the like) and that the enforcement of publicity rights in court (as well as the state's enactment of publicity laws in the first place) constitutes state action for purposes of First Amendment law. (Indeed, if that were not the case, the Court could have reversed the Ohio Supreme Court's decision in *Zacchini* on one or the other of these grounds.) To define exactly what *Zacchini* means for the interplay of publicity rights and the First Amendment, however, requires considerable further analysis.

Recall from Chapter 9 that content-based regulations of noncommercial speech are generally subject to strict scrutiny; regulations of commercial speech, as well as content-neutral regulations, are subject to some form of intermediate scrutiny. *Zacchini* involved noncommercial speech, but the case arose before the Supreme Court had fully developed the distinction between content-based and content-neutral regulations. If a similar case arose today, how would the Court analyze it? Should the lower courts read *Zacchini* broadly (insulating publicity claims from First Amendment scrutiny most or all of the time) or narrowly (insulating those claims only sometimes, or perhaps only rarely)?

At present, there is no consensus on these questions. According to some commentators, the right of publicity falls squarely within the definition of a content-based regulation (because it cannot be "justified without reference to the content of the speech") and therefore potentially is subject to strict scrutiny, *Zacchini* notwithstanding. *See, e.g.*, F. Jay Dougherty, *All the World's a Stooge: The "Transformativeness" Test for Analyzing a Right Amendment Defense to a Right of Publicity Claim Against Distribution of a Work of Art*, 27 COLUM. J.L. & ARTS 1 (2003); Eugene Volokh, *Freedom of Speech and Intellectual Property: Some Thoughts After* Eldred, Bartnicki, *and* 33 Liquormart, 40 HOUS. L. REV. 697 (2003). Other observers, however, contend that the First Amendment does not affect most applications of publicity rights, because (1) publicity rights are a form of property, and (2) the First Amendment generally does not guarantee speakers the right to use another person's property to express the speaker's point of view, *see* Lloyd Corp., Ltd. v. Tanner, 407 U.S. 551, 570 (1972). On this view, publicity rights are analogous to time, place, and manner restrictions and thus are subject only to intermediate scrutiny. *See* Mark S. Lee, *Agents of Chaos: Judicial Confusion in Defining the Right of Publicity-Free Speech Interface*, 23 LOYOLA L.A. ENT. L. REV. 471 (2003); Rebecca Kwok, Comment, Cardtoons v. Major League Baseball Players Association: *Fair Use or Foul Play?*, 5 UCLA ENT. L. REV. 315 (1998). Critics of this argument counter that the states cannot restrict expression merely by characterizing certain interests as "property." *See* Mark A. Lemley & Eugene Volokh, *Freedom of Speech and Injunctions in Intellectual Property Cases*, 48 DUKE L.J. 147, 183 (1998) (arguing that "content-based laws, specifically targeted at speech, must be seen as speech restrictions regardless of whether one frames them as 'property' rules").

Another argument against subjecting publicity rights to strict scrutiny is that other intellectual property rights, such as copyrights, generally are not subjected to such heightened scrutiny. *See, e.g.*, Eldred v. Ashcroft, 537 U.S. 186, 221 (2003) (stating that "when . . . Congress has not altered the traditional contours of copyright protection, further First Amendment scrutiny is unnecessary"); Golan v. Holder, 611 F. Supp. 2d 1165 (D. Colo. 2009) (applying intermediate scrutiny to strike down law restoring terminated copyrights to qualifying foreign authors). Copyright law, however, is authorized by the same Constitution that forbids laws restricting freedom of speech; and it is usually viewed as advancing the same governmental interest (the creation and publication of speech) as the First Amendment. *See* Harper & Row Publishers, Inc. v. Nation Enters., 471 U.S. 539, 545-60 (1985); Neil Weinstock Netanel, *Locating Copyright within the First Amendment Skein*, 54 STAN. L. REV. 1, 49-54 (2001) (arguing that these features of copyright, among others, lead to the conclusion that copyright rules should be subject to intermediate, not strict, scrutiny). State publicity rights, by contrast, have no basis in the U.S. Constitution, and their speech-inducing effects are probably minimal in comparison with copyright. *See* Dougherty, *supra*, at 51.

Of course, even if publicity rights are a form of content-based regulation, traditional applications of the right occur within the context of commercial speech and thus would be subject only to *Central Hudson*'s version of intermediate scrutiny. *See* Central Hudson Gas & Electric Corp. v. Public Service Commission, 447 U.S. 557, 565 (1980) (holding that, in evaluating the constitutionality of commercial speech regulation, courts should inquire (1) whether the speech is misleading or promotes illegal transactions; (2) whether the regulation serves an important government interest; (3) whether the regulation directly advances the government interest; and (4) whether the regulation is narrowly tailored to achieve its goals and does not restrict more speech than necessary). Does the right of publicity directly advance important governmental interests? Does it restrict more speech than is necessary? Even if, as a general matter, the answer to the first question is "yes" and to the second "no," does it follow that *all* applications of publicity rights in the context of commercial speech survive *Central Hudson* scrutiny? Is Vanna White's claim against Samsung valid under *Central Hudson*? Note that Judge Kozinski accuses the majority in that case of ignoring the *Central Hudson* inquiry altogether.

2. Notwithstanding the preceding analysis, some applications of the right of publicity certainly do involve noncommercial speech. *Zacchini* is an obvious example, but there are others. For example, suppose that a celebrity objects to the marketing of T-shirts or posters or other merchandise that bears her likeness. (The claims at issue in the Marilyn Monroe litigation described above involved merchandise depicting

Monroe's photographic image.) Such "expressive merchandise" probably doesn't qualify as commercial speech under the applicable criteria as developed by the Supreme Court. *See* Bolger v. Young Drug Products Corp., 463 U.S. 60, 68 (1983) (finding three factors relevant though not necessarily dispositive, namely whether the speech occurs in the context of advertising, refers to a specific product, and is made pursuant to an economic motivation); *see also* Comedy III Prods., Inc. v. Gary Saderup, Inc., *infra* (holding that T-shirts depicting the Three Stooges were noncommercial speech). Would the application of the right of publicity in the context of expressive merchandise satisfy strict scrutiny? If not, are such applications unconstitutional? Or is strict scrutiny (for whatever reason) not the appropriate standard in this context?

What if Comedy III had asserted a claim for false endorsement as well as for violation of the right of publicity, in connection with Saderup's marketing of his Three Stooges T-shirts? Would such a claim make sense, given that the Stooges are deceased? Is it constitutional for courts to ban noncommercial speech on the ground that it threatens to confuse consumers as to sponsorship, affiliation, or endorsement? Courts do this all time, don't they? *See* Lisa Ramsey, *Increasing First Amendment Scrutiny of Trademark Law*, 61 SMU L. Rev. 381 (2008) (arguing that, while "courts have generally not applied strict scrutiny analysis to trademark laws regulating non-commercial speech," they should do so; and questioning whether eliminating confusion as to sponsorship, as opposed to source, would be a compelling state interest).

3. What if a state law purported to render the unauthorized use of a person's name or other indicia of identity unlawful, even when the use occurs in connection with a work of fiction or biography? On this issue, most of the relevant authorities are in agreement. To avoid First Amendment conflicts in this context, many state laws (as well as the *Restatement of Unfair Competition*) simply define these types of uses as not being "for purposes of trade." Of course, there is a bit of a legal fiction here: Money surely changes hands when consumers buy books, magazines, films, and other expressive works. Defining such uses as not "for purposes of trade" nevertheless enables courts to dodge the constitutional issue in many of these of cases. According to the *Restatement*:

> The name, likeness, and other indicia of a person's identity are used "for purposes of trade" under the rule stated in § 46 if they are used in advertising the user's goods or services, or are placed on merchandise marketed by the user, or are used in connection with services rendered by the user. However, use "for purposes of trade" does not ordinarily include the use of a person's identity in news reporting, commentary, entertainment, works of fiction or nonfiction, or in advertising that is incidental to such uses.

Restatement (Third) of Unfair Competition § 47. Under this principle, the right of publicity ordinarily would not forbid authors from publishing unauthorized biographies; from using the biography subject's photo on the cover of the book; or from using the subject's name to advertise the book. Nor would it ordinarily forbid the marketing of a motion picture using actors to depict real people, or the publication of news stories involving real people, or the inclusion of real people as characters in works of fiction. *See id.* cmts. a, c.

Note, however, the *Restatement*'s use of the word "ordinarily" in the language quoted above ("use 'for purposes of trade' does not *ordinarily* include the use of a person's identity in news reporting, commentary, entertainment, works of fiction or nonfiction, or in advertising that is incidental to such uses") (emphasis added). The phrasing suggests that there may be *some* circumstances in which the use of a person's identity in an expressive work *will* violate the person's right of publicity, and the *Restatement* itself identifies a few such circumstances. First, the *Restatement* takes the position that expressive merchandise of the type described in Comments and Questions No. 2 above is "ordinarily actionable as an infringement of the right of publicity." *Id.* § 47 cmt. b. We will come back to this issue in connection with the *Comedy III* case excerpted below.

Second, the *Restatement* cautions that "if the name or likeness is used solely to attract attention to a work that is not related to the identified person, the user may be subject to liability for a use of the other's identity in advertising." Restatement (Third) of Unfair Competition, § 47 cmt. c. In one case arguably involving this type of fact pattern, a federal district court concluded that the hip-hop band OutKast was entitled to use civil rights icon Rosa Parks's name by marketing a recording of a song titled "Rosa Parks" that, on its face, appeared to have nothing to do with either Ms. Parks or civil rights (though it did contain the line "everyone move to the back of the bus."). The Sixth Circuit reversed, however, finding a genuine issue of material fact whether the use at issue was "solely to attract attention" to a song that was not related to Ms. Parks. *See* Parks v. LaFace Records, 329 F.3d 437, 460-61 (6th Cir. 2003), *rev'g* 76 F. Supp. 2d 775 (E.D. Mich. 1999).

Third, the *Restatement* asserts that "if a photograph of the plaintiff is included in the defendant's publication merely for the purpose of appropriating the plaintiff's commercial value as a model rather than as part of a news or other communicative use, the defendant may be subject to liability for a merchandising use of the plaintiff's identity." Restatement (Third) of Unfair Competition, § 47 cmt. c. Consistent with this statement, some courts have concluded that the publication of photographs in (often sexually explicit) magazines, videos, or Web sites, without the photographic subjects' authorization, constituted an appropriation of modeling services. *See, e.g.*, Douglass v. Hustler Magazine, 769 F.2d 1128, 1138-39 (7th Cir. 1985); KNB Enters. v. Matthews, 92 Cal. Rptr. 2d 713, 717 (Ct. App. 2000). In other cases, however, courts have ruled for defendants on a variety of theories. *See, e.g.*, Almeida v. Amazon.com, Inc., 456 F.3d 1316, 1326 (11th Cir. 2006) (holding that bookseller was not liable for selling a photography book that displayed plaintiff's image on the cover); Ann-Margret v. High Soc'y Mag., Inc., 498 F. Supp. 401, 403-07 (S.D.N.Y. 1980). On this logic, would a painting, sculpture, or "fine art" photograph of a real person constitute a nonactionable expressive work, or an actionable appropriation of modeling services? Is there any principled way of drawing such distinctions? *Compare* Hoepker v. Kruger, 200 F. Supp. 2d 340, 354 (S.D.N.Y. 2002) (holding that museum reproductions of works of art incorporating plaintiff's photographic image, even in formats such as T-shirts and refrigerator magnets, did not violate plaintiff's right of publicity under New York law, because such reproductions retained an "essential nature of artistic expression"); Brinkley v. Casablancas, 438 N.Y.S.2d 1038 (App. Div. 1981) (holding that unauthorized distribution of mass market posters depicting model Christie Brinkley violated Brinkley's right of publicity under New York law); Simoneov v. Tiegs, 602 N.Y.S.2d 1014, 1018 (N.Y. City Civ. Ct. 1993) (in a case involving sculptural works depicting model Cheryl Tiegs, stating that "an artist may make a work of art that includes a recognizable likeness of a person without her or his written consent and sell at least a limited number of copies thereof without violating" N.Y. Civil Rights Law § 51). What about a mass market poster depicting a famous athlete such as Tiger Woods? *See* ETW Corp. v. Jireh Publ'g,

Inc., 332 F.3d 915, 936-37 (6th Cir. 2003) (concluding that the defendant's limited edition serigraphs and lithographs, depicting Tiger Woods golfing at the 1997 Masters Tournament while other legendary golfers appear in the background, had sufficient transformative elements to outweigh Woods' assertion of the right of publicity). Or a T-shirt depicting the Three Stooges? Is the artist appropriating Tiger Woods's (or Larry, Curly, and Moe's) modeling services?

In the opinion of the drafters of the *Restatement*, the principle discussed in the preceding paragraph also provides a basis — though perhaps only a tenuous one — for *Zacchini*. Referring to *Zacchini*, *Restatement* § 47 cmt. d provides:

> Liability has been imposed . . . in connection with an unauthorized broadcast of the plaintiff's performance or a sustained imitation of the plaintiff's performing style or performing persona that is marketed by the defendant as a simulation of the plaintiff's performance. If the defendant's appropriation falsely suggests the participation or endorsement of the plaintiff, liability may be imposed under the rules prohibiting deceptive marketing. . . . If the defendant has appropriated a work of authorship owned by the plaintiff, liability may be imposed for an infringement of federal statutory or state common law copyright. . . . Broader restrictions on the use of another's identity in entertainment, news, or other creative works threaten significant public and constitutional interests. In an effort to balance the personal and proprietary interests recognized by the right of publicity with the public interests in free expression and in the creation of original works, some courts have engaged in an analysis analogous to the determination of fair use in copyright law. The substantiality and market effect of the appropriation have been analyzed in light of the informational or creative content of the defendant's use. In cases of imitation, the public interest in competition and in avoiding the monopolization of successful styles, together with the interest in the production of new works including parody and satire, will ordinarily outweigh any adverse effect on the plaintiff's market. When the defendant's appropriation consists, not of an imitation, but of an unauthorized broadcast or other reproduction of an actual performance by the plaintiff, the greater likelihood of commercial injury to the plaintiff and the reduced public interest in permitting the use may justify relief in exceptional circumstances. Since the personal and proprietary interests underlying the right of publicity (see § 46, Comment c) diminish after death, more substantial appropriations may be permissible after the death of the identified person even in jurisdictions in whichthe right is descendible. Statutes in some states can be interpreted to permit the use of another's identity in news reporting or other specified works without regard to the substantiality of the use or its effect on the plaintiff.
>
> **Illustrations:**
>
> 7. B, the operator of a television station, broadcasts on its local news program a videotape of a "human cannonball" act performed by A, with favorable commentary. The videotape was made despite A's objection at one of a series of performances by A scheduled throughout the duration of the local county fair. The broadcast by B includes A's entire performance. A court may properly conclude in light of the substantiality and likely market effect of the appropriation that B is subject to liability to A for infringement of A's right of publicity under the rule stated in § 46.
>
> 8. The facts being otherwise as stated in Illustration 7, the broadcast by B occurs two years after A's death as part of a feature story on the history of the county fair. A's right of publicity is owned by A's son, C. A court may properly conclude in light of the absence of any injury to the personal interests of A and the minimal market effect of the appropriation on C that B is not subject to liability to C.

Is the *Restatement*'s interpretation of *Zacchini* persuasive? As the commentary suggests, courts *could* interpret *Zacchini* narrowly by focusing on its peculiar facts: that (1) the defendant appropriated the plaintiff's *actual* performance, (2) *in its entirety*, (3) the performer sought only damages, not an injunction,[9] and (4) the performer was still alive (and thus had an interest in preserving his ability to make a living). The commentary therefore disapproves of cases that have imposed liability for *imitation* performances, such as unauthorized Beatles tribute bands or Elvis impersonators. *See* Apple Corps Ltd. v. A.D.P.R., Inc. 843 F. Supp. 342 (M.D. Tenn. 1992); Apple Corps Ltd. v. Leber, 229 U.S.P.Q. 1015 (Cal. Super. Ct. 1986); Estate of Presley v. Russen, 513 F. Supp. 1339 (D.N.J. 1981); *but see* Joplin Enters. v. Allen, 795 F. Supp. 349 (W.D. Wash. 1992) (permitting a play based on the life of Janis Joplin, including one act that replicated a Joplin concert, to proceed); J. Thomas McCarthy & Paul M. Anderson, *Protection of the Athlete's Identity: The Right of Publicity, Endorsements and Domain Names*, 11 MARQ. SPORTS L. REV. 195, 198 (2001) (stating that the right of publicity "cannot prevent use of identity in an entertainment parody or satire, such as that of imitator Rich Little and satirical programs such as Saturday Night Live"). Should such imitation performances be actionable? Is there a meaningful distinction between free-riding on Zacchini's actual performance by broadcasting that performance as captured on tape, and free-riding on John Lennon's performance at a 1964 concert by an actor's depicting Lennon on stage?

Fourth, some state publicity laws might impose liability for expressive uses beyond the limits recommended by the *Restatement.* Cases imposing liability for unauthorized imitation performances would be one example. In addition, some state laws do not contain express exemptions for certain types of expressive uses that the *Restatement* would permit. The California statute, for instance, does not explicitly exempt the unauthorized use of a living person's identity in books, motion pictures, and other audiovisual works. *See* CAL. CIV. CODE § 3344(d) (exempting uses "in connection with any news, public affairs, or sports broadcast or account, or any political campaign"). In addition, courts in a few jurisdictions have imposed liability for the unauthorized inclusion of a person's identity in an expressive work, particularly where the use distorts the truth in some material way. *See* Messenger ex rel. Messenger v. Gruner + Jahr Printing & Publ'g, Inc., 727 N.E.2d 549, 555 (N.Y. 2000) (stating that "invented biographies" may be "so infected with fiction, dramatization or embellishment that [they] cannot be said to fulfill the purpose of the newsworthiness exception" to liability under New York law); Cason v. Baskin, 20 So. 2d 243, 244-53 (Fla. 1945) (holding that plaintiff stated a claim based on author's description of her in the book *Cross Creek*). Are these rulings consistent with contemporary First Amendment law? *Cf.* Cantrell v. Forest City Publ'g Co., 419 U.S. 245, 249 (1974); Time, Inc. v. Hill, 385 U.S. 374, 387-88 (1967) (both cases applying an "actual malice" standard to claims for false light invasion of privacy involving matters of public interest). *See also* Matthews v. Wozencraft, 15 F.3d 432 (5th Cir. 1994) (Texas right of publicity does not allow plaintiff to block a fictionalized biographical narrative, even though plaintiff can be identified from the book).

4. Is even the limited reading of *Zacchini* recommended by the *Restatement* viable? Can courts always determine what constitutes an "entire" performance? Would the appropriation of substantially an entire performance be actionable (and

9. A fact the Court noted three times in the course of the opinion. *See Zacchini*, 433 U.S. at 565, 573-74, 578.

if so, what constitutes a substantial appropriation?) *Cf. Zacchini*, 433 U.S. at 579-81 & n.1 (Powell, J., dissenting) (questioning courts' abilities to make such distinctions in any principled fashion). Would the Court's recitation of economic incentive-type arguments as justifications for the right of publicity satisfy strict scrutiny if the case arose today? Did Zacchini really need the economic incentive of a right of publicity to engage in his livelihood? Is the case better understood as vindicating Zacchini's autonomy interest (that is, his interest in deciding when and for whom to perform)? Would that interest suffice today? Consider that, in Bartnicki v. Vopper, 532 U.S. 514 (2001), the Supreme Court held that the First Amendment precluded the application of federal and state laws prohibiting the disclosure of illegally intercepted communications by a person who knows or should know that the communications have been illegally intercepted, where the defendants did not participate in the interception and the communications at issue involved a matter of public concern. (The disclosed communications at issue were telephone conversations during the course of which one of the speakers made threatening statements about school board officials, in connection with a labor dispute.) Does *Bartnicki* overrule *Zacchini* to the extent that the communication of Zacchini's performance was "newsworthy" or a matter of "public concern"?[10] Like Zacchini, the speakers in *Bartnicki* presumably did not want their "performance" to be made available to the general public. Or are the two cases distinguishable in light of the "unusual public concern," *Bartnicki*, 532 U.S. at 536 (Breyer, J., concurring), at issue in *Bartnicki*?

Of course, unless and until the Supreme Court chooses to overrule *Zacchini*, lower courts remain bound to follow the decision.

5. Apropos of use "for purposes of trade," some courts have held that "fleeting," "incidental," "insignificant," or "de minimis" uses of names and other indicia of identity are not actionable because they are likely to have no commercial impact. Consider, for example, Aligo v. Time-Life Books, Inc., No. C 94-20707 JW, 1994 WL 715605 (N.D. Cal. Dec. 19, 1994). In April 1969, a photograph of Police Officer James Aligo holding a billy club over a student protester appeared on the cover of *Rolling Stone* magazine. In 1993, Time-Life aired a 29-minute television infomercial touting the "Rolling Stone Collection" of music from the 1960s. Six minutes into the infomercial, and lasting for four seconds, the cover of the April 1969 issue of *Rolling Stone* on which Aligo's image was captured appeared on screen. Aligo filed suit for violation of his right of publicity, but the court dismissed:

> The contours of the incidental use doctrine are not well-defined in California. However, the general rule is that incidental use of a name or likeness does not give rise to liability for invasion of privacy by appropriation. The rationale for this rule is that an incidental use has no commercial value. Furthermore, allowing anyone briefly depicted or referred to for commercial purposes would unduly burden expressive activity.
>
> Whether the incidental use doctrine is applicable is determined by the role that the use plays with respect to the entire publication. A number of factors are relevant in this regard: (1) whether the use has a unique quality or value that would result in commercial profit to the defendant, (2) whether the use contributes something of significance; (3) the relationship between the reference to the plaintiff and the purpose and subject of the work; and (4) the duration, prominence or repetition of the name or likeness relative to the rest of the publication.

10. *See* Pamela Samuelson, *Reviving* Zacchini: *Analyzing First Amendment Defenses in Right of Publicity and Copyright Cases*, 57 Tul. L. Rev. 836, 858 (1983) (noting that Zacchini had conceded the "newsworthiness" of his act). What exactly is a "newsworthy" event? A matter of "public concern"?

> Defendants' use of Plaintiff's picture in the infomercial is incidental and, therefore, does not state either a common law claim or a claim under section 3344. The photograph appears in the 29-minute program once, and for only four seconds. It is one of dozens of Rolling Stone covers used in the program and is insignificant to the commercial purpose of selling the music anthology. It is inconceivable that commercial profits could inure to Defendants as a result of this fleeting and inconsequential use.

The incidental use doctrine appears to be a close cousin of the de minimis doctrine in copyright law. *See, e.g.*, Sandoval v. New Line Cinema Corp., 147 F.3d 215, 217 (2d Cir. 1998) (defining de minimis copying as "so trivial 'as to fall below the quantitative threshold of substantial similarity' "); Ringgold v. Black Entm't Television, Inc., 126 F.3d 70, 74 (2d Cir. 1997). For discussion and citations to other relevant case law, see 2 J. THOMAS MCCARTHY, THE RIGHTS OF PUBLICITY AND PRIVACY, § 7.20 (2009).

Comedy III Productions, Inc. v. Gary Saderup, Inc.
25 Cal. 4th 387, 21 P.3d 797, 106 Cal. Rptr. 2d 126 (2001)

MOSK, J.

A California statute grants the right of publicity to specified successors in interest of deceased celebrities, prohibiting any other person from using a celebrity's name, voice, signature, photograph, or likeness for commercial purposes without the consent of such successors. The United States Constitution prohibits the states from abridging, among other fundamental rights, freedom of speech. (U.S. CONST., 1st and 14th Amends.) In the case at bar we resolve a conflict between these two provisions. The Court of Appeal concluded that the lithographs and silkscreened T-shirts in question here received no First Amendment protection simply because they were reproductions rather than original works of art. As will appear, this was error: reproductions are equally entitled to First Amendment protection. We formulate instead what is essentially a balancing test between the First Amendment and the right of publicity based on whether the work in question adds significant creative elements so as to be transformed into something more than a mere celebrity likeness or imitation. Applying this test to the present case, we conclude that there are no such creative elements here and that the right of publicity prevails. On this basis, we will affirm the judgment of the Court of Appeal. . . .

II. Facts

Plaintiff Comedy III Productions, Inc. (hereafter Comedy III), brought this action against defendants Gary Saderup and Gary Saderup, Inc. (hereafter collectively Saderup), seeking damages and injunctive relief for violation of section 990 [the predecessor to § 3344.1] and related business torts. The parties waived the right to jury trial and the right to put on evidence, and submitted the case for decision on the following stipulated facts: Comedy III is the registered owner of all rights to the former comedy act known as The Three Stooges, who are deceased personalities within the meaning of the statute.

Saderup is an artist with over 25 years' experience in making charcoal drawings of celebrities. These drawings are used to create lithographic and silkscreen masters, which in turn are used to produce multiple reproductions in the form, respectively, of lithographic prints and silkscreened images on T-shirts. Saderup creates the original drawings and is actively involved in the ensuing lithographic and silkscreening processes. Without securing Comedy III's consent, Saderup sold lithographs and T-shirts bearing a likeness of The Three Stooges reproduced from a charcoal drawing he had made. These lithographs and T-shirts did not constitute an advertisement, endorsement, or sponsorship of any product.

Saderup's profits from the sale of unlicensed lithographs and T-shirts bearing a likeness of The Three Stooges was $75,000 and Comedy III's reasonable attorney fees were $150,000.

On these stipulated facts the court found for Comedy III and entered judgment against Saderup awarding damages of $75,000 and attorney fees of $150,000 plus costs. The court also issued a permanent injunction restraining Saderup from violating the statute by use of any likeness of The Three Stooges in lithographs, T-shirts, "or any other medium by which the [Saderup's] art work may be sold or marketed." The injunction further prohibited Saderup from "Creating, producing, reproducing, copying, distributing, selling or exhibiting any lithographs, prints, posters, t-shirts, buttons, or other goods, products or merchandise of any kind, bearing the photograph, image, face, symbols, trademarks, likeness, name, voice or signature of The Three Stooges or any of the individual members of The Three Stooges." The sole exception to this broad prohibition was Saderup's original charcoal drawing from which the reproductions at issue were made.

Saderup appealed. The Court of Appeal modified the judgment by striking the injunction. The court reasoned that Comedy III had not proved a likelihood of continued violation of the statute, and that the wording of the injunction was overbroad because it exceeded the terms of the statute and because it "could extend to matters and conduct protected by the First Amendment. . . ."

The Court of Appeal affirmed the judgment as thus modified, however, upholding the award of damages, attorney fees, and costs. In so doing, it rejected Saderup's contentions that his conduct (1) did not violate the terms of the statute, and (2) in any event was protected by the constitutional guaranty of freedom of speech.

We granted review to address these two issues.

III. Discussion

A. *The Statutory Issue*

[The court held that the statute extends to the sale of products featuring a deceased personality's likeness as well as advertisements.]

B. *The Constitutional Issue*

Saderup next contends that enforcement of the judgment against him violates his right of free speech and expression under the First Amendment. He raises a difficult issue, which we address below.

The right of publicity is often invoked in the context of commercial speech when the appropriation of a celebrity likeness creates a false and misleading impression that the celebrity is endorsing a product. (See Waits v. Frito-Lay, Inc. (9th Cir. 1992) 978 F.2d 1093; Midler v. Ford Motor Co. (9th Cir. 1988) 849 F.2d 460.) Because the First Amendment does not protect false and misleading commercial speech (Central Hudson Gas & Elec. Corp. v. Public Serv. Com'n (1980) 447 U.S. 557, 563-564), and because even nonmisleading commercial speech is generally subject to somewhat lesser First Amendment protection (*Central Hudson*, at p. 566), the right of publicity may often trump the right of advertisers to make use of celebrity figures.

But the present case does not concern commercial speech. As the trial court found, Saderup's portraits of The Three Stooges are expressive works and not an advertisement for or endorsement of a product. Although his work was done for financial gain, "[t]he First Amendment is not limited to those who publish without charge. . . . [An expressive activity] does not lose its constitutional protection because it is undertaken for profit." (Guglielmi v. Spelling-Goldberg Productions (1979) 25 Cal. 3d 860, 868, 160 Cal. Rptr. 352, 603 P.2d 454 (conc. opn. of Bird, C.J.) (*Guglielmi*).)

The tension between the right of publicity and the First Amendment is highlighted by recalling the two distinct, commonly acknowledged purposes of the latter. First, " 'to preserve an uninhibited marketplace of ideas' and to repel efforts to limit the 'uninhibited, robust and wide-open debate on public issues.' " (*Guglielmi*, supra, 25 Cal. 3d at p. 866, 160 Cal. Rptr. 352, 603 P.2d 454.) Second, to foster a "fundamental respect for individual development and self-realization. The right to self-expression is inherent in any political system which respects individual dignity. Each speaker must be free of government restraint regardless of the nature or manner of the views expressed unless there is a compelling reason to the contrary." (Ibid., fn. omitted; see also EMERSON, THE SYSTEM OF FREEDOM OF EXPRESSION (1970) pp. 6-7.)

The right of publicity has a potential for frustrating the fulfillment of both these purposes. Because celebrities take on public meaning, the appropriation of their likenesses may have important uses in uninhibited debate on public issues, particularly debates about culture and values. And because celebrities take on personal meanings to many individuals in the society, the creative appropriation of celebrity images can be an important avenue of individual expression. As one commentator has stated: "Entertainment and sports celebrities are the leading players in our Public Drama. We tell tales, both tall and cautionary, about them. We monitor their comings and goings, their missteps and heartbreaks. We copy their mannerisms, their styles, their modes of conversation and of consumption. Whether or not celebrities are 'the chief agents of moral change in the United States,' they certainly are widely used — far more than are institutionally anchored elites — to symbolize individual aspirations, group identities, and cultural values. Their images are thus important expressive and communicative resources: the peculiar, yet familiar idiom in which we conduct a fair portion of our cultural business and everyday conversation." (Madow, *Private Ownership of Public Image: Popular Culture and Publicity Rights* (1993) 81 CAL. L. REV. 125, 128 (italics and fns. omitted).)

As Madow further points out, the very importance of celebrities in society means that the right of publicity has the potential of censoring significant expression by suppressing alternative versions of celebrity images that are iconoclastic, irreverent, or otherwise attempt to redefine the celebrity's meaning. (Madow, supra, 81 Cal. L. Rev. at pp. 143-145; see also Coombe, *Author/izing the Celebrity: Publicity Rights, Postmodern Politics, and Unauthorized Genders* (1992) 10 CARDOZO ARTS AND ENT. L.J. 365, 377-388.) A majority of this court recognized as much in *Guglielmi:* "The right of publicity derived from public prominence does not confer a shield to ward off caricature, parody and satire. Rather, prominence invites creative comment." (*Guglielmi*, supra, 25 Cal. 3d at p. 869, 160 Cal. Rptr. 352, 603 P.2d 454.)

For similar reasons, speech about public figures is accorded heightened First Amendment protection in defamation law. As the United States Supreme Court held in Gertz v. Robert Welch, Inc. (1974) 418 U.S. 323, public figures may prevail in a libel action only if they prove that the defendant's defamatory statements were made with actual malice, i.e., actual knowledge of falsehood or reckless disregard for the truth, whereas private figures need prove only negligence. (Id. at pp. 328, 342, 344-45.) The rationale for such differential treatment is, first, that the public figure has greater access to the media and therefore greater opportunity to rebut defamatory statements, and second, that those who have become public figures have done so voluntarily and therefore "invite attention and comment." (Id. at pp. 344-345, 94 S. Ct. 2997.) Giving broad scope to the right of publicity has the potential of allowing a celebrity to accomplish through the vigorous exercise of that right the censorship of unflattering commentary that cannot be constitutionally accomplished through defamation actions.

Nor do Saderup's creations lose their constitutional protections because they are for purposes of entertaining rather than informing. As Chief Justice Bird stated in *Guglielmi*, invoking the dual purpose of the First Amendment: "Our courts have often observed that entertainment is entitled to the same constitutional protection as the exposition of ideas. That conclusion rests on two propositions. First, '[t]he line between informing and entertaining is too elusive for the protection of the basic right. Everyone is familiar with instances of propaganda through fiction. What is one man's amusement, teaches another doctrine.'" (*Guglielmi*, supra, 25 Cal. 3d at p. 867, 160 Cal. Rptr. 352, 603 P.2d 454, fn. omitted.) "Second, entertainment, as a mode of self-expression, is entitled to constitutional protection irrespective of its contribution to the marketplace of ideas. 'For expression is an integral part of the development of ideas, of mental exploration and of the affirmation of self. The power to realize his potentiality as a human being begins at this point and must extend at least this far if the whole nature of man is not to be thwarted.'" (Ibid.)

Nor does the fact that expression takes a form of nonverbal, visual representation remove it from the ambit of First Amendment protection. In Bery v. City of New York (2d Cir. 1996) 97 F.3d 689, the court overturned an ordinance requiring visual artists — painters, printers, photographers, sculptors, etc. — to obtain licenses to sell their work in public places, but exempted the vendors of books, newspapers or other written matter. As the court stated: "Both the [district] court and the City demonstrate an unduly restricted view of the First Amendment and of visual art itself. Such myopic vision not only overlooks case law central to First Amendment jurisprudence but fundamentally misperceives the essence of visual communication and artistic expression. Visual art is as wide ranging in its depiction of ideas, concepts and emotions as any book, treatise, pamphlet or other writing, and is similarly entitled to full First Amendment protection. . . . One cannot look at Winslow Homer's paintings on the Civil War without seeing, in his depictions of the boredom and hardship of the individual soldier, expressions of anti-war sentiments, the idea that war is not heroic." (Id. at p. 695.)

Moreover, the United States Supreme Court has made it clear that a work of art is protected by the First Amendment even if it conveys no discernable message: "[A] narrow, succinctly articulable message is not a condition of constitutional protection, which if confined to expressions conveying a 'particularized message,' [citation], would never reach the unquestionably shielded painting of Jackson Pollock, music of Arnold Schoenberg, or Jabberwocky verse of Lewis Carroll." (Hurley v. Irish-American Gay, Lesbian and Bisexual Group of Boston, Inc. (1995) 515 U.S. 557, 569.)

Nor does the fact that Saderup's art appears in large part on a less conventional avenue of communications, T-shirts, result in reduced First Amendment protection. As Judge Posner stated in the case of a defendant who sold T-shirts advocating the legalization of marijuana, "its T-shirts . . . are to [the seller] what the *New York Times* is to the Sulzbergers and the Ochs — the vehicle of her ideas and opinions." (Ayres v. City of Chicago (7th Cir. 1997) 125 F.3d 1010, 1017; see also Cohen v. California (1971) 403 U.S. 15, [jacket with words "Fuck the Draft" on the back is protected speech].) First Amendment doctrine does not disfavor nontraditional media of expression.

But having recognized the high degree of First Amendment protection for noncommercial speech about celebrities, we need not conclude that all expression that trenches on the right of publicity receives such protection. The right of publicity, like copyright, protects a form of intellectual property that society deems to have some social utility. "Often considerable money, time and energy are needed to develop one's prominence in a particular field. Years of labor may be required before one's skill, reputation, notoriety or virtues are sufficiently developed to permit an economic return through some medium of commercial promotion. [Citations.] For some, the investment may eventually create considerable commercial value in one's identity." (*Lugosi*, supra, 25 Cal. 3d at pp. 834-835, 160 Cal. Rptr. 323, 603 P.2d 425 (dis. opn. of Bird, C.J.).)

The present case exemplifies this kind of creative labor. Moe and Jerome (Curly) Howard and Larry Fein fashioned personae collectively known as The Three Stooges, first in vaudeville and later in movie shorts, over a period extending from the 1920's to the 1940's. (See FLEMING, THE THREE STOOGES: AMALGAMATED MORONS TO AMERICAN ICONS (1999) pp. 10-46.) The three comic characters they created and whose names they shared — Larry, Moe, and Curly — possess a kind of mythic status in our culture. Their journey from ordinary vaudeville performers to the heights (or depths) of slapstick comic celebrity was long and arduous. (Ibid.) Their brand of physical humor — the nimble, comically stylized violence, the "nyuk-nyuks" and "whoop-whoop-whoops," eye-pokes, slaps and head conks (see, e.g., *Three Little Pigskins* (Columbia Pictures 1934), *Hoi Polloi* (Columbia Pictures 1935), *A Gem of a Jam* (Columbia Pictures 1943), *Micro Phonies* (Columbia Pictures 1945)) — created a distinct comedic trademark. Through their talent and labor, they joined the relatively small group of actors who constructed identifiable, recurrent comic personalities that they brought to the many parts they were scripted to play. "Groucho Marx just being Groucho Marx, with his moustache, cigar, slouch and leer, cannot be exploited by others. Red Skelton's variety of self-devised roles would appear to be protectible, as would the unique personal creations of Abbott and Costello, Laurel and Hardy and others of that genre. . . . '[W]e deal here with actors portraying themselves and developing their own characters.' " (*Lugosi*, supra, 25 Cal. 3d at pp. 825-826, 160 Cal. Rptr. 323, 603 P.2d 425 (conc. opn. of Mosk, J.).)

In sum, society may recognize, as the Legislature has done here, that a celebrity's heirs and assigns have a legitimate protectible interest in exploiting the value to be obtained from merchandising the celebrity's image, whether that interest be conceived as a kind of natural property right or as an incentive for encouraging creative work. (See 1 McCarthy, The Rights of Publicity and Privacy (2d ed. 2000) §§ 2.2-2.7, pp. 2-1 to 2-22 (McCarthy).) Although critics have questioned whether the right of publicity truly serves any social purpose (see, e.g., Madow, supra, 81 Cal. L. Rev. at pp. 178-238), there is no question that the Legislature has a rational basis for permitting celebrities and their heirs to control the commercial exploitation of the celebrity's likeness.

Although surprisingly few courts have considered in any depth the means of reconciling the right of publicity and the First Amendment, we follow those that have in concluding that depictions of celebrities amounting to little more than the appropriation of the celebrity's economic value are not protected expression under the First Amendment. . . .

It is admittedly not a simple matter to develop a test that will unerringly distinguish between forms of artistic expression protected by the First Amendment and those that must give way to the right of publicity. Certainly, any such test must incorporate the principle that the right of publicity cannot, consistent with the First Amendment, be a right to control the celebrity's image by censoring disagreeable portrayals. Once the celebrity thrusts himself or herself forward into the limelight, the First Amendment dictates that the right to comment on, parody, lampoon, and make other expressive uses of the celebrity image must be given broad scope. The necessary implication of this observation is that the right of publicity is essentially an economic right. What the right of publicity holder possesses is not a right of censorship, but a right to prevent others from misappropriating the economic value generated by the celebrity's fame through the merchandising of the "name, voice, signature, photograph, or likeness" of the celebrity. (§ 990.)

Beyond this precept, how may courts distinguish between protected and unprotected expression? Some commentators have proposed importing the fair use defense from copyright law (17 U.S.C. § 107), which has the advantage of employing an established doctrine developed from a related area of the law. (See Barnett, *First Amendment Limits on the Right of Publicity* (1995) 30 Tort & Ins. L.J. 635, 650-657; Coyne, *Toward a Modified Fair Use Defense in Right of Publicity Cases* (1988) 29 Wm. & Mary L. Rev. 781, 812-820.) Others disagree, pointing to the murkiness of the fair use doctrine and arguing that the idea/expression dichotomy, rather than fair use, is the principal means of reconciling copyright protection and First Amendment rights. (2 McCarthy, supra, § 8.38, pp. 8-358 to 8-360; see also Kwall, *The Right of Publicity vs. The First Amendment: A Property and Liability Rule Analysis* (1994) 70 Ind. L.J. 47, 58, fn. 54.)

We conclude that a wholesale importation of the fair use doctrine into right of publicity law would not be advisable. At least two of the factors employed in the fair use test, "the nature of the copyrighted work" and "the amount and substantiality of the portion used" (17 U.S.C. § 107(2), (3)), seem particularly designed to be applied to the partial copying of works of authorship "fixed in [a] tangible medium of expression" (17 U.S.C. § 102); it is difficult to understand why these factors would be especially useful for determining whether the depiction of a celebrity likeness is protected by the First Amendment.

Nonetheless, the first fair use factor — "the purpose and character of the use" (17 U.S.C. § 107(1)) — does seem particularly pertinent to the task of reconciling the rights of free expression and publicity. As the Supreme Court has stated, the central purpose of the inquiry into this fair use factor "is to see, in Justice Story's words, whether the new work merely 'supersede[s] the objects' of the original creation [citations], or instead adds something new, with a further purpose or different character, altering the first with new expression, meaning, or message; it asks, in other words, whether and to what extent the new work is 'transformative.' Although such transformative use is not absolutely necessary for a finding of fair use, the goal of copyright, to promote science and the arts, is generally furthered by the creation of transformative works." (Campbell v. Acuff-Rose Music, Inc. (1994) 510 U.S. 569, 579, fn. omitted.)

This inquiry into whether a work is "transformative" appears to us to be necessarily at the heart of any judicial attempt to square the right of publicity with the First Amendment. As the above quotation suggests, both the First Amendment and copyright law have a common goal of encouragement of free expression and creativity, the former by protecting such expression from government interference, the latter by protecting the creative fruits of intellectual and artistic labor. (See 1 NIMMER ON COPYRIGHT (2000 ed.) § 1.10, pp. 1-66.43 to 1-66.44 (NIMMER).) The right of publicity, at least theoretically, shares this goal with copyright law. (1 MCCARTHY, supra, § 2.6, pp. 2-14 to 2-19.) When artistic expression takes the form of a literal depiction or imitation of a celebrity for commercial gain,[9] directly trespassing on the right of publicity without adding significant expression beyond that trespass, the state law interest in protecting the fruits of artistic labor outweighs the expressive interests of the imitative artist. (See *Zacchini*, supra, 433 U.S. at pp. 575-576.)

On the other hand, when a work contains significant transformative elements, it is not only especially worthy of First Amendment protection, but it is also less likely to interfere with the economic interest protected by the right of publicity. As has been observed, works of parody or other distortions of the celebrity figure are not, from the celebrity fan's viewpoint, good substitutes for conventional depictions of the celebrity and therefore do not generally threaten markets for celebrity memorabilia that the right of publicity is designed to protect. (See Cardtoons, L.C. v. Major League Baseball Players Association (10th Cir. 1996) 95 F.3d 959, 974 (*Cardtoons*).) Accordingly, First Amendment protection of such works outweighs whatever interest the state may have in enforcing the right of publicity. The right-of-publicity holder continues to enforce the right to monopolize the production of conventional, more or less fungible, images of the celebrity.[10] *Cardtoons*, supra, 95 F.3d 959, cited by Saderup, is consistent with this "transformative" test. There, the court held that the First Amendment

9. Inquiry into the "purpose and character" of the work in copyright law also includes "whether such use is of a commercial nature or is for nonprofit educational purposes." (17 U.S.C. § 107(1).) It could be argued that reproduction of a celebrity likeness for noncommercial use — e.g., T-shirts of a recently deceased rock musician produced by a fan as a not-for-profit tribute — is a form of personal expression and therefore more worthy of First Amendment protection. This is an issue, however, that we need not decide in this case. It is undisputed that Saderup sold his reproductions for financial gain.

10. There is a fourth factor in the fair use test not yet mentioned, "the effect of the use upon the potential market for or value of the copyrighted work" (17 U.S.C. § 107(4)), that bears directly on this question. We do not believe, however, that consideration of this factor would usefully supplement the test articulated here. If it is determined that a work is worthy of First Amendment protection because added creative elements significantly transform the celebrity depiction, then independent inquiry into whether or not that work is cutting into the market for the celebrity's images — something that might be particularly difficult to ascertain in the right of publicity context (see Madow, supra, 81 CAL. L. REV. at pp. 221-222) — appears to be irrelevant. Moreover, this "potential market" test has been criticized for circularity: it could be argued that if a defendant has capitalized in any way on a celebrity's image, he or she has found a potential market and therefore could be liable for such work. (See 4 NIMMER, supra, § 13.05[A][4] at pp. 13-183 to 13-184.) The "transformative" test elaborated in this opinion will, we conclude, protect the right-of-publicity holder's core interest in monopolizing the merchandising of celebrity images without unnecessarily impinging on the artists' right of free expression.

protected a company that produced trading cards caricaturing and parodying well-known major league baseball players against a claim brought under the Oklahoma right of publicity statute. The court concluded that "[t]he cards provide social commentary on public figures, major league baseball players, who are involved in a significant commercial enterprise, major league baseball," and that "[t]he cards are no less protected because they provide humorous rather than serious commentary." (*Cardtoons*, at p. 969.) The *Cardtoons* court weighed these First Amendment rights against what it concluded was the less-than-compelling interests advanced by the right of publicity outside the advertising context—especially in light of the reality that parody would not likely substantially impact the economic interests of celebrities—and found the cards to be a form of protected expression. (*Cardtoons*, at pp. 973-976.) While *Cardtoons* contained dicta calling into question the social value of the right of publicity, its conclusion that works parodying and caricaturing celebrities are protected by the First Amendment appears unassailable in light of the test articulated above.

We emphasize that the transformative elements or creative contributions that require First Amendment protection are not confined to parody and can take many forms, from factual reporting (see, e.g., Rosemont Enterprises, Inc. v. Random House, Inc. (N.Y. Sup. Ct. 1968) 58 Misc. 2d 1, 294 N.Y.S.2d 122, 129, affd. mem. (1969) 32 A.D.2d 892, 301 N.Y.S.2d 948) to fictionalized portrayal (*Guglielmi*, supra, 25 Cal. 3d at pp. 871-872, 160 Cal. Rptr. 352, 603 P.2d 454; see also Parks v. LaFace Records (E.D. Mich. 1999) 76 F. Supp. 2d 775, 779-782 [use of civil rights figure Rosa Parks in song title is protected expression][11]), from heavy-handed lampooning (see Hustler Magazine v. Falwell (1988) 485 U.S. 46) to subtle social criticism (see COPLANS ET AL., ANDY WARHOL (1970) pp. 50-52 [explaining Warhol's celebrity portraits as a critique of the celebrity phenomenon]).

Another way of stating the inquiry is whether the celebrity likeness is one of the "raw materials" from which an original work is synthesized, or whether the depiction or imitation of the celebrity is the very sum and substance of the work in question. We ask, in other words, whether a product containing a celebrity's likeness is so transformed that it has become primarily the defendant's own expression rather than the celebrity's likeness. And when we use the word "expression," we mean expression of something other than the likeness of the celebrity.

We further emphasize that in determining whether the work is transformative, courts are not to be concerned with the quality of the artistic contribution—vulgar forms of expression fully qualify for First Amendment protection. (See, e.g., Hustler Magazine v. Falwell, supra, 485 U.S. 46, 99 L. Ed. 2d 41; see also Campbell v. Acuff-Rose Music, Inc., supra, 510 U.S. at p. 582.) On the other hand, a literal depiction of a celebrity, even if accomplished with great skill, may still be subject to a right of publicity challenge. The inquiry is in a sense more quantitative than qualitative, asking whether the literal and imitative or the creative elements predominate in the work.

Furthermore, in determining whether a work is sufficiently transformative, courts may find useful a subsidiary inquiry, particularly in close cases: does the marketability and economic value of the challenged work derive primarily from the fame of the celebrity depicted? If this question is answered in the negative, then there would

11. [The *Parks* case was reversed on appeal. *See* Parks v. LaFace Records, 329 F.3d 427 (6th Cir. 2003).—EDS.]

generally be no actionable right of publicity. When the value of the work comes principally from some source other than the fame of the celebrity—from the creativity, skill, and reputation of the artist—it may be presumed that sufficient transformative elements are present to warrant First Amendment protection. If the question is answered in the affirmative, however, it does not necessarily follow that the work is without First Amendment protection—it may still be a transformative work.

In sum, when an artist is faced with a right of publicity challenge to his or her work, he or she may raise as affirmative defense that the work is protected by the First Amendment inasmuch as it contains significant transformative elements or that the value of the work does not derive primarily from the celebrity's fame.

Turning to the present case, we note that the trial court, in ruling against Saderup, stated that "the commercial enterprise conducted by [Saderup] involves the sale of lithographs and T-shirts which are not original single works of art, and which are not protected by the First Amendment; the enterprise conducted by the [Saderup] was a commercial enterprise designed to generate profits solely from the use of the likeness of The Three Stooges which is the right of publicity . . . protected by section 990." Although not entirely clear, the trial court seemed to be holding that *reproductions* of celebrity images are categorically outside First Amendment protection. The Court of Appeal was more explicit in adopting this rationale: "Simply put, although the First Amendment protects speech that is sold, reproductions of an image, made to be sold for profit do not per se constitute speech." But this position has no basis in logic or authority. No one would claim that a published book, because it is one of many copies, receives less First Amendment protection than the original manuscript. It is true that the statute at issue here makes a distinction between a single and original work of fine art and a reproduction. (§990, subd. (n)(3).) Because the statute evidently aims at preventing the illicit merchandising of celebrity images, and because single original works of fine art are not forms of merchandising, the state has little if any interest in preventing the exhibition and sale of such works, and the First Amendment rights of the artist should therefore prevail. But the inverse—that a reproduction receives no First Amendment protection—is patently false: a reproduction of a celebrity image that, as explained above, contains significant creative elements is entitled to as much First Amendment protection as an original work of art. The trial court and the Court of Appeal therefore erred in this respect.

Rather, the inquiry is into whether Saderup's work is sufficiently transformative. Correctly anticipating this inquiry, he argues that all portraiture involves creative decisions, that therefore no portrait portrays a mere literal likeness, and that accordingly all portraiture, including reproductions, is protected by the First Amendment. We reject any such categorical position. Without denying that all portraiture involves the making of artistic choices, we find it equally undeniable, under the test formulated above, that when an artist's skill and talent is manifestly subordinated to the overall goal of creating a conventional portrait of a celebrity so as to commercially exploit his or her fame, then the artist's right of free expression is outweighed by the right of publicity. As is the case with fair use in the area of copyright law, an artist depicting a celebrity must contribute something more than a "merely trivial" variation, [but must create] something recognizably "his own" (L. Batlin & Son, Inc. v. Snyder (2d Cir. 1976) 536 F.2d 486, 490), in order to qualify for legal protection.

On the other hand, we do not hold that all reproductions of celebrity portraits are unprotected by the First Amendment. The silkscreens of Andy Warhol, for example, have as their subjects the images of such celebrities as Marilyn Monroe, Elizabeth

Taylor, and Elvis Presley. Through distortion and the careful manipulation of context, Warhol was able to convey a message that went beyond the commercial exploitation of celebrity images and became a form of ironic social comment on the dehumanization of celebrity itself. (See COPLANS ET AL., supra, at p. 52.) Such expression may well be entitled to First Amendment protection. Although the distinction between protected and unprotected expression will sometimes be subtle, it is no more so than other distinctions triers of fact are called on to make in First Amendment jurisprudence. (See, e.g., Miller v. California (1973) 413 U.S. 15, 24, [requiring determination, in the context of work alleged to be obscene, of "whether the work, taken as a whole, lacks serious literary, artistic, political, or scientific value"].)[12]

Turning to Saderup's work, we can discern no significant transformative or creative contribution. His undeniable skill is manifestly subordinated to the overall goal of creating literal, conventional depictions of The Three Stooges so as to exploit their fame. Indeed, were we to decide that Saderup's depictions were protected by the First Amendment, we cannot perceive how the right of publicity would remain a viable right other than in cases of falsified celebrity endorsements.

Moreover, the marketability and economic value of Saderup's work derives primarily from the fame of the celebrities depicted. While that fact alone does not necessarily mean the work receives no First Amendment protection, we can perceive no transformative elements in Saderup's works that would require such protection.

Saderup argues that it would be incongruous and unjust to protect parodies and other distortions of celebrity figures but not wholesome, reverential portraits of such celebrities. The test we articulate today, however, does not express a value judgment or preference for one type of depiction over another. Rather, it reflects a recognition that the Legislature has granted to the heirs and assigns of celebrities the property right to exploit the celebrities' images, and that certain forms of expressive activity protected by the First Amendment fall outside the boundaries of that right. Stated another way, we are concerned not with whether conventional celebrity images should be produced but with who produces them and, more pertinently, who appropriates the value from their production. Thus, under section 990, if Saderup wishes to continue to depict The Three Stooges as he has done, he may do so only with the consent of the right-of-publicity holder.

IV. Disposition

The judgment of the Court of Appeal is affirmed.

12. The novelist Don DeLillo gives this fictional account of an encounter with Warhol's reproductions of images of Mao Zedong: "He moved along and stood finally in a room filled with images of Chairman Mao. Photocopy Mao, silk-screen Mao, wallpaper Mao, synthetic-polymer Mao. A series of silk screens was installed over a broader surface of wallpaper serigraphs, the Chairman's face a pansy purple here, floating nearly free of its photographic source. Work that was unwitting of history appealed to [him]. He found it liberating. Had he ever realized the deeper meaning of Mao before he saw these pictures?" (DELILLO, MAO II (1991) p. 21.)

Appendix

FIGURE 10-2
The Three Stooges T-shirt image

COMMENTS AND QUESTIONS

1. The court in *Saderup* concludes (correctly, it seems) that the T-shirts at issue are noncommercial speech. Does the court state what level of scrutiny it is applying? Would the application of California's right of publicity statute in this context withstand strict scrutiny? Intermediate scrutiny?

In answering this question, ask yourself: What exactly is the state interest justifying application of the right of publicity in *Saderup*? Larry, Curly, and Moe were all deceased at the time *Saderup* was decided, so it's hard to see how a privacy or autonomy interest is at stake.[12] Would the state's interest in preventing consumers from being deceived into thinking that the Stooges endorsed the T-shirts be a compelling state interest? Some consumers may not have been aware that the Stooges were dead, after all. *See also* 1 J. Thomas McCarthy, McCarthy on Trademarks and Unfair Competition §28:15, at 28-28 (4th ed. 2009) (raising, but not answering, the question whether "use of the identity of a deceased person" would constitute actionable false endorsement, if consumers think that the "product was endorsed by the person while alive"). But the case obviously doesn't hinge on (indeed, doesn't even discuss) the issue of consumer confusion. Should California's interest in conferring upon performers an economic incentive to create unique performances, or to manage their fame so as to prevent its premature dissipation, be sufficient to overcome a First Amendment challenge? Does California have a compelling interest in vindicating the investment of labor or personality that goes into creating memorable performances? Is that labor in fact captured by Saderup's T-shirt? Is it relevant that none of the Stooges were alive when California extended right of publicity protection to deceased performers in 1984?

12. Curly died in 1952; Larry and Moe in 1975. "Shemp" Howard, who replaced Curly, died in 1955. Four other actors occasionally appeared as "Stooges" at other times, but none of them are depicted on the T-shirts.

2. Does the court's test adequately protect the freedom of expression? Is the court saying that art needs to go beyond literal interpretation and not be mass marketed? Or possibly that the stature of the artist (e.g., Warhol) must be balanced against the popularity of the target? Would it be legal under the court's opinion to make and mass market a statue of Bill Clinton?

3. The California Supreme Court's framework rests upon two relatively subjective pillars: fair use analysis and art criticism. Is the analysis too subjective? The court's protestations notwithstanding, does the decision require judges to perform the role of art critics? Does it discriminate against literal depictions?

Subsequent cases illustrate the unpredictability of this balancing framework. In a case that comes close to the conventional portrayal and direct commercial exploitation in *Saderup*, the majority of a divided Sixth Circuit panel ruled that a limited edition painting featuring Tiger Woods was immune from a right of publicity claim under Ohio common law on freedom of expression grounds. *See* ETW Corp. v. Jireh Publ'g, Inc., 332 F.3d 915 (6th Cir. 2003).

Just two years after its *Saderup* decision, the California Supreme Court revisited the interplay of the right of publicity and the First Amendment. Johnny and Edgar Winter, well-known musicians (their 1973 album "They Only Come Out at Night" featured the #1 hit instrumental "Frankenstein" and the top 15 single "Free Ride") with albino complexions and long white hair, brought a right of publicity action against D.C. Comics for its publication of a comic book featuring the characters "Johnny and Edgar Autumn," half-worm, half-human creatures with pale faces and long white hair. The comic book series portrayed them as "vile, depraved, stupid, cowardly, subhuman individuals who engage in wanton acts of violence, murder and bestiality for pleasure and who should be killed." Applying the *Saderup* balancing framework, the California Supreme Court concluded that the expressive qualities of the work afforded D.C. Comics First Amendment protection from a right of publicity claim. Winter v. D.C. Comics, 30 Cal. 4th 881, 134 Cal. Rptr. 2d 634, 69 P.3d 473 (Cal. S. Ct. 2003). For another case reaching a similar outcome, see Kirby v. Sega of Am., Inc., 50 Cal. Rptr. 3d 607 (Ct. App. 2006) (holding that video game character was sufficiently transformative to overcome singer's right of publicity claim).

By contrast, the Missouri Supreme Court in John Doe, a/k/a Tony Twist v. TCI Cablevision, 110 S.W.3d 363 (Mo. 2003), adopted a much more plaintiff-friendly standard. The plaintiff, former professional hockey player Tony Twist, objected to the defendants' inclusion of a mobster character named Anthony "Tony Twist" Twistelli in its *Spawn* comic book series. The court rejected *Comedy III*'s transformativeness test as being insufficiently protective of plaintiffs' interests in controlling the use of their names and likenesses. In place of the *Comedy III* standard, the court adopted a "predominant purpose" test, which focuses on whether the defendant's predominant purpose for using the plaintiff's name or identity was commercial or expressive. Applying this test, the court concluded that the defendant's predominant purpose in appropriating the plaintiff's name and image (as a tough guy, "enforcer" type) was commercial—to sell comic books—and therefore that "free speech must give way to the right of publicity." Is this standard preferable to the transformative use test? Is it more predictable? Does it focus too much on the defendant's intent? Does it give sufficient weight to defendants' free speech interests?

In some other cases, courts have given greater emphasis to free speech concerns. For example, in Cardtoons, L.C. v. Major League Baseball Players Ass'n, 95 F.3d 959

(10th Cir. 1996), the court, after weighing all of the asserted policy reasons for recognizing a right of publicity, concluded that none of them sufficed to overcome the declaratory judgment plaintiff's interest in marketing a line of parody baseball cards skewering real-life stars such as Barry Bonds. More recently, in C.B.C. Distrib. & Mktg., Inc. v. Major League Baseball Advanced Media, L.P., 505 F.3d 818 (8th Cir. 2007), the Eighth Circuit concluded that a declaratory judgment plaintiff's First Amendment interest in marketing a fantasy baseball league, using real players' names and statistics, outweighed the players' right to control the unauthorized use of their names and other identifying characteristics.[13] Both cases engaged in an ad hoc balancing of competing interests, without articulating any particular test or the appropriate level of First Amendment scrutiny. Would it be preferable in cases like *Cardtoons* and *C.B.C.* to craft some sort of "fair use" exception instead? Or is wholesale adoption of the fair use doctrine not a good idea, for the reasons the California Supreme Court cited in *Saderup*?

Is there any other approach to balancing the tension between the right of publicity and the First Amendment? What about the use of disclaimers to the effect that a work of art was not authorized, sponsored, or endorsed by the target celebrity (or the holders of his or her postmortem right of publicity)? If the right of publicity is predominantly an economic right, should society be deeply concerned about the economic plight of celebrities? Or is the right based on other interests, such as personal autonomy and identity? Do the facts in the *Winter* case suggest the need for a broader foundation for protection?

4. *Artistic Advertising*. In its March 1997 "Fabulous Hollywood Issue!," *Los Angeles Magazine* featured an article entitled "Grand Illusions," which used digitally altered film stills to make it appear that the actors were wearing Spring 1997 fashions. The 16 familiar scenes included movies and actors such as *Rear Window* (Grace Kelly and Jimmy Stewart), *The Seven Year Itch* (Marilyn Monroe), and *Thelma and Louise* (Susan Sarandon and Geena Davis). The feature also included an image from the film *Tootsie* in which Dustin Hoffman's head was digitally superimposed atop a picture of another model. The caption read "Dustin Hoffman isn't a drag in a butter-colored silk gown by Richard Tyler and Ralph Lauren heels." Hoffman sued, claiming violation of his right of publicity as well as Lanham Act and other state law claims. The Ninth Circuit reversed an award in excess of $3 million on the ground that *L.A. Magazine*'s appropriation of Hoffman's identity was "communicative" rather than "commercial" and hence was entitled to the highest level of protection under the First Amendment. More precisely, the court held that, because the magazine edition at issue was not purely commercial speech, Hoffman (a public figure) needed (and failed) to show "actual malice" in the sense that the defendant knew that the depiction was false or acted in reckless disregard of its truth or falsity, in order to recover under the right of publicity. *See* Hoffman v. Capital Cities/ABC, Inc., and L.A. Magazine, Inc., 255 F.3d 1180 (9th Cir. 2001). The court never explained why Hoffman would have to show

13. *See also* CBS Interactive Inc. v. Nat'l Football Players Ass'n, Civil No. 08-5097 ADM/SRN, 2009 WL 1151982, at *21 (D. Minn. Apr. 28, 2009) (following *C.B.C.* in a case involving a fantasy football game); Jenna Ross, *Yahoo! Sues for Fantasy Football Info*, MINNEAPOLIS STAR-TRIBUNE (June 3, 2009) (discussing similar lawsuit filed by Yahoo!). Some other cases involving fantasy sports games have gone the other way, however. *See* Uhlaender v. Henricksen, 316 F. Supp. 1277, 1278-83 (D. Minn. 1970); Palmer v. Schonhorn Enters., 232 A.2d 458, 459-62 (N.J. Super. 1967); *see also* Gridiron.com, Inc. v. National Football League Player's Ass'n, Inc., 106 F. Supp. 2d 1309 (S.D. Fla. 2000) (enjoining unauthorized use of players' images in connection with fantasy football game).

falsity (or reckless disregard) with respect to a cause of action for which falsity is not an element.[14] The court seems to have assumed that consumer confusion is the proper rationale for the right of publicity. The Supreme Court has imposed such a requirement in at least one other context that normally does not require proof of falsity. *See* Hustler Magazine v. Falwell, 485 U.S. 46, 56 (1988) (involving a public figure's claim for intentional infliction of emotional distress). *See also* Stewart v. Rolling Stone LLC, 105 Cal. Rptr. 908 (Cal. App. 2010) (dismissing musicians' right of publicity claim against magazine, where musicians failed to prove actual malice in connection with magazine's use of musicians' images in close proximity to cigarette ad).

Can you square the *Hoffman* result with the California Supreme Court's analytical framework in *Saderup?* Can freedom of expression and marketing be treated separately or are they inextricably intertwined? Will future Dustin Hoffmans abandon careers in acting (or otherwise alter their creative and commercial choices) as a result of this case? If not, doesn't this case suggest that we need not be so solicitous of right of publicity claimants? What other justifications might support celebrities in such cases?

5. *Artistic Relevance.* How relevant must a creative work be to a person before the author can use their name in the title? In Rogers v. Grimaldi, 875 F.2d 994 (2d Cir. 1989), the court held that the maker of a movie about two cabaret dancers who imitated Fred Astaire and Ginger Rogers in their act could title the movie "Ginger and Fred" over the objections of the real Ginger Rogers.[15] A similar issue arose when the rap group OutKast titled a song "Rosa Parks," after the woman who helped trigger the civil rights movement by refusing to sit in the back of the bus. The only reference to Parks in the song is the line "Ah-ha, hush that fuss. Everybody move to the back of the

14. In Eastwood v. Superior Court, 198 Cal. Rptr. 342 (1983), a case in which actor Clint Eastwood alleged that the *National Enquirer* violated his right of publicity by publishing a (false) article about him, the court suggested that a true story would not be actionable at all, but (citing New York precedent) that a "deliberate fictionalization" could be, albeit only on a showing of actual malice. *See id.* at 352. *See also* Thomas F. Cotter & Irina Dmitrieva, *Integrating the Right of Publicity with First Amendment and Copyright Preemption Analysis*, 33 COLUM. J.L. & ARTS 165, 174 & n.50 (2010) (noting that, under the *Restatement* approach, "the publication of news stories involving real people or the inclusion of real people as characters in works of fiction" is not ordinarily a violation of the right of publicity, but that according to some courts " 'invented biographies' may be 'so infected with fiction, dramatization or embellishment that [they] cannot be said to fulfill the purpose of the newsworthiness exception' to liability") (quoting Messenger ex rel. Messenger v. Gruner + Jahr Printing & Publ., Inc., 727 N.E.2d 549, 555 (N.Y. 2000)). Do these interpretations make sense, or should aggrieved plaintiffs be left to their remedies, if any, under such doctrines as defamation and false light?

15. When, as in *Rogers*, the plaintiff also asserts a Lanham Act claim, a court may exhibit similar deference to the plaintiff's choice of title. *See Rogers*, 875 F.2d at 1000 ("Where a title with at least some artistic relevance to the work is not explicitly misleading as to the content of the work, it is not false advertising under the Lanham Act"); ETW Corp. v. Jireh Publ'g Inc., 332 F.3d 915, 928 (6th Cir. 2003) (holding that, if the defendant's use has artistic relevance, the plaintiff must show that "the public interest in avoiding confusion outweighs the public interest in free expression," i.e., "the public interest in free expression should prevail if the use of the celebrity's image has artistic relevance, unless it is used in such a way that it explicitly misleads as to the source of the work"). In the context of false endorsement cases, some courts also may be amenable to a nominative use defense if (1) the plaintiff is not readily identifiable without the use of the attribute; (2) only so much of the attribute is used as is reasonably necessary to identify the plaintiff; and (3) the defendant has done nothing that would, in conjunction with the image, suggest sponsorship or endorsement by the plaintiff. *See* Cairns v. Franklin Mint Co., 292 F.3d 1139, 1151-55 (holding that Franklin Mint could market collectors' plates bearing the image of the late Princess Diana, because Princess Diana was not readily identifiable without use of her likeness, the entire likeness was necessary to identify her, and Franklin Mint did not do anything to mislead the public as to endorsement; note also that Diana's right of publicity claim, under British law, terminated at her death); Abdul-Jabbar v. General Motors Corp., 85 F.3d 407, 412-13 (9th Cir. 1996) (genuine issue of material fact whether consumers would be confused into thinking that Kareem Abdul-Jabbar endorsed Oldsmobiles, following defendant's use in a TV commercial of footage of him playing basketball).

bus." Parks sued, alleging false advertising and violation of the right of publicity. After the appellate court overturned a grant of summary judgment for the defendants on the ground that a reasonable jury could find violations of the Lanham Act and the common law right of publicity, *see* Parks v. LaFace Records, 329 F.3d 437 (6th Cir. 2003), the parties settled, with OutKast and its record label paying an undisclosed sum and agreeing to "enlighten today's youth about the significant role Rosa Parks played in making America a better place for all races" by working with Parks and the Rosa and Raymond Parks Institute for Self Development to promote Parks's legacy. (The record labels and OutKast admitted no wrongdoing.) Other songs lack even the tenuous connection that may have existed in *Rogers* and *Parks. Hear, e.g.*, Gorillaz, "Clint Eastwood."

Can the title alone ever give political content to a song not otherwise obviously about a famous person?

6. *Newsworthiness Exception.* Reflecting freedom of speech and First Amendment protections, right of publicity statutes as well as common law rulings recognize a newsworthiness exception. *See, e.g.*, CAL. CIV. CODE § 3344(d) (exempting "use of a name, voice, signature, photograph, or likeness in connection with any news, public affairs, or sports broadcast or account, or any political campaign"). The scope of this exception can be difficult to gauge, however. In Montana v. San Jose Mercury News, 34 Cal. App. 4th 790, 40 Cal. Rptr. 2d 639 (1995), for example, the court held that the *San Jose Mercury News* had a right to reprint its news story about and picture of football star Joe Montana on promotional posters "for the purpose of showing the quality and content of the newspaper." In a sense, the newspaper was using the name and likeness of the newsworthy figure to gain a commercial advantage in the form of increased sales, but this was still held to be a permissible use.

Consider as well the following recent case. Following the murder of a female professional wrestler by her husband, a well-known professional wrestler who committed suicide following the crime, *Hustler Magazine* advertised on the cover of its issue: "WRESTLER CHRIS BENOIT'S MURDERED WIFE NUDE." The table of contents listed "NANCY BENOIT Exclusive Nude Pics of Wrestler's Doomed Wife." Neither the cover nor the table of contents made any reference to the accompanying article entitled "NANCY BENOIT Au Naturel: The long-lost images of wrestler Chris Benoit's doomed wife." The title and page frame, which read "EXCLUSIVE PICS! EXCLUSIVE PICS!," comprise about one third of the first page. A second third of the page was devoted to two nude photographs of Benoit. The final third of the page discussed Benoit's murder and her nude photo shoot, twice referencing her brief desire to be a model. The second page of the article was entirely devoted to photographs, displaying eight additional photographs of Benoit. After the victim's mother and administrator of the estate sued for violation of her daughter's right of publicity, the lower court determined that this use fell squarely within the newsworthiness exception. On appeal, the Eleventh Circuit, applying Georgia law, reversed, holding that the publication "of private, nude photographs were not incident to a newsworthy article; rather, the brief biography was incident to the photographs. Additionally, these photographs were neither related in time nor concept to the current incident of public interest." As a result, publication of these photographs fell outside of the newsworthiness exception to the right of publicity. Toffoloni v. LFP Publishing Group, LLC, 572 F.3d 1201 (11th Cir. 2009), *cert. denied*, 130 S. Ct. 1689 (2010).

In reaching this result, the court stated that, on the facts of the case, the right of publicity could be viewed as serving both a privacy and an economic interest. Curiously, the court seemed to equate the privacy interest at issue in some right of publicity cases with the constitutional right of privacy invoked in cases such as *Roe v. Wade*. *See Toffoloni*, 572 F.3d at 1207-08 ("Both the rights to freedom of speech and freedom of the press, as guaranteed by the First Amendment, and the right to privacy, as guaranteed by the Due Process Clause, are fundamental constitutional rights. The Constitution directs no hierarchy between them. Thus, courts are required to engage in a fact-sensitive balancing, with an eye toward that which is reasonable and that which resonates with our community morals, in order to protect the Constitution as a whole"). Is the court saying that the right of publicity is constitutionally *required*? Would such an interpretation make sense? The court also appeared to hold that, under Georgia law, the privacy interest at issue can be asserted postmortem. *See Toffoloni*, 572 F.3d at 1206, 1211-12. The majority of jurisdictions, however, do not view privacy interests as surviving death. *See* 1 J. THOMAS MCCARTHY, THE RIGHTS OF PUBLICITY AND PRIVACY § 9:1, at 381 (2009) (stating, with some exaggeration perhaps, that "[b]oth the commentators and the cases unanimously support" the rule that privacy rights terminate at death). Can a state overcome a First Amendment challenge to a right of publicity claim by simply extending privacy protection postmortem? Could the decedent's surviving family members' interest in relational privacy support application of the right of publicity in a case of this nature?

In addition, the court cited *Zacchini* for the proposition that the right of publicity also promotes performers' economic interests. *See Toffoloni*, 572 F.3d at 1207. In *Toffoloni*, however, the plaintiffs' motivation for filing suit is not to vindicate any interest in the economic value of the photographs, but rather (understandably) to prevent their publication. Can the economic interests underlying the right of publicity be invoked to support the subject's interest in censorship? Should it matter if the photographs were legally obscene?

PROBLEMS

Problem 10-3. John Riggins is a former professional football player who played for the New York Jets and Washington Redskins. He was inducted in the Pro Football Hall of Fame in 1992. In 1991, Riggins and his wife Mary Lou Riggins divorced. John Riggins conveyed his ownership interest in the marital home, in suburban Washington, D.C., to Mary Lou Riggins. A few months later, Mary Lou Riggins put the house up for sale. To advertise the property, Mary Lou Riggins arranged for the printing and distribution of an 8½ × 11 inch handbill that included a photograph of the property and the statement, in large, bold-faced lettering "Come see John Riggins's former home." John Riggins did not consent to this use of his name on the handbill. He files suit against Mary Lou Riggins and her real estate broker for violation of John Riggins's right of publicity. What result? Is there a viable First Amendment defense?

Would John Riggins have a claim for violation of his right of publicity based on our use of this hypothetical (which is based on a real case) in this casebook?

Problem 10-4. John Facenda was a long-time radio and television announcer for the Philadelphia Eagles football team. He achieved national fame, however, for his work doing narration for NFL Films, Inc., which produces and distributes films of professional football "highlights." In this regard, Facenda was known for his distinctive, recognizable baritone voice.

Shortly before his death in 1984, Facenda signed a "standard release" contract stating that NFL Films enjoys "the unequivocal rights to use the audio and visual film sequences recorded of me, or any part of them . . . in perpetuity and by whatever media or manner NFL Films . . . sees fit, provided, however, such use does not constitute an endorsement of any product or service." In 2005, NFL Films produced "The Making of Madden NFL 06" about a soon-to-be released annual update of a video game that simulates NFL games. This production was 22 minutes long and was shown on the NFL Network eight times in a three-day span leading up to the release of the video game to retail stores. It featured interviews with NFL players, the game's producers, and others. It also included several sequences comparing the video game's virtual environment with the actual NFL environment, extolling the realism of everything from the stadiums to the game play. The program also used sound recordings, taken from earlier NFL Films' productions, of three sentences read by Facenda: (1) "Pro Football, the game for the ear and the eye," (2) "This sport is more than spectacle, it is a game for all seasons," and (3) "X's and O's on the blackboard are translated into aggression on the field." These excerpts totaled 13 seconds of the program. The NFL admitted that these excerpts were chosen "to underscore the degree to which the video game authentically recreates the NFL experience."

Facenda's Estate files suit against NFL Films for violation of Facenda's right of publicity and for false endorsement. What result? Can a false endorsement claim be premised on the unauthorized use of a deceased person's identity?

Problem 10-5. In the long-running *Seinfeld* television show, the fictional character George Costanza was a long-time friend of the lead character, Jerry Seinfeld. During the course of the series, George Costanza encountered numerous problems relating to employment, romance, and conflicts with his parents; his character was notably self-absorbed, self-centered, and unreliable. While the show was still being produced, a man whose real name is Michael Costanza filed suit against the producers of the Seinfeld series for violation of, among other things, his right of publicity. Michael Costanza claimed that he knew Jerry Seinfeld in college; and that, like the fictional George Costanza, he was short, fat, bald, and hailed from Queens, New York. He concluded that the show was intended to depict him. Did Michael Costanza have a viable cause of action? Does it matter whether Seinfeld admits that he based George Costanza's character on the plaintiff?

11 Trade Secrets

A. INTRODUCTION

1. History

The idea that information should be protected against "theft" (which may include the physical taking of tangible goods containing information or simply the copying or memorization of data) is a venerable one in the law. One scholar traces the earliest legal protection against "misappropriation of trade secrets" to the Roman empire.[1] The Roman courts created a cause of action called "actio servi corrupti"—literally, an action for corrupting a slave. According to Schiller, the actio servi corrupti was used to protect slave owners from third parties who would "corrupt" slaves (by bribery or intimidation) into disclosing their owners' confidential business information. The law made such third parties liable to the slave owner for twice the damages he suffered as a result of the disclosure.

1. Arguably, trade secrets existed before this time, albeit in unusual forms. *Consider* Mark C. Suchman, *Invention and Ritual: Notes on the Interrelation of Magic and Intellectual Property in Preliterate Societies*, 89 Colum. L. Rev. 1264, 1274 (1989):

> [L]et us imagine a hypothetical preliterate inventor who, through diligence or good fortune, discovers that her maize crop is larger when she plants a small fish next to each kernel of corn. . . . Clearly, this technique has economic value and could garner its creator material and social rewards if she could monopolize it and license it for a fee. Unfortunately, the odds of keeping such a discovery secret are slight. . . . [T]he procedure is so simple that even a casual observer could replicate the process. . . . Magic, however, provides a way out of the dilemma. By claiming, for example, that the power of the fish is activated by a talisman that she alone possesses, the inventor can remove her idea from the public domain. . . . [T]he magicked process is far easier to monopolize than the simple technology alone.

While recent scholarship has cast some doubt on the enforcement of trade secret protection in the Roman empire,[2] the concept that so-called business or "trade secrets" were entitled to legal protection spread rapidly throughout the world. As early as the Renaissance, most European nation-states had laws that protected businesses (notably, the guild cartels) from those who used their secret processes and ideas without permission. These early laws were translated during the Industrial Revolution into statutes that protected "industrial secrets." Many of these statutes are still in force today, albeit in modified form.

The roots of trade secrecy in slavery law were further evident in the treatment of employees in the centuries before the Industrial Revolution. Both commerce and foreign policy included a strong dose of "mercantilism." Governments and private guilds attempted to keep "their" intellectual property within their grasp, using a combination of rewards to inventors and rules that reduced employee mobility. These developments are well traced in CARLO M. CIPOLLA, BEFORE THE INDUSTRIAL REVOLUTION: EUROPEAN ECONOMY AND SOCIETY 1000-1700 (2d ed. 1980); DAVID J. JEREMY, TRANSATLANTIC INDUSTRIAL REVOLUTION: THE DIFFUSION OF TEXTILE TECHNOLOGIES BETWEEN BRITAIN AND AMERICA, 1790-1830's, at 185-89 (MIT Press 1981). The authors provide such examples as restrictive British secrecy laws, city rewards to woollen craftsmen in thirteenth-century Bologna and, on the other side, the kidnapping of skilled Swedish ironworkers by France in 1660.

This patchwork of public and private regulation arguably served as a substitute for strong intellectual property protection by protecting a country's or a corporation's "human capital" and so encouraging investment in employee skills and training. The guild system of apprenticeship and mandatory periods of servitude operated to prevent excessive "spillovers" of guild knowledge to competitors and hence may have encouraged innovation. On this point, compare Paul A. David, *Intellectual Property and the Panda's Thumb: Patents, Copyrights, and Trade Secrets in Economic Theory and History*, *in* GLOBAL DIMENSIONS OF INTELLECTUAL PROPERTY RIGHTS IN SCIENCE AND TECHNOLOGY 19, 45 (Nat'l Acad. Press 1993) (guild system encouraged investment in innovation) with Cipolla, *supra*, at 261 (guilds restricted competition and therefore restrained business and technological progress). In effect, guilds and countries solved the public goods problem by doing their best to privatize the good — keeping information secret from prying eyes.

Unfortunately, this form of private protection comes at a price. Companies (or countries) that must rely on current and former employees to keep secrets run into a host of problems. Companies may not disclose to employees all the information they need to know. They may take inefficient physical security precautions. They may hire employees based on their loyalty rather than their productivity. And finally, they may simply choose to prey on other companies rather than investing in innovation themselves. Robert Sherwood makes the case that many of these problems occurred in the recent past in Mexico and Brazil as a result of inadequate trade secret protection. *See* ROBERT M. SHERWOOD, INTELLECTUAL PROPERTY AND ECONOMIC DEVELOPMENT 113 (1990).

2. For a discussion of the Roman law, see A. Arthur Schiller, *Trade Secrets and the Roman Law: The Actio Servi Corrupti*, 30 COLUM. L. REV. 837 (1930). For a dissenting view on the role of Roman law in protecting trade secrets, see Alan Watson, *Trade Secrets and Roman Law: The Myth Exploded*, 11 TUL. EUR. & CIV. L.F. 19 (1996).

Obviously, it would be preferable to have a legal system that could protect an employer's secrets while allowing employee mobility and the dissemination of information through licensing. And such rules have generally developed as legal systems and norms became stable enough to support them. European countries, for example, developed trade secret protection quite early.[3]

By contrast, Anglo-American jurisprudence was a relative latecomer to the protection of trade secrets. English and American courts first recognized a cause of action for damages for misappropriation of trade secrets in 1817 and 1837, respectively[4]; injunctive relief against actual or threatened misappropriation came still later.[5] These early decisions concerned issues that are still debated in trade secret cases today: the circumstances in which an employee may continue her business after departing her employer, the circumstances in which a competitor may copy another's publicly sold product, and whether courts will enforce a contract requiring that business information be kept confidential.

Trade secret litigation is particularly important to small companies. A study of 530 manufacturing firms in Massachusetts found that small firms spent a greater proportion of their litigation resources on trade secret cases than did large firms, perhaps because of the enormous cost associated with patent litigation or because of the delay in obtaining patents. Forty-three percent of the intellectual property disputes involving these firms had a trade secret component. Josh Lerner, *The Importance of Trade Secrecy: Evidence from Civil Litigation* (Harv. Bus. School working paper #95-043), *available at* http://ssrn.com/abstract=6089. Lerner's data indicate that trade secrets, though important to all firms, are most important for the small companies that drive innovation in many developing fields. Since the time of his study, however, patent litigation has been growing in significance relative to trade secrecy.

2. Overview of Trade Secret Protection

Today, every one of the United States protects trade secrets in some form or another. Improper use or disclosure of a trade secret was traditionally a common law tort. In the twentieth century, the principal document setting forth the "law" of trade secrets was the *Restatement of Torts*, published in 1939. Sections 757 and 758 of the *Restatement* set forth basic principles of trade secret law that were adopted by courts in most states in the country. National protection for trade secrets is also compelled by United States adherence to the intellectual property agreement in the Uruguay Round of the General Agreement on Tariffs and Trade (GATT) Trade-Related Aspects of Intellectual Property Rights (TRIPs) in 1994. GATT TRIPs article 39 requires member nations to protect trade secrets.

3. Interestingly, Japan has only recently enacted a trade secret protection statute. *See* Hideo Nakoshi, *New Japanese Trade Secret Act*, 75 J. PAT. & TRADEMARK OFF. SOC'Y 631 (1993). Nakoshi provides some interesting thoughts on why Japan considered such a trade secret statute unnecessary for so long. He argues that cultural norms of assumed trust made it socially uncomfortable to insist on formal confidentiality agreements, and that long-term or lifetime employment eliminated many trade secret issues associated with employee mobility.

4. *See* Newberry v. James, 35 Eng. Rep. 1011, 1013 (Ct. Ch. 1817); Vickey v. Welch, 36 Mass. 523, 527 (1837).

5. *See* Yovett v. Winyard, 37 Eng. Rep. 525 (Ct. Ch. 1820); Taylor v. Blanchard, 95 Mass. 370 (1866).

The *Restatement* protected as a trade secret any information "used in one's business" that gives its owner "an opportunity to obtain an advantage over competitors who do not know or use it," so long as the information was in fact a secret. RESTATEMENT §757, cmt *b*.

When the *Restatement (Second) of Torts* was published in 1979, the authors decided not to include sections 757 and 758, on the grounds that the law of trade secrets had developed into an independent body of law that no longer relied on general principles of tort law. The influence of the original *Restatement* remained, however, because it had been adopted by so many courts.[6]

Beginning in 1979, the National Conference of Commissioners on Uniform State Laws promulgated a model state statute, the Uniform Trade Secrets Act, which differed in some respects from the common law. The Uniform Trade Secrets Act (UTSA) has now been enacted (in one form or another) by 44 states and the District of Columbia. *See* RESTATEMENT (THIRD) OF UNFAIR COMPETITION § 39, at 437-38 (listing state statutes). Because of the Uniform Act's importance, we reproduce its primary provisions here.

Uniform Trade Secrets Act, with 1985 Amendments

§ 1. Definitions

As used in this [Act], unless the context requires otherwise:

(1) "Improper means" includes theft, bribery, misrepresentation, breach or inducement of a breach of a duty to maintain secrecy, or espionage through electronic or other means;

(2) "Misappropriation" means:

(i) acquisition of a trade secret of another by a person who knows or has reason to know that the trade secret was acquired by improper means; or

(ii) disclosure or use of a trade secret of another without express or implied consent by a person who

(A) used improper means to acquire knowledge of the trade secret; or

(B) at the time of disclosure or use, knew or had reason to know that his knowledge of the trade secret was

(I) derived from or through a person who had utilized improper means to acquire it;

(II) acquired under circumstances giving rise to a duty to maintain its secrecy or limit its use; or

(III) derived from or through a person who owed a duty to the person seeking relief to maintain its secrecy or limit its use; or

(C) before a material change of his [or her] position, knew or had reason to know that it was a trade secret and that knowledge of it had been acquired by accident or mistake. . . .

(4) "Trade secret" means information, including a formula, pattern, compilation, program, device, method, technique, or process, that:

(i) derives independent economic value, actual or potential, from not being generally known to, and not being readily ascertainable by proper

6. The authors of the *Restatement (Third) of Unfair Competition*, published in 1994, once again included a section on the law of trade secrets. The section is organized to follow the Uniform Act, and many of its provisions are consistent with the act. Nonetheless, there are some differences between the act and the *Restatement*. They are discussed below.

means by, other persons who can obtain economic value from its disclosure or use, and

(ii) is the subject of efforts that are reasonable under the circumstances to maintain its secrecy.

A trade secret claim can be broken down into three essential elements. First, the subject matter involved must qualify for trade secret protection: It must be the type of knowledge or information that trade secret law was meant to protect, and it must not be generally known to all. On eligible subject matter, the current trend, exemplified once again by the UTSA, is to protect as a trade secret *any* valuable information so long as the information is capable of adding economic value to the plaintiff. The requirement that the information not be generally known follows from the label trade *secret*. The requirement is meant to ensure that no one claims intellectual property protection for information commonly known in a trade or industry.

The second element to be established by the plaintiff in a trade secret case is that the plaintiff, holder of the trade secret, took *reasonable precautions* under the circumstances to prevent its disclosure. Courts have shown some confusion over the rationale for this requirement. Some see in it evidence that the trade secret is valuable enough to bother litigating; others argue that where reasonable precautions are taken, chances are that a defendant acquired the trade secret wrongfully. Whatever the justification, it is clear that no one may let information about products and operations flow freely to competitors at one time and then later claim that competitors have wrongfully acquired valuable trade secrets. To establish the right to sue later, one must be consistently diligent in protecting information. As always, however, the presence of the term "reasonable" ensures close cases and difficult line-drawing for courts, a theme reflected in several of the cases that follow.

Finally, a trade secret plaintiff also must prove that the defendant acquired the information wrongfully — in a word, that the defendant *misappropriated* the trade secret. Just because a person's information is valuable does not make it wrong for another to use it or disclose it. But use or disclosure is wrong, in the eyes of trade secret law, when the information is acquired through deception, skullduggery, or outright theft. As we will see in the cases that follow, close cases abound in this area because of the creativity of competitors in rooting out information about their rivals' businesses and products.

In many cases, a defendant's use or disclosure is wrongful because of a preexisting obligation to the plaintiff not to disclose or appropriate the trade secret. Such an obligation can arise in either of two ways: explicitly, by contract; and implicitly, because of an *implied duty*. A classic example of an implied duty is the case of an employee. Even in the absence of an explicit contract, most employees are held to have a duty to protect their employers' interests in the employers' secret practices, information, and the like. Even where the duty arises by explicit contract, however, public policy limitations on the scope and duration of the agreement will often come into play, in some cases resulting in substantial judicial modification of the explicit obligations laid out in the contract.

3. Theory of Trade Secrets

Legal protection for trade secrets is premised primarily on two theories that are only partly complementary. The first is utilitarian. Under this view, protecting against the theft of proprietary information encourages investment in such information. This idea is sometimes associated with the view that trade secrets are a form of property. The second theory emphasizes deterrence of wrongful acts and is therefore sometimes described as a tort theory. Here the aim of trade secret law is to punish and prevent illicit behavior, and even to uphold reasonable standards of commercial behavior. *Cf.* KIM LANE SCHEPPELE, LEGAL SECRETS: EQUALITY AND EFFICIENCY IN THE COMMON LAW (1988) (arguing that cases involving legal secrets—including trade secrets cases—are better explained in terms of principles all would be willing to agree to rather than in the efficiency terms of law and economics). Although under the tort theory trade secret protection is not explicitly about encouraging investments, it is plain that one consequence of deterring wrongful behavior would be to encourage investment in trade secrets. Hence, despite their conceptual differences, the tort and property/incentive approaches to trade secrets may well push in the same direction.

Property Rights. Some jurists have conceptualized "intellectual property" as a species of the broader concept of "property." The Supreme Court adopted this view of trade secret law in Ruckelshaus v. Monsanto Co., 467 U.S. 986, 1001-04 (1984). There the Court faced the question (considered in more detail below) of whether a federal law that required Monsanto to publicly disclose its trade secrets was a "taking of private property" for which the Fifth Amendment required compensation. The Court, in finding that trade secrets were "property," reasoned in part that "[t]rade secrets have many of the characteristics of more tangible forms of property. A trade secret is assignable. A trade secret can form the res of a trust, and it passes to a trustee in bankruptcy." *Id.* at 1002-04. Treatment of trade secrets as property rights vested in the trade secret "owner" is consistent with a view of trade secrets law as providing an additional incentive to innovate, beyond those provided in patent law. The Supreme Court has offered some support for this incentive view in cases such as Kewanee Oil Co. v. Bicron Corp., 416 U.S. 470, 481-85 (1974).[7]

Mark Lemley argues that trade secrets make sense not so much as real property, but as *intellectual* property—that is, as government policy designed to promote innovation and, ironically, to encourage efficient disclosure of secrets. Mark A. Lemley, *The Surprising Virtues of Treating Trade Secrets as IP Rights*, 61 STAN. L. REV. 311 (2008).

Tort Law. An alternate explanation for much of trade secrets law is what might be described as a "duty-based" theory, or what Melvin Jager calls "the maintenance of commercial morality." 1 MELVIN JAGER, TRADE SECRETS LAW § 1.03, at 1-4. The Supreme Court adopted this view in a famous early decision:

> The word "property" as applied to trademarks and trade secrets is an unanalyzed expression of certain secondary consequences of the primary fact that the law makes some rudimentary requirements of good faith. Whether the plaintiffs have any valuable secret or

7. In *Kewanee*, the Court held that:

> Certainly the patent policy of encouraging invention is not disturbed by the existence of another form of incentive to invention. In this respect the two systems are not and never would be in conflict. . . .
>
> Trade secret law will encourage invention in areas where patent law does not reach, and will prompt the independent innovator to proceed with the discovery and exploitation of his invention. Competition is fostered and the public is not deprived of the use of valuable, if not quite patentable, invention.

> not, the defendant knows the facts, whatever they are, through a special confidence that he accepted. The property may be denied, but the confidence cannot be. Therefore the starting point for the present matter is not property or due process of law, but that the defendant stood in confidential relations with the plaintiffs. . . .

E.I. duPont deNemours Powder Co. v. Masland, 244 U.S. 100, 102 (1917).[8] Closely related to *Masland*'s theory of "breach of confidence" is the contract basis for trade secret law. While not always applicable, many trade secret cases arise out of a "duty" explicitly stated in a contract, such as a technology license or an employment agreement. The tort-based theory of breach of duty merges in those cases with a standard common law action for breach of contract.

For an argument that there is no theoretical justification for trade secret law, and that other contract and tort doctrines can do just fine in protecting confidential information, see Robert G. Bone, *A New Look at Trade Secret Law: Doctrine in Search of Justification*, 86 CAL. L. REV. 241 (1998).

The different theories of trade secret law reflect different views of the nature of intellectual property law as a whole, discussed in Chapter 1 *supra*. These debates recur throughout this book, because the reason that we protect intellectual property turns out to matter a great deal in deciding whether and to what extent we protect it.

Keep in mind the different rationales for trade secret protection as you read the material that follows. Consider the extent to which each of these theories can explain the law of trade secrets.

B. SUBJECT MATTER

1. Defining Trade Secrets

Metallurgical Industries Inc. v. Fourtek, Inc.
790 F.2d 1195 (5th Cir. 1986)

GEE, Circuit Judge:

Today's case requires us to review Texas law on the misappropriation of trade secrets. Having done so, we conclude that the district court misconceived the nature and elements of this cause of action, a misconception that led it to direct a verdict erroneously in favor of appellee Bielefeldt. We also conclude that the court abused its discretion in excluding certain evidence. Accordingly, we affirm in part, reverse in part, and remand the case for a new trial.

8. The *Monsanto* Court attempted to distinguish *Masland* in a footnote, claiming that "Justice Holmes did not deny the existence of a property interest; he simply deemed determination of the existence of that interest irrelevant to the resolution of the case." *Monsanto*, 467 U.S. 1004 n.9.

I. Facts of the Case

We commence with a brief description of the scientific process concerned. Tungsten carbide is a metallic compound of great value in certain industrial processes. Combined with the metal cobalt, it forms an extremely hard alloy known as "cemented tungsten carbide" used in oil drills, tools for manufacturing metals, and wear-resistant coatings. Because of its great value, reclamation of carbide from scrap metals is feasible. For a long time, however, the alloy's extreme resistance to machining made reclamation difficult. In the late 1960's and early 1970's, a new solution — known as the zinc recovery process — was devised, a solution based on carbide's reaction with zinc at high temperatures. In the crucibles of a furnace, molten zinc will react with the cobalt in the carbide to cause swelling and cracking of the scrap metal. After this has occurred, the zinc is distilled from the crucible, leaving the scrap in a more brittle state. The carbide is then ground into a powder, usable in new products as an alternative to virgin carbide. This process is the generally recognized modern method of carbide reclamation.

Metallurgical Industries has been in the business of reclaiming carbide since 1976, using the more primitive "cold-stream process." In the mid-1970's, Metallurgical began to consider using the zinc recovery process. In that connection, it came to know appellee Irvin Bielefeldt, a representative of Therm-O-Vac Engineering & Manufacturing Company (Therm-O-Vac). Negotiations led to a contract authorizing Therm-O-Vac to design and construct two zinc recovery furnaces, the purchase order for the first being executed in July 1976.

The furnace arrived in April 1977. Dissatisfied with its performance, Metallurgical modified it extensively. First, it inserted chill plates in one part of the furnace to create a better temperature differential for distilling the zinc. Second, Metallurgical replaced the one large crucible then in place with several smaller crucibles to prevent the zinc from dispersing in the furnace. Third, it replaced segmented heating elements which had caused electric arcing with unitary graphite heating elements. Last, it installed a filter in the furnace's vacuum-pumps, which zinc particles had continually clogged. These efforts proved successful and the modified furnace soon began commercial operation.

. . . [M]etallurgical returned to Therm-O-Vac for its second furnace. A purchase order was signed in January 1979, and the furnace arrived that July. Further modifications again had to be made, but commercial production was allegedly achieved in January 1980.

In 1980, after Therm-O-Vac went bankrupt, Bielefeldt and three other former Therm-O-Vac employees — Norman Montesino, Gary Boehm, and Michael Sarvadi — formed Fourtek, Incorporated. Soon thereafter, Fourtek agreed to build a zinc recovery furnace for appellee Smith International, Incorporated (Smith). . . .

Metallurgical . . . brought a diversity action against Smith, Bielefeldt, Montesino, Boehm, and Sarvadi in November 1981. In its complaint, Metallurgical charged the defendants with misappropriating its trade secrets. . . . [Trial] testimony indicated Metallurgical's frequent notices to Bielefeldt that the process was a secret and that the disclosures to him were made in confidence. Another witness recounted meetings in which the modifications were agreed to. Bielefeldt was allegedly unconvinced about the efficacy of these changes and contributed little to the discussion. Metallurgical also presented evidence that it had expended considerable time, effort, and money to modify the furnaces.

[The district court nonetheless granted defendants' motions for directed verdicts.] The principal reason advanced was the court's conclusion that no trade secret is involved. At trial, Metallurgical acknowledged that the individual changes, by themselves, are not secrets; chill plates and pump filters, for example, are well-known. Metallurgical's position instead was that the process, taken as a whole, is a trade secret in the carbide business. The court, however, refused to recognize any protection Texas law provides to a modification process. It also concluded that the information Bielefeldt obtained from working with Metallurgical is too general to be legally protected. Finally, it ruled that "negative know-how"—the knowledge of what not to do—is unprotected. . . .

III. Defining a "Trade Secret"

We begin by reviewing the legal definition of a trade secret. Of course, to qualify as one, the subject matter involved must, in fact, be a secret; "matters of general knowledge in an industry cannot be appropriated by one as his secret." Wissman v. Boucher, 150 Tex. 326, 240 S.W.2d 278, 280 (Tex. 1951); see also Zoecon Industries v. American Stockman Tag Co., 713 F.2d 1174, 1179 (5th Cir. 1983) ("a customer list of readily ascertainable names and addresses will not be protected as a trade secret"). Smith emphasizes the absence of any secret because the basic zinc recovery process has been publicized in the trade. Acknowledging the publicity of the zinc recovery process, however, we nevertheless conclude that Metallurgical's particular modification efforts can be as yet unknown to the industry. A general description of the zinc recovery process reveals nothing about the benefits unitary heating elements and vacuum pump filters can provide to that procedure. That the scientific principles involved are generally known does not necessarily refute Metallurgical's claim of trade secrets.

Metallurgical, furthermore, presented evidence to back up its claim. One of its main witnesses was Arnold Blum, a consultant very influential in the decisions to modify the furnaces. Blum testified as to his belief that Metallurgical's changes were unknown in the carbide reclamation industry. The evidence also shows Metallurgical's efforts to keep secret its modifications. Blum testified that he noted security measures taken to conceal the furnaces from all but authorized personnel. The furnaces were in areas hidden from public view, while signs warned all about restricted access. Company policy, moreover, required everyone authorized to see the furnace to sign a nondisclosure agreement. These measures constitute evidence probative of the existence of secrets. One's subjective belief of a secret's existence suggests that the secret exists. Security measures, after all, cost money; a manufacturer therefore presumably would not incur these costs if it believed its competitors already knew about the information involved. In University Computing Co. v. Lykes-Youngstown Corp., 504 F.2d 518, 535 (5th Cir. 1974), we regarded subjective belief as a factor to consider in determining whether secrecy exists. Because evidence of security measures is relevant, that shown here helps us conclude that a reasonable jury could have found the existence of the requisite secrecy.

Smith argues, however, that Metallurgical's disclosure to other parties vitiated the secrecy required to obtain legal protection. Metallurgical revealed its information to Consarc Corporation in 1978; it also disclosed information in 1980 to La Floridienne, its European licensee of carbide reclamation technology. Because both these disclosures occurred before Bielefeldt allegedly misappropriated the knowledge of modifications, others knew of the information when the Smith furnace was built. This being so, Smith argues, no trade secret in fact existed.

Although the law requires secrecy, it need not be absolute. Public revelation would, of course, dispel all secrecy, but the holder of a secret need not remain totally silent:

> He may, without losing his protection, communicate to employees involved in its use. He may likewise communicate it to others pledged to secrecy. . . . Nevertheless, a substantial element of secrecy must exist, so that except by the use of improper means, there would be difficulty in acquiring the information.

RESTATEMENT OF TORTS, § 757 Comment b (1939). We conclude that a holder may divulge his information to a limited extent without destroying its status as a trade secret. To hold otherwise would greatly limit the holder's ability to profit from his secret. If disclosure to others is made to further the holder's economic interests, it should, in appropriate circumstances, be considered a limited disclosure that does not destroy the requisite secrecy. The only question is whether we are dealing with a limited disclosure here. . . .

Looking . . . to the policy considerations involved, we glean two reasons why Metallurgical's disclosures to others are limited and therefore insufficient to extinguish the secrecy Metallurgical's other evidence has suggested. First, the disclosures were not public announcements; rather, Metallurgical divulged its information to only two businesses with whom it was dealing. This case thus differs from Luccous v. J.C. Kinley Co., 376 S.W.2d 336 (Tex. 1964), in which the court concluded that the design of a device could not be a trade secret because it had been patented — and thus revealed to all the world — before any dealing between the parties. Second, the disclosures were made to further Metallurgical's economic interests. Disclosure to Consarc was made with the hope that Consarc could build the second furnace. A long-standing agreement gave La Floridienne the right, as a licensee, to the information in exchange for royalty payments. Metallurgical therefore revealed its discoveries as part of business transactions by which it expected to profit.

Metallurgical's case would have been stronger had it also presented evidence of confidential relationships with these two companies, but we are unwilling to regard this failure as conclusively disproving the limited nature of the disclosures. Smith correctly points out that Metallurgical bears the burden of showing the existence of confidential relationships. Contrary to Smith's assertion, however, confidentiality is not a requisite; it is only a factor to consider. Whether a disclosure is limited is an issue the resolution of which depends on weighing many facts. The inference from those facts, construed favorably to Metallurgical, is that it wished only to profit from [disclosure of] its secrets to the public. We therefore are unpersuaded by Smith's argument.

Existing law, however, emphasizes other requisites for legal recognition of a trade secret. In *Huffines*, 314 S.W.2d 763, a seminal case of trade secret law, Texas adopted the widely-recognized pronouncements of the American Law Institute's *Restatement of the Law*. The Texas Supreme Court quoted the *Restatement*'s definition of a trade secret:

> A trade secret may consist of any formula, pattern, device, or compilation of information which is used in one's business, and which gives him an opportunity to obtain an

> advantage over competitors who do not know or use it. It may be a chemical compound, a process of manufacturing, treating or preserving materials, a pattern for a machine or other device or a list of customers.

Id. at 776, quoting RESTATEMENT OF TORTS, § 757 Comment b (1939). From this the criterion of value to the holder of the alleged secret arises. . . .

Metallurgical met the burden of showing the value of its modifications. Lawrence Lorman, the company's vice president, testified that the zinc recovery process gave Metallurgical an advantage over its two competitors by aiding in the production of the highest quality reclaimed carbide powder. The quality of the powder, in fact, makes it an alternative to the more costly virgin carbide. Lorman testified that customers regarded Metallurgical's zinc reclaimed powder as a better product than that reclaimed by the coldstream process used by others. This evidence clearly indicates that the modifications that led to the commercial operation of the zinc recovery furnace provided a clear advantage over the competition.

Another requisite is the cost of developing the secret device or process. In *Huffines'* companion case, K&G Oil, Tool & Service Co. v. G&G Fishing Tool Service, 158 Tex. 594, 314 S.W.2d 782, 790, 117 U.S.P.Q. (BNA) 471 (Tex. 1958), the court recognized the cost involved in developing the device in question; "the record shows . . . that much work and ingenuity have been applied to the development of a practical and successful device." See also *Zoecon Industries*, 713 F.2d at 1179 ("even if the names and addresses were readily ascertainable through trade journals as the defendants allege, the other information could be compiled only at considerable expense"). No question exists that Metallurgical expended much time, effort, and money to make the necessary changes. It clearly has met the burden of demonstrating the effort involved in making a complex manufacturing process work.

That the cost of devising the secret and the value the secret provides are criteria in the legal formulation of a trade secret shows the equitable underpinnings of this area of the law. It seems only fair that one should be able to keep and enjoy the fruits of his labor. If a businessman has worked hard, has used his imagination, and has taken bold steps to gain an advantage over his competitors, he should be able to profit from his efforts. Because a commercial advantage can vanish once the competition learns of it, the law should protect the businessman's efforts to keep his achievements secret. As is discussed below, this is an area of law in which simple fairness still plays a large role.

We do not say, however, that all these factors need exist in every case. Because each case must turn on its own facts, no standard formula for weighing the factors can be devised. Secrecy is always required, of course, but beyond that there are no universal requirements. In a future case, for example, should the defendant's breach of confidence be particularly egregious, the injured party might still seek redress in court despite the possibility that the subject matter was discovered at little or no cost or that the object of secrecy is not of great value to him. The definition of "trade secret" will therefore be determined by weighing all equitable considerations. It is easy to recognize the possibility of a trade secret here, however, because Metallurgical presented evidence of all three factors discussed above.

Appellees posit two other reasons why Metallurgical's modification process cannot be defined as a trade secret. The first is premised on characterizing the process in question as the installation of various devices all well known to modern manufacturing. This being so, the argument runs, the process itself can be no secret, either. The technologies of chill plates, multiple crucibles, pump filters, and unitary graphite heating elements are all said to be public knowledge. This may well be so, but it does not prevent Metallurgical from seeking legal protection. Ventura Manufacturing Co. v. Locke, 454 S.W.2d 431 (Tex. Civ. App. 1970), involved a process of finding and cleaning small yet valuable titanium scraps lost during the manufacturing of airplanes. Appellee Locke refined a previously unsuccessful process by implementing new procedures, none of which was innovative. The court nevertheless found that his efforts could constitute a trade secret:

> Obviously, the basic proposition involved in the cleaning of dirty parts by commercial detergents involves no trade secret. Also, the use of production line techniques as such must be considered as a matter of general knowledge. On the other hand, we cannot say that the details of the procedure followed in the cleaning of these fasteners are matters of general knowledge. To the contrary, the record demonstrates that such details as the types and amounts of chemicals to be used and the times and temperatures for cleaning the fasteners were developed by Ventura through extensive trial and error and at considerable expense.

Id. at 434. Similarly, in *Sikes*, 665 F.2d 731, 736, we quoted with approval the following passage from Water Services, Inc. v. Tesco Chemicals, 410 F.2d 163, 173 (5th Cir. 1969).

It is clear that the theory of the Treat-A-Matic was not new to the industry. The court also found that the design was apparent from inspection, and that the system had been sold and advertised without restriction. These findings are supported by the evidence. But these findings are not conclusive. The trade secret here was the application of known techniques and the assembly of available components to create the first successful system in the industry. . . . As the Second Circuit stated in Imperial Chemical, Ltd. v. National Distillers & Chemical Corp. (2 Cir. 1965) 342 F.2d 737, 742, "a trade secret can exist in a combination of characteristics and components each of which, by itself, is in the public domain, but the unified process, design and operation of which in unique combination, affords a competitive advantage and is a protectible secret." We believe these cases cogently refute appellees' assertions to the contrary.

The second defense advances a supposed concept of "negative know how" in reliance on one sentence from Hurst v. Hughes Tool Co., 634 F.2d 895 (5th Cir.) cert. denied, 454 U.S. 829, 102 S. Ct. 123, 70 L. Ed. 2d 105 (1981). The court there ruled that Hughes Tool Company did not really use the information Hurst provided; "Hurst's information, while of some benefit, provided only negative, 'what not to do,' input to Hughes." Id. at 899. Both the district court and Smith interpret this to mean that negative know-how cannot constitute a trade secret. The sentence in *Hurst*, however, has nothing to do with whether the information was a trade secret. It is not found in the section of the opinion dealing with the existence of a trade secret; rather, we were determining whether Hughes Tool Company could be found to have used commercially any secrets Hurst conveyed.

Regardless of this misreading, the argument that negative know-how is involved here is unpersuasive. We do not understand how the changes that we have described can be seen as only showing what not to do. Metallurgical's evidence shows that it encountered many problems with the furnaces Therm-O-Vac delivered. Striving to solve these problems, Metallurgical took several steps to modify the furnaces.

Installing unitary heating elements, chill plates, multiple crucibles, and pump filters are all "positive" steps resulting from conclusions on what to do. These changes allegedly turned unusable furnaces into ones fit for commercial operation. One may say, of course, that these actions result from realizations of what not to do; but so does every human process: the selection of one action at a given moment involves the rejection of every other conceivable one that might have been chosen. Using multiple crucibles, for example, stems from the conclusion that a single large crucible should not be used. This characterization, however, can always describe the invention or modification of a device. Knowing what not to do often leads automatically to knowing what to do. Although we decline to hold that this distinction will always be unavailing, in this case at least we regard the distinction between "positive" and "negative" knowledge to be unintelligible. Because this final claim of Smith is unpersuasive, we conclude that the evidence which was presented at trial could have led a reasonable jury to believe a trade secret existed.

COMMENTS AND QUESTIONS

1. Sales of goods in mass retail markets are made to further the seller's economic interests. Under the rationale in *Fourtek*, why do such sales destroy the value of the secret?

2. If the defendants had acquired information about Metallurgical's process from Consarc or La Floridienne — the Metallurgical licensees — would the case have come out differently? Should it matter whether they acquired the information with knowledge that Metallurgical still considered it a trade secret?

3. The categories of information *eligible* for protection as trade secrets are quite expansive. As *Fourtek* makes clear, they include secret combinations of items which by themselves are publicly known. They also include both scientific and technical information and business information, such as customer lists and business plans. Can you think of any type of information that should be ineligible for trade secret protection?

Note that eligibility for protection is only the first of many hurdles required to establish the existence of a trade secret. Many alleged trade secrets that are *eligible* for protection do not in fact receive protection because they do not meet one of the other standards described in this section. Courts have frequently held certain basic ideas or concepts incapable of protection as secrets on the grounds that they were too well known to derive value from secrecy. For example, in Buffets, Inc. v. Klinke, 73 F.3d 765 (9th Cir. 1996), the court held that the plaintiff could not claim its relatively straightforward recipes for barbequed chicken and macaroni and cheese as trade secrets. On the other hand, in Camp Creek Hospitality Inns v. Sheraton Franchise Corp., 139 F.3d 1396 (11th Cir. 1997), the court held that a hotel could protect information about its prices, discounts, and occupancy levels as a trade secret where it was closely guarded information in the industry.

4. Courts have made it clear that strict novelty is not required for trade secret protection. The idea may have occurred to someone before; it may even be in use by another. But if it is not generally known or readily ascertainable to the competitors in an industry, it may still qualify for trade secret protection. One widely cited decision described the standard for protectable ideas as follows:

> [U]niqueness in the patent law sense is not an essential element of a trade secret, for the patent laws are designed to encourage invention, whereas trade secret law is designed to

protect against a breach of faith. However, the trade secret must "possess at least that modicum of originality which will separate it from everyday knowledge." Cataphote Corporation v. Hudson, 444 F.2d 1313, 1315 (5th Cir. 1971). As stated in an authoritative treatise on this subject:

> As distinguished from a patent, a trade secret need not be essentially new, novel or unique; therefore, prior art is a less effective defense in a trade secret case than it is in a patent infringement case. The idea need not be complicated; it may be intrinsically simple and nevertheless qualify as a secret, unless it is in common knowledge and, therefore, within the public domain.

2 Callman, Unfair Competition, Trademarks and Monopolies § 52.1 (3d ed. 1968).

Forest Laboratories v. The Pillsbury Co., 425 F.2d 621, 624 (7th Cir. 1971). Some courts have gone even further, suggesting that "[a] trade secret may be no more than 'merely a mechanical improvement that a good mechanic can make.'" SI Handling Systems, Inc. v. Heisley, 753 F.2d 1244, 1256 (3d Cir. 1985).

Why not require novelty in order to protect a trade secret? That is, why should the law protect the "secrecy" of a piece of information if others have already discovered it?

5. The *Restatement of Torts* offers further guidance in determining whether information constitutes a trade secret. It lists six factors to be considered:

- The extent to which the information is known outside the claimant's business.
- The extent to which it is known by employees and others involved in the business.
- The extent of measures taken by the claimant to guard the secrecy of the information.
- The value of the information to the business and its competitors.
- The amount of effort or money expended by the business in developing the information.
- The ease or difficulty with which the information could be properly acquired or duplicated by others.

Each of these factors is open-ended. Together, they provide the basis for an inquiry into how secret the information really is. This is also the point of *Forest Laboratories'* truncated inquiry into novelty. To be protectable, information must not be "generally known" or "readily ascertainable" by competitors in an industry. *See* Burbank Grease Servs. LLC v. Sokolowski, 693 N.W.2d 89 (Wis. App. 2005) (Burbank's list of potential customers was readily ascertainable from the Internet, trade associations, and by asking customers who to contact), *reversed on other grounds*, 717 N.W.2d 781 (Wis. 2006).

6. Why should we bother to protect secrets that were stumbled upon with little or no investment in research but that happen to have "value"? Does the economic rationale for intellectual property suggest that such secrets will be underproduced absent protection?

7. Why is secrecy required at all? Trade secrets are not misappropriated unless information is taken by improper means or from a confidential relationship. Why aren't those tortious elements enough? It is certainly possible to envision a "misappropriation" tort that punishes diversion of information, whether or not it is secret.[9] Indeed, a

9. For suggestions along these lines, *see* Dennis Karjala, *Misappropriation as a Third Intellectual Property Paradigm*, 94 Colum. L. Rev. 2594 (1994); J.H. Reichman, *Legal Hybrids Between the Patent and Copyright Paradigms*, 94 Colum. L. Rev. 2432 (1994).

number of controversial cases discussed in Chapter 6 have created just such a common law tort. In addition to the cases cited there, *see* United States Sporting Products v. Johnny Stewart Game Calls, 865 S.W.2d 214 (Tex. Ct. App. 1993) (publicly sold uncopyrighted recordings protectable under a "labor theory"); Note, *The "Genetic Message" from the Cornfields of Iowa: Expanding the Law of Trade Secrets*, 38 DRAKE L. REV. 631 (1989) (describing a similar case involving publicly sold grain).

One possible objection to such a scheme is that it may chill the legitimate acquisition of information from competitors. But the only information protected by a misappropriation tort that is not also protected by trade secret law is public information. Since it is public, the need for competitors to acquire it directly from another company or through dubious means is presumably low.[10]

But there may be a wide gulf between "secret" information and "public" information. If three large companies all use the same process but guard it closely, is it a secret? If a company guards a process closely as a secret, but an account of the process is available in an obscure published source, does the company have a protectable trade secret? Does it matter how obscure the published source is, if the defendant in fact obtains the information from the plaintiff rather than going to the public source? What theory of trade secrets would support a finding of liability in such a case? For an argument that the secrecy requirement actually encourages wider disclosure, by allowing companies to rely on the law rather than on more stringent physical protections, see Mark A. Lemley, *The Surprising Virtues of Treating Trade Secrets as IP Rights*, 61 STAN. L. REV. 311 (2008).

In Rohm & Haas Co. v. Adco Chemical Co., 689 F.2d 424 (3d Cir. 1982), defendant Harvey was a former Rohm & Haas employee who was hired by Adco to duplicate a process for producing "paint delivery vehicles," the chemicals added to paint that allow it to be applied to surfaces easily. There seems no question in the case that Harvey did in fact memorize the plaintiff's formula and take it to Adco. In their defense, the defendants offered evidence that Rohm & Haas's "secret" process was in fact disclosed in a series of prior publications. The court nonetheless concluded that it was a protectable trade secret, in part because the defendants *did not in fact* obtain the information from those publications. Why should this matter? Certainly the defendants' conduct proves that they took the information from the plaintiff, but that should be irrelevant if the plaintiff does not have a protectable secret. Has the *Rohm & Haas* court in effect abolished the requirement of secrecy by requiring only that the defendants in fact obtain the information from the plaintiff?

Rohm & Haas is at the center of a critical debate in trade secret law. At issue is whether information must actually be "known" to competitors or merely be "knowable" for the court to conclude that it is not secret. Many courts following the

10. Another reason for limiting common law protection to secret information may be concern over preemption of state common law by the federal intellectual property laws. While the course of the law is not completely clear, federal courts have generally held that state laws that create property rights in public information are preempted by the patent and copyright laws. The policy being served by preemption is to protect the balance struck by federal intellectual property laws. *See, e.g.*, Synercom Technology v. University Computing Co., 474 F. Supp. 37 (N.D. Tex. 1979) (state unfair competition laws cannot prevent copying of public information).

There are two rationales for such preemption. First, it may be that the federal laws reflect a judgment that unpatentable inventions ought to belong to the public. On this rationale, see Bonito Boats v. Thunder Craft Boats, 489 U.S. 141 (1989). Second, preemption may serve to erect barriers between different types of intellectual property protection, "channeling" inventions into one or another form of protection. We discuss federal preemption in more detail in Chapter 6 *supra*.

Restatement of Torts have taken the former view, as *Rohm & Haas* does. This view gives broad scope to trade secret law, because it allows a plaintiff to protect information that could have been acquired properly but in fact was not. It also underscores the unfair competition rationale for trade secret protection—the problem is not that the defendant acquired the information at all, but the way in which it was acquired.

In a significant break with the old *Restatement* rule, the Uniform Trade Secrets Act provides that information is not a trade secret if it is "generally known" or "readily ascertainable by proper means."[11] Under this view, once a secret is readily available through public sources, it loses all trade secret protection. At this point, the defendant is free to obtain the information from the public source *or from the plaintiff herself. See* RESTATEMENT (THIRD) OF UNFAIR COMPETITION § 39 cmt. *f*, at 433 ("When the information is readily ascertainable from such [public] sources, however, actual resort to the public domain is a formality that should not determine liability.").

Even jurisdictions that follow the *Restatement of Torts* view place some limit on what can qualify for trade secret protection. If information is generally known to the public, or even within a specialized industry, it does not qualify for protection. No company can claim that "$E = mc^2$" is a trade secret, for example, even if it keeps the formula under lock and key, and even if the defendant steals it from the company rather than obtaining it elsewhere. *See* Spring Indus. v. Nicolozakes, 58 U.S.P.Q.2d 1794 (Ohio App. 2000) (information on gravel mining not a trade secret despite efforts to keep it confidential). We consider the rather different issue of whether two parties could *agree* to treat the formula as a secret in section D *infra*.

8. What relevance do the competing theories of trade secret protection have for the known versus knowable debate? If the purpose of trade secret law is to promote innovation, why should a company be entitled to protect an idea that already exists in the literature and can readily be found there? On the other hand, doesn't the tort theory compel the conclusion that a company should be able to protect an idea against being stolen *from it*, even if the idea is commonly known elsewhere?

9. The *Restatement* factors used in *Forest Labs* seem to focus on how widely the information is known, suggesting that information used by many people cannot be a secret. The secrecy requirement, therefore, may reflect a policy judgment in favor of the distribution of information once it has reached a certain "critical mass." *Metallurgical Industries*, by contrast, focuses on attempts to prevent disclosure of the information. This approach suggests that even widely known information (or published information, as that in *Metallurgical Industries* was) may receive trade secret protection.

Compare the definition of a trade secret offered in the new *Restatement (Third) of Unfair Competition*:

> A trade secret is any information that can be used in the operation of a business or other enterprise and that is sufficiently valuable and secret to afford an actual or potential economic advantage over others.

RESTATEMENT (THIRD) OF UNFAIR COMPETITION § 39. Under the new *Restatement*, many different companies can possess the same information and each protect it as a

11. Some states, however, refused to accede to this change and have modified the language of the Act to remove the reference to "readily ascertainable" information. California is one prominent example. *See* CAL. CIV. CODE § 3426.1(d)(1); ABBA Rubber Co. v. Seaquist, 286 Cal. Rptr. 518 (Ct. App. 1991) (customer list qualified for trade secret protection even though information was available in trade directories). California law does permit proof of ready ascertainability as a defense, however.

secret. *Id.* at illustration 1.[12] In a comment interpreting this provision, the drafters note that "[t]he concept of a trade secret as defined in this Section is intended to be consistent with the definition of 'trade secret' in § 1(4) of the [Uniform Trade Secrets] Act." Is it?

PROBLEMS

Problem 11-1. Company *X* possesses a valuable piece of information about the process for making its product. That information is not known at all outside company *X*. Suppose *X* discloses the information to two companies, *A* and *B*. *A* receives the information in confidence, and subject to a written agreement that it will not use or disclose the information outside the bounds of the relationship. *B* receives the information without any restrictions whatever on its use. Does *X* have a protectable trade secret that it can assert against *A*? Against *B*? Against *C*, who steals the information from *X*'s computer network?

Does your answer change if *X*, *A*, *B*, and *C* are the only companies in the industry?

Problem 11-2. StartUp, Inc., is the only participant in a new market. The market is based on a product for which StartUp has a nonexclusive license from the inventor; that is, StartUp cannot prevent others from obtaining a similar license. Nonetheless, StartUp has exhaustively researched the demand for the product, has concluded that a market exists, and has worked to stimulate demand. As a result, it has both "made" a market for the product and developed a comprehensive list of customers.

Thaddeus, a sales representative for StartUp, leaves to found his own company. He gets a license to make the product from its inventor. He takes with him from StartUp the customer list he worked with as an employee, his personal knowledge of and contacts with specific customers, and StartUp's knowledge of the market. StartUp sues Thaddeus for misappropriation of trade secrets. What result?

Problem 11-3. Research Co. is a *major* pharmaceutical company working on a cure for certain types of cancer. Derek is a molecular biologist employed by Research. After several years on the job, Derek leaves Research for Conglomerate, Inc., another pharmaceutical company, which has decided to work on the same cancer cure. At the time Derek leaves, Research has not been successful in finding a cancer cure. However, as a result of his work at Research, Derek is able to help Conglomerate avoid several unproductive avenues of research. Aided in part by this knowledge, Conglomerate (using scientists other than Derek) develops a cancer cure before Research. Research sues Conglomerate, alleging misappropriation of trade secrets. Does Research have a case?

12. The *Restatement* does note, however, that "[w]hen information is no longer sufficiently secret to qualify for protection as a trade secret, its use should not serve as a basis for the imposition of liability," *id.* at 433 cmt. *f*, suggesting that at some point information is not secret even though companies protect it as if it were.

Problem 11-4. The Church of True Belief is a religious group founded around a set of closely guarded scriptural materials *supposedly* handed down to Church's elders from Church's deity. After a bitter theological dispute, a group of adherents leaves the church to form the House of Absolute Belief. They take with them a copy of Church's confidential scriptures, which they rely on in gaining adherents and founding the new House. Church sues House for misappropriation of trade secrets.

At trial, the issue is whether the scriptures qualify as a trade secret. The evidence indicates that the scriptures had never before been removed from the confines of Church, that both Church and House are tax-exempt nonprofit organizations that rely on donations for their funding, and that Church (but not House) *rations* access to the scriptures in proportion to the size of an adherent's donation.

Can the scriptures qualify as a trade secret? Does your answer *depend* on whether the governing law is the UTSA, the *Restatement of Torts*, or the *Restatement (Third) of Unfair Competition*?

Problem 11-5. Pear Computer Corporation, known for its obsessive secrecy, password protects all its files. Can the password itself be a trade secret? Does it matter whether the UTSA or the *Restatement* applies?

2. Reasonable Efforts to Maintain Secrecy

Besides the existence of a trade secret, plaintiffs must show under the Uniform Act that they have taken "reasonable measures" to protect the secrecy of their idea. Certainly, a plaintiff cannot publicly disclose the secret and still expect to protect it. But precautions must go further than that. Generally, they must include certain efforts to prevent theft or use of the idea by former employees.

Rockwell Graphic Systems, Inc. v. DEV Industries, Inc.
925 F.2d 174 (7th Cir. 1991)

POSNER, Circuit Judge:

This is a suit for misappropriation of trade secrets. Rockwell Graphic Systems, a manufacturer of printing presses used by newspapers, and of parts for those presses, brought the suit against DEV Industries, a competing manufacturer, and against the president of DEV, who used to be employed by Rockwell. . . .

When we said that Rockwell manufactures both printing presses and replacement parts for its presses — "wear parts" or "piece parts," they are called — we were speaking approximately. Rockwell does not always manufacture the parts itself. Sometimes when an owner of one of Rockwell's presses needs a particular part, or when Rockwell anticipates demand for the part, it will subcontract the manufacture of it to an independent machine shop, called a "vendor" by the parties. When it does this it must give the vendor a "piece part drawing" indicating materials, dimensions, tolerances, and methods of manufacture. Without that information the vendor could not manufacture the part. Rockwell has not tried to patent the piece parts. It believes that the purchaser cannot, either by inspection or by "reverse engineering" (taking something apart in an effort to figure out how it was made), discover how to manufacture the part; to do that you need the piece part drawing, which contains much information concerning methods of manufacture, alloys, tolerances, etc. that cannot be gleaned from the part itself. So Rockwell tries — whether hard enough is the central issue in the case — to keep the piece part drawings secret, though not of course from the vendors; they could not manufacture the parts for Rockwell without the drawings. DEV points out that some of the parts are for presses that Rockwell no longer manufactures. But as long as the presses are in service — which can be a very long time — there is a demand for replacement parts.

Rockwell employed Fleck and Peloso in responsible positions that gave them access to piece part drawings. Fleck left Rockwell in 1975 and three years later joined DEV as its president. Peloso joined DEV the following year after being fired by Rockwell when a security guard caught him removing piece part drawings from Rockwell's plant. This suit was brought in 1984, and pretrial discovery by Rockwell turned up 600 piece part drawings in DEV's possession, of which 100 were Rockwell's. DEV claimed to have obtained them lawfully, either from customers of Rockwell or from Rockwell vendors, contrary to Rockwell's claim that either Fleck and Peloso stole them when they were employed by it or DEV obtained them in some other unlawful manner, perhaps from a vendor who violated his confidentiality agreement with Rockwell. Thus far in the litigation DEV has not been able to show which customers or vendors lawfully supplied it with Rockwell's piece part drawings.

The defendants persuaded the magistrate and the district judge that the piece part drawings weren't really trade secrets at all, because Rockwell made only perfunctory efforts to keep them secret. Not only were there thousands of drawings in the hands of the vendors; there were thousands more in the hands of owners of Rockwell presses, the customers for piece parts. The drawings held by customers, however, are not relevant. They are not piece part drawings, but assembly drawings. . . . An assembly drawing shows how the parts of a printing press fit together for installation and also how to integrate the press with the printer's other equipment. Whenever Rockwell sells a printing press it gives the buyer assembly drawings as well. These are the equivalent of instructions for assembling a piece of furniture. Rockwell does not claim that they contain trade secrets. It admits having supplied a few piece part drawings to customers, but they were piece part drawings of obsolete parts that Rockwell has no interest in manufacturing and of a safety device that was not part of the press as originally delivered but that its customers were clamoring for; more to the point, none of these drawings is among those that Rockwell claims DEV misappropriated.

. . . DEV's main argument is that Rockwell was impermissibly sloppy in its efforts to keep the piece part drawings secret.

On this, the critical, issue, the record shows the following. (Because summary judgment was granted to DEV, we must construe the facts as favorably to Rockwell as is reasonable to do.) Rockwell keeps all its engineering drawings, including both piece part and assembly drawings, in a vault. Access not only to the vault, but also to the building in which it is located, is limited to authorized employees who display identification. These are mainly engineers, of whom Rockwell employs 200. They are required to sign agreements not to disseminate the drawings, or disclose their contents, other than as authorized by the company. An authorized employee who needs a drawing must sign it out from the vault and return it when he has finished with it. But he is permitted to make copies, which he is to destroy when he no longer needs them in his work. The only outsiders allowed to see piece part drawings are the vendors (who are given copies, not originals). They too are required to sign confidentiality agreements, and in addition each drawing is stamped with a legend stating that it contains proprietary material. Vendors, like Rockwell's own engineers, are allowed to make copies for internal working purposes, and although the confidentiality agreement that they sign requires the vendor to return the drawing when the order has been filled, Rockwell does not enforce this requirement. The rationale for not enforcing it is that the vendor will need the drawing if Rockwell reorders the part. Rockwell even permits unsuccessful bidders for a piece part contract to keep the drawings, on the theory that the high bidder this round may be the low bidder the next. But it does consider the ethical standards of a machine shop before making it a vendor, and so far as appears no shop has ever abused the confidence reposed in it.

The mere fact that Rockwell gave piece part drawings to vendors — that is, disclosed its trade secrets to "a limited number of outsiders for a particular purpose" — did not forfeit trade secret protection. On the contrary, such disclosure, which is often necessary to the efficient exploitation of a trade secret, imposes a duty of confidentiality on the part of the person to whom the disclosure is made. But with 200 engineers checking out piece part drawings and making copies of them to work from, and numerous vendors receiving copies of piece part drawings and copying them, tens of thousands of copies of these drawings are floating around outside Rockwell's vault, and many of these outside the company altogether. Although the magistrate and the district judge based their conclusion that Rockwell had not made adequate efforts to maintain secrecy in part at least on the irrelevant fact that it took no efforts at all to keep its assembly drawings secret, DEV in defending the judgment that it obtained in the district court argues that Rockwell failed to take adequate measures to keep even the piece part drawings secret. Not only did Rockwell not limit copying of those drawings or insist that copies be returned; it did not segregate the piece part drawings from the assembly drawings and institute more secure procedures for the former. So Rockwell could have done more to maintain the confidentiality of its piece part drawings than it did, and we must decide whether its failure to do more was so plain a breach of the obligation of a trade secret owner to make reasonable efforts to maintain secrecy as to justify the entry of summary judgment for the defendants.

The requirement of reasonable efforts has both evidentiary and remedial significance, and this regardless of which of the two different conceptions of trade secret protection prevails. . . . [T]he two different conceptions of trade secret protection are better described as different emphases. The first emphasizes the desirability of deterring efforts that have as their sole purpose and effect the redistribution of wealth from one firm to another. The second emphasizes the desirability of encouraging inventive activity by protecting its fruits from efforts at appropriation that are, indeed, sterile wealth-redistributive — not productive — activities. The approaches differ, if at all, only in that the second does not limit the class of improper means to those that fit a preexisting pigeonhole in the law of tort or contract or fiduciary duty — and it is by no means clear that the first approach assumes a closed class of wrongful acts, either.

Under the first approach, at least if narrowly interpreted so that it does not merge with the second, the plaintiff must prove that the defendant obtained the plaintiff's trade secret by a wrongful act, illustrated here by the alleged acts of Fleck and Peloso in removing piece part drawings from Rockwell's premises without authorization, in violation of their employment contracts and confidentiality agreements, and using them in competition with Rockwell. Rockwell is unable to prove directly that the 100 piece part drawings it got from DEV in discovery were stolen by Fleck and Peloso or obtained by other improper means. But if it can show that the probability that DEV could have obtained them otherwise — that is, without engaging in wrongdoing — is slight, then it will have taken a giant step toward proving what it must prove in order to recover under the first theory of trade secret protection. The greater the precautions that Rockwell took to maintain the secrecy of the piece part drawings, the lower the probability that DEV obtained them properly and the higher the probability that it obtained them through a wrongful act; the owner had taken pains to prevent them from being obtained otherwise.

Under the second theory of trade secret protection, the owner's precautions still have evidentiary significance, but now primarily as evidence that the secret has real value. For the precise means by which the defendant acquired it is less important under the second theory, though not completely unimportant; remember that even the second theory allows the unmasking of a trade secret by some means, such as reverse engineering. If Rockwell expended only paltry resources on preventing its piece part drawings from falling into the hands of competitors such as DEV, why should the law, whose machinery is far from costless, bother to provide Rockwell with a remedy? The information contained in the drawings cannot have been worth much if Rockwell did not think it worthwhile to make serious efforts to keep the information secret.

The remedial significance of such efforts lies in the fact that if the plaintiff has allowed his trade secret to fall into the public domain, he would enjoy a windfall if permitted to recover damages merely because the defendant took the secret from him, rather than from the public domain as it could have done with impunity. Brunswick Corp. v. Outboard Marine Corp., supra, 79 Ill. 2d at 479, 404 N.E.2d at 207; Van Products Co. v. General Welding & Fabricating Co., 419 Pa. 248, 267-68, 213 A.2d 769, 779-80 (1965) (repudiating the interpretation of Pennsylvania law that this court had adopted in Smith v. Dravo Corp., 203 F.2d 369, 374-75 (7th Cir. 1953)). It would be like punishing a person for stealing property that he believes is owned by another but that actually is abandoned property. If it were true, as apparently it is not, that Rockwell had given the piece part drawings at issue to customers, and it had done so without requiring the customers to hold them in confidence, DEV could have obtained the drawings from the customers without committing any wrong. The harm to Rockwell would have been the same as if DEV had stolen the drawings from it, but it would have had no remedy, having parted with its rights to the trade secret. This is true whether the trade secret is regarded as property protected only against wrongdoers or (the logical extreme of the second conception, although no case — not even *Christopher* — has yet embraced it and the patent statute may preempt it) as property protected against the world. In the first case, a defendant is perfectly entitled to obtain the property by lawful conduct if he can, and he can if the property is in the hands of persons who themselves committed no wrong to get it. In the second case the defendant is perfectly entitled to obtain the property if the plaintiff has abandoned it by giving it away without restrictions.

It is easy to understand therefore why the law of trade secrets requires a plaintiff to show that he took reasonable precautions to keep the secret a secret. If analogies are needed, one that springs to mind is the duty of the holder of a trademark to take reasonable efforts to police infringements of his mark, failing which the mark is likely to be deemed abandoned, or to become generic or descriptive (and in either event be unprotectable). The trademark owner who fails to police his mark both shows that he doesn't really value it very much and creates a situation in which an infringer may have been unaware that he was using a proprietary mark because the mark had drifted into the public domain, much as DEV contends Rockwell's piece part drawings have done.

But only in an extreme case can what is a "reasonable" precaution be determined on a motion for summary judgment, because the answer depends on a balancing of costs and benefits that will vary from case to case and so require estimation and measurement by persons knowledgeable in the particular field of endeavor involved. On the one hand, the more the owner of the trade secret spends on preventing the secret from leaking out, the more he demonstrates that the secret has real value deserving of legal protection, that he really was hurt as a result of the misappropriation of it, and that there really was misappropriation. On the other hand, the more he spends, the higher his costs. The costs can be indirect as well as direct. The more Rockwell restricts access to its drawings, either by its engineers or by the vendors, the harder it will be for either group to do the work expected of it. Suppose Rockwell forbids any copying of its drawings. Then a team of engineers would have to share a single drawing, perhaps by passing it around or by working in the same room, huddled over the drawing. And how would a vendor be able to make a piece part—would Rockwell have to bring all that work in house? Such reconfigurations of patterns of work and production are far from costless; and therefore perfect security is not optimum security.

There are contested factual issues here, bearing in mind that what is reasonable is itself a fact for purposes of Rule 56 of the civil rules. Obviously Rockwell took some precautions, both physical (the vault security, the security guards—one of whom apprehended Peloso in flagrante delicto) and contractual, to maintain the confidentiality of its piece part drawings. Obviously it could have taken more precautions. But at a cost, and the question is whether the additional benefit in security would have exceeded that cost. We do not suggest that the question can be answered with the same precision with which it can be posed, but neither can we say that no reasonable jury could find that Rockwell had done enough and could then go on to infer misappropriation from a combination of the precautions Rockwell took and DEV's inability to establish the existence of a lawful source of the Rockwell piece part drawings in its possession.

This is an important case because trade secret protection is an important part of intellectual property, a form of property that is of growing importance to the competitiveness of American industry. Patent protection is at once costly and temporary, and therefore cannot be regarded as a perfect substitute. If trade secrets are protected only if their owners take extravagant, productivity-impairing measures to maintain their secrecy, the incentive to invest resources in discovering more efficient methods of production will be reduced, and with it the amount of invention. . . .

Reversed and remanded.

COMMENTS AND QUESTIONS

1. There is an intuitive relationship between the existence of a secret and reasonable efforts to protect a secret. After all, if something is not a secret, there would not seem to be any point to protecting it. And the fact that an idea is well protected may be evidence that it is in fact a secret. Nonetheless, the requirements are conceptually distinct. Information in the public domain cannot be turned into a secret merely by

treating it like a secret, a point that lawyers and even courts sometimes forget. This distinction is made clear in the Uniform Trade Secrets Act, which defines a trade secret as information that is both "not generally known" *and* the subject of reasonable efforts to maintain secrecy. UTSA § 1(4).

Consider whether the opinion in *Rockwell* conflates these two into a single requirement. The court seems to emphasize the evidentiary significance of the precautions Rockwell took in proving misappropriation. Since it was clear (to the court, anyway) that the DEV employees did in fact take the information from Rockwell, the court did not consider the precautions to be that important. This approach was apparently followed in the *Restatement (Third) of Unfair Competition.* Unlike the Uniform Act, the new *Restatement* does not contain a requirement that plaintiffs take reasonable precautions to protect their secrets. The comment to section 39 takes the position that, while "[p]recautions taken to maintain the secrecy of information are relevant in determining whether the information qualifies for protection as a trade secret," "if the value and secrecy of the information are clear, evidence of specific precautions taken by the trade secret owner may be unnecessary." RESTATEMENT (THIRD) OF UNFAIR COMPETITION § 39, cmt. *g*, at 435-36.

Contrast *Rockwell* with the Minnesota Supreme Court's decision in Electro-Craft Corp. v. Controlled Motion, Inc., 332 N.W.2d 890 (Minn. 1983), a case that also involved information taken by former employees and used in starting a competing company. The court found that the information the employees took was not generally known or readily ascertainable in the industry. However, it found that the information did not constitute a trade secret:

> (c) Reasonable efforts to maintain secrecy. It is this element upon which [plaintiff Electro-Craft Corp., or "ECC"]'s claim founders. The district court found that, even though ECC had no "meaningful security provisions," ECC showed an intention to keep its data and processes secret. This finding does not bear upon the statutory requirement that ECC use "efforts that are reasonable under the circumstances to maintain . . . secrecy." MINN. STAT. § 325C.01, subd. 5(ii). . . . [E]ven under the common law, more than an "intention" was required—the plaintiff was required to show that it had manifested that intention by making some effort to keep the information secret.
>
> This element of trade secret law does not require maintenance of absolute secrecy; only partial or qualified secrecy has been required under the common law. What is actually required is conduct which will allow a court acting in equity to enforce plaintiff's rights. . . .
>
> In the present case, even viewing the evidence most favorably to the findings below, we hold that ECC did not meet its burden of proving that it used reasonable efforts to maintain secrecy as to [the subject matter of the suit, a product called the ECC 1125]. We acknowledge that ECC took minimal precautions in screening its Handbook and publications for confidential information and by requiring some of its employees to sign a confidentiality agreement, but these were not enough.
>
> First, ECC's physical security measures did not demonstrate any effort to maintain secrecy. By "security" we mean the protection of information from discovery by outsiders. Security was lax in this case. For example, the main plant had a few guarded entrances, but seven unlocked entrances existed without signs warning of limited access. Employees were at one time required to wear badges, but that system was abandoned by the time of the events giving rise to this case. The same was generally true of the Amery, Wisconsin plant where ECC 1125 and brushless motors were manufactured. One sign was posted at each plant, however, marking the research and development lab at Hopkins and the machine shop at Amery as restricted to "authorized personnel." Discarded drawings and plans for

motors were simply thrown away, not destroyed. Documents such as motor drawings were not kept in a central or locked location, although some design notebooks were kept locked.

The relaxed security by itself, however, does not preclude a finding of reasonable efforts by ECC to maintain secrecy. Other evidence did not indicate that industrial espionage is a major problem in the servo motor industry. Therefore, "security" measures may not have been needed, and the trial court could have found trade secrets if ECC had taken other reasonable measures to preserve secrecy.

However, ECC's "confidentiality" procedures were also fatally lax, and the district court was clearly in error in finding ECC's efforts to be reasonable. By "confidentiality" in this case we mean the procedures by which the employer signals to its employees and to others that certain information is secret and should not be disclosed. Confidentiality was important in this case, for testimony demonstrated that employees in the servo motor business frequently leave their employers in order to produce similar or identical devices for new employers. ECC has hired many employees from other corporations manufacturing similar products.[16] If ECC wanted to prevent its employees from doing the same thing, it had an obligation to inform its employees that certain information was secret.

ECC's efforts were especially inadequate because of the non-intuitive nature of ECC's claimed secrets here. The dimensions, etc., of ECC's motors are not trade secrets in as obvious a way as a "secret formula" might be. ECC should have let its employees know in no uncertain terms that those features were secret.

Instead, ECC treated its information as if it were not secret. None of its technical documents were marked "Confidential," and drawings, dimensions and parts were sent to customers and vendors without special marking. Employee access to documents was not restricted. ECC never issued a policy statement outlining what it considered to be secret. Many informal tours were given to vendors and customers without warnings as to confidential information. Further, two plants each had an "open house" at which the public was invited to observe manufacturing processes. . . .

In summary, ECC has not met its burden of proof in establishing the existence of any trade secrets. The evidence does not show that ECC was ever consistent in treating the information here as secret.

In a part of the opinion not reprinted here, the court noted that the information in question was not in fact known at all outside ECC. Given that, why shouldn't the company be able to prevent its employees from using the information they acquired there? Should the laxity of ECC's precautions matter if no one other than the defendants in fact took advantage of it?

2. In *Rockwell*, the court apparently assumed that the manufacturer was in a confidential relationship with the subcontractors that it sent drawings to. Is it reasonable to assume that there was an implied relationship of confidentiality in the absence of an express agreement? Two decisions by the Ninth Circuit set the parameters of this debate. In Entertainment Research Group v. Genesis Creative Group, 122 F.3d 1211 (9th Cir. 1997), the court found no confidential relationship between a manufacturer of inflatable costumes and the marketing firm hired to distribute them. By contrast, in IMAX Corp. v. Cinema Technologies, 152 F.3d 1161 (9th Cir. 1998), the court concluded that the proprietor of an IMAX movie theater had a duty to IMAX to

16. One ECC employee actually prided himself on the information he had brought with him from his former employer. One day, just before that employee left ECC to join another company, the president of ECC found him copying documents after hours. ECC never questioned the employee or warned him or his new employer that certain information was confidential.

protect the specifications of the projector as trade secrets from a competitor who was attempting to reverse engineer the IMAX technology.

3. How much effort should be required of trade secret owners? Obviously, the best way to protect a secret is not to tell anyone at all. In the modern commercial world, however, this is normally impractical. Companies with trade secrets must tell the secret to their employees, their business partners, and often their distributors and customers as well. But the risk of *inadvertent* use or disclosure can be reduced in a number of ways: for example, by requiring employees, licensees, and even customers to sign confidentiality agreements; by investing in physical security measures against theft, such as fences, safes, and guards; and by designing products themselves so that they do not reveal their secrets upon casual (or even detailed) inspection. The First Circuit has held that "affirmative steps" to protect secrecy, not merely "ordinary discretion," are required. Incase Inc. v. Timex Corp., 488 F.3d 46 (1st Cir. 2007).

4. Will reasonable precautions *always* be a question of fact? Or are certain activities (publishing a secret formula, for example) so inconsistent with trade secret protection that they automatically preclude a successful trade secret suit? *See* section B.3 *infra*, discussing disclosure of trade secrets.

One issue that arises frequently is whether companies that sell products on the open market that embody their trade secret have disclosed the secret. As we shall see, customers who buy a product on the open market are entitled to break it apart to see how it works. This process is called "reverse engineering" the product. Trade secret law does not protect owners against legitimate purchasers who discover the secret through reverse engineering, absent a valid nondisclosure agreement. But does the possibility that a product might be reverse-engineered foreclose *any* trade secret protection, even against people who have not actually reverse-engineered the product? At least one court has said no. In Data General Corp. v. Grumman Systems Support Corp., 825 F. Supp. 340, 359 (D. Mass. 1993), the court upheld a jury's verdict that Grumman had misappropriated trade secrets contained in object code form in Data General's computer program, despite the fact that many copies of the program had been sold on the open market. The court reasoned: "With the exception of those who lawfully licensed or unlawfully misappropriated MV/ADEX, Data General enjoyed the exclusive use of MV/ADEX. Even those who obtained MV/ADEX and were able to *use* MV/ADEX were unable to discover its trade secrets because MV/ADEX was distributed only in its object code form, which is essentially unintelligible to humans."

Data General suggests that reasonable efforts to protect the secrecy of an idea contained in a commercial product — such as locks, black boxes, or the use of unreadable code — may suffice to maintain trade secret protection even after the product itself is widely circulated. Does this result make sense?

On the basis of the reasoning in *Data General* — that the source code, which contained the secrets, was not widely disclosed — would the distribution of the Data General software in object code form to the general public constitute misappropriation of those trade secrets?

5. If the idea is to encourage investment in trade secrets, why require any degree of "reasonable precautions" at all? One sometimes hears in this regard that *all* "fencing" expenditures are inefficient. *Cf.* Edmund W. Kitch, *The Law and Economics of Rights in Valuable Information*, 9 J. Legal Stud. 683 (1980) (arguing that reasonable precautions make sense only as evidence of the existence of a trade secret). Why not simply require explicit notice — large neon signs, stamps on all documents, or publication of a

secrecy policy—in place of physical precautions? For a suggestion that proceeds along these lines to some extent, see J.H. Reichman, *Legal Hybrids Between the Patent and Copyright Paradigms*, 94 COLUM. L. REV. 2432 (1994).

Is it appropriate to punish the creator of a valuable secret who has not invested in "reasonable precautions"? What value is there in a legal rule that requires investment in precautions up to the level that would be rational *in the absence of* the legal rule? Are prospective trade secret thieves actually encouraged by the reasonable precautions argument to steal ideas when they observe a lapse in security, and does this rule give them an incentive to search out such lapses? Professor Kitch asks the related question of why these expenses should be required in addition to the expense of bringing a trade secret lawsuit.

David Friedman, William Landes & Richard Posner, *Some Economics of Trade Secret Law*, 5 J. ECON. PERSP. 61, 67 (1991), makes the related point that a trade secret cause of action that yields a legal remedy ought to be available when it is cheaper than the physical precautions that would be necessary to protect a piece of information. They also state:

> Where on the contrary the social costs of enforcing secrecy through the legal system would be high, the benefits of shared information are likely to exceed the net benefits of legal protection.

Should it be a defense to a trade secret action that the plaintiff could more easily have protected the secret through physical precautions?

Kitch notes by way of analogy that we do not prohibit criminal complaints for larceny just because a property owner was careless. (On the other hand, many states do reduce recovery in tort suits on the basis of "comparative negligence.") He also suggests that reasonable precautions are required only to put prospective infringers on notice about the existence of a right and to serve as evidence of the fact that the secret is worth protecting legally. The fencing thus serves a notice function, akin to "marking" products with patent numbers, copyright symbols, or trademark symbols. Kitch, *supra*, at 698.

The Court in E.I. duPont deNemours & Co. v. Christopher, 431 F.2d 1012 (5th Cir. 1970), *cert. denied*, 400 U.S. 1024 (1971), pays significant attention to the role of fencing costs in trade secrets suits. We will return to that case when we consider misappropriation of trade secrets in section C *infra*.

One might imagine other rationales for requiring reasonable protection. For example, one might treat the requirement of reasonable precautions as serving a gatekeeper function that helps to weed out frivolous trade secret claims by requiring evidence of investment by the plaintiff in protecting the secret.

PROBLEMS

Problem 11-6. Smith, a bar owner in rural Alabama, develops by accident one night the relatively simple formula for a new alcoholic beverage. The drink is simply a mixture of three common ingredients. Smith begins selling the drink, which he calls "Mobile Mud," in his bar. However, he instructs his bartenders not to reveal the formula to anyone and has them premix "Mud" in the back of the bar, out of sight of customers. Smith is outraged when he learns that Jimmy Dean, an international distributor of alcoholic beverages, has copied his formula and is marketing it under a different name. At trial, Dean employees and independent experts unanimously testify that it is possible for someone with experience in the beverage industry to determine the formula for Mud by looking at, smelling, and tasting the drink.

Has Smith taken reasonable precautions? What more could he have done to protect the "secret formula" of Mobile Mud? Is the secret so obvious to consumers that selling the product on the open market destroys protection? Does your opinion of the case change if you learn that Dean's representative went to Smith's bar and bribed a bartender to disclose the formula?

Problem 11-7. MidContinent is a small manufacturer of signs and decals. It has only five employees, two of whom are father and son and two more of whom are family friends. The company describes itself as having a "relaxed, congenial" working atmosphere. In order to avoid what the president considers excessive formality, the employees have never been required to sign confidentiality agreements, and documents kept within the company aren't stamped confidential. The company has never conducted "exit interviews" or instructed its employees about trade secrecy. According to the company president, "we trust our employees, and that trust has never been misplaced." On the other hand, the company does take certain steps to keep outsiders from accessing its customer lists and its adhesive manufacturing process. And there is little history of economic espionage in the decal-manufacturing business.

Has MidContinent taken reasonable efforts to protect its secrets? Should it matter whether the party accused of stealing those secrets is an employee or an outsider?

3. Disclosure of Trade Secrets

It is axiomatic that public disclosure of a trade secret destroys the "secret," and therefore ends protection forever. The corollary to this rule is that as long as a trade secret remains secret, it is protectable. Thus, trade secrets do not last for a specific term of years but continue indefinitely until the occurrence of a particular event—the public disclosure of the secret.

But when does a use of a trade secret in one's business turn into a disclosure of the secret? Consider the following case.

Data General Corp. v. Digital Computer Controls, Inc.

297 A.2d 433 (Del. Ct. Ch. 1971), aff'd, 297 A.2d 437 (Del. S. Ct. 1972)

Marvel, Vice Chancellor:

Data General Corporation seeks an order preliminarily enjoining the defendant Digital Computer Controls from making use of claimed trade secrets allegedly contained in design drawings which accompany certain sales of plaintiff's Nova 1200 computer, defendant having acquired such a computer with accompanying drawings from one of plaintiff's customers. This is the decision of the Court on plaintiff's motion for a preliminary injunction as well as on defendants' cross-motion for summary judgment of dismissal of the present action.

The relevant facts thus far adduced are as follows: During the past several years plaintiff has developed and marketed successfully small general-purpose computers to which they have given the name Nova, a large part of plaintiff's research and development budget for the past several years having been allocated to the development of such small computers, which, the parties agree, are the only ones of their type presently being profitably marketed, there having been no device on the market comparable to plaintiff's machines until defendant's entry on the scene.

When a sale of a Nova 1200 computer is made, plaintiff makes available at no extra cost to those customers who wish to do their own maintenance the design or logic drawings of the device sold, in this case a Nova 1200 computer. Such type of maintenance has been found to be desired by some customers in order to avoid periods of unproductive delay while waiting for repairs to be made by plaintiff's trained personnel.

Design drawings made available to customers are furnished subject to the terms of a non-disclosure clause contained in a paper which accompanies a purchase agreement. Furthermore, all drawings bear a legend to the effect that they contain proprietary information of the plaintiff which is not to be used by a purchaser for manufacturing purposes. However, the Nova 1200 is not patented, and its design drawings have not been copyrighted.

In April, 1971, the defendant Ackley, the president of Digital, purchased for his company from a customer of Data General, namely Mini-Computer Systems, Inc., a Nova 1200 computer which the latter had earlier acquired from plaintiff. Although the exact circumstances surrounding such sale are not entirely clear on the present record, the corporate defendant's president, in consummating such purchase, acquired a set of design drawings of the Nova 1200, said drawings having been furnished to MiniComputer by the plaintiff in order to facilitate maintenance by the former of its Nova 1200's. The corporate defendant thereafter proceeded to use such design drawings as a pattern for the construction of a competing machine which it is now about to market, the corporate defendant's president conceding that only minor changes have been made in the basic design of plaintiff's device in the course of the development of defendant's comparable computer. . . .

II

Defendants' other arguments are accordingly based on the law of trade secrets. . . .

Defendants insist, however, that plaintiff has not maintained that degree of secrecy which will preserve its right to relief, either by publicly selling an article alleged to contain a trade secret, or by failing to restrict access to the design drawings for its device, arguing that matters of common knowledge in an industry may not be claimed as trade secrets.

It has been recognized in similar cases that even though an unpatented article, device or machine has been sold to the public, and is therefore subject to examination and copying by anyone, the manner of making the article, device or machine may yet constitute a trade secret until such a copy has in fact been made, Schulenburg v. Signatrol, Inc., 33 Ill. 2d 379, 212 N.E.2d 865, and Tabor v. Hoffman, N.Y., 118 N.Y. 30, 23 N.E. 12.

Defendants contend, however, that the issuance by plaintiff of copies of design drawings to its customers was made without safeguards designed properly to maintain the secrecy requisite to the existence of a trade secret. In other words, it is contended that plaintiff's attempts to maintain secrecy merely consisted of (1) not giving copies of the design drawings to those customers who did not need them for maintenance of their computer, (2) obtaining agreements not to disclose the information from those customers who were given copies of the drawings, and (3) printing a legend on the drawings which contained the allegedly confidential information which identified the drawing as proprietary information, the use of which was restricted. Plaintiff argues, however, that disclosure of the design drawings to purchasers of the computer is necessary properly to maintain its device, that such disclosure was required by the very nature of the machine, and that reasonable steps were taken to preserve the secrecy of the material released. I conclude at this preliminary stage of the case that it cannot be held as a matter of law that such precautions were inadequate, a factual dispute as to the adequacy of such precautions having clearly been raised. Defendants' motion for summary judgment must accordingly be denied.

Finally, I am satisfied that if plaintiff were to prevail at final hearing, it would only be entitled to injunctive relief during that undetermined period of time which would be required for defendants substantially to reproduce the plaintiff's device without its accompanying drawings. Such period of time would, on the present record, vary according to the number of man hours devoted to so-called reverse engineering. Thus, the granting of a preliminary injunction at this juncture would grant plaintiff all the relief it might hope ultimately to obtain after final hearing. Compare Thomas C. Marshall, Inc. v. Holiday Inn, Inc., 40 Del. Ch. 77, 174 A.2d 27. In addition, while plaintiff has presented evidence of its attempts to preserve the secrecy of the alleged secrets it now seeks to have protected by injunction, it has not adduced sufficient evidence to establish that likelihood of ultimate success on final hearing which would entitle it to the issuance of a preliminary injunction.

COMMENTS AND QUESTIONS

1. Disclosure of a once-protected trade secret can occur in a number of ways:

- First, a trade secret owner may publish the secret, whether in an academic journal or any other forum. In that case, secrecy is lost, at least provided the publication is accessible to those interested in the subject matter. This loss might reasonably be considered a substantial disincentive to publication of scientific or technical advances. But publication of secret information regularly occurs, either because the inventors have not thought through the consequences of their actions or because the value or prestige of first publication is deemed to outweigh the potential loss of commercial trade secret protection.

  One common form of disclosure is the publication of an issued patent. Because (as we shall see) patent law requires the public disclosure of an invention with sufficient specificity to enable one of ordinary skill in the art to make it, obtaining a patent on an invention destroys trade secret protection. *See* Ferroline Corp. v. General Aniline & Film Corp., 207 F.2d 912 (7th Cir. 1953), *cert. denied*, 347 U.S. 953 (1954). Thus an inventor must "elect" either patent or trade secret protection, for the two cannot protect the same invention simultaneously.

The Federal Circuit applied a notable exception to this seemingly absolute rule in Rhone-Poulenc Agro v. DeKalb Genetics Corp., 272 F.3d 1335 (Fed. Cir. 2001). In that case, the defendant had stolen the plaintiff's trade secrets and published them in its own patent application. The court concluded that in those circumstances the trade secret owner hadn't had the opportunity to "elect" to give up trade secret protection, and so ruled that the publication of the defendant's patent hadn't disclosed plaintiff's trade secrets. This result seems equitable to the plaintiff. But does it really comport with the principle that information must be secret to be protected? For a contrary rule, see Evans v. General Motors, 125 F.3d 1448 (Fed. Cir. 1997) (holding that publication by a thief started the one-year clock running for patenting an invention, and reasoning that because the trade secret owner knew of the theft he could have acted to seek patent protection within a reasonable period of time).

- Second, a trade secret owner may in some cases disclose the secret by selling a commercial product that embodies the secret. As one court explained, both the *Restatement of Torts* and the Uniform Trade Secrets Act "necessarily compel the conclusion that a trade secret is protectable only so long as it is kept secret by the party creating it. If a so-called trade secret is fully disclosed by the products produced by use of the secret then the right to protection is lost." Vacco Indus. v. Van den Berg, 6 Cal. Rptr. 2d 602, 611 (Ct. App. 1992) (citations omitted). Further, disclosure may occur even without sale of the product itself, if the secret is disclosed freely and without restriction during the manufacturing or development processes.

  However, sales of a product to the public do not necessarily disclose a trade secret simply because the product embodies the trade secret. Rather, the question is whether the secret is apparent from the product itself. Secrets that are apparent to the buyers of a product are considered disclosed by the product, but secrets contained in undecipherable form within the product (such as object code in a computer program) are considered secret even when the product is sold.

  Of what relevance is the motivation behind the disclosure of a secret? Recall that in *Metallurgical Industries*, the court found the fact that Metallurgical had disclosed its secrets only for profit to weigh in favor of trade secret status. Why should this be the case? On the one hand, licensing is evidence that a secret has value and is worth protecting. On the other hand, one could argue that the fact that a secret holder has sold its information for profit suggests that it is not trying to keep this information secret at all but rather is attempting to profit from its disclosure. Which of these arguments you find persuasive may depend on the view you take of the reasons for trade secret protection.

- Third, trade secrets may be publicly disclosed (through publication or the sale of a product) by someone other than the trade secret owner. Commonly, this occurs when someone other than the trade secret owner has independently developed or discovered the secret. Call the first trade secret "owner" *A*, and the independent developer *B*. *A* has no control over what *B* does with her independent discovery; if she chooses to publish the secret, she defeats not only her rights to trade secret protection, but *A*'s rights as well. Suppose *B* did not develop the secret independently of *A* but in fact stole it from *A*. What happens if *B* publishes the secret? Can *A* still protect it? If so, what happens to *C*, who began using the secret after reading *B*'s publication? This issue was addressed in Religious Technology Center v. Lerma, 908 F. Supp. 1362 (E.D. Va. 1995). In that case, the Church of Scientology sued (among others) the *Washington Post*, which had quoted from part of its confidential scriptures. The court concluded that the fact that the scriptures were posted on a Usenet newsgroup for ten days defeated any claim of trade secrecy:

> [For ten days, the documents] remained potentially available to the millions of Internet users around the world.
>
> As other courts who have dealt with similar issues have observed, "posting works to the Internet makes them generally known" at least to the relevant people interested in the news group. Once a trade secret is posted on the Internet, it is effectively part of the public domain, impossible to retrieve. Although the person who originally posted a trade secret on the Internet may be liable for trade secret misappropriation, the party who merely down loads Internet information cannot be liable for misappropriation because there is no misconduct involved in interacting with the Internet.

908 F. Supp. at 1368; *accord* American Red Cross v. Palm Beach Blood Bank Inc., 143 F.3d 1407 (11th Cir. 1998) (Red Cross donor list lost trade secret status because it was posted on a publicly accessible computer bulletin board). *But see* Silicon Image Inc. v. Analogix Semiconductor Inc., 2008 WL 166950 (N.D. Cal. Jan. 17, 2008) (presence of information on the Internet does not destroy secrecy absent evidence that competitors knew about it).

Should the obscurity of the Web site matter? What if it is not indexed in a search engine? In DVD Copy Control Ass'n v. Bunner, 116 Cal. App. 4th 241, 10 Cal. Rptr. 3d 185 (Ct. App. 2004), the court found disclosure of a secret on the Internet only because it was "quickly and widely republished to an eager audience," and cautioned that it did not assume that the secrets were lost merely because they were put on the Internet. *See infra* section F for further discussion of *Bunner*. For an argument that disclosure on the Internet should not destroy a secret irrevocably, see Elizabeth A. Rowe, *Introducing a Takedown for Trade Secrets on the Internet*, 2007 WISC. L. REV. 1042; Elizabeth A. Rowe, *Saving Trade Secret Disclosures on the Internet Through Sequential Preservation*, 42 WAKE FOREST L. REV. 1 (2007).

- Fourth, trade secrets may be disclosed inadvertently (for example, by being left on a train or elsewhere in public view). While the case law on this issue is sparse, it seems reasonable to argue that a truly accidental disclosure should not defeat trade secret protection if reasonable precautions have been taken. On the other hand, if the inadvertent disclosure is widespread, it would seem unfair (as well as impracticable) to require the public as a whole to "give back" the secret. Note that section 1(2)(ii)(C) of the Uniform Trade Secrets Act provides that it is misappropriation for someone to disclose a secret that they have reason to know has been acquired "by accident or mistake." The *Restatement (Third) of Unfair*

Competition § 40(b)(4) takes the same position, "unless the [accidental] acquisition was the result of the [trade secret owner]'s failure to take reasonable precautions to maintain the secrecy of the information." *See also* Williams v. Curtis-Wright Corp., 681 F.2d 161 (3d Cir. 1982) (user of secrets disclosed by mistake was liable for misappropriation because he had constructive notice of the secrecy of the information). But in DVD Copy Control Ass'n v. Bunner, 116 Cal. App. 4th 241, 10 Cal. Rptr. 3d 185 (Ct. App. 2004), the court rejected the idea that "once the information became *publicly* available everyone else would be liable under the trade secret laws simply because they knew about its unethical origins." "This," the court said, "is not what trade secret law is designed to do."

- Finally, government agencies sometimes require the disclosure of trade secrets by private parties in order to serve some other social purpose. *See* Corn Products Refining Co. v. Eddy, 249 U.S. 427 (1919) (requiring a food manufacturer to label its product with an accurate list of ingredients). Health and environmental concerns are a very common reason for the government to require disclosure of product contents. For example, the Federal Insecticide, Fungicide and Rodenticide Act (FIFRA), 7 U.S.C. §§ 136 *et seq.*, requires disclosure of the contents of pesticides as well as a great deal of other information. FIFRA makes two concessions to trade secret protection, however. First, it limits public disclosure of information concerning manufacturing processes and inert (as opposed to active) contents. Second, it provides for compensation to be paid to the inventors of trade secrets that the government appropriates by public disclosure. *See also* Ruckelshaus v. Monsanto Co., 467 U.S. 986 (1984) (federal requirement that private parties disclose trade secrets may constitute a taking under the Fifth Amendment); Philip Morris Inc. v. Reilly, 312 F.3d 24 (1st Cir. 2002) (Massachusetts law requiring labeling of cigarette ingredients was a taking of tobacco companies' trade secrets).

2. The plaintiff in *Data General* sold over 500 Nova computers to the general public. Each purchaser who requested one got a copy of the "confidential" design drawings. Why are these drawings still considered a secret? Does widespread disclosure compromise the secrecy claim at some point, even though all disclosures are made under an agreement of confidentiality? This issue arises frequently today in the software industry. As computers have become ubiquitous in business and quite common in the home, the numbers of "secret" programs in circulation may be counted in the millions rather than the hundreds. *Data General* implicitly concludes that even a relatively widespread disclosure to customers does not compromise the secrecy of the computer design. For cases addressing this issue in the context of computer software, compare Management Science of Am. v. Cyborg Sys., Inc., 1977-1 Trade Cas. (CCH) ¶ 61,472 (N.D. Ill. 1977) (holding that distribution of 600 copies of a program under a confidentiality agreement did not destroy secrecy) with Young Dental Mfg. Co. v. Q3 Special Prods., Inc., 891 F. Supp. 1345 (E.D. Mo. 1995) (characterizing as "completely frivolous" plaintiff's claim that its publicly sold software was a trade secret).

A closely related question involves attempts by the owners of information to "contract around" the requirement of secrecy. If the parties agree to treat a piece of information as secret, is the licensee bound not to use or disclose the information under contract principles regardless of whether or not it is in fact in the public domain? This issue is a recurring one in intellectual property law, and a problem that has never adequately been addressed.

Under what circumstances does the sale of a commercial product embodying a trade secret destroy the secret? Is the answer different for a commercially available product produced by a secret manufacturing process? In this regard, computer software may present a special case. While a particular computer program may be widely distributed, in fact all that is sold to the consumer is a disk containing object code. Object code is virtually impossible for humans to read without machine assistance.[13] Because of this, computer software is in some sense unlike a physical product whose design is evident to the casual observer. Even after it is publicly distributed, object code is meaningless to the casual observer. Only a complex process of reverse engineering (sometimes called "disassembly" or "decompilation") can enable the user to decipher the source code that was originally written for the program.

Should it matter that a computer program is distributed only in object code form? Consider the following case, in which the defendant was accused of misappropriating a computer program in object code form:

> The source code can and does qualify as a trade secret. . . .
>
> Whether the object code is a trade secret is a more difficult question.[8] Atkinson first contends that the object code cannot be a trade secret because it does not derive independent economic value from its secrecy, and therefore fails the first definitional requirement of a trade secret. This argument has no merit. Trandes generates most of its revenues by providing computer services. . . . Armed with a copy of the object code, an individual would have the means to offer much the same engineering services as Trandes. . . .
>
> Atkinson next argues that the object code cannot be a trade secret because Trandes did not keep it secret. . . . Atkinson asserts that the Tunnel System has been widely disclosed as a mass-marketed product and that its existence and its abilities are not secret. [The court concluded that the object code remained secret because it had only been distributed to two customers, and both of them signed licenses agreeing to keep the program a secret.]

Trandes Corp. v. Guy F. Atkinson Co., 996 F.2d 655, 663-64 (4th Cir. 1993). Consider the court's footnote. Can object code be a trade secret if it can easily be duplicated (whether or not the copier understands what he is copying)? Is the plaintiff in this case really trying to leverage copyright protection out of a trade secret claim? In other cases, such as Integrated Cash Management Services, Inc. v. Digital Transactions, Inc., 920 F.2d 171 (2d Cir. 1990), and Comprehensive Technologies Int'l, Inc. v. Software Artisans, Inc., 3 F.3d 730 (4th Cir. 1993), the alleged trade secret at issue was not the source or object code of the computer program itself but certain high-level design features of the program (its "architecture"). Suppose that, rather than using what they had learned of the architecture of the program while employed by the company, Integrated Cash Management's former employees had copied the object code of the program altogether. (Leave aside for a moment questions of copyright

13. It is possible to "reverse engineer" object code in some cases to create a kind of rough estimate of what must have been in the original source code. The process, however, is demanding and time consuming even for expert programmers. *See, e.g.*, Andrew Johnson-Laird, *Technical Demonstration of "Decompilation,"* paper presented at the Computer Law Association's 1993 International Computer Law Retreat, Oct. 21-23, 1993, at 29.

8. This case presents an unusual set of facts. In the ordinary case, the owner of trade secret computer software will maintain the secrecy of the source code but freely distribute the object code. *See, e.g.*, Q-Co Indus. v. Hoffman, 625 F. Supp. 608, 617 (S.D.N.Y. 1985) (program secret where source code secret, even though object code not secret). In such cases, the owner of the software cannot claim trade secret protection for the object code because its disclosure to the public destroyed its secrecy. In this case, however, Trandes maintained the secrecy of the source code and the object code, as we explain below.

infringement, and consider only the trade secret issue.) Would they be liable for misappropriating the trade secrets contained in the program architecture on the grounds that copying the program in its entirety necessarily copied the architecture? Or would the fact that the object code was publicly disclosed protect them from liability? How would the courts in *Trandes* and the *Data General* cases answer this question? Does the answer suggest a problem with relying on trade secrecy to protect computer programs?

3. Until 1999, patent applications were kept secret by the U.S. Patent Office unless and until the patent issued. *See* 35 U.S.C. § 122. If a patent application was not actively prosecuted, or if the patent did not issue, it was declared abandoned by the Patent Office. *See* 37 C.F.R. § 114 (1995). Abandoned applications were *not* available to the public. In fact, the application itself was destroyed after 20 years. *Id.*

In Europe, Japan, and elsewhere, patent applications are published 18 months after they are filed, regardless of whether the patent has yet issued. Normally, however, an applicant is notified before the application is published, allowing him or her to "elect" whether to continue to pursue a patent (and have the application be disclosed to the world) or to forgo prosecuting the patent (and retain the secrecy of the application). In 1999, Congress changed U.S. law to require that some (but not all) patent applications be published after 18 months. Since it takes almost three years on average for a patent to issue, many applicants will face an election not between patent and trade secret protection, but between trade secret protection and the prospect of future patent protection.

The notion of an "election" between trade secret and patent protection assumes that the patent application actually describes all the details of an invention. For more on this issue — known as the "enablement" requirement in patent law — see 35 U.S.C. § 112, and Chapter 3 *supra*. Certainly there is evidence that firms sometimes make precisely such an election. For an interesting historical example, see Henry Petroski, The Pencil 114-15 (1990) (describing how the family of Henry David Thoreau kept its pencil-making technology secret rather than disclose it by obtaining a patent). Most patent licenses also allow the licensee to use trade secrets and know-how related to or associated with the patent. If both a patent and its associated secrets are licensed, should there be any limits on the duration of the license? Do these licenses suggest that an inventor can avoid the "election" doctrine and "have it both ways" in some respects? *See* United States v. Pilkington plc, No. 94-345-TUC-WDB (D. Ariz. May 25, 1994) (government antitrust action against a company that sought to enforce trade secrets against competitors after a related patent had expired).

4. To what extent does the incorporation of a secret in a public governmental record preclude trade secret protection? *See* Frazee v. U.S. Forest Service, 97 F.3d 367 (9th Cir. 1996) (information was not a trade secret because it could be obtained from the government under the Freedom of Information Act); Weygand v. CBS, Inc., 43 U.S.P.Q.2d 1120 (C.D. Cal. 1997) (depositing a work with the U.S. Copyright Office destroys trade secrecy).

C. MISAPPROPRIATION OF TRADE SECRETS

Not all uses of another's trade secrets constitute misappropriation. Acquisition or use of a trade secret is illegal only in two basic situations: where it is done through improper means, or where it involves a breach of confidence. Uniform Trade Secrets Act § 1; RESTATEMENT (THIRD) OF UNFAIR COMPETITION § 40.

1. Improper Means

E. I. duPont deNemours & Co. v. Rolfe Christopher et al.
431 F.2d 1012 (5th Cir. 1970)

GOLDBERG, Circuit Judge:

This is a case of industrial espionage in which an airplane is the cloak and a camera the dagger. The defendants-appellants, Rolfe and Gary Christopher, are photographers in Beaumont, Texas. The Christophers were hired by an unknown third party to take aerial photographs of new construction at the Beaumont plant of E.I. duPont deNemours & Company, Inc. Sixteen photographs of the DuPont facility were taken from the air on March 19, 1969, and these photographs were later developed and delivered to the third party.

DuPont employees apparently noticed the airplane on March 19 and immediately began an investigation to determine why the craft was circling over the plant. By that afternoon the investigation had disclosed that the craft was involved in a photographic expedition and that the Christophers were the photographers. DuPont contacted the Christophers that same afternoon and asked them to reveal the name of the person or corporation requesting the photographs. The Christophers refused to disclose this information, giving as their reason the client's desire to remain anonymous.

Having reached a dead end in the investigation, DuPont subsequently filed suit against the Christophers, alleging that the Christophers had wrongfully obtained photographs revealing DuPont's trade secrets which they then sold to the undisclosed third party. DuPont contended that it had developed a highly secret but unpatented process for producing methanol, a process which gave DuPont a competitive advantage over other producers. This process, DuPont alleged, was a trade secret developed after much expensive and time-consuming research, and a secret which the company had taken special precautions to safeguard. The area photographed by the Christophers was the plant designed to produce methanol by this secret process, and because the plant was still under construction parts of the process were exposed to view from directly above the construction area. Photographs of that area, DuPont alleged, would enable a skilled person to deduce the secret process for making methanol. DuPont thus contended that the Christophers had wrongfully appropriated DuPont trade secrets by taking the photographs and delivering them to the undisclosed third party. In its suit DuPont asked for damages to cover the loss it had already sustained as a result of the wrongful disclosure of the trade secret and sought temporary and permanent injunctions prohibiting any further circulation of the photographs already taken and prohibiting any additional photographing of the methanol plant. . . .

. . . [T]he Christophers argue that for an appropriation of trade secrets to be wrongful there must be a trespass, other illegal conduct, or breach of a confidential relationship. We disagree.

It is true, as the Christophers assert, that the previous trade secret cases have contained one or more of these elements. However, we do not think that the Texas courts would limit the trade secret protection exclusively to these elements. On the contrary, in Hyde Corporation v. Huffines, 1958, 158 Tex. 566, 314 S.W.2d 763, the Texas Supreme Court specifically adopted the rule found in the Restatement of Torts which provides:

> One who discloses or uses another's trade secret, without a privilege to do so, is liable to the other if
>
> (a) he discovered the secret by improper means, or
> (b) his disclosure or use constitutes a breach of confidence reposed in him by the other in disclosing the secret to him. . . .

RESTATEMENT OF TORTS § 757 (1939). Thus, although the previous cases have dealt with a breach of a confidential relationship, a trespass, or other illegal conduct, the rule is much broader than the cases heretofore encountered. Not limiting itself to specific wrongs, Texas adopted subsection (a) of the *Restatement* which recognizes a cause of action for the discovery of a trade secret by any "improper" means. . . .

The question remaining, therefore, is whether aerial photography of plant construction is an improper means of obtaining another's trade secret. We conclude that it is and that the Texas courts would so hold. The Supreme Court of that state has declared that "the undoubted tendency of the law has been to recognize and enforce higher standards of commercial morality in the business world." Hyde Corporation v. Huffines, supra, 314 S.W.2d at 773. That court has quoted with approval articles indicating that the proper means of gaining possession of a competitor's secret process is "through inspection and analysis" of the product in order to create a duplicate. K & G Tool & Service Co. v. G & G Fishing Tool Service, 1958, 158 Tex. 594, 314 S.W.2d 782, 783, 788. Later another Texas court explained:

> The means by which the discovery is made may be obvious, and the experimentation leading from known factors to presently unknown results may be simple and lying in the public domain. But these facts do not destroy the value of the discovery and will not advantage a competitor who by unfair means obtains the knowledge without paying the price expended by the discoverer.

Brown v. Fowler, Tex. Civ. App. 1958, 316 S.W.2d 111, 114, *writ ref'd n.r.e.*

We think, therefore, that the Texas rule is clear. One may use his competitor's secret process if he discovers the process by reverse engineering applied to the finished product; one may use a competitor's process if he discovers it by his own independent research; but one may not avoid these labors by taking the process from the discoverer without his permission at a time when he is taking reasonable precautions to maintain its secrecy. To obtain knowledge of a process without spending the time and money to discover it independently is improper unless the holder voluntarily discloses it or fails to take reasonable precautions to ensure its secrecy.

In the instant case the Christophers deliberately flew over the DuPont plant to get pictures of a process which DuPont had attempted to keep secret. The Christophers delivered their pictures to a third party who was certainly aware of the means by which they had been acquired and who may be planning to use the information contained therein to manufacture methanol by the DuPont process. The third party has a right to use this process only if he obtains this knowledge through his own research efforts, but thus far all information indicates that the third party has gained this knowledge solely by taking it from DuPont at a time when DuPont was making reasonable efforts to preserve its secrecy. In such a situation DuPont has a valid cause of action to prohibit the Christophers from improperly discovering its trade secret and to prohibit the undisclosed third party from using the improperly obtained information.

We note that this view is in perfect accord with the position taken by the authors of the *Restatement*. In commenting on improper means of discovery the savants of the *Restatement* said:

> f. Improper means of discovery. The discovery of another's trade secret by improper means subjects the actor to liability independently of the harm to the interest in the secret. Thus, if one uses physical force to take a secret formula from another's pocket, or breaks into another's office to steal the formula, his conduct is wrongful and subjects him to liability apart from the rule stated in this Section. Such conduct is also an improper means of procuring the secret under this rule. But means may be improper under this rule even though they do not cause any other harm than that to the interest in the trade secret. Examples of such means are fraudulent misrepresentations to induce disclosure, tapping of telephone wires, eavesdropping or other espionage. A complete catalogue of improper means is not possible. In general they are means which fall below the generally accepted standards of commercial morality and reasonable conduct.

RESTATEMENT OF TORTS § 757, Comment *f* at 10 (1939).

In taking this position we realize that industrial espionage of the sort here perpetrated has become a popular sport in some segments of our industrial community. However, our devotion to free-wheeling industrial competition must not force us into accepting the law of the jungle as the standard of morality expected in our commercial relations. Our tolerance of the espionage game must cease when the protections required to prevent another's spying cost so much that the spirit of inventiveness is dampened. Commercial privacy must be protected from espionage which could not have been reasonably anticipated or prevented. We do not mean to imply, however, that everything not in plain view is within the protected vale, nor that all information obtained through every extra optical extension is forbidden. Indeed, for our industrial competition to remain healthy there must be breathing room for observing a competing industrialist. A competitor can and must shop his competition for pricing and examine his products for quality, components, and methods of manufacture. Perhaps ordinary fences and roofs must be built to shut out incursive eyes, but we need not require the discoverer of a trade secret to guard against the unanticipated, the undetectable, or the unpreventable methods of espionage now available.

In the instant case DuPont was in the midst of constructing a plant. Although after construction the finished plant would have protected much of the process from view, during the period of construction the trade secret was exposed to view from the air. To require DuPont to put a roof over the unfinished plant to guard its secret would impose an enormous expense to prevent nothing more than a school boy's trick. We introduce here no new or radical ethic since our ethos has never given moral sanction to piracy. The market place must not deviate far from our mores. We should not require a person or corporation to take unreasonable precautions to prevent another from doing that which he ought not do in the first place. Reasonable precautions against predatory eyes we may require, but an impenetrable fortress is an unreasonable requirement, and we are not disposed to burden industrial inventors with such a duty in order to protect the fruits of their efforts. "Improper" will always be a word of many nuances, determined by time, place, and circumstances. We therefore need not proclaim a catalogue of commercial improprieties. Clearly, however, one of its commandments does say "thou shall not appropriate a trade secret through deviousness under circumstances in which countervailing defenses are not reasonably available." . . .

COMMENTS AND QUESTIONS

1. Improper means has a substantial basis in other torts. See Comment *f* to the *Restatement*, cited in *duPont*, and the *Restatement (Third) of Unfair Competition* § 43 (defining improper means as including "theft, fraud, unauthorized interception of communications, inducement of or knowing participation in a breach of confidence, and other means either wrongful in themselves or wrongful under the circumstances of the case.").

DuPont itself provides an example of conduct prohibited by trade secret law that is probably not otherwise tortious. Should otherwise legitimate conduct be prohibited because it will disclose a trade secret? Most people would probably say yes in the context of the *duPont* case. As Judge Posner noted in *Rockwell*, misappropriation of trade secrets is largely redundant if it does not reach any further than other torts. Nonetheless, the reach of the case is troubling. Consider the last sentence of the *duPont* opinion. What is wrong with "deviousness"? Is reverse engineering (which is legal under both the *Restatement* and the Uniform Act) any less devious than aerial photography? And why should "countervailing defenses" enter the picture?

2. There is general agreement that "reverse engineering"—that is, buying a product and taking it apart to see how it works—is not a misappropriation of a trade secret.[14] But while it is easy to see how to reverse engineer a product, how does one reverse engineer a process? Are there realistic alternatives to the sort of espionage condemned in *duPont* for those who seek to reproduce a process? Should there be some legally protected way of discovering a competitor's process?

3. Note how the decision in *duPont* dovetails with the discussion of precautions in section B.2 *supra*. DuPont could have protected itself against aerial photography by building a roof over its plant area before beginning internal construction. The Fifth Circuit rejected this alternative because it would "impose an enormous expense to prevent nothing more than a school boy's trick." On the other hand, the courts are clearly willing to put duPont to *some* expense to protect its secrets from prying eyes. If duPont had allowed its engineers to leave copies of the plant blueprints on subways, the result of the case might be very different.

How much expense is duPont required to incur to protect itself? The uniform answer of the courts is that only "reasonable" precautions must be taken. While this is not a terribly helpful answer, it may be a fairly practical one in any given industry, where companies can protect themselves by taking those precautions that are customary in that industry.

On the other hand, consider the Second Circuit's statement in Franke v. Wiltschek, 209 F.2d 493, 495 (2d Cir. 1953):

> It matters not that the defendants could have gained their knowledge from a study of the expired patent and plaintiff's publicly marketed product. The fact is they did not. Instead

14. As we shall see, however, reverse engineering of a patented invention is generally not permissible.

> they gained it from plaintiffs via their confidential relationship, and in doing so incurred a duty not to use it to plaintiff's detriment. This duty they have breached.

Is this consistent with the UTSA?

4. An interesting case involving only circumstantial evidence of misappropriation is Pioneer Hi-Bred International v. Holden Foundation Seeds, Inc., 35 F.3d 1226, 31 U.S.P.Q.2d 1385 (8th Cir. 1994). Plaintiff Pioneer could not establish a specific act of misappropriation, but it did show (through the use of three sophisticated scientific tests) that it was highly unlikely that defendant's hybrid seeds had been developed independently of plaintiff's seeds. Instead, due to genetic similarities, Pioneer showed that it was much more likely that those seeds were "derived from" a popular Pioneer hybrid. Pioneer was found to have maintained reasonable measures to guard against disclosure, including putting experimental seeds in bags marked with a secret code, allowing seeds to be grown only under strict nondisclosure arrangements, and leaving unmarked the fields in which the seeds had been planted. Pioneer was awarded $46.7 million in damages.

By contrast, the Fourth Circuit in Othentec Ltd. v. Phelan, 526 F.3d 135 (4th Cir. 2008) made it clear that speculation of theft based on the defendant's speed in entering the market was not enough. The court required "actual objective evidence" of misappropriation.

PROBLEMS

Problem 11-8. Suppose that, at trial in the *duPont* case, the Christophers proved that they could have discovered the secrets contained in the layout of the duPont plant by careful viewing of images available on Google Earth. Are the Christophers then relieved from liability for misappropriation of trade secrets? Would your answer change if they had in fact obtained the photos by sneaking onto duPont property on the ground?

Problem 11-9. Professional athletes and coaches often use signals to convey confidential information to other members of the team. In baseball, for example, the catcher often signals the pitcher what pitch to throw next; the third base coach may signal the batter whether to take the next pitch, attempt a bunt or a hit and run, and so on. Alternatively, the way a pitcher holds his fingers on the ball just prior to pitching it will often indicate what pitch is on its way. Opposing players may try to observe the signals and fingerings from the field or the bench and decipher them, but leagues often forbid teams from employing more extensive methods of signal stealing (such as the use of concealed cameras). Teams that violate league rules relating to signal stealing may be subject to league-imposed penalties, but stories persist that elaborate methods of signal stealing have long been a part of professional sports. Suppose that a baseball or football team violates a league rule forbidding signal stealing by means of surreptitious videotaping. In addition to being liable for violating the league rule, would there be a plausible argument that the signal stealing constitutes a misappropriation of trade secrets? Even if such a claim is theoretically possible, would it be worthwhile to file suit?

Problem 11-10. Elise, Company X's vice president for marketing, is in the habit of taking home confidential materials relating to Company X's upcoming campaigns so that she can work at home in the evenings and on weekends. Some of these materials are in the form of paper copies, while others are stored on a flash drive in Word files. One day Elise accidentally leaves her briefcase on the subway when she gets off at her accustomed destination in Brooklyn Heights. The briefcase is retrieved by Merle, an executive of X's archrival Company Y, who happens to be riding in the same subway car on his way home to Park Slope. Without disclosing the source of his information to anyone at Company Y, Merle uses that information to help Company Y craft an effective countercampaign to Company X's launch of a new soft drink. Suspecting that someone at Company Y has acquired the materials contained in the lost briefcase, Company X files suit against Company Y. What result under the Uniform Trade Secret Act?

2. Confidential Relationship

The previous section concerned misappropriation of trade secrets by improperly obtaining them from their owner. But secrets that have been properly obtained may still be misappropriated if they are improperly used or disclosed. Most often, this occurs when the secrets are used or disclosed in violation of a confidential relationship.

What is a confidential relationship? Obviously, the easiest way to create a confidential relationship is to sign a contract to that effect. Agreements to keep certain information confidential are generally enforceable, at least if the information meets the definition of a trade secret. *See* RESTATEMENT (THIRD) OF UNFAIR COMPETITION § 39 cmt. *d*, at 430. But confidential relationships may also arise without any express agreement. Consider the following case.

Smith v. Dravo Corp.
203 F.2d 369 (7th Cir. 1953)

LINDLEY, J.

Plaintiffs appeal from a judgment for defendant entered at the close of a trial by the court without a jury. The complaint is in four counts: 1 and 2 charge an unlawful appropriation by defendant of plaintiffs' trade secrets relating to the design and construction and selling and leasing of freight containers; 3 and 4 aver infringement of plaintiffs' patents Nos. 2,457,841 and 2,457,842. . . .

In the early 1940s Leathem D. Smith, now deceased, began toying with an idea which, he believed, would greatly facilitate the ship and shore handling and transportation of cargoes. As he was primarily engaged in the shipbuilding business, it was quite natural that his thinking was chiefly concerned with water transportation and dock handling. Nevertheless his overall plan encompassed rail shipping as well. He envisioned construction of ships especially designed to carry their cargo in uniformly sized steel freight containers. These devices (which, it appears, were the crux of his idea) were: equipped with high doors at one end; large enough for a man to enter easily; weather and pilfer proof; and bore collapsible legs, which (1) served to lock them (a) to the deck of the ship by fitting into recesses in the deck, or (b) to each other, when stacked, by reason of receiving sockets located in the upper four corners of each container, and (2) allowed sufficient clearance between deck and container or container and container for the facile insertion of a fork of a lift tractor, and (3) were equipped with lifting eyelets, which, together with a specially designed hoist, made possible placement of the containers upon or removal from a ship, railroad car or truck, while filled with cargo. The outer dimensions of the devices were such that they would fit compactly in standard gauge North American railroad cars, or narrow gauge South American trains, and in the holds of most water vessels.

[At the end of World War II, Smith's company—Safeway Containers—had some success building and selling such containers.]

On June 23, 1946, Smith died in a sailing accident. The need for cash for inheritance tax purposes prompted his estate to survey his holdings for disposable assets. It was decided that the container business should be sold. Devices in process were completed but no work on new ones was started.

Defendant was interested in the Safeway container, primarily, it appears, for use by its subsidiary, the Union Barge Lines. In October 1946 it contacted Agwilines [one of Smith's customers] seeking information. It watched a loading operation in which Agwilines used the box. At approximately the same time, defendant approached the shipbuilding company and inquired as to the possibility of purchase of a number of the containers. It was told to communicate with Cowan, plaintiffs' eastern representative. This it did, and, on October 29, 1946, in Pittsburgh, Cowan met with defendant's officials to discuss the proposed sale of [containers]. But, as negotiations progressed, defendant demonstrated an interest in the entire container development. Thus, what started as a meeting to discuss the purchase of individual containers ended in the possible foundation for a sale of the entire business.

Based upon this display of interest, Cowan sent detailed information to defendant concerning the business. This included: (1) patent applications for both the "knock-down" and "rigid" crates; (2) blue prints of both designs; (3) a miniature Safeway container; (4) letters of inquiry from possible users; (5) further correspondence with prospective users. In addition, defendant's representatives journeyed to Sturgeon Bay, Wisconsin, the home of the shipbuilding company, and viewed the physical plant, inventory and manufacturing operation.

Plaintiffs quoted a price of $150,000 plus a royalty of $10 per unit. This was rejected. Subsequent offers of $100,000 and $75,000 with royalties of $10 per container were also rejected. Negotiations continued until January 30, 1947, at which time defendant finally rejected plaintiffs' offer.

On January 31, 1947 defendant announced to Agwilines that it "intended to design and produce a shipping container of the widest possible utility" for "coastal steamship application . . . [and] use . . . on the inland rivers and . . . connecting highway and rail carriers." Development of the project moved rapidly, so that by February 5, 1947 defendant had set up a stock order for a freight container which was designed, by use of plaintiffs' patent applications, so as to avoid any claim of infringement. One differing feature was the use of skids and recesses running the length of the container, rather than legs and sockets as employed in plaintiffs' design. However, Agwilines rejected this design, insisting on an adaptation of plaintiffs' idea. In short defendant's final product incorporated many, if not all, of the features of plaintiffs' design. So conceived, it was accepted by the trade to the extent that, by March 1948, defendant had sold some 500 containers. Many of these sales were made to firms who had shown considerable prior interest in plaintiffs' design and had been included in the prospective users disclosed to defendant.

One particular feature of defendant's container differed from plaintiffs: its width was four inches less. As a result plaintiffs' product became obsolete. Their container could not be used interchangeably with defendant's; they ceased production. Consequently the prospects of disposing of the entire operation vanished.

The foregoing is the essence of plaintiffs' cause of action. Stripped of surplusage, the averment is that defendant obtained, through a confidential relationship, knowledge of plaintiffs' secret designs, plans and prospective customers, and then wrongfully breached that confidence by using the information to its own advantage and plaintiffs' detriment.

[The court found that, notwithstanding certain disclosures of information during the operation of Safeway, plaintiffs' information about how to design its containers remained a trade secret.]

(3) Was Defendant in a Position of Trust and Confidence at the Time of the Disclosure?

Mr. Justice Holmes once said that the existence of the confidential relationship is the "starting point" in a cause of action such as this. E.I. DuPont de Nemours Powder Co. v. Masland, 244 U.S. 100, 102, 37 S. Ct. 575, 61 L. Ed. 1016. While we take a slightly different tack, there is no doubt as to the importance of this element of plaintiffs' case.

Certain it is that a non-confidential disclosure will not supply the basis for a law suit. Plaintiffs' information is afforded protection because it is secret. Promiscuous disclosures quite naturally destroy the secrecy and the corresponding protection. But this is not true where a confidence has been reposed carrying with it communication of an idea.

It is clear that no express promise of trust was exacted from defendant. There is, however, the further question of whether one was implied from the relationship of the parties. Pennsylvania has not provided us with a decision precisely in point but Pressed Steel Car Co. v. Standard Car Co., 210 Pa. 464, 60 A. 4, furnishes abundant guideposts. There plaintiff delivered its blue prints to customers in order that they might acquaint themselves more thoroughly with the railroad cars they were purchasing; from these customers, defendant obtained the drawings. In holding that the customers held the plans as a result of a confidence reposed in them by plaintiff, and that the confidence was breached by delivery of the blue prints to defendant, the court said, 60 A. at page 10: "While there was no expressed restriction placed on the ownership of the prints, or any expressed limitation as to the use to which they were to be put, it is clear . . . that the purpose for which they were delivered by the plaintiff was understood by all parties. . . ."

The quoted language is applicable and determinative. Here plaintiffs disclosed their design for one purpose, to enable defendant to appraise it with a view in mind of purchasing the business. There can be no question that defendant knew and understood this limited purpose. Trust was reposed in it by plaintiffs that the information thus transmitted would be accepted subject to that limitation. "[T]he first thing to be made sure of is that the defendant shall not fraudulently abuse the trust reposed in him.

It is the usual incident of confidential relations. If there is any disadvantage in the fact that he knew the plaintiffs' secrets, he must take the burden with the good." E.I. DuPont de Nemours Powder Co. v. Masland, 244 U.S. 100 at page 102, 37 S. Ct. 575, at page 576, 61 L. Ed. 1016.

Nor is it an adequate answer for defendant to say that the transactions with plaintiffs were at arms length. So, too, were the overall dealings between plaintiffs and defendants in Booth v. Stutz Motor Car Co., 7 Cir., 56 F.2d 962; Allen-Qualley Co. v. Shellmar Products Co., D.C., 31 F.2d 293, affirmed, 7 Cir., 36 F.2d 623 and Schavoir v. American Rebonded Leather Co., 104 Conn. 472, 133 A. 582. That fact does not detract from the conclusion that but for those very transactions defendant would not have learned, from plaintiffs, of the container design. The implied limitation on the use to be made of the information had its roots in the "arms-length" transaction.

(4) The Improper Use by Defendant of the Secret Information

Defendant's own evidence discloses that it did not begin to design its container until after it had access to plaintiffs' plans. Defendant's engineers admittedly referred to plaintiffs' patent applications, as they said, to avoid infringement. It is not disputed that, at the urging of Agwilines, defendant revised its proposed design to incorporate the folding leg and socket principles of plaintiffs' containers. These evidentiary facts, together with the striking similarity between defendant's and plaintiffs' finished product, were more than enough to convict defendant of the improper use of the structural information obtained from plaintiffs.

COMMENTS AND QUESTIONS

1. Since the shipping containers were available on the open market, couldn't Dravo have argued that they were not a trade secret? Did Smith's agent, Cowan, disclose anything that was *not* readily apparent from inspection of the containers?

2. In Van Prod. Co. v. General Welding & Fabricating Co., 213 A.2d 769, 779-80 (Pa. 1965), the Pennsylvania Supreme Court criticized *Smith* for focusing on the existence of a confidential relationship to the exclusion of whether there was a trade secret at all. The court said: "The starting point in every case of this sort is not whether there was a confidential relationship, but whether, in fact, there was a trade secret to be misappropriated."

3. Compare Smith v. Dravo with Omnitech Int'l v. Clorox Co., 29 U.S.P.Q.2d 1665 (5th Cir. 1994), *cert. denied*, 115 S. Ct. 71 (1994), where the court held that it was not an actionable "use" of a trade secret for the defendant to *evaluate* it in the course of trying to decide whether to (a) acquire the company or (b) take a license to use the trade secret. A finding of no liability here makes sense, because it allows the potential licensee to make an informed judgment and therefore promotes efficient licensing. But how far does it extend? Is the potential licensee entitled to replicate the research or build models in an effort to evaluate it? Are there special limits that should be placed on companies engaged in a "make or buy" decision — that is, who are

considering *either* licensing the plaintiff's technology *or* entering the market themselves?

Smith and *Omnitech* both involved disclosures in the course of licensing negotiations. Cases such as these form part of the amorphous law of "precontractual liability." *See* E. Allen Farnsworth, *Precontractual Liability and Preliminary Agreements: Fair Dealing and Failed Negotiations*, 87 COLUM. L. REV. 217 (1987). Both the *Smith* and *Omnitech* cases present the problem of Arrow's Information Paradox. What the plaintiff has to sell to the defendant is information that is valuable only because it is secret. If there is no legal protection and if the plaintiff discloses the secret to the defendant, its value will be lost. But the defendant cannot be expected to pay for information unless it can see the information to determine its value. Thus, absent some form of legal protection for confidential disclosures, sale or licensing of trade secrets may not occur. Note that this problem does not arise in other areas of intellectual property, such as patent law, since the inventions being licensed are already publicly disclosed.

4. The *Restatement (Third) of Unfair Competition* §41 holds that a confidential relationship is established in the following circumstances:

> (a) the person made an express promise of confidentiality prior to the disclosure of the trade secret; or
>
> (b) the trade secret was disclosed to the person under circumstances in which the relationship between the parties to the disclosure or the other facts surrounding the disclosure justify the conclusions that, at the time of the disclosure,
>
> > (1) the person knew or had reason to know that the disclosure was intended to be in confidence, and
> >
> > (2) the other party to the disclosure was reasonable in inferring that the person consented to an obligation of confidentiality.

On the issue of knowledge, compare this "had reason to know" standard with the Eleventh Circuit's decision in Bateman v. Mnemonics, Inc., 79 F.3d 1532 (11th Cir. 1996). In that case, the court indicated that it was "wary" of trade secret claims based on implied confidential relationships because they were subject to abuse. The court rejected Bateman's allegation that such a relationship existed because Bateman had not "made it clear to the parties involved that there was an expectation and obligation of confidentiality." Thus the court seemed to create a standard of actual knowledge on the part of the recipient of confidential information that the discloser of such information intended the disclosure to be confidential. At the other extreme, the Fifth Circuit in Phillips v. Frey, 20 F.3d 623, 631-32 (5th Cir. 1994), found an implied confidential relationship to exist in the course of negotiations over the sale of a business, despite the fact that the disclosing party never even requested that the information remain confidential.

Which approach makes more sense? Who is in the best position to clarify the question, the discloser or the recipient?

5. Is there any way for a potential licensee to prevent the formation of a confidential relationship in such a situation?

6. The defendant in *Smith* actually sold a device that was not identical to the plaintiff's. Under what circumstances can a defendant be liable for misappropriation without literally copying the trade secret? In Mangren Resources & Dev. Corp. v. National Chem. Co., 87 F.3d 937 (7th Cir. 1996), the court defined improper "use" broadly, stating that "the user of another's trade secret is liable even if he uses it with

modifications or improvements upon it effected by his own efforts, so long as the substance of the process used by the actor is derived from the other's secret. . . . If trade secret law were not flexible enough to encompass modified or even new products that are substantially derived from the trade secrets of another, the protections that the law provides would be hollow indeed." To similar effect as *Mangren* is Texas Tanks Inc. v. Owens-Corning Fiberglas Corp., 99 F.3d 740 (5th Cir. 1997). In *Texas Tanks*, the Fifth Circuit held that any improper "exercise of control and domination" over a secret constituted a commercial use of that secret. It rejected the defendant's argument that it could not be liable for taking a secret unless the secret was actually incorporated in a commercial product. The court noted that Owens-Corning's awareness of the secret would likely influence the development of its own competing product, and that this was enough to demonstrate improper "use" of the secret.

PROBLEMS

Problem 11-11. Solomon, a regular customer of ToolCo's products, comes up with an idea for a new tool. He sends the idea to ToolCo, suggesting that they manufacture it. ToolCo does in fact produce and sell the new tool. Is Solomon entitled to compensation for ToolCo's use of his idea? Does it make any difference if (1) ToolCo actively solicited the idea from Solomon? (2) Solomon sent the suggestion to ToolCo along with a letter saying he wanted to open negotiations over a possible licensing arrangement to use the idea? (3) ToolCo has in the past had an informal, unwritten policy of compensating inventors who submit good ideas?

Problem 11-12. VenCo, a venture capitalist in the business of financing start-up companies, investigates TechCo in an effort to decide whether or not to finance it. To aid in its investigation, VenCo asks for and receives confidential information about TechCo's products and *market* position. VenCo eventually decides not to finance TechCo because of concerns about its management, but it does finance a start-up competitor of TechCo in the same field. Are VenCo or the start-up liable to TechCo? What obligations, if any, does VenCo undertake as a result of its exposure to TechCo's secrets?

Problem 11-13. MegaGene (MG) is a genomics company: a company whose business is to isolate and identify individual human genes. Founded in 1996, MG was originally conceived as a company that would accumulate patents on various genes and partial gene sequences. The idea was that as researchers—either within MG or outside of it—figured out what particular proteins were *produced* ("coded for") by individual genes, some of those genes would be very valuable. Some might code for important proteins that some humans needed as disease therapies; others might contain errors that caused diseases, and thereby be useful in diagnosing or treating the diseases.

MG's original strategy was to obtain patents on as many genes and partial gene sequences as it could. Today it has over 100 such patents, almost exclusively on full gene sequences. These patents were acquired because MG was able to establish the *actual* function of each of the genes. Legal changes—most notably a tighter interpretation of patentable "utility" (*see* Chapter 3 *supra*)—precluded MG from acquiring any patents on partial gene sequences, however.

Although some of the full-gene patents may someday be valuable, none are as yet. So to try to generate cash in the short term, MG has been pursuing another approach to the genomics business: It charges users for access to its database of gene sequences and related *information*. The database has been painstakingly assembled not only from information in MG's own 100 patents, but also from various public domain sources. It includes a great deal of information from the publicly funded Human Genome Project. For example, it includes information on many "markers" that help researchers determine which individual chromosome certain sequences come from. It also contains a great deal of information about individual genes: when they are expressed or repressed, and what they code for in various tissue samples and patient populations. This information helps researchers identify which genetic sequences are part of genes that may be important—because they are associated with a disease, for example.

IceGene is a company based in Iceland that has designed a highly promising approach to genomics. IceGene has combined a vast genetic database with detailed information on disease incidence in specific people. This is made possible by the fact that for many years detailed genealogical records have been kept for the highly homogenous Icelandic population. Now, IceGene has compiled a large database of tissue samples from individual Icelanders. Its business goal is to identify, from genealogical records, specific individuals whose family histories show they may be at risk for certain diseases and other conditions. Then, with access to the genetic code of the individual in question, IceGene can locate specific genetic variations and mutations that might be associated with the disease or condition. Once a correlation or association is established, specific genes and genetic problems can be identified for future research. (Much of this information is derived with reference to public data, including the Human Genome Project data.) IceGene plans to pursue some of these research opportunities itself, but there will be too many for the firm to research all of them. So it too plans to establish a database of genes and individual genetic variations that will be accessible (for a fee) to other companies doing genomics research.

Both MG and IceGene have established Web-based access to their databases. The Web pages are accessible only by subscribers of the firms' respective services, but customers can subscribe online using an interactive signup menu. The signup procedure requires users to agree to a "Database and Trade Secrecy Access Agreement," which includes these two provisions:

> [1] Customer, upon accepting this Access Agreement, agrees that the Genetic Data accessible hereon is and will be a Trade Secret of Company, and further agrees not to disclose, publish, or otherwise disseminate said Genetic Data to any other company, person, or institution. Customer also agrees that payment under the Payment provision herein will continue as provided for in this Agreement, notwithstanding the subsequent disclosure, publication, or other dissemination of any portion of said Genetic Data by a third party not subject to this Agreement. . . .
>
> [2] Customer agrees to pay to the Company a royalty of 5 per cent of the gross selling price of any diagnostic kit, therapeutic drug, or other commercial product developed as a result of Customer's access to or use of the Genetic Data contained herein.

MG becomes the dominant genomics database firm, with over 8,000 subscribers. It is widely known in the industry that virtually every serious researcher uses MG data in his or her genomics research. Meanwhile, IceGene has become an accepted source for information about the relationship between certain gene mutations and actual human diseases. Gene O'Mick, a researcher based in Europe, is a subscriber to both the MG and the IceGene databases. In the course of his research, Gene discovers a gene, called "Cobb1," that he believes is linked to a rare genetic disorder called Ty Cobb syndrome. (Sufferers are mentally unstable and often kleptomaniacs.) Although Gene is an MG subscriber, he contends that he did not use the database in locating the Cobb1 gene; his published research on the subject reveals that he used the publicly available Human Genome Project database to first home in on the gene's location and then sequence it. Gene now wants to confirm the link between the Cobb1 gene and Ty Cobb syndrome, by running an analysis using the IceGene database. He balks, however, when he comes to clause [2] above in the IceGene Access Agreement. Gene believes that the rarity of Ty Cobb's disease will make it very difficult to interest pharmaceutical firms in developing a therapy to deal with it. (This could, for example, take the form of a chemical compound that inhibits expression of the Cobb1 gene, effectively suppressing the disorder.) Because of this, Gene wants to keep the cost of any Cobb1 therapy as low as possible. So he objects to the "reach through" or "pass through" royalty called for in clause [2] above.

Gene has asked you to argue his position with MG and IceGene. What arguments would you marshal on his behalf?

3. Reverse Engineering

Not all use or disclosure of someone's secret is actionable misappropriation. Rather, as the commissioners who drafted the Uniform Trade Secrets Act noted, there are several categories of "proper means" of obtaining a trade secret. We classify these "proper means" as defenses, because they do not directly deny the existence of a trade secret or the defendant's use of that secret. Rather, they are *legitimate* uses of trade secrets by a competitor.

The commissioners' Comment to section 1 of the Act had this to say on the subject of defenses:

> One of the broadly stated policies behind trade secret law is "the maintenance of standards of commercial ethics." The *Restatement of Torts*, Section 757, Comment (f), notes: "A complete catalogue of improper means is not possible," but Section 1(1) includes a partial listing.
>
> Proper means include:
>
> 1. Discovery by independent invention;
>
> 2. Discovery by "reverse engineering," that is, by starting with the known product and working backward to find the method by which it was developed. The acquisition of the known product must, of course, also be by a fair and honest means, such as purchase of the item on the open market, for reverse engineering to be lawful; . . .
>
> 4. Observation of the item in public use or on public display;
>
> 5. Obtaining the trade secret from published literature.

See also Restatement (Third) of Unfair Competition § 43 ("Independent discovery and analysis of publicly available products or information are not improper means of acquisition.").

Kadant, Inc. v. Seeley Machine, Inc.
244 F. Supp. 2d 19 (N.D.N.Y. 2003)

Hurd, District Judge.

II. Facts

Kadant is a publicly traded corporation with yearly sales eclipsing $100 million. Kadant AES ("AES") is a division of Kadant located in Queensbury, New York. For twenty-eight years, AES has manufactured and sold to customers worldwide products that clean and condition papermaking machines and filter water used in the papermaking process. "There are three main products areas of the business of AES: shower and spray devices and nozzles; foil blades to remove water from the paper during the papermaking process; and structures that hold foils and filters for straining water utilized in the papermaking process so that it can be reused." . . . Plaintiff occupies a dominant place in the national papermaking market.

Corlew was hired by AES in July of 1995 as a machinist. Nearly three years later, in April of 1998, he was promoted to a position in the engineering department. In that capacity, Corlew would be provided with a refined customer order, made by an AES engineer and a customer, and it was his job to create a "manufacturing drawing (with instructions and a bill of materials — i.e., the 'recipe') for the order." In order to create such a drawing, Corlew used a computer assisted drawing machine. The computer assisted drawing machine contained "the recipes for the AES products and generate[d] drawings and bills of materials." Plaintiff contends that AES took steps to protect the secrecy of the information contained in the computer assisted drawing machine. In June of 1999, Corlew was promoted again and now had the responsibility to assist the engineers in designing customer orders. Corlew was terminated in the summer of 2001.

During his tenure at AES, Corlew had access to plaintiff's "recipes" ("design specifications") for its products and to plaintiff's computerized database of prospective customers, which includes "names, addresses, and e-mails for all potential customers in the papermaking industry, including the names of individuals key to these companies' purchasing orders." Plaintiff contends that one of Corlew's final assignments while at AES was to coordinate this database with the database containing information on all current AES customers and their purchasing histories. Corlew had access to AES's entire computer system, which apparently included both databases as well as the computer assisted drawing machine containing the design specifications. At the end of his employment, Corlew's access to AES's computer system was terminated, and his laptop was wiped clean of AES information, and/or access thereto. Throughout his employment with AES, Corlew was subject to a signed confidentiality agreement, in which he agreed not to disclose or use to his benefit any confidential information, including information about AES customers.

Following his termination, Corlew formed APE "to outsource the manufacture of his own line of products for sale to the pulp and papermaking industry." According to defendants, APE was not a successful venture, forcing Corlew to begin working for Cambridge Valley Machine, Inc. ("CVM"). In April or May of 2002, Corlew resigned from CVM. Defendants contended in their moving papers that, as a condition of his resignation, Corlew was required to relinquish the rights to the name APE to CVM.

Near the end of April of 2002, Corlew began working for Seeley, "developing and marketing a new line of Seeley products for sale to the pulp and papermaking industry." According to defendants, "[t]he products comprising this new line were reverse-engineered from existing products, freely available in the public domain and unprotected by published patent applications, in-force patents or trade secrets." According to plaintiff, the only way defendants could have developed and put out for sale this new line of products in so short of time is not by reverse engineering, which it alleges is time consuming, expensive, and requiring technical skill, but by Corlew's theft of AES's trade secrets — its design specifications and the customer databases — and infringement of its trademark.

Specifically, claims plaintiff, using as a frame of reference defendants' own expert, it would take defendants 1.7 years to reverse engineer all of plaintiff's nozzles. Defendants maintain, however, that only a small fraction, not all, of plaintiff's products were reverse engineered. The parties also dispute how much time would be associated with the manufacturing process. . . .

III. Discussion

Plaintiff has moved for preliminary injunctive relief pursuant to Fed. R. Civ. P. 52(a). . . .

In order for plaintiff to successfully move for a preliminary injunction, it must demonstrate: 1) a likelihood of irreparable harm if the injunction is not granted; and 2) either a likelihood of success on the merits of its claims, or the existence of serious questions going to the merits of its claims plus a balance of the hardships tipping decidedly in its favor. Bery v. City of New York, 97 F.3d 689, 693-94 (2d Cir. 1996). Because the issuance of a preliminary injunction is a drastic remedy, plaintiff is required to make a "clear showing" of these requirements. *See* Mazurek v. Armstrong, 520 U.S. 968, 972, 117 S. Ct. 1865, 138 L. Ed. 2d 162 (1997). . . .

B. Trade Secret Theft/Misappropriation

1. Likelihood of Success on the Merits

To establish misappropriation of a trade secret, a plaintiff must prove: 1) that "it possessed a trade secret; and 2) that defendants are using that trade secret in breach of an agreement, confidence, or duty, or as a result of discovery by improper means." Integrated Cash Management Services, Inc. v. Digital Transactions, Inc., 920 F.2d 171, 173 (2d Cir. 1990); *see also* Carpetmaster of Latham v. Dupont Flooring Systems, 12 F. Supp. 2d 257, 261 (N.D.N.Y. 1998). . . .

b. Design Specifications

Secrecy again takes center stage and is dispositive when determining whether plaintiff's product design specifications are entitled to trade secret protection for the purposes of obtaining preliminary injunctive relief. If secrecy is lost when a product is placed on the market, there is no trade secret protection. *See LinkCo*, 230 F. Supp. 2d at 498-99 (collecting cases). The primary issue with respect to this alleged trade secret is whether plaintiff's products could be reverse engineered in the time span between Corlew's hiring at Seeley and defendants' marketing and putting out their products for sale.[11] As will be shown, *infra*, the parties disagree about every material fact that goes toward resolving this debate.

"Trade secret law . . . does not offer protection against discovery by . . . so-called reverse engineering[.]" Kewanee Oil Co. v. Bicron Corp., 416 U.S. 470, 476, 94 S. Ct. 1879, 40 L. Ed. 2d 315 (1974). However, "the term 'reverse engineering' is not a talisman that may immunize the theft of trade secrets." Telerate Systems, Inc. v. Caro, 689 F. Supp. 221, 233 (S.D.N.Y. 1988). The relevant inquiry is whether the means to obtain the alleged trade secret were proper or "honest," as opposed to being obtained by virtue of a confidential relationship with an employer. *See* Franke v. Wiltschek, 209 F.2d 493, 495 (2d Cir. 1953); *Telerate*, 689 F. Supp. at 233. Reverse engineering a product to determine its design specifications is therefore permissible so long as the means used to get the information necessary to reverse engineer is in the public domain, and not through the confidential relationship established with the maker or owner of the product.

One court, not satisfied with this distinction, has held that even where a product is out in the public domain, and was thus subject to being reverse engineered by a purchaser, trade secret status remains intact because the defendant's former employment with the plaintiff was the only basis for the defendants being "able to select particular items from a vast sea of public information." *See* Monovis, Inc. v. Aquino, 905 F. Supp. 1205, 1228 (W.D.N.Y. 1994). This view of the law would effectively eviscerate any benefit reverse engineering would provide in the preliminary injunction analysis as applied to trade secrets, forestall healthy notions of commercial competitiveness, and heavily contribute to an inert marketplace where products can only be developed and sold under an impenetrable cloak of originality. It is therefore rejected.

Plaintiff has presented no evidence that the means used by defendants to obtain the alleged trade secret were improper or dishonest. In short, it has no evidence Corlew actually stole the design specifications. It instead necessarily relies upon an inference — that the only way defendants could develop, market, and sell their products in so short of time is if Corlew stole the design specification information — that is, as far as the evidence to this point shows, is unjustified. Plaintiff does not seem to argue that reverse engineering is impossible, just that it would take a great deal of time, skill, and expense, and that the lack thereof demonstrates that the design specifications must have been stolen. Defendants have argued that the plaintiff's products were simple, consisting of non-technical and few parts, that reverse engineering would take little time, and that, in any event, they only reverse engineered a small fraction, not all, of plaintiff's products. Plaintiff has not sufficiently rebutted these contentions.

11. "Reverse engineering is the process by which an engineer takes an already existing product and works backward to re-create its design and/or manufacturing process." United Technologies Corp. by Pratt & Whitney v. F.A.A., 102 F.3d 688, 690 n.1 (2d Cir. 1996).

Thus, because plaintiff has failed to make a clear showing that defendants improperly obtained and reverse engineered its products, trade secret protection at this stage of the litigation is improper. *See, e.g.*, Bridge C.A.T. Scan Associates v. Technicare Corp., 710 F.2d 940, 946-47 (2d Cir. 1983) (lack of evidence that means to receive information that plaintiff claimed was trade secret were improper mandated denying preliminary injunctive relief).

COMMENTS AND QUESTIONS

1. Why is reverse engineering lawful? If, as the Commissioners suggested, one purpose of trade secret law is to promote standards of commercial ethics, doesn't there seem to be something wrong with taking apart a competitor's product in order to figure out how to copy it? Does reverse engineering benefit only those competitors who are not smart enough to develop ideas or products for themselves?

In Chicago Lock Co. v. Fanberg, 676 F.2d 400 (9th Cir. 1982), the plaintiff, a company that made locks, sued a locksmith who compiled a list of master key codes for the plaintiff's locks by soliciting information from those who had picked the locks on behalf of their clients. The court rejected the claim, holding that the owners of the individual locks had the right to open them, and therefore to authorize others to reverse engineer the key codes:

> A lock purchaser's own reverse-engineering of his own lock, and subsequent publication of the serial number-key code correlation, is an example of the independent invention and reverse engineering expressly allowed by trade secret doctrine.[4] Imposing an obligation of nondisclosure on lock owners here would frustrate the intent of California courts to disallow protection to trade secrets discovered through "fair and honest means." See id. Further, such an implied obligation upon the lock owners in this case would, in effect, convert the Company's trade secret into a state-conferred monopoly akin to the absolute protection that a federal patent affords. Such an extension of California trade secrets law would certainly be preempted by the federal scheme of patent regulation.
>
> Appellants, therefore, cannot be said to have procured the individual locksmiths to breach a duty of nondisclosure they owed to the Company, for the locksmiths owed no such duty.

2. Does reverse engineering by one or a few firms mean that the plaintiff's information is no longer secret? *See* Barr-Mullin, Inc. v. Browning, 442 S.E.2d 226 (Ct. App. N.C. 1993). In Reingold v. Swiftships, 126 F.3d 645 (5th Cir. 1997), the court rejected a claim that a boat hull mold could not be a trade secret because it could readily be reverse engineered. While reverse engineering may protect one who engages in it, the court held, it does not protect those who actually acquire the secret by improper means. Should it matter whether the reverse engineering is very difficult or easy enough that any competitor could do it?

Reverse engineering may be explained as a legal rule designed to weaken trade secret protection relative to patent protection. Can you think of reasons why we would

4. If a group of lock owners, for their own convenience, together published a listing of their own key codes for use by locksmiths, the owners would not have breached any duty owed to the Company. Indeed, the Company concedes that a lock owner's reverse engineering of his own lock is not "improper means."

want to weaken trade secret protection? *See* Kewanee Oil Co. v. Bicron Corp., 416 U.S. 470 (1974) (patent law does not preempt trade secret law, in part because the reverse engineering rule "weakens" trade secret law).

3. Consider the recurring question of whether the parties can agree to override trade secret law. Suppose that the owner of a trade secret includes in a license or sale contract a provision prohibiting the buyer from reverse engineering the product. Is that contractual provision enforceable? The courts are split. *Compare* K & G Oil & Tool Service Co. v. G & G Fishing Tool Service, 158 Tex. 94, 314 S.W.2d 782, 785-86 (1958) (contract preventing disassembly of tools to protect trade secrets was enforceable), *with* Vault Corp. v. Quaid Software, Ltd., 847 F.2d 255, 265-67 (5th Cir. 1988) (contract provision prohibiting reverse engineering of software void as against public policy).

4. Trade secret law does not protect owners against legitimate purchasers who discover the secret through reverse engineering. But does the possibility that a product might be reverse engineered foreclose *any* trade secret protection? In Data General Corp. v. Grumman Systems Support Corp., 825 F. Supp. 340, 359 (D. Mass. 1993), the court upheld a jury's verdict that Grumman had misappropriated trade secrets contained in object code form in Data General's computer program, despite the fact that many copies of the program had been sold on the open market. The court reasoned: "With the exception of those who lawfully licensed or unlawfully misappropriated MV/ADEX, Data General enjoyed the exclusive use of MV/ADEX. Even those who obtained MV/ADEX and were able to *use* MV/ADEX were unable to discover its trade secrets because MV/ADEX was distributed only in its object code form, which is essentially unintelligible to humans." The court noted that Data General took significant steps to preserve the secrecy of MV/ADEX, requiring that all users of the program sign licenses agreeing not to disclose the program to third parties. Under this decision, a defendant may have to prove that they had some sort of legitimate access to the plaintiff's information — for example, by demonstrating that they reverse-engineered it from a publicly available product — even though the product containing the secret is widely distributed.

The *Data General* cases suggest that reasonable efforts to protect the secrecy of an idea contained in a commercial product — such as locks, black boxes, or the use of unreadable code — may suffice to maintain trade secret protection even after the product itself is widely circulated. Does this result make sense? For a different approach, see Videotronics v. Bend Electronics, 564 F. Supp. 1471, 1476 (D. Nev. 1983) (holding that software cannot be a trade secret if it is publicly distributed and can be readily copied).

5. If a company is looking for a piece of information — say, the solution to a given technical problem — society is very much concerned that the company be allowed free access to information in the public domain. The reason is that minimizing the search costs of the company is thought to be a social good, consistent with some level of protection for the prior investment of others. In a similar vein, suppose the costs of obtaining that information from the public domain are very high, but the costs (to the company) of stealing it from a competitor are very low. Should society punish — and therefore deter — the theft? Wouldn't that simply create an inefficiency, since the company could get the information but would have to incur greater search costs? *Cf.* David Friedman, William Landes & Richard Posner, *Some Economics of Trade Secret Law*, 5 J. Econ. Persp. 61, 62 (1991) (arguing that trade secret law prohibits only costly means of obtaining competitors' information, while encouraging cheaper

forms of obtaining information such as reverse engineering). Are there other considerations that militate in favor of requiring such a search?

PROBLEMS

Problem 11-14. Atech and Alpha both manufacture complex medical devices used in diagnosing a variety of ailments. These devices are sold almost exclusively to hospitals, since they cost in excess of $100,000 each. There are several hundred Atech devices currently in use in hospitals throughout the country. Atech, which claims a trade secret in the internal workings of its device, carefully monitors the purchasers of its device. Alpha pays a third party to buy a device from Atech without disclosing that it will be given to Alpha. Once it has obtained the device, Alpha disassembles it and studies it in order to compare it to Alpha's own device. In the course of opening it up, Alpha's engineers pick two internal padlocks on the Atech device. When Atech discovers that Alpha has obtained the device, it demands the unit's return, offering to refund the purchase price. Alpha refuses, and Atech sues for misappropriation of trade secrets.

a) Assume that Atech's trade secrets were worth $5 million. Assume further that the padlocks cost $5 each, and that it costs $100 per lock to pick these padlocks. Has Atech taken reasonable precautions to preserve its secrets? What other security measures must Atech take—and at what cost—both to deter Alpha (and others) from reverse engineering and to preserve its secrecy? Does Atech's sale of the products on the open market automatically preclude a finding of secrecy?

b) Assume Atech has presented the buyer of the machine with a contract that licenses (rather than sells) the machine, subject to the following restrictions: (a) the buyer is prohibited from disclosing anything she learns during the course of using the machine; (b) the buyer is prohibited from reselling the machine; and (c) the buyer is liable for Atech's damages in the event that any third party learns of Atech's secrets from the buyer or the buyer's machine. Is such an agreement enforceable? Would you advise a client thinking of licensing an Atech machine to sign this contract? How would you redraft the agreement to protect the buyer?

c) Assume that after Alpha's engineers picked the padlocks, they gained access to the inner workings of the machine. Assume further that they discovered numerous flaws in the imaging mechanism that caused potentially serious defects in the images (and hence the diagnoses) *stemming* from the Atech machine. Finally, assume that Alpha's engineers not only fixed these problems but significantly improved on Atech's design and hence the reliability of the machine. Should these facts affect Alpha's liability? Atech's remedy?

Problem 11-15. Bonnie Bluenote, a world-famous blues guitarist, is noted for her distinctive sound, which she gets by tuning her guitar specially every time before she plays. Although the *guitar* itself is a standard professional model, Bonnie's adjustments of settings on the guitar, amplifier, and sound system combine to produce a distinctive sound. Because the sound is so important to her image, Bonnie guards it carefully. While she is tuning her guitar, only band members and close associates are allowed in the room. When she records in a new studio, she has the sound engineers sign nondisclosure agreements.

One day Freddie Fender-Rhodes, a big fan of Bonnie's and a budding bluesman himself, is hanging around outside the studio where Bonnie is recording her newest album. He happens to see an ID tag, worn by all guests in the studio, in the wastebasket. He fills in his name and walks into the studio. The band members and recording engineers, seeing the tag, let Freddie stay. He observes how Bonnie tunes her guitar, sees the sound board settings, and makes extensive mental notes.

Five months later, *Bonnie* is shocked to see in a record store a CD by Freddie titled "The Bonnie Bluenote Sound." Then she discovers that Freddie is planning to publish an article in *Blues Guitar* magazine revealing the secrets to Bonnie's sound. Does she have any recourse against Freddie? What additional precautions should she have taken?

4. The Special Case of Departing Employees

Many of the thorniest issues in trade secret (and contract) law arise when employees leave a company in order either to start their own business or to take a job elsewhere. Such cases present a fundamental clash of rights between an employee and an employer, as Judge Adams suggests in the following excerpt from SI Handling Systems v. Heisley, 753 F.2d 1244, 1266-69 (3d Cir. 1985) (Adams, J., concurring):

> When deciding the equitable issues surrounding the request for a trade secret injunction, it would seem that a court cannot act as a pure engineer or scientist, assessing the technical import of the information in question. Rather, the court must also consider economic factors since the very definition of "trade secret" requires an assessment of the competitive advantage a particular item of information affords to a business. Similarly, among the elements to be weighed in determining trade secret status are the value of the information to its owner and to competitors, and the ease or difficulty with which the information may be properly acquired or duplicated.
>
> While the majority may be correct in suggesting that the trial court need not always "engage in extended analysis of the public interest," the court on occasion must apply the elements of sociology. This is so since trade secret cases frequently implicate the important countervailing policies served on one hand by protecting a business person from unfair competition stemming from the usurpation of trade secrets, and on the other by permitting an individual to pursue unhampered the occupation for which he or she is best suited. "Trade secrets are not . . . so important to society that the interests of employees, competitors and competition should automatically be relegated to a lower position whenever trade secrets are proved to exist." Robison, *The Confidence Game: An Approach to the Law About Trade Secrets*, 25 Ariz. L. Rev. 347, 382 (1983).
>
> These observations take on more force, I believe, when a case such as the present one involves the concept of "know-how." Under Pennsylvania law an employee's general knowledge, skill, and experience are not trade secrets. Thus in theory an employer generally may not inhibit the manner in which an employee uses his or her knowledge, skill, and experience—even if these were acquired during employment. When these attributes of the employee are inextricably related to the information or process that constitutes an employer's competitive advantage—as increasingly seems to be the case in newer,

> high-technology industries—the legal questions confronting the court necessarily become bound up with competing public policies.
>
> It is noteworthy that in such cases the balance struck by the Pennsylvania courts apparently has favored greater freedom for employees to pursue a chosen profession. The courts have recognized that someone who has worked in a particular field cannot be expected to forego the accumulated skills, knowledge, and experience gained before the employee changes jobs. Such qualifications are obviously very valuable to an employee seeking to sell his services in the marketplace. A person leaving one employer and going into the marketplace will seek to compete in the area of his or her greatest aptitude. In light of the highly mobile nature of our society, and as the economy becomes increasingly comprised of highly skilled or high-tech jobs, the individual's economic interests will more and more be buffeted by competitive advantage. Courts must be cautious not to strike a balance that unduly disadvantages the individual worker. . . .
>
> In my view a proper injunction necessarily would impose the minimum restraint upon the free utilization of employee skill consistent with denying unfaithful employees an advantage from misappropriation of information. Thus, as I see it, the district court, on remand, should fashion an injunction that extends only so long as is essential to negate any unfair advantage that may have been gained by the appellants.

The majority opinion in *SI Handling* partially upheld a finding that two former employees had misappropriated trade secrets, but it vacated an injunction against them in order for the district court to reconsider its scope.

a. Employee Trade Secrets

Note on the Common Law Obligation to Assign Inventions

At common law, ownership of inventions—including ownership of patent rights—was determined according to an employee's status under a long line of common law employee invention cases. In general, employees fall into one of three categories: (1) employees "hired to invent," which results in employer ownership of the invention; (2) employees who invent on the employer's time or using its resources, which results in a limited, nonexclusive "shop right" on the part of the employer to practice the invention; and (3) an employee's "independent invention," in which case the employee owns the invention. *See generally* United States v. Dubilier Condenser Corp., 289 U.S. 178 (1933); John C. Stedman, *Employer-Employee Relations, in* FREDRIK NEUMEYER, THE EMPLOYED INVENTOR IN THE UNITED STATES 30, 40-41 (1971).

The first category is relatively straightforward. It seems logical to extend this treatment to consultants and others who are not "employees" in the strict sense. *Cf.* McElmurry v. Arkansas Power & Light Co., 27 U.S.P.Q.2d 1129, 1135 n.15 (Fed. Cir. 1993) (upholding shop right in employer where inventor/patentee was a consultant); Robert P. Merges, *Intellectual Property and the Costs of Commercial Exchange: A Review Essay*, 93 MICH. L. REV. 1570 (1995) (highlighting the role of intellectual property in structuring non-employment-based organizations, such as consulting companies and joint ventures). Category (2) reflects situations where employers have less than a complete claim to the invention, but where the employer's facilities or resources are combined with the inventor's talent and industry to produce the invention. The employee owns it, but the employer is compensated by receiving a limited right to practice the invention. Category (3) covers cases where the employee invents on his or her own time, outside the field of employment. See *Dubilier, supra.*

An employee's obligation to refrain from using an employer's trade secrets looks more onerous when it is the employee herself who came up with the secret. In Wexler v. Greenberg, 160 A.2d 430 (Pa. 1960), the Pennsylvania Supreme Court went out of its way to conclude that a departing employee was entitled to take formulas he had himself developed at his prior employer to work for a competitor. Despite the fact that the employee, Greenberg, was the chief chemist at the plaintiff, the court concluded that he was not in fact "hired to invent" and therefore owned the inventions he made.

Even in Pennsylvania *Wexler* is not always followed. *See* Healthcare Affiliated Services v. Lippancy, 701 F. Supp. 1142, 1155 (W.D. Pa. 1988) (rejecting *Wexler* analysis, emphasizing that although defendant developed inventions on his own, he did so using knowledge and information made available by the plaintiff employer). *But see* Fidelity Fund v. DiSanto, 500 A.2d 431 (Sup. Ct. Pa. 1985) (denying recovery against ex-employee salesman partly on the basis that he developed client contacts himself during employment).

Does the *Wexler* court confuse an employee's *general* knowledge and skills with specific inventions developed by the employee while at work *based* on that knowledge and skills? If an employee's job involves two tasks, working on established products (covered by trade secrets) and developing new ones, what effect will the *Wexler* rule have on the employee's allocation of time between these tasks?

Note on Contracts That Restrict the Use of Trade Secrets

Wexler is explicitly based on the absence of a written agreement between employer and employee.[15] Suppose that Greenberg had signed a contract when he was hired which stated that "all discoveries, inventions, or intellectual property rights stemming from employee's work at Buckingham are the exclusive property of Buckingham." Would such a contract be enforceable? Does it matter whether Greenberg's "discoveries" were new formulas or ways to copy competitors' formulas?

An example of the more common situation, in which the court finds either an express or implied agreement to assign an employee's own inventions, is Winston Research Corp. v. 3M Co., 350 F.2d 134 (9th Cir. 1965). There, the court dismissed an argument akin to Greenberg's as follows:

> Winston argues that information is protected from disclosure only if communicated to the employee by the employer who is seeking protection, and that the information involved in this case was not disclosed by [3M] to the employees subsequently hired by Winston, but rather was developed by these employees themselves, albeit while employed by [3M].
>
> We need not examine the soundness of the rule for which Winston contends, or its applicability to a case such as this in which a group of specialists engaged in related facets of

15. The absence of such an agreement can be significant even in situations in which it might be assumed that the "employer" had a reasonable claim to the employee's invention. *Cf.* Lariscey v. United States, 20 U.S.P.Q.2d 1845 (Fed. Cir. 1991) (prison inmate owns rights to a secret process he developed while working in a prison shop).

> a single development project change their employer. . . . [A]n obligation not to disclose may arise from circumstances other than communication in confidence by the employer. It may also rest upon an express or implied agreement. In the present case, an agreement not to disclose might be implied from [3M]'s elaborate efforts to maintain the secrecy of its development program, and the employees' knowledge of those efforts and participation in them. In any event, [3M] and its employees entered into express written agreements binding the latter not to disclose confidential information, and these agreements did not exclude information which the employee himself contributed.

Id. at 140.

Most companies require their employees to sign some sort of employment agreement, either when they are hired or at some point during their tenure. Employment agreements generally fall into one or more of three categories: confidentiality agreements, invention assignments, and noncompetition agreements. Confidentiality agreements, with which we are concerned here, generally recite that the employee will receive confidential information during her employment, and that she undertakes to keep it secret and not to use it for anyone other than the employer. Invention assignments give the employer the right to intellectual property created by the employee while she was employed. Noncompetition agreements limit the circumstances in which former employees can compete for customers with their former employers.

Presumably, employers may require their employees to agree not to use or disclose trade secrets to which they have access during employment. Virtually all employers do so. A variant on the departing employee who wishes to take her own inventions is the departing sales representative who wishes to "take" a list of customers (either a written list or one that they have memorized) in order to call on those customers for a competitor.[16] Customer lists are generally protectable as trade secrets, but enjoining employees from calling on customers with whom they have had long-standing relationships raises serious concerns about employee mobility. Two California cases frame the dispute. In Moss, Adams & Co. v. Shilling, 179 Cal. App. 3d 124 (1986), the court drew a line between an employee announcing her departure to start a competing company and actively soliciting old clients to follow her. The former was permissible, but the latter was not. This compromise was thrown into doubt by the decision in Morlife Inc. v. Perry, 66 Cal. Rptr. 2d 731 (Ct. App. 1997), where the court held that the passage of the Uniform Trade Secrets Act in California superseded *Moss, Adams* and that continuing personal relationships with former customers could constitute misappropriation of a trade secret.

On the other hand, *Restatement (Third) of Unfair Competition* § 41, cmt. d states:

> The reasonableness of an agreement that merely prohibits the use or disclosure of particular information depends primarily upon whether the information protected by the agreement qualifies as a trade secret. If the information qualifies for protection

16. Merely memorizing a trade secret rather than taking physical documents will not preclude a finding of misappropriation, though it may make misappropriation harder to detect. *See* Ed Nowogroski Ins. Inc. v. Rucker, 971 P. 2d 936 (Wash. 1999). In Stampede Tool Warehouse Inc. v. May, 651 N.E.2d 209 (Ill. Ct. App. 1995), for example, the plaintiff alleged that former employees who started a competing business had misappropriated its trade secrets by memorizing a list of plaintiff's customers and soliciting those customers. The court found the defendants liable, reasoning that "memorization is one method of misappropriation." But if the case involved merely a former employee contacting those she knew from experience to be potential customers, rather than explicitly attempting to memorize a list of customers, it is hard to fault the employee's conduct.

> under the rule stated in § 39, a contract prohibiting its use or disclosure is generally enforceable according to its terms. Although in some cases courts have enforced nondisclosure agreements directed at information found ineligible for protection as a trade secret, many of these decisions merely reflect a more narrow definition of trade secret than that adopted in § 39. However, a nondisclosure agreement that encompasses information that is generally known or in which the promisee has no protectable interest, such as a former employee's promise not to use information that is part of the employee's general skill and training (see § 42, Comment d), may be unenforceable as an unreasonable restraint of trade. Agreements that deny the promisor the right to use information that is in the public domain are ordinarily enforceable only if justified on the basis of interests other than the protection of confidential information.

Where should the line be drawn between permissible work and impermissible use of "secret" lists of customers? To whom does the value inherent in personal relationships belong?

A more difficult problem arises when employers attempt to limit an employee's use of information that does not constitute a trade secret under the legal standards described above. Can employers and employees "agree" that the employee will not use *any* information obtained during employment, whether it is public or not? This question parallels the problem of restrictive license provisions — are employers limited by the intellectual property laws to protecting only trade secrets that meet the statutory requirements, or are they free to impose additional restrictions on their employees so long as they do so by agreement? Courts struggle with this issue, with the majority concluding that "reasonable" contract restrictions on employees are enforceable even in the absence of a protectable trade secret. *See* Bernier v. Merrill Air Engineers, 770 A.2d 97 (Me. 2001); 12 Roger Milgrim, Milgrim on Trade Secrets § 3.05[1][a], at 3-209 to 3-210. One state has even gone so far as to enact a statute that automatically assigns inventions to an employer provided they were developed in the course of employment and relate to the scope of the employee's work. Nev. Rev. Stat. § 600.500.

On the other hand, in an attempt to alleviate the disparity in bargaining power between the employer and the inventor/employee, several states have adopted "freedom to create" statutes restricting the instances in which employers may compel assignment through contract. *See* Minn. Stat. Ann. § 181.78 (1980); N.C. Gen. Stat. § 66-57.1 to 57.2 (1981); Wash. Rev. Code Ann. § 49.44.140 (1987); Cal. Labor Code § 2870 (West 1987). These statutes provide that any employee invention assignment agreement that purports to give employers greater rights than they have under the statute is against public policy and unenforceable. The California statute is a good example. It provides that contracts may not require assignment of "invention[s] that the employee developed entirely on his or her own time without using the employer's equipment, supplies, facilities, or trade secret information" unless the invention relates to the employer's current or demonstrably anticipated business. Cal. Labor Code § 2870.

One commentator has argued that the United States is slipping in technological innovation because this country's inventors (the vast majority of whom are employed) have lost their incentive to create partially due to assignment agreements. After labeling the state legislation described above as "a step forward," the author writes: "Comprehensive federal legislation is necessary to provide employed inventors greater control over, and interests in, their inventions in order to create the psychological and financial incentives required to increase technological innovation in the United States. . . . Federal legislation would obviate the need for state reform and would bring uniformity that would solve the potential problem of inventors employed by multistate corporations." Henrik D. Parker, *Reform for Rights of Employed Inventors*, 57 S. CAL. L. REV. 603 (1984). *But see* Robert P. Merges, *The Law and Economics of Employee Inventions*, 13 HARV. J.L. & TECH. 1 (1999).

PROBLEM

Problem 11-16. Helen, an employee of CarTech, is assigned to work on solving a particular problem in car design. She works for two years on that problem for CarTech, without success. Two months after Helen leaves CarTech to start her own company, she puts out a product that incorporates a solution to the same problem. CarTech sues Helen for misappropriation of trade secrets. At trial, CarTech proves that Helen came up with her system while at CarTech and that she decided to start her own company to exploit her invention rather than disclose it to CarTech. As a result, CarTech had no knowledge of the idea until Helen came out with her product. Should CarTech prevail in its trade secret suit, assuming that there was no employment or invention contract between the parties?

Note on Trailer Clauses

The common law rules just described apply in the absence of contracts, as stated; but they also have some relevance even when written agreements are in place. This is so because, under principles similar to those applied in the law of noncompetition agreements, the law limits the ability of employers to claim ownership by contract of all employee inventions no matter how tenuously related to the employment relationship. A case study in the limits of invention assignment agreements involves the "trailer clause," a contractual provision that requires employees to assign their rights not only in inventions made during the period of employment but also for a certain time thereafter. Trailer clauses developed in response to a number of cases which held that, absent contractual provisions to the contrary, an employee's ideas did not belong to the employer unless they were written down in tangible form (such as a patent disclosure statement) before the employee left work. *See* Jamesbury Corp. v. Worcester Valve Co., 443 F.2d 205 (1st Cir. 1971).

Of course, even if an employer uses a trailer clause, there is always the risk that the former employee will simply wait out the duration of the term and then conveniently make the discovery upon the trailer clause's expiration. Such a strategy was attempted by an inventor in at least one case. Fortunately for the employer, the court did not believe the defendant inventor's story that the conception date for his flow meter was five days after the expiration of the six months specified in the trailer clause:

> The perfection of a flow meter proved to be a painstakingly intricate process involving extensive testing. It is therefore difficult to believe that after a long and distinguished career with Plaintiff, Mr. Halmi in his musing five days after the trailer clause expired for the first time came up with the idea for the NTV. Although the word "Eureka!" has allegedly been uttered by more than one inventor over the years, the concept at issue does not lend itself to such sudden discovery. The court finds that the concept of the '434

> patent must have existed in Mr. Halmi's mind before his employment with GSC ended. Mr. Halmi therefore violated his agreement with GSC.

General Signal Corp. v. Primary Flow Signal, Inc., 1987 U.S. Dist. LEXIS 6929, at *10 (D.R.I. July 27, 1987).

Generally, trailer clauses are enforceable only to the extent that they are "reasonable." Although trailer clauses are generally enforceable, clauses of particularly long or indefinite duration may run afoul of the antitrust laws as well as being unenforceable. *See* United Shoe Machinery Co. v. La Chapelle, 212 Mass. 467, 99 N.E. 289 (1912). One court expressed the requirement of reasonableness as follows:

> Hold-over clauses are simply a recognition of the fact of business life that employees sometimes carry with them to new employers inventions or ideas so related to work done for a former employer that in equity and good conscience the fruits of that work should belong to that former employer. In construing and applying hold-over clauses, the courts have held that they must be limited to *reasonable times* . . . and to *subject matter* which an employee worked on or had knowledge of during his employment. . . . Unless expressly agreed otherwise, an employer has no right under a holdover clause to inventions made outside the scope of the employee's former activities, and made on and with a subsequent employer's time and funds.

Dorr-Oliver, Inc. v. United States, 432 F.2d 447, 452 (Ct. Cl. 1970). Corporations may have trouble enforcing restrictions that are broader in scope. *See* Applied Materials, Inc. v. Advanced Micro-Fabrication Equipment (Shanghai) Co., 2009 WL 1481147 (N.D. Cal. May 20, 2009) (rejecting one-year trailer clause as an invalid noncompete agreement). This is particularly true of large conglomerates that attempt to require the assignment of any invention related to their (diverse) fields of business. *See* Ingersoll-Rand Co. v. Ciavatta, 110 N.J. 609, 542 A.2d 879, 896 n.6 (1988).

b. Noncompetition Agreements

Employees inevitably learn a great deal about a business on the job. They may learn the trade secrets of their employer, but they may also learn such basic information as how many people it takes to make a product, who is likely to buy the product, where to advertise, etc. Further, employees develop personal relationships with vendors, customers, and others that are immensely useful in business. For this reason, many employers would like to prevent their employees from competing against them at all. Such employers often ask their employees to sign "noncompetition agreements," which prevent the employee from competing with his former employer for customers for a set period of time. Should such agreements be enforceable?

Edwards v. Arthur Andersen LLP

81 Cal. Rptr. 3d 282 (Sup. Ct. 2008)

CHIN, J.

We granted review to address the validity of noncompetition agreements in California and the permissible scope of employment release agreements. We limited our review to the following issues: To what extent does Business and Professions Code section 16600 prohibit employee noncompetition agreements. . . .

We conclude that section 16600 prohibits employee noncompetition agreements unless the agreement falls within a statutory exception. . . . We therefore affirm in part and reverse in part the Court of Appeal judgment.

Facts

In January 1997, Raymond Edwards II (Edwards), a certified public accountant, was hired as a tax manager by the Los Angeles office of the accounting firm Arthur Andersen LLP (Andersen). Andersen's employment offer was made contingent upon Edwards's signing a noncompetition agreement, which prohibited him from working for or soliciting certain Andersen clients for limited periods following his termination. The agreement was required of all managers, and read in relevant part: "If you leave the Firm, for eighteen months after release or resignation, you agree not to perform professional services of the type you provided for any client on which you worked during the eighteen months prior to release or resignation. This does not prohibit you from accepting employment with a client. [¶] For twelve months after you leave the Firm, you agree not to solicit (to perform professional services of the type you provided) any client of the office(s) to which you were assigned during the eighteen months preceding release or resignation. [¶] You agree not to solicit away from the Firm any of its professional personnel for eighteen months after release or resignation." Edwards signed the agreement.

Between 1997 and 2002, Edwards continued to work for Andersen, moving into the firm's private client services practice group, where he handled income, gift, and estate tax planning for individuals and entities with large incomes and net worth. Over this period he was promoted to senior manager and was on track to become a partner. In March 2002, the United States government indicted Andersen in connection with the investigation into Enron Corporation, and in June 2002, Andersen announced that it would cease its accounting practices in the United States. In April 2002, Andersen began selling off its practice groups to various entities. In May 2002, Andersen internally announced that HSBC USA, Inc. (a New York-based banking corporation), through a new subsidiary, Wealth and Tax Advisory Services (WTAS), would purchase a portion of Andersen's tax practice, including Edwards's group.

In July 2002, HSBC offered Edwards employment. Before hiring any of Andersen's employees, HSBC required them to execute a "Termination of Non-compete Agreement" (TONC) in order to obtain employment with HSBC. Among other things, the TONC required employees to, inter alia, (1) voluntarily resign from Andersen; (2) release Andersen from "any and all" claims, including "claims that in any way arise from or out of, are based upon or relate to Employee's employment by, association with or compensation from" defendant; (3) continue indefinitely to preserve confidential information and trade secrets except as otherwise required by a court or governmental agency; (4) refrain from disparaging Andersen or its related entities or partners; and (5) cooperate with Andersen in connection with any investigation of, or litigation against, Andersen. In exchange, Andersen would agree to accept Edwards's resignation, agree to Edwards's employment by HSBC, and release Edwards from the 1997 noncompetition agreement. . . .

Edwards signed the HSBC offer letter, but he did not sign the TONC. In response, Andersen terminated Edwards's employment and withheld severance benefits. HSBC withdrew its offer of employment to Edwards.

Procedural History

On April 30, 2003, Edwards filed a complaint against Andersen, HSBC and WTAS for intentional interference with prospective economic advantage and anticompetitive business practices under the Cartwright Act (BUS. & PROF. CODE, § 16720 *et seq.*). Edwards alleged that the Andersen noncompetition agreement violated section 16600, which states "[e]xcept as provided in this chapter, every contract by which anyone is restrained from engaging in a lawful profession, trade, or business of any kind is to that extent void." . . .

The trial court heard argument from both parties, but took no evidence. The court determined all issues of law in favor of Andersen on the merits, and entered judgment in its favor. The court specifically decided that the noncompetition agreement did not violate section 16600 because it was narrowly tailored and did not deprive Edwards of his right to pursue his profession. . . . Thus, requiring him to sign these documents was not unlawful. Edwards appealed the trial court's decision. . . .

In the published part of its opinion, the Court of Appeal held: (1) the noncompetition agreement was invalid under section 16600, and requiring Edwards to sign the TONC as consideration to be released from it was an independently wrongful act for purposes of the elements of Edwards's claim for intentional interference with prospective economic advantage. . . .

Discussion

A. *Section 16600*

Under the common law, as is still true in many states today, contractual restraints on the practice of a profession, business, or trade, were considered valid, as long as they were reasonably imposed. (Bosley Medical Group v. Abramson (1984) 161 Cal. App. 3d 284, 288, 207 Cal. Rptr. 477.) This was true even in California. (Wright v. Ryder (1868) 36 Cal. 342, 357 [relaxing original common law rule that all restraints on trade were invalid in recognition of increasing population and competition in trade].) However, in 1872 California settled public policy in favor of open competition, and rejected the common law "rule of reasonableness," when the Legislature enacted the Civil Code. (Former CIV. CODE, § 1673, repealed by Stats. 1941, ch. 526, § 2, p. 1847, and enacted as BUS. & PROF. CODE, § 16600, Stats. 1941, ch. 526, § 1, p. 1834; *Bosley*, supra, 161 Cal. App. 3d at p. 288, 207 Cal. Rptr. 477.) Today in California, covenants not to compete are void, subject to several exceptions discussed briefly below.

Section 16600 states: "Except as provided in this chapter, every contract by which anyone is restrained from engaging in a lawful profession, trade, or business of any kind is to that extent void." The chapter excepts noncompetition agreements in the sale or dissolution of corporations (§ 16601), partnerships (ibid.; § 16602), and limited liability corporations (§ 16602.5). In the years since its original enactment as Civil Code section 1673, our courts have consistently affirmed that section 16600 evinces a settled legislative policy in favor of open competition and employee mobility. (See D'sa v. Playhut, Inc. (2000) 85 Cal. App. 4th 927, 933, 102 Cal. Rptr. 2d 495.) The law protects Californians and ensures "that every citizen shall retain the right to pursue any lawful employment and enterprise of their choice." (Metro Traffic Control, Inc. v. Shadow Traffic Network (1994) 22 Cal. App. 4th 853, 859, 27 Cal. Rptr. 2d 573.) It protects "the important legal right of persons to engage in businesses and occupations of their choosing." (Morlife, Inc. v. Perry (1997) 56 Cal. App. 4th 1514, 1520, 66 Cal. Rptr. 2d 731.)

This court has invalidated an otherwise narrowly tailored agreement as an improper restraint under section 16600 because it required a former employee to forfeit his pension rights on commencing work for a competitor. (Muggill v. Reuben H. Donnelley Corp. (1965) 62 Cal. 2d 239, 242-243, 42 Cal. Rptr. 107, 398 P.2d 147 (*Muggill*); Chamberlain v. Augustine (1916) 172 Cal. 285, 289, 156 P. 479 [invalidating contract with partial trade restriction].) In *Muggill*, the court reviewed an adverse judgment against a company's retired employee whose pension plan rights were terminated after the former employee commenced work for a competitor. (*Muggill*, at p. 240, 42 Cal. Rptr. 107, 398 P.2d 147.) The retired employee had sued the former employer, seeking declaratory relief on the ground that the provision in the pension plan that terminated the retirement payments because the retiree went to work for a competitor was "against public policy and unenforceable." (Ibid.) *Muggill* held that, with exceptions not applicable here, section 16600 invalidates provisions in employment contracts and retirement pension plans that prohibit "an employee from working for a competitor after completion of his employment or imposing a penalty if he does so [citations] unless they are necessary to protect the employer's trade secrets [citation]." (*Muggill*, at p. 242, 42 Cal. Rptr. 107, 398 P.2d 147.)[4] In sum, following the Legislature, this court generally condemns noncompetition agreements. (*See, e.g.*, Armendariz v. Foundation Health Psychcare Services, Inc. (2000) 24 Cal. 4th 83, 123, fn.12, 99 Cal. Rptr. 2d 745, 6 P.3d 669 [such restraints on trade are "illegal"].)

Under the statute's plain meaning, therefore, an employer cannot by contract restrain a former employee from engaging in his or her profession, trade, or business unless the agreement falls within one of the exceptions to the rule. (§ 16600.) Andersen, however, asserts that we should interpret the term "restrain" under section 16600 to mean simply to "prohibit," so that only contracts that totally prohibit an employee from engaging in his or her profession, trade, or business are illegal. It would then follow that a mere limitation on an employee's ability to practice his or her vocation would be permissible under section 16600, as long as it is reasonably based.

Andersen contends that some California courts have held that section 16600 (and its predecessor statutes, Civil Code former sections 1673, 1674, and 1675) are the statutory embodiment of prior common law, and embrace the rule of reasonableness in evaluating competitive restraints. (*See, e.g.*, South Bay Radiology Medical Associates v. Asher (1990) 220 Cal. App. 3d 1074, 1080, 269 Cal. Rptr. 15 (*South Bay Radiology*) [§ 16600 embodies common law prohibition against restraints on trade]; Vacco Industries, Inc. v. Van Den Berg (1992) 5 Cal. App. 4th 34, 47-48, 6 Cal. Rptr. 2d 602 (*Vacco*) [§ 16600 is codification of common law reasonable restraint rule].) Andersen claims that these cases show that section 16600 "prohibits only broad agreements that prevent a person from engaging entirely in his chosen business, trade or profession. Agreements that do not have this broad effect — but merely regulate some

4. We do not here address the applicability of the so-called trade secret exception to section 16600, as Edwards does not dispute that portion of his agreement or contend that the provision of the noncompetition agreement prohibiting him from recruiting Andersen's employees violated section 16600.

aspect of post-employment conduct, e.g., to prevent raiding [employer's personnel]—are not within the scope of [s]ection 16600."

As Edwards observes, however, the cases Andersen cites to support a relaxation of the statutory rule simply recognize that the statutory exceptions to section 16600 reflect the same exceptions to the rule against noncompetition agreements that were implied in the common law. . . .

As the present Court of Appeal recognized, "Fairly read, the foregoing authorities suggest section 16600 embodies the original, strict common law antipathy toward restraints of trade, while the section 16601 and 16602 exceptions incorporated the later common law 'rule of reasonableness' in instances where those exceptions apply."

We conclude that Andersen's noncompetition agreement was invalid. As the Court of Appeal observed, "The first challenged clause prohibited Edwards, for an 18-month period, from performing professional services of the type he had provided while at Andersen, for any client on whose account he had worked during 18 months prior to his termination. The second challenged clause prohibited Edwards, for a year after termination, from 'soliciting,' defined by the agreement as providing professional services to any client of Andersen's Los Angeles office." The agreement restricted Edwards from performing work for Andersen's Los Angeles clients and therefore restricted his ability to practice his accounting profession. (See Thompson v. Impaxx, Inc. (2003) 113 Cal. App. 4th 1425, 1429, 7 Cal. Rptr. 3d 427 [distinguishing "trade route" and solicitation cases that protect trade secrets or confidential proprietary information].) The noncompetition agreement that Edwards was required to sign before commencing employment with Andersen was therefore invalid because it restrained his ability to practice his profession. (See *Muggill*, supra, 62 Cal. 2d at pp. 242-243, 42 Cal. Rptr. 107, 398 P.2d 147.)

B. *Ninth Circuit's Narrow-restraint Exception*

Andersen asks this court to adopt the limited or "narrow-restraint" exception to section 16600 that the Ninth Circuit discussed in Campbell v. Trustees of Leland Stanford Jr. Univ. (9th Cir. 1987) 817 F.2d 499 (*Campbell*), and that the trial court relied on in this case in order to uphold the noncompetition agreement. In *Campbell*, the Ninth Circuit acknowledged that California has rejected the common law "rule of reasonableness" with respect to restraints upon the ability to pursue a profession, but concluded that section 16600 "only makes illegal those restraints which preclude one from engaging in a lawful profession, trade, or business." (*Campbell*, supra, 817 F.2d at p. 502.) The court remanded the case to the district court in order to allow the employee to prove that the noncompetition agreement at issue completely restrained him from practicing his "profession, trade, or business within the meaning of section 16600." (*Campbell*, at p. 503.)

The confusion over the Ninth Circuit's application of section 16600 arose in a paragraph in *Campbell*, in which the court noted that some California courts have excepted application of section 16600 " 'where one is barred from pursuing only a small or limited part of the business, trade or profession.' " (*Campbell*, supra, 817 F.2d at p. 502.) . . .

Andersen is correct, however, that *Campbell* has been followed in some recent Ninth Circuit cases to create a narrow-restraint exception to section 16600 in federal court. For example, International Business Machines Corp. v. Bajorek (9th Cir. 1999) 191 F.3d 1033, upheld an agreement mandating that an employee forfeits stock options if employed by a competitor within six months of leaving employment. General Commercial Packaging v. TPS Package (9th Cir. 1997) 126 F.3d 1131, held that a bargained-for contractual provision barring one party from courting a specific named customer was not an illegal restraint of trade prohibited by section 16600, because it did not "entirely preclude[ ]" the party from pursuing its trade or business. (General Commercial Packaging v. TPS Package, supra, 126 F.3d at p. 1133.)

Contrary to Andersen's belief, however, California courts have not embraced the Ninth Circuit's narrow-restraint exception. Indeed, no reported California state court decision has endorsed the Ninth Circuit's reasoning, and we are of the view that California courts "have been clear in their expression that section 16600 represents a strong public policy of the state which should not be diluted by judicial fiat." (Scott v. Snelling and Snelling, Inc. (N.D. Cal. 1990) 732 F. Supp. 1034, 1042.) Section 16600 is unambiguous, and if the Legislature intended the statute to apply only to restraints that were unreasonable or overbroad, it could have included language to that effect. We reject Andersen's contention that we should adopt a narrow-restraint exception to section 16600 and leave it to the Legislature, if it chooses, either to relax the statutory restrictions or adopt additional exceptions to the prohibition-against-restraint rule under section 16600. . . .

Disposition

We hold that the noncompetition agreement here is invalid under section 16600, and we reject the narrow-restraint exception urged by Andersen. Noncompetition agreements are invalid under section 16600 in California even if narrowly drawn, unless they fall within the applicable statutory exceptions of sections 16601, 16602, or 16602.5. . . .

We therefore affirm in part and reverse in part the Court of Appeal judgment, and remand the matter for proceedings consistent with the views expressed above.

Comprehensive Technologies Int'l v. Software Artisans, Inc., 3 F.3d 730 (4th Cir. 1993). CTI brought suit for copyright infringement and misappropriation of trade secrets against a group of former employees who left the company to form a competing company, which shortly thereafter came out with a new product. The court concluded that the departing employees had not infringed CTI's copyrights or misappropriated any CTI trade secrets. Nonetheless, the court enforced an agreement signed by one of the employees, Dean Hawkes. The agreement provided that for a period of 12 months after he left CTI, Hawkes would not

> engage directly or indirectly in any business within the United States (financially as an investor or lender or as an employee, director, officer, partner, independent contractor, consultant or owner or in any other capacity calling for the rendition of personal services or acts of management, operation or control) which is in competition with the business of

> CTI. For purposes of this Agreement, the "business of CTI" shall be defined as the design, development, marketing, and sales of CLAIMS EXPRESS- and EDI LINK-type PC-based software with the same functionality and methodology. . . .

The court stated the general legal standard governing covenants not to compete:

> Virginia has established a three-part test for assessing the reasonableness of restrictive employment covenants. Under the test, the court must ask the following questions:
>
> (1) Is the restraint, from the standpoint of the employer, reasonable in the sense that it is no greater than is necessary to protect the employer in some legitimate business interest?
> (2) From the standpoint of the employee, is the restraint reasonable in the sense that it is not unduly harsh and oppressive in curtailing his legitimate efforts to earn a livelihood?
> (3) Is the restraint reasonable from the standpoint of a sound public policy?
>
> Blue Ridge Anesthesia & Critical Care, Inc. v. Gidick, 239 Va. 369, 389 S.E.2d 467, 469 (Va. 1990). If a covenant not to compete meets each of these standards of reasonableness, it must be enforced. As a general rule, however, the Virginia courts do not look favorably upon covenants not to compete, and will strictly construe them against the employer. The employer bears the burden of demonstrating that the restraint is reasonable.

The court found that Hawkes's agreement, which prevented him from competing with CTI anywhere in the United States, was reasonable because CTI had offices, clients, or prospects in many (though not all) states throughout the country. Further, the court noted:

> . . . As the individual primarily responsible for the design, development, marketing and sale of CTI's software, Hawkes became intimately familiar with every aspect of CTI's operation, and necessarily acquired information that he could use to compete with CTI in the marketplace. When an employee has access to confidential and trade secret information crucial to the success of the employer's business, the employer has a strong interest in enforcing a covenant not to compete because other legal remedies often prove inadequate. It will often be difficult, if not impossible, to prove that a competing employee has misappropriated trade secret information belonging to his former employer. On the facts of this case, we conclude that the scope of the employment restrictions is no broader than necessary to protect CTI's legitimate business interests.

COMMENTS AND QUESTIONS

1. The California rule set out in section 16600 is the minority rule. Most states apply an overarching requirement of "reasonableness" to covenants not to compete, as the Virginia court did in *CTI. See* MICH. COMP. LAWS § 445.774a (noncompetition agreements enforceable if the agreement is "reasonable as to its duration, geographical area, and type of employment or line of business"). They may disagree, however, on what restrictions are reasonable. In Gateway 2000 Inc. v. Kelley, 9 F. Supp. 2d 790 (E.D. Mich. 1998), the court invalidated an agreement that was similar to the one upheld in *CTI.* The court relied in part on the fact that the company had later adopted a less restrictive noncompetition provision, suggesting that the older, broader provision was not necessary to protect its interests. And the Virginia Supreme

Court has held unreasonable a noncompetition agreement that prevented the defendant from working for a competitor in any capacity, rather than specifying particular positions the defendant could not take. Modern Environments, Inc. v. Stinnett, 561 S.E.2d 694 (Va. 2002).

Some courts have limited the enforcement of noncompetition agreements to situations where trade secrets are likely to be used or disclosed if an employee is allowed to compete. The New York Court of Appeals, for example, took the following view:

> Undoubtedly judicial disfavor of these covenants is provoked by "powerful considerations of public policy which militate against sanctioning the loss of a man's livelihood" (*Purchasing Assoc. v. Weitz. . . .*) Indeed, our economy is premised on the competition engendered by the uninhibited flow of services, talent and ideas. Therefore, no restrictions should fetter an employee's right to apply to his own best advantage the skills and knowledge acquired by the overall experience of his previous employment. This includes those techniques which are but "skillful variations of general processes known to the particular trade" (RESTATEMENT, AGENCY 2D, § 396 Comment *b*).
>
> Of course, the courts must also recognize the legitimate interest an employer has in safeguarding that which has made his business successful and to protect himself against deliberate surreptitious commercial piracy. Thus restrictive covenants will be enforceable to the extent necessary to prevent the disclosure or use of trade secrets or confidential customer information. In addition injunctive relief may be available where an employee's services are unique or extraordinary and the covenant is reasonable. This latter principle has been interpreted to reach agreements between members of the learned professions.

Reed Roberts Assocs. v. Strauman, 40 N.Y.2d 303, 353 N.E.2d 590 (Ct. App. 1976). Does the *Reed Roberts* approach in essence hold noncompetition agreements unenforceable, since it allows them to operate only when trade secret laws also provide relief? Are there sound reasons to enforce an employer-employee agreement that prevents the employee from competing after termination? State statutes that address the issue have generally been interpreted to allow such "reasonable" employee agreements, regardless of how the statutes themselves are worded. Of course, what agreements are "reasonable" is far from clear in this context, and is the subject of considerable litigation. Many states have invalidated noncompetition agreements on the ground that they were unreasonable. *See, e.g.*, Mutual Service Casualty Ins. Co. v. Brass, 625 N.W.2d 648 (Wisc. App. 2001); Brentlinger Enters. v. Curran, 752 N.E.2d 994 (Ohio App. 2001); Harvey Barnett, Inc. v. Shidler, 143 F. Supp. 2d 1247 (D. Colo. 2001); Mertz v. Pharmacists Mutual Ins., 625 N.W.2d 197 (Neb. 2001); City Slickers, Inc. v. Douglas, 40 S.W.3d 805 (Ark. App. 2001).

2. The New York Court of Appeals interpreted *Reed Roberts* in a somewhat narrower fashion in BDO Seidman v. Hirshberg, 690 N.Y.S.2d 854 (Ct. App. 1999). Hirshberg, an accountant employed by BDO Seidman, had agreed that if he served a former client of BDO's Buffalo, New York, office within 18 months of the termination of his employment, "he would compensate BDO 'for the loss and damages suffered' in an amount equal to 1 1/2 times the fees BDO had charged that client over the last fiscal year of the client's patronage." *Id.* at 387. Hirshberg left the firm in 1993. BDO filed suit, claiming that in the year after Hirshberg's departure he had billed $138,000 worth of business to 100 former BDO clients. (Hirshberg countered that he had brought many of the clients to BDO himself, and that with respect to others he had not been the primary contact person at BDO.) The court noted, first, that while the agreement did not literally prevent the

defendant from competing against the plaintiff, its purpose and effect was indistinguishable from a noncompete. *See id.* at 388. The court also noted that in *Reed Roberts* it had strictly limited the enforceability of noncompetes. *See id.* Nevertheless, the court appeared open to the possibility that in some cases noncompetes among professionals (including accountants)[17] might be more broadly enforceable:

> With agreements not to compete between professionals, however, we have given greater weight to the interests of the employer in restricting competition within a confined geographical area. In Gelder Med. Group v. Webber, 41 N.Y.2d 680, 394 N.Y.S.2d 867, 363 N.E.2d 573, and Karpinski v. Ingrasci, 28 N.Y.2d 45, 320 N.Y.S.2d 1, 268 N.E.2d 751, we enforced total restraints on competition, in limited rural locales, permanently in *Karpinski* and for five years in *Gelder*. The rationale for the differential application of the common-law rule of reasonableness expressed in our decisions was that professionals are deemed to provide "unique or extraordinary" services (see Reed, Roberts Assocs. v. Strauman, supra, 40 N.Y.2d, at 308, 386 N.Y.S.2d 677, 353 N.E.2d 590).

On the facts of the case, however, the agreement nevertheless was only partly enforceable:

> This Court's rationale for giving wider latitude to covenants between members of a learned profession because their services are unique or extraordinary (Reed, Roberts Assocs. v. Strauman, supra) does not realistically apply to the actual context of the anti-competitive agreement here. In the instant case, BDO is a national accounting firm seeking to enforce the agreement within a market consisting of the entirety of a major metropolitan area. Moreover, defendant's unchallenged averments indicate that his status in the firm was not based upon the uniqueness or extraordinary nature of the accounting services he generally performed on behalf of the firm, but in major part on his ability to attract a corporate clientele. Nor was there any proof that defendant possessed any unique or extraordinary ability as an accountant that would give him a competitive advantage over BDO. Moreover, the contexts of the agreements not to compete in *Karpinski* and *Gelder Medical Group* were entirely different. In each case, the former associate would have been in direct competition with the promisee-practitioner for referrals from a narrow group of primary health providers in a rural geographical market for their medical or dental practice specialty.
>
> Thus, our learned profession precedents do not obviate the need for independent scrutiny of the anti-competitive provisions of the Manager's Agreement under the tripartite common-law standard. Close analysis of paragraph SIXTH of the agreement under the first prong of the common-law rule, to identify the legitimate interest of BDO and determine whether the covenant is no more restrictive than is necessary to protect that interest, leads us to conclude that the covenant as written is overbroad in some respects. BDO claims that the legitimate interest it is entitled to protect is its entire client base, which it asserts a modern, large accounting firm expends considerable time and money building and maintaining. However, the only justification for imposing an employee agreement not to compete is to forestall unfair competition (see Columbia Ribbon & Carbon Mfg. Co. v. A-I-A Corp., 42 N.Y.2d, supra, at 499, 398 N.Y.S.2d 1004, 369 N.E.2d 4). It seems self-evident that a former employee may be capable of fairly competing for an employer's clients by refraining from use of unfair means to compete. If the employee abstains from unfair means in competing for those clients, the employer's

17. But not lawyers. *See BDO Seidman*, 690 N.Y.S.2d at 857 n.1 ("Law firm partnership agreements represent an exception to the liberality with which we have previously treated restraints on competition in the learned professions").

interest in preserving its client base against the competition of the former employee is no more legitimate and worthy of contractual protection than when it vies with unrelated competitors for those clients.

Legal scholars and courts have more circumspectly identified the employer's legitimate interest in employee anti-competitive agreements than that of preservation of the employer's entire client base where, as here, there is no evidence that the employee obtained a competitive advantage by using confidential information. Professor Blake, in his seminal article in the *Harvard Law Review*, explains that the legitimate purpose of an employer in connection with employee restraints is "to prevent competitive use, for a time, of information or relationships which pertain peculiarly to the employer and which the employee acquired in the course of the employment" (Blake, op. cit., at 647 [emphasis supplied]). Protection of customer relationships the employee acquired in the course of employment may indeed be a legitimate interest (id., at 653). "The risk to the employer reaches a maximum in situations in which the employee must work closely with the client or customer over a long period of time, especially when his services are a significant part of the total transaction" (id., at 661). Then, the employee has been enabled to share in the goodwill of a client or customer which the employer's over-all efforts and expenditures created. The employer has a legitimate interest in preventing former employees from exploiting or appropriating the goodwill of a client or customer, which had been created and maintained at the employer's expense, to the employer's competitive detriment (see, Technical Aid Corp. v. Allen, supra, 134 N.H., at 9, 591 A.2d, at 266; Peat Marwick Main & Co. v. Haass, 818 S.W.2d 381, 387 [Tex. Sup. Ct.]).

It follows from the foregoing that BDO's legitimate interest here is protection against defendant's competitive use of client relationships which BDO enabled him to acquire through his performance of accounting services for the firm's clientele during the course of his employment (Blake, op. cit., at 647-661). Extending the anti-competitive covenant to BDO's clients with whom a relationship with defendant did not develop through assignments to perform direct, substantive accounting services would, therefore, violate the first prong of the common-law rule: it would constitute a restraint "greater than is needed to protect" these legitimate interests (Restatement [Second] of Contracts § 188[1][a]). . . .

To the extent, then, that paragraph SIXTH of the Manager's Agreement requires defendant to compensate BDO for lost patronage of clients with whom he never acquired a relationship through the direct provision of substantive accounting services during his employment, the covenant is invalid and unenforceable. By a parity of reasoning, it would be unreasonable to extend the covenant to personal clients of defendant who came to the firm solely to avail themselves of his services and only as a result of his own independent recruitment efforts, which BDO neither subsidized nor otherwise financially supported as part of a program of client development. Because the goodwill of those clients was not acquired through the expenditure of BDO's resources, the firm has no legitimate interest in preventing defendant from competing for their patronage. Indeed, enforcement of the restrictive covenant as to defendant's personal clients would permit BDO to appropriate goodwill created and maintained through defendant's efforts, essentially turning on its head the principal justification to uphold any employee agreement not to compete based on protection of customer or client relationships.

Except for the overbreadth in the foregoing two respects, the restrictions in paragraph SIXTH do not violate the tripartite common-law test for reasonableness. The restraint on serving BDO clients is limited to 18 months, and to clients of BDO's Buffalo office. The time constraint appears to represent a reasonably brief interlude to enable the firm to replace the client relationship and goodwill defendant was permitted to acquire with some of its clients. Defendant is free to compete immediately for new business in any market and, if the overbroad provisions of the covenant are struck, to retain his personal clients and those clients of BDO's that he had not served to any significant extent

> while employed at the firm. He has averred that BDO's list of lost accounts contains a number of clients in both categories. Thus, there is scant evidence suggesting that the covenant, if cured of overbreadth, would work an undue hardship on defendant.
>
> Moreover, given the likely broad array of accounting services available in the greater Buffalo area, and the limited remaining class of BDO clientele affected by the covenant, it cannot be said that the restraint, as narrowed, would seriously impinge on the availability of accounting services in the Buffalo area from which the public may draw, or cause any significant dislocation in the market or create a monopoly in accounting services in that locale. These factors militate against a conclusion that a reformed paragraph SIXTH would violate the third prong of the common-law test, injury to the public interest (see Gelder Med. Group v. Webber, supra, 41 N.Y.2d, at 685, 394 N.Y.S.2d 867, 363 N.E.2d 573; Blake, op. cit., at 686-687; Restatement [Second] of Contracts § 188, comment g). . . .

The court then proceeded to sever the enforceable from the unenforceable portions of the contract. States differ in their approach to the severability issue, with some permitting courts to enforce the divisible portions of a noncompete; others permitting them even to rewrite the offensive portions so as to render them enforceable (e.g., by changing the term from an overly long to an acceptable time period); and others striking the covenant in its entirety if any portion of it is unenforceable. For discussion, *see, e.g.*, Michael J. Garrison & John T. Wendt, *The Evolving Law of Employee Noncompete Agreements: Recent Trends and an Alternative Policy Approach*, 45 Am. Bus. L.J. 57 (2007); *see also* Star Direct, Inc. v. Del Pra, 767 N.W.2d 898 (Wis. 2009) (discussing different approaches taken by the Wisconsin state courts over the years).

3. In *Comprehensive Technologies*, there seems to be no question in the court's mind that none of the defendants misappropriated any CTI trade secrets, infringed any copyrights, or otherwise "took" anything belonging to CTI in starting Software Artisans. Why doesn't that dispose of the case? What social purpose is served by enjoining former employees from pursuing their livelihood? Shouldn't the mobility and liberty of individuals be the paramount consideration, as California courts have suggested?

4. Despite the absolute nature of the California statute, California courts have interpreted this statute to bar noncompetition agreements altogether in employee contracts but to permit such agreements if they are ancillary to the sale of a business, so long as the terms of the agreement are "reasonable." *See* Monogram Indus., Inc. v. SAR Indus., Inc., 64 Cal. App. 3d 692, 134 Cal. Rptr. 714, 718 (1976). Further, while California courts will not enforce a noncompetition agreement, they will prevent departing employees from using or disclosing their former employer's trade secrets. *See* State Farm Mutual Automobile Ins. Co. v. Dempster, 344 P.2d 821 (Cal. App. 1959); Gordon v. Landau, 49 Cal. 2d 690, 321 P.2d 456 (Cal. 1958). Other states, including Alabama, Louisiana, Montana, and North Dakota, also forbid noncompetition agreements. Still other states, including Colorado, Delaware, Massachusetts, and Tennessee, forbid them in professional settings but allow them in other contexts. *See, e.g.*, Murfreesboro Med. Clinic v. Udom, 166 S.W.3d 674 (Tenn. 2005). *But see* Central Indiana Podiatry PC v. Krueger, 882 N.E.2d 723 (Ind. 2008) (noncompete agreement enforceable against physician if reasonable).

5. The strength of California's commitment to the free movement of employees was demonstrated in The Application Group, Inc. v. The Hunter Group, Inc., 72 Cal. Rptr. 2d 73 (Ct. App. 1998). There, the California Court of Appeals held that § 16600 precluded the enforcement of a noncompetition agreement entered into in Maryland between a Maryland employer and employee, where the employee subsequently left to

take a job telecommuting from Maryland for a California company. Despite the fact that Maryland courts would enforce the agreement, the California court concluded that California's interests were "materially stronger" than Maryland's in this case. *See also* D'Sa v. Playhut, Inc., 85 Cal. App. 4th 927, 102 Cal. Rptr. 2d 495 (2000) (disregarding choice of law provision in holding a noncompete agreement unenforceable).

California's strong public policy has led to conflicts with other states. The most notable example is Advanced Bionics v. Medtronic, 87 Cal. App. 4th 1235 (2001), in which both California and Minnesota courts asserted that their law should control, with the Minnesota court enjoining the departing employee and the California court enjoining the employer from proceeding with the suit. The California Supreme Court ultimately reversed, not because it didn't consider the policy of employee mobility important but because it thought the specter of conflicting judgments unseemly. Advanced Bionics v. Medtronic, 29 Cal. 4th 697, 128 Cal. Rptr. 2d 172 (2002). But doing so may simply subjugate California's policy to the law of any other state that would enforce a noncompete agreement, even if the employee doesn't work in that state. *See* IBM Corp. v. Bajorek, 191 F.3d 1033 (9th Cir. 1999) (applying New York law to enjoin competition against New York company by employee in California, and disregarding California policy to the contrary). For a contrary ruling giving nationwide effect to a refusal to enforce a noncompete agreement under Georgia law, see Palmer & Cay v. Marsh & McLennan, 404 F.3d 1297 (11th Cir. 2005).

Is there a reasoned way to resolve such conflicts in public policy? Or will the inevitable result be a "race to the courthouse"?

6. What are the competing policy interests at stake in noncompetition clauses? On the one hand, such restrictions seem onerous burdens to impose on employees. Imagine how you would feel as an attorney if you left a firm only to find that you were prevented from practicing law in the same field or geographic region for the next two years. (In this regard, it is significant that even *Reed Roberts* expressed the view that the "learned professions" were properly subject to noncompetition agreements.) In addition, it is not completely clear that such provisions benefit companies in the long run. Strauman, the defendant in *Reed Roberts*, came to Reed Roberts after having worked for a competitor for four years. He was hired in part because of his valuable experience in the industry. What if Strauman's former employer had required him to sign an enforceable noncompete agreement?

On the other hand, it seems unfair to employers to simply allow their employees to do whatever they want upon leaving. Particularly where the employees were in positions of importance, their knowledge of the employer's trade secrets may leave the former employer at a competitive disadvantage. In a competitive industry, preventing the disclosure of trade secrets is far preferable to suing for misappropriation after they have already been disclosed. A noncompetition agreement may be a reasonable way for an employer to prevent a problem — and a lawsuit — before it starts. *See* Eden Hannon & Co. v. Sumitomo Trust & Banking Co., 914 F.2d 556 (4th Cir. 1990):

> There are several problems with trying to prevent former employees from illegally using the former employer's trade secrets, and these problems are caused by the status of the law regarding the misappropriation of trade secrets. First . . . it is difficult to prove that the trade secret was actually used. Second, the former employee tends to get "one free bite" at the trade secret. Most courts will refuse to enjoin the disclosure or use of a trade secret until its illegal use is imminent or until it has already occurred. By that time, much of

> the damage may be done. Third, even if a clearly illegal use of the trade secret by a former employee can be shown, most courts will not enjoin that person from working for the competition on that basis. Instead, they will merely enjoin future disclosure of the trade secret. Yet, policing the former employee's compliance with that injunction will be difficult. Finally, even if the employee does not maliciously attempt to use his former employer's trade secrets in the new employer's workplace, avoiding this use can be difficult. It would be difficult for the employee to guard the trade secret of the former employer and be effective for the new employer.

In the views of some other courts and commentators, however, noncompetes are problematic precisely because (as the name suggests) they are anticompetitive in nature. But what exactly does this mean? If noncompetes were anticompetitive in the sense that term is used in antitrust law—that is, if they enabled firms to expand or maintain market power within a given industry, without an offsetting efficiency justification—they would routinely run afoul of federal and state antitrust laws. In fact, however, most noncompetes probably do not enable firms to acquire or maintain market power (roughly, the ability to control price or output in a given market). There appear to be very few cases in which noncompetes have led to the imposition of antitrust liability, and some commentators have argued that the typical noncompete is no more anticompetitive than other types of exclusive dealing arrangements (which are evaluated, and typically withstand scrutiny, under antitrust law's rule of reason). *See, e.g.*, Edmund W. Kitch, *The Law and Economics of Rights in Valuable Information*, 9 J. LEGAL STUD. 683, 387-88 (1980); Maureen B. Callahan, Comment, *Post-Employment Restraint Agreements: A Reassessment*, 52 U. CHI. L. REV. 703, 712-18 (1985). For an overview of some of the economics literature on noncompetes, see Orly Lobel, *Intellectual Property and Restrictive Covenants*, http://ssrn.com/abstract=1226463, at 4-9 (Aug. 17, 2008).

One author has suggested that there is a more practical economic motivation for precluding such noncompetition agreements. She argues that the relative success of California's Silicon Valley compared to Boston's Route 128 is directly attributable to the prevalence of noncompetition agreements in Route 128 companies, which prevented the free movement of employees and therefore discouraged start-up companies. *See* ANNALEE SAXENIAN, REGIONAL ADVANTAGE: CULTURE AND COMPETITION IN SILICON VALLEY AND ROUTE 128 (1994).

7. In states that enforce covenants not to compete, one possible problem is the inconsistency and unpredictability with which different judges might evaluate the reasonableness of similar restraints. To address this problem, in 1996 Florida enacted a statute that governs the enforceability of noncompetes within that state. *See* FLA. STAT. § 542.335. The statute goes into considerable detail concerning what types of justifications for noncompetes qualify as legitimate business interests, and how long in duration a noncompete may last before it becomes presumptively unreasonable. For example, if the noncompete is intended to protect the employer's trade secrets, "a court shall presume reasonable in time any restraint of 5 years or less and shall presume unreasonable in time any restraint of more than 10 years. All such presumptions shall be rebuttable presumptions." FLA. STAT. § 542.335(e). If, on the other hand, an employer seeks to enforce a noncompete against a former employee based on the protection of certain other interests, such as "substantial relationships with specific prospective or existing customers, patients, or clients," the noncompete is presumed reasonable only if it lasts for six months or less, and is presumed unreasonable if it

extends for more than two years. *See id.* § 542.335(d). Interestingly, in determining the enforceability of a noncompete courts are forbidden from considering any individualized economic or other hardship that might accrue to the employee; from employing any rule of contract construction that would require them to construe the contract against the drafter; and from refusing enforcement based on public policy, subject to certain qualifications. *See id.* § 542.335(g), (h), (i).

Does Florida's statutory approach to noncompetes make sense? Is it really reasonable to restrict employees from taking a new job for five years? Is it best that noncompetes be interpreted (relatively) uniformly and predictably, even if the specific time limits set forth in the statute seem somewhat arbitrary? Or does such an approach unduly interfere with a court's equitable discretion or enable employer overreaching?

8. When a firm requires a new employee to sign an employment agreement containing a covenant not to compete, the employee is giving up something substantial. What is the employer giving up? Some cases have raised the issue of consideration (in the contract law sense) in such an agreement on the part of the employer; they generally conclude that there is consideration, on one theory or another. *See, e.g.*, Central Adjustment Bureau v. Ingram, 678 S.W.2d 28 (Tenn. 1984) (consideration in the form of continuous employment over a long period of time); Alex Sheshunoff Mgmt. Servs. v. Johnson, 209 S.W.3d 644, 646 (Tex. 2006) (same; rejecting prior Texas case law).

Why not require, out of fairness, that an employer who insists on such a covenant must pay the employee's salary during the term of the noncompete provision?[18] How would this change the behavior of an ex-employer vis-à-vis the newly departed employee? Would you expect the rate of employee mobility to be higher under such a system?

9. Can an employer avoid state laws restricting noncompetition agreements by requiring the employee to sign an agreement that does not forbid employment, but calls for the payment of a "liquidated damage" penalty if the employee goes to work for a competitor? Is such a monetary penalty effectively the same as enforcing a noncompete?

Note on the "Inevitable Disclosure" of Trade Secrets

Are there circumstances in which an employee's use or disclosure of trade secrets is "inevitable"? On the other hand, the Seventh Circuit ordered the issuance of a preliminary injunction preventing Quaker Oats Co. from employing Redmond, a former general manager for PepsiCo North America. Redmond was general manager of PepsiCo's California business unit for ten years until, in 1994, he accepted Quaker's offer to become the chief operating officer of its Gatorade and Snapple Co. divisions. The court held that Redmond would inevitably be forced to use PepsiCo trade secrets for his new employer:

> PepsiCo asserts that Redmond cannot help but rely on PCNA [PepsiCo North America] trade secrets as he helps plot Gatorade and Snapple's new course, and that these secrets will enable Quaker to achieve a substantial advantage by knowing exactly how

18. German law requires just this. *See Abschn. Handlungsgehilfen and Handlungslehrlinge* § 74, *in* HANDELSGESETZBUCH 27 (2001). In the United States, some companies have adopted such a rule voluntarily. *See* Marcam Corp. v. Orchard, 885 F. Supp. 294 (D. Mass. 1995) (enforcing a contractual provision preventing Orchard from working for any competitor in the country for one year, provided that Marcam paid 110 percent of the salary offered by the competitor).

> PCNA will price, distribute, and market its sports drinks and new age drinks and being able to respond strategically. This type of trade secret problem may arise less often, but it nevertheless falls within the realm of trade secret protection under the present circumstance.
>
> Quaker and Redmond assert that they have not and do not intend to use whatever confidential information Redmond has by virtue of his former employment. They point out that Redmond has already signed an agreement with Quaker not to disclose any trade secrets or confidential information gleaned from his earlier employment. They also note with regard to distribution systems that even if Quaker wanted to steal information about PCNA's distribution plans, they would be completely useless in attempting to integrate the Gatorade and Snapple beverage lines.
>
> The defendants' arguments fall somewhat short of the mark. Again, the danger of misappropriation in the present case is not that Quaker threatens to use PCNA's secrets to create distribution systems or coopt PCNA's advertising and marketing ideas. Rather, PepsiCo believes that Quaker, unfairly armed with knowledge of PCNA's plans, will be able to anticipate its distribution, packaging, pricing, and marketing moves. Redmond and Quaker even concede that Redmond might be faced with a decision that could be influenced by certain confidential information that he obtained while at PepsiCo. In other words, PepsiCo finds itself in the position of a coach, one of whose players has left, playbook in hand, to join the opposing team before the big game. Quaker and Redmond's protestations that their distribution systems and plans are entirely different from PCNA's are thus not really responsive. . . .
>
> Quaker and Redmond do not assert that the confidentiality agreement is invalid; such agreements are enforceable when supported by adequate consideration.[10] Rather, they argue that "inevitable" breaches of these contracts may not be enjoined. The case on which they rely, however, R.R. Donnelley & Sons Co. v. Fagan, 767 F. Supp. 1259 (S.D.N.Y. 1991) (applying Illinois law), says nothing of the sort. The *R.R. Donnelley* court merely found that the plaintiffs had failed to prove the existence of any confidential information or any indication that the defendant would ever use it. Id. at 1267. The threat of misappropriation that drives our holding with regard to trade secrets dictates the same result here.

PepsiCo, Inc. v. Redmond, 54 F.3d 1262, 35 U.S.P.Q.2d 1010 (7th Cir. 1995). The court distinguished two prior cases refusing to find that an ex-employee's disclosure of trade secrets was inevitable:

> In *Teradyne*, Teradyne alleged that a competitor, Clear Communications, had lured employees away from Teradyne and intended to employ them in the same field. In an insightful opinion, Judge Zagel observed that "threatened misappropriation can be enjoined under Illinois law" where there is a "high degree of probability of inevitable and immediate . . . use of . . . trade secrets." *Teradyne*, 707 F. Supp. at 356. Judge Zagel held, however, that Teradyne's complaint failed to state a claim because Teradyne did not allege "that defendants have in fact threatened to use Teradyne's secrets or that they will inevitably do so." [The *Teradyne* court held]:
>
> > the defendants' claimed acts, working for Teradyne, knowing its business, leaving its business, hiring employees from Teradyne and entering the same field (though in a market not yet serviced by Teradyne) do not state a claim of threatened misappropriation. All that is

10. The confidentiality agreement is also not invalid for want of a time limitation. *See* 765 ILCS 1065/8(b)(1) ("[A] contractual or other duty to maintain secrecy or limit use of a trade secret shall not be deemed to be void or unenforceable solely for lack of durational or geographic limitation on the duty."). Nor is there any question that the confidentiality agreement covers much of the information PepsiCo fears Redmond will necessarily use in his new employment with Quaker.

> alleged, at bottom, is that defendants could misuse plaintiff's secrets, and plaintiffs fear they will. This is not enough. It may be that little more is needed, but falling a little short is still falling short.

Id. at 357.

In *AMP* we affirmed the denial of a preliminary injunction on the grounds that the plaintiff AMP had failed to show either the existence of any trade secrets or the likelihood that defendant Fleischhacker, a former AMP employee, would compromise those secrets or any other confidential business information. AMP, which produced electrical and electronic connection devices, argued that Fleischhacker's new position at AMP's competitor would inevitably lead him to compromise AMP's trade secrets regarding the manufacture of connectors. *AMP*, 823 F.2d at 1207. In rejecting that argument, we emphasized that the mere fact that a person assumed a similar position at a competitor does not, without more, make it "inevitable that he will use or disclose . . . trade secret information" so as to "demonstrate irreparable injury." Id.

The ITSA, *Teradyne*, and *AMP* lead to the same conclusion: a plaintiff may prove a claim of trade secret misappropriation by demonstrating that defendant's new employment will inevitably lead him to rely on the plaintiff's trade secrets. See also 1 Jager, . . . §7.02[2][a] at 7-20 (noting claims where "the allegation is based on the fact that the disclosure of trade secrets in the new employment is inevitable, whether or not the former employee acts consciously or unconsciously"). . . .

PepsiCo presented substantial evidence at the preliminary injunction hearing that Redmond possessed extensive and intimate knowledge about PCNA's strategic goals for 1995 in sports drinks and new age drinks. The district court concluded on the basis of that presentation that unless Redmond possessed an uncanny ability to compartmentalize information, he would necessarily be making decisions about Gatorade and Snapple by relying on his knowledge of PCNA trade secrets. It is not the "general skills and knowledge acquired during his tenure with" PepsiCo that PepsiCo seeks to keep from falling into Quaker's hands, but rather "the particularized plans or processes developed by [PCNA] and disclosed to him while the employer-employee relationship existed, which are unknown to others in the industry and which give the employer an advantage over his competitors." *AMP*, 823 F.2d at 1202. The *Teradyne* and *AMP* plaintiffs could do nothing more than assert that skilled employees were taking their skills elsewhere; PepsiCo has done much more.

Id.

COMMENTS AND QUESTIONS

1. What Pepsi trade secrets are threatened by Redmond's "defection" to Quaker? The information Redmond possesses includes (1) new flavor and product packaging information; (2) pricing strategies; (3) Pepsi's "attack plans" for specific markets; and (4) Pepsi's new distribution plan, being pilot tested in California. What advantages would Quaker obtain by knowing this information? How long would it take Quaker to find out about each in the absence of inside knowledge from Redmond? If all these items would become readily apparent the moment Pepsi's plans were implemented, does this circumstance suggest a limit on the appropriate remedy?

Assuming that Quaker will learn of Pepsi's strategies from Redmond unless enjoined, how expensive would it be for Pepsi to develop a new marketing strategy? Could the new strategy take advantage of the fact that Quaker *thinks* it knows what Pepsi will do? How would this possibility affect Quaker's use of the information?

2. Assume that the market for sports and new age drinks is increasingly concentrated in the hands of two companies, Pepsi and Quaker. Should this affect the outcome of the case? Given the court's decision, what can one predict about future salary and benefits negotiations in this industry for employees like Redmond?

3. Is it fair to preclude former employees from doing any work for a competitor simply because they would be incapable of not using the information they obtained from their former employer? Note that the Seventh Circuit upheld an injunction against Redmond's employment for only six months. At the same time, the court issued a permanent injunction against the disclosure of Pepsi's trade secrets. Does this result make sense? If the theory of inevitable disclosure is that Redmond *must* use Pepsi's secrets in his employment, could he go to work for Quaker at the end of six months without violating the permanent injunction? Perhaps the court was implicitly seeking to balance Redmond's interests in employment mobility, reasoning that the business secrets would be less important after that time.

4. Is there any way that that employee can "keep separate" the ideas and projects he was working on for his old employer from the ideas and projects he will be asked to develop for his new employer? If not, should the employer be entitled to prevent the employee from competing even if it cannot show that the employee *intends* to use its trade secrets? *Cf.* Al Minor & Assocs. v. Martin, 881 N.E.2d 850 (Ohio 2008) (holding that the fact that a defendant had the plaintiff's secrets in his memory rather than on a disk or document did not preclude a finding of misappropriation).

IBM made just this argument when one of its disk drive specialists, Peter Bonyhard, left IBM to work for Seagate Technology in the same field. A preliminary injunction granted by the district court against Bonyhard's employment was reversed by the Eighth Circuit in an unpublished decision. IBM v. Bonyhard, 962 F.2d 12 (8th Cir. 1992). Several other decisions have also rejected inevitable disclosure as a basis for an injunction against employment. Campbell Soup Co. v. Giles, 47 F.3d 467 (1st Cir. 1995); FMC Corp. v. Cyprus Foote Mineral Co., 899 F. Supp. 1477 (W.D.N.C. 1995). In *Campbell*, the court grounded its rejection of inevitable disclosure theory in the public policy that favors employee mobility. It quoted the district court opinion in the case, holding that public policy "counsels against unilateral conversion of non-disclosure agreements into non-competitive agreements. If Campbell wanted to protect itself against the competition of former employees, it should have done so by contract. This court will not afford such protection after the fact." *See also* Carolina Chem. Equip. Co. v. Muckenfuss, 471 S.E.2d 721 (S.C. App. 1996) (agreement entitled "Covenant Not to Divulge Trade Secrets" was actually an overly broad and unenforceable covenant not to compete, because the definition of trade secrets in the agreement was so broad as to effectively prevent any competition).

The judicial debate over the appropriateness of the inevitable disclosure doctrine has continued. Several cases have followed *PepsiCo* and enjoined employment absent either proof of trade secret misappropriation or an enforceable noncompetition agreement. *See* Uncle B's Bakery v. O'Rourke, 920 F. Supp. 1405 (N.D. Iowa 1996) (enjoining former plant manager at a bagel manufacturer from working for any competing business within a 500-mile radius); National Starch & Chem. Corp. v. Parker Chem. Corp., 530 A.2d 31 (N.J. App. 1997) (citing *PepsiCo* with approval). By contrast, one court has adopted what might be called a "partial inevitable disclosure" injunction. In Merck & Co. v. Lyon, 941 F. Supp. 1443 (M.D.N.C. 1996), the court enjoined a pharmaceutical marketing director from discussing his former employer's products or pricing for a period of two years, but refused to enjoin him from competing employment altogether absent a "showing of bad faith." Another court has accepted an inevitable disclosure theory, but issued an injunction limited to nine months, reasoning that the secrets likely to be disclosed would turn stale over time. Novell Inc. v. Timpanogos Research Group, 46 U.S.P.Q.2d 1197 (D. Utah 1998). And other courts, particularly those in California, continue to reject inevitable disclosure altogether. *See, e.g.*, GlobeSpan, Inc. v. O'Neill, 151 F. Supp. 2d 1229 (C.D. Cal. 2001); Danjaq, LLC v. Sony Corp., 50 U.S.P.Q.2d 1638 (C.D. Cal. 1999), *aff'd on other grounds*, 263 F.3d 942 (9th Cir. 2001); Bayer Corp. v. Roche Molecular Sys., 72 F. Supp. 2d 1111, 1120 (N.D. Cal. 1999); Cardinal Health Staffing Network v. Bowen, 106 S.W.3d 452 (Tex. App. 2004); Del Monte Fresh Produce Co. v. Dole Food Co., 148 F. Supp. 2d 1326, 1337-39 (S.D. Fla. 2001); LeJeune v. Coin Acceptors, 849 A.2d 451 (Md. App. 2004); Whyte v. Schlage Lock Co., 101 Cal. App. 4th 1443, 125 Cal. Rptr. 2d 277 (Ct. App. 2002).

5. From the plaintiff's perspective, how much additional leverage does the inevitable disclosure doctrine really provide? Section 2(a) of the UTSA expressly states that "[a]ctual or *threatened* misappropriation may be enjoined" (emphasis added). Thus, according to some courts, if the plaintiff can prove that the former employee is *likely* to use or disclose the plaintiff's trade secrets in his new job, the plaintiff should be able to prevail on a threatened misappropriation theory. *See* Bimbo Bakeries USA, Inc. v. Botticella, 613 F.3d 102, 114 (3d Cir. 2010) (stating that, under Pennsylvania law, the standard for "determining whether to grant an injunction to prevent the threatened disclosure of trade secrets is not whether a defendant inevitably will disclose a trade secret . . . but instead whether 'there is sufficient likelihood, or substantial threat, of defendant doing so in the future' ") (citations omitted). From this standpoint, requiring the plaintiff to prove that the use or disclosure is *inevitable* might make it more difficult for the plaintiff to prevail. Alternatively, some courts view inevitable disclosure as one way of proving "threatened misappropriation." *See* Interbake Foods, L.L.C. v. Tomasiello, 461 F. Supp. 2d 943, 972-73 (N.D. Iowa 2006) (citing with approval an earlier case holding that "[t]he inevitable disclosure doctrine appears to be aimed at preventing disclosures despite the employee's best intentions, and the threatened disclosure doctrine appears to be aimed at preventing disclosures based on the employee's intentions"; and stating that "inevitable disclosure . . . is just one way of showing a threatened disclosure in cases where additional evidence showing the existence of a substantial threat of impending injury is unavailable to the movant"). Yet another possibility, adopted by some courts, is to characterize inevitable disclosure as a third theory of recovery *in addition to* actual or threatened misappropriation. On this view, even if the plaintiff cannot prove that the former employee is likely to use or disclose (or has already used or disclosed) specific trade secrets in his new job, the plaintiff nevertheless may succeed in showing that the former employee inevitably will rely on his knowledge of the plaintiff's trade secrets when providing advice to his new employer. *See Del Monte*, 184 F. Supp. 2d at 1337-40 (rejecting the inevitable disclosure doctrine, which the court interpreted as a third theory of liability, and holding that threatened misappropriation requires proof of "a substantial threat of impending injury," "inevitability-plus"); Jennifer N. Saulito, Note, *Locating Inevitable Disclosure's Place in Trade Secret Analysis*, 100 MICH. L. REV. 1184 (2002). From this perspective, the inevitable disclosure doctrine, if adopted, would make it easier for the plaintiff to prevail in some cases. Roughly speaking, then, the first theory (as reflected in *Bimbo Bakeries*) suggests that inevitable disclosure is a stricter standard

than is necessary to prove threatened misappropriation; the second and third theories view it as a lower standard. Which view is correct?

In addition, perhaps in some cases involving inevitable disclosure courts would be more likely to grant broad injunctions, forbidding the former employee from taking the new job altogether for a period of time (as in *PepsiCo*) rather than merely from using or disclosing specific trade secrets. Even courts that do not require proof of inevitable disclosure, however, may broadly enjoin the defendant from taking the new job for a period of time. *See Bimbo Bakeries*, 613 F.3d at 112 (noting that "[a]n injunction against employment . . . is simply one weapon in an equity court's arsenal to prevent the threatened misappropriation of trade secrets").

6. Ronald Coase famously argued that, in the absence of transaction costs or other obstacles to bargaining, the initial allocation of rights (or any other default rule) is irrelevant to the attainment of economic efficiency, because the parties to a contemplated transaction can always bargain to the efficient outcome. *See* Ronald Coase, *The Problem of Social Cost*, 3 J.L. & Econ. 1 (1960). The initial allocation of rights may matter for distributional justice reasons, however. And when transaction costs (or other bargaining obstacles) *are* present—that is to say, in many real-world settings—the initial allocation can matter because (among other reasons) departing from that allocation may be prohibitively costly.

What implications might the Coase Theorem have for the inevitable disclosure doctrine? Consider: In practical terms, the inevitable disclosure doctrine creates a sort of noncompete agreement by default, one that cannot be changed by contract. Creating such a mandatory rule might make sense if we think it would be more costly to require parties who would voluntarily bargain *for* a noncompete to do so formally than it would be to require parties who would *not* agree to a noncompete to bargain the default rule away. But is this likely to be the case? On the one hand, for those parties who would likely agree to a noncompete the inevitable disclosure might conserve on transaction costs a bit by making it less important for them to reach a formal agreement. But the reduction in costs may be small or nonexistent if the employer would have imposed a noncompete agreement as a matter of course anyway. On the other hand, if the privately efficient outcome would be the *absence* of a noncompete, the inevitable disclosure doctrine in effect gives the parties something they wouldn't have bargained for voluntarily *and probably cannot easily bargain away.* Can you imagine an employee negotiating for the inclusion in his or her job contract of a promise on the part of the employer not to enforce the inevitable disclosure doctrine at some point in the distant future? Would such an agreement be enforceable in any event? If this analysis is correct, it suggests that the inevitable disclosure is less efficient than would be a rule that requires parties to negotiate a noncompete *ex ante* if doing so is in their mutual interest.

Note on Nonsolicitation Agreements

If the departing employees can avoid using the employer's trade secrets when they leave, the question becomes a rather different one—is it acceptable to hire away a group of employees? In Diodes, Inc. v. Franzen, 260 Cal. App. 2d 244, 67 Cal. Rptr. 19 (1968), the president and vice-president of Diodes left to form a competing company, called Semtech. Before they left, the officers solicited a number of Diodes employees to join them. Diodes sued the departing employees, alleging a number of claims centering on unfair competition and breach of fiduciary duty. The court dismissed the complaint, stating:

> As a general principle, one who unjustifiably interferes with an advantageous business relationship to another's damage may be held liable therefor. The product is bottled under a variety of labels, including unfair competition, interference with advantageous relations, contract interference, and inducing breach of contract.
>
> Even though the relationship between an employer and his employee is an advantageous one, no actionable wrong is committed by a competitor who solicits his competitor's employees or who hires away one or more of his competitor's employees who are not under contract, so long as the inducement to leave is not accompanied by unlawful action. In the employee situation the courts are concerned not solely with the interests of the competing employers, but also with the employee's interest. The interests of the employee in his own mobility and betterment are deemed paramount to the competitive business interests of the employers, where neither the employee nor his new employer has committed any illegal act accompanying the employment change.

67 Cal. Rptr. at 25-26 (citations omitted). *See also* Reeves v. Hanlon, 33 Cal. 4th 1140 (2004) (a competitor who uses only lawful means to solicit at-will employees does not tortiously interfere with economic advantage).

Can employers change this result by forcing their employees to sign "nonsolicitation agreements" that prevent a departing employee from soliciting other employees to join him? What if such agreements also prohibit departing employees from soliciting their former customers? In a case that has been heavily criticized on other grounds, the Ninth Circuit has upheld (albeit without discussion) an injunction against solicitation of employees or customers based on such a nonsolicitation agreement. *See* MAI Systems Corp. v. Peak Computing, Inc., 991 F.2d 511, 523 (9th Cir. 1993). Other courts and commentators take a more guarded approach, prohibiting solicitation only where there is active inducement or where departing employees have taken a customer list that is itself a trade secret. *Cf.* James H.A. Pooley, *Restrictive Employee Covenants in California*, 4 Santa Clara Computer & High Tech. L.J. 251, 259 (1988).

Should former employees be allowed to compete for the business of their old customers? Should they be allowed to hire away their coworkers? Does your answer depend on whether the employees are using trade secrets in the solicitation? On whether the employee has signed a nonsolicitation agreement?

Should the dominance of the employer in the industry matter? In Wood v. Acordia of West Virginia, 2005 WL 1567337 (W. Va. 2005), the court upheld a two-year agreement preventing insurance agents from soliciting any of Acordia's current, former, or prospective customers. In dissent, Justice Starcher pointed out that Acordia was so dominant in the West Virginia insurance market that "every prospect in the market has been spoken for by an Acordia salesman." The agreement at issue thus effectively prevents all competition.

PROBLEM

Problem 11-17. You have been offered a position with a high-technology start-up company. They ask you to sign the following agreement. Do you sign it? Is it enforceable?

EMPLOYMENT, CONFIDENTIAL INFORMATION, AND INVENTION ASSIGNMENT AGREEMENT

As a condition of my employment with Science Company, its subsidiaries, affiliates, successors, or assigns (together the "Company"), and in consideration of my employment with the Company and my receipt of the compensation now and hereafter paid to me by the Company, I agree to the following:

1. Confidential Information

(a) *Company Information.* I agree at all times during the term of my employment and thereafter, to hold in strictest confidence, and not to use, except for the benefit of the Company, or to disclose to any person, firm, or corporation without written authorization of the Board of Directors of the Company, any Confidential Information of the Company. I understand that "**Confidential Information**" means any Company proprietary information, technical data, trade secrets or know-how, including, but not limited to, research, product plans, products, services, customer lists and customers (including, but not limited to, customers of the Company on whom I called or with whom I became acquainted during the term of my employment), markets, software, developments, inventions, processes, formulas, technology, designs, drawings, engineering, hardware configuration information, marketing, finances, or other business information disclosed to me by the Company either directly or indirectly in writing, orally, or by drawings or observation of parts or equipment. I further understand that Confidential Information does not include any of the foregoing items which has become publicly known and made generally available through no wrongful act of mine or of others who were under confidentiality obligations as to the item or items involved.

(b) *Third Party Information.* I recognize that the Company has received and in the future will receive from third parties their confidential or proprietary information subject to a duty on the Company's part to maintain the confidentiality of such information and to use it only for certain limited purposes. I agree to hold all such confidential or proprietary information in the strictest confidence and not to disclose it to any person, firm, or corporation or to use it except as necessary in carrying out my work for the Company consistent with the Company's agreement with such third party.

2. Inventions

I agree that I will promptly make full written disclosure to the Company, will hold in trust for the sole right and benefit of the Company, and hereby assign to the Company, or its designee, all my right, title, and interest in and to any and all inventions, original works of authorship, developments, concepts, improvements or trade secrets, whether or not patentable or registrable under copyright or similar laws, which I may solely or jointly conceive or develop or reduce to practice, or cause to be conceived or developed or reduced to practice (collectively referred to as "Inventions"), during the period of time I am in the employ of the Company and for three months thereafter, except as provided below. I further acknowledge that all original works of authorship which are made by me (solely or jointly with others) within the scope of and during the period of my employment with the Company and which are protectable by copyright are "works made for hire," as that term is defined in the United States Copyright Act.

3. Conflicting Employment

I agree that, during the term of my employment with the Company and for a period of one year thereafter, I will not engage in any other employment, occupation, consulting, or other business activity in competition with or directly related to the business in which the Company is now involved or becomes involved during the term of my employment, nor will I engage in any other activities that conflict with my obligations to the Company.

4. Returning Company Documents

I agree that at the time of leaving the employ of the Company, I will deliver to the Company (and will not keep in my possession, recreate or deliver to anyone else) any and all devices, records, data, notes, reports, proposals, lists, correspondence, specifications, drawings, blueprints, sketches, materials, equipment, other documents or property, or reproductions of any aforementioned items developed by me pursuant to my employment with the Company or otherwise belonging to the Company, its successors or assigns.

5. Notification to New Employer

In the event that I leave the employ of the Company, I hereby grant consent to notification by the Company to my new employer about my rights and obligations under this Agreement.

6. Solicitation of Employees

I agree that for a period of twelve (12) months immediately following the termination of my relationship with the Company for any reason, whether with or without cause, I shall not either directly or indirectly solicit, induce, recruit or encourage any of the Company's employees to leave their employment, or take away such employees, or attempt to solicit, induce, recruit, encourage, or take away employees of the Company, either for myself or for any other person or entity.

D. AGREEMENTS TO KEEP SECRETS

As we have seen, trade secret law imposes certain limitations on the owner of a trade secret. To qualify for trade secret protection, information must not be generally known, must be valuable, and must not be disclosed. But can an owner of information avoid those restrictions by requiring others to *agree* to keep the information secret, whether or not the information meets the requirements for protection? The question is fundamental in intellectual property law.

Licenses are generally considered good from an economic standpoint because they promote efficiency. The company (or individual) that develops a new product may not be in the best position to market it, particularly if the invention has uses in several different fields. Absent licenses, that company would either have to sell the product outright, use it incompletely or inefficiently, enter a new field itself, or not use it at all. Private contract remedies allow the market to reorder itself efficiently and still determine the appropriate reward for invention. But we cannot always rely on the market to determine an efficient outcome. Indeed, intellectual property in general is an example of pervasive market failure, a failure that may color the role of contract law.

Warner-Lambert Pharmaceutical Co. v. John J. Reynolds, Inc.
178 F. Supp. 655 (S.D.N.Y. 1959)

BRYAN, District Judge.

Plaintiff sues under the Federal Declaratory Judgment Act, 28 U.S.C. §§ 2201 and 2202, for a judgment declaring that it is no longer obligated to make periodic payments to defendants based on its manufacture or sale of the well known product "Listerine," under agreements made between Dr. J.J. Lawrence and J.W. Lambert in 1881, and between Dr. Lawrence and Lambert Pharmacal Company in 1885. Plaintiff also seeks to recover the payments made to defendants pursuant to these agreements since the commencement of the action.

Plaintiff is a Delaware corporation which manufactures and sells Listerine, among other pharmaceutical products. It is the successor in interest to Lambert and Lambert Pharmacal Company which acquired the formula for Listerine from Dr. Lawrence under the agreements in question. Defendants are the successors in interest to Dr. Lawrence.

Jurisdiction is based on diversity of citizenship.

For some seventy-five years plaintiff and its predecessors have been making the periodic payments based on the quantity of Listerine manufactured or sold which are called for by the agreements in suit. The payments have totaled more than twenty-two million dollars and are presently in excess of one million five hundred thousand dollars yearly. . . .

[J.J. Lawrence developed the formula for Listerine in 1880. He licensed the secret formula exclusively to Lambert (later Warner-Lambert) in 1881 under a contract which provided that

> I, Jordan Lambert, hereby agree for myself, my heirs, executors and assigns to pay monthly to Dr. Lawrence, his heirs, executors or assigns, the sum of twenty dollars for each and every gross of said Listerine hereafter sold by myself, my heirs, executors or assigns.

The amount was reduced by subsequent agreement to $6.00 per gross.]

The agreements between the parties contemplated, it is alleged, "the periodic payment of royalties to Lawrence for the use of a trade secret, to wit, the secret formula for" Listerine. After some modifications made with Lawrence's knowledge and approval, the formula was introduced on the market. The composition of the compound has remained the same since then and it is still being manufactured and sold by the plaintiff.

It is then alleged that the "trade secret" (the formula for Listerine) has gradually become a matter of public knowledge through the years following 1881 and prior to 1949, and has been published in the United States Pharmacopo[e]ia, the National Formulary and the Journal of the American Medical Association, and also as a result of proceedings brought against plaintiff's predecessor by the Federal Trade Commission. Such publications were not the fault of plaintiff or its predecessors. . . .

(1)

The plaintiff seems to feel that the 1881 and 1885 agreements are indefinite and unclear, at least as to the length of time during which they would continue in effect. I do not find them to be so. These agreements seem to me to be plain and unambiguous. . . .

The obligation to pay on each and every gross of Listerine continues as long as this preparation is manufactured or sold by Lambert and his successors. It comes to an end when they cease to manufacture or sell the preparation. . . . The plain meaning of the language used in these agreements is simply that Lambert's obligation to pay is co-extensive with manufacture or sale of Listerine by him and his successors. . . .

(3)

However, plaintiff urges with vigor that the agreement must be differently construed because it involved the conveyance of a secret formula. The main thrust of its argument is that despite the language which the parties used the court must imply a limitation upon Lambert's obligation to pay measured by the length of time that the Listerine formula remained secret.

To sustain this theory plaintiff relies upon a number of cases involving the obligations of licensees of copyrights or patents to make continuing payments to the owner or licensor, and argues that these cases are controlling here. . . .

. . . [A]ll [these cases hold] is that when parties agree upon a license under a patent or copyright the court will assume, in the absence of express language to the contrary, that their actual intention as to the term is measured by the definite term of the underlying grant fixed by statute.

It is quite plain that were it not for the patent and copyright features of such license agreements the term would be measured by use. . . .

In the patent and copyright cases the parties are dealing with a fixed statutory term and the monopoly granted by that term. This monopoly, created by Congress, is designed to preserve exclusivity in the grantee during the statutory term and to release the patented or copyrighted material to the general public for general use thereafter. This is the public policy of the statutes in reference to which such contracts are made and it is against this background that the parties to patent and copyright license agreements contract.

Here, however, there is no such public policy. The parties are free to contract with respect to a secret formula or trade secret in any manner which they determine for their own best interests. A secret formula or trade secret may remain secret indefinitely. It may be discovered by someone else almost immediately after the agreement is entered into. Whoever discovers it for himself by legitimate means is entitled to its use.

But that does not mean that one who acquires a secret formula or a trade secret through a valid and binding contract is then enabled to escape from an obligation to which he bound himself simply because the secret is discovered by a third party or by the general public. I see no reason why the court should imply such a term or condition in a contract providing on its face that payment shall be co-extensive with use. To do so here would be to rewrite the contract for the parties without any indication that they intended such a result. . . .

One who acquires a trade secret or secret formula takes it subject to the risk that there be a disclosure. The inventor makes no representation that the secret is non-discoverable. All the inventor does is to convey the knowledge of the formula or process which is unknown to the purchaser and which in so far as both parties then know is unknown to any one else. The terms upon which they contract with reference to this subject matter are purely up to them and are governed by what the contract they enter into provides.

If they desire the payments or royalties should continue only until the secret is disclosed to the public it is easy enough for them to say so. But there is no justification for implying such a provision if the parties do not include it in their contract, particularly where the language which they use by fair intendment provides otherwise. . . .

COMMENTS AND QUESTIONS

1. The scope of trade secret protection is limited, not by a fixed term of years but by the length of time the information remains secret. Indeed, trade secrets become a part of the public domain once secrecy is lost, and their owner cannot prevent even direct copying. It seems odd that contract law would require royalty payments from Warner-Lambert for 80 years (or presumably 130 or more years, as Listerine is still sold commercially), while every other competitor can copy the formula for free. Are there sound reasons for such a rule?

One such reason may be the economic value of freedom of contract. If a party chooses to contract to pay royalties for as long as it uses a product, it is free to do so. Presumably the amount of the royalty payments as well as their duration will reflect the value of the secret to the buyer, discounted by the likelihood of public disclosure. But doesn't this argument also apply to extensions of the patent or copyright term as well? Compare Meehan v. PPG Indus., 802 F.2d 881, 886 (7th Cir. 1986), and Boggild v. Kenner Prods., 776 F.2d 15, 1320-21 (6th Cir. 1985), which hold that it is illegal patent or copyright misuse to agree to extend a patent or copyright beyond its term. Why does contract law appear to override trade secret law but not patent or copyright law?

Could a licensee evade its royalty obligations by acquiring the now-public secret from an independent source? The answer seems to depend on the way in which the particular license is written. *But cf.* Aronson v. Quick Point Pencil Co., 440 U.S. 257 (1979) (holding that the contract obligated licensee to continue paying royalties on an invention even though licensor's patent application had been rejected).

2. The *Warner-Lambert* result is controversial. The *Restatement (Third) of Unfair Competition* takes the position that nondisclosure agreements which purport to protect information in the public domain may be unenforceable as an unreasonable restraint on trade. *See* §41, cmt. *d*, at 472. Further, the *Restatement* notes that

"because of the public interest in preserving access to information that is in the public domain, such an agreement will not ordinarily estop a defendant from contesting the existence of a trade secret." § 39, cmt. *d*, at 430. A number of cases support this view, which seems at odds with *Warner-Lambert. See, e.g.*, Gary Van Zeeland Talent, Inc. v. Sandas, 267 N.W.2d 242 (Wis. 1978); Sarkes Tarzian, Inc. v. Audio Devices, Inc., 166 F. Supp. 250 (S.D. Cal. 1958), *aff'd*, 283 F.2d 695 (9th Cir. 1960).

On the other hand, the *Restatement* also can be read as approving the result reached in *Warner-Lambert*, at least in cases in which the information remains secret at the time the contract is negotiated. *See* RESTATEMENT (THIRD) OF UNFAIR COMPETITION § 41, cmt. *d* (suggesting that, if a contract is interpreted to require *A* to continue paying royalties to *B* even after the trade secret process has fallen into the public domain and others begin to use it, *B* may continue to enforce the agreement even if it doesn't have a trade secret claim). Moreover, the Federal Circuit has seemingly endorsed the *Warner-Lambert* approach, holding that the issuance of a patent did not extinguish the confidentiality obligation imposed by a nondisclosure agreement, even though the issuance of the patent destroyed the trade secret that was the basis for the agreement. Celeritas Technologies v. Rockwell Int'l Corp., 150 F.3d 1354 (Fed. Cir. 1998). The equities in that case might be thought to favor the plaintiff: The patent was held invalid, and so offered the plaintiff no relief against a theft of its technology. But isn't that the risk a trade secret owner takes in deciding to patent (and therefore disclose) her invention? The Seventh Circuit has held that courts had no power to review business nondisclosure agreements for reasonableness, even though employee agreements were subject to a reasonableness requirement. IDX Systems v. Epic Systems, 285 F.3d 581 (7th Cir. 2002). And in Bernier v. Merrill Air Engineers, 770 A.2d 97 (Me. 2001), the Maine Supreme Court held that an employee violated a nondisclosure agreement by disclosing information that did not qualify as a trade secret.

3. Should such restrictions be governed by intellectual property law—making them unenforceable—or by contract law, which presumably would enforce them? The answer to that question will determine whether intellectual property laws (including trade secret laws) constitute binding governmental rules balancing competing interests or merely "default" rules that parties may opt to change. In practice, the courts have walked a hazily defined middle line, refusing to hold that intellectual property statues preempt contracts that alter their terms, but also refusing to enforce certain contracts that go "too far" in upsetting the balance the intellectual property laws have struck.

4. Many licensing agreements are between competitors in an industry, since firms in the same industry are generally those who will be interested in a particular invention. Agreements between competitors, though, are generally considered suspect under the antitrust laws. So too are common license restrictions that limit the use the licensee can make of the technology. For discussion, *see, e.g.*, U.S. Dep't of Justice & Fed. Trade Comm'n, Antitrust Guidelines for the Licensing of Intellectual Property (1995).

E. FIRST AMENDMENT CONSIDERATIONS

Most of the defenses that arise in trade secret law (aside from arguments that certain types of agreements are unenforceable, as discussed in the preceding two sections) consist of trying to negate the plaintiff's evidence that, for example, the information at issue is secret, or confers a competitive advantage, or has been misappropriated (as opposed to independently acquired or reverse engineered). Occasionally, however, defendants accused of trade secret misappropriation raise the First Amendment as a defense, on the theory that if a court were to enjoin the defendant from disclosing information based upon the information's content (or otherwise penalize such conduct) the court order would amount to state action infringing the defendant's freedom of speech. To date, cases raising serious First Amendment challenges to the enforcement of trade secret rights have been less common that one might expect. As Pam Samuelson notes, the enforcement of trade secret rights often raises no First Amendment problems because, among other things, (1) "many trade secrets are 'things' that do not implicate First Amendment interests," such as products, tools, and chemical processes; (2) "most trade secret injunctions aim to regulate illegal or unethical conduct," such as wiretapping, which also does not implicate the First Amendment; (3) "[c]aselaw suggests that injunctive relief to enforce non-disclosure obligations arising from a contract or deriving from confidential receipt of the information as against competitors is generally consistent with the First Amendment"; and (4) often neither party seeks the public disclosure of the subject information, because both parties expect to derive economic benefits from its continuing secrecy. In addition, "[i]nsofar as trade secret injunctions aim to stop private use or disclosure harmful to the plaintiff's economic interests, First Amendment interests are less weighty because the secrets are matters of private concern." *See* Pamela Samuelson, *Principles for Resolving Conflicts Between Trade Secrets and the First Amendment*, 58 Hastings L.J. 777, 780-88 (2006). *See also* Mark A. Lemley & Eugene Volokh, *Freedom of Speech and Injunctions in Intellectual Property Cases*, 48 Duke L.J. 147, 229-32 (1998) (arguing that trade secret litigation often does not implicate serious First Amendment issues, but that preliminary injunctions against disclosure of trade secret information may constitute prior restraints on speech). Professor Samuelson nevertheless expects conflicts between trade secret and First Amendment interests to increase, due in part to "increased use of mass-market licenses aimed at maintaining secrecy for information that would otherwise be lawful to acquire and disclose," and to "proposal to strengthen trade secret rights to safeguard them from threats posed by the Internet." *Id.* at 778. The following case is illustrative of the type of conflict she identifies.

DVD Copy Control Ass'n v. Bunner

75 P.3d 1 (Cal. 2005)

Brown, J.:

Today we resolve an apparent conflict between California's trade secret law (Civ. Code, § 3426 *et seq.*) and the free speech clauses of the United States and California Constitutions. In this case, a Web site operator posted trade secrets owned by another on his Internet Web site despite knowing or having reason to know that the secrets were acquired by improper means. The trial court found that the operator misappropriated these trade secrets in violation of section 3426.1 and issued a preliminary injunction pursuant to section 3426.2, subdivision (a), prohibiting the operator from disclosing these secrets. Accepting as true the trial court's findings, we now consider whether this preliminary injunction violates the First Amendment of the United States Constitution and article I, section 2, subdivision (a) of the California Constitution. We conclude it does not.

I.

A.

Digital versatile discs (DVD's) "are five-inch wide disks capable of storing more than 4.7 [Gigabytes] of data. In the application relevant here, they are used to hold full-length motion pictures in digital form. They are the latest technology for private home viewing of recorded motion pictures and result in drastically improved audio and visual clarity and quality of motion pictures shown on televisions or computer screens." (Universal City Studios, Inc. v. Reimerdes (S.D.N.Y. 2000) 111 F. Supp. 2d 294, 307, fn. omitted (*Reimerdes*).)

"[T]he improved quality of a movie in a digital format brings with it the risk that a virtually perfect copy, i.e., one that will not lose perceptible quality in the copying process, can be readily made at the click of a computer control and instantly distributed to countless recipients throughout the world over the Internet." (Universal City Studios, Inc. v. Corley (2d Cir. 2001) 273 F.3d 429, 436 (*Corley*).) Recognizing this risk of widespread piracy, the motion picture industry insisted that a viable protection system be made available to prevent users from making copies of motion pictures in digital form. Without such protection, it would not have agreed to release movies on DVD's.

To provide this protection, two companies, Toshiba and Matsushita Electric Industrial Co., Ltd., developed the Content Scrambling System (CSS). "CSS is an encryption scheme that employs an algorithm configured by a set of 'keys' to encrypt a DVD's contents. The algorithm is a type of mathematical formula for transforming the contents of the movie file into gibberish; the 'keys' are in actuality strings of 0's and 1's that serve as values for the mathematical formula. Decryption in the case of CSS requires a set of '[master] keys' contained in compliant DVD players, as well as an understanding of the CSS encryption algorithm. Without the [master] keys and the algorithm, a DVD player cannot access the contents of a DVD. With the [master] keys and the algorithm, a DVD player can display the movie on a television or a computer screen, but does not give a viewer the ability to use the copy function of the computer to copy the movie or to manipulate the digital content of the DVD." (*Corley*, supra, 273 F.3d at pp. 436-437.)

. . . Jon Johansen, a Norwegian resident, acquired the proprietary information embodied in the technology — including the master keys and algorithms — by reverse engineering software created by a licensee, Xing Technology Corporation (Xing). Xing's software is licensed to users under a license agreement, which specifically prohibits reverse engineering. Using the proprietary information culled from this software, Johansen wrote a program called DeCSS that decrypts movies stored on DVD's and enables users to copy and distribute these movies. According to DVD CCA, DeCSS "embodies, uses, and/or is a substantial derivation of confidential proprietary information" found in the CSS technology. Johansen posted the source code of DeCSS on an Internet Web site in October 1999.

Soon thereafter, DeCSS appeared on other Web sites, including a Web site maintained by Andrew Bunner. Bunner posted DeCSS on his Web site allegedly because "it would enable 'Linux' users to use and enjoy 'DVDs' available for purchase or rental in video stores" and "make 'Linux' more attractive and viable to consumers." Bunner also claimed he wanted "to ensure [that] programmers would have access to the information needed to add new features, fix existing defects and, in general, improve the '[D]eCSS' program."

B.

. . . In the complaint, DVD CCA did not seek damages. Instead, it only sought an order "enjoining and restraining [d]efendants . . . from making any further use or otherwise disclosing or distributing, on their web sites or elsewhere, or 'linking' to other web sites which disclose, distribute, or 'link' to any proprietary property or trade secrets relating to the CSS technology and specifically enjoining [d]efendants . . . from copying, duplicating, licensing, selling, distributing, publishing, leasing, renting or otherwise marketing the DeCSS computer program and all other products containing, using and/or substantially derived from CSS proprietary property or trade secrets. . . ."

Following a hearing and after considering written declarations submitted by the parties, the trial court issued a preliminary injunction. The injunction enjoined the named defendants, including Bunner, from "[p]osting or otherwise disclosing or distributing, on their [W]eb sites or elsewhere, the DeCSS program, the master keys or algorithms of the Content Scrambling System . . . , or any other information derived from this proprietary information." The court, however, refused to enjoin the defendants from "linking to other [Web sites] which contain the protected materials" because "such an order [would be] overbroad and extremely burdensome."

In issuing the injunction, the court concluded that DVD CCA was likely to prevail on the merits and would suffer irreparable harm without injunctive relief. First, the court concluded that the CSS technology contained protectable trade secrets because it derived independent economic value from its secrecy and because DVD CCA made reasonable efforts to maintain its secrecy. Second, the court found that Johansen had obtained these trade secrets through reverse engineering in violation of a license agreement and therefore acquired these secrets by improper means. Third, the court found that the defendants, including Bunner, knew or should have known that Johansen acquired these trade secrets by improper means when they posted DeCSS on their Web sites. Fourth, the court held that the trade secret status of the CSS technology had not been destroyed because it had been posted on the Internet. Fifth, the court concluded that DVD CCA would suffer irreparable harm without an injunction. "If the Court does not immediately enjoin the posting of this proprietary information, [DVD CCA's] right to protect this information as secret will surely be lost. . . ." The court then observed that an injunction would cause minimal harm to the defendants. Finally, the court acknowledged potential enforcement problems, but held that "a possibility or even a likelihood that an order may be disobeyed or not enforced in other jurisdictions is not a reason to deny the relief sought."

Only Bunner appealed, and the Court of Appeal reversed. Rather than review the trial court's findings in support of injunctive relief, the Court of Appeal assumed that DVD CCA was likely to prevail on the merits and would suffer irreparable harm.

The court then held that the preliminary injunction, even if justified under California's trade secret law, violated the First Amendment. According to the Court of Appeal, DeCSS was "pure speech," and the injunction was an invalid prior restraint on pure speech. . . . We granted review to decide this important constitutional question.

II.

. . . [W]e follow the lead of the Court of Appeal and assume as true the trial court findings in support of the preliminary injunction. Specifically, we accept for purposes of this appeal that DVD CCA is likely to prevail on its claims that (1) the CSS technology and its master keys and algorithms are trade secrets; (2) publication of these trade secrets on the Internet has not destroyed their trade secret status; (3) publication of DeCSS discloses these trade secrets; (4) the creator of DeCSS acquired these trade secrets by improper means; and (5) Bunner knew or had reason to know that DeCSS disclosed trade secrets acquired by improper means.[5] We also assume that DVD CCA will suffer irreparable harm without injunctive relief and that the injunction will cause minimal harm to Bunner. Thus, the narrow question before us is whether the preliminary injunction violates Bunner's right to free speech under the United States and California Constitutions even though DVD CCA is likely to prevail on its trade secret claim against Bunner.

III.

A.

In answering this question, we must first determine whether restrictions on the dissemination of computer codes in the form of DeCSS are subject to scrutiny under the First Amendment. We conclude they are.

" '[A]ll ideas having even the slightest redeeming social importance,' including those concerning 'the advancement of truth, science, morality, and arts' have the full protection of the First Amendment.". . . .

As such, "[i]t cannot seriously be argued that any form of computer code may be regulated without reference to First Amendment doctrine." (*Reimerdes*, supra, 111 F. Supp. 2d at p. 326.) "A computer program states or represents a procedure or algorithm in a programming language. The same algorithm could be written in a natural language like English or a programming language like C or LISP, but it remains the same algorithm." (Tien, *Publishing Software as a Speech Act* (2000) 15 Berkeley Tech. L.J. 629, 633, fn. omitted.) . . .

5. Therefore, we need not decide whether the proprietary CSS technology is part of the public domain and no longer a protectable trade secret or whether Johansen acquired the trade secrets by improper means when he reverse engineered the Xing software in violation of a license agreement. We also decline to address Bunner's contention that the preliminary injunction violates the intellectual property clause of the United States Constitution (U.S. Const., art. I, § 8) because DVD CCA's trade secrets have been publicly disclosed and are no longer secret. We leave the resolution of these issues for the Court of Appeal on remand.

B.

"As computer code . . . is a means of expressing ideas, the First Amendment must be considered before its dissemination may be prohibited or regulated. . . . But that conclusion still leaves for determination the level of scrutiny to be applied in determining the constitutionality of" an injunction prohibiting the dissemination of computer code. (*Reimerdes*, supra, 111 F. Supp. 2d at p. 327.) In determining the appropriate level of scrutiny, the critical question is whether the injunction is content neutral or content based. Content-based injunctions are subject to "the level of heightened scrutiny set forth in Perry Ed. Assn. [v. Perry Local Educators Assn. (1983)] 460 U.S. [37,] 45 [103 S. Ct. 948]." (*Madsen*, at pp. 763-764, 114 S. Ct. 2516.) By contrast, content-neutral injunctions are subject to the lesser level of scrutiny set forth in *Madsen*, supra, 512 U.S. at page 765, 114 S. Ct. 2516. In this case, we conclude that the preliminary injunction issued by the trial court is content neutral and should be reviewed under the standard articulated in *Madsen*.

"Our principal inquiry in determining content neutrality is whether the government has adopted a regulation of speech 'without reference to the content of the regulated speech.'" "[L]iteral or absolute content neutrality" is not necessary. "The government's purpose is the controlling consideration," and a governmental regulation of speech is only content based if the government adopted the regulation "because of disagreement with the message it conveys." This is true for "speech cases generally. . . ." Thus, an injunction "that serves purposes unrelated to the content of expression is deemed neutral, even if it has an incidental effect on some speakers or messages but not others." However, injunctions "that by their terms distinguish favored speech from disfavored speech on the basis of the ideas or views expressed are content based." (Turner Broadcasting System, Inc. v. FCC (1994) 512 U.S. 622, 643, 114 S. Ct. 2445, 129 L. Ed. 2d 497.)

Applying this standard, we conclude that the preliminary injunction at issue here is content neutral. The underlying basis for the injunction is the trial court's holding that Bunner misappropriated DVD CCA's property—its trade secrets—in violation of California's trade secret law. (See Ruckelshaus v. Monsanto Co. (1984) 467 U.S. 986, 1003-1004, 104 S. Ct. 2862, 81 L. Ed. 2d 815 (*Monsanto*) [holding that trade secrets are a "property right . . . protected by the Taking Clause of the Fifth Amendment"].) In issuing the injunction, the court therefore relied on the fact that DVD CCA made reasonable efforts to keep the information secret (§3426.1, subd. (d)(2)), and that DVD CCA received a "competitive advantage over others . . . by virtue of its exclusive access to the" information (*Monsanto*, at p.1012, 104 S. Ct. 2862). Thus, the injunction singled out Bunner's communications because of DVD 'CA's efforts to maintain the secrecy of the CSS technology and the competitive advantage it enjoyed from those efforts-and not because of the communications' subject matter or any disagreement with Bunner's message or viewpoint. In other words, the trial court issued the injunction to protect DVD CCA's statutorily created property interest in information-and not to suppress the content of Bunner's communications. Because the injunction is justified without reference to the content of Bunner's communications, it is content neutral. (See *Bartnicki*, supra, 532 U.S. at p. 526, 121 S. Ct. 1753 [finding a statute that singled out communications "by virtue of the fact that they were illegally intercepted . . . rather than the subject matter" is content neutral].)

Indeed, the governmental purpose behind protecting trade secrets like the CSS technology through injunctive relief is wholly unrelated to their content. "Trade secret law promotes the sharing of knowledge, and the efficient operation of industry; it permits the individual inventor to reap the rewards of his labor by contracting with a company large enough to develop and exploit it." (Kewanee Oil Co. v. Bicron Corp. (1974) 416 U.S. 470, 493, 94 S. Ct. 1879, 40 L. Ed. 2d 315 (*Kewanee*).) The law also maintains important standards of commercial ethics. (Id. at p. 481, 94 S. Ct. 1879.) Assuming, as we do, that the trial court properly applied California's trade secret law, the preliminary injunction necessarily serves the broader governmental purpose behind the law. Because the injunction does not purport to restrict DVD CCA's trade secrets based on their expressive content, the injunction's restrictions on Bunner's speech "properly are characterized as incidental to the primary" purpose of California's trade secret law—which is to promote and reward innovation and technological development and maintain commercial ethics.

The fact that the preliminary injunction identifies the prohibited speech by its content does not make it content based. "An injunction, by its very nature, applies only to a particular group (or individuals) and regulates the activities, and perhaps the speech, of that group. It does so, however, because of the group's past actions in the context of a specific dispute between real parties. The parties seeking the injunction assert a violation of their rights; the court hearing the action is charged with fashioning a remedy for a specific deprivation, not with the drafting of a statute addressed to the general public." (*Madsen*, supra, 512 U.S. at p. 762, 114 S. Ct. 2516.) In this case, the specific deprivation to be remedied is the misappropriation of a property interest in information. Thus, any injunction remedying this deprivation must refer to the content of that information in order to identify the property interest to be protected. Such an injunction remains content neutral so long as it serves significant governmental purposes unrelated to the content of the proprietary information. (See *SFA & A*, supra, 483 U.S. at pp. 536-537, 107 S. Ct. 2971 [finding that an injunction that specifically prohibits the defendant's use of the word "Olympic" is content neutral because its restrictions serve "the primary congressional purpose of encouraging and rewarding the [United States Olympic Committee's] activities"].) Because the preliminary injunction at issue here does not "involve government censorship of subject matter or governmental favoritism among different viewpoints," it is content neutral and not subject to strict scrutiny. (*Los Angeles Alliance*, supra, 22 Cal. 4th at p. 377, 93 Cal. Rptr. 2d 1, 993 P.2d 334.) . . .

C.

Under the *Madsen* test, "when evaluating a content-neutral injunction . . . [w]e must ask . . . whether the challenged provisions of the injunction burden no more speech than necessary to serve a significant government interest." (*Madsen*, supra, 512 U.S. at p. 765, 114 S. Ct. 2516.) This test requires "a balance between the governmental interest and the magnitude of the speech restriction." (*SFA & A*, supra, 483 U.S. at p. 537, fn.16, 107 S. Ct. 2971.) As explained below, we conclude that the preliminary injunction issued by the trial court achieves the requisite balance and burdens "no more speech than necessary to serve" the government interests at stake here. (*Madsen*, at p. 765, 114 S. Ct. 2516.)

By creating a limited property right in information, trade secret law "acts as an incentive for investment in innovation." . . .

Assuming, as we do, that the trial court properly granted injunctive relief under California's trade secret law, its preliminary injunction burdens no more speech than necessary to serve these significant government interests. First, prohibiting the disclosure of trade secrets acquired by improper means is the only way to preserve the property interest created by trade secret law and its concomitant ability to encourage invention. . . .

The First Amendment does not prohibit courts from incidentally enjoining speech in order to protect a legitimate property right. (See *SFA & A*, supra, 483 U.S. at pp. 526, 537-540, 107 S. Ct. 2971 [holding that a statutory injunction prohibiting promotional uses of the word "Olympic" without a showing of a likelihood of confusion does not violate the First Amendment].) And "[t]he mere fact that" Bunner "claims an expressive . . . purpose does not give [him] a First Amendment right to 'appropriat[e] to [himself] the harvest of those who have sown.' " (Id. at p. 541, 107 S. Ct. 2971, quoting International News Service v. Associated Press (1918) 248 U.S. 215, 239-240, 39 S. Ct. 68, 63 L. Ed. 211.) Indeed, the protection of trade secrets and the benefits to research and development derived from the government's recognition of this property right depend on the judiciary's power to enjoin disclosures by those who know or have reason to know of their misappropriation. Bunner proffers, and we can think of, no less restrictive way of protecting an owner's constitutionally recognized property interest in its trade secrets. Thus, the preliminary injunction burdens no more speech than necessary to serve the government's interest in encouraging innovation and development.

Second, prohibiting Bunner—who knew or had reason to know that the trade secrets were acquired by improper means—from disclosing those secrets upholds the standard of commercial ethics maintained by trade secret law. . . .

By prohibiting Bunner from exploiting and destroying DVD CCA's trade secrets because of his actual or constructive knowledge of its illegal acquisition, the preliminary injunction merely applies this venerable standard of commercial ethics to a constitutionally recognized property interest in information. Because a person who knowingly exploits the illegal acquisition of property owned by another should be in "no better position than" the illegal acquirer himself, the injunction burdens no more speech than necessary to serve the government's important interest in maintaining commercial ethics. . . .

In this case, the content of the trade secrets neither involves a matter of public concern nor implicates the core purpose of the First Amendment. "Whether . . . speech addresses a matter of public concern must be determined by the content, form, and context of a given statement, as revealed by the whole record." (Connick v. Myers (1983) 461 U.S. 138, 147-148, 103 S. Ct. 1684, 75 L. Ed. 2d 708, fn. omitted.) DVD CCA's trade secrets in the CSS technology are not publicly available and convey only technical information about the method used by specific private entities to protect their intellectual property. Bunner posted these secrets in the form of DeCSS on the Internet so Linux users could enjoy and use DVD's and so others could improve the functional capabilities of DeCSS. He did not post them to comment on any public issue or to participate in any public debate. Indeed, only computer encryption enthusiasts are likely to have an interest in the expressive content—rather than the uses—of DVD CCA's trade secrets. Thus, these trade secrets, as disclosed by Bunner, address matters of purely private concern and not matters of public importance.

The mere fact that DVD CCA's trade secrets may have some link to a public issue does not create a legitimate public interest in their disclosure. Disclosure of this highly technical information adds nothing to the public debate over the use of encryption software or the DVD industry's efforts to limit unauthorized copying of movies on DVD's. And the injunction does not hamper Bunner's ability to "discuss and debate" these issues as he has "in the past in both an educational, scientific, philosophical and political context." . . .

D.

Although the preliminary injunction issued by the trial court survives the *Madsen* test, we must still determine whether the prior restraint doctrine bars it. Because the injunction is content neutral and was issued because of Bunner's prior unlawful conduct, we conclude it is not a prior restraint and therefore does not violate the First Amendment.

"[P]rior restraints on speech and publication are the most serious and the least tolerable infringement on First Amendment rights." (Nebraska Press Assn. v. Stuart (1976) 427 U.S. 539, 559, 96 S. Ct. 2791, 49 L. Ed. 2d 683.) "The term prior restraint is used 'to describe administrative and judicial orders forbidding certain communications when issued in advance of the time that such communications are to occur.' [Citation.] Temporary restraining orders and permanent injunctions—i.e., court orders that actually forbid speech activities—are classic examples of prior restraints." (Alexander v. United States (1993) 509 U.S. 544, 550, 113 S. Ct. 2766, 125 L. Ed. 2d 441.) Nonetheless, the United States Supreme Court "has never held that all injunctions are impermissible." (Pittsburgh Press Co. v. Pittsburgh Comm'n on Human Relations (1973) 413 U.S. 376, 390, 93 S. Ct. 2553, 37 L. Ed. 2d 669.) "The special vice of a prior restraint is that communication will be suppressed, either directly or by inducing excessive caution in the speaker, before an adequate determination that it is unprotected by the First Amendment." (Ibid.) Thus, "[n]ot all injunctions that may incidentally affect expression . . . are 'prior restraints'. . . ." (*Madsen*, supra, 512 U.S. at p. 763, fn. 2, 114 S. Ct. 2516.)

Despite these pronouncements, the United States Supreme Court has "neither defined prior restraint, nor explained precisely why injunctions fit within a definition of prior restraint." Nonetheless, the court has provided some guiding principles. For example, the court has recently held that only content-based injunctions are subject to prior restraint analysis. Based on our review of high court decisions, we have also observed that "[a] prior restraint is a content-based restriction on speech prior to its occurrence." Consistent with these guiding principles, the United States Supreme Court has declined to apply prior restraint analysis to a permanent injunction and a preliminary injunction "issued not because of the content of petitioners' expression . . . but because of their prior unlawful conduct" (*Madsen*, at p. 763, fn. 2, 114 S. Ct. 2516; see also *Schenck*, at p. 374, fn. 6, 117 S. Ct. 855).

Applying these principles, we find that the preliminary injunction at issue here is not a prior restraint. The injunction is content neutral and the trial court found that Bunner had previously disclosed DVD CCA's trade secrets in violation of California law. The court therefore issued the content-neutral injunction because of Bunner's "prior unlawful conduct." . . .

CBS Inc. v. Davis (1994) 510 U.S. 1315, 114 S. Ct. 912, 127 L. Ed. 2d 358 is inapposite. In *CBS*, a federal district court issued an injunction "prohibiting CBS from airing videotape footage taken at the factory of Federal Beef Processors, Inc." because the tape disclosed Federal's " 'confidential and proprietary practices and processes. . . .' " Concluding that the injunction was an unconstitutional prior restraint, Justice Blackmun stayed its enforcement. As a single justice order, *CBS* is arguably not binding on this court. In any event, it is distinguishable. Justice Blackmun, in finding a prior restraint, relied on the lack of clear evidence establishing that CBS had acquired Federal's proprietary information by improper means. In contrast, we assume for purposes of this appeal that Bunner knew or had reason to know that DVD CCA's trade secrets were acquired by improper means. Moreover, unlike the trade secrets at issue here, the videotape footage at issue in *CBS* appeared to address a matter of public concern-"unsanitary practices in the meat industry" (*CBS*, at p. 1315, 114 S. Ct. 912). . . .

Disposition

We reverse the judgment of the Court of Appeal and remand for further proceedings consistent with this opinion.

George, C.J., Baxter, J., Rivera, J., and Robie, J., concur.

Concurring Opinion by Moreno, J.:

I concur in the majority's narrow holding, which, as I understand it, is that the First Amendment does not categorically prohibit preliminary injunctions to enjoin the publication of trade secrets. I further agree that the First Amendment requires independent appellate review of such preliminary injunctions, rather than the deferential review usually accorded such injunctions. I write separately for two reasons. First, I believe there is a need to clarify how the prior restraint doctrine under the First Amendment applies to the publication of alleged trade secrets. Second, I would forgo further proceedings in the Court of Appeal and simply affirm that court's judgment. In my view, the DVD Copy Control Association's (DVD CCA) trade secret claim against Bunner is patently without merit for the reasons explained below.

I.

. . . The preliminary injunction in this case is subject-matter censorship — entirely prohibiting Bunner from publishing a particular type of information related to the DVD CCA's content scrambling system (CSS) and the descrambling program (DeCSS), not a content-neutral time, place, and manner regulation. If the alleged trade secret is not in fact a trade secret, then the court will be enjoining protected speech. A preliminary injunction issued prior to an adjudication on the merits would therefore pose the precise danger of prior restraint identified in Pittsburgh Press Co., i.e., "the special vice . . . that communication will be suppressed . . . before an adequate determination that it is unprotected by the First Amendment.'" But that particular "special vice" would not threaten in the case of time, place, and manner restrictive injunctions or ordinances, where speech is not being entirely suppressed; instead, the special vice of those regulations is that their restrictions may be stricter than needed to accomplish the government objective.

It should also be noted that the Court of Appeal properly rejected the DVD CCA's reliance on copyright cases in arguing that preliminary injunctions should be routinely granted. As the Court of Appeal stated: "Protections for trade secrets . . . are not comparable to protections for copyrights with respect to the First Amendment. First, since both the First Amendment and the constitutional authority underlying the Copyright Act are contained in the United States Constitution, the resolution of a conflict between free speech and copyright involves a delicate balancing of two federal constitutional protections. . . . The [Uniform Trade Secrets Act], on the other hand, lacks any constitutional foundation. . . . [¶] Second, injunctions in copyright infringement cases have been upheld 'on the ground that First Amendment concerns are protected by and coextensive with the [Copyright Act's] fair use doctrine.' (Nihon Keizai Shimbun, Inc. v. Comline Business Data (2d Cir. 1999) 166 F.3d 65, 74.) . . . In contrast, the UTSA contains no exception for 'fair use' or any other vehicle for safeguarding First Amendment concerns."

But concluding that prior restraint analysis applies in the case of preliminary injunctions of alleged trade secret publications is not the same as concluding that all such injunctions are prohibited. Both the United States Supreme Court and this court have recognized that the First Amendment right to free expression may be legitimately circumscribed by state law intellectual property rights. Trade secret law is an indisputably important means of protecting a certain form of intellectual property for the benefit of society as a whole. . . . Because the very existence of a trade secret is destroyed by its disclosure, a categorical inability by trade secret holders to obtain preliminary injunctive relief against the publication of trade secrets could significantly undermine their property rights. . . . Furthermore, as the majority suggests, the fact that publication of most trade secrets does not address matters of public concern is a factor that may somewhat lighten the heavy presumption against the constitutional validity of a prior restraint.

The question, then, is how should a court balance First Amendment protections with an alleged trade secret holder's property rights when asked to issue a preliminary injunction against publication? The answer lies in requiring the plaintiff to make a sufficient evidentiary showing before the injunction is granted. . . .

In my view, the need to safeguard the First Amendment right against prior restraint, while not barring trade secret holders from obtaining preliminary injunctions, requires that we make the standard for granting such injunctions more rigorous. As Professor Redish has stated: "[B]ecause such prior restraints are imposed by a judicial officer following some form of adversarial judicial process, the heavy negative presumption traditionally associated with the prior restraint doctrine is inappropriate. Nevertheless, because prior restraints are issued following only an abbreviated judicial inquiry, they are properly employed only if the asserted governmental interest could not be adequately protected by regulation following a full adversarial trial and only if the court determines that a strong likelihood exists that the government will be able to establish that the challenged expression is regulable under substantive first amendment standards. . . . The traditional equitable principle that the issuance of such preliminary relief is largely a matter of the court's discretion . . . would have to change. Such broad discretion is not consistent with first amendment concerns, and any court issuing such preliminary relief against expression should expect no deference in the course of appellate review." (Redish, supra, 70 VA. L. REV. at pp. 88-89, fns. omitted.)

II.

. . . As explained in the majority opinion, Bunner is alleged to have downloaded from the Internet and republished the DeCSS source code incorporating CSS, the DVD CCA's proprietary information. The general rule is that "[o]nce the secret is out, the rest of the world may well have a right to copy it at will; but this should not protect the misappropriator or his privies." DeCSS was not demonstrably secret in this case when Bunner republished it, and Bunner was neither alleged to be the original misappropriator nor to be in privity with any such misappropriators. . . .

Therefore, had Bunner obtained DeCSS information from a computer magazine or a newspaper, the information would be considered "readily ascertainable" and not a trade secret. Instead, he learned of DeCSS from a computer discussion group and downloaded it from a Web site on the Internet. The date of Bunner's initial posting is unclear from the record, and the availability of DeCSS on the Internet at the time of the posting is also not clear. The DVD CCA's attorney declared that at the time the complaint against Bunner and others was filed in December 1999, approximately two months after the initial posting, at least 118 Web sites had been identified that either contained proprietary information related to CSS or provided links to other Web sites with such information. How can information published in a computer magazine be regarded as "readily ascertainable" but not information published on numerous Web sites? Nor is it at all clear that information published in a trade journal would have greater permanency than information published on the Internet.[3]

Courts that have considered the matter have agreed that, generally speaking, a party not involved in the initial misappropriation of a trade secret cannot be prosecuted under trade secret law for downloading and republishing proprietary information posted on the Internet, primarily because the information is in the public domain and is no longer secret. This conclusion is also consistent with the principle that the First Amendment generally prohibits limitations, absent some extraordinary showing of governmental interest, on the publication of information already made public. . . . Thus, both trade secret law and the First Amendment are in accord that information republished on the Internet after having been made public on the Internet generally cannot be sanctioned. . . .

That is not to say that a trade secret is automatically lost any time it is posted on the Internet. Amici curiae Intellectual Property Law Professors et alia argue, for example, that information posted on an obscure Internet site and detected quickly should not lose trade secret status. This position is consistent with case law holding that minor disclosures of a trade secret followed by a brief delay in withdrawing it from

3. I note that since the time the preliminary injunction went into effect, it appears that the DVD CCA's proprietary information has been widely distributed. According to several uncontradicted declarations attached to Bunner's motion to dismiss for mootness, filed in this court on February 7, 2003, DeCSS remains available at hundreds of locations on the Internet. Moreover, CSS and its algorithms and keys have been the subject of extensive academic research and discussion, including technical papers describing and analyzing CSS, and computer science courses in which the methods and flaws of CSS encryption are taught.

the public domain do not cause trade secret status to be lost. But a plaintiff carries the burden of showing that the trade secret remains a secret despite the Internet posting. In the present case, nothing in the record indicates that the DVD CCA met that burden. . . .

COMMENTS AND QUESTIONS

1. On remand, the California Court of Appeals again reversed the order granting the preliminary injunction. The court concluded that the plaintiff DVD CCA had not demonstrated a likelihood of success on the merits (one of the requirements for granting preliminary relief), because (1) by the time Bunner first posted DeCSS on his Web site, it may already have been distributed by others to a worldwide audience; and (2) it was unclear to the court whether the Norwegian teenager who decrypted CSS had acquired the information by improper means. In addition, the court concluded that DVD CCA was not faced with irreparable harm justifying a preliminary injunction prohibiting disclosure if the information was no longer secret. *See* DVD Copy Control Ass'n v. Bunner, 10 Cal. Rptr. 3d 185 (Ct. App. 2004). This terminated the litigation because, while the appeal was pending, DVD CCA voluntarily dismissed its complaint. *See id.* at 187 n.2.

2. The *Bunner* majority characterizes the preliminary injunction issued by the trial court as "content neutral," because "the governmental purpose behind protecting trade secrets . . . through injunctive relief is wholly unrelated to their content." Is that right? Isn't the governmental purpose inextricably linked to the information's content? If the injunction is characterized as a content-based regulation of speech, it is subject to strict scrutiny. Can the prevention of trade secret misappropriation qualify as a compelling state interest? Note the similarity of the debate over trade secrets as a form of speech regulation and the debate over the right of publicity as a form of speech regulation, discussed in Chapter 10 *supra*. Trade secrets, however, have a longer pedigree than publicity rights, and there is much more of a consensus among courts and commentators in favor of protecting trade secrets than there is with respect to publicity rights. *See also* Samuelson, *supra*, at 814-33 (arguing that a heavy presumption against issuance of preliminary injunctions should *not* apply in ordinary trade secret cases, but that courts should invoke the presumption against prior restraints when third-party recipients propose to disclose newsworthy confidential information).

3. The court also makes much of trade secrets' status as "property," citing in various portions of the opinion Ruckelshaus v. Monsanto Co., 467 U.S. 986 (1984), which held that trade secrets were property for purposes of the Fifth Amendment's Takings Clause. As suggested earlier in this chapter, the characterization of trade secrets as property nevertheless remains controversial. *See, e.g.*, Oren Bar-Gill & Gideon Parchomovsky, *Law and the Boundaries of Technology-Intensive Firms*, 157 U. PA. L. REV. 1649, 1675 (2009) (noting that "several commentators . . . argue that trade secrets constitute at best quasi property or incomplete property rights," and that "trade secrets lack some of the defining characteristics of property rights"); Mark A. Lemley, *The Surprising Virtues of Treating Trade Secrets as IP Rights*, 61 STAN. L. REV. 311 (2008) (arguing that trade secrets are best characterized not as traditional property but as intellectual property); Samuelson, *supra*, at 805-08 (arguing that trade secrets are not akin to conventional property). Can states evade First Amendment scrutiny by cloaking information in the guise of property interests? *See* Lemley &

Volokh, *supra*, at 182-85 (arguing that they cannot; noting as an example of the problem with this theory an effort by Congress to declare flag burning to be copyright infringement in order to ban it).

4. As Pam Samuelson notes, the court in *DVD Copy Control* "left for another day . . . the question whether DVD CCA should be able to use mass market license to override the reverse engineering privilege of trade secret law and to bind the whole world not to reverse engineer globally distributed DVD players it did not manufacture through multiple layers of license requirements reaching down to the end-user." Samuelson, *supra*, at 794. As noted in other portions of this book, the enforceability of mass market licenses such as shrinkwrap or clickwrap licenses remains unclear. Assuming, for the sake of argument, that such a license would be enforceable as a matter of general contract law, should it nevertheless be unenforceable because of the important role that reverse engineering plays in the law of trade secrets? Justice Moreno notes in his concurring opinion that the ability to reverse engineer is one of the characteristics that keeps trade secret law from being preempted by federal patent law. *See* DVD Copy Control Ass'n v. Bunner, 75 P.3d 1, 28 n.5 (Cal. 2003) (Moreno, J., concurring) ("if trade secret law did allow alleged trade secret holders to redefine 'improper means' to include reverse engineering, it would likely be preempted by federal patent law, which alone grants universal protection for a limited time against the right to reverse engineer." (*See* Bonito Boats, Inc. v. Thunder Craft Boats, Inc. (1989) 489 U.S. 141, 155, 109 S. Ct. 971, 103 L. Ed. 2d 118.)"); see also Chapter 15, *infra*, discussing preemption.

On the other hand, in other litigation involving DeCSS a federal district court in New York held that the posting of DeCSS on a Web site violated the Digital Millennium Copyright Act (DMCA), which forbids (among other things) trafficking in technology that is primarily designed to circumvent technological measures that control access to copyrighted works; and that the DMCA's very limited exception for reverse engineering did not apply on the facts of the case. *See* United States v. Reimerdes, 111 F. Supp. 2d 294, 319-20 (S.D.N.Y. 2000), *aff'd*, 273 F.3d 429 (2d Cir. 2001). If a type of reverse engineering is lawful as a matter of trade secret law, but unlawful as a matter of copyright law, would reverse engineering that results in the acquisition of trade secret information constitute proper or improper means under the UTSA?

5. Because of the risk of loss of trade secrecy through Internet posting, companies have been more aggressive in suing individuals who post information they consider confidential. *See* O'Grady v. Superior Court, 44 Cal. Rptr. 3d 72 (Ct. App. 2006); Ford v. Lane (67 F. Supp. 2d 745 (E.D. Mich. 1999)). In some of these cases, notably *O'Grady*, the company knows only that the information has been disclosed, and not who has done so. Do such lawsuits present First Amendment issues? Several have involved claims by the defendant that they are being sued for reporting legitimate news. *See* Franklin B. Goldberg, Ford Motor Co. v. Lane, 16 BERKELEY TECH. L.J. 271 (2001). And *O'Grady* held that bloggers who disclosed Apple's trade secrets were entitled to First Amendment protection as reporters, so their identity could not be disclosed by subpoena. For criticism of the district court's refusal to enter a preliminary injunction against the disclosure of alleged trade secret information in *Lane*, see Richard A. Epstein, *Privacy, Publication, and the First Amendment: The Dangers of First Amendment Exceptionalism*, 52 STAN. L. REV. 1003, 1035-46 (2000).

F. INTERNATIONAL CONSIDERATIONS

The law of other countries with respect to trade secrets, confidential information, and other forms of "know how" varies considerably from one place to another, and international law on trade secrets remains sparse. Article 10bis of the Paris Convention requires member states to assure to nationals of other member states "effective protection against unfair competition," and states that "[a]ny act of competition contrary to honest practices in industrial or commercial matters constitutes an act of unfair competition." Paris Convention art. 10bis (1), (2). The Convention does not provide a more precise definition of the term "unfair competition," however, and although article 10bis (3) requires member states to afford some measure of protection against passing off, false advertising, and commercial disparagement, it says nothing specifically about trade secrets.

In the 1990s, however, the United States became a party to two important trade-related agreements: the North American Free Trade Agreement (NAFTA), the other parties to which are Canada and Mexico; and the Agreement on Trade-Related Aspects of Intellectual Property Rights (TRIPs). Of the two, TRIPs is the more important, because all member nations of the World Trade Organization (WTO) are obligated to abide by TRIPs.

Section 7 of the TRIPs Agreement, titled "Protection of Undisclosed Information," contains a single provision, article 39, which reads as follows:

> 1. In the course of ensuring effective protection against unfair competition as provided in Article 10*bis* of the Paris Convention (1967), Members shall protect undisclosed information in accordance with paragraph 2 and data submitted to governments or governmental agencies in accordance with paragraph 3.
>
> 2. Natural and legal persons shall have the possibility of preventing information lawfully within their control from being disclosed to, acquired by, or used by others without their consent in a manner contrary to honest commercial practices[10] so long as such information:
>
> (a) is secret in the sense that it is not, as a body or in the precise configuration and assembly of its components, generally known among or readily accessible to persons within the circles that normally deal with the kind of information in question;
>
> (b) has commercial value because it is secret; and
>
> (c) has been subject to reasonable steps under the circumstances, by the person lawfully in control of the information, to keep it secret.
>
> 3. Members, when requiring, as a condition of approving the marketing of pharmaceutical or of agricultural chemical products which utilize new chemical entities, the submission of undisclosed test or other data, the origination of which involves a considerable effort, shall protect such data against unfair commercial use. In addition, Members shall protect such data against disclosure,

10. For the purpose of this provision, "a manner contrary to honest commercial practices" shall mean at least practices such as breach of contract, breach of confidence and inducement to breach, and includes the acquisition of undisclosed information by third parties who knew, or were grossly negligent in failing to know, that such practices were involved in the acquisition.

except where necessary to protect the public, or unless steps are taken to ensure that the data are protected against unfair commercial use.

Paragraph 2 of TRIPs, referenced in article 39(1), requires members to comply with the substantive provisions of the Paris Convention, while paragraph 3 of TRIPS generally requires that members afford national treatment to nationals of other member states.

How do these provisions compare to the Uniform Trade Secret Act? Are member nations free to enact trade secret laws that are stronger than the UTSA (e.g., that would penalize reverse engineering of trade secret information)? Are they free to enact laws that are substantially weaker than the UTSA?

For useful discussion of certain aspects of the international and comparative law of trade secrets, including the TRIPs and NAFTA provisions cited above, see Doris Estelle Long & Anthony D'Amato, A Coursebook in International Intellectual Property 243-80, 350-54 (2000). *See also* UNCTAD-ICTSD, Resource Book on TRIPs and Development: An Authoritative and Practical Guide to the TRIPs Agreement, ch. 28 (June 1, 2005) (providing an overview of TRIPs article 39, but noting that there is thus far no WTO case law on the subject), *available at* http://www.iprsonline.org/unctadictsd/docs/RB_2.28_update.pdf.

G. REMEDIES

As might be expected given the fluidity of doctrine in trade secret law, there are disparate remedies for trade secret misappropriation stemming from different remedial concerns. The Uniform Trade Secrets Act sets forth the following remedies for misappropriation:

Section 2

(a) Actual or threatened misappropriation may be enjoined. Upon application to the court, an injunction shall be terminated when the trade secret has ceased to exist, but the injunction may be continued for an additional reasonable period of time in order to eliminate commercial advantage that otherwise would be derived from the misappropriation.

(b) If the court determines that it would be unreasonable to prohibit future use, an injunction may condition future use upon payment of a reasonable royalty for no longer than the period of time the use could have been prohibited.

(c) In appropriate circumstances, affirmative acts to protect a trade secret may be compelled by court order.

Section 3

(a) In addition to or in lieu of injunctive relief, a complainant may recover damages for the actual loss caused by misappropriation. A complainant also may recover for the unjust enrichment caused by misappropriation that is not taken into account in computing damages for actual loss.

(b) If willful and malicious misappropriation exists, the court may award exemplary damages in an amount not exceeding twice any award made under subsection (a).

Section 4

If (i) a claim of misappropriation is made in bad faith, (ii) a motion to terminate an injunction is made or resisted in bad faith, or (iii) willful and malicious misappropriation exists, the court may award reasonable attorney's fees to the prevailing party.

What motivates this hodgepodge of remedial measures? As we shall see in the chapters to come, most intellectual property statutes operate on the basis of "property rules." That is, as in cases involving real property, the owner of the intellectual property right is entitled to judicial assistance in protecting the right from future interference. Normally this assistance comes in the form of injunctive relief. By contrast, most tort and contract cases do not involve injunctive relief but rather damages designed to make the plaintiff "whole" in the sense of restoring her to the position she occupied before the tort, or to the position she expected to occupy if the contract had been performed.

Section 2 of the Uniform Trade Secrets Act seems to entitle trade secret plaintiffs to property-like protection, as least so long as their secret remains a secret. But section 2(b) holds open the possibility that courts may refuse to grant such an injunction, settling instead for a reasonable "royalty" (presumably a court's attempt to approximate what the parties might have agreed to pay in a licensing transaction). This provision casts some doubt on the "property entitlement" a trade secret owner might expect.

Similar doubt pervades the provisions on damages. Concepts like "reasonable royalty," "lost profits," and limited-time injunctions designed to "eliminate commercial advantage" all sound like restitutionary measures, aimed at making the plaintiff whole after a loss without necessarily punishing or deterring the defendant. But further provisions permit trade secret plaintiffs to recover for "unjust enrichment" on the part of defendants, and to recover treble damages and attorney fees in the case of willful misappropriation. And in some circumstances misappropriation of trade secrets can be a criminal offense, an idea that is certainly more consistent with a property entitlement rule than a tort or contract rule.

Generally, injunctions are available as a remedy in trade secret cases. Since injunctions offer only prospective relief, however, damages for pre-injunction activities may also be collected. Since, unlike patents and copyrights, trade secrets have no definite term, the length of the injunction is often a difficult issue. The following case illustrates the use of one important measure of trade secret injunctions, the "head start" theory.

Winston Research Corp. v. 3M Co.

350 F.2d 134 (9th Cir. 1965)

Browning, Circuit Judge:

For some uses of precision tape recorder/reproducers, the time interval between coded signals must be recorded and reproduced with great accuracy. To accomplish this, the tape must move at as constant a speed as possible during both recording and reproduction, and any changes in tape speed during recording must be duplicated as nearly as possible during reproduction. The degree to which a particular tape recorder/reproducer accomplishes, this result is measured by its "time-displacement error."

An electronic device known as a "servo" system is commonly used to reduce time-displacement error by detecting fluctuations in tape speed and immediately adjusting the speed of the motor. Machines prior to the Mincom machine employed a flywheel to inhibit fluctuation in tape speed by increasing the inertia of the system. However, the flywheel reduced the effectiveness of the servo system since the increased inertia prevented rapid adjustments in the speed of the motor.

The effectiveness of the servo system in prior machines was also reduced by resonances created by the moving parts. The range of sensitivity of the servo system was limited to exclude the frequencies of the interfering resonances. This had the disadvantage of limiting the capacity of the servo system to respond to a full range of variations in the speed of the tape.

To solve these problems Mincom eliminated the flywheel and reduced the mass of all other rotating parts. This reduced the inertia of the tape transport system, permitting rapid adjustments in tape speed. Interfering resonances were eliminated by mechanical means. This permitted use of a servo system sensitive to a wide range of frequencies, and hence capable of rapid response to a wide range of variations in tape speed. After four years of research and development based upon this approach, Mincom produced a successful machine with an unusually low time-displacement error.

In May 1962, when Mincom had substantially completed the research phase of its program and was beginning the development of a production prototype, Johnson, who was in charge of Mincom's program, left Mincom's employment. He joined Tobias, who had previously been discharged as Mincom's sales manager, in forming Winston Research Corporation. In late 1962, Winston contracted with the government to develop a precision tape reproducer. Winston hired many of the technicians who had participated in the development of the Mincom machine to work on the design and development of the Winston machine.

In approximately fourteen months, Winston completed a machine having the same low time-displacement error as the Mincom machine.

Conflicting policy considerations come into play in deciding what limitations should be imposed upon an employee in the use and disclosure of information acquired in the course of a terminated employment relationship—or, conversely, what protection should be extended to the former employer against use and disclosure of such information.

On the one hand, restrictions upon the use and disclosure of such information limit the employee's employment opportunities, tie him to a particular employer, and weaken his bargaining power with that employer. Such restrictions interfere with the employee's movement to the job in which he may most effectively use his skills. They inhibit an employee from either setting up his own business or from adding his strength to a competitor of his employer, and thus they diminish potential competition. Such restrictions impede the dissemination of ideas and skills throughout industry. The burdens that they impose upon the employee and society increase in proportion to the significance of the employee's accomplishments, and the degree of his specialization.

On the other hand, restrictions upon an employee's disclosure of information that was developed as a result of the employer's initiative and investment, and which was entrusted to the employee in confidence, are necessary to the maintenance of decent standards of morality in the business community. Unless protection is given against unauthorized disclosure of confidential business information by employees, employee-employer relationships will be demoralized; employers will be compelled to limit communication among employees with a consequent loss in efficiency; and business, espionage, deceit, and fraud among employers will be encouraged. . . .

The federal patent statutes require full disclosure of the invention as a condition to the grant of monopoly so that at the end of the period of monopoly the development may be freely available to all. Thus, the federal patent statutes would seem to reflect a congressional determination that any individual or social interests that may be served by secrecy are outweighed by those served by full disclosure. And it would seem to follow that state law providing protection for trade secrets cannot be applied to serve a premise that the balance of interests favors secrecy. Thus, state law protecting trade secrets cannot be based "on a policy of rewarding or otherwise encouraging the development of secret processes or devices. The protection is merely against breach of faith and reprehensible means of learning another's secret." RESTATEMENT, TORTS § 757, comment b.

The district court found, and Winston concedes, that Johnson and the other former Mincom employees based Winston's development program upon the same approach to the problem of achieving a low time-displacement error as they had pursued in developing the Mincom machine. The district court further found that this general approach was not a trade secret of Mincom's. Finally, the district court found that the particular embodiment of these general concepts in the Mincom machine was Mincom's trade secret, and had been improperly utilized by the former Mincom employees in developing the Winston machine.

Mincom contends that the court defined Mincom's trade secrets too narrowly; Winston, that the court's definition was too broad.

In describing Mincom's trade secrets in the judgment, the district court first outlined the general approach which both Mincom and Winston followed in the development of their machines, closing with the phrase, "as accomplished and adopted by" Mincom. The court then set out the detailed specifications of the various elements of the Mincom machine. Winston reads the court's initial outline of the general approach as a determination that this was itself a Mincom trade secret, and then vigorously attacks this supposed determination.

We read the initial description of the general approach as merely introductory to, and limited by, the detailed specifications that follow. We think the district court rejected Mincom's contention that the general approach itself was a Mincom trade secret — and properly so. There was expert testimony that if a technician in the field were asked to design a machine having the time-displacement error achieved by the Mincom machine he would adopt the general approach of reducing the inertia of rotating parts and utilizing a wide band servo system — that this approach was dictated by well known principles of physics. It was therefore not protectable under accepted trade secret doctrine. It was not "secret," for it consisted essentially of general engineering principles in the public domain and part of the intellectual equipment of technical employees. Its disclosure could not be treated as betrayal of a confidence placed by Mincom in its technical employees.

Winston points out that the basic mechanical elements of the Mincom machine were found in various publicly known recorder-reproducers, and that all of them were disclosed in a patent issued to Johnson and assigned to Mincom in 1961. But there was substantial evidence that the specifications of these basic mechanical elements and their relationship to each other embodied in the Mincom machine and detailed in the district court's judgment were not publicly known, and were arrived at by Mincom only after painstaking research and extensive trial and error.

As we read the findings and judgment, it was these specifications and relationships that the court found to constitute Mincom's trade secret, and not the general approach itself or the basic mechanical elements as such. We think this determination was correct.

Winston also suggests that the specifications were "mere choices of engineering design," and not of critical importance. Even if this were so, they were choices made first by Mincom, and gave Mincom product having superior characteristics that Winston achieved only by utilizing elements with substantially the same specifications.

Winston argues that information is protected from disclosure only if communicated to the employee by the employer who is seeking protection, and that the information involved in this case was not disclosed by Mincom to the employees subsequently hired by Winston, but rather was developed by these employees themselves, albeit while employed by Mincom.

We need not examine the soundness of [this argument], or its applicability to a case such as this, in which a group of specialists engaged in related facets of a single development project change their employer. The argument is apparently based upon the notion that unless the first employer conveys the information to the employee, subsequent disclosure by the employee cannot be a breach of a duty of confidence owed that employer. Futurecraft Corp. v. Clary Corp., 23 Cal. Rptr. 198. As the court in *Futurecraft* recognized, an obligation not to disclose may arise from circumstances other than communication in confidence by the employer. It may also rest upon an express or implied agreement. In the present case, an agreement not to disclose might be implied from Mincom's elaborate efforts to maintain the secrecy of its development program, and the employees' knowledge of these efforts and participation in them. In any event, Mincom and its employees entered into express written agreements binding the latter not to disclose confidential information, and these agreements did not exclude information which the employee himself contributed.

The district court enjoined Winston Research Corporation, Johnson, and Tobias from disclosing or using Mincom's trade secrets in any manner for a period of two years from the date of judgment. The court also required the assignment of certain patent applications to Mincom. No damages were awarded. . . . Mincom argues that the injunction should have been permanent, or at least for a substantially longer period. Winston contends that no injunctive relief was appropriate.

Mincom was, of course, entitled to protection of its trade secrets for as long as they remained secret. The district court's decision to limit the duration of injunctive relief was necessarily premised upon a determination that Mincom's trade secrets would shortly be fully disclosed, through no fault of Winston, as a result of public announcements, demonstrations, and sales and deliveries of Mincom machines. Mincom has not seriously challenged this implicit finding, and we think the record fully supports it. . . .

We think the district court's approach was sound. A permanent injunction would subvert the public's interest in allowing technical employees to make full use of their knowledge and skill and in fostering research and development. On the other hand, denial of any injunction at all would leave the faithless employee unpunished where, as here, no damages were awarded; and he and his new employer would retain the benefit of a headstart over legitimate competitors who did not have access to the trade secrets until they were publicly disclosed. By enjoining use of the trade secrets for the approximate period it would require a legitimate Mincom competitor to develop a successful machine after public disclosure of the secret information, the district court denied the employees any advantage from their faithlessness, placed Mincom in the position it would have occupied if the breach of confidence had not occurred prior to the public disclosure, and imposed the minimum restraint consistent with the realization of these objectives upon the utilization of the employees' skills. . . .

Winston also challenges the district court's determination that "knowledge of the reasons for" the particular specifications of the Mincom machine, and "knowledge of what not to do . . . and how not to make the same mistakes" as Mincom had made in arriving at these specifications, were Mincom trade secrets. [Although we agree with the district court's conclusion that such "negative know-how" is a trade secret, in the circumstances of this case we can see no way to prohibit Mincom's former employees from using such knowledge without prohibiting them from using their general knowledge and experience at the same time. In an appropriate case, this kind of knowledge can be protected by an injunction or even an award of damages, but this is not such a case.] . . .

Mincom argues that the district court should have awarded money damages as well as injunctive relief. We think the district court acted well within its discretion in declining to do so. Since Winston sold none of its machines, it had no profits to disgorge. The evidence as to possible future profits was at best highly speculative. To enjoin future sales and at the same time make an award based on future profits from the prohibited sales would result in duplicative and inconsistent relief, and the choice that the district court made between these mutually exclusive alternatives was not an unreasonable one. There was evidence that Winston would probably sell its machine and realize profits after the injunction expired, but these sales and profits, as we have seen, would not be tainted by breach of confidence, since Winston could by that time have developed its machine from publicly disclosed information. . . .

Finally, Mincom's employment contracts required its employees to assign to Mincom inventions conceived during employment, and inventions conceived within one year of termination of employment that were "based upon" confidential information. Mincom sought to require the assignment of one patent and a number of patent applications. The district court received evidence as to when each invention was conceived and its relationship to Mincom's secrets.

The district court found that three patent applications involved inventions conceived during the inventors' employment by Mincom, and ordered assignment on that basis. The court also found that a patent and some other patent applications involving inventions conceived after the employees left Mincom and went to Winston were not based on Mincom's confidential trade secrets. [The mere fact that they were conceived after the employees moved to Winston was not the reason for this finding — the reason was that these later inventions simply were not based on Mincom's confidential information.] We think these findings have support in the record and are not clearly erroneous. [Judgment affirmed.]

COMMENTS AND QUESTIONS

1. Should injunctions issue as a matter of course in trade secret cases? The general rule in IP law does not make injunctions automatic, but applies a four-factor balancing test that asks whether the plaintiff will be irreparably injured absent an injunction,

whether the grant or denial of an injunction would impose more hardship, and where the public interest lies. *See* eBay, Inc. v. MercExchange LLC, 547 U.S. 388 (2006). Because the public disclosure of a trade secret can destroy the secret altogether, courts and commentators have traditionally thought injunctions appropriate to prevent an injury that truly is irreparable. But in the wake of *eBay* some courts have denied injunctive relief. *See, e.g.*, Faiveley Transport Malmo AB v. Wabtec Corp., 559 F.3d 110 (2d Cir. 2009); Am. Airlines, Inc. v. Imhof, 2009 WL 1531098 (S.D.N.Y. June 3, 2009) (refusing to presume irreparable injury; plaintiff did not show that the defendant was likely to disclose the documents he took to his new employer).

2. "Head-start injunctions" are available to plaintiffs who have published or otherwise disclosed their secret at some point after it was misappropriated. Suppose Anne possesses a secret that she is in the process of commercializing. Suppose further that it takes Anne two years after developing the secret to bring the product to market, at which point the secret is disclosed. If Benjamin steals Anne's idea during the development process (say, at month 12), Benjamin will be able to get to market one year earlier than if he had waited until the information became public. In such a case, courts will issue a "head-start" injunction for a period of one year, putting Benjamin in the same position he would have been in without the secret. *See, e.g.*, Verigy US Inc. v. Mayder, 2008 WL 564634 (N.D. Cal. Feb. 29, 2008) (granting a five-month injunction to account for the lag time defendant would have faced in getting to market absent misappropriation).

Even if such an injunction is impossible (for example, because Benjamin has already entered the market), courts may allow him to continue using the former secret but require him to pay a "reasonable royalty" to Anne. The reasonable royalty is presumably set by the court, in an effort to approximate the royalty Anne might have charged Benjamin in a voluntary transaction.

Is a reasonable royalty a fair solution in such a situation? *See* Mid-Michigan Comp. Sys. v. Marc Glassman Inc., 416 F.3d 505 (6th Cir. 2005) (basing damages for misappropriation of computer software on a reasonable royalty). At least one commentator has suggested that such a remedy "is peculiarly inappropriate to redress a situation where injunctive relief ought to be applied." *See* 12 ROGER MILGRIM, MILGRIM ON TRADE SECRETS § 1.01[2][a], at 1-36 n.20 (citing a district court decision concluding that limiting relief to a reasonable royalty invites misappropriation).

3. In Kewanee Oil Co. v. Bicron Corp., 416 U.S. 470, 473 (1974), the former employees had signed confidentiality agreements. The Court upheld the district court's granting of a permanent injunction against the disclosure or use by respondents of 20 of the 40 claimed trade secrets until such time as the trade secrets had been released to the public, had otherwise generally become available to the public, or had been obtained by respondents from sources having the legal right to convey the information. *Id.* at 473-74. *See also* Henry Hope X-Ray Prods., Inc. v. Marron Carrel, Inc., 674 F.2d 1336, 1342 (9th Cir. 1982) (the limitation on confidential information contains the implicit temporal limitation that information may be disclosed when it ceases to be confidential). *But see* Howard Schultz & Assocs. v. Broniec, 239 Ga. 181, 236 S.E.2d 265, 270 (1977) ("The nondisclosure covenant here contains no time limitation and hence it is unenforceable"); Gary Van Zeeland Talent, Inc. v. Sandas, 54 Wis. 2d 202, 267 N.W.2d 242, 250 (1978) (unlimited duration of agreement not to disclose trade secret customer list makes the agreement per se void).

The Eighth Circuit in Sigma Chemical Co. v. Harris, 794 F.2d 371, 375 (8th Cir. 1986), explained, in the course of rejecting a "temporally unlimited" injunction, the rationale for limiting injunctions in time:

> [E]xtending the injunction beyond the time needed for independent development would give the employer "a windfall protection and would subvert the public interest in fostering competition and in allowing employees to make full use of their knowledge and ability."
>
> We believe the part of the injunction prohibiting disclosure of trade secrets must be limited in duration and, accordingly, reverse in part and remand the case to the district court for consideration of the time it would take a "legitimate competitor" to independently reproduce the information contained in the product and vendor files. On remand, the district court should also modify the language of the injunction to expressly state that Harris may use that information which is already in the public domain.

4. Should there be a presumption that injunctive relief is appropriate? Such a presumption is typical of cases involving real property, but no such rule exists in most tort cases, and certainly not in typical contract cases. Are damages sufficient to protect trade secret owners? Perhaps not, since trade secrets are often hard to value, and misappropriation by one party can destroy the secret altogether. On the other hand, perhaps the parties could contract for injunctive relief, at least in employment cases, using noncompetition or confidentiality agreements. Should the law impose obligations the parties have not undertaken voluntarily? Should it refuse to enforce contract terms that the parties have agreed to? *See* East v. Aqua Gaming Inc., 805 So. 2d 932 (Fla. App. 2001) (affirming injunction against use of trade secrets, but vacating injunction that prevented competition in the absence of an enforceable noncompete agreement).

One problem with such "automatic" injunctive relief is that it is difficult—and costly—to enforce. Is it an appropriate use of judicial resources to supervise employer-employee relationships on an ongoing basis? Is there a more cost-effective alternative to such supervision?

Who should be enjoined? Several courts have refused to hold the new employer liable for an employee's malfeasance where they were unaware of it. *See* Infinity Prods. v. Quandt, 810 N.E.2d 1028 (Ind. 2004) (no respondeat superior liability for trade secret law); BEA Sys. v. WebMethods, Inc., 595 S.E.2d 87 (Ga. App. 2004).

Note on Criminal Trade Secret Statutes

Misappropriation of trade secrets is not only a tort; in some circumstances, it is a crime. *See generally* Eli Lederman, *Criminal Liability for Breach of Confidential Commercial Information*, 38 EMORY L.J. 921 (1989) (summarizing criminal laws governing misappropriation of confidential information). A series of well-publicized criminal prosecutions of computer executives accused of taking trade secrets to their new employers have raised the consciousness of industry professionals about trade secrets. The prosecutions have also raised ethical and political questions about the propriety of trade secret prosecutions "engineered" by the real parties in interest, often major companies such as Intel or Borland.

Criminal trade secret cases differ from civil ones in several respects. Obviously, the complaining party is the government rather than the injured company. However, the injured companies are the "real parties in interest" and usually have some presence in the case. Even though they are not parties to the criminal proceeding, they at least supply a significant number of the witnesses and enjoy a high level of communication with the district attorney.

Just as obviously, the burden of proof is higher than in a civil case. Some cases that could be won by the plaintiffs as civil cases will be lost in criminal court. This situation is even more likely because several states have definitions of trade secrets in their criminal laws that are more limited than their civil counterparts. For example, Cal. Penal Code §499c, which governs theft of trade secrets, historically limited the definition of a trade secret to "scientific or technical" information. (The constitutionality of this definition of trade secrets was upheld against a vagueness attack in People v. Serrata, 133 Cal. Rptr. 144 (Ct. App. 1976).) But in 1996, the California legislature amended its criminal trade secret statute to be coextensive with the definition of trade secrets in the Uniform Trade Secrets Act.

Defendants accused of stealing trade secrets may be charged with other offenses as well. For example, defendants who acquire a secret through improper means, as opposed to acquisition in a confidential relationship, may be guilty of larceny, receiving stolen property, or a host of similar crimes. *See* People v. Gopal, 217 Cal. Rptr. 487, 493-94 (Ct. App. 1985), *cert. denied*, 476 U.S. 1105 (1986). Further, the growth of computer technology has expanded the federal role in prosecuting theft of trade secrets, since data taken over a computer network is considered to cross state lines. *See* United States v. Riggs, 739 F. Supp. 414 (N.D. Ill. 1990) (allowing indictment of computer hackers who published data from a Bell South computer text file for wire fraud and interstate transportation of stolen property).

The prosecution of a criminal (rather than civil) trade secret case has other effects on the parties involved. First, criminal trade secret courtrooms are the scene of constant battles over the publication of information. The real parties in interest will naturally oppose the disclosure in a public courtroom of the very secrets the defendant is accused of stealing. This concern runs headlong into the defendant's constitutional right to a public trial.[19] Second, civil cases are generally stayed pending the outcome of a criminal prosecution. Thus a criminal prosecution may actually delay injunctive relief—the kind of remedy a civil plaintiff is often most interested in.

COMMENTS AND QUESTIONS

1. Given the stay imposed on a parallel civil action and the higher burden of proof in a criminal case, why would a civil plaintiff ever seek a criminal prosecution?

2. Should theft of trade secrets be a criminal offense? Does the presence of criminal sanctions have any effect on the optimal level of deterrence provided in damages suits, and therefore on the damages that should be awarded in a civil suit?

19. There is no such right in civil cases. To avoid the very real danger that a misappropriation action will result in disclosure of the very secrets the plaintiff seeks to protect, civil trade secret actions will almost invariably include protective orders limiting the disclosure of information produced in discovery. Such orders are usually agreed to by the parties but may sometimes be imposed by the court. They will sometimes go so far as to prevent the parties themselves (as opposed to the attorneys and hired experts) from reviewing the other side's documents. In such a case, should in-house counsel be given access to discovery documents? *See* Brown Bag Software v. Symantec Corp., 960 F.2d 1465, 1470 (9th Cir. 1992).

Do you see any problems with California's inclusion of business information in the criminal trade secret statute? Are there reasons to treat theft of scientific information more harshly than theft of business information?

Note on Federal Criminal Liability for Trade Secret Misappropriation[20]

Prior to the passage of the Economic Espionage Act of 1996, there was only a single, very limited federal statute that directly prohibited the misappropriation of a trade secret. When confronted with an allegation that an individual had misappropriated a valuable trade secret, federal prosecutors were forced to turn to a number of federal statutes that were clearly not designed to cover trade secrets. In particular, prosecutors attempted to use the Depression-era Interstate Transportation of Stolen Property Act (ITSP) and the wire fraud and mail fraud statutes. However, a recent court decision severely curtails the use of ITSP, and the use of the mail and wire fraud statutes has always been limited because the theft often does not involve the use of mail or wire. In addition, since a thief usually merely copies information and does not necessarily "defraud" the victim permanently of the data, prosecutions are further limited. These shortcomings of federal law, coupled with testimony about the threat of economic espionage sponsored by foreign governments, underlie Congress's decision to enact the Economic Espionage Act of 1996 (EEA), 18 U.S.C. §§ 1831 *et seq.*

The structure of the EEA reflects its rather disparate origins and the confusion that surrounded major changes made in the last days of the 1996 Congressional session. The EEA contains a definition of trade secrets that is taken, with only minor modifications, from the definition in the Uniform Trade Secrets Act. At the same time, the sections defining misappropriation are entirely new, and have no parallels in existing trade secret law.

Sections 1831(a) and 1832(a) contain identical language regarding acts of misappropriation, punishing a specified individual who:

> (1) steals, or without authorization appropriates, takes, carries away, or conceals, or by fraud, artifice or deception obtains a trade secret;
> (2) without authorization copies, duplicates, sketches, draws, photographs, downloads, uploads, alters, destroys, photocopies, replicates, transmits, delivers, sends, mails, communicates, or conveys a trade secret;
> (3) receives, buys, or possesses a trade secret, knowing the same to have been stolen or appropriated, obtained, or converted without authorization . . .

These provisions are significantly broader in some respects than corresponding civil trade secret laws such as the Uniform Act.

Section (a)(1) lists a number of means of improper acquisition of a trade secret. In general, the provisions in this section seem to track the "improper means" of acquisition punished in civil cases. In particular, the references to stealing, concealment, fraud, artifice, and deception are reminiscent of the civil law's prohibition

20. This section is adapted from James H.A. Pooley et al., *Understanding the Economic Espionage Act of 1996*, 5 Tex. Intell. Prop. L.J. 177 (1997).

against both illegal and immoral business conduct. However, the provision also makes it a crime to "appropriate" or "take" a secret without authorization from the trade secret owner. These terms might be thought to encompass the sort of lawful business espionage that has long been permitted by civil trade secret law—conduct on the order of observing a competitor's property from across the street. There is some suggestion in the legislative history that the EEA is not intended to inhibit robust competition.[21] While this might be enough to declare broad categories of competitive intelligence gathering proper and therefore lawful, the ambiguity of some of the terms in section (a)(1) is troubling.

Broader still is section (2), which gives the trade secret owner the right to control a whole host of activities on the order of duplication, transportation, or destruction of a trade secret. This provision encompasses more than its civil counterparts. Section (2) is not by its terms limited to secrets acquired by "improper means" like those listed in section (1). Even legally acquired secrets can be misappropriated under the EEA if they are analyzed or duplicated in one of the ways listed in section (2). The civil law does prohibit some such uses of a lawfully acquired trade secret, but limits its reach to disclosure or use of a secret in violation of a confidential relationship. By contrast, there is no requirement of such a confidential relationship in the EEA. So long as the requirements of secrecy are satisfied, the trade secret owner is apparently entitled to seek the aid of the Justice Department in preventing the world from engaging in any of the enumerated acts in section (2), even if the secret is contained in a product that the defendant lawfully acquired.[22] As a result, the EEA effectively implies a confidential relationship between the trade secret owner and the world at large, something trade secret law has never before attempted and an indication that Congress believes trade secrets law is based in property theory, not tort or contract. Further, some of the specific provisions in section (2), such as the prohibition against "altering" or "destroying" a trade secret, are outside the normal reach of trade secret law.[23]

The most troubling thing about 18 U.S.C. §1831(a)(2) is that it arguably prohibits many forms of heretofore lawful reverse engineering activity. While reverse engineering is not expressly prohibited under this section, neither is it expressly permitted. Rather, its legality appears to be judged according to whether the reverse engineer engages in any of the prohibited acts.[24] To be sure, some types of reverse engineering, such as looking at or tasting a lawfully acquired product in order to determine what is in it, will not be illegal under the EEA. On the other hand, several of the restrictions in section (2) will, if read literally, encompass some forms of reverse engineering. For example, reverse engineering of computer software by "decompilation" almost always involves the making of a prohibited "copy" of the program. Reverse engineering of mechanical devices and computer hardware may well involve prohibited "sketching, drawing, or photographing" of the trade secret contained in

21. S. Rep. No. 142-12212 ("Other companies can and must have the ability to determine the elements of a trade secret through their own inventiveness, creativity and hard work. . . . [P]arallel development of a trade secret cannot and should not constitute a violation of this statute.").

22. *See* H.R. Rep. No. 104-788 ("The concept of control also includes the mere possession of the information, regardless of the manner by which the non-owner gained possession of the information.").

23. "Destroying" a secret might mean "destroying its value by publishing it to the world," in which case civil law does provide a remedy. Alternatively, it might mean the physical destruction of valuable information, which is not covered by the Uniform Act.

24. *See* S. Rep. No. 142-12212.

the publicly sold device. It is even possible that the prohibition against "altering" a trade secret will be interpreted to prevent chemical analysis of a trade secret product if such analysis involves the use of chemical reactants that bond to secret chemicals or that precipitate out certain elements from the formula.

The legislative history of the EEA is not encouraging to reverse engineers. The Senate report suggests that "the important thing is to focus on whether the accused has committed one of the prohibited acts of this statute rather than whether he or she has 'reverse engineered.' If someone has lawfully gained access to a trade secret and can replicate it without violating copyright, patent *or this law*, then that form of 'reverse engineering' should be fine."[25] The report goes on to suggest that observing a lawfully purchased product, or drinking a Coca-Cola, are legitimate activities.[26] On the other hand, there appears to be no reverse engineering defense protecting any of the forms of analysis suggested above. A computer programmer has the right to decompile a software program in certain circumstances under the Uniform Act, copyright law, and the common law without fear of civil liability. Under the EEA, though, that programmer has arguably committed a felony.

The Justice Department is actively prosecuting cases under the EEA. As of this writing, over three dozen cases had been filed. In United States v. Hsu, 155 F.3d 189 (3d Cir. 1998), the first appellate decision interpreting the Act, the court concluded that the defendants (who were the subject of a sting operation) could be found guilty of conspiring and attempting to misappropriate information that was not in fact a trade secret, because the crime of attempt did not require proof that the information the defendants tried to steal was in fact a secret. This is an issue that has recurred in the cases. *Consider* United States v. Lange, 312 F.3d 263 (7th Cir. 2002):

> § 1832(a)(4) makes it a crime to attempt to sell trade secrets without the owner's permission. Even if Lange did not have real trade secrets in his possession, the argument goes, he *thought* he did and therefore may be penalized for an attempted sale. The argument finds support in *Hsu*, which held that in order to avoid graymail-the threat that to obtain a conviction the prosecutor must disclose the secret by putting it in the trial record-a case may be based on § 1832(a)(4) without disclosing all details of the trade secret. Accord United States v. Pin Yen Yang, 281 F.3d 534, 543-44 (6th Cir. 2002). We agree with the general approach of these decisions. *Hsu* analogized the attempted sale of information believed to be a trade secret to an attempt such as shooting a corpse, believing it to be alive, or selling sugar, believing it to be cocaine. Events of this sort underlie the maxim that factual impossibility is no defense to a prosecution for attempt. See United States v. Bailey, 227 F.3d 792, 797 (7th Cir. 2000); United States v. Saunders, 166 F.3d 907, 916 (7th Cir. 1999); United States v. Cotts, 14 F.3d 300, 307 (7th Cir. 1994). This does not mean, however, that the defendant's belief *alone* can support a conviction. All attempt prosecutions depend on demonstrating that the defendant took a substantial step toward completion of the offense, which could have been carried out unless thwarted. Braxton v. United States, 500 U.S. 344, 111 S. Ct. 1854, 114 L. Ed. 2d 385 (1991). Although the American Law Institute recommends a definition of attempt linked closely to intent, Model Penal Code § 5.01(1)(c), the Supreme Court has not embraced this view and demands in cases under federal law that the prosecutor establish a probability of success. See, e.g., Spectrum Sports, Inc. v. McQuillan, 506 U.S. 447, 113 S. Ct. 884, 122 L. Ed. 2d 247 (1993) ("dangerous probability" of success is an ingredient of attempted monopolization).

25. S. Rep. No. 142-12212, at 12-13 (emphasis added).
26. *Id.* at 12213. *Cf.* Mason v. Jack Daniels Distillery, 518 So. 2d 130 (Ala. Ct. App. 1987).

An attempted murder may be thwarted by substituting a sack of flour for the intended victim; a sale of drugs may be thwarted by substituting sugar for cocaine, or rock candy for crack. These situations present a good chance of success, but for the intervention. So does "the disgruntled former employee who walks out of his former company with a computer diskette full of engineering schematics" (*Hsu*, 155 F.3d at 201)—a fair description of Lange's conduct (though diskettes are obsolete). See also United States v. Martin, 228 F.3d 1, 10-12 (1st Cir. 2000). A sale of trade secrets may be thwarted by substituting a disk with the collected works of Shakespeare for the disk that the defendant believed contained the plans for brake assemblies, or by an inadvertent failure to download the proper file. The attempted sale of the disk is a culpable substantial step. But it is far less clear that sale of information already known to the public could be deemed a substantial step toward the offense, just because the defendant is deluded and does not understand what a trade secret is. Selling a copy of *Zen and the Art of Motorcycle Maintenance* is not attempted economic espionage, even if the defendant thinks that the tips in the book are trade secrets; nor is sticking pins in voodoo dolls attempted murder. Booksellers and practitioners of the occult pose no social dangers, certainly none of the magnitude of those who are tricked into shooting bags of sand that have been substituted for targets of assassination. Lange was more dangerous than our bookseller but much less dangerous than our hypothetical assassin. Perhaps data purloined from an ex-employer is sufficiently *likely* to contain trade secrets to justify calling the preparation for sale a substantial step toward completion of the offense, and thus a culpable attempt, even if the employee stole the wrong data file and did not get his hands on the commercially valuable information. We need not pursue the subject beyond noting the plausibility of the claim and its sensitivity to the facts—what kind of data did the employee think he stole, and so on. For it is not necessary to announce a definitive rule about how dangerous the completed acts must be in trade secret cases: the judge was entitled to (and did) find that Lange had *real* trade secrets in his possession.

Lange wants us to proceed as if all he tried to sell were measurements that anyone could have taken with calipers after disassembling an original-equipment part. Such measurements could not be called trade secrets if, as Lange asserts, the assemblies in question were easy to take apart and measure. But no one would have paid $100,000 for metes and bounds, while Lange told his customers that the data on offer were worth more than that asking price. Which they were. What Lange had, and tried to sell, were the completed specifications and engineering diagrams that reflected all the work completed *after* the measurements had been taken: the metallurgical data, details of the sintering, the results of the tests, the plans needed to produce the finished goods, everything required to get FAA certification of a part supposedly identical to one that had been approved. Those details "derive[d] independent economic value, actual or potential, from not being generally known to, and not being readily ascertainable through proper means by, the public[.]" Every firm other than the original equipment manufacturer and RAPCO had to pay dearly to devise, test, and win approval of similar parts; the details unknown to the rivals, and not discoverable with tape measures, had considerable "independent economic value . . . from not being generally known". A sensible trier of fact could determine that Lange tried to sell trade secrets.

Id. at 268-69.

12

Legal Protection for Facts, Uncopyrightable Factual Compilations, and Ideas

One of the major bodies of IP law, copyright, confers protection on original works of authorship that are fixed in a tangible medium of expression. "Originality" is a low threshold, requiring only a modicum of independent creativity. "Work of authorship" is a broad construct that includes subject matter such as literary works, musical compositions, and motion pictures. This combination of a low originality standard and a broad "work of authorship" standard means that, at any given time, copyright subsists in a very large number of creative works. Copyright is not limitless, however. Importantly, copyright does not subsist in either facts or ideas. Indeed, the Supreme Court has held that the Constitution prohibits Congress from extending copyright protection to unoriginal factual compilations, no matter how much "sweat of the brow" goes into their creation. *See* Feist v. Rural Tel. Co., 499 U.S. 340 (1991) (holding uncopyrightable a comprehensive alphabetical listing of names and phone numbers for a given geographical area, as found in the white pages of a telephone directory). Many commentators believe that the uncopyrightability of facts (and ideas) is good policy as well, because facts and ideas are the essential building blocks to which all creators need access. Put another way, the theory is that the social benefits of extending copyright protection to facts and ideas (for example, possibly inducing more people to discover new facts and to develop new ideas) would be outweighed by the social costs of inhibiting access.

Not everyone agrees, however, that facts and ideas should be relegated to the public domain under all circumstances. With respect to facts in particular, some scholars have argued that failure to extend protection (whether it takes the form of copyright protection or something else) to unoriginal but labor-intensive databases threatens to discourage the optimal production of such databases, as a result of free-rider problems. (Others strongly disagree, as the Comments and Questions portions of this chapter demonstrate.) Sections A and B of this chapter focus on two possible legal responses, one sounding in the common law of unfair competition and the other in contract, to the desire on the part of some content providers to attain some type of protection in uncopyrightable factual material. Section C discusses parallel developments with respect to the protection of uncopyrightable ideas. As you read through these materials, ask yourself which side — the high or low protectionists — appears to have the better of the policy argument.

A. THE TORT OF MISAPPROPRIATION

International News Service v. Associated Press
248 U.S. 215 (1918)

Justice PITNEY delivered the opinion of the court.

The parties are competitors in the gathering and distribution of news and its publication for profit in newspapers throughout the United States. The Associated Press, which was complainant in the District Court, is a cooperative organization, incorporated under the Membership Corporations Law of the State of New York, its members being individuals who are either proprietors or representatives of about 950 daily newspapers published in all parts of the United States. . . . Complainant gathers in all parts of the world, by means of various instrumentalities of its own, by exchange with its members, and by other appropriate means, news and intelligence of current and recent events of interest to newspaper readers and distributes it daily to its members for publication in their newspapers. The cost of the service, amounting approximately to $3,500,000 per annum, is assessed upon the members and becomes a part of their costs of operation, to be recouped, presumably with profit, through the publication of their several newspapers. Under complainant's by-laws each member agrees upon assuming membership that news received through complainant's service is received exclusively for publication in a particular newspaper, language, and place specified in the certificate of membership, that no other use of it shall be permitted, and that no member shall furnish or permit anyone in his employ or connected with his newspaper to furnish any of complainant's news in advance of publication to any person not a member. And each member is required to gather the local news of his district and supply it to the Associated Press and to no one else.

Defendant is a corporation organized under the laws of the State of New Jersey, whose business is the gathering and selling of news to its customers and clients, consisting of newspapers published throughout the United States, under contracts by which they pay certain amounts at stated times for defendant's service. It has widespread news-gathering agencies; the cost of its operations amounts, it is said, to more than $2,000,000 per annum; and it serves about 400 newspapers located in the various cities of the United States and abroad, a few of which are represented, also, in the membership of the Associated Press.

The parties are in the keenest competition between themselves in the distribution of news throughout the United States; and so, as a rule, are the newspapers that they serve, in their several districts.

Complainant in its bill, defendant in its answer, have set forth in almost identical terms the rather obvious circumstances and conditions under which their business is conducted. The value of the service, and of the news furnished, depends upon the promptness of transmission, as well as upon the accuracy and impartiality of the news; it being essential that the news be transmitted to members or subscribers as early or earlier than similar information can be furnished to competing newspapers by other news services, and that the news furnished by each agency shall not be furnished to newspapers which do not contribute to the expense of gathering it. And further, to quote from the answer:

> Prompt knowledge and publication of world-wide news is essential to the conduct of a modern newspaper, and by reason of the enormous expense incident to the gathering and distribution of such news, the only practical way in which a proprietor of a newspaper can obtain the same is, either through cooperation with a considerable number of other newspaper proprietors in the work of collecting and distributing such news, and the equitable division with them of the expenses thereof, or by the purchase of such news from some existing agency engaged in that business.

The bill was filed to restrain the pirating of complainant's news by defendant in three ways: First, by bribing employees of newspapers published by complainant's members to furnish Associated Press news to defendant before publication, for transmission by telegraph and telephone to defendant's clients for publication by them; Second, by inducing Associated Press members to violate its by-laws and permit defendant to obtain news before publication; and Third, by copying news from bulletin boards and from early editions of complainant's newspapers and selling this, either bodily or after rewriting it, to defendant's customers.

The District Court, upon consideration of the bill and answer, with voluminous affidavits on both sides, granted a preliminary injunction under the first and second heads; but refused at that stage to restrain the systematic practice admittedly pursued by defendant, of taking news bodily from the bulletin boards and early editions of complainant's newspapers and selling it as its own. The court expressed itself as satisfied that this practice amounted to unfair trade, but as the legal question was one of first impression it considered that the allowance of an injunction should await the outcome of an appeal. 240 Fed. Rep. 983, 996. Both parties having appealed, the Circuit Court of Appeals sustained the injunction order so far as it went, and upon complainant's appeal modified it and remanded the cause with directions to issue an injunction also against any bodily taking of the words or substance of complainant's news until its commercial value as news had passed away. 245 Fed. Rep. 244, 253. The present writ of certiorari was then allowed. 245 U.S. 644.

The only matter that has been argued before us is whether defendant may lawfully be restrained from appropriating news taken from bulletins issued by complainant or any of its members, or from newspapers published by them, for the purpose of selling it to defendant's clients. Complainant asserts that defendant's admitted course of conduct in this regard both violates complainant's property right in the news and constitutes unfair competition in business. And notwithstanding the case has proceeded only to the stage of a preliminary injunction, we have deemed it proper to consider the underlying questions, since they go to the very merits of the action and are presented upon facts that are not in dispute. As presented in argument, these questions are: 1. Whether there is any property in news; 2. Whether, if there be property in news collected for the purpose of being published, it survives the instant of its publication in the first newspaper to which it is communicated by the news-gatherer; and 3. Whether defendant's admitted course of conduct in appropriating for commercial use matter taken from bulletins or early editions of Associated Press publications constitutes unfair competition in trade.

The federal jurisdiction was invoked because of diversity of citizenship, not upon the ground that the suit arose under the copyright or other laws of the United States. Complainant's news matter is not copyrighted. It is said that it could not, in practice, be copyrighted, because of the large number of dispatches that are sent daily; and, according to complainant's contention, news is not within the operation of the copyright act. Defendant, while apparently conceding this, nevertheless invokes the analogies of the law of literary property and copyright, insisting as its principal contention that, assuming complainant has a right of property in its news, it can be maintained (unless the copyright act be complied with) only by being kept secret and confidential, and that upon the publication with complainant's consent of uncopyrighted news by any of complainant's members in a newspaper or upon a bulletin board, the right of property is lost, and the subsequent use of the news by the public or by defendant for any purpose whatever becomes lawful. . . .

In considering the general question of property in news matter, it is necessary to recognize its dual character, distinguishing between the substance of the information and the particular form or collocation of words in which the writer has communicated it.

No doubt news articles often possess a literary quality, and are the subject of literary property at the common law; nor do we question that such an article, as a literary production, is the subject of copyright by the terms of the act as it now stands. In an early case at the circuit Mr. Justice Thompson held in effect that a newspaper was not within the protection of the copyright acts of 1790 and 1802 (Clayton v. Stone, 2 Paine, 382; 5 Fed. Cas. No. 2872). But the present act is broader; it provides that the works for which copyright may be secured shall include "all the writings of an author," and specifically mentions "periodicals, including newspapers." Act of March 4, 1909, c. 320, §§4 and 5, 35 Stat. 1075, 1076. Evidently this admits to copyright a contribution to a newspaper, notwithstanding it also may convey news; and such is the practice of the copyright office, as the newspapers of the day bear witness. See Copyright Office Bulletin No. 15 (1917), pp. 7, 14, 16-17.

But the news element—the information respecting current events contained in the literary production—is not the creation of the writer, but is a report of matters that ordinarily are publici juris; it is the history of the day. It is not to be supposed that the framers of the Constitution, when they empowered Congress "to promote the progress of science and useful arts, by securing for limited times to authors and inventors the exclusive right to their respective writings and discoveries" (Const., Art. I, §8, par. 8), intended to confer upon one who might happen to be the first to report a historic event the exclusive right for any period to spread the knowledge of it.

We need spend no time, however, upon the general question of property in news matter at common law, or the application of the copyright act, since it seems to us the case must turn upon the question of unfair competition in business. And, in our opinion, this does not depend upon any general right of property analogous to the common-law right of the proprietor of an unpublished work to prevent its publication without his consent; nor is it foreclosed by showing that the benefits of the copyright act have been waived. We are dealing here not with restrictions upon publication but with the very facilities and processes of publication. The peculiar value of news is in the spreading of it while it is fresh; and it is evident that a valuable property interest in the news, as news, cannot be maintained by keeping it secret. Besides, except for matters improperly disclosed, or published in breach of trust or confidence, or in violation of law, none of which is involved in this branch of the case, the news of current events may be regarded as common property. What we are concerned with is the business of making it known to the world, in which both parties to the present suit are engaged. That business consists in maintaining a prompt, sure, steady, and reliable service designed to place the daily events of the world at the breakfast table of the millions at a price that, while of trifling moment to each reader, is sufficient in the aggregate to afford compensation for the cost of gathering and distributing it, with the added profit so necessary as an incentive to effective action in the commercial world. The service thus performed for newspaper readers is not only innocent but extremely useful in itself, and indubitably constitutes a legitimate business. The parties are competitors in this field; and, on fundamental principles, applicable here as elsewhere, when the rights or privileges of the one are liable to conflict with those of the other, each party is under a duty so to conduct its own business as not unnecessarily or unfairly to injure that of the other. Hitchman Coal & Coke Co. v. Mitchell, 245 U.S. 229, 254.

Obviously, the question of what is unfair competition in business must be determined with particular reference to the character and circumstances of the business. The question here is not so much the rights of either party as against the public but their rights as between themselves. See Morison v. Moat, 9 Hare, 241, 258. And although we may and do assume that neither party has any remaining property interest as against the public in uncopyrighted news matter after the moment of its first publication, it by no means follows that there is no remaining property interest in it as between themselves. For, to both of them alike, news matter, however little susceptible of ownership or dominion in the absolute sense, is stock in trade, to be gathered at the cost of enterprise, organization, skill, labor, and money, and to be distributed and sold to those who will pay money for it, as for any other merchandise. Regarding the news, therefore, as but the material out of which both parties are seeking to make profits at the same time and in the same field, we hardly can fail to recognize that for this purpose, and as between them, it must be regarded as quasi property, irrespective of the rights of either as against the public.

In order to sustain the jurisdiction of equity over the controversy, we need not affirm any general and absolute property in the news as such. The rule that a court of equity concerns itself only in the protection of property rights treats any civil right of a pecuniary nature as a property right (In re Sawyer, 124 U.S. 200, 210; In re Debs, 158 U.S. 564, 593); and the right to acquire property by honest labor or the conduct of a lawful business is as much entitled to protection as the right to guard property already acquired. Truax v. Raich, 239 U.S. 33, 37-38; Brennan v. United Hatters, 73 N.J.L. 729, 742; Barr v. Essex Trades Council, 53 N.J. Eq. 101. It is this right that furnishes the basis of the jurisdiction in the ordinary case of unfair competition. . . .

Not only do the acquisition and transmission of news require elaborate organization and a large expenditure of money, skill, and effort; not only has it an exchange value to the gatherer, dependent chiefly upon its novelty and freshness, the regularity of the service, its reputed reliability and thoroughness, and its adaptability to the public needs; but also, as is evident, the news has an exchange value to one who can misappropriate it.

The peculiar features of the case arise from the fact that, while novelty and freshness form so important an element in the success of the business, the very processes of distribution and publication necessarily occupy a good deal of time. Complainant's service, as well as defendant's, is a daily service to daily newspapers; most of the foreign news reaches this country at the Atlantic seaboard, principally at the City of New York, and because of this, and of time differentials due to the earth's rotation, the distribution of news matter throughout the country is principally from east to west; and, since in speed the telegraph and telephone easily outstrip the rotation of the earth, it is a simple matter for defendant to take complainant's news from bulletins or early editions of complainant's members in the eastern cities and at the mere cost of telegraphic transmission cause it to be published in western papers issued at least as early as those served by complainant. Besides this, and irrespective of time differentials, irregularities in telegraphic transmission on different lines, and the normal consumption of time in printing and distributing the newspaper, result in permitting pirated news to be placed in the hands of defendant's readers sometimes simultaneously with the service of competing Associated Press papers, occasionally even earlier.

Defendant insists that when, with the sanction and approval of complainant, and as the result of the use of its news for the very purpose for which it is distributed, a portion of complainant's members communicate it to the general public by posting it upon bulletin boards so that all may read, or by issuing it to newspapers and distributing it indiscriminately, complainant no longer has the right to control the use to be made of it; that when it thus reaches the light of day it becomes the common possession of all to whom it is accessible; and that any purchaser of a newspaper has the right to communicate the intelligence which it contains to anybody and for any purpose, even for the purpose of selling it for profit to newspapers published for profit in competition with complainant's members.

The fault in the reasoning lies in applying as a test the right of the complainant as against the public, instead of considering the rights of complainant and defendant, competitors in business, as between themselves. The right of the purchaser of a single newspaper to spread knowledge of its contents gratuitously, for any legitimate purpose not unreasonably interfering with complainant's right to make merchandise of it, may be admitted; but to transmit that news for commercial use, in competition with complainant — which is what defendant has done and seeks to justify — is a very different matter. In doing this defendant, by its very act, admits that it is taking material that has been acquired by complainant as the result of organization and the expenditure of labor, skill, and money, and which is salable by complainant for money, and that defendant in appropriating it and selling it as its own is endeavoring to reap where it has not sown, and by disposing of it to newspapers that are competitors of complainant's members is appropriating to itself the harvest of those who have sown. Stripped of all disguises, the process amounts to an unauthorized interference with the normal operation of complainant's legitimate business precisely at the point where the profit is to be reaped, in order to divert a material portion of the profit from those who have earned it to those who have not; with special advantage to defendant in the competition because of the fact that it is not burdened with any part of the expense of gathering the news. The transaction speaks for itself, and a court of equity ought not to hesitate long in characterizing it as unfair competition in business.

The underlying principle is much the same as that which lies at the base of the equitable theory of consideration in the law of trusts — that he who has fairly paid the price should have the beneficial use of the property. Pom. Eq. Jur., §981. It is no answer to say that complainant spends its money for that which is too fugitive or evanescent to be the subject of property. That might, and for the purposes of the discussion we are assuming that it would, furnish an answer in a common-law controversy. But in a court of equity, where the question is one of unfair competition, if that which complainant has acquired fairly at substantial cost may be sold fairly at substantial profit, a competitor who is misappropriating it for the purpose of disposing of it to his own profit and to the disadvantage of complainant cannot be heard to say that it is too fugitive or evanescent to be regarded as property. It has all the attributes of property necessary for determining that a misappropriation of it by a competitor is unfair competition because contrary to good conscience.

The contention that the news is abandoned to the public for all purposes when published in the first newspaper is untenable. Abandonment is a question of intent, and the entire organization of the Associated Press negatives such a purpose. The cost of the service would be prohibitive if the reward were to be so limited. No single newspaper, no small group of newspapers, could sustain the expenditure. Indeed, it is one of the most obvious results of defendant's theory that, by permitting indiscriminate publication by anybody and everybody for purposes of profit in competition with the news-gatherer, it would render publication profitless, or so little profitable as in effect to cut off the service by rendering the cost prohibitive in comparison with the return. The practical needs and requirements of the business are reflected in complainant's by-laws which have been referred to. Their effect is that publication by each member must be deemed not by any means an abandonment of the news to the world for any and all purposes, but a publication for limited purposes; for the benefit of the readers of the bulletin or the newspaper as such; not for the purpose of making merchandise of it as news, with the result of depriving complainant's other members of their reasonable opportunity to obtain just returns for their expenditures.

It is to be observed that the view we adopt does not result in giving to complainant the right to monopolize either the gathering or the distribution of the news, or, without complying with the copyright act, to prevent the reproduction of its news articles; but only postpones participation by complainant's competitor in the processes of distribution and reproduction of news that it has not gathered, and only to the extent necessary to prevent that competitor from reaping the fruits of complainant's efforts and expenditure, to the partial exclusion of complainant, and in violation of the principle that underlies the maxim sic utere tuo, etc.

It is said that the elements of unfair competition are lacking because there is no attempt by defendant to palm off its goods as those of the complainant, characteristic of the most familiar, if not the most typical, cases of unfair competition. Howe Scale Co. v. Wyckoff, Seamans & Benedict, 198 U.S. 118, 140. But we cannot concede that the right to equitable relief is confined to that class of cases. In the present case the fraud upon complainant's rights is more direct and obvious. Regarding news matter as the mere material from which these two competing parties are endeavoring to make money, and treating it, therefore, as quasi property for the purposes of their business because they are both selling it as such, defendant's conduct differs from the ordinary case of unfair competition in trade principally in this that, instead of selling its own goods as those of complainant, it substitutes misappropriation in the place of misrepresentation, and sells complainant's goods as its own.

Besides the misappropriation, there are elements of imitation, of false pretense, in defendant's practices. The device of rewriting complainant's news articles, frequently resorted to, carries its own comment. The habitual failure to give credit to complainant for that which is taken is significant. Indeed, the entire system of appropriating complainant's news and transmitting it as a commercial product to defendant's clients and patrons amounts to a false representation to them and to their newspaper readers that the news transmitted is the result of defendant's own investigation in the field. But these elements, although accentuating the wrong, are not the essence of it. It is something more than the advantage of celebrity of which complainant is being deprived. . . .

The decree of the Circuit Court of Appeals will be Affirmed.

HOLMES, J., concurring:

When an uncopyrighted combination of words is published there is no general right to forbid other people repeating them — in other words there is no property in the combination or in the thoughts or facts that the words express. Property, a creation of law, does not arise from value, although exchangeable — a matter of fact. Many exchangeable values may be destroyed intentionally without compensation. Property depends upon exclusion by law from interference, and a person is not excluded from using any combination of words merely because someone has used it before, even if it took labor and genius to make it. If a given person is to be prohibited from making the use of words that his neighbors are free to make some other ground must be found. One such ground is vaguely expressed in the phrase unfair trade. This means that the words are repeated by a competitor in business in such a way as to convey a misrepresentation that materially injures the person who first used them, by appropriating credit of some kind which the first user has earned. The ordinary case is a representation by device, appearance, or other indirection that the defendant's goods come from the plaintiff. But the only reason why it is actionable to make such a representation is that it tends to give the defendant an advantage in his competition with the plaintiff and that it is thought undesirable that an advantage should be gained in that way. Apart from that the defendant may use such unpatented devices and uncopyrighted combinations of words as he likes. The ordinary case, I say, is palming off the defendant's product as the plaintiff's, but the same evil may follow from the opposite falsehood — from saying, whether in words or by implication, that the plaintiff's product is the defendant's, and that, it seems to me, is what has happened here.

Fresh news is got only by enterprise and expense. To produce such news as it is produced by the defendant represents by implication that it has been acquired by the defendant's enterprise and at its expense. When it comes from one of the great news-collecting agencies like the Associated Press, the source generally is indicated, plainly importing that credit; and that such a representation is implied may be inferred with some confidence from the unwillingness of the defendant to give the credit and tell the truth. If the plaintiff produces the news at the same time that the defendant does, the defendant's presentation impliedly denies to the plaintiff the credit of collecting the facts and assumes that credit to the defendant. If the plaintiff is later in western cities it naturally will be supposed to have obtained its information from the defendant. The falsehood is a little more subtle, the injury a little more indirect, than in ordinary cases of unfair trade, but I think that the principle that condemns the one condemns the other. It is a question of how strong an infusion of fraud is necessary to turn a flavor into a poison. The dose seems to me strong enough here to need a remedy from the law. But as, in my view, the only ground of complaint that can be recognized without legislation is the implied misstatement, it can be corrected by stating the truth; and a suitable acknowledgment of the source is all that the plaintiff can require. I think that within the limits recognized by the decision of the Court the defendant should be enjoined from publishing news obtained from the Associated Press for __ hours after publication by the plaintiff unless it gives express credit to the Associated

Press; the number of hours and the form of acknowledgment to be settled by the District Court. . . .

BRANDEIS, J., dissenting: . . .

News is a report of recent occurrences. The business of the news agency is to gather systematically knowledge of such occurrences of interest and to distribute reports thereof. The Associated Press contended that knowledge so acquired is property, because it costs money and labor to produce and because it has value for which those who have it not are ready to pay; that it remains property and is entitled to protection as long as it has commercial value as news; and that to protect it effectively the defendant must be enjoined from making, or causing to be made, any gainful use of it while it retains such value. An essential element of individual property is the legal right to exclude others from enjoying it. If the property is private, the right of exclusion may be absolute; if the property is affected with a public interest, the right of exclusion is qualified. But the fact that a product of the mind has cost its producer money and labor, and has a value for which others are willing to pay, is not sufficient to ensure to it this legal attribute of property. The general rule of law is, that the noblest of human productions — knowledge, truths ascertained, conceptions, and ideas — become, after voluntary communication to others, free as the air to common use. Upon these incorporeal productions the attribute of property is continued after such communication only in certain classes of cases where public policy has seemed to demand it. These exceptions are confined to productions which, in some degree, involve creation, invention, or discovery. But by no means all such are endowed with this attribute of property. The creations which are recognized as property by the common law are literary, dramatic, musical, and other artistic creations; and these have also protection under the copyright statutes. The inventions and discoveries upon which this attribute of property is conferred only by statute, are the few comprised within the patent law. There are also many other cases in which courts interfere to prevent curtailment of plaintiff's enjoyment of incorporeal productions; and in which the right to relief is often called a property right, but is such only in a special sense. In those cases, the plaintiff has no absolute right to the protection of his production; he has merely the qualified right to be protected as against the defendant's acts, because of the special relation in which the latter stands or the wrongful method or means employed in acquiring the knowledge or the manner in which it is used. Protection of this character is afforded where the suit is based upon breach of contract or of trust or upon unfair competition.

The knowledge for which protection is sought in the case at bar is not of a kind upon which the law has heretofore conferred the attributes of property; nor is the manner of its acquisition or use nor the purpose to which it is applied, such as has heretofore been recognized as entitling a plaintiff to relief. . . .

The means by which the International News Service obtains news gathered by the Associated Press is also clearly unobjectionable. It is taken from papers bought in the open market or from bulletins publicly posted. No breach of contract such as the court considered to exist in Hitchman Coal & Coke Co. v. Mitchell, 245 U.S. 229, 254; or of trust such as was present in Morison v. Moat, 9 Hare, 241; and neither fraud nor force, is involved. The manner of use is likewise unobjectionable. No reference is made by word or by act to the Associated Press, either in transmitting the news to subscribers or by them in publishing it in their papers. Neither the International News Service nor its subscribers is gaining or seeking to gain in its business a benefit from the reputation of the Associated Press. They are merely using its product without making compensation. See Bamforth v. Douglass Post Card & Machine Co., 158 Fed. Rep. 355; Tribune Co. of Chicago v. Associated Press, 116 Fed. Rep. 126. That, they have a legal right to do; because the product is not property, and they do not stand in any relation to the Associated Press, either of contract or of trust, which otherwise precludes such use. The argument is not advanced by characterizing such taking and use a misappropriation.

It is also suggested, that the fact that defendant does not refer to the Associated Press as the source of the news may furnish a basis for the relief. But the defendant and its subscribers, unlike members of the Associated Press, were under no contractual obligation to disclose the source of the news; and there is no rule of law requiring acknowledgment to be made where uncopyrighted matter is reproduced. The International News Service is said to mislead its subscribers into believing that the news transmitted was originally gathered by it and that they in turn mislead their readers. There is, in fact, no representation by either of any kind. Sources of information are sometimes given because required by contract; sometimes because naming the source gives authority to an otherwise incredible statement; and sometimes the source is named because the agency does not wish to take the responsibility itself of giving currency to the news. But no representation can properly be implied from omission to mention the source of information except that the International News Service is transmitting news which it believes to be credible.

. . . The great development of agencies now furnishing country-wide distribution of news, the vastness of our territory, and improvements in the means of transmitting intelligence, have made it possible for a news agency or newspapers to obtain, without paying compensation, the fruit of another's efforts and to use news so obtained gainfully in competition with the original collector. The injustice of such action is obvious. But to give relief against it would involve more than the application of existing rules of law to new facts. It would require the making of a new rule in analogy to existing ones. The unwritten law possesses capacity for growth; and has often satisfied new demands for justice by invoking analogies or by expanding a rule or principle. This process has been in the main wisely applied and should not be discontinued. Where the problem is relatively simple, as it is apt to be when private interests only are involved, it generally proves adequate. But with the increasing complexity of society, the public interest tends to become omnipresent; and the problems presented by new demands for justice cease to be simple. Then the creation or recognition by courts of a new private right may work serious injury to the general public, unless the boundaries of the right are definitely established and wisely guarded. In order to reconcile the new private right with the public interest, it may be necessary to prescribe limitations and rules for its enjoyment; and also to provide administrative machinery for enforcing the rules. It is largely for this reason that, in the effort to meet the many new demands for justice incident to a rapidly changing civilization, resort to legislation has latterly been had with increasing frequency.

The rule for which the plaintiff contends would effect an important extension of property rights and a corresponding curtailment of the free use of knowledge and of ideas; and the facts of this case admonish us of the danger involved in recognizing such a property right in news, without imposing upon news-gatherers corresponding obligations. . . .

Courts are ill-equipped to make the investigations which should precede a determination of the limitations which should be set upon any property right in news or of the circumstances under which news gathered by a private agency should be deemed affected with a public interest. Courts would be powerless to prescribe the detailed regulations essential to full enjoyment of the rights conferred or to introduce the machinery required for enforcement of such regulations. Considerations such as these should lead us to decline to establish a new rule of law in the effort to redress a newly-disclosed wrong, although the propriety of some remedy appears to be clear.

National Basketball Association v. Motorola, Inc.

105 F.3d 841 (1997)

WINTER, Circuit Judge:

Motorola, Inc. and Sports Team Analysis and Tracking Systems ("STATS") appeal from a permanent injunction entered by Judge Preska. The injunction concerns a handheld pager sold by Motorola and marketed under the name "SportsTrax," which displays updated information of professional basketball games in progress. The injunction prohibits appellants, absent authorization from the National Basketball Association and NBA Properties, Inc. (collectively the "NBA"), from transmitting scores or other data about NBA games in progress via the pagers, STATS's site on America On-Line's computer dial-up service, or "any equivalent means."

The crux of the dispute concerns the extent to which a state law "hot-news" misappropriation claim based on International News Service v. Associated Press, 248 U.S. 215 (1918) ("INS"), survives preemption by the federal Copyright Act and whether the NBA's claim fits within the surviving INS-type claims. We hold that a narrow "hot-news" exception does survive preemption. However, we also hold that appellants' transmission of "real-time" NBA game scores and information tabulated from television and radio broadcasts of games in progress does not constitute a misappropriation of "hot news" that is the property of the NBA. . . .

I. Background

The facts are largely undisputed. Motorola manufactures and markets the SportsTrax paging device while STATS supplies the game information that is transmitted to the pagers. The product became available to the public in January 1996, at a retail price of about $200. SportsTrax's pager has an inch-and-a-half by inch-and-a-half screen and operates in four basic modes: "current," "statistics," "final scores" and "demonstration." It is the "current" mode that gives rise to the present dispute. In that mode, SportsTrax displays the following information on NBA games in progress: (i) the teams playing; (ii) score changes; (iii) the team in possession of the ball; (iv) whether the team is in the free-throw bonus; (v) the quarter of the game; and (vi) time remaining in the quarter. The information is updated every two to three minutes, with more frequent updates near the end of the first half and the end of the game. There is a lag of approximately two or three minutes between events in the game itself and when the information appears on the pager screen.

SportsTrax's operation relies on a "data feed" supplied by STATS reporters who watch the games on television or listen to them on the radio. The reporters key into a personal computer changes in the score and other information such as successful and missed shots, fouls, and clock updates. The information is relayed by modem to STATS's host computer, which compiles, analyzes, and formats the data for retransmission. The information is then sent to a common carrier, which then sends it via satellite to various local FM radio networks that in turn emit the signal received by the individual SportsTrax pagers. . . .

The district court dismissed all of the NBA's claims except the first-misappropriation under New York law. . . . Finding Motorola and STATS liable for misappropriation, Judge Preska entered the permanent injunction, reserved the calculation of damages for subsequent proceedings, and stayed execution of the injunction pending appeal. Motorola and STATS appeal. . . .

[The court first concludes that federal copyright law does not preempt the "hot news" doctrine as construed by the court. We excerpt this portion of the court's opinion in Chapter 15 *infra.*]

In our view, the elements central to an INS claim are: (i) the plaintiff generates or collects information at some cost or expense; (ii) the value of the information is highly time-sensitive; (iii) the defendant's use of the information constitutes free-riding on the plaintiff's costly efforts to generate or collect it; (iv) the defendant's use of the information is in direct competition with a product or service offered by the plaintiff; (v) the ability of other parties to free-ride on the efforts of the plaintiff would so reduce the incentive to produce the product or service that its existence or quality would be substantially threatened.

INS is not about ethics; it is about the protection of property rights in time-sensitive information so that the information will be made available to the public by profit seeking entrepreneurs. If services like AP were not assured of property rights in the news they pay to collect, they would cease to collect it. The ability of their competitors to appropriate their product at only nominal cost and thereby to disseminate a competing product at a lower price would destroy the incentive to collect news in the first place. The newspaper-reading public would suffer because no one would have an incentive to collect "hot news." . . .

We conclude that Motorola and STATS have not engaged in unlawful misappropriation under the "hot-news" test set out above. To be sure, some of the elements of a "hot-news" INS claim are met. The information transmitted to SportsTrax is not precisely contemporaneous, but it is nevertheless time-sensitive. Also, the NBA does provide, or will shortly do so, information like that available through SportsTrax. It now offers a service called "Gamestats" that provides official play-by-play game sheets and half-time and final box scores within each arena. It also provides such information to the media in each arena. In the future, the NBA plans to enhance Gamestats so that it will be networked between the various arenas and will support a pager product analogous to SportsTrax. SportsTrax will of course directly compete with an enhanced Gamestats.

However, there are critical elements missing in the NBA's attempt to assert a "hot-news" INS-type claim. As framed by the NBA, their claim compresses and confuses three different informational products. The first product is generating the information by playing the games; the second product is transmitting live, full descriptions of those games; and the third product is collecting and retransmitting strictly factual information about the games. The first and second products are the NBA's primary business: producing basketball games for live attendance and licensing copyrighted broadcasts of those games. The collection and retransmission of strictly factual material about the games is a different product: e.g., box-scores in newspapers, summaries of statistics on television sports news, and real-time facts to be transmitted to pagers. In our view, the NBA has failed to show any competitive effect whatsoever from

SportsTrax on the first and second products and a lack of any free-riding by SportsTrax on the third.

With regard to the NBA's primary products-producing basketball games with live attendance and licensing copyrighted broadcasts of those games-there is no evidence that anyone regards SportsTrax or the AOL site as a substitute for attending NBA games or watching them on television. In fact, Motorola markets SportsTrax as being designed "for those times when you cannot be at the arena, watch the game on TV, or listen to the radio . . ."

The NBA argues that the pager market is also relevant to a "hot-news" INS-type claim and that SportsTrax's future competition with Gamestats satisfies any missing element. We agree that there is a separate market for the real-time transmission of factual information to pagers or similar devices, such as STATS's AOL site. However, we disagree that SportsTrax is in any sense free-riding off Gamestats.

An indispensable element of an INS "hot-news" claim is free riding by a defendant on a plaintiff's product, enabling the defendant to produce a directly competitive product for less money because it has lower costs. SportsTrax is not such a product. The use of pagers to transmit real-time information about NBA games requires: (i) the collecting of facts about the games; (ii) the transmission of these facts on a network; (iii) the assembling of them by the particular service; and (iv) the transmission of them to pagers or an on-line computer site. Appellants are in no way free-riding on Gamestats. Motorola and STATS expend their own resources to collect purely factual information generated in NBA games to transmit to SportsTrax pagers. They have their own network and assemble and transmit data themselves.

To be sure, if appellants in the future were to collect facts from an enhanced Gamestats pager to retransmit them to SportsTrax pagers, that would constitute free-riding and might well cause Gamestats to be unprofitable because it had to bear costs to collect facts that SportsTrax did not. If the appropriation of facts from one pager to another pager service were allowed, transmission of current information on NBA games to pagers or similar devices would be substantially deterred because any potential transmitter would know that the first entrant would quickly encounter a lower cost competitor free-riding on the originator's transmissions.

However, that is not the case in the instant matter. SportsTrax and Gamestats are each bearing their own costs of collecting factual information on NBA games, and, if one produces a product that is cheaper or otherwise superior to the other, that producer will prevail in the marketplace. This is obviously not the situation against which INS was intended to prevent: the potential lack of any such product or service because of the anticipation of free-riding.

For the foregoing reasons, the NBA has not shown any damage to any of its products based on free-riding by Motorola and STATS. . . .

COMMENTS AND QUESTIONS

1. Both the majority and the dissent in *International News* seem to agree that there is no traditional intellectual property right in published news. Copyright law—the most likely candidate for protecting works of authorship—protects only the original expression, selection, or arrangement of facts or ideas, and not the ideas themselves. In addition, copyright formalities that existed in 1918 (e.g., mandatory notice and registration) may have made it very difficult for AP to assert a copyright

claim even if INS copied AP's expression verbatim. Moreover, the majority's reference to "unfair competition" suggests that its theory is grounded in a tort of wrongful appropriation. But the tort analogy runs into difficulty as well, since (as Justice Brandeis observes) it is hard to fault the conduct at issue in the case. (Note that the Supreme Court did not consider AP's claim that INS had bribed AP newspapers or employees, an allegation which if true seems much more likely to support a tort action for interference with contract. *See* Chapter 14 *infra.*) Instead, the Court seems to settle into what it calls a theory of "quasi-property" that entitles its owner to protection only against direct competitors.

2. How should courts following *International News* determine whether two companies are direct competitors who are then subject to this quasi-property right? For example, suppose that a single newspaper (not a member of AP) had appropriated information from published AP reports. Does the single paper compete with AP in news gathering? Does it matter whether the paper competes directly with one of AP's members, or has its own city monopoly? Or should the test be whether AP could have expected licensing revenues from the paper, whether or not they are in competition? *Cf.* National Football League v. Delaware, 435 F. Supp. 1372 (D. Del. 1977) (NFL cannot prevent Delaware from implementing a lottery based on NFL games, because the lottery is a "collateral service" rather than one in competition with the NFL).

3. How long does this quasi-property right last? The Court suggests one answer: until AP has appropriated its news value as a return on its news-gathering activities. Justice Holmes's concurrence suggests that this would be a matter of hours. But is that necessarily true? What happens when different news media compete? Should there be different rules for CNN, scheduled television news, daily newspapers, and weekly and monthly news magazines? Is AP entitled to protect its news not only from appropriation by "immediate" news sources, but also from the weeklies and monthlies that seek to use its news reports?

4. What if INS or its newspapers had credited AP with reporting the story? In that case, AP would presumably have received some value for its news—credit for the "scoop." But its member papers would still have faced competition from nonmembers that they would prefer to avoid. Should attribution be enough? Justice Holmes says yes, but neither the majority nor Justice Brandeis' dissent sees this as the major issue (although the majority notes that INS's failure to attribute the news to AP "accentuates" the unfairness of its competition). Note that attribution should solve any Lanham Act problem that might otherwise arise, since there is no danger that INS or its member papers will be "passing off" AP stories as their own if the source of the story is clearly identified. (Query: Would the misattribution be actionable under the current Lanham Act as a false designation of origin? As false advertising? Review Chapter 9 *supra.*)

This fact points up a significant difference between the tort of misappropriation and trademark infringement. Trademark law is premised on harm to consumers stemming from a "likelihood of confusion." Absent consumer confusion, trademarks (and trade dress) are generally not protectable. *International News* cuts a much broader swath. If it is not based on consumer protection, what is the rationale for the tort of misappropriation? Is it incentive theory? If so, what exactly is the Court trying to encourage?

5. As the *NBA* case suggests, until recently the *International News* decision has not fared well in the courts. Early decisions by lower courts attempted to construe the decision narrowly. Indeed, in 1929 Judge Learned Hand went so far as to say: "While

it is of course true that the law ordinarily speaks in general terms, there are cases where the occasion is at once the justification for, and the limit of, what is decided. [*International News*] appears to us such an instance; we think that no more was covered than situations substantially similar to those then at bar." Cheney Bros. v. Doris Silk Corp., 35 F.2d 279 (2d Cir. 1929). Judge Hand went on to characterize the problems with the Court's decision as "insuperable," and to state that it "flagrantly conflict[ed]" with the federal statutory intellectual property laws. *Id.* Moreover, after Erie R.R. Co. v. Tompkins, 304 U.S. 64 (1938), abolished federal common law in diversity cases (the grounds on which *International News* was decided), it seemed to many that the *International News* misappropriation doctrine was dead. *See, e.g.*, James Treece, *Patent Policy and Pre-emption: The* Stiffel *and* Compco *Cases*, 32 U. CHI. L. REV. 80 (1964).

But to paraphrase Mark Twain, rumors of the doctrine's death (arguably) have been exaggerated. Courts have invoked the doctrine in a number of cases besides *NBA v. Motorola. See, e.g.*, United States Golf Ass'n v. St. Andrews Systems, 749 F.2d 1028 (3d Cir. 1984) (*International News* was based on direct competition between the parties; court refused to apply it absent such direct competition); Imax Corp. v. Cinema Technologies, Inc., 152 F.3d 1161 (9th Cir. 1998) (owner of movie projector equipment could recover on a common law misappropriation theory for the use of information disclosed in confidence, despite the fact that the plaintiff could not prevail on its trade secret claim); Ettore v. Philco Television Broadcasting Corp., 229 F.2d 481 (3d Cir. 1956) (producer of boxing match could recover damages from television station which broadcast the match without permission). And as content producers increasingly shift from analog to digital media, the misappropriation doctrine may come to play a correspondingly important role in the years ahead. At present, several lawsuits involving the misappropriation doctrine have met with judicial approval, at least at the pleading stage. *See* Banxcorp v. Costco Wholesale Corp., ____ F. Supp. 2d ____ (S.D.N.Y. 2010) (denying motion to dismiss, *inter alia*, hot news misappropriation claim involving use of money market and CD rate indices); Barclays Capital Inc. v. Theflyonthewall.com, 700 F. Supp. 2d 310 (S.D.N.Y. 2010) (enjoining the defendant from redistributing plaintiff's stock recommendations for one half-hour after the opening of the New York Stock Exchange or 10 A.M., whichever is later); Associated Press v. All Headline News Corp., 608 F. Supp. 2d 454 (S.D.N.Y. 2009) (denying motion to dismiss AP's complaint, alleging misappropriation of hot news and other theories, against Internet news aggregator). *But see* Agora Fin., LLC v. Samler, ____ F. Supp. 2d ____ (D. Md. 2010) (disagreeing with much of the *Barclays* court's analysis). As of this writing, the *Barclays* case is on appeal to the Second Circuit.

Does the hot news doctrine as interpreted by the Second Circuit in *NBA v. Motorola* protect an important interest, even if only in a small number of cases? Do the benefits outweigh the costs?

6. As noted at the beginning of this chapter, in Feist v. Rural Telephone Service, 499 U.S. 340 (1991), the Supreme Court held that a comprehensive alphabetical listing of names and phone numbers for a given geographical area, as found in the white pages of a telephone directory, was insufficiently original to qualify for federal copyright protection. Suppose, however, that the plaintiff had brought a claim for misappropriation and unfair competition rather than a copyright claim. Should the plaintiff prevail under *International News*? Under *NBA v. Motorola*? It certainly would be able to claim that it had invested substantial time and effort in putting together a telephone directory, and that defendant (a direct competitor) had merely copied that

information as soon as it became public. Assuming this is enough to show unfair competition under *International News*, what does that fact suggest about the interaction between the copyright laws and the unfair competition doctrine? Does it make sense that the rule in *Feist* should coexist with unfair competition law?

7. One solution to the inconsistency between *Feist* and *International News* would be to create an explicit (presumably statutory) property right in factual compilations. Strong arguments in favor of such protection were made in the copyright context both before and after *Feist*. (Thus far, Congress has rejected efforts to craft some sort of federal statutory protection for unoriginal databases; the member states of the European Union, by contrast, do accord databases some measure of protection as a result of the EC's 1996 Database Directive, *see* Council Directive 96/9 1996 O.J. (L077) 20 (EC).) Doesn't the Court in *International News* have a valid point about the incentive to invest in a productive activity (collecting news) whose benefits will immediately be dissipated by imitators? Isn't that precisely the justification for the patent system?

On the other hand, what problems do you foresee with such a new federal intellectual property regime? Would it overwhelm patent and copyright as means of protecting intellectual property? What effect would it have on businesses? Would it encourage factual research and compilation, or just encourage monopolization of facts? On this subject, see also Leo J. Raskind, *The Misappropriation Doctrine as a Competitive Norm of Intellectual Property Law*, 75 MINN. L. REV. 875, 876-77 (1991). Raskind argues that:

> when courts hear patent, copyright, and trademark cases in which statutory protection is inappropriate, but nonetheless the conduct of a party is characterized as "chiseling," "piracy," "unethical," or the like, they should begin their analysis by considering the competitive relationship from which the claim originates. The clear legislative expression of a preference for competition contained in federal antitrust laws warrants this approach. Moreover, courts in these cases should recognize the Supreme Court's continued emphasis on the preemptive effect given federal legislation relating to competition. Ancillary doctrines that impinge on competition, such as misappropriation, should be invoked sparingly. From this perspective, courts should consider allegedly "inappropriate" conduct as an element of behavior in a competitive market context; within that framework, courts should view such conduct as an element of cost that a seller, as a competitor, considers when determining how much of a particular product to offer.

8. To what extent was the Court in *International News* merely enforcing the norms of commercial reasonableness in the newspaper industry? *See* Richard Epstein, *International News Service v. Associated Press: Custom and Law as Sources of Property Rights in News*, 78 VA. L. REV. 85 (1992) (noting the different customary rules in the news trade under which "lifting" stories was wrong, but following up on another paper's "tips" to report the same story was acceptable; and concluding that, partially unwittingly, Justice Pitney ended up affirming these customary rules in his opinion); Douglas G. Baird, *Common Law Intellectual Property and the Legacy of* International News Service v. Associated Press, 50 U. CHI. L. REV. 411 (1983). *But see* Stephen L. Carter, *Custom, Adjudication, and Petrushevsky's Watch: Some Notes from the Intellectual Property Front*, 78 VA. L. REV. 129, 132 (1992) ("Even courts inclined to enforce private orderings might not be very good at anthropology. The judge, after all, is on the outside, looking in. Even assuming—and there is no reason to do so—that the parties tell the whole truth, it will not always be so easy for a court to discern an industry's customs.").

9. Another issue in some cases involving application of the hot news doctrine is whether enjoining the defendant from publishing uncopyrightable facts can be reconciled with the First Amendment. Copyright claims generally withstand First Amendment challenges precisely because copyright maintains a distinction between copyrightable expression and uncopyrightable ideas and facts (and because copyright has a fair use doctrine). *See* Eldred v. Ashcroft, 537 U.S. 186, 219-20 (2003); Harper & Row Publishers, Inc. v. Nation Enters., 471 U.S. 539, 560 (1985). Moreover, the Constitution itself authorizes Congress to enact copyright laws. Neither justification applies to state-law claims involving the misappropriation of facts. Some commentators therefore have argued that at least hot news claims are constitutionally suspect. *See* Note, *Nothing But Internet*, 110 HARV. L. REV. 1143, 1155-60 (1997). The district court in the recent *Barclay's Capital* decision, involving financial service firms' successful application of the hot news doctrine against the distribution of their equity research recommendations by theflyonthewall.com, an online subscription newsfeed, addressed these sorts of concerns as follows:

> It was undisputed at this trial, and explicitly conceded by Fly, that the production of equity research in general, and its production by the plaintiff Firms specifically, is a valuable social good. Such research plays a vital role in modern capital markets by helping to disclose information material to the market, to price stocks more fairly and, as a result, to produce a more efficient allocation of capital. Although the gains from immediate trading and rapid stock movement based on knowledge of Recommendations may be realized initially only by sophisticated investors, all market participants benefit from a market operating to align prices with underlying value as quickly as possible. . . . Because the availability of the detailed and sophisticated analysis that can appear in research reports, which are the basis for the Recommendations, depends upon their producer's ability to reap a benefit from producing it, research reports' analyses of corporations will be underproduced unless the Firms can achieve an economic return on their investment.
>
> It is also worth bearing in mind that the Recommendations are not objective facts, but rather, subjective judgments based on complex and imperfect evidence. In this sense, the Recommendations produced by the Firms represent the kinds of information to which the Court of Appeals has seen fit to extend protection under copyright laws. Such information has been described as "soft facts" or "soft ideas infused with taste or opinion," and explicitly includes items such as subjective valuations or target prices.
>
> The public interest in the production of equity research notwithstanding, there is also a competing, and no less important, public interest in "unrestrained access to information," particularly when the information is heavily fact-based. Widespread access to information is critical to "the progress of Science and the useful Arts," U.S. Const. art. I, § 8, cl. 8, and it is in part for this reason that Congress and the courts have declined to extend copyright protection to pure facts. . . . For this reason, the Firms appropriately conceded at trial that there is, and should be, an "ordinary presumption in favor of the free flow of information." Plaintiffs seek only that the incentives be preserved to create the activity that generates that information in the first place.
>
> Ultimately, the purpose of the *INS* tort, like the traditionally accepted goal of intellectual property law more generally, is to provide an incentive for the production of socially useful information without either under-or over-protecting the efforts to gather such information. A balance must be struck between establishing rewards to stimulate socially useful efforts on the one hand, and permitting maximum access to the fruits of those efforts to facilitate still further innovation and progress on the other. . . .
>
> The balance of these considerations strongly supports the injunctive relief that will be ordered in this action. This injunction . . . will not grant plaintiffs an effective monopoly over a particular financial concept, formula, or line of business. Anyone, including Fly,

> remains free to conduct equity research, write research reports, and make Recommendations. Nor will Fly be restrained with respect to any element of its newsfeed that does not involve reporting the Firms' Recommendations or conference call access information. An injunction with a limited period of exclusivity for the dissemination of a Firm's Recommendations will, however, preserve the incentive to create equity research and ultimately spread the benefits of that research to all investors through the operation of the markets. . . .
>
> The length of time for which the Firms should be protected from unauthorized redistribution or repetition of their Recommendations is the most important question to be determined. Ordinarily, "[t]he originator of valuable information . . . has an opportunity to exploit the advantage of a lead time in the market," thereby "provid[ing] the originator with an opportunity to recover the costs of development and . . . encourag[ing] continued investment." RESTATEMENT § 38 cmt. c. In *INS*, the Supreme Court described this lead time for exploitation of the news as the period "until its commercial value as news to the complainant and all of its members has passed away." *Id.* at 245 (emphasis omitted).
>
> In this case, the goal is a period of lead time long enough to enable the Firms to conduct a reasonable sales effort and to retain the advantage of being the first to reach key institutional investors who may react promptly to a Firm's Recommendation. Where the investor will require a more sustained consultation with the Firm or wish to ponder the research report in more depth, however, it is unnecessary to restrict unauthorized dissemination of the Recommendations. In those instances, the research reports themselves retain value even though their Recommendations may be widely known. With the right lead time, the Firms will retain an incentive to create their research, but they will not be given a vise to squeeze every last cent out of their efforts to the exclusion of others.
>
> Plaintiffs seek an injunction against reporting a Recommendation for four hours from the release of a research report or until 12:00 P.M., whichever is later in time. They contend that only this length of time is able to restore "breathing room for a reasonable sales and trading effort." Fly, without conceding liability, argues that the injunction should last no longer than ten minutes from the release of the report to a Firm's customers, which is usually hours before the market opens.

The court went on to consider three possible time frames for an injunction: "(1) for some length of time ending before the 9:30 A.M. market opening; (2) for some relatively limited period ending just after the 9:30 A.M. market opening; and (3) for a period of hours after market opening, up to the two-and-one-half hours requested by the Firms." The court concluded that option (2) was superior, because it would "preserve[ ] incentives for the Firms to create and disseminate research reports to their investor clients, while still recognizing the inevitable, fast-moving, and widespread informal communication of Recommendations on Wall Street. Because this time frame will not fully insulate the Firms from the pressures of adjusting to the rapidly evolving informational marketplace, it will also motivate the Firms to continue to explore ways to improve and expedite the dissemination of their research." Barclay's Capital Inc. v. Theflyonewall.com, 700 F. Supp. 2d 310, 343-47 (S.D.N.Y. 2010).

Is the court's opinion sufficiently sensitive to the interest in public access to market information? Does it extend sufficient protection to the plaintiff firms? As of this writing, the case remained pending on appeal to the Second Circuit.

10. In a 2003 essay, Judge Posner doubts the need for a separate misappropriation doctrine. *See* Richard A. Posner, *Misappropriation: A Dirge*, 40 HOUS. L. REV. 621 (2003). He does not believe that its core principle—discouraging free-riding—is itself a necessary or sufficient condition for IP protection. *See generally* Mark A.

Lemley, *Property, Intellectual Property, and Free Riding*, 83 TEX. L. REV. 1031 (2005). Upon reviewing the major reported cases, Judge Posner concludes that unsuccessful claimants were properly rejected and that successful claimants could have prevailed under other doctrines (such as copyright law, contract law, or trespass to chattels). He is "hard pressed to find a case in which a claim of misappropriation should have succeeded." Posner, 40 HOUS. L. REV. 621 at 633.

PROBLEM

Problem 12-1. The rise of the Internet has imperiled many traditional news gathering organizations. Sites like Craiglist have reduced the market for classified advertising. The success of Google's AdSense — its keyword-triggered advertising platforms — cut deeply into the revenue that had traditionally flowed into print advertising. And the revenue models for many newspaper Web sites have been hampered by news aggregator sites, news search engines, and bloggers who repackage news. To some extent, newspapers created the latter set of problems by not choosing the subscription model path (as, for example, the *Wall Street Journal* did). Just as misappropriation law bolstered AP's lead-time nearly a century ago, Judge Richard Posner suggests that a similar approach (through an amendment to copyright law) could improve the quantity and quality of news gathering today:

> News, as well the other information found in newspapers, is available online for nothing, including at the websites of the newspapers themselves, who thus are giving away content. The fact that online viewing is rising as print circulation is falling indicates a shift of consumers from the paid to the free medium. . . . [M]any of the people who have switched under economic pressure to the free medium may find themselves as happy or happier. . . .
>
> Moreover, while in many industries a reduction in output need not entail any reduction in the quality of the product, in newspaper it does entail a reduction in quality. Most of the costs of a newspaper are fixed costs, that is, costs invariant to output — for they are journalists' salaries. A newspaper with shrinking revenues can shrink its costs only by reducing the number of reporters, columnists, and editors, and when it does that quality falls, and therefore demand, and falling demand means falling revenues and therefore increased pressure to economize — by cutting the journalist staff some more. This vicious cycle, amplified by the economic downturn, may continue until very little of the newspaper industry is left.
>
> So what will happen to news and information? Online news is free for two reasons. First, in the case of a newspaper, the marginal cost of providing content online is virtually zero, since it is the same content (or a selection of the content) in a different medium. Second, online providers of news who are not affiliated with a newspaper can provide links to newspaper websites and paraphrase articles in newspapers, in neither case being required to compensate the newspaper.
>
> As newspaper revenues decline, newspaper content becomes thinner and thinner — but by the same token so does the linked or paraphrased newspaper content found in web sites that have no affiliation with a newspaper. If eventually newspapers vanish, online providers will have higher advertising revenues (because newspaper advertising will have disappeared) and may decide to charge for access to their online news, and so the critical question is whether online advertising

revenues will defray the costly news-gathering expenses incurred at this time by newspapers. Imagine if the New York Times migrated entirely to the World Wide Web. Could it support, out of advertising and subscriber revenues, as large a news-gathering apparatus as it does today? This seems unlikely, because it is much easier to create a web site and free ride on other sites than to create a print newspaper and free ride on other print newspapers, in part because of the lag in print publication; what is staler than last week's news. Expanding copyright law to bar online access to copyrighted materials without the copyright holder's consent, or to bar linking to or paraphrasing copyrighted materials without the copyright holder's consent, might be necessary to keep free riding on content financed by online newspapers from so impairing the incentive to create costly news-gathering operations that news services like Reuters and the Associated Press would become the only professional, nongovernmental sources of news and opinion.

See Richard A. Posner, *The Future of Newspapers*, THE BECKER-POSNER BLOG (June 23, 2009), http://www.becker-posner-blog.com/2009/06/the-future-of-newspapers—posner.html. What counter-arguments would you offer? Do you agree with Judge Posner's prescription?

B. CONTRACTUAL PROTECTION OF FACTS

Inventors and creators can also use contract law to achieve some of the goals they might otherwise use intellectual property rights to obtain. Contracts are fundamentally intertwined with intellectual property, because rights owners use contracts to license those rights to others. But companies who are dissatisfied with the protections intellectual property affords may also seek to use contract law to create their own private intellectual property rights, or to modify or expand the rights the law gives them. In this section, we discuss a number of circumstances in which creators have sought to do just that.

When private parties seek the help of state courts to vary the rules of intellectual property, courts must decide whether such efforts are preempted by the federal intellectual property scheme. We discuss the possible preemption of contract claims in Chapter 15 *infra*.

1. Shrinkwrap Licenses

ProCD, Inc. v. Zeidenberg
86 F.3d 1447 (7th Cir. 1996)

EASTERBROOK, Circuit Judge.

Must buyers of computer software obey the terms of shrinkwrap licenses? The district court held not, for two reasons: first, they are not contracts because the licenses are inside the box rather than printed on the outside; second, federal law forbids enforcement even if the licenses are contracts. 908 F. Supp. 640 (W.D. Wis. 1996).

The parties and numerous amici curiae have briefed many other issues, but these are the only two that matter—and we disagree with the district judge's conclusion on each. Shrinkwrap licenses are enforceable unless their terms are objectionable on grounds applicable to contracts in general (for example, if they violate a rule of positive law, or if they are unconscionable). Because no one argues that the terms of the license at issue here are troublesome, we remand with instructions to enter judgment for the plaintiff.

I

ProCD, the plaintiff, has compiled information from more than 3,000 telephone directories into a computer database. We may assume that this database cannot be copyrighted, although it is more complex, contains more information (nine-digit zip codes and census industrial codes), is organized differently, and therefore is more original than the single alphabetical directory at issue in Feist Publications, Inc. v. Rural Telephone Service Co., 499 U.S. 340, 113 L. Ed. 2d 358, 111 S. Ct. 1282 (1991). See Paul J. Heald, *The Vices of Originality*, 1991 Sup. Ct. Rev. 143, 160-68. ProCD sells a version of the database, called SelectPhone (trademark), on CD-ROM discs. (CD-ROM means "compact disc—read only memory." The "shrinkwrap license" gets its name from the fact that retail software packages are covered in plastic or cellophane "shrinkwrap," and some vendors, though not ProCD, have written licenses that become effective as soon as the customer tears the wrapping from the package. Vendors prefer "end user license," but we use the more common term.) A proprietary method of compressing the data serves as effective encryption too. Customers decrypt and use the data with the aid of an application program that ProCD has written. This program, which is copyrighted, searches the database in response to users' criteria (such as "find all people named Tatum in Tennessee, plus all firms with 'Door Systems' in the corporate name"). The resulting lists (or, as ProCD prefers, "listings") can be read and manipulated by other software, such as word processing programs.

The database in SelectPhone (trademark) cost more than $10 million to compile and is expensive to keep current. It is much more valuable to some users than to others. The combination of names, addresses, and SIC codes enables manufacturers to compile lists of potential customers. Manufacturers and retailers pay high prices to specialized information intermediaries for such mailing lists; ProCD offers a potentially cheaper alternative. People with nothing to sell could use the database as a substitute for calling long distance information, or as a way to look up old friends who have moved to unknown towns, or just as a electronic substitute for the local phone book. ProCD decided to engage in price discrimination, selling its database to the general public for personal use at a low price (approximately $150 for the set of five discs) while selling information to the trade for a higher price. It has adopted some intermediate strategies too: access to the SelectPhone (trademark) database is available via the America Online service for the price America Online charges to its clients (approximately $3 per hour), but this service has been tailored to be useful only to the general public.

If ProCD had to recover all of its costs and make a profit by charging a single price—that is, if it could not charge more to commercial users than to the general public—it would have to raise the price substantially over $150. The ensuing reduction in sales would harm consumers who value the information at, say, $200. They get consumer surplus of $50 under the current arrangement but would cease to buy if the price rose substantially. If because of high elasticity of demand in the consumer segment of the market the only way to make a profit turned out to be a price attractive to commercial users alone, then all consumers would lose out—and so would the commercial clients, who would have to pay more for the listings because ProCD could not obtain any contribution toward costs from the consumer market.

To make price discrimination work, however, the seller must be able to control arbitrage. An air carrier sells tickets for less to vacationers than to business travelers, using advance purchase and Saturday-night-stay requirements to distinguish the categories. A producer of movies segments the market by time, releasing first to theaters, then to pay-per-view services, next to the videotape and laserdisc market, and finally to cable and commercial TV. Vendors of computer software have a harder task. Anyone can walk into a retail store and buy a box. Customers do not wear tags saying "commercial user" or "consumer user." Anyway, even a commercial-user-detector at the door would not work, because a consumer could buy the software and resell to a commercial user. That arbitrage would break down the price discrimination and drive up the minimum price at which ProCD would sell to anyone.

Instead of tinkering with the product and letting users sort themselves—for example, furnishing current data at a high price that would be attractive only to commercial customers, and two-year-old data at a low price—ProCD turned to the institution of contract. Every box containing its consumer product declares that the software comes with restrictions stated in an enclosed license. This license, which is encoded on the CD-ROM disks as well as printed in the manual, and which appears on a user's screen every time the software runs, limits use of the application program and listings to non-commercial purposes.

Matthew Zeidenberg bought a consumer package of SelectPhone (trademark) in 1994 from a retail outlet in Madison, Wisconsin, but decided to ignore the license. He formed Silken Mountain Web Services, Inc., to resell the information in the SelectPhone (trademark) database. The corporation makes the database available on the Internet to anyone willing to pay its price—which, needless to say, is less than ProCD charges its commercial customers. Zeidenberg has purchased two additional SelectPhone (trademark) packages, each with an updated version of the database, and made the latest information available over the World Wide Web, for a price, through his corporation. ProCD filed this suit seeking an injunction against further dissemination that exceeds the rights specified in the licenses (identical in each of the three packages Zeidenberg purchased). The district court held the licenses ineffectual because their terms do not appear on the outside of the packages. The court added that the second and third licenses stand no different from the first, even though they are identical, because they might have been different, and a purchaser does not agree to—and cannot be bound by—terms that were secret at the time of purchase. 908 F. Supp. at 654.

II

Following the district court, we treat the licenses as ordinary contracts accompanying the sale of products, and therefore as governed by the common law of contracts and the Uniform Commercial Code. Whether there are legal differences between "contracts" and "licenses" (which may matter under the copyright doctrine of first sale) is a subject for another day. See Microsoft Corp. v. Harmony Computers & Electronics, Inc., 846 F. Supp. 208 (E.D.N.Y. 1994). Zeidenberg does not argue that Silken Mountain Web Services is free of any restrictions that apply to Zeidenberg himself, because any effort to treat the two parties as distinct would put Silken Mountain behind the eight ball on ProCD's argument that copying the application program onto its hard disk violates the copyright laws. Zeidenberg does argue, and the district court held, that placing the package of software on the shelf is an "offer," which the customer "accepts" by paying the asking price and leaving the store with the goods. Peters v. State, 154 Wis. 111, 142 N.W. 181 (1913). In Wisconsin, as elsewhere, a contract includes only the terms on which the parties have agreed. One cannot agree to hidden terms, the judge concluded. So far, so good — but one of the terms to which Zeidenberg agreed by purchasing the software is that the transaction was subject to a license. Zeidenberg's position therefore must be that the printed terms on the outside of a box are the parties' contract — except for printed terms that refer to or incorporate other terms. But why would Wisconsin fetter the parties' choice in this way? Vendors can put the entire terms of a contract on the outside of a box only by using microscopic type, removing other information that buyers might find more useful (such as what the software does, and on which computers it works), or both. The "Read Me" file included with most software, describing system requirements and potential incompatibilities, may be equivalent to ten pages of type; warranties and license restrictions take still more space. Notice on the outside, terms on the inside, and a right to return the software for a refund if the terms are unacceptable (a right that the license expressly extends), may be a means of doing business valuable to buyers and sellers alike. See E. ALLAN FARNSWORTH, 1 FARNSWORTH ON CONTRACTS § 26 (1990); RESTATEMENT (2D) OF CONTRACTS § 211 comment a (1981) ("Standardization of agreements serves many of the same functions as standardization of goods and services; both are essential to a system of mass production and distribution. Scarce and costly time and skill can be devoted to a class of transactions rather than the details of individual transactions."). Doubtless a state could forbid the use of standard contracts in the software business, but we do not think that Wisconsin has done so.

Transactions in which the exchange of money precedes the communication of detailed terms are common. Consider the purchase of insurance. The buyer goes to an agent, who explains the essentials (amount of coverage, number of years) and remits the premium to the home office, which sends back a policy. On the district judge's understanding, the terms of the policy are irrelevant because the insured paid before receiving them. Yet the device of payment, often with a "binder" (so that the insurance takes effect immediately even though the home office reserves the right to withdraw coverage later), in advance of the policy, serves buyers' interests by accelerating effectiveness and reducing transactions costs. Or consider the purchase of an airline ticket. The traveler calls the carrier or an agent, is quoted a price, reserves a seat, pays, and gets a ticket, in that order. The ticket contains elaborate terms, which the traveler can reject by canceling the reservation. To use the ticket is to accept the terms, even terms that in retrospect are disadvantageous. See Carnival Cruise Lines, Inc. v. Shute, 499 U.S. 585 (1991); see also Vimar Seguros y Reaseguros, S.A. v. M/V Sky Reefer, 515 U.S. 528 (1995) (bills of lading). Just so with a ticket to a concert. The back of the ticket states that the patron promises not to record the concert; to attend is to agree. A theater that detects a violation will confiscate the tape and escort the violator to the exit. One could arrange things so that every concertgoer signs this promise before forking over money, but that cumbersome way of doing things not only would lengthen queues and raise prices but also would scotch the sale of tickets by phone or electronic data service.

Consumer goods work the same way. Someone who wants to buy a radio set visits a store, pays, and walks out with a box. Inside the box is a leaflet containing some terms, the most important of which usually is the warranty, read for the first time in the comfort of home. By Zeidenberg's lights, the warranty in the box is irrelevant; every consumer gets the standard warranty implied by the UCC in the event the contract is silent; yet so far as we are aware no state disregards warranties furnished with consumer products. Drugs come with a list of ingredients on the outside and an elaborate package insert on the inside. The package insert describes drug interactions, contra-indications, and other vital information — but, if Zeidenberg is right, the purchaser need not read the package insert, because it is not part of the contract.

Next consider the software industry itself. Only a minority of sales take place over the counter, where there are boxes to peruse. A customer pay place an order by phone in response to a line item in a catalog or a review in a magazine. Much software is ordered over the Internet by purchasers who have never seen a box. Increasingly software arrives by wire. There is no box; there is only a stream of electrons, a collection of information that includes data, an application program, instructions, many limitations ("MegaPixel 3.14159 cannot be used with Byte-Pusher 2.718"), and the terms of sale. The user purchases a serial number, which activates the software's features. On Zeidenberg's arguments, these unboxed sales are unfettered by terms — so the seller has made a broad warranty and must pay consequential damages for any shortfalls in performance, two "promises" that if taken seriously would drive prices through the ceiling or return transactions to the horse-and-buggy age.

According to the district court, the UCC does not countenance the sequence of money now, terms later. (Wisconsin's version of the UCC does not differ from the Official Version in any material respect, so we use the regular numbering system. Wis. Stat. §402.201 corresponds to UCC §2-201, and other citations are easy to derive.) One of the court's reasons — that by proposing as part of the draft Article 2B a new UCC §2-2203 that would explicitly validate standard-form user licenses, the American Law Institute and the National Conference of Commissioners on Uniform Laws have conceded the invalidity of shrinkwrap licenses under current law, see 908 F. Supp. at 655-66 — depends on a faulty inference. To propose a change in a law's text is not necessarily to propose a change in the law's effect. New words may be designed to fortify the current rule with a more precise text that curtails uncertainty. To judge by the flux of law review articles discussing shrinkwrap licenses, uncertainty is much in need of reduction — although businesses seem to feel less uncertainty than do scholars, for only three cases (other than ours) touch on the subject, and none directly addresses it. See Step-Saver Data Systems, Inc. v. Wyse Technology, 939 F.2d 91 (3d Cir. 1991); Vault Corp. v. Quaid Software Ltd., 847 F.2d 255, 268-70 (5th Cir. 1988); Arizona Retail Systems, Inc. v. Software Link, Inc., 831 F. Supp. 759 (D. Ariz. 1993). As their titles suggest, these are not consumer transactions. *Step-Saver* is a battle-of-the-forms case, in which the parties exchange incompatible forms and a court must decide which prevails. See Northrop Corp. v. Litronic Industries, 29 F.3d 1173 (7th Cir. 1994) (Illinois law); Douglas G. Baird & Robert Weisberg, *Rules, Standards, and the Battle of the Forms: A Reassessment of §2-207*, 68 Va. L. Rev. 1217, 1227-31 (1982). Our case has only one form; UCC §2-207 is irrelevant. *Vault* holds that Louisiana's special shrinkwrap-license statute is preempted by federal law, a question to which we return.

And *Arizona Retail Systems* did not reach the question, because the court found that the buyer knew the terms of the license before purchasing the software.

What then does the current version of the UCC have to say? We think that the place to start is § 2-204(1): "A contract for sale of goods may be made in any manner sufficient to show agreement, including conduct by both parties which recognizes the existence of such a contract." A vendor, as master of the offer, may invite acceptance by conduct, and may propose limitations on the kind of conduct that constitutes acceptance. A buyer may accept by performing the acts the vendor proposes to treat as acceptance. And that is what happened. ProCD proposed a contract that a buyer would accept by using the software after having an opportunity to read the license at leisure. This Zeidenberg did. He had no choice, because the software splashed the license on the screen and would not let him proceed without indicating acceptance. So although the district judge was right to say that a contract can be, and often is, formed simply by paying the price and walking out of the store, the UCC permits contracts to be formed in other ways. ProCD proposed such a different way, and without protest Zeidenberg agreed. Ours is not a case in which a consumer opens a package to find an insert saying "you owe us an extra $10,000" and the seller files suit to collect. Any buyer finding such a demand can prevent formation of the contract by returning the package, as can any consumer who concludes that the terms of the license make the software worth less than the purchase price. Nothing in the UCC requires a seller to maximize the buyer's net gains.

Section 2-606, which defines "acceptance of goods," reinforces this understanding. A buyer accepts goods under § 2-606(1)(b) when, after an opportunity to inspect, he fails to make an effective rejection under § 2-602(1). ProCD extended an opportunity to reject if a buyer should find the license terms unsatisfactory; Zeidenberg inspected the package, tried out the software, learned of the license, and did not reject the goods. We refer to § 2-606 only to show that the opportunity to return goods can be important; acceptance of an offer differs from acceptance of goods after delivery, see Gillen v. Atalanta Systems, Inc., 997 F.2d 280, 284 n.1 (7th Cir. 1993); but the UCC consistently permits the parties to structure their relations so that the buyer has a chance to make a final decision after a detailed review.

Some portions of the UCC impose additional requirements on the way parties agree on terms. A disclaimer of the implied warranty of merchantability must be "conspicuous." UCC § 2-316(2), incorporating UCC § 1-201(10). Promises to make firm offers, or to negate oral modifications, must be "separately signed." UCC §§ 2-205, 2-209(2). These special provisos reinforce the impression that, so far as the UCC is concerned, other terms may be as inconspicuous as the forum-selection clause on the back of the cruise ship ticket in *Carnival Lines*. Zeidenberg has not located any Wisconsin case — for that matter, any case in any state — holding that under the UCC the ordinary terms found in shrinkwrap licenses require any special prominence, or otherwise are to be undercut rather than enforced. In the end, the terms of the license are conceptually identical to the contents of the package. Just as no court would dream of saying that Select-Phone (trademark) must contain 3,100 phone books rather than 3,000, or must have data no more than 30 days old, or must sell for $100 rather than $150 — although any of these changes would be welcomed by the customer, if all other things were held constant — so, we believe, Wisconsin would not let the buyer pick and choose among terms. Terms of use are no less a part of "the product" than are the size of the database and the speed with which the software compiles listings.

Competition among vendors, not judicial revision of a package's contents, is how consumers are protected in a market economy. Digital Equipment Corp. v. Uniq Digital Technologies, Inc., 73 F.3d 756 (7th Cir. 1996). ProCD has rivals, which may elect to compete by offering superior software, monthly updates, improved terms of use, lower price, or a better compromise among these elements. As we stressed above, adjusting terms in buyers' favor might help Matthew Zeidenberg today (he already has the software) but would lead to a response, such as a higher price, that might make consumers as a whole worse off.

COMMENTS AND QUESTIONS

1. Courts are split on the enforceability of shrinkwrap licenses. *ProCD* was the first court to enforce a shrinkwrap license; a number of courts before that time had refused to enforce them. *See* Step-Saver v. Wyse Technology, 939 F.3d 91 (3d Cir. 1991); Vault Corp. v. Quaid Software, Ltd., 847 F.2d 255 (5th Cir. 1988); Arizona Retail Sys. v. Software Link, Inc., 831 F. Supp. 759 (D. Ariz. 1993); *cf.* Foresight Resource Corp. v. Pfortmiller, 719 F. Supp. 1006 (D. Kan. 1989) (dictum).

Since *ProCD*, a majority of courts have enforced shrinkwrap licenses. *See* M.A. Mortenson Co. v. Timberline Software Corp., 998 P.2d 305 (Wash. 2000); Information Handling Servs. v. LRP, 2000 Copyright L. Decisions ¶28,177 (E.D. Pa. Sept. 20, 2000); Peerless Wall & Window Coverings v. Synchronics, 85 F. Supp. 2d 519 (W.D. Pa. 2000); Adobe v. One Stop Micro, 84 F. Supp. 2d 1086 (N.D. Cal. 2000); Davidson & Assocs. v. Jung, 422 F.3d 630 (8th Cir. 2005); Bowers v. Baystate Technologies, 320 F.3d 1317 (Fed. Cir. 2003).

A minority of cases since *ProCD* have refused to enforce shrinkwrap licenses, however. *See* Novell v. Network Trade Center, 25 F. Supp. 1218 (D. Utah 1997); Klocek v. Gateway, Inc., 104 F. Supp. 2d 1332 (D. Kan. 2000). *Cf.* Morgan Labs, Inc. v. Micro Data Base Sys., 41 U.S.P.Q.2d 1850 (N.D. Cal. 1997) (refusing to allow a shrinkwrap license to modify a prior signed contract). The reasoning of these cases differs. Some courts (*Arizona Retail*, for instance) follow the rationale of *Step-Saver*, holding that the shrinkwrap license should be treated as a "battle of the forms" under U.C.C. 2-207. Other courts (*Pfortmiller*, the district court in *Vault*) conclude that shrinkwrap licenses are unenforceable as "contracts of adhesion." And the Fifth Circuit in *Vault* relied on the federal intellectual property laws to preempt contrary provisions in shrinkwrap licenses.

The "contract of adhesion" rationale is suspect. Under traditional doctrines of contract law, a contract of adhesion is a standardized contract prepared entirely by one party and, due to the disparity in bargaining power between the parties, is effectively offered on a "take-it-or-leave-it" basis. Contrary to the holding of the district court in *Vault*, contracts of adhesion are generally enforceable unless certain other factors (such as "unconscionability") are present. According to the *Restatement (Second) of Contracts*, §211(3), "[w]here the other party has reason to believe that the party manifesting such assent would not do so if he knew that the writing contained a particular term, the term is not part of the agreement." Comment f states that "[r]eason to believe [that the adherent would not knowingly have signed] may be inferred from the fact that the term is bizarre or oppressive, from the fact that it eviscerates the nonstandard terms explicitly agreed to, or from the fact that it eliminates the dominant purpose of the transaction."

On the other hand, a "shrinkwrap license" is not an ordinary contract of adhesion. Unlike most form contracts, in this case the party bound by the contract does not even sign or otherwise manifest consent to the terms that bind her. Indeed, in many cases she may not be aware of them.

2. Why did shrinkwrap licenses develop in the software context? They were certainly a fixture of the mass market software industry by the early 1980s. One answer may be that shrinkwrap licenses serve (or once served) as a declaration of the vendor's rights. Generally, proprietary rights provisions of shrinkwrap licenses assert that the information contained in the accompanying computer software is confidential and proprietary to the vendor, and may not be copied or disclosed without the vendor's permission. Software vendors who needed proof that they were not in fact disclosing their trade secrets by selling copies to whoever wanted them created the legal fiction that they were really licensing rather than selling their software. Because the "license" contained provisions that required customers to keep the software confidential, the trade secrets contained therein could be protected under decisions like *Data General.*

This rationale has much less force today, when it is clear that patent and copyright law are available to protect software sold on the mass market. Unlike trade secrets, patent and copyright law operate against the world, and do not require proof of tortious conduct or of a confidential relationship (or indeed any relationship at all) between the parties.

3. Judge Easterbrook points out that certain special contract terms have special contract formation procedures and requirements under the U.C.C. Finding none for shrinkwrap contracts, he reverts to the general formation procedure under Article 2. But is the code section he relies on — section 2-204 — the right one? Other courts have characterized shrinkwrap licenses under U.C.C. 2-207 (dealing with the "battle of the forms") or U.C.C. 2-209 (dealing with modifications to an existing contract). The last provision seems particularly appropriate for a common class of shrinkwrap licenses, which give no indication of the license terms until after the consumer has purchased the product and left the store.

Is *ProCD* such a case? The box containing the ProCD disks did not disclose the license terms but did at least indicate that there *were* additional terms contained in the box. Should this make a difference in deciding whether to enforce the terms?

4. In Judge Easterbrook's view, ProCD's business model relied heavily on the ability to price discriminate between different classes of users.[1] Judge Easterbrook argues the benefits of this practice and of contracts to carry it out. *Cf.* Frank H. Easterbrook, *Cyberspace and the Law of the Horse*, 1996 U. CHI. LEGAL F. 205. Are there counterarguments or limits to the degree to which law ought to enable price discrimination? *See* Wendy J. Gordon, *Intellectual Property as Price Discrimination: Implications for Contract*, 73 CHI.-KENT L. REV. 1367 (1998).

2. "Clickwrap" Licenses and Electronic Commerce

ProCD and other shrinkwrap license cases have all been based on a rather traditional model of software distribution, in which software is sold off the shelf in a

1. In fact, there was no evidence introduced in the case that indicated ProCD would be willing to authorize a use such as Zeidenberg's at any price. The price discrimination rationale is a construct based on Judge Easterbrook's assumption about what a rational actor might do.

storefront, or delivered in a box via the mail. Increasingly, however, software is not distributed by these means at all. Rather, software (as well as other forms of digital information) is likely to be distributed over the Internet directly. This new distribution mechanism has a number of implications for the contract rules that govern the transactions.

Specht v. Netscape Communications Corp.

306 F.3d 17 (2d Cir. 2002)

SOTOMAYOR, Circuit Judge:

This is an appeal from a judgment of the Southern District of New York denying a motion by defendants-appellants Netscape Communications Corporation and its corporate parent, America Online, Inc. (collectively, "defendants" or "Netscape"), to compel arbitration and to stay court proceedings. In order to resolve the central question of arbitrability presented here, we must address issues of contract formation in cyberspace. Principally, we are asked to determine whether plaintiffs-appellees ("plaintiffs"), by acting upon defendants' invitation to download free software made available on defendants' webpage, agreed to be bound by the software's license terms (which included the arbitration clause at issue), even though plaintiffs could not have learned of the existence of those terms unless, prior to executing the download, they had scrolled down the webpage to a screen located below the download button. We agree with the district court that a reasonably prudent Internet user in circumstances such as these would not have known or learned of the existence of the license terms before responding to defendants' invitation to download the free software, and that defendants therefore did not provide reasonable notice of the license terms. In consequence, plaintiffs' bare act of downloading the software did not unambiguously manifest assent to the arbitration provision contained in the license terms. . . .

We therefore affirm the district court's denial of defendants' motion to compel arbitration and to stay court proceedings.

Background

I. Facts

In three related putative class actions, plaintiffs alleged that, unknown to them, their use of SmartDownload transmitted to defendants private information about plaintiffs' downloading of files from the Internet, thereby effecting an electronic surveillance of their online activities in violation of two federal statutes, the Electronic Communications Privacy Act, 18 U.S.C. §§ 510 et seq., and the Computer Fraud and Abuse Act, 18 U.S.C. § 1030.

Specifically, plaintiffs alleged that when they first used Netscape's Communicator—a software program that permits Internet browsing—the program created and stored on each of their computer hard drives a small text file known as a "cookie" that functioned "as a kind of electronic identification tag for future communications" between their computers and Netscape. Plaintiffs further alleged that when they installed SmartDownload—a separate software "plug-in" that served to enhance Communicator's browsing capabilities — SmartDownload created and stored on their computer hard drives another string of characters, known as a "Key," which similarly functioned as an identification tag in future communications with Netscape. According to the complaints in this case, each time a computer user employed Communicator to download a file from the Internet, SmartDownload "assume[d] from Communicator the task of downloading" the file and transmitted to Netscape the address of the file being downloaded together with the cookie created by Communicator and the Key created by SmartDownload. These processes, plaintiffs claim, constituted unlawful "eavesdropping" on users of Netscape's software products as well as on Internet websites from which users employing SmartDownload downloaded files.

In the time period relevant to this litigation, Netscape offered on its website various software programs, including Communicator and SmartDownload, which visitors to the site were invited to obtain free of charge. It is undisputed that five of the six named plaintiffs — Michael Fagan, John Gibson, Mark Gruber, Sean Kelly, and Sherry Weindorf — downloaded Communicator from the Netscape website. These plaintiffs acknowledge that when they proceeded to initiate installation of Communicator, they were automatically shown a scrollable text of that program's license agreement and were not permitted to complete the installation until they had clicked on a "Yes" button to indicate that they accepted all the license terms.[4] If a user attempted to install Communicator without clicking "Yes," the installation would be aborted. All five named user plaintiffs expressly agreed to Communicator's license terms by clicking "Yes." The Communicator license agreement that these plaintiffs saw made no mention of SmartDownload or other plug-in programs, and stated that "[t]hese terms apply to Netscape Communicator and Netscape Navigator" and that "all disputes relating to this Agreement (excepting any dispute relating to intellectual property rights)" are subject to "binding arbitration in Santa Clara County, California."

Although Communicator could be obtained independently of SmartDownload, all the named user plaintiffs, except Fagan, downloaded and installed Communicator in connection with downloading SmartDownload. Each of these plaintiffs allegedly arrived at a Netscape webpage captioned "SmartDownload Communicator" that urged them to "Download With Confidence Using SmartDownload!" At or near the bottom of the screen facing plaintiffs was the prompt "Start Download" and a tinted button labeled "Download." By clicking on the button, plaintiffs initiated the download of SmartDownload. Once that process was complete, SmartDownload, as its first plug-in task, permitted plaintiffs to proceed with downloading and installing Communicator, an operation that was accompanied by the clickwrap display of Communicator's license terms described above.

The signal difference between downloading Communicator and downloading SmartDownload was that no clickwrap presentation accompanied the latter operation.

4. This kind of online software license agreement has come to be known as "clickwrap" (by analogy to "shrinkwrap," used in the licensing of tangible forms of software sold in packages) because it "presents the user with a message on his or her computer screen, requiring that the user manifest his or her assent to the terms of the license agreement by clicking on an icon. The product cannot be obtained or used unless and until the icon is clicked." *Specht*, 150 F. Supp. 2d at 593-94 (footnote omitted). Just as breaking the shrinkwrap seal and using the enclosed computer program after encountering notice of the existence of governing license terms has been deemed by some courts to constitute assent to those terms in the context of tangible software, see, e.g., ProCD, Inc. v. Zeidenberg, 86 F.3d 1447, 1451 (7th Cir. 1996), so clicking on a webpage's clickwrap button after receiving notice of the existence of license terms has been held by some courts to manifest an Internet user's assent to terms governing the use of downloadable intangible software, see, e.g., Hotmail Corp. v. Van Money Pie Inc., 47 U.S.P.Q.2d 1020, 1025 (N.D. Cal. 1998).

Instead, once plaintiffs Gibson, Gruber, Kelly, and Weindorf had clicked on the "Download" button located at or near the bottom of their screen, and the downloading of SmartDownload was complete, these plaintiffs encountered no further information about the plug-in program or the existence of license terms governing its use. The sole reference to SmartDownload's license terms on the "SmartDownload Communicator" webpage was located in text that would have become visible to plaintiffs only if they had scrolled down to the next screen.

Had plaintiffs scrolled down instead of acting on defendants' invitation to click on the "Download" button, they would have encountered the following invitation: "Please review and agree to the terms of the *Netscape SmartDownload software license agreement* before downloading and using the software." Plaintiffs Gibson, Gruber, Kelly, and Weindorf averred in their affidavits that they never saw this reference to the SmartDownload license agreement when they clicked on the "Download" button. They also testified during depositions that they saw no reference to license terms when they clicked to download SmartDownload, although under questioning by defendants' counsel, some plaintiffs added that they could not "remember" or be "sure" whether the screen shots of the SmartDownload page attached to their affidavits reflected precisely what they had seen on their computer screens when they downloaded SmartDownload.[10]

In sum, plaintiffs Gibson, Gruber, Kelly, and Weindorf allege that the process of obtaining SmartDownload contrasted sharply with that of obtaining Communicator. Having selected SmartDownload, they were required neither to express unambiguous assent to that program's license agreement nor even to view the license terms or become aware of their existence before proceeding with the invited download of the free plug-in program. Moreover, once these plaintiffs had initiated the download, the existence of SmartDownload's license terms was not mentioned while the software was running or at any later point in plaintiffs' experience of the product.

Even for a user who, unlike plaintiffs, did happen to scroll down past the download button, SmartDownload's license terms would not have been immediately displayed in the manner of Communicator's clickwrapped terms. Instead, if such a user had seen the notice of SmartDownload's terms and then clicked on the underlined invitation to review and agree to the terms, a hypertext link would have taken the user to a separate webpage entitled "License & Support Agreements." The first paragraph on this page read, in pertinent part:

> The use of each Netscape software product is governed by a license agreement. You mustread and agree to the license agreement terms BEFORE acquiring a product. Please click on the appropriate link below to review the current license agreement for the product of interest to you before acquisition. For products available for download, you must read and agree to the license agreement terms BEFORE you install the software. If you do not agree to the license terms, do not download, install or use the software.

Below this paragraph appeared a list of license agreements, the first of which was "*License Agreement for Netscape Navigator and Netscape Communicator Product Family* (Netscape Navigator, Netscape Communicator and Netscape SmartDownload)." If the

10. In the screen shot of the SmartDownload webpage attached to Weindorf's affidavit, the reference to license terms is partially visible, though almost illegible, at the bottom of the screen. In the screen shots attached to the affidavits of Gibson, Gruber, and Kelly, the reference to license terms is not visible.

user clicked on that link, he or she would be taken to yet another webpage that contained the full text of a license agreement that was identical in every respect to the Communicator license agreement except that it stated that its "terms apply to Netscape Communicator, Netscape Navigator, and Netscape SmartDownload." The license agreement granted the user a nonexclusive license to use and reproduce the software, subject to certain terms:

> BY CLICKING THE ACCEPTANCE BUTTON OR INSTALLING OR USING NETSCAPE COMMUNICATOR, NETSCAPE NAVIGATOR, OR NETSCAPE SMARTDOWNLOAD SOFTWARE (THE "PRODUCT"), THE INDIVIDUAL OR ENTITY LICENSING THE PRODUCT ("LICENSEE") IS CONSENTING TO BE BOUND BY AND IS BECOMING A PARTY TO THIS AGREEMENT. IF LICENSEE DOES NOT AGREE TO ALL OF THE TERMS OF THIS AGREEMENT, THE BUTTON INDICATING NON-ACCEPTANCE MUST BE SELECTED, AND LICENSEE MUST NOT INSTALL OR USE THE SOFTWARE.

Among the license terms was a provision requiring virtually all disputes relating to the agreement to be submitted to arbitration:

> Unless otherwise agreed in writing, all disputes relating to this Agreement (excepting any dispute relating to intellectual property rights) shall be subject to final and binding arbitration in Santa Clara County, California, under the auspices of JAMS/EndDispute, with the losing party paying all costs of arbitration. . . .

II. *Proceedings Below*

In the district court, defendants moved to compel arbitration and to stay court proceedings pursuant to the Federal Arbitration Act ("FAA"), 9 U.S.C. § 4, arguing that the disputes reflected in the complaints, like any other dispute relating to the SmartDownload license agreement, are subject to the arbitration clause contained in that agreement. Finding that Netscape's webpage, unlike typical examples of clickwrap, neither adequately alerted users to the existence of SmartDownload's license terms nor required users unambiguously to manifest assent to those terms as a condition of downloading the product, the court held that the user plaintiffs had not entered into the SmartDownload license agreement. *Specht*, 150 F. Supp. 2d at 595-96.

[Defendants appealed]

Discussion . . .

III. *Whether the User Plaintiffs Had Reasonable Notice of and Manifested Assent to the SmartDownload License Agreement*

Whether governed by the common law or by Article 2 of the Uniform Commercial Code ("UCC"), a transaction, in order to be a contract, requires a manifestation of agreement between the parties. See Windsor Mills, Inc. v. Collins & Aikman Corp., 101 Cal. Rptr. 347, 350 (Cal. Ct. App. 1972) ("[C]onsent to, or acceptance of, the arbitration provision [is] necessary to create an agreement to arbitrate."); see also CAL. COM. CODE § 2204(1) ("A contract for sale of goods may be made in any manner sufficient to show agreement, including conduct by both parties which recognizes the existence of such a contract.").[13] Mutual manifestation of assent, whether by written or spoken word or by conduct, is the touchstone of contract. Binder v. Aetna Life Ins. Co., 89 Cal. Rptr. 2d 540, 551 (Cal. Ct. App. 1999); cf. RESTATEMENT (SECOND) OF CONTRACTS § 19(2) (1981) ("The conduct of a party is not effective as a manifestation of his assent unless he intends to engage in the conduct and knows or has reason to know that the other party may infer from his conduct that he assents."). Although an onlooker observing the disputed transactions in this case would have seen each of the user plaintiffs click on the SmartDownload "Download" button, see Cedars Sinai Med. Ctr. v. Mid-West Nat'l Life Ins. Co., 118 F. Supp. 2d 1002, 1008 (C.D. Cal. 2000) ("In California, a party's intent to contract is judged objectively, by the party's outward manifestation of consent."), a consumer's clicking on a download button does not communicate assent to contractual terms if the offer did not make clear to the consumer that clicking on the download button would signify assent to those terms, see *Windsor Mills*, 101 Cal. Rptr. at 351 ("[W]hen the offeree does not know that a proposal has been made to him this objective standard does not apply."). California's common law is clear that "an offeree, regardless of apparent manifestation of his consent, is not bound by inconspicuous contractual provisions of which he is unaware, contained in a document whose contractual nature

13. The district court concluded that the SmartDownload transactions here should be governed by "California law as it relates to the sale of goods, including the Uniform Commercial Code in effect in California." *Specht*, 150 F. Supp. 2d at 591. It is not obvious, however, that UCC Article 2 ("sales of goods") applies to the licensing of software that is downloadable from the Internet. Cf. Advent Sys. Ltd. v. Unisys Corp., 925 F.2d 670, 675 (3d Cir.1991) ("The increasing frequency of computer products as subjects of commercial litigation has led to controversy over whether software is a 'good' or intellectual property. The [UCC] does not specifically mention software."); Lorin Brennan, *Why Article 2 Cannot Apply to Software Transactions*, PLI PATENTS, COPYRIGHTS, TRADEMARKS, & LITERARY PROPERTY COURSE HANDBOOK SERIES (Feb.-Mar. 2001) (demonstrating the trend in case law away from application of UCC provisions to software sales and licensing and toward application of intellectual property principles). There is no doubt that a sale of tangible goods over the Internet is governed by Article 2 of the UCC. See, e.g., Butler v. Beer Across Am., 83 F. Supp. 2d 1261, 1263-64 & n.6 (N.D. Ala. 2000) (applying Article 2 to an Internet sale of bottles of beer). Some courts have also applied Article 2, occasionally with misgivings, to sales of off-the-shelf software in tangible, packaged formats. See, e.g., *ProCD*, 86 F.3d at 1450 ("[W]e treat the [database] licenses as ordinary contracts accompanying the sale of products, and therefore as governed by the common law of contracts and the Uniform Commercial Code. Whether there are legal differences between 'contracts' and 'licenses' (which may matter under the copyright doctrine of first sale) is a subject for another day."); i.LAN Sys., Inc. v. NetScout Serv. Level Corp., 183 F. Supp. 2d 328, 332 (D. Mass. 2002) (stating, in the context of a dispute between business parties, that "Article 2 technically does not, and certainly will not in the future, govern software licenses, but for the time being, the Court will assume that it does").

Downloadable software, however, is scarcely a "tangible" good, and, in part because software may be obtained, copied, or transferred effortlessly at the stroke of a computer key, licensing of such Internet products has assumed a vast importance in recent years. Recognizing that "a body of law based on images of the sale of manufactured goods ill fits licenses and other transactions in computer information," the National Conference of Commissioners on Uniform State Laws has promulgated the Uniform Computer Information Transactions Act ("UCITA"), a code resembling UCC Article 2 in many respects but drafted to reflect emergent practices in the sale and licensing of computer information. UCITA, prefatory note (rev. ed. Aug. 23, 2001) (available at www.ucitaonline.com/ucita.html). UCITA—originally intended as a new Article 2B to supplement Articles 2 and 2A of the UCC but later proposed as an independent code—has been adopted by two states, Maryland and Virginia. See MD. CODE ANN. COM. LAW §§ 22-101 et seq.; VA. CODE ANN. §§ 59.1-501.1 et seq.

We need not decide today whether UCC Article 2 applies to Internet transactions in downloadable products. The district court's analysis and the parties' arguments on appeal show that, for present purposes, there is no essential difference between UCC Article 2 and the common law of contracts. We therefore apply the common law, with exceptions as noted.

is not obvious." Id.; see also Marin Storage & Trucking, Inc. v. Benco Contracting & Eng'g, Inc., 107 Cal. Rptr. 2d 645, 651 (Cal. Ct. App. 2001) (same).

Arbitration agreements are no exception to the requirement of manifestation of assent. "This principle of knowing consent applies with particular force to provisions for arbitration." *Windsor Mills*, 101 Cal. Rptr. at 351. . . .

A. The Reasonably Prudent Offeree of Downloadable Software

Defendants argue that plaintiffs must be held to a standard of reasonable prudence and that, because notice of the existence of SmartDownload license terms was on the next scrollable screen, plaintiffs were on "inquiry notice" of those terms. We disagree with the proposition that a reasonably prudent offeree in plaintiffs' position would necessarily have known or learned of the existence of the SmartDownload license agreement prior to acting, so that plaintiffs may be held to have assented to that agreement with constructive notice of its terms. See CAL. CIV. CODE § 1589 ("Avoluntary acceptance of the benefit of a transaction is equivalent to a consent to all the obligations arising from it, so far as the facts are known, or ought to be known, to the person accepting."). It is true that "[a] party cannot avoid the terms of a contract on the ground that he or she failed to read it before signing." *Marin Storage & Trucking*, 107 Cal. Rptr. 2d at 651. But courts are quick to add: "An exception to this general rule exists when the writing does not appear to be a contract and the terms are not called to the attention of the recipient. In such a case, no contract is formed with respect to the undisclosed term." Id.; cf. Cory v. Golden State Bank, 157 Cal. Rptr. 538, 541 (Cal. Ct. App. 1979) ("[T]he provision in question is effectively hidden from the view of money order purchasers until after the transactions are completed. . . . Under these circumstances, it must be concluded that the Bank's money order purchasers are not chargeable with either actual or constructive notice of the service charge provision, and therefore cannot be deemed to have consented to the provision as part of their transaction with the Bank."). . . .

[R]eceipt of a physical document containing contract terms or notice thereof is frequently deemed, in the world of paper transactions, a sufficient circumstance to place the offeree on inquiry notice of those terms. "Every person who has actual notice of circumstances sufficient to put a prudent man upon inquiry as to a particular fact, has constructive notice of the fact itself in all cases in which, by prosecuting such inquiry, he might have learned such fact." CAL. CIV. CODE § 19. These principles apply equally to the emergent world of online product delivery, pop-up screens, hyperlinked pages, clickwrap licensing, scrollable documents, and urgent admonitions to "Download Now!". What plaintiffs saw when they were being invited by defendants to download this fast, free plug-in called SmartDownload was a screen containing praise for the product and, at the very bottom of the screen, a "Download" button. Defendants argue that under the principles set forth in the cases cited above, a "fair and prudent person using ordinary care" would have been on inquiry notice of SmartDownload's license terms. *Shacket*, 651 F. Supp. at 690.

We are not persuaded that a reasonably prudent offeree in these circumstances would have known of the existence of license terms. Plaintiffs were responding to an offer that did not carry an immediately visible notice of the existence of license terms or require unambiguous manifestation of assent to those terms. Thus, plaintiffs' "apparent manifestation of . . . consent" was to terms "contained in a document whose contractual nature [was] not obvious." *Windsor Mills*, 101 Cal. Rptr. at 351. Moreover, the fact that, given the position of the scroll bar on their computer screens, plaintiffs may have been aware that an unexplored portion of the Netscape webpage remained below the download button does not mean that they reasonably should have concluded that this portion contained a notice of license terms. In their deposition testimony, plaintiffs variously stated that they used the scroll bar "[o]nly if there is something that I feel I need to see that is on — that is off the page," or that the elevated position of the scroll bar suggested the presence of "mere[ ] formalities, standard lower banner links" or "that the page is bigger than what I can see." Plaintiffs testified, and defendants did not refute, that plaintiffs were in fact unaware that defendants intended to attach license terms to the use of SmartDownload.

We conclude that in circumstances such as these, where consumers are urged to download free software at the immediate click of a button, a reference to the existence of license terms on a submerged screen is not sufficient to place consumers on inquiry or constructive notice of those terms. The SmartDownload webpage screen was "printed in such a manner that it tended to conceal the fact that it was an express acceptance of [Netscape's] rules and regulations." *Larrus*, 266 P.2d at 147. Internet users may have, as defendants put it, "as much time as they need[ ]" to scroll through multiple screens on a webpage, but there is no reason to assume that viewers will scroll down to subsequent screens simply because screens are there. When products are "free" and users are invited to download them in the absence of reasonably conspicuous notice that they are about to bind themselves to contract terms, the transactional circumstances cannot be fully analogized to those in the paper world of arm's-length bargaining. In the next two sections, we discuss case law and other legal authorities that have addressed the circumstances of computer sales, software licensing, and online transacting. Those authorities tend strongly to support our conclusion that plaintiffs did not manifest assent to SmartDownload's license terms.

B. Shrinkwrap Licensing and Related Practices

Defendants cite certain well-known cases involving shrinkwrap licensing and related commercial practices in support of their contention that plaintiffs became bound by the SmartDownload license terms by virtue of inquiry notice. [The Court discusses *Hill*, *ProCD*, and *Mortenson*.]

These cases do not help defendants. To the extent that they hold that the purchaser of a computer or tangible software is contractually bound after failing to object to printed license terms provided with the product, *Hill* and *Brower* do not differ markedly from the cases involving traditional paper contracting discussed in the previous section. Insofar as the purchaser in *ProCD* was confronted with conspicuous, mandatory license terms every time he ran the software on his computer, that case actually undermines defendants' contention that downloading in the absence of conspicuous terms is an act that binds plaintiffs to those terms. In *Mortenson*, the full text of license terms was printed on each sealed diskette envelope inside the software box, printed again on the inside cover of the user manual, and notice of the terms appeared on the computer screen every time the purchaser executed the program. *Mortenson*, 970 P.2d at 806. In sum, the foregoing cases are clearly distinguishable from the facts of the present action.

C. Online Transactions

Cases in which courts have found contracts arising from Internet use do not assist defendants, because in those circumstances there was much clearer notice than in the present case that a user's act would manifest assent to contract terms. [The court discussed several clickwrap license cases, and also referred to UCITA as a relevant statement of analogous rules.]

After reviewing the California common law and other relevant legal authority, we conclude that under the circumstances here, plaintiffs' downloading of SmartDownload did not constitute acceptance of defendants' license terms. Reasonably conspicuous notice of the existence of contract terms and unambiguous manifestation of assent to those terms by consumers are essential if electronic bargaining is to have integrity and credibility. We hold that a reasonably prudent offeree in plaintiffs' position would not have known or learned, prior to acting on the invitation to download, of the reference to SmartDownload's license terms hidden below the "Download" button on the next screen. We affirm the district court's conclusion that the user plaintiffs, including Fagan, are not bound by the arbitration clause contained in those terms.

Conclusion

For the foregoing reasons, we affirm the district court's denial of defendants' motion to compel arbitration and to stay court proceedings.

COMMENTS AND QUESTIONS

1. Clickwrap and browsewrap licenses differ in significant respects from shrinkwrap licenses. First, bits sent over a modem seem less like traditional, tangible "goods" to which Article 2 has traditionally applied. This doesn't necessarily mean that the information in question is "licensed" of course. Software sold over the Internet is still distributed in the form of "copies," at least in a copyright law sense; it's just that those copies are created at the buyer's site, rather than being shipped there in physical form. Further, most of the indicia of sale in a mass market transaction—the possession of one copy, with perpetual use rights in exchange for a single lump-sum payment—are still present in an online transaction. But even if the transaction looks more like a sale than a lease (or "license"), it is more and more difficult to apply Article 2 to such a deal, except perhaps by analogy.

Second, the nature of online sales gives vendors an opportunity to avoid the problems of shrinkwrap licenses entirely, by disclosing terms to buyers and obtaining agreement to those terms before the purchase is completed. It is relatively common for Web sites to require agreement to certain terms and conditions by asking the user to click "OK" before proceeding. Such an agreement, entered into before the vendor sells the software or other information, is certainly a "contract of adhesion." The buyer has no realistic choice, other than "take it or leave it." But it is not a shrinkwrap license. The buyer has the opportunity to read and agree to the terms before she pays her money. It is not surprising, therefore, that such "clickwrap" licenses are easier to enforce than their shrinkwrap counterparts. *See* Davidson & Assocs. v. Internet Gateway, 420 F.3d 630 (8th Cir. 2005); i.Lan Systems v. Netscout, 183 F. Supp. 328 (D. Mass. 2002); Caspi v. Microsoft Network LLC, 732 A.2d 528 (N.J. App. Div. 1999); Hotmail Corp. v. Van Money Pie, 47 U.S.P.Q.2d 1020 (N.D. Cal. 1998) (assuming such an agreement was enforceable, without discussing the issue).

2. Do consumers really benefit from being able to see the terms in advance, if they still have no choice regarding what those terms are? Is the real objection to shrinkwrap licenses their immutable, monolithic character, and not how they are presented to the consumer? *Cf.* Robert P. Merges, *Intellectual Property and the Costs of Commercial Exchange: A Review Essay*, 93 MICH. L. REV. 1570, 1612 (1995) (suggesting that shrinkwrap license terms should be preempted when there is sufficient uniformity in the industry that the terms in effect amount to "private legislation" by software vendors); Florencia Marotta-Wurgler, *Are "Pay Now, Terms Later" Contracts Worse for Buyers? Evidence from Software License Agreements*, 38 J. LEGAL STUD. 309 (2009) (presenting an empirical study of software license agreements, and arguing that software publishers that use "pay now, terms later" contracts for their online sales "do not offer more one-sided terms than those who make their licenses available prior to purchase"); Maureen A. O'Rourke, *Copyright Preemption After the* ProCD *Case: A Market-Based Approach*, 12 BERKELEY TECH. L.J. 53 (1997).

3. Despite the obvious legal advantages to giving consumers terms to review and approve before entering into a contract, many Web sites (like the one in *Specht*) do not in fact require purchasers to read and agree to their terms. Not surprisingly, many courts have refused to enforce such unilateral statements as contracts. In addition to *Specht* and the cases it discusses, see Campbell v. General Dynamics, 407 F.3d 546 (1st Cir. 2005); Westcode, Inc. v. RBE Electronics, Inc., 2000 WL 124566 (E.D. Pa. Feb. 1, 2000). But a surprising number of courts have enforced such "browsewrap" agreements, often in the context of claims for invasion of property by electronic robots. *See, e.g.*, Register.com v. Verio, Inc., 356 F.3d 393 (2d Cir. 2004); Ticketmaster Corp. v. Tickets.com, 2003 WL 21406289 (C.D. Cal. Mar. 7, 2003); Pollstar v. Gigmania, Ltd., 170 F. Supp. 2d 974 (E.D. Cal. 2000). For a discussion of the enforceability of browsewrap terms, see Mark A. Lemley, *Terms of Use*, 91 MINN. L. REV. 459 (2006).

In 2010, the American Law Institute published its Principles of the Law of Software Contracts. (The "Principles" project is similar in format to a *Restatement*, but according to the Institute the law is at a sufficiently early stage that it would be premature to attempt to "restate" it. The "Principles" project therefore "accounts for the case law and recommends best practices, without unduly hindering the law's adaptability to future developments.") Section 2.02, titled "Standard-Form Transfers of Generally Available Software: Enforcement of the Standard Form," states:

> (a) This Section applies to standard-form transfers of generally available software as defined in § 1.01(l).
>
> (b) A transferee adopts a standard form as a contract when a reasonable transferor would believe the transferee intends to be bound to the form.
>
> (c) A transferee will be deemed to have adopted a standard form as a contract if
>
> (1) the standard form is reasonably accessible electronically prior to initiation of the transfer at issue;
>
> (2) upon initiating the transfer, the transferee has reasonable notice of and access to the standard form before payment or, if there is no payment, before completion of the transfer;

(3) in the case of an electronic transfer of software, the transferee signifies agreement at the end of or adjacent to the electronic standard form, or in the case of a standard form printed on or attached to packaged software or separately wrapped from the software, the transferee does not exercise the opportunity to return the software unopened for a full refund within a reasonable time after the transfer; and

(4) the transferee can store and reproduce the standard form if presented electronically.

(d) Subject to § 1.10 (public policy), § 1.11 (unconscionability), and other invalidating defenses supplied by these Principles or outside law, a standard term is enforceable if reasonably comprehensible.

(e) If a transferee asserts that it did not adopt a standard form as a contract under subsection (b) or asserts a failure of the transferor to comply with subsection (c) or (d), the transferor has the burden of production and persuasion on the issue of compliance with the subsections.

As § 2.02 and the accompanying comments make clear, the Principles generally approve of shrinkwrap and clickwrap licenses where (as in *ProCD*) the transferee has the opportunity to return the software unopened, or the transferee has the opportunity to read and agree to terms before purchase. The Reporters' Notes cite *Specht* for the proposition that "Browsewrap is more problematic because it does not require transferees to see the terms before 'agreeing to them,'" but also cites cases such as *Register.com* for the proposition that some courts have enforced them. Comment (b) clarifies that § 2.02(b) "does not establish a bright-line rule for enforcement requiring, for example, clicking 'I agree' at the end of an electronic standard form." In addition, comment (c) refers to § 2.02(c) as a provision that "prescribes best practices and constitutes a safe-harbor provision for transferors."

Should courts defer to the Institute's approach as set forth in § 2.02, or should they take a more aggressive approach in policing contract formation? Can you think of any reason not to require a consumer to click "I agree"? What does such a policy say about the importance of the terms to the vendor? To the transaction? If merely posting terms on a Web site creates a contract with anyone who visits the Web site, is there any way for a consumer to avoid entering into such a contract? What happens when companies post conflicting terms of use on their Web sites?

C. LEGAL PROTECTION OF IDEAS

Courts have struggled over the years with whether and under what circumstances a person who supplies a valuable idea to another may obtain legal redress. *See* Lionel S. Sobel, *The Law of Ideas, Revisited*, 1 UCLA Ent. L. Rev. 9 (1994). On the one hand, as the preceding chapter noted, copyright law expressly disavows protection for ideas, *see* 17 U.S.C. § 102(b), and patent law imposes stringent requirements—examination, novelty, non-obviousness, utility, and disclosure—before affording protection. Therefore, it would seem incongruous for state law to protect ideas. On the other hand, we protect valuable information through state trade secret law. Should there be some role for state law to protect promises to pay for an idea that is not a trade secret?

What if the idea is communicated without a formal contract being entered into? Without such protection, people with good ideas might lack the legal and economic security to exchange such information with those in a position to develop products, movies, and other valuable works. But if unpatented, nonsecret ideas are protectable, what is left of the public domain?

Nadel v. Play-by-Play Toys & Novelties, Inc.

208 F.3d 368 (2d Cir. 2000)

SOTOMAYOR, Circuit Judge.

Plaintiff-appellant Craig P. Nadel ("Nadel") brought this action against defendant-appellee Play-By-Play Toys & Novelties, Inc. ("Play-By-Play") for breach of contract, quasi contract, and unfair competition. The thrust of Nadel's complaint was that Play-By-Play took his idea for an upright, sound-emitting, spinning plush toy and that, contrary to industry custom, Play-By-Play used the idea in its "Tornado Taz" product without paying him compensation. . . .

Background

Nadel is a toy idea man. Toy companies regularly do business with independent inventors such as Nadel in order to develop and market new toy concepts as quickly as possible. To facilitate the exchange of ideas, the standard custom and practice in the toy industry calls for companies to treat the submission of an idea as confidential. If the company subsequently uses the disclosed idea, industry custom provides that the company shall compensate the inventor, unless, of course, the disclosed idea was already known to the company.

In 1996, Nadel developed the toy concept at issue in this case. He transplanted the "eccentric mechanism"[1] found in several hanging Halloween toys then on the market-such as "Spooky Skull" and "Shaking Mutant Pumpkin"—and placed the mechanism inside of a plush toy monkey skin to develop the prototype for a new table-top monkey toy. This plush toy figure sat upright, emitted sound, and spun when placed on a flat surface.

In October 1996, Nadel met with Neil Wasserman, an executive at Play-By-Play who was responsible for the development of its plush toy line. According to Nadel, he showed his prototype monkey toy to Wasserman, who expressed interest in adapting the concept to a non-moving, plush Tazmanian Devil toy that Play-By-Play was already producing under license from Warner Bros. Nadel contends that, consistent with industry custom, any ideas that he disclosed to Wasserman during their October 1996 meeting were subject to an agreement by Play-By-Play to keep such ideas confidential and to compensate Nadel in the event of their use.

Nadel claims that he sent his prototype monkey toy to Wasserman as a sample and awaited the "Taz skin" and voice tape, which Wasserman allegedly said he would send, so that Nadel could make a sample spinning/laughing Tazmanian Devil toy for

1. An eccentric mechanism typically consists of a housing containing a motor with an eccentric weight attached to the motor shaft. When the motor is activated, the motor rotates the weight centrifugally, causing the housing to shake or spin.

Play-By-Play. Wasserman never provided Nadel with the Taz skin and voice tape, however, and denies ever having received the prototype monkey toy from Nadel.

Notwithstanding Wasserman's denial, his secretary, Melissa Rodriguez, testified that Nadel's prototype monkey toy remained in Wasserman's office for several months. According to Ms. Rodriguez, the monkey toy was usually kept in a glass cabinet behind Wasserman's desk, but she remembered that on one occasion she had seen it on a table in Wasserman's office. Despite Nadel's multiple requests, Wasserman did not return Nadel's prototype monkey toy until February 1997, after Play-by-Play introduced its "Tornado Taz" product at the New York Toy Fair.

The parties do not dispute that "Tornado Taz" has the same general characteristics as Nadel's prototype monkey toy. Like Nadel's toy, Tornado Taz is a plush toy that emits sounds (including "screaming," "laughing," "snarling," and "grunting"), sits upright, and spins by means of an internal eccentric vibration mechanism.

Nadel claims that, in violation of their alleged agreement, Play-By-Play used his idea without paying him compensation. Play-By-Play contends, however, that it independently developed the Tornado Taz product concept and that Nadel is therefore not entitled to any compensation. Specifically, Play-By-Play maintains that, as early as June or July of 1996, two of its officers — Wasserman and Slattery — met in Hong Kong and began discussing ways to create a spinning or vibrating Tazmanian Devil, including the possible use of an eccentric mechanism. Furthermore, Play-By-Play claims that in late September or early October 1996, it commissioned an outside manufacturing agent — Barter Trading of Hong Kong — to begin developing Tornado Taz.

Play-By-Play also argues that, even if it did use Nadel's idea to develop Tornado Taz, Nadel is not entitled to compensation because Nadel's concept was unoriginal and non-novel to the toy industry in October 1996. In support of this argument, Play-By-Play has submitted evidence of various toys, commercially available prior to October 1996, which used eccentric motors and allegedly contained the same characteristics as Nadel's prototype monkey toy. . . .

Discussion

I. Nadel's Claims

On January 21, 1999, the district court granted Play-By-Play's motion for summary judgment dismissing Nadel's claims for breach of contract, quasi contract, and unfair competition. Interpreting New York law, the district court stated that "a party is not entitled to recover for theft of an idea unless the idea is novel or original." Nadel v. Play By Play Toys & Novelties, Inc., 34 F. Supp. 2d 180, 184 (S.D.N.Y. 1999). Applying that principle to Nadel's claims, the district court concluded that, even if the spinning toy concept were novel to Play-By-Play at the time Nadel made the disclosure to Wasserman in October 1996, Nadel's claims must nonetheless fail for lack of novelty or originality because "numerous toys containing the characteristics of [Nadel's] monkey were in existence prior to[ ] October 1996." Id. at 185. In essence, the district court interpreted New York law to require that, when a plaintiff claims that a defendant has either (1) misappropriated his idea (a "property-based claim") or (2) breached an express or implied-in-fact contract by using such idea (a "contract-based claim"), the idea at issue must be original or novel generally. See id. at 184 n.1.

Thus, according to the district court, a finding that an idea was novel as to Play By Play—i.e., novel to the buyer—cannot suffice to sustain any of Nadel's claims. See id.

On appeal, Nadel challenges the district court's conclusion that a showing of novelty to the buyer—i.e., that Nadel's idea was novel to Play-By-Play at the time of his October 1996 disclosure—cannot suffice to sustain his claims for breach of contract, quasi contract, and unfair competition under New York law. Nadel claims, moreover, that the record contains a genuine issue of material fact concerning whether his toy idea was novel to Play-By-Play at the time of his October 1996 disclosure to Wasserman and that the district court therefore erred in granting Play-By-Play's motion for summary judgment.

Nadel's factual allegations present a familiar submission-of-idea case: (1) the parties enter into a pre-disclosure confidentiality agreement; (2) the idea is subsequently disclosed to the prospective buyer; (3) there is no post-disclosure contract for payment based on use; and (4) plaintiff sues defendant for allegedly using the disclosed idea under either a contract-based or property-based theory. For the reasons that follow, we conclude that a finding of novelty as to Play-By-Play can suffice to provide consideration for Nadel's contract claims against Play-By-Play. Accordingly, because we also find that there exists a genuine issue of material fact as to whether Nadel's idea was novel to Play-By-Play at the time of his October 1996 disclosure, we vacate the district court's grant of summary judgment on Nadel's contract claims. With respect to Nadel's misappropriation claim, we similarly vacate the district court's grant of summary judgment and remand for further proceedings to determine whether Nadel's idea was original or novel generally.

A. Submission-of-Idea Cases Under New York Law

Our analysis begins with the New York Court of Appeals' most recent discussion of the law governing idea submission cases, Apfel v. Prudential-Bache Securities, Inc., 81 N.Y.2d 470, 600 N.Y.S.2d 433, 616 N.E.2d 1095 (1993). In *Apfel*, the Court of Appeals discussed the type of novelty an idea must have in order to sustain a contract-based or property-based claim for its uncompensated use. Specifically, *Apfel* clarified an important distinction between the requirement of "novelty to the buyer" for contract claims, on the one hand, and "originality" (or novelty generally) for misappropriation claims, on the other hand.

Under the facts of *Apfel*, the plaintiff disclosed his idea to the defendant pursuant to a confidentiality agreement and, subsequent to disclosure, entered into another agreement wherein the defendant agreed to pay a stipulated price for the idea's use. See id. at 474. The defendant used the idea but refused to pay plaintiff pursuant to the post-disclosure agreement on the asserted ground that "no contract existed between the parties because the sale agreement lacked consideration." Id. at 475. The defendant argued that an idea could not constitute legally sufficient consideration unless it was original or novel generally and that, because plaintiff's idea was not original or novel generally (it had been in the public domain at the time of the post-disclosure agreement), the idea provided insufficient consideration to support the parties' post-disclosure contract. See id. at 474-75.

In rejecting defendant's argument, the Court of Appeals held that there was sufficient consideration to support plaintiff's contract claim because the idea at issue had value to the defendant at the time the parties concluded their post-disclosure agreement. See id. at 476. The *Apfel* court noted that "traditional principles of contract law" provide that parties "are free to make their bargain, even if the consideration exchanged is grossly unequal or of dubious value," id. at 475, and that, so long as the "defendant received something of value" under the contract, the contract would not be void for lack of consideration, id. at 476. See also id. at 478 ("[T]he buyer knows what he or she is buying and has agreed that the idea has value, and the Court will not ordinarily go behind that determination.").

The *Apfel* court explicitly rejected defendant's contention that the court should carve out "an exception to traditional principles of contract law" for submission-of-idea cases by requiring that an idea must also be original or novel generally in order to constitute valid consideration. Id. at 477. In essence, the defendant sought to impose a requirement that an idea be novel in absolute terms, as opposed to only the defendant buyer, in order to constitute valid consideration for the bargain. In rejecting this argument, the *Apfel* court clarified the standards for both contract-based and property-based claims in submission-of-idea cases. That analysis guides our decision here.

The *Apfel* court first noted that "novelty as an element of an idea seller's claim" is a distinct element of proof with respect to both (1) "a claim based on a property theory" and (2) "a claim based on a contract theory." Id. at 477. The court then proceeded to discuss how the leading submission-of-idea case — Downey v. General Foods Corp., 31 N.Y.2d 56, 334 N.Y.S.2d 874, 286 N.E.2d 257 (1972) — treated novelty with respect to property-based and contract-based claims. First, the *Apfel* court explained that the plaintiff's property-based claims for misappropriation were dismissed in Downey because "the elements of novelty and originality [were] absent," i.e., the ideas were so common as to be unoriginal and known generally. *Apfel*, 81 N.Y.2d at 477 (quoting *Downey*, 31 N.Y.2d at 61) (alteration in original); accord *Downey*, 31 N.Y.2d at 61-62 (holding that the submitted idea — marketing Jell-O to children under the name "Mr. Wiggle" — was "lacking in novelty and originality" because the idea was merely the "use of a word ('wiggley' or 'wiggle') descriptive of the most obvious characteristic of Jell-O, with the prefix 'Mr.' added"). Second, the *Apfel* court explained that the plaintiff's contract claims in Downey had been dismissed on the separate ground that the "defendant possessed plaintiff's ideas prior to plaintiff's disclosure [and thus], the ideas could have no value to defendant and could not supply consideration for any agreement between the parties." *Apfel*, 81 N.Y.2d at 477; accord *Downey*, 31 N.Y.2d at 62 (finding that, where defendant had used the words "wiggles" and "wigglewam" in prior advertising, defendant could "rel[y] on its own previous experience" and "was free to make use of 'Mr. Wiggle' without being obligated to compensate the plaintiff").

By distinguishing between the two types of claims addressed in *Downey* and the different bases for rejecting each claim, the New York Court of Appeals clarified that the novelty requirement in submission-of-idea cases is different for misappropriation of property and breach of contract claims. . . .

Thus, the *Apfel* court refused to read *Downey* and "similar decisions" as requiring originality or novelty generally in all cases involving disclosure of ideas. See *Apfel*, 81 N.Y.2d at 476-77 ("These decisions do not support [the] contention that novelty [in absolute terms] is required in all cases involving disclosure of ideas."). Rather, the *Apfel* court clarified that the longstanding requirement that an idea have originality or general novelty in order to support a misappropriation claim does not apply to contract claims. See Oasis Music, Inc. v. 900 U.S.A., Inc., 161 Misc. 2d 627, 614 N.Y.S.2d 878, 881 (1994) (noting that "the *Apfel* court did not repudiate the long line of cases requiring novelty in certain situations[,] . . . the *Apfel* court merely clarified that novelty is not required in all cases"). For contract-based claims in submission-of-idea cases, a showing of novelty to the buyer will supply sufficient consideration to support a contract.

Moreover, *Apfel* made clear that the "novelty to the buyer" standard is not limited to cases involving an express post-disclosure contract for payment based on an idea's use. The *Apfel* court explicitly discussed the pre-disclosure contract scenario present in the instant case, where "the buyer and seller contract for disclosure of the idea with payment based on use, but no separate post-disclosure contract for the use of the idea has been made." *Apfel*, 81 N.Y.2d at 477-78. In such a scenario, a seller might, as Nadel did here, bring an action against a buyer who allegedly used his ideas without payment, claiming both misappropriation of property and breach of an express or implied-in-fact contract.[5] Of course, the mere disclosure of an unoriginal idea to a defendant, to whom the idea is novel, will not automatically entitle a plaintiff to compensation upon the defendant's subsequent use of the idea. An implied-in-fact contract "requires such elements as consideration, mutual assent, legal capacity and legal subject matter." Id. (internal quotation marks omitted). The existence of novelty to the buyer only addresses the element of consideration necessary for the formation of the contract. Thus, apart from consideration, the formation of a contract implied-in-fact will depend on the presence of the other elements. The element of mutual assent, for example, must be inferred from the facts and circumstances of each case, including such factors as the specific conduct of the parties, industry custom, and course of dealing. Cf. id. at 94. The *Apfel* court recognized that these cases present courts with the difficult problem of determining "whether the idea the buyer was using was, in fact, the seller's." Id. at 478. Specifically, the court noted that, with respect to a misappropriation of property claim, it is difficult to "prove that the buyer obtained the idea from [the seller] and nowhere else." Id. With respect to a breach of contract claim, the court noted that it would be inequitable to enforce a contract if "it turns out upon disclosure that the buyer already possessed the idea." Id. The court then concluded that, with respect to these cases, "[a] showing of novelty, at least novelty as to the buyer" should address these problems.[6]

We note, moreover, that the "novelty to the buyer" standard comports with traditional principles of contract law. While an idea may be unoriginal or non-novel in a general sense, it may have substantial value to a particular buyer who is unaware of it and therefore willing to enter into contract to acquire and exploit it. See *Apfel*,

5. Where the pre-disclosure agreement is not an express contract to pay for the disclosed idea, an idea seller may argue in the alternative, cf. Watts v. Columbia Artists Mgmt. Inc., 188 A.D.2d 799, 591 N.Y.S.2d 234, 236 (3d Dep't 1992) (noting that express contract and implied-in-fact contract theories are mutually exclusive), that the parties entered into an agreement implied-in-fact. See Robbins v. Frank Cooper Assocs., 14 N.Y.2d 913, 252 N.Y.S.2d 318, 200 N.E.2d 860 (1964) (finding an implied-in-fact contract for the reasonable value of plaintiff's idea for a television program format where the parties had failed to reduce their agreement to writing). Unlike an express contract, an implied-in-fact contract arises "when the agreement and promise have simply not been expressed in words," but "a court may justifiably infer that the promise would have been explicitly made, had attention been drawn to it." Maas v. Cornell Univ., 94 N.Y.2d 87, 93-94, 699 N.Y.S.2d 716, 721 N.E.2d 966 (1999).

6. We note that this particular sentence could be read out of context to suggest that novelty to the buyer will alone support a misappropriation claim under New York law. However, nothing in *Apfel* otherwise suggests that the Court of Appeals meant to supplant the longstanding requirement that originality or novelty generally must be shown to support a misappropriation claim. . . .

81 N.Y.2d at 475-76; Robert Unikel, *Bridging the "Trade Secret" Gap: Protecting "Confidential Information" Not Rising to the Level of Trade Secrets*, 29 Loy. U. Chi. L.J. 841, 877 n.151 (1998) (noting that, if a valuable idea is already known to an industry but has not yet been acquired by a prospective buyer, one of two circumstances may exist: "(1) the person[ ] ha[s] not identified the potential value of the easily acquired information; or (2) the person[ ] ha[s] not identified the means, however easy or proper, for obtaining the valuable information"). As the *Apfel* court emphasized, "the buyer may reap benefits from such a contract in a number of ways — for instance, by not having to expend resources pursuing the idea through other channels or by having a profit-making idea implemented sooner rather than later." *Apfel*, 81 N.Y.2d at 478. . . .

In contrast to contract-based claims, a misappropriation claim can only arise from the taking of an idea that is original or novel in absolute terms, because the law of property does not protect against the misappropriation or theft of that which is free and available to all. See Murray v. National Broad. Co., 844 F.2d 988, 993 (2d Cir. 1988) ("Since . . . non-novel ideas are not protectible as property, they cannot be stolen."); cf. Ed Graham Prods., Inc. v. National Broad. Co., 75 Misc. 2d 334, 347 N.Y.S.2d 766, 769 (1973) ("Ideas such as those presented by the plaintiff are in the public domain and may freely be used by anyone with impunity."); Educational Sales Programs, Inc. v. Dreyfus Corp., 65 Misc. 2d 412, 317 N.Y.S.2d 840, 843 (1970) ("An idea is impalpable, intangible, incorporeal, yet it may be a stolen gem of great value, or mere dross of no value at all, depending on its novelty and uniqueness.").

Finally, although the legal requirements for contract-based claims and property-based claims are well-defined, we note that the determination of novelty in a given case is not always clear. Cf. AEB & Assocs. Design Group, Inc. v. Tonka Corp., 853 F. Supp. 724, 734 (S.D.N.Y. 1994) ("In establishing an idea's originality, a plaintiff cannot rest on mere assertions, but must demonstrate some basis in fact for its claims."). The determination of whether an idea is original or novel depends upon several factors, including, inter alia, the idea's specificity or generality (is it a generic concept or one of specific application?), its commonality (how many people know of this idea?), its uniqueness (how different is this idea from generally known ideas?), and its commercial availability (how widespread is the idea's use in the industry?). Cf. *Murray*, 844 F.2d at 993 ("In assessing whether an idea is in the public domain, the central issue is the uniqueness of the creation."); *AEB & Assocs.*, 853 F. Supp. at 734 ("[N]ovelty cannot be found where the idea consists of nothing more than a variation on a basic theme."); *Educational Sales Programs*, 317 N.Y.S.2d at 844 (noting that an idea "must show[ ] genuine novelty and invention, and not a merely clever or useful adaptation of existing knowledge" in order to be considered original or novel). Thus, for example, a once original or novel idea may become so widely disseminated over the course of time that it enters the body of common knowledge. When this occurs, the idea ceases to be novel or original. See, e.g., *Murray*, 844 F.2d at 989, 991-92 (affirming district court's finding that plaintiff's idea for a television sitcom about "Black American family life" was not novel or original because it "merely combined two ideas which had been circulating in the industry for a number of years — namely, the family situation comedy, which was a standard formula, and the casting of black actors in non-stereotypical roles," even though "the portrayal of a nonstereotypical black family on television was indeed a breakthrough").

Moreover, in assessing the interrelationship between originality and novelty to the buyer, we note that in some cases an idea may be so unoriginal or lacking in novelty that its obviousness bespeaks widespread and public knowledge of the idea, and such knowledge is therefore imputed to the buyer. See *Soule*, 195 N.Y.S. at 575 (noting that the idea that an increase in the wholesale price of groceries would result in an increase in profits was "not new" in 1922, "not original," and left the court "at a loss to understand how it could be deemed valuable"). In such cases, a court may conclude, as a matter of law, that the idea lacks both the originality necessary to support a misappropriation claim and the novelty to the buyer necessary to support a contract claim. See id. at 576 ("No person can by contract monopolize an idea that is common and general to the whole world."); *Ed Graham Prods.*, 347 N.Y.S.2d at 769 ("[W]here plaintiff's idea is wholly lacking in novelty, no cause of action in contract or tort can stand. . . .") (emphasis added); *Educational Sales Programs*, 317 N.Y.S.2d at 843-44 ("Nothing is bestowed if the facts of a 'secret' imparted in confidence are already the subject of general knowledge.").

In sum, we find that New York law in submission-of-idea cases is governed by the following principles: Contract-based claims require only a showing that the disclosed idea was novel to the buyer in order to find consideration.[10] Such claims involve a fact-specific inquiry that focuses on the perspective of the particular buyer. By contrast, misappropriation claims require that the idea at issue be original and novel in absolute terms. This is so because unoriginal, known ideas have no value as property and the law does not protect against the use of that which is free and available to all. Finally, an idea may be so unoriginal or lacking in novelty generally that, as a matter of law, the buyer is deemed to have knowledge of the idea. In such cases, neither a property-based nor a contract-based claim for uncompensated use of the idea may lie.

In light of New York's law governing submission-of-idea cases, we next consider whether Nadel's toy idea was original or novel in absolute terms so as to support his misappropriation claim and whether his idea was novel as to Play-By-Play so as to support his contract claims.

B. Nadel's Misappropriation Claim

This Court reviews a district court's grant of summary judgment de novo. See Quinn v. Green Tree Credit Corp., 159 F.3d 759, 764 (2d Cir. 1998). In so doing, we must consider the evidence in the record in a light most favorable to the non-movant, drawing all reasonable inferences in its favor. See id. at 764-65. Summary judgment is appropriate only where there is no genuine issue of material fact. See id.

In this case, the district court did not decide whether Nadel's idea—a plush toy that sits upright, emits sounds, and spins on a flat surface by means of an internal eccentric motor—was inherently lacking in originality. See *Nadel*, 34 F. Supp. 2d at 185 ("[We] need [not] reach the issue of whether combining elements of two commercially available toys to make another toy may be novel or is, as a matter of law, merely a 'clever adaptation of existing technology,' for Play-By-Play has demonstrated that plaintiff's idea was one which was already in use in the industry at the time that it

10. Of course, the mere formation of a contract in a submission-of-idea case does not necessarily mean that the contract has been breached by the defendant upon his use of the idea. In order to recover for breach of contract, a plaintiff must demonstrate some nexus or causal connection between his or her disclosure and the defendant's use of the idea, i.e., where there is an independent source for the idea used by the defendant, there may be no breach of contract, and the plaintiff's claim for recovery may not lie. . . .

was submitted"). We therefore remand this issue to the district court to determine whether Nadel's idea exhibited "genuine novelty or invention" or whether it was "a merely clever or useful adaptation of existing knowledge." *Educational Sales Programs*, 317 N.Y.S.2d at 844.

Moreover, insofar as the district court found that Nadel's idea lacked originality and novelty generally because similar toys were commercially available prior to October 1996, we believe that there remains a genuine issue of material fact on this point. While the record contains testimony of Play-By-Play's toy expert — Bert Reiner — in support of the finding that Nadel's product concept was already used in more than a dozen different plush toys prior to October 1996, the district court cited the "Giggle Bunny" toy as the only such example. See *Nadel*, 34 F. Supp. 2d at 185. Nadel disputes Reiner's contention and claims, furthermore, that the district court erroneously relied on an undated video depiction of the Giggle Bunny toy to conclude that upright, sound-emitting, spinning plush toys were commercially available prior to October 1996.

With respect to the Giggle Bunny evidence, we agree with Nadel that the Giggle Bunny model depicted in the undated video exhibit is physically different from the earlier Giggle Bunny model known to be commercially available in 1994. Drawing all factual inferences in Nadel's favor, we cannot conclude as a matter of law that the upright, sound-emitting, spinning plush Giggle Bunny shown in the video exhibit was commercially available prior to October 1996, and we certainly cannot conclude based on this one exhibit that similar toys were in the public domain at that time.

Moreover, although we find highly probative Mr. Reiner's testimony that numerous toys with the same general characteristics of Nadel's toy idea were commercially available prior to October 1996, his testimony and related evidence are too ambiguous and incomplete to support a finding of unoriginality as a matter of law. Mr. Reiner's testimony fails to specify precisely which (if any) of the enumerated plush toys were designed to (1) sit upright, (2) on a flat surface, (3) emit sounds, and (4) spin or rotate (rather than simply vibrate like "Tickle Me Elmo," for example). Without this information, a reasonable finder of fact could discount Mr. Reiner's testimony as vague and inconclusive.

On remand, the district court is free to consider whether further discovery is warranted to determine whether Nadel's product concept was inherently original or whether it was novel to the industry prior to October 1996. A finding of unoriginality or lack of general novelty would, of course, preclude Nadel from bringing a misappropriation claim against Play-By-Play. Moreover, in evaluating the originality or general novelty of Nadel's idea in connection with his misappropriation claim, the district may consider whether the idea is so unoriginal that Play-By-Play should, as a matter of law, be deemed to have already possessed the idea, and dismiss Nadel's contract claims on that ground.

C. Nadel's Contract Claims

Mindful that, under New York law, a finding of novelty as to Play-By-Play will provide sufficient consideration to support Nadel's contract claims, we next consider whether the record exhibits a genuine issue of material fact on this point.

Reading the record in a light most favorable to Nadel, . . . we conclude that there exists a genuine issue of material fact as to whether Nadel's idea was, at the time he disclosed it to Wasserman in early October 1996, novel to Play-By-Play. Notably, the timing of Play-By-Play's development and release of Tornado Taz in relation to Nadel's October 1996 disclosure is, taken alone, highly probative. Moreover, although custom in the toy industry provides that a company shall promptly return all samples if it already possesses (or does not want to use) a disclosed idea, Play-By-Play in this case failed to return Nadel's prototype monkey toy for several months, despite Nadel's multiple requests for its return. According to Wasserman's secretary, Melissa Rodriguez, Nadel's sample was not returned until after the unveiling of "Tornado Taz" at the New York Toy Fair in February 1997. Ms. Rodriguez testified that from October 1996 through February 1997, Nadel's sample was usually kept in a glass cabinet behind Wasserman's desk, and on one occasion, she remembered seeing it on a table in Wasserman's office. These facts give rise to the reasonable inference that Play-By-Play may have used Nadel's prototype as a model for the development of Tornado Taz.

None of the evidence adduced by Play-By-Play compels a finding to the contrary on summary judgment. With regard to the discussions that Play-By-Play purportedly had in June or July of 1996 about possible ways to create a vibrating or spinning Tazmanian Devil toy, those conversations only lasted, according to Mr. Slattery, "a matter of five minutes." Play-By-Play may have "discussed the concept," as Mr. Slattery testified, but the record provides no evidence suggesting that, in June or July of 1996, Play-By-Play understood exactly how it could apply eccentric motor technology to make its Tazmanian Devil toy spin rather than, say, vibrate like Tickle Me Elmo. Similarly, although Play-By-Play asserts that it commissioned an outside manufacturing agent — Barter Trading of Hong Kong — to begin developing Tornado Taz in late September or early October of 1996, Play-By-Play admits that it can only "guess" the exact date. Play-By-Play cannot confirm that its commission of Barter Trading pre-dated Nadel's alleged disclosure to Wasserman on or about October 9, 1996. Nor has Play-By-Play produced any documents, technical or otherwise, relating to its purported business venture with Barter Trading or its independent development of a spinning Tornado Taz prior to October 1996. Based on this evidence, a jury could reasonably infer that Play-By-Play actually contacted Barter Trading, if at all, after learning of Nadel's product concept, and that Play-By-Play's development of Tornado Taz is attributable to Nadel's disclosure.

We therefore conclude that there exists a genuine issue of material fact as to whether Nadel's idea was, at the time he disclosed it to Wasserman in early October 1996, novel to Play-By-Play. . . .

COMMENTS AND QUESTIONS

1. *Idea Submission Causes of Action.* As the *Nadel* case reflects, idea submission cases must be brought within some property, contract, or tort cause of action. Contract law has proven the most resilient basis for protecting ideas. *Nadel* discusses the availability of express and implied contract rights for the disclosure of an idea. In addition, some courts have protected ideas under the law of confidential relationships (and the related body of trade secret protection). *See, e.g.*, Ralph Andrews Prods. v. Paramount Pictures, 222 Cal. App. 3d 676, 271 Cal. Rptr. 797 (1990) (trade secret suit alleging that a former employee stole an idea for a game show and sold it to Paramount Pictures). The misappropriation cause of action derives from property and tort principles. As noted in section A, *supra*, it is quite narrow. Misappropriation and other property-type claims (e.g., conversion) no longer exist as to ideas for copyrightable works — stories, movies, songs. Some states jettisoned such protection

expressly. *See, e.g., Desny* ("California does not now accord individual property type protection to abstract ideas"), excerpted below. State laws protecting such subject matter as of January 1, 1978, were preempted by the 1976 Copyright Act. *See* Nash v. CBS, Inc., 704 F. Supp. 823, 833-35 (N.D. Ill. 1989), *aff'd*, 899 F.2d 1537 (7th Cir. 1990) (rejecting claim that CBS had misappropriated ideas from plaintiff's book, *The Dillinger Report*, in an episode of the television drama "Simon and Simon").

2. *Requirements.* Based upon the *Nadel* case, under what circumstances can ideas be protected? What elements must one who submits an idea to another prove in order to recover?

3. *Semantics.* The *Nadel* court uses words familiar from the study of patent and copyright law — originality, novelty, and obviousness. But do these intellectual property words of art have the same meaning in the law of idea submissions? What does the court mean by "original," "novel," and "obvious"? How do these meanings compare to the definitions from copyright and patent law? Does the court suggest that the "novelty" requirement for a misappropriation claim incorporates a broader conception of non-obviousness than patent law?

4. The novelty requirement was central to the Second Circuit's decision rejecting an idea submission claim in Murray v. National Broadcasting Co., 844 F.2d 988 (2d Cir. 1988). In that case, Murray (an NBC employee) submitted a two-page proposal to NBC for a show entitled "Father's Day" that would "combine humor with serious situations in a manner similar to that of the old Dick Van Dyke Show" but with a "Black perspective" and "a contemporary, urban setting." The proposal specifically identified Bill Cosby as the lead actor. NBC informed Murray that it was not interested in pursuing his proposal. When "The Cosby Show" aired four years later, starring Bill Cosby as Dr. Cliff Huxtable living in a contemporary urban setting with his lawyer-spouse and their five children, Murray sued. The court rejected Murray's claim for lack of novelty:

> [W]e believe, as a matter of law, that plaintiff's idea embodied in his "Father's Day" proposal was not novel because it merely represented an "adaptation of existing knowledge" and of "known ingredients" and therefore lacked "genuine novelty and invention." *Educational Sales Programs*, 317 N.Y.S.2d at 844.
>
> We recognize of course that even novel and original ideas to a greater or lesser extent combine elements that are themselves not novel. Originality does not exist in a vacuum. Nevertheless, where, as here, an idea consists in essence of nothing more than a variation on a basic theme — in this case, the family situation comedy — novelty cannot be found to exist. . . .
>
> Appellant would have us believe that by interpreting New York law as we do, we are in effect condoning the theft of ideas. On the contrary, ideas that reflect "genuine novelty and invention" are fully protected against unauthorized use. But those ideas that are not novel "are in the public domain and may freely be used by anyone with impunity." Since such non-novel ideas are not protectible as property, they cannot be stolen. Id. at 992-93.

How does this use of the term "novelty" compare to the patent law's definition?[2] Wouldn't a new combination of known elements be considered novel under the patent

2. It should be noted that Murray's claim of novelty would have surely failed under a patent law standard. Evidence at the trial revealed that Cosby himself had been quoted in a newspaper article 20 years earlier stating that it was his "dream" to appear in a situation comedy along the lines of "The Dick Van Dyke Show," but featuring an African-American family. *Id.* at 989. The court did not base its decision on this evidence, which would have gone to the question of whether NBC had independently developed the idea for the show.

law's standards? Isn't the court really saying that the idea was obvious? How would this determination be made under the patent law's standards? Was there a suggestion or motivation to combine? Don't secondary considerations — especially commercial success — weigh against a finding of obviousness? Would the law of idea submissions be improved by adopting the patent law's framework for judging novelty and non-obviousness?

5. *The Novelty to the User Standard and Diffusion of Ideas.* Idea protection today is based upon an express or implied contract between an idea purveyor and a potential user. Under *Apfel* and *Nadel*, the idea purveyor need only show that the idea was not known *to the defendant* in order to satisfy the novelty element. This element provides the consideration necessary for there to be a valid contract. The court notes, however, that "in some cases an idea may be so unoriginal or lacking in novelty that its obviousness bespeaks widespread and public knowledge of the idea, and such knowledge is therefore imputed to the buyer." Should protection for ideas turn on the sophistication of the buyer?

One justification for such a doctrine is to reward diffusion of ideas to those best situated to commercialize them. As we discussed in Chapter 1, economic historians and theorists find that diffusion of knowledge is a crucial element in the creation of social benefit flowing from innovation. This doctrine rewards not the inventor but those who have the insight and possibly the connections to diffuse (or market) information. Certainly a true inventor can benefit, because being first ensures that the idea will be novel to others. Should the intellectual property system reward diffusion of ideas in this way?

6. *Concreteness.* Some courts consider whether an idea is sufficiently "concrete" in determining liability based on breach of implied contract and confidential relationship causes of action, although not in express contract claims. In the words of one court, "[i]deas are the most intangible of property rights, and their lineage is uniquely difficult to trace. Paternity can be claimed in the most casual of ways, and once such a claim is lodged, definitive blood tests are notoriously lacking." Burten v. Milton Bradley Co., 592 F. Supp. 1021, 1031 (D.R.I. 1984), *rev'd on other grounds*, 763 F.2d 461 (1st Cir. 1985). In assessing a claim to protect the idea of organizing and sponsoring radio broadcasts of student talent shows, the court in Hamilton Nat'l Bank v. Belt, 210 F.2d 706 (D.C. Cir. 1953), noted that "[t]he law shies away from according protection to vagueness, and must do so especially in the realm of ideas with the obvious dangers of a contrary rule." *Id.* at 708. Does this amount to an indefinite claiming doctrine? Or is it more akin to a rejection under Section 101 of the Patent Act for claiming only an abstract idea?

7. *Contract Analysis; Comparison to Trade Secret.* How does the contract analysis in *Nadel* compare to that in the trade secret/breach of confidence cases involving contracts, such as *Smith v. Dravo Corp.*, discussed in Chapter 11? What (if any) differences are there in the relationship of the parties, the duties of the idea/information recipient, and the nature of the idea or information? In the remedies?

8. *Defenses: Waiver/Release.* Many companies and film production studios require that those who submit ideas sign waivers or releases from liability. The release used in the *Downey* case, 286 N.E.2d 257 (N.Y. Ct. App. 1972), stated:

> I submit this suggestion with the understanding, which is conclusively evidenced by my use and transmittal to you of this form, that this suggestion is not submitted to you in confidence, that no confidential relationship has been or will be established between us

> and that the use, if any, to be made of this suggestion by you and the compensation to be paid therefor, if any, if you use it, are matters resting solely in your discretion.

Suppose that the recipient used the idea without paying any compensation. Should such a clause be enforceable? Consider the argument put forth by Lon Sobel favoring enforcement in the context of script submissions: "If courts were to refuse to enforce releases, it is likely that unrepresented writers would be unable to get their material read at all — a consequence more harmful to aspiring writers than the possibility that releases will bar some of them from suing for the suspected theft of their ideas." *See* Lionel S. Sobel, *The Law of Ideas, Revisited*, 1 UCLA Ent. L. Rev. 9, 91 (1994).

9. *Remedies.* What should be the remedy for the misappropriation of an idea or breach of a contract to pay for an idea? Assuming that Nadel prevails on his liability claims (misappropriation and contract) at trial, what should be the measure of damages? Assuming that Murray had carried his burden of proof on the novelty of "The Cosby Show," should he be entitled to all of the profits from the show?

10. For further scholarly discussion of the law of idea submission, see, e.g., Larissa Katz, *A Power-Based Approach to the Protection of Ideas*, 23 Cardozo Arts & Ent. L.J. 687 (2006); Mary LaFrance, *Something Borrowed, Something New: The Changing Role of Novelty in Idea Protection Law*, 34 Seton Hall. L. Rev. 485 (2004); Arthur R. Miller, *Common Law Protection for Products of the Mind: An "Idea" Whose Time Has Come*, 119 Harv. L. Rev. 703 (2006).

Desny v. Wilder

46 Cal. 2d 715, 299 P.2d 257, 110 U.S.P.Q. 433 (Cal. Sup. Ct. 1956)

Schauer, Justice.

Plaintiff appeals from a summary judgment rendered against him in this action to recover the reasonable value of a literary composition, or of an idea for a photoplay, a synopsis of which composition, embodying the idea, he asserts he submitted to defendants for sale, and which synopsis and idea, plaintiff alleges, were accepted and used by defendants in producing a photoplay. . . .

[W]e have concluded, for reasons hereinafter stated, that the summary judgment in favor of defendants was erroneously granted and should be reversed. . . .

[I]t appears from the present record that defendant [Billy] Wilder [a famous director] at the times here involved was employed by defendant Paramount Pictures Corporation . . . either as a writer, producer or director, or a combination of the three. In November, 1949, plaintiff telephoned Wilder's office. Wilder's secretary, who was also employed by Paramount, answered, and plaintiff stated that he wished to see Wilder. At the secretary's insistence that plaintiff explain his purpose, plaintiff "told her about this fantastic unusual story. . . . I told her that it was the life story of Floyd Collins who was trapped and made sensational news for two weeks . . . and I told her the plot." . . . Two days later plaintiff, after preparing a three or four page outline of the story, telephoned Wilder's office a second time and told the secretary the synopsis was ready. The secretary requested plaintiff to read the synopsis to her over the telephone so that she could take it down in shorthand, and plaintiff did so. . . . Plaintiff on his part told the secretary that defendants could use the story only if they paid him "the reasonable value of it." . . . She said that if Billy Wilder of Paramount uses the story, "naturally we will pay you for it." . . . Plaintiff's only subsequent contact with the secretary was a telephone call to her in July, 1950, to protest the alleged use of his composition and idea in a photoplay produced and exhibited by defendants. The photoplay, as hereinafter shown in some detail, closely parallels both plaintiff's synopsis and the historical material concerning the life and death of Floyd Collins.

Defendants concede, as they must, that "the act of disclosing an unprotectible idea, if that act is in fact the bargained for exchange for a promise, may be consideration to support the promise." They then add, "But once the idea is disclosed without the protection of a contract, the law says that anyone is free to use it. Therefore, subsequent use of the idea cannot constitute consideration so as to support a promise to pay for such use." And as to the effect of the evidence defendants argue that plaintiff "disclosed his material before . . . (defendants) did or could do anything to indicate their willingness or unwillingness to pay for the disclosure. The act of using the idea, from which appellant attempts to imply a promise to pay, came long after the disclosure." . . .

Generally speaking, ideas are as free as the air. . . . But there can be circumstances when neither air nor ideas may be acquired without cost. The diver who goes deep in the sea, even as the pilot who ascends high in the troposphere, knows full well that for life itself he, or someone on his behalf, must arrange for air. . . . The theatrical producer likewise may be dependent for his business life on the procurement of ideas from other persons as well as the dressing up and portrayal of his self-conceptions; he may not find his own sufficient for survival. As counsel for the Writers Guild aptly say, ideas "are not freely usable by the entertainment media until the latter are made aware of them." The producer may think up the idea himself, dress it and portray it; or he may purchase either the conveyance of the idea alone or a manuscript embodying the idea in the author's concept of a literary vehicle giving it form, adaptation and expression. It cannot be doubted that some ideas are of value to a producer.

An idea is usually not regarded as property, because all sentient beings may conceive and evolve ideas throughout the gamut of their powers of cerebration and because our concept of property implies something which may be owned and possessed to the exclusion of all other persons. We quote as an accurate statement of the law in this respect the following language of Mr. Justice Brandeis, dissenting in International News Service v. Associated Press (1918), 248 U.S. 215, 250:

> An essential element of individual property is the legal right to exclude others from enjoying it. [. . .] But the fact that a product of the mind has cost its producer money and labor, and has a value for which others are willing to pay, is not sufficient to ensure to it this legal attribute of property. The general rule of law is, that the noblest of human productions, knowledge, truths ascertained, conceptions, and ideas become, after voluntary communication to others, free as the air to common use.

The principles above stated do not, however, lead to the conclusion that ideas cannot be a subject of contract. As Mr. Justice Traynor stated in his dissenting opinion in Stanley v. Columbia Broadcasting System (1950), 35 Cal. 2d 653, 674, 221 P.2d 73:

> The policy that precludes protection of an abstract idea by copyright does not prevent its protection by contract. Even though an idea is not property subject to exclusive ownership, its disclosure may be of substantial benefit to the person to whom it is disclosed. That disclosure may therefore be consideration for a promise to pay. . . . Even though the

idea disclosed may be "widely known and generally understood" (citation), it may be protected by an express contract providing that it will be paid for regardless of its lack of novelty.

The lawyer or doctor who applies specialized knowledge to a state of facts and gives advice for a fee is selling and conveying an idea. In doing that he is rendering a service. The lawyer and doctor have no property rights in their ideas, as such, but they do not ordinarily convey them without solicitation by client or patient. Usually the parties will expressly contract for the performance of and payment for such services, but, in the absence of an express contract, when the service is requested and rendered the law does not hesitate to infer or imply a promise to compensate for it. In other words the recovery may be based on contract either express or implied. The person who can and does convey a valuable idea to a producer who commercially solicits the service or who voluntarily accepts it knowing that it is tendered for a price should likewise be entitled to recover. In so holding we do not fail to recognize that free-lance writers are not necessarily members of a learned profession and as such bound to the exalted standards to which doctors and lawyers are dedicated. So too we are not oblivious of the hazards with which producers of the class represented here by defendants and their related amici are confronted through the unsolicited submission of numerous scripts on public domain materials in which public materials the producers through their own initiative may well find nuclei for legitimately developing the "stupendous and colossal." The law, however, is dedicated to the proposition that for every wrong there is a remedy. . . . To that end the law of implied contracts assumes particular importance in literary idea and property controversies. . . .

[W]e conclude that conveyance of an idea can constitute valuable consideration and can be bargained for before it is disclosed to the proposed purchaser, but once it is conveyed, i.e., disclosed to him and he has grasped it, it is henceforth his own and he may work with it and use it as he sees fit. In the field of entertainment the producer may properly and validly agree that he will pay for the service of conveying to him ideas which are valuable and which he can put to profitable use. Furthermore, where an idea has been conveyed with the expectation by the purveyor that compensation will be paid if the idea is used, there is no reason why the producer who has been the beneficiary of the conveyance of such an idea, and who finds it valuable and is profiting by it, may not then for the first time, although he is not at that time under any legal obligation so to do, promise to pay a reasonable compensation for that idea, that is, for the past service of furnishing it to him and thus create a valid obligation. . . . But, assuming legality of consideration, the idea purveyor cannot prevail in an action to recover compensation for an abstract idea unless (a) before or after disclosure he has obtained an express promise to pay, or (b) the circumstances preceding and attending disclosure, together with the conduct of the offeree acting with knowledge of the circumstances, show a promise of the type usually referred to as "implied" or "implied-in-fact." . . .

Such inferred or implied promise, if it is to be found at all, must be based on circumstances which were known to the producer at and preceding the time of disclosure of the idea to him and he must voluntarily accept the disclosure, knowing the conditions on which it is tendered. . . . The idea man who blurts out his idea without having first made his bargain has no one but himself to blame for the loss of his bargaining power. . . . So, if the plaintiff here is claiming only for the conveyance of the idea of making a dramatic production out of the life of Floyd Collins he must fail unless in conformity with the above stated rules he can establish a contract to pay.

From plaintiff's testimony, as epitomized above . . . it does not appear that a contract to pay for conveyance of the abstract photoplay idea had been made, or that the basis for inferring such a contract from subsequent related acts of the defendants had been established, at the time plaintiff disclosed his basic idea to the secretary. Defendants, consequently, were at that time and from then on free to use the abstract idea if they saw fit to engage in the necessary research and develop it to the point of a usable script. Whether defendants did that, or whether they actually accepted and used plaintiff's synopsis, is another question.

. . . Literary property which is protectible may be created out of unprotectible material such as historical events. It has been said (and does not appear to have been successfully challenged) that "There are only thirty-six fundamental dramatic situations, various facets of which form the basis of all human drama." (GEORGES POLTI, 'THE THIRTY-SIX DRAMATIC SITUATIONS'; see also, HENRY ALBERT PHILLIPS, 'THE UNIVERSAL PLOT CATALOG'; ERIC HEATH, 'STORY PLOTTING SIMPLIFIED.') It is manifest that authors must work with and from ideas or themes which basically are in the public domain. . . . Events from the life of Floyd Collins were avowedly the basic theme of plaintiff's story. . . .

[A]ny literary composition, conceivably, may possess value in someone's estimation and be the subject of contract. . . . Obviously the defendants here used someone's script in preparing and producing their photoplay. That script must have had value to them. As will be hereinafter shown, it closely resembles plaintiff's synopsis. Ergo, plaintiff's synopsis appears to be a valuable literary composition. Defendants had an unassailable right to have their own employees conduct the research into the Floyd Collins tragedy (an historical event in the public domain) and prepare a story based on those facts and to translate it into a script for the play. But equally unassailable (assuming the verity of the facts which plaintiff asserts) is plaintiff's position that defendants had no right except by purchase on the terms he offered to acquire and use the synopsis prepared by him.

[Affirmed in part, reversed in part, and remanded.]

CARTER, Justice [concurring in result]. . . .

When we consider the difference in economic and social backgrounds of those offering such merchandise for sale and those purchasing the same, we are met with the inescapable conclusion that it is the seller who stands in the inferior bargaining position. It should be borne in mind that producers are not easy to contact. . . . It should also be borne in mind that writers have no way of advertising their wares that, as is most graphically illustrated by the present opinion, no producer, publisher, or purchaser for radio or television, is going to buy a pig in a poke. And, when the writer, in an earnest endeavor to sell what he has written, conveys his idea or his different interpretation of an old idea, to such prospective purchaser, he has lost the result of his labor, definitely and irrevocably. And, in addition, there is no way in which he can protect himself. If he says to whomever he is permitted to see, or, as in this case, talk with over the telephone, "I won't tell you what my idea is until you promise to pay me for it," it takes no Sherlock Holmes to figure out what the answer will be! This case is a beautiful example of the practical difficulties besetting a writer with something to sell. . . .

I disagree with the statement in the majority opinion that: "The idea man who blurts out his idea without having first made his bargain has no one but himself to blame for the loss of his bargaining power." It seems to me that in the ordinary situation, when the so-called "idea man" has an opportunity to see, or talk with, the prospective purchaser, or someone in his employ, that it is at that time, without anything being said, known to both parties that the one is there to sell, and the other to buy. This is surely true of a department store when merchandise is displayed on the counter; it is understood by anyone entering the store that the merchandise so displayed is for sale. [I]t is completely unnecessary for the storekeeper, or anyone in his employ, to state to anyone entering the store that all articles there are for sale. I am at a loss to see why any different rules should apply when it is ideas for sale rather than the normal run of merchandise.

COMMENTS AND QUESTIONS

1. The concurring opinion makes an interesting point: "[W]hen the writer, in an earnest endeavor to sell what he has written, conveys his idea or his different interpretation of an old idea, to [a] prospective purchaser, he has lost the result of his labor." This general feature of the "market for information" was noted by Kenneth Arrow, in an article entitled *Economic Welfare and the Allocation of Resources for Invention*, *in* THE RATE AND DIRECTION OF INVENTIVE ACTIVITY 615 (1962). Indeed, the phenomenon is sometimes called "Arrow's paradox of information." Without a property right, Arrow pointed out, the seller of information is in a pickle: If in trying to strike a deal she discloses the information, she has nothing left to sell, but if she does not disclose anything the buyer has no idea what is for sale. Arrow pointed out that when the information involves an invention, patents protect the seller so she can confidently offer her idea for sale. In other words, patents solve Arrow's Paradox. Does the opinion above prove that property rights are necessary to overcome the information paradox?

One problem with giving property rights to abstract ideas is that it can put the recipients of idea submissions in a bind. They are just as bound by Arrow's information paradox as plaintiffs—if they don't listen to the idea "pitch," they will never know whether the idea was worth paying for. The point of intellectual property protection in this situation is to encourage such idea submissions by making the plaintiff confident in her ability to protect her idea. But suppose that a defendant hears a "pitch" for an idea that is old, that she has already come up with herself, or that someone else has already pitched to her. If intellectual property protection extends to idea submissions, the recipient may be forced to pay for an idea she already has! Arguably, therefore, awarding property rights in idea submissions merely changes the nature of Arrow's paradox, rather than eliminating it entirely.

2. Wendy Gordon has explored the notion that a central problem of intellectual property law is to compensate creators of works who bestow benefits on those who follow, up to some socially justifiable point. In this analysis, the basic structure of intellectual property law is closely akin to the law of restitution, which seeks to determine when someone who bestows unbargained-for benefits deserves compensation. *See, e.g.*, Wendy J. Gordon, *On Owning Information: Intellectual Property and the Restitutionary Impulse*, 78 VA. L. REV. 149 (1992); Wendy J. Gordon, *Of Harms and Benefits: Torts, Restitution and Intellectual Property*, 21 J. LEGAL STUD. 449 (1992). On restitution generally, see Saul Levmore, *Explaining Restitution*, 71 VA. L. REV. 65 (1985). Does this literature help explain the need for a remand in the *Desny* case? Recall that the purpose of the remand is to determine how much Desny's idea contributed to the profits of Wilder's film.

3. The holding in *Desny* has been applied and extended in a number of cases. For instance, in Blaustein v. Burton, 88 Cal. Rptr. 319, 9 Cal. App. 3d 161 (Cal. Ct. App. 1970), the plaintiff Blaustein orally "pitched" the idea of using Richard Burton and Elizabeth Taylor in a film version of Shakespeare's "Taming of the Shrew." Although there was little novel in the pitch, the court held that there were triable issues of fact concerning the enforceability of an implied contract for the idea. The case is notable in that the "pitch" was protectable even though it was never reduced to writing.

4. The oral presentation of ideas for movies, TV series, etc., is a well-recognized part of the entertainment industry. Recent cases show that it can be a dangerous practice, however, for the "pitch-person." A number of recent cases find no liability for the uncompensated use of "pitched" ideas. *See, e.g.*, Selby v. New Line Cinema Corp., 96 F. Supp. 2d 1053 (C.D. Cal. 2000) (refusing to enforce implied-in-fact contract for use of a movie idea, holding that enforcement of such a contract is preempted by the Copyright Act). *But see* Firoozye v. Earthlink Network, 153 F. Supp. 2d 1115 (N.D. Cal. 2001) (finding implied-in-fact contract claims, in case involving ongoing relationship between computer programmer and customer, not preempted by the Copyright Act). The courts may be reacting to the flood of lawsuits (mostly meritless) against major movie studios in which plaintiffs allege that the idea for the movie was originally theirs.

PROBLEM

Problem 12-2. The Washington humorist and columnist Art Buchwald submitted an eight-page summary of a film idea entitled "It's a Crude, Crude World" to executives at Paramount. The summary described in some detail the storyline, which involved a third-world prince who came to America for "a state visit." Buchwald gave a two-page overview of the plot to Paramount Pictures. Paramount subsequently entered into a contract with Buchwald whereby Paramount bought the rights to Buchwald's story and concept, with the aim of making a movie, starring Eddie Murphy, to be called "King for a Day." Another person would write the actual script, but "King for a Day" was to be based on "It's a Crude, Crude World." Because of various production difficulties, Paramount abandoned the project in March 1985. In May 1986, Buchwald gave an option on his film idea to the Warner Brothers Studio. In the summer of 1987, Paramount began development of a similar script by Eddie Murphy. In this movie—which became the successful film *Coming to America*—Murphy portrayed an African prince who comes to America in search of a suitable woman to marry.

The two scripts have been contrasted as follows:

> In Buchwald's treatment, a rich, educated, arrogant, extravagant, despotic African potentate comes to America for a state visit. After being taken on a grand tour of the United States, the potentate arrives at the White House. A gaff[e] in remarks made by the President infuriates the African leader. His sexual desires are rebuffed by a black woman State Department officer assigned to him. She is requested by the President to continue to serve as the potentate's United States escort. While in the United States, the potentate is deposed, deserted by his entourage and left destitute. He ends up in the Washington ghetto, is stripped of his clothes, and befriended by a black lady. The potentate experiences a number of

> incidents in the ghetto, and obtains employment as a waiter. In order to avoid extradition, he marries the black lady who befriended him, becomes the emperor of the ghetto and lives happily ever after.
>
> In "Coming to America" the pampered prince of a mythical African Kingdom (Zamunda) wakes up on his 21st birthday to find that the day for his prearranged marriage has arrived. Discovering his bride to be very subservient and being unhappy about that fact, he convinces his father to permit him to go to America for the ostensible purpose of sewing [sic] his "royal oats." In fact, the prince intends to go to America to find an independent woman to marry. The prince and his friend go to Queens, New York, where their property is stolen and they begin living in a slum area. The prince discovers his true love, Lisa, whose father—McDowell—operates a fast-food restaurant for whom the prince and his friend begin to work. The prince and Lisa fall in love, but when the King and Queen come to New York and it is disclosed who the prince is, Lisa rejects the prince's marriage invitation. The film ends with Lisa appearing in Zamunda, marrying the prince and apparently living happily ever after.

Because of *Coming to America*, Warner Brothers decided not to pursue Buchwald's story. Buchwald then sued Paramount. The contract between Buchwald and Paramount provided in pertinent part:

> "Work" means the aforementioned Material and includes all prior, present and future versions, adaptations and translations thereof (whether written by Author or by others), its theme, story, plot, characters and their names, its title or titles and subtitles, if any, . . . and each and every part of all thereof. "Work" does not include any material written or prepared by Purchaser or under Purchaser's Authority. . . .
>
> ["Contingent consideration":]
>
> For the first theatrical motion picture (the "Picture"): If, but only if, a feature length theatrical motion picture shall be produced *based upon Author's Work.* [Emphasis Added.]

How should the court rule?

COMMENTS AND QUESTIONS

1. If you were an independent scriptwriter, how would you protect your ideas while trying to market them? Under what circumstances would the career damage from obtaining a reputation for litigiousness be worth it?

2. If you were a film studio or television production company, how could you guard against suits by people like Buchwald, or by people who claim to have submitted ideas that no one in your company ever recalls seeing? Recall Sobel's argument favoring judicial enforcement of waivers and release clauses imposed as conditions for idea submissions. Under some cases habitual rejection and return of unsolicited ideas eliminates the prospect of liability. *See, e.g.*, Davis v. General Foods Corp., 21 F. Supp. 445 (S.D.N.Y. 1937) (plaintiff's unsolicited recipe returned with form letter); Whitfield v. Lear, 751 F.2d 90 (2d Cir. 1984) (noting, in decision reversing summary judgment for defendant, plaintiff's evidence that it was customary in the television industry for a studio not desiring outside submissions to say so explicitly and to return scripts so

submitted without opening them). Is it desirable for firms to routinely reject submissions, some of which may be worth pursuing, for fear of spurious lawsuits? Is this an example of nuisance lawsuits undermining an otherwise mutually beneficial market? Is it an example of the "market for lemons," where bad idea submissions (i.e., ones that lead to spurious suits) drive out the good ones? Is it enough that studios and production companies can rely on trusted middlepersons such as agents to obtain ideas from proven submitters? *See* Julie Salamon, *Bookshelf: Celluloid Immortals and Literary He-Men*, WALL ST. J., July 29, 1992, p. A7, col. 1:

> Whatever the outcome, the suit has made Hollywood acutely aware of where it gets its ideas. "Producers are going to have to be very careful what submissions they read, and that makes it harder in the way they conduct business," says producer Howard Rosenman, co-president of Sandollar Productions, adding, "I never accept any unsolicited material. Ever."

3. Some cases involving the alleged unauthorized use of submitted ideas have indeed resulted in substantial judgments. *See, e.g.*, *Judge Awards Whole Enchilada*, ASSOCIATED PRESS, Sept. 12, 2003 (discussing $41.9 million judgment against Taco Bell, for alleged unauthorized use of plaintiffs' "Psycho Chihuahua" ad campaign idea); *Disney Loses $240 Million Suit*, CNN, Aug. 11, 2000 (discussing $240 million judgment against Disney for alleged unauthorized use of plaintiffs' "Wide World of Sports" theme park idea). If a plaintiff can avoid dismissal and summary judgment, even a small risk of catastrophic liability makes settlement an attractive option for defendants, doesn't it?

4. *The Hollywood Script Registry.* The Writer's Guild of America, West, developed a "Script Registry" to lower the risks to both aspiring writers and studios. Writers deposit a copy of a script they are going to submit with the Registry, which date-stamps it and stores it for five years. The Registry also operates an arbitration service for resolving disputes over writing credits.

PROBLEM

Problem 12-3. Lohr, an eccentric engineer, mails an idea she has had for a new invention to several engineering companies. The idea is mailed in a "double envelope." The outer envelope contains a confidentiality agreement, indicating that the contents of a second, sealed envelope are the property of Lohr and may not be used unless the user pays Lohr 10 percent of any profit that results. If the recipient does not agree to these terms, he is instructed to mail back the sealed, stamped, self-addressed envelope containing the idea. The "agreement" clearly provides that by opening the envelope, the recipient agrees to the terms.

Dupco receives the agreement and opens the inner envelope. The next day, Dupco discovers that Lohr has posted the complete text of her idea on the Internet with no confidentiality restriction. Can Dupco use Lohr's idea without compensating her? Does it matter how novel or original the idea was on the day Dupco opened the envelope?

13 Cybertrespass

Until fairly recently, few statutes explicitly addressed the question of liability for allegedly harmful interferences with computer systems, Web sites, domain names, and other related subject matter. Owners of such subject matter have sometimes urged courts to adapt concepts from the law of personal property (specifically, the doctrines of trespass to chattels and of conversion) to fill these perceived gaps in the law. As you read through the following materials, ask yourself whether these adaptations are sound. Does the law of personal property provide an adequate fit for subject matter that, it is fair to say, no one could have foreseen when these doctrines arose at common law? Do the courts' adaptations go far enough in protecting the subject matter at issue?

A. TRESPASS TO CHATTELS

eBay, Inc. v. Bidder's Edge, Inc.
100 F. Supp. 2d 1058 (N.D. Cal. 2000)

WHYTE, District Judge.

Plaintiff eBay, Inc.'s ("eBay") motion for preliminary injunction was heard by the court on April 14, 2000. The court has read the moving and responding papers and heard the argument of counsel. For the reasons set forth below, the court preliminarily enjoins defendant Bidder's Edge, Inc. ("BE") from accessing eBay's computer systems by use of any automated querying program without eBay's written authorization.

I. Background

eBay is an Internet-based, person-to-person trading site. eBay offers sellers the ability to list items for sale and prospective buyers the ability to search those listings and bid on items. The seller can set the terms and conditions of the auction. The item is sold to the highest bidder. The transaction is consummated directly between the buyer and seller without eBay's involvement. A potential purchaser looking for a particular item can access the eBay site and perform a key word search for relevant auctions and bidding status. eBay has also created category listings that identify items in over 2500 categories, such as antiques, computers, and dolls. Users may browse these category listing pages to identify items of interest.

Users of the eBay site must register and agree to the eBay User Agreement. Users agree to the seven page User Agreement by clicking on an "I Accept" button located at the end of the User Agreement. The current version of the User Agreement prohibits the use of "any robot, spider, other automatic device, or manual process to monitor or copy our web pages or the content contained herein without our prior expressed written permission." It is not clear that the version of the User Agreement in effect at the time BE began searching the eBay site prohibited such activity, or that BE ever agreed to comply with the User Agreement.

eBay currently has over 7 million registered users. Over 400,000 new items are added to the site every day. Every minute, 600 bids are placed on almost 3 million items. Users currently perform, on average, 10 million searches per day on eBay's database. Bidding for and sales of items are continuously ongoing in millions of separate auctions.

A software robot is a computer program which operates across the Internet to perform searching, copying and retrieving functions on the web sites of others. A software robot is capable of executing thousands of instructions per minute, far in excess of what a human can accomplish. Robots consume the processing and storage resources of a system, making that portion of the system's capacity unavailable to the system owner or other users. Consumption of sufficient system resources will slow the processing of the overall system and can overload the system such that it will malfunction or "crash." A severe malfunction can cause a loss of data and an interruption in services.

The eBay site employs "robot exclusion headers." A robot exclusion header is a message, sent to computers programmed to detect and respond to such headers, that eBay does not permit unauthorized robotic activity. Programmers who wish to comply with the Robot Exclusion Standard design their robots to read a particular data file, "robots.txt," and to comply with the control directives it contains . . . .

eBay identifies robotic activity on its site by monitoring the number of incoming requests from each particular IP [(Internet Protocol)] address. Once eBay identifies an IP address believed to be involved in robotic activity, an investigation into the identity, origin and owner of the IP address may be made in order to determine if the activity is legitimate or authorized. If an investigation reveals unauthorized robotic activity, eBay may attempt to ignore ("block") any further requests from that IP address. Attempts to block requests from particular IP addresses are not always successful.

Organizations often install "proxy server" software on their computers. Proxy server software acts as a focal point for outgoing Internet requests. Proxy servers conserve system resources by directing all outgoing and incoming data traffic through a centralized portal. . . . Information requests sent through such proxy servers cannot easily be traced back to the originating IP address and can be used to circumvent attempts to block queries from the originating IP address. Blocking queries from innocent third party proxy servers is both inefficient, because it creates an endless game of hide-and-seek, and potentially counterproductive, as it runs a substantial risk of blocking requests from legitimate, desirable users who use that proxy server. . . .

BE does not host auctions. BE is an auction aggregation site designed to offer on-line auction buyers the ability to search for items across numerous on-line auctions without having to search each host site individually. As of March 2000, the BE web site contained information on more than five million items being auctioned on more than one hundred auction sites. BE also provides its users with additional auction-related services and information. The information available on the BE site is contained in a database of information that BE compiles through access to various auction sites such as eBay. When a user enters a search for a particular item at BE, BE searches its database and generates a list of every item in the database responsive to the search, organized by auction closing date and time. Rather than going to each host auction site one at a time, a user who goes to BE may conduct a single search to obtain information about that item on every auction site tracked by BE. It is important to include information regarding eBay auctions on the BE site because eBay is by far the biggest consumer to consumer on-line auction site. . . .

[The parties attempted to agree on terms for BE's access to the eBay site, but were unable to do so.] As a result, eBay attempted to block BE from accessing the eBay site; by the end of November, 1999, eBay had blocked a total of 169 IP addresses it believed BE was using to query eBay's system. BE elected to continue crawling eBay's site by using proxy servers to evade eBay's IP blocks.

Approximately 69% of the auction items contained in the BE database are from auctions hosted on eBay. BE estimates that it would lose one-third of its users if it ceased to cover the eBay auctions.

The parties agree that BE accessed the eBay site approximately 100,000 times a day. eBay alleges that BE activity constituted up to 1.53% of the number of requests received by eBay, and up to 1.10% of the total data transferred by eBay during certain periods in October and November of 1999. BE alleges that BE activity constituted no more than 1.11% of the requests received by eBay, and no more than 0.70% of the data transferred by eBay. . . . eBay has not alleged any specific incremental damages due to BE activity.

It appears that major Internet search engines, such as Yahoo!, Google, Excite and AltaVista, respect the Robot Exclusion Standard.[5]

eBay now moves for preliminary injunctive relief preventing BE from accessing the eBay computer system based on nine causes of action: trespass, false advertising, federal and state trademark dilution, computer fraud and abuse, unfair competition, misappropriation, interference with prospective economic advantage and unjust enrichment. However, eBay does not move, either independently or alternatively, for injunctive relief that is limited to restricting how BE can use data taken from the eBay site.[6] . . .

5. BE appears to argue that this cannot be the case because searches performed on each of these search engines will return results that include eBay web pages. However, this does not establish that these sites do not respect robot exclusion headers. There are numerous ways in which search engines can obtain information in compliance with exclusion headers, including: obtaining consent, abiding by the robot.txt file guidelines, or manually searching the sites. BE did not present any evidence of any site ever complaining about the activities of any of these search engines.

6. The bulk of eBay's moving papers and declarations address the alleged misuse of the eBay mark and the information BE obtains from the eBay computers. The court does not address the facts specific to these claims, nor the merits of these claims.

III. Analysis

A. *Balance of Harm*

According to eBay, the load on its servers resulting from BE's web crawlers represents between 1.11% and 1.53% of the total load on eBay's listing servers. eBay alleges both economic loss from BE's current activities and potential harm resulting from the total crawling of BE and others. In alleging economic harm, eBay's argument is that eBay has expended considerable time, effort and money to create its computer system, and that BE should have to pay for the portion of eBay's system BE uses. eBay attributes a pro rata portion of the costs of maintaining its entire system to the BE activity. However, eBay does not indicate that these expenses are incrementally incurred because of BE's activities, nor that any particular service disruption can be attributed to BE's activities. eBay provides no support for the proposition that the pro rata costs of obtaining an item represent the appropriate measure of damages for unauthorized use. In contrast, California law appears settled that the appropriate measure of damages is the actual harm inflicted by the conduct:

> Where the conduct complained of does not amount to a substantial interference with possession or the right thereto, but consists of intermeddling with or use of or damages to the personal property, the owner has a cause of action for trespass or case, and may recover only the actual damages suffered by reason of the impairment of the property or the loss of its use.

Zaslow v. Kroenert, 29 Cal. 2d 541, 551, 176 P.2d 1 (1946). Moreover, even if BE is inflicting incremental maintenance costs on eBay, potentially calculable monetary damages are not generally a proper foundation for a preliminary injunction. See e.g., Sampson v. Murray, 415 U.S. 61, 90, 94 S. Ct. 937, 39 L. Ed. 2d 166 (1974). Nor does eBay appear to have made the required showing that this is the type of extraordinary case in which monetary damages may support equitable relief. . . .

eBay's allegations of harm are based, in part, on the argument that BE's activities should be thought of as equivalent to sending in an army of 100,000 robots a day to check the prices in a competitor's store. This analogy, while graphic, appears inappropriate. Although an admittedly formalistic distinction, unauthorized robot intruders into a "brick and mortar" store would be committing a trespass to real property. There does not appear to be any doubt that the appropriate remedy for an ongoing trespass to business premises would be a preliminary injunction. See e.g., State v. Carriker, 5 Ohio App. 2d 255, 214 N.E.2d 809, 811-12 (1964) (interpreting Ohio criminal trespass law to cover a business invitee who, with no intention of making a purchase, uses the business premises of another for his own gain after his invitation has been revoked); General Petroleum Corp. v. Beilby, 213 Cal. 601, 605, 2 P.2d 797 (1931). More importantly, for the analogy to be accurate, the robots would have to make up less than two out of every one-hundred customers in the store, the robots would not interfere with the customers' shopping experience, nor would the robots even be seen by the customers. Under such circumstances, there is a legitimate claim that the robots would not pose any threat of irreparable harm. However, eBay's right to injunctive relief is also based upon a much stronger argument.

If BE's activity is allowed to continue unchecked, it would encourage other auction aggregators to engage in similar recursive searching of the eBay system such that eBay would suffer irreparable harm from reduced system performance, system unavailability, or data losses. BE does not appear to seriously contest that reduced system performance, system unavailability or data loss would inflict irreparable harm on eBay consisting of lost profits and lost customer goodwill. Harm resulting from lost profits and lost customer goodwill is irreparable because it is neither easily calculable, nor easily compensable and is therefore an appropriate basis for injunctive relief. See, e.g., People of California ex rel. Van De Kamp v. Tahoe Reg'l Planning Agency, 766 F.2d 1316, 1319 (9th Cir. 1985). Where, as here, the denial of preliminary injunctive relief would encourage an increase in the complained of activity, and such an increase would present a strong likelihood of irreparable harm, the plaintiff has at least established a possibility of irreparable harm.

In the patent infringement context, the Federal Circuit has held that a preliminary injunction may be based, at least in part, on the harm that would occur if a preliminary injunction were denied and infringers were thereby encouraged to infringe a patent during the course of the litigation. See Atlas Powder Co. v. Ireco Chemicals, 773 F.2d 1230, 1233 (Fed. Cir. 1985). In the absence of preliminary injunctive relief, "infringers could become compulsory licensees for as long as the litigation lasts." Id. The Federal Circuit's reasoning is persuasive. "The very nature of the patent right is the right to exclude others. . . . We hold that where validity and continuing infringement have been clearly established, as in this case, immediate irreparable harm is presumed. To hold otherwise would be contrary to the public policy underlying the patent laws." Smith Int'l, Inc. v. Hughes Tool Co., 718 F.2d 1573, 1581 (Fed. Cir. 1983) (footnotes omitted). Similarly fundamental to the concept of ownership of personal property is the right to exclude others. See Kaiser Aetna v. United States, 444 U.S. 164, 176, 100 S. Ct. 383, 62 L. Ed. 2d 332 (1979) (characterizing "the right to exclude others" as "one of the most essential sticks in the bundle of rights that are commonly characterized as property"). If preliminary injunctive relief against an ongoing trespass to chattels were unavailable, a trespasser could take a compulsory license to use another's personal property for as long as the trespasser could perpetuate the litigation.

BE correctly observes that there is a dearth of authority supporting a preliminary injunction based on an ongoing to trespass to chattels. In contrast, it is black letter law in California that an injunction is an appropriate remedy for a continuing trespass to real property. See Allred v. Harris, 14 Cal. App. 4th 1386, 1390, 18 Cal. Rptr. 2d 530 (1993) (citing 5 B.E. Witkin, Summary of California Law, Torts § 605 (9th ed. 1988)). If eBay were a brick and mortar auction house with limited seating capacity, eBay would appear to be entitled to reserve those seats for potential bidders, to refuse entrance to individuals (or robots) with no intention of bidding on any of the items, and to seek preliminary injunctive relief against non-customer trespassers eBay was physically unable to exclude. The analytic difficulty is that a wrongdoer can commit an ongoing trespass of a computer system that is more akin to the traditional notion of a trespass to real property, than the traditional notion of a trespass to chattels, because even though it is ongoing, it will probably never amount to a conversion. The court concludes that under the circumstances present here, BE's ongoing violation of eBay's fundamental property right to exclude others from its computer system potentially causes sufficient irreparable harm to support a preliminary injunction. . . .

If eBay's irreparable harm claim were premised solely on the potential harm caused by BE's current crawling activities, evidence that eBay had licensed others to crawl the eBay site would suggest that BE's activity would not result in irreparable harm to eBay. However, the gravamen of the alleged irreparable harm is that if BE is allowed to continue to crawl the eBay site, it may encourage frequent and unregulated crawling to the point that eBay's system will be irreparably harmed. There is no evidence that eBay has indiscriminately licensed all comers. Rather, it appears that eBay has carefully chosen to permit crawling by a limited number of aggregation sites that agree to abide by the terms of eBay's licensing agreement. "The existence of such a [limited] license, unlike a general license offered to all comers, does not demonstrate a decision to relinquish all control over the distribution of the product in exchange for a readily computable fee." Ty, Inc. v. GMA Accessories, Inc., 132 F.3d 1167, 1173 (7th Cir. 1997) (discussing presumption of irreparable harm in copyright infringement context). eBay's licensing activities appear directed toward limiting the amount and nature of crawling activity on the eBay site. Such licensing does not support the inference that carte blanche crawling of the eBay site would pose no threat of irreparable harm. . . .

B. Likelihood of Success . . .

1. Trespass

Trespass to chattels "lies where an intentional interference with the possession of personal property has proximately cause injury." Thrifty-Tel v. Bezenek, 46 Cal. App. 4th 1559, 1566, 54 Cal. Rptr. 2d 468 (1996). Trespass to chattels "although seldom employed as a tort theory in California" was recently applied to cover the unauthorized use of long distance telephone lines. Id. Specifically, the court noted "the electronic signals generated by the [defendants'] activities were sufficiently tangible to support a trespass cause of action." Id. at n.6. Thus, it appears likely that the electronic signals sent by BE to retrieve information from eBay's computer system are also sufficiently tangible to support a trespass cause of action.

In order to prevail on a claim for trespass based on accessing a computer system, the plaintiff must establish: (1) defendant intentionally and without authorization interfered with plaintiff's possessory interest in the computer system; and (2) defendant's unauthorized use proximately resulted in damage to plaintiff. See *Thrifty-Tel*, 46 Cal. App. 4th at 1566, 54 Cal. Rptr. 2d 468; see also Itano v. Colonial Yacht Anchorage, 267 Cal. App. 2d 84, 90, 72 Cal. Rptr. 823 (1968) ("When conduct complained of consists of intermeddling with personal property 'the owner has a cause of action for trespass or case, and may recover only the actual damages suffered by reason of the impairment of the property or the loss of its use.' ") (quoting Zaslow v. Kroenert, 29 Cal. 2d 541, 550, 176 P.2d 1 (1946)). Here, eBay has presented evidence sufficient to establish a strong likelihood of proving both prongs and ultimately prevailing on the merits of its trespass claim.

a. BE's Unauthorized Interference

eBay argues that BE's use was unauthorized and intentional. eBay is correct. BE does not dispute that it employed an automated computer program to connect with and search eBay's electronic database. BE admits that, because other auction aggregators were including eBay's auctions in their listing, it continued to "crawl" eBay's web site even after eBay demanded BE terminate such activity.

BE argues that it cannot trespass eBay's web site because the site is publicly accessible. BE's argument is unconvincing. eBay's servers are private property, conditional access to which eBay grants the public. eBay does not generally permit the type of automated access made by BE. In fact, eBay explicitly notifies automated visitors that their access is not permitted. "In general, California does recognize a trespass claim where the defendant exceeds the scope of the consent." Baugh v. CBS, Inc., 828 F. Supp. 745, 756 (N.D. Cal. 1993).

Even if BE's web crawlers were authorized to make individual queries of eBay's system, BE's web crawlers exceeded the scope of any such consent when they began acting like robots by making repeated queries. See City of Amsterdam v. Daniel Goldreyer, Ltd., 882 F. Supp. 1273, 1281 (E.D.N.Y. 1995) ("One who uses a chattel with the consent of another is subject to liability in trespass for any harm to the chattel which is caused by or occurs in the course of any use exceeding the consent, even though such use is not a conversion."). Moreover, eBay repeatedly and explicitly notified BE that its use of eBay's computer system was unauthorized. The entire reason BE directed its queries through proxy servers was to evade eBay's attempts to stop this unauthorized access. The court concludes that BE's activity is sufficiently outside of the scope of the use permitted by eBay that it is unauthorized for the purposes of establishing a trespass. See Civic Western Corp. v. Zila Industries, Inc., 66 Cal. App. 3d 1, 17, 135 Cal. Rptr. 915 (1977) ("It seems clear, however, that a trespass may occur if the party, entering pursuant to a limited consent . . . proceeds to exceed those limits. . . .") (discussing trespass to real property).

eBay argues that BE interfered with eBay's possessory interest in its computer system. Although eBay appears unlikely to be able to show a substantial interference at this time, such a showing is not required. Conduct that does not amount to a substantial interference with possession, but which consists of intermeddling with or use of another's personal property, is sufficient to establish a cause of action for trespass to chattel. See *Thrifty-Tel*, 46 Cal. App. 4th at 1567, 54 Cal. Rptr. 2d 468 (distinguishing the tort from conversion). Although the court admits some uncertainty as to the precise level of possessory interference required to constitute an intermeddling, there does not appear to be any dispute that eBay can show that BE's conduct amounts to use of eBay's computer systems. Accordingly, eBay has made a strong showing that it is likely to prevail on the merits of its assertion that BE's use of eBay's computer system was an unauthorized and intentional interference with eBay's possessory interest.

b. Damage to eBay's Computer System

A trespasser is liable when the trespass diminishes the condition, quality or value of personal property. See CompuServe, Inc. v. Cyber Promotions, 962 F. Supp. 1015 (S.D. Ohio 1997). The quality or value of personal property may be "diminished even though it is not physically damaged by defendant's conduct." Id. at 1022. The *Restatement* offers the following explanation for the harm requirement:

> The interest of a possessor of a chattel in its inviolability, unlike the similar interest of a possessor of land, is not given legal protection by an action for nominal damages for harmless intermeddlings with the chattel. In order that an actor who interferes with another's chattel may be liable, his conduct must affect some other and more important interest of the possessor. Therefore, one who intentionally intermeddles with another's chattel is subject to liability only if his intermeddling is harmful to the possessor's

> materially valuable interest in the physical condition, quality, or value of the chattel, or if the possessor is deprived of the use of the chattel for a substantial time, or some other legally protected interest of the possessor is affected. . . . Sufficient legal protection of the possessor's interest in the mere inviolability of his chattel is afforded by his privilege to use reasonable force to protect his possession against even harmless interference.

Restatement (Second) of Torts § 218 cmt. e (1977).

eBay is likely to be able to demonstrate that BE's activities have diminished the quality or value of eBay's computer systems. BE's activities consume at least a portion of plaintiff's bandwidth and server capacity. Although there is some dispute as to the percentage of queries on eBay's site for which BE is responsible, BE admits that it sends some 80,000 to 100,000 requests to plaintiff's computer systems per day. Although eBay does not claim that this consumption has led to any physical damage to eBay's computer system, nor does eBay provide any evidence to support the claim that it may have lost revenues or customers based on this use, eBay's claim is that BE's use is appropriating eBay's personal property by using valuable bandwidth and capacity, and necessarily compromising eBay's ability to use that capacity for its own purposes. See *CompuServe*, 962 F. Supp. at 1022 ("any value [plaintiff] realizes from its computer equipment is wholly derived from the extent to which that equipment can serve its subscriber base.").

BE argues that its searches represent a negligible load on plaintiff's computer systems, and do not rise to the level of impairment to the condition or value of eBay's computer system required to constitute a trespass. However, it is undisputed that eBay's server and its capacity are personal property, and that BE's searches use a portion of this property. Even if, as BE argues, its searches use only a small amount of eBay's computer system capacity, BE has nonetheless deprived eBay of the ability to use that portion of its personal property for its own purposes. The law recognizes no such right to use another's personal property. Accordingly, BE's actions appear to have caused injury to eBay and appear likely to continue to cause injury to eBay. If the court were to hold otherwise, it would likely encourage other auction aggregators to crawl the eBay site, potentially to the point of denying effective access to eBay's customers. If preliminary injunctive relief were denied, and other aggregators began to crawl the eBay site, there appears to be little doubt that the load on eBay's computer system would qualify as a substantial impairment of condition or value. California law does not require eBay to wait for such a disaster before applying to this court for relief. The court concludes that eBay has made a strong showing that it is likely to prevail on the merits of its trespass claim, and that there is at least a possibility that it will suffer irreparable harm if preliminary injunctive relief is not granted. eBay is therefore entitled to preliminary injunctive relief. . . .

COMMENTS AND QUESTIONS

1. The tort of trespass to chattels traditionally requires proof not just that the defendant "intermeddled" with a chattel, but that the defendant's use actually caused injury to the chattel or injured the owner by depriving it of the benefit of using the chattel. The chattel in this case is eBay's server, so the *Restatement* approach would seem to require proof that eBay's servers were damaged, or at least that eBay lost the use of its servers. But eBay could not prove either of those things. eBay's servers did not

crash, nor did they need more frequent repair because Bidder's Edge sent a large number of requests to the servers. Nor was eBay deprived of the use of the server. eBay customers weren't kicked out, nor did they have their requests delayed, by reason of Bidder's Edge's use.

Judge Whyte's opinion points to two sorts of injury attributable to Bidder's Edge's conduct. First, Judge Whyte pointed out that when Bidder's Edge sent its flood of requests (normally in the middle of the night), it used just over 1 percent of eBay's capacity. The court worried that if dozens of other companies sent similar bulk requests at exactly the same time, eBay's server could crash. Second, Judge Whyte seemed to undo the injury requirement altogether by concluding that any use of the plaintiff's server was necessarily an interference with eBay's exclusive right of control, even if the use didn't prevent eBay from doing whatever it wanted with its server. Significantly, it is the second rationale that every subsequent court has pointed to in finding trespass to chattels even absent any possible injury to the chattel itself. [But note that it is no longer good law in California after the *Intel v. Hamidi* case discussed *infra.*]

Does *eBay*'s analysis of injury make sense? Or is the court really applying the rather different tort of trespass to land, which punishes intermeddling directly whether or not there is injury? *See* Dan L. Burk, *The Trouble with Trespass*, 4 J. SMALL & EMERGING BUS. L. 27 (2000) (criticizing trespass cases for confusing the two doctrines).

2. Might eBay have anti-competitive motives for preventing Bidder's Edge from truthfully reporting the prices of various goods on different auction sites? If auction aggregators don't exist, it becomes harder for consumers to comparison shop, and they may just buy from the auction site with the largest brand name—eBay. Law professors opposed to the *eBay* decision made this point on appeal:

> Established online merchants have a substantial incentive to use the doctrine of trespass to interfere with the flow of price and product information on the Internet. The district court's decision places the flow of information within their control, as it allows them to circumscribe the use of tools that gather information and present the results in a usable format. These tools are essential to make the process of gathering information both feasible and useful to the average consumer. Without information about online alternatives, competition on the Internet will be reduced. Like eBay, many sites may have a motive to prevent such competition. eBay would rather not have a site like Bidder's Edge tell consumers that they can get the same product cheaper at a competing auction site. Similarly, online sellers of music, books, videos, toys and countless other sites that don't have the lowest prices won't want to participate in a price-comparison service. This is especially true of companies like eBay with large market shares, because they may believe that they could shut down a data aggregator altogether by choosing not to participate. Such companies will instead rely on their strong brand name to keep consumers coming to their site—and ignorant of the cheaper prices or better service that may be available elsewhere. The district court's opinion gives these companies the power to block such a price-comparison service altogether. While the promise of ecommerce is to improve consumer information and lower transaction costs, under a trespass theory many of those benefits will disappear.[4]

4. Consumers can obtain price information in the physical world by reading advertisements and catalogs or using existing comparison-shopping products like *Consumer Reports.* While in theory a store might be legally justified in excluding anyone who works for *Consumer Reports* from entering their store or buying their products, as a practical matter it would be difficult for them to do so. eBay, by contrast, has found in its trespass theory a perfect mechanism for preventing information-gathering.

Is this a fair criticism? Should the doctrine of trespass to chattels take the plaintiff's motive into account? Note that some of the successful applications of trespass to chattels have been against price-comparison sites. *See* Southwest Airlines Co. v. Farechase, Inc., 318 F. Supp. 2d 435 (N.D. Tex. 2004); American Airlines v. Farechase, Inc., No. 067-194022-02 (Tex. Dist. Ct. Mar. 8, 2003).

3. While the trespass to chattels cause of action has only recently been applied to the Internet, a number of decisions have used the tort to permit the owners of servers to prevent unwanted access. These cases fall into two basic categories. One set of cases — including *eBay* — involves a Web site owner's attempt to limit or prevent access to data the Web site owner has itself made open to the public.[1] In addition to *eBay*, courts in Register.com, Inc. v. Verio, Inc., 356 F.3d 393 (2d Cir. 2004), and Oyster Software, Inc. v. Forms Processing, 2001 WL 1736382 (N.D. Cal. Dec. 6, 2001), have held that a public Web site can prevent automated access, even to information (such as the WHOIS database in *Verio*) that the Web site is obligated to make available to the public. *Oyster Software* did not require any proof of burden on the server. Rather, the court followed the second theory in *eBay*, holding that any access to the server deprived the Web site owner of its right of dominion. By contrast, the Second Circuit opinion in *Register.com* affirmed the district court's finding of trespass only because Verio's search "consumed a significant portion of the capacity of Register's computer systems," so that even though "Verio's robots alone would not incapacitate Register's systems . . . it was 'highly probable' that other Internet service providers would devise similar programs to access Register's data, and that the system would be overtaxed and would crash." 356 F.3d at 404.

The second set of cases involves not the collection of data from a Web site, but the sending of data to a mail server. The first applications of trespass to chattels to the Internet involved spam. *See* CompuServe, Inc. v. Cyber Promotions, Inc., 962 F. Supp. 1015 (S.D. Ohio 1997); America Online v. National Health Care Discount, Inc., 174 F. Supp. 2d 890 (N.D. Iowa 2001). In these cases, the court found that bulk e-mail was overwhelming the servers of the plaintiff Internet service providers, and the court concluded that sending such bulk e-mail trespassed on the ISP servers.

After *Verio*, can you think of any electronic transmission to a public server that doesn't require advance permission?

The California courts have rejected trespass to chattels claims in the absence of evidence of actual harm to the chattel in question — the computer server. Ticketmaster Corp. v. Tickets.com, 2000 Copyright L. Decs. ¶28,146 (C.D. Cal. Aug. 10, 2000). In *Ticketmaster*, the court concluded that tickets.com was not trespassing on Ticketmaster's server by "scraping" the data from the Ticketmaster server, and then linking directly to places on the Ticketmaster site where users could buy tickets to various events.[2] The court was skeptical of the entire theory of trespass to chattels as applied to the Internet, but it distinguished *eBay* on the ground that Ticketmaster could not show actual harm to its servers. And in Intel Corp. v. Hamidi, 30 Cal. 4th 1342, 71 P.3d 296, 1 Cal. Rptr. 3d 32 (2003), the court limited the rationale of the spam trespass cases by requiring the plaintiff to prove damage to or dispossession of the

1. The protection of information not open to the public — private or password-controlled servers — presents a different set of issues. The Computer Fraud and Abuse Act, 18 U.S.C. §1030, precludes unauthorized access to a networked computer, and there is no need to apply trespass to preclude such conduct.

2. Presumably the linking claim would have to be based on some theory of contributory trespass, since it is Ticketmaster customers rather than tickets.com who are actually sending data to the Ticketmaster site.

chattel. In that case, the trial court enjoined Hamidi, a former employee of Intel, from sending e-mails to current Intel employees complaining about the company. The California Supreme Court reversed, noting that there was clearly no harm to or burden on the servers — they were not shut down and Intel's e-mail was not delayed. The court held that the requirement for injury could not be met merely by proof that Intel employees spent company time reading the e-mails:

> After reviewing the decisions analyzing unauthorized electronic contact with computer systems as potential trespasses to chattels, we conclude that under California law the tort does not encompass, and should not be extended to encompass, an electronic communication that neither damages the recipient computer system nor impairs its functioning. Such an electronic communication does not constitute an actionable trespass to personal property, i.e., the computer system, because it does not interfere with the possessor's use or possession of, or any other legally protected interest in, the personal property itself. The consequential economic damage Intel claims to have suffered, i.e., loss of productivity caused by employees reading and reacting to Hamidi's messages and company efforts to block the messages, is not an injury to the company's interest in its computers — which worked as intended and were unharmed by the communications — any more than the personal distress caused by reading an unpleasant letter would be an injury to the recipient's mailbox, or the loss of privacy caused by an intrusive telephone call would be an injury to the recipient's telephone equipment.
>
> Our conclusion does not rest on any special immunity for communications by electronic mail; we do not hold that messages transmitted through the Internet are exempt from the ordinary rules of tort liability. To the contrary, e-mail, like other forms of communication, may in some circumstances cause legally cognizable injury to the recipient or to third parties and may be actionable under various common law or statutory theories. Indeed, on facts somewhat similar to those here, a company or its employees might be able to plead causes of action for interference with prospective economic relations, see Guillory v. Godfrey 134 Cal. App. 2d 628, 630-632, 286 P.2d 474 (1955) (defendant berated customers and prospective customers of plaintiffs' cafe with disparaging and racist comments), interference with contract, see Blender v. Superior Court, 55 Cal. App. 2d 24, 25-27, 130 P.2d 179 (1942) (defendant made false statements about plaintiff to his employer, resulting in plaintiff's discharge) or intentional infliction of emotional distress, see Kiseskey v. Carpenters' Trust for So. California 144 Cal. App. 3d 222, 229-230, 192 Cal. Rptr. 492 (1983) (agents of defendant union threatened life, health, and family of employer if he did not sign agreement with union). And, of course, as with any other means of publication, third party subjects of e-mail communications may under appropriate facts make claims for defamation, publication of private facts, or other speech-based torts. See, e.g., Southridge Capital Management v. Lowry, 188 F. Supp. 2d 388, 394-396 (S.D.N.Y. 2002) (allegedly false statements in e-mail sent to several of plaintiff's clients support actions for defamation and interference with contract).Intel's claim fails not because e-mail transmitted through the Internet enjoys unique immunity, but because the trespass to chattels tort — unlike the causes of action just mentioned — may not, in California, be proved without evidence of an injury to the plaintiff's personal property or legal interest therein.
>
> Nor does our holding affect the legal remedies of Internet service providers (ISP's) against senders of unsolicited commercial bulk e-mail (UCE), also known as "spam." See Ferguson v. Friendfinders, Inc., 94 Cal. App. 4th 1255, 1267, 115 Cal. Rptr. 2d 258 (2002). A series of federal district court decisions, beginning with CompuServe, Inc. v. Cyber Promotions, Inc. 962 F. Supp. 1015 (S.D. Ohio 1997), has approved the use of trespass to chattels as a theory of spammers' liability to ISP's, based upon evidence that the vast quantities of mail sent by spammers both overburdened the

> ISP's own computers and made the entire computer system harder to use for recipients, the ISP's customers. See id. at pp. 1022-1023. In those cases, discussed in greater detail below, the underlying complaint was that the extraordinary quantity of UCE impaired the computer system's functioning. In the present case, the claimed injury is located in the disruption or distraction caused to recipients by the contents of the e-mail messages, an injury entirely separate from, and not directly affecting, the possession or value of personal property.

The court went on to reject a policy argument that trespass law should be expanded by treating Web sites like real property:

> We discuss this debate among the amici curiae and academic writers only to note its existence and contours, not to attempt its resolution. Creating an absolute property right to exclude undesired communications from one's e-mail and Web servers might help force spammers to internalize the costs they impose on ISP's and their customers. But such a property rule might also create substantial new costs, to e-mail and e-commerce users and to society generally, in lost ease and openness of communication and in lost network benefits. In light of the unresolved controversy, we would be acting rashly to adopt a rule treating computer servers as real property for purposes of trespass law.

Justice Brown dissented. She took a broad view of Intel's property rights:

> Intel has invested millions of dollars to develop and maintain a computer system. It did this not to act as a public forum but to enhance the productivity of its employees. Kourosh Kenneth Hamidi sent as many as 200,000 e-mail messages to Intel employees. The time required to review and delete Hamidi's messages diverted employees from productive tasks and undermined the utility of the computer system. "There may . . . be situations in which the value to the owner of a particular type of chattel may be impaired by dealing with it in a manner that does not affect its physical condition." REST. 2D TORTS, § 218, com. h, p. 422. This is such a case.
>
> The majority repeatedly asserts that Intel objected to the hundreds of thousands of messages solely due to their content, and proposes that Intel seek relief by pleading content-based speech torts. This proposal misses the point that Intel's objection is directed not toward Hamidi's message but his use of Intel's property to display his message. Intel has not sought to prevent Hamidi from expressing his ideas on his Web site, through private mail (paper or electronic) to employees' homes, or through any other means like picketing or billboards. But as counsel for Intel explained during oral argument, the company objects to Hamidi's using Intel's property to advance his message.
>
> Of course, Intel deserves an injunction even if its objections are based entirely on the e-mail's content. Intel is entitled, for example, to allow employees use of the Internet to check stock market tables or weather forecasts without incurring any concomitant obligation to allow access to pornographic Web sites.

4. As the *Intel* court suggests, many of the cases decided under the rubric of trespass to chattels could also be decided under other statutes. For example, many state laws now ban spam. *See, e.g.*, CAL. BUS. & PROF. CODE § 17538.4. And many of the data cases, such as *eBay* and *Ticketmaster*, are really efforts to protect uncopyrightable data by creating a new form of intellectual property law. The intuitive case for protection of data compilations may motivate courts to rule for the plaintiffs on a trespass theory in order to effectively create a form of intellectual property for data

protection. Does this result make sense? Or should the courts be careful to avoid undermining copyright law's limits? Note that copyright law may preempt state torts that create copyright-like rights within the constitutional field of copyright. *See Ticketmaster, supra*, in which the court held various state torts preempted by federal copyright law. For a fuller discussion of copyright preemption, see Chapter 15 *infra*.

5. The broad application of trespass to the Internet effectively creates a consent standard for using the Internet. Web sites and even e-mail recipients have an effective veto over the sending or collecting of data. Rather than simply deciding to make information open to the public or keep it private, a Web site owner can declare that information is public but that particular specified individuals are barred from using it.

Understanding the trespass cases in this light puts the focus on how those declarations are made and communicated. In some cases, such as *eBay*, this is not much of an issue: It was quite clear to Bidder's Edge that eBay objected to its collection of data from the eBay Web site. But in other cases, courts have held that terms and conditions placed on a Web site — or even the use of an automated Robot Exclusion Header — constitute sufficient notice that a particular user is unwanted.

Does it make sense to give a Web site owner the right to post an announcement excluding certain users or anyone who would make certain uses? The alternative is for the Web site owner to rely on technical blocking alternatives. For example, after Ticketmaster lost its case, it reconfigured its Web site to block deep links from tickets.com. Should the courts stay out of such disputes and let the parties engage in their own technological competition? Or will the result be a wasteful technological "arms race"? David McGowan argues that Web site owners should have such a right. He doesn't worry that giving them such a right will interfere with the operation of the Internet because the vast majority of them will have incentives to permit most "trespasses" to their server by search engines, consumers, and others, although likely not by competitors. *See* David McGowan, *Website Access: The Case for Consent*, 35 Loy. U. Chi. L. Rev. 341 (2003).

6. The concept of trespass in cyberspace depends heavily on a conception of a Web site or mail server as "property" from which, like land, the owner ought to have the right to exclude others. If a Web site is like land, the trespass to land rules (which don't require proof of injury to the land for liability) seem like the ones to apply. But a number of commentators have challenged the metaphor of an Internet site as a "place" akin to land. *See, e.g.*, Dan Hunter, *Cyberspace as Place and the Tragedy of the Digital Anticommons*, 91 Cal. L. Rev. 439 (2003); Mark A. Lemley, *Place and Cyberspace*, 91 Cal. L. Rev. 521 (2003); Maureen A. O'Rourke, *Property Rights and Competition on the Internet: In Search of an Appropriate Analogy*, 16 Berkeley Tech. L.J. 561 (2001); *see also* Catherine M. Sharkey, *Trespass Torts and Self-Help for an Electronic Age*, 45 Tulsa L. Rev. 677 (2010). Hunter suggests that the metaphor is psychologically quite powerful, but troubling as a policy matter. Lemley argues that courts can and should focus on the ways the Internet is *not* like land. He also points out that treating the Internet like land does not necessarily mean that the owner should get an absolute right to exclude others. In the real world, the law gives many different sorts of rights of varying strengths to land owners. Similarly, a court might decide that an absolute right of exclusion is not the right legal analogy.

Are property principles relevant to the Internet at all? If so, how should a court decide which analogy is the right one to apply?

PROBLEM

Problem 13-1. Infoplex is a search engine. In order to run a comprehensive search engine, Infoplex must collect and index data from over 1 billion Web sites. In order to keep its search engine up-to-date, Infoplex must revisit those pages at least once a week, and often more frequently. To do this, Infoplex uses automated software robots called "spiders." These spiders crawl the Web, automatically downloading all of the information on all of the Web sites it can find. Because of the practical impossibility of entering into contracts with the owners of all these Web sites — among other things, millions of new pages are added each year — Infoplex has configured its spiders to collect any data it can from any site that is open to the public.

Do any of the following plaintiffs have a claim against Infoplex for trespass to chattels based on its indexing of their sites?

a) Site A, which has a written "terms of use" statement precluding any collection of all or substantially all of its data by any for-profit company.
b) Site B, which uses a Robot Exclusion Header in the source code of its Web page. Such a header signals to robots that they are not welcome on the site. Not all robots recognize or respect such a header, though, and Infoplex has configured its robots to ignore such headers.
c) Site C, an Internet service provider which has sent a letter to the general counsel of Infoplex demanding that Infoplex pay it $1,000 per month for the right to index any of its customers' pages.

B. CONVERSION

Kremen v. Cohen
337 F.3d 1024 (2003)

KOZINSKI, Circuit Judge.

We decide whether Network Solutions may be liable for giving away a registrant's domain name on the basis of a forged letter.

Background

"Sex on the Internet?," they all said. "That'll never make any money." But computer-geek-turned-entrepreneur Gary Kremen knew an opportunity when he saw it. The year was 1994; domain names were free for the asking, and it would be several years yet before Henry Blodget and hordes of eager NASDAQ day traders would turn the Internet into the Dutch tulip craze of our times. With a quick e-mail to the domain name registrar Network Solutions, Kremen became the proud owner of sex.com.

He registered the name to his business, Online Classifieds, and listed himself as the contact.

Con man Stephen Cohen, meanwhile, was doing time for impersonating a bankruptcy lawyer. He, too, saw the potential of the domain name. Kremen had gotten it first, but that was only a minor impediment for a man of Cohen's boundless resource and bounded integrity. Once out of prison, he sent Network Solutions what purported to be a letter he had received from Online Classifieds. It claimed the company had been "forced to dismiss Mr. Kremen," but "never got around to changing our administrative contact with the internet registration [sic] and now our Board of directors has decided to abandon the domain name sex.com." Why was this unusual letter being sent via Cohen rather than to Network Solutions directly? It explained:

> Because we do not have a direct connection to the internet, we request that you notify the internet registration on our behalf, to delete our domain name sex.com. Further, we have no objections to your use of the domain name sex.com and this letter shall serve as our authorization to the internet registration to transfer sex.com to your corporation.

Despite the letter's transparent claim that a company called "Online Classifieds" had no Internet connection, Network Solutions made no effort to contact Kremen. Instead, it accepted the letter at face value and transferred the domain name to Cohen. When Kremen contacted Network Solutions some time later, he was told it was too late to undo the transfer. Cohen went on to turn sex.com into a lucrative online porn empire.

And so began Kremen's quest to recover the domain name that was rightfully his. He sued Cohen and several affiliated companies in federal court, seeking return of the domain name and disgorgement of Cohen's profits. The district court . . . ordered the domain name returned to Kremen. It also told Cohen to hand over his profits, invoking the constructive trust doctrine and California's "unfair competition" statute, Cal. Bus. & Prof. Code § 17200 et seq. It awarded $40 million in compensatory damages and another $25 million in punitive damages.

Kremen, unfortunately, has not had much luck collecting his judgment. The district court froze Cohen's assets, but Cohen ignored the order and wired large sums of money to offshore accounts. His real estate property, under the protection of a federal receiver, was stripped of all its fixtures — even cabinet doors and toilets — in violation of another order. The court commanded Cohen to appear and show cause why he shouldn't be held in contempt, but he ignored that order, too. The district judge finally took off the gloves — he declared Cohen a fugitive from justice, signed an arrest warrant and sent the U.S. Marshals after him.

Then things started getting really bizarre. Kremen put up a "wanted" poster on the sex.com site with a mug shot of Cohen, offering a $50,000 reward to anyone who brought him to justice. Cohen's lawyers responded with a motion to vacate the arrest warrant. They reported that Cohen was under house arrest in Mexico and that gunfights between Mexican authorities and would-be bounty hunters seeking Kremen's reward money posed a threat to human life. The district court rejected this story as "implausible" and denied the motion. Cohen, so far as the record shows, remains at large.

Given his limited success with the bounty hunter approach, it should come as no surprise that Kremen seeks to hold someone else responsible for his losses. That someone is Network Solutions, the exclusive domain name registrar at the time of Cohen's antics. Kremen sued it for mishandling his domain name, invoking four theories at issue here. He argues that he had an implied contract with Network Solutions, which it breached by giving the domain name to Cohen. He also claims the transfer violated Network Solutions's cooperative agreement with the National Science Foundation — the government contract that made Network Solutions the .com registrar. His third theory is that he has a property right in the domain name sex.com, and Network Solutions committed the tort of conversion by giving it away to Cohen. Finally, he argues that Network Solutions was a "bailee" of his domain name and seeks to hold it liable for "conversion by bailee."

The district court granted summary judgment in favor of Network Solutions on all claims. Kremen v. Cohen, 99 F. Supp. 2d 1168 (N.D. Cal. 2000). It held that Kremen had no implied contract with Network Solutions because there was no consideration: Kremen had registered the domain name for free. Id. at 1171-72. It rejected the third-party contract claim on the ground that the cooperative agreement did not indicate a clear intent to grant enforceable contract rights to registrants. Id. at 1172.

The conversion claims fared no better. The court agreed that sex.com was Kremen's property. It concluded, though, that it was intangible property to which the tort of conversion does not apply. Id. at 1173. The conversion by bailee claim failed for the additional reason that Network Solutions was not a bailee. Id. at 1175.

Kremen appeals, and we consider each of his four theories in turn.

Breach of Contract

Kremen had no express contract with Network Solutions, but argues that his registration created an implied contract, which Network Solutions breached. A defendant is normally not liable for breach of contract, however, if he promised to do something for free. The party claiming breach must show that, in return for the promise, it conferred some benefit the other party was not already entitled to receive, or suffered some prejudice it was not already bound to endure. CAL. CIV. CODE § 1605. The adequacy of consideration doesn't matter, but it must be "something of real value." Herbert v. Lankershim, 9 Cal. 2d 409, 475, 71 P.2d 220 (1937) (internal quotation marks omitted). . . .

Kremen did not give consideration for his domain name, so he had no contract with Network Solutions. Cf. Oppedahl & Larson v. Network Solutions, Inc., 3 F. Supp. 2d 1147, 1160-61 (D. Colo. 1998).

[The court goes on to reject the claim that Kremen was a third-party beneficiary of the Network Solutions-NSF contract.]

Conversion

Kremen's conversion claim is another matter. To establish that tort, a plaintiff must show "ownership or right to possession of property, wrongful disposition of the property right and damages." G.S. Rasmussen & Assocs., Inc. v. Kalitta Flying Serv., Inc., 958 F.2d 896, 906 (9th Cir. 1992). The preliminary question, then, is whether registrants have property rights in their domain names. Network Solutions all but concedes that they do. This is no surprise, given its positions in prior litigation. See Network Solutions, Inc. v. Umbro Int'l, Inc., 259 Va. 759, 529 S.E.2d 80, 86

(2000) ("[Network Solutions] acknowledged during oral argument before this Court that the right to use a domain name is a form of intangible personal property."); Network Solutions, Inc. v. Clue Computing, Inc., 946 F. Supp. 858, 860 (D. Colo. 1996) (same). The district court agreed with the parties on this issue, as do we.

Property is a broad concept that includes "every intangible benefit and prerogative susceptible of possession or disposition." Downing v. Mun. Court, 88 Cal. App. 2d 345, 350, 198 P.2d 923 (1948) (internal quotation marks omitted). We apply a three-part test to determine whether a property right exists: "First, there must be an interest capable of precise definition; second, it must be capable of exclusive possession or control; and third, the putative owner must have established a legitimate claim to exclusivity." *G.S. Rasmussen*, 958 F.2d at 903 (footnote omitted). Domain names satisfy each criterion. Like a share of corporate stock or a plot of land, a domain name is a well-defined interest. Someone who registers a domain name decides where on the Internet those who invoke that particular name — whether by typing it into their web browsers, by following a hyperlink, or by other means — are sent. Ownership is exclusive in that the registrant alone makes that decision. Moreover, like other forms of property, domain names are valued, bought and sold, often for millions of dollars, see Greg Johnson, *The Costly Game for Net Names*, L.A. TIMES, Apr. 10, 2000, at A1, and they are now even subject to in rem jurisdiction, see 15 U.S.C. §1125(d)(2).

Finally, registrants have a legitimate claim to exclusivity. Registering a domain name is like staking a claim to a plot of land at the title office. It informs others that the domain name is the registrant's and no one else's. Many registrants also invest substantial time and money to develop and promote websites that depend on their domain names. Ensuring that they reap the benefits of their investments reduces uncertainty and thus encourages investment in the first place, promoting the growth of the Internet overall. See *G.S. Rasmussen*, 958 F.2d at 900.

Kremen therefore had an intangible property right in his domain name, and a jury could find that Network Solutions "wrongful[ly] dispos[ed] of" that right to his detriment by handing the domain name over to Cohen. Id. at 906. The district court nevertheless rejected Kremen's conversion claim. It held that domain names, although a form of property, are intangibles not subject to conversion. This rationale derives from a distinction tort law once drew between tangible and intangible property: Conversion was originally a remedy for the wrongful taking of another's lost goods, so it applied only to tangible property. See PROSSER AND KEETON ON THE LAW OF TORTS §15, at 89, 91 (W. Page Keeton ed., 5th ed. 1984). Virtually every jurisdiction, however, has discarded this rigid limitation to some degree. See id. at 91. Many courts ignore or expressly reject it. See *Kremen*, 325 F.3d at 1045-46 n.5 (Kozinski, J., dissenting) (citing cases); Astroworks, Inc. v. Astroexhibit, Inc., 257 F. Supp. 2d 609, 618 (S.D.N.Y. 2003) (holding that the plaintiff could maintain a claim for conversion of his website); Val D. Ricks, *The Conversion of Intangible Property: Bursting the Ancient Trover Bottle with New Wine*, 1991 B.Y.U. L. REV. 1681, 1682. Others reject it for some intangibles but not others. The *Restatement*, for example, recommends the following test:

> (1) Where there is conversion of a document in which intangible rights are merged, the damages include the value of such rights.

> (2) One who effectively prevents the exercise of intangible rights of the kind customarily merged in a document is subject to a liability similar to that for conversion, even though the document is not itself converted.

Restatement (Second) of Torts § 242 (1965) (emphasis added). An intangible is "merged" in a document when, "by the appropriate rule of law, the right to the immediate possession of a chattel and the power to acquire such possession is represented by [the] document," or when "an intangible obligation [is] represented by [the] document, which is regarded as equivalent to the obligation." Id. cmt. a (emphasis added).[6] The district court applied this test and found no evidence that Kremen's domain name was merged in a document.

The court assumed that California follows the *Restatement* on this issue. Our review, however, revealed that "there do not appear to be any California cases squarely addressing whether the 'merged with' requirement is a part of California law." *Kremen*, 325 F.3d at 1042. We invoked the California Supreme Court's certification procedure to offer it the opportunity to address the issue. Id. at 1043; Cal. Rules of Court 29.8. The Court declined, Kremen v. Cohen, No. S112591 (Cal. Feb. 25, 2003), and the question now falls to us.

We conclude that California does not follow the *Restatement*'s strict merger requirement. Indeed, the leading California Supreme Court case rejects the tangibility requirement altogether. In Payne v. Elliot, 54 Cal. 339, 1880 WL 1907 (1880), the Court considered whether shares in a corporation (as opposed to the share certificates themselves) could be converted. It held that they could, reasoning: "[T]he action no longer exists as it did at common law, but has been developed into a remedy for the conversion of every species of personal property." Id. at 341 (emphasis added). While *Payne's* outcome might be reconcilable with the *Restatement*, its rationale certainly is not: It recognized conversion of shares, not because they are customarily represented by share certificates, but because they are a species of personal property and, perforce, protected. Id. at 342.[7]

Notwithstanding *Payne*'s seemingly clear holding, the California Court of Appeal held in Olschewski v. Hudson, 87 Cal. App. 282, 262 P. 43 (1927), that a laundry route was not subject to conversion. It explained that *Payne*'s rationale was "too broad a statement as to the application of the doctrine of conversion." Id. at 288, 262 P. 43. Rather than follow binding California Supreme Court precedent, the court retheorized *Payne* and held that corporate stock could be converted only because it was "represented by" a tangible document. Id.; see also Adkins v. Model Laundry Co., 92 Cal. App. 575, 583, 268 P. 939 (1928) (relying on *Olschewski* and holding that no property right inhered in "the intangible interest of an exclusive privilege to collect laundry").

Were *Olschewski* the only relevant case on the books, there might be a plausible argument that California follows the *Restatement*. But in Palm Springs-La Quinta

6. The *Restatement* does note that conversion "has been applied by some courts in cases where the converted document is not in itself a symbol of the rights in question, but is merely essential to their protection and enforcement, as in the case of account books and receipts." Id. cmt. b.

7. Intangible interests in real property, on the other hand, remain unprotected by conversion, presumably because trespass is an adequate remedy. See Goldschmidt v. Maier, 73 P. 984, 985 (Cal. 1903) (per curiam) ("[A] leasehold of real estate is not the subject of an action of trover."); Vuich v. Smith, 140 Cal. App. 453, 455, 35 P.2d 365 (1934) (same). Some California cases also preserve the traditional exception for indefinite sums of money. See 5 Witkin Torts § 614.

Development Co. v. Kieberk Corp., 46 Cal. App. 2d 234, 115 P.2d 548 (1941), the court of appeal allowed a conversion claim for intangible information in a customer list when some of the index cards on which the information was recorded were destroyed. The court allowed damages not just for the value of the cards, but for the value of the intangible information lost. See id. at 239, 115 P.2d 548. Section 242(1) of the *Restatement*, however, allows recovery for intangibles only if they are merged in the converted document. Customer information is not merged in a document in any meaningful sense. A Rolodex is not like a stock certificate that actually represents a property interest; it is only a means of recording information.

Palm Springs and *Olschewski* are reconcilable on their facts — the former involved conversion of the document itself while the latter did not. But this distinction can't be squared with the *Restatement*. The plaintiff in *Palm Springs* recovered damages for the value of his intangibles. But if those intangibles were merged in the index cards for purposes of section 242(1), the plaintiffs in *Olschewski* and *Adkins* should have recovered under section 242(2) — laundry routes surely are customarily written down somewhere. "Merged" can't mean one thing in one section and something else in the other.

California courts ignored the *Restatement* again in A & M Records, Inc. v. Heilman, 75 Cal. App. 3d 554, 142 Cal. Rptr. 390 (1977), which applied the tort to a defendant who sold bootlegged copies of musical recordings. The court held broadly that "such misappropriation and sale of the intangible property of another without authority from the owner is conversion." Id. at 570, 142 Cal. Rptr. 390. It gave no hint that its holding depended on whether the owner's intellectual property rights were merged in some document. One might imagine physical things with which the intangible was associated — for example, the medium on which the song was recorded. But an intangible intellectual property right in a song is not merged in a phonograph record in the sense that the record represents the composer's intellectual property right. The record is not like a certificate of ownership; it is only a medium for one instantiation of the artistic work.

In short, California does not follow the *Restatement*'s strict requirement that some document must actually represent the owner's intangible property right. On the contrary, courts routinely apply the tort to intangibles without inquiring whether they are merged in a document and, while it's often possible to dream up some document the intangible is connected to in some fashion, it's seldom one that represents the owner's property interest. To the extent *Olschewski* endorses the strict merger rule, it is against the weight of authority. That rule cannot be squared with a jurisprudence that recognizes conversion of music recordings, radio shows, customer lists, regulatory filings, confidential information and even domain names.

Were it necessary to settle the issue once and for all, we would toe the line of *Payne* and hold that conversion is "a remedy for the conversion of every species of personal property." 54 Cal. at 341. But we need not do so to resolve this case. Assuming arguendo that California retains some vestigial merger requirement, it is clearly minimal, and at most requires only some connection to a document or tangible object — not representation of the owner's intangible interest in the strict *Restatement* sense.

Kremen's domain name falls easily within this class of property. He argues that the relevant document is the Domain Name System, or "DNS" — the distributed electronic database that associates domain names like sex.com with particular computers connected to the Internet. We agree that the DNS is a document (or perhaps more accurately a collection of documents). That it is stored in electronic form rather than on ink and paper is immaterial. See, e.g., *Thrifty-Tel*, 46 Cal. App. 4th at 1565, 54 Cal. Rptr. 2d 468 (recognizing conversion of information recorded on floppy disk); *A & M Records*, 75 Cal. App. 3d at 570, 142 Cal. Rptr. 390 (same for audio record); *Lone Ranger Television*, 740 F.2d at 725 (same for magnetic tape). It would be a curious jurisprudence that turned on the existence of a paper document rather than an electronic one. Torching a company's file room would then be conversion while hacking into its mainframe and deleting its data would not. That is not the law, at least not in California.[11]

The DNS also bears some relation to Kremen's domain name. We need not delve too far into the mechanics of the Internet to resolve this case. It is sufficient to observe that information correlating Kremen's domain name with a particular computer on the Internet must exist somewhere in some form in the DNS; if it did not, the database would not serve its intended purpose. Change the information in the DNS, and you change the website people see when they type "www.sex.com."

Network Solutions quibbles about the mechanics of the DNS. It points out that the data corresponding to Kremen's domain name is not stored in a single record, but is found in several different places: The components of the domain name ("sex" and "com") are stored in two different places, and each is copied and stored on several machines to create redundancy and speed up response times. Network Solutions's theory seems to be that intangibles are not subject to conversion unless they are associated only with a single document.

Even if Network Solutions were correct that there is no single record in the DNS architecture with which Kremen's intangible property right is associated, that is no impediment under California law. A share of stock, for example, may be evidenced by more than one document. . . . Network Solutions's "single document" theory is unsupported.

Network Solutions also argues that the DNS is not a document because it is refreshed every twelve hours when updated domain name information is broadcast across the Internet. This theory is even less persuasive. A document doesn't cease being a document merely because it is often updated. If that were the case, a share registry would fail whenever shareholders were periodically added or dropped, as would an address file whenever business cards were added or removed. Whether a document is updated by inserting and deleting particular records or by replacing an old file with an entirely new one is a technical detail with no legal significance.

Kremen's domain name is protected by California conversion law, even on the grudging reading we have given it. Exposing Network Solutions to liability when it gives away a registrant's domain name on the basis of a forged letter is no different from holding a corporation liable when it gives away someone's shares under the same circumstances. See Schneider v. Union Oil Co., 6 Cal. App. 3d 987, 992, 86 Cal. Rptr. 315 (1970); Ralston v. Bank of Cal., 112 Cal. 208, 213, 44 P. 476 (1896). We have not "creat[ed] new tort duties" in reaching this result. Cf. Moore v. Regents of the Univ. of Cal., 51 Cal. 3d 120, 146, 271 Cal. Rptr. 146, 793 P.2d 479 (1990). We have only applied settled principles of conversion law to what the parties and the district court all agree is a species of property.

11. The *Restatement* requires intangibles to be merged only in a "document," not a tangible document. Restatement (Second) of Torts § 242. Our holding therefore does not depend on whether electronic records are tangible. Compare eBay, Inc. v. Bidder's Edge, Inc., 100 F. Supp. 2d 1058, 1069 (N.D. Cal. 2000) ("[I]t appears likely that the electronic signals sent by [Bidder's Edge] to retrieve information from eBay's computer system are . . . sufficiently tangible to support a trespass cause of action."), with Intel Corp. v. Hamidi, 30 Cal. 4th 1342 (2003) (implying that electronic signals are intangible).

The district court supported its contrary holding with several policy rationales, but none is sufficient grounds to depart from the common law rule. The court was reluctant to apply the tort of conversion because of its strict liability nature. This concern rings somewhat hollow in this case because the district court effectively exempted Network Solutions from liability to Kremen altogether, whether or not it was negligent. Network Solutions made no effort to contact Kremen before giving away his domain name, despite receiving a facially suspect letter from a third party. A jury would be justified in finding it was unreasonably careless.

We must, of course, take the broader view, but there is nothing unfair about holding a company responsible for giving away someone else's property even if it was not at fault. Cohen is obviously the guilty party here, and the one who should in all fairness pay for his theft. But he's skipped the country, and his money is stashed in some offshore bank account. Unless Kremen's luck with his bounty hunters improves, Cohen is out of the picture. The question becomes whether Network Solutions should be open to liability for its decision to hand over Kremen's domain name. Negligent or not, it was Network Solutions that gave away Kremen's property. Kremen never did anything. It would not be unfair to hold Network Solutions responsible and force it to try to recoup its losses by chasing down Cohen. This, at any rate, is the logic of the common law, and we do not lightly discard it.

The district court was worried that "the threat of litigation threatens to stifle the registration system by requiring further regulations by [Network Solutions] and potential increases in fees." *Kremen*, 99 F. Supp. 2d at 1174. Given that Network Solutions's "regulations" evidently allowed it to hand over a registrant's domain name on the basis of a facially suspect letter without even contacting him, "further regulations" don't seem like such a bad idea. And the prospect of higher fees presents no issue here that it doesn't in any other context. A bank could lower its ATM fees if it didn't have to pay security guards, but we doubt most depositors would think that was a good idea.

The district court thought there were "methods better suited to regulate the vagaries of domain names" and left it "to the legislature to fashion an appropriate statutory scheme." Id. The legislature, of course, is always free (within constitutional bounds) to refashion the system that courts come up with. But that doesn't mean we should throw up our hands and let private relations degenerate into a free-for-all in the meantime. We apply the common law until the legislature tells us otherwise. And the common law does not stand idle while people give away the property of others.

The evidence supported a claim for conversion, and the district court should not have rejected it. [The court then concludes that Kremen's claim for "conversion by bailee" is "not a distinct tort, but merely the tort of conversion committed by one who is a bailee. . . . To prove 'conversion by bailee,' Kremen must establish all the elements of conversion but, having done so, he gains nothing by also showing that Network Solutions is a bailee."]

Kremen had a viable claim for conversion. The judgment of the district court is reversed on this count, and the case is remanded for further proceedings.

COMMENTS AND QUESTIONS

1. Having been cheated out of sex.com, Kremen achieved considerable financial success by founding the popular Internet dating site match.com. Meanwhile, in 2005

Mexican police arrested Stephen Cohen in Tijuana, where he reportedly had been living for several years, and handed him over to U.S. authorities.

2. Does the "merger doctrine" as applied in the context of the common law of conversion serve a valid purpose? Should it be as easy to satisfy as the Ninth Circuit believes it to be? If so, is there any point in retaining it at all?

3. Federal and state statutes such as the Controlling the Assault of Non-Solicited Pornography and Marketing (CAN-SPAM) Act, 15 U.S.C. §§7701 et seq., and the Computer Fraud and Abuse Act, 18 U.S.C. §1030, address a variety of computer-related offenses, but they do not reach all of the conduct discussed in this section. Absent statutory coverage, *Kremen* and the cases on trespass to chattels all involve courts searching for common law tools for dealing with problems generated by new technologies. In a sense, this shouldn't seem so strange. Modifying the common law in light of new economic and technological developments is precisely what common law courts have been doing for centuries. Are such solutions preferable to statutory solutions, because the latter are susceptible to industry capture? To being outdated within a short time? Or is a statutory approach preferable, because legislatures can (at least in theory) provide a more informed, and narrowly tailored, approach to evolving issues?

Is there a risk that too many *state* statutes addressing Internet activities will lead to an inefficient patchwork of regulation? Does the application of state common law raise similar concerns, or not? *See* Peter S. Menell, *Regulating "Spyware": The Limitations of State "Laboratories" and the Case for Federal Preemption of State Unfair Competition Laws*, 20 BERKELEY TECH. L.J. 1363 (2005).

PROBLEM

Problem 13-2. Ozzie Scientific makes test kits for various types of biowarfare agents. After Ozzie incurs financial difficulties, Adderly Corp. agrees to acquire all of the shares of Ozzie as part of a corporate restructuring; Adderly also decides to terminate the contract of Bodick, Ozzie's chief scientist. Hearing of these impending events, Bodick allegedly alters the formulas for Ozzie's biowarfare testing solutions by tampering with a computer disk that stores those formulas. As a result of Bodick's action, the formulas stored on the disk are rendered useless. Adderly sues Bodick for conversion. What result under California law? Under the *Restatement (Second) of Torts*?

14 Tortious Interference and RICO

In many of the cases we have discussed throughout this book, as well as many others having nothing to do with intellectual property or unfair competition law as such, litigants have asserted a variety of miscellaneous business tort claims, either as their principal claims or as fallbacks. This chapter focuses mostly on a body of state law relating to tortious interference with contract (also known as inducement of breach of contract) and tortious interference with prospective business relations (also known as interference with prospective business advantage or business expectancy).[1] We also devote some (limited) attention to the law of fraud, including its modern-day incarnation in the context of civil RICO claims.

A. TORTIOUS INTERFERENCE

Suppose that Party A and Party B enter a valid contract under which Party B promises to perform a service for Party A in exchange for a fee. If Party B materially breaches the contract, Party A may file suit against Party B for breach of contract. Should Party A also have a claim against a nonparty to the contract (call him C) who in some sense *caused* B to breach the contract? Should A have a claim against C merely for interfering with A's *expectation* of a future business or contractual relationship with C? Does extending liability to C serve any valid social purpose, or does it threaten to erase important boundaries between the domains of contract and tort?

1. Courts occasionally note a possible distinction between tortious interference with prospective *contractual* relations and tortious interference with prospective *business* relations or business expectancy. *See, e.g.*, Benefit Resource, Inc. v. Apprize Tech. Solutions, Inc., Civ. No. 07-4199 (JNE/FLN), 2008 WL 2080977, at *10 (D. Minn. May 15, 2008) (stating that the Minnesota Supreme Court thus far has explicitly recognized only the former). The *Restatement of Torts*, however, does not appear to distinguish the two. *See* RESTATEMENT (SECOND) OF TORTS, § 766B cmts. b, c.

The principle that C may be liable to A, depending on the facts, for causing B to forgo an advantageous business relationship with A has a long pedigree. *See* RESTATEMENT (SECOND) OF TORTS § 766B cmt. b (citing cases dating back to the late Middle Ages). The principle that C may be liable to A for causing B to breach B's contract with A, on the other hand, appears to be of more recent vintage. The first reported decision on point is Lumley v. Gye, 118 Eng. Rep. 749 (Q.B. 1853). Plaintiff Benjamin Lumley had engaged an opera singer named Johanna Wagner (niece of the composer Richard Wagner) to perform at the Queen's Theatre in London for three months. Defendant Frederick Gye intentionally induced Wagner to breach her contract with Lumley and to agree to perform instead at the Royal Opera House, Covent Garden, which Gye managed. Lumley sued Gye, who filed a demurrer (motion to dismiss). The Court of Queen's Bench held that Lumley had stated a cause of action for Gye's alleged maliciously procuring the singer to breach her contract exclusively to provide personal services for Lumley for a specified time.[2]

Both the torts of interference with contract and interference with prospective business relations have made their way into U.S. law over the years. Their precise contours nevertheless remain somewhat variable from one jurisdiction to another, and sometimes generate confusion, as the cases in this section demonstrate.

Tuttle v. Buck

119 N.W. 946 (1909)

This appeal was from an order overruling a general demurrer to a complaint in which the plaintiff alleged: That for more than 10 years last past he has been and still is a barber by trade, and engaged in business as such in the village of Howard Lake, Minn., in said county, where he resides, owning and operating a shop for the purpose of his said trade. That until the injury hereinafter complained of his said business was prosperous, and plaintiff was enabled thereby to comfortably maintain himself and family out of the income and profits thereof, and also to save a considerable sum per annum, to wit, about $800. That the defendant, during the period of about 12 months last past, has wrongfully, unlawfully, and maliciously endeavored to destroy plaintiff's said business and compel plaintiff to abandon the same. That to that end he has persistently and systematically sought, by false and malicious reports and accusations of and concerning the plaintiff, by personally soliciting and urging plaintiff's patrons no longer to employ plaintiff, by threats of his personal displeasure, and by various other unlawful means and devices, to induce, and has thereby induced, many of said patrons to withhold from plaintiff the employment by them formerly given. That defendant is possessed of large means, and is engaged in the business of a banker in said village of Howard Lake, at Dassel, Minn., and at divers other places, and is nowise interested in the occupation of a barber; yet in the pursuance of the wicked, malicious, and unlawful purpose aforesaid, and for the sole and only purpose of injuring the trade of the plaintiff, and of accomplishing his purpose and threats of ruining the plaintiff's said

2. As a result of the ensuing dispute, Wagner wound up returning to Germany and not performing at Covent Garden either. Two years later, however, she returned to England and gave several performances at the Queen's Theatre.

business and driving him out of said village, the defendant fitted up and furnished a barber shop in said village for conducting the trade of barbering. That failing to induce any barber to occupy said shop on his own account, though offered at nominal rental, said defendant, with the wrongful and malicious purpose aforesaid, and not otherwise, has during the time herein stated hired two barbers in succession for a stated salary, paid by him, to occupy said shop, and to serve so many of plaintiff's patrons as said defendant has been or may be able by the means aforesaid to direct from plaintiff's shop. That at the present time a barber so employed and paid by the defendant is occupying and nominally conducting the shop thus fitted and furnished by the defendant, without paying any rent therefor, and under an agreement with defendant whereby the income of said shop is required to be paid to defendant, and is so paid in partial return for his wages. That all of said things were and are done by defendant with the sole design of injuring the plaintiff, and of destroying his said business, and not for the purpose of serving any legitimate interest of his own. That by reason of the great wealth and prominence of the defendant, and the personal and financial influence consequent thereon, he has by the means aforesaid, and through other unlawful means and devices by him employed, materially injured the business of the plaintiff, has largely reduced the income and profits thereof, and intends and threatens to destroy the same altogether, to plaintiff's damage in the sum of $10,000.

ELLIOTT, J. (after stating the facts as above).

It has been said that the law deals only with externals, and that a lawful act cannot be made the foundation of an action because it was done with an evil motive. . . .

We do not intend to enter upon an elaborate discussion of the subject, or become entangled in the subtleties connected with the words 'malice' and 'malicious.' We are not able to accept without limitations the doctrine above referred to, but at this time content ourselves with a brief reference to some general principles. It must be remembered that the common law is the result of growth, and that its development has been determined by the social needs of the community which it governs. It is the resultant of conflicting social forces, and those forces which are for the time dominant leave their impress upon the law. It is of judicial origin, and seeks to establish doctrines and rules for the determination, protection, and enforcement of legal rights. Manifestly it must change as society changes and new rights are recognized. To be an efficient instrument, and not a mere abstraction, it must gradually adapt itself to changed conditions. Necessarily its form and substance has been greatly affected by prevalent economic theories. For generations there has been a practical agreement upon the proposition that competition in trade and business is desirable, and this idea has found expression in the decisions of the courts as well as in statutes. But it has led to grievous and manifold wrongs to individuals, and many courts have manifested an earnest desire to protect the individuals from the evils which result from unrestrained business competition. The problem has been to so adjust matters as to preserve the principle of competition and yet guard against its abuse to the unnecessary injury to the individual. So the principle that a man may use his own property according to his own needs and desires, while true in the abstract, is subject to many limitations in the concrete. Men cannot always, in civilized society, be allowed to use their own property as their interests or desires may dictate without reference to the fact that they have neighbors whose rights are as sacred as their own. The existence and well-being of society requires that each and every person shall conduct himself consistently with the fact that he is a social and reasonable person. The purpose for which a man is using his own property may thus sometimes determine his rights . . . .

. . . In Plant v. Woods, 176 Mass. 492, 57 N.E. 1011, 51 L. R. A. 339, 79 Am. St. Rep. 330, Mr. Justice Hammond said: "It is said, also, that, where one has the lawful right to do a thing, the motive by which he is actuated is immaterial. One form of this statement appears in the first headnote in Allen v. Flood, as reported in [1898] A. C. 1, as follows: 'An act lawful in itself is not converted by a malicious or bad motive into an unlawful act, so as to make the doer of the act liable to a civil action.' If the meaning of this and similar expressions is that, where a person has the lawful right to do a thing irrespective of his motive, his motive is immaterial, the proposition is a mere truism. If, however, the meaning is that where a person, if actuated by one kind of a motive, has a lawful right to do a thing, the act is lawful when done under any conceivable motive, or that an act lawful under one set of circumstances is therefore lawful under every conceivable set of circumstances, the proposition does not commend itself to us as either logically or legally accurate." Similar language was used by Mr. Justice Wells in Walker v. Cronin, 107 Mass. 555; by Lord Coleridge in Mogul Steamship Co. v. McGregor, 21 Q. B. D. 544-533. . . .

It is freely conceded that there are many decisions contrary to this view; but, when carried to the extent contended for by the appellant, we think they are unsafe, unsound, and illy adapted to modern conditions. To divert to one's self the customers of a business rival by the offer of goods at lower prices is in general a legitimate mode of serving one's own interest, and justifiable as fair competition. But when a man starts an opposition place of business, not for the sake of profit to himself, but regardless of loss to himself, and for the sole purpose of driving his competitor out of business, and with the intention of himself retiring upon the accomplishment of his malevolent purpose, he is guilty of a wanton wrong and an actionable tort. In such a case he would not be exercising his legal right, or doing an act which can be judged separately from the motive which actuated him. To call such conduct competition is a perversion of terms. It is simply the application of force without legal justification, which in its moral quality may be no better than highway robbery.

Nevertheless, in the opinion of the writer this complaint is insufficient. It is not claimed that it states a cause of action for slander. No question of conspiracy or combination is involved. Stripped of the adjectives and the statement that what was done was for the sole purpose of injuring the plaintiff, and not for the purpose of serving a legitimate purpose of the defendant, the complaint states facts which in themselves amount only to an ordinary everyday business transaction. There is no allegation that the defendant was intentionally running the business at a financial loss to himself, or that after driving the plaintiff out of business the defendant closed up or intended to close up his shop. From all that appears from the complaint he may have opened the barber shop, energetically sought business from his acquaintances and the customers of the plaintiff, and as a result of his enterprise and command of capital obtained it, with the result that the plaintiff, from want of capital, acquaintance, or enterprise, was unable to stand the competition and was thus driven out of business. The facts thus alleged do not, in my opinion, in themselves, without reference to the way in which they are characterized by the pleader, tend to show a malicious and wanton wrong to the plaintiff.

A majority of the Justices, however, are of the opinion that, on the principle declared in the foregoing opinion, the complaint states a cause of action, and the order is therefore affirmed.

Affirmed.

JAGGARD, J., dissents.

COMMENTS AND QUESTIONS

1. In *Tuttle*, Justice Elliott states that the plaintiff did not "state a cause of action for slander," and that he did not allege "that the defendant was intentionally running the business at a financial loss to himself." Slander, of course, would be an actionable tort in its own right.[3] And under modern-day antitrust law, pricing below cost can under some circumstances constitute predatory pricing in violation of section 2 of the Sherman Act (although those circumstances would not, by any stretch of the imagination, have been present in *Tuttle v. Buck*). Moreover, it seems unlikely that the defendant induced anyone to breach a contract with the plaintiff; people don't normally enter into long-term contracts with their barbers. Thus, the cause of action at issue in this case is not tortious interference with *contract*, but rather what has come to be known as tortious interference with prospective economic advantage.

2. What exactly is the holding of *Tuttle v. Buck*? Do a majority of the justices believe that the plaintiff stated a claim upon which relief may be granted, or not? Does *Tuttle* stand for the proposition that a defendant's act of competing against the plaintiff, though otherwise lawful, can be rendered unlawful due to the defendant's motive of malice or ill will toward the plaintiff?

To the extent this interpretation is correct, does it make sense? Suppose that in a neighboring town another wealthy banker had funded another barber shop to compete against the only barber in *that* town; but that the second banker's motivation was that the incumbent barber simply wasn't doing an adequate job cutting the townsfolk's hair. (In the words of the fictional Vito Corleone, "it's nothing personal, just business.") The fictional banker would escape liability, whereas the real-world banker did not, even though the *effect* of their conduct—driving the incumbent barber in their respective towns out of business—appears to be precisely the same.

3. The court twice notes that, according to the complaint, the defendant's *only* motive for setting up a competing barber shop was to injure the plaintiff. *See Tuttle*, 119 N.W. at 147 (according to the complaint, "all of said things were and are done by defendant with the sole design of injuring the plaintiff"); *id.* at 151 ("when a man starts an opposition place of business . . . for the sole purpose of driving his competitor out of business, and with the intention of himself retiring upon the accomplishment of his malevolent purpose, he is guilty of a wanton wrong and an actionable tort"). The phrasing would suggest that, in a case in which the defendant was motivated even in

3. The complaint *does* state that the defendant had sought "by false and malicious reports and accusations of and concerning the plaintiff . . . to induce . . . patrons to withhold from plaintiff the employment by them formerly given," but apparently this barebones allegation wasn't adequate under the code pleading rules of 1909.

part by the desire to serve his own economic interest, and not exclusively by ill will toward the plaintiff, he would escape liability (unless his conduct was independently tortious or criminal, or induced a breach of contract). As you can imagine, courts that take this language at face value have been hard pressed to find many real-world instances in which the defendant's conduct was motivated exclusively by ill will. *See* RESTATEMENT (THIRD) OF UNFAIR COMPETITION, § 1 cmt. c. Alternatively, though, as we will see some courts phrase the inquiry as whether the defendant's *predominant* motive was ill will or spite (as opposed to the defendant's own economic self-interest). This alternative phrasing, if taken seriously, suggests that courts somehow must weigh a defendant's subjective motivations to determine which one dominates. Are courts well positioned to make this sort of inquiry?

Another possibility would be to impose as an additional requirement proof that the defendant intended to cease doing business after the plaintiff went out of business. *See, e.g.*, Dunshee v. Standard Oil Co., 132 N.W. 371, 375 (1911) ("If . . . there was no real purpose or desire to establish a competing business, but, under the guise or pretense of competition, to accomplish a malicious purpose to ruin [plaintiff's company] or drive it out of business, intending themselves to retire therefrom when their end had been secured, then they can claim no immunity under the rules of law which recognize and protect competition between dealers in the same line of business seeking in good faith the patronage of the same people"); RESTATEMENT OF TORTS, § 709. According to Justice Elliott, the plaintiff made no such allegation in *Tuttle v. Buck*. Would the addition of such a requirement eliminate the risk of discouraging new entrants from competing against incumbents?

4. In *Tuttle v. Buck*, the defendant's conduct toward the plaintiff was clearly (alleged to be) intentional. Other cases have had to address the question of whether a tortious interference plaintiff must plead and prove that the defendant acted intentionally, or whether merely *negligent* conduct can give rise to liability for causing a breach of contract or the breaking off of advantageous economic relations. Almost all courts follow the rule that intent is an element of a claim for tortious interference with contract. *See, e.g.*, Fifield Manor v. Finston, 354 P.2d 1073 (Cal. 1960); Witte Transp. Co. v. Murphy Motor Freight Lines, Inc., 193 N.W.2d 148 (Minn. 1971). A few jurisdictions, however, including California, permit claims to go forward for negligent interference with prospective business advantage. *See* J'Aire Corp. v. Gregory, 598 P.2d 60 (Cal. 1979). In these latter jurisdictions, the tort to some extent overrules the common law economic loss rule, doesn't it? *See* Daniel London, *Is the Economic Loss Rule in Peril?*, 71 DEF. COUNSEL J., 379 (2004); Robert L. Rabin, *Tort Recovery for Negligently Inflicted Economic Loss: A Reassessment*, 37 STAN. L. REV. 1513 (1985). Is there any defensible rationale for permitting claims to go forward for negligent interference with prospective business advantage, but not for negligent interference with contract?

5. The defendant in *Tuttle*, Cassius M. Buck, was a prominent Minnesota banker and politician. From 1903 to 1905, Buck served as state senator representing Faribault (pronounced "FAIR-boh"), a town about 50 miles south of Minneapolis-St. Paul, where he had an elegant home. Earlier in his career, Buck had organized a bank in Howard Lake, a small town about 80 miles northwest of Faribault. Apparently Buck retained his business connections with Howard Lake, where plaintiff Tuttle had his barber shop in the early twentieth century. Exactly what lay at the root of the feud between barber Tuttle and banker Buck, however, remains a mystery.

Katz v. Kapper

44 P.2d 1060 (1935)

SHINN, Justice pro tem.

This is an appeal by plaintiff from a judgment in favor of defendants after an order sustaining a demurrer to the complaint.

Plaintiff and defendants were rival wholesale fish dealers in the city of Los Angeles. The defendants Kapper, Isenberg, Baker, and Simon comprised a single firm doing business under the name of "Central Market." The action is for damages alleged to have been sustained to plaintiff's business by reason of the acts of defendants, and for exemplary damages. The complaint alleges that plaintiff had a well-established wholesale fish business, the good will of which was valuable; that with the sole intention "to put the plaintiff out of business, ruin him, deprive him of his customers and custom, and to take away from him all of his business and trade, together with the good will, without any benefit to themselves," the defendants maliciously called meetings of the customers of plaintiff, threatened them that they would be driven out of business and ruined if they continued to purchase fish from plaintiff, but promised that if they purchased fish from defendants, they would be given substantial reductions in price, so that they could successfully compete with plaintiff and drive him out of business; that if said customers continued to buy from plaintiff, the defendants would open a retail store and would sell fish to the customers of plaintiff's customers at such low prices that plaintiff's customers would be driven out of business. It was further alleged that the defendants did open such a store, did widely advertise and sell fish at lower prices than either plaintiff or defendants could purchase the same, and at a loss to the defendants; that all of said acts were done for the purpose of driving plaintiff out of business; and that as a result thereof "a considerable number of said retailers and peddlers and customers ceased from doing business with plaintiff and made their purchases from these defendants to plaintiff's damage," etc.

To this complaint, defendants interposed a general and special demurrer, which was sustained by the court, and plaintiff declining to amend, judgment of dismissal was entered. The general demurrer presents the questions whether the purposes of the defendants were unlawful, and, if lawful, whether they were sought to be accomplished by unlawful means. . . .

There are cases relied upon by appellant, of which Dunshee v. Standard Oil Co., 152 Iowa, 618, 132 N.W. 371, 36 L.R.A. (N.S.) 263, is a leading one, in which interference with business is held actionable. In that case, the defendant pursued a policy of selling gasoline and oil to plaintiff's customers from tank wagons purchased and used solely for that purpose, initiating the practice for the purpose of driving the plaintiff out of business, and with the intention of discontinuing it when such purpose was accomplished. An action was held to lie because the object of the defendant was not to engage in real competition or to build up its own business but to ruin a business rival. The cases that follow this doctrine proceed on the theory that an act lawful in itself becomes unlawful if induced by a wrong motive. This principle is not generally recognized by English or American authorities. In California the Supreme Court in Boyson v. Thorn, 98 Cal. 578, 33 P. 492, 21 L.R.A. 233, adopted the rule that an act lawful in itself does not become unlawful because of a malicious or wrongful motive. People v. Schmitz, 7 Cal. App. 330, 94 P. 407, 419, 15 L.R.A. (N.S.) 717, and *Parkinson Co. v. Building Trades Council*, supra, follow this principle. We may apply either rule to the facts of the present case with the same result because they both recognize the principle that detriment to business which is incidental to lawful competition is damnum absque injuria.

It very clearly appears from the allegations of the complaint that the primary purpose of the defendants was to acquire for themselves the business of plaintiff's customers, and that the detriment which would result to plaintiff's business from the accomplishment of defendants' purpose was incidental thereto. This view must be taken of the complaint, notwithstanding the allegation that the sole purpose was to drive plaintiff out of business. The defendants are not charged with making any effort to deprive plaintiff of his trade except by transferring the same to themselves. This is essentially business competition. The defendants did or threatened to do nothing other than to gain a business advantage proportionate to the losses sustained by plaintiff, and by the accomplishment of that end their purposes would have been satisfied. It cannot be said that the methods used by the defendants were unlawful. They threatened plaintiff's customers with the ruination of their businesses if they continued to trade with plaintiff, but a threat is not unlawful if it is to do a lawful thing. . . .

The threats alleged in general terms are identified and particularized by the allegations that the defendants threatened to and did undersell the plaintiff and his customers at retail prices less than the wholesale prices at which the commodities could be purchased. These must be taken as the only acts of coercion either threatened or done, since no others are alleged. They were not unlawful nor were they committed in an unlawful manner. They related solely to the aims of the defendants to engage in business competition with plaintiff for the resulting business advantage to themselves. The fact that the methods used were ruthless, or unfair, in a moral sense, does not stamp them as illegal. It has never been regarded as the duty or province of the courts to regulate practices in the business world beyond the point of applying legal or equitable remedies in cases involving acts of oppression or deceit which are unlawful. Any extension of this jurisdiction must come through legislative action. In this case no questions of statutory law are involved. The alleged acts of defendants do not fall within the category of business methods recognized as unlawful, and hence they are not actionable. The demurrer to the complaint was properly sustained.

The judgment is affirmed.

Imperial Ice Co. v. Rossier
112 P.2d 631 (1941)

TRAYNOR, Justice.

The California Consumers Company purchased from S.L. Coker an ice distributing business, inclusive of good will, located in territory comprising the city of Santa Monica and the former city of Sawtelle. In the purchase agreement Coker contracted as follows: "I do further agree in consideration of said purchase and in connection therewith, that I will not engage in the business of selling and or distributing ice, either directly or indirectly, in the above described territory so long as the purchasers, or anyone deriving title to the good will of said business from said purchasers, shall be engaged in a like business therein." Plaintiff, the Imperial Ice Company, acquired from the successor in interest of the California Consumers Company full title to this ice distributing business, including the right to enforce the covenant not to compete. Coker subsequently began selling in the same territory in violation of the contract ice supplied to him by a company owned by W. Rossier, J. A. Matheson, and Fred Matheson. Plaintiff thereupon brought this action in the superior court for an injunction to restrain Coker from violating the contract and to restrain Rossier and the Mathesons from inducing Coker to violate the contract. The complaint alleges that Rossier and the Mathesons induced Coker to violate his contract so that they might sell ice to him at a profit. The trial court sustained without leave to amend a demurrer to the complaint of the defendants Rossier and Matheson and gave judgment for those defendants. Plaintiff has appealed from the judgment on the sole ground that the complaint stated a cause of action against the defendants Rossier and the Mathesons for inducing the breach of contract.

The question thus presented to this court is under what circumstances may an action be maintained against a defendant who has induced a third party to violate a contract with the plaintiff.

It is universally recognized that an action will lie for inducing breach of contract by resort to means in themselves unlawful such as libel, slander, fraud, physical violence, or threats of such action. . . .

Such justification exists when a person induces a breach of contract to protect an interest which has greater social value than insuring the stability of the contract. RESTAT. TORTS, sec. 767. Thus, a person is justified in inducing the breach of a contract the enforcement of which would be injurious to health, safety, or good morals. The interest of labor in improving working conditions is of sufficient social importance to justify peaceful labor tactics otherwise lawful, though they have the effect of inducing breaches of contracts between employer and employee or employer and customer. In numerous other situations, justification exists (see RESTAT. TORTS, secs. 766 to 774) depending upon the importance of the interest protected. The presence or absence of ill-will, sometimes referred to as "malice," is immaterial, except as it indicates whether or not an interest is actually being protected.

It is well established, however, that a person is not justified in inducing a breach of contract simply because he is in competition with one of the parties to the contract and seeks to further his own economic advantage at the expense of the other. Whatever interest society has in encouraging free and open competition by means not in themselves unlawful, contractual stability is generally accepted as of greater importance than competitive freedom. Competitive freedom, however, is of sufficient importance to justify one competitor in inducing a third party to forsake another competitor if no contractual relationship exists between the latter two. Katz v. Kapper, 7 Cal. App. 2d 1, 44 P.2d 1060. A person is likewise free to carry on his business, including reduction of prices, advertising, and solicitation in the usual lawful manner although some third party may be induced thereby to breach his contract with a competitor in favor of dealing with the advertiser. Again, if two parties have separate contracts with a third, each may resort to any legitimate means at his disposal to secure performance of his contract even though the necessary result will be to cause a breach of the other contract. A party may not, however, under the guise of competition actively and affirmatively induce the breach of a competitor's contract in order to secure an economic advantage over that competitor. The act of inducing the breach must be an intentional one. If the actor had no knowledge of the existence of the contract or his actions were not intended to induce a breach, he cannot be held liable though an actual breach results from his lawful and proper acts.

In California the case of *Boyson v. Thorn* has been considered by many as establishing the proposition that no action will lie in this state for inducing breach of contract by means which are not otherwise unlawful. In that case the manager of a hotel induced the owner of the hotel to evict plaintiffs in violation of a contract. The complaint expressly alleged the existence of malicious motives on the part of the manager. This court affirmed a judgment entered on an order which sustained a demurrer without leave to amend, stating that an act otherwise lawful was not rendered unlawful by the existence of "malice." It is clear that the confidential relationship which existed between the manager of the hotel and the owner justified the manager in advising the owner to violate his contract with plaintiffs. His conduct thus being justified, it was lawful despite the existence of ill-will or malice on his part. The statements to the effect that no interference with contractual relations is actionable if the means employed are otherwise lawful were not necessary to the decision and should be disregarded. . . . The case of Katz v. Kapper, 7 Cal. App. 2d 1, 44 P.2d 1060, 1061, relied upon by defendants, held only that a person by the use of lawful means could interfere with advantageous business relationships of a competitor by inducing customers to trade with him instead. The case did not involve a breach of contract, and the court specifically stated: "In deciding whether the conduct of defendants alleged in the complaint is actionable, it is necessary to apply certain well-settled rules relating to competition in business. These may be generally stated as follows: 'Competition in business, though carried to the extent of ruining a rival, is not ordinarily actionable, but every trader is left to conduct his business in his own way, so long as the methods he employs do not involve wrongful conduct such as fraud, misrepresentation, intimidation, coercion, obstruction, or molestation of the rival or his servants or workmen, *or the procurement of the violation of contractual relations. . . .*' " (Italics added.) In California, therefore, an action will lie for unjustifiably inducing a breach of contract.

The complaint in the present case alleges that defendants actively induced Coker to violate his contract with plaintiffs so that they might sell ice to him.

The contract gave to plaintiff the right to sell ice in the stated territory free from the competition of Coker. The defendants, by virtue of their interest in the sale of ice in that territory, were in effect competing with plaintiff. By inducing Coker to violate his contract, as alleged in the complaint, they sought to further their own economic advantage at plaintiff's expense. Such conduct is not justified. Had defendants merely sold ice to Coker without actively inducing him to violate his contract, his distribution of the ice in the forbidden territory in violation of his contract would not then have rendered defendants liable. They may carry on their business of selling ice as usual without incurring liability for breaches of contract by their customers. It is necessary to prove that they intentionally and actively induced the breach. Since the complaint alleges that they did so and asks for in injunction on the grounds that damages would be inadequate, it states a cause of action, and the demurrer should therefore have been overruled.

The judgment is reversed.

COMMENTS AND QUESTIONS

1. *Katz v. Kapper* holds that intentionally causing customers to transfer business from the plaintiff to the defendants is permissible, even though the defendants know that plaintiff will suffer financial injury as a result, and even if the defendants' methods are "ruthless, or unfair, in a moral sense." Competition, therefore, appears to be a valid justification for interfering with another's prospective business advantage, at least

where the means employed are not independently unlawful. (In a sense, it would be hard to imagine the rule being otherwise in a mostly capitalist economy, wouldn't it?) In *Katz*, did it matter that the defendants' "primary purpose . . . was to acquire for themselves the business of plaintiff's customers," or would the case have come out the same way even if the plaintiff could have proven that the defendants' primary (or sole?) motivation was ill will towards the plaintiff? Didn't the plaintiff allege that this was their motivation? Was it proper to dismiss the action on the pleadings, or is the court implicitly rejecting the rule from *Tuttle v. Buck*?

2. *Imperial Ice*, by contrast, flatly says that competition generally is *not* a valid justification for inducing a breach of contract—though there might be some justifications, such as inducing the breach of a contract the enforcement of which would be injurious to health or safety, or incident to peaceful labor tactics—that would suffice. More generally, Justice Traynor says that the means employed by the defendant are less relevant to claims for tortious interference with contract than to tortious interference with prospective business advantage. Under Justice Traynor's approach, even the use of otherwise lawful means to induce a breach of contract is generally not permitted, though such means probably would privilege merely interfering with prospective business relations. Subsequent case law tends to agree. *See, e.g.*, Della Penna v. Toyota Motor Sales, U.S.A., Inc., 902 P.2d 740, 750-51 (Cal. 1995); Guard-Life Corp. v. S. Parker Hardware Mfg. Corp., 406 N.E.2d 445, 448-49 (N.Y. 1980). *But see* Jesse Max Creed, Note, *Integrating Preliminary Agreements into the Interference Torts*, 110 Colum. L. Rev. 1253, 1260-61 (2010) (noting that some jurisdictions may still require plaintiff to prove that the interference with contract was improper, beyond the fact of the interference itself). Does this divergence between the two branches of the tort make sense, because of the need for stability in contractual relationships? What about the efficient breach theory? See the Note on the Economics of Tortious Interference at the end of this section.

Note that the contract with which the defendant unlawfully interfered in *Imperial Ice* was a covenant not to compete. As you learned in a preceding chapter, California courts generally don't enforce noncompetes except in connection with the sale of a business (as in *Imperial Ice*). If the underlying contract had been void, would it still have been unlawful for the defendant to interfere with it?

3. At this point, it probably would be helpful more formally to enumerate the elements of a claim for tortious interference. In a typical jurisdiction, these elements are: (1) the existence of a contract, or prospective business relations, between the plaintiff and another; (2) the defendant knowingly and intentionally (3) caused either the plaintiff or (more commonly) the other person to breach the contract or forgo the prospective relations, or caused the plaintiff's performance to be more expensive or burdensome that it otherwise would have been; (4) the defendant acted improperly (without justification, without privilege); and (5) the plaintiff suffered actual damages as a result.

As for element (1), as we've seen the law doesn't necessarily require there to be an existing contract between the plaintiff and another; inducing a termination of reasonably certain business relations is good enough if all the other elements are met. How "reasonably certain" the relations must be, however, may vary somewhat from one court to another. *Compare* Day Distributing Co. v. Nantucket Allserve, Inc., No. 07-CV-1132 (PJS/RLE), 2008 WL 2945442, at *9 (D. Minn. July 25, 2008) (granting summary judgment to defendant, where "plaintiffs do not identify any existing or prospective contracts with any specificity"), *with* Rainforest Café, Inc. v. Amazon,

Inc., 86 F. Supp. 2d 886, 908 (D. Minn. 1999) (stating that, although counterclaimant presented no evidence that counterclaim defendant "was aware of the specific prospective contractual relationship with which it allegedly interfered . . . a genuine issue of fact exists as to whether the [counterclaim defendant] was 'substantially certain' that investors, formerly predisposed to finance the [counterclaimant] would abandon such designs upon learning of the [counterclaim defendant's] expansion").

Can a defendant be liable for causing another to terminate a contract at will? *See* Speakers of Sport, Inc. v. ProServ, Inc., 178 F.3d 862, 865 (7th Cir. 1999) (yes, under the same conditions that a defendant could be liable for interfering with prospective business advantage); Guard-Life Corp. v. S. Parker Hardware Mfg. Corp., 406 N.E.2d 445, 450-51 (N.Y. 1980); RESTATEMENT (SECOND) OF TORTS § 766 cmt. g. What about a contract that is voidable for a reason such as noncompliance with the statute of frauds? Again, many courts say yes. *See, e.g.*, Harris v. Perl, 197 A.2d 359, 363 (N.J. 1964); RESTATEMENT (SECOND) OF TORTS, § 766 cmt. f ("The defendant actor is not . . . free to interfere with performance of the contract before it is avoided"). *Cf.* Northern Plumbing & Heating, Inc. v. Henderson Bros., 268 N.W.2d 296, 299 (Mich. App. 1978) (noting a division of authority). Should interference with voidable contracts be analyzed as interferences with prospective economic advantage?

How should courts deal with interferences with "preliminary agreements" (that is, agreements to negotiate towards a final agreement)? For an interesting discussion, see Jesse Max Creed, Note, *Integrating Preliminary Agreements into the Interference Torts*, 110 COLUM. L. REV. 1253 (2010) (proposing that courts analyze such instances as analogous to interferences with at-will contracts; require proof of an independent wrong; and award only reliance, not expectation, damages). Creed argues, accordingly, that the case of Texaco, Inc. v. Pennzoil Co., 729 S.W.2d 768 (Tex. App. 1987)—in which a jury found that Texaco induced Getty Oil to accept a takeover bid from Texaco after having in principle agreed to a merger with Pennzoil, and awarded Pennzoil an $11 *billion* judgment—should have resulted in a much smaller damages award. Creed also notes that, in the wake of *Texaco*, firms involved in M & A negotiations often include a "Texaco clause" stating their intent not to be legally bound by the terms of a preliminary agreement.

4. To satisfy the knowledge element, the plaintiff must prove that the defendant was aware of the existence of the contract or business relations, and that the defendant knew or should have known that his conduct was likely to cause them to terminate. RESTATEMENT (SECOND) OF TORTS, § 766 cmts. k, l; *id.* § 767 cmt. d. In addition, and as noted above, in most but not all states the defendant must intend for the breach or breaking off of business relations to occur. *See id.* § 766B cmt. d (stating that "[t]he interference with the other's prospective contractual relation is intentional if the actor desires to bring it about or if he knows that the interference is certain or substantially certain to occur as a result of his action").

As for causation, the plaintiff must prove that the defendant's conduct was both the cause-in-fact and the proximate cause of the breach of contract or forgoing of prospective relations. *See, e.g.*, Super Future Equities, Inc. v. Wells Fargo Bank Minn., N.A., 553 F. Supp. 2d 680, 694 (N.D. Tex. 2008) (citations omitted); RESTATEMENT (SECOND) OF TORTS, § 767 cmt. h.

5. *Without Justification (Privilege).* As we've seen, competition generally is a justifiable reason for interfering with prospective business advantage; it is not for interfering with contract. Beyond these rules, determining what counts as a

justification or privilege, and who has the burden of pleading and proving it, is subject to wide variation among jurisdictions.

One possibility would be to place the burden of pleading and proving justification/privilege on the *defendant* in all cases. (This would be analogous to the practice followed by some states of presuming actual malice, and thus requiring the defendant to prove an applicable privilege, upon the plaintiff's pleading of the standard five elements of a common law commercial disparagement claim discussed *supra* in Chapter 9.) This is sometimes referred to as the "prima facie" tort approach. One consequence of this approach, however, is that everyday competition — under which one firm attracts customers away from another by offering those customers a better deal — is prima facie tortious. Of course, this doesn't mean that lawful competition is illegal, even in prima facie tort states. Under cases such as *Katz v. Kapper*, the defendant could successfully plead and prove the competitor's privilege. Nevertheless, it has long struck many observers as odd — and potentially subject to anticompetitive abuse — that competition can be even prima facie tortious. *See, e.g.*, Della Penna v. Toyota Motor Sales, U.S.A., Inc., 902 P.2d 740, 744-45 (Cal. 1995); Zechariah Chafee, Jr., *Unfair Competition*, 53 HARV. L. REV. 1289, 1304 (1940). Relatively few jurisdictions follow this approach today.

At the other end of the spectrum, one could require the *plaintiff* to plead and prove a lack of justification or privilege in every case. The question then arises what this means. Does the plaintiff have to prove a lack of justification under some sort of totality of the circumstances standard? Or can the plaintiff's burden be made more predictable in its operation? If so, might there still be some specific privileges that the defendant could come forward with in an appropriate case? Excerpts from the following two cases may be helpful in guiding your thinking on these issues.

Leigh Furniture & Carpet Co. v. Isom

657 P.2d 293 (1982)

OAKS, Justice:

In 1970, Leigh Furniture and Carpet Co., a corporation, sold a furniture business in St. George to T. Richard Isom on a contract specifying a $20,000 down payment for immediate possession, with the balance of $60,000 at $500 per month plus interest for ten years.

In 1975, when the contract balance was $27,000, Leigh Furniture (hereafter "the Leigh Corporation") brought this action against Isom to repossess the business, terminate his interest under the contract, and obtain a deficiency judgment for any sums due after liquidation. Isom denied that he was in default under the agreement, alleged his tender and the Leigh Corporation's refusal to accept the sum due under the contract, and counterclaimed for $100,000 damages caused when the Corporation intentionally and maliciously forced him out of business and into bankruptcy. Isom also sought punitive damages.

The jury found for Isom in all respects, including compensatory damages of $65,000 and punitive damages. . . .

The issues on this appeal are exclusively concerned with Isom's recovery on the counterclaim. They are: (1) whether Utah has a cause of action for intentional interference with prospective economic relations; and, if so, (2) whether that tort was proved on the facts of this case. . . .

Leigh Furniture, a closely held family corporation, operated a main store in Cedar City and branch stores in Kanab and St. George. The principal owner and chief executive officer was W.S. "Dub" Leigh (hereafter "Leigh"). In 1969, Leigh decided to sell the St. George store. He contacted T. Richard Isom ("Isom"), a Utah native then living in Washington State but desirous of returning to Utah, as a possible buyer. Discussions ensued, and Isom moved to St. George and began working as an employee in the Leigh store. On May 14, 1970, Isom signed the contract to buy the St. George store from the Leigh Corporation. Isom agreed to maintain the inventory, together with cash and accounts receivable, at a level of at least $60,000, and to provide the Leigh Corporation with an inventory each quarter and a financial statement each month. . . .

For one year, relations between the contracting parties were peaceful, but in June and July of 1971, Leigh began to complain about the contract and to state that he wanted to sell the entire building but prospective buyers would not purchase it subject to Isom's long-term lease and option to buy. In a letter to Isom, Leigh complained that Isom was in default on his payments and was allowing his inventory to drop below $60,000. (Isom was behind in his payments at that time but was within the 60-day grace period in the contract and therefore was not in default.) At that same time, Leigh visited Isom in the store, verbally attacking him while he was with a customer and causing the customer to leave the store.

Beginning in July, 1971, Leigh, his wife, and the Corporation's bookkeeper, acting as the Leigh Corporation's agents, began a continuous pattern of visiting Isom at least once a week while he was working in his store, questioning him concerning his operation of the business, and making demands and accusations. In addition to the visits, Leigh wrote defendant letters criticizing various aspects of the business. In one week in the summer of 1971, Isom received four letters from Leigh, his wife, and his bookkeeper complaining about the furnace, the heat, and the delay in receiving the monthly financial statements. All of this conduct on Leigh's part had the cumulative effect of demoralizing and upsetting Isom and his employees, reducing their productivity, and impairing their ability to deal with the public and to conduct their business. At the same time, despite the existing contract with Isom, Leigh attempted to sell the building to two of Isom's employees.

[The opinion goes on to recount Leigh's alleged harassment of Isom. According to the court, over the next three and a half years, Leigh repeatedly visited the store, questioned Isom, made abusive demands, and embarrassed Isom in front of customers; refused to allow Isom to select the business partner Isom wanted, then refused to allow Isom to enter into a contract with the partner Leigh had recommended; and filed two frivolous lawsuits against Isom.]

On February 24, 1975, without notifying Isom of any default, Leigh filed the complaint in this case, seeking to repossess the premises and terminate Isom's interest under the contract. Three days later, unaware that the complaint had been filed, Isom tendered to Leigh the $27,000 balance due. He requested that Leigh give a receipt for the payment, appoint an appraiser to facilitate his exercise of the purchase option, and approve Brent Talbot as his business associate under the existing lease if the purchase of the building were not accomplished.

Isom learned of the lawsuit before he was served with process. Though demoralized, he nevertheless continued to negotiate with Leigh and to operate the business through February, 1975. Leigh never responded to Isom's tender of the remaining $27,000, although he again told Isom's attorney that he would never approve Talbot's association with Isom under the long-term lease, even for the few months required to finance a purchase of the building, nor would he permit a sale of the property for its appraised value of $130,000. When confronted by Isom's attorney and accused of being recalcitrant so that Isom's business would fail and Leigh could reacquire the business and property, Leigh made no denial.

In March, 1975, while talking to a customer in his store, Isom was served with Leigh's complaint. This service of process despite his continuing efforts to negotiate, surprised and upset Isom so much that he dismissed the customer he had been helping. Upon reading the complaint, he noted that it appeared to be the same complaint Leigh had threatened to file in 1972 and that it reopened the disputes which the supplemental agreement and the prepayment of $20,000 had been intended to resolve. Because of the complaint's prayer for an order restraining Isom from doing further business until an audit could be conducted to determine if he was maintaining adequate security for the $27,000 balance, Isom concluded he could do no further business. He therefore closed the store immediately after being served. Within the next week, Isom's suppliers contacted him to request return of their furniture. Isom replied that at that time he was unable to determine whether he would remain in business, but that he could not release any of his inventory until the dispute with Leigh was finally resolved. Isom declared bankruptcy shortly thereafter.

At trial, there was expert testimony that the value of Isom's leasehold was $45,000, and the net value of Isom's furniture retailing business as of March, 1975, was $59,300. Isom testified that he paid the Leigh Corporation a total of $53,000 plus interest on the total $80,000 purchase price, none of which he recouped. He further testified that because of his bankruptcy he was never able to exercise his option to purchase the building. The record further indicates that through bankruptcy proceedings, the Leigh Corporation, as secured party, finally achieved its goal of reacquiring the business, including inventory, accounts receivable, and the leased premises.

II. Interference with Contract

Leigh Furniture first contends that Isom's recovery cannot be sustained as an interference with contract because the evidence showed no conduct which "intentionally and improperly interferes with the performance of a contract . . . between another and a third person by inducing or otherwise causing the third person not to perform the contract." RESTATEMENT (SECOND) OF TORTS § 766 (1979). See also Bunnell v. Bills, 13 Utah 2d 83, 90, 368 P.2d 597, 602 (1962); W. PROSSER, HANDBOOK OF THE LAW OF TORTS § 129 at 929-30 (4th ed. 1971); Annot., 26 A.L.R.2d 1227 (1952). In this case, the only contract in evidence was the contract between Isom and the Leigh Corporation. It is settled that one party to a contract cannot be liable for the tort of interference with contract for inducing a breach by himself or the other contracting party Isom having failed to prove a cause of action for intentional interference with contract, we cannot sustain the verdict on that theory.

However, the right of action for interference with a specific contract is but one instance, rather than the total class, of protections against wrongful interference with advantageous economic relations. We therefore proceed to consider whether the jury's verdict for Isom can be sustained on the basis of the related tort of interference with prospective economic relations.

III. Interference with Prospective Economic Relations

A. History and Elements of the Tort

The tort of intentional interference with prospective economic relations reaches beyond protection of an interest in an existing contract and protects a party's interest in prospective relationships of economic advantage not yet reduced to a formal contract (and perhaps not expected to be). Although previously faced with arguments or circumstances presenting the issue, e.g., Searle v. Johnson, Utah, 646 P.2d 682, 683 (1982); Soter v. Wasatch Development Corp., 21 Utah 2d 224, 443 P.2d 663 (1968), we have never expressly resolved the question of whether Utah recognizes this tort. We now resolve that question, in the affirmative.

The plethora of decided cases and abundant literature on the tort of intentional interference with prospective economic relations has been helpful in our consideration. In summarizing the history of this tort, the *Restatement (Second) of Torts*, ch. 37, "Interference with Contract or Prospective Contractual Relation" (1979), observes that its elements are a curious blend of the principles of liability for intentional torts (in which the plaintiff proves a prima facie case of liability, subject to the defendant's proof of justification) and for negligent torts (in which the plaintiff must prove liability based on the interplay of various factors). The disagreement and confusion incident to this blend of intentional and negligent tort principles has produced two different approaches to the definition of this tort.

Influenced by the model of the intentional tort, many jurisdictions and the first *Restatement of Torts* define the tort of intentional interference with prospective economic relations as a prima facie tort, subject to proof of privilege as an affirmative defense. To recover, the plaintiff need only prove a prima facie case of liability, i.e., that the defendant intentionally interfered with his prospective economic relations and caused him injury. As with other intentional torts, the burden of going forward then shifts to the defendant to demonstrate as an affirmative defense that under the circumstances his conduct, otherwise culpable, was justified and therefore privileged. . . .

The problem with the prima facie-tort approach is that basing liability on a mere showing that defendant intentionally interfered with plaintiff's prospective economic relations makes actionable all sorts of contemporary examples of otherwise legitimate persuasion, such as efforts to persuade others not to eat certain foods, use certain substances, engage in certain activities, or deal with certain entities. The major issue in the controversy—justification for the defendant's conduct—is left to be resolved on the affirmative defense of privilege. In short, the prima facie approach to the tort of interference with prospective economic relations requires too little of the plaintiff.

Under the second approach, which is modeled after other negligent torts, the plaintiff must prove liability based on the interplay of various factors. The *Restatement (Second) of Torts* now defines an actionable interference with prospective economic relations as an interference that is both "intentional" and "improper." Id. at § 766B.[5]

5. One who intentionally and improperly interferes with another's prospective contractual relation (except a contract to marry) is subject to liability to the other for the pecuniary harm resulting from loss of the benefits of the relation, whether the interference consists of

(a) inducing or otherwise causing a third person not to enter into or continue the prospective relation or
(b) preventing the other from acquiring or continuing the prospective relation.

Under this approach, the trier of fact must determine whether the defendant's interference was "improper" by balancing and counterbalancing seven factors, including the interferor's motive, the nature of his conduct and interests, and the nature of the interests with which he has interfered. Id. at §767. In those jurisdictions which have followed the negligence model, the plaintiff bears the burden of proving that in view of all of these factors the defendant's interference was improper. This obviously imposes a very significant burden on the plaintiff and magnifies the difficulty of resolving some contested issues on the pleadings. So far as we have been able to discover, only four states have specifically adopted the *Restatement (Second)* definition of the elements of this tort, though others have apparently applied some portion of the *Restatement* formulation in their own definitions.

In short, there is no generally acknowledged or satisfactory majority position on the definition of the elements of the tort of intentional interference with prospective economic relations. In its historical review, the *Restatement (Second) of Torts* states that "the law in this area has not fully congealed but is still in a formative stage" so that the "several forms of the tort . . . are often not distinguished by the courts, and cases have been cited among them somewhat indiscriminately." Id., Introductory Note to ch. 37 at 5. We concur in the *Restatement (Second)*'s rejection of the prima facie tort approach because it leaves too much uncertainty about the requirements for a recognized privilege and the defendant's burden of pleading and proving these and other matters. Id. But we also reject the *Restatement (Second)*'s definition of the tort because of its complexity. We seek a better alternative.

Oregon has outlined a middle ground by defining the tort of interference with prospective economic relations so as to require the plaintiff to allege and prove more than the prima facie tort, but not to negate all defenses of privilege. Privileges remain as affirmative defenses. This approach originated with Justice Linde's opinion in Top Service Body Shop, Inc. v. Allstate Insurance Co., 283 Or. 201, 582 P.2d 1365 (1978). After summarizing the history of this tort and specifically refusing to require a plaintiff to prove that the interference was "improper" under the balancing-of-factors approach specified in the *Restatement (Second)*, the court defined the cause of action for "wrongful interference with economic relationships" as follows:

> Either the pursuit of an improper objective of harming plaintiff or the use of wrongful means that in fact cause injury to plaintiff's contractual or business relationships may give rise to a tort claim for those injuries. . . . In summary, such a claim is made out when interference resulting in injury to another is wrongful by some measure beyond the fact of the interference itself. Defendant's liability may arise from improper motives or from the use of improper means.

Top Service Body Shop, Inc., 283 Or. at 205, 209, 582 P.2d at 1368, 1371. . . .

We recognize a common-law cause of action for intentional interference with prospective economic relations, and adopt the Oregon definition of this tort. Under this definition, in order to recover damages, the plaintiff must prove (1) that the defendant intentionally interfered with the plaintiff's existing or potential economic relations, (2) for an improper purpose or by improper means, (3) causing injury to the plaintiff. Privilege is an affirmative defense, Searle v. Johnson, Utah, 646 P.2d 682 (1982), which does not become an issue unless "the acts charged would be tortious on the part of an unprivileged defendant." *Top Service Body Shop, Inc.*, 283 Or. at 210, 582 P.2d at 1371. . . .

C. *Evidence of Intentional Interference and Causation*

Reviewing the record, we conclude that there was sufficient evidence to sustain the jury's verdict against the Leigh Corporation for intentional interference with prospective economic relations that caused injury to Isom.

There was ample evidence that Isom had business relationships with various customers, suppliers, and potential business associates, and that Leigh, the former owner of the business, understood the value of those relationships. There was also substantial competent evidence that the Corporation, through Leigh, his wife, and his bookkeeper, intentionally interfered with and caused a termination of some of those relationships (actual or potential). Their frequent visits to Isom's store during business hours to confront him, question him, and make demands and inquiries regarding the manner in which he was conducting his business repeatedly interrupted sales activities, caused his customers to comment and complain, and more than once caused a customer to leave the store. Driving away an individual's existing or potential customers is the archetypical injury this cause of action was devised to remedy. E.g., Guillory v. Godfrey, 134 Cal. App. 2d 628, 286 P.2d 474 (1955); Tuttle v. Buck, 107 Minn. 145, 119 N.W. 946 (1909); W. Prosser, Handbook of the Law of Torts § 130 (4th ed. 1971); Restatement (Second) of Torts § 766B(a).

Other actions by which the Leigh Corporation imposed heavy demands on Isom's time and financial resources to the detriment of his ability to attract and retain customers and conduct the other activities of his business included: numerous letters of complaint, Leigh's demand for an audit of Isom's books and inventory during the busy holiday season, his continued threats to cancel the contract and sell the building and business to another buyer, his refusal to pay the contracted share of the heating bills or the cost of repairing the furnace and the store's broken window, his refusal of the tendered payment of the balance due under the contract, and his suit for repossession, termination, and injunction. Leigh's refusals also prevented Isom from consummating potentially advantageous business associations with Hunter, with Talbot, and finally with Applegate, all experienced retailers able to contribute expertise and additional capital to Isom's business.

Taken in isolation, each of the foregoing interferences with Isom's business might be justified as an overly zealous attempt to protect the Corporation's interests under its contract of sale. As such, none would establish the intentional interference element of this tort, though some might give rise to a cause of action for breach of specific provisions in the contract or of the duty of good faith performance which inheres in every contractual relation. Even in small groups, these acts might be explained as merely instances of aggressive or abrasive — though not illegal or tortious — tactics, excesses that occur in contractual and commercial relationships. But in total and in cumulative effect, as a course of action extending over a period of three and one-half years and culminating in the failure of Isom's business, the Leigh Corporation's acts cross the threshold beyond what is incidental and justifiable to what is tortious. The Corporation's acts provide sufficient evidence to establish two of the elements in the definition of this tort: an intentional interference with present or prospective economic relations that caused injury to the plaintiff.

Focusing on the issue of causation, the Leigh Corporation argues that Isom's losses resulted from his inadequate working capital or from his unilateral decision to close his store immediately after being served with the complaint and to file for bankruptcy shortly thereafter. These arguments are unavailing because there was substantial evidence of causation to support the jury's verdict. For example, the jury could have found that the initiation of this lawsuit was but another instance of the Corporation's ongoing pattern of harassment, which made it impossible for Isom to continue to operate his business with any anticipation of success or profit. The parties had reached an impasse: Leigh had refused to accept Isom's tender of payment in full and had refused to permit Isom to exercise his option to purchase the building or to associate himself with experienced partners. Upon being served with the complaint, Isom could reasonably have concluded that the Corporation's interference and harassment would continue to thwart his commercial efforts for the foreseeable future. On analogous facts, a California court held in a case involving a seller's malicious interference with his buyer's business that "it was reasonable for [the buyer] to have elected to close rather than to continue to accumulate operating expenses without receipts coming in to meet them." Drouet v. Moulton, 245 Cal. App. 2d 667, 54 Cal. Rptr. 278, 282 (1966).

The evidence was also sufficient to support the verdict under the requirement that the intentional interference with prospective economic relations (in this case, Isom's relations with his customers, suppliers, and potential business associates) must have been for an improper purpose or by the use of improper means. These two alternatives are discussed in the next two sections.

D. *Improper Purpose*

The alternative of improper purpose (or motive, intent, or objective) will support a cause of action for intentional interference with prospective economic relations even where the defendant's means were proper. . . .

Because it requires that the improper purpose predominate, this alternative takes the long view of the defendant's conduct, allowing objectionable short-run purposes to be eclipsed by legitimate long-range economic motivation. Otherwise, much competitive commercial activity, such as a businessman's efforts to forestall a competitor in order to further his own long-range economic interests, could become tortious. In the rough and tumble of the marketplace, competitors inevitably damage one another in the struggle for personal advantage. The law offers no remedy for those damages — even if intentional — because they are an inevitable byproduct of competition. Problems inherent in proving motivation or purpose make it prudent for commercial conduct to be regulated for the most part by the improper means alternative, which typically requires only a showing of particular conduct.[9]

The alternative of improper purpose will be satisfied where it can be shown that the actor's predominant purpose was to injure the plaintiff. . . . .

As noted earlier, there is substantial evidence that the Leigh Corporation deliberately injured Isom's economic relations. But that injury was not an end in itself. It was an intermediate step toward achieving the long-range financial goal of profitably reselling the building free of Isom's interest. Because that economic interest seems to have been controlling, we must conclude that the evidence in this case would not

9. On this same point, the *Restatement (Second) of Torts* holds that a competitor's interference with a prospective contractual relation is not improper if, among other things, "his purpose is at least in part to advance his interest in competing with the other." Id. §768(d). . . .

support a jury finding that the Corporation's predominant purpose was to injure or ruin Isom's business merely for the sake of injury alone.

However, because we will affirm the judgment on the general verdict on any ground for which there is substantial factual support in the record, *Berger v. Southern Pacific Co.* and other authorities cited in Part II, supra, we must examine the record to determine whether the verdict can be supported on the basis of the alternative that the Corporation's interference was accomplished by improper means.

E. Improper Means

The alternative requirement of improper means is satisfied where the means used to interfere with a party's economic relations are contrary to law, such as violations of statutes, regulations, or recognized common-law rules. Such acts are illegal or tortious in themselves and hence are clearly "improper" means of interference, Searle v. Johnson, Utah, 646 P.2d 682 (1982) (secondary boycott); Gammon v. Federated Milk Producers Association, Inc., 14 Utah 2d at 295-96, 383 P.2d at 405-06 (1963) (price fixing), unless those means consist of constitutionally protected activity, like the exercise of First Amendment rights. NAACP v. Claiborne Hardware Co., 458 U.S. 886, 102 S. Ct. 3409, 73 L. Ed. 2d 1215 (1982). "Commonly included among improper means are violence, threats or other intimidation, deceit or misrepresentation, bribery, unfounded litigation, defamation, or disparaging falsehood." *Top Service Body Shop, Inc.*, 582 P.2d at 1371 & n.11. Means may also be improper or wrongful because they violate "an established standard of a trade or profession." Id. at 1371.

By forcing Isom to defend what appear to have been two groundless lawsuits, the Leigh Corporation was clearly employing an improper means of interference with Isom's business. Such use of civil litigation as a weapon to damage another's business, besides being an intolerable waste of judicial resources, may give rise to independent causes of action in tort for abuse of process and malicious prosecution. Crease v. Pleasant Grove City, 30 Utah 2d 451, 455, 519 P.2d 888, 890 (1974) (abuse of process); Baird v. Intermountain School Federal Credit Union, Utah, 555 P.2d 877, 878 (1976) (malicious prosecution); Johnson v. Mount Ogden Enterprises, Inc., 23 Utah 2d 169, 169-73, 460 P.2d 333, 334-46 (1969) (malicious prosecution); W. Prosser, Handbook of the Law of Torts §§ 120, 121 (4th ed. 1971). The jury's verdict can therefore be sustained on the ground that the Leigh Corporation intentionally interfered with Isom's economic relations by improper means.

There is also another basis for affirming that verdict on the basis of improper means.

A deliberate breach of contract, even where employed to secure economic advantage, is not, by itself, an "improper means." Because the law remedies breaches of contract with damages calculated to give the aggrieved party the benefit of the bargain, there is no need for an additional remedy in tort (unless the defendant's conduct would constitute a tort independent of the contract).[10]

Neither a deliberate breach of contract nor an immediate purpose to inflict injury which does not predominate over a legitimate economic end will, by itself, satisfy this

10. Likewise, for reasons discussed in the preceding section, a party whose immediate purpose is to inflict injury does not satisfy the element of "improper purpose" so long as the long-range or predominant purpose is to further a legitimate economic end.

element of the tort. However, they may do so in combination. This is so because contract damages provide an insufficient remedy for a breach prompted by an immediate purpose to injure, and that purpose does not enjoy the same legal immunity in the context of contract relations as it does in the competitive marketplace. As a result, a breach of contract committed for the immediate purpose of injurying the other contracting party is an improper means that will satisfy this element of the cause of action for intentional interference with economic relations. . . .

In the case at bar, the Leigh Corporation breached its contract in various ways.

It breached its implied duty to exercise all of its rights under the contract reasonably and in good faith. Cahoon v. Cahoon, Utah, 641 P.2d 140, 144 (1982); Rio Algom Corp. v. Jimco Ltd., Utah, 618 P.2d 497, 505 (1980); Ferris v. Jennings, Utah, 595 P.2d 857, 859 (1979). Leigh's unexplained refusal to approve Isom's prospective business partners without consideration of their merits indicates an absence of good faith and provides evidence that the Corporation's breach was intended to deprive Isom's business of additional capital and valuable expertise which (at least with regard to Talbot) Leigh himself had repeatedly urged Isom to acquire. Similar refusals to approve prospective subtenants under a contract clause in order to injure the tenant's business have been held to constitute tortious interference with economic relations. Homa-Goff Interiors, Inc. v. Cowden, Ala., 350 So. 2d 1035 (1977); Nizzo v. Amoco Oil Co., Fla. Dist. Ct. App., 333 So. 2d 491 (1976). In addition, Leigh, his wife, and his bookkeeper continually interrupted sales activities with their visits, letters, threats, and demands, causing customers to comment and complain and sometimes to leave. Although the contract entitled the Corporation, as lessor and secured party, to reasonable supervision of Isom's business, the jury had sufficient evidence to conclude that this conduct constituted an unreasonable exercise of contract rights and/or was done in bad faith for the purpose of injuring Isom's business relations.

The Corporation also breached its contractual duty by refusing Isom's tender of the balance of the purchase price and by refusing to appoint an appraiser to establish a price for the sale of the entire building, thereby preventing Isom from exercising his purchase option. There is evidence of Leigh's purpose in the fact that he openly regretted his contract with Isom and frequently expressed his desire to "get Richard out" of the business and building. Furthermore, he continually contacted prospective buyers for the building, even approaching two of Isom's employees for this purpose.

All of the above provide substantial evidence from which the jury could have concluded that the Corporation breached its express and implied contractual duties for the purpose of ruining Isom's business and obtaining possession of the building in order to sell it more profitably elsewhere. By themselves, the Corporation's breaches would not satisfy the requirement of "improper means," but they could do so when coupled with the improper purpose of injuring Isom. In combination, a breach of contract and an intent to injure satisfy the improper means requirement for the cause of action for intentional interference with prospective economic relations.

F. *Summary*

In defining the tort of intentional interference with prospective economic relations, we reject the two extremes of the prima facie tort and the balancing-of-factors approach. Instead, we adopt the Oregon definition, under which the plaintiff must prove that the intentional interference with existing or potential economic relations that caused injury to the plaintiff was done for an improper purpose or by improper means. The jury instructions in this case, which in effect required a finding that the Corporation's conduct was "wrongful or malicious," were sufficiently in harmony with this definition to permit the jury to return a verdict under it. There was sufficient evidence of intentional interference and causation.

To satisfy the alternative of improper purpose, the defendant's purpose to injure the plaintiff must predominate over all other purposes, including the long-range purpose of achieving some personal economic gain. Under this definition, the evidence is insufficient to justify a verdict against Leigh Corporation on the basis of improper purpose. Improper means refers primarily to actions that are contrary to law, such as violations of statutes, regulations, or recognized common-law rules. The Leigh Corporation's pursuit of two groundless lawsuits against Isom was an improper means. A deliberate breach of contract for the purpose of injuring the contracting party is also an improper means, and there is also sufficient evidence to sustain the jury's verdict on that basis.

Speakers of Sport, Inc. v. ProServ, Inc.
178 F.3d 862 (1999)

Posner, Chief Judge.

The plaintiff, Speakers of Sport, appeals from the grant of summary judgment to the defendant, ProServ, in a diversity suit in which one sports agency has charged another with tortious interference with a business relationship and related violations of Illinois law. The essential facts, construed as favorably to the plaintiff as the record will permit, are as follows. Ivan Rodriguez, a highly successful catcher with the Texas Rangers baseball team, in 1991 signed the first of several one-year contracts making Speakers his agent. ProServ wanted to expand its representation of baseball players and to this end invited Rodriguez to its office in Washington and there promised that it would get him between $2 and $4 million in endorsements if he signed with ProServ—which he did, terminating his contract (which was terminable at will) with Speakers. This was in 1995. ProServ failed to obtain significant endorsement for Rodriguez and after just one year he switched to another agent who the following year landed him a five-year $42 million contract with the Rangers. Speakers brought this suit a few months later, charging that the promise of endorsements that ProServ had made to Rodriguez was fraudulent and had induced him to terminate his contract with Speakers.

The parties agree that the substantive issues in this diversity suit are governed by Illinois law, and we do not look behind such agreements so long as they are reasonable, Spinozzi v. ITT Sheraton Corp., 174 F.3d 842, 849 (7th Cir. 1999), as this one is. . . .

Speakers could not sue Rodriguez for breach of contract, because he had not broken their contract, which was, as we said, terminable at will. Nor, therefore, could it accuse ProServ of inducing a breach of contract, as in J.D. Edwards & Co. v. Podany, 168 F.3d 1020, 1022 (7th Cir. 1999). But Speakers did have a contract with Rodriguez, and inducing the termination of a contract, even when the termination is not a breach because the contract is terminable at will, can still be actionable under the tort law of Illinois, either as an interference with prospective economic advantage or as an interference with the contract at will itself. Nothing turns on the difference in characterization.

There is in general nothing wrong with one sports agent trying to take a client from another if this can be done without precipitating a breach of contract. That is the process known as competition, which though painful, fierce, frequently ruthless, sometimes Darwinian in its pitilessness, is the cornerstone of our highly successful economic system. Competition is not a tort, Keeble v. Hickeringill, 11 East. 574, 103 Eng. Rep. 1127 (K.B. 1706 or 1707); Frandsen v. Jensen-Sundquist Agency, Inc., 802 F.2d 941, 947 (7th Cir. 1986), but on the contrary provides a defense (the "competitor's privilege") to the tort of improper interference. It does not privilege inducing a breach of contract, Soderlund Bros., Inc. v. Carrier Corp., *supra*, 215 Ill. Dec. 251, 663 N.E.2d at 8 — conduct usefully regarded as a separate tort from interfering with a business relationship without precipitating an actual breach of contract — but it does privilege inducing the lawful termination of a contract that is terminable at will. Sellers (including agents, who are sellers of services) do not "own" their customers, at least not without a contract with them that is not terminable at will. Ingle v. Glamore Motor Sales, Inc., 73 N.Y.2d 183, 538 N.Y.S.2d 771, 535 N.E.2d 1311, 1313-14 (1989).

There would be few more effective inhibitors of the competitive process than making it a tort for an agent to promise the client of another agent to do better by him, Triangle Film Corp. v. Artcraft Pictures Corp., 250 F. 981 (2d Cir. 1918) (L. Hand, J.) — which is pretty much what this case comes down to. It is true that Speakers argues only that the competitor may not make a promise that he knows he cannot fulfill, may not, that is, compete by fraud. Because the competitor's privilege does not include a right to get business from a competitor by means of fraud, it is hard to quarrel with this position in the abstract, but the practicalities are different. If the argument were accepted and the new agent made a promise that was not fulfilled, the old agent would have a shot at convincing a jury that the new agent had known from the start that he couldn't deliver on the promise. Once a case gets to the jury, all bets are off. The practical consequence of Speakers' approach, therefore, would be that a sports agent who lured away the client of another agent with a promise to do better by him would be running a grave legal risk.

This threat to the competitive process is blocked by the principle of Illinois law that promissory fraud is not actionable unless it is part of a scheme to defraud, that is, unless it is one element of a pattern of fraudulent acts. By requiring that the plaintiff show a pattern, by thus not letting him rest on proving a single promise, the law reduces the likelihood of a spurious suit; for a series of unfulfilled promises is better (though of course not conclusive) evidence of fraud than a single unfulfilled promise.

Criticized for vagueness, e.g., *id.* at 1354; Stamatakis Industries, Inc. v. King, 165 Ill. App. 3d 879, 117 Ill. Dec. 419, 520 N.E.2d 770, 772-73 (1987) (and think only of the difficulty that courts have had in defining "pattern" under the RICO statute), and rejected in most states, e.g., Engalla v. Permanente Medical Group, Inc., 15 Cal. 4th 951, 64 Cal. Rptr. 2d 843, 938 P.2d 903, 917 (1997); Palm Harbor Homes, Inc. v. Crawford, 689 So. 2d 3, 9 (Ala. 1997); 2 FOWLER V. HARPER, FLEMING JAMES, JR. & OSCAR S. GRAY, THE LAW OF TORTS § 7.10, p. 447-448 n.19 (2d ed. 1986), the Illinois rule yet makes sense in a case like this, if only as a filter against efforts to use the legal process to stifle competition. Consider in this connection the characterization by Speakers' own chairman of ProServ's promise to Rodriguez as "pure fantasy and gross exaggeration" — in other words, as puffing. Puffing in the usual sense signifies meaningless superlatives that no reasonable person would take seriously, and so it is not actionable as fraud. Noll v. Peterson, 338 Ill. 552, 170 N.E. 756, 761 (1930); Evanston Hospital v. Crane, 254 Ill. App. 3d 435, 193 Ill. Dec. 870, 627 N.E.2d 29, 36 (1993); All-Tech Telecom, Inc. v. Amway Corp., 174 F.3d 862, 867-68

(7th Cir. 1999). Rodriguez thus could not have sued ProServ (and has not attempted to) in respect of the promise of $2-$4 million in endorsements. If Rodriguez thus was not wronged, we do not understand on what theory Speakers can complain that ProServ competed with it unfairly.

The promise of endorsements was puffing not in the most common sense of a cascade of extravagant adjectives but in the equally valid sense of a sales pitch that is intended, and that a reasonable person in the position of the "promisee" would understand, to be aspirational rather than enforceable — an expression of hope rather than a commitment. It is not as if ProServ proposed to employ Rodriguez and pay him $2 million a year. That would be the kind of promise that could found an enforceable obligation. ProServ proposed merely to get him endorsements of at least that amount. They would of course be paid by the companies whose products Rodriguez endorsed, rather than by ProServ. ProServ could not force them to pay Rodriguez, and it is not contended that he understood ProServ to be warranting a minimum level of endorsements in the sense that if they were not forthcoming ProServ would be legally obligated to make up the difference to him.

It is possible to make a binding promise of something over which one has no control; such a promise is called a warranty. But it is not plausible that this is what ProServ was doing — that it was guaranteeing Rodriguez a minimum of $2 million a year in outside earnings if he signed with it. The only reasonable meaning to attach to ProServ's so-called promise is that ProServ would try to get as many endorsements as possible for Rodriguez and that it was optimistic that it could get him at least $2 million worth of them. So understood, the "promise" was not a promise at all. But even if it was a promise (or a warranty), it cannot be the basis for a finding of fraud because it was not part of a scheme to defraud evidenced by more than the allegedly fraudulent promise itself.

It can be argued, however, that competition can be tortious even if it does not involve an actionable fraud (which in Illinois would not include a fraudulent promise) or other independently tortious act, such as defamation, or trademark or patent infringement, or a theft of a trade secret; that competitors should not be allowed to use "unfair" tactics; and that a promise known by the promisor when made to be unfulfillable is such a tactic, especially when used on a relatively unsophisticated, albeit very well to do, baseball player. Considerable support for this view can be found in the case law. But the Illinois courts have not as yet embraced the doctrine, and we are not alone in thinking it pernicious. Della Penna v. Toyota Motor Sales, U.S.A., Inc., 11 Cal. 4th 376, 45 Cal. Rptr. 2d 436, 902 P.2d 740, 760-63 (1995) (concurring opinion). The doctrine's conception of wrongful competition is vague — "wrongful by reason of . . . an established standard of a trade or profession," Yoakum v. Hartford Fire Ins. Co., *supra*, 923 P.2d at 423, or "a violation of recognized ethical rules or established customs or practices in the business community," RTL Distributing, Inc. v. Double S Batteries, Inc., *supra*, 545 N.W.2d at 591, or "improper because they [the challenged competitive tactics] violate an established standard of a trade or profession, or involve unethical conduct, . . . sharp dealing[, or] overreaching." Duggin v. Adams, *supra*, 360 S.E.2d at 837. Worse, the established standards of a trade or profession in regard to competition, and its ideas of unethical competitive conduct, are likely to reflect a desire to limit competition for reasons related to the self-interest of the trade or profession rather than to the welfare of its customers or clients. We agree with Professor Perlman that the tort of interference with business relationships should be confined to cases in which the defendant employed unlawful means to stiff a competitor, Harvey S. Perlman, *"Interference With Contract and Other Economic Expectancies: A Clash of Tort and Contract Doctrine,"* 49 U. Chi. L. Rev. 61 (1982), and we are reassured by the conclusion of his careful analysis that the case law is generally consistent with this position as a matter of outcomes as distinct from articulation.

Invoking the concept of "wrongful by reason of . . . an established standard of a trade or profession," Speakers points to a rule of major league baseball forbidding players' agents to compete by means of misrepresentations. The rule is designed to protect the players, rather than their agents, so that even if it established a norm enforceable by law Speakers would not be entitled to invoke it; it is not a rule designed for Speakers' protection. In any event its violation would not be the kind of "wrongful" conduct that should trigger the tort of intentional interference; it would not be a violation of law. . . .

We add that even if Speakers could establish liability under either the common law of torts or the deceptive practices act, its suit would fail because it cannot possibly establish, as it seeks to do, a damages entitlement (the only relief it seeks) to the agent's fee on Rodriguez's $42 million contract. That contract was negotiated years after he left Speakers, and by another agent. Since Rodriguez had only a year-to-year contract with Speakers-terminable at will, moreover-and since obviously he was dissatisfied with Speakers at least to the extent of switching to ProServ and then when he became disillusioned with ProServ of *not* returning to Speakers' fold, the likelihood that Speakers would have retained him had ProServ not lured him away is too slight to ground an award of such damages. Such an award would be the best example yet of puffing in the pie-in the-sky sense.

AFFIRMED.

COMMENTS AND QUESTIONS

1. In *Leigh Furniture*, the Utah Supreme Court concludes, first, that Isom did not prove an intentional interference with *contract*. Why not?

As for the intentional interference with prospective business advantage claim, the Utah court rejects the *Restatement of Torts* approach to the justification element as being too burdensome. In place of the *Restatement* approach, the court requires the plaintiff to plead and prove either "improper purpose" or "improper means." As for improper purpose, at one portion of the opinion the court states the inquiry as whether the defendant's "predominant purpose" was to injure the plaintiff; in another, it cites the *Restatement* for the proposition that that purpose is not improper where the defendant was motivated "at least in part" by its interest in competing with the plaintiff. Are these two standards equivalent? Which is preferable? Did Isom prove that Leigh's predominant purpose was ill will toward Isom?

In *Speakers of Sport*, by contrast, Judge Posner doesn't refer to "improper purpose" at all, and he states instead that "the tort of interference with business relationships should be confined to cases in which the defendant employed unlawful means to stiff a competitor." He also cites with approval an article by Professor Harvey Perlman arguing that plaintiffs *should* have to prove improper means in tortious interference with prospective business advantage cases. (Professor Perlman was a reporter for the *Restatement (Third) of Unfair Competition*, and his views on this matter are reflected in § 1, comment c of that *Restatement*.) Should a plaintiff be allowed to proceed on an improper purpose theory alone, as in *Tuttle v. Buck*? Consider again the question whether conduct that is not otherwise unlawful should be rendered unlawful because its motivation is morally repugnant.

2. In *Leigh Furniture*, the court defines "improper means" as means that are contrary to law or that violate an established standard of a trade or profession. Judge Posner takes issue with this definition, in part. How would Judge Posner limit the meaning of "improper means"? Whose definition is better?

If the term "improper means" includes only conduct that is independently unlawful (such as fraud, defamation, patent or trademark infringement, or trade secret misappropriation), and if Judge Posner is correct in rejecting "improper purpose" as an alternative basis for finding defendants liable, does the tort of interference with prospective business advantage become redundant? Presumably the victim of the independently unlawful act could sue the defendant for committing that act. The tortious interference plaintiff, however, might not have standing to assert a claim against the defendant premised solely on the defendant's commission of the independently unlawful act. In *Speakers of Sport*, for example, suppose that the plaintiff had proven that ProServ caused Ivan Rodriguez to walk away from his terminable-at-will contract by committing some sort of actionable fraud against Rodriguez (or, worse yet, by threatening him or his family). In such a case, Speakers of Sport would not have had a claim against ProServ for fraud (or extortion), but it may well have had a valid claim for tortious interference with prospective business advantage. Thus, even under Judge Posner's somewhat restrictive interpretation of the tort, tortious interference is hardly redundant in all cases. Of course, if ProServ had induced Rodriguez to abandon Speakers of Sport by feeding him false rumors about Speakers' competence, Speakers itself would have been the immediate victim of the improper means. Any claims it may have had against ProServ for commercial disparagement or defamation might have rendered an additional claim for tortious interference redundant.

3. On the facts of *Leigh Furniture*, the Utah court concluded that the evidence supported a finding of improper means under two different theories. What was the first theory? Were the means relevant to this theory the cause-in-fact of Isom's financial injury?

The second theory is cast as an exception to the general rule that a deliberate breach of contract is *not* an "improper means" for causing someone to forgo prospective business relations. Why is this the general rule? What is the exception to the rule, as crafted by the Utah court, and why does it apply on the facts of *Leigh Furniture*? Does the exception make economic sense?

4. Should justification/privilege be a question of fact or a question of law?

5. Even if a plaintiff succeeds in proving improper means or improper purpose, along with the other elements of the case, can you imagine any reasons why the defendant nevertheless should be immune from liability? *See* RESTATEMENT (SECOND) OF TORTS, §§769 et seq. (discussing various privileges analogous to the privileges available to defamation and commercial disparagement defendants). *See also* NAACP v. Claiborne Hardware Co., 458 U.S. 886, 913-15 (1982) (First Amendment precludes liability for tortious interference, where defendants' calls for boycotts of white-owned businesses caused plaintiffs to suffer economic harm).

6. Under the standard recitation of the elements of the tortious interference torts as presented above, the plaintiff must prove that it suffered actual damages. As a general matter, a successful tortious interference plaintiff is entitled to the normal range of tort damages for injuries proximately caused by the defendant's conduct.

See, e.g., RESTATEMENT (SECOND) OF TORTS § 774A (stating that the plaintiff may recover for "the pecuniary loss of the benefits of the contract or the prospective relations," "consequential losses for which the interference is a legal cause," and "emotional distress or actual harm to reputation if they are reasonably to be expected to result from the interference"; and that the fact that another person is liable to the plaintiff for breach of contract "does not affect the amount of damages awardable against the" tortious interference defendant, though "any damages in fact paid by the third person will reduce the damages actually recoverable on the judgment"). Punitive damages also are available in appropriate cases. *See id.* cmt. a. Occasionally courts award equitable remedies as well. *See id.* cmt. f (noting the possibility of an injunction against a future violation); Advantage Digital Sys. v. Digital Imaging Serv., 870 So. 2d 111, 115-16 (Fla. App. 2003) (stating the conditions under which an injunction would be appropriate).

PROBLEMS

Problem 14-1. Malvar, a citizen and resident of the Kingdom of Fredonia, is hired to manage a Fredonian start-up company (Fredonian Suspended Ceiling Company, or FSCC) that will make and sell acoustic ceiling tiles in the Middle East. FSCC contracts with Cotco, a U.S. company that makes and sells (among other products) acoustic ceiling tiles, for assistance in setting up operations. FSCC licenses some of Cotco's trade secrets subject to a strict confidentiality agreement. Three years later, FSCC decides expand its production line and invites representatives of Knox International, one of Cotco's competitors, to tour the Fredonian facility and make recommendations. Cotco becomes suspicious that FSCC has disclosed Cotco's trade secrets to Knox and wants to initiate legal action against FSCC for breach of contract and trade secret misappropriation. Under the terms of Cotco's agreement with FSCC, however, any and all disputes between the parties are subject to arbitration in London. Cotco invokes its right to arbitration, but while the arbitration is pending Cotco also serves Malvar with process while Malvar is on a business trip in the United States. Cotco's complaint alleges that Malvar, as president of FSCC, intentionally induced FSCC to breach its confidentiality agreement with Cotco, and that Malvar is therefore personally liable for tortious interference with contract. What result?

Problem 14-2. Same facts as above, but suppose instead that Cotco sues FSCC's parent company (a global conglomerate, Fredonia Inc.) and is prepared to show that Fredonia Inc.'s management takes an active role in managing the affairs of its subsidiary FSCC. Can Fredonia Inc. be liable in tort for causing its subsidiary to breach a contract? What if Fredonia Inc. is a major shareholder but FSCC is a publicly traded company?

Problem 14-3. Recall Problem 9-15 from the chapter on false advertising: Novelist Alec Blaine is upset that the *Fredonia Times-Dispatch* erroneously left his name off of its weekly best-sellers list. Assume that Blaine can establish that the error probably resulted in a loss of $100,000 worth of sales of his book. Does he have a claim against the newspaper for tortious interference with prospective business advantage?

Suppose instead that Blaine files suit for defamation, based on the newspaper's publication of a story falsely implicating Blaine in a sex and drugs scandal. Because Blaine is a public figure and the matter in controversy is deemed to be a matter of public concern, the court requires Blaine to prove actual malice by clear and convincing evidence (*see* Chapter 9 *supra*). Unable to make the requisite showing of actual malice, Blaine amends his complaint to state a claim for tortious interference with prospective business advantage. In particular, Blaine claims that he can prove that the newspaper's publication of the false story caused his long-time publisher to terminate negotiations over Blaine's proposed authorship of a series of "thrillers" for children and teens. Blaine argues that liability for tortious interference does not require proof of actual malice even if he is a public figure and the matter in controversy is of public concern. What result?

Problem 14-4. Recall Problem 13-2 from the chapter on cybertrespass. Would Adderly have a claim against Bodick for tortious interference with contract?

A Note on the Economics of Tortious Interference

Returning to the hypothetical with which we began this chapter, suppose that B breaches a contract with A. A has the option of suing B for breach of contract, but what happens if B is partially or entirely judgment-proof, or if for some other reason pursuing a claim against B does not appear cost-effective (for example, maybe B has fled the country or there are other jurisdictional problems)? If A had foreseen these contingencies ex ante, she might have taken various steps to counteract them. For example, A could have attempted to purchase insurance against B's inability to pay or nonamenability to suit; or she might have insisted that B himself provide a surety of some sort — that is, another party who would agree to step into B's shoes and perform, or pay damages, in the event that B could not or would not. (Have any of you ever had a parent cosign a loan?) But sometimes parties don't foresee these contingencies, or else they don't think it to be worthwhile to insure against them. In such instances, the law could simply leave A without a remedy. But now assume, as we proposed earlier in this section, that nonparty-to-the-transaction C caused the breach. Does economic reasoning shed any light on whether, or under what circumstances, A should be able to pursue a tort claim against C?

Alternatively, should A have a claim against C merely for interfering with A's reasonable expectation of future business dealings with B? As in the preceding example, there are (in theory, at least) various options A may have had ex ante to insure against the loss of B's patronage or services, including negotiating an enforceable long-term contract with B. Of course, in many commonplace settings, such long-term contracts would be highly unusual. Customers don't normally enter into long-term contracts with their favorite barbers or bartenders, for example; and, in rare circumstances, long-term exclusive dealing contracts themselves can violate the antitrust laws.

The preceding examples may suggest analogies from other bodies of law. You may recall from torts or criminal law, for instance, that inducing someone to commit a tort or crime is itself sometimes an independent tortious or criminal act. And if you've taken other intellectual property courses, you probably recall that patent, copyright, and trademark law all have evolved doctrines of "indirect" liability (under names such as contributory infringement, active inducement, and vicarious infringement), the theory being that doctrines of this type are necessary to preserve the value of the intellectual asset. So maybe allowing A to sue C in our hypotheticals above would promote analogous interests — that is, it would help to preserve the value of a contractual relationship that otherwise would be at risk in the event B's breach of contract left A without any effective remedy against B. On the other hand, allowing the recovery of monetary damages against C might seem to undermine the common law economic loss rule, under which purely economic losses are not compensable in tort absent some sort of personal injury or injury to tangible property. *See, e.g.*, Rickards v. Sun Oil Co., 41 A.2d 267 (N.J. Super. 1945). Moreover, the theory of "efficient breach" holds that, because contract law generally awards only reasonably foreseeable compensatory damages, it encourages the efficient use of resources. To illustrate, in the example above suppose that A and B each expect to benefit in the amount of $10,000 from B's performance under her contract with A; but that before B has performed she realizes that she could earn a $20,000 profit from performing for C instead. Under these circumstances, the efficient solution is for B to breach her contract with A, pay compensatory damages to A of $10,000, and perform for C. Contract law generally facilitates this sequence of events by awarding A her reasonably foreseeable compensatory damages of only $10,000. *See* RICHARD A. POSNER, ECONOMIC ANALYSIS OF LAW § 4.10, at 120 (7TH ed. 2007). Allowing A to recover damages against C in tort (where damages are not necessarily limited to that which is reasonably foreseeable at the time of contract, and may even include a punitive component) risks deterring such efficient breaches. Or does it simply mean that C would have to negotiate with A to buy out A's interest in B's performance?

Nevertheless, allowing A to recover damages from C might make sense if the risk of B being judgment-proof is substantial. And, unlike the situation presented in economic loss cases, A's injury may be foreseeable to both B and C — indeed, under the standard enumeration of the elements of the inducement tort, C *must* know or have reason to know of the existing contract or relationship between A and B. For further discussion, pro and con, of the economic wisdom of the inducement tort, see Lillian R. BeVier, *Reconsidering Inducement*, 76 VA. L. REV. 877 (1990); Richard A Epstein, *Inducement of Breach of Contract as a Problem of Ostensible Ownership*, 16 J. LEGAL STUD. 1 (1987); Fred S. McChesney, *Tortious Interference with Contract Versus "Efficient" Breach: Theory and Empirical Evidence*, 82 J. LEGAL STUD. 131 (1999); Gary Myers, *The Differing Treatment of Efficiency and Competition in Antitrust and Tortious Interference Law*, 77 MINN. L. REV. 1097 (1993); Note, *An Analysis of the Formation of Property Rights Underlying Tortious Interference with Contracts and Other Economic Relations*, 50 U. CHI. L. REV. 1116 (1983); Harvey S. Perlman, *Interference with Contract and Other Economic Expectancies: A Clash of Tort and Contract Doctrine*, 49 U. CHI. L. REV. 61 (1982); POSNER, *supra*, at § 8.2, at 254-55; and Richard A. Posner, *Common Law Economic Torts: An Economic and Legal Analysis*, 48 ARIZ. L. REV. 735, 743-44 (2006). Analysts who favor the existence of tortious interference with contract claims view them as in effect conferring upon Party A a property interest in Party B's performance, for which equitable remedies such as pre-breach injunctions and post-breach restitution may be appropriate. *See* McChesney, *supra*, at 167-70.

B. FRAUD AND CIVIL RICO

Fraud is a fluid concept, and the law renders many different types of fraud potentially actionable. Misrepresentations that result in personal injuries, for example, may breach the common law duty of care, subjecting the party making the misrepresentation to damages. Misrepresentations resulting in economic harms may be actionable at tort under the common law of fraud (deceit, fraudulent misrepresentation), and may also in an appropriate case provide a basis for rescission and restitution of a contract entered into in reliance on the fraud. As a general matter, the common law tort requires proof that the defendant knowingly made a material misrepresentation of fact for the purpose of inducing another to act or refrain from acting; justifiable reliance on the part of the plaintiff; causation; and pecuniary damages. *See, e.g.*, RESTATEMENT (SECOND) OF TORTS §§ 525, 526 (1977). In some circumstances, negligent or even innocent omissions may be actionable as well. *See id.* §§ 552, 552C. The common law generally did not impose a duty to disclose (caveat emptor!), though contemporary law sometimes may, depending on the circumstances. *See id.* § 551. Throughout the course of the twentieth century and into the present, Congress and the states also have enacted many different statutes imposing liability for certain types of fraud, including securities fraud, mail fraud, and wire fraud.[4] Some of these statutes, such as those relating to securities fraud, impose substantial affirmative duties to disclose. And, of course, many of the topics covered earlier in this casebook, including the law of trademarks, false advertising, consumer fraud, and commercial disparagement, either evolved from or share some affinities with the common and statutory law of fraud.

In 1970, Congress enacted the Organized Crime Control Act, a portion of which is known as the Racketeer Influenced and Corrupt Organizations Act (RICO). The RICO Act was intended to make it easier for the federal government to prosecute persons associated with organized crime, and in this respect it appears to have succeeded. Over the years, the criminal RICO Act has enabled the federal government to prosecute several high-profile organized crime cases; in the 1980s, for example, as U.S. Attorney for the Southern District of New York, Rudolph Giuliani made a name for himself in part by securing RICO convictions against alleged members of New York's

4. In relevant part, the federal mail fraud statute, 18 U.S.C. § 1341, states:

> Whoever, having devised or intending to devise any scheme or artifice to defraud . . . for the purpose of executing such scheme or artifice or attempting so to do, places in any post office or authorized depository for mail matter, any matter or thing whatever to be sent or delivered by the Postal Service, or deposits or causes to be deposited any matter or thing whatever to be sent or delivered by any private or commercial interstate carrier . . . shall be fined under this title or imprisoned not more than 20 years, or both.

The federal wire fraud statute, 18 U.S.C. § 1343, states:

> Whoever, having devised or intending to devise any scheme or artifice to defraud . . . transmits or causes to be transmitted by means of wire, radio, or television communication in interstate or foreign commerce, any writings, signs, signals, pictures, or sounds for the purpose of executing such scheme or artifice, shall be fined under this title or imprisoned not more than 20 years, or both.

"Five Families." Like many criminal statutes, RICO also authorizes civil actions based on conduct that violates the statute's substantive provisions. Until the 1980s, however, civil litigants made little use of these provisions. That began to change as litigants slowly realized that, depending on how the statutory terms are read, RICO could provide a convenient vehicle for securing treble damages judgments for various types of civil fraud having little or no connection with any form of organized crime.

This casebook will not provide a thorough analysis of this complex statute and the case law that has grown up around it.[5] It is important, however, for a student of business torts to have some general understanding of how the RICO statute works and why it sometimes is applicable in commonplace business disputes. The following discussion presents some key statutory provisions and a few of the more important decisions interpreting the act.

For civil litigation purposes, the most important provision of the statute is 18 U.S.C. § 1962(c), which in relevant part states "It shall be unlawful for any person employed by or associated with any enterprise engaged in, or the activities of which affect, interstate or foreign commerce, to conduct or participate, directly or indirectly, in the conduct of such enterprise's affairs through a pattern of racketeering activity. . . ." Section 1961(1) defines the term "racketeering activity" to include a wide variety of illegal activities, including (among many, many others) mail and wire fraud; bribery; and extortion. The statute defines a person to include "any individual or entity capable of holding a legal or beneficial interest in property," *id.* § 1961(3); an enterprise to include "any individual, partnership, corporation, association, or other legal entity, and any union or group of individuals associated in fact although not a legal entity," *id.* § 1961(4); and a "pattern of racketeering activity" as "requir[ing] at least two acts of racketeering activity, one of which occurred after the effective date of this chapter and the last of which occurred within ten years (excluding any period of imprisonment) after the commission of a prior act of racketeering activity," *id.* § 1961(5). Using language patterned after federal antitrust law's Clayton Act, § 1964(c) authorizes private civil actions, stating "Any person injured in his business or property by reason of a violation of Section 1962 . . . may sue therefore in any appropriate United States district court and shall recover threefold the damages he sustains and the cost of the suit, including a reasonable attorney's fee. . . ."

Early case law under civil RICO focused on questions such as (1) whether the private plaintiff must prove that the defendant has been criminally convicted of the predicate racketeering activity (or must otherwise prove each predicate act beyond a reasonable doubt); (2) whether the statute is limited to racketeering activity occurring in connection with organized crime (or otherwise requires proof of "racketeering injury" distinct from the injury caused by the predicate acts); and (3) whether a pattern of racketeering activity requires proof of multiple schemes. In Sedima, S.p.r.L. v. Imrex Co., 473 U.S. 479, 496 (1985), the Supreme Court answered the first two of these questions in the negative, holding that a violation of § 1962(c) only "requires (1) conduct (2) of an enterprise (3) through a pattern (4) of racketeering activity. . . . In addition, the plaintiff only has standing if, and can only recover to the extent that, he has been injured in his business or property by the conduct constituting

5. For those interested in more detailed discussions, there are several RICO treatises on the market, including Paul Batista, Civil Rico Practice Manual (3d ed. 2009); Gregory P. Joseph, Civil RICO: A Definitive Guide (3d ed. 2010); and R. Douglas Rees et al., RICO: A Guide to Civil RICO Litigation in Federal Court (2009).

the violation." Thus, although the dispute at issue (involving a defendant purchaser who allegedly violated federal mail and wire fraud statutes by, among other things, submitting bills to the plaintiff for nonexistent expenses) struck the dissenting justices as alleging nothing more than "garden-variety fraud," *Sedima*, 473 U.S. at 525 (Powell, J., dissenting), the majority could find nothing in the statutory text or history to suggest that civil RICO requires proof of ties to organized crime or a distinct "racketeering injury." Four years later, in H.J. Inc. v. Northwestern Bell Telephone Co., 492 U.S. 229 (1989) (Brennan, J.), the Court once again read the statute expansively, concluding that a RICO "pattern" does not require proof of multiple schemes (though by the same token, a pattern is not necessarily present merely upon completion of two predicate acts). Instead, a pattern consists of two elements, "continuity" and "relationship." The predicate acts are "related" if they "have the same or similar purposes, results, participants, victims, or methods of commission, or otherwise are interrelated by distinguishing characteristics and are not isolated events." *Id.* at 240 (quoting, as persuasive authority, another portion of the Organized Crime Control Act of 1970, 18 U.S.C. §3575(e)). As for the remaining element:

> "Continuity" is both a closed- and open-ended concept, referring either to a closed period of repeated conduct, or to past conduct that by its nature projects into the future with a threat of repetition. It is, in either case, centrally a temporal concept—and particularly so in the RICO context, where *what* must be continuous, RICO's predicate acts or offenses, and the *relationship* these predicates must bear one to another, are distinct requirements. A party alleging a RICO violation may demonstrate continuity over a closed period by proving a series of related predicates extending over a substantial period of time. Predicate acts extending over a few weeks or months and threatening no future criminal conduct do not satisfy this requirement: Congress was concerned in RICO with long-term criminal conduct. Often a RICO action will be brought before continuity can be established in this way. In such cases, liability depends on whether the *threat* of continuity is demonstrated. See S. Rep. No. 91-617, at 158.
>
> Whether the predicates proved establish a threat of continued racketeering activity depends on the specific facts of each case. Without making any claim to cover the field of possibilities—preferring to deal with this issue in the context of concrete factual situations presented for decision—we offer some examples of how this element might be satisfied. A RICO pattern may surely be established if the related predicates themselves involve a distinct threat of long-term racketeering activity, either implicit or explicit. Suppose a hoodlum were to sell "insurance" to a neighborhood's storekeepers to cover them against breakage of their windows, telling his victims he would be reappearing each month to collect the "premium" that would continue their "coverage." Though the number of related predicates involved may be small and they may occur close together in time, the racketeering acts themselves include a specific threat of repetition extending indefinitely into the future, and thus supply the requisite threat of continuity. In other cases, the threat of continuity may be established by showing that the predicate acts or offenses are part of an ongoing entity's regular way of doing business. Thus, the threat of continuity is sufficiently established where the predicates can be attributed to a defendant operating as part of a long-term association that exists for criminal purposes. Such associations include, but extend well beyond, those traditionally grouped under the phrase "organized crime." The continuity requirement is likewise satisfied where it is shown that the predicates are a regular way of conducting defendant's ongoing legitimate business (in the sense that it is not a business that exists for criminal purposes), or of conducting or participating in an ongoing and legitimate RICO "enterprise."

As in *Sedima*, the majority opinion provoked a vigorous dissent — this time from Justice Scalia, who described the phrase "continuity plus relationship" (which the majority took from the statute's legislative history, not from the statute itself) as "about as helpful . . . as 'life is a fountain.'" *H.J.*, 492 U.S. at 252. Conceding that he could do no better in defining the term "pattern," Justice Scalia predicted that RICO might be vulnerable to constitutional challenge on vagueness grounds, *see id.* at 255-56, but so far no such challenge has succeeded.

Other hotly contested elements in civil RICO actions include the elements of causation, the meaning of the term "enterprise," and what sort of harms qualify as injuries to "business or property" for purposes of § 1964(c). The following case, and the Comments and Questions that follow, shed some light on these issues.

Hemi Group, LLC v. City of New York

130 S. Ct. 983 (2010)

Chief Justice ROBERTS delivered the opinion of the Court in part.

The City of New York taxes the possession of cigarettes. Hemi Group, based in New Mexico, sells cigarettes online to residents of the City. Neither state nor city law requires Hemi to charge, collect, or remit the tax, and the purchasers seldom pay it on their own. Federal law, however, requires out-of-state vendors such as Hemi to submit customer information to the States into which they ship the cigarettes.

Against that backdrop, the City filed this lawsuit under the Racketeer Influenced and Corrupt Organizations Act (RICO), alleging that Hemi failed to file the required customer information with the State. That failure, the City argues, constitutes mail and wire fraud, which caused it to lose tens of millions of dollars in unrecovered cigarette taxes. Because the City cannot show that it lost the tax revenue "by reason of" the alleged RICO violation, 18 U.S.C. § 1964(c), we hold that the City cannot state a claim under RICO. We therefore reverse the Court of Appeals' decision to the contrary. . . .

New York State authorizes the City of New York to impose its own taxes on cigarettes. Under that authority, the City has levied a $1.50 per pack tax on each standard pack of cigarettes possessed within the City for sale or use. When purchasers buy cigarettes from in-state vendors, the seller is responsible for charging, collecting, and remitting the tax. Out-of-state vendors, however, are not. Instead, the City is responsible for recovering, directly from the customers, use taxes on cigarettes sold outside New York. That can be difficult, as those customers are often reluctant to pay and tough to track down. One way the City can gather information that would assist it in collecting the back taxes is through the Jenkins Act, 63 Stat. 884, as amended by 69 Stat. 627. That Act requires out-of-state cigarette sellers to register and to file a report with state tobacco tax administrators listing the name, address, and quantity of cigarettes purchased by state residents. 15 U.S.C. §§ 375-78. . . .

Hemi Group is a New Mexico company that sells cigarettes online. Hemi, however, does not file Jenkins Act information with the State. The City alleges that this failure has cost it "tens if not hundreds of millions of dollars a year in cigarette excise tax revenue." Record A996. Based on Hemi's failure to file the information with the State, the City filed this federal RICO claim. . . .

The City alleges that Hemi's "interstate sale of cigarettes and the failure to file Jenkins Act reports identifying those sales" constitute the RICO predicate offenses of mail and wire fraud in violation of § 1962(c), for which § 1964(c) provides a private cause of action. Record A980. Invoking that private cause of action, the City asserts that it has suffered injury in the form of lost tax revenue — its "business or property" in RICO terms — "by reason of" Hemi's fraud.

Hemi does not contest the City's characterization of the Jenkins Act violations as predicate offenses actionable under § 1964(c). (We therefore assume, without deciding, that failure to file Jenkins Act material can serve as a RICO predicate offense.) Instead, Hemi argues that the City's asserted injury — lost tax revenue — is not "business or property" under RICO, and that the City cannot show that it suffered any injury "by reason of" the failure to file Jenkins Act reports.

The District Court dismissed the City's RICO claims, determining that Hemi owner and officer Kai Gachupin did not have an individual duty to file Jenkins Act reports, and thus could not have committed the alleged predicate acts. City of New York v. Nexicon, Inc., No. 03 CV 383(DAB), 2006 WL 647716, *7-*8 (S.D.N.Y., Mar. 15, 2006). The District Court therefore held that the City could not establish that Hemi and Gachupin formed an "enterprise" as required to establish RICO liability. Id., at *7-*10. Because it dismissed on that ground, the District Court did not address whether the City's loss of tax revenue constitutes an injury to its "business or property" under § 1964, or whether that injury was caused "by reason of" Hemi's failure to file the Jenkins Act reports. . . .

II

Though framed as a single question, Hemi's petition for certiorari raises two distinct issues: First, whether a loss in tax revenue is "business or property" under 18 U.S.C. § 1964(c); and second, whether the City's asserted injury came about "by reason of" the allegedly fraudulent conduct, as required by § 1964(c). We determine that the City cannot satisfy the causation requirement-that any injury the City suffered must be "by reason of" the alleged frauds-and therefore do not decide whether the City's allegations of lost tax revenue constitute an injury to its "business or property."

A

In Holmes v. Securities Investor Protection Corporation, 503 U.S. 258 (1992), we set forth the standard of causation that applies to civil RICO claims. In that case, we addressed a RICO claim brought by Securities Investor Protection Corporation (SIPC) against defendants whom SIPC alleged had manipulated stock prices. SIPC had a duty to reimburse customers of certain registered broker-dealers in the event the broker-dealers were unable to meet their financial obligations. When the conspiracy by the stock manipulators was detected, stock prices collapsed, and two broker-dealers were unable to meet their obligations to their customers. SIPC, as insurer against that loss, ultimately was on the hook for nearly $13 million to cover the customers' claims. The Court held that SIPC could not recover against the conspirators because it could not establish that it was injured "by reason of" the alleged fraud, as that phrase is used in RICO.

We explained that, to state a claim under civil RICO, the plaintiff is required to show that a RICO predicate offense "not only was a 'but for' cause of his injury, but was the proximate cause as well." Id., at 268. Proximate cause for RICO purposes, we made clear, should be evaluated in light of its common-law foundations; proximate cause thus requires "some direct relation between the injury asserted and the injurious conduct alleged." Ibid. A link that is "too remote," "purely contingent," or "indirec[t]" is insufficient. Id., at 271.

Applying that standard, we rejected SIPC's RICO claim. The alleged conspiracy, we held, directly harmed only the broker-dealers; SIPC's injury, on the other hand, was "purely contingent" on that harm. Id. at 271. The connection between the alleged conspiracy and SIPC's injury was therefore "too remote" to satisfy RICO's direct relationship requirement.

The City's causal theory is far more attenuated than the one we rejected in *Holmes*. According to the City, Hemi committed fraud by selling cigarettes to city residents and failing to submit the required customer information to the State. Without the reports from Hemi, the State could not pass on the information to the City, even if it had been so inclined. Some of the customers legally obligated to pay the cigarette tax to the City failed to do so. Because the City did not receive the customer information, the City could not determine which customers had failed to pay the tax. The City thus could not pursue those customers for payment. The City thereby was injured in the amount of the portion of back taxes that were never collected. See Record A996.

But as we reiterated in *Holmes*, "[t]he general tendency of the law, in regard to damages at least, is not to go beyond the first step." Our cases confirm that the "general tendency" applies with full force to proximate cause inquiries under RICO. *Holmes*, supra, at 271-272, 112 S. Ct. 1311; see also Bridge v. Phoenix Bond & Indemnity Co., 553 U.S. ____, ____, 128 S. Ct. 2131, 2144-45, 170 L. Ed. 2d 1012 (2008); Anza v. Ideal Steel Supply Corp., 547 U.S. 451, 460-461, 126 S. Ct. 1991, 164 L. Ed. 2d 720 (2006). Because the City's theory of causation requires us to move well beyond the first step, that theory cannot meet RICO's direct relationship requirement.

Our decision in *Anza*, supra, confirms that the City's theory of causation is far too indirect. There we considered a RICO claim brought by Ideal Steel Supply against its competitor, National Steel Supply. Ideal alleged that National had defrauded New York State by failing to charge and remit sales taxes, and that National was thus able to undercut Ideal's prices. The lower prices offered by National, Ideal contended, allowed National to attract customers at Ideal's expense. Id., at 458, 126 S. Ct. 1991.

Finding the link between the fraud alleged and injury suffered to be "attenuated," we rejected Ideal's claim. Id., at 459, 126 S. Ct. 1991. "The direct victim of this conduct," we held, was "the State of New York, not Ideal." Id., at 458, 126 S. Ct. 1991. . . .

The City's claim suffers from the same defect as the claim in *Anza*. Here, the conduct directly responsible for the City's harm was the customers' failure to pay their taxes. And the conduct constituting the alleged fraud was Hemi's failure to file Jenkins Act reports. Thus, as in *Anza*, the conduct directly causing the harm was distinct from the conduct giving rise to the fraud. See id., at 458, 126 S. Ct. 1991. . . .

The City's theory thus requires that we extend RICO liability to situations where the defendant's fraud on the third party (the State) has made it easier for a fourth party (the taxpayer) to cause harm to the plaintiff (the City). Indeed, the fourth-party taxpayers here only caused harm to the City in the first place if they decided not to pay taxes they were legally obligated to pay. Put simply, Hemi's obligation was to file the Jenkins Act reports with the State, not the City, and the City's harm was directly caused by the customers, not Hemi. We have never before stretched the causal chain of a RICO violation so far, and we decline to do so today.

One consideration we have highlighted as relevant to the RICO "direct relationship" requirement is whether better situated plaintiffs would have an incentive to sue. See *Holmes*, supra, at 269-270, 112 S. Ct. 1311. The State certainly is better situated than the City to seek recovery from Hemi. . . . We do not opine on whether the State could bring a RICO action for any lost tax revenue. Suffice it to say that the State would have concrete incentives to try.

The dissent would have RICO's proximate cause requirement turn on foreseeability, rather than on the existence of a sufficiently "direct relationship" between the fraud and the harm. It would find that the City has satisfied that requirement because "the harm is foreseeable; it is a consequence that Hemi intended, indeed desired; and it falls well within the set of risks that Congress sought to prevent." *Post*, at 997-998 (opinion of BREYER, J.). If this line of reasoning sounds familiar, it should. It is precisely the argument lodged against the majority opinion in *Anza*. There, the dissent criticized the majority's view for "permit[ting] a defendant to evade liability for harms that are not only foreseeable, but the intended consequences of the defendant's unlawful behavior." 547 U.S., at 470, 126 S. Ct. 1991 (THOMAS, J., concurring in part and dissenting in part). But the dissent there did not carry the day, and no one has asked us to revisit *Anza*.

The concepts of direct relationship and foreseeability are of course two of the "many shapes [proximate cause] took at common law," *Holmes*, supra, at 268, 112 S. Ct. 1311. Our precedents make clear that in the RICO context, the focus is on the directness of the relationship between the conduct and the harm. Indeed, *Anza* and *Holmes* never even mention the concept of foreseeability.

B

The City . . . relies on *Bridge*, 553 U.S. _____, 128 S. Ct. 2131. *Bridge* reaffirmed the requirement that there must be "a sufficiently direct relationship between the defendant's wrongful conduct and the plaintiff's injury." Id., at 2144. The case involved competing bidders at a county tax-lien auction. Because the liens were profitable even at the lowest possible bid, multiple bidders offered that low bid. (The bidding took the form of the percentage tax penalty the bidder would require the property owner to pay, so the lowest possible bid was 0%.) To decide which bidder would be awarded the lien, the county devised a plan to allocate the liens "on a rotational basis." Id., at 2135-36 (internal quotation marks omitted). But as we noted in that case, this created a "perverse incentive": "Bidders who, in addition to bidding themselves, sen[t] agents to bid on their behalf [would] obtain a disproportionate share of liens." Ibid. The county therefore prohibited bidders from using such agents. Ibid.

A losing bidder alleged that a competitor had defrauded the county by employing shadow bidders to secure a greater proportion of liens than it was due. We held that the bidder-plaintiff had met RICO's causation requirement. Distinguishing that claim from the one at issue in *Anza*, we noted that the plaintiff's theory of causation in *Bridge* was "straightforward": Because of the zero-sum nature of the auction, and because the county awarded bids on a rotational basis, each time a fraud-induced bid was awarded, a particular legitimate bidder was necessarily passed over. 553

U.S., at _____, 128 S. Ct., at 2144. The losing bidders, moreover, "were the only parties injured by petitioners' misrepresentations." Ibid. The county was not; it received the same revenue regardless of which bidder prevailed.

The City's theory in this case is anything but straightforward: Multiple steps, as we have detailed, separate the alleged fraud from the asserted injury. And in contrast to *Bridge*, where there were "no independent factors that account[ed] for [the plaintiff's] injury," ibid., here there certainly were: The City's theory of liability rests on the independent actions of third and even fourth parties. . . .

It bears remembering what this case is about. It is about the RICO liability of a company for lost taxes it had no obligation to collect, remit, or pay, which harmed a party to whom it owed no duty. It is about imposing such liability to substitute for or complement a governing body's uncertain ability or desire to collect taxes directly from those who owe them. And it is about the fact that the liability comes with treble damages and attorney's fees attached. This Court has interpreted RICO broadly, consistent with its terms, but we have also held that its reach is limited by the "requirement of a direct causal connection" between the predicate wrong and the harm. *Anza*, 547 U.S., at 460, 126 S. Ct. 1991. The City's injuries here were not caused directly by the alleged fraud, and thus were not caused "by reason of" it. The City, therefore, has no RICO claim. . . .

[Concurring opinion of Justice GINSBURG, and dissenting opinion of Justice BREYER, omitted.]

COMMENTS AND QUESTIONS

1. The opinion in *Hemi Group* provides a short but useful overview of the Court's other principal RICO opinions on causation: Bridge v. Phoenix Bond & Indemnity Co., 128 S. Ct. 2131 (2008), Anza v. Ideal Steel Supply Corp., 547 U.S. 451 (2006), and Holmes v. Securities Investor Protection Corp., 503 U.S. 258 (1992). *Bridge* also put to rest a circuit conflict on the question of whether a plaintiff alleging a RICO violation premised on predicate acts of mail or wire fraud must prove that it reasonably relied on the fraudulent misrepresentations. *See Bridge*, 128 S. Ct. at 2139 (holding that no such requirement exists).

2. The Court in *Hemi Group* does not reach the issue of the City's interest in receiving lawfully assessed tax revenue qualifies as "business or property," and the Court's other RICO opinions have never specifically addressed the meaning of this statutory element. Lower court opinions agree that concrete financial losses generally qualify as injuries to business or property, but the extent to which injuries to intangible interests are remediable under RICO can sometimes be difficult to ascertain. For example, although "a scheme or artifice to deprive another of the intangible right of honest services," *see* 18 U.S.C. § 1346, can result in a violation of the mail or wire fraud statutes,[6] and although mail and wire fraud can qualify as RICO predicate acts, lower courts generally have held that the loss of the right to honest services comprises an injury to business or property under RICO only if it results in a concrete financial loss. *See* Ove v. Gwinn, 264 F.3d 817, 825 (9th Cir. 2001) ("[P]laintiffs fail

6. In Skilling v. United States, 130 S. Ct. 2896 (2010), however, the Supreme Court cut back somewhat on the broad use of the honest services statute, holding that the statute is violated only when the defendant engages in bribery or kickbacks.

to allege injury: They do not allege any financial loss to *their* business or property and the deprivation of 'honest services' does not constitute concrete financial loss."); Doe v. Roe, 958 F.2d 763, 769 n.5 (7th Cir. 1992); Township of Marlboro v. Scannapieco, 545 F. Supp. 2d 452, 458-59 (D.N.J. 2008) ("A governmental agency's allegations that it suffered amorphous injuries to a right to its employees' honest services are *not* 'concrete financial loss[es]' recoverable under RICO. Rather, a municipality like Marlboro must establish some 'type of actual monetary loss that is sufficient to satisfy RICO's injury requirement.' ") (citation omitted). In addition, the lower courts are divided on the question of whether a loss of business reputation or customers constitutes a RICO injury. *Compare* Clark v. Stipe Law Firm, L.L.P., 320 F. Supp. 2d 1207, 1213-14 (W.D. Okla. 2004) (discussing the split of authority and concluding that, at least on a motion to dismiss, allegations of harm to business reputation were sufficient under RICO); Guerrero v. Gates, 110 F. Supp. 2d 1287, 1293 (C.D. Cal. 2000) ("[L]oss of business opportunities[] and damage to professional reputation have been . . . held to constitute [a] cognizable injur[y] to business or property for purposes of RICO . . . ."); In re Am. Honda Motor Co. Dealerships Relations Litig., 941 F. Supp. 528, 541 (D. Md. 1996) (observing that courts have treated loss of customers as an injury to business or property), *with* Hamm v. Rhone-Poulenc Rorer Pharms., Inc., 187 F.3d 941, 954 (8th Cir. 1999) (holding that damage to business reputation does not constitute injury to business or property under RICO); City of Chicago Heights v. Lobue, 914 F. Supp. 279, 285 (N.D. Ill. 1996) (same); In re Teledyne Def. Contracting Derivative Litig., 849 F. Supp. 1369, 1372 n.1 (C.D. Cal. 1993) ("Plaintiffs also allege injury to the Company's 'business reputation.' However, injury to such an intangible property interest is not cognizable under RICO in this circuit.").

3. Whether the defendant participated in the affairs of an "enterprise" also can be a disputed issue in some cases. As noted above, § 1961(4) defines an enterprise broadly to "include any individual, partnership, corporation, association, or other legal entity, and any union or group of individuals associated in fact although not a legal entity." Thus in the early case of United States v. Turkette, 452 U.S. 576, 580 (1981), the Court held that a RICO enterprise includes "a group of persons associated together for a common purpose of engaging in a course of conduct." More recently, in Boyle v. United States, 129 S. Ct. 2237, 2244-45 (2009), the Court rejected the argument that RICO enterprises include only "business-like entities." The Court explained:

> . . . [T]he specific question on which we granted certiorari is whether an association-in-fact enterprise must have "an ascertainable structure beyond that inherent in the pattern of racketeering activity in which it engages." Pet. for Cert. i. We will break this question into three parts. First, must an association-in-fact enterprise have a "structure"? Second, must the structure be "ascertainable"? Third, must the "structure" go "beyond that inherent in the pattern of racketeering activity" in which its members engage?
>
> "*Structure.*" We agree with petitioner that an association-in-fact enterprise must have a structure. . . .
>
> From the terms of RICO, it is apparent that an association-in-fact enterprise must have at least three structural features: a purpose, relationships among those associated with the enterprise, and longevity sufficient to permit these associates to pursue the enterprise's purpose. As we succinctly put it in *Turkette*, an association-in-fact enterprise is "a group of persons associated together for a common purpose of engaging in a course of conduct." 452 U.S., at 583, 101 S. Ct. 2524.
>
> That an "enterprise" must have a purpose is apparent from meaning of the term in ordinary usage, i.e., a "venture," "undertaking," or "project." WEBSTER'S THIRD NEW

International Dictionary 757 (1976). The concept of "associat[ion]" requires both interpersonal relationships and a common interest. Section 1962(c) reinforces this conclusion and also shows that an "enterprise" must have some longevity, since the offense proscribed by that provision demands proof that the enterprise had "affairs" of sufficient duration to permit an associate to "participate" in those affairs through "a pattern of racketeering activity." . . .

"*Ascertainable.*" Whenever a jury is told that it must find the existence of an element beyond a reasonable doubt, that element must be "ascertainable" or else the jury could not find that it was proved. Therefore, telling the members of the jury that they had to ascertain the existence of an "ascertainable structure" would have been redundant and potentially misleading.

"*Beyond that inherent in the pattern of racketeering activity.*" This phrase may be interpreted in least two different ways, and its correctness depends on the particular sense in which the phrase is used. If the phrase is interpreted to mean that the existence of an enterprise is a separate element that must be proved, it is of course correct. As we explained in *Turkette*, the existence of an enterprise is an element distinct from the pattern of racketeering activity and "proof of one does not necessarily establish the other." 452 U.S., at 583, 101 S. Ct. 2524.

On the other hand, if the phrase is used to mean that the existence of an enterprise may never be inferred from the evidence showing that persons associated with the enterprise engaged in a pattern of racketeering activity, it is incorrect. We recognized in *Turkette* that the evidence used to prove the pattern of racketeering activity and the evidence establishing an enterprise "may in particular cases coalesce." Ibid. . . .

The crux of petitioner's argument is that a RICO enterprise must have structural features in addition to those that we think can be fairly inferred from the language of the statute. Although petitioner concedes that an association-in-fact enterprise may be an " 'informal' " group and that "not 'much' " structure is needed, Reply Brief for Petitioner 24, he contends that such an enterprise must have at least some additional structural attributes, such as a structural "hierarchy," "role differentiation," a "unique modus operandi," a "chain of command," "professionalism and sophistication of organization," "diversity and complexity of crimes," "membership dues, rules and regulations," "uncharged or additional crimes aside from predicate acts," an "internal discipline mechanism," "regular meetings regarding enterprise affairs," an "enterprise 'name,' " and "induction or initiation ceremonies and rituals." Id., at 31-35; see also Brief for Petitioner 26-28, 33; Tr. of Oral Arg. 6, 8, 17.

We see no basis in the language of RICO for the structural requirements that petitioner asks us to recognize. As we said in *Turkette*, an association-in-fact enterprise is simply a continuing unit that functions with a common purpose. . . .

4. The "enterprise" element nevertheless can still remain difficult to apply in some cases. For example, in In re Actiq Sales & Marketing Practices Litigation, Civil Action No. 07-4492, 2009 WL 1444443 (E.D. Pa. May 22, 2009) (*Actiq I*), a group of insurers alleged that Cephalon, Inc., a pharmaceutical company, pursued a deceptive marketing scheme involving the marketing of a prescription drug (Actiq) for uses not approved by the federal Food and Drug Administration. The insurers claimed that, as a result of the scheme, they were obligated to pay excessive prescription costs for the off-label uses of the drug. The district court dismissed the insurers' RICO claim on the ground that the insurers had

failed to establish facts sufficient to infer the existence of an enterprise as required by the statute. First, Plaintiffs have failed to set forth sufficient details in more than vague terms to identify the alleged enterprise. Plaintiffs state that "the enterprise is an

> association-in-fact consisting of Defendant . . . and pain management specialists, CME speakers, paid speakers, and doctors paid to publish studies and the marketing and publication firms employed by Defendant to promote Actiq for off-label uses." Am. Compl. at ¶82. Plaintiff further states that "Defendant and the other members of the Enterprise created and maintained systematic links for a common purpose to aid in marketing Actiq for off-label uses. Am. Compl. at ¶83. Yet, these statements are merely conclusory and open-ended, such that they fail to sufficiently identify the structure of the alleged entity, as well as names or titles of the individuals involved. Courts have established that the mere statement that individuals performed a particular roles and were aware of each other's roles will not suffice to plead the existence of an enterprise. The allegations of the Amended Complaint simply do not provide sufficient details which support the existence of an ongoing organization which functions as a continuous unit.
>
> Second, Plaintiffs have not established that the alleged enterprise has an existence separate and apart from the pattern of activity in which it engages. Plaintiffs assert that "the enterprise was created precisely to make it appear to the public that Defendant did not have a hand in any discussions or promotion of off-label use." Am. Compl. at ¶94. Such a statement establishes both that the enterprise that Plaintiffs allege existed has no legitimate purpose beyond the racketeering activity, but further that Plaintiffs have affirmatively negated that which they attempt to prove, namely that the enterprise existed beyond committing the alleged predicate acts. Consequently, Plaintiffs have failed to plead adequate facts to support the existence of a RICO enterprise.

Id. at **4-5. In a related action filed by health and welfare trust funds that provide prescription drug coverage to union members, the plaintiffs alleged that Cephalon had engaged in a similarly deceptive scheme by promoting two other drugs, Provigil and Gabitril, for unapproved uses for which the plaintiffs bore the cost. This time, however, the same judge held that the plaintiffs *had* adequately pleaded a RICO enterprise:

> Using the *Boyle* Court's reasoning, Plaintiffs argue that their complaint sets forth sufficient allegations to establish the three structural features necessary for an association-in-fact, and that a hub and spoke organizational, decision-making structure is visible, or can be inferred. This Court finds Plaintiffs' arguments persuasive.
>
> Plaintiffs' complaint provides allegations which identify the structure in question in more than vague terms, as well as particular members of the enterprise and details regarding the actual operation of the enterprise. Defendant argues that Plaintiffs' Complaint is "virtually identical" to the Actiq Complaint, however, this Court disagrees. While Plaintiffs' complaint unquestionably contains some allegations that are similar to the Actiq complaint, the gradations in Plaintiffs' complaint are sufficient to nudge the allegations over the line from that which is merely "speculative" and "conceivable," to that which states "a claim to relief that is plausible on its face." *Twombly*, 127 S. Ct. at 1974. Here, Plaintiffs have not only alleged a decision-making structure that goes beyond surface descriptions of the enterprise and associate roles, but also details about the ongoing functions of the alleged enterprise, descriptions of monetary and other incentives used to attract speakers and other participants to the enterprise, specifics regarding the manner in which presentations are created to allegedly mislead physicians about the efficacy of Provigil and Gabitril for certain conditions, and how sales representatives were utilized in the course of Defendant's national marketing scheme. Furthermore, Plaintiffs have provided sufficient allegations to address the three structural elements that the Boyle Court required.
>
> Defendant is adamant that *Boyle* does not relieve Plaintiffs of the burden to adequately plead the existence of a structure, and that to infer a structure from allegations that Defendant engaged in off-label promotion and had relationships with speakers is

> implausible. Yet, it is not merely the allegations of off-label promotion or outside relationships from which an association-in-fact enterprise can be inferred. Rather, an association-in-fact can be inferred from such allegations in conjunction with Plaintiffs' allegations regarding deceptive and misleading marketing tactics allegedly utilized by Defendant, such as omitting critical information about side-effects, training speakers and representatives to continue omitting such information in presentations, and allegedly re-directing marketing strategies away from FDA regulatory oversight. Taken together, this Court finds that Plaintiffs' allegations state a claim for relief that is plausible on its face, and therefore, will deny Defendant's Motion.

In re Actiq Sales & Marketing Practices Litig., Civil Action Nos. 07-4492, 09-431, 2009 WL 2581717, at *4 (E.D. Pa. Aug. 21, 2009) (*Actiq II*). The Supreme Court's decision in *Boyle* came out in between *Actiq I* and *Actiq II*. The district court nevertheless adhered to its decision in *Actiq I*, choosing to distinguish rather than revisit that decision in *Actiq II*. Does *Boyle* require a different outcome in *Actiq I*?

Although it did not affect the outcome of the case, in *Actiq I* the court also held that the plaintiffs *had* adequately pleaded proximate cause/standing in light of *Bridge*. After *Hemi Group* (decided in 2010), did the court rule correctly on the causation issue?

5. As noted above, the RICO statute (like the federal antitrust laws) provides for the successful plaintiff to recover treble damages and attorney fees. The Supreme Court has yet to determine whether private plaintiffs (as opposed to the United States as civil plaintiff) may obtain injunctive relief, however, and the lower courts remain divided on this question. *Compare* Nat'l Org. for Women, Inc. v. Scheidler, 267 F.3d 687, 695-700 (7th Cir. 2001) (holding that RICO allows private plaintiffs to sue for injunctive relief), *rev'd on other grounds*, Scheidler v. Nat'l Org. for Women, Inc., 537 U.S. 393 (2003); Chambers Dev. Co. v. Browning-Ferris Indus., 590 F. Supp. 1528, 1541 (W.D. Pa. 1984) ("[P]rivate claimants in RICO cases may seek equitable relief."), *with* Religious Tech. Ctr. v. Wollersheim, 796 F.2d 1076, 1079-89 (9th Cir. 1986) (concluding, after an extensive analysis, "that Congress did not intend to give private RICO plaintiffs any right to injunctive relief"); In re Fredeman Litig., 843 F.2d 821, 828 (5th Cir. 1988); *see also* Minter v. Wells Fargo Bank, N.A., 593 F. Supp. 2d 788, 794-96 (D. Md. 2009) (noting the ongoing split).

6. For purposes of § 1962(c), the "person" and the "enterprise" must be distinct legal entities. *See* Cedric Kushner Promotions v. King, 533 U.S. 158, 160 (2001). A corporation therefore cannot be both the § 1962(c) defendant and a member of the RICO enterprise. *See* Riverwoods Chappaqua Corp. v. Marine Midland Bank, N.A., 30 F.3d 339, 344 (2d Cir. 1994) ("We have made clear that, by virtue of the distinctness requirement, a corporate entity may not be both the RICO person and the RICO enterprise under section 1962(c)."); Kehr Packages, Inc. v. Fidelcor, Inc., 926 F.2d 1406, 1411 (3d Cir. 1991); Haroco, Inc. v. Am. Nat'l Bank & Trust Co. of Chi., 747 F.2d 384, 400-02 (7th Cir. 1984). A corporate employee, however, may be liable for participating through a pattern of racketeering activity in the affairs of the corporation for which she works. *See King*, 533 U.S. at 161 (holding that the president/sole shareholder of a personal corporation could violate RICO by participating in the affairs of the corporate enterprise; the two were legally distinct entities); *see also* Reves v. Ernst & Young, 507 U.S. 170, 184-85 (1993) (stating that "one is not liable under [§ 1962(c)] unless one has participated in the operation or management of the enterprise itself," but that the "enterprise also might be 'operated' or 'managed'

by others 'associated with' the enterprise who exert control over it as, for example, by bribery").[7] Moreover, courts are split on the question of whether an employer can be vicariously liable for its employee's violation of the RICO Act. According to some, the employer can be liable if it is the beneficiary, but not the victim, of the predicate racketeering acts. *See* Oki Semiconductor Co. v. Wells Fargo Bank, Nat'l Ass'n, 298 F.3d 768, 774-77 (9th Cir. 2002) ("Under RICO . . . respondeat superior liability attaches only if an employer benefitted from its employee's RICO violation."); Liquid Air Corp. v. Rogers, 834 F.2d 1297, 1306-07 (7th Cir. 1987) ("Vicarious liability . . . has only limited application to civil RICO to avoid holding vicariously liable a corporation that was the *victim* of a RICO violation. . . . [T]he doctrine may apply only when 1) the corporation has derived some benefit from the RICO violation and 2) imposing vicarious liability is not inconsistent with the intent of Congress. . . . [T]he express language of subsection (c) has been read to proscribe vicarious liability. . . . *Respondeat superior* is therefore entirely appropriate under both subsections (a) and (b), so long as [the defendant] derived a benefit from the violations.") (citation omitted); Design Pallets, Inc. v. GrayRobinson, P.A., 515 F. Supp. 2d 1246, 1256-57 (M.D. Fla. 2007) ("A corporation can be liable for the RICO violations of its employees when the corporation is actually the direct or indirect beneficiary of the pattern of racketeering activity, but not when it is merely the victim, prize, or passive instrument of racketeering.") (internal quotation marks and citation omitted); *see also* Cox v. Adm'r U.S. Steel & Carnegie, 17 F.3d 1386, 1403-08 (11th Cir. 1994) (noting that "some courts have recognized a narrow exception to vicarious liability under RICO," surveying different approaches among the circuits, and ultimately rejecting most limitations on vicariously liability and instead holding that the defendant union could be vicariously liable under the theory of respondeat superior for the acts of its employees).

7. Litigation against the tobacco industry in recent years has involved not only relatively familiar tort theories such as product liability, but also a variety of business tort claims. In United States v. Philip Morris USA, Inc., 449 F. Supp. 2d 1 (D.D.C. 2006), for example, Judge Gladys Kessler issued a *1,742-page* opinion (987 pages as published in F. Supp. 2d) finding the major tobacco companies liable for RICO violations arising from a decades-long scheme to, among other things, misrepresent the link between cigarette smoking and disease. Judge Kessler enjoined the companies from deceptively marketing their products and required corrective advertising.[8] The D.C. Circuit affirmed most of the court's rulings on liability and remedies. *See* United States v. Philip Morris USA, Inc., 566 F.3d 1095 (D.C. Cir. 2009) (per curiam), *cert. denied*, 130 S. Ct. 3502 (2010). Other major tobacco cases in recent years have been premised on false advertising and consumer fraud claims of the type discussed *supra* in Chapter 9. *See, e.g.*, Altria Group, Inc. v. Good, 129 S. Ct. 538 (2009) (holding that Federal Cigarette Labeling and Advertising Act did not preempt claim under Maine Unfair Trade Practices Act that advertising cigarettes as "light" and having "lowered tar and nicotine" was deceptive); In re Light Cigarettes Mktg. Sales Practices Litig., 691 F. Supp. 2d 239 (D. Me. 2010) (declining to give issue preclusive effect to

7. The Court in *Reves* noted, however, that outsiders may be liable for violations of one or more of RICO's other substantive provisions. *See Reves*, 507 U.S. at 185 & n.10 (noting possibility of outsider liability under § 1962(a), (b), or (d)).

8. The D.C. Circuit had earlier ruled that disgorgement of the defendants' profits was not an available remedy under § 1964(a). *See* United States v. Philip Morris USA, Inc., 396 F.3d 1190 (D.C. Cir. 2005).

the findings in *United States v. Philip Morris*); Clinton v. Brown & Williamson Holdings, Inc., 652 F. Supp. 2d 528 (S.D.N.Y. 2009) (vacating summary judgment for defendant post-*Altria* in a case alleging common law fraud); Aspinall v. Philip Morris, Inc., 902 N.E.2d 421, 422, 426 (Mass. 2009) (holding, in a "class action alleging that the defendants engaged in unfair or deceptive practices, in violation of" Massachusetts law, that the defendants failed to show that "they were given affirmative permission to use the descriptors at issue" and thus concluding that the state statutory exemption from liability did not apply).

PROBLEM

Problem 14-5. Groucho Corp. and Harpo Inc. are competitors in the business of arranging vacations to Fredonia. Groucho alleges that, for a period of over one year, Harpo's CEO Wendell used telephone and e-mail services to communicate materially false information (that Groucho was on the verge of bankruptcy) to potential customers in violation of the federal wire fraud statute. Groucho files suit against Wendell under § 1962(c) of the RICO Act; Wendell moves to dismiss. Who wins? What other claims, if any, might Groucho have?

15 Federal and State Preemption of Unfair Competition Claims

Many of the doctrines we have considered in this second half of the casebook are creatures of state law: For example, common law commercial disparagement, the right of publicity, trade secret law, and tortious interference with contract. As such, they are potentially subject to federal preemption by virtue of the Constitution's Supremacy Clause. *See* U.S. CONST. art. VI ("This Constitution, and the Laws of the United States which shall be made in Pursuance thereof . . . shall be the supreme Law of the Land"). As we will see, sometimes it may be the case that the Constitution itself preempts state unfair competition laws that threaten to undermine the Constitution's allocation of exclusive power over certain subject matter to the federal government. Alternatively, sometimes it may be a matter of a federal statute expressly or implicitly preempting a conflicting state law. In such a case, although the Constitution would tolerate the state regulation at issue, Congress itself has chosen (legitimately?) to preempt the regulation at issue. Finally, although less commonly, sometimes state trade secret law preempts other state laws that cover the same subject matter. In this chapter, we consider these various facets of preemption doctrine as it relates to unfair competition law. We begin with four cases addressing federal patent preemption of state unfair competition laws. We then present case excerpts discussing whether federal copyright law preempts the misappropriation ("hot news" doctrine), state contract law, and the right of publicity. We conclude with a case presenting radically different interpretations of the preemption provision of the Uniform Trade Secrets Act.

A. PATENT PREEMPTION

Sears, Roebuck & Co. v. Stiffel Co.
376 U.S. 225 (1964)

Mr. Justice BLACK delivered the opinion of the Court.

The question in this case is whether a State's unfair competition law can, consistently with the federal patent laws, impose liability for or prohibit the copying of an article which is protected by neither a federal patent nor a copyright. The respondent, Stiffel Company, secured design and mechanical patents on a "pole lamp" — a vertical tube having lamp fixtures along the outside, the tube being made so that it will stand upright between the floor and ceiling of a room. Pole lamps proved a decided commercial success, and soon after Stiffel brought them on the market Sears, Roebuck & Company put on the market a substantially identical lamp, which it sold more cheaply, Sears' retail price being about the same as Stiffel's wholesale price. Stiffel then brought this action against Sears in the United States District Court for the Northern District of Illinois, claiming in its first count that by copying its design Sears had infringed Stiffel's patents and in its second count that by selling copies of Stiffel's lamp Sears had caused confusion in the trade as to the source of the lamps and had thereby engaged in unfair competition under Illinois law. There was evidence that identifying tags were not attached to the Sears lamps although labels appeared on the cartons in which they were delivered to customers, that customers had asked Stiffel whether its lamps differed from Sears', and that in two cases customers who had bought Stiffel lamps had complained to Stiffel on learning that Sears was selling substantially identical lamps at a much lower price.

The District Court, after holding the patents, invalid for want of invention, went on to find as a fact that Sears' lamp was "a substantially exact copy" of Stiffel's and that the two lamps were so much alike, both in appearance and in functional details, "that confusion between them is likely, and some confusion has already occurred." On these findings the court held Sears guilty of unfair competition, enjoined Sears "from unfairly competing with (Stiffel) by selling or attempting to sell pole lamps identical to or confusingly similar to" Stiffel's lamp, and ordered an accounting to fix profits and damages resulting from Sears' "unfair competition."

The Court of Appeals affirmed. . . .

Before the Constitution was adopted, some States had granted patents either by special act or by general statute, but when the Constitution was adopted provision for a federal patent law was made one of the enumerated powers of Congress because, as Madison put it in *The Federalist No. 43*, the States "cannot separately make effectual provision" for either patents or copyrights. That constitutional provision is Art. I, s 8, cl. 8, which empowers Congress "To promote the Progress of Science and useful Arts, by securing for limited Times to Authors and Inventors the exclusive Right to their respective Writings and Discoveries." Pursuant to this constitutional authority, Congress in 1790 enacted the first federal patent and copyright law, 1 Stat. 109, and ever since that time has fixed the condition upon which patents and copyrights shall be granted, see17 U.S.C. §§ 1-216; 35 U.S.C. §§ 1-293. These laws, like other laws of the United States enacted pursuant to constitutional authority, are the supreme law of the land. When state law touches upon the area of these federal statutes, it is "familiar doctrine" that the federal policy "may not be set at naught, or its benefits denied" by the state law. Sola Elec. Co. v. Jefferson Elec. Co., 317 U.S. 172, 173, 176, 63 S. Ct. 172, 173, 87 L. Ed. 165 (1942). This is true, of course, even if the state law is enacted in the exercise of otherwise undoubted state power.

The grant of a patent is the grant of a statutory monopoly; indeed, the grant of patents in England was an explicit exception to the statute of James I prohibiting monopolies. Patents are not given as favors, as was the case of monopolies given by the Tudor monarchs, see The Case of Monopolies (Darcy v. Allein), 11 Co. Rep. 84, b., 77 Eng. Rep. 1260 (K.B. 1602), but are meant to encourage invention by rewarding the inventor with the right, limited to a term of years fixed by the patent, to exclude others from the use of his invention. During that period of time no one may make use, or sell the patented product without the patentee's authority. 35 U.S.C. § 271. But in rewarding useful invention, the "rights and welfare of the community must be fairly dealt with and effectually guarded." Kendall v. Winsor, 21 How. 322, 328, 16 L. Ed. 165 (1859). To that end the prerequisites to obtaining a patent are strictly observed, and when the patent has issued the limitations on its exercise are equally strictly enforced. To begin with, a genuine "invention" or "discovery" must be demonstrated "lest in the constant demand for new appliances the heavy hand of tribute be laid on each slight technological advance in an art." Cuno Engineering Corp. v. Automatic Devices Corp., 314 U.S. 84, 92, 62 S. Ct. 37, 41, 86 L. Ed. 58 (1941). Once the patent issues, it is strictly construed. [I]t cannot be used to secure any monopoly beyond that contained in the patent, the patentee's control over the product when it leaves his hands is sharply limited, and the patent monopoly may not be used in disregard of the antitrust laws. Finally, and especially relevant here, when the patent expires the monopoly created by it expires, too, and the right to make the article—including the right to make it in precisely the shape it carried when patented—passes to the public.

Thus the patent system is one in which uniform federal standards are carefully used to promote invention while at the same time preserving free competition.[7] Obviously a State could not, consistently with the Supremacy Clause of the Constitution, extend the life of a patent beyond its expiration date or give a patent on an article which lacked the level of invention required for federal patents. To do either would run counter to the policy of Congress of granting patents only to true inventions, and then only for a limited time. Just as a State cannot encroach upon the federal patent laws directly, it cannot, under some other law, such as that forbidding unfair competition, give protection of a kind that clashes with the objectives of the federal patent laws.

In the present case the "pole lamp" sold by Stiffel has been held not to be entitled to the protection of either a mechanical or a design patent. An unpatentable article, like an article on which the patent has expired, is in the public domain and may be made and sold by whoever chooses to do so. What Sears did was to copy Stiffel's design and to sell lamps almost identical to those sold by Stiffel. This it had every right to do under the federal patent laws. That Stiffel originated the pole lamp and made it popular is immaterial. "Sharing in the goodwill of an article unprotected by patent or trade-mark is the exercise of a right possessed by all-and in the free exercise of which the consuming public is deeply interested." Kellogg Co. v. National Biscuit Co., supra, 305 U.S. at 122, 59 S. Ct. at 115. To allow a State by use of its law of unfair competition to prevent the copying of an article which represents too slight an advance to be patented would be to permit the State to block off from the public something which federal law has said belongs to the public. The result would be that while federal law grants only 14 or 17 years' protection to genuine inventions, see 35 U.S.C. §§ 154, 173, States could allow perpetual protection to articles too lacking in novelty to merit any patent at all

7. The purpose of Congress to have national uniformity in patent and copyright laws can be inferred from such statutes as that which vests exclusive jurisdiction to hear patent and copyright cases in federal courts, 28 U.S.C. § 1338(a), and that section of the Copyright Act which expressly saves state protection of unpublished writings but does not include published writings, 17 U.S.C. § 2.

under federal constitutional standards. This would be too great an encroachment on the federal patent system to be tolerated.

Sears has been held liable here for unfair competition because of a finding of likelihood of confusion based only on the fact that Sears' lamp was copied from Stiffel's unpatented lamp and that consequently the two looked exactly alike. Of course there could be "confusion" as to who had manufactured these nearly identical articles. But mere inability of the public to tell two identical articles apart is not enough to support an injunction against copying or an award of damages for copying that which the federal patent laws permit to be copied. Doubtless a State may, in appropriate circumstances, require that goods, whether patented or unpatented, be labeled or that other precautionary steps be taken to prevent customers from being misled as to the source, just as it may protect businesses in the use of their trademarks, labels, or distinctive dress in the packaging of goods so as to prevent others, by imitating such markings, from misleading purchasers as to the source of the goods. But because of the federal patent laws a State may not, when the article is unpatented and uncopyrighted, prohibit the copying of the article itself or award damages for such copying. Cf. G. Ricordi & Co. v. Haendler, 194 F.2d 914, 916 (C.A.2d Cir. 1952). The judgment below did both and in so doing gave Stiffel the equivalent of a patent monopoly on its unpatented lamp. That was error, and Sears is entitled to a judgment in its favor.

Reversed.

Compco Corp. v. Day-Brite Lighting, Inc.
376 U.S. 234 (1964)

Mr. Justice BLACK delivered the opinion of the Court.

As in Sears, Roebuck & Co. v. Stiffel Co., 376 U.S. 225, 84 S. Ct. 784, the question here is whether the use of a state unfair competition law to give relief against the copying of an unpatented industrial design conflicts with the federal patent laws. . . .

. . . Here Day-Brite's fixture has been held not to be entitled to a design or mechanical patent. Under the federal patent laws it is, therefore, in the public domain and can be copied in every detail by whoever pleases. It is true that the trial court found that the configuration of Day-Brite's fixture identified Day-Brite to the trade because the arrangement of the ribbing had, like a trademark, acquired a "secondary meaning" by which that particular design was associated with Day-Brite. But if the design is not entitled to a design patent or other federal statutory protection, then it can be copied at will.

As we have said in Sears, while the federal patent laws prevent a State from prohibiting the copying and selling of unpatented articles, they do not stand in the way of state law, statutory or decisional, which requires those who make and sell copies to take precautions to identify their products as their own. A State of course has power to impose liability upon those who, knowing that the public is relying upon an original manufacturer's reputation for quality and integrity, deceive the public by palming off their copies as the original. That an article copied from an unpatented article could be made in some other way, that the design is "nonfunctional" and not essential to the use of either article, that the configuration of the article copied may have a "secondary meaning" which identifies the maker to the trade, or that there may be "confusion" among purchasers as to which article is which or as to who is the maker, may be relevant evidence in applying a State's law requiring such precautions as labeling; however, and regardless of the copier's motives, neither these facts nor any others can furnish a basis for imposing liability for or prohibiting the actual acts of copying and selling. . . .

[Concurring opinion of Mr. Justice HARLAN omitted.]

Kewanee Oil Co. v. Bicron Corp.
416 U.S. 470 (1974)

Mr. Chief Justice BURGER delivered the opinion of the Court.

We granted certiorari to resolve a question on which there is a conflict in the courts of appeals: whether state trade secret protection is pre-empted by operation of the federal patent law. In the instant case the Court of Appeals for the Sixth Circuit held that there was preemption. The Courts of Appeals for the Second, Fourth, Fifth, and Ninth Circuits have reached the opposite conclusion. . . .

Petitioner brought this diversity action in United States District Court for the Northern District of Ohio seeking injunctive relief and damages for the misappropriation of trade secrets. The district Court, applying Ohio trade secret law, granted a permanent injunction against the disclosure or use by respondents of 20 of the 40 claimed trade secrets until such time as the trade secrets had been released to the public, had otherwise generally become available to the public, or had been obtained by respondents from sources having the legal right to convey the information.

The Court of Appeals for the Sixth Circuit held that the findings of fact by the District Court were not clearly erroneous, and that it was evident from the record that the individual respondents appropriated to the benefit of Bicron secret information on processes obtained while they were employees at Harshaw. Further, the Court of Appeals held that the District Court properly applied Ohio law relating to trade secrets. Nevertheless, the Court of Appeals reversed the District Court, finding Ohio's trade secret law to be in conflict with the patent laws of the United States. The Court of Appeals reasoned that Ohio could not grant monopoly protection to processes and manufacturing techniques that were appropriate subjects for consideration under 35 U.S.C. § 101 for a federal patent but which had been in commercial use for over one year and so were no longer eligible for patent protection under 35 U.S.C. § 102(b).

We hold that Ohio's law of trade secrets is not preempted by the patent laws of the United States, and accordingly, we reverse. . . .

III

The first issue we deal with is whether the States are forbidden to act at all in the area of protection of the kinds of intellectual property which may make up the subject matter of trade secrets. . . .

In the 1972 Term, in Goldstein v. California, 412 U.S. 546 (1973), we held that the cl. 8 grant of power to Congress was not exclusive and that, at least in the case of writings, the States were not prohibited from encouraging and protecting the efforts of those within their borders by appropriate legislation. The States could, therefore, protect against the unauthorized rerecording for sale of performances fixed on records or tapes, even though those performances qualified as "writings" in the constitutional sense and Congress was empowered to legislate regarding such performances and could pre-empt the area if it chose to do so. This determination was premised on the great diversity of interests in our Nation — the essentially nonuniform character of the appreciation of intellectual achievements in the various States. Evidence for this came from patents granted by the States in the 18th century. 412 U.S., at 557.

Just as the States may exercise regulatory power over writings so may the States regulate with respect to discoveries. States may hold diverse viewpoints in protecting intellectual property relating to invention as they do in protecting the intellectual property relating to the subject matter of copyright. The only limitation on the States is that in regulating the area of patents and copyrights they do not conflict with the operation of the laws in this area passed by Congress, and it is to that more difficult question we now turn.

IV

The question of whether the trade secret law of Ohio is void under the Supremacy Clause involves a consideration of whether that law "stands as an obstacle to the accomplishment and execution of the full purposes and objectives of Congress." Hines v. Davidowitz, 312 U.S. 52, 67 (1941). See Florida Avocado Growers v. Paul, 373 U.S. 132, 141 (1963). We stated in Sears, Roebuck & Co. v. Stiffel Co., 376 U.S. 225, 229 (1964), that when state law touches upon the area of federal statutes enacted pursuant to constitutional authority, "it is 'familiar doctrine' that the federal policy 'may not be set at naught, or its benefits denied' by the state law. Sola Elec. Co v. Jefferson Elec. Co., 317 U.S. 173, 176 (1942). This is true, of course, even if the state law is enacted in the exercise of otherwise undoubted state power." . . .

The stated objective of the Constitution in granting the power to Congress to legislate in the area of intellectual property is to "promote the Progress of Science and useful Arts." The patent laws promote this progress by offering a right of exclusion for a limited period as an incentive to inventors to risk the often enormous costs in terms of time, research, and development. . . .

The maintenance of standards of commercial ethics and the encouragement of invention are the broadly stated policies behind trade secret law. "The necessity of good faith and honest, fair dealing, is the very life and spirit of the commercial world." . . .

As we noted earlier, trade secret law protects items which would not be proper subjects for consideration for patent protection under 35 U.S.C. § 101. As in the case of the recordings in *Goldstein v. California*, Congress, with respect to nonpatentable subject matter, "has drawn no balance; rather, it has left the area unattended, and no reason exists why the State should not be free to act." *Goldstein v. California*, supra, at 570 (footnote omitted).

Since no patent is available for a discovery, however useful, novel, and nonobvious, unless it falls within one of the express categories of patentable subject matter of 35 U.S.C. § 101, the holder of such a discovery would have no reason to apply for a patent whether trade secret protection existed or not. Abolition of trade secret protection would, therefore, not result in increased disclosure to the public of discoveries in the area of nonpatentable subject matter. . . .

Congress has spoken in the area of those discoveries which fall within one of the categories of patentable subject matter of 35 U.S.C. § 101 and which are, therefore, of a nature that would be subject to consideration for a patent. Processes, machines, manufactures, compositions of matter, and improvements thereof, which meet the tests of utility, novelty, and nonobviousness are entitled to be patented, but those which do not, are not. The question remains whether those items which are proper subjects for consideration for a patent may also have available the alternative protection accorded by trade secret law.

Certainly the patent policy of encouraging invention is not disturbed by the existence of another form of incentive to invention. In this respect the two systems are not and never would be in conflict. Similarly, the policy that matter once in the public domain must remain in the public domain is not incompatible with the existence of trade secret protection. By definition a trade secret has not been placed in the public domain. . . .

. . . Trade secret law will encourage invention in areas where patent law does not reach, and will prompt the independent innovator to proceed with the discovery and exploitation of his invention. Competition is fostered and the public is not deprived of the use of valuable, if not quite patentable, invention. . . .

The final category of patentable subject matter to deal with is the clearly patentable invention, i.e., that invention which the owner believes to meet the standards of patentability. It is here that the federal interest in disclosure is at its peak. . . .

Trade secret law provides far weaker protection in many respects than the patent law. While trade secret law does not forbid the discovery of the trade secret by fair and honest means, e.g., independent creation or reverse engineering, patent law operates "against the world," forbidding any use of the invention for whatever purpose for a significant length of time. The holder of a trade secret also takes a substantial risk that the secret will be passed on to his competitors, by theft or by breach of a confidential relationship, in a manner not easily susceptible of discovery or proof. Painton & Co. v. Bourns, Inc., 442 F.2d, at 224. Where patent law acts as a barrier, trade secret law functions relatively as a sieve. The possibility that an inventor who believes his invention meets the standards of patentability will sit back, rely on trade secret law, and after one year of use forfeit any right to patent protection, 35 U.S.C. § 102(b), is remote indeed.

Nor does society face much risk that scientific or technological progress will be impeded by the rare inventor with a patentable invention who chooses trade secret protection over patent protection. The ripeness-of-time concept of invention, developed from the study of the many independent multiple discoveries in history, predicts that if a particular individual had not made a particular discovery others would have, and in probably a relatively short period of time. If something is to be discovered at all very likely it will be discovered by more than one person. . . .

. . . Trade secret law and patent law have co-existed in this country for over one hundred years. Each has its particular role to play, and the operation of one does not take away from the need for the other. . . . Congress, by its silence over these many years, has seen the wisdom of allowing the States to enforce trade secret protection. Until Congress takes affirmative action to the contrary, States should be free to grant protection to trade secrets. . . .

Mr. Justice MARSHALL, concurring in the result.

Unlike the Court, I do not believe that the possibility that an inventor with a patentable invention will rely on state trade secret law rather than apply for a patent is "remote indeed." Ante, at 1890. State trade secret law provides substantial protection to the inventor who intends to use or sell the invention himself rather than license it to others, protection which in its unlimited duration is clearly superior to the 17-year monopoly afforded by the patent laws. I have no doubt that the existence of trade secret protection provides in some instances a substantial disincentive to entrance into the patent system, and thus deprives society of the benefits of public disclosure of the invention which it is the policy of the patent laws to encourage. This case may well be such an instance.

But my view of sound policy in this area does not dispose of this case. Rather, the question presented in this case is whether Congress, in enacting the patent laws, intended merely to offer inventors a limited monopoly in exchange for disclosure of their invention, or instead to exert pressure on inventors to enter into this exchange by withdrawing any alternative possibility of legal protection for their inventions. I am persuaded that the former is the case. State trade secret laws and the federal patent laws have co-existed for many, many years. During this time, Congress has repeatedly demonstrated its full awareness of the existence of the trade secret system, without any indication of disapproval. Indeed, Congress has in a number of instances given explicit federal protection to trade secret information provided to federal agencies. See, e.g., 5 U.S.C. §552(b)(4); 18 U.S.C. §1905; see generally Appendix to Brief for Petitioner. Because of this, I conclude that there is "neither such actual conflict between the two schemes of regulation that both cannot stand in the same area, nor evidence of a congressional design to pre-empt the field." Florida Lime & Avocado Growers v. Paul, 373 U.S. 132, 141, 83 S. Ct. 1210, 1217, 10 L. Ed. 2d 248 (1963). I therefore concur in the result reached by the majority of the Court.

Mr. Justice DOUGLAS, with whom Mr. Justice BRENNAN concurs, dissenting.

Today's decision is at war with the philosophy of Sears, Roebuck & Co. v. Stiffel Co., 376 U.S. 225, and Compco Corp. v. Day-Brite Lighting, Inc., 376 U.S. 234. Those cases involved patents — one of a pole lamp and one of fluorescent lighting fixtures — each of which was declared invalid. The lower courts held, however, that though the patents were invalid the sale of identical or confusingly similar products to the products of the patentees violated state unfair competition laws. We held that when an article is unprotected by a patent, state law may not forbid others to copy it, because every article not covered by a valid patent is in the public domain. Congress in the patent laws decided that where no patent existed, free competition should prevail; that where a patent is rightfully issued, the right to exclude others should obtain for no longer than 17 years, and that the States may not "under some other law, such as that forbidding unfair competition, give protection of a kind that clashes with the objectives of the federal patent laws," 376 U.S., at 231. . . .

The conflict with the patent laws is obvious. The decision of Congress to adopt a patent system was based on the idea that there will be much more innovation if discoveries are disclosed and patented than there will be when everyone works in secret. Society thus fosters a free exchange of technological information at the cost of a limited 17-year monopoly. . . .

A suit to redress theft of a trade secret is grounded in tort damages for breach of a contract — a historic remedy, Cataphote Corp. v. Hudson, 422 F.2d 1290. Damages for breach of a confidential relation are not pre-empted by this patent law, but an injunction against use is pre-empted because the patent law states the only monopoly over trade secrets that is enforceable by specific performance; and that monopoly exacts as a price full disclosure. A trade secret can be protected only by being kept secret. Damages for breach of a contract are one thing; an injunction barring disclosure does service for the protection accorded valid patents and is therefore pre-empted. . . .

Bonito Boats, Inc. v. Thunder Craft Boats, Inc.

489 U.S. 141 (1989)

Justice O'CONNOR delivered the opinion of the Court. . . .

In September 1976, petitioner Bonito Boats, Inc., a Florida corporation, developed a hull design for a fiberglass recreational boat which it marketed under the trade name Bonito Boat Model 5VBR. Designing the boat hull required substantial effort on the part of Bonito. A set of engineering drawings was prepared, from which a hardwood model was created. The hardwood model was then sprayed with fiberglass to create a mold, which then served to produce the finished fiberglass boats for sale. The 5VBR was placed on the market sometime in September 1976. There is no indication in the record that a patent application was ever filed for protection of the utilitarian or design aspects of the hull, or for the process by which the hull was manufactured. The 5VBR was favorably received by the boating public, and "a broad interstate market" developed for its sale.

In May 1983, after the Bonito 5VBR had been available to the public for over six years, the Florida Legislature enacted Fla. Stat. § 559.94 (1987). The statute makes "it . . . unlawful for any person to use the direct molding process to duplicate for the purpose of sale any manufactured vessel hull or component part of a vessel made by another without the written permission of that other person." § 559.94(2). The statute also makes it unlawful for a person to "knowingly sell a vessel hull or component part of a vessel duplicated in violation of subsection (2)." § 559.94(3). Damages, injunctive relief, and attorney's fees are made available to "any person who suffers injury or damage as the result of a violation" of the statute. § 559.94(4). The statute was made applicable to vessel hulls or component parts duplicated through the use of direct molding after July 1, 1983. § 559.94(5).

On December 21, 1984, Bonito filed this action in the Circuit Court of Orange County, Florida. The complaint alleged that respondent here, Thunder Craft Boats, Inc., a Tennessee corporation, had violated the Florida statute by using the direct molding process to duplicate the Bonito 5VBR fiberglass hull, and had knowingly sold such duplicates in violation of the Florida statute. . . .

III

We believe that the Florida statute at issue in this case so substantially impedes the public use of the otherwise unprotected design and utilitarian ideas embodied in unpatented boat hulls as to run afoul of the teaching of our decisions in *Sears* and *Compco.* It is readily apparent that the Florida statute does not operate to prohibit "unfair competition" in the usual sense that the term is understood. The law of unfair competition has its roots in the common-law tort of deceit: its general concern is with protecting *consumers* from confusion as to source. . . .

With some notable exceptions, including the interpretation of the Illinois law of unfair competition at issue in *Sears* and *Compco* . . . the common-law tort of unfair competition has been limited to protection against copyright of nonfunctional aspects of consumer products which have acquired secondary meaning such that they operate as a designation of source. . . .

In contrast to the operation of unfair competition law, the Florida statute is aimed directly at preventing the exploitation of the design and utilitarian conceptions embodied in the product itself. The sparse legislative history surrounding its enactment indicates that it was intended to create an inducement for the improvement of boat hull designs. See Tr. of Meeting of Transportation Committee, Florida House of Representatives, May 3, 1983 ("There is no inducement for [a] quality boat manufacturer to improve these designs and secondly, if he does, it is immediately copied. This would prevent that and allow him recourse in circuit court"). To accomplish this goal, the Florida statute endows the original boat hull manufacturer with rights against the world, similar in scope and operation to the rights accorded a federal patentee. Like the patentee, the beneficiary of the Florida statute may prevent a competitor from "making" the product in what is evidently the most efficient manner available and from "selling" the product when it is produced in that fashion. Compare 35 U.S.C. § 154. The Florida scheme offers this protection for an unlimited number of years to all boat hulls and their component parts, without regard to their ornamental or technological merit. Protection is available for subject matter for which patent protection has been denied or has expired, as well as for designs which have been freely revealed to the consuming public by their creators. That the Florida statute does not remove all means of reproduction and sale does not eliminate the conflict with the federal scheme. See *Kellogg*, 305 U.S., at 122. In essence, the Florida law prohibits the entire public from engaging in a form of reverse engineering of a product in the public domain. This is clearly one of the rights vested in the federal patent holder, but has never been a part of state protection under the law of unfair competition or trade secrets. . . .

Moreover, as we noted in *Kewanee*, the competitive reality of reverse engineering may act as a spur to the inventor, creating an incentive to develop inventions that meet the rigorous requirements of patentability. 416 U.S., at 489-490. The Florida statute substantially reduces this competitive incentive, thus eroding the general rule of free competition upon which the attractiveness of the federal patent bargain depends. . . . The Florida statute is aimed directly at the promotion of intellectual creation by substantially restricting the public's ability to exploit ideas that the patent system mandates shall be free for all to use. Like the interpretation of Illinois unfair competition law in *Sears* and *Compco*, the Florida statute represents a break with the tradition of peaceful coexistence between state market regulation and federal patent policy. The Florida law substantially restricts the public's ability to exploit an unpatented design in general circulation, raising the specter of state-created monopolies in a host of useful shapes and processes for which patent protection has been denied or is otherwise unobtainable. It thus enters a field of regulation which the patent laws have reserved to Congress. The patent statute's careful balance between public right and private monopoly to promote certain creative activity is a "scheme of federal regulation . . . so pervasive as to make reasonable the inference that Congress left no room for the States to supplement it." Rice v. Santa Fe Elevator Corp., 331 U.S. 218, 230 (1947). . . .

COMMENTS AND QUESTIONS

1. The rule set forth by Sears, Roebuck & Co v. Stiffel Co., 376 U.S. 225 (1964), was fairly clear: Patent law reflects a compromise between the goal of promoting innovation and the danger of condoning monopoly. Supplementing the scope of patent law may upset that balance, and is therefore prohibited. Supplementing *enforcement* of the federal intellectual property laws was condoned in dictum at the end of Compco Corp. v. Day-Brite Lighting, Inc., 376 U.S. 234 (1964), and in Justice Harlan's concurrence in both cases. After these cases, state law served a very limited function in the scheme of intellectual property protection. States could work to further the goals of federal protection, but they had to work within the parameters set down by federal law. As a result, both *Sears* and *Compco* struck down state statutes providing design protection to unpatentable utilitarian articles.

The *Kewanee* opinion takes a remarkably different tack. Chief Justice Burger's opinion for the Court emphasizes only one of the two policies shaping the patent laws: the goal of promoting innovation. The opinion does not discuss the dangers intellectual property protection poses for free competition. As a result, the *Kewanee* Court finds no problem with trade secret protection that extends beyond the scope of the patent laws. Note that the Court seems to approve not only state laws that protect nonpatentable subject matter (an area in which it could be argued that the federal government has no interest),[1] but also the protection of inventions not patentable for some other reason (i.e., suppression, misuse, lack of novelty, or obviousness).

Is *Kewanee* reconcilable with *Sears*? The *Kewanee* Court did not overrule *Sears* or *Compco*; indeed, it cited them in support of its holding. Thus state laws preventing copying were treated differently from trade secret laws after *Kewanee*. The latter, although broader in scope (they prevented far more than just outright copying of products), were permissible; the former were not. For an argument that *Kewanee* "closed the circle" on the open-ended preemption analysis of *Sears* and *Compco*, see Paul Goldstein, Kewanee Oil Co. v. Bicron Corp.: *Notes on a Closing Circle*, 1974 Sup. Ct. Rev. 81 (1974).

2. Is preemption a good idea? That depends on what you think of the balance the federal laws have struck. If you are more concerned about injury to competition by conferring monopoly rights on patentees, you are likely to favor the result in *Sears*. If on the other hand you think that innovation is underrewarded, it is reasonable to oppose federal preemption. One way to reconcile these cases may be to read *Sears* and *Compco* as expressing a federal policy in favor of reverse engineering of products in the public domain. If that is the overarching federal goal, it is logical to strike down the laws in *Sears* and *Compco* but not *Kewanee*, since trade secrets statutes (unlike the unfair competition laws we have discussed) generally allow reverse engineering. This result is also consistent with the reading of trade secret laws as merely an application of tort and contract principles.

3. Do *Sears* and *Compco* hold that the *Constitution* forbids the states from enacting laws like the Illinois statute at issue in those cases? Or is it the *Patent Act* that forbids this? If the latter, what part? Is Justice O'Connor's characterization (in *Bonito*

1. Even in this area, though, a federal interest may be discerned. If Congress has declared some subject matter unpatentable, that could reflect a federal determination that that matter is unworthy of protection, a determination that state law should not be allowed to upset.

Boats) of these two cases as having turned on Illinois's protection of functional designs accurate?

4. Does the result in *Bonito Boats* make sense? Is it consistent with *Kewanee*? *Bonito Boats* can be reconciled with trade secrets statutes if one accepts the reverse engineering rationale described above. Whatever one thinks of the *Bonito* result, the last sentence remains troubling. Characterizing patent law as "pervasive federal regulation" suggests that it might preempt the field, automatically striking down all state laws that attempt to regulate intellectual property. If taken seriously, that approach would leave no room at all for state protection of inventions.

5. Note the similarity between the statutes struck down in *Sears* and *Bonito Boats*. In both cases, what was prohibited was the direct copying of a competitor's design. The *Bonito Boats* statute is more limited than that in *Sears*, since it prohibits only one particular method of copying. Nonetheless, the Court struck it down. Why should the courts be concerned about these comparatively narrow statutes when they allowed the far broader statute in *Kewanee* to pass muster?

6. The *Bonito Boats* decision has been roundly criticized. *See, e.g.*, John S. Wiley, Jr., Bonito Boats: *Uninformed But Mandatory Federal Innovation Policy*, 1989 SUP. CT. REV. 283. *Cf.* Symposium, *Product Simulation: A Right or a Wrong?*, 64 COLUM. L. REV. 1178 (1964) (articles criticizing the analogous decisions in *Sears* and *Compco*). Does this criticism make sense? Or is *Bonito Boats* a needed barrier to the creation of state laws that would undo the balance struck by Congress?

A different form of criticism of the result in *Bonito Boats* was offered by Congress in 1998. As part of the Digital Millennium Copyright Act, Congress created a new federal intellectual property right protecting "original" boat hull designs. 17 U.S.C. §§ 1301 *et seq.* We discuss this statute in more detail in Chapter 4 *supra*. Can Congress lawfully accomplish here what the states cannot? Does *Bonito Boats* suggest some sort of constitutional limitation on any form of protection (state or federal) in this area?

7. As noted in Chapter 9 *supra*, on some occasions the Federal Circuit has held that federal patent law preempts state unfair competition law premised on a false assertion of patent or other intellectual property rights, absent proof that the defendant's conduct was both objectively and subjectively in bad faith. *See* 800 Adept, Inc. v. Murex Sec., Ltd., 539 F.3d 1354, 1370 (Fed. Cir. 2008) (stating that plaintiff asserting tortious interference claims arising out of alleged false claim of patent infringement must prove both objective and subjective bad faith); Dominant Semiconductors SDN BHD v. Osram GmbH, 524 F.3d 1254, 1260 n.5 (Fed. Cir. 2008). The court has extended this bad faith requirement to claims based on *federal* unfair competition as well, even though these claims are not, technically, subject to preemption by other federal laws. *See, e.g.*, Zenith Elecs. Corp. v. Exzec, Inc., 182 F.3d 1340, 1352-55 (Fed. Cir. 1999).

Sometimes the requisite showing of bad faith is present. *See, e.g.*, Dow Chemical v. Exxon Corp., 139 F.3d 1470 (Fed. Cir. 1998) (unfair competition claims by accused infringer based on alleged inequitable conduct not preempted); Univ. of Colorado Found. v. American Cyanamid, Inc., 196 F.3d 1366 (Fed. Cir. 1999) (state claims of fraud and unjust enrichment against patentee who stole invention from plaintiff not preempted). The court has, however, required that state claims that touch on areas of federal patent interest be judged by federal, not state, standards, so that they do not upset the balance struck by patent law. *See Univ. of Colorado*, *supra*; Midwest Industries v. Karavan Trailers, 175 F.3d 1356 (Fed. Cir. 1999). Is this a reasonable compromise?

8. In a number of cases, restrictions on the content of licensing contracts are said to raise preemption issues. One might question whether contracts are equivalent to state statutes for preemption purposes. On at least one occasion, the Supreme Court has suggested that protection of unpatentable goods (which would be prohibited under state misappropriation statutes) is permissible under contract law. *See, e.g.*, Aronson v. Quick Point Pencil, 440 U.S. 257 (1979). On the other hand, there are a variety of circumstances in which federal patent policy simply precludes the parties from contracting to the contrary. *See, e.g.*, Brulotte v. Thys Co., 379 U.S. 29 (1964) (holding unenforceable patent licensed in agreement that extends beyond patent's then 17-year term); Lear, Inc. v. Adkins, 395 U.S. 653 (1969) (contracts estopping licensee from challenging the validity of a patent are void); Everex Systems Inc. v. Cadtrak Corp., 89 F.3d 673 (9th Cir. 1996) (federal policy precluding assignment of nonexclusive patent licenses prevailed over state doctrine permitting such assignments). Note that in some of these cases, such as *Everex*, federal preemption actually works to the benefit of the intellectual property owner.

9. Regardless of the particular limitations federal law imposes on licensing agreements, patent licensing in general is a question of state (not federal) law. The Federal Circuit reaffirmed this in Gjerlov v. Schuyler Labs. Inc., 131 F.3d 1016 (Fed. Cir. 1997).

B. COPYRIGHT PREEMPTION

Cases in which defendants argue that federal copyright law preempts the plaintiff's state law claim raise some additional issues. In the *Goldstein* case excerpted below, the Supreme Court focused on whether the Constitution or federal copyright law preempted a California law that prohibited the copying of sound recordings. At the time the case began, sound recordings were not among the class of copyrightable works under federal copyright law.

A few years after the *Goldstein* decision, Congress enacted the 1976 Copyright Act, which (unlike the Patent Act and previous Copyright Acts) contains an express preemption provision, 17 U.S.C. § 301. In relevant part, this statute provides:

> (a) . . . all legal or equitable rights that are equivalent to any of the exclusive rights within the general scope of copyright as specified by section 106 in works of authorship that are fixed in a tangible medium of expression and come within the subject matter of copyright as specified by sections 102 and 103 . . . are governed exclusively by this title.
>
> (b) Nothing in this title annuls or limits any rights or remedies under the common law or statutes of any State with respect to — (1) subject matter that does not come within the subject matter of copyright as specified by sections 102 and 103, including works of authorship not fixed in any tangible medium of expression; or . . . (3) activities violating legal or equitable rights that are not equivalent to any of the exclusive rights within the general scope of copyright as specified by section 106. . . .

Most cases today in which copyright preemption is at issue focus on the meaning of § 301. As we will see, however, conflict preemption (the type of preemption at issue in *Goldstein*) may still retain some vitality in specific types of cases.

1. Conflict Preemption

Goldstein v. California
412 U.S. 546 (1973)

Mr. Chief Justice BURGER delivered the opinion of the Court.

We granted certiorari to review petitioners' conviction under a California statute making it a criminal offense to "pirate" recordings produced by others.

In 1971, an information was filed by the State of California, charging petitioners in 140 counts with violating § 653h of the California Penal Code. The information charged that, between April 1970 and March 1971, petitioners had copied several musical performances from commercially sold recordings without the permission of the owner of the master record or tape.[1] Petitioners moved to dismiss the complaint on the grounds that s 653h was in conflict with Art. I, § 8, cl. 8, of the Constitution, the "Copyright Clause," and the federal statutes enacted thereunder. Upon denial of their motion, petitioners entered pleas of nolo contendere to 10 of the 140 counts. . . .

I

Petitioners were engaged in what has commonly been called "record piracy" or "tape piracy" — the unauthorized duplication of recordings of performances by major musical artists. . . .

The challenged California statute forbids petitioners to transfer any performance fixed on a tape or record onto other records or tapes with the intention of selling the duplicates, unless they have first received permission from those who, under state law, are the owners of the master recording. Although the protection afforded to each master recording is substantial, lasting for an unlimited time, the scope of the proscribed activities is narrow. No limitation is placed on the use of the music, lyrics, or arrangement employed in making the master recording. Petitioners are not precluded from hiring their own musicians and artists and recording an exact imitation of the performance embodied on the master recording. Petitioners are even free to hire the same artists who made the initial recording in order to duplicate the performance. In essence, the statute thus provides copyright protection solely for the specific expressions which compose the master record or tape.

Petitioners' attack on the constitutionality of § 653h has many facets. First, they contend that the statute establishes a state copyright of unlimited duration, and thus conflicts with Art. I, § 8, cl. 8, of the Constitution. Second, petitioners claim that the state statute interferes with the implementation of federal policies inherent in the federal copyright statutes. 17 U.S.C. § 1 et seq. According to petitioners, it was the intention of Congress, as interpreted by this Court in Sears, Roebuck & Co. v. Stiffel Co., 376 U.S. 225, 84 S. Ct. 784, 11 L. Ed. 2d 661 (1964), and Compco Corp. v. Day-Brite Lighting, 376 U.S. 234, 84 S. Ct. 779, 11 L. Ed. 2d 669 (1964), to establish a uniform law throughout the United States to protect original writings.

1. In pertinent part, the California statute provides: "(a) Every person is guilty of a misdemeanor who:(1) Knowingly and willfully transfers or causes to be transferred any sounds recorded on a phonograph record, . . . tape, . . . or other article on which sounds are recorded, with intent to sell or cause to be sold, . . . such article on which such sounds are so transferred, without the consent of the owner. . . ."

As part of the federal scheme, it is urged that Congress intended to allow individuals to copy any work which was not protected by a federal copyright. Since § 653h effectively prohibits the copying of works which are not entitled to federal protection, petitioners contend that it conflicts directly with congressional policy and must fall under the Supremacy Clause of the Constitution. . . .

We note at the outset that the federal copyright statutes to which petitioners refer were amended by Congress while their case was pending in the state courts. In 1971, Pub. L. 92-140, 85 Stat. 391, 17 U.S.C. §§ 1(f), 5(n), 19, 20, 26, 101(e), was passed to allow federal copyright protection of recordings. However, § 3 of the amendment specifically provides that such protection is to be available only to sound recordings "fixed, published, and copyrighted" on and after February 15, 1972. . . . The recordings which petitioners copied were all "fixed" prior to February 15, 1972. . . .

II

Petitioners' first argument rests on the premise that the state statute under which they were convicted lies beyond the powers which the States reserved in our federal system. If this is correct, petitioners must prevail, since the States cannot exercise a sovereign power which, under the Constitution, they have relinquished to the Federal Government for its exclusive exercise.

A

. . . The clause of the Constitution granting to Congress the power to issue copyrights does not provide that such power shall vest exclusively in the Federal Government. Nor does the Constitution expressly provide that such power shall not be exercised by the States. . . .

Article I, § 8, cl. 8, of the Constitution gives to Congress the power—

> To promote the Progress of Science and useful Arts, by securing for limited Times to Authors and Inventors the exclusive Rights to their respective Writings and Discoveries. . . .

. . . The objective of the Copyright Clause was clearly to facilitate the granting of rights national in scope. . . . The national system which Madison supported eliminates the need for multiple applications and the expense and difficulty involved. In effect, it allows Congress to provide a reward greater in scope than any particular State may grant to promote progress in those fields which Congress determines are worthy of national action.

Although the Copyright Clause thus recognizes the potential benefits of a national system, it does not indicate that all writings are of national interest or that state legislation is, in all cases, unnecessary or precluded. . . . [I]t is unlikely that all citizens in all parts of the country place the same importance on works relating to all subjects. Since the subject matter to which the Copyright Clause is addressed may thus be of purely local importance and not worthy of national attention or protection, we cannot discern such an unyielding national interest as to require an inference that state power to grant copyrights has been relinquished to exclusive federal control.

The question to which we next turn is whether, in actual operation, the exercise of the power to grant copyrights by some States will prejudice the interests of other States. As we have noted, a copyright granted by a particular State has effect only within its boundaries. If one State grants such protection, the interests of States which do not are not prejudiced since their citizens remain free to copy within their borders those works which may be protected elsewhere. The interests of a State which grants copyright protection may, however, be adversely affected by other States that do not; individuals who wish to purchase a copy of a work protected in their own State will be able to buy unauthorized copies in other States where no protection exists. However, this conflict is neither so inevitable nor so severe as to compel the conclusion, that state power has been relinquished to the exclusive jurisdiction of the Congress. Obviously when some States do not grant copyright protection — and most do not — that circumstance reduces the economic value of a state copyright, but it will hardly render the copyright worthless. The situation is no different from that which may arise in regard to other state monopolies, such as a state lottery, or a food concession in a limited enclosure like a state park; in each case, citizens may escape the effect of one State's monopoly by making purchases in another area or another State. Similarly, in the case of state copyrights, except as to individuals willing to travel across state lines in order to purchase records or other writings protected in their own State, each State's copyrights will still serve to induce new artistic creations within that State-the very objective of the grant of protection. We do not see here the type of prejudicial conflicts which would arise, for example, if each State exercised a sovereign power to impose imposts and tariffs; nor can we discern a need for uniformity such as that which may apply to the regulation of interstate shipments.

Similarly, it is difficult to see how the concurrent exercise of the power to grant copyrights by Congress and the States will necessarily and inevitably lead to difficulty. At any time Congress determines that a particular category of "writing" is worthy of national protection and the incidental expenses of federal administration, federal copyright protection may be authorized. Where the need for free and unrestricted distribution of a writing is thought to be required by the national interest, the Copyright Clause and the Commerce Clause would allow Congress to eschew all protection. In such cases, a conflict would develop if a State attempted to protect that which Congress intended to be free from restraint or to free that which Congress had protected. However, where Congress determines that neither federal protection nor freedom from restraint is required by the national interest, it is at liberty to stay its hand entirely.[16] Since state protection would not then conflict with federal action, total relinquishment of the States' power to grant copyright protection cannot be inferred.

As we have seen, the language of the Constitution neither explicitly precludes the States from granting copyrights nor grants such authority exclusively to the Federal Government. The subject matter to which the Copyright Clause is addressed may at times be of purely local concern. No conflict will necessarily arise from a lack of uniform state regulation, nor will the interest of one State be significantly prejudiced by the actions of another. No reason exists why Congress must take affirmative action either to authorize protection of all categories of writings or to free them from all restraint. We therefor conclude that, under the Constitution, the States have not relinquished all power to grant to authors "the exclusive Right to their respective Writings."

16. For example, Congress has allowed writings which may eventually be the subject of a federal copyright, to be protected under state law prior to publication. 17 U.S.C. § 2.

B

Petitioners base an additional argument on the language of the Constitution. The California statute forbids individuals to appropriate recordings at any time after release. From this, petitioners argue that the State has created a copyright of unlimited duration, in violation of that portion of Art. I, § 8, cl. 8, which provides that copyrights may only be granted "for limited Times." Read literally, the text of Art. I does not support petitioners' position. Section 8 enumerates those powers which have been granted to Congress; Whatever limitations have been appended to such powers can only be understood as a limit on congressional, and not state, action. Moreover, it is not clear that the dangers to which this limitation was addressed apply with equal force to both the Federal Government and the States. When Congress grants an exclusive right or monopoly, its effects are pervasive; no citizen or State may escape its reach. As we have noted, however, the exclusive right granted by a State is confined to its borders. Consequently, even when the right is unlimited in duration, any tendency to inhibit further progress in science or the arts is narrowly circumscribed. The challenged statute cannot be voided for lack of a durational limitation.

III

Our conclusion that California did not surrender its power to issue copyrights does not end the inquiry. We must proceed to determine whether the challenged state statute is void under the Supremacy Clause. No simple formula can capture the complexities of this determination; the conflicts which may develop between state and federal action are as varied as the fields to which congressional action may apply. "Our primary function is to determine whether, under the circumstances of this particular case, (the state) law stands as an obstacle to the accomplishment and execution of the full purposes and objectives of Congress." Hines v. Davidowitz, 312 U.S., 52, 67, 61 S. Ct. 399, 404, 85 L. Ed. 581 (1941). We turn, then, to federal copyright law to determine what objectives Congress intended to fulfill.

By Art. I, § 8, cl. 8, of the Constitution, the States granted to Congress the power to protect the "Writings" of "Authors." These terms have not been construed in their narrow literal sense but, rather, with the reach necessary to reflect the broad scope of constitutional principles. While an "author" may be viewed as an individual who writes an original composition, the term, in its constitutional sense, has been construed to mean an "originator," "he to whom anything owes its origin." Burrow-Giles Lithographic Co. v. Sarony, 111 U.S. 53, 58, 4 S. Ct. 279, 281, 28 L. Ed. 349 (1884). Similarly, although the word "writings" might be limited to script or printed material, it may be interpreted to include any physical rendering of the fruits of creative intellectual or aesthetic labor. Ibid.; *Trade-Mark Cases*, 100 U.S. 82, 94, 25 L. Ed. 550 (1879). Thus, recordings of artistic performances may be within the reach of Clause 8.

While the area in which Congress many act is broad, the enabling provision of Clause 8 does not require that Congress act in regard to all categories of materials which meet the constitutional definitions. Rather, whether any specific category of "Writings" is to be brought within the purview of the federal statutory scheme is left to the discretion of the Congress. The history of federal copyright statutes indicates that the congressional determination to consider specific classes of writings is dependent, not only on the character of the writing, but also on the commercial importance of the product to the national economy. As our technology has expanded the means available for creative activity and has provided economical means for reproducing manifestations of such activity, new areas of federal protection have been initiated.

Petitioners contend that the actions taken by Congress in establishing federal copyright protection preclude the States from granting similar protection to recordings of musical performances. According to petitioners, Congress addressed the question of whether recordings of performances should be granted protection in 1909; Congress determined that any individual who was entitled to a copyright on an original musical composition should have the right to control to a limited extent the use of that composition on recordings, but that the record itself, and the performance which it was capable of reproducing were not worthy of such protection.

[The Court then examines the legislative history of the 1909 Copyright Act, and concludes that nothing in it "indicate[s] that Congress considered records as anything but a component part of a machine, capable of reproducing an original composition or that Congress intended records, as renderings of original artistic performance, to be free from state control." It also concludes that Congress has not "so occupied the field of copyright protection as to pre-empt all comparable state action. . . . In regard to this category of 'Writings,' Congress has drawn no balance; rather, it has left the area unattended, and no reason exists why the State should not be free to act."]

Affirmed.

Mr. Justice DOUGLAS, with whom Mr. Justice BRENNAN and Mr. Justice BLACKMUN concur, dissenting. . . .

Prior to February 25, 1972, copyright protection was not extended to sound recordings. *Sears* and *Compco* make clear that the federal policy expressed in Art. I, § 8, cl. 8, is to have "national uniformity in patent and copyright laws," 376 U.S., at 231 n.7, 84 S. Ct., at 788 n.7, a policy bolstered by Acts of Congress which vest "exclusive jurisdiction to hear patent and copyright cases in federal courts . . . and that section of the Copyright Act which expressly saves state protection of unpublished writings but does not include published writings." Ibid. . . .

I would reverse the judgment below.

[Dissenting opinion of Justice MARSHALL, in which Justices BRENNAN and BLACKMUN joined, is omitted.]

COMMENTS AND QUESTIONS

1. Is the *Goldstein* Court's rationale for distinguishing *Sears* and *Compco* persuasive? In his dissenting opinion, Justice Marshall noted that in *Sears* "the Court repeatedly referred to the patent and copyright statutes as if the same rules of interpretation applied to both." He's correct, isn't he?

2. On what basis did the Court in *Goldstein* infer that Congress was indifferent with respect to state protection for sound recordings, whereas state protection for unpatented designs would "disturb[ ] the careful balance" between innovation and competition implicit in the Patent Act? Is there such a ground? Recall that in *Kewanee Oil* Justice Marshall (in his concurring opinion) found it relevant that Congress had

long tolerated state trade secret law. Has Congress long tolerated some aspects of state copyright law, even if not the specific law at issue in *Goldstein*?

3. How important are changes in personnel on the Supreme Court to the outcome of these preemption cases? In between *Sears/Compco* and *Goldstein*, Chief Justice Burger had replaced Chief Justice Warren, and Justice Powell had replaced Justice Black (among other changes in personnel). *Goldstein* was a 5-4 decision.

4. Is the Court in *Goldstein* implicitly stating (as the Court later explicitly states in *Bonito Boats*) that federal law preempts state laws that "substantially interfere[ ]" with the federal scheme? If so, what does it mean to "substantially interfere"?

2. Express Preemption

National Basketball Association v. Motorola, Inc.

105 F.3d 841 (1997)

[The facts of this case are set forth in Chapter 12 *supra*.]

When Congress amended the Copyright Act in 1976, it provided for the preemption of state law claims that are interrelated with copyright claims in certain ways. Under 17 U.S.C. § 301, a state law claim is preempted when: (i) the state law claim seeks to vindicate "legal or equitable rights that are equivalent" to one of the bundle of exclusive rights already protected by copyright law under 17 U.S.C. § 106-styled the "general scope requirement"; and (ii) the particular work to which the state law claim is being applied falls within the type of works protected by the Copyright Act under Sections 102 and 103—styled the "subject matter requirement." . . .

The subject matter requirement is met when the work of authorship being copied or misappropriated "fall[s] within the ambit of copyright protection." Harper & Row, Publishers, Inc. v. Nation Enter., 723 F.2d 195, 200 (1983), rev'd on other grounds, 471 U.S. 539, 105 S. Ct. 2218, 85 L. Ed. 2d 588 (1985). We believe that the subject matter requirement is met in the instant matter. . . . Although game broadcasts are copyrightable while the underlying games are not, the Copyright Act should not be read to distinguish between the two when analyzing the preemption of a misappropriation claim based on copying or taking from the copyrightable work. We believe that:

> [O]nce a performance is reduced to tangible form, there is no distinction between the performance and the recording of the performance for the purposes of preemption under § 301(a). Thus, if a baseball game were not broadcast or were telecast without being recorded, the Players' performances similarly would not be fixed in tangible form and their rights of publicity would not be subject to preemption. By virtue of being videotaped, however, the Players' performances are fixed in tangible form, and any rights of publicity in their performances that are equivalent to the rights contained in the copyright of the telecast are preempted.

Baltimore Orioles, 805 F.2d at 675 (citation omitted).

Copyrightable material often contains uncopyrightable elements within it, but Section 301 preemption bars state law misappropriation claims with respect to uncopyrightable as well as copyrightable elements. . . .

Under the general scope requirement, Section 301 "preempts only those state law rights that 'may be abridged by an act which, in and of itself, would infringe one of the exclusive rights' provided by federal copyright law." Computer Assoc. Int'l, Inc. v. Altai, Inc., 982 F.2d 693, 716 (2d Cir. 1992) (quoting *Harper & Row*, 723 F.2d at 200). However, certain forms of commercial misappropriation otherwise within the general scope requirement will survive preemption if an "extra-element" test is met. As stated in *Altai*:

> But if an "extra element" is "required instead of or in addition to the acts of reproduction, performance, distribution or display, in order to constitute a state-created cause of action, then the right does not lie 'within the general scope of copyright,' and there is no preemption."

Id. (quoting 1 Nimmer on Copyright § 1.01[B] at 1-15). . . .

We turn, therefore, to the question of the extent to which a "hot-news" misappropriation claim based on INS involves extra elements and is not the equivalent of exclusive rights under a copyright. Courts are generally agreed that some form of such a claim survives preemption. Financial Information, Inc. v. Moody's Investors Service, Inc., 808 F.2d 204, 208 (2d Cir. 1986), cert. denied, 484 U.S. 820, 108 S. Ct. 79, 98 L. Ed. 2d 42 (1987) ("*FII*"). . . .

. . . *Computer Associates Intern., Inc. v. Altai Inc.* indicated that the "extra element" test should not be applied so as to allow state claims to survive preemption easily. 982 F.2d at 717. "An action will not be saved from preemption by elements such as awareness or intent, which alter 'the action's scope but not its nature'. . . . Following this 'extra element' test, we have held that unfair competition and misappropriation claims grounded solely in the copying of a plaintiff's protected expression are preempted by section 301." Id. (citation omitted).

Our conclusion, therefore, is that only a narrow "hot-news" misappropriation claim survives preemption for actions concerning material within the realm of copyright.[6] See also 1 McCarthy on Trademarks and Unfair Competition (4th ed. 1996), § 10:69, at 10-134 (discussing National Exhibition Co. v. Fass, 133 N.Y.S.2d 379 (Sup. Ct. 1954), *Muzak*, 30 N.Y.S.2d 419, and other cases relied upon by NBA that pre-date the 1976 amendment to the Copyright Act and concluding that after the amendment, "state misappropriation law would be unnecessary and would be preempted: protection is solely under federal copyright").

[The court states that the elements of an *INS* claim are (i) the plaintiff generates or collects information at some cost or expense; (ii) the value of the information is highly time-sensitive; (iii) the defendant's use of the information constitutes free-riding on the plaintiff's costly efforts to generate or collect it; (iv) the defendant's use of the information is in direct competition with a product or service offered by the plaintiff; and (v) the ability of other parties to free-ride on the efforts of the plaintiff would so reduce the incentive to produce the product or service that its existence or quality would be substantially threatened. It then concludes that "the extra elements — those in addition to the elements of copyright infringement — that allow a "hot-news" claim to survive preemption are: (i) the time-sensitive value of factual information, (ii) the

6. State law claims involving breach of fiduciary duties or trade-secret claims are not involved in this matter and are not addressed by this discussion. These claims are generally not preempted because they pass the "extra elements" test. See *Altai*, 982 F.2d at 717.

free-riding by a defendant, and (iii) the threat to the very existence of the product or service provided by the plaintiff."]

COMMENTS AND QUESTIONS

1. How would you articulate the test Judge Winter applies in *Motorola*? With respect to the "subject matter" prong, is the court asking whether the information at issue has been extracted from a copyrightable work of authorship? What would be the danger of focusing instead on whether the information at issue is itself copyrightable expression, selection, or arrangement?

2. Would the case come out the same way if the Court applied conflict preemption (as in *Goldstein*) as opposed to express preemption?

ProCD, Inc. v. Zeidenberg

86 F.3d 1447 (7th Cir. 1996)

EASTERBROOK, Circuit Judge.

[The facts of this case are set forth in Chapter 12 *supra*.]

III

The district court held that, even if Wisconsin treats shrinkwrap licenses as contracts, § 301(a) of the Copyright Act, 17 U.S.C. § 301(a), prevents their enforcement. 908 F. Supp. at 656-59. The relevant part of § 301(a) preempts any "legal or equitable rights [under state law] that are equivalent to any of the exclusive rights within the general scope of copyright as specified by section 106 in works of authorship that are fixed in a tangible medium of expression and come within the subject matter of copyright as specified by sections 102 and 103." ProCD's software and data are "fixed in a tangible medium of expression," and the district judge held that they are "within the subject matter of copyright." The latter conclusion is plainly right for the copyrighted application program, and the judge thought that the data likewise are "within the subject matter of copyright" even if, after *Feist*, they are not sufficiently original to be copyrighted. 908 F. Supp. at 656-57. Baltimore Orioles, Inc. v. Major League Baseball Players Ass'n, 805 F.2d 663, 676 (7th Cir. 1986), supports that conclusion, with which commentators agree. E.g., PAUL GOLDSTEIN, III COPYRIGHT § 15.2.3 (2d ed. 1996); MELVILLE B. NIMMER & DAVID NIMMER, NIMMER ON COPYRIGHT § 101[B] (1995); WILLIAM F. PATRY, II COPYRIGHT LAW AND PRACTICE 1108-09 (1994). One function of § 301(a) is to prevent states from giving special protection to works of authorship that Congress has decided should be in the public domain, which it can accomplish only if "subject matter of copyright" includes all works of a type covered by sections 102 and 103, even if federal law does not afford protection to them. Cf. Bonito Boats, Inc. v. Thunder Craft Boats, Inc., 489 U.S. 141, 103 L. Ed. 2d 118, 109 S. Ct. 971 (1989) (same principle under patent laws).

But are rights created by contract "equivalent to any of the exclusive rights within the general scope of copyright"? Three courts of appeals have answered "no." National

Car Rental Systems, Inc. v. Computer Associates International, Inc., 991 F.2d 426, 433 (8th Cir. 1993); Taquino v. Teledyne Monarch Rubber, 893 F.2d 1488, 1501 (5th Cir. 1990); Acorn Structures, Inc. v. Swantz, 846 F.2d 923, 926 (4th Cir. 1988). The district court disagreed with these decisions, 908 F. Supp. at 658, but we think them sound. Rights "equivalent to any of the exclusive rights within the general scope of copyright" are rights established by law — rights that restrict the options of persons who are strangers to the author. Copyright law forbids duplication, public performance, and so on, unless the person wishing to copy or perform the work gets permission; silence means a ban on copying. A copyright is a right against the world. Contracts, by contrast, generally affect only their parties; strangers may do as they please, so contracts do not create "exclusive rights." Someone who found a copy of SelectPhone (trademark) on the street would not be affected by the shrinkwrap license — though the federal copyright laws of their own force would limit the finder's ability to copy or transmit the application program.

Think for a moment about trade secrets. One common trade secret is a customer list. After *Feist*, a simple alphabetical list of a firm's customers, with address and telephone numbers, could not be protected by copyright. Yet Kewanee Oil Co. v. Bicron Corp., 416 U.S. 470, 40 L. Ed. 2d 315, 94 S. Ct. 1879 (1974), holds that contracts about trade secrets may be enforced — precisely because they do not affect strangers' ability to discover and use the information independently. If the amendment of § 301(a) in 1976 overruled *Kewanee* and abolished consensual protection of those trade secrets that cannot be copyrighted, no one has noticed — though abolition is a logical consequence of the district court's approach. Think, too, about everyday transactions in intellectual property. A customer visits a video store and rents a copy of Night of the Lepus. The customer's contract with the store limits use of the tape to home viewing and requires its return in two days. May the customer keep the tape, on the ground that § 301(a) makes the promise unenforceable?

A law student uses the LEXIS database, containing public-domain documents, under a contract limiting the results to educational endeavors; may the student resell his access to this database to a law firm from which LEXIS seeks to collect a much higher hourly rate? Suppose ProCD hires a firm to scour the nation for telephone directories, promising to pay \$100 for each that ProCD does not already have. The firm locates 100 new directories, which it sends to ProCD with an invoice for \$10,000. ProCD incorporates the directories into its database; does it have to pay the bill? Surely yes; Aronson v. Quick Point Pencil Co., 440 U.S. 257, 59 L. Ed. 2d 296, 99 S. Ct. 1096 (1979), holds that promises to pay for intellectual property may be enforced even though federal law (in *Aronson*, the patent law) offers no protection against third-party uses of that property. See also Kennedy v. Wright, 851 F.2d 963 (7th Cir. 1988). But these illustrations are what our case is about. ProCD offers software and data for two prices: one for personal use, a higher price for commercial use. Zeidenberg wants to use the data without paying the seller's price; if the law student and Quick Point Pencil Co. could not do that, neither can Zeidenberg.

Although Congress possesses power to preempt even the enforcement of contracts about intellectual property — or railroads, on which see Norfolk & Western Ry. v. Train Dispatchers, 499 U.S. 117 (1991) — courts usually read preemption clauses to leave private contracts unaffected. American Airlines, Inc. v. Wolens, 115 S. Ct. 817 (1995), provides a nice illustration. A federal statute preempts any state "law, rule, regulation, standard, or other provision . . . relating to rates, routes, or services of any air carrier." 49 U.S.C. App. § 1305(a)(1). Does such a law preempt the law of contracts — so that, for example, an air carrier need not honor a quoted price (or a contract to reduce the price by the value of frequent flyer miles)? The Court allowed that it is possible to read the statute that broadly but thought such an interpretation would make little sense. Terms and conditions offered by contract reflect private ordering, essential to the efficient functioning of markets. 115 S. Ct. at 824-25. Although some principles that carry the name of contract law are designed to defeat rather than implement consensual transactions, id. at 826 n.8, the rules that respect private choice are not preempted by a clause such as § 1305(a)(1). Section 301(a) plays a role similar to § 1301(a)(1): it prevents states from substituting their own regulatory systems for those of the national government. Just as § 301(a) does not itself interfere with private transactions in intellectual property, so it does not prevent states from respecting those transactions. Like the Supreme Court in *Wolens*, we think it prudent to refrain from adopting a rule that anything with the label "contract" is necessarily outside the preemption clause: the variations and possibilities are too numerous to foresee. *National Car Rental* likewise recognizes the possibility that some applications of the law of contract could interfere with the attainment of national objectives and therefore come within the domain of § 301(a). But general enforcement of shrinkwrap licenses of the kind before us does not create such interference.

Aronson emphasized that enforcement of the contract between Aronson and Quick Point Pencil Company would not withdraw any information from the public domain. That is equally true of the contract between ProCD and Zeidenberg. Everyone remains free to copy and disseminate all 3,000 telephone books that have been incorporated into ProCD's database. Anyone can add SIC codes and zip codes. ProCD's rivals have done so. Enforcement of the shrinkwrap license may even make information more readily available, by reducing the price ProCD charges to consumer buyers. To the extent licenses facilitate distribution of object code while concealing the source code (the point of a clause forbidding disassembly), they serve the same procompetitive functions as does the law of trade secrets. Rockwell Graphic Systems, Inc. v. DEV Industries, Inc., 925 F.2d 174, 180 (7th Cir. 1991). Licenses may have other benefits for consumers: many licenses permit users to make extra copies, to use the software on multiple computers, even to incorporate the software into the user's products. But whether a particular license is generous or restrictive, a simple two-party contract is not "equivalent to any of the exclusive rights within the general scope of copyright" and therefore may be enforced.

Reversed and remanded.

COMMENTS AND QUESTIONS

1. Section 301 is designed to prevent states from passing or enforcing laws "equivalent" to copyright. Whether a particular law is equivalent to copyright can be difficult to determine, however. Courts generally do not ask whether a body of law as a whole (contract or trade secrets, say) is equivalent to copyright. Rather, the question is whether the application of a state law to a particular factual circumstance would create a state-law right equivalent to copyright. Even *ProCD*, which takes a fairly categorical approach to section 301 preemption, is careful to note that it is not holding that section 301 will never preempt contract terms.

Nonetheless, Judge Easterbrook sees a categorical difference between enforcement of contract law and enforcement of other state laws. The court reasoned:

> Rights "equivalent to any of the exclusive rights within the general scope of copyright" are rights established *by law*—rights that restrict the options of persons who are strangers to the author. Copyright law forbids duplication, public performance, and so on, unless the person wishing to copy or perform the work gets permission; silence means a ban on copying. A copyright is a right against the world. Contracts, by contrast, generally affect only their parties; strangers may do as they please, so contracts do not create "exclusive rights." Someone who found a copy of [the plaintiff's software product] on the street would not be affected by the shrinkwrap license. . . .

Is this distinction between judicial enforcement of contracts and other state laws persuasive? Commentators have been skeptical. Radin and Wagner point out that the Legal Realist movement in the last century exploded the myth that contracts are purely "private" creatures; they depend on the legal system for their enforcement. Margaret Jane Radin & R. Polk Wagner, *The Myth of Private Ordering: Rediscovering Legal Realism in Cyberspace*, 73 CHI.-KENT L. REV. 1295 (1998). And Lemley observes that "even truly 'private' contracts affect third parties who haven't agreed to the contract terms. Many contracts have significant negative externalities." Mark A. Lemley, *Beyond Preemption: The Law and Policy of Intellectual Property Licensing*, 87 CAL. L. REV. 111 (1999). Whatever the validity of the general distinction, the court in *ProCD* applied it to validate a "shrinkwrap license," a peculiar form of contract that is drafted by the creator of the product and that purports to bind to its terms anyone who uses the product. While it is technically true in such a case that only "parties" to the contract are bound by it, anyone who has access to the product will automatically become such a party. Scholars argue that shrinkwrap licenses accordingly look less like contracts in the pure sense, and more like examples of private legislation:

> [T]he viability of the distinction between private contracts and public legislation is diminishing day by day. One of the main changes [*ProCD* and its progeny] would make in current law would be to render enforceable contract "terms" to which the parties did not agree in the classic sense, and indeed of which one party may be entirely unaware. [They] would also enable the enforcement of such contract terms "downstream"—that is, against whomever later acquires the software—despite the fact that a first sale under both patent and copyright law would free the purchaser from upstream contractual restrictions. Technology facilitates this change by allowing a vendor to interpose contract terms even in a downstream transaction that would not ordinarily be thought to demonstrate privity between the "contracting" parties.

Lemley, *supra*.

2. Does copyright preemption of state contract law depend on the remedy asserted for breach of contract? Should federal law be more concerned if a party seeks by contract to bring the weapons of copyright law to bear? For example, the House Committee Notes to section 109(a) of the Copyright Act (the "first sale" doctrine) provide that a contract limiting a user's first sale rights may be enforceable by an action for breach of contract, but do not give rise to an action for copyright infringement. Contract remedies are ordinarily limited to expectation damages, rather than the consequential damages, statutory damages, attorney fees, and injunctions available under the copyright law. But suppose a license agreement provided that *resale*

of a copyrighted work—permissible under copyright law—voids the entire license, rendering the reseller liable for copyright infringement. Should such a contract be preempted by copyright law? If not, is there anything left in practice of the first sale doctrine?

3. After *ProCD*, is there any set of circumstances in which section 301 will preempt a contract? Suppose that a contract provided that the buyer of a book could not make fair use of the book. Should such a contract term be enforced? Would section 301 stand in the way? Should the context of the contract (whether it was a shrinkwrap, whether the product was widely sold, whether the buyer was a consumer) matter?

4. While we have so far discussed copyright preemption of contract claims, copyright preemption also applies to a variety of state statutes and common law causes of action. Indeed, in *ProCD* itself, the district court held state tort claims for unfair competition, misappropriation, and violation of the Wisconsin Computer Crimes Act to be preempted, because all three claims were based on Zeidenberg's copying of uncopyrightable data. ProCD, Inc. v. Zeidenberg, 908 F. Supp. 640 (W.D. Wis. 1996). The Seventh Circuit let these findings stand on appeal. The Eleventh Circuit has held claims for unfair competition and deceptive trade practices preempted where those claims were made in an effort to protect uncopyrightable databases. Lipscher v. LRP Publications, 266 F.3d 1305 (11th Cir. 2001). On copyright preemption of trade secret claims, see Computer Associates Int'l v. Altai, Inc., 982 F.2d 693, 715-17 (2d Cir. 1992) (copyright and trade secret claims could co-exist regarding the use of the same computer program, as long as misappropriation of trade secrets is based on a defendant's breach of a duty of trust or confidence). *See also* Automated Drawing Systems v. Integrated Network Services, 447 S.E.2d 109 (Ga. Ct. App. 1994) (copyright law did not preempt Georgia Computer Systems Protection Act, which prohibited the "misappropriation" of source code and provided tort damages).

5. *The "Additional Element" Test for Preemption Under Section 301.* Courts attempting to determine whether a right was "equivalent" to copyright have introduced a seemingly straightforward test for federal preemption of state laws in the general domain of copyright: the so-called extra element test. Under this test, if state law provides a cause of action that requires proof of at least one element in addition to those required for a copyright infringement claim, the state law survives. The test tries to state simply, in terms of required pleadings for an effective cause of action, the basic idea that a state can proscribe activities in the general domain of intellectual property as long as those activities are qualitatively different from the ones that are the subject of federal protection. Claims for breach of implied contract in the context of idea submissions (as seen in *Desny v. Wilder*) survive federal preemption as they turn "not upon the existence of a [copyright] . . . but upon the implied promise to pay the reasonable value of the material disclosed." Grosso v. Miramax Film Corp., 383 F.3d 965, 968 (9th Cir. 2004) (quoting Landsberg v. Scrabble Crossword Game Players, Inc., 802 F.2d 1193, 1196 (9th Cir. 1986)).

As applied, the "additional element" test has an elastic quality. In National Car Rental System v. Computer Associates, 991 F.2d 426 (8th Cir. 1993), for example, the court held that a claim for breach of a license to use a computer program was not preempted under section 301 because the claim involved "use" of the program, and "use" of a computer program was not one of the rights conferred by the Copyright Act. If read broadly, so that an allegation of use *in addition to* copying of a copyrighted work survives preemption, *National Car Rental* doesn't leave much of section 301 preemption. Other examples of courts reaching to find an extra element include Taco

Bell Corp. v. Wrench LLC, 256 F.3d 446 (6th Cir. 2001) (holding that the requirement of an "expectation of compensation" in a claim for implied-in-fact contract saved the claim from preemption).

6. *Supremacy Clause Preemption.* Section 301 is not all there is to copyright preemption. Congress enacted section 301 because it intended to "preempt the field" of copyright law, precluding states from passing laws that mimicked the federal statute. But even where Congress has not preempted the field, state statutes will still be preempted if they conflict with the specific mandate of federal law, or if they stand as an obstacle to the purposes of a federal statute. In copyright law, such "conflicts" or "Supremacy Clause" preemption obviously occurs when a state law prevents the enforcement of a federal copyright. For example, if the State of California were to pass a law stating that the Copyright Act did not apply to citizens of California, the law would arguably survive section 301 preemption, since it contains an "extra element" (citizenship) and does not create a right equivalent to copyright. But it would surely be struck down by the courts as an interference with the federal scheme.

Not all interferences are so straightforward. In ASCAP v. Pataki, 930 F. Supp. 873 (S.D.N.Y. 1996), the court invalidated a state statute regulating the activities of performing rights societies such as ASCAP and BMI. The state statute required, among other things, that such groups provide owners of establishments performing music with written notice of an investigation within 72 hours after it is initiated, thus making it difficult for ASCAP and others to conduct "undercover" investigations for violations of the copyright laws. The court's opinion addressed only the issue of "conflict preemption, which occurs either where compliance with both federal and state regulations is a physical impossibility, or where state law stands as an obstacle to the accomplishment and execution of the full purposes and objectives of Congress." *Id.* The court found that the state statutory provisions "hinder the realization of the federal copyright scheme" for several reasons: the statute made it more difficult for copyright owners to enforce their rights; it effectively established a "statute of limitations" on copyright investigations that was shorter than the federal statute; and it gave copyright defendants a counterclaim that they could use to offset copyright damages. *See also* College Entrance Examination Board v. Pataki, 889 F. Supp. 554 (N.D.N.Y. 1995) (state law requiring disclosure of standardized test questions and answers preempted by Copyright Act because it conflicted with the rights of copyright owners to restrict distribution of copyrighted material).

Because the Copyright Act is an attempt by Congress to balance the interests of creators and users of intellectual property, state laws that give *too much* protection to copyrighted works may also interfere with the objectives of Congress. *See, e.g.*, United States ex rel. Berge v. Trustees of the University of Alabama, 104 F.3d 1453 (4th Cir. 1997) ("The shadow actually cast by the Act's preemption is notably broader than the wing of its protection."). As the Supreme Court explained in *Goldstein v. California*, *supra*, the question is whether Congress intended to place a particular work or use in the public domain. Although *Goldstein* was decided before the enactment of section 301, conflicts preemption is still a significant part of copyright law. Several cases have gone beyond section 301 to a general preemption analysis along the lines of the patent preemption cases such as *Kewanee* and *Bonito Boats.* In Associated Film Distribution Corp. v. Thornburgh, 520 F. Supp. 971 (E.D. Pa. 1981), *rev'd and remanded on other grounds*, 683 F.2d 808, 817 (3d Cir. 1982), the court held preempted a state statute regulating the procedure by which film exhibitors licensed major motion pictures from film distribution arms of the major movie companies. The court went beyond section 301, stating that the "more general question of conflict between the two statutory schemes under the supremacy clause is decisive." 520 F. Supp. at 993. *See also* Orson, Inc. v. Miramax Film Corp., 189 F.3d 377 (3d Cir. 1999) (en banc) (a Pennsylvania statute that prohibited an exclusive license of a first-run film for longer than six weeks was preempted by the Copyright Act); *but see* Allied Artists Pictures Corp. v. Rhodes, 496 F. Supp. 408 (S.D. Ohio 1980), *aff'd and remanded in part*, 679 F.2d 656, 665 (6th Cir. 1982) (reaching the opposite conclusion).

A number of cases have in fact preempted contract terms that conflict with federal patent and copyright policy. For example, contract terms that purport to extend a patent or copyright beyond its expiration have repeatedly been held unenforceable. On the distinction between "conflicts preemption" and copyright field preemption in the contract area, see David Nimmer et al., *The Metamorphosis of Contract into Expand*, 87 CAL. L. REV. 17 (1999).

7. Is *ProCD* in fact a case of conflict between copyright and contract? The stage for such a conflict is set by the Supreme Court decision in *Feist*, which held that the telephone white pages at issue in *ProCD* were constitutionally ineligible for copyright protection. Does the fact that ProCD's shrinkwrap license gives, if anything, even greater protection than copyright would suggest there is a conflict here? In ProCD v. Zeidenberg, 908 F. Supp. 640 (W.D. Wis. 1996), the district court reasoned in dictum that state contract law could not be used to prevent the copying of telephone white pages, which the Supreme Court had determined in *Feist* were uncopyrightable. The district court applied a constitutional copyright preemption analysis similar to the patent analysis undertaken in *Bonito Boats*. The Seventh Circuit reversed the district court's decision, concluding that under section 301 of the Copyright Act state contract law could not be preempted in this case. ProCD v. Zeidenberg, 86 F.3d 1447 (7th Cir. 1996). Judge Easterbrook's opinion did not mention Supremacy Clause preemption at all, even though the issue was briefed and was necessary to the decision, leaving the issue in some doubt.

Courts to consider the question of whether shrinkwrap licenses can be preempted when they conflict with federal policy are split. One court concluded that a state statute permitting enforcement of shrinkwrap licenses was invalid under the Supremacy Clause where the shrinkwrap license at issue forbad reverse engineering that was permissible under the Copyright Act. Vault Corp. v. Quaid Software, Ltd., 847 F.2d 255 (5th Cir. 1988). *See also* Bowers v. Baystate Technologies, 320 F.3d 1317, 1337 (Fed. Cir. 2003) (Dyk, J., dissenting) (endorsing this result). On the other hand, two more recent decisions have found no distinction between shrinkwrap licenses and negotiated contracts, and permitted copyright owners to block reverse engineering using a shrinkwrap provision. Davidson & Assocs. v. Jung, 422 F.3d 630 (8th Cir. 2005); Bowers v. Baystate Technologies, 320 F.3d 1317 (Fed. Cir. 2003).

If the federal copyright scheme intends unoriginal works like the telephone white pages to be in the public domain, is there any way to prevent the sort of use Zeidenberg made of this data? States presumably would lack the power to do so. There is some question whether Congress could avoid the constitutional limitation of originality in the Copyright Clause by enacting protection for databases under the Commerce Clause. In United States v. Moghadam, 175 F.3d 1269 (11th Cir. 1999), the court concluded that Congress could protect unfixed works under the Commerce Clause because it perceived no conflict between the anti-bootlegging statute at issue there and the policies of copyright law. But a Congressional effort to overrule *Feist* might be more problematic. *See* Paul J. Heald & Suzanna Sherry, *Implied Limits on the*

Legislative Power: The Intellectual Property Clause as an Absolute Constraint on Congress, 2000 U. Ill. L. Rev. 1119.

PROBLEM

Problem 15-1. Presco is in the business of printing and selling academic journals to university libraries. When Presco receives a subscription request, it sends a form contract to the requestor. The requesting library is required to sign the contract before Presco will start the subscription. Presco's form contract provides in part that: "Independent of and in addition to any provisions of state or federal law, the parties agree that Subscriber will not make, cause to be made, or allow to be made any copies of any Presco journals without the prior express written consent of Presco."

Is the contract provision preempted? Does it matter whether the subscriber's copying would constitute fair use under the copyright laws?

3. Copyright Preemption of Right of Publicity Claims

Many applications of the right of publicity — such as the unauthorized use of a celebrity's name to endorse a product — easily survive federal preemption by the Copyright Act because enforcement of the right in such circumstances does not implicate a copyrighted work. Several contexts, however, strain the tests for federal preemption. Consider the analysis presented in the following two cases.

Laws v. Sony Music Entertainment, Inc.

448 F.3d 1134 (2006)

Bybee, Circuit Judge.

Plaintiff Debra Laws ("Laws") brought suit against defendant Sony Music Entertainment, Inc. ("Sony") for misappropriating her voice and name in the song "All I Have" by Jennifer Lopez and L.L. Cool J. The district court found that Sony had obtained a license to use a sample of Laws's recording of "Very Special" and held that Laws's claims for violation of her common law right to privacy and her statutory right of publicity were preempted by the Copyright Act, 17 U.S.C. § 101-1332. We agree with the district court that the Copyright Act preempts Laws's claims, and we affirm.

I. Facts and Proceedings

In 1979, professional vocalist and recording artist Debra Laws and Spirit Productions ("Spirit") entered into a recording agreement with Elektra/Asylum Records ("Elektra") to produce master recordings of Laws's vocal performances for Elektra. The agreement gave Elektra the "sole and exclusive right to copyright such master recordings" and "the exclusive worldwide right in perpetuity . . . to lease, license, convey or otherwise use or dispose of such master recordings." Elektra also secured the right "to use and to permit others to use your name, the Artist's name . . . likeness, other identification, and biographical material concerning the Artist . . . in connection with such master recordings." Notwithstanding these provisions, Elektra agreed that "we shall not, without your prior written consent, utilize or authorize others to utilize the Masters in any so-called 'audio-visual' or 'sight and sound' devices intended primarily for home use," and "we or our licensees shall not, without your prior written consent, sell records embodying the Masters hereunder for use as premiums or in connection with the sale, advertising or promotion of any other product or service." In 1981, Laws recorded the song "Very Special," which was released on Laws's album on the Elektra label. Elektra copyrighted the song that same year.

In November 2002, Elektra's agent, Warner Special Products, Inc., entered into an agreement with Sony Music Entertainment, Inc. ("Sony") to grant Sony a non-exclusive license to use a sample of Debra Laws's recording of "Very Special" in the song "All I Have," performed by recording artists Jennifer Lopez and L.L. Cool J. The agreement required Sony to include a credit stating, "Featuring samples from the Debra Laws recording 'Very Special'" in any reproduction. Warner, Elektra's agent, did not seek permission from Laws or Spirit before it released the disc and video, and neither Laws nor Spirit was compensated.

Sony subsequently released a Jennifer Lopez compact disc and music video incorporating brief samples of "Very Special" into her recording of "All I Have." The sampled portions include a segment approximately ten seconds in length at the beginning of "All I Have," and shorter segments repeated in the background throughout the song. Sony included the required credit in the booklet accompanying the compact disc. The song and Lopez's album, "This is Me . . . Then," became a huge commercial success, netting over forty-million dollars. At one time "All I Have" was the number one song in the United States.

[Laws filed suit, alleging violation of her right of publicity in violation of California law. The district court granted Sony's motion for summary judgment on preemption grounds. Laws appealed.]

III. Analysis

. . . We have adopted a two-part test to determine whether a state law claim is preempted by the [Copyright] Act. We must first determine whether the "subject matter" of the state law claim falls within the subject matter of copyright as described in 17 U.S.C. §§ 102 and 103. Second, assuming that it does, we must determine whether the rights asserted under state law are equivalent to the rights contained in 17 U.S.C. § 106, which articulates the exclusive rights of copyright holders. . . .

A. The "Subject Matter" of Copyright

We first consider whether the subject matter of Laws's misappropriation claim is within the subject matter of the Copyright Act. We conclude that it is. Sections 102 and 103 of the Act identify the works of authorship that constitute the "subject matter" of copyright. Section 102 of the Act extends copyright protection to "original works of authorship fixed in any tangible medium of expression . . . from which they can be . . . reproduced, . . . either directly or with the aid of a machine or device." 17 U.S.C. § 102(a). That section defines a "work of authorship" to include "sound recordings." *Id.* § 102(a)(7). "A work is 'fixed' in a tangible medium of expression when its embodiment in a copy or phonorecord, by or under the authority of the author, is sufficiently permanent or stable to permit it to be perceived, reproduced, or otherwise communicated for a period of more than transitory duration." *Id.* § 101. Laws's master recordings held by Elektra are plainly within these definitions.

Laws nevertheless contends that the subject matter of a copyright claim and a right of publicity claim are substantively different. She argues that a copyright claim protects ownership rights to a work of art, while a right of publicity claim concerns the right to protect one's persona and likeness. Sony, by contrast, contends that the subject matter of a right of publicity in one's voice is not different from a copyright claim when the voice is embodied within a copyrighted sound recording. Sony argues that once a voice becomes part of a sound recording in a fixed tangible medium it comes within the subject matter of copyright law.

Our jurisprudence provides strong guidance to the resolution of this question. In Sinatra v. Goodyear Tire & Rubber Co., 435 F.2d 711 (9th Cir. 1970), Nancy Sinatra filed suit against Goodyear Tire on the basis of an advertising campaign that featured "These Boots Are Made for Walkin'," a song that Sinatra made famous. Goodyear Tire had obtained a license from the copyright proprietor for the use of music, lyrics, and arrangement of the composition. Goodyear Tire subsequently used the music and lyrics in its ads, which were sung by unknown vocalists. She alleged the song had taken on a "secondary meaning" that was uniquely injurious to her. We rejected her claim:

> [A]ppellant's complaint is not that her sound is uniquely personal; it is that the sound in connection with the music, lyrics and arrangement, which made her the subject of popular identification, ought to be protected. But as to these latter copyrightable items she had no rights. Presumably, she was required to obtain permission of the copyright owner to sing "Boots," and to make an arrangement of the song to suit her own tastes and talents. Had she desired to exclude all others from use of the song so that her "secondary meaning" with the song could not be imitated she could have purchased those rights from the copyright proprietor. One wonders whether her voice . . . would have been identifiable if another song had been presented, and not "her song," which unfortunately for her was owned by others and licensed to the defendants.

Id. at 716. Although *Sinatra* was decided prior to passage of the modern-day preemption provision in section 301, we nonetheless ruled that the Copyright Act impliedly preempted Sinatra's state law claim. *Id.* at 717-18. We later confirmed this holding in Midler v. Ford Motor Co., 849 F.2d 460, 462 (9th Cir. 1988), when we observed that "[t]o give Sinatra damages for [defendants'] use of the song would clash with federal copyright law."

In *Midler*, recording and performing artist Bette Midler filed suit against an advertising agency and its client when a professional "sound alike" was used to imitate Midler's voice from her hit song "Do You Want to Dance." The agency did not acquire a license to use Midler's recording; instead, it had obtained a license from the song's copyright holder and then attempted to get Midler to do the commercial. When Midler's agent advised the agency that she was not interested, the agency hired someone who had been a backup singer for Midler and could imitate her voice and style. Indeed, the singer was instructed to sound as much like Bette Midler as possible. We held that Midler's common law misappropriation claim was not preempted by copyright law because the "thing" misappropriated, her voice, was not copyrightable in that instance. We explained:

> Midler does not seek damages for [the defendant's] use of "Do You Want To Dance," and thus her claim is not preempted by federal copyright law. Copyright protects "original works of authorship fixed in any tangible medium of expression." A voice is not copyrightable. The sounds are not "fixed." What is put forward as protectible here is more personal than any work of authorship.

Id. at 462 (citation omitted). What Midler sought was relief from an unauthorized vocal imitation for advertising purposes, and that was not the subject of copyright.

We subsequently applied *Midler* in Waits v. Frito-Lay, Inc., 978 F.2d 1093 (9th Cir. 1992). The voice of Tom Waits, a professional singer, songwriter, and actor, was imitated and then broadcast in a commercial for Frito-Lay. Waits filed a right of publicity claim under California law. We held that the claim was not preempted by copyright law because it was "for infringement of voice, not for infringement of a copyrightable subject such as sound recording or musical composition." *Id.* at 1100. Thus, the issues in *Waits* were "whether the defendants had deliberately imitated Waits' voice rather than simply his style and whether Waits' voice was sufficiently distinctive and widely known to give him a protectible right in its use. These elements are 'different in kind' from those in a copyright infringement case challenging the unauthorized use of a song or recording." *Id.*

In this case, Laws's voice misappropriation claim is plainly different from the claims in *Midler* and *Waits* and falls within the subject matter of copyright. In contrast to *Midler* and *Waits*, where the licensing party obtained only a license to the song and then imitated the artist's voice, here Sony obtained a license to use Laws's recording itself. Sony was not imitating "Very Special" as Laws might have sung it. Rather, it used a portion of "Very Special" as sung by Debra Laws. *See also* Brown v. Ames, 201 F.3d 654, 658 (5th Cir. 2000) ("The crucial difference between [this case and Daboub v. Gibbons, 42 F.3d 285 (5th Cir. 1995),] is that in *Daboub* the basis of the misappropriation claim . . . was the song itself, bringing it within section 301's ambit, whereas here the basis of the misappropriation claim was defendants' use of plaintiffs' names and/or likenesses.").

Laws does not dispute Sony's contention that the recording of "Very Special" was a copyrighted sound recording fixed in a tangible medium of expression. Laws's right of publicity claim is based exclusively on what she claims is an unauthorized duplication of her vocal performance of the song "Very Special." Although California law recognizes an assertable interest in the publicity associated with one's voice, we think it is clear that federal copyright law preempts a claim alleging misappropriation of one's voice when the entirety of the allegedly misappropriated vocal performance is contained within a copyrighted medium. Our conclusion is consistent with our holdings in *Midler* and *Waits*, where we concluded that the voice misappropriation claim was not preempted, because the alleged misappropriation was the imitation of the plaintiffs' voices. Neither of those imitations was contained in a copyrighted vocal performance. Moreover, the fact that the vocal performance was copyrighted demonstrates that what is put forth here as protectible is *not* "more personal than any work of authorship." *Midler*, 849 F.2d at 462.

Laws points to two cases for support. Both cases, however, involve photographs used in advertising, and are distinguishable from this case. In *Downing*, 265 F.3d 994, we held that a claim based on the right of publicity was not preempted by the Copyright Act. In *Downing*, retailer Abercrombie & Fitch was developing a surfing theme — "Surf Nekkid" — for its subscription catalog. Abercrombie published a photo of the plaintiffs, who were participants in a surf championship in Hawaii in 1965. Abercrombie ran the photo, which it had purchased from the photographer (who held the copyright), and it identified the plaintiffs by name. Abercrombie went well beyond mere republication of the photograph. Without obtaining plaintiffs' consent to use their names and images, it also offered t-shirts exactly like those worn by the plaintiffs in the photo. We noted that the photograph itself was within the subject matter protected by the Copyright Act. But Abercrombie had not merely published the photograph. Rather, it published the photo in connection with a broad surf-themed advertising campaign, identified the plaintiffs-surfers by name, and offered for sale the same t-shirts worn by the plaintiffs in the photo. By doing so, it had suggested that the surfers had endorsed Abercrombie's t-shirts. Accordingly, we concluded that "it is not the publication of the photograph itself, as a creative work of authorship, that is the basis for[plaintiffs'] claims, but rather, it is the use of the [plaintiffs'] likenesses and their names pictured in the published photograph." *Id.* at 1003; *see also Brown*, 201 F.3d at 656-57 (no preemption where the record company used the names and likenesses of musicians, song writers, and producers on compact disks, tapes, catalogs and posters). We thus concluded that the claim was not within the subject matter of copyright because "[a] person's name or likeness is not a work of authorship within the meaning of 17 U.S.C. § 102." *Downing*, 265 F.3d at 1004.

Laws also relies on a second case, Toney v. L'Oreal USA, Inc., 406 F.3d 905 (7th Cir. 2005), in which the Seventh Circuit held that a claim under the Illinois Right of Publicity Act was not preempted by the Copyright Act. Toney was a model who had posed for photographs used to promote hair-care products on packaging and in national advertisements. Defendants owned the copyright for the photograph of Toney that was used, and had a right to use it from November 1995 to November 2000; any other use would be negotiated separately. In apparent violation of their understanding, defendants continued to use the photographs in their advertising beyond 2000. Toney alleged that this use violated her right of publicity under Illinois law. The Seventh Circuit concluded that

> Toney's identity is not fixed in a tangible medium of expression. There is no "work of authorship" at issue in Toney's right of publicity claim. A person's likeness — her persona — is not authored and it is not fixed. The fact that an image of the person might be fixed in a copyrightable photograph does not change this. . . . The fact that the photograph itself could be copyrighted, and that defendants owned the copyright to the photograph that was used, is irrelevant to the [right of publicity] claim. . . . The defendants did not have her consent to continue to use the photograph. . . .

Id. at 910. The fact that the photograph was copyrighted could not negate the fact that Toney had reserved artistic control over her image for any period beyond the contractual time frame. The Seventh Circuit concluded that Toney's claim was not preempted.[4]

4. *Toney* differs from this case in a significant way: Toney brought her right of publicity claim against L'Oreal U.S.A., Inc., the Wella Corp., and Wella Personal Care of North America, Inc., which each at some point held the copyright and had agreed not to use Toney's likeness after 2000. The facts of this case would

In contrast, Jennifer Lopez's song "All I Have" incorporated samples of Deborah Laws's "Very Special" and gave her the attribution negotiated by Elektra and Sony. Sony did not use Laws's image, name, or the voice recording in any promotional materials. Her state tort action challenges control of the artistic work itself and could hardly be more closely related to the subject matter of the Copyright Act.

We find more to the point, and quite persuasive, the California Court of Appeal's decision in Fleet v. CBS, Inc., 50 Cal. App. 4th 1911, 58 Cal. Rptr. 2d 645 (1996). There, defendant CBS owned the exclusive rights to distribute a motion picture in which plaintiffs performed. A third party who financed the operation of the movie refused to pay plaintiffs their previously agreed-to salaries. Plaintiffs brought suit against CBS alleging, *inter alia*, that by airing the motion picture using their names, pictures, and likenesses without their consent, CBS had violated their statutory right of publicity. The Court of Appeal held that the Copyright Act preempted the action. As the court observed, "it was not merely [plaintiffs'] likenesses which were captured on film — it was their dramatic performances which are . . . copyrightable." *Id.* at 651. "[O]nce [plaintiffs'] performances were put on film, they became 'dramatic work[s]' 'fixed in[a] tangible medium of expression. . . .' At that point, the performances came within the scope or subject matter of copyright law protection," and the claims were preempted. *Id.* at 650; *see also Downing*, 265 F.3d at 1005 n.4 ("In *Fleet*, the plaintiffs were actors in a copyrighted film. The claims of the plaintiffs were based on their dramatic performance in a film CBS sought to distribute. . . . This is clearly distinguishable from this case where the Appellants' claim is based on the use of their names and likenesses, which are not copyrightable."). In effect, the plaintiffs' right of publicity claim was a question of control over the distribution, display or performance of a movie CBS owned. Since CBS's use of plaintiffs' likenesses did not extend beyond the use of the copyrighted material it held, there was no right of publicity at issue, aside from the actors' performances. Had the court held otherwise, each actor could claim that any showing of the film violated his right to control his image and persona.

Laws makes much of the fact that she possessed a right of first refusal in all future uses of "Very Special" under the original production agreement with Elektra. She contends that this right expressly gives her control over the use of her name and voice in connection with any use of "Very Special." She also contends that "[i]f the copyright holder itself, Elektra/Asylum, was not ceded such rights, then as a matter of law its licensee does not possess those rights." In effect, Laws contends that her contractual reservation gives her an interest in the copyright and, concomitantly, renders Elektra's copyright partially subject to her control.

We express no view as to the effect of Laws's reservation in the production agreement and no view as to any remedies that Laws may have against Elektra. Whether or not the two parties contracted around the actual use of a copyright does not affect our preemption analysis. To the extent that Laws has enforceable, contractual rights regarding the use of Elektra's copyright, her remedy may lie in a breach of contract claim against Elektra for licensing "Very Special" without her authorization. *See* Grosso v. Miramax Film Corp., 383 F.3d 965, 968 (9th Cir. 2004).

---

be analogous to *Toney* if Laws had brought her right of publicity claim against Elektra, which holds the copyright to the song and may have agreed to licensing limitations. We express no views on the correctness of *Toney* or its application to any claims against Elektra.

In sum, we hold that Laws's cause of action is within the subject matter of copyright.

B. Equivalent Rights

We must next determine whether the rights she asserts under California law are equivalent to the rights protected under the Copyright Act. We conclude that they are. In Del Madera Props. v. Rhodes & Gardner, 820 F.2d 973 (9th Cir. 1987), *overruled on other grounds*, Fogerty v. Fantasy, Inc., 510 U.S. 517, 114 S. Ct. 1023, 127 L. Ed. 2d 455 (1994), we outlined the test for determining whether state rights were "equivalent" to those under the Copyright Act:

> To satisfy the "equivalent rights" part of the preemption test . . . the . . . alleged misappropriation . . . must be equivalent to rights within the general scope of copyright as specified by section 106 of the Copyright Act. Section 106 provides a copyright owner with the exclusive rights of reproduction, preparation of derivative works, distribution, and display. To survive preemption, the state cause of action must protect rights which are qualitatively different from the copyright rights. The state claim must have an extra element which changes the nature of the action.

Id. at 977 (quotations and citations omitted). . . .

Laws contends that her right of publicity claim under California Civil Code § 3344 requires proof of a use for a "commercial purpose," which is not an element of a copyright infringement claim. She concedes that a right which is the "equivalent to copyright" is one that is infringed by the mere act of reproduction; however, she argues that her claim is not based on Sony's mere act of reproduction, but "is for the use of . . . Laws'[s] voice, the combination of her voice with another artist, and the commercial exploitation of her voice and name in a different product without her consent."

Sony argues that Laws's claims are based exclusively on the reproduction of "Very Special" in "All I Have." It asserts that the rights protected under Laws's voice misappropriation claim are not qualitatively different from the rights protected under copyright law because the sole basis for her voice misappropriation claim is the unauthorized reproduction of her copyrighted vocal performance.

The essence of Laws's claim is, simply, that she objects to having a sample of "Very Special" used in the Jennifer Lopez-L.L. Cool J recording. But Laws gave up the right to reproduce her voice — at least insofar as it is incorporated in a recording of "Very Special" — when she contracted with Elektra in 1981 and acknowledged that Elektra held the "sole and exclusive right to copyright such master recordings," including the right "to lease, license, convey or otherwise use or dispose of such master recordings." At that point, Laws could have either retained the copyright, or reserved contractual rights in Elektra's use of the recording. Indeed, Laws claims that the latter is precisely what she did. But if Elektra licensed "Very Special" to Sony in violation of its contract with Laws, her remedy sounds in contract against Elektra, not in tort against Sony.

The mere presence of an additional element ("commercial use") in section 3344 is not enough to qualitatively distinguish Laws's right of publicity claim from a claim in copyright. The extra element must transform the nature of the action. Although the elements of Laws's state law claims may not be identical to the elements in a copyright action, the underlying nature of Laws's state law claims is part and parcel of a copyright claim. *See Fleet*, 58 Cal. Rptr. 2d at 649. Under the Act, a copyright owner has the exclusive right "to reproduce the copyrighted work." 17 U.S.C. § 106(1). Laws's claims are based on the premise that Sony reproduced a sample of "Very Special" for commercial purposes without her permission. But Sony obtained a limited license from the copyright holder to use the copyrighted work for the Lopez album. The additional element of "commercial purpose" does not change the underlying nature of the action. *See* Motown Record Corp. v. George A. Hormel & Co., 657 F. Supp. 1236, 1239-40 (C.D. Cal. 1987).

IV. Conclusion

. . . To be clear, we recognize that not every right of publicity claim is preempted by the Copyright Act. Our holding does not extinguish common law or statutory rights of privacy, publicity, and trade secrets, as well as the general law of defamation and fraud (or any other similar causes of action), so long as those causes of action do not concern the subject matter of copyright and contain qualitatively different elements than those contained in a copyright infringement suit. Elektra copyrighted Laws's performance of "Very Special" and licensed its use to Sony. If Laws wished to retain control of her performance, she should (and may) have either retained the copyright or contracted with the copyright holder, Elektra, to give her control over its licensing. In any event, her remedy, if any, lies in an action against Elektra, not Sony.

We therefore agree with the district court's conclusion that Laws's right of publicity claims are preempted by the Copyright Act. The judgment is

AFFIRMED.

Facenda v. N.F.L. Films, Inc.

542 F.3d 1007 (2008)

AMBRO, Circuit Judge.

John Facenda, a Philadelphia broadcasting legend, provided his voice to many productions of NFL Films, Inc. before his death in 1984. These well-known productions recounted tales of the National Football League with filmed highlights, background music, and Facenda's commanding narration. More than two decades after Facenda's death, NFL Films used small portions of his voice-over work in a cable-television production about the football video game "Madden NFL 06." That production, entitled "The Making of Madden NFL 06," sparked this controversy.

Facenda's Estate ("the Estate") sued NFL Films, the National Football League, and NFL Properties (which we refer to collectively, where appropriate, as "the NFL") in the United States District Court for the Eastern District of Pennsylvania. . . . The Estate . . . claims that the program was an unauthorized use of Facenda's name or likeness in violation of Pennsylvania's "right of publicity" statute. In its defense the NFL argued, among other things, that its copyrights in the original NFL Films productions that Facenda narrated gave it the exclusive right to use portions of those productions' soundtracks as it saw fit, including in the television piece at issue.

We must resolve this clash between parties claiming different types of intellectual property. . . . We affirm . . . the District Court's grant of summary judgment to the Estate on the Pennsylvania right-of-publicity claim.

I. Facts

Facenda won national acclaim for his NFL Films work. His Estate credits that fame to the special qualities of his voice. In various depositions, several representatives for NFL Films described Facenda's deep baritone voice as "distinctive," "recognizable," "legendary," and as known by many football fans as "the Voice of God." As recently as 1999, NFL Films released works branded as featuring "the Legendary Voice of John Facenda."

For decades, Facenda worked on a session-by-session basis under an oral agreement, receiving a per-program fee. But shortly before he died from cancer in 1984, Facenda signed a "standard release" contract stating that NFL Films enjoys "the unequivocal rights to use the audio and visual film sequences recorded of me, or any part of them . . . in perpetuity and by whatever media or manner NFL Films . . . sees fit, provided, however, such use does not constitute an endorsement of any product or service."

In 2005, NFL Films produced "The Making of Madden NFL 06" about the soon-to-be released annual update of the video game that simulates NFL games. This production is 22 minutes long and was shown on the NFL Network eight times in a three-day span leading up to the release of the video game to retail stores. It featured interviews with NFL players, the game's producers, and others. It also included several sequences comparing the video game's virtual environment with the actual NFL environment, extolling the realism of everything from the stadiums to the game play. The end of the program featured a countdown to the video game's release.

The District Court found that not a single critical observation was made in this video regarding Madden NFL 06; all the commentary was positive. Other media, outside of the NFL Network, also covered the release of the game and addressed similar topics (albeit with the inclusion of the occasional criticism or recitation of the game's perceived faults).

The program used sound recordings, taken from earlier NFL Films' productions, of three sentences read by Facenda: (1) "Pro Football, the game for the ear and the eye," (2) "This sport is more than spectacle, it is a game for all seasons," and (3) "X's and O's on the blackboard are translated into aggression on the field." These excerpts from his NFL Films work total 13 seconds of the program. In its opening brief to our Court, the NFL admits that these excerpts were chosen "to underscore the degree to which the video game authentically recreates the NFL experience."

The producers of the program used the excerpts in a slightly altered form. The sound waves in the original recording of Facenda's voice were digitally filtered to sound more like the synthesized speech one might hear from a computer. (NFL Films President Steve Sabol described the results of this aesthetic choice by the show's producers as "awful.")

The NFL has an agreement with EA Sports, the makers of Madden NFL 06, which provides the NFL with royalty revenue in return for the use of the NFL's intellectual property. Various e-mail messages in the record suggest that NFL Films sought to create the television program as a promotion for Madden NFL 06, describing it as the "Madden Promo" or as "the Advertisements" in actors' release forms. But in their depositions, many NFL Films executives testified that the program was a documentary and denied that it was a commercial or that it was motivated by promotional considerations. . . .

VI. Unauthorized Use of Name or Likeness Under Pennsylvania Law

Pennsylvania law grants individuals the exclusive right to their name and likeness, which includes voice. 42 PA. CONS. STAT. ANN. § 8316. "Any natural person whose name or likeness has commercial value and is used for any commercial or advertising purpose" without consent may sue for an injunction and damages. Id. § 8316(a). A deceased person's estate may bring such an action, id. § 8316(b)(3), although the right only lasts until thirty years after the person's death, id. § 8316(c).

The District Court held that the NFL violated this statute with its use of Facenda's voice because (a) his voice's commercial value was not disputed, (b) the NFL used his voice for a commercial purpose, and (c) the standard release Facenda signed did not consent to the use of his voice in endorsements. *Facenda*, 488 F. Supp. 2d at 502. . . .

We agree that the NFL has violated § 8316 on its face for precisely the reasons provided by the District Court, and we see no disputed issues of material fact on that question. On appeal, the NFL instead focuses on another argument it raised in the District Court — that copyright law preempts the Estate's right-of-publicity claim.

A. *The NFL's Copyright in the Sound Clips*

A threshold issue for the NFL's preemption defense is whether the NFL has a valid copyright in the sound recordings of Facenda's voice. The NFL notes that it excerpted the sound clips at issue from copyrighted productions of NFL Films. Moreover, the sound clips represent Facenda's readings of copyrighted NFL scripts, making the clips "derivative works" (of the scripts) in which a distinct copyright exists. See 17 U.S.C. § 106(2) (granting copyright holders the exclusive right to prepare derivative works); id. § 102(a)(7) (allowing copyrights in sound recordings, which are separate and distinct from the copyrights in musical compositions of § 102(a)(2)). Either way, the NFL had the copyright in the sound clips.

By using the sound clips of Facenda's voice in "The Making of Madden NFL 06," the NFL was exercising its exclusive right to make derivative works of those sound clips under § 106(2). In effect, it was "sampling" itself, making a collage, taking a small piece of an old work and using it in a new work — as when a hip-hop group samples the drum part from James Brown's "Funky Drummer." It is well-established that copyrights extend to samples, even brief samples. See, e.g., Grand Upright Music Ltd. v. Warner Bros. Records, Inc., 780 F. Supp. 182, 183 (S.D.N.Y. 1991). For instance, no third party to this case may use those recordings unless a limitation on or exception to the NFL's § 106 rights applies, such as the fair use doctrine of 17 U.S.C. § 107. See Campbell v. Acuff-Rose Music, Inc., 510 U.S. 569, 571-72, 579-80, 114 S. Ct. 1164, 127 L. Ed. 2d 500 (1994) (holding a parody of Roy Orbison's "Oh, Pretty

Woman" may be a fair use). Thus, the NFL is correct that copyright law, taken in isolation, gives it the exclusive right (absent a limitation or exception) to use the sound recordings of Facenda's voice in the way that it did.

The question for us is how the NFL's (federal) copyright relates to Facenda's (state-law) right of publicity. Does the state-law right of publicity exist irrespective of the federal copyright? Put another way, does federal copyright law preempt the right of publicity claim under Pennsylvania law?

B. *Express Preemption*

* * *

1. Equivalent to an Exclusive Right?

. . . Under the first prong of express copyright preemption analysis, some courts have looked to the elements of a state-law cause of action. The presence of an "additional element" required to state a cause of action under state law, beyond what a copyright-infringement claim would require, renders the state-law cause of action not equivalent to a copyright. See Dielsi v. Falk, 916 F. Supp. 985, 991-93 (C.D. Cal. 1996).

Pennsylvania's right-of-publicity statute requires a showing of commercial value, defined as a "[v]aluable interest in a natural person's name or likeness that is developed through the investment of time, effort and money." 42 PA. CONS. STAT. ANN. § 8316(e). The requirement under the statute that Facenda's voice have "commercial value," id. § 8316(a), provides an additional element beyond what a copyright-infringement claim requires, see 1 NIMMER ON COPYRIGHT § 1.01[B][1][c], at 1-29 to -30 ("Invasion of privacy may sometimes occur by acts of reproduction, distribution, performance, or display, but inasmuch as the essence of the tort does not lie in such acts, pre-emption should not apply. The same may be said of the right of publicity."); accord 2 MCCARTHY, RIGHTS OF PUBLICITY AND PRIVACY § 11:50, at 785. Because the Estate's right-of-publicity claim relied on an element not equivalent to any of the exclusive rights granted to federal copyright holders, we hold that the first prong of § 301(a) is not satisfied here.

2. Copyrightable Subject Matter?

Looking to the second prong of 17 U.S.C. § 301(a), does Facenda's voice fall under the subject matter of copyright? The Court of Appeals for the Ninth Circuit has stated, in the context of vocal imitations, that "[a] voice is not copyrightable. The sounds are not 'fixed.' What is put forward as protectible [sic] here is more personal than any work of authorship." Midler v. Ford Motor Co., 849 F.2d 460, 462 (9th Cir. 1988). One can fix Facenda's voice in a tangible medium by recording it, but one cannot divorce his distinctive voice itself from the Facenda identity (or persona). See 1 NIMMER ON COPYRIGHT § 1.01[B][1][c], at 1-30 ("The 'work' that is the subject of the right of publicity is the persona, i.e., the name and likeness of a celebrity or other individual. A persona can hardly be said to constitute a 'writing' of an 'author' within the meaning of the Copyright Clause of the Constitution."); 2 McCarthy, Rights of Publicity and Privacy § 11:53, at 802 ("The sound in plaintiff's recording is merely an indicium by which the listening public can identify plaintiff's persona and identity."). We hold that Facenda's voice is outside the subject matter of copyright. Thus, the second prong of § 301(a) is not satisfied.

V.

* * *

We conclude thus that copyright's express preemption provision, 17 U.S.C. § 301(a), does not bar the Estate's right-of-publicity claim. Thus, we affirm the holding of the District Court to this effect.

C. *Conflict Preemption*

Our analysis, however, does not stop there. We also consider whether federal copyright law impliedly preempts the Estate's right-of-publicity claim.

The analysis works as follows. Copyright law does not expressly preempt the right of publicity because an individual's identity or persona is outside the subject matter of copyright. See, e.g., *Waits*, 978 F.2d at 1100; *Midler*, 849 F.2d at 462. Yet in some situations, including this case, the right of publicity clashes with the exploitation of a defendant's copyright. Unlike the plaintiffs in cases involving vocal imitations, see, e.g., *Midler*, 849 F.2d at 460, Facenda collaborated with the NFL to create the copyrighted sound recordings at issue. In our view, this gives the NFL a stronger preemption defense than the vocal-imitation defendants, for example. Where a defendant in a right-of-publicity claim obtained a copyright in a work featuring the plaintiff, courts must separate legitimate exploitations of what Congress intended to be a copyright holder's exclusive rights from particular uses that infringe the right of publicity. Otherwise, few copyright holders would be safe from suits by performers who agreed to appear in the holders' works. See 2 McCarthy, Rights of Publicity and Privacy § 11:55, at 817 ("[W]hen another reproduces a recorded performance in an expressive, non-advertising medium, this should not be the concern of right of publicity law.").

Conflict preemption is a particular species of implied preemption that "renders state law 'without effect' when, without 'express congressional command,' state law conflicts with federal law." Pa. Employees Benefit Trust Fund v. Zeneca Inc., 499 F.3d 239, 247 (3d Cir. 2007) (citing Cipollone v. Liggett Group, Inc., 505 U.S. 504, 516, 112 S. Ct. 2608, 120 L. Ed. 2d 407 (1992)). As one copyright treatise puts it:

> Therefore, even apart from Section 301, the general proposition pertains in copyright law, as elsewhere, that a state law is invalid that "stands as an obstacle to the accomplishment of the full purposes and objectives of Congress." Such "conflict pre-emption" equally pertains when compliance with both federal and state mandates is a physical impossibility.

1 Nimmer on Copyright § 1.01[B][3][a], at 1-77. The Estate's claim, if successful, will constrain the NFL's ability to exercise its full array of exclusive rights under the Copyright Code. Yet federal copyrights are not absolute.

Courts have found conflict preemption where state laws interfere with federal copyright law's goal of leaving some works, or uses of works, in the public domain. See id. § 1.01[B][1][c], at 1-33 (citing Brown v. Ames, 201 F.3d 654, 660-61 (5th Cir. 2000)). For example, these concerns might arise with respect to state laws offering protection for "sound-alike" sound recordings, which copyright does not protect. See id. § 1.01[B][3][b][i], at 1-82 to -83 (discussing *Midler*, 849 F.2d at 460); see also Vault Corp. v. Quaid Software Ltd., 847 F.2d 255, 269-70 (5th Cir. 1988) (holding that a Louisiana state law permitting a software producer to prohibit disassembly of its computer program conflicted with rights Congress left to software purchasers [under what is now 17 U.S.C. § 117(a) of the federal Copyright Code] and was therefore unenforceable).

Our case presents a different kind of potential conflict. Here we are concerned with the conflict between copyright law and the right of publicity. When does the right of individuals to avoid commercial exploitation of their identities interfere with the rights of copyright owners to exploit their works? In addition, we must confront the role of the standard release contract. Does a contract acknowledging a right-of-publicity for defendant's copyright in a work containing a plaintiff's identity mean that the defendant may use that work in any way it sees fit?

David Nimmer has proposed a two-part framework for handling cases at the intersection of copyright, the right of publicity, and contract. First, we look to how the copyrighted work featuring the plaintiff's identity is used. Surveying the case law, Nimmer finds that when defendants use the work "for the purposes of trade," such as in an advertisement, plaintiffs' right-of-publicity claims have not been held to be preempted. See 1 Nimmer on Copyright § 1.01[B][3][b][iv][I], at 1-88.2(9)-(11). On the other hand, when defendants' uses constitute "expressive works," right-of-publicity claims have been preempted. See id. § 1.01[B][3][b][iv][I], at 1-88.2(11). The rationale is that state law has a role in regulating practices of trade, including advertising. But limiting the way that material can be used in expressive works extends beyond the purview of state law and into the domain of copyright law.

Seale v. Gramercy Pictures was Nimmer's inspiration for this framework, and illustrates the distinction he draws. 949 F. Supp. 331 (E.D. Pa. 1996). Seale's right-of-publicity claim for use of his likeness to make a "docudrama" about the Black Panthers failed as a matter of law. Id. at 337-38. Nimmer contends that this claim should have been preempted because it targeted an expressive work. See 1 Nimmer on Copyright § 1.01[B][3][b][iv] [I], at 1-88.2(12). On the other hand, Seale's claim based on the use of his image to sell compact discs (on which he did not perform) went to trial, *Seale*, 949 F. Supp. at 337 (although the defendants ultimately prevailed, *Seale*, 964 F. Supp. at 931). Nimmer suggests that this claim should not have been preempted even though it proved unsuccessful. See 1 Nimmer on Copyright § 1.01[B][3][b][iv][I], at 1-88.2(12) to -88.2(13).

The NFL used the sound recordings of Facenda's voice in a television production promoting the video game Madden NFL 06. This kind of use, in what amounts to a 22-minute promotional piece akin to advertising, does not count as an expressive work. Following the case law, this suggests that conflict preemption is inappropriate in our case.

The second part of Nimmer's framework addresses the way that contracts affect the preemption analysis. Nimmer proposes that courts should examine the purpose of the use to which the plaintiff initially consented when signing over the copyright in a contract. He argues that the proper question in cases involving advertising and a contract between the plaintiff and the defendant-such as our case-is whether the plaintiff "collaborated in the creation of a copyrighted advertising product." 1 NIMMER ON COPYRIGHT § 1.01[B][3][b][iv][II], at 1-88.2(20). If the plaintiff did collaborate in that fashion, then the party holding the copyright is in a very strong position to contend that allowing the plaintiff to assert a right of publicity against use of its likeness in advertising would interfere with the rights it acquired. If, on the other hand, the plaintiff did not collaborate specifically in the creation of advertising content, then the plaintiff is in a strong position to assert continuing control over the use of his image.

Three cases, along with the District Court's opinion in our case, provide the most important background case law for the second part of Nimmer's analysis. *Fleet v. CBS, Inc.* involved a right-of-publicity claim by actors seeking to prevent a movie-distribution company from distributing a film in which they appeared. 50 Cal. App. 4th 1911, 58 Cal. Rptr. 2d 645, 646-47 (1996). The actors had contracted away their rights in the film, but had not received compensation. They apparently hoped to obtain leverage in seeking payment by enjoining distribution of the film. The California Court of Appeal held that the actors' claim was preempted, stating that "a party who does not hold the copyright in a performance captured on film cannot prevent the one who does from exploiting it by resort to state law." Id. at 652-53.

The Ninth Circuit Court of Appeals in *Laws v. Sony Music Entertainment, Inc.*, evaluated singer Debra Laws's claims that Sony had violated her right of publicity by using a sample of one of her recordings in a song by Jennifer Lopez and LL Cool J. 448 F.3d at 1135-36. A third party, Elektra Asylum Records, owned the copyright in the original sound recording that featured Laws. Elektra granted Sony a license to use the sample in the J. Lo-LL Cool J song. Laws's recording contract with Elektra gave Elektra the right to grant licenses, subject to contractual conditions. In that context, whether Laws authorized the sample license was a contract issue between Laws and Elektra. But Laws sued Sony, the end user of the sample. See id. at 1143 ("To the extent that Laws has enforceable, contractual rights regarding the use of Elektra's copyright, her remedy may lie in a breach of contract claim against Elektra for licensing [her song] 'Very Special' without her authorization."). Even though Laws might have been able to state a contract claim against Elektra, her right-of-publicity claim against Sony was preempted by § 301(a).

In *Toney v. L'Oreal U.S.A., Inc.*, the plaintiff, a model, sued L'Oreal for the unauthorized use of her image on product packaging. 406 F.3d at 907. The plaintiff had a contract with L'Oreal's corporate predecessor to use her image in that way, but it had expired. The Court of Appeals for the Seventh Circuit held that the plaintiff's claim was not preempted. Id. at 911. "There is no 'work of authorship' at issue in Toney's right of publicity claim. A person's likeness — her persona — is not authored and it is not fixed. The fact that an image of the person might be fixed in a copyrightable photograph does not change this." Id. at 910. Thus, the second express-preemption requirement of § 301(a) (that the state law at issue purports to protect something that falls within the subject matter of copyright) was not met, and accordingly Toney's claim was not preempted.

To illustrate this second part of his framework, Nimmer puts the fact situations in FLEET, LAWS, and TONEY on one side, and the fact situation of our case (which he uses as his main counter-example, based on the District Court's opinion) on the other:

> Fleet acted in a movie; for that reason, he could not complain when that very movie was later exploited, by being broadcast on television. Laws sang for a recording; for that

> reason, she could not complain when that very recording was later exploited, by being used as background for Jennifer Lopez. Toney posed for the packaging of "Ultra Sheen Supreme." Parallel reasoning indicates that she should not be able to complain about subsequent exploitation of that very work. The defendants in that case, in short, did not "appropriate[ ] the commercial value of a [Toney]'s identity by using [it] without consent." Far from it — they simply did exactly what she agreed to. In that regard, they stand poles apart from the NFL, when it took anchorman Facenda's sports commentary and transmuted it into part of a pitch for a computer game.

1 NIMMER ON COPYRIGHT § 1.01[B][3][b][iv][II], at 1-88.2(18). Thus, with regard to Toney's claim, Nimmer answers the question "Did she collaborate in the production of a copyrighted advertising product?" in the affirmative. He argues that her case should have been an exception to the usual rule that right-of-publicity claims for uses in advertisements would not be preempted (and thus the Seventh Circuit erred). But in our case, Nimmer suggests that preemption is not appropriate. Facenda consented to participation in films documenting NFL games, not an advertisement for a football video game. The release form Facenda signed did not implicitly waive his right to publicity, the core of which is the right not to have one's identity used in advertisements. See, e.g., 1 MCCARTHY, RIGHTS OF PUBLICITY AND PRIVACY § 1:3, at 3. In fact, the release specifically preserved that right by carving out endorsements.

The NFL argues that Facenda's only remedy should lie in contract. While we agree that Facenda could state a claim for breach of contract, we believe that he also retained his tort-derived remedy for violation of Pennsylvania's right-of-publicity statute. Parties may waive tort remedies via contract. It follows that they may also preserve them. Cf. 1 NIMMER ON COPYRIGHT § 1.01 [B][3][b][iv][II], at 1-88.2(16) (discussing the relationship between "copyright, contract, and the right of publicity"). While performing artists should have the burden of reserving publicity rights when contracting away any rights under copyright law they might have, we hold that Facenda successfully bore that burden here and preserved his state-law right-to-publicity claim.

Despite our holding, we emphasize that courts must circumscribe the right of publicity so that musicians, actors, and other voice artists do not get a right that extends beyond commercial advertisements to other works of artistic expression. If courts failed to do so, then every record contract or movie contract would no longer suffice to authorize record companies and movie studios to distribute their works. In addition to copyrights, entertainment companies would need additional licenses for artists' rights of publicity in every case.

Thus, we believe that *Laws* was rightly decided — Debra Laws sought to enforce a right that she had contracted away. We do not intend to express any disagreement with the Ninth Circuit Court of Appeals by distinguishing the facts of our case from those of *Laws.* Our case simply presents a different scenario than *Laws.* Just as Facenda did not, in the standard release contract, waive the right to bring a false-endorsement claim, see supra Section V.B.1, he did not grant the NFL the right to use his voice in a promotional television program. This contrasts with the situation in *Laws.* Debra Laws's voice was not used in an endorsement, but in a work of artistic expression.

In the endorsement context, an individual's identity and credibility are put directly on point. Advertisements are special in the way they implicate an individual's identity. Precisely what Pennsylvania's right of publicity is meant to protect is a citizen's prerogative not to have his or her name, likeness, voice, or identity used in a commercial advertisement, whether that citizen is a celebrity or not.

In our case, we have no precedent to hold that the right of publicity in an individual's voice is analogous to the public domain. In this void, we believe state-law protection of an individual's voice will not upset copyright law's balance as long as the state law is not construed too broadly. Pennsylvania's § 8316 focuses solely on the commercial-advertising context. It is targeted at endorsements, not the full universe of creative works. The Estate's claim lies at the heart of the statute's focus. For these reasons, the state-law right of publicity does not conflict with federal copyright law in this case.

* * *

We hold that neither express nor implied conflict preemption bars the Estate's right-of-publicity claim under Pennsylvania law. We affirm the District Court's grant of summary judgment to the Estate on that claim.

COMMENTS AND QUESTIONS

1. Should federal copyright law be viewed as preempting *any* right of publicity claims? *All* right of publicity claims? Only *some* claims? If so, which ones?

2. Was the Third Circuit right to look beyond § 301 of the Copyright Act and to consider whether Facenda's claim was preempted under principles of conflict preemption? Applying the conflict preemption analysis set forth in *Goldstein v. California*, would you find Facenda's claim preempted? What about Laws's claim?

3. In *Facenda*, the Third Circuit quotes a portion of *Nimmer on Copyright* in which the authors argue that the publicity claims brought by Debra Laws and by June Toney were preempted because in both cases the plaintiffs had previously consented to the *type* of use at issue. Presumably in such instances, the plaintiffs could pursue state-law claims for breach of contract, assuming that the statute of limitations had not run and that the breaching party was amenable to service of process. Is this a sensible accommodation of federal and state rights, or does it give too little weight to the interests of Laws and Toney in their personas? What adverse consequences, if any, might there be if defendants routinely had to discern whether the consent given to the first party in the chain was valid and still in effect?

4. In right of publicity cases, two independent bodies of legal doctrine — the First Amendment and copyright preemption — may have a bearing on whether the plaintiff's claim may proceed to judgment. Is there any way to integrate these two bodies of law into a coherent analytical framework? For one proposed framework, see Thomas F. Cotter & Irina Dmitrieva, *Integrating the Right of Publicity with First Amendment and Copyright Preemption Analysis*, 33 Colum. J.L. & Arts 165 (2010). Cotter and Dmitrieva propose a three-step inquiry. First, echoing Nimmer's suggestion above, the court should consider whether the plaintiff consented to the *type* of use at issue. If so, the court should enter judgment for the defendant. If not, the second step is to ask whether the use at issue was "for purposes of trade" as defined in the *Restatement (Third) of Unfair Competition*. If not, the court should enter judgment for the defendant; if so, then the court should consider whether the defendant's First Amendment interest outweighs the state interest underlying the exercise of publicity rights at issue, taking into account the use's status as commercial or noncommercial speech. Only a claim that survives all three steps may proceed to trial. Does this framework strike the right balance, or does it screen out too many publicity claims? Too few? Does it collapse the First

Amendment and preemption issues into one? Is there any principled way to apply to step (3) or is the inquiry inevitably ad hoc?

PROBLEM

Problem 15-2. In the late 1980s, the New Kids on the Block were an enormously successful pop music group, especially among the younger teen market. Capitalizing on this success, the New Kids sold over 500 products or services bearing their trademarked name. Among those services were "900 numbers" that fans could call to learn more about the New Kids, or to talk to the New Kids themselves.

During the height of the New Kids craze, the newspaper *USA Today* conducted a telephone poll that allowed readers to "vote" for their favorite New Kid (or for "none of the above" if they did not like the band at all) by calling a *USA Today* 900 number. As a part of the poll, the paper included captioned pictures of each of the band members. Suppose that the New Kids on the Block sued *USA Today* for infringement of their right of publicity. Do they have a claim under California law?

C. PREEMPTION OF OTHER STATE LAWS UNDER THE UTSA

Burbank Grease Servs. LLC v. Sokolowski

717 N.W.2d 781 (Wis. 2006)

Patience Drake ROGGENSACK, J.

This case requires us to determine whether the trade secret statute, Wis. Stat. § 134.90 (2003-04), precludes all civil law remedies based on the misappropriation of confidential information that falls outside of the statutory definition of a trade secret. . . . We conclude that § 134.90(6)(a) does not preclude all other civil remedies based on the misappropriation of confidential information, if the information does not meet the statutory definition of a trade secret under § 134.90(1)(c). Accordingly, in the case before us, § 134.90(6)(b)2 permits civil tort remedies based on the misappropriation of confidential information. Therefore, because the plaintiff's complaint stated other common law claims and because material facts relevant to those claims are disputed, it was error to dismiss the complaint. . . .

I. Background

Burbank Grease Services, LLC (Burbank) is engaged in the business of collecting and processing used restaurant fry grease, trap grease, and industrial grease. . . .

Larry Sokolowski (Sokolowski) was employed by Burbank in various management positions from November 1997 to April 2001. When he resigned from Burbank, Sokolowski was territory manager. His duties in that position included the oversight of sales people, the management of customer relations with industrial clients and the preparation of spreadsheets and billings for Burbank's accountant.

Burbank distributed a code of conduct in regard to confidential information that it required all managers to acknowledge and to follow. The code provided that "[n]o . . . employee shall disclose any confidential or privileged information to any person within the Company who does not have a need to know or to any outside individual or organization except as required in the normal course of business." Sokolowski was aware of this provision.

All Burbank employees received an employee handbook that contained a provision requiring non-disclosure of trade secret and confidential business information. The handbook provided that disclosure could result in disciplinary action, including termination. The handbook provision also stated that employees might be required to sign a non-disclosure agreement as a condition of employment. Sokolowski acknowledged in writing that he received and understood this provision.

On April 15, 2001, Sokolowski signed an employment agreement with United Liquid Waste Recycling, Inc. (United Liquid), and on April 20, 2001, he resigned from Burbank. Prior to resigning, he obtained confidential information from Burbank's computer system. He took the following information with him when he left: (1) a hardcopy of a list of Burbank's grease trap customers, containing about 2,400 names, phone numbers and addresses, contact persons, total gallons for each grease trap, and pricing Burbank had applied to each customer; (2) a spreadsheet of Burbank's industrial clients that showed the amount of grease collected from each customer times the market rate less a processing fee, which determined what Burbank would pay the customer for the material collected; and (3) a computerized spreadsheet showing the amount of collections and revenues per customer for certain drivers, organized by the driver's route. Sokolowski took the information with him when he left Burbank's employ, without Burbank's permission and with the knowledge that Burbank considered all of this information confidential.

On April 25, 2001, Sokolowski began working for United Liquid as a sales and customer service representative. United Liquid provided waste and cake sludge hauling and glass, metal, and plastic recycling services to industrial, municipal, and commercial clients throughout Wisconsin. Sokolowski and United Liquid later formed United Grease, LLC (United Grease), which began collecting fry grease, trap grease and industrial grease in direct competition with Burbank.

Sokolowski had Burbank's confidential information entered into United Liquid's computer system. Sokolowski used this confidential information to solicit customers for United Grease.

Subsequently, United Grease acquired about 80 fry grease customers, which were mostly former Burbank customers, and 157 grease trap customers, the majority of which were former Burbank customers. United Grease also managed to acquire one or two of Burbank's former industrial customers.

When Burbank became aware that Sokolowski was soliciting its customers, it filed this action alleging that Sokolowski misappropriated Burbank's trade secrets in violation of Wis. Stat. § 134.90; breached his duty of loyalty to Burbank, which he owed as Burbank's agent; intentionally interfered with Burbank's business relationships; and committed computer crimes in violation of Wis. Stat. § 943.70(2).

The complaint also alleged that United Grease and United Liquid had aided and abetted Sokolowski in the breach of his duty of loyalty; had conspired to deprive Burbank of its customers; and had intentionally interfered with Burbank's business relationships.

Both parties filed motions for summary judgment. The circuit court granted the defendants' motion and dismissed the complaint. The circuit court concluded that Burbank's confidential information was not protected by Wis. Stat. § 134.90(6), the trade secret statute, because the information did not meet the statutory definition of a trade secret. The circuit court also concluded that by enacting § 134.90(6), all common law tort claims based on the misappropriation of confidential information were precluded, except those that involved information that met the statutory definition of a trade secret. . . .

II. Discussion

. . . Wisconsin Stat. § 134.90(1)(c) defines the term "trade secret" and § 134.90(2) prohibits any person from misappropriating a trade secret through a variety of specific acts set forth in the statute. The statute also permits courts to grant injunctions, § 134.90(3), and to award damages in addition to, or in lieu of, injunctive relief, § 134.90(4).

Previous judicial decisions that Burbank has not appealed have concluded, for purposes of this case, that Burbank's confidential information Sokolowski, United Grease and United Liquid used did not qualify under Wis. Stat. § 134.90(1)(c) as trade secrets. Accordingly, we do not decide whether the confidential information that Sokolowski took from Burbank would qualify as trade secrets under § 134.90(1)(c). Instead, we are asked to construe subsec. (6) of § 134.90 to determine if it precludes Burbank's other claims for relief, even though what was taken did not qualify as trade secrets.

Wisconsin Stat. § 134.90(6) states:

> Effect on other laws. (a) Except as provided in par. (b), this section displaces conflicting tort law, restitutionary law and any other law of this state providing a civil remedy for misappropriation of a trade secret.
>
> (b) This section does not affect any of the following:
>
> 1. Any contractual remedy, whether or not based upon misappropriation of a trade secret.
> 2. Any civil remedy not based upon misappropriation of a trade secret.
> 3. Any criminal remedy, whether or not based upon misappropriation of a trade secret.*

Burbank argues that the statutory language explicitly preserved its common law claims, because those claims were not based on the misappropriation of a trade secret and therefore, fit squarely within Wis. Stat. § 134.90(6)(b)2. The defendants, on the other hand, urge us to adopt the court of appeals ruling, that all of Burbank's claims are pre-empted by § 134.90(6)(a). They argue that the legislative intent underlying the

* [Under the standard codification of the Uniform Trade Secret Act, the language quoted above is found in section 7. — Eds.]

statute was to encompass all claims based upon confidential business information, even when a claim does not allege or depend on determining that the confidential information met the statutory definition of a trade secret.

We begin our statutory construction by examining the plain language of the statute. *Kalal*, 271 Wis.2d 633, ¶¶45-46, 681 N.W.2d 110. When we examine the language of para. (6)(a) and subd. (6)(b)2 in the context of Wis. Stat. § 134.90, we first focus on the term "trade secret." This is because the "effect on other laws" provision, para. (6)(a), specifically states that the statute displaces "any other law of this state providing a civil remedy for misappropriation of a trade secret." (Emphasis added.) "Trade secret" is defined in para. (1)(c) of § 134.90, and as we explained above, Burbank has not appealed the conclusion that its confidential information that Sokolowski took was not a trade secret, as defined in § 134.90(1)(c).

Accordingly, the plain language of Wis. Stat. § 134.90(6)(a) appears to have the effect of making § 134.90 the exclusive remedy for civil claims based on the misappropriation of a statutorily-defined trade secret. However, what is at issue here is whether para. (6)(a) precludes Burbank's other tort claims, which were not based on the theory that the confidential information Sokolowski took constituted a trade secret, as defined in § 134.90(1)(c).

Wisconsin Stat. § 134.90(6)(a) prefaces its preclusive language with "[e]xcept as provided in par. (b)," indicating that despite the expressed intent of one paragraph of the trade secret statute to displace other remedies for trade secret misappropriation, another paragraph of the statute expressly states that there remain claims based on the misappropriation of confidential information that will not be affected by § 134.90. For example, subd. (6)(b)2 provides that subsec. (6) does not affect "[a]ny civil remedy not based upon misappropriation of a trade secret." (Emphasis added.)

Focusing on the common word "any" in Wis. Stat. § 134.90(6)(b)2, we use a dictionary definition for assistance. See *Garcia*, 273 Wis. 2d 612, ¶14, 682 N.W.2d 365. "Any" is defined as: "one or some indiscriminately of whatever kind"; and "unmeasured or unlimited in amount, number, or extent." WEBSTER'S NEW COLLEGIATE DICTIONARY 51 (5th ed. 1977). "Any" is a very broad term. Accordingly, we conclude that its use evinces a broad range of civil remedies that are not precluded by para. (6)(a). Subdivision (6)(b)2 excepts from the class of unaffected remedies only those remedies based on the misappropriation of a statutorily-defined trade secret. It leaves available all other remaining civil remedies for the protection of confidential information.

The statutory term "civil remedy" is a technical term that is given its technical, legal meaning. *Kalal*, 271 Wis. 2d 633, ¶45, 681 N.W.2d 110. *Black's Law Dictionary* aids us in this regard. It defines "remedy" as:

> The means of enforcing a right or preventing or redressing a wrong; legal or equitable relief.

BLACK'S LAW DICTIONARY 1320 (8th ed. 1990). We conclude the sum effect of the statutory terms is that civil claims for relief are not abrogated by Wis. Stat. § 134.90(6)(b)2, with the exception of those civil tort claims that require the use of a statutorily-defined trade secret. It follows that all other types of civil tort claims that Burbank may assert in regard to the misuse of its confidential information remain available to it under the directive of § 134.90(6)(b)2.

Furthermore, to adopt the court of appeals' view, that para. (6)(a) in combination with subd. (6)(b)2 precludes all Burbank's common law claims, would require us to read into the statute the following underlined language:

> (b) This section does not affect any of the following:
> . . . 2. Any civil remedy not based upon misappropriation of a trade secret and not based on confidential business information.

However, the legislature did not choose the language employed by the court of appeals, and we are not free to add it. . . .

The defendants also urge us to conclude that subsec. (7) of Wis. Stat. § 134.90, the uniformity clause, supports the court of appeals' interpretation. Subsection (7) states:

> Uniformity of application and construction. This section shall be applied and construed to make uniform the law relating to misappropriation of trade secrets among states enacting substantially identical laws.

The plain language of subsec. (7) relates only to the "misappropriation of trade secrets," which, according to our analysis of subd. (6)(b)2 and the plain meaning of subsec. (7), requires a statutorily-defined trade secret as a prerequisite. Our construction in this regard is in accord with the promotion of uniformity by subsec. (7), because the statutory definition of a trade secret is made uniform throughout the states enacting a version of the Uniform Trade Secrets Act (UTSA), and our application of that definition has been in accord with other UTSA jurisdictions. See, e.g., *Minuteman*, 147 Wis. 2d at 851, 434 N.W.2d 773; Electro-Craft Corp. v. Controlled Motion, Inc., 332 N.W.2d 890, 899 (Minn. 1983); Convolve, Inc. v. Compaq Computer Corp., No. 00CV5141 (GBD), 2006 WL 839022, at *5-6 (S.D.N.Y. March 31, 2006). . . .

Our analysis of the plain language of Wis. Stat. § 134.90(6)(b)2 results in only one reasonable interpretation; therefore, the statute is not ambiguous. Our interpretive inquiry would normally stop here. *Kalal*, 271 Wis. 2d 633, ¶ 45, 681 N.W.2d 110. However, we also note that we can use legislative history to confirm a plain-meaning interpretation. Id., ¶ 50, 681 N.W.2d 110. The legislative history does so here.

The Special Committee on the UTSA, established and directed by the Legislative Council to investigate the desirability of incorporating uniform trade secret protections into state law, issued a 1984 Staff Brief that explained the various implications of the potential adoption of the UTSA. That report cited comments of the UTSA Commissioners to explain the purpose of its effect on other law:

> Section 7(a) of the [Uniform Trade Secrets] Act states that it "displaces conflicting tort, restitutionary, and other law of [the enacting state] pertaining to civil liability for misappropriation of a trade secret." Section 7(b) provides that the law does not affect contractual or other civil liability or relief that is not based on misappropriation of a trade secret or criminal liability for misappropriation of a trade secret.
>
> The Commissioners' Comments state that the [Uniform Trade Secrets] Act is not intended to be a comprehensive remedy. According to the Comment, it applies to duties imposed by law in order to protect competitively significant secret information. The Act does not apply to duties voluntarily assumed through an express or an implied-in-fact contract. For example, the enforceability of covenants not to disclose trade secrets, and covenants not to compete that are intended to protect trade secrets, are governed by other

> law. Also, the Act does not apply to duties imposed by law which are not dependent upon the existence of competitively significant secret information, like an agent's duty of loyalty to his or her principal.

Wis. Legis. Council, Staff Brief 84-9, Uniform Trade Secrets Act, at 8 (Aug. 14, 1984) (emphasis added). The commissioners' comment that the UTSA was not enacted to be the exclusive remedy for misappropriation of confidential information is a confirmation that our plain meaning analysis accurately interprets Wis. Stat. § 134.90. . . .

In sum . . . the plain language of Wis. Stat. § 134.90(6)(a) and (b)2, taken together, are meant to do the following: (1) replace all pre-existing definitions of "trade secret" and remedies for tort claims dependent solely on the existence of a specific class of information statutorily defined as "trade secrets"; and (2) leave available all other types of civil actions that do not depend on information that meets the statutory definition of a "trade secret." Therefore, any civil tort claim not grounded in a trade secret, as defined in the statute, remains available to Burbank. Accordingly, we overrule the contrary conclusion of the court of appeals, and we withdraw language from any case that relied on the holding of Burbank in regard to § 134.90(6)(a) and (b)2. See, e.g., Aon Risk Servs., Inc. v. Liebenstein, 2006 WI App 4, ¶ 10, 289 Wis. 2d 127, 710 N.W.2d 175. . . .

Ann Walsh Bradley, J. (dissenting).

This court is not interpreting Wis. Stat. § 134.90 in a vacuum. Section 134.90 is based on the Uniform Trade Secrets Act (UTSA), which 44 states have adopted in some form. See Unif. Trade Secrets Act (amended 1985), 14 U.L.A. 529 (Master ed. 2005). Many states have already weighed in on the interpretation of this uniform law.

What is remarkable about the majority opinion is its disregard of the legislative directive that § 134.90 be interpreted to "make uniform the law relating to misappropriation of trade secrets among the states." Section 134.90(7). . . . Why does the majority ignore the legislative directive that § 134.90 be construed to further a uniform interpretation of UTSA among the states?

The majority unabashedly answers the question. It does not think that the uniformity goal is all that important, so it casts it aside. Rather, what is of prime importance to the majority is its own purported plain-language construction of the statute: "cases from other jurisdictions cannot substitute for our construction of the relevant Wisconsin Statute." Majority op., ¶ 32. Lest the reader think that this disregard of the legislative directive is an isolated statement in its opinion, such disregard permeates the majority's analysis.

Not only does the majority disregard the directive of the legislature on how this statute should be interpreted, but also it concludes that its own purported plain-language interpretation is the only "reasonable interpretation." Id., ¶ 28. In the wake of its conclusion, the majority discards what the court of appeals and legal commentators describe as the correct or prevailing interpretation. Because the majority's approach undermines the uniformity goal of UTSA, I respectfully dissent.

One essential goal of UTSA is to make uniform the law of the states adopting it. Indeed, the legislature specifically adopted this goal as a directive in § 134.90(7): "This section shall be applied and construed to make uniform the law relating to misappropriation of trade secrets among states enacting substantially identical laws." Both the drafters of UTSA and the legislature have recognized the need for uniformity in a world of business where transactions occur between states as frequently as within one state's borders. . . .

Of course other states have the same language in the statute. That is the nature of uniform laws. The question is not whether other states have the same language, but rather how do other states interpret that language and why do they interpret it that way?

The majority does not seem to care about the answer. Concluding that its analysis of the plain language of the statute "results in only one reasonable interpretation," it declares that the "statute is not ambiguous." Id., ¶ 28. What about states that interpret the statute differently than does the majority? Why is the interpretation given by courts in those states unreasonable?

The majority weakly attempts to address these questions. It does not analyze the interpretations of other states observing only that "cases from other jurisdictions cannot substitute for our construction of the relevant Wisconsin Statute." Id., ¶ 32. . . .

The court of appeals determined that if common law claims for unauthorized use of confidential information that did not meet the statutory definition of a trade secret were permitted, the result would undermine the uniformity and clarity that motivated the creation and passage of UTSA. Id., ¶ 30, 693 N.W.2d 89. It further determined that the prevailing rule in most UTSA jurisdictions is that UTSA is meant to replace tort claims for unauthorized use of confidential information with a single statutory cause of action. Id., ¶ 35, 693 N.W.2d 89.

The court of appeals found this rule persuasive. It therefore concluded that § 134.90(6) preempts common law claims, however denominated, that are based solely on allegations or evidence of unauthorized use of confidential information, regardless of whether that information meets the statutory definition of a trade secret. Id., ¶ 37, 693 N.W.2d 89. . . .

The court of appeals' interpretation of UTSA's preemption provision is contrary to the majority's interpretation but consistent with that of legal commentators. One such commentator, Robert Unikel, explains in detail. He divides the case law in UTSA jurisdictions into three views. See Robert Unikel, *Bridging the "Trade Secret" Gap: Protecting "Confidential Information" Not Rising to the Level of Trade Secrets*, 29 Loy. U. Chi. L.J. 841, 886-87 (Summer 1998). Under the first view, which is the view adopted by the court of appeals and rejected by the majority opinion, there is preemption of all non-UTSA claims for the protection of both trade secrets and other confidential information. Id. at 886. Unikel explains that, absent contrary legislative guidance by a state, this view "is the most reasonable." Id. at 887. Contrast the majority opinion: "Our analysis . . . results in only one reasonable interpretation." Majority op., ¶ 28.

Are Unikel and the court of appeals unreasonable, or is the majority? Here is Unikel's explanation for why the interpretation of UTSA applied by the court of appeals is the more reasonable:

> Permitting litigants in UTSA states to assert common-law claims for the misappropriation or misuse of confidential data would reduce the UTSA to just another basis for recovery and leave prior law effectively untouched. Further, by expressly exempting "contractual remedies, whether or not based upon misappropriation of a trade secret" and "other civil remedies that are not based upon misappropriation of a trade secret" from its preemptive penumbra, the UTSA makes clear that only those claims addressing or arising out of

> wrongs distinct from pure information piracy survive passage of the trade secret statute. Indeed, contrary interpretations of the UTSA's "Effect on Other Law" provision [§ 134.90(6) in Wisconsin], such as those embodied in the second and third views of UTSA preemption, effectively negate the UTSA's goal of promoting uniformity in "trade secrets" law. Additionally, these contrary interpretations render the statutory preemption provision effectively meaningless.

Bridging the "Trade Secret" Gap, at 888 (emphasis added; footnotes omitted).

Thus, the majority opinion has adopted one of the views that Unikel says "render[s] the statutory preemption provision effectively meaningless." Id. That does not sound very reasonable to me. . . .

II

The problem with the majority opinion is amplified by its approach to the definition of "trade secret" in § 134.90(1)(c). Although this court was not asked to review whether Burbank's customer information was a "trade secret" under the statutory definition, the scope of that definition is pivotal in interpreting the preemption provisions in UTSA. This much the majority seems to recognize. See majority op., ¶ 19.

The majority concludes, however, that § 134.90(6) does not preempt civil remedies based on misappropriation of "confidential information" that falls outside the statutory definition of a "trade secret." Majority op., ¶ 1. The majority thereby distinguishes between "statutorily-defined" trade secrets as actionable under UTSA and other "confidential information" as actionable under Wisconsin common law. Id., ¶ 24. Such a distinction, however, may be just what the drafters of UTSA (and the Wisconsin legislature in adopting UTSA) sought to avoid.

The majority's conclusion again appears to be at odds with the interpretation given UTSA by legal commentators. According to one commentator, UTSA was intended to divide information into two categories: (1) actionable "trade secrets" and (2) unprotected knowledge or skill. For example, one commentator writes:

> The *Restatement of Unfair Competition*, following the lead of the Uniform Trade Secrets Act and cases following the Act, eliminates the distinction between information that is a trade secret and other confidential information. All secret information of economic value falls within the definition of trade secrets. Trade secrets are protected against any misappropriation.

Edmund W. Kitch, *The Expansion of Trade Secrecy Protection and the Mobility of Management Employees: A New Problem for the Law*, 47 S.C. L. Rev. 659, 662 (Summer 1996) (emphasis added; footnotes omitted).

Similarly, Unikel states that UTSA reflects a " 'two-tiered' approach to the protection of commercial knowledge—an approach in which information is classified only as either a protected 'trade secret' or unprotected 'general skill and knowledge.' " *Bridging the "Trade Secret" Gap*, at 868.

To the extent these commentators are correct, the majority's construction of § 134.90 is not. If these commentators are correct, it would appear that common law causes of action for misappropriation of "confidential information" that is not a "trade secret" under UTSA are no longer available in UTSA states such as Wisconsin.

The majority's construction of § 134.90(6) would undermine uniformity if courts in other states gave their analogous provisions of UTSA such a construction. If litigants in the various states could maintain common law claims for misappropriation of "confidential information" that does not rise to the level of a UTSA-defined "trade secret," then trade secret law across jurisdictions would continue to depend on the varying common law rules as to misappropriation of economically-valuable secret information. The majority does not endeavor to explain how this could have been the intent of either the drafters of UTSA or the legislature. . . .

COMMENTS AND QUESTIONS

1. Which side has the better of the argument in *Burbank Grease*? Does the UTSA preempt claims for the misappropriation of confidential, proprietary, but non-trade secret information? Given the breadth of the definition of "trade secret" found in the UTSA, is there any social value in protecting information that doesn't satisfy the statutory definition?

2. It seems reasonably clear that the UTSA preempts claims for "trade secret misappropriation" that otherwise might be brought under the common law or other statutes. It also seems reasonably clear that if a claim for conversion, unjust enrichment, quantum meruit, or the like is just a trade secret claim in disguise, it should be preempted. If the *Burbank Grease* majority is correct, however, in concluding that the statute does not preempt claims for the misappropriation of non-trade secret information, what effect might this have on trial practice? Could plaintiffs plead and offer evidence on both theories (trade secret and non-trade secret misappropriation) and let the jury sort it out, or should the plaintiff be required to elect one or the other theory in advance of trial?

3. Does the UTSA preempt trade secret misappropriation claims against a faithless employee's new employer premised on the doctrine of respondeat superior? Why or why not? What about tortious interference claims? Cybertrespass?

Table of Cases

Principal cases are in italics.

Index